MW00777001

THEOLOGY
YOU CAN COUNT ON

THEOLOGY

YOU CAN COUNT ON

TONY EVANS

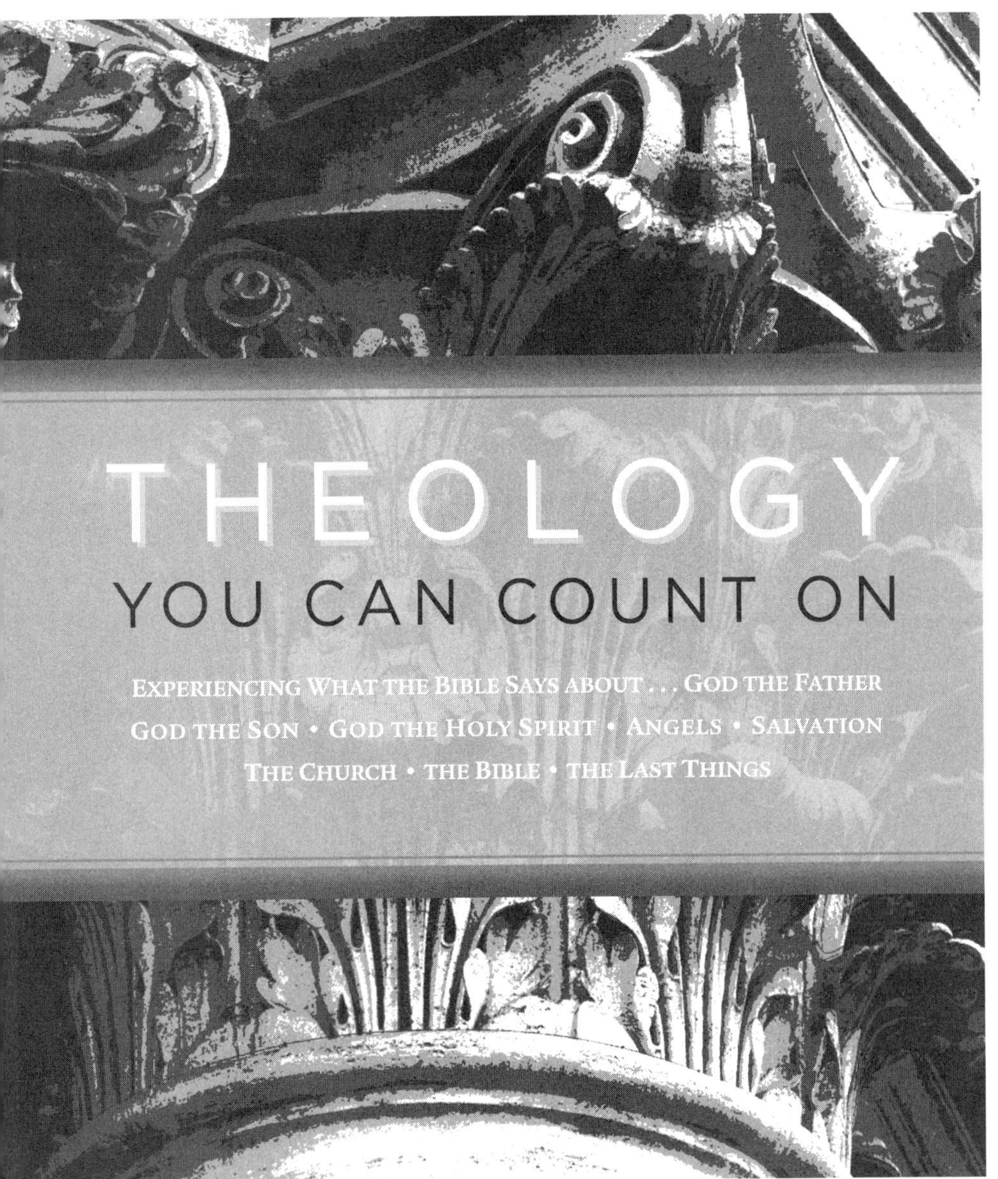

THEOLOGY

YOU CAN COUNT ON

EXPERIENCING WHAT THE BIBLE SAYS ABOUT . . . GOD THE FATHER
GOD THE SON • GOD THE HOLY SPIRIT • ANGELS • SALVATION
THE CHURCH • THE BIBLE • THE LAST THINGS

MOODY PUBLISHERS
CHICAGO

This work is a condensation of eight books in the Understanding God series: *The Battle Is the Lord's, The Best Is Yet to Come, God's Glorious Church, Our God Is Awesome, The Promise, Totally Saved, The Transforming Word,* and *Who Is This King of Glory?*

Editors: Phil Rawley, Jim Vincent
Personal and Group Study Material: Dana Gould
Interior and Cover Design: Smartt Guys design
Cover Photo: Roberto A. Sanchez, iStock

Library of Congress Cataloging-in-Publication Data

Evans, Tony.
Theology you can count on : experiencing what the Bible says about God the Father, God the Son, God the Holy Spirit, angels, salvation, the church, the Bible, the last things / Tony Evans.
p. cm.
Includes bibliographical references and index.
ISBN 978-0-8024-6653-2
ISBN-10: 0-8024-6653-2
1. Theology, Doctrinal—Popular works. I. Title.

BT77.E79 2008
230—dc22

2008009402

We hope you enjoy this book from Moody Publishers. Our goal is to provide high-quality, thought-provoking books and products that connect truth to your real needs and challenges. For more information on other books and products written and produced from a biblical perspective, go to www.moodypublishers.com or write to:

Moody Publishers
820 N. LaSalle Boulevard
Chicago, IL 60610

1 3 5 7 9 10 8 6 4 2

Printed in the United States of America

This book is gratefully dedicated to
my good friend and editor,
Philip Rawley
who has steadfastly worked with me
in the completion of the entire
applied theology series, of
which this book is a summary.

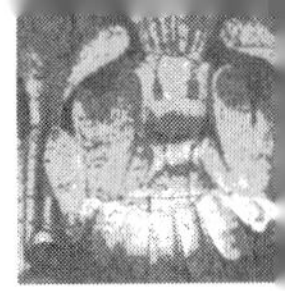

CONTENTS

Part 2: CHRISTOLOGY
The Doctrine of God the Son

Part 3: PNEUMATOLOGY
The Doctrine of God the Holy Spirit

PART 4: ANGELOLOGY
The Doctrine of Angels

Part 5: SOTERIOLOGY
The Doctrine of Salvation

Part 6: ECCLESIOLOGY
The Doctrine of the Church

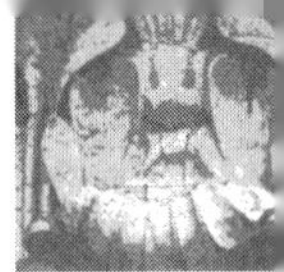

ACKNOWLEDGMENTS

No work of this magnitude can be achieved by one person alone. I want to acknowledge the people who have played a strategic role in bringing this book to fruition. They include the team at Moody Bible Institute and Moody Publishers: vice-president Greg Thornton, who was instrumental in the conception and execution of this project, editor Jim Vincent, and many other people at Moody who helped in the production of this book.

I also want to thank Mr. Dana Gould, who contributed his skills and insights to the "For Group Study" sections that follow each chapter in this theology, as well as most of the "Personal Application for Life" in the chapters in Parts 2–8, a tremendous amount of work. A final word of thanks goes to my friend and editor, Phil Rawley—who also drew on the assistance of his two children and coworkers, Philip and Bethany Rawley. God bless you all!

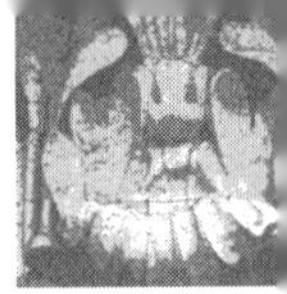

INTRODUCTION

Theology may be defined as learning, organizing, and communicating the truths about God as revealed in His Word. For many people the word *theology* suggests seminary-educated scholars who sit in ivory towers, isolated from the real world, studying the Bible. Such study is often viewed as esoteric and unrelated to the world where men and women live, work, play, raise families, and struggle with the realities of day-to-day life.

Theology need not be that remote, however, and that is not God's intent in the Scriptures. Instead, the Bible is written to real people living in a real world, facing real problems, and needing a real, practical word from God. That's one reason the Scriptures are not given to us in a systematized way. Rather, the truths about God are presented in the context of the realities of life where different authors communicated to different groups over different periods of time with contemporary messages from God. It is in this context of biblical theology that we discover in Scripture the truths that God wants us to know about Himself

The challenge then is to organize those truths in a way that communicates a clear understanding of the Bible's teaching on any subject it addresses. This organizing process is called *systematic theology*. Since readers of the holy Scriptures cannot go just to one verse, one passage, or even one book to discover the full biblical revelation on any subject, the various teachings on a particular truth must be brought together and harmonized in an orderly way.

This volume, like all systematic theologies, has been written to present the major categories of theology. However, the particular distinctive of this work is to put theology on the "lower shelf," where it can be accessed and understood by all. That is where the organized truths of God are communicated in a simple and practical way. The goal of this volume is not only to make theology easily understood, but also to show how it applies to the lives of those who learn its truths. This is why you will find points of illustration and application within each of the eight parts. It is also why each chapter ends with a section for personal application as well as questions for group discussion. I encourage you to use this book as part of a discussion and study in a Sunday morning class or in a small group setting.

Theology, when properly understood, ought to be challenging, inspiring, transforming, and even fun. To have the privilege of learning truth about God and seeing that truth transform our lives is the greatest pursuit in life. The goal of learning sound doctrine (2 Timothy 4:3; Titus 1:9) is to lead us into holy living (Philippians 1:9–11; Colossians 1:9–10). It is my hope that this book will assist you in achieving this goal, whether you are a pastor, student, scholar, or layperson.

PART 1

THEOLOGY PROPER

The Doctrine of God the Father

SECTION I

The Subject of God

1. THE STUDY OF GOD
2. THE NATURE OF GOD

1

THE STUDY OF GOD

It's hard to know where to begin when your subject is God Himself, a subject more important than anything else we could ever study. Nothing can fully express the subject, especially since God is more than the sum total of His attributes. King David said, "Such knowledge [of God] is too wonderful for me" (Psalm 139:6). But God invites us to know Him. He wants us to contemplate all that He is, because nothing else matters without Him.

I like what the great English preacher Charles Spurgeon told his church one Sunday (and J. I. Packer cites in his book *Knowing God*):

> I believe . . . that the proper study of God's elect is God; the proper study of a Christian is the Godhead. The highest science, the loftiest speculation, the mightiest philosophy, which can ever engage the attention of a child of God, is the name, the nature, the person, the work, the doings, and the existence of the great God whom he calls his Father.

No study of God can be said to be comprehensive for three reasons. The first has to do with the sheer limitation of the human mind. A finite mind cannot fully grasp an infinite being. Second is the moral problem. The presence of sin, even in our converted state, has limited our capacity for understanding spiritual truth. Third, we have a resource problem. God has simply not told us everything about Himself. What He has told us we can know, but He has not revealed everything.

Because of the greatness of our subject, I will be taking you to many portions of Scripture. But due to the limitations of space and my own finiteness, we will neither exhaust the subject nor be able to give equal attention to all of these Scriptures.

THE STUDY OF GOD

My thesis in this introductory chapter can be stated simply: The study of the knowledge of God is the most important pursuit in life.

Of all the things that matter in our lives, to know God through a purposeful study of His nature, His character, and His perfections should be our driving force. Only then will we be able to define everything else accurately. But let me make three clarifications right now before we get into the heart of this chapter and the book.

More than Awareness

First of all, when I talk about the study of the knowledge of God, I am not referring to an awareness of God. Simply to say there is a God doesn't say a whole lot about Him, because it would be hard to miss Him entirely when you understand that He is an all-encompassing Being. So when I talk about knowing God, I mean more than that you are aware He exists.

More than Information

Second, when I talk about knowing God, I mean more than that you have information about God; that is, knowing that He is the Creator or powerful or big or grand or majestic.

More than Religion

Knowing God also means more than having a religious experience with God or saying that we feel Him. It is valid to have an emotional and religious experience with God, but to know Him involves more than that.

To know God is to have Him rub off on you, to enter into relationship with God so that who He is influences who you are. One of the great tragedies today is that you can go to church and be aware of God; you can go to church and have information about God; and if your church has a great choir, you can even go to church and "feel" God; but you can leave church with Him never having rubbed off on you.

LIFE'S MOST MEANINGFUL PURSUIT

The study of God is the most meaningful pursuit in life. Jeremiah 9:23–24 expresses the importance of knowing God better than I ever could:

> Thus says the Lord, "Let not a wise man boast of his wisdom, and let not the mighty man boast of his might, let not a rich man boast of his riches; but let him who boasts boast of this, that he understands and knows Me."

The Right Kind of Bragging

It's amazing how many things we brag about. Some of us can brag about our educational achievements. We've gone through school and we've done well. We've got a bachelor's degree. We've earned a master's degree. Perhaps we even graduated magna cum laude.

Perhaps you started on the bottom rung of the ladder at your company. You've grown up through the company and now you've become a supervisor; you've "graduated" to become a manager. You own your own business, your own success. Now extra money is in the account. The home looks nice. The cars are modern. The suits are authentic.

But God says, "If you are going to brag, if you really want something to shout about, can you brag that you know Me? Because if you can't talk about that, you don't have much to brag about."

Hitting the Right Target

A man once went to visit a farmer and noticed something very odd. On the side of the farmer's barn were a number of targets with holes dead center in each bull's-eye. The visitor said, "My goodness! Every single hole is right in the center of every single bull's-eye! I didn't know you were that good."

His farmer friend said, "I'm really not."

"Wait a minute. I see a hole in the center of every single bull's-eye. How could you not be that good and shoot that well?"

The farmer replied, "It's like this. I shoot the hole into the barn first, then I draw me a bull's-eye."

That's the way a lot of us live our lives. We shoot for riches, power, or education and then draw the meaning of life around these things. Then we go around saying, "I hit a bull's-eye!" We give the impression that we know how to shoot, when in actuality we don't know what in the world we are doing. We are as confused as those around us.

But God says, "If you are going to brag, can you brag on the fact that I have rubbed off on you; that My thinking has become your thinking; that My way of living and walking and moving and functioning has become your way? Only when that happens can you say that you know Me." And so we need to say, "We will boast in the name of the Lord, our God" (Psalm 20:7).

LIFE'S MOST AUTHENTIC PURSUIT

The study of God is also life's most authentic pursuit. In John 17, Jesus gave His high priestly prayer in which He prays on behalf of His disciples, including you and me:

> Jesus spoke these things; and lifting up His eyes to heaven, He said, "Father, the hour has come; glorify Your Son, that the Son may glorify You, even as You gave Him authority over all flesh, that to all whom You have given Him, He may give eternal life. This is eternal life, that they may know You, the only true God, and Jesus Christ whom You have sent." (vv. 1–3)

Authentic Life

According to Jesus, authentic life is eternal life. Jesus is not referring to how long you are going to live. He's talking about a quality of life in verse 3. Eternal life means knowing God. Life can never be what it was intended to be for you or me unless that life consists of God's life being lived out in us.

Jesus says in verse 3 that the only way you will get eternal life experience in this life is in the knowledge of God. To know God is to live life as it was meant to be lived. That's why Jesus said He came to give us life and to give it to us more abundantly.

To understand life, you have to understand a very simple principle: Eternal life, or the quality of life that God has intended for us, equals the knowledge of Him. Jesus makes a comparative statement in John 17:3. If you want to live, He says, don't go looking for life. Look for the knowledge of God, because authentic life means knowing Him.

Telling the Truth

Only one standard of information clarifies what life is all about: the Word of God. Jesus said to the Father in His prayer in John 17, "Your word is truth" (v. 17). If we are going to live life authentically, we need someone who will tell us the truth. We don't do that with each other. We don't tell people the truth because we don't want to offend them. We don't tell them the truth because we don't want them mad at us. We don't tell them the truth because people like being lied to. Therefore, our relationships are often shallow and never get to where they are supposed to be.

You don't have that problem with God. God calls it as He sees it. He will not tell you, "I'm OK, you're OK." He tells you, "You were dead in your trespasses and in your sins, and you lived according to the flesh, according to the lust of this age." He's not going to make it comfortable or convenient for you. He will tell you the truth, like a good doctor.

The Real You

That's the downside of our study. When God unveils who He is, the knowledge will also unveil who we are. We're faced with the problem Peter had when he ran into Jesus Christ and found out who he was. The revelation of Jesus Christ made Peter fall on his face and say, "I am a sinful man" (Luke 5:8).

The prophet Isaiah saw the Lord and cried out, "Woe is me!" (Isaiah 6:5). Why? Because if you want the real deal, if you really want the truth, God will give you the truth. When you see God as He is, when He unveils Himself, when the true knowledge of God is revealed, it shows you for who you are.

The Real World

The knowledge of God also shows the world for what it is. People spend much time analyzing our world. Philosophers analyze society because people want answers to the fundamental questions of life, such as, Who is man? Where did man come from? Where is he going?

Other people pursue the social analysis of man: how man functions in communication and communion with others, how people relate to each other, how people can stop themselves from hurting one another, and how they can live in peace with one another. The result is often political attempts to make the world right. But when you have the Word of God, you understand the rules of society because God tells the truth about the world.

God also tells the truth about sex, about money, and about all the ingredients that relate to life. He tells the truth about who you are. And so who you are, where you came from, why you are here, and where you are going all come from the knowledge of God.

LIFE'S MOST BENEFICIAL PURSUIT

Nothing will benefit you more in day-to-day living than the knowledge of God. Daniel 11:32 says this: "The people who know their God will display strength and take action."

Daniel was a captive in Babylon, an ungodly nation that was turned over to the Medes and the Persians. Daniel was constantly under oppression. He was constantly being victimized, but he says, "The people who know God even in the midst of a bad situation will know the right steps to take in confronting the issues of life."

Confidence

The knowledge of God gives the ability to make the correct response to the circumstances of life. The people who know their God will have the confidence and ability to do the right thing. You see, the problem today with people who want to correct the social or political order, who want to change this and fix that, is that they want to do good things, but they don't know the right way.

But the people who know their God will move forward with confidence, and take action. Knowledge of God is not passive. It's not something you do on the sidelines. It really frees you up to do something, but to do the right something.

Security

The knowledge of God also gives security in life. Look at Psalm 46:1–3:

> God is our refuge and strength, a very present help in trouble. Therefore we will not fear, though the earth should change and though the mountains slip into the heart of the sea; though its waters roar and foam, though the mountains quake at its swelling pride.

The psalmist says that even when earthquakes shake things up, those who know God will be secure. When the ground under you starts shaking, there isn't much around you to hold onto.

Wisdom

The knowledge of God also gives wisdom. Paul prays in Ephesians 1:17 "that the God of our Lord Jesus Christ, the Father of glory, may give to you a spirit of wisdom and of revelation in the knowledge of Him." Wisdom is spiritual insight for earthly application, the ability to know what God wants and the know-how to apply it where you live. Wisdom is to truth as a shoe is to shoe leather. Wisdom means the ability to take a divine, spiritual perspective and turn it into an earthly, functional application.

Proverbs 9:10 puts it this way: "The fear of the Lord is the beginning of wisdom, and the knowledge of the Holy One is understanding." Solomon says God will show you how to live a wise life. A lot of us have book sense, but we don't have common sense.

It's not that we don't have information; it's just that we don't have wisdom, the ability to apply the knowledge we have. But the knowledge of God can give us wisdom, Proverbs says, the ability to make the right decisions in life.

Order

The apostle Peter says the knowledge of God can give you a well-ordered life:

> Grace and peace be multiplied to you in the knowledge of God and of Jesus our Lord; seeing that His divine power has granted to us everything pertaining to life and godliness, through the true knowledge of Him who called us. (2 Peter 1:2–3)

Peter says the knowledge of God will give you grace, peace, and power. What more could you ask for? A grace life, a peace life, and a divinely powerful life is a well-ordered life, but Peter says it only comes by the true knowledge of God.

Spiritual Fruit

If you allow God to work in your life and transform it, He will give you spiritual development:

> For this reason also, since the day we heard of it, we have not ceased to pray for you and to ask that you may be filled with the knowledge of His will in all spiritual wisdom and understanding, so that you may walk in a manner worthy of the Lord, to please Him in all respects, bearing fruit in every good work and increasing in the knowledge of God. (Colossians 1:9–10)

Paul says that the knowledge of God will change the way you walk. When you know God, you walk differently. You move differently. You act differently. You think differently. Why? Because you are filled with the knowledge of God. With this knowledge comes the knowledge of His will, and the knowledge of His will transforms your life. As He transforms your life, you bear spiritual fruit.

Fruit has two characteristics. First, it always reflects the character of the tree of which it is a part. When you bear spiritual fruit, you begin to look like Christ. Second, fruit is never borne for itself. It is always borne so someone else can take a bite. When you start bearing fruit, other people want to take a bite out of your life. Other people want to be like you, because you are a productive person for the purposes of God.

LIFE'S MOST CHALLENGING PURSUIT

Finally, the study of God is the most challenging pursuit in life:

> Oh, the depth of the riches both of the wisdom and knowledge of God! How unsearchable are His judgments and unfathomable His ways! For who has known the mind of the Lord, or who became His counselor? Or who has first given to Him that it might be paid back to him again? For from Him and through Him and to Him are all things. To Him be the glory forever. Amen. (Romans 11:33–36)

An Eternal Challenge

Do you want a challenge? Decide to get to know God. It's a challenge first because verse 33 says getting to know God will never end. God is never, and will never be, fully comprehensible to man, not only in time, but in eternity.

Any married person can relate to this. You can live with a woman or a man for fifty years and still discover new information. Now, if you can do that with another person over a lifetime, think about our infinite God. It will take eternity and then some to understand Him. The knowledge of God will always be a challenge because you will never learn it all.

A Revealing Challenge

Second, the knowledge of God challenges us because getting to know someone demands that he reveal himself to us and grant us the privilege of that knowledge. It's like a guy who comes up to a lady and says, "My name is John. What's your name?"

Now John may want to get to know her, but is she as interested in knowing him as he is in knowing her? In other words, the knowledge of another person is not just contingent on one person's desire to have that information, but on the other's desire to reveal it. God has made it very clear that He has a passionate desire to reveal Himself to us. In Hosea 6:6, God Himself says, "For I delight in loyalty rather than sacrifice, and in the knowledge of God rather than burnt offerings."

So if you do not come to know God, it is not God's fault because He has made Himself available to be known. And although we can never know

God exhaustively, we can know Him intimately. Anyone who has ever dated and gotten serious with someone knows that as two people get to know each other, a growing process of intimacy develops. A transformation occurs over time. That's what happens with God. As you come to know Him, you will discover a growing process of intimacy, a closeness where you feel that you know Him and you want to know Him more.

A Priority Challenge

Knowing God is also a challenge because it must be your priority. Deuteronomy 4:29 says that you must search for God with all your heart if you would find Him. The sage says that the knowledge of God is like a man searching for silver (Proverbs 2:4). Where can silver be found? Underneath the ground, so dig.

Why has God not made it easy? Because He wants to know, "How serious are you? You get up and work out because you're serious. But when you've got to get up and spend time with Me, you're too tired. You need that extra fifteen minutes of sleep. Are you serious? You have time to watch your favorite TV show, but you are always too tired to spend time with Me. Are you serious?"

Getting to know God is a challenge because it's hard work to make it a priority. So where do you start? First of all, you must start with a desire to know God. Moses said in Exodus 33:13, "Let me know Your ways that I may know You." David said, "As the deer pants for the water brooks, so my soul pants for You, O God" (Psalm 42:1). Paul said his greatest longing was "that I may know Him" (Philippians 3:10). Jesus said, "Blessed are those who hunger and thirst for righteousness, for they shall be satisfied" (Matthew 5:6).

All of them say the same thing. God only feeds hungry people. If you are not hungry, ask God to give you a new spiritual appetite as you study this book.

PERSONAL APPLICATION FOR LIFE

1. The true beginning point in knowing God is entering into a relationship with Him through the Lord Jesus Christ. If you have never trusted Christ as your Savior, or if you are unsure of your standing before God, all you need to do is admit that you are a sinner (see Romans 3:9–10:23) and cannot save yourself (Acts 4:12). Acknowledge that Jesus paid for your sin on the cross (Romans 5:8), and put your faith in Him alone to save you. Call upon Him to save you today (Romans 10:13), receive Him as your Savior (1 John 1:12)—and welcome to the family. Be sure to tell your pastor or a Christian friend about your decision.

2. All of us cling to things that give us a sense of identity and importance, whether job titles, family heritage, bank accounts, or material possessions. List three of the things that are most important to you, and ask yourself what would happen if you lost them. Could you give them up and still say things are OK because you know the true God and that's enough? It's worth thinking about as you read this book.

3. Perhaps you know a step of obedience and faith that God wants you to take, but you're holding back for fear of what people will think or what the outcome might be. If so, remember that the people who know their God can be strong and take action. Take that needed step, and trust God for the consequences. He will bless you for taking Him at His Word.

4. Speaking of the Word, there's no better way to know God than to hide His Word in your heart and mind. Proverbs 9:10 would be a great verse to memorize over the next few days or weeks: "The fear of the Lord is the beginning of wisdom, and the knowledge of the Holy One is understanding." It captures the theme of this book. If it helps, write it on a card and carry it with you for review until you know the verse well.

FOR GROUP STUDY

Questions for Group Discussion

1. The knowledge of God can give us wisdom to help make the right decisions in our lives. In what areas of life may we apply the wisdom that comes from the knowledge of God?

2. One by-product of the knowledge of God is that it has the power to transform our lives, if we allow it. The Bible uses the analogy of bearing fruit when describing spiritual development. What are some of the characteristics of fruit? What are the results of bearing spiritual fruit? Discuss Galatians 5:22 and John 15:5.

3. Dr. Evans says that knowing God has to be a priority for us. What are some practical ways we can meet this challenge and make knowing God a priority in the midst of busy lifestyles? Where do we start?

4. One of the benefits of the knowledge of God is security in the midst of the upheavals of life. Psalm 46:1 describes God as our "refuge," "strength," and "a very present help in trouble." Do a study on what those images tell us about God and how they relate to a believer's security in life.

PICTURE THIS

What we already have learned about God should create a greater desire to know Him. There is always something new to know about God and, as we discover, our knowledge of Him becomes increasingly enriching.

THE WEALTH OF BENEFITS FROM KNOWING GOD

BENEFIT	SCRIPTURE PASSAGE	WAYS WE BENEFIT
Power	Daniel 11:32	The circumstances of life cannot hold us down.
Peace	1 Peter 1:2	A growing sense of inner peace and comfort.
Wisdom	John 1:17	Making the right choices and better decisions.
Growth	Colossians 1:9–10	Spiritual growth and productivity.
Freedom	Galatians 4:8–9	Assurance and confidence to live freely from the circumstances and emotions that can enslave us.

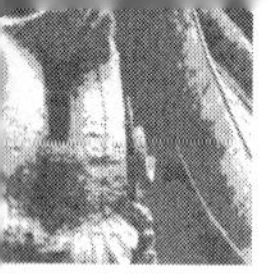

2

THE NATURE OF GOD

Once upon a time a scorpion needed to cross a pond. Wondering how he would get to the other side, he noticed a frog nearby. "Mr. Frog, will you please hop me across this pond?"

The kind, gentle frog said, "Certainly, Mr. Scorpion. I will be glad to do so."

So Mr. Scorpion jumped onto Mr. Frog's back as Mr. Frog hopped from pod to pod, bringing Mr. Scorpion to the other side of the pond. But just as the frog said, "Well, Mr. Scorpion, here we are," he felt an excruciating pain in his back. Mr. Scorpion had stung him.

As Mr. Frog lay dying, he looked up at Mr. Scorpion and said, "How could you do this? I brought you from one side of the pond to the other and now you sting me so that I die."

Mr. Scorpion looked at Mr. Frog and said, "I can't help it. It's my nature."

It's important to know the nature of the one you are dealing with. If you think you are getting one thing, but when you get it it's not what you thought it was, you could be in trouble. That happens today with a lot of errant teaching about who God is. God has been so misdefined, tragically redefined, and even dismissed that people do not understand His true nature.

When we talk about the nature of something, we mean what is intrinsic to its being. When we talk about the nature of God, we speak of characteristics intrinsic to His being. What does He do naturally? To some people God appears a tyrant, so they are waiting for their next whipping. To others, He's a joke. To still others, God seems like a nice grandfather with a long, white beard, kind of gentle to be around but with very little influence. Or He's just a bigger, better version of man.

But if we are going to have an intimate walk with God, we must understand what makes Him tick—His true nature. That's what I want to do in this chapter—consider the character of God, His nature, by looking at five areas that will help us grasp the greatness of our God.

GOD IS A TRANSCENDENT BEING

God exists above His creation. A key passage for this wonderful truth is Isaiah 40. Verse 18 asks, "To whom then will you liken God? Or what likeness will you compare with Him?" The prophet then goes on in verses 19–25 to contrast the true God to idols made by man and gives an awesome description of God's limitless power.

When we say that God is transcendent, we mean that He is totally distinct from His creation. The word *distinct* is a synonym for transcendent. God is unique. He is one of a kind. You can make no comparison that will give you an understanding of God unless He grants that comparison, because there is nothing you can compare Him to.

Distinct in His Thoughts

The Bible declares that God is distinct from us in His thoughts. In Isaiah 55 the Lord says:

> "My thoughts are not your thoughts, neither are your ways My ways," declares the Lord. "For as the heavens are higher than the earth, so are My ways higher than your ways and My thoughts than your thoughts." (vv. 8–9)

Many times you hear people say, "Well, I don't believe God will do that." How do they know, if His thoughts are not like their thoughts? God is transcendent in His thinking. He does things totally differently than the way we do things. He operates in a totally different way than anything we've ever seen before.

Distinct in His Person

Psalm 50:21 says that God is totally unlike man. He looks at man and says, "I am not like you." So when you deal with God, you are not dealing with an elevated man. The great French agnostic Voltaire said, "God created man in His own image, and man returned the favor." God created man, and we've reduced our unique God to just a Superman. But He remains totally, utterly, absolutely transcendent.

Distinct in His Deity

Psalm 97:9 says God is "exalted far above all gods." He is also "exalted above all the peoples" (Psalm 99:2). God is absolute deity, and He cannot be compared with anything you've ever seen or known before. That truth contains heavy implications relative to the transcendent nature or distinctiveness of God. The first of the Ten Commandments says we are to have no other god because there is only one true God. Then the second commandment says we are not to make any likeness of God (Exodus 20:3–4).

This means we must not paint pictures of God. Now let me explain. I'm sure you are familiar with those photo booths they have in the malls. You go in, put in some coins, sit down, and draw the curtain. The light comes on, you get in your pose, and the camera snaps. Some ugly pictures come out of those machines, don't they?

Someone says to you, "Show me a picture of your girlfriend (or wife or husband)." You dig in your wallet or purse and pull out the picture, and then you always say, "This isn't a good shot. If you really saw what she looks like in real life, you would understand. This just gives you a general idea."

We apologize for a bad picture. God says, "Don't make any likeness of Me, because anything you come up with will make Me look bad." We are to make no likenesses of God to enable us to worship Him other than those He prescribes. When people paint pictures of God—or even Jesus, since we don't know what He looked like—and then use those pictures as objects to enhance worship, that's idolatry. When we put up crosses to help us worship God better, that's idolatry.

If you want to buy something to decorate your wall, or because you enjoy its artistic value or because it's just jewelry to you, that's one thing. But you cannot use any emblems or symbols to enhance your worship other than the ones God prescribes, like the bread and wine. These are designed to show forth the death and resurrection of Christ, and they are legitimate parts of corporate worship because God prescribes them. Otherwise, He says, "You cannot create, on your own, likenesses of Me because I am totally distinct and you would limit My glory if you did that."

GOD IS A SPIRIT BEING

During Jesus' encounter with the Samaritan woman in John 4, He makes a very important statement about His essential nature. They are talking about worship, and Jesus says, "An hour is coming, and now is, when the true worshipers will worship the Father in spirit and truth; for such people the Father seeks to be His worshipers. God is spirit . . ." (vv. 23–24a).

Please notice that "spirit" has no article. God is not "the" Spirit, God is spirit; that is, spirit is His essence, who He is. This phrase comes at the front of the sentence in Greek for emphasis, so Jesus is saying, "I want to emphasize why you must worship God in spirit and truth."

God Is Immaterial

"God is spirit." What does it mean to say something is spirit? First of all, it means that God is nonmaterial. He is immaterial; that is, He does not have a body. Jesus said in Luke 24:39 that spirits don't have bodies.

Jesus does have a body, but that's because He became man, not because of His eternal essence. God's essence is immaterial. Now, the God of the Bible knows that we have trouble with that because we function in a world that needs bodies for us to understand things. So the Bible contains many *anthropomorphisms*, a word for your theological dictionary. This term is made up of two Greek words: *anthropos*, which means "man"; and *morphos*, which means "form."

In other words, God speaks to us in "man-forms." The Bible may say, "The hand of the Lord is mighty to save," or, "The eye of the Lord can see." The Bible may talk about God's back, His face, or His ears. Those are anthropomorphisms, the use of human descriptions to help us relate to a spirit being we could not relate to otherwise.

But even though God allows Himself to be described in human terms, when it comes to worship He says, "You must worship Me in My essence." God is spirit, even though He speaks and uses material objects to make clear who He is.

God Is a Person

The second thing you need to know about God as spirit is that He is a person. John 4:24 says, "Those who worship *Him*" (italics added). God is a person who has the three attributes of personhood: emotions or feelings, intellect or the mind, and will or the power to choose. Those three things make people distinct from the rest of creation. God is a person because He feels, thinks, and chooses.

So when I speak of God as spirit, I do not mean that He's not a person. He is an immaterial person. The classic statement of God's personhood is His answer to Moses in Exodus 3:14. Moses wanted to know what he should tell the children of Israel when they asked who had sent him. God said "I AM WHO I AM. . . . Thus shall you say to the sons of Israel, 'I AM has sent me to you.'"

God Is Invisible

If God is spirit, not only is He immaterial, not only is He a person, but He is also invisible: "No one has seen God at any time" (John 1:18). That verse means just what it says. No one has ever seen God. Moses once prayed, "Show me Your glory" (Exodus 33:18). But the Bible says that God had to hide Moses "in the cleft of the rock" lest Moses see God and die (v. 22).

That's why when you go to heaven, you must have a new body. This body can't stand the heat. I know some people run around saying they have seen God. No, they just had too much pizza. "No one has seen God at any time." The only revelation of God in terms of full visibility—although clothed in humanity—is the person of Christ.

But that's also why prayer gets boring unless your spirit is growing, because you can't see anything. Your spirit can see because prayer is spirit to spirit, but if you're not developing spiritually, you won't have much dynamic with God because He does not exist as a physical being, someone you can see.

GOD IS AN ETERNAL BEING

A third truth we need to know about the nature of our great God is that He is eternal. Moses declared:

> Lord, Thou hast been our dwelling place in all generations. Before the mountains were born, or Thou didst give birth to the earth and the world, even from everlasting to everlasting, Thou art God. (Psalm 90:1–2)

He Has No Beginning

"From everlasting to everlasting"—that's a long time! When did God begin? From everlasting—but if you exist from everlasting, you have no starting point. To put it another way, there has never been a time when God was not. Now don't try to figure that one out or it will drive you stark raving mad. I remember when I was a young Christian, I just stood in my room one day thinking about the fact that God has no beginning. But how can something not have a beginning?

We are creatures of history because we are linear creatures. By that I mean we go from point A to point B to point C, from one to ten. We go from this event to that event to the next event, one after the other. We are creatures of the past, the present, and the future. We are linear, successive creatures, but that is irrelevant to God. He knows about history because He's the God of history, but history doesn't control Him. Remember that He told Moses, "I AM WHO I AM."

That verb *am* is very important because it means that God forever lives in the present tense. He has no past. He has no future.

He Is Independent

The eternality of God also means, as we've seen already, that God is independent. Everything created needs something outside of itself to exist. But God depends on nothing outside Himself to exist. He is self-generating. Before there was earth or anything else, God was. When the earth was created, God had already existed millions of years. In fact, even that is an understatement, since one can go back into eternity forever and never find a time when God did not exist.

GOD IS AN IMMUTABLE BEING

God is not only transcendent, eternal spirit, He is also immutable. Immutability means not having the ability to change. "Every good thing bestowed and every perfect gift is from above, coming down from the Father of lights, with whom there is no variation, or shifting shadow" (James 1:17).

Changeless in His Person

God cannot, does not, will not change. That makes Him unlike everything else in creation. The second law of thermodynamics says that every transformation of energy is accompanied by a loss of available energy, so that future use of that energy is no longer available to the same degree. We change constantly, but God does not change. His Word does not change (Psalm 119:89).

Changeless in His Purpose

The writer of Hebrews testifies that God's purpose is unchangeable (immutable, incapable of change), and to prove it God swore "by two unchangeable [immutable] things, in which it is impossible for God to lie" (Hebrews 6:17–18). God's character does not change. Neither does His love (Jeremiah 31:3). The Son of God does not change, for "Jesus Christ is the same yesterday and today, yes and forever" (Hebrews 13:8). God's plans do not change (Psalm 33:11), and His knowledge is the same today as it was on the day He created the world. Do you get the point? God does not, cannot, and will not ever change!

Changeless in His Character

Whenever we talk about God's immutability, someone always says, "Wait a minute. The Bible talks about God changing His mind. In fact, He changed His mind about destroying Israel after Aaron built the golden calf."

That's true as far as it goes. The Bible does say that God was going to destroy the people for their sin (Exodus 32:10). But Moses pleaded with God not to do it, "so the Lord changed His mind about the harm which He said He would do to His people" (v. 14). So we've got a problem here.

If God doesn't change, how can He change His mind?

Although God's character does not ever change, His methods may. Here's what I mean. God's character is constant; however, if a change on man's part affects another part of God's character, God is then free to relate to that person out of that part of His character rather than out of the previous part of His character. For example, God was going to destroy Nineveh because of its sin. When the people there repented, God did not change His mind about sin. In their repentance they appealed to another part of God's character, His grace. God had been dealing with them from one part of His character, His wrath against sin. Now their repentance brought them another part of His character.

By the way, God has given us proof that He will never change: the rainbow. The rainbow was God's promise to Noah that He would never destroy the earth by water again. Destroying mankind in the flood hurt God so badly that He said, "I'll never do it again, and to let you know I'll give you a rainbow as a sign in the heavens." Every time you see a rainbow, you need to say, "Thank You, Lord. You don't change. You are constant." God is immutable. He does not change.

GOD IS A TRIUNE BEING

This is the final truth we want to examine. Let me set the parameters to begin. There is only one God. Deuteronomy 6:4 affirms, "The Lord is our God, the Lord is one." God Himself declares, "Besides Me there is no God" (Isaiah 45:5). The apostle Paul says the same thing: "There is no God but one" (1 Corinthians 8:4).

One God in Three Persons

However, this one God is made up of three distinct Persons: Father, Son, and Holy Spirit. The word we use for this is *Trinity*. This word does not appear in the Bible, but the teaching of the "threeness" of God shows up all through the Bible. This is difficult for many people to understand.

But it shouldn't be any problem for us. Do you know why? Because God is transcendent. He's not like us. Many Bible teachers have struggled to illustrate this. Some use water, which can be liquid, ice, or steam, but all three have the same two parts hydrogen, one part oxygen. Others try to illustrate the concept of the Trinity with the egg. An egg has a shell, a white, and a yolk, but it's all one egg.

We can also illustrate the Trinity by means of a simple pretzel which has three holes, each distinct from the other two, yet all intimately tied together into one whole. The Father is not the Son or the Spirit, but all three Persons make up one God because they all share the same divine essence, or attributes.

The Trinity in Creation

The Bible gives us a lot of information about the Trinity. First of all, we see the plurality of God in creation. "In the beginning God created the heavens and the earth" (Genesis 1:1). The Hebrew word for God here is *Elohim*, a plural word.

He shows this in the creation of man, because in Genesis 1:26, God says, "Let *Us* make man in *Our* image" (italics added). But then the very next verse says, "God created man in *His* own image" (italics added). The text moves freely from plural to singular and back to plural. Why? Because our one God is made up of three Persons.

We also get a glimpse of the Trinity in Isaiah 48:16, where the preincarnate Christ says, "The Lord God has sent Me, and His Spirit," associating God the Father with the Son and the Holy Spirit. That's why you can have Jesus on the cross saying to the Father, "Why hast Thou forsaken Me?" They are two different Persons. The Father is not the Son; the Son is not the Spirit. But the Father is God, the Son is God, and the Spirit is God. All three are equal in essence as part of the singular Godhead while remaining distinct from each other in their personhood.

The plurality of God also appears in the descriptions of God. The Father is called God (Galatians 1:1, 3; Ephesians 1:2–3). The Son is called God (John 20:28). The Holy Spirit is called God (Acts 5:3–4). In fact, in Hebrews 1:8, God the Father calls God the Son "God."

Thus all three act in unity, one God in three Persons, equal in essence though distinct in function. So how do we conclude? With 1 Timothy 1:17, where Paul writes to this young preacher: "Now to the King eternal, immortal, invisible, the only God, be honor and glory forever and ever. Amen."

PERSONAL APPLICATION FOR LIFE

1. Let God be God. This may sound elementary, but we often fall into the trap of trying to confine God to our perceptions of Him. One sign of this common malady is thinking or saying things like, "God would never allow that." If this is a problem for you, go to the Lord in prayer and give Him permission to be Lord in your heart.

2. Related to our tendency to box God in is our inclination to make bargains with Him. They may be well-meaning bargains and sometimes they are even unspoken, but we cannot put God on a performance basis. We can't say, "I'll give to Your work with the understanding that You will bless my finances." God may want to bless you anyway, but He doesn't do deals. Got any "deals" working with God right now? Cancel them.

3. Sometimes we turn things around the other way and put ourselves on a performance basis, figuring that the better we are, the more God will love us. But Colossians 2 says you are already complete in Christ in terms of your standing before Him. You don't have to work harder to make yourself more acceptable to Him. Rejoice in that wonderful truth; let it sink deep into your soul. Then enjoy the fact that you are free to serve Him out of love and gratitude, not because it's your duty.

4. If you want to make knowing God a priority in your life, it means you're going to have to say no to some things, even good things. Have you said no to anything lately so you can say yes to God's invitation to know Him intimately?

FOR GROUP STUDY

Questions for Group Discussion

1. Have group members share the insights they have gained from observing God at work in their lives. The insights of one member can be an encouragement to the entire group. How do your insights relate to the nature of God discussion of this current lesson?

2. As Dr. Evans warns, we must be careful not to paint pictures of God. Our proper "view" of God comes from having a personal relationship with His Son, Jesus Christ. As a basis for this discussion, read Isaiah 40:18.

   Do you always view God as He really is? It's easy for us to "assign" human traits to God and have a very limited view of His nature. During the course of a normal day, what are some ways you knowingly or unknowingly compare God's responses to human behavior? When you experience a crisis, how do you view God? What steps might we all take to correct and realign our thinking about God with regard to His nature?

3. In 1 Timothy 1:17, the apostle Paul gives us a doxology loaded with meaning—a mini-lesson on God's nature. Using your Bible as its own commentary, trace the key words of this doxology. For starters, *immortal* (Romans 1:23); *invisible* (Colossians 1:15); *only God* (Romans 16:27; John 5:44; 17:3); *glory* (1 Chronicles 29:11); *forever and ever* (Ephesians 3:21).

4. In Exodus 3:14, God described Himself as "I AM WHOM I AM." That description tells us that He forever lives in the present tense. Focus on the present tense verb "am" and how the incarnate Son of God applied this "I am" theme to His teaching. From John's gospel, include in your study: 6:41; 8:12; 10:9; 11:25; and 14:6.

PICTURE THIS

We are to "worship the Father in spirit and truth" (John 4:23-24). How can a human being relate to God who is spirit? God has created within each person the capacity to relate to Him. We all possess the "image of God" (Genesis 1:26-27). That image within us includes at least an intellect, a volition, and emotion. It is with these elements of our personality that we can relate to God's truth.

RELATING TO THE GOD OF THE UNIVERSE

IMAGE OF GOD IN US	SCRIPTURE PASSAGE	HOW WE RELATE TO GOD'S TRUTH
Our intellect	"Your Word is truth" (John 17:17)	With our minds we learn the truth and think God's thoughts after Him.
Our emotions	The Son is truth (John 14:6)	With our hearts we embrace the truth and express our love for God's Son.
Our volition	The Spirit is truth (John 14:17)	With our wills we obey the truth and respond to the ministry of the Holy Spirit.

SECTION II

The Attributes of God

3. The Sufficiency of God
4. The Holiness of God
5. The Sovereignty of God
6. The Glory of God
7. The Omniscience of God
8. The Omnipresence of God
9. The Omnipotence of God
10. The Wisdom of God
11. The Goodness of God
12. The Wrath of God
13. The Love of God
14. The Grace of God

3

THE SUFFICIENCY OF GOD

Because God is a person, He bears all the attributes of personhood in absolute perfection. We share some of His attributes, such as love and anger, but God also possesses divine attributes that belong to Him alone. In chapters 3–14, we will look at twelve unique attributes of God—distinct qualities that make God uniquely God. We begin with the attribute known as God's sufficiency.

This attribute of God means He is totally and absolutely complete within Himself. Nothing can be added to or taken away from God. That thought defies comprehension because we don't know anything else like that in our universe. But that explains why the Bible says nothing compares to God.

It frustrates autonomous men that they can't put a limit on God. They can't box Him in. The test tubes don't work when it comes to Him. The mathematical formulas don't equate when it comes to God because His sufficiency means that all that makes God who He is already resides within Him.

That doesn't mean we Christians have God figured out. Trying to comprehend the subject of God overwhelms us because it only reveals how little we know. Sometimes I think it's better if I don't study it so I won't know how ignorant I am. The study of God can be intimidating because it lets us know how great He is, and in the process it lets us know how small we are. But He invites us to know Him. So I want to observe four truths about the sufficiency of God.

GOD IS RESPONSIBLE FOR HIS CREATION

The sufficiency of God means that He is totally responsible for all of creation. Colossians 1, in a reference to the second Person of the Trinity, puts it so clearly:

> And He is the image of the invisible God, the first-born of all creation. For by Him all things were created, both in the heavens and on earth, visible and invisible, whether thrones or dominions or rulers or authorities—all things have been created by Him and for Him. (vv. 15–16)

Creation Reveals His Person

These verses tell us that the glory of God's all-inclusiveness can be realized by all the variety that exists within His creation. If you want to see how glorious God is, He invites you, "Look at what I have done." If you really want to know how sufficient, how good, how complete something is, look at what it produces. If it produces glorious results, then the one responsible for that production must be more glorious than the thing produced. All of us can look at nature and see that "the heavens are telling of the glory of God" (Psalm 19:1).

That's why God does not spend time trying to prove His existence to atheists. Only a fool would reject the existence of God after looking at a creation as complex and orderly as this world. All the things that make life what it is prove that we have an all-sufficient God and that none is like Him. God asked Job, "Where were you when I created the universe?" God was saying to Job that by virtue of His creation, the greatness of who He is becomes evident.

Creation Reveals His Pleasure

Do you ever do anything just because it makes you feel good? You don't have to do it. You have no need to do it, but you just enjoy doing it. God created the universe out of His own good pleasure. In fact, Ephesians 1:5 says that God does all things out of Himself simply because it pleases Him to do so. God's self-sufficiency shows in the fact that when He wants to do something, He does it.

God has a patent on creation because creation comes from Him. God can create because He is sufficient within Himself to produce anything He wants to exist.

And when God creates, He only has to speak the word. He doesn't have to go through trauma, draw up blueprints, or form construction companies. Within Himself He holds the power to pull off anything.

GOD IS INDEPENDENT OF HIS CREATION

One of the great passages of Scripture is Paul's sermon to the Greeks in Athens as they were groping after the true God. Paul begins, "While I was passing through and examining the objects of your worship, I also found an altar with this inscription, 'TO AN UNKNOWN GOD.' Therefore what you worship in ignorance, this I proclaim to you" (Acts 17:23).

In this classic passage Paul explains to people who want to know the true God, the God who created heaven and earth and everything in it, that this God is independent of His creation. By independent I mean that God does not need anything from His created order to enable Him to continue being God. God does not function out of necessity.

No Outside Influences

All of us can explain who we are by virtue of the influences in our lives. I can describe where I am today by pointing to the influence of my parents. I can tell you the schools I went to that educated me, expanded my vocabulary, and gave me a perspective of different sciences. I can explain the clothes on my back by talking about someone who took animal skins or pieces of cloth and stitched them together.

But God has no such explanation. No influences have ever made God what He is. All that God is and always was He always will be. You cannot offer anything that will enhance Him, nor can you take anything away that will detract from Him.

No Necessary Relationships

This understanding can enhance our worship of God, because while God has a voluntary relationship to everything, He has a necessary relationship to nothing. In other words, God relates to His creation because He chooses to, not because He needs to. For example, if you show up for worship at your church, that's good and God is glad to see you. But He will not be worse off if you stay home. He's not going to panic.

Several reasons may help explain this. First, God's worship is within Himself. God adores Himself already. He's not like people, who want compliments. One time my wife told me, "You didn't say anything about my new dress." I didn't see her new dress. I didn't even know it was a new dress.

God does not need to be noticed. He does not need recognition. It is not God's privilege that we get to worship, but our privilege. We come to worship God because He's asked us to, not because He needs us to. You do not add to God, because if you don't worship Him, someone else will.

In Isaiah 6:2–3, the Bible tells us absolutely clearly that God has beings in heaven who worship Him twenty-four hours a day. That's all the seraphim do, and guess what? They're tickled to death to do it! They don't sleep, they don't slumber, all they do is exalt the name of God.

No External Needs

So God does not need you or me. We need Him. God is sufficient, complete within Himself. He does not need anything in His created order to make Him feel better about being God. Job 22:2–3 says that God receives no benefit from man.

Job underscores that again by reminding us that man at his best offers nothing of benefit to God (Job 35:7–8). Jesus said that even our best, when it's placed against God, makes us "unworthy slaves" (Luke 17:10). This is true for entire nations too. "The nations are like a drop from a bucket . . . a speck of dust on the scales" to God (Isaiah 40:15). He simply blows on them and they cease to exist.

God's self-sufficiency also means He is answerable to no one. He does not need our permission to do what He plans to do. Our complaints don't make a difference either. God can do this because He is the self-sufficient, independent, self-existent God who has life within Himself. Since nothing is greater than God that could produce God, He is the greatest Being that has ever existed.

Some Implications

What are the implications of God's independence? First, it means that you cannot help God out. God will do what He is going to do no matter what you do. Therefore, He cannot be intimidated. You can't threaten Him.

Second, God does not need to be defended. He can defend Himself. He can move people and nations. He can shut down and raise up things.

Third, God's independence means that He does not depend on us. He enjoys us and wants our worship and fellowship, as we will see. But when you come to know God, you have to bank on Him, not the other way around.

WE ARE DEPENDENT ON GOD'S SUFFICIENCY

Here we see the other side of the equation. God's creation is not independent of Him. Let's look again at Paul's sermon in Acts 17:

> He made from one man every nation of mankind to live on all the face of the earth, having determined their appointed times, and the boundaries of their habitation, that they should seek God, if perhaps they might grope for Him and find Him, though He is not far from each one of us; for in Him we live and move and exist. (vv. 26–28)

Our Reference Point

In God we move and have our being. Paul makes the point that we cannot know ourselves apart from God. You will never know who you are, where you came from, why you are here, or where you are going apart from God. In Him, you live. In Him, you move. In Him, you exist. God appointed when you were born, and He has appointed when you will die. I don't care how much you jog; you will not postpone that date. It is determined and appointed by God.

Our Inescapable God

When men rebel against God, they only create an environment where, instead of enjoying His love, they must endure His wrath. Even in hell men will not get away from God. You can do nothing to get rid of God. Since you can't beat God or get away from Him, rather than resisting God, why not be a cooperator under Him so that you can enjoy His benefits? We are all dependent on God.

Even if you couldn't see it, the sun would still shine. You can't get mad at the sun and say, "I can't see you, sun, so stop shining." The sun will shine because that's what the sun does. God is going to be God because that's what God does.

If you don't believe in God, if you reject Him, He's still God. If you don't want Him to be God, He's still God. If you curse Him, He's still God. If you don't acknowledge Him, He's still God because God is not dependent on us; we are dependent on Him. If anyone has to jump, we have to jump—not God.

Let me summarize. God is sufficient within Himself. He is responsible for everything we see, all of creation, yet He is independent of His creation. He can do whatever He wants. By virtue of the fact that we live, move, and have our being in Him, we are utterly dependent on Him. All that we are is because of all that He is.

WE FIND OUR COMPLETENESS ONLY IN GOD

I don't know of any more important statement I can make than this: God's sufficiency means that we can find our completeness only in Him. This truth appears all through the Bible, but I want to take one of the most beautiful poetic passages in Scripture to make this final, all-important point.

David wrote Psalm 23 while reflecting on his old occupation as a shepherd. David knew God. The Psalms reflect his intimacy with God and his knowledge of God. God Himself said that David was a man after His own heart (Acts 13:22). As he reflected, David realized that what he as a shepherd was to his sheep, God was to him.

So David wrote, "The Lord is my shepherd, I shall not want" (Psalm 23:1). He says that if you simply let God be God, you will have no lack. Many of us are failing in our lives because we want to make God into a man. David is saying, "Let God be God."

When sheep try to make shepherds into sheep, the sheep are going to be confused. But as long as sheep let the shepherd be the shepherd, they will have someone to lead them where they ought to go.

Stop trying to get God to be like you, and simply let God be God. When you do that, He will let you be you as you ought to be.

Spiritual Needs

"He makes me lie down in green pastures; He leads me beside quiet waters. He restores my soul" (vv. 2–3a). David says if the Lord is your shepherd, He will meet your spiritual needs. He is not referring to drinking water or eating green grass here, because if you were drinking the water, it wouldn't be quiet. And if you ate the grass, the pasture wouldn't be green but bare.

No, a carpet of green grass and quiet waters is a picture of rest. David's point is that God gives you back your life. Life is full of frustration. But if you will let God be God even in the midst of life's pressures and pain, when you submit who you are to who He is, He gives you back your soul. He gives you spiritual rejuvenation

The Bible tells us about two roads. The broad way leads to destruction. The other way is narrow and leads to life. The broad road is crowded. A lot of parties happen on that road. A lot of traffic comes down that road, a lot of good times. But no filling stations can be seen on the broad road. When you run out of gas, you are finished. You have to pull over to the side.

The narrow road looks less pretty and less crowded. You don't have as much fanfare, but Jesus Christ moves up and down the narrow road. Yes, you might have to pull over in a ditch, but He refuels your tank so you can keep on keeping on. He restores your soul. He meets your spiritual needs.

Directional Needs

David continues, "He guides me in the paths of righteousness for His name's sake" (v. 3b). When David led sheep, every now and then a dumb sheep would wander off on the wrong road. David would leave the flock and find that one sheep, pick it up, put it on his shoulder, and take it by the right path back to the fold.

What David did for sheep, God does for His sheep; that is, He can take a lost sheep and make it found. He can take wrong decisions and make them right. He can take you going down the wrong road in life and, if you will reconnect with Him, put you on the right road. He can take a bad situation and make it good.

If the Lord is your shepherd, He will meet your directional needs. He guides you in life. Maybe you didn't know you would be where you are today, but the Good Shepherd knows the right road for His sheep. If you will simply let God be God, He will restore your soul. If you will let Him be the sufficient God, stop giving Him advice and simply do what He says, He will direct you down the right road.

Emotional Needs

"Even though I walk through the valley of the shadow of death, I fear no evil; for You are with me; Your rod and Your staff, they comfort me" (v. 4).

When sheep get lost, they come between two mountains or two crevices and if it is the right time of day, the sun casts a shadow over the path. Not being very smart, the sheep see the shadow and think night is coming. Of course, sheep are afraid at night. David says that when the shadows of life come over us and we think we have no hope and things are out of kilter, God stands by us with His rod and staff.

The rod was a club the shepherd had designed to pulverize the hyenas and foxes that tried to prey on the sheep. The staff was a long stick with a hook on it so the shepherd could reach into the bushes and pull a sheep out when it got caught in the thicket.

David had gotten caught in the thickets of life because of his immorality. He had committed adultery with Bathsheba and murdered her husband. He was all tangled up. The shadow of death came over him, but when he dealt with his sins and returned to God, God's rod protected him. God's staff pulled him back in, and God's grace covered him. If the Lord is your shepherd, He can keep fear from overwhelming you.

When the Lord is your shepherd, He takes care of your emotional needs. As the psalmist puts it, "He giveth his beloved sleep" (Psalm 127:2 KJV). He gives you the ability to sleep regardless of the circumstances around you. God will meet your emotional needs so that you can say, "I will fear no evil."

Physical Needs

God will also meet your physical needs, according to Psalm 23:5: "You prepare a table before me in the presence of my enemies; You have anointed my head with oil; my cup overflows."

Inside the belt shepherds wore was a little cloth and a pouch. In the pouch were fodder and grains, so whenever David found a lost sheep he would spread the cloth on the ground and put the food from his little pouch on the cloth. That was the "table" for the sheep. Foxes and hyenas hung around, but not only could they not eat the sheep, they could not eat what the sheep was eating because of the shepherd's presence.

He would also take a cup that he carried on his belt, dip it in water, and as he walked over to the sheep the water would splash out the top of the cup. The cup would be running over, letting the sheep know that there was going to be more than enough water to satisfy his thirst.

God is saying that what David was to his sheep, He is to His children. He is so sufficient that the running over of your cup does not depend on what the economy does. It does not depend on recession or inflation. It does not depend on who is laying off or who is hiring. When you stay in God's will and God's way, He gives you your daily bread. He meets your needs.

Eternal Needs

Finally, God is sufficient for your eternal needs. "Surely goodness and lovingkindness will follow me all the days of my life, and I will dwell in the house of the Lord forever" (v. 6). God is good not only for time, but for eternity. If you know Jesus Christ, He's sufficient!

If you are down, He's what you need to lift you up. If you don't know which decision to make, He's who you need to direct your path. If you are afraid about how the world is going, He is able to give you sleep. If you are not sure about where you are going to live forever, He's all you need to get your eternal destiny straight.

Now I have a question: Is there any issue in your life that doesn't fit into one of these categories? Your needs are either spiritual, directional, emotional, physical, or eternal. God is sufficient for all of them. Everything you need can be covered by the sufficiency of God as you live under His authority, according to His will, and in concert with His Word. If you come to know Him and live in Him obediently, willingly, and voluntarily, God will demonstrate to you His sufficiency.

So the only question on the floor is, Is the Lord your shepherd? Only if you let Him be your Shepherd will you learn that He is sufficient for your needs. God is sufficient by virtue of His creation. God is sufficient by virtue of His independence. God is sufficient by virtue of our dependence. Therefore, we can find our completeness only in Him.

PERSONAL APPLICATION FOR LIFE

1. How long has it been since you thought about the fact that God created you out of His good pleasure? He wanted to create you. You are incredibly valuable to Him. Thank the Lord that He loves you so much—and ask Him to help you see other people in this light.

2. List the three biggest trials or challenges you're facing right now. Beside each trial, write down at least one way that you know God is sufficient to meet your need. Ask Him to deal with each need in the way He sees best.

3. Maybe you're the independent type. Can you find any area of your life where you've excluded God, even unconsciously, because you feel perfectly capable of handling that area? Give this question some prayerful, heart-searching thought, and be prepared to respond to whatever God shows you.

4. Take the psalmist-shepherd's advice and find a carpet of green grass and quiet waters. In other words, take a retreat to get alone and commune with God—whether it's a day away from the routine, an early-morning walk, or just a few minutes alone in your office or bedroom where you pull the blinds and shut the door for a brief time of uninterrupted solitude.

FOR GROUP STUDY

Questions for Group Discussion

1. As Psalm 23 teaches, we find our completeness in God. This very familiar psalm has many great lessons. In verse 1, because of the Shepherd's care, the psalmist concludes, "I shall not want." Our needs fit into five categories: spiritual, directional, emotional, physical, and eternal. Discuss how God meets our general or your specific needs. What verse or verses can you claim from Psalm 23?

2. Dr. Evans makes the point that God's creation reveals His person. If we want to see how glorious God is, God invites us to look at what He has done. Certainly all of us have looked at a clear night sky and seen that "the heavens are telling of the glory of God" (Psalm 19:1). Have group members take a turn relating something they have observed about God's creation that made them stop and think about the Creator. Perhaps it was the design and complexity of the human body. Or the sheer beauty of a breathtaking outdoor venue. What are your impressions of the Creator?

3. Colossians 1:15–16 refers to God the Son and teaches us that God is totally responsible for His creation. Do a study on these verses and their context. What is the meaning of the phrase "firstborn of all creation"? What is the significance of these categories: "both in the heavens and on earth," "visible and invisible," "whether thrones or dominions or rulers or authorities"?

4. Focus on Psalm 23, the key passage of this chapter's study. Drawing from the imagery the psalmist uses, what are our characteristic needs as "sheep"? What are the qualities of the Great Shepherd, and in what ways does He care for His sheep?

PICTURE THIS

In this life, we are a "work in progress." And, during our walk of faith, our lives can sometimes become "fragmented." As Dr. Evans explains, "God is sufficient by virtue of our dependence. Therefore, we can find our completeness only in Him." God is sufficient for our every need.

Our Completeness in God As Pictured in Psalm 23

OUR NEED	PSALM 23	GOD'S SUFFICIENCY
Spiritual	Verses 2–3a	In the midst of life's frustrations and detours, God restores and rejuvenates our souls.
Directional	Verse 3b	The Good Shepherd will guide us in the decisions and turns of life.
Emotional	Verse 4	When circumstances and the "shadows" of life seem to overwhelm us, God can calm our fears.
Physical	Verse 5	When we stay in God's will, He meets our daily needs.
Eternal	Verse 6	God is sufficient not only during our earthly existence, but for eternity as well.

4

THE HOLINESS OF GOD

One year we had a problem with our television picture. It was full of fuzz, so I called the repairman who told me we had a reception problem. Our antenna and wiring were just not doing the job.

That's what may happen when you try to study God. If your antenna is not working right, you won't get a clear picture. He won't come in clear. He won't be sharp, not because something is wrong with Him, but because something has gone wrong with your receiver.

Since Adam's fall, our ability to pick up the "God channel" has been greatly disturbed. As a result, we stare into the picture of the "Holy Other," our great God, but somehow He just doesn't come into clear focus.

Of all the things about God hard for us to focus on, one of the most difficult is His holiness. Holiness is one of those uncomfortable attributes because it reminds us how much unlike God we are.

Let's start with a definition: The holiness of God is His intrinsic and transcendent purity, the standard of righteousness to which the whole universe must conform.

God does not conform to any standard created by others. He is the standard. Therefore, He demands that His creation conform to His standard.

Some atheists say there could not be a God, given the existence and prevalence of evil. Actually, the opposite is true. You can call evil evil only if there is a holy God against whose standard you can measure evil.

GOD'S CENTRAL ATTRIBUTE

Holiness is the centerpiece of God's attributes. At the center of His being, He is holy. Exodus 15 shows a great picture of God's holiness as Moses and the "sons of Israel" sing about their deliverance from Pharaoh and his army.

Majestic in Holiness

In verse 8, the singers begin reciting what we might call poetic anthropomorphisms. We have already talked about this figure of speech, which uses human language to define God since we don't have spirit language that makes sense to us. Moses says, "At the blast of Your nostrils the waters were piled up," describing the parting of the Red Sea. God doesn't have nostrils, of course. Moses was saying in a poetic fashion that when God blew, so to speak, the waters parted.

Verse 10 also uses this language to picture the great deliverance Israel had experienced: "You blew with Your wind, the sea covered them; they sank like lead in the mighty waters."

Having recited Israel's great deliverance, Moses then says, "Who is like You among the gods, O Lord? Who is like You, *majestic in holiness,* awesome in praises, working wonders?" (v. 11, italics added). Moses says that if you want to understand the majesty, the distinctiveness, the uniqueness of God, you have to understand it in concert with His holiness.

The Key to God's Nature

God's holiness unlocks the door to understanding and making sense out of everything else about Him. This attribute infiltrates all the other attributes.

God even calls Himself holy. Throughout the Old and New Testaments He is called "The Holy One." When Mary was reciting her praise to God at the news that she would be the mother of the Savior, she said in Luke 1:49: "The Mighty One has done great things for me; and holy is His name."

God's holiness is central to understanding who and what He is. He is never emphatically called by any name except one: "Holy, Holy, Holy, is the

Lord of hosts" (Isaiah 6:3). Whenever you see three words like this, you are reading an emphatic statement meaning that this is something you don't want to miss.

God swears by His holiness (Psalm 89:35) because it is the fullest expression of His character. It most fully explains who He is. The Bible declares that God's law is holy (Romans 7:12), and that God is holy in all of His being (Leviticus 19:2).

GOD'S HOLINESS SEPARATES HIM FROM CREATION

The prophet Isaiah writes:

> For thus says the high and exalted One who lives forever, whose name is Holy, "I dwell on a high and holy place, and also with the contrite and lowly of spirit in order to revive the spirit of the lowly and to revive the heart of the contrite." (Isaiah 57:15)

The Hebrew word *holy* means "separate." It's the same root word from which we get the words *saint* and *sanctified*. All three of these carry the meaning "to be separate or distinct."

Perfect in Holiness

That's why God told Moses at the burning bush, "Remove your sandals from your feet, for the place on which you are standing is holy ground" (Exodus 3:5). When you come to understand how high and holy God is, you will come to understand how little we are.

The Bible makes clear in Romans 10:3 that people are ignorant of the holiness of God. They do not understand that "God is light, and in Him there is no darkness at all" (1 John 1:5). He is perfect in holiness. James 1:13–14 says that God cannot sin. He cannot even be tempted to sin, and He cannot tempt someone else to sin. The very idea of sin either in God or coming from God is inconceivable because of His purity.

We must understand this because we get really confused here. We grade sin by degrees. We say, "He's a bad sinner, a murderer, a rapist."

Then we climb the ladder a little bit and say, "Well, he's an OK sinner.

He's not all that hot, but he's not like that bad sinner."

Then we climb up a little higher and come to the "good" sinner. He's a nice guy. He's not perfect, but he's cool.

Finally, we come to the "excellent" sinner. That's where most of us think we stand. We say, "Yeah, I'm not perfect, but Lord have mercy, I'm good!"

No Degrees of Sin

We make these measurements, but God recognizes no such measurement. He has no degrees of sin. Now don't misunderstand me. There are degrees of consequences. Every sin doesn't deserve the same penalty, but evil does not have degrees. The man on death row is no different in the sight of a holy God than the person who goes through all of his life and tells one lie. This is fundamental. God does not have a grading system for sin because He is totally, absolutely perfect in all of His ways.

That ticks us off. We don't like a God who puts us on the same level as a criminal. We may not like it, but we'd better understand it. It's critical that we understand this in order to have a right view of God and a right view of ourselves. The Bible says, "There is none righteous, not even one" (Romans 3:10). "All have sinned and fall short of the glory of God" (v. 23).

The great naturalist and writer Henry David Thoreau epitomized most people's attitude toward sin. Near the end of his life, Thoreau was urged to make his peace with God. "I did not know that we had ever quarreled," was his response.

There has been a quarrel, all right! God has a quarrel with us, because we have all offended His holiness. All men need to be saved because everyone has the same problem.

Someone might object, "But that's not fair."

Sure it is. Suppose you were sick, and as the doctor was getting ready to operate on you, he said, "All my scalpels are dirty. I've got one that I just picked up out of the mud. It's real dirty. I've got another one here that I cleaned, but I smeared some of the dirt on it. It's a little better, but it's still dirty. But I've got this one scalpel that's just got a little spot of dirt on it. So I think we can chance this operation on you with this scalpel that has only a little spot."

But that little spot can be as bad as the thick dirt. Why? Because it only takes a few germs to contaminate your whole body. You want to make sure that the doctor's scalpel has been sterilized. You want absolute cleanliness when it comes to cutting you open. God is so holy, His scalpel so absolutely clean, that He is as offended by an evil thought as He is by murder. While there are differences in the consequences of sin, there is no difference in essence.

Encountering a Holy God

That's how holy God is, how totally unlike us. We have to do the adjusting. He's not going to change. When you come to understand the holiness of God, something has to happen. When the prophet Habakkuk ran into the holiness of God, he said, "My inward parts trembled . . . my lips quivered. Decay enters my bones" (Habakkuk 3:16). He had a different view of himself.

When Isaiah beheld God's holiness, he could only say, "Woe is me!" (Isaiah 6:5). Here was a great prophet, but all he could say was "Woe is me!" Isaiah was announcing a curse on himself. He was saying, "Cursed am I." Then he said, "I am ruined," or undone. The word *ruined* means "to unravel." Isaiah said "I'm coming apart" because he saw God in all His awesome holiness.

When you come face-to-face with God, He affects your self-esteem. You discover you are not what you thought you were when you see God. We do not take living the Christian life seriously enough because we forget who God is, so we try anything.

If we are going to be serious about walking with God, we have to understand who He is and who we are in light of Him. We must go low because He sits high.

GOD'S HOLINESS AND SIN

The holiness of God demands that He judge sin. This is repeated all through the Bible. God has always judged sin, and He has a future judgment in store, which is the Great Tribulation as described in Revelation 16:1–5.

Natural and Necessary

God judges man and creation because a holy God cannot skip over sin. God's holiness means sin must be taken seriously and always will be judged.

Even health and holiness go together. The Bible says some Christians who live a rebellious life get sick (1 Corinthians 11:30; James 5:13–16). On the other hand, unholiness and decay go together. Where there is unholiness, there is decay.

When we talk about the wrath or judgment of God, we do not mean mere emotional outbursts. We get mad because someone ticked us off. We get mad because we're having a bad day. God doesn't have bad days, and He doesn't just blow up. God's wrath is His natural and necessary reaction to anything and everything that is opposed to His holiness.

Comprehensive

God's judgment against sin is also comprehensive. The Bible declares that God has judged and will judge Satan, and He will judge men. In fact, the Bible puts men and Satan together under judgment in Matthew 25:41. There Jesus says: "Then [God] will also say to those on His left, 'Depart from Me, accursed ones, into the eternal fire which has been prepared for the devil and his angels.'"

God did not create hell for people. He created hell for the Devil. Then why do people go there? Because they choose to follow the Devil. If you choose to reject God and His salvation, you get the curse and the wrath that has been assigned to Satan.

God is so holy that He even judged His Son. Men crucified Jesus "by the predetermined plan and foreknowledge of God" (Acts 2:23). God's holiness is terrible. The Bible says, "Our God is a consuming fire" (Hebrews 12:29). He cannot be trifled with.

We are dealing with a very holy Being who demands to be taken seriously and who stands distinct from anything that is impure. Think about it. For one sin, Adam was put out of the garden. For one sin, Cain and his progeny were cursed. For one sin, Moses was kept out of the Promised Land. For one sin, Elijah's servant got leprosy. For one sin, Ananias and Sapphira were killed. That's "a consuming fire."

God must always have by nature a judgment for sin. A lot of people think, for example, that David got away with his sin. They say, "David sinned grievously, and God was gracious." That's true. David did sin and

God was gracious, because David should have been executed. But did God skip over David's sin? No, He just took the lives of four of David's children in his place.

In other words, David lived because someone else died. After David sinned with Bathsheba, the baby died. I know that's hard to swallow because it is so unlike what we think God ought to be like. The tension comes when we wrestle with the reality that God judges sin while simultaneously loving the sinner.

God Loves the Sinner

God does not wipe us all out because while He despises and judges sin, He is intensely in love with the sinner. God wants to destroy the sin without destroying the sinner. Anyone who has ever had cancer understands this. You want to nail that cancer, but you want to be able to walk away.

So God's holiness is directed against sin, but He loves the sinner. The problem is He cannot overlook the sinner in judging the sin, because the sinner is the one doing it. The seriousness of this business of God and His holiness should shake us down to our socks. The Bible says that when God came down to the children of Israel, Mount Sinai shook. He had not even said anything yet. Just His holy presence made the mountain shake violently (Exodus 19:16–18).

Then God told Moses, "Go down, warn the people, lest they break through to the Lord to gaze, and many of them perish" (v. 21). God said, "If these folk hang around the foot of this mountain, they are going to be in trouble. If they even try to take a peek at Me, they shall surely die." That's our holy God.

When God moves, mountains shake. How come we are not shaking? If mountains shake when God moves, why don't we quiver at the thought of God? Why are we not reverential toward God? Why don't we hold Him in awe? Because we have forgotten who He is. We must take God seriously!

GOD'S HOLINESS AND HIS TERMS

The holiness of God means that we can only approach Him on His terms. That's what the book of Hebrews is all about. Hebrews spends a lot of time contrasting the old covenant with the new covenant. The old way of approaching God and the new way of approaching God are contrasted most graphically in Hebrews 9:21–22:

> In the same way he sprinkled both the tabernacle and all the vessels of the ministry with the blood. And according to the Law, one may almost say, all things are cleansed with blood, and without shedding of blood there is no forgiveness.

The fundamental principle is this: The only thing that can satisfy the demands of a holy God is "the shedding of blood." God requires a sacrifice, but why He chose this arrangement, I cannot fully say. All I know is that this is what God says. The very first thing that happened when Adam and Eve sinned was that God killed an animal to provide them a covering, physically and redemptively.

Israel's Tabernacle

In the Old Testament, God established a comprehensive and somewhat complicated system of worship because people could not just barge into His presence. Some years ago, when the elder George Bush was president, I was invited to the White House along with others for a briefing from the president. Can you picture me going into the White House doing my little Dallas thing and saying, "Is Mr. Prez in? I need to see him now."

They would say, "I'm sorry, sir, you can't see him."

"No, you don't know who I am. Tony Evans of Dallas, Texas. Pastor of Oak Cliff Bible Fellowship Church. We've got a radio program. I'm sure you've heard it."

They would say, "No, you don't understand. He's the president."

Because of who the president is and what he represents you don't just barge into his office. You come by invitation and by permission only. It's the same with God.

God established a place and a process of worship for Israel called the tabernacle. The tabernacle was designed to let Israel know who God was; to let them know that He was distinct from them, yet He wanted to be present with them.

The tabernacle had three different compartments, divided by three curtains. One curtain hung across the outside entrance into the court. Another curtain covered the entrance into the holy place where the sacrifices were made. The third blocked entrance into the "holiest of all" where God's presence was. Only the high priest was allowed to go in there, and only once a year.

That's how serious God's holiness is. You see, unless blood was on that altar covering your sin, you'd better not try to go past that curtain because sinful men cannot waltz into the presence of a holy God. He doesn't allow it.

Our Tabernacle

You say, "But wait a minute. How come we don't have a tabernacle?" We do! Listen to the writer of Hebrews:

> For Christ did not enter a holy place made with hands, a mere copy of the true one, but into heaven itself, now to appear in the presence of God for us; nor was it that He should offer Himself often, as the high priest enters the holy place year by year with blood not his own. (9:24–25)

But he goes on to say in verse 28: "So Christ also, having been offered once to bear the sins of many, shall appear a second time for salvation without reference to sin, to those who eagerly await Him." Do you know why you can waltz into God's presence today? Because Jesus put His shed blood on that altar for you.

The only reason you can approach God today is that Jesus Christ split the curtain separating us from the holiest of all. Christ opened the way so that now we have access to God through Christ (Ephesians 2:18). When God sees you coming before Him, He only lets you come into His presence because He sees you through the lens of Jesus. God's condition for approaching Him is a blood sacrifice, and Jesus made that sacrifice for us.

GOD'S HOLINESS AND OUR LIFESTYLE

Finally, the holiness of God demands that Christians reflect His character in their lifestyles. First Peter 1 puts it so well: "As obedient children, do not be conformed to the former lusts which were yours in your ignorance, but like the Holy One who called you, be holy yourselves" (vv. 14–16).

Pleasing Our God

God says, "Because of who I am, that is who you should strive to be." The holiness of God demands that holiness be the goal of the believer. Paul says, "Let everyone who names the name of the Lord abstain from wickedness" (2 Timothy 2:19). Hebrews 12:10 says that God is so eager for our holiness He "spanks" His children "that we may share His holiness," just like we spank our children that they might be partakers of our rules and regulations and guidelines.

Pursuing Holiness

You don't build a chicken coop on the foundation of a skyscraper. However, many Christians build junky lives on the foundation of the cross. You can't excuse sin. You can't say, "Oh, everyone does it." No, you don't know who God is.

You don't just pass it by or ignore your sin. You fall down like Isaiah and say, "Woe is me! I am undone! I am a man/woman of unclean lips. Woe is me!" When Isaiah did that, an angel took a coal from the altar and put it on his lips. God cleaned Isaiah up.

Getting Clean

Have you ever been real dirty and stepped into a nice, hot shower? You are filthy, but you get in that shower, turn on the hot water, and say, "Ahhhhh!"

God will tell you that you are dirty. If you will just admit you are dirty and stop thinking you are clean, He'll come alongside you and scrub you up so you can walk away clean, saying "Ahhhhh!"

But not only that, after God has cleaned you up, He will fix you up so that He can use you up. That's what happened to Isaiah, and that's what God will do with you if you come clean with Him.

So our prayer must be like that of David: "Create in me a clean heart,

O God" (Psalm 51:10). In other words, "Lord, give me a clean heart. I'm dirty. I'm sinful. I've messed up, but if You will scrub me, I will be clean. Then You can dress me and send me on my way."

PERSONAL APPLICATION FOR LIFE

1. How's the "God reception" in your home and family right now? Is He coming in clear or fuzzy? Here's an interesting experiment you can perform to help you get a handle on things. Over the next few days, sit down and listen to your home. Take note of the conversations, the level of the electronic noise coming in, things like that. You may discover that a lot of "atmospheric interference" blocks your family's ability to hear and respond to God. If needed, make some adjustments to eliminate and tune out some of the static.

2. If you are holding other people accountable to live up to your mental list of dos and don'ts, tear up that list and set those people free to respond to God as He leads them. Remember: God's standards seldom match ours.

3. Here's an idea you can use in your witnessing as people throw out their objections to believing in God. Many will say, "God isn't fair." Instead of challenging that and putting yourself on the defensive, agree. "You're right, God isn't fair, and I'm glad. If He were fair, you and I wouldn't be here today. We'd be in hell. What we really need is not God's fairness, but His mercy."

4. Since holiness is such a foreign concept to the human heart, ask God to help you live each day in a healthy awareness of His awesome holiness. Pray that God will make the truth of 1 Peter 1:15–16, "Be holy yourselves also in all your behavior; because it is written, 'You shall be holy,'" a reality in your heart and life.

FOR GROUP STUDY

Questions for Group Discussion

1. As a group, read Psalm 51. This is a psalm of David, and the result of David's sin with Bathsheba (2 Samuel 11–12). What does this psalm reveal about our human nature? What does it reveal about the cost of sinning?

2. The lifestyle of the believer needs to align with God's demand for holiness. Second Timothy 2:19 tells us, "Let everyone who names the name of the Lord abstain from wickedness." How does Hebrews 12:10 relate to our abstaining from sin? Abstaining is one part of our lifestyle; we need also pursue holiness. Discuss 1 Peter 1:14–16 and Romans 12:2.

3. As Dr. Evans indicates, the Hebrew word for *holy* in Isaiah 57:15 means "separate." Associated with this concept is the quality of a believer's life and conduct. God is perfect in His holiness (Leviticus 19:2; 1 John 1:5; James 1:13–14). How should the holiness of God make us think about our own sin? (See Isaiah 6:3, 5; Luke 5:8).

4. What was the purpose of the tabernacle? What were the limitations for access to God's presence? Read Hebrews 9:21–22, 24–25, 28 and Ephesians 2:18. What is different about our access to God today? What has made that difference?

PICTURE THIS

As Dr. Evans has shown, if we are going to be serious about walking with God, we must gain a full understanding of who He is and who we are in the light of His holiness. He demands holiness, and it is we who must align to His standard.

THE DEMANDS OF GOD'S HOLINESS

GOD'S HOLINESS AND . . .	SCRIPTURE PASSAGE	DEMANDS
His creation	Isaiah 57:15	God's holiness separates Him from His creation.
The presence of sin	1 Corinthians 11:30	The holiness of God demands that He judge sin.
Our access to God	Hebrews 9:21-22, 24–25	Access is possible through the shedding of blood.
Our lifestyle	1 Peter 1:14–16	Christians must reflect God's holy character.

5

THE SOVEREIGNTY OF GOD

The God most of us worship is too small. The God of most Christians seems anemic, weak, and limited. He does not have the capacity to make a difference, to turn things around. The God most of us serve resembles more the flickering of a candle than the burning of the noonday sun.

One reason for this is that we do not understand God's sovereignty. We have allowed God to be everywhere but on His throne, and we have paid dearly in our own spiritual failure and weakness and limited power because the God we talk about has little to do with the sovereign God of the universe.

GOD'S ABSOLUTE RULE

God's sovereignty concerns His absolute rule and control over all of His creation, including the affairs of men. He sits on the throne of the universe as Lord. Everything that happens comes about because He either directly causes it or consciously allows it. Nothing enters into history or could ever exist outside of history that does not come under the complete control of God.

Only when you understand that this is the kind of God with whom we have to do will you take seriously the issue of His authority. I know that many people do not like the doctrine of God's sovereignty. They don't want a sovereign God. Certainly non-Christians, and unfortunately many times we as Christians, don't want a sovereign God because we don't want anyone ruling over us. We want to be autonomous.

Perhaps you have teenagers in your home like that. When they get to a certain age, they want to be free. I remember as a teenager telling my dad whenever I wanted to do something and he said no, "But Dad, I'm almost a man." Now, I wasn't crazy. I would always say "almost" because I wasn't ready to pay rent and make car payments!

In the same way, people do not want to be under the authority of God. They want a "jack-in-the-box" God who will pop up whenever they call Him. But until they need Him, they say, "Don't call us. We'll call You."

Satan knows this propensity well. He has it himself. He did not want to serve God, but he wanted to be autonomous. When he tempted Eve in the garden, Satan said, "God knows that the day you eat of this fruit, you will be like Him—autonomous. You'll be able to think your own thoughts, go your own places, and be your own person. Stop letting God stifle you. Become autonomous."

But once you understand God's sovereignty, you realize nobody can be autonomous from Him.

GOD DOES WHAT HE PLEASES

The sovereignty of God means that He exercises His prerogative to do whatever He pleases with His creation. Why? Because, "The earth is the Lord's, and all it contains, the world, and those who dwell in it" (Psalm 24:1).

God Rules

Suppose you came into my home and said, "Evans, I don't like your furniture. I don't particularly appreciate the art on your walls. The way you've got your bedroom organized is really an eyesore to me. You need to move this vanity over here, the bed over there. Your kitchen utensils, plates, and saucers really don't fit my taste. I wish you would do something about it."

I would only have one response to you: "When you start buying the furniture and paying the bills, then we can entertain your viewpoint. But as long as I'm spending the money, your viewpoint carries no clout in my house."

When you start making universes, creating planets, and giving life, perhaps then you can start dictating how God ought to run the universe. But until and unless you get that divine clout, you cannot exercise that divine prerogative. The prerogative always belongs to God, never to us, and He does whatever He chooses. This does not just appear as a fleeting thought in the Bible, but as an overwhelming doctrine.

Job says that "what [God's] soul desires, that He does" (Job 23:13). Job 42:2 puts it this way: "I know that You can do all things, and that no purpose of Yours can be thwarted."

According to Psalm 115:3, "Our God is in the heavens; He does whatever He pleases." Psalm 135:6 tells us, "Whatever the Lord pleases, He does, in heaven and in earth, in the seas and in all deeps."

Listen to Proverbs 16:4: "The Lord has made everything for its own purpose, even the wicked for the day of evil."

And in Isaiah 45:7, God says He is "the One forming light and creating darkness, causing well-being and creating calamity; I am the Lord who does all these."

The New Testament does not remain silent either. Paul says in Ephesians 1:11 that God works all things "after the counsel of His will." Romans 11:36 testifies, "For from Him and through Him and to Him are all things. To Him be the glory forever. Amen."

Not even evil and unrighteousness can escape the all-controlling hand of God. I love Revelation 19:6, which says, "For the Lord our God, the Almighty, reigns." God rules! Even when it looks like He's not ruling, He's ruling. When chaos appears, He's ruling the chaos. When things are falling apart, He's ruling the falling apart of those things.

God Decides

Our God is sovereign. That means there's no such thing as luck. The word ought to be expunged from the dictionary. You are never lucky or unlucky. Under God, no chance happenings occur. Anything that happens to you, good or bad, must pass through His fingers first. There are no accidents with God.

I like the story of the cowboy who applied for health insurance. The agent routinely asked him, "Have you ever had any accidents?"

The cowboy replied, "Well no, I've not had any accidents. I was bitten by a rattlesnake once, and a horse did kick me in the ribs. That laid me up for a while, but I haven't had any accidents."

The agent said, "Wait a minute. I'm confused. A rattlesnake bit you, and a horse kicked you. Weren't those accidents?"

"No, they did that on purpose."

That cowboy had the right idea. Things don't just happen. Everything that occurs, occurs under the hand of a sovereign God. Once you understand that, all of life takes on a different shape and perspective.

Our Decisions

Not the smallest detail of our lives escapes God—none. That creates a problem for us, because this question must now be answered: If in fact God is this kind of God, then why do my decisions matter? If He is sovereign and has already determined everything that will happen according to what pleases Him, then why do I need to choose? Why not just sit back, relax, and let Him do what He's going to do since He's going to do it anyway?

In theology we call this an *antinomy*; that is, parallel truths which run side by side and do not appear to cross each other. On the one hand, we have a sovereign God who "works all things after the counsel of His will" (Ephesians 1:11). On the other hand, I get to choose. But if I get to choose, then how much is He really in control? And if He's really in control, why do I need to choose?

I don't propose to have the last word on the subject; however, I do have a word on it. Suppose I were to go downtown in Dallas, with my destination being city hall. That is my determined purpose, but I am not limited to just one option for getting there. Depending on traffic or other factors, I could go several different ways.

God has determined in His sovereign will where He's going to wind up. But within the context of His will, He has many ways of getting there. He allows you to make choices. Your choices will not determine whether God winds up where He wants to go. He will arrive at His destination, but your choices affect which route He takes. When it is all said and done, the route you choose will be the one He sovereignly uses in order to achieve His intended purposes.

For example, God has determined that in all eternity, men will bring Him glory. The primary end toward which God moves is that all men who were ever created will for all time give glory to His name. Some of us will be giving glory to God's name in heaven for all eternity as we live with Him in the joyousness of His kingdom.

Another group of people will be doing the very same thing in hell, giving God glory forever and ever. Hell has no atheists. Nobody there doubts the existence of God. All men will, for all time, do exactly what God has ordained men will do. But He has given them a choice as to which route they will take, and which place they will occupy for all eternity to bring Him that glory.

Sovereignty and Prayer

What about prayer? God has determined what He's going to do, but He will not do certain things until we make the choice to pray. "You do not have because you do not ask" (James 4:2). God has determined what He's going to do, but on some of those things He says, "I won't do it until I hear 'Daddy.'" When we call on Him, He responds.

So God has given us options within His sovereignty to determine how we will fit into the outworking of His sovereignty. No one will thwart the plan of God. All we can do is cooperate with it.

Created for Him

The sovereignty of God means first of all that God exercises His prerogative to do with His creation whatever He chooses. Consider 1 Corinthians 8:6, which says:

> For us there is but one God, the Father, from whom are all things, and we exist for Him; and one Lord, Jesus Christ, by whom are all things, and we exist through Him.

You exist for God. That is why you were created. You were not made just to get a good job, to live happily ever after, to get married, and to have kids.

Those you call bonuses. You were created to bring God glory and to accomplish His purposes on earth. That's why you will find no rest in life until you find your rest in Him.

GOD'S GLORY AND WILL

The sovereignty of God involves the exercise of His attributes in order to maintain His glory and accomplish His will. Men have often tried to do a coup d'etat against God. That can never work because of God's attributes, which guarantee that no one will knock Him off His sovereign throne.

Forever Sovereign

God will always be sovereign because He always has His eternal attributes to guarantee it. You can't plan a revolt against Him because He's all-powerful. He can put down the revolt. You can't get in a secret room and plan to knock Him off His throne because He's all-knowing. He's in the room at the meeting with you while you plan to get rid of Him.

You can't plan to do something in one place to catch Him by surprise somewhere else because He's omnipresent. He's at both places at the same time. You can't box Him in, you can't confine Him, because He's independent. God's attributes guarantee His sovereign rule.

Sovereignty and Status

Do you get the point? No matter how high you climb, no matter what name you get, no matter how much money you accumulate, our God is sovereign. That means that while you respect people, no person intimidates you. You give people the honor due them, but you recognize that underneath God, everyone is nothing. That's why you can't be overly proud of your race. You are only black because God made you that way; you are only white because God made you that way. You can't get too proud about how God made you unless you think He endowed you with something that makes you better than the next man.

Black and white people and all colors in between will live both in heaven and in hell, because God is no respecter of persons. Like Paul, you can only say, "I am what I am by the grace of God."

GOD'S SOVEREIGNTY AND OUR SIN

One might mention at this point the question of the origin of evil. Since God is sovereign, why did He allow the existence and proliferation of evil, especially in light of the fact that God hates sin (Romans 1:18), is completely holy (Isaiah 6:3), and cannot sin (Psalm 5:4; 1 John 1:5) or tempt others to do so (John 1:13)?

We must begin by asserting that the Bible teaches clearly that God cannot sin Himself, and neither does He ever cause us to sin (James 1:13). Thus, sin is allowed by God, but not created by Him. Since God does everything for His greatest glory (Ephesians 1:11–12), we must naturally conclude that God will get more glory with the existence of sin than without it. This makes sense because some of God's attributes are most clearly demonstrated against the backdrop of sin.

The greatness of His love shows most clearly in contrast to our sinfulness (Romans 5:8). God's holiness and wrath, two indispensable aspects of His nature, could never be fully seen without the reality of sin (Romans 1:18; 9:22–23). Most important, the magnificence of His grace could hardly be measured except against the ugliness of sin (Ephesians 2:1–7). Thus, in allowing sin, the glory of God's attributes and character is most visibly displayed.

Second, in allowing the existence of evil, God is allowing everything that can be attempted to thwart His kingdom so that throughout the ages to come, it will be unquestionably clear that no enemy or scheme can succeed against the Almighty One. God's comprehensive defeat of evil will be a primary basis for His people giving Him praise (Revelation 19:1–6).

Finally, God allows evil because of His love. He does not wish to coerce obedience. For God to coerce obedience would invalidate the authentic nature of that obedience, especially since God looks at the heart (Romans 8:27), which remains disobedient. In order for man to function authentically as God's image-bearer with a moral will, the possibility of evil must exist. For God to have negated that possibility would be for Him to nullify the very thing He created—namely, beings with the ability to choose. And choice, of necessity, requires options. By allowing His creatures to have choice, God made evil and sin possible. But mankind made it real by making wrong choices.

We must, therefore, conclude that God permits sin by allowing His creatures, whom He has endowed with a moral will (and given responsibility to manage the affairs of earth, Psalm 115:16), to rebel against His authority. He then sovereignly overrules and uses their evil to accomplish His predetermined purposes. In the allowance of evil, God demonstrates how great He really is.

GOD'S SOVEREIGNTY AND OUR PERSPECTIVE

The sovereignty of God provides the Christian with the proper perspective in which to view all of life. If you ever get the sovereignty of God straight, your life will begin to take shape.

Strength

Paul says, "I can do all things through Him who strengthens me" (Philippians 4:13). That's the proper kind of positive thinking. As Christ supplies, I can do.

Comfort in Circumstances

God's sovereignty also gives comfort in the midst of life's circumstances. Life is bittersweet. One day you can wake up and be on top of the world. But all of that can change in five seconds.

But when you have a sovereign God, it means that the negative and the positive do not come by chance. The flat tire that made you miss the interview you were banking on to get that job was part of God's sovereign plan. The situation you thought was going to work out a certain way, the job you were sure was yours which was given to someone else, was all a part of God's sovereign plan.

Confidence

His sovereignty means He allows no chance, no luck, no mistakes, no accidents. You can have confidence: "Lord, You did what I thought You weren't going to do. That's because You want to do something else in my life, and I'm excited to see how You are going to use what You just did to do what You want to do."

God is up to something good in your life. He's taking the bad and the good and mixing them through the Holy Spirit, and when He finishes the trials and brings you through them, you will come out fine. That's what Romans 8:28 means: "God causes all things to work together for good to those who love God, to those who are called according to His purpose."

The Whole Picture

When you walk with God, when you live under His control, when you are in His hands, nothing can stifle you. God has allowed the negative, and He's going to use it to propel you. It's not evident at first because we have limited perspective.

It all depends on what you see. From our perspective we see one piece of the puzzle at a time because we live one day at time. But God sees the whole picture and He can put the whole thing together. When you understand the sovereignty of God, you believe in the power of prayer because you are convinced of what God can do.

Certain things you don't get just because you want them and you've done the best you can. Certain things only come because you've prayed about them to the point of giving up the craving of your appetite to get them. Unless you've understood the sovereignty of God, then God appears to be just a nice person who does things every now and then.

Sovereignty and Impossibilities

If I'm excited about one doctrine in my own life and ministry, it is God's sovereignty. I don't believe He can give me a vision to do anything that can't be done as long as it is in His will. Since I have that view, the obstacles seem irrelevant to me. I find the fact that it's never been done before irrelevant. The fact that no one else believes it can be done is irrelevant because the Bible says nothing is impossible with God (Luke 1:37).

Have you ever met people you think even God can't save? We are talking about sinful sinners. But Hebrews 7:25 says that God can save to the uttermost. That person you think will never become a Christian? Bring him or her to God in prayer and He can melt that heart of stone.

I like the confidence of Paul. He says in 2 Timothy 1:12, "I know whom I have believed and I am convinced that He is able to guard what I have entrusted to Him until that day."

GOD'S SOVEREIGNTY AND WORSHIP

The sovereignty of God should lead us to enthusiastic worship of Him. You know what ought to draw us to church on Sunday? The fact that the sovereign God, who holds up the universe by the word of His power, wants to have a meeting with us; that this great God, who gives us the air we breathe every day, who provides us everything we need, wants to meet with us.

Giving God Honor

Worship is the proper response to God's sovereignty. First Chronicles 29 brings this out. David is in a building program, and Israel is getting ready to build God a house. David challenges the people to bring their offerings for the temple they will build for God, and the people respond generously (vv. 6–7). David then offered a prayer in which he praised God and gave Him the honor due His name (vv. 10–13).

That's what ought to draw you to church on Sunday—to praise God's glorious name, because what king is like our God? He deserves your worship, your homage. He deserves your bowing before His face, glorifying His name. He deserves our worship—and the good news is that God *wants* our dedicated, committed worship.

PERSONAL APPLICATION FOR LIFE

1. If worship is the proper response to God's sovereignty, then it is time to measure your "Worship Quotient" (WQ). For example, do you see worship as something you do once a week? Or do you see your daily work as an act of worship to God? Can you worship when things are a little rocky, or does everything have to be smooth before you can genuinely offer God worship? Take a reading of your WQ, and make any necessary adjustments.

2. Read today's newspaper or watch this evening's newscast in light of the truth of God's sovereignty. Is anything going on in our world that might scare you out of your socks if you didn't know and believe that God had a firm grip on this place? Thank Him that ABC, CBS, NBC, or CNN can show you nothing that YHWH (the "I AM" God) can't handle.

3. If God is sovereign, that means He's capable of helping you do whatever He's called you to do. Make the affirmation of Philippians 4:13 personal by completing this statement: "I can do __________ through Him who strengthens me."

4. King Nebuchadnezzar of Babylon concluded his power and success were his doing (Daniel 4:29–30); God showed him otherwise (vv.31–33). Is there a "Nebuchadnezzar" in your family or circle of acquaintances who you know is heading for a collision with our sovereign God? Tell God you're available to be used in that person's life to snap him or her awake and avoid the crash.

FOR GROUP STUDY

Questions for Group Discussion

1. In general, what does God's sovereignty mean? Discuss Psalm 24:1 and Job 23:13.

2. That man is his own god is a lie that can be traced back to the garden of Eden. The two closing lines of the poem "Invictus," by William Ernest

Henley, epitomize this autonomous attitude: "I am the master of my fate. / I am the captain of my soul." How does this attitude conflict with what Scripture teaches about God's sovereignty? What will be the result of such an attitude?

3. Consider the problem of God's sovereignty and our freedom of will. How might you resolve this apparent contradiction in your thinking? Each group member should contribute a few thoughts to the discussion.

4. How does prayer work within the framework of God's sovereignty? Quoting James 4:2, Dr. Evans addresses this topic. Do a study on this topic. Here are a few verses to anchor your discussion: James 1:5; 5:16; Isaiah 7:12; Matthew 7:7- 8; Luke 11:9-13; John 4:10; 16:24. Why are our prayers effective? Are there conditions we need to observe?

PICTURE THIS

Dr. Evans points out that one of the reasons we do not understand God's sovereignty is that we allow Him to be everywhere but on His throne. As a result of the walk of faith, the believer continually grows in his or her understanding of God's sovereignty. Here are some of the ways God's sovereignty impacts the believer's life.

GOD'S SOVEREIGNTY AND THE LIFE OF THE CHRISTIAN

ARENA OF LIFE	SCRIPTURE PASSAGES	THE IMPACT ON OUR LIVES
Our existence	1 Corinthians 8:6	We were created to bring glory to God and accomplish His purposes on earth.
Our sin	Romans 1:18; 5:8; Ephesians 2:1–7	We see God's attributes of love, holiness, wrath, and grace clearly displayed against the backdrop of our sin.
Our lives	Philippians 4:13; Romans 8:28	We gain perspective in our view of life in terms of strength, comfort, and confidence.
Our worship	1 Chronicles 29:10–13	We should wholeheartedly worship God.

6

THE GLORY OF GOD

NBA superstar Michael Jordan disappointed lots of fans in October 1993 when he announced he was retiring. The man who had taken professional basketball to another level was hanging up his sneakers.

Fans and media alike mourned the news. And TV stations across America showed clips of "Air Jordan" in action, going up high, tongue hanging low, hitting the crucial shot to win the game. Some would show the replay I like: Jordan coming down the court, getting to the top of the key, feet lifting off the floor, moving in mid-air. As he dunked the ball, the commentator would say, "Ladies and gentlemen, you are watching living poof that men can fly."

Michael had glory. He had the unique ability to transcend the admirable (play all-star-quality pro basketball) and do what many would feel is supernatural: play gracefully above the rim, making aerodynamic soaring dunks and clutch jump shots as time wound down.

Michael returned to basketball less than two years later (after an inglorious run at Major League baseball). Once again he led the Chicago Bulls to three more NBA championships. But eventually Jordan's glory faded: His final two years with the Washington Wizards were lackluster, and today his magnificence can only be relived through a "Best of Michael" highlights DVD.

In contrast, God's glory never fades—it always is. The glory of God is best described as the visible manifestation of His attributes, His character, His perfections. The word translated *glory* in the Old Testament is very interesting. It means "to be weighted, to be heavy." We would use the word *awesome*. When we discuss God's glory, we talk about someone with an awesome reputation because He has awesome splendor. God is glorious.

GOD'S GLORY MANIFESTED IN HIS NATURE

When I talk about the glory of God, I mean the composite nature, the comprehensive grouping of all that makes Him who He is; the sum of His being. Exodus 33 brings this to light well. As Moses leads the people of Israel toward the Promised Land, he makes three requests of God.

In verse 13, Moses says, "I pray You, if I have found favor in Your sight, let me know Your ways that I may know You." If you want to know God, you must know His ways. You must say to Him, "Help me to know Your ways so that I might understand You, because You do things differently than I."

Notice how the Lord answered Moses: "My presence shall go with you" (v. 14). In other words, "Don't worry about it, Moses. I will be with you. You will see Me do My thing."

Then Moses makes a second request in verse 15: "If Your presence does not go with us, do not lead us up from here." Moses is saying, "If you don't go before me into the Promised Land, I would rather stay here in the wilderness." Here we see another important principle. It's better to be in an apartment with God than in a house without Him!

God responded to Moses, "I will also do this thing of which you have spoken; for you have found favor in My sight, and I have known you by name" (v. 17).

Then Moses makes his third and final request: "I pray You, show me Your glory!" (v. 18). God answered this prayer too (vv. 19-20, 22-23). Moses only got to see the backside of God's glory because God said Moses couldn't see His essence and live.

God is glorious by nature. We are only glorious when we are made to feel glorious; that is, we have ascribed glory. But God's glory exists whether or not you ever say something about it or recognize it. He has glory by virtue of who He is, not by virtue of what you say. God's glory is unique, so distinct that He says He will not share it with anyone (Isaiah 42:8). The psalmist writes, "Not to us, O Lord, not to us, but to Your name give glory" (Psalm 115:1).

The glory of God, then, has to do with His intrinsic character, who He is at the core of His being. It is not predicated on what He does, but on who He is. Psalm 29:3 calls Him the "God of glory."

GOD'S GLORY MANIFESTED IN HISTORY

We also know that God is glorious because He has manifested Himself gloriously in human history. God's internal essence is made known externally by what He does. The Jews had a word for this: *shekinah* glory. The word *shekinah* means "to dwell or reside with," the glory of God residing with men so men can see it.

This is a very important point, and I want to do it justice theologically without overstating the case. If you could pull out the nucleus of God, so to speak, His internal essence would be a huge, radiating light. Listen to the apostle Paul describing to Timothy God's inner essence as he discusses the second coming of Jesus Christ:

> He . . . is the blessed and only Sovereign, the King of kings and Lord of lords, who alone possesses immortality and dwells in unapproachable light, whom no man has seen or can see. To Him be honor and eternal dominion! Amen. (1 Timothy 6:15–16)

God's inner core is a radiating, unapproachable light. This explains why God created the sun with its "unapproachable light" to rule the day. Now you understand what God meant when He said, "No man can see Me and live." You would disintegrate because at His core, God is light (1 John 1:5). That's why whenever God shows up in history, it's always in relation to light.

For example, when Ezekiel saw the glory of God, he said it was like a "surrounding radiance" and the prophet fell on his face (Ezekiel 1:28).

When the shepherds were in the field at the birth of Jesus, "the glory of the Lord shone around them" (Luke 2:9). And concerning the New Jerusalem, the Bible says, "The city has no need of the sun or of the moon to shine on it, for the glory of God has illumined it" (Revelation 21:23).

Revealed in Creation

God reveals the light of His glory in a number of ways. The first of these is creation. In Psalm 19, the classic passage on this truth, the psalmist says,

> The heavens are telling of the glory of God; and their expanse is declaring the work of His hands. Day to day pours forth speech, and night to night reveals knowledge. . . . Their line has gone out through all the earth, and their utterances to the end of the world. In them He has placed a tent for the sun, which is as a bridegroom coming out of his chamber; it rejoices as a strong man to run his course. Its rising is from one end of the heavens, and its circuit to the other end of them; and there is nothing hidden from its heat. (vv. 1–2, 4–6)

In the same way that nothing is hidden from the sun, nothing can hide from God's glory. God says, "If you want to see how great I am, go outside. The heavens tell of My glory." We get confused because we talk about Mother Nature, not Father God. You've only got to go outside, and the heavens will tell you a story about the glory of God.

God's glory can be seen in the vastness of space, and it's also seen in life's particulars. It's seen when snowflakes fall. It's seen in the fact that no two people have the same fingerprints. It's seen in the fact that when the earth spins on its axis, it doesn't spin too fast lest we be thrown off. It doesn't spin too slow lest we feel it and become dizzy to death. It spins just right so we neither fall off nor feel dizzy because it spins at the same rate as our ability to function within the force of gravity. How could that happen? We have a glorious God.

Revealed in the Tabernacle

God's passion is for His glory, that there be a visible recognition that He alone is God. His glory was visible to Israel at the tabernacle. Israel built a tabernacle which wasn't particularly exciting to look at on the outside. But after they built it, the glory of the Lord came in the "glory cloud." Exodus 40 tells us about it:

> Then the cloud covered the tent of meeting, and the glory of the Lord filled the tabernacle. Moses was not able to enter the tent of meeting because the cloud had settled on it, and the glory of the Lord filled the tabernacle. (vv. 34-35)

God came down and rested on the tabernacle as the glory cloud filled the Holy of Holies and all of the tabernacle. The reason God had to come in a cloud was because He had to veil His glory. He could not reveal His inner core, His full inner light. But the beauty of the glory cloud was that when the cloud moved, Israel moved. When the glory cloud stopped, Israel stopped.

When you live your life for the glory of God, you don't have to worry about His will. The glory cloud leads you. So don't look for God's will; look for His glory, and you will find His will.

Revealed in the Temple

Later, Israel built a permanent residence for the glory of God called the temple. At the temple's dedication, the glory cloud so filled the place that the priests couldn't do their work (1 Kings 8:10-11). God now had a permanent resting place for His presence among His people.

When God's presence was among His people, it meant His attributes were among His people. So they had the power of God, the knowledge of God, the presence of God, the truth of God, the revelation of God, the Spirit of God, the guidance of God, and anything else necessary because to have the glory of God is to have God, to have all His attributes at work for you.

Conversely, when the people disobeyed God, the Bible says that over Israel was written "*Ichabod*," which means "The glory has departed from Israel" (1 Samuel 4:21). When the glory cloud leaves you, you are in trouble because you have no presence of God.

Revealed in Christ

But neither creation, the tabernacle, nor the temple was the ultimate revelation of God's glory in history. God's visible glory was most fully seen in the person of Jesus Christ:

> In the beginning was the Word, and the Word was with God, and the Word was God. . . . And the Word became flesh, and dwelt among us, and we beheld His glory, glory as of the only begotten from the Father, full of grace and truth. . . . No man has seen God at any time; the only begotten God [Jesus] who is in the bosom of the Father, He has explained [revealed] Him. (John 1:1, 14, 18)

In His earthly life, Jesus Christ was God's glory in human flesh. That's why He did what only God could do: heal the blind and the sick, raise the dead, read people's minds, know what was happening ahead of time. Jesus was the visible manifestation of God in human flesh. His glory was veiled, though, because no one can look on God and live.

But in Matthew 17 Jesus took Peter, James, and John up to a mountain. There Christ zipped down His humanity, so to speak. He took off the veil of flesh for just a minute, and the Bible says that bursting out of His humanity was a bright light. Jesus Christ is God incarnate, the magnificent revelation of God in terms human beings can understand because He was God become Man.

Revealed in the Church

God has not only manifested His glory in nature, in the tabernacle, in the temple, and in Christ. God's glory is also manifested in the church:

> Now to Him who is able to do far more abundantly beyond all that we ask or think, according to the power that works within us, to Him be the glory in the church. (Ephesians 3:20–21)

Not only is there to be glory in the Son of God; there is to be glory through the people of God. We should reflect the attributes of God in our world. The church is designed to be a unique gathering of God's people through whom God mirrors His glory. This world should see our glorious God when they see the functioning of His people.

GOD'S GLORY DEMANDS A RESPONSE

Only two groups of beings won't voluntarily glorify God: fallen men and fallen angels. Both will be discarded from His presence because throughout all eternity, God will only fellowship with those who voluntarily bring Him glory.

You see, your claim to esteem God will be validated by how you respond to the God you say you esteem. The proof that you glorify God, that you recognize His intrinsic value, will be the value that you ascribe to His glory.

Sing to Him

How should we respond to God's glory? Psalm 96 gives us some great answers:

> Sing to the Lord a new song; sing to the Lord, all the earth. Sing to the Lord, bless His name; proclaim good tidings of His salvation from day to day. Tell of His glory among the nations. . . . Ascribe to the Lord, O families of the peoples, ascribe to the Lord glory and strength. Ascribe to the Lord the glory of His name; bring an offering and come into His courts. Worship the Lord in holy attire. (vv. 1-3, 7–9a)

Even your clothing ought to be whistling the glory of God. Watch how you dress when you worship. "Tremble before Him, all the earth" (v. 9b). That's what people do who glorify God. They don't come and mumble little words. Even if they can't sing, they break out in song because the ability to make a joyful noise was given by God.

Praise Him

The Bible says that all of creation resonates with the glory of God except people. God demands and deserves glory. We can't give Him glory, because He already has it. It's intrinsic. We ascribe to Him the glory that He's due.

A judge becomes glorious when he puts on his robe. But when he takes off the robe, he's just another man. A policeman is glorious when he has on a badge and a blue uniform, but take off the badge and the uniform and he's just another person. God is always glorious because He never takes off His "uniform." He never takes off His robe of glory. He is the King of the universe. He is glorious.

How much should we do this thing called glorifying God? Psalm 113:3–4 puts it this way: "From the rising of the sun to its setting the name of the Lord is to be praised. The Lord is high above all nations; His glory is above the heavens." In other words, when you open your eyes in the morning, praise Him. When you go into the bathroom and look in the mirror, praise Him. When you go to the breakfast table, praise Him. When you get in your car, praise Him. When He takes you safely to work, praise Him.

When the day ends and you are still alive to go back home, praise Him. When you get home and have dinner, praise Him. When you see the rest of your family that He brought safely home, praise Him. When you retire for the night, praise Him. The Bible says the Lord is enthroned on the praises of His people (Psalm 22:3).

Glorify Him

One day Jesus came upon ten lepers who cried out "Have mercy on us!" (Luke 17:13). The Lord had pity on them and said, "Go and show yourselves to the priests" (v. 14). As they went, their skin became like babies' skin. The leprosy was gone.

Nine of the lepers kept going, but one—a foreigner, a Samaritan—turned around, came back, fell on his knees before Jesus, and glorified Him. Jesus looked at him and said, "Were there not ten cleansed? But the nine—where are they?" (v. 17).

He asked a great question. Where are all the people to whom God has given life, health, and strength? How can we stay in bed on Sunday morning when God has given us strength? How can we be too tired for Him when, if it were not for Him, we wouldn't be here at all? How can we not give Him glory?

God deserves glory, not only in terms of our worship but by what we do each day. The Bible contains many examples:

1. God is glorified when we "bear much fruit"—show Christlike character (John 15:8).
2. God is glorified when we do good works—apply biblical truths to human situations (Matthew 5:16).
3. God is glorified by our sexual purity (1 Corinthians 6:18–20).
4. God is glorified when we confess our sins (Joshua 7:19).
5. God is glorified when we live by faith and not by sight (Romans 4:19–21).
6. God is glorified when we proclaim His Word (2 Thessalonians 3:1).
7. God is glorified when we appeal to His glory in our suffering (1 Peter 4:14–16).
8. God is glorified when we do His will (John 17:4).
9. God is glorified when we confess His Son (Philippians 2:10).
10. God is glorified when we reflect the character of Christ (Romans 15:6).

I said earlier that unbelievers don't voluntarily glorify God. But God still gets what He wants—glory to Himself—even out of them. Remember what Pharaoh said to Moses in Egypt? "I'm not going to let you and your people go."

However, God told Moses, "Don't worry about Pharaoh. His heart is hard. I'm going to make it harder. I'm going to make him so mad at Me that he will do exactly what I want him to do. I will harden Pharaoh's heart and still get glory from him" (see Exodus 14:17).

So the issue is really not whether we will give God glory. Whether we give it to Him voluntarily or He has to squeeze it out of us against our wills, we are going to give God glory. God will get glory, but given the fact of all that He's done for us, doesn't He deserve it? Shouldn't we be hurrying to give Him glory?

GOD'S GLORY TRANSFORMS THOSE WHO RESPOND

Second Corinthians 3:18 is another beautiful passage of Scripture: "But we all, with unveiled face, beholding as in a mirror the glory of the Lord, are being transformed into the same image from glory to glory, just as from the Lord, the Spirit."

Do you want to transform yourself? Do you have things in your life that need to be changed? Catch hold of the glory of God. Do you want to change your mate? Don't nag him or her. Point the person to the glory of God.

A Temporary Glow

To understand what Paul's talking about, we need to go back to verse 13: "Moses . . . used to put a veil over his face that the sons of Israel would not look intently at the end of what was fading away." Paul is referring to an incident in Exodus 34, which continues the text discussed at the opening of this chapter.

On that mountain, Moses saw the backside of the glory of God. Then as Moses came down the mountain, his face started to shine because he had been in God's presence. But the farther he went, the more the shine started to fade. By the time he got to the people, he had only a little shine left. Moses covered his face so the people wouldn't see his shine fading.

We're sort of like that. When we walk out of church on Sunday morning, most of us are shining because we've been in God's presence and have seen His glory. But by the time we get home and sit down for lunch, we have lost our shine.

A Permanent Glow

When Jesus Christ saved you, He put a new covering on you so that when you're exposed to the light of the glory of God, it will put a glow in your life. But when you remove yourself from God's glory, your glow begins to diminish. When you find that happening, you need to wrap yourself around the light of God's glory. Then the transforming work of God can begin to glow in you again.

So what's the bottom line? "Whether, then, you eat or drink or whatever you do, do all to the glory of God" (1 Corinthians 10:31). God says, "If you would just remember to thank Me every time you do anything, you will begin to shine and the glory cloud will transform your life." If you want to be transformed, submit to God's glory. Stop trying to share His glory, let Him be God, and let the light of the glory of God transform you.

PERSONAL APPLICATION FOR LIFE

1. Take another look at your schedule for the next week or so in light of God's glory. How much of what you hope and plan to do will in some way enhance the glory of God? That doesn't mean everything you do has to be a "spiritual" or church activity. You can bring Him glory mopping the floors. If your schedule doesn't reflect your desire to glorify God as much as you'd like, you may need to make some additions—or cancellations.

2. Is there anyone you're working hard to change these days? Only God can change hearts. Why not begin praying instead that your "project" will be touched and transformed by the glory of God? After all, God will do a lot better job than you will anyway.

3. Feeling a little crushed or beaten down right now? Go to God and ask Him to clear away some of the haze so that you can see the "glory cloud" again. Make a renewed commitment to be faithful to Him regardless of the circumstances.

4. First Corinthians 10:13, God's promise of sufficient strength for any trial, is another of those key verses you need to file in your spiritual inventory. Commit this great verse to memory if you haven't done so already.

FOR GROUP STUDY

Questions for Group Discussion

1. Take a moment to consider the ways God has made known His glory to you. In what ways have you been especially impacted? Share your thoughts with the group.

2. Dr. Evans suggests at least ten ways we can glorify God in our lives. Have the group leader briefly go over these, making certain the group embraces associated Scripture passages. Acknowledge group members who have been encouraging by the ways they glorify God in their lives. Explore new ways we can glorify God in our daily routines.

3. How does God reveal His glory through His church? Why is Ephesians 1:12 important to every believer?

4. From Exodus 40:34–38, Dr. Evans extracted a very important principle for Christian living. What does this passage teach us about God's glory and what we can expect when we live for His glory?

PICTURE THIS

Scripture has recorded the ongoing revelation of God's glory to mankind. The following is snapshot of how God has chosen to reveal His glory.

GOD'S GLORY REVEALED IN HISTORY

SOURCE	SCRIPTURE PASSAGE	ACCOMPLISHMENT
Creation	Psalm 19:1–2, 3–4	God's creation constantly reveals His glory.
The tabernacle	Exodus 40:34–38	God demonstrated His glory to Israel.
The temple	1 Kings 8:10–11	God's glory had a permanent resting place among His people.
Christ	John 1:1, 14, 18	God revealed His visible glory in the person of His Son, Jesus Christ.
The church	Ephesians 3:20–21	God reveals His glory through His people.

7

THE OMNISCIENCE OF GOD

If your grade school was anything like mine, you had a "know-it-all" in your class. He or she seemed to have every answer, and whatever the subject, Mister or Miss Know-it-all could expound at length about it. Nothing made you madder than to see that kid who acted like he or she knew everything, because you knew he or she didn't know half of it.

The universe only contains one "know-it-all." The only one who knows everything is the great God whose perfections we have been studying. One of the attributes of our God is His *omniscience*, a word made up of two words: *omni*, which means "all," and *science*, which has to do with knowledge.

So when we talk about the omniscience of God, we are referring to His "all-knowingness," what God knows. A simple definition is that God's omniscience refers to His perfect knowledge of all things both actual and potential.

Let's put it down straight right up front. The omniscience of God means that there is absolutely nothing He doesn't know; that no informational system or set of data exists anywhere outside of God's knowledge—nothing. He depends on no one outside Himself for any knowledge about anything. The author of Hebrews said, "All things are open and laid bare in the eyes of Him with whom we have to do" (Hebrews 4:13).

That's so unlike us. We all are dependent on someone else's knowledge. In fact, we sometimes stake our lives on the fact that someone knows something. Every time you fill a prescription at the pharmacy, you trust your life to the assumption that your pharmacist went to school and that he doesn't confuse medicines. Every time you get on an airplane, you assume your pilot has done this before. You hope all those switches mean something to him. When you go to school, you depend on the fact that your teacher has been to school, although sometimes you may doubt it. We depend heavily on the knowledge that other people possess.

I like the story of the very wealthy grandfather who was getting up in age. He was going deaf, but he went to the doctor and was fitted with a unique hearing aid. It not only overcame the old man's deafness, but it allowed him to hear perfectly. When he went back to the doctor for a checkup, the doctor commented, "Well, your family must be extremely happy to know that you can now hear."

The grandfather said, "No, I haven't told them about my hearing aid. I just sit around and listen to the conversations. I've already changed my will twice."

When folks don't think you know, it will greatly affect what they say and do. So we had better understand that God knows everything, because it will affect everything we say and do.

GOD'S OMNISCIENCE IS INTUITIVE

In Isaiah 40:13–14, the prophet gives us this very valuable piece of information about God's perfect knowledge:

> Who has directed the Spirit of the Lord, or as His counselor has informed Him? With whom did He consult and who gave Him understanding? And who taught Him in the path of justice and taught Him knowledge and informed Him of the way of understanding?

To put it in our terms, where did the Lord go to school? Isaiah raises the question to illustrate a fundamental principle that God does not gain His knowledge by learning. He does not need to study, read, and analyze. He knows what He knows simply because He knows it. He did not learn it.

As finite creatures, the more we learn the more we know that we don't know all that we need to know. That's a real dilemma, but God does not have this problem because everything that can be known, everything that has ever been known, and everything that will ever be known, He already knows.

God has innate knowledge of all data at all times. He never forgets, so He doesn't ever have to remember. After God had miraculously intervened in her life to give her a baby, Hannah offered Him a prayer of thanksgiving for little Samuel. In her praise she gave God glory and said, "The Lord is a God of knowledge" (1 Samuel 2:3).

That's who He is. Because God is an eternal being, whatever He knows, He knows immediately and simultaneously. Because He is eternal, He does not have to look back to the past to remember or look forward to the future to project. Because God is infinite, "His understanding is infinite" (Psalm 147:5).

GOD'S OMNISCIENCE IS COMPREHENSIVE

Nothing can be hidden from God. He knows our feelings, our desires, our excuses, and our personalities. He knows everything and anything, and He knows it comprehensively. Nothing sits outside of the body of information He possesses. According to Acts 15:18, He has known everything from the very beginning.

No Detail Overlooked

God's comprehensive knowledge also includes a moral element. Proverbs 15:3 says that "the eyes of the Lord are in every place, watching the evil and the good." No detail escapes His all-encompassing knowledge.

Jesus said, "Not one [sparrow] will fall to the ground apart from your Father" (Matthew 10:29). The legendary Baptist preacher Dr. Robert G. Lee once said, "God is the only One who attends a sparrow's funeral." According to Psalm 50:11, God knows every beast and every bird of the air. That's comprehensive knowledge!

God's omniscience isn't confined to things on earth. The psalmist says every star among the billions of stars that inhabit all of the galaxies has been numbered and named by Him (Psalm 147:4).

God sees what's done in secret and what's done in the light. God is the eternal, cosmic X-ray machine. David says in Psalm 139:12 that the day and the night are alike to God. Moses reminds us that our secret sins are brought to light in His presence (Psalm 90:8). This is powerful information because it means all of our lives are totally known to God.

According to Psalm 73:8–11, because men don't want this kind of God, they dismiss Him by telling themselves, "God doesn't know what we're doing." But their denial does not change God's omnipotence.

What Could Have Been

God not only knows what is; He knows what could have been. It's one thing for a person to know actual events, but it's a whole different ballgame for a person to know potential events as well. In Matthew 11, we find Jesus pronouncing this judgment, which reveals His comprehensive knowledge, because Jesus is God:

> Woe to you, Chorazin! Woe to you, Bethsaida! For if the miracles had occurred in Tyre and Sidon which occurred in you, they would have repented long ago in sackcloth and ashes. Nevertheless I say to you, it shall be more tolerable for Tyre and Sidon in the day of judgment than for you. And you, Capernaum . . . will descend to Hades; for if the miracles had occurred in Sodom which occurred in you, it would have remained to this day. Nevertheless I say to you that it shall be more tolerable for the land of Sodom in the day of judgment, than for you. (vv. 21–24)

Jesus says if this would have happened, then the people would have done that. That's not what happened, but Jesus said if it would have happened, this would have been the certain result. This shows how comprehensive God's omniscience is. He knows the potential as well as the actual events and outcomes of history.

For example, people often speculate that if Gen. Stonewall Jackson had not been killed early in the Civil War, he might have led the Confederacy to victory. Someone else has said that if Adolf Hitler had only listened to the Jewish scientists in Germany, the Nazis might have had the atomic bomb first and ruled the world.

We'll never know about these things, but God knows. He also knows your potential history. What if you had been born at another time, in another place, of another race? What if you had married that person instead of this one? God knows what could have been, and because of that you can rest in what is.

Why? Because God could have made your life totally different. But since He allowed you to be as you are, you can have confidence that He didn't change it because He didn't want to change it.

Now don't misread me here. I realize that life often brings us pain and grief: a failed marriage, the loss of a child, a loved one stricken with a deadly illness. When I say that God didn't change your circumstances because He didn't want to, I do not mean He is sitting up in heaven letting you suffer needlessly. God permits trials for reasons we don't always understand, but He is able to bring good out of even the worst circumstances. That's what Joseph learned (Genesis 50:20).

GOD'S OMNISCIENCE IS PERSONAL

The omniscience of God is not only intuitive and comprehensive, but intensely personal. Psalm 139 brings this home in a very graphic way. The psalmist David begins, "O Lord, You have searched me and known me. You know when I sit down and when I rise up" (vv. 1–2a).

God Knows Us

I don't know of a more mundane activity than sitting down and rising up. But the Bible says that God is acutely aware of the smallest detail of our lives.

David goes on to say, "You understand my thought from afar" (v. 2b). God is acutely aware of our thinking. Ezekiel 11:5 says that God knows the things that come in our mind. He knows where they came from and how they wound up there. The Bible says that God reads our hearts. He understands every thought and intent of the heart (1 Samuel 16:7).

The psalmist also says, "You scrutinize my path and my lying down, and are intimately acquainted with all my ways" (Psalm 139:3). In other words, "You scrutinize my direction in life. You look at the way I am traveling." That's why when you are lost, you can pray for God's guidance because God knows the right path to get you back on the right road.

"Even before there is a word on my tongue, behold, O Lord, You know it all" (v. 4). God knows your thought before it even gets into your mind. Once you have the thought, He knows how it's going to be expressed before it ever reaches your tongue. So by the time the first word gets out of your mouth, God has already waxed eloquent on that information.

No wonder David observes in verse 5: "You have enclosed me behind and before, and laid Your hand upon me." He's saying, "I'm locked in by Your knowledge." To put it another way, we have nowhere to run, nowhere to hide. God knows all things related to our personal lives. But that's good news, because God not only knows. He *understands* us.

Psalm 103:14 says God knows that "we are but dust." He knows we are weak. He knows we can't do all that He commands us to do, even though that ought to be our passion and our goal. He knows we are dust. That's not an excuse, it's reality.

God Sees Through Us

God also knows when we act as hypocrites, wearing our masks. He knows when we look one way on the outside but are totally different on the inside. The Sadducees and Pharisees of Jesus' day went around fooling the people with their righteous talk, their righteous prayers, and their righteous fasting. But then they ran into Jesus. Being God in the flesh, He looked at them and said, "You are like whitewashed tombs . . . full of dead men's bones" (Matthew 23:27).

Jesus was referring to the Jewish law which said that anyone who touched a grave would be defiled. To avoid defilement, they would whitewash the tombs to mark them clearly so travelers could avoid them. But whitewashing a tomb didn't change the reality that it held dead people's bones.

That grave was still a place of death. It was just a place of death that looked good on the outside. If we're not careful, we can become whitewashed tombs. Some folks are all painted up lovely on the outside, but if we could open their hearts, we'd find rot, treachery, and immorality. You can fool some of the people some of the time, but you can fool God none of the time.

When my mother thought I was doing something wrong, she used to look at me and say, "Son, you can jive the baker because he'll give you a bun, but you can't jive me, because I ain't got none."

She was saying to me, "I'm your mother and I know you."

God says, "I'm your Father and I know you." So it's imperative that we come clean with God because He knows what's on the inside.

GOD'S KNOWLEDGE IS PURPOSEFUL

God doesn't use His omniscience to win contests. He doesn't play *Jeopardy* or spin the *Wheel of Fortune*. Everything God knows is plugged into His eternal purposes.

In Relation to Salvation

Ephesians 1 brings this out in relationship to our salvation. God wants us to know that our salvation was not by luck or chance. Instead,

> He chose us in Him before the foundation of the world, that we would be holy and blameless before Him. In love He predestined [predetermined] us to adoption as sons . . . to the praise of the glory of His grace. (vv. 4–6)

God does what He does for reasons. His omniscience is purposeful. The Bible says of Jesus' crucifixion that while unregenerate men killed Him, Jesus was crucified by "the predetermined plan and foreknowledge of God" (Acts 2:23). God was responsible for the death of Jesus even though the means He used was ungodly men. God's purpose in this was that His Son would pay for the sins of the world on the cross.

So God's knowledge is intricately tied to His purposes. This raises the very complex question of the interplay of God's election, predestination, and foreknowledge, particularly as they relate to our salvation.

There are two extremes in my view. The hyper-Calvinistic view says God has already determined everything that will happen, meaning that we have no real choice in anything. We are more like robots carrying out God's predetermined will than agents of moral choice who have legitimate and meaningful decisions to make. But that seems to negate the many clear commands to us in Scripture to do this and avoid that. Those commands also have real consequences attached.

The other extreme is the Arminian view, which postures God as sitting in heaven biting His fingernails, if you will, basing His actions and plans on what He knows we are going to do. Based on what we do, He develops and builds His agenda. But He's not quite sure what we will do. I have overstated the case a little, but the Arminian view waters down God's omniscience. Arminianism separates God's omniscience from His sovereignty and omnipotence.

The tension remains there, no doubt about it. How do we handle the reality that God has determined the events of history and at the same time has made us free moral agents with real choices to make?

Many Christians think that because the Bible teaches both God's absolute foreknowledge and our capacity to choose, there has to be some sort of contradiction.

But the Bible clearly teaches two important facts. First, "[God] desires all men to be saved" (1 Timothy 2:4). This is the burden of His heart. He is not "wishing for any to perish but for all to come to repentance" (2 Peter 3:9).

Second, God did something about His desire. He made provision for everyone to be saved. Jesus tasted death for every person (Hebrews 2:9). "For God so loved the world, that He gave His only begotten Son" for the world (John 3:16). Jesus was not only the propitiation for the saints, but for the world (1 John 2:2). Therefore, it is not God's fault that some people are not saved.

Yet on the opposite side, the Bible also clearly teaches that God has elected some to be saved (Ephesians 1:4). We will discuss this in more detail in our chapter on salvation and God's grace (chapter 64). Suffice it to say at this point that God's knowledge is so comprehensive that it includes the choices people make. And those choices are incorporated into God's comprehensive plan in such a way that He remains sovereign and human beings have free moral choice.

In other words, God's knowledge and His eternal purposes intersect with human choice in such a way that we have real choices to make, and yet those choices fulfill God's purpose to accomplish His goal.

We must accept the clear teaching of the Bible that all men who die separated from God will be held accountable because Jesus Christ paid for their sins on Calvary. And those of us who are on our way to heaven can never brag, since we will get there only because He called us back to Himself.

So God has made provision for all but guaranteed the salvation of some, leaving us with a choice but guaranteeing His plan.

In Relation to Daily Living

The interplay of God's purposes with our freedom appears not only in salvation, but in our day-to-day Christian life. We find a great example in Luke 22, during the Last Supper. In the middle of the meal Jesus turns to Peter and says: "Simon, Simon, behold, Satan has demanded permission to sift you like wheat; but I have prayed for you, that your faith may not fail; and you, when once you have turned again, strengthen your brothers" (vv. 31–32).

Peter responds immediately. "Lord, with You I am ready to go both to prison and to death!" (v. 33). But in the very next verse, Jesus predicts Peter's failure. He says, "You are going to blow it. You are going to deny Me before all of these people. Satan is going to use your self-confidence to drive you to spiritual defeat. I know this in advance, so I've been praying for you."

Thankfully, the story of Peter doesn't end in Luke 22 but continues in John 21, where Jesus gently forgave and restored Peter. And Jesus still says to us today, "I love you." Paul writes, "But God demonstrates His own love toward us, in that while we were yet sinners, Christ died for us" (Romans 5:8). He knew our mess up, yet He's willing to make up. He's the all-knowing, all-wise, all-loving God.

PERSONAL APPLICATION FOR LIFE

1. If sin is a problem for you right now, run to the Father. He already knows about it, so don't try to hide it. Lay it on the table. Confess your sin and claim His forgiveness (1 John 1:9).

2. Thank God that He knows you so thoroughly and loves you so completely. No one will ever know you better or love you more!

3. Give to the Lord that situation in which you were misunderstood, that incident in which someone misread your motives. Forgive the people involved if that's needed, and rest your case with God, realizing that He knows your heart.

4. Read Psalm 139:1–18, then take a look at yourself in the mirror today. Remember that you were created by a God whose knowledge is infinite and who had an infinite number of options to choose from. He knew exactly what He was doing when He chose to create you. Nothing about you is an afterthought!

FOR GROUP STUDY

Questions for Group Discussion

1. God's knowledge is tied to His purposes. One of the eternal purposes of God's knowledge is our salvation. Focus on Ephesians 1:4–6. What is the main point of this passage? Expand your study by examining Acts 2:23. How do we reconcile the reality that God has determined events of history while making us free moral agents with decision-making ability?

2. Hebrews 4:13 tells us that "there is no creature hidden from His sight, but all things are open and laid bare to the eyes of Him with whom we have to do." God's "eye," (an anthropomorphism, or assigning human characteristics to God) involves more than the process of seeing; it also involves understanding. Do a study on the phrase "eyes of the Lord" to discover just how penetrating they are. Include in your study Proverbs 15:3; 5:21; 2 Chronicles 16:9; Job 34:21–22; and Jeremiah 16:17; 23:24; 32:19.

3. The Bible tells us that God's knowledge is intuitive (Isaiah 40:13–14). He has innate knowledge of all data at all times. Do we always pray with that in mind? When we bring out concerns and requests in prayer to God, it obviously is not to inform Him about the facts surrounding our needs. He knows all about them. Why do you think God wants us to come to Him in prayer and listens to what we know and perceive about our lives? Note Hannah's prayer of thanksgiving and praise to God (1 Samuel 2:3).

4. Examine the these passages from the Bible: Isaiah 40:13–14 (God's intuitive knowledge); Psalm 147:5 (God's infinite knowledge); Psalm 139 (God's personal knowledge). What new insights about God's all-knowingness can we gain from those passages?

PICTURE THIS

An aspect of God's omniscience, and perhaps surprising to some, is that it is intensely personal. We are part of God's knowledge, and it embraces us in our day-to-day living.

GOD'S KNOWLEDGE AND US

WHAT GOD'S KNOWLEDGE DOES	SCRIPTURE PASSAGES	WHAT IT TEACHES US
It knows us.	Ezekiel 11:5; 1 Samuel 16:7	God knows every thought of our minds and every intent of our hearts.
It understands us.	Job 23:101; Psalm 103:14	God knows we are made of dust and fallible. He knows our every pain and heartache.
It sees through us.	Matthew 23:37	God looks past what we say and do and sees the state of our inner being.

8

THE OMNIPRESENCE OF GOD

There's a story told about a man who was walking in the marketplace of Damascus and came face-to-face with Death. The man noticed an expression of surprise on Death's face. The man himself was terrified, looking Death in the face, knowing that it had come for him. So he took off running and went to a wise friend for advice. "In the marketplace I just saw Death, and he was staring me right in the face. What should I do?"

The wise man said, "What you've got to do is run to the city of Aleppo. Go to that city and get away from Death."

So the man got on his horse and reached Aleppo in record time to get away from Death. When he arrived, he wiped his brow and congratulated himself that he had escaped Death. But just then, Death came up to him and tapped him on the shoulder. "Excuse me, but I have come for you."

The man looked at him and said, "How can this be? I thought I met you in Damascus yesterday."

Death looked at him and said, "Exactly! That's why I looked so surprised when I saw you, because I was scheduled to meet you in Aleppo today."

That's what it's like to try and escape an omnipresent God. When you run from Him and you get to where you were going, you bump into Him.

There is nowhere to run, nowhere to hide. There is no place in creation where God does not exist—and exist in all His divine fullness. That's why David asked, "Where can I go from Your Spirit? Or where can I flee from Your presence?" (Psalm 139:7). We'll see his answer below.

Omnipresence is the second in the trilogy of God's "omni" attributes. The word *omnipresence* is very simple to understand: *Omni* means "all," as we learned in chapter 7. *Presence* is a common word, having to do with locality. The omnipresence of God means that His complete essence is fully present in all places at all times.

PEOPLE WANT TO LIMIT GOD

Most people are not comfortable with an omnipresent God. That's why people like idols: They can see them, touch them, and, most important, control them. Even some people who go to church do not want to worship the God of the Bible.

Some have taken this to extremes and created entire theological systems in an attempt to confine, limit, or control God. You are probably familiar with pantheism, which teaches that God is an impersonal force. This idea was popularized in the Star Wars movie series, where God was the impersonal "force" and was identified with nature.

In pantheism, everything partakes of God. The trees are a part of God; the mountains are a part of God; and the lakes, streams, and oceans are a part of God. Of course, we are a part of God too, so nobody can sin or be separated from Him or need salvation. God becomes merely the harmless, amoral sum total of all natural elements. That is heresy!

The other extreme is deism. Deism says we have seen God's power, but we don't know much of His presence. God set the universe in motion according to fixed laws, then He turned His attention elsewhere. He is not involved in the daily affairs of this world. He exists way out there, an absentee landlord who has little real involvement with His creation. Deism is also a heresy.

The omnipresence of God says that our God dwells intimately in history and yet exists totally outside of history. He is both transcendent and immanent at the same time.

GOD IS FREE OF LIMITATIONS

In 1 Kings 8, Solomon dedicated the magnificent temple he built as a dwelling place for the glory of God so that Israel will know it is God's house. But Solomon did not want the people to get confused and think that God's presence was limited to their building. So he prayed in verses 26–27:

> Now therefore, O God of Israel, let Your word, I pray, be confirmed which You have spoken to Your servant, my father David. But will God indeed dwell on the earth? Behold, heaven and the highest heaven cannot contain You, how much less this house which I have built!

No Limitations of Space

God's presence is in the sphere of immensity and infinitude. *Infinitude*, or infinity, means "that which is without limit." *Immensity* refers to that which cannot be contained. God's presence is so vast that not only is He everywhere in the known universe, but He bursts through the limits of the universe and fills everything we do not even know about.

Many of us understand the problem of immensity as we gain weight. We search through the closet and put on clothes, and we begin bursting out of them. When man tries to stuff God into the universe, Solomon says to God, "You burst out of it. It cannot contain You."

God's presence is immense. He cannot be contained. God's presence is also distinct in that all of Him exists everywhere. He is not broken up into parts. Each little piece of the universe has the entire presence of God. We know this because God's being possesses what theologians call simplicity. That is, He cannot be divided. God is spirit; therefore, He exists everywhere at the same time.

No Limitations of Flesh

"God is spirit," Jesus said in John 4:24. He's an uncompounded being. So everything everywhere is encompassed by the full presence of God. So, for instance, you don't have to worry that I am drawing on His omniscience while someone else is using His omnipotence; that you have His omnipresence while someone else is borrowing His power. God is present everywhere in all the fullness of His deity.

The problem is, sometimes we don't feel that God is with us. We can't see Him, so we wonder if He's there. But we experience many things we don't see, like a chilly morning or the blowing of the wind. We know the wind is blowing because we see and feel its effects all around us. We have to put on a coat to keep off the chill, or struggle to keep the wind from turning our umbrellas inside out.

This is why the Bible declares it takes a fool to say, "There is no God" (Psalm 14:1). Only a fool would say to himself, *It's not chilly,* or *It's not windy,* when all the evidence pointed to the contrary.

It's obvious to anyone who goes outside that God's presence is everywhere. Just as light and air fill a room, God fills the universe and more. He is omnipresent. We can trick ourselves into thinking otherwise by becoming spiritual ostriches.

God Is with Us

God is in all the nooks and crannies and crevices of life. Some people say, for example, "I don't think my prayers are getting past the ceiling." They don't have to get even that high. God stands in the room with us. We are dealing with a Being unlike anyone we've ever met because He lives in infinity. We are limited to space. We can only be in one place at a time. He has none of these limitations.

It's important to understand that Satan is not omnipresent. He is a created being who can be only one place at a time. But if Satan is limited, how can he seem to be everywhere, causing so much trouble all the time? Because he's the ruler of a demonic kingdom (Ephesians 2:2). He has a vast army to whom he issues orders, and Satan is so effective because his followers do what God's followers too often don't. They obey, and in their obedience they wreak havoc.

But Satan is not omnipresent. That's why John can declare, "Greater is He who is in you than he who is in the world" (1 John 4:4). "He who is in you" is everywhere equally all the time. That's the God we have.

GOD IS INTIMATELY INVOLVED WITH CREATION

After David raised the question we quoted previously in Psalm 139:7, he provided the answer:

> If I ascend to heaven, You are there; if I make my bed in Sheol, behold, You are there. If I take the wings of the dawn, if I dwell in the remotest part of the sea, even there Your hand will lead me, and Your right hand will lay hold of me. (vv. 8–10)

Too Big to Avoid

David says to God, "No matter where I go, I run into You." But this is good news to the psalmist, because he goes on to say in verses 11–12:

> If I say, "Surely the darkness will overwhelm me, and the light around me will be night," even the darkness is not dark to You, and the night is as bright as the day. Darkness and light are alike to You.

No matter where he went, David knew that he would run into the sustaining hand and presence of God.

Too Close to Ignore

God is so close you can't get away from Him. That means He's near you today. I don't know what you are facing, but He's right beside you—and because He's omniscient, He knows what's going on. He's not a "do nothing" God.

A man in Scripture tried to run from God. Jonah was a prophet, a man whose job it was to carry the truth of God to people who needed to hear it. But when God told him to go to the Ninevites, Israel's cruel enemies, Jonah didn't want to do it. So Jonah basically said no to God and bought a ticket to go to Tarshish in the opposite direction (Jonah 1:1–3).

Jonah thought he had run away from God, but he forgot something. You can't run from God without running through Him and winding up running toward Him. Jonah got on that ship, but God took care of the problem by ordering the sea to track Jonah down. A fierce storm erupted on the sea. The waves rose and pointed a finger right at Jonah.

Jonah was trying to go two thousand miles west to Tarshish when he should have gone just five hundred miles east to Nineveh. When you run from God, the trip is always longer and harder than it would be if you stayed with Him.

But that was just the beginning. After the sailors tossed Jonah overboard, God sent him a "whale-o-gram," a fish to pick him up out of the water. God brought Jonah back and finally got him to Nineveh. The people repented, but Jonah wasn't happy about it and took off again, going out east of the city to pout over God's sparing of Israel's enemies (Jonah 4:5).

What a lineup God used to go after Jonah this time: a plant, a worm, and a "scorching east wind" (4:8). It's all at His command, and God can tell the waves or the wind what to do with you when you get to where you think you have moved beyond His presence.

Too Caring to Ignore Us

God knows where He wants to take us and how He wants to get us there. God calls on us to understand that He is intimately involved with us. Having a God who is everywhere and associated with everything means we have nothing we can't bring to His attention. He is acutely aware because He's intimately there. He can identify with the hurts, the struggles, and the pain. He can identify with our difficulties because He is intimately associated with each of us.

GOD'S OMNIPRESENCE BRINGS SPECIAL BENEFITS

We need to be clear on this one. Even though God is equally present everywhere in all of His fullness, He is not equally related to everyone and everything. In other words, we have an equality of essence but not of relationship.

The Bible teaches that God adjusts His presence, so to speak, to things and people based on how He is related to them. Read Isaiah 43:1-7 and you'll see this very clearly. God takes care of His own. He is present with His children in a way that He is not present with those who don't know Him. If you know Jesus Christ, God treats you as His child, as part of His family. You enjoy the special, relational presence of God. Here are some of the benefits of His special presence.

Guidance

God's children benefit from His special guidance. Jacob found that out in a dramatic way in Genesis 28. He was fleeing from Esau after stealing his birthright. On his flight he stopped for the night. With a stone for a pillow, he went to sleep and had his famous dream of the ladder going from earth to heaven and the angels of God ascending and descending on the ladder.

In his dream, Jacob also saw God standing above the ladder. God reaffirmed His covenant promises to Jacob (vv. 13–14), then He declared, "I am with you and will keep you wherever you go and will bring you back to this land; for I will not leave you until I have done what I have promised you" (v. 15).

Victory over Temptation

Another benefit you get as a child of God is victory over temptation. Paul says in 1 Corinthians 10:13 that "no temptation has overtaken you but such as is common to man; and God is faithful, who will . . . provide the way of escape also, so that you may be able to endure it."

How does God's presence bear on your temptations? Paul says that "your body is a temple of the Holy Spirit" (1 Corinthians 6:19). Wherever you go, God goes; whatever you do, God does; you can go no place where He is not. That's why He can provide a way of escape. He knows what door you need to run through. He's with you when you are being tempted.

But this is also a call to holiness because it means that God stays with you when you fail, when you sin. In the context of the verse I just quoted, Paul says that when you engage in a sexual relationship outside of marriage, you have engaged God in the affair. Why? Because "you are not your own" (v. 19).

Now you haven't contaminated God, but His presence is associated with us when we sin. We've got to understand that when we sin, it's as if we were doing it in God's throne room. He watches us do what we're doing, think what we're thinking, say what we're saying, act like we're acting. He asks us, "How could you do that with Me standing here?"

That's why when we do sin, we must confess it because God is already in on it. He watched the whole act and heard the whole conversation. He was there during your time of temptation. He's in us, around us, over us, under us, and beside us. He is the all-present God.

Provision for Needs

God's special, relational presence is also available to us in our needs. For example, have you ever had bills you can't pay, financial turmoil you can't handle? Hebrews 13:5 has a glorious promise for you, but an important condition is attached to it: "Make sure that your character be free from the love of money, being content with what you have. For He Himself has said, 'I will never desert you, nor will I ever forsake you.'"

The problem is that we are often not content. We would be further along financially today if we had been more content yesterday. But because we weren't content yesterday, we got into debt yesterday that we can't pay today. It's not because God didn't supply. It's because we weren't content with what He gave us.

You may say, "But I don't see where the money will come from to pay my bills." You don't see God either, do you? But you know He's there. You don't have to see Him to know that He's at work. But first He has to get you free from the love of money. Otherwise, it won't do any good to deliver you from financial bondage because you'll soon be right back.

You see, some of us love money so much we don't have time to go to church. We love money so much we can't give any to the Lord because we are paying the bills we ran up satisfying our own pleasure. We don't work to live, we live to work, but we are never content. God can tell us to be content because He has promised us His presence.

Here's another great promise. Paul says, "My God will supply all your needs according to His riches in glory in Christ Jesus" (Philippians 4:19). But the context of this promise discusses liberal giving to God's work.

Freedom from the love of money and contentment are what keep us from trying to turn God's promises of supply into a "health and wealth gospel." You can't command God to make you wealthy. It won't do you any good to run up a bunch of bad bills and then bring them to church in a wheelbarrow for someone to pray over them and demand that God pay them. It doesn't work like that.

I'm not saying don't try to improve or get ahead. I'm saying to be content on the way there. Paul gives us invaluable insight on this in Philippians 4:11–13. He calls what he learned a "secret," and it must be a secret because so few folk seem to know about it. Whether he had nothing or was abundantly supplied, Paul had learned to be content with what God provided because he had learned, "I can do all things through Him who strengthens me" (v. 13).

Freedom from Anxiety

God lets you get lonely so you will discover what kind of friend He can really be. The truth is, some of us haven't gotten lonely enough yet. We don't run to God when no one else is around. Instead, we go looking for someone else instead of saying, "Lord, let me snuggle up to You."

No, you can't see God, but you don't have to see Him to know He is there. As I said earlier, you don't have to see the wind for it to affect you. If it's blowing hard enough, it will turn your umbrella inside out, pull your coat off your back, make your car swerve as you drive down the road.

You don't need to see God to know that He's right by your side. He only has to let the wind of His Spirit blow by you in that lonely room, or wherever you are. The good news of God's relational presence is that you can talk to Him no matter what you are doing, no matter what the time of day, no matter what your circumstance.

In Isaiah 41:10, God makes this wonderful promise: "Do not fear, for I am with you; do not anxiously look about you, for I am your God. I will strengthen you, surely I will help you, surely I will uphold you with My righteous right hand."

So what's the bottom line? Philippians 4:6–7 tells us:

> Be anxious for nothing, but in everything by prayer and supplication with thanksgiving let your requests be made known to God. And the peace of God, which surpasses all comprehension, will guard your hearts and your minds in Christ Jesus.

PERSONAL APPLICATION FOR LIFE

1. One way to make the truth of God's omnipresence real in your life this week is to be sure there are no distractions that would keep you from hearing His voice. Turn off the TV or lay aside the newspaper a little earlier than usual for the next few days, and spend those extra minutes enjoying His presence.

2. Perhaps you're angry at God right now because it seems He has forgotten or abandoned you. If so, don't let another day go by without dealing with your hurt. Be honest before Him; He can handle the truth. If it would help, discuss your problem with your pastor or a trusted friend, and ask for prayer support.

3. The reality of God's presence should renew your confidence in prayer. Look at your prayer list today and pick out your toughest circumstance, greatest need, or biggest fear. Thank God that He is present in this situation, and ask Him for the grace to continue praying about it and awaiting His answer.

4. Be sure you are taking full advantage of God's presence and promise of victory in spiritual warfare. Read over the Christian's list of armor in Ephesians 6 and "polish up" any piece of your armor that may have become a little rusty.

FOR GROUP STUDY

Questions for Group Discussion

1. Take a moment to think of one or two freedoms you experience or exercise as an individual, and then to observe their limitations. Contrast your experiences of limitation with that of God's unlimited omnipresence. What are some of your thoughts?

2. Being the finite creatures we are, it's easy for us to limit our vision of God, to consciously or unknowingly place Him in a "box." As you dwell on the concept of God's unlimited presence, consider some of the ways

we tend to box in God. What about your prayer life? How about your dealing with circumstances? As a result of this discussion, might there be promises of God's Word that you might want to reclaim in a renewed way?

3. First John 4:4 tells us that "greater is He who is in you than he who is in the world." The latter part of verse 4 refers to Satan and his demonic kingdom. Satan's presence and power are limited. Not only is God everywhere we are, His indwelling Holy Spirit resides within and ministers to the believer. As we deal with temptation and strive to live a holy life, what encouragements can we draw from the fact that our God is unlimited and Satan is not?

4. Dr. Evans points out that Isaiah 43:1–7 teaches that God adjusts His presence to things and people based on how He is related to them. He goes on to point out several benefits believers enjoy because of God's relational presence. Study these seven verses in Isaiah. What encouragements and promises can you draw from this passage?

PICTURE THIS

As children of God, we are part of His family. We enjoy God's special, relational presence. Below is a snapshot of some of the benefits of His special presence.

Benefits of God's Omnipresence

BENEFIT	SCRIPTURE PASSAGES	BENEFIT REALIZED
Special guidance	Genesis 28:13–15	God constantly leads us. Even the negatives are part of His positive program.
Victory over temptation	1 Corinthians 10:13	God is with us when we are tempted and will help us find a way of escape.
Provision for needs	Hebrews 13:5–6; Philippians 4:11–13	God's relational presence is available to us in our needs. He controls provisions and circumstances.
Freedom from anxiety	Isaiah 41:10; Philippians 4:6-7	In the midst of difficulties, God is with us and strengthens us.

9

THE OMNIPOTENCE OF GOD

Did you know that I can lift a ton? You may not believe it, but I can. So now you're going to say, "Show me." All right, just let me hitch a ride on the next space probe that lands on the moon. Then turn on your television and watch me lift a ton.

How can I do that? Because the law of gravity is vastly different on the moon than it is on Earth. What would be impossible for me on Earth is easy on the moon because I'm standing on a different sphere and I have different power. On the moon I am less limited by the law that says, "What goes up must come down."

In other words, if you change my environment, I can do things I can't do here on earth. We have problems with the power of God because we keep Him in our environment. We try to limit Him to what we know on earth, so we just know that He can't do this or that. But God lives in a realm far beyond us, and His power operates according to vastly different rules.

As we look at the omnipotence of God, we once again enter a realm far beyond anything we have ever experienced before. All of us are concerned at one level or another with the issue of power. People want political power. Our generation has seen the power of atomic energy unleashed. In the past few years we have seen the power of nature in unforgettable ways as water, wind, fire, and earthquakes have wreaked havoc on this planet.

But none of these can even begin to compare to the power, the omnipotence, of God. We already know that *omni* means "all." Therefore, God is all-powerful. But His omnipotence involves more than just raw power. God's omnipotence includes the exercise of His choice to use His unlimited power to reflect His divine glory and accomplish His sovereign will. Jesus taught us to pray, "Yours is . . . the power . . . forever" (Matthew 6:13).

Like His other attributes, God's omnipotence has a moral base. He uses His power to magnify His glory and accomplish His perfect will. He's not strutting His stuff—but make no mistake, God is powerful. The sum total of all the power in all the universe would be like a toenail on the person of God.

GOD'S POWER IS UNLIMITED

Because God is infinite, He is infinitely powerful. Isaiah asks, "Do you not know? Have you not heard? The Everlasting God, the Lord, the Creator of the ends of the earth does not become weary or tired. His understanding is inscrutable" (Isaiah 40:28).

The psalmists agree. David declares, "Power belongs to God" (Psalm 62:11). "Great is our Lord, and abundant in strength," the writer says in Psalm 147:5.

Creative Power

All that has ever been made or that will ever be made was created by the power of God. According to Psalm 89:11, "The heavens are Yours, the earth also is Yours; the world and all it contains, You have founded them." God can create a universe because He has no limitations. He has made things we haven't even discovered yet. And when we add to this the fact that God is infinitely greater than all of His creation, we are talking about someone who is unbelievable in power.

Autonomous man has turned away in rebellion from this fact and taken refuge in science. In science classes at every level of education, especially in college and postgraduate work, you find that puny, independent, insignificant, rebellious, on-his-way-to-the-grave man has dismissed God from the discussion and decided to take His place.

But true science is the process of observing the consistency of God. Scientists look for consistent patterns. When they see that a pattern does not change, they call it a law. But then they give nature the credit for this law when they have really only discovered that God is consistent. He never meant for us to take credit for His work or to give the credit to some ambiguous entity called nature.

"Out of Nothing" Power

God is not only unlimited in what He can do. He is unlimited in how He gets it done. God's power is so limitless that He can create *ex nihilo*, meaning "out of nothing." He did not need raw material to put together His creation.

The Bible declares that God "calls into being that which does not exist" (Romans 4:17). That's power!

Self-generating Power

God's power is self-generating. It can be compared to a generator that always runs and never needs fueling or fixing. God never needs anything outside of Himself to generate or sustain His power. His omnipotence is such that by His speaking the word, "the heavens were made" (Psalm 33:6). "He spoke, and it was done" (v. 9), because God generates His power within Himself.

People often say that God has to show them His power before they'll believe. But He has shown us His power. The evidence of it surrounds us. God asked Job a very interesting question: "Where were you when I laid the foundation of the earth?" (Job 38:4). God was saying, "I didn't have to get advice or help from you to pull any of this off."

Think about this. It takes no more effort for God to create a universe than it does for Him to create an ant. All He has to do is say, "Ant be," and you've got an ant. He says, "Universe be," and you've got a universe. No effort is involved here.

Some time ago, I came out to my kitchen late at night and found a roach on my counter. But this was unlike any other roach I had ever seen. This was a "jump bad in your face, get down" roach. I walked up to the roach, but this brother didn't run away. He just stood there as if to say, "Look, this is my house."

I couldn't believe it. It was amazing to look at this thing. I would move my hand in front of it, and it did not move. Obviously, he did not know who I was, because I squashed that boy flat!

That's what autonomous man does. He gets "roachy" on God. He pops back like he is someone, like he has a little power. He's got a little degree behind his name. He's got some machines that can take him into outer space, and he thinks he's got some power. But it's suicide to "jump bad" against God. He has unlimited power.

GOD'S OMNIPOTENCE IS BROAD IN SCOPE

The prophet Jeremiah says, "Ah Lord God! Behold, You have made the heavens and the earth by Your great power and by Your outstretched arm! Nothing is too difficult for You" (Jeremiah 32:17).

Once you know God can make the universe, nothing else is hard. If He can pull that off, He can do anything because the universe includes everything.

Power over Nature

If you don't believe God has power over nature, ask Pharaoh. Ask the children of Israel, who went through the Red Sea and saw God hold back nature and then collapse it on the Egyptians. Ask the people of Sodom and Gomorrah after the brimstone fell from heaven to destroy those two cities. Ask Noah's family after it rained for forty days and forty nights. Ask the disciples who were in the boat with Jesus when He said, "Peace, be still!"

God's power over nature is so broad that it sustains as well as creates things: "He [Jesus] is the radiance of His [the Father's] glory and the exact representation of His nature, and upholds all things by the word of His power" (Hebrews 1:3).

The word *upholds* means "to sustain." We don't fly off the earth because God sustains the law of gravity. The earth doesn't spin out of its orbit because He keeps it intact. We don't burn or freeze to death because God keeps the sun at just the right distance from us.

Power to Give Life

Psalm 139 talks about all three of God's "omni" attributes, including His omnipotence. David says in verses 13–14: "You formed my inward parts; You wove me in my mother's womb. I will give thanks to You, for I am fearfully and wonderfully made."

Any doctor will tell you that the two cells which come together in a mother's womb already carry the DNA code to determine the baby's race, height, and every other trait down to the shape of its nose. God has to know what He's doing to pull that off! He has to be powerful.

Power over the Enemy

God's power is also seen in His ability to handle the other side of life—the demons. In Matthew 8:28–34, Jesus came upon two demon-possessed men. They had lost their minds and turned violent as a result of this demonic oppression. The demons saw Jesus and cried out, knowing what His power could do to them. So the demons asked Jesus for permission to leave the men and go into a herd of pigs nearby. Jesus dismissed the demons, who entered the herd of pigs and destroyed them.

The Devil wants to destroy you, but one Person has more power than the Devil and his entire realm, and that is God. He is the only One who can dismiss those things that will drive you crazy and tear you apart.

Power over Illness

God also has power over illness. Luke 9:11 says the people brought their sick ones to Jesus, and He healed them. I could give multiple examples here, but it would take the rest of the chapter.

Power over Circumstances

This is another of the wonderful lessons that Jeremiah wrote about in chapter 32. God told the prophet, "I'm going to judge Israel by bringing the Babylonians in to destroy the nation and carry you off." But with the city of Jerusalem under siege by the Babylonians, God told Jeremiah to buy himself a plot of land (Jeremiah 32:6–9).

Jeremiah obeyed and bought the land, although it seemed to make about as much sense as arranging deck chairs on the *Titanic*. In verse 25, he expressed his misgivings to God. After all, wasn't Israel about to be carried off into captivity? What good would a piece of land do Jeremiah?

The prophet was distressed. His circumstances were bad, but God had another word for him. First, though, the Lord needed to establish some ground rules. So He asked Jeremiah, "Behold, I am the Lord, the God of all flesh; is anything too difficult for Me?" (v. 27). This was not a multiple-choice question, so Jeremiah knew the answer had to be no.

Why did God make this declaration of His omnipotence? Because He was about to tell Jeremiah that when the captivity of Israel was finished, He would bring the nation back to its land and the people would enjoy prosperity again (vv. 36–44). Then Jeremiah's deed would mean something. The negative was not the last word because God has power over circumstances.

Power over Death

God is even more powerful than death. By His power every man, woman, boy, and girl who has ever lived and trusted Jesus for forgiveness of their sins will be raised from the dead.

Whenever Jesus said to a dead person, "Get up!" that person got up. He called Lazarus from the grave, and Lazarus came out bound in grave clothes even though he had been dead for three days.

Now that's good news, because when the doctor says to your family, "He's gone," if you know Jesus, He is going to say at the same time, "Get up! Come on out of there and come home." Because only God has power over life and death and everything in between, no one else can offer you that hope.

GOD'S OMNIPOTENCE IS PURPOSEFUL

In Genesis 17:1–5, we read about a man who up to this point was known as Abram. God told him, "No longer shall your name be called Abram, but your name shall be Abraham; for I will make you the father of a multitude of nations" (v. 5).

We've got a problem here. God promises a ninety-nine-year-old childless man that entire nations will come from him and his eighty-nine-year-old wife, Sarah, who has been unable to have children. Ask any nursing home worker, and he or she will tell you that you have a problem on your hands when you make that kind of promise.

But that's exactly what God did. In Genesis 18:10, the Lord told Abraham: "I will surely return to you at this time next year; and behold, Sarah your wife shall have a son."

The idea of getting pregnant at her age, especially when she looked at old Abraham, struck Sarah as so improbable that she laughed at God. But Sarah did give birth to Isaac, and Abraham did father a nation called Israel.

Now if you are eighty-nine years old and pray, "Lord, I want to get pregnant," you may have a problem. It's not that God can't do with you what He did with Sarah, but in His purposes it is not necessary. He had a specific purpose in Sarah's pregnancy. Her child was the fulfillment of God's covenant promise. He was building a great nation through which He would show the world His mighty power and grace, and starting that nation through a miraculous birth showed His ability to keep the other promises related to the nation of Israel.

You can never detach God's omnipotence from His sovereignty. Revelation 19:6 puts it this way: "Hallelujah! For the Lord our God, the Almighty, reigns." That is, His omnipotence is tied to His rule, and His rule is tied to His will. So to get His power, you must be tied to His will.

Jesus understood this. According to Hebrews 5:7, Jesus cried out to His Father, knowing that the Father had the power to deliver Him from death. Jesus did not want to die on that cross, but in the garden of Gethsemane we find Him praying, "Yet not what I will, but what You will" (Mark 14:36). With God, it's never a question of power. The issue is matching His power with His will.

So the question is always, What is God's will? That should be our major concern, finding and getting in line with the will of God. God's desires are never more extensive than His powers. He says in Isaiah 46:10, "My purpose will be established, and I will accomplish all My good pleasure."

GOD'S OMNIPOTENCE IS PERSONAL

Here's the best part. The ones who really get to see God's power are His people. In Ephesians 3:19–20 Paul prays that we might comprehend the love of

Christ and "be filled up to all the fullness of God." Then in verse 20 Paul says, "Now to Him *who is able* to do far more abundantly beyond all that we ask or think, according to the power that works within us" (italics added).

If you ever forget the word *omnipotent*, if the word *power* doesn't do anything for you, just do what the writers of the Bible did. They reached back to an old phrase and simply said, "He's able." If you lose the theology of it, if you don't know how to match omnipotence with sovereignty, just remember this phrase: "He's able."

He's Able to Save

The Bible says, first of all, that God is able to save you forever (Hebrews 7:25). Not only that, but "[God] is able to guard what I have entrusted to Him until that day" (2 Timothy 1:12). You can't lose your salvation once you are truly saved, not because you are holding on to God, but because He's able to hold on to you.

If we had to maintain our own salvation, we'd be saved one day, lost the next day; saved one minute, lost the next minute. I'm grateful that God is able because if He weren't, I would be living in fear of committing a sin and being lost forever. But now that I know He's able, I realize my salvation does not depend on me. It's not me holding God's hand, it's God holding my hand.

He's Able to Meet Needs

God is also able to meet all of your needs. In 2 Corinthians 9:8 Paul writes, "God is able to make all grace abound to you, so that always having all sufficiency in everything, you may have an abundance for every good deed." You need to understand that he is speaking to Christians who have honored God and not robbed Him in giving, who have not given God the leftovers and then come to Him later for a blessing.

God is able, Paul says, to take care of those bills. He's able to pay off those credit cards. He's able to handle that mortgage note. He's able to deal with the finances of those who are following Him, who are His people.

He's Able to Heal

God is also able to heal. In Matthew 9:27–29, two blind men followed Jesus crying out, "Have mercy on us, Son of David!"

Jesus looked at them and had just one question: "Do you believe that I am able to do this?"

They said, "Yes, Lord."

That's all it took. Jesus said, "It shall be done to you according to your faith," and He healed them.

He's Able to Deliver

The Bible says God is able to deliver us. And so, when King Nebuchadnezzar threatened to throw Shadrach, Meshach, and Abednego into the fiery furnace, they replied, "Our God whom we serve is able to deliver us from the furnace of blazing fire" (Daniel 3:17).

Later, Daniel himself was thrown into the lions' den (Daniel 6). The king came down the next day, removed the stone, peered in, and asked Daniel, "Has your God, whom you constantly serve, been able to deliver you from the lions?" (v. 20).

Daniel's answer (paraphrased), "He's able. He delivered me."

He's Able to Keep You

Listen to the opening of a great benediction: "Now to Him who is able to keep you from stumbling, and to make you stand in the presence of His glory blameless with great joy" (Jude 24).

God may let you trip, but He won't let you fall because He's able. He may allow you to have some difficulty, but He will hold your hand. If your marriage is falling apart, God can put it back together because He's able. If you've got a habit of any sort that you can't handle, bring it to God because He's able to help you beat it.

In light of this, we need to do what Paul advised the Ephesians to do: "Be strong in the Lord, and in the strength of His might" (Ephesians 6:10). Remember, God's ability to do "exceeding abundantly beyond all that we ask or think" is "according to the power that works within us."

If you don't have any power at work in you, then you won't see any power at work through you. The biggest problem with seeing God's power is that Christians aren't committed. They aren't submissive to His will, so they don't believe God has all this power. But if He can create the universe, He can handle your problems!

PERSONAL APPLICATION FOR LIFE

1. In light of what we have learned, are you in a situation where you have been pushing too hard, trying to arrange things or make something happen on your own? If so, you could be blocking God from exercising His power. Step back from your efforts for a while, and ask God to show you His power.

2. Take some time to recall recent occasions when God revealed Himself to you in a mighty way. Try to be specific; it doesn't have to be a major event. Discuss your findings with your spouse, your family, or a friend. If your list is blank, maybe it's time to get alone with God on your knees.

3. What about that person, situation, or need you've given up on as impossible? If God can create a universe, He can do the impossible in your universe. Take that "impossible dream" and put it at the top of your prayer list. Do so exercising faith in God's power and in His sovereignty. If you need to, do like that distraught father and pray, "I do believe; help my unbelief" (Mark 9:24).Remember, a powerful God can act even on weak faith.

4. Turn to a great passage like Isaiah 40:28–31, or one of the psalms we have looked at, and read God's Word back to Him. He loves to hear it. Make the verses your prayer, saying, for example, "Lord, I need new strength. I need to mount up with wings like an eagle; I need the stamina to run and not get weary."

FOR GROUP STUDY

Questions for Group Discussion

1. Read Genesis 18:9–14. Do you remember responding to God's promises in a similar way as Sarah did? Share an example of God's power in your life that surprised you.

2. Dr. Evans points out that God's wisdom can order our lives. The Bible is replete with illustrations of this truth. Discuss the following biblical

accounts: Joseph and his brothers (Genesis 50:20); Esther and her cousin Mordecai (Esther 4); and the apostle Paul's "thorn in the flesh" (2 Corinthians 1:4–5; 12:7–9). What is the point of each, and what lessons might we draw from these about allowing God to order our own lives?

3. To get an accurate picture of God's omnipotence, it helps to take a look at the broad scope of His power. Examine each of the following elements of God's power and their accompanying Scripture passages: over nature (Hebrews 1:3); to give life (Psalm 139); over the enemy (Matthew 8:28–34); over illness (Luke 9:11); over circumstances (Jeremiah 32); over death (Hebrews 2:14). What existing ideas about the scope of God's power did you reinforce or expand upon? Were there any new discoveries?

4. What are the purposes for which God exercises His power? To begin, examine the accounts in Genesis 17:1–5 (God's covenant with Abram) and Genesis 18:10–12 (Sarah and Abraham). Also examine Revelation 19:6; Mark 14:36; and Isaiah 46:10. List the purposes you find that are linked to God's exercise of His power.

PICTURE THIS

God, in His wisdom, makes it possible for His people to experience and benefit from His power personally. Below are some ways God's omnipotence touches and changes the lives of His people.

God's Omnipotence Made Personal

GOD'S ABILITY	SCRIPTURE PASSAGES	GOD'S POWER REALIZED
Able to save	Hebrews 7:25; 2 Timothy 1:12	God saves us and guards our salvation.
Able to meet needs	2 Corinthians 9:8	God is able to meet all our needs.
Able to heal	Matthew 9:27–29	God, the Great Physician, has the power to heal.
Able to deliver	Daniel 3:17; 6:20	God can deliver us from the midst of our most difficult circumstances.
Able to keep	Jude 24; Ephesians 6:10	Although we may stumble, God gives strength to keep us from falling.

10

THE WISDOM OF GOD

The wisdom of God is His unique ability to so interrelate His attributes that He accomplishes His predetermined purpose by the best means possible. This definition contains a lot of parts, so let's break it down a little.

God's ability to use His attributes in perfect wisdom is unique because He is the only one who can do it. And we know from our study of God's sovereignty that He has a predetermined plan and purpose He is bringing about for His glory. His power and perfections guarantee that He will always accomplish His plan by the best means possible.

When we talk about wisdom, we refer to more than just knowledge. Wisdom is more than having information. All of us know people who are well educated but just plain dumb when it comes to day-to-day living. They have a lot of book sense but no common sense. So simply accumulating data is not having wisdom. Wisdom has to do with the use of the information we have rather than just its possession.

A good example of this use of wisdom appears in Exodus 31:1–5. Israel was building the tabernacle, and one of the skilled artisans doing the work was a man named Bezalel. The Lord told Moses that He had filled Bezalel with "the Spirit of God in wisdom" for all kinds of craftsmanship. In other words, Bezalel knew how to use his skills in the best way possible to make the most of his work and help achieve God's plan for the tabernacle.

When we talk about wisdom, we must consider a specific goal, the best means to reach that goal, and the materials necessary to get there. All three components are embodied in the idea of wisdom. Wisdom is the ability to work with information in such a way that you accomplish the right purpose with that data in the right way. With this in mind, I want to show you five things about the wisdom of God.

GOD'S WISDOM AND ETERNAL PURPOSE

God's wisdom does not operate outside of His purpose. Paul makes this clear in Ephesians 1:7–11:

> In Him we have redemption through His blood, the forgiveness of our trespasses, according to the riches of His grace, which He lavished upon us. In all wisdom and insight He made known to us the mystery of His will, according to His kind intention which He purposed in Him with a view to an administration suitable to the fullness of the times, that is, the summing up of all things in Christ, things in the heavens and things on the earth. In Him also we have obtained an inheritance, having been predestined according to His purpose who works all things after the counsel of His will.

God's wisdom is tied to His purpose. And Paul states His eternal purpose to be "the summing up of all things in Christ" for His glory. Everything God does in wisdom propels creation toward that one purpose, which is the same in history as it is throughout eternity: His own glory.

No One Wiser

That upsets a lot of people. They say, "Who does God think He is, constructing all events for all times just so that He might be glorified and Christ might be exalted? It's all Him, Him, Him: His will, His glory, and His Son. It's all Him!"

The best explanation I can offer is that God exists for Himself. The reason is simple: There is nothing or no one greater than Him for whom He could exist. God exists for Himself because He is the highest possible goal or end that could ever be reached. No one expressed it any better than Paul in the great benediction of Romans 11:33-36.

Everything that God constructs, He constructs with that goal in mind. Now remember the ingredients of wisdom. Wisdom is arranging things so they meet a goal in the best way possible. God's wisdom so constructs circumstances and people that they all wind up achieving His goal because there is no higher goal to which they could ever go. God is unique in this.

No wonder He is called "the only wise God" (Romans 16:27)! No one else could take all the events of history and so arrange them that they achieve one solitary, all-encompassing purpose.

No One Greater

You don't have to embrace God's goal. You don't even have to like it—but God will reach it anyway. You could only stop God from reaching His goal by being greater than He is, by having more attributes than He has. Since most of us know better than to try and checkmate God, we'd be much better off to cooperate with Him in achieving the goal His wisdom has set.

Did you know that God will ultimately achieve His purpose even in hell? The people in hell will help achieve the purpose of God, for they will glorify God throughout all eternity.

GOD'S WISDOM IS UNIQUE

God's wisdom is His unique ability to use His attributes in perfect harmony and balance: to blend them together, to take two attributes out over here and add two more over there, and so correlate them that they achieve exactly what He desires.

A Revealing Wisdom

Daniel 2 shows us this interworking in an interesting way. Daniel has just been given the interpretation of the king's dream, and he praises God for it. Notice that Daniel uses the term *wisdom* coupled with another of God's attributes to show how they operate together: "Then the mystery was revealed to Daniel in a night vision. Then Daniel blessed the God of heaven;

Daniel answered and said, 'Let the name of God be blessed forever and ever, for wisdom and power belong to Him'" (vv. 19–20).

An Ordering Wisdom

In His wisdom, God rearranges people, nations, and situations. Because God knows all things, He knows the best choices to make in the outworking of His plan. It takes infinite wisdom guiding perfect attributes. I'm not up to that, and neither are you. Only God can do it. Acts 15:18 puts it this way: "Known unto God are all his works from the beginning of the world" (KJV).

A Detailed Wisdom

I'm glad we've got a wise God putting it all together instead of leaving it up to us, because most people don't care about the details. When we see a machine with a lot of little parts in it, most of us are not concerned with the parts but simply with whether the machine works.

Your watch is a perfect example. When you want to know the time, you don't worry about the details of how a watch works. You just look at it because you only care about the goal: the time.

But God knows the details of all of His works so well that we can have confidence He's going to reach His goal and get there by the best means possible. As Hebrews 4:13 reminds us, "There is no creature hidden from His sight." God's wisdom is unique because it allows Him to interrelate His attributes.

GOD'S WISDOM IS EVIDENT

Let me cite four activities in history through which we see the wisdom of God.

In Creation

Psalm 104:24 says that "in wisdom" God made all of His works. God's wisdom is clearly seen by creation. In the same way as we can see the wisdom of the watchmaker in the watch, we can see the wisdom of the Earthmaker in the earth. David declares, "The heavens are telling of the glory of God" (Psalm 19:1).

In Salvation

God's wisdom manifests itself in a glorious way in the plan He devised for our salvation. In 1 Corinthians 1, Paul throws some jabs at folk who think they are smart:

> It is written, "I will destroy the wisdom of the wise, and the cleverness of the clever I will set aside." Where is the wise man? Where is the scribe? Where is the debater of this age? Has not God made foolish the wisdom of the world? (vv. 19–20)

None of us would have ever come up with the plan of salvation that God did. In our "wisdom" we would have made it much more confusing, complex, and inequitable. Earn your way to heaven. We would have devised a "layaway" salvation plan. But God designed a salvation free for all, available to all, by sending His Son to die for our sins.

God had a superior plan, even though the cross looks foolish to a dying world that prefers to depend on its own wisdom:

> For since in the wisdom of God the world through its wisdom did not come to know God, God was well-pleased through the foolishness of the message preached to save those who believe. . . . Because the foolishness of God is wiser than men, and the weakness of God is stronger than men. . . . But God has chosen the foolish things of the world to shame the wise, and God has chosen the weak things of the world to shame the things which are strong, and the base things of the world and the despised God has chosen . . . that no man may boast before God. (vv. 21, 25, 27–29)

God doesn't want to share His glory, so He chooses the thing that you would least think of to get the job done. That's why so many things in the Bible don't make sense. You and I wouldn't do it that way. Why does God do it that way? So that He gets the greatest glory.

In Jesus Christ

Jesus Christ is the wisdom of God in the flesh. The Bible says that in Him "are hidden all the treasures of wisdom and knowledge" (Colossians 2:3), and Christ "became to us wisdom from God" (1 Corinthians 1:30).

You get smart when you know Christ. Atheists are some of the most brilliant and yet dumbest people you ever want to meet. Their brilliance can explain the world, but their ignorance lets them explain the world in a way that explains God away.

In the Church

Here is another way in which God demonstrates His infinite wisdom:

> To me . . . this grace was given, to preach among the Gentiles the unfathomable riches of Christ, and to bring to light what is the administration of the mystery which for ages has been hidden in God, who created all things; so that the manifold wisdom of God might now be made known through the church. (Ephesians 3:8–10)

Paul says that God's wisdom, which is tied to His purpose, is manifold, the Greek word that means "multicolored," or "variegated," or many-sided.

As the wisdom of God shines through the church, the church becomes a prism that reveals all the colors and textures of His wisdom. Open the doors of any church, and you will see a collection of people who, despite all their faults and failures, are the living body of Christ.

GOD'S WISDOM IS GENEROUSLY AVAILABLE

The apostle James made one of the greatest offers in the Bible when he invited us to tap into the wisdom of God: "If any of you lacks wisdom, let him ask of God, who gives to all men generously and without reproach, and it will be given to him" (James 1:5).

In Trials

Verses 2–4 of James 1 tell us that this offer of wisdom is related to our trials. When God brings a trial into your life, His eternal purpose is that through this test you might bring Him glory. But you bring Him glory by passing the test, not by ducking it or just coasting through.

But God knows that this creates a problem for us. How do we handle the trials He sends? That's why the promise of James 1:5 is so important. God offers us His wisdom, and He offers it generously!

Notice, however, that God does not offer you His wisdom so you can figure out how to beat the system and avoid problems. Wisdom has to do with the response you need to make for His glory in the midst of problems. Many people pray the wrong prayer: "Lord, get me out of this trial!"

That's why James cautions, "Let endurance have its perfect result" (v. 4). God will keep you in His classroom until you finish His test. Now if you have taken tests like the ones I've taken, you sit in the room and try to outwait the teacher. But in this case, that can't happen. You will not outwait God. God is going to stay until you finish the test and you pass. If you fail, you get to retake the test. So you might as well study the first time so you can finish the test and move on.

Let God finish doing what He's doing, because He will give you the wisdom you need to pass the test. That's why Ephesians 5:17 says, "Do not be foolish, but understand what the will of the Lord is." God will show you how to bring Him the most glory by showing you what His will is for you in your time of testing.

In Our Constant Need

Now let me explain a few things about the wisdom God gives. First, we need it constantly. Every day we face important issues of life, so every day we need to be praying for wisdom. God says, "I will grant you My wisdom for handling trials if you will pray for it and be committed to it."

When We Ask

Second, we need to ask in faith. A double-minded person (James 1:8) is by definition uncommitted because he is trying to go in two directions at once. He's not sure if he's going to do what God wants done when God reveals it, and God's not going to waste His revelation on people who want to debate Him about it.

Many of us don't get our prayers for wisdom answered because we are double-minded. We have not decided ahead of time that we will do what God asks us to do.

One Dose at a Time

A third thing you need to know about God's wisdom is that He gives it one need or trial at a time. To pray "Lord, give me wisdom for this year" or "Help me to live my life wisely" doesn't really get you anywhere.

When We Want Answers

Fourth, getting God's wisdom does not guarantee that you will figure out why He allowed the trial. "The secret things belong to the Lord our God" (Deuteronomy 29:29). But God does guarantees us the wisdom to steer our lives over the twisting and sometimes treacherous roads of life. The famous Highway 1 along the California coast is an exciting drive, with some great views of the Pacific Ocean and coastline. But it's also a treacherous piece of road. At times you ride near the edge of the cliff with no guardrails—and the cliff drops nearly a mile straight down. It's called a "scenic highway." I call it "Suicide Road."

Once, when my kids were small, I drove Highway 1. They demanded, "Get off this thing at the next exit!" They were basically saying, "Dad, we have a fundamental problem with your driving skills on regular highways, so we certainly don't want to be at your mercy on Highway 1."

You know what's interesting about driving on roads like that? When you come to a treacherous curve, you don't get into a discussion of why they built this highway like this, why they put this curve here. You don't ask that. Your only concern is to negotiate the curve properly. Getting God's wisdom doesn't mean you get all the answers. But it will help you negotiate the curve that God has put in your path.

God's wisdom reveals what His will is for us while we are going through our trial. That often means that He has to spend a lot of time resisting our will. We move out in our own direction, and then we get ourselves all tangled up and wonder why we can't move forward. God has to resist us even though we are trying to go the right way, so we wind up praying, "Lord, I'm trying. How come You're resisting me?"

He's resisting us so He can get us untangled from ourselves. Only God in His wisdom can move us forward so that we can achieve His glory.

GOD'S WISDOM AND THE WORLD'S WISDOM

James 3 lays down another fundamental truth about God's wisdom. You cannot mix human wisdom and divine wisdom. God's wisdom is different from the wisdom of this world: "Who among you is wise and understanding? Let him show by his good behavior his deeds in the gentleness of wisdom" (v. 13).

Visibly Different

To be wise biblically doesn't necessarily mean to be educated and be able to crank out a lot of knowledge. That's why if you need advice, you shouldn't necessarily go to the most educated person you know. You may get only sophisticated-sounding ignorance. God's wisdom is walk, not talk. Here's how James distinguishes between God's wisdom and the world's wisdom:

> But if you have bitter jealousy and selfish ambition in your heart, do not be arrogant and so lie against the truth. This wisdom is not that which comes down from above, but is earthly, natural, demonic. For where jealousy and selfish ambition exist, there is disorder and every evil thing. (James 3:14–16)

Just as there is heavenly wisdom, there is hellish wisdom. James says, "It's the way everyone thinks, but it's straight from hell." Notice how he couples the words *natural* and *demonic.* So if it's the normal way unsaved people think, then it's born in hell. You'd expect a child of the Devil to think like his daddy.

This wisdom has visible results. It produces jealousy and selfish ambition. It promotes itself, pushing others down so it can climb up. It's prideful and deceitful. It produces divisiveness instead of unity. The result of worldly wisdom is "disorder and every evil thing."

Experientially Different

Do you know why our homes have disorder? Because too many of our marriages and families operate out of envy and ambition. Instead of everyone upholding the central goal of the home, every family member wants his or her agenda. What else can you have but discord? That's earthly wisdom.

But James offers us another kind of wisdom, the "wisdom from above" (v. 17), which he says is first of all "pure." That means it's authentic, transparent, clean, like God's Word. Psalm 19:8 says, "The commandment of the Lord is pure."

God's wisdom is also "peaceable," promoting unity and not strife; "gentle," meaning considerate; "reasonable," willing to take instruction, ready to listen to people who make sense; "full of mercy and good fruits," giving practical help to others; "unwavering," taking a stand on principles instead of flowing one way today and another way tomorrow; and "without hypocrisy," not wearing a mask. That's what a wise person looks like.

PERSONAL APPLICATION FOR LIFE

Here are four things you can do to get wisdom from our all-wise God who has made His wisdom available to us:

1. Admit that you need it. Proverbs 11:2 says that wisdom is given only to the humble. You've got to admit that you don't know what you thought you knew. Make this your prayer: "Lord, I need You. I don't know how negotiate the turns in the road of my life today."

2. Fear the Lord. The Bible declares again and again that "the fear of the Lord is the beginning of wisdom" (Psalm 111:10). That doesn't mean to be petrified of God, but to stand in awe of Him, believing that He knows what He's talking about. It means to reverence God. God doesn't want to give you His wisdom if it's going to be treated like leftover information. Come to God recognizing who He is.

3. Study the Word. Read Psalm 119:97–100 and you'll see that David's study of God's Word gave him wisdom and made him wiser than his enemies, and even wiser than his elders and his teachers. Only God can make you wiser than all of those folks. How are you doing in your personal Bible study. No number of books can replace that.

4. Pray for wisdom. Go back to James 1:5 where we're told to ask God for His wisdom. If you don't ask for it, He's not going to give it to you, because you don't want it enough.

FOR GROUP STUDY

Questions for Group Discussion

1. Have the group leader ask each member to take a moment to consider the concept of wisdom and to write his or her own working definition of wisdom. After comparing your thoughts with what you learned about God's wisdom from this lesson, what were your ideas and insights?

2. When asking God for wisdom, James 1:6 tells us, "But he must ask in faith without any doubting, for the one who doubts is like the surf of

the sea, driven and tossed by the wind." This verse paints a picture of restless swaying to and fro on the surface of the sea, being blown by the shifting ocean breezes. The word *doubt* in the original Greek text means "to be at variance with oneself; to hesitate, waver." Read James 1:1–7 and discuss the proper way to approach God for wisdom. Read also Romans 4:20 for an example of one who did not waver.

3. How is God's wisdom unique? (See Daniel 2:19–23.) Dr. Evans mentions several ways God's wisdom is unique: it is revealing, ordering, and detailed. How do these unique features work their way into our lives?

4. As Dr. Evans points out, God's wisdom is generously available. At times, experiences and trials in life will create a special need for God's wisdom. Generally, we need God's wisdom to make the right decisions in life. As God's wisdom is generously available to us, what steps can we take to ensure that we are available and in a position to receive it? James 1:2–6 is a good starting point.

PICTURE THIS

God's wisdom is not hidden from the world, but in full view. In fact, it is constantly evident in all of creation and evident in ongoing activities resulting from landmark events orchestrated by God throughout history.

God's Wisdom Revealed Throughout History

INSTRUMENT	SCRIPTURE PASSAGES	WISDOM'S REVELATION
Creation	Psalm 104:2–4; 19:1	Creation constantly pouring forth evidence of God's wisdom.
Salvation	1 Corinthians 1:19–29	God's design in His plan of salvation.
Incarnation of Jesus Christ	Colossians 2:3; 1 Corinthians 1:30	Jesus Christ is the wisdom of God in the flesh for all the world to see.
The church	Ephesians 3:8–11	The wisdom of God shining through His people.
Ordering of life	Genesis 50:20; 2 Corinthians 1:4–5; 12:7–9	God's ordering of the lives of His people to align them with His purposes.

11

THE GOODNESS OF GOD

Many of us grew up singing a little chorus that proclaims, "God is so good." That song actually contains some profound theology, for the goodness of God is one of the infinite attributes of His character.

God's goodness can be defined as the collective perfections of His nature and the benevolence of His acts. To put it in the words of Psalm 119:68, "You are good and do good." God is good by nature and good in what He does.

We live in a time when people question the goodness of God. This is not a new problem, however. It really goes back all the way to the garden of Eden, when Satan informed Eve that the only reason God didn't want her to eat from the tree in the middle of the garden was that God was selfish (Genesis 3:1–7). He wasn't good, in other words.

Once Satan got Eve to focus on the one tree she couldn't eat from rather than the hundreds she could enjoy, she lost sight of God's goodness and plunged herself, her family, and the rest of the world into sin. To help remedy our problem, I want to discuss five important truths about the goodness of God.

GOD'S GOODNESS IS THE STANDARD

The goodness of God is the standard by which anything called good must be judged. Mark 10 makes this remarkably clear because in that chapter we are confronted with the foundation of goodness. A rich, young ruler had it all: wealth, youth, and power, all the things that most people fight to get. But he knew he had a hole inside of him. Something was missing. So one day he ran up to Jesus and asked the famous question, "Good Teacher, what shall I do to inherit eternal life?" (v. 17).

Either No Good—or God

Jesus' answer in verse 18 is instructive: "Why do you call Me good? No one is good except God alone." The young man was using the term *good* without realizing the full implications of what he was saying or the person he was talking to. He needed a quick theology lesson, so Jesus challenged him, "How do you know I'm good? By what standard are you using this term? You need to understand that no one is really good except God."

Jesus' point was simply this: "Either I'm no good, or I'm God." Jesus was bringing the young man in through the "back door" to realize His deity. Aside from this man's particular need, Jesus makes the broader point that anything called "good" must find its source in God.

All Good from God

The Bible declares in James 1:17, "Every good thing given and every perfect gift is from above, coming down from the Father of lights." Anything authentically good has its source in God.

One day I ran into a man who rejected the concept of a good God. His argument was a familiar one: "How can there be a good God when He allowed six million Jews to be slaughtered in the Nazi Holocaust? I can't believe in a God who would allow six million people to be killed."

I said to him, "OK, let's suppose your conclusion is right. Let's suppose God does not exist. Now tell me, who killed those six million Jews? You see, getting rid of God doesn't solve your problem. You've still got six million people dead."

You address these issues by understanding that if it is not good, it didn't have its source in God. Yes, God is sovereign and He allows things for reasons we don't always understand, but the Bible makes clear that God does not participate in sin in any way. There is no defect in Him.

GOD'S GOODNESS IS EXPRESSED IN HIS ATTRIBUTES

The goodness of God is expressed in and through His attributes. In other words, you know God is good by simply looking at who He is. In Exodus 33:18, Moses asked to see God's glory, and in response the Lord says, "I Myself will make all My goodness pass before you" (v. 19). Now compare that with Exodus 34:5–7:

> And the Lord descended in the cloud and stood there with him as he called upon the name of the Lord. Then the Lord passed by in front of him and proclaimed, "The Lord, the Lord God, compassionate and gracious, slow to anger, and abounding in lovingkindness and truth; who keeps lovingkindness for thousands, who forgives iniquity, transgression and sin; yet He will by no means leave the guilty unpunished, visiting the iniquity of fathers on the children and on the grandchildren to the third and fourth generations."

God tells Moses, "I will let My goodness pass by before you," and then when it happens God says, in essence, "Look at My character."

God expresses His goodness to us by attaching one of His characteristics to the circumstances of our lives. Because God is good, for example, He is patient. In the Bible, patience means not avenging wrong done to you even though you have the power and the right to do so.

You say, "I've got it bad, so God can't be good." No, if God were not good, you wouldn't have anything at all. Because if God were not good, He would not demonstrate patience toward you. And if that were the case, the moment you even thought about a sin, you would drop dead because God is so holy that He has to punish every sin.

God's goodness is seen in His love by which He identified with sinful humanity. God is so good, He sent Jesus to die for you and me. He's full of grace. Grace means giving your absolute best to someone who deserves your absolute worst.

He's also merciful, which means removing your misery. He's truthful.

He's the only One who will give you the straight story all the time. He forgives you of things that other people will hold against you until they go to their graves.

The goodness of God also shows in the fact that He will apply the appropriate part of His character to your situation. Some people like to point out that God once destroyed the whole world with a flood, and they ask, "How could God do that if He's good?"

But they ignore the rest of the story. For 120 years, God warned those people through Noah, "It's going to rain." Noah builds the ark on dry land, a huge ship almost as big as two football fields. He goes into town every day, preaching the same four-word sermon: "It's going to rain." Over and over, year after year, Noah faithfully delivered God's warning.

And if I were there, even if I didn't believe Noah, when I saw the animals lining up two by two to get on that ark, I would figure something was getting ready to happen. When Mr. & Mrs. Giraffe and Mr. & Mrs. Anteater start saying by their actions, "It's going to rain," I think I would check out what Noah was saying a little closer. All the signs were present, for 120 years!

God is good. That's not the problem. The problem is that people don't want His goodness because they want to make it on their own, to rely on their own goodness.

GOD'S GOODNESS IS DEMONSTRATED IN HIS PROVISION

According to the opening chapter of Genesis, God in His goodness not only created you and me, but He also created everything for us (see Genesis 1:27–31).

Earthly Provisions

In other words, God didn't create the plants, animals, or fish just to have them around. He created them for the benefit of mankind, to give us a home to enjoy. In Genesis 1:29, God told Adam that He had given mankind "every plant" and "every tree" for food. Every day when you get up and see the sun shine and say, "What a beautiful day!" God sits back and says, "How do you think that happened? Today didn't just jump up here by itself. It's a beautiful day because I'm a good God."

Every time I pick up a piece of fried chicken, I am reminded that God is good. Every time you see a rose, God says, "I don't want you just talking about how pretty those roses are, or you miss the point. The point is I know what I'm doing when I make flowers because I am a good God."

Goodness to All

God's goodness is not equal. God is good to all in some ways, but He's good to some in all ways.

Matthew 5:45 gives an example of how God is good to all: "He causes His sun to rise on the evil and the good, and sends rain on the righteous and the unrighteous." You don't have to be a Christian to get God's rain because He has ordained that certain aspects of His goodness be available to all people.

Goodness to His People

On the other hand, God has provided Christians with the ability to enjoy His goodness in ways that the world can never appreciate. He's given us His revelation, His Holy Spirit to guide us, and a divine perspective on life that opens our eyes to see and enjoy His goodness.

If you are a Christian, you can participate in and benefit from the goodness of God like no unregenerate person can. Romans 8:32 says, "He who did not spare His own Son, but delivered Him up for us all, how will He not also with Him freely give us all things?"

Now I realize that to talk about enjoying things makes some Christians nervous. So I want you to consider two verses that may be shocking if you're not used to the idea of Christians having a good time. Paul wrote: "Everything created by God is good, and nothing is to be rejected, if it is received with gratitude; for it is sanctified by means of the word of God and prayer" (1 Timothy 4:4–5).

Paul was refuting those who try to lay all kinds of restrictions and rules on God's people. But here's a revolutionary thought: It's a sin not to enjoy the goodness of God when He has provided it for us! It gets even better in 1 Timothy 6: "Instruct those who are rich in this present world not to be conceited or to fix their hope on the uncertainty of riches, but on God, *who richly supplies us with all things to enjoy*" (v. 17, italics added).

So if we're receiving God's goodness with gratitude and our focus is fixed on Him, we are free to enjoy His blessings. Where does it say sinners get to have the most fun? Many of us were raised to think that when you become a Christian, you enter into a boring existence while sinners enjoy all the good stuff. It's a demonic doctrine that says to be a Christian is to live an empty, boring, purposeless, and dull life of denial. It's false because God says, "Everything that I created is good and meant to be enjoyed by those who know the truth."

Believers should be enjoying nature more than nonbelievers because we know who the Maker is. We should be enjoying relationships more than anyone. We should be enjoying a good meal more than anyone. We should be enjoying the flowers more than anyone. We should be enjoying creation more than anyone because we know the Creator.

GOD'S GOODNESS TRANSCENDS THE NEGATIVE

You and I live in a contaminated world, and it rubs off. We have to shower/wash up every day because we get dirty, and what is true in the physical realm is true in the spiritual realm. We get dirty. The effects of a sinful world rub off on us. That's what makes heaven so great. Heaven will be heaven because no sin will be there.

But because of sin, we live in a very painful world of cancer, AIDS, personality conflicts, attitude battles, and racial strife. We live in a world where if a sinner decides to pick up a gun, a Christian could be in trouble. Much in our world is not good, but it's not because God is not good. It's because man is not good.

Some people will always try to pin the blame on God for the bad things. No, the blame goes to the people who are doing those bad things. We have to understand that even though God is good, bad things are still going to happen. Creation was completely good when it came from God's hand, but it has been contaminated by sin. Therefore, we live in a world where many bad things happen.

Have you ever had your house all clean and then had people come in and mess it up? It's still a good house, but it looks like a mess because of the guests who've invaded it. God created a good world, but it appears to be a mess because the people He has put here to occupy it have been the worst kind of "guests" possible.

How do you feel when you have guests like that? You may whisper to your mate, "I sure will be glad when they leave." I imagine God feels like saying, "I sure will be glad when they leave because they are messing up My house. They throw their clothing of sin all over the place and the mess rubs off on everyone."

Turning Bad into Good

How then can God be good when negative circumstances make up so much a part of life in this world? The Bible says, "God causes all things to work together for good to those who love [Him]" (Romans 8:28). God's goodness does not show only when He prevents problems. It also appears in the fact that even when they do happen, a good God will transcend those negative things and ultimately work out that which will be for His glory and our benefit.

When my oldest son, Anthony Jr., was very small, he had an asthma attack. We took him to the doctor and laid him on the table. The doctor needed to give him a shot, and the needle he brought out was long and intimidating. Anthony saw the doctor beginning to fill the syringe and did a Superman leap off that table and reached out to me. I tried to tell him, "Son, you're sick and the doctor needs to do this."

Then he began crying, "Daddy, no, no!"

The doctor looked at me and said, "You are going to have to hold him down."

I tried to talk to Anthony a little while longer, but he didn't understand. So I had to hold him down, and I will never forget the look on his face, which said, "How can you do this to me? How can you join forces with the enemy? How can you help the doctor hurt me?"

I did it because it was good. Painful, yes—but good. Could Anthony understand it? Absolutely not; he was too young, too inexperienced. Could I understand it? Absolutely. I'd been that route before. I'd had those asthma needles when I was growing up. I understood that Anthony's temporary pain was necessary to produce long-term health.

Becoming Conquerors

So even when "tribulation, or distress, or persecution, or famine, or nakedness, or peril, or sword" (Romans 8:35) come along, God so constructs the trial that when it finishes, good results. And through it we become overwhelming conquerors (v. 37).

Nothing is more exciting than to see a dying Christian who is an overwhelming conqueror. I don't know when I'm going to die, but I sure want to die as a conqueror. I want to go like a friend of mine who knew he was dying and knew there was no medical hope. He looked up and said, "This is my crowning day. Come quickly, Lord Jesus!"

Don't let anyone tell you that God's goodness has to mean bad things shouldn't happen. God is good because He takes the bad things that happen to us and brings eternal good out of them.

GOD'S GOODNESS SHOULD MOTIVATE WORSHIP

The goodness of God should motivate His people to worship Him. Listen to Psalm 107:1–2a: "Oh give thanks to the Lord, for He is good; for His lovingkindness is everlasting. Let the redeemed of the Lord say so." We can say so through talk, celebration, and saying thank you to Him.

Talk about It

We talk about everything else, don't we? When the big game plays, people aren't afraid to let their voices be heard when their team scores. They burst out with praise. Later, they gather together to celebrate their team's victory.

Then God tells us to talk up His goodness and His redemption and we say, "He already knows I'm grateful." But God doesn't just want to read your mind or heart. He wants to hear your lips praise and thank Him.

Celebrate His Goodness

We are also to come together and celebrate God's goodness. According to Psalm 107:2–3, the people who were to tell of God's goodness were those He had "redeemed from the hand of the adversary, and gathered from the lands, from the east and from the west, from the north and from the south."

Someone will always answer, "I don't have to go to church to be a Christian." You sure don't. Going to church doesn't make you a Christian. But if you are a grateful Christian, you will go there to celebrate God's goodness. You won't mind singing to His glory. You will shout it out. Why? Because He's been good to you.

Verse 7 of this psalm says that God also leads His people. Therefore, the psalmist's advice is, "Give thanks to the Lord" (v. 8). In verse 9 the writer declares that God gives food to the hungry and water to the thirsty. Then he says if you are in sin, repent because God has been good (vv. 13–14).

Say "Thank You"

God wants to be praised. You've probably taught your children to say "Thank you." But do you just teach them to say it once a week or once a year? Or do you want them to learn to say "Thank you" as a way of life, so that it's the exception when they don't express thanks? We say to our kids when they receive something, "I didn't hear you say thank you. What do you say?"

God says to us, "What do you say? I can't hear you. I don't hear the thanksgiving." Praise is not complete until it has been expressed. The goodness of God gives us ample opportunities to be thankful. Psalm 34:8 invites us, "O taste and see that the Lord is good."

PERSONAL APPLICATION FOR LIFE

1. If you are allowing or practicing something in your life that may not be good by God's definition of goodness, apply this simple test to it. See if you can pray, "God, I know this is a gift from You, and You want me to have it because it is good," without experiencing any conviction. If so, you may be on the right track. But if you can't thank God for it with a clear heart and conscience, it's best to dump it!

2. Maybe you've got a negative circumstance knocking the props out of your life right now. Write it down on a card or piece of paper. Now under it write Romans 8:28—not as a way of just pretending it isn't bad, but as a promise from your good God. Put that card where you'll see it every day. When you do, thank God that He can bring good out of bad. Do that for a while, and see if that circumstance doesn't begin to look a lot different.

3. What have you received—or avoided!—in the last month or so that was purely a gift of grace from a good God? Reflect on it, and thank Him again for it. Can't think of anything? Better check your spiritual batteries to see if you're still running.

4. If you have a church where you gather regularly with God's people to worship and thank Him, keep up the good work. But if you're trying to fly solo right now in your Christian life, make it a priority to find a good church before you crash-land somewhere. Ask a trusted Christian friend for the name of a church where God is worshiped and His Word is taught.

FOR GROUP STUDY

Questions for Group Discussion

1. What do you envision when you think of God's *goodness*? Make a list of the thoughts that come to mind. It's safe to say that we tend to apply to God the highest human traits of goodness we can think of. Does your list include a few human traits? Share your conclusions with the group.

2. God's goodness should motivate us to worship Him. As a group, read Psalm 107. In what ways does this passage inspire you to worship?

3. Read in Mark 10 the account of Jesus' encounter with the rich young ruler (vv. 17–23). What was wrong with the rich young ruler's use of the term *good* in verse 17? What was the point of Jesus' reply?

4. How does God's goodness help His people live productive spiritual lives in a contaminated world? Use Romans 8:28–37 as your central passage. What truths and promises can you draw from this passage? What steps can we take, as God's people, to align with the teaching of Romans 8?

PICTURE THIS

God has demonstrated His goodness to all the world through His generous provisions. Below are the basic provisions we enjoy. Because of our relationship with the Creator, God's people are in a special position to acknowledge God and express our gratitude.

God's Good Provisions for Us

PROVISION	SCRIPTURE PASSAGES	WHO BENEFITS?
Earthy provisions	Genesis 1	God created all things for the benefit of all mankind.
Goodness to all	Matthew 5:45	The righteous and unrighteous alike benefit from God's provision of goodness.
Goodness to His people	1 Timothy 4:1–5; Psalm 31:19; 84:11	Because of their perspective, God's people are able to enjoy God's goodness in greater ways and, as a result, express their gratitude.

12

THE WRATH OF GOD

What would you say about a father who failed to warn his children of impending danger? You would have to conclude that he was not being a good parent.

How about a doctor who knew you had a life-threatening illness, but simply told you, "Take two aspirin, go home, and rest"? His compassion for you as your doctor would be in serious question.

I could go on, but let me ask you just one more question. What would you say about a pastor who told you about God's love and forgiveness and patience, but never warned you of His wrath? I'd like to answer that one myself. That pastor would be doing you a great disservice.

God's wrath is not an easy subject to talk about. But it's as integral to His nature as any of His other perfections. If I failed to teach about it, I would be doing my readers a great disservice. Any discussion of God's character that does not include His characteristic called wrath is an incomplete study. Worse yet, it may even be an errant study of God, because one of the inescapable truths about our great God is that He is a God of wrath.

In fact, the Bible has more to say about God's wrath than it does about His love. Of course God is good, kind, loving, and forgiving. But if you put a period there, you haven't got the complete story. God's wrath must be taken seriously. So let's begin by defining our subject. The wrath of God is His necessary, just, and righteous retribution against sin.

God's wrath against sin arises by necessity because of the justice of His law and the righteousness of His character. God must judge sin, although He takes no pleasure in punishing the unrighteous (Ezekiel 33:11).

Psalm 18:8 puts it this way: "Smoke went up out of [God's] nostrils" as He huffed with anger at the presence of sin. Moses writes in Exodus 34:7 that God will not let the guilty go unpunished. In Deuteronomy 32:41, Moses records God's declaration, "I will render vengeance on My adversaries." Peter reminds us that God is impartial and will judge all men according to their deeds (1 Peter 1:17).

We can find no way around it, nowhere to run from it. God is a God of wrath. I want to give you the straight scoop because it's better to have a headache now than a "hell ache" later. The Greek words for *wrath* indicate God's intense displeasure at sin and His judgment against it. God does not throw temper tantrums. He doesn't pitch fits, but He has intense anger against sin: big sin, little sin, medium-size sin. He does not make a distinction between white and black lies, between felonies and misdemeanors. All sin is repulsive to Him.

GOD'S WRATH IS ONE OF HIS PERFECTIONS

I mentioned this above, but let's look at it in more detail. Romans 11:22 helps us here:

> Behold then the kindness and severity of God; to those who fell, severity, but to you, God's kindness, if you continue in His kindness; otherwise you also will be cut off.

God's Severity

The word *severity* is the Greek word that means "to be cut off." This is a description of God's wrath. When His patience against sin expires, God cuts people off from His kindness. God's kindness is perfectly balanced with His severity. Both are part of who He is.

The prophet Nahum describes God as "a jealous and avenging God" (Nahum 1:2a). And the prophet's words get stronger: "The Lord takes vengeance on His adversaries, and He reserves wrath for His enemies. The Lord is slow to anger and great in power, and the Lord will by no means leave the guilty unpunished" (vv. 2b–3a).

But after painting a picture like this, Nahum begins verse 7 by saying, "The Lord is good." God is good, but don't mistake His goodness for weakness or indifference toward sin. God is so good He must address evil.

God's Righteous Wrath

God's wrath is not at all like ours. Probably one reason people run from the subject of God's anger is that they think God gets mad the way people get mad. We get ticked off when someone does us wrong—or if we think someone has done us wrong. And, too often, we unload on them with both barrels.

That's not how God responds. The wrath of God is His response to that which in its essence is against His nature. God's wrath is not cruel but just. Prison isn't a fun place, but we lock up people who have committed crimes to keep them from committing those crimes again because we want justice and order in society. That's a reflection—although a very poor and imperfect one—of God's righteous anger.

God wants justice and order in His universe, which means He must respond to the crime called sin. The only way you can get God not to respond to you is not to be a sinner. But if you say you are not a sinner, you prove you are because you just lied (see 1 John 1:8). God responds to sin by cutting the sinner off from His goodness. The Bible says these two sides of God must be always held in tension. "You have loved righteousness and hated wickedness" (Psalm 45:7).

GOD'S WRATH DISPLAYS HIS JUSTICE

The wrath of God is the ongoing display of His justice in history. Romans 1:18 contains the most concise statement of God's wrath in the Bible: "For the wrath of God is revealed from heaven against all ungodliness and unrighteousness of men who suppress the truth in unrighteousness."

Notice that God does not hide His wrath. He does not put it under a bushel. His wrath is revealed so that we can know this is part of His nature. Some people act as though God is apologetic about His anger toward sin and doesn't want us to know about it.

No, the Bible says God actively reveals His wrath. He tells us in advance that this is part of who He is. We have to adjust, because God says, "I, the Lord, do not change" (Malachi 3:6).

Romans 1:18 means there is no time when God is not reacting to sin. The problem is that people suppress or hold down the truth. They don't want to deal with it. But we've got to tell the truth, pointing out that God's holy indignation reacts against sin every time and everywhere it shows up. The verb in verse 18 is a present tense, meaning God's wrath "keeps on being revealed" against sin.

Paul then continues to explain why God reveals His wrath against the unrighteousness of men:

> Because that which is known about God is evident within them; for God made it evident to them. For since the creation of the world His invisible attributes, His eternal power and divine nature, have been clearly seen, being understood through what has been made, so that they are without excuse. (vv. 19–20)

So while we can't see God's essence, we can see God's effect, just like we see the wind's effect. Between the truth God put within us and what is evident around us, we are left without excuse. God has made His reality crystal clear. That's why no matter where you go in the world, you will find people worshiping something.

God's Character Distorted

Our problem is not evolution, it's devolution. Evolution says that man started small and grew great. But the truth is that man started great but has been growing smaller spiritually and morally ever since. Why? Because even though people knew God, "they did not honor Him as God, or give thanks; but they became futile in their speculations, and their foolish heart was darkened" (Romans 1:21). Sinful man has distorted God's character. The result is that we didn't treat God like He was God.

The problem gets worse in verse 23: "[They] exchanged the glory of the incorruptible God for an image in the form of corruptible man and of birds and four-footed animals and crawling creatures"—and of cars and of houses and of money and on and on. God has been exchanged. We've taken Him back like a Christmas present that doesn't fit and we've said, "We want our money back." Rather than glorifying God, people have elevated other things in His place.

God's "Giving Up"

So what does God do with people like that? It's stated three times in Romans 1 (vv. 24, 26, 28). He gives up on those who insist on perverting the knowledge of Him. That means He unleashes these people to fulfill their wildest dreams and enjoy the consequences thereof. God takes His hand of restraint off and says, "You want it, you've got it."

What kind of things do people seek when they refuse to acknowledge God? "Women exchanged the natural function for that which is unnatural" (v. 26). That's lesbianism. "And in the same way also the men abandoned the natural function of the woman and burned in their desire toward one another, men with men committing indecent acts and receiving in their own persons the due penalty of their error" (v. 27). That's homosexuality. One penalty or payment for their sin is called AIDS.

Because of this, innocent people have to suffer early and agonizing deaths through things like AIDS-contaminated blood transfusions, as men and women come up with every kind of device imaginable to fulfill their passions.

But we still haven't hit bottom. We have not arrived at the worst stage yet, which is described in Romans 1:28: "And just as they did not see fit to acknowledge God any longer, God gave them over to a depraved mind, to do those things which are not proper."

God will let people get so crazy in their sin that they can no longer think right or act right. They go stark-raving mad spiritually, morally, physically, ethically, and every other way. This madness shows itself in so many horrible ways that Paul merely needs to list them and we get the message (vv. 28–32).

GOD'S WRATH DISPLAYS HIS JUSTICE IN ETERNITY

We see God's wrath executing His justice in history right now, but this is not the end of it. The wrath of God will continue in eternity: "But because of your stubbornness and unrepentant heart you are storing up wrath for yourself in the day of wrath and revelation of the righteous judgment of God" (Romans 2:5).

Stored-up Wrath

Sometimes we get upset because evil people seem to keep getting away with evil. But the truth is their sin account just keeps growing. Many people will never have much trouble in this life. But if you could only see the bill awaiting them in eternity! The psalmist pictured the wrath of God like a bow being drawn back (Psalm 7:12). The more sinners sin, the farther God pulls back the bow.

God says that when He lets His arrow go, it's going to penetrate the unrighteous with great agony. That's why the Bible cautions us not to become envious of the wicked. God just hasn't let His arrow go yet.

Evil people are storing up God's wrath, and the Bible says that God will let His arrow fly at the judgment. This will usher in eternity, which will mean hell for those under His wrath. I would prefer that hell not be part of the deal, but I'm not making the rules. And God has said there is a place where those who reject Him will be housed forever.

So critical is this doctrine that John the Baptist warned, "Flee from the wrath to come" (Matthew 3:7). Jesus said that in hell, "their worm does not die" (Mark 9:48). In other words, there is no death there, no time when the conscience is at ease. Hell is a place of desolation and great pain.

In Revelation 20:10–15, John describes the great and final judgment when Satan and those who reject Christ will be thrown in the "lake of fire" along with "death and Hades" (the abode of the dead, a "holding tank" for those awaiting judgment). The lake of fire is eternal punishment, for its inhabitants will be "tormented day and night forever and ever" (v. 10).

Eternal Wrath Illustrated

The Bible's most descriptive story about eternal punishment isn't designed to make us feel good. But when you have cancer and need radical treatment, making you feel good is not the doctor's first goal. Sin is a cancer, and God's eternal wrath will be the outcome of it unless we have radical surgery to remove it.

The story is in Luke 16:19–31, and since it fell from the lips of Jesus we need to give it careful attention. It's the account of the rich man and Lazarus. When both men die, Jesus peels back the corners of eternity and gives us a look at both sides. Lazarus was carried by angels who put him in Abraham's bosom, what we would call paradise or heaven.

The rich man, called Dives by tradition, died and went to Hades (v. 23), the abode of the evil dead until the final judgment. There he was in "agony" in the flames (v. 24), which means he could feel pain.

He could see too. Jesus says that Dives looked up "and saw Abraham far away, and Lazarus in his bosom" (v. 23). He saw what he was missing. The great tragedy of hell is not only what you are going through, but what you could have had and are missing. This definitely gives the lie to the notion that hell is where the party is. God throws the party in heaven.

Dives then asks Abraham to send Lazarus with just a fingerful of water to ease his pain. Whenever you feel like one drop of water will change your existence, you are in bad shape.

But Abraham answered, "I'm sorry. A great gulf is fixed between us and you. We can't come over there and you can't come over here" (see vv. 25–26).

Eternal Wrath Experienced

Do you know the worst part of hell? It will be the eternal torment of remembering that on such and such a day, the person sat in church, heard that preacher say this place was real, and didn't do anything about it. Hell is knowing that you could have but never did address the issue of your eternal destiny. You didn't take seriously the wrath of God.

No help came for Dives. He remained fully conscious. He had his memory, his conscience, and all of his physical senses intact, but it was all agony. And his plea to go back and warn his brothers of that awful place was denied by Abraham (Luke 16:31).

A man once told me, "I'm not into that hell stuff. I don't believe in the wrath of God. But even if hell is true, I'm going to turn the place out because all my 'homies' are going to be there. We are going to go down there, get with the Devil, and boogie down."

He obviously didn't get the picture, so I said, "Do me a favor. When you go home today, turn on a burner on your stove and wait till it gets real hot. Then sit on that burner and try to get a party going at the same time. Let's see how you do."

He did not understand that hell is a place of solitary confinement. Hell has no fellowship, no parties, no get-togethers, no buffets. God will eternally quarantine all those who are not rightly related to Him in the pit of the universe so they won't mess up the enjoyment of heaven for those who are rightly related to Him.

GOD'S WRATH COMES WHEN HIS PATIENCE IS IGNORED

God does not just come out of nowhere and lower the boom on unsuspecting people who had no chance to do anything about their eternal destiny. Paul points out that God endures "with much patience" even those people who are "vessels of wrath prepared for destruction" (Romans 9:22), people we might call hell-bent.

Wrath and Mercy

As we saw earlier, God is long-suffering. "The Lord . . . is patient toward you, not wishing for any to perish but for all to come to repentance" (2 Peter 3:9). God is not wrathful because He wants to injure. He's wrathful because He's just. But He is also merciful.

God's patience lasts a lifetime. He waits on us, He forgives us, He doesn't give us what we deserve, He holds back His wrath toward us. He says, "Come to Me now." But we keep putting Him off, not submitting and turning to Christ.

We say, "Not now. Tomorrow. Before I die." And the clock runs out.

The End of Patience

But you say no one knows his death date. You're right—and that's why today is always the day of salvation (2 Corinthians 6:2; Hebrews 4:7–15). You don't put this thing off. God is patient, so come to Him while you can.

How patient is God? Numbers 14 tells about the unbelief of Israel when the people refused to believe God and take the Promised Land. God was hot. He wanted to destroy those rebels and start over with Moses (vv. 11–12). But Moses reminded God of His patience, and He granted the nation a stay of execution, so to speak (vv. 18–20).

But read the rest of Numbers 14 and you'll see that God did judge His people. Too many make the mistake described in Ecclesiastes 8:11, which says that people take God's delay in judging sin as an excuse to sin more. They figure they're home free. They think God has slackened up (2 Peter 3:9).

Kids make this mistake all the time. You haven't spanked them yet, so they figure you aren't ever going to do anything. Because God hasn't done anything yet, we think He's never going to do anything about sin. But God is a wrathful God, and when the clock strikes midnight, it's over.

Hebrews 9:27 says, "It is appointed for men to die once and after this comes judgment." No second chance, no slack or a reprieve, but judgment. Romans 2:4 says it this way: "Do you think lightly of the riches of His kindness and forbearance and patience, not knowing that the kindness of God leads you to repentance?" If He hasn't judged you yet, you should be running to Him in repentance.

ESCAPING GOD'S WRATH

A choice must be made. Anyone who goes to hell goes by his or her choice, not because God is an ogre. God made hell for Satan and his angels, not for people, the Bible says (Matthew 25:41). His justice demands payment for sin, but in His mercy He provided a substitute to take our punishment for us.

This is good news! God's system of justice allows for a substitute. That's why 1 Thessalonians 1:10 says Jesus "delivers us from the wrath to come." According to Romans 5:8–9:

> God demonstrates His own love toward us, in that while we were yet sinners, Christ died for us. Much more then, having now been justified by His blood, we shall be saved from the wrath of God through Him.

You are not saved by attending church, by being a nice person, or by doing good in the community. You will be saved from the wrath to come only by the eternal provision of Jesus Christ.

PERSONAL APPLICATION FOR LIFE

1. Have you got a family member or friend who is dangling over the open mouth of hell? Get on the phone, pick up a pen and paper, make a lunch appointment, or do whatever else you have to do to get with that person and share the truth of God's love—and wrath—with him or her.

2. Sometimes as Christians we get upset because the wicked in our world seem to have things their way. If you've ever felt this way, you're in good company. Read Psalm 73 carefully. The psalmist began lamenting the ease of the wicked and got himself really worked up about it. But notice the first word of verse 17: "Until." Thank God that this world isn't the last word, and that you belong to Him.

3. Here is another line of thought you can use in your witnessing when someone rejects the idea of God's wrath. Ask that person how he would feel if he gave someone a gift that cost him dearly, only to have the recipient snort in disgust, throw the gift back in his face, and walk away.

   Most people wouldn't have any problem admitting they would be hurt and angry. Now take your friend a step further and ask him to imagine this happening again and again as he kept offering his priceless gift to the receiver. How many times would he allow himself to be rejected and insulted before he would withdraw his offer? We can't appreciate God's wrath until we see what a great offense our rejection of Christ is.

4. If you have any doubt about where you stand before God, flee His wrath and embrace the pardon offered in Jesus Christ. Don't put it off. Don't count on your church membership or good deeds to save you. Don't guess about your eternal destiny!

FOR GROUP STUDY

Questions for Group Discussion

1. Have each group member take a moment to list his or her impressions about God's wrath and to address the questions: What is God's wrath?

Why does God exercise His wrath? Allow your group leader to use your insights and discoveries as discussion points.

2. God's wrath is one of His perfections. His justice demands payment for sin. Drawing from Dr. Evans's teaching is this chapter, discuss these three aspects: His severity, His goodness, and His righteous wrath. Begin your discussion by reading and examining Romans 11:22 and then exploring Nahum 1:2–6. How do we explain these aspects in the context of God's perfection?

3. In the Bible, we have a record of God's demand for justice as displayed by His wrath throughout history. Examine what Scripture says about God's ongoing display of wrath in history. Include in your study these passages: Malachi 3:6; Romans 1:18–32; and Psalm 7:11. What can we conclude from what Scripture teaches about God's wrath displaying His justice?

4 God's wrath is not limited to human involvement on earth. The Bible teaches that He displays His justice even into eternity. Continue your study, starting with Romans 2:5, Psalm 7:12; Matthew 3:7; Mark 9:48; and Revelation 20:10–15. The story of Dives in Luke 16:19–31 provides an excellent illustration of God's eternal wrath.

PICTURE THIS

God's wrath is real and is recorded in the pages of Scripture. The Bible clearly teaches that He brings justice by executing His wrath. Some might try to ignore it, while others might try to excuse it or evade it. But every person must address this attribute.

THE CERTAINTY OF GOD'S WRATH

EVIDENCE	SCRIPTURE PASSAGE	SIGNIFICANCE
Wrath is one of His perfections.	Romans 11:22	God's wrath is His response to that which in its essence is against His nature.
It is displayed by His justice.	Romans 1:18; 2:5	God is holy and cannot permit ungodliness.
God judges His people.	Numbers 14	God does judge sin.
God's patience has limits.	Hebrews 9:27	Those who are unsaved will not escape God's wrath.

13

THE LOVE OF GOD

Everyone wants to be loved. Love is the crying need of the human heart. But when you ask people to define love, they hem and haw, trying to come up with words that work. For some it's a fuzzy feeling in the pit of the stomach. For others, it's a deep caring. For others, it's excitement over something they value highly.

The concept of love has been so used, abused, and misused today that you can put almost anything under it and it will work. That's because most people are desperately looking for love in all the wrong places. They know they need it, they know they've got to have it, but where to find it and how to know it's authentic, that's another question.

If you feel like that, or know someone who does, I have good news for you: "God is love" (1 John 4:8). The love of God is His joyful self-determination to reflect the goodness of His will and glory by meeting the needs of mankind.

That's a big definition, but I believe it includes the key elements of what the Bible means by God's love. And the Bible makes this absolutely clear: No definition of love means anything unless it is rooted in God. No matter how you define love, if you can't root your definition in God, it is flawed.

It will either be incomplete or imbalanced, but it will not be correct because God is the definition of love.

THE JOYFUL OVERFLOW OF GOD'S WILL AND GLORY

One fundamental principle of God's love is that it is inextricably tied to His own glory. Ephesians 1:4–6 highlights this connection:

> [God] chose us in [Christ] before the foundation of the world, that we should be holy and blameless before Him. In love He predestined us to adoption as sons through Jesus Christ to Himself, according to the kind intention of His will, to the praise of the glory of His grace.

God's Love and His Glory

These verses make clear that God's activity in love always coincides with His will, which verse 6 shows to be "the praise of the glory of His grace." The working out of God's will in love results in His glory. And Paul doesn't stop there, because this is important. Again in verses 12 and 14, he caps off God's work in saving us and sealing us with the Holy Spirit by saying all of it is for "the praise of His glory."

How does this fact relate to God's love? First, we need to realize that God did not become love after He made the world and mankind. God's love is eternal. In and of Himself, God is love.

Now if God's love existed before the foundation of the world because *He* existed before the foundation of the world, what was there for God to love in eternity past? We can draw only one conclusion: The object of God's love was Himself. God is absorbed in His own glory.

Here is one major difference between God and us. If we become absorbed in our own glory, we've got a problem. First, because we focus on untrue things. We begin to deceive ourselves. Second, we start forgetting about things we can't do. We begin to think we can leap tall buildings. Third, we focus on things that are flawed by sin. We begin to mess with stuff better left alone.

But God can pursue His own glory because He has perfect glory. God does not pursue His glory to gain something He lacks. God has everything He needs. He pursues His own glory because He could aspire to no greater goal than Himself.

Since God's love precedes creation, the only way God could express His love was within Himself. Therefore, for God to love, He must seek Himself. And in order for God to seek Himself, He must seek His own will and glory.

If we simply let God be God, we will be halfway to unraveling what sounds like a complicated truth. Since nothing greater than our perfect God could possibly exist, it shouldn't surprise us that His glory is the focus of His love.

God's Love and You

Make no mistake. Nothing I've said about how much God loves Himself and delights in His glory is meant to imply that God is selfish with His love, hoarding it for Himself. God forbid! But the only reason God can be for you is that God is for Himself. If God were only for you and not for Himself, there would be limits on what He could do.

But since God is pursuing His own glory, when He brings you under the umbrella of His love, you are in the very best position possible. Why? Because as God unfolds His will to achieve His glory in your life, you get to enjoy the blessings of His grace, power, purpose, and joy.

When you get the love of God, you will be loved like you've never been loved before—or ever could be. God said to His people Israel, "I have loved you with an everlasting love" (Jeremiah 31:3).

GOD'S LOVE MANIFEST

God's love finds its fullest manifestation in Christ's provision for the salvation of sinful men. "God demonstrates His own love toward us, in that while were yet sinners, Christ died for us" (Romans 5:8).

If you really want to understand love, don't listen to "rap" music. Don't listen to people who throw the term "love" around. If you want to get to the depths of what it means to love and be loved, look to the death of Christ, because there God's love came to mankind.

What God did for us in Christ is the starting and ending point of any definition of love. Love must have these six criteria to be genuine.

Visibly Expressed

True love does not just say, "I love you." That's rap. True love is always visibly expressed. Invisible love is no love at all. If people have to read your mind to know you love them, they will never really know they've been loved. True love always can be pointed to. Its activity constantly says, "I love you." God so loved that He gave us His Son (John 3:16).

Always Sacrificial

True love is always willing to pay a price for the benefit of another. John 3:16 reminds us how deeply sacrificial God's love is. If you want to measure your love for someone, or his or her love for you, look at the price tag each person is willing to pay for love. If a man will not sacrifice anything for the woman he claims to love and wishes to marry, he's not the one. If he doesn't want to be inconvenienced, he's not the one. True love is sacrificial.

A great price tag is attached to true love. Just look at the price paid by Christ. Too many people, though, do not understand or appreciate the price of Calvary. That's why God doesn't get much love back from us. Some people even dare to question whether God loves them. But He says, "Look at the price I paid for you. Look at the fact that when you were hopeless, when you were sinful, when salvation was totally out of your reach, I gave My Son for you. That's how much I love you." God's love is forever, for the Bible promises that nothing "will be able to separate us from the love of God, which is in Christ Jesus our Lord" (Romans 8:39).

Always Beneficial

True love always seeks to benefit the one loved. It does not ask first, "What am I going to get out of this?" but "What am I going to put into this so that the one I love can get something out of it?" Godly love "does not seek its own" (1 Corinthians 13:5), but rather that which is beneficial to another.

Romans 5:9 reveals a tremendous benefit that Christ purchased for us when He demonstrated God's love. He died for us to save us from "the wrath of God." He had our interest in mind.

Unconditional

God's love is not tied to the worth of the person being loved. If that were the case, none of us would have been saved because Romans 5:8 tells us what our "worth" was before God: "We were yet sinners."

Jesus didn't wait until we got better to die for us. He died when we were in our most unlovely state. The person who doesn't deserve love actually needs love more, not less. If you know someone unworthy of love, that's great! You now have a chance to emulate Christ, because the essence of His love is unconditional.

Judicial

The fact that God's love is unconditional doesn't make it weak and accepting of everything. Here we find a major difference between divine love and what so often passes for human love. God's love always makes judgment calls. Paul put it this way: Love "does not rejoice in unrighteousness, but rejoices with the truth" (1 Corinthians 13:6). Love hates what is wrong and embraces what is right.

Some people believe that if you love them, you have to accept anything they want to do. No, love always makes judgment calls. That's why parents who love have to spank sometimes. Hebrews 12:6 says, "Whom the Lord loveth, He spanketh" (Evans translation). Love does not tolerate wrong, so the loving thing to do is to correct. You do not love when you do not correct.

Emotional

Don't let anyone tell you that love does not feel. True love always feels. Emotion by itself doesn't equal love, but you can't have true love without feeling. God feels His love. The Bible says He takes great joy in His love for us. Sometimes we emphasize the caring aspect of *agape* love so much we negate the emotion of it.

Paul told the Philippians that he longed for them with "the affection of Christ Jesus" (1:8). Any definition of love is incomplete that does not include joy and deep feeling. It doesn't mean you feel good all the time, but it means that your love is marked by an overriding principle of joy.

GOD'S LOVE AND OUR WELFARE

The love of God reflects in His determination to see to the comprehensive welfare of His children. This takes us back to Romans 8:

> What then shall we say to these things? If God is for us, who is against us? He who did not spare His own Son, but delivered Him up for us all, how will He not also with Him freely give us all things? (vv. 31–32)

These are rhetorical questions. If God is for you, who can be against you? Answer: Nobody! Not your employer, your circumstances, or your enemies. If He did the hard thing and gave up His Son for you, will He not also freely give you any good thing you need? Answer: Of course He will.

Nothing Overlooked

This means that when God loves, He loves in such a way that He is not just concerned about getting you to heaven. He cares about your comprehensive well-being, every minute detail of your life. He checks into all the nooks and crannies of your existence.

No area goes unloved by God because if He gave you Jesus, He's not going to hold back anything else. He has invested too much in you to overlook anything.

Closing the Loop

Therefore, when your life is falling apart, when your world is crumbling, you can appeal to the love of God. Now this may raise a few questions in your mind, because when we look around, things don't look as good as Romans 8 makes them sound, right? Why don't we experience the love of God more or feel it more deeply, since feeling is involved? Why don't we have a greater sense that God loves us like this passage says He loves us?

There is a reason. We don't sense God's love more because we break the loop of His love. I said earlier that the love of God is the overflow of His glory. You and I live in a world where our negative circumstances often obscure His love. But when we live for His glory (which is what He loves), when we are passionately consumed with living for God's glory, then we close the loop of His love.

The "secret" is in our passion to live for God's glory. The psalmist said, "Delight yourself in the Lord" (Psalm 37:4). Find your chief joy in life in Him. Paul wrote, "Rejoice in the Lord always; again I will say, rejoice!" (Philippians 4:4). In other words, when we seek God's glory in every circumstance of life, when we take what He does in our lives and aim it back toward His glory, God finds great joy in our taking His glory seriously.

God's Joy

True love is only activated when the glory of God is the goal of our lives, because that's what His love is designed to achieve. If you live only for yourself and not for the glory of God, He will not share His joy with you.

If you are not living for God's joy, marriage won't help you. You will have a husband or a wife and no joy. The idea is to become dominated with God's joy whether you have a mate or not; whether you have a job or not; whether you have money or not; whether your circumstances are good or not.

Consumed with His Love

Knowing Christ means we have His guarantee that in every situation in life, He loves us. When our world falls apart, we can say, "Lord, I don't know why I'm going through this. I don't understand it, but I'm sure glad to know You love me. How can I glorify You right now?"

You say, "How do I know God is loving me at times like that?"

Because when you "exult" in your trials and bear up under them with perseverance, God pours His joy into your heart in such abundance that it just spills all over the place (Romans 5:1–5). His joy consumes you. This means you don't have to fear anymore. "Perfect love casts out fear" (1 John 4:18). Are there legitimate reasons for concern? Of course. But you don't let these things consume you. Why? Because God loves you.

GOD'S LOVE IS THE MEASURE

We measure authentic love for others against the love of God. John says this: "Every one who loves is born of God and knows God" (1 John 4:7). "Born of God" is salvation; "knows God" is intimacy.

John is saying, "If you have learned love, you learned it from God because He is the only One who can give you this kind of love." You can't learn this kind of love from watching *As the World Turns. All My Children* won't teach you this.

John goes on to say in verse 8: "The one who does not love does not know God, for God is love." You can't have God and not have love. If you are getting close to God, it's going to rub off on you.

So if you are hateful, ornery, irritable, or frustrated; if you are not a "happy camper," your problem isn't that people keep messing with you. Your problem is you don't know God. I am convinced that a lot of the problems I see in relationships, especially between husbands and wives, come because someone doesn't know God here. When God consumes you, He says, "You will love."

Loving Others

That's the beautiful thing about admitting "I can't love so-and-so." You are absolutely right. You can't, but that's not the question. The question is, Can God love this person? Then you'd better get hooked up with Him.

In 1 John 4:19–20, John concludes, "We love, because He first loved us. If someone says, 'I love God,' and hates his brother, he is a liar; for the one who does not love his brother whom he has seen, cannot love God whom he has not seen." Anyone who says he loves God and can't love others is lying through his two front teeth. You can't be consumed with God and not love other sinners. He doesn't like what they do, but He loves sinners.

When you get consumed by the love of God, it overflows you and spills out onto others. If God has poured His overflowing love into your heart, others can't help getting hit by the splash.

PERSONAL APPLICATION FOR LIFE

1. Besides your words, can you point to something you've done in the past week to demonstrate your love to your spouse, your child, or some other loved one or friend? If you have to scratch your head to come up with something, it's time to get busy.

2. If you're like most of us, somewhere along the way God has brought an unlovely person into your life—someone very hard for you to love. Try a "sneak attack." At your next opportunity, startle that person with an act of kindness or a helping hand at the moment he or she least expects or deserves it. It may take a while to plan this one, but God will make it worth the effort.

3. Since God has promised to carry you from spiritual birth (no condemnation) all the way to heaven and His presence (no separation), nothing in between can take you out! If that assurance makes you just a little bit happy, why not spend the next few minutes telling God how wonderful His love is?

4. You may be carrying a heavy load right now. At times like this, the *daily* presence and assurance of God's love means the most. No matter what the load or how long you've been carrying it, do you believe God can give you the grace and strength to carry it one more day or week or month? Do you believe He's eager to give you what you need? Then ask Him for it today . . . and tomorrow.

FOR GROUP STUDY

Questions for Group Discussion

1. Take a moment to read Ephesians 1:4–6. To open discussion, have group members contribute their thoughts about the important concepts and truths they found in those three verses.

2. John 3:16 is one of the most well-known and often-quoted verses of the Bible. Although very simple to understand, it is the world's most pro-

found statement of love. Take a moment to examine this verse closely and be reminded of what it teaches. What great truths and promises does it give us? If time allows, have group members share how this verse has impacted their lives.

3. Dr. Evans devotes a section of this chapter to how God makes His love manifest. Discuss ways you have experienced God's love in your life, and perhaps ways you have seen God's love in the lives of others.

4. Dr. Evans notes that God's love is *the* true measure of authentic love. Examine 1 John 4. What does this kind of love entail for God's people to live out such love in their lives?

PICTURE THIS

The love of God is reflected in His determination to ensure the comprehensive welfare of His children. He cares about each of us and manifests His love to us in several ways. Below are a few of those ways.

GOD'S LOVE AND OUR WELFARE

FOCUS OF HIS LOVE	SCRIPTURE PASSAGES	LOVE'S ENABLEMENT
Involves our entire existence	Romans 8:31–37	God gives us the courage and strength to "overcome the world."
Open to our passion for Him	Psalm 37:4; Philippians 4:4	When we delight in the Lord in the midst of life's circumstances, He allows us to experience His joy.
Gives us joy in the midst of trials.	Romans 5:1–5; 1 John 4:18	No matter what trials we face, God fills us and consumes us with His joy.

14
THE GRACE OF GOD

What would you think if you went to buy a car and the salesman told you that you either had to push the car everywhere you went or pay extra for an engine? You'd know something was wrong because cars come equipped with their own supply of power to get you where you're going. The engine is part of the purchase price of the car.

You do have a responsibility to turn on the ignition and steer, but your effort does not supply the power for the trip. When I see so many Christians failing in their Christian life, living defeated lives day after day, month after month, and year after year, it soon becomes apparent they "push" their Christian lives. They don't realize that the power for the Christian life is already under the hood.

That power is the grace of God, His inexhaustible supply of goodness by which He does for us what we could never do for ourselves. Some of us live under the misconception that we have the power to pull off the Christian life. If that were true, we would be no different than a non-Christian who keeps the Ten Commandments. It's all human effort.

But God has supplied every true believer with a magnificent provision of grace. We can't earn it, we don't deserve it, but He has made it abundantly available.

Grace means God doesn't have to do anything. He is totally self-sufficient and in need of nothing. Grace means that all you are and all you have comes because He chooses to give it, not because you can demand it or deserve it.

We have to understand that. God owes us nothing. Yet in grace, He has given us everything. "My grace is sufficient for you" (2 Corinthians 12:9) is not only a promise of sufficiency in trials, but in all things.

GRACE IS POSSIBLE BECAUSE OF CHRIST

The grace of God is possible because of the sacrifice His Son made for the salvation of sinful mankind. We are only alive today and not consumed because of what Jesus did. And we will only go to heaven because of what Jesus did.

If it were not for the sacrifice of Jesus Christ, we would have been wiped out in judgment. But Christ's death on the cross freed God up to shower us with His grace rather than pour out His holy and justly deserved wrath on us.

But God's goodness is only available because of grace. The reason we worship the Lord Jesus Christ is that because of Him, God's grace was unleashed. We worship Christ because He dealt with the one thing which kept God from extending His grace to us: our sin.

Romans 5 contrasts the first Adam with the last Adam (Christ). Paul says, "Just as through one man sin entered into the world, and death through sin, and so death spread to all men, because all sinned" (v. 12). In other words, "In Adam all die" (1 Corinthians 15:22). We will die because Adam sinned. We were "in Adam" when he sinned. Adam was our titular head; that is, he was our representative.

Now someone may say, "Wait a minute. I didn't choose Adam to represent me. I want to represent myself in this thing. I'm a pretty good person."

But God says, "If you want to represent yourself, you've got a problem. You've sinned too, just like Adam. You haven't done any better than he did."

Even if Adam hadn't messed up, we would have because "all have sinned" (Romans 3:23). Turning back to Romans 5, listen to what Paul says about the grace of God in Christ that takes the sting out of death: "But the free gift is not like the transgression. For if by the transgression of the one the many died, much more did the grace of God and the gift by the grace of the one Man, Jesus Christ, abound to the many" (v. 15).

Thanks to God's "gift of grace" in Christ, we as Christians don't have to fear death. The Bible describes the death of a Christian as "sleep" (1 Corinthians 15:51). Non-Christians die; Christians sleep. The moment you close your eyes, "to be absent from the body [is] to be at home with the Lord" (2 Corinthians 5:8).

Common Grace

The work of Jesus Christ also brings general benefits to all people. *Original sin* means that we are all born into this world with the mark of condemnation on us. But the atonement of Jesus Christ for the sins of all men has neutralized the effects of the Adamic curse and satisfied the demands of a holy God, so that God is now free to be good even to sinful people. This is called common grace.

For instance, Jesus says that God causes the sun to shine and the rain to fall on the unrighteous as well as the righteous (Matthew 5:45). That's part of God's common grace to all. So is the air. You don't have to be a Christian to get oxygen.

Please note, I did not say that all people are automatically saved by Christ's death. Every person will be judged on the basis of what he did with Christ. Those who reject Him will face condemnation. Common grace has rendered all people "savable" by dealing with original sin, so that now people are condemned because of their personal sin and refusal to accept God's way of salvation.

Special Grace

God gives common grace to the whole human race (see Matthew 5:45), but the benefits of His special grace come only to His children. Again, these flow to us through our relationship with Jesus Christ.

Non-Christians will not always thank God for the air, water, and sunshine that keep them alive, but everyone who names the name of Christ should wake up each morning thanking God for His grace. We know it's all because Jesus Christ satisfied the demands of a holy God.

GOD'S GRACE BRINGS US MERCY

God's mercy is distinct from His grace in that grace means giving a person something he doesn't deserve, while mercy is identifying with someone's misery. According to Ephesians 2:4–5: "God, being rich in mercy, because of His great love with which He loved us, even when we were dead in our transgressions, made us alive together with Christ (by grace you have been saved)."

Here Paul beautifully juxtaposes grace and mercy. In mercy, God's heart went out to us in our helpless condition. In grace, He gave us what we didn't deserve—salvation. Mercy is what a mother shows when she cuddles her sick child.

Every misery we experience in life is to some degree related to sin: either our own sin, someone else's sin, or just the contaminated, sinful world in which we live. Because He is "rich in mercy," when God sees our pain, He feels it. He experiences it with us. But grace must precede mercy because God can't help us with our misery until He first deals with our sin.

That's why John wrote to Christians, "If we confess our sins, He is faithful and righteous to forgive us our sins and to cleanse us from all unrighteousness" (1 John 1:9). Confession of your sin frees God to show you His mercy. If you are miserable, you need God's mercy. But you can't have His mercy until you have allowed His grace to take away your sin. Once you've come clean with God, He is able to help you with the things that bring hurt.

The Bible says that God's mercies are "new every morning" (Lamentations 3:23). Every day, God has something new to show you as He deals with some aspect of your life. And why can God show us mercy? Because of grace. Because He looks at Jesus Christ and is so satisfied He's able to deal with us in mercy and pity us in our pain. No one wants what he or she deserves. A guilty person doesn't throw himself on the justice of the court, but on the *mercy* of the court.

That's what we do when we cry out to God and say, "Lord, I messed up. It was my sin that got me in here, or the sin of someone else, but I plead the blood of Jesus Christ. Have mercy on me!"

The Israelites cried out to God from the misery of Egyptian slavery, and their cry reached not only His ear, but His heart. So He sent Moses to deliver them (Exodus 3:9–10). Those Israelite slaves wanted mercy. So should we.

GOD'S GRACE IS SUFFICIENT FOR EVERY NEED

You should memorize this verse: "And God is able to make all grace abound to you, that always having all sufficiency in everything, you may have an abundance for every good deed" (2 Corinthians 9:8). God's got something for everything you need. There is no such thing as insufficient grace.

Most of us have suffered the embarrassment of bouncing a check because of insufficient funds. But God has no problem covering His checks. The Bible says that God's grace is so inexhaustible, so awesome in its supply, it never runs out. Grace is designed not only to save you, but to keep you. When you became a Christian, God supplied you everything you need for spiritual life and growth.

That's why Peter says, "Grow in the grace and knowledge of our Lord and Savior Jesus Christ" (2 Peter 3:18). Peter is saying, "Grow in your understanding of grace. The more you understand about grace, the more you enjoy the Christian life." Don't let anyone stop you from growing in your understanding of the awesome supply of God's grace.

I think when a lot of us get to heaven, God will say, "All of your answers were available in My grace. But you didn't grow in grace and never came to understand My sufficiency."

Many Christians live pauper lives because they haven't grown in their understanding of God's great, inexhaustible supply that was provided in Christ. Don't let anyone stop you from maximizing your Christian experience, because God says, "My grace is sufficient for you" (2 Corinthians 12:9).

GOD'S GRACE TRAINS US FOR VICTORY

The grace of God also trains us in how to live the victorious Christian life. Paul says, "For the grace of God has appeared, bringing salvation to all men, instructing us to deny ungodliness and worldly desires and to live sensibly, righteously and godly in the present age" (Titus 2:11–12).

Grace instructs us in how to live. Grace will give you victory where you didn't have victory. Grace will give you power where you didn't have power. Grace will give you the ability to keep on keeping on when you want to give up.

Grace teaches us how to live. It not only gives us the right information, but the right enablement with it. With grace comes power. A lot of people can give out right information. After all, we're on the "information superhighway." Trouble is, this highway has no gas stations. Where do we get the power to pull this off?

"Grace gives it to you," Paul says. He explained it to the Galatians this way: "I have been crucified with Christ; and it is no longer I who live, but Christ lives in me; and the life which I now live in the flesh I live by faith in the Son of God, who loved me, and delivered Himself up for me" (2:20). In other words, "I have exchanged my life for Christ's life living in me." Notice he goes on to say in verse 21 that this kept him from "nullify[ing] the grace of God."

Living the Christian life in your own power nullifies the grace of God. If you try to pull yourself up spiritually by your own good works, by positive thinking, or by sheer determination, you cancel out God's grace.

It's no accident that Paul wrote this way to the believers in Galatia. In the very next sentence he said, "You foolish Galatians, who has bewitched you, before whose eyes Jesus Christ was publicly portrayed as crucified?" (3:1). They were being tricked by people who had exchanged inner spiritual power for outward religious conformity. If you're making that same exchange today, you have been tricked.

What's the solution? Paul reveals it in Galatians 5:1: "It was for freedom that Christ set us free; therefore keep standing firm and do not be subject again to a yoke of slavery." You are free now. Don't let anyone tie you up.

Some Christians are tied up in knots trying to live by other people's religious rules rather than by grace. Paul says, "Let grace govern your lives, not people."

It's possible for us as Christians to go back to an external rule of conformity, and in so doing to cancel the power of Christ in our lives. Some of us who are trying to do good have cut off the power of Christ because we operate by our external conformity and determination rather than by the inner dynamic of grace.

It's much like marriage. To newlyweds, it's pure joy to do things for one another. The daily chores that come with married life aren't a burden but a delight, because the energy to do them is generated from within, from the power and newness of that love relationship.

But what happens five years later? He's lucky to get a meal. Meantime, he doesn't open the car door for her—she's lucky he doesn't take off while she's trying to get in the car. If the work still gets done, it's because they have to, not because they want to. What happened? The internal motivation has been replaced by external conformity. Whenever that happens, you have no inner joy or dynamic. You just have a job.

Like a joyless marriage, the Christian life becomes miserable whenever you try to live it by your own determination rather than by the supply of divine energy from within. The Christian life can only be lived when you remain in vital relationship with Jesus Christ, your power source. That's why Paul goes on to say in Galatians 5:16: "Walk by the Spirit, and you will not carry out the desire of the flesh."

Now don't get me wrong. Nothing is wrong with rules. Rules are necessary, but the power to obey them must come from within. The idea is not to get rid of legitimate rules, but to get back into relationship with Christ so that we will have the proper motivation to do the right thing.

Grace never means people hold no responsibility. That's called lawlessness. The difference between living under grace and living under law is that under grace we are motivated to obey by the proper power source, which is the Spirit. That's the engine underneath the hood. The Bible calls it "the filling of the Holy Spirit" (see Ephesians 5:18).

As our relationship with Christ is cultivated, we grow in grace. Then the supply of grace, energized by the power of the Holy Spirit, gives us spiritual victory. When grace starts operating, we'll begin to sing when it's not Sunday, serve without being asked, and know how to speak to others with a voice of grace (Colossians 4:6). We give grace because we've got grace.

GOD GIVES GRACE ON HIS TERMS

The grace of God is only experienced by those who receive it on His terms. James 4:1–2 says:

> What is the source of quarrels and conflicts among you? Is not the source your pleasures that wage war in your members? You lust and do not have; so you commit murder. And you are envious and cannot obtain; so you fight and quarrel. You do not have because you do not ask.

The first way you get God's grace is by asking for it. But too many of us try to make things happen on our own, fussing and fighting to get what we want. How many husbands and wives fight to change one another? Or struggle to make things happen? "You are warring," James says, "when all you have to do is ask."

It is of course possible to ask "with wrong motives, so that you may spend it on your pleasures" (v. 3). We tend to think of this as asking for material things. We think, "Sure, I can understand God not giving me a sports car." But this can apply to all kinds of prayers we make that are designed not to glorify Him, but to benefit us.

James says, "One reason you don't have a lot of things necessary for you to be victorious is that you don't ask. And when you do ask, you ask too often only to benefit yourself. You are using human methods. Ask, but with the right motives."

Then he says in verse 4, "You adulteresses, do you not know that friendship with the world is hostility toward God? Therefore whoever wishes to be a friend of the world makes himself an enemy of God." You can't love the world and love God at the same time. You have to make a choice. "You can't have the world and God too; that's spiritual adultery," James warns.

Our God is jealous of His work in us (v. 5). He won't share us with another spiritual suitor—and He shouldn't have to!

Then James makes a statement about grace: "But He gives a greater grace. Therefore it says, 'God is opposed to the proud, but gives grace to the humble'" (v. 6).

If you think you can do it yourself, God says, "OK, do it yourself. If you can't do it yourself, come to Me." That's humility, recognizing that I have a need I can't meet by myself.

God opposes the proud, and you don't want God opposing you. He will make it impossible for you to do what you want to do through the methods you are trying to use. He's going to resist you because God will resist His children who operate independently of Him, who don't ask, who compromise with the world. But the humble cry, "I can't. I need You. I'm desperate!" To them He gives more grace.

Hebrews 4:16 says, "Let us therefore draw near with confidence to the throne of grace, that we may receive mercy and may find grace to help in time of need." You can go to a place called the "throne room of grace." In this throne room God dispenses grace, but only upon request.

God says, "Do you need grace? Then draw near that you may receive mercy and grace in the time of need." How long do you stay there? Until you get what you need. If it's important enough, you will stay. This is the provision of God's grace.

PERSONAL APPLICATION FOR LIFE

1. Here's a great verse to memorize: "And God is able to make all grace abound to you, that always having all sufficiency in everything, you may have an abundance for every good deed" (2 Corinthians 9:8).

2. What have you done in the past week, month, or even year that can only be explained as the power of God working through you? If you have trouble answering that, it may be time to get alone with God and allow His Spirit to do some heart searching.

3. Anytime is a good time to measure your growth in grace. Before too much longer, take some time to put your life up against a "spiritual growth chart" like Galatians 5:22–23, the fruit of the Spirit, and mark your progress. For every sign of new growth you see, thank the Lord. For every area of growth needed, humbly ask for His grace.

4. Based on what we have learned from James 4 about asking with the wrong motives, we probably ought to thank God more often for unanswered prayer. Have you prayed any prayers like that lately? Is it possible you're praying for something right now that would not be good for you or glorify God? Those questions are worth thinking seriously about.

FOR GROUP STUDY

Questions for Group Discussion

1. Read Ephesians 2:1–10 and have group members jot down key points. What do verses 4 and 5 mean? Have members share their insights and ideas with the group.

2. Dr. Evans notes that God's grace trains us in how to live the victorious Christian life, focusing on Titus 2:11–12. Read that passage and discuss how grace instructs us in living the Christian life victoriously. Other passages that support this discussion are Galatians 2:20; 3:1; 5:1.

3. Dr. Evans points out that God gives His grace on His terms. Examine

James 4:1–6. Drawing from this passage, what are God's terms? What do we learn additionally from Hebrews 4:16?

4. How does God's grace result in spiritual growth? Begin your study with 2 Peter 3:18. The apostle Paul speaks of grace that leads to growth (2 Corinthians 12:7–9). What does his experience teach us?

PICTURE THIS

From the text of Romans 5 we see a contrast between the first Adam with the "last" Adam (Jesus Christ). The apostle Paul sums us this contrast in 1 Corinthians 15:22: "For as all die in Adam, so all will be made alive in Christ."

THE TWO ADAMS CONTRASTED

THE FIRST ADAM	CONTRAST ⟷	THE SECOND ADAM (JESUS CHRIST)
A man who wanted to be like God (Genesis 3:4–6)	⟷	God who became man (John 1:14)
Disobeyed (Genesis 3:17)	⟷	Obeyed (Philippians 2:6–8)
Believed a lie (John 8:44)	⟷	Is the Truth (John 1:17; 14:6)
Brought death (Romans 5:12)	⟷	Brought life (1 Corinthians 15:21–22)

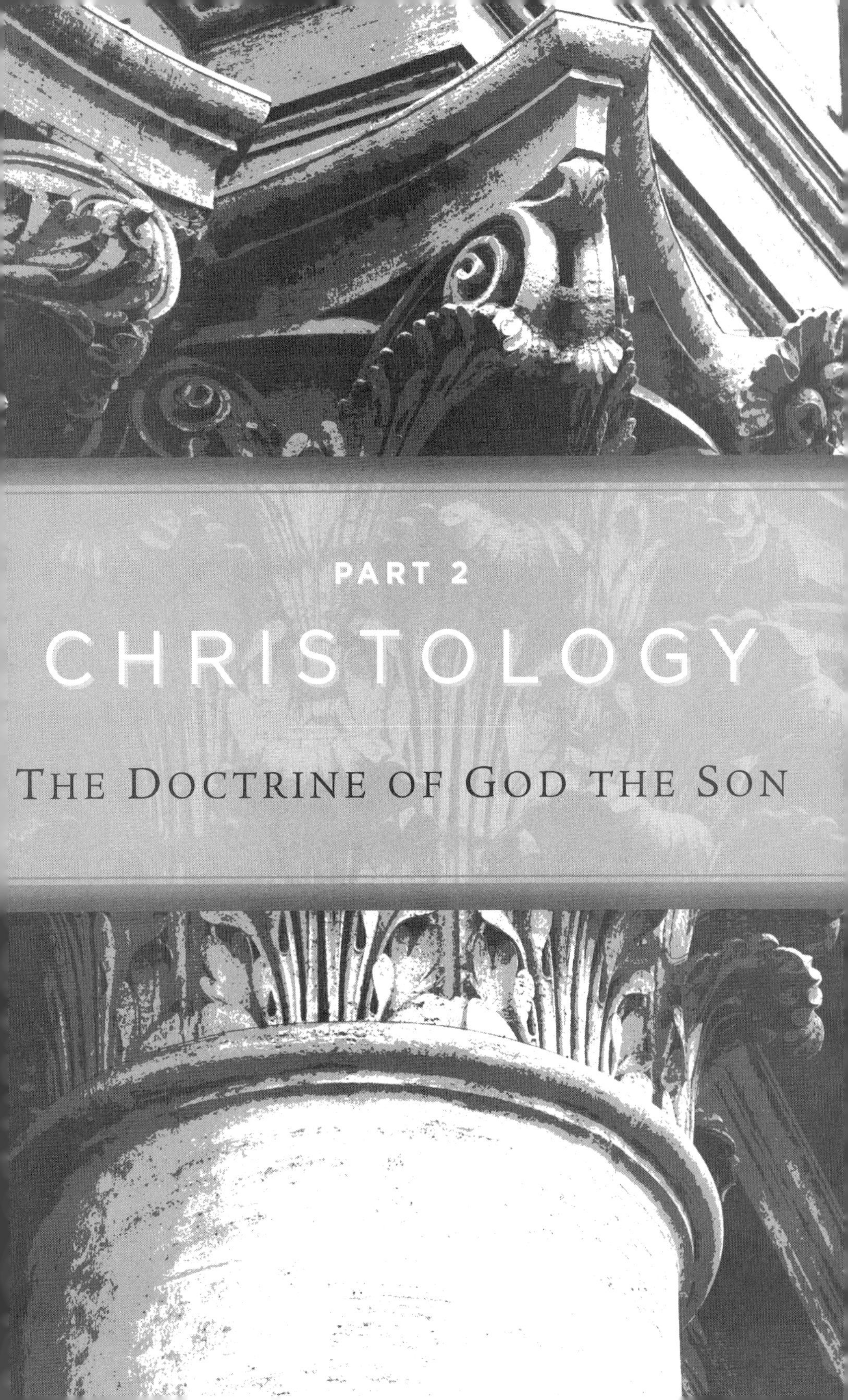

PART 2

CHRISTOLOGY

The Doctrine of God the Son

SECTION I

THE UNIQUENESS OF CHRIST

15

THE UNIQUENESS OF THE PERSON OF CHRIST

Jesus Christ is *the* unique, one-of-a-kind person in all of history. His appearance on earth was so monumental that history divided around His life, B.C. and A.D. Time only has meaning to us as it is defined by the presence of Jesus Christ in history.

On one occasion Jesus' disciples voiced the question that people have been asking about Him for two thousand years. Having witnessed His miraculous calming of the sea, the Twelve looked at one another and asked in amazement, "What kind of a man is this?" (Matthew 8:27). The Gospels and the rest of the New Testament were written to answer that most important of all questions and explain its implications for our lives.

Jesus is unique because He is the only person who existed before He was born and who is today what He has always been. He is the only person whose conception had no relationship to His origin, yet He was not a man before His incarnation. By virtue of His birth as a man, Jesus Christ is now both Son of God and Son of Man. He is deity, and He is humanity. Jesus is the God-man.

JESUS CHRIST'S DEITY

Jesus Christ is "very God of very God," to use a phrase theologians use to try to declare Christ's divine nature. A lot of people respect Christ as a great person, an inspiring teacher, and a great leader, but reject His deity. This is heresy. You cannot hold Jesus in high regard while denying He is the eternal God, a point Jesus Himself made to the rich young man (Mark 10:17–18).

Jesus clearly and directly claimed to be God when He said, "I and the Father are one" (John 10:30). This statement is significant because the word *one* is neuter in form meaning that He and the Father were one, perfect in nature and unified in essence. This was a personal claim of total equality with the Father. Those who heard this statement clearly understood it to be a claim to deity, for they immediately tried to stone Him for blasphemy because He made Himself equal to God (v. 33).

Christ's Preexistence

We have already said that Christ existed before His birth. The prophet stated Christ's preexistence this way: "As for you, Bethlehem Ephrathah, too little to be among the clans of Judah, from you One will go forth for Me to be ruler in Israel. His goings forth are from long ago, from the days of eternity" (Micah 5:2).

This is a significant verse for several reasons, not the least of which is Micah's accuracy in prophesying Jesus' birthplace. Notice also that the prophet said that this One had no beginning; His existence reaches back into eternity past.

Isaiah gave Jesus Christ the title "Eternal Father" (Isaiah 9:6), or "Father of eternity," in his prophecy of Jesus' first and second comings. Since Jesus is the Father of eternity, He is also the Father or initiator of time.

But the only way Jesus could be the initiator of time is if He existed before time. This verse speaks of His preexistence and tells us that Christ is of a different nature than anyone else who has ever lived.

The prophets were not the only ones who taught Jesus' preexistence. Jesus declared it Himself in an exchange that stunned and infuriated His Jewish detractors.

They had accused Jesus of having a demon (John 8:52) because He claimed that anyone who believed in Him would not see death. They reviled Him and asked this question: "Whom do You make Yourself out to be?" (v. 53).

That's a great question, but they didn't like Jesus' answer: "Your father Abraham rejoiced to see My day" (v. 56). The Jews replied, "You are not yet fifty years old, and have You seen Abraham?" (v. 57). They were getting upset because Jesus was making claims no man had ever made before.

Then Jesus made this crucial statement: "Truly, truly, I say to you, before Abraham was born, I am" (v. 58).

Don't miss the importance of the verb tenses Jesus used here. He did not say, "Before Abraham was born, I *was*," but "I am." This is significant because "I AM" is the name God gave Himself when He sent Moses to redeem Israel from Egypt. "God said to Moses . . . 'Thus you shall say to the sons of Israel, "I AM has sent me to you"'" (Exodus 3:14).

This is the name we transliterate as *Yahweh*, the self-existing God. This name describes God's personal self-sufficient and eternal nature. The eternal God has no past, so He cannot say "I was." He has no future, so cannot say "I will be." God exists in an eternal now. Time is only meaningful to us because we are not independently self-sufficient and eternal.

When Jesus told the Jews that He predated Abraham, He was claiming not only preexistence, but deity.

Jesus' Equality with God the Father

There is another important claim in what Jesus told His Jewish opponents in John 8. By taking to Himself the most personal and hallowed name of God, Jesus was making Himself equal with God.

His hearers understood this perfectly, because they picked up stones to stone Jesus for blasphemy (John 8:59).

Jesus' claim is even stronger in John 5:17–18. "'My Father is working until now, and I Myself am working.' For this reason therefore the Jews were seeking all the more to kill Him, because He not only was breaking the Sabbath, but also was calling God His own Father, making Himself equal with God."

These people understood Jesus to mean that He was placing Himself on equal standing with God because He was claiming to be of the same essence as God.

The Bible elsewhere equates Jesus with God. Genesis 1:1 says that God created the world. But Colossians 1:16 says that by Jesus Christ "all things where created." Either we have two Creators, or the God of Genesis 1 is the God of Colossians 1.

John made the identical claim for Jesus when he began his gospel by declaring, "In the beginning was the Word, and the Word was with God, and the Word *was* God" (John 1:1, italics added). So the Word is distinct from God, yet the Word is equal with God.

John doesn't leave us in doubt about the identity of the Word. "And the Word became flesh, and dwelt among us, and we saw His glory, glory as of the only begotten from the Father, full of grace and truth" (John 1:14).

Then verse 18 adds, "No man has seen God at any time; the only begotten God who is in the bosom of the Father, He has explained Him." And in Hebrews 1:8, God Himself is the speaker. "Of the Son He says, 'Your throne, O God, is forever and ever.'" God the Father is calling His Son "God." Nothing could be clearer or more direct than that. This cannot be said about anyone else. Jesus claimed equality with God, and the writers of Scripture consistently support that claim.

Christ's Membership in the Trinity

The Bible teaches that Jesus Christ is the Son of God, and yet He is fully God. It also teaches that God the Father is God. The question the early church grappled with was how Jesus could be God but also be distinct from the Father as the Son.

A child at our church in Dallas once asked me, "Pastor, if Jesus is God, then who was He talking to on the cross when He said, 'My God, My God, why have You forsaken Me?' Was He talking to Himself?"

That's a very perceptive question. Jesus was not talking to Himself on the cross, but to the Father. We can say this with confidence because the Bible teaches that the Godhead is composed of three distinct yet coequal persons who share the same divine substance: Father, Son, and Holy Spirit. The term *Trinity* is used for this foundational truth.

So when we talk about God, we could be talking about either the Godhead corporately or about any one of the three persons who make up the

Godhead. God's Word teaches Jesus' deity because it presents Him as a member of the Godhead, the divine Trinity.

Jesus identified Himself as distinct from the Father when He called Himself "the Son of God" (John 10:36). Yet, just a few minutes before He said that, He also said, "I and the Father are one" (v. 30).

The unity of the Trinity, and yet the distinction of its three members, is evident in Jesus' commission to His disciples. He told us to baptize people "in the name of the Father and the Son and the Holy Spirit" (Matthew 28:19). Normally we would expect to read the word *names* (plural) here, because Jesus mentioned three names. But He used the singular, *name*, on purpose because the three members of the Godhead make up one entity.

The name of God is singular because the triune God is one God. This is the consistent teaching of Scripture. Paul closed one of his letters with this benediction: "The grace of the Lord Jesus Christ, and the love of God, and the fellowship of the Holy Spirit, be with you all" (2 Corinthians 13:14). The biblical doctrine of the Trinity establishes the full deity of Jesus Christ. He is God.

Christ's Own Statements of His Deity

Another proof of Christ's deity is the way He spoke of it Himself, without any self-consciousness or hesitation. Jesus made several claims to His own deity in one exchange with His Jewish opponents. In their course of their discussion, Jesus said to them: "If I glorify Myself, My glory is nothing; it is My Father who glorifies Me, of whom you say, 'He is our God'" (John 8:54). Here Jesus clearly said that the God of Israel was His Father.

But then Jesus claimed not only to be the Son of God, but to be *equal* with God: "'Your father Abraham rejoiced to see My day, and he saw it and was glad.' So the Jews said to Him, 'You are not yet fifty years old, and have You seen Abraham?' Jesus said to them, 'Truly, truly, I say to you, before Abraham was born, I am'" (vv. 56–58). The Jews knew Jesus was claiming to be the same Yahweh who spoke to Moses at the burning bush (Exodus 3), and they sought to stone Him for blasphemy.

And if this was not a clear enough claim for His equality with God, Jesus later declared, "I and the Father are one" (John 10:30).

JESUS CHRIST'S HUMANITY

Jesus is also man. He partakes of the nature of deity because He is the Son of God. He also partakes of the nature of humanity because He is the "Son of Man." In fact, this was Jesus' favorite title for Himself.

In this section we want to talk about Jesus' humanity, because it is this union of deity and humanity that makes Jesus unique in history. Jesus left heaven to take on human flesh, which is what we mean by the term *incarnation*. Jesus became flesh and blood, an event that was prophesied in Scripture hundreds of years before Jesus was ever born.

The Key Distinctive of His Human Nature

The most important distinctive of Jesus' human nature is that He was born of a virgin. In Isaiah 7:14 the prophet wrote, "The Lord Himself will give you a sign: Behold, a virgin will be with child and bear a son, and she will call His name Immanuel."

Then in a verse we have already noted, Isaiah 9:6, we read: "A child will be born to us, a son will be given to us." Notice how careful the Holy Spirit is with the language here.

The Son is "given," not born. Why? Because as the Son of God, Jesus already existed. But the child is "born," a reference to Jesus' birth in Bethlehem. God the Father gave the Son to us through a supernaturally wrought conception in human flesh through the process of a human birth.

Paul brought these prophecies from Isaiah together when he wrote, "When the fullness of the time came, God sent forth His Son, born of a woman, born under the Law" (Galatians 4:4).

God "sent forth" the Son because the Son is given (Isaiah 9:6). Jesus was "born of a woman" because a child was to be born. This is the incarnation of Jesus Christ.

Make no mistake, Jesus was fully human. He was the God who made everything, the God who never becomes weary or needs to sleep. Yet in His humanity He could be tired and thirsty (John 4:6–7). We know Jesus had human emotions because He wept at Lazarus's grave (John 11:35) and felt compassion for people (Matthew 9:36). He also loved us with an everlasting love. And He had a human soul and spirit (Matthew 26:38; Luke 23:46), which all human beings have.

The Perfections of His Human Nature

Some people have a problem with Jesus' human nature because they assume if He was human, He had to be sinful. Not when the Holy Spirit oversees the birth process. We have already noted that Jesus was conceived by the Holy Spirit, bypassing the sinful human nature of Joseph as the father.

The same objection is raised about the Bible. If the Bible was written by human beings, the argument goes, it must have errors in it. That might be true except for one thing: The Holy Spirit oversaw the writing of Scripture to preserve it from error (2 Peter 1:21).

What the Spirit did with the written Word of God, He did with the incarnate Word of God, Jesus Christ. The Spirit superintended the conception of both the written and the incarnate Word so that there was no human contamination in either.

Lest you think all of this is just the musings of theologians, you need to realize that everything Jesus did, and is doing, for you and me is tied to His sinless humanity.

Paul said that God made Jesus, "who knew no sin," to become sin on our behalf so we might partake of God's righteousness (2 Corinthians 5:21). If Jesus were just a sinful human being, His death would have done nothing to save us.

According to Hebrews 4:15, Jesus' present ministry in heaven as our Great High Priest is also dependent upon His sinlessness. He could not help us in our weakness if He were as sinful and weak as we are.

THE PERFECT UNION OF CHRIST'S TWO NATURES

The two natures of Jesus Christ form what theologians call the *hypostatic union*. This is a big term that simply means undiminished deity and perfect humanity united forever in one person.

In other words, Jesus was no less God when He became a perfect Man. He was fully human, but without sin. It's important that we understand Jesus is one person, not two. He is the God-man, not sometimes God and sometimes man. He is one person with two natures.

Jesus has a perfect human and divine nature, which makes Him unique. Nobody else is God become a man—God in the flesh.

A Picture of Jesus' Humanity

When Jesus became a man, He "emptied Himself, taking the form of a bond-servant, and being made in the likeness of men" (Philippians 2:7). Does this mean that Jesus emptied Himself of His deity?

Not at all. It was impossible that Jesus Christ could cease being God. This famous verse is not talking about what Jesus emptied Himself of, but what He emptied Himself into.

It's like pouring something from one pitcher into another. Jesus took all of His deity and poured it into another vessel, the "form of a bond-servant." He didn't stop being who He is, but He changed the form of who He is.

When He came to earth, Jesus moved from His preexistent, glorified form and poured the fullness of His deity into a human form.

Simply becoming a human being was enough of a step down for the Son of God. But Jesus became a "bond-servant," a slave, the lowest possible position on the social ladder in that day. We could say that He who is very God of very God became "very slave of very slave."

Jesus came as a lowly servant, which is good news for us because that means there is no one with whom Jesus cannot identify. If you are not very high on the social ladder, Jesus understands because He has been there. And no matter how high you may be, Jesus has been higher because He is the Son of God.

When Jesus took on flesh, He was "made in the likeness of men," as we read above. That simply means that even though Jesus was much more than just a man, those who saw Him would think He was just a man.

Jesus didn't go around with a halo around His head. He looked like a man. Luke 2:52 says Jesus grew in the same ways as other people: physically, spiritually, emotionally, and socially.

Jesus was not only born in humble circumstances, but "He humbled Himself by becoming obedient to the point of death, even death on a cross" (Philippians 2:8). In His sacrifice for our sins, Jesus humbly accepted the most painful, humiliating form of death the Romans could inflict.

In Jesus' crucifixion we get an idea of what is meant when the Bible says He emptied Himself. Jesus chose to lay aside the independent use of His divine attributes, submitting Himself completely to His Father's will.

How do we know this? Because when Peter attacked the high priest's servant, Jesus told Peter He could call more than twelve legions of angels to rescue Him if He desired (Matthew 26:53).

But Jesus did not do that because in order for His sacrifice to be effective for sin, He had to suffer and die and defeat Satan as a perfect Man. He could not simply call on His divine power to wipe out Satan, but had to submit Himself to death.

The Only Sensible Response

But Philippians 2 does not end with verse 8. Because Jesus was obedient to death, "God highly exalted Him, and bestowed on Him the name which is above every name, that at the name of Jesus every knee will bow . . . and that every tongue will confess that Jesus Christ is Lord, to the glory of God the Father" (vv. 9–11).

When we understand the uniqueness of Jesus Christ, only one response makes sense—to fall on our knees and confess Him as Savior and Lord.

There are two ways we can do this. We can either bow in humble submission today, confessing Jesus and receiving Him as our Savior, or we will be forced to bow to Him at the judgment. But every creature in heaven, on earth, and in hell is going to bow to Jesus Christ.

When you bow to Jesus in repentance and submission, He becomes Lord of your life. And when He becomes Lord of your life, He takes over. That means He deserves all of your respect, honor, and obedience because of who He is and what He has done for you.

Jesus is King of the universe and Lord of our lives. He is the unique God-man to whom every knee will someday bow. The wisest thing you and I can do is bow to Him today!

PERSONAL APPLICATION FOR LIFE

1. "And the Word became flesh, and dwelt among us, and we saw His glory, glory as of the only begotten from the Father, full of grace and truth" (John 1:14). Without question, the incarnation of Jesus Christ is one of the greatest events in all of human history. That God lived among us in human form should give us pause. For believers, it is also one of the most exciting truths, and it gives us a reason to shout for joy! Do you remember to thank God for sending His Son?

2. When you bow to Jesus in repentance and submission, He becomes Lord of your life. That means He deserves all of your respect, honor, and obedience because of who He is and what He has done for you. Is Jesus Lord of your life? Someday every knee will bow to Jesus. The wisest thing we can do is bow to Him today!

3. Praise God for the sinlessness of Jesus. Had He been a sinful human being as ourselves, His death would have done nothing to save us. Take comfort in knowing Jesus' present ministry is in heaven as our Great High Priest (Hebrews 4:15). Not only does He know our weakness, but also because of His sinlessness, He is able to help in our weakness. Be encouraged that Jesus is constantly interceding for you as you continue in your walk of faith.

4. As we are caught up in the duties of our busy lifestyles, it is so easy to regard our Christian heritage lightly. Are you a believer? If so, your sins have been cleansed by the blood of our sinless Savior! Not only was God interested in saving you, He also wants to guide you through his life and into His glory. You are a citizen of God's kingdom; make every minute and every day count for His glory.

FOR GROUP STUDY

Questions for Group Discussion

1. Jesus is truly the unique person of all time. Discuss Dr. Evans's main points regarding Christ's deity: His preexistence, His equality with the

Father, and His membership in the Trinity. To the Jews, what was the significance of Jesus' statement, "Before Abraham was born . . . I am"?

2. Read Micah 5:2, the prophet's statement about Christ's preexistence. What is especially significant about his prophecy?

3. In 2 Corinthians 5:21, the apostle Paul tells us that Jesus "knew no sin." In what ways was He sinless? According to this passage, why was it important that Jesus be sinless and remain sinless?

4. Theologians refer to the union of Christ's two natures, His deity and His perfect humanity, as the *hypostatic union*. Read Philippians 2:6–11. From that passage, what do we learn about that union? In light of this passage, what should be our response to Jesus?

PICTURE THIS

What makes Jesus *the* unique individual is His dual natures. Not only does He possess a human nature, but also a divine nature. The Bible clearly teaches that Jesus is deity as the following Scripture passages emphasize.

JESUS CHRIST'S DEITY

FOCUS	SCRIPTURE PASSAGES	WHAT IT MEANS
His preexistence	Micah 5:2; Isaiah 9:6; John 1:1; 3:53–58	Jesus is Deity because He existed with God the Father before the creation of the world and time.
His equality with God the Father	John 1:1, 14; 5:17–18; Colossians 1:16; Hebrews 1:8	Jesus is Deity the same as God the Father.
His membership in the Trinity	John 10:30, 36; Matthew 28:19; 2 Corinthians 13:14	Jesus is Deity because He is a full member of the Godhead.

16

THE UNIQUENESS OF CHRIST IN PROPHECY AND TYPOLOGY

Biblical prophecy and typology are related in the sense that both of them present us with pictures of Christ before He came to earth. Prophecy foretells the coming of Christ the first time to be the Savior from sin and the second time to rule as King.

Prophecy is found in both the Old and New Testaments. Typology is also a study for which we need both testaments. That's because the pictures or types are the means by which the Old Testament foreshadows the person and work of Christ. A type is an Old Testament picture that reveals and points forward to a New Testament truth. The New Testament is the fulfillment of the type, the reality behind the shadow.

The central truth of prophecy as it relates to Jesus Christ is the fact that He is both the prophesied Messiah of the Old Testament and the prophesied King who will rule not only over Israel, but over the world.

John the Baptist hit the issue of prophecy squarely on the head when he sent some disciples from his prison cell to ask Jesus, "Are You the Expected One, or do we look for someone else?" (Luke 7:19).

John was asking Jesus if He was the prophesied Messiah. If not, John and his disciples needed to be looking elsewhere for God's redemption. John wavered in doubt for a minute, and Jesus reassured him. But the point I want you to see is that prophecy is critical to our understanding of who Jesus Christ is.

My purpose here is to show you that Jesus is the focus of Bible prophecy and is, therefore, unique.

THE SUBJECT OF PROPHECY

There is a familiar passage of Scripture in which the risen Christ Himself teaches about His central place in prophecy. It is found in Luke 24, during a walk Jesus took with two of His disciples to the village of Emmaus the very evening of resurrection day.

The two men on the Emmaus road were talking about the recent uproar in Jerusalem over this Man named Jesus. This was not just another ordinary weekend. The whole town was in pandemonium over Jesus, who was called "King of the Jews" and who claimed to be the Son of God, but who had been crucified a few days earlier. Now it was reported that He was alive again. His grave was empty.

The Things about Jesus

The Bible says that as they walked, "Jesus Himself approached, and began traveling with them. But their eyes were prevented from recognizing Him" (Luke 24:15- 16).

Jesus asked them, "What are these words that you are exchanging with one another?" (v. 17). Cleopas (v. 18) and the other disciple must have been having quite a discussion, because the word *exchanging* means a heated debate. They couldn't believe Jesus did not know about what had happened in Jerusalem.

So they said, "The things about Jesus the Nazarene, who was a prophet mighty in deed and word in the sight of God and all the people, and how the chief priests and our rulers delivered Him to the sentence of death, and crucified Him. But we were hoping that it was He who was going to redeem Israel" (vv. 19-21).

The men went on to tell Jesus how some women had gone to the tomb early that morning and found it empty, and how some other disciples had gone to verify the story (vv. 21–24). The thing to note is the disappointment in these disciples' voices (v. 21). Evidently, they didn't think the reports of Jesus' resurrection were really true.

The Prophetic Teacher

The problem is these disciples were uninformed about the truth of the events they had just experienced. Their lack of faith had caused them either to forget, or misunderstand, the prophetic word concerning the Messiah. So Jesus began to enlighten them:

> "O foolish men and slow of heart to believe in all that the prophets have spoken! Was it not necessary for the Christ to suffer these things and to enter into His glory?" Then beginning with Moses and with all the prophets, He explained to them the things concerning Himself in all the Scriptures. (vv. 25–27)

You can't get a better situation than this. Here are people who are thoroughly confused and discouraged because things didn't work out the way they should have, and it seems as if God's prophetic plan has backfired. But Jesus Himself comes along to clarify the situation.

Luke says Jesus enlightened these men by using the Old Testament to explain His coming and His ministry—"the things concerning Himself in all the Scriptures."

As they walked, Jesus walked these men through the Scriptures to bring them to an understanding of who He was, what was happening, and how they were to perceive the events they had just experienced.

In other words, Jesus taught from the Scriptures that prophesied about Him. Even though we do not know exactly what He said to them, we know that everything Jesus taught was about Himself because He is the subject of prophecy.

The two disciples from Emmaus had the greatest Teacher teaching from the greatest Book about the greatest person—Himself. And there were only two in the congregation. The problem was that they were slow to believe. Later, Jesus said to the group of followers, "Why are you troubled, and why do doubts arise in your hearts?" (Luke 24:38). If you are going to understand the prophetic Word, you must be willing to give God your heart, not only your head.

THE CONTENT OF PROPHECY

After Jesus revealed Himself to the pair in Emmaus and then vanished, they hurried back to Jerusalem that same night. There they found the apostles and others, and as they were telling their story, Jesus came into the room and conversed with them. First He said, "All things which are written about Me in the Law of Moses and the Prophets and the Psalms must be fulfilled" (Luke 24:44). Here Jesus declared that the entire Old Testament spoke prophetically of Him.

Jesus' summary of these prophecies included these facts: "Thus it is written, that the Christ should suffer and rise again from the dead on the third day; and that repentance for forgiveness of sins should be proclaimed in His name to all the nations, beginning from Jerusalem" (vv. 46–47).

The Prophecies Announced

The death and resurrection of "the Christ," the Messiah, for the forgiveness of sin is the summary and the heart of prophecy. The entire Old Testament can be summed up as looking forward to the coming of the Messiah. This prophecy was first given at the very beginning, when God told Satan that the Seed would come which would crush Satan's head (Genesis 3:15).

The patriarch Israel said this Seed would come from the tribe of Judah (Genesis 49:10). And God told David that his throne would endure forever (2 Samuel 7:16) because David would have a greater Son, the Messiah, who would rule and reign. So the Old Testament prophecies concerning Messiah were very specific.

Prophecies of Christ's Birth

Now let's "fast-forward" to the opening chapter of the New Testament, Matthew 1:1–17, the genealogy of Jesus Christ. This is the part most people skip over so they can get to the Christmas story.

Big mistake! This record and the genealogy in Luke are critical to the unfolding of the prophetic story concerning Jesus. They demonstrate that

Jesus' claim to be Messiah and King, the ruler from the line of David, was legitimate, because He was the Son of David both legally and biologically.

These written records were especially important for the Jews who would come along after Jesus. This is because in A.D. 70 all of Israel's genealogical records were lost when the Roman army under Titus sacked Jerusalem and burned the temple, where the records were stored.

Someone who was claiming to be Messiah, the rightful ruler from the line of David, needed to be able to trace his lineage back to David (2 Samuel 7:12–16; Isaiah 11:1–10). Therefore, God preserved the genealogical record of Jesus even though everyone else's records were destroyed.

Luke 3 takes Jesus' genealogy all the way back to Adam (v. 38). Why is it important that Jesus be connected to the garden of Eden? Because of the prophecy of the righteous Seed that would come and crush Satan (Genesis 3:15). God is removing all doubt that Jesus is the fulfillment of prophecy.

Prophecies of Christ's Death

The Old Testament prophecies also deal with Christ's death.

One classic prophecy that describes the Messiah's death for sin is Isaiah 53. I want to pick up a few key verses from this great passage and then see how they were fulfilled in Jesus. Of the Messiah, Isaiah wrote:

> He was despised and forsaken of men, a man of sorrows, and acquainted with grief. . . . Surely our griefs He Himself bore, and our sorrows He carried; yet we ourselves esteemed Him stricken, smitten of God, and afflicted. But He was pierced through for our transgressions, He was crushed for our iniquities; the chastening for our well-being fell upon Him, and by His scourging we are healed. (vv. 3–5)

Psalm 22 contains another great prophecy that the New Testament applies to Jesus Christ in His death on the cross. The psalm opens with the cry, "My God, my God, why have You forsaken me?" (v. 1), the very cry Jesus uttered from the cross.

The psalmist also said, "I am a worm, and not a man, a reproach of men and despised by the people. All who see me sneer at me; they separate with the lip, they wag the head, saying, 'Commit yourself to the Lord; let Him deliver him; let Him rescue him, because He delights in him'" (vv. 6–8).

Luke said that when Jesus was on the cross, "even the rulers were sneering at Him, saying, 'He saved others; let Him save Himself if this is the Christ of God'" (Luke 23:35).

Look back at Psalm 22. "I am poured out like water, and all my bones are out of joint" (v. 14). "They pierced my hands and my feet" (v. 16). "They divide my garments among them, and for my clothing they cast lots" (v. 18).

When a person hung on a cross through crucifixion, the weight of his own body dislocated his joints. Psalm 22 speaks prophetically of the manner of Jesus' death. He was pierced through His hands and feet. The soldiers gambled for His clothing (Matthew 27:35). Jesus' death was clearly prophesied, and He fulfilled every prophecy to the detail.

Prophecies of Christ's Resurrection

The final point of prophecy I want to mention is prophecy concerning Jesus' resurrection.

Jesus predicted His own resurrection on several occasions, both to His disciples (Matthew 17:23; 20:19) and to unbelieving Jews (John 2:18–21). John said that after Jesus was raised, the disciples remembered what He said, and they believed (v. 22).

In his Pentecost sermon, Peter drew on an Old Testament prophecy to prove that Jesus was the Messiah (Acts 2:25–28). The passage Peter quoted is Psalm 16:8–11, in which David wrote:

> I have set the Lord continually before me; because He is at my right hand, I will not be shaken. Therefore my heart is glad and my glory rejoices; my flesh also will dwell securely. For You will not abandon my soul to Sheol; nor will You allow Your Holy One to undergo decay. (vv. 8-10)

In Acts 2:29–32 Peter made it clear that the fulfillment of this passage was in the life of Jesus Christ. David looked ahead and spoke prophetically about the Christ, the Messiah. David wasn't the one resurrected; Jesus was.

And, Peter said, "We are all witnesses" to the fact that God raised Christ from the dead.

This is the uniqueness of Christ in prophecy. When you see the many ways the prophetic Word about Christ was fulfilled in His first coming, you can have confidence in the prophecies about His second coming and glorious rule (Daniel 7:14; 1 Peter 1:10–11).

THE SUBJECT OF TYPOLOGY

We could say that typology is the other side of the coin of prophecy. The two are related, because just as God gave us a prophetic map in Scripture that points to Jesus, He also gave us pictures in the Old Testament that point to Jesus and remind us of Him. Remember, Christ is the theme of the Old Testament (Matthew 5:17; Luke 24:27, 44; John 5:39).

That's what a type is, an Old Testament picture of a New Testament reality. Many of the Old Testament's ceremonies, regulations, and even people were types of Christ in that they illustrated various aspects of His person and work.

Jesus on Typology

Jesus was intensely interested in the Old Testament's typology about Himself. We can see that in Luke 24, the passage we studied at the beginning of this chapter.

When Jesus took those two disciples through the Old Testament and explained what the Scriptures said about Himself (vv. 27, 44), He was talking about typology as well as prophecy. We can say that because He began with "the Law of Moses" (v. 44), the first five books of the Old Testament, which are full of types of Jesus Christ.

The tabernacle in the wilderness was a type of Christ, as was the entire sacrificial system. A lot of the events that happened in the books of Moses typified Jesus (John 3:14–15). Moses himself as the deliverer was a type of Christ.

The point is that Jesus explained His life and ministry using events that happened hundreds of years earlier. He could do this because these things pictured Him, anticipated Him, and pointed forward to Him.

That's why Jesus could make this astounding statement: "Do not think that I came to abolish the Law or the Prophets; I did not come to abolish, but to fulfill" (Matthew 5:17). Jesus came to bring the Old Testament to its God-intended consummation.

The Better Things of Christ

In Colossians 2:17, Paul said the things of the Old Testament were "a mere shadow of what is to come; but the substance belongs to Christ." Now tell me, would you rather hug a shadow or a person?

There's nothing like the real thing. To embrace the Old Testament alone is to embrace the shadow. To embrace Jesus Christ is to embrace the substance of the shadow, the reality behind the type.

One of the favorite words of the author of Hebrews was *better*, which he uses thirteen times to show how the old covenant pointed ahead to something better in Christ.

For example, the writer said Jesus is "much better than the angels, as He has inherited a more excellent name than they" (Hebrews 1:4). If you settle for the glory of angels you settle for second best.

Hebrews 7:22 says, "Jesus has become the guarantee of a better covenant." The Old Testament law was a cumbersome way to live. It involved a complicated system of rituals and sacrifices. Jesus is a better way than the old covenant.

Besides, according to Hebrews 7:19, "the Law made nothing perfect." But Jesus introduced "a better hope," something we can hold on to and be confident in as we approach God.

The writer of Hebrews continued. Because the old covenant had become useless (see 7:18) in justifying sinners before God, it was necessary for a better sacrifice to be offered (9:23). This was the sacrifice Jesus made on the cross. The good news of the gospel is that the final sacrifice for sin has already been made. Thanks to what Christ has done for us, God has prepared a city called heaven for us (Hebrews 11:16). The Promised Land of Canaan was a type of heaven, but the Israelites' best day in Canaan cannot begin to compare with what Jesus has prepared for us (John 14:1–3). We have a better home.

Here's one more "better thing" in Hebrews. "God had provided something better for us, so that apart from us they would not be made perfect" (11:40). We have a better salvation. The "antetype," the New Testament fulfillment, is better than the type, the picture in the Old Testament.

TYPOLOGICAL PEOPLE

Now let's look at some of the biblical characters who became types of Christ. The fact that Jesus Christ was the only person whose life was foreshadowed in types tells us that He is unique in history.

We mentioned briefly above that Moses was a type of Christ in that Moses was the redeemer who liberated his people from slavery to Egypt, while Jesus liberated us from slavery to sin. I want to mention several other prominent types in the Old Testament.

Adam as a Type of Christ

Paul wrote in Romans 5:14, "Death reigned from Adam until Moses, even over those who had not sinned in the likeness of the offense of Adam, who is a type of Him who was to come."

Then the apostle said in 1 Corinthians 15:45, "'The first man, Adam, became a living soul.' The last Adam became a life-giving spirit."

In each case, Paul was comparing the two Adams, the Adam of creation and Christ. What is the relationship? Adam acted as the head of the human race when he sinned in Eden. He was our representative, so in the first Adam we all died when he died.

We got life through the first Adam, because it was through him that all of us are here. But we also inherited death from him.

However, the last Adam, Jesus Christ, is the head of a new race. And He did not sin. He was obedient to God, so through His death we have eternal life. That's why Peter called the church a new race of people (1 Peter 2:9). Whereas we got our first life, physical life, from the first Adam, we get our spiritual life from the last Adam.

So Adam is a type of Christ because both Adams give life. But the last Adam is better than the first because although the first Adam gave us life, he also dealt us death when he sinned (Romans 6:23).

But while the first Adam was a death-dealer, the last Adam is a life-giver. People who are related only to the first Adam will only see physical life. Their future is eternal death.

But people who are related to the last Adam not only have the life of the first Adam physically, they have the life of the last Adam eternally, which is a better life.

Aaron as a Type of Christ

A second person who served as a type of Christ was Moses' brother, Aaron, the high priest of Israel. We'll deal more with Christ's priesthood in a later chapter when we talk about His present work of intercession, but I want to reference this type now because it is so foundational.

In Hebrews 5:1–6, the writer mentioned two priesthoods and two types, that of Aaron and Melchizedek. Aaron and his priesthood came into being when the Law was given from Mt. Sinai. Aaron was called of God and anointed as high priest, and the tribe of Levi was chosen for priestly service.

Aaron and the other priests served as mediators between God and the people, because sinful people could not come directly into the presence of a holy God. The priest acted as a mediator by offering sacrifices to cover sins, and the high priest offered the main sacrifice once a year on the Day of Atonement. This blood sacrifice addressed the people's sins for one year, but it had to be repeated every year.

In his ministry as mediator between God and man, Aaron served as a type of Christ. But Christ was also a better mediator than Aaron. Why? Because Aaron had to offer a sacrifice for his own sins as well as for the people's sins (Hebrews 5:3). A priest could not approach God on behalf of others if his own sin was not atoned for.

But the Bible says that Jesus, our High Priest, was without sin (Hebrews 4:15). Therefore, He didn't have to offer a sacrifice for Himself. The full benefit of His death was applied to our sin account. Jesus perfectly fulfilled the type of high priest foreshadowed in Aaron and the Levitical priesthood.

Jesus Christ fulfilled the type of the priesthood because He was a better priest serving in a better temple, the eternal temple in heaven (Hebrews 9:24). He offered His own blood, not the blood of animals (Hebrews 9:12).

He entered the holy place to make His sacrifice once for all instead of just once a year (Hebrews 9:25-26).

In other words, a system of sacrifice that went on for more than a thousand years was wrapped up in one person. That makes Jesus Christ unique. He is the only One qualified to fulfill the type of Aaron's priesthood.

Melchizedek as a Type of Christ

The book of Hebrews also introduces us to Melchizedek, another priest with a very different priesthood. Melchizedek is the Bible's mystery man, mentioned only in Hebrews 5-7, Genesis 14:18-20, and Psalm 110:4. He is also a type of Christ. Interestingly, Hebrews 7:1 says that was both a priest and a king. That would normally be a problem, so what was happening here?

The explanation is that Melchizedek had nothing to do with the kings of Israel or Judah. He was of a different origin, so he could bring together in himself the offices of king and priest. Melchizedek was the only man in history, *other than Jesus Christ,* who could pull this off.

Melchizedek also typified Jesus as a king-priest because as far as history is concerned, Melchizedek had no beginning or ending of life. Who does that sound like?

Of course, the Bible is not saying Melchizedek had no father or mother or genealogy. There was simply no record of his birth, death, or parentage. He was unique and the founder of a unique priesthood that did not depend on the Law of Moses for its existence or authority.

Melchizedek's priesthood is perpetual. So Jesus Christ was designated by God as a member of this eternal priesthood—not the temporary priesthood of Aaron.

Hebrews 7:11-17 gives us the payoff for all of this. If Jesus Christ had to qualify for His priesthood through the Law, He would be out. Why? Because Jesus was from the tribe of Judah, not Levi, and all priests under the Law had to be Levites (7:13-14). So Jesus could not be our Great High Priest by human descent.

Second, we need an eternal priest, not a temporary one. The Levitical priesthood was rendered obsolete when Jesus died on the cross to offer the once-for-all, final sacrifice for sin. So if Jesus were a Levitical priest, His ministry would be over.

But Christ is a priest in the order of Melchizedek. Therefore, His priesthood is eternal, based not on the Law but on "the power of an indestructible life" (7:16).

That means Jesus is always on the job in heaven. We know that Satan is always there to accuse us, but whenever he tries to cut us off from God, Jesus steps in and says, "Father, those accusations are invalid. My blood has cleansed that person. He belongs to Me."

This is why you can't lose your salvation! Jesus never misses a day on the job as your High Priest. He never dies, like the Old Testament priests did. If He ever took a second off, you and I would be in deep trouble. But don't worry, Jesus is a "priest *forever* according to the order of Melchizedek" (v. 17, italics added).

TYPOLOGICAL ITEMS AND EVENTS

Besides people, many other things in the Old Testament served as types of Christ and demonstrated His uniqueness. I want to highlight a few of these as we close this chapter.

Israel's Sacrifices

The Israelites offered five basic kinds of sacrifices under the Law. They were the burnt offering, the grain offering, the peace offering, the sin offering, and the trespass offering.

The first three offerings had to do with dedication to God, while the last two had to do with atonement. But Jesus Christ is pictured in all the sacrifices.

Jesus fulfilled the type represented by the first three sacrifices through His life of total submission and complete obedience to God the Father. Jesus' declaration on earth was, "Behold, I have come (in the scroll of the book it is written of Me) to do Your will, O God" (Hebrews 10:7).

If Jesus had disobeyed God even once, He would have been disqualified from being our Savior. But once again, He is unique among all people because He obeyed God perfectly.

The sin offering and trespass offering were fulfilled by Christ's death.

We have already discussed the sacrificial nature of His death pretty thoroughly, so we just need to note it here.

The Tabernacle

The study of the tabernacle as a type of Christ is worth a book in itself. God specified in the book of Exodus how He wanted this place built, and every detail pointed ahead to Christ in some fashion.

Before the temple was built, the tabernacle was the dwelling place of God, the location of His *shekinah*, His glory. If you wanted to hang out with God, you had to hang out in the tabernacle.

Here are just a few of the ways Jesus fulfilled the type of the tabernacle. There was one door in the tabernacle. Jesus said He was the way (John 14:6). The tabernacle contained a brass altar for sacrifice. Jesus said in Mark 10:45 that He came to give His life as a ransom or sacrifice for many.

In the tabernacle was a laver where the priest washed his hands. Jesus told Peter, "If I do not wash you, you have no part with Me" (John 13:8). The tabernacle also contained a light, and we know that Jesus said, "I am the light of the world" (John 8:12).

Also in the tabernacle was a table on which sat some consecrated bread. Jesus called Himself "the bread of life" (John 6:48). The priest burned incense in the tabernacle to symbolize the prayers that went up to God. Jesus acted as our High Priest when He prayed for us (John 17:9).

Again, in the tabernacle there hung a veil that separated the outer chambers from the inner part, the Holy of Holies. It signified that full access to God was not yet achieved. But when Jesus died, the veil in the temple was torn in half (Matthew 27:51). The writer of Hebrews said the veil was Christ's body (Hebrews 10:20).

Finally, in the Holy of Holies was the ark of God with its covering called the mercy seat, where the blood of the sacrificial lamb was sprinkled to atone for sin. Jesus said in John 10:15, "I lay down My life."

Do you get the idea? The tabernacle, which was a tent, housed the presence and glory of God. When Jesus came, the Bible says, "The Word became flesh, and dwelt [literally, "tabernacled"] among us, and we beheld His glory" (John 1:14).

The word *dwelt* meant to pitch a tent, like the tabernacle. The connection between Christ and the tabernacle could not be clearer. The purpose of the tabernacle was to display God's glory, and when Jesus came people could see God's glory in Him. Jesus uniquely and perfectly fulfilled this type as well.

PERSONAL APPLICATION FOR LIFE

1. According to Colossians 2:17, what had been a mere shadow of what was to come found substance in Christ. The writer of the book of Hebrews spoke of the "better things" of Christ. Among the many better things we have is a better covenant, a better hope, and a better salvation. Because of these "better things," we can embrace the hope of better things to come. Take on a special confidence in your walk of faith, allowing the promises of God's Word to anchor your hope and shape your future in Christ.

2. When Jesus died on the cross, His made a once-and-for-all, final sacrifice for sin. As a result, His priesthood is eternal. So whenever Satan accuses you before God, know that your sins have been paid for, covered by Christ's sacrifice. Are you struggling with guilt over a sin you have committed? Right now, confess your sin before God and restore your fellowship with Him. Never let the Devil get you down with guilt over a sin paid by Christ's sacrifice.

3. As we learned in this chapter, the tabernacle is a type of Christ in many ways. The veil that separated the temple's outer chambers from the Holy of Holies was torn in half when Jesus died on the cross. No longer was access to God limited to a human high priest. Because of Christ's death, you have access to the Father. Hebrews 4:16 exhorts us to "draw near with confidence to the throne of grace, so that we may receive mercy and find grace to help in time of need." Do you have a personal or family need? Approach your heavenly Father with the confidence that He will address your need.

4. We can read about Christ in prophecy and see the many ways the prophetic Word about Christ was fulfilled in His first coming. Do you also have confidence in the prophecies about His second coming and glorious rule? (See Daniel 7:14; 1 Peter 1:10–11.) Ask God to help you live confidently and victoriously today in view of His second coming.

FOR GROUP STUDY

Questions for Group Discussion

1. Read John the Baptist's question to Jesus in John 7:19. What is the central truth of prophecy as it relates to Jesus Christ? What did Jesus teach about His place in prophecy? (See John 24.)

2. As outlined by Dr. Evans, what are the four main facts about the content of prophecy relating to Jesus? What is the relevance of each?

3. What is a *type*? How is a type different from a prophecy? What are their purposes as they relate to Jesus? Discuss the prophetic aspects of Psalm 22.

4. In what ways is the tabernacle a type of Christ? In his gospel, what are some of the ways the apostle John uses elements of the tabernacle as types of Christ? Also discuss how Israel's sacrifices are a type of Christ.

PICTURE THIS

The Bible presents several Old Testament characters as types of Christ. Below are three characters whose lives and functions typified Christ. Each shows a unique characteristic of Christ.

BIBLICAL CHARACTERS AS TYPES OF CHRIST

CHARACTER	SCRIPTURE PASSAGES	SIGNIFICANCE
Adam	1 Corinthians 15:45; Romans 6:23	Adam's sin brought death; Christ's death brings salvation and life.
Aaron	Hebrews 5:1–6.; 4:15; 9:24–26)	Aaron was a mediator between God and man, requiring blood sacrifices; Christ's sacrificial death qualifies Him to be our eternal priest.
Melchizedek	Hebrews 7:11–17	Melchizedek's priesthood is perpetual; Christ's priesthood is eternal, forever.

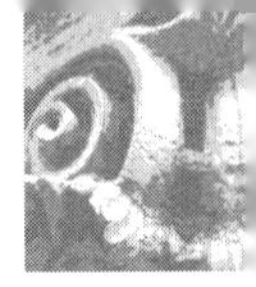

17

THE UNIQUENESS OF CHRIST IN HIS HUMILIATION

The word *humiliation* is a theological term that describes the steps downward Jesus Christ took in leaving the highest position in heaven for the lowest position on earth. That required a level of self-humbling you and I will never fully understand.

The implications of Jesus' humiliation in coming to earth and dying on the cross are staggering. In one short chapter, the best we can hope to do is get a basic understanding of this great truth as taught in Philippians 2:5–11, a passage that provides us with the crucial details of Christ's humiliation.

THE EXTENT OF CHRIST'S HUMILIATION

We can only begin to appreciate how far down Jesus was willing to come when we realize how exalted He is. Jesus "existed in the form of God" (v. 6).

Jesus' Full Deity

There never has been a time when Jesus did *not* exist as God. Philippians 2:6 affirms His deity. The word *form* means inner essence or being. Hebrews 13:8 says Jesus Christ is the same yesterday, today, and forever. Who Jesus is today, He always has been. Who Jesus was yesterday, He forever will be. And who Jesus forever will be, He is today.

Philippians 2 continues about this One who was and is fully God. "[Jesus] did not regard equality with God a thing to be grasped" (2:6). He did not hold on selfishly to all the glory and delights of heaven. Even though we will never understand completely what all this means, we need to come to grips with what Jesus did, because Paul commanded us to have the same attitude.

One thing we know is that Jesus was not insecure about letting go of the privileges of Deity. It's not as if someone else was going to usurp His place in heaven. Jesus had nothing to worry about there.

Jesus also did not need to hold on to His privileged position in heaven to maintain His position because none of His deity was diminished, compromised, or impaired in the slightest when He became a man. One thing we must understand is that whatever the humiliation and self-emptying of Jesus means, it does not mean He laid aside His deity.

The reason Jesus was willing to leave heaven and take on human form is because of the mind-set He had. He did not object to giving up His prerogatives for the greater good and glory of God.

Jesus could have said, "I don't want to be nailed to a tree to pay for the sins of those rebels." He could have said, "Send someone else."

But in eternity past, Jesus Christ made a decision to act on our behalf. No wonder John said, "We love, because He first loved us" (1 John 4:19).

Jesus' Self-Emptying

In verse 7 of Philippians 2, we get into the heart of what it meant for Christ to humble Himself. This is a somewhat controversial passage, because there are differences of opinion over what is included in Christ's emptying, or *kenosis* (the Greek term). Let's review the verse and then study it carefully.

The text says Christ "emptied Himself, taking the form of a bond-servant, and being made in the likeness of men." We need to compare verses 6–7 to see the extent of Christ's humiliation. He was "in the form of God," but took on "the form of a bond-servant," a slave.

Paul's use of this term is important. Why didn't he just say Jesus took on the form of a human being? That would be humiliation enough for God. There's a Greek word for humanity in general Paul could have used here, or he could have used the word that meant a male as opposed to a female.

But Paul used neither of these. Instead, he chose the more specific term *doulos*, which means "slave." In other words, Jesus became a particular kind of man, a slave, the lowest position a person could become in the Roman world.

This is good news for us. No matter what we go through, no matter how low we may get, we can never sink so far that Jesus cannot get under us and lift us up. He can identify with us in any situation, no matter how hard: poverty, loneliness, homelessness, rejection, you name it.

Jesus' Humanity

Philippians 2:7 goes on to say that Jesus was "made in the likeness of men." That means He looked like an ordinary man. He didn't go around with a halo around His head, floating above the ground. He looked like a servant, because that's what He was.

Jesus Himself said He came not to be served—which was His right and prerogative as God—but to serve, which is what a slave does (Mark 10:45). A slave doesn't have any rights. So when Jesus took on a human body, He also volunteered to accept the limitations of being human. He lived as a man without using His deity for His personal comfort or benefit or to avoid having to face the hardships and temptations of everyday human life.

In other words, Jesus did not use His divine power to solve a problem for His humanity. One example of this is in His temptation, when He was hungry and the Devil tempted Him to turn stones into bread (Matthew 4:3).

But the greatest example is in the garden of Gethsemane, when Jesus rebuked Peter for drawing his sword, telling him that if He chose, He could call "more than twelve legions of angels" to deliver Him (Matthew 26:53).

Now don't misunderstand. Jesus did use His divine power on a number of occasions. We call them miracles. But they were always done for the benefit of the kingdom and the blessing of others, not to make Jesus' life easier.

The reason is that Jesus had to experience every pain and temptation we face (Hebrews 4:15) so He could reverse the first Adam's failure and win the spiritual battle Adam lost for mankind in Eden. Jesus lived out the will of God on earth that He might be an acceptable substitute for man.

When Jesus Christ emptied Himself, He poured His deity into a container called a human body. This is what we call the incarnation, Jesus taking on human flesh. The second person of the Trinity was encased in a body that God prepared for Him through the virgin birth, when the Holy Spirit conceived a baby in Mary's womb.

Notice again that Jesus did the emptying Himself. It was voluntary. He didn't have to do it, but He did it to save people like you and me, just because He loved us.

Deity on Display

We'll go back to Philippians 2 in a little while, but we need to visit a biblical event that shows that Christ did not stop being God when He became a man.

The transfiguration revealed the Deity that was veiled, or hidden, in Christ's humanity. Matthew 17:1 says Jesus took Peter, James, and John with Him to a mountain. Let's pick up the story:

> And He was transfigured before them; and His face shone like the sun, and His garments became as white as light. And behold, Moses and Elijah appeared to them, talking with Him. Peter said to Jesus, "Lord, it is good for us to be here; if You wish, I will make three tabernacles here, one for You, and one for Moses, and one for Elijah." While he was still speaking, a bright cloud overshadowed them, and behold, a voice out of the cloud said, "This is My beloved Son, with whom I am well-pleased; listen to Him!" (vv. 2–5)

On this occasion, Jesus Christ revealed His deity. When He did so, Jesus' body blazed with a light so brilliant it was hard to describe (Mark struggled to find words to describe it—see Mark 9:3). This was nothing less than the glory of Deity.

That was a tremendous witness of Jesus' deity to the disciples. But two other people showed up to testify, Moses and Elijah. The selection of these men for this task was not accidental. They represented the Old Testament, often referred to as the Law and the Prophets, to declare that the Old Testament looked forward to Christ.

The New Testament was also represented by the presence of the three apostles. So in the Transfiguration we have the whole Bible coming together, with Jesus in the center. Both testaments witnessed to the fact that this ordinary-looking Man standing on a mountaintop is really God in all of His glory.

And to top off this testimony, the disciples heard the voice of God Himself, speaking from heaven to identify His Son.

Jesus' Power

Remember I said earlier that Jesus did not use His deity to ease His way through life or make problems go away. But that does not mean He lived a powerless life. Not at all. He lived the most powerful, victorious life any person has ever lived.

If Jesus did not just draw on His own deity to live above the realm of the ordinary, how did He do it? The answer is given to us in an amazing sequence of events in Luke 4.

Luke 4:1 says that when Jesus went into the wilderness to be tempted by Satan, the most cataclysmic confrontation and spiritual battle any human being could ever face, He went "full of the Holy Spirit."

Then, when Jesus had decisively defeated Satan and was ready to commence His public ministry, the Bible says, "Jesus returned to Galilee in the power of the Spirit" (v. 14). And the power in His ministry was apparent to all (v. 15).

But there's more. When Jesus went to His hometown of Nazareth and spoke in the synagogue, His first words were from Isaiah 61:1: "The Spirit of the Lord is upon Me, because He anointed Me to preach the gospel to the poor. He has sent Me to proclaim release to the captives, and recovery of sight to the blind, to set free those who are oppressed, to proclaim the favorable year of the Lord" (vv. 18–19).

You can't miss the message. Jesus operated in total dependence on the power of the Holy Spirit to accomplish the will of God. He said Himself He was Spirit anointed and Spirit sent.

THE PURPOSE OF CHRIST'S EMPTYING

Now we can move on to Philippians 2:8, which tells us that Jesus took on human flesh and became a bond-servant for a very specific purpose: "Being found in appearance as a man, He humbled Himself by becoming obedient to the point of death, even death on a cross."

A Sacrifice for Sin

We can say right off that Christ did not go to the cross because His humanity wanted to go. Remember His prayer in Gethsemane? "My Father, if it is possible, let this cup pass from Me" (Matthew 26:39).

How difficult was it for Jesus to face the cross? So difficult an angel had to strengthen Him in the garden of Gethsemane as He bore the agony of it (Luke 22:43–44).

What was it about the cross that caused Jesus such agony? Was it the physical torture and pain He would have to endure?

Crucifixion was a horrible way to die, for sure. The weight of the victim's body hanging from his wrists caused his joints to dislocate as he tried to push up on his feet to breathe and keep from suffocating. Eventually, the victim was no longer able to push himself up and finally suffocated.

Jesus endured that horrible trauma, not to mention the spikes through His wrists or the pain of the cross's rough wood scraping against His back, shredded from the beating He had received with a cat-o'-nine-tails.

Jesus suffered as no one else, but it wasn't the physical pain that caused Him the most suffering. Neither was it the taunting and humiliation He endured from His enemies as they watched Him die.

The true agony Jesus endured on the cross was the abandonment He suffered as God the Father turned His back on His Son. The Bible says when Jesus was on the cross, "about the ninth hour Jesus cried out with a loud voice, saying, 'Eli, Eli, lama sabachthani?' that is, 'My God, My God, why have You forsaken Me?'" (Matthew 27:46).

This was the agony of the cross for Jesus. This was the suffering He endured by becoming obedient to death. The Bible says that God made Jesus, who knew no sin, to be sin for us (2 Corinthians 5:21). The sins of the world were laid on Jesus on the cross, and God had to turn His back on the Son with whom He had enjoyed unbroken fellowship from all eternity.

To give you an idea of the depth of Jesus' suffering, being abandoned by God is the definition of hell. Hell is broken fellowship with God for all eternity. The suffering of hell is not first and foremost the fire, but the horrible reality of knowing that you are abandoned by God forever.

Jesus was abandoned by God on the cross, and in those hours He endured all the hell that all sinners will ever endure. Jesus had to go through this to bear your sin and mine. Jesus and His Father had enjoyed eternal fellowship. What happened on the cross had never happened before, not in all of eternity.

There had never been a disagreement, a moment of irritation or frustration between Father and Son. But on the day of Jesus' crucifixion, He had to bear the sins of the world. And for an unbelievably agonizing few hours, God could not bear to look at His Son.

We don't completely understand what was being transacted on the cross between God the Father and Jesus, because it has eternal implications. But we know that Jesus was offering Himself as a sacrifice for our sins, and we know that God accepted that payment.

Jesus cried out just before His death, "It is finished!" (John 19:30). The declaration is one word in Greek, meaning the debt is paid in full.

Jesus did not give up His spirit until He had said this, so there would be no doubt that the payment for sin was complete. Jesus died after making this announcement because His work on the cross was done.

Jesus was obedient to death, "even death on a cross" (Philippians 2:8). In the garden of Gethsemane, after asking that the cross might be lifted from Him, Jesus prayed, "Yet not what I will, but what You will" (Mark 14:36).

We are to have the same attitude in ourselves. Jesus did not have to go to the cross. But when He came to the greatest crisis of His life, He submitted Himself to God's will and was obedient to death because of His love for us.

A Mediator between God and Man

Another aspect of the purpose behind Jesus Christ's humiliation and self-emptying is this: It put Him in position to be the mediator we need.

In 1 Timothy 2 Paul told us to pray for everyone. Then he said, "This is good and acceptable in the sight of God our Savior, who desires all men to be saved and to come to the knowledge of the truth. For there is one God, and one mediator also between God and men, the man Christ Jesus, who gave Himself as a ransom for all" (vv. 3–6).

A mediator is a go-between, someone who can stand between two parties who are at odds with each other and bring them together. On the cross, Jesus literally hung between two estranged parties, His Father and the human race, to bring us to God.

The concept of a mediator is an old one. In Job, considered the oldest book of the Bible, the patriarch sensed his need for a go-between with God so he could plead his case.

Job was struggling and hurting, as we know. He was desperate for help as his three friends accused him of sin. At one point, Job said, "How can a man be in the right before God? If one wished to dispute with Him, he could not answer Him once in a thousand times" (Job 9:2–3).

How can a human argue with God? That's what Job was asking. In verses 32–33 of the same chapter Job said of God, "He is not a man as I am that I may answer Him, that we may go to court together. There is no umpire between us, who may lay his hand upon us both."

Job wanted a go-between that the *New American Standard Version* translates as "umpire." This is the same principle as a mediator.

In order to be an effective mediator between a perfect, holy God and sinners, someone would have to know how God feels and thinks—someone like God, in other words. And this mediator would have to know how we think and feel—someone like us.

I need a God-man, and so do you. Jesus Christ uniquely fulfills that requirement. That's why the Bible says He is the *one* Mediator who can stand between God and us.

THE EXALTATION OF JESUS CHRIST

Now we're ready to talk about Philippians 2:9–11, where Paul wrote:

> For this reason also, God highly exalted Him, and bestowed on Him the name which is above every name, so that at the name of Jesus every knee will bow, of those who are in heaven and on earth and under the earth, and that every tongue will confess that Jesus Christ is Lord, to the glory of God the Father.

Jesus' humiliation is not the end of the story. God raised Jesus up from the grave of His humanity and exalted Him in heaven as the God-man.

When you and I meet Jesus in heaven, we will not see the preincarnate Jesus. We will see the resurrected Jesus, the God-man. I don't know if we will see God the Father in heaven, since He is pure spirit. But I can tell you, Jesus Christ is exalted above everyone and everything in the universe.

PERSONAL APPLICATION FOR LIFE

1. Because of our sin, every human being needs spiritual help. The good news is that because of Christ's humiliation, we have a Mediator between a holy God and our sinful selves. Our Mediator, Jesus Christ, knows how we think, how we feel, and how we hurt. He knows our weakness. What is your need? Forgiveness? Strength? Whatever your need, come confidently to God through Christ, the perfect Mediator.

2. Here is a great encouragement for every child of God. Luke 4:1 tells us that Jesus was "full of the Holy Spirit" when He went into the wilderness to be tempted by Satan. Jesus depended on the power of the Holy Spirit to resist and defeat the temptations of Satan and accomplish God's will. Use His example and call upon the Spirit to do the same!

3. Much of the unbelieving world claims there is no God. It is blind to the fact that Jesus lived among us as God in human form. Not only did Jesus reveal His veiled glory (Matthew 17:1–5), He lived a sinless life before the world. God's glory shone throughout Jesus' words and action on earth as recorded in the Gospel accounts. How might Jesus handle your situation? How might He get a grip on your problem? Make it a point to study regularly the Gospels to learn more about Jesus, the glorious God-man.

4. Are you going through a tough time right now? Poverty, loneliness, homelessness, or rejection can be very painful. The good news is that no matter what we go through, no matter how low we may get, we can never sink so far that Jesus cannot get under us and lift us up. He can identify with us in any situation we might find ourselves in, no matter how hard. Ask God for the next step in working through your situation.

FOR GROUP STUDY

Questions for Group Discussion

1. Read Philippians 2:5–11. Theologically speaking, what do we mean by the term *humiliation*? In what ways—and to what extent—was Christ humiliated?

2. What did the apostle Paul mean when he said that Christ emptied Himself? To what extent did He empty Himself? Discuss Paul's description in Philippians 2:6–7. What was the purpose of Christ's self-emptying?

3. From what we can gather from Scripture, what happened on the cross? What are a few of the many implications of His death on the cross? In John 19:30, what is the meaning of the phrase, "It is finished"?

4. Read Philippians 2:9–11. What was the result of Christ's humiliation? How will the world eventually respond to a resurrected Savior?

PICTURE THIS

Christ's humiliation involved all aspects of who He is. Philippians 2:5–11 focuses on the four areas represented below.

THE EXTENT OF CHRIST'S HUMILIATION
Philippians 2:5–11

POINT OF HUMILIATION	SCRIPTURE PASSAGE	WHAT IT MEANS
Leaving behind the exercise of His full Deity	verse 6	Jesus left heaven, giving up His prerogatives, to take on human form and its limitations.
His self-emptying	verses 6–7	Jesus emptied Himself to take the form of a bond-servant, or slave.
His humanity	verse 7; Hebrews 4:15	Jesus did not use His divine power to solve problems for His humanity.
His power	Luke 4:1	Jesus depended on the power of the Holy Spirit to accomplish God's will.

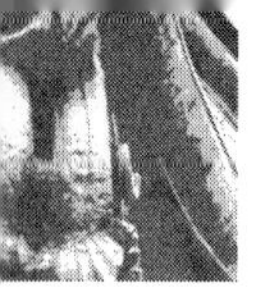

18

THE UNIQUENESS OF CHRIST IN HIS DEATH

My guess is that if you asked a large sample of people what symbol or image comes to mind when they think of Jesus Christ, a high percentage would say the cross.

The cross became a symbol for Christianity centuries ago. It's one of the things that sets Jesus Christ apart, that makes Him unique among all religious figures in the world. The cross marked a defining moment in Christ's life because, as we read earlier in Mark 10:45, Jesus said He came to die.

Jesus Christ was certainly not the only person to die by crucifixion. But His death was unique, because He is the one-and-only Son of God.

THE NECESSITY OF CHRIST'S DEATH

The Bible treats the subject of Jesus' death from a number of different perspectives, which are important because we must understand why Jesus had to die.

The Contamination of Sin

The Bible says, "Through one man sin entered into the world, and death through sin, and so death spread to all men, because all sinned" (Romans 5:12).

Sin entered the world through Adam. His human nature, and Eve's too, were contaminated through sin, and they passed the contamination on through the procreation of the race. So every time a baby is born, a sin nature is passed on to that baby, just as surely as its hair and eye color and other traits are transmitted by the parents. This is how sin has "spread to all men."

The doctrine Paul is teaching here is that of imputation, or crediting something to a person's account. Our plastic-crazy society can understand that. Adam's sin was charged to the account of his offspring, the human race. This teaching has been the subject of a lot of theological debate. But Paul said all of us have sinned, so don't worry about whether you are going to have to pay for Adam's sin. We have our own sin to deal with.

Sin's contamination is universal. David wrote, "I was brought forth in iniquity, and in sin my mother conceived me" (Psalm 51:5). Paul said of himself, "I know that nothing good dwells in me, that is, in my flesh; for the willing is present in me, but the doing of the good is not" (Romans 7:18).

The final result of sin's contamination is death. We usually think of physical death, but actually the Bible teaches three kinds of death.

There is physical death, the separation of the body from the spirit; spiritual death, in which a person is separated from fellowship with God; and eternal death, in which a person is separated from God forever. Notice that the key element is always separation.

Jesus Christ had to die because sin is so pervasive and so corrupting that nothing short of His death could eradicate it.

The Essence of Sin

Sin also separates—the attitude that is the very essence of sin. At the heart of sin is the desire to be independent of God, to do things our own way. Our human desire for independence from God is a reaction of rebellion. We don't want to be answerable to Him. The Bible describes this attitude in Romans 1:

> Even though they [unbelievers] knew God, they did not honor Him as God or give thanks, but they became futile in their speculations, and their foolish

> heart was darkened. . . . Just as they did not see fit to acknowledge God any longer, God gave them over to a depraved mind, to do those things which are not proper. (vv. 21, 28)

Independence says, "I don't want to honor God. I want to do *my* thing. I want to be my own boss." Maybe you recognize this attitude, because it originated in the heart and mind of the angel Lucifer, who said, "I will make myself like the Most High" (Isaiah 14:14). Any attempt on our part to be independent of God is an expression of sin.

The Standard That Defines Sin

Romans 3:23 says the standard against which sin is measured is "the glory of God." In other words, when God measures this problem called sin, He measures it against Himself, not your neighbor or the person at work. God doesn't say, "You are a pretty good person"; He says, "You are not as good as Me."

Most non-Christians either don't understand or don't believe that, so they don't think sin is a big deal. They don't see why someone has to die to answer for sin. They think God judges using scales to weigh our good deeds against our bad deeds, or else grades on the curve.

But the Bible says everyone falls short or fails to measure up to the standard, because the standard is God's perfection. God's glory is the manifestation of His person and purity, so Paul used it to describe the target we had to reach to please God. And no one has ever made it.

Imagine two travelers missing their flight at the airport. One traveler misses the flight by just five seconds, while the other person is forty-five minutes late. Is the first person any better off? No, it's irrelevant how far short of the standard the two people fell. They are both stuck at the airport. In the same way, God determined that we have fallen short of heaven, and it doesn't matter whether we miss heaven by an inch or a mile.

God must respond to sin because His controlling attribute is holiness. The prophet Habakkuk said, "Your eyes are too pure to approve evil, and You can not look on wickedness with favor" (1:13). That's why the cross was necessary.

When even righteous people in the Bible came face-to-face with God's holiness, they weren't casual about it.

Isaiah, an obedient prophet, still cried out in the presence of a holy God, "Woe is me, for I am ruined!" (Isaiah 6:5), a word that means he was coming apart at the seams. Job—who had been commended by God (Job 1:8)—met an awesome God after his testing and realized his sinfulness: "Now my eye sees You; therefore I retract, and I repent in dust and ashes" (Job 42:5b–6).

Stand in Job's or Isaiah's sandals for a minute, and you'll understand why Jesus had to die for sin and why no one else but Jesus could make that payment.

THE NATURE OF CHRIST'S DEATH

Since God is the offended party when we sin, it is His prerogative to determine on what basis sin shall be atoned for and forgiven. That basis is clearly spelled out in Hebrews 9:22: "According to the Law, one may almost say, all things are cleansed with blood, and without shedding of blood there is no forgiveness."

A Blood Sacrifice

There it is. The means by which God forgives sin is the shedding of blood. Anything less than that doesn't get the job done. All of the moaning and groaning and promising and turning over new leaves that people do will not remove sin. It is a capital offense. It carries the death penalty.

Why did God decree that blood was the required payment for sin? Because the shedding of blood requires death, since the life of the flesh is in the blood (Leviticus 17:11). God had told Adam that the day he sinned, he would die (Genesis 2:17).

Obviously, God is not saying there is some magical chemical in blood that washes away sin. But the requirement of blood to deal with sin goes all the way back to Eden, when God killed an animal to cover Adam and Eve after they sinned (Genesis 3:21). The animal's death satisfied God's requirement and substituted for their deaths.

Christ's death was, therefore, a blood atonement. He offered Himself as a sacrificial substitution for the death our sins deserved.

Death on a Cross

The apostle Peter, who was present at Jesus' crucifixion, made this great statement: "He Himself bore our sins in His body on the cross" (1 Peter 2:24).

Why did Jesus have to die on the cross? The Bible explains why, and when you see it you'll be grateful for the cross.

The Bible says, "Christ redeemed us from the curse of the Law, having become a curse for us—for it is written, 'Cursed is everyone who hangs on a tree'" (Galatians 3:13).

Notice that the Law of Moses had a curse attached to it. Just three verses earlier Paul had written, quoting Deuteronomy 27:26, "Cursed is everyone who does not abide by all things written in the book of the law, to perform them" (Galatians 3:10).

So if you failed in one point of the Law, you blew the whole thing and came under the Law's curse (James 2:10).

That's very bad, but here's something very good. Jesus took our curse for us by hanging on a tree, another term for the cross. To demonstrate his point, Paul quoted Deuteronomy 21:23, which pronounced a curse on anyone who hung on a tree.

In Old Testament days, a person who committed a capital crime would be executed, usually by stoning. If the crime was particularly hideous, the dead criminal would then be hung from a tree as the ultimate form of disgrace and shame. This also served as a warning to others, as you can imagine.

This was not crucifixion, but the central idea was to bring shame to the criminal, because for the Jews to be hung up like that was disgraceful. It was obvious to all that a person hung on a tree was cursed.

So why death on a cross for Jesus? Because God wanted to demonstrate to the world that Jesus was bearing the curse of the Law for us. Jesus hung on a tree as an object of open shame so it would be clear beyond any doubt that God was allowing the death blow of His curse to fall on His Son. All so that you and I could go free.

A Full Payment

The good news is that God accepted Christ's death as payment in full for our sins (see John 19:30). Let's look at the payment from the standpoint of the doctrine of imputation. God was not "counting" or imputing or charging our sins against our account (2 Corinthians 5:19).

How could God not do that? Because "He [God the Father] made Him who knew no sin to be sin on our behalf, that we might become the righteousness of God in Him" (v. 21). God charged our sins to Jesus' account and credited Jesus' perfect righteousness to our account. That's good news!

THE MOTIVATION FOR CHRIST'S DEATH

Anytime we are discussing salvation, it is good to step back and remind ourselves why God was willing to send His Son to the cross and why Jesus was willing to die. If anything sets Jesus Christ apart from all others and makes Him unique, it is His love for sinners like us apart from anything we did to deserve that love.

This is very hard for us to appreciate because it is so opposite to human nature. Think about it. Would you offer to sacrifice your child for a roach? That may sound hard, but that's the equivalent of what God did for us in Christ.

We were not a pretty sight to God, but He loved us even at our worst. "We were yet sinners" (Romans 5:8) when Christ went to the cross. That's why if you don't understand the cross, you will never fully understand love.

God's love for us was not a feeling of butterflies in the stomach. His love is His joyful self-determination to reflect His goodness and glory by meeting the needs of mankind. That's a big definition, so let me put it in some everyday terms.

First of all, God's love is always visible. God so loved that He *gave* His Son (John 3:16).

God's love is also sacrificial. If you haven't loved someone to the point of paying a price for that person, you haven't fully loved yet.

The love of Calvary is also unconditional. According to Romans 5:8, Christ died for us before we got our act cleaned up. In fact, God doesn't want you cleaning up your own act, because you are going to miss some spots. He didn't put any conditions on His love. Jesus died for us when we were sinners, period.

Another feature of God's love is its benefits. In Romans 5:9 Paul said,

"We shall be saved from the wrath of God through [Christ]." We are delivered from judgment because of Christ's death on our behalf in the present.

Finally, God's love is judicial. The cross is also a judicial statement of God's holy determination to punish sin.

Some people have the mistaken idea that love means never having to discipline or confront anyone. That's not biblical, though. Parents who say they don't discipline their children because they love them aren't showing real love. Love always makes a distinction between right and wrong. The Bible says in effect, "Whom the Lord loveth, He spanketh" (my "translation" of Hebrews 12:6).

THE ACCOMPLISHMENTS OF CHRIST'S DEATH

I want to cover this final point by looking at some key theological terms that tell us what Christ's death accomplished. We have already discussed some of these, but let's review them again. (They are discussed in greater detail in chapters 59–61 and 64.)

Christ's Death Brought Justification

Romans 5:1 makes a great declaration of our standing in Jesus Christ. "Having been justified by faith, we have peace with God through our Lord Jesus Christ."

Justification is a legal term that means to acquit, to find the defendant not guilty. More than that, in the New Testament it means to declare the former defendant righteous. The picture here is a courtroom in which you and I stand condemned by our sin. God has found us guilty beyond a shadow of a doubt.

But Jesus, as our "Advocate" (1 John 2:1), our defense attorney, steps in and applies His blood to our sins. He assumes our guilt, and we go free.

The reason we have peace with God once we are justified is that neither Satan nor anyone else can ever go back and bring up those sins against us again. Paul asked, "Who will bring a charge against God's elect?" (Romans 8:33a).

That's a legal question, the answer to which is no one, because "God is the one who justifies" (v. 33b). So when someone tries to accuse you and me before God, He says, "Not in My court. I have declared that person righteous."

Justification is a pardon from a death penalty. It's like sitting in the electric chair and having the phone ring five seconds before the switch was to be thrown. The message comes over the phone that you have been pardoned; you are free to walk out of the prison.

Paul said of Abraham, "If Abraham was justified by works, he has something to boast about; but not before God" (Romans 4:2). But since Abraham was justified by faith, he has nothing to brag about. Neither do we. We are only saved because the telephone rang in the execution chamber just in the nick of time.

Christ's Death Brought Redemption

Redemption means to deliver through the payment of a price (Mark 10:45; 1 Peter 1:18–19). Christ's death was the price God demanded to redeem us from slavery to sin (Galatians 1:4; Titus 2:14).

When I was growing up in Baltimore, our family saved the green stamps we got at various stores. We put them into books, and when the books were full we could purchase things from the company's redemption catalog, or even go to a redemption store to buy things with the stamps.

That's a picture of the redemption Jesus Christ accomplished for us. He paid the price that God demanded for sin. God never skips sin. Someone has to pay the price—either you or a substitute.

That's why 1 Corinthians 6:20 says, "You have been bought with a price."

Christ's Death Brought Propitiation

First John 2:2 says, "He Himself is the propitiation for our sins; and not for ours only, but also for those of the whole world."

I want to highlight again Christ's work of *propitiation*, a word that means to make satisfaction. God was righteously angry with us because of our sin, but Christ through His death has appeased or satisfied God's wrath against us. God was so satisfied with Christ's sacrifice on the cross that He averted the wrath that was due us.

Christ's Death Brought Reconciliation

Jesus also accomplished our reconciliation with God when He died on the cross. Reconciliation has to do with resolving conflict between people and bringing them back into harmony with one another.

Our sin put us "on the outs" with God. We were the ones who caused the rupture in relationship with God, so we are the ones who needed to be reconciled with Him.

But we were helpless to heal the breach in our relationship with God, so "[He] reconciled us to Himself through Christ" (2 Corinthians 5:18). God did not count our sins against us (v. 19).

God said, "You have sinned against Me and offended Me. But because of what My Son did on the cross, I do not count your sins against you. When I look at you, I will see Him. Our relationship is restored" (see Romans 5:10).

Christ's Death Brought Sanctification

Besides taking care of our sin problem, the death of Jesus Christ also has the power to help us grow and become mature in Christ—the process the Bible calls sanctification.

The Bible says, "By [God's] will we have been sanctified through the offering of the body of Jesus Christ once for all" (Hebrews 10:10). Then in verse 14 we read, "For by one offering He has perfected for all time those who are sanctified."

To be sanctified means you are now set apart. You are special, because your life is reserved for God and His glory. The key to your sanctification or Christian growth is to identify with the cross of Christ, because it was the cross that broke the power of Satan (Colossians 2:15).

That's why Paul said, "I have been crucified with Christ" (Galatians 2:20). Jesus told us to deny ourselves, take up our cross, and follow Him (Luke 9:23). Jesus' cross must become your cross as you die to your own interests and desires.

Christ's Death Brought Adoption

Nobody in the body of Christ is fatherless or motherless, because we were adopted as God's children when we came to Christ (Ephesians 1:5).

In the ancient world, adoption took place when a person was an adult, not an infant. Adoption conferred on the adoptee the full rights and privileges that came with being the child of the adoptive parent.

Your adoption as a child of God was also purchased at the cross. Jesus said He was going to His Father's house to prepare a place for you (John 14:1–3). The reason you are going to heaven is because that's where your Daddy lives. It's home.

Adoption also put the adopted child in line to be a full heir of the father. Most of us leave our stuff to our children after we are gone because they are family. God has bequeathed all of the riches of heaven to you because you are family now!

PERSONAL APPLICATION FOR LIFE

1. The Bible teaches that while we were yet sinners, Jesus died for us. He placed no conditions on His love. As a result, the apostle Paul tells us that "we shall be saved from the wrath of God through [Christ]" (Romans 5:9). We are delivered from judgment because of Christ's death on our behalf in the present. Praise God that we are spared from His wrath by His unconditional love! Never take sin lightly. It was paid for with an enormous price.

2. It is God's nature to punish sin. Be assured that God will discipline His children when they sin (Hebrews 12:6). Have you been "spanked" lately? If so, it's a sign that you are a child of God and that He is exercising His love toward you. Always remember that you are a child of the King, and be careful to conduct your life accordingly.

3. To be sanctified means you are now set apart and your life is reserved for God and His glory. Jesus instructed us to deny ourselves, take up our cross, and follow Him (Luke 9:23). That means you must die to your own interests and desires and focus on heavenly and eternal values (Colossians 3:2). Make it a point to daily read and study God's Word, and you will find yourself thinking God's thoughts after Him and aligning your life with His will.

4. The essence of sin is that it separates. As unbelievers, because we were contaminated with sin, we were separated from any fellowship with God. Because of Christ's death, as believers we can fellowship with God. However, when we allow sin to creep in, that fellowship is broken and must be restored by confession and forgiveness. Be vigilant. Don't let the Devil rob you of your fellowship with God.

FOR GROUP STUDY

Questions for Group Discussion

1. What made Christ's death unique? Why did He need to die? What perspectives does the Bible give us?

2. By what standard does the Bible define sin? By what standards do many in the world define sin? Why do the world's standards fall short?

3. What is the "curse of the law"? Read Deuteronomy 21:23; 1 Peter 2:24; Galatians 3:10, 13. To the Jews, what was the significance of Jesus dying on a *cross*, rather than simply dying? What motivated Jesus to die on the cross?

4. Christ' sacrificial death was full of purpose. What important accomplishments came as a result of Christ's death? (Use the chart on the next page to aid your discussion.)

PICTURE THIS

Christ's death on the cross accomplished several of God's eternal purposes. The following is a breakdown of the theological terms the author uses to describe the accomplishments of the cross.

ACCOMPLISHMENTS OF CHRIST'S DEATH ON THE CROSS

ACCOMPLISHMENT	SCRIPTURE PASSAGES	WHAT IT MEANS
It brought justification.	Romans 5:1; 1 John 2:1	Through Jesus Christ, we have a pardon from the penalty of sin and peace with God.
It brought redemption.	Mark 10:45; 1 Peter 1:18–19; Galatians 1:4; Titus 2:14; 1 Corinthians 6:20	Christ delivered payment for our sin through His death.
It brought propitiation.	John 2:2	Christ's death has satisfied God's wrath against us.
It brought reconciliation.	2 Corinthians 5:18–19; Romans 5:10	Our relationship to God is restored.
It brought sanctification.	Hebrews 10:10, 14; Colossians 2:15; Galatians 2:20; Luke 9:23	We are set apart and reserved for God and His glory.
It brought adoption.	Ephesians 1:5; John 14:1–3	We are the adopted children of God and full heirs to the riches of heaven.

19

THE UNIQUENESS OF CHRIST IN HIS RESURRECTION

Through ancient and modern history there have been many teachers and religious leaders—some great, some near-great, and some not so great. These leaders taught various worldviews and philosophies, and many of them acquired great followings. Some even died for their cause, which sometimes made them seem larger than life.

But there is a dramatic difference between all of these leaders and Jesus Christ. Despite the claims of some to represent God, or even to *be* God Himself, these leaders are dead, buried, and gone. But Jesus Christ is alive! He stepped out of His grave on the third day.

Without the resurrection, Christianity would have been stillborn. You can't have a living faith if all you have is a dead savior. Without the resurrection, the Christian faith might be a commendable way of life, but Jesus would be just another great teacher who lived His life and returned to dust. Christianity would not be *the* truth from God if Jesus did not rise from the dead.

The resurrection of Jesus Christ makes Him unique. Other religions can compete with Christianity on some things. They can say, for example, "Your founder gave you a holy book? Our founder gave us a holy book. Your founder has a large following? So does ours. You have buildings where people come to worship your God? We have buildings where people come to worship our god."

But only Christians can say, "All of that may be true, but our Founder rose from the dead!"

That's the uniqueness of the resurrection. In this chapter, I want to talk about the validity, the value, and the victory of Christ's resurrection.

THE VALIDITY OF THE RESURRECTION

We confidently believe and teach that George Washington and Abraham Lincoln existed because we have reliable, written documentation of their lives. We have their own words recorded for us to read, and we have the testimony of others who saw and heard them and lived alongside them.

No one alive today has seen George Washington in the flesh. None of us was present when America won its independence from Britain. But we accept these people and events as true because of the reliability of the documentation. The same argument holds true for Jesus Christ. The documentation validates His resurrection.

Let me give you a number of proofs that validate the resurrection. This evidence can stand beside the evidence for any historical event or person.

The Empty Tomb

The first proof of Jesus' resurrection is His empty tomb. This is a huge problem for those who doubt and reject the resurrection.

The issue is simple. If Jesus died and stayed dead, then why did His tomb turn up empty? Christianity could have been stopped before it got started if Jesus' enemies had simply produced His dead body. After all, they were the ones who had control over the tomb.

"Oh," some people say, "that's easy to explain. Any number of things could have happened to the body." There are several theories put forth to explain the empty tomb of Jesus.

One of these is the so-called swoon theory. This argues that Jesus did not die on the cross but simply lapsed into deep unconsciousness. Since the people of that day were medically unsophisticated, they assumed Jesus was dead and buried Him, but the coolness of the tomb revived Jesus. He got up, shook off the effects of all His horrible injuries, unwrapped His grave clothes, pushed aside the stone without disturbing the Roman guards, and snuck away, then reappeared to claim He had been raised from the dead.

The best argument against this theory is the action of Jesus' enemies themselves. They made *sure* He was dead. When the Roman soldiers came to finish off the men on the crosses, they saw that Jesus was already dead. But just to make sure, "one of the soldiers pierced His side with a spear" (John 19:34). When Pilate heard Jesus was dead, he checked with the centurion to make sure (Mark 15:44–45). There is no question that Jesus died on the cross.

Another theory is that the disciples went to the wrong tomb when they reported that Jesus was alive, because it was dark and they were confused and upset. But even if that happened, all the Jews and Pilate had to do was take the disciples to the right tomb and show them Jesus' body.

Another theory that was popular for a while was the idea that the disciples stole Jesus' body and then claimed His resurrection. But this theory ignores all the precautions that Pilate took to make sure that did not happen.

The Jews feared that very thing, so they went to Pilate and said, "Sir, we remember that when He was still alive that deceiver said, 'After three days I am to rise again.' Therefore, give orders for the grave to be made secure until the third day, otherwise His disciples may come and steal Him away and say to the people, 'He has risen from the dead'" (Matthew 27:63–64).

So Pilate gave them a Roman detail to guard the tomb and permission to seal the tomb with a Roman seal (vv. 65–66). To steal Jesus' body, eleven civilian disciples would have had to overpower a well-armed detail of up to sixteen Roman soldiers and remove a stone that weighed more than a ton to get to Jesus.

But more than that, the disciples would have had to break that official Roman seal, which was a death penalty offense. It would have been suicidal for the disciples to try to steal Jesus' body. Besides, where could they have hidden a dead body so no one would detect it? And if they did pull a deception like that, why would the disciples then go out and give their lives for what they knew was a lie?

The Witness of the Grave Clothes

When John first arrived at Jesus' tomb and looked in, he saw "the linen wrappings lying there, and the face-cloth which had been on His head, not lying with the linen wrappings, but rolled up in a place by itself" (John 20:6–7). That was enough for John to believe in Jesus' resurrection.

The reason is the way the grave clothes were arranged. In biblical days corpses were wrapped with one cloth around the body and a different piece of cloth around the head. The cloths were wound around the body and the head so that the headpiece was like a turban. Then the body was laid face-up on a shelf in the tomb.

What John described was a scene in which the grave clothes were lying undisturbed. The headpiece was not unwound, but still wrapped and lying in a separate place from the other wrappings.

The only way these grave clothes could still be in position with no body in them is if Jesus came right through them. If He had not died, but revived and escaped as some say, He would have had to unwrap to get out. The clothes would have been piled in a heap on the floor of the tomb. But Jesus came through those grave clothes in His resurrected, glorified body.

The Disciples' Transformation

Another "convincing proof" that validates the resurrection is the transformation that took place in the lives of the disciples.

Peter denied he knew Jesus three times at the crucifixion. But just a few weeks later, Peter "[took] his stand with the eleven, raised his voice and declared" the gospel fearlessly on the Day of Pentecost (Acts 2:14).

It took a lot of courage for Peter to declare, "This Man . . . you nailed to a cross by the hands of godless men and put Him to death. But God raised Him up again" (v. 23–24). Don't think he would put himself in jeopardy like that for a lie. A couple of chapters later in Acts, Peter and the apostles were getting beaten for their message. James lost his life, and Peter wound up in jail under a death sentence (Acts 12).

What about Paul, formerly known as Saul, the persecutor of the church? Saul was present at the stoning of Stephen, giving his approval (Acts 7:58; 8:1). Saul was determined to eradicate this new sect called

Christians. And he was good at it too (Philippians 3:6).

What happened to Saul? He saw the risen Jesus, first of all (1 Corinthians 15:8). After the risen Christ met Saul on the Damascus road (Acts 9:5), he was never the same. He became the apostle Paul, who would become so convinced of the truth of the resurrection that he would put his life on the line for it, because his former Jewish pals tried to kill him after he became a Christian.

THE VALUE OF CHRIST'S RESURRECTION

The resurrection of Jesus Christ is not only validated, but it is incredibly valuable. I want to mention just a handful of the benefits of the fact that Jesus' tomb is empty.

The Resurrection Verifies Prophecy

Since the Old Testament prophesied Jesus' resurrection (Psalm 16:10), the Bible is validated as the absolute and inerrant revelation of God.

Remember also that Jesus personally prophesied His resurrection on several occasions. "From that time Jesus began to show His disciples that He must go to Jerusalem, and suffer many things from the elders and chief priests and scribes, and be killed, and be raised up on the third day" (Matthew 16:21).

Later, Jesus told the disciples they were going to Jerusalem, where He would suffer many things and be delivered to the Gentiles, who would "mock and scourge and crucify Him, and on the third day He will be raised up" (Matthew 20:18–19).

Then on resurrection day, Mary Magdalene came to the tomb and met an angel, who told her, "He is not here, for He has risen, just as He said" (Matthew 28:6).

If Jesus were wrong about His resurrection, then we should not believe anything else He said. If He did rise from the dead, then we can believe everything else He said. So when Jesus said, "I go and prepare a place for you" (John 14:3), we can take that to the bank.

The Resurrection Confirms Our Salvation

Jesus' resurrection also confirms our salvation. It is the divine guarantee, God's "receipt," that Jesus' death satisfied the payment demanded for sin.

Paul said in Romans 4:25 that Jesus was delivered to the cross for our sins and "was raised because of our justification." When He cried, "It is finished!" on the cross (John 19:30), He was announcing that the price for sin had been paid in full.

Therefore, if you have received Jesus Christ as your Savior by faith, His resurrection is your guarantee that your salvation is secure.

The Resurrection Conquers Death

In his Pentecost sermon, Peter said of Jesus, "God raised Him up again, putting an end to the agony of death, since it was impossible for Him to be held in its power" (Acts 2:24).

Death was unable to hold Christ, not only because He is God, but because His death broke the power of sin. Sin is the only power that can hold a person in death. Death only exists because of sin, so when sin is done away with, death has lost its hold on us (1 Corinthians 15:55–56).

When Jesus rose from the dead, He broke the power of sin for all time. And since we are attached to Jesus by faith, since we hold the "receipt" that shows our sins have been paid for, we will not stay dead either. It is impossible for us to be held in death's power because it was impossible for Christ to be held in death's power.

THE VICTORY OF CHRIST'S RESURRECTION

We have seen the validity and the value of Christ's resurrection. But there's also personal victory because He walked out of the tomb.

Victory over Sin's Power

This is the other side of the truth we discussed above. In His resurrection, Jesus gave us victory over sin. That's true in the future, when the grave has to let go of us. On our resurrection day we will be free from the very presence of sin because we will be in heaven.

But Christ's resurrection also gives us victory over sin today, in the here and now. That's what Paul said in Romans 6:1–5, a crucial passage in which he explained that when you accepted Christ you were identified completely with Him, both in His death and in His resurrection. So when Christ was raised from the dead, you also were raised to a new way of life.

We need this new connection to Christ because of our old connection to Adam. When Adam sinned, his death sentence was passed on to all of us, as we learned earlier, because all of us have sinned.

So our connection to Adam brought death, and death is a reality for all of us. But when we believe in Jesus, we get connected to Him. And when we get connected to Jesus, we get connected to His resurrection life in the same way we were plugged in to death through Adam.

Therefore, if you and I have sin in our lives that is overcoming us and beating us down, it is because we have adopted faulty thinking. We are living as if Christ's resurrection life within us is theoretical and not real.

The analogy is this. If death is real and not just theoretical, then your new life in Christ and your new power over sin are real and not theoretical. If you will learn to identify with your new life in Christ (Ephesians 2:5), rather than with your old life in Adam, you will have new victory in Christ rather than old defeat in Adam.

You and I need to learn to think in terms of, "I am not what I used to be, so I don't have to act like I used to act."

Some of us have it backward. We say, "OK, I'm going to stop doing this." So we take a deep breath and give it our best shot. We make all the resolutions, but in a few days or weeks we're back where we started. Self-effort is not the answer. If it were, you could have stopped a long time ago.

What's needed is to say to God, "I can't do it. I can't stop. I can't help myself. But here and now, I thank You that You have already given me the victory over this in Christ. I thank You that because He rose from the dead, You have given me the strength I need to live above this sin. So by faith, I am going to walk in the victory You gave me—and not in the old defeat I have when I try it on my own."

That's the only way you can tap into resurrection power that is yours in Christ. When Jesus said, "Apart from Me you can do nothing" (John 15:5), that's just what He meant.

When you connect yourself to Christ as a daily reality, you experience His resurrection power and His victory over sin. That's the key, because the Christian life is "Christ in you, the hope of glory" (Colossians 1:27).

Victory over Sin's Penalty

We have already established the fact that Christ's resurrection is part of the victory He gives us over the penalty of sin.

In Acts 17:31, Paul said that God is going to judge the world "through a Man whom He has appointed, having furnished proof to all men by raising Him from the dead." This Man is Jesus, because He is the only One who has been raised from the dead. One day all people will appear before God's judgment bar. But if you have received Christ as your Savior, you won't be judged for your sin as far as salvation is concerned because you have already been judged and declared righteous in Christ. And you have your "receipt," His resurrection, to prove it!

Victory over Limitations

Another victory we have through the resurrection is that someday we will have glorified, resurrected bodies just like Jesus' body.

"Our citizenship is in heaven, from which also we eagerly wait for a Savior, the Lord Jesus Christ; who will transform the body of our humble state into conformity with the body of His glory, by the exertion of [His] power" (Philippians 3:20–21).

When you are raised from the dead, you will have a body that conforms to Christ's—which means a body like you never had before. Jesus could come through His grave clothes and walk through closed doors because His resurrected body was not subject to human limitations. Your body will also be set free from its limitations someday through resurrection.

Victory over Death

This is the final victory we will enjoy because of Christ's resurrection.

Paul gave this promise to a group of Christians who were worried that their dead fellow believers were gone forever: "If we believe that Jesus died and rose again, even so God will bring with Him those who have fallen asleep in Jesus" (1 Thessalonians 4:14).

First Corinthians 15 is the Bible's Magna Carta on the subject of death and resurrection. Paul said in verse 20, "But now Christ has been raised from the dead, the first fruits of those who are asleep." This means He is the first of many more to come. What happened to Him will happen to us.

Paul also wrote concerning our victory over death, "As in Adam all die, so also in Christ all shall be made alive" (v. 22). And then he capped his teaching in this long chapter with a ringing declaration of victory (vv. 54–57).

When you know Jesus Christ, the Bible says to be absent from the body is to be at home with the Lord (2 Corinthians 5:8). How fast will that happen? "In a moment, in the twinkling of an eye . . . the dead will be raised imperishable" (1 Corinthians 15:52). Faster than you can blink, you'll have your new body and be in the presence of Jesus when you die. When your spirit leaves your body, you will be in heaven so fast you won't even have time to know you are dead!

PERSONAL APPLICATION FOR LIFE

1. We cannot prevent the ultimate impact of sin taking its toll on our bodies. We will die. However, we can stop sin from dominating our lives because we are connected to Jesus who gives us resurrection power today to be victorious over sin. In your daily walk in Christ, take to heart Paul's command in Romans 6:12: "Do not let sin reign in your mortal body."

2. Because of Christ's victory over sin's power, you have a new life in Christ (Ephesians 2:5) to rule over your old life in Adam. Begin to think in terms of "I am not what I used to be, so I don't have to act like I used to act." Remember that through Christ you have the power to win over temptation and guilt from any memories of old, forgiven sins Satan might try to use to keep you down.

3. The Christian life is a supernatural life. Therefore, as others look at us they ought to see something that cannot be accounted for in purely natural terms: our love, our peace, our joy, our generosity, and so on. Ask yourself this question: Is there anything about my life that can't be explained except by the power of the Holy Spirit working in me?

4. After reading this chapter, write down three truths or promises about the resurrection that especially encouraged you. These may have been truths new to you or ones you might not have especially considered before. Ask God to help you realize the power of those in your life today.

FOR GROUP STUDY

Questions for Group Discussion

1. Discuss Dr. Evans's three main proofs for the validity of Christ's resurrection. Why does each provide validity to the resurrection?

2. What are some of ways Christ's resurrection is valuable to us? What would be the state of Christianity without the fact of the resurrection?

3. Discuss the ways the resurrection is victorious. (Use the chart below as an aid.) From the associated Scripture passages, what do we learn about the part each victory plays?

4. Read Romans 6:1–7, a crucial passage about the impact of the resurrection in the life of the believer. What truths can your group glean from this passage? What are some obvious applications of those truths?

PICTURE THIS

Christ's resurrection was powerful and provided victory over many things. Below are a few of the specific victories we gain because of His resurrection.

OUR VICTORIES BECAUSE OF CHRIST'S RESURRECTION

VICTORY	SCRIPTURE PASSAGES	WHAT WE GAIN
Victory over sin's power	Romans 6:1–5; Ephesians 2:5	We experience resurrection power and His victory over sin.
Victory over sin's penalties	Acts 17:31	We have been judged and declared righteous in Christ.
Victory over limitations	Philippians 3:20–21	We will have resurrection bodies not subject to human limitations.
Victory over death	1 Corinthians 15	We will be in the presence of Jesus when we die.

20

THE UNIQUENESS OF CHRIST IN HIS ASCENSION AND PRESENT MINISTRY

Every four years the United States government stages the closest thing our country has to the coronation of a king or queen—the inauguration of a president.

Government officials gather in Washington, D.C., for the ceremony, while the nation watches this bestowing of authority on television. The inauguration is the moment when the new or returning president is publicly recognized as the leader of the nation.

A presidential inauguration is impressive. The old newsreel showing the coronation of Britain's Queen Elizabeth in 1953 is even more impressive. But none of these events can begin to compare with the enthronement of Jesus Christ at the right hand of God, the coronation with which He was honored when He ascended back to heaven after His resurrection.

THE IMPORTANCE OF CHRIST'S ASCENSION

The first thing to understand about the ascension is its importance. Jesus' return in the clouds to heaven is an important confirmation of the truth of Scripture, and it has staggering implications for us today.

Its Prophetic Importance

In his great sermon to the Jews on the day of Pentecost, the apostle Peter indicted the nation for rejecting Jesus and putting Him to death. Then Peter said:

> This Jesus God raised up again, to which we are all witnesses. Therefore having been exalted to the right hand of God, and having received from the Father the promise of the Holy Spirit, He has poured forth this which you both see and hear. For it was not David who ascended into heaven, but he himself says: "The Lord said to my Lord, 'Sit at My right hand, until I make Your enemies a footstool for Your feet.'" (Acts 2:32–35)

Peter's quotation is from Psalm 110:1, a prophecy made almost one thousand years before Jesus was born. David looked ahead and prophesied that Christ would ascend to God and be seated at His right hand. So the ascension is an important validation of God's prophetic Word in the Old Testament.

Jesus' ascension also validated His own prophetic utterances. Just as He prophesied His death and resurrection, Jesus also foretold His ascension.

In John 6, some of Jesus' followers were grumbling because He had been teaching some hard things. So He asked, "Does this cause you to stumble? What then if you should see the Son of Man ascending where He was before?" (vv. 61–62). During the Last Supper with His disciples, Jesus said, "Now I am going to Him who sent Me" (John 16:5).

Then after His resurrection, Jesus fulfilled prophecy by leaving this earth and returning to God the Father in the ascension (Acts 1:9–11). The Bible says Jesus "was lifted up." A cloud "received Him." He was "departing" in the cloud. The angels said He was "taken up."

In other words, Jesus' ascension was gradual, visible, and physical. This was not a mirage, not a trick or the result of any hocus-pocus. In the same way that Jesus arose bodily, He ascended bodily. The Bible prophesied His ascension, and in the presence of His disciples, Jesus ascended back to heaven.

Its Importance for Us Today

The ascension and present ministry of Jesus are all-important for you and me and every believer as we seek to live the dynamic, victorious, Spirit-filled Christian life that is God's will for us.

During the Last Supper, after predicting His ascension, Jesus told the disciples, "I tell you the truth, it is to your advantage that I go away; for if I do not go away, the Helper will not come to you; but if I go, I will send Him to you" (John 16:7).

This, of course, is Jesus' promise to send the Holy Spirit, of whom Jesus had said, "He abides with you, and will be in you" (John 14:17). Jesus said His ascension would initiate the ministry of the Holy Spirit and that this would be even better for the disciples than His physical presence.

How can this be? Because when Jesus was on earth, He functioned in one location at a time. So when someone needed Jesus to meet a serious need, as happened on several occasions, He had to leave where He was and go with the person who needed Him.

But because the Holy Spirit lives within each believer, He goes with us wherever we go. And He is always present in full power with each believer in the world, all at the same time. The Holy Spirit is not subject to the limitations of human flesh to which Jesus voluntarily submitted so He could be our Savior. That's part of the good news of Jesus' ascension.

Its Importance for Us Tomorrow

Jesus' ascension is also at the heart of one of the most precious promises in the Bible. The night before His death, Jesus assured His followers, "In My Father's house are many dwelling places; if it were not so, I would have told you; for I go to prepare a place for you. And if I go and prepare a place for you, I will come again, and receive you to Myself; that where I am, there you may be also" (John 14:2–3).

The ascension is vitally important to our hope for tomorrow and for eternity. Jesus not only ascended to return to His Father and send us the promised Holy Spirit, but to prepare heaven for our occupancy someday. Because Jesus went somewhere, we have somewhere to go. And just as Christ ascended to heaven, you and I will leave this earth someday and ascend to heaven because Jesus is coming back for us. If the ascension is true, then heaven is true.

THE ACCOMPLISHMENTS OF CHRIST'S ASCENSION

The second aspect of the ascension we need to see is its accomplishments. What is true today because Jesus ascended to the Father?

It Enthroned Jesus in the Place of Authority

When Jesus ascended and was enthroned at God's right hand, every power in the universe was made subject to Him—particularly the spirit realm, both the holy angels and the demonic world.

Peter wrote that Christ is "at the right hand of God, having gone into heaven, after angels and authorities and powers had been subjected to Him" (1 Peter 3:22).

The writer of Hebrews also established the authority of the risen and ascended Christ: "When He had made purification of sins, He sat down at the right hand of the Majesty on high, having become as much better than the angels, as He has inherited a more excellent name than they" (Hebrews 1:3–4).

Christ was exalted over the angelic realm in His ascension, and that has huge implications for you and me. Paul said that because of our identification with Christ, we are raised up with Him and "seated . . . with Him in the heavenly places" (Ephesians 2:6). We are rulers in the heavenly realm with Christ! In His ascension, redeemed mankind was elevated to a position of authority over the angelic world.

It Gives Us Authority

The ascension of Jesus, and our identification with Him, also gives us tremendous authority for service to Him.

Just before His ascension, Jesus told His disciples, "All authority has been given to Me in heaven and on earth" (Matthew 28:18). Then He commissioned them, and us, to make disciples of all nations.

The authority of Jesus Christ abides today in His church. "He [God] put all things in subjection under His [Jesus'] feet, and gave Him as head over all things to the church, which is His body, the fullness of Him who fills all in all" (Ephesians 1:22–23).

When we understand the limitless spiritual authority we have in Christ, we will realize that none of the weapons of Satan formed against us can defeat us. If they do, it is because we let Satan win, not because he has more power than Christ.

THE UNIQUENESS OF CHRIST IN HIS PRESENT MINISTRY

The fact that Jesus Christ is ascended and enthroned in heaven leads naturally to the question, What is He doing in heaven today as He awaits His return? I want to answer that with seven biblical portraits that convey the present ministry of Christ.

The Leader of a New Creation

Portrait number one of Christ's present ministry is His role as leader of a new, redeemed creation.

The key here is the contrast Paul presents in 1 Corinthians 15: "As in Adam all die, so also in Christ all will be made alive" (v. 22). As he explains later: "'The first man, Adam, became a living soul.' The last Adam became a life-giving spirit. . . . The first man is from the earth, earthy; the second man is from heaven" (vv. 45, 47).

Adam's sin not only plunged the human race into sin and death, but it also put the whole creation under a curse of sin because Adam was placed in rulership over creation. Now, all of creation groans under the curse of sin (Romans 8:20–22). But as the last Adam or new Adam, Jesus Christ is in the process of undoing the destruction wrought by the first Adam.

Just as Adam's sin brought death and deterioration to mankind and his environment, Christ's complete obedience brings life and hope and restoration to the environment that had been cursed.

Jesus Christ reversed the sin curse of Adam. Adam once ruled as earthly head of the race. But now Jesus sits on the heavenly throne as the Head of a redeemed and transformed people, those who have put their faith in Him and have passed from spiritual death to spiritual life (1 John 3:14).

The Head of His Body, the Church

Colossians 1:18 says that Jesus is the "head of the body, the church." He is the head "from whom the entire body, being supplied and held together by the joints and ligaments, grows with a growth which is from God" (Colossians 2:19).

Headship over the church is a second aspect of Christ's present work. The metaphor of the head and the body is Paul's favorite analogy of the present relationship between Christ and His church (see 1 Corinthians 12:12–31).

Jesus is the authoritative head of the church. And just as a human body looks to its head for direction, so the members of Christ's body, the church, look to Him for direction.

In Colossians 1:18 we find the goal of Christ's headship over the body: "So that He Himself will come to have first place in everything." That's what Jesus is after in His ministry as head of the church, in the church collectively and in us individually.

The Shepherd of the Sheep

This is the third of our word portraits that describe Jesus' present ministry, and it is one of the most reassuring.

Jesus said, "Truly, truly, I say to you, I am the door of the sheep. . . . If anyone enters through Me, he shall be saved, and shall go in and out, and find pasture. . . . I am the good shepherd; the good shepherd lays down His life for the sheep" (John 10:7, 9, 11). Jesus Christ is our Good Shepherd today. He is also our "great Shepherd" (Hebrews 13:20) and our "Chief Shepherd" (1 Peter 5:4).

Jesus' present ministry as our shepherd involves His *provision* for us. A shepherd in Jesus' day provided everything his sheep needed. And this is what we must have today, because left to themselves sheep are about the most helpless and directionless of all God's creatures.

For example, our Shepherd provides us with *security* or protection. In Jesus' days the sheepfold had an opening through which the sheep went in and out to pasture. The shepherd would literally lie across that opening at night to keep the sheep in and the predators out.

In addition, our Shepherd provides us with *salvation* (John 10:9). We know that Jesus is the only way to heaven (John 10:1; 14:6).

Jesus is not only providing us with salvation and security today, but we also have *satisfaction* in Him. We shall "find pasture" (v. 9).

Sheep need pasture both for nourishment and as a place where they can lie down for refreshment and rest. Jesus supplies us with all the satisfaction we could ever want. He put it this way, "I came that they might have life, and might have it abundantly" (John 10:10). Psalm 23:1 says, "The Lord is my shepherd, I shall not want."

As our Shepherd, Jesus also provides us with *direction*. "He makes me lie down in green pastures; He leads me beside quiet waters" (Psalm 23:2).

Along with direction, Jesus provides us with *peace*, even when we walk "through the valley of the shadow of death" (v. 4). What a wonderful thing to be in a fearful situation and yet not be afraid. Only Jesus can provide that.

Another provision of our Shepherd is *comfort*. "Your rod and Your staff, they comfort me" (v. 4).

Take the first line of Psalm 23, "The Lord is my shepherd," put it with the last lines, "all the days of my life" and "I will dwell in the house of the Lord forever," and that covers this life and eternity and everything in between.

The Vine Supporting the Branches

A fourth word picture or analogy that describes Jesus Christ's present ministry is that of the vine and the branches.

At the Last Supper, Jesus said, "I am the true vine, and My Father is the vinedresser. Every branch in Me that does not bear fruit, He takes away; and every branch that bears fruit, He prunes it, that it may bear more fruit" (John 15:1–2).

Then He told the disciples, "I am the vine, you are the branches; he who abides in Me, and I in him, he bears much fruit. . . . I chose you, and appointed you, that you would go and bear fruit, and that your fruit would remain" (vv. 5, 16).

The fruit Jesus was talking about here is spiritual—the good works God has ordained for us (Ephesians 2:10) as part of our growth to spiritual maturity. Notice the progression from "fruit" to "more fruit" to "remaining fruit." That's what God wants from us.

The Foundation and Cornerstone

Jesus Christ is also the foundation and cornerstone of the church today—anchoring His church, tying the parts of the building together, and giving it stability.

Paul wrote in 1 Corinthians 3, "Like a wise master builder I laid a foundation, and another is building on it. But let each man be careful how he builds upon it. For no man can lay a foundation other than the one which is laid, which is Jesus Christ" (vv. 10–11).

You know how important the foundation is to the superstructure of a building. It determines whether the building will stand or not. It determines the building's size and shape. If the foundation is weak, it doesn't matter how pretty a building looks, because when the storm hits the building will topple.

Jesus is the only foundation that will stand. No one can supplant Jesus as your foundation. Whenever you abandon the kind of dependence on Christ talked about above, your life is in trouble. Paul told the Corinthians, "Be imitators of me, just as I also am of Christ" (1 Corinthians 11:1).

"Be careful how you build on the foundation," Paul cautions us. In other words, don't build a cheap building on the strong foundation of Jesus Christ. Use "gold, silver, precious stones" (1 Corinthians 3:12).

Jesus Christ is also the cornerstone of the church. "Behold I lay in Zion a choice stone, a precious corner stone, and he who believes in Him shall not be disappointed." (1 Peter 2:6) The cornerstone is the alignment stone, the stone the builder uses to properly align the other stones in the building. By saying that Jesus Christ is the church's cornerstone, Peter was talking about the unity of the church.

We are the living stones God is using to build His church. The only way the church can be built properly and fit together the way God intended is if we are aligned with Christ. Jesus Christ the cornerstone must be our standard.

The Bridegroom of the Church

The relationship between the ascended and reigning Jesus Christ and His people is a love relationship, and nothing captures that more than the biblical portrait of Christ as the church's bridegroom.

Human marriage is an illustration of Christ's husbandly love for the church. "Husbands, love your wives, just as Christ also loved the church and gave Himself up for her" (Ephesians 5:25).

Marriage includes a time of engagement or betrothal, the wedding ceremony, and then the wedding banquet or reception. The same thing is true of Christ and the church. He betrothed us to Himself in salvation, He is coming to take us for Himself as His bride at the rapture, and then will come "the marriage supper of the Lamb" (Revelation 19:7–9).

The wedding ceremony and marriage supper of Christ and His church are still future. We are in the period of betrothal or engagement. And in preparation for the wedding, Christ is preparing for Himself a pure and attractive bride.

We have a lot of stains and wrinkles and ugly spots on us. But Christ is sanctifying us, cleaning us up "by the washing of water with the word, that He might present to Himself the church in all her glory, having no spot or wrinkle or any such thing; but that she would be holy and blameless" (Ephesians 5:26–27).

The High Priest

Our final word picture is a glorious one. Jesus Christ in heaven today is serving as our High Priest, our intercessor before God.

The high priest in Israel was the mediator, the intercessor, the go-between who stood before God and offered sacrifice for the people's sins, to make them acceptable to God (Hebrews 5:1).

That's what Jesus did for us when He offered Himself on the cross, and He is presently standing in the temple in heaven, interceding with God for us and applying the benefits of His blood sacrifice to our sins.

Hebrews 7:26 describes the kind of high priest we have. Jesus is "holy, innocent, undefiled, separated from sinners and exalted above the heavens." Human high priests had to offer sacrifices for their own sins first, and human priests died off and had to be replaced. Plus, their animal sacrifices could not permanently deal with sin.

But Jesus has none of these defects. His sacrifice was perfect and once-and-for-all, and He serves in heaven as our perfect High Priest forever.

And best of all, even though Jesus Christ is perfect and separated from sinners in that He had no sin, He is able to identify with us because He became a man like us (Hebrews 2:17). Therefore, we have a high priest who can "sympathize with our weaknesses" (Hebrews 4:15).

That's good news. Jesus "has been tempted in all things as we are, yet without sin" (v. 15). We can come to Him with our needs, "For since He Himself was tempted in that which He has suffered, He is able to come to the aid of those who are tempted" (Hebrews 2:18).

So no matter what you are facing right now, or what Satan is trying to do to you, you are not alone. Your High Priest in heaven is praying for you, asking the Father to give you all the strength you need.

This is Jesus Christ . . . stepping on a cloud and ascending to heaven, receiving a crown as the King and being seated at the Father's right hand in the place of highest power and authority, yet getting up from His throne to serve as our Great High Priest.

APPLICATION FOR LIFE

1. What is your first response to Christ's ascension? According to Philippians 2:9–10, our response should be to exalt Jesus' name and honor Him. Make it a point to align all you do with the goal of enhancing His glory (Colossians 3:23).

2. Jesus is our Good Shepherd who watches over His flock. That is a good thing because we are prone to wander just like sheep. Have you ever wandered off on your own, trying your own way rather than the Shepherd's way, only to get lost and wind up in a ditch? Stop trying to make your own way and follow the Shepherd. He will guide you along the right paths.

3. Christ is the head of the church collectively as well as the head over us individually. Does He have first place with everything in your life? The degree to which Jesus is prioritized in your life is the degree to which you will grow into the spiritual maturity that is His will for you. Don't look to yourself; look to the Head as your divine reference point.

4. Hebrews 4:15 tells us that Jesus "has been tempted in all things as we are, yet without sin." And, "For since He Himself was tempted in that which He has suffered, He is able to come to the aid of those who are tempted" (2:18). That means you can come to Him with your needs, no matter what you are facing right now. Give a prayer of thanksgiving to your High Priest, who is now in heaven asking the Father to give you all the strength you need.

FOR GROUP STUDY

Questions for Group Discussion

1. Discuss the important points of Christ's ascension as outlined in this chapter. How is each point relevant to us? What is noteworthy about the prophecy in Psalm 110:1?

2. What did Christ accomplish with His ascension? Read Ephesians 1:22–23. What does His ascension mean for believers today?

3. Using a word picture, Jesus said that He is the vine supporting the branches (John 15:1–2, 5, 16). What is He teaching here? What "fruit" is He talking about? (See also Ephesians 2:10.) What are the characteristics of the fruit?

4. In John 10:7, 9, 11, Jesus used the analogy of being the Good Shepherd. (See also 1 Peter 5:4 and Hebrews13:20.) What provisions does Jesus provide us as the Good Shepherd?

PICTURE THIS

Christ's present position is manifold with many unique ministries. Listed below are seven of those ministries.

THE UNIQUENESS OF CHRIST'S PRESENT MINISTRY

UNIQUE POINT	SCRIPTURE PASSAGES	WHY IT IS UNIQUE
The leader of a new creation	1 Corinthians 15	Jesus reversed the sin curse of Adam and wants to re-create us inside.
The head of His body, the church	Colossians 1:18	Jesus is the authoritative head of the church, which takes its direction from Him.
The Shepherd of the sheep	John 10:7, 9, 11	Jesus is the Shepherd who guides and provides for His sheep.
The Vine supporting the branches	John 15:1–2, 5, 16	As the Vine, Jesus helps us bear spiritual fruit that displays the character of Christ.
The Foundation and Cornerstone	1 Corinthians 3:10–11	Jesus anchors His church, giving it the stability that enables it to grow.
The Bridegroom of the church	Ephesians 5:25; Revelation 19:7–9	Jesus will one day take His church as His bride.
The Great High Priest	Hebrews 4:15	Jesus is our Great High Priest, our Intercessor before God.

21

THE UNIQUENESS OF CHRIST IN HIS RETURN AND MILLENNIAL RULE

When Jesus got ready to leave this earth, He promised His disciples that He would return for them (John 14:3). That promise was restated and reinforced at Jesus' ascension when the angels said, "This Jesus, who has been taken up from you into heaven, will come in just the same way as you have watched Him go into heaven" (Acts 1:11). No one else has ever left this earth by ascension the way Jesus left it, and no one is coming back the way Jesus is coming back. That makes Him unique in His return, which is the next item on God's future program.

The Bible says that Jesus will first return for us. That's the rapture. Then He will return with us. That's the event most often referred to as the second coming. We'll talk about that at the end of this chapter. But the first aspect of Christ's return is the rapture.

THE RAPTURE OF THE CHURCH

In 1 Thessalonians 4:17, Paul said believers will be "caught up" someday to be with the Lord forever. The term *rapture* comes from the Latin translation of this phrase.

The background to this teaching is found right in the text. The church had been around long enough that some believers in Thessalonica had died.

This was very upsetting to the surviving believers there, since the church did not know what would happen to these people and since the church in that day was expecting Christ to return at any time. So Paul had to address the question of whether dead believers would miss out on the return of Christ.

His answer begins in verse 13. "We do not want you to be uninformed, brethren, about those who are asleep, so that you will not grieve, as do the rest who have no hope."

Hope in Spite of Grief

We have grief when we lose a loved one. But there is a big difference between grief and hopelessness. Since those who are outside of Christ have no hope for the future, it's not surprising that their grief at death takes on a sense of hopelessness and despair.

But because Christ is returning for His own, we can grieve *in* hope instead of *without* hope. The Thessalonians were ignorant of this truth, so they were grieving over their dead as if they would never see them again. Ignorance of biblical truth can lead to emotional instability.

Paul addressed this need by referring to dead believers as "those who are asleep." This is a term we need to understand, because it describes the death of all Christians. The word is never used of non-Christians in the Bible, only of God's people.

The "Sleep" of Death

We use the term *death* to describe the cessation of life because from the human perspective, death is the end. But in the Bible, physical death never means the end of a person's existence.

Some groups of people who may come to your door will use 1 Thessalonians 4 to teach "soul sleep," the idea that the believing dead exist in an unconscious, sleeplike state until Christ returns. But that is uninformed teaching, because that is not what the Bible says.

When a person dies, the body goes to sleep, but not the spirit. The person whose body has ceased to function is still alive and functioning in another realm. For unbelievers, that realm is the torment of hell. But for Christians, physical death or sleep means that we go immediately to be in God's presence.

We can demonstrate that in 1 Thessalonians 4: "God will bring with Him those who have fallen asleep in Jesus" (v. 14).

Paul had just said that dead believers were asleep. If they were simply buried in the ground awaiting the resurrection, how could Christ bring them *back* from heaven with Him at the rapture? You can't come back with someone unless you are already with him. And Paul clearly said that sleeping saints will come back with Jesus when He returns.

Here is proof that at the instant of death, while the body falls asleep the soul and spirit of a Christian go to be with Jesus. In other words, you will be very much alive after your body dies—and a lot better off, even though we still await our resurrection bodies (2 Corinthians 5:4).

Our Guarantee of Jesus' Return

Someone may say, "How do we know all of this is true?" The answer takes us back to the uniqueness of Jesus Christ.

We can trust the word of the One who died and rose again when He said He will return for us. Jesus' promise to return from heaven and catch away His people is as sure as the truth of His death and resurrection. These events stand or fall together. We can't say we believe in the death and resurrection of Jesus Christ but we don't know what's going to happen to us when we die. We must give the rapture the same weight we give to these other doctrines.

This ought to give you hope! It ought to change how you think about this fearful thing called death. Death is fearful for us, because it is the unknown.

But Jesus has been to death and back, so death is not unknown to Him. And if He said He is coming back to raise the dead, you can stake your eternal destiny on it.

Otherwise, we have no real hope, because Paul said, "If we have hoped in Christ in this life only, we are of all men most to be pitied" (1 Corinthians 15:19). Believing in Christ is not only good for time, but for eternity.

The signs announcing the rapture are described in 1 Thessalonians 4:15–16 and are detailed in chapter 109 (see pages 1253–54). Those details, including a shout, an archangel's voice, and a trumpet blast, tell us that Christ's return is a sure thing.

Our Preparation for the Rapture

The return of Jesus Christ is sure, it's wonderful, and it could happen anytime. It's like a telephone answering machine that tells you, "I'm not home now, but when I return I will call you."

If the person we have called is reliable, we can expect a return call even though we don't know whether it will be five minutes or five hours before it comes. Jesus is coming back. What should we be doing now to prepare ourselves for His coming and live in the light of it?

Every year I go to a clinic in Dallas for my annual checkup. It's a time when I find out how well I have taken care of my body during the year. When I remember that this time of evaluation is coming, I get serious about watching what I eat and exercising. When I forget about this time of evaluation, I get slothful.

Paul tells us: "For the grace of God has appeared, bringing salvation to all men, instructing us to deny ungodliness and worldly desires and to live sensibly, righteously and godly in the present age, looking for the blessed hope and the appearing of the glory of our great God and Savior, Christ Jesus" (Titus 2:11–13). We should be looking for and anticipating Christ's return every day. We are looking for the "upper taker," not the undertaker! But during the waiting period, at least two things should characterize us.

First, Paul said that while we are looking for Jesus to return, the best way to prepare for Christ's coming is to live a life that pleases Him, one characterized by godliness and righteousness.

John said the hope of Christ's return should have a purifying effect on us (1 John 3:2–3). Looking for Jesus to return does not mean just sitting and staring into the sky or living in some dreamy world. It means you are so aware of His presence and so focused on seeing Him someday that you want to live like Him now, so you won't disappoint Him at His coming.

Second, looking for Jesus Christ to return should also deepen our love for Him. God does not want us to be focused on an event, but on a person. We are looking forward to the return of Someone we love, not just the occurrence of an event.

Peter puts it in perspective when he said, "Though you have not seen [Christ], you love Him, and though you do not see Him now, but believe in

Him, you greatly rejoice with joy inexpressible and full of glory" (1 Peter 1:8). You don't have to see Jesus Christ to love Him. And your love for Him will only intensify your desire to see Him.

THE JUDGMENT SEAT OF CHRIST

Once Christ returns for His church, He oversees what the Bible calls "the judgment seat of Christ" (2 Corinthians 5:10). I am connecting this event with the rapture because this is the first order of business on Christ's agenda for the church after we are caught away to be with Him.

Evaluation for Rewards

Even though this event is called a judgment, it is not a judgment for salvation. Anyone who is not saved did not make this trip. The judgment seat of Christ is an evaluation of us as believers to determine the rewards, or lack of rewards, we will receive based on the quality of our Christian lives and service.

Don't think that because your eternal destiny is not at stake here this review is not important. It was of great concern to the apostle Paul. Just before he declared that we must all appear at this judgment, Paul wrote, "We also have as our ambition, whether at home or absent, to be pleasing to Him" (2 Corinthians 5:9).

The Greek term for "judgment seat" is *bēma*, which was a platform erected for the judges during the Isthmian Games, a first-century version of the Olympics that were held near Corinth. The judges sat on the *bema* to determine who won and who lost, or who was disqualified (see 1 Corinthians 9:24–27). The prizes given to the winners were also handed out at the *bema*.

A Serious Occasion

Let me give you the full statement in 2 Corinthians 5:10. "For we must all appear before the judgment seat of Christ, so that each one may be recompensed for his deeds in the body, according to what he has done, whether good or bad."

Does this sound serious to you? It does to me. Anyone who says, "Well, I don't really care whether I get any rewards or not as long as I make it to heaven," doesn't understand what's going on here.

There is a lot at stake here. Our degree of authority and privilege in heaven will be determined at Christ's judgment seat. The kind of Christian life we have lived will be revealed there. We will have to stand before Jesus Christ and give account for how we have managed the gifts and resources He entrusted to us.

This is serious stuff. Paul wrote, "Each one of us will give account of himself to God" (Romans 14:12).

So let me say it again. The judgment seat is important. (For more on the purposes and our preparation for the judgment seat, see chapter 110). The Bible uses at least three analogies to help us see what we will be judged for at the *bēma* of Christ.

The Analogy of a Steward

In Luke 16:1–13, Jesus told the parable of a steward who was dishonest in the way he handled his master's business and was fired from his position. We are more familiar with the word *manager*, but the concept is the same. A steward is responsible for the resources his master entrusts to his care.

In Jesus' story, when the master realized his steward was cheating him, he said, "Give an account of your stewardship" (Luke 16:2). Stewardship always involves accountability.

Peter said, "As each one has received a special gift, employ it in serving one another, as good stewards of the manifold grace of God" (1 Peter 4:10). Spiritual gifts are part of the stewardship for which we will give account at the *bēma* of Christ. Our material resources, our families, and the opportunities for ministry God gives us are also included in our stewardship. Even our bodies are given to us by God and are included in the responsibility of stewardship (1 Corinthians 9:27).

Our goal as God's stewards or managers is to do the best possible job we can with what He has given us. And the standard by which we will be measured is clear: "It is required of stewards that one be found trustworthy" (1 Corinthians 4:2).

The Analogy of a Builder

The second analogy Paul used for our stewardship is that of a builder. I encourage you to read 1 Corinthians 3:10–15, where Paul said we are builders in God's kingdom, and we have been given the most magnificent foundation ever laid for a building—Jesus Christ Himself.

With a foundation like that, you don't want to build junk. The quality of our work for Christ will be revealed at "the day," which is a reference to Christ's judgment seat.

The test will be the quality of our work—not just the quantity, or the flashiness, or the busyness of what we tried to do for Christ. The question will be, Did you give God the leftovers of your life or the best you had? Did you invest the precious things of life in His service, or were you content with any old building material you could find?

Building with gold, silver, and precious stones is another way of saying you gave Christ the place of supreme value in your life. That commitment will be rewarded at the *bema*.

The Analogy of an Athlete

Paul also compared the Christian life to an athletic contest. "Do you not know that those who run in a race all run, but only one receives the prize? Run in such a way that you may win" (1 Corinthians 9:24). Then he said that when it comes to serving Christ, he is running to win (v. 26).

How do you win the prize Jesus Christ has for you? By running the race of life in such a way that you fulfill God's will and hear Jesus' commendation, "Well done." In other words, "Congratulations, you won the race. Here's your prize."

I know you don't want to read what follows, but it's inescapable. If you want to win the race, you have to get in shape (see vv. 25–27). And that means saying no to a lot of things that are not wrong in themselves, and saying yes to a lot of exercise and sweating when you don't feel like exercising and sweating.

Paul told Timothy, "Discipline yourself for the purpose of godliness" (1 Timothy 4:7). It won't happen automatically. The Spirit of God is not going to levitate you out of bed tomorrow morning and float you into a chair with your Bible. You have to discipline yourself to get up.

Paul said if athletes in the Isthmian Games exercised strict self-discipline to win a wreath of leaves that would fade away, we should be much more willing to discipline ourselves to win the "imperishable" prize Jesus will give us at His *bēma* (1 Corinthians 9:25). This should motivate us to get in shape and run the race to win.

A BATTLE AND A WEDDING

Christ's return *with* us will occur at the battle of Armageddon (Revelation 19:17–21). After Christ Jesus wins that final battle, He will consummate His marriage to His waiting bride. The church is seen preparing herself for her bridegroom by putting on her wedding garments, "fine linen, bright and clean" (v. 8).

This marriage supper will take place during the glorious, millennial rule of Jesus Christ. His thousand-year reign will be ushered in when He returns in what the theologians call His second advent, the event most people have in mind when they talk about the second coming or return of Christ. This is when sin and Satan are judged and righteousness is established.

This marriage supper is something like a reception. It is basically a party, a celebration when people gather together to congratulate the newlyweds and celebrate their union.

Well, the marriage supper of Jesus Christ is a *real* party! I say that because this bash is going to last one thousand years. The millennial reception will bring time to an end and usher in eternity. (For an in-depth look at Christ's millennial kingdom, see chapter 114).

THE PURPOSE OF CHRIST'S MILLENNIAL REIGN

Why did God ordain and decree in His eternal plan that there would be a thousand-year period on earth that His Son would rule with absolute, sovereign control and perfect righteousness?

To Vindicate Jesus

One reason is to vindicate Christ. Jesus was rejected by the nation Israel when He came the first time to be their King. But it is impossible that the second person of the Trinity could ultimately be prevented from taking His rightful throne.

That's why Jesus will rule His kingdom with Jerusalem as His capital. Remember the magi asked, "Where is He who has been born King of the

Jews?" (Matthew 2:2). That title was written over Jesus' cross, and it still belongs to Him. During the millennium, He will finally claim His throne and receive all the glory that is His due.

To Vindicate God's Plan

The millennial kingdom will also prove the wisdom of God's original plan for mankind. God created man to rule the earth in His behalf (see Psalm 8:5–6; Hebrews 2:7) in response to the conflict in heaven when Satan and one-third of the angels rebelled and were booted out of heaven.

God wanted to demonstrate His glory to the angels by fashioning human beings, creatures inferior to the angels, whom He would use to rule the earth and overcome the sin and ruin caused by the angel Lucifer, or Satan. This will happen during the millennium, the "world to come" (Hebrews 2:5) that the writer of Hebrews said will be ruled by Christ and His redeemed people.

So in the millennial kingdom, mankind will realize his original destiny and purpose to rule and reign with Christ for a thousand years (Revelation 20:6).

THE PROCESS OF CHRIST'S MILLENNIAL REIGN

With the bride of Christ adorned and ready for her marriage, Jesus Christ will ride out of heaven to inaugurate His kingdom and begin the wedding reception (Revelation 19:11–14). We are with Him, because no bridegroom goes to his reception without his bride.

But in order to inaugurate His thousand-year rule, Jesus Christ must deal with His enemies. So His first task will be judgment. That's the purpose of the army following Him and the sword coming from His mouth, described in Revelation 19:16.

Jesus Christ is coming back from His throne in heaven to rid Himself of all opposition as He sets up His throne on earth. The battle of Armageddon, which will take place at the end of the tribulation, will begin with the capture of the Antichrist and the False Prophet. After those two are judged and thrown into the lake of fire, King Jesus will defeat the armies. Finally Satan will be bound and put into the abyss for one thousand years. The details of this awesome battle and Christ's great triumph are found in chapter 113.

Then King Jesus will reign in a peace-filled kingdom on earth for a millennium.

APPLICATION FOR LIFE

1. Are you ready for the rapture? According to 1 John 3:2–3, the imminent return of Jesus should have a purifying effect on us. Are you denying ungodliness and living in ways that are pleasing to God? Don't be caught off guard when Jesus returns!

2. Jesus Christ has won each believer as part of His bride, His church. We know He is coming back because He promised to return. We have the Bible, God's love letter to His church. Approach your Bible as if it is God's love letter to *you*. Before you begin reading, ask the Lord to open your heart and help you make a heart response to what you read.

3. The Bible teaches that our resurrection bodies will be new, glorified bodies—perfect and no longer subjected to the limitations of time, illness, or injury. Philippians 3:21 teaches that our bodies will be like Jesus' glorified body. Those who have gone before us will receive their bodies first. The rapture could happen at any moment. As believers, we should live each day in anticipation of this glorious event.

4. Christian stewardship is a key issue for any believer. God will hold us accountable for what He has given us (1 Corinthians 4:2). Are you a good steward of the resources God has entrusted to you? It's always a good exercise to occasionally take inventory of yourself in this regard. Are you investing your resources for the furtherance of God's kingdom? Do you use your skills and talents to help others? Ask God to help you look for opportunities for ministry. A new "to do" list might effectively help you re-channel your resources in more effective ways.

FOR GROUP STUDY

Questions for Group Discussion

1. Read 1 Thessalonians 4:17. What is the doctrine of the rapture of the church? What prompted the apostle Paul to teach this doctrine?

2. According to 1 Thessalonians 4:15–16, what three events will take place during the rapture? What encouragements do you draw from this passage?

3. In preparation for discussion, read Titus 2:11–13; 1 John 3:2–3; and 1 Peter 1:8. Although the Bible teaches that the rapture is imminent, what might we do to prepare for it?

4. Second Corinthians 5:10 speaks of the "judgment seat of Christ." Also read 1 Corinthians 9:24–27. Describe the judgment seat of Christ. What is its purpose, and what happens at this event? Discuss the analogies Scripture uses to describe stewardship. (Use the chart below as an aid to your discussion.)

PICTURE THIS

Scripture presents the following three analogies to illustrate Christian stewardship.

PICTURES OF CHRISTIAN STEWARDSHIP

ANALOGY	SCRIPTURE PASSAGES	OUR RESPONSIBILITY
Analogy of a steward	Luke 16:1–13; 1 Peter 4:10; 1 Corinthians 9:27	God wants us to do our best with what He has given us.
Analogy of a builder	1 Corinthians 3:10–15	God will test the quality of our walk and Christian service for Him.
Analogy of an athlete	1 Corinthian 9:24–27	We must run our race to win and in a way that fulfills God's will.

SECTION II

The Authority of Christ

22

THE AUTHORITY OF CHRIST OVER NATURE

Beyond God the Son's uniqueness, there is His authority. In the remaining chapters of Part 2, we will see that just as Christ's uniqueness as the Son of God extends to every area of life and to every corner of earth and heaven, so His authority over every other force and power on earth or under the earth is complete, absolute, and never ending.

Let's begin by looking at Christ's authority over nature, using one of my favorite stories in the gospel of Mark (4:35–41). This is a confrontation between Jesus and the forces of nature that served notice on the disciples, and serves notice on all of us, that Jesus Christ is in a class by Himself.

THE PLAN

Jesus had been teaching from a boat at the edge of the Sea of Galilee (Mark 4:1). At the end of a long day, He turned to the disciples and said, "Let us go over to the other side" (v. 35). He was referring to the western shore of the Sea of Galilee opposite the Galilee side, about a seven-and-a-half mile trip. That was the plan.

When that boat set out on its trip, Jesus was very tired. He had been teaching the multitudes and answering the disciples' questions and finally evening approached. You need to read Mark 4:1–34 to get the picture of the kind of exhausting day Jesus had experienced. Jesus lay down in the boat and was asleep as soon as His head hit the cushion (v. 38).

THE PROBLEM

Even though Jesus had made a simple statement of His intention to go with His disciples to the other side of the lake, they obviously weren't listening.

The Threat of the Storm

We know that they weren't listening because as soon as they got out on the water, a storm came up and they panicked, thinking for sure they were going to drown right there.

The Sea of Galilee is situated in such a way that the winds can come sweeping down from the surrounding mountains and create ferocious storms. This is the kind of storm that engulfed the boat carrying Jesus and the disciples. "There arose a fierce gale of wind, and the waves were breaking over the boat so much that the boat was already filling up" (Mark 4:37).

These men had heard Jesus say they were going to the other side, but all of a sudden their experience was not matching Jesus' word. They began to see that they were in danger of not making it to the other side. They had a major problem.

So the disciples did what you and I probably would have done in the same situation. They looked at Jesus asleep in the back of the boat, "awoke Him and said to Him, 'Teacher, do You not care that we are perishing?'" (v. 38).

This was a serious situation, not some minor inconvenience. Jesus must have been getting wet, but He was still asleep.

The Fear at Jesus' Seeming Unconcern

Have you ever been in a circumstance like this? You believe you are acting in God's will, but then hell attacks. When you call on Jesus, it seems like He is asleep. No one picks up on the other end of the line.

The disciples felt like that, and they asked themselves, "How could Jesus sleep at a time like this?" So they woke Him up to inform Him of the terrible problem they had. As far as they could see, they were about to die, and Jesus didn't even care.

The disciples were saying, "Jesus, even if You don't care that much about us, You ought to at least care about Yourself, because if this boat goes down, You are going down with us."

It wasn't the storm or the danger that woke Jesus. It was the disciples who woke Him up, because they were beginning to allow their circumstances to control their theology. They were measuring the love of Christ by the amount of water in the bottom of the boat.

The disciples forgot what Jesus had said when it was calm and began to doubt His care based on their problem. They suddenly developed a "circumstantial theology" in the middle of that storm. They determined what they believed by what they were going through.

But the middle of a storm is not the place to work out your theology. You need to determine what you believe in the good times, so you'll know what to believe when the bad times hit. You need to decide who Jesus Christ is when everything's going right, so you'll know who He is when everything's going wrong.

The disciples forgot what they had learned about Jesus when the sea was calm, so they raised a very serious question: "Jesus, don't You care?"

THE PROVISION

The dangerous storm and the disciples' question led to a miraculous provision by Jesus Christ, who exercised His authority over the natural world He had created.

Jesus Calms the Sea

"And He got up and rebuked the wind and said to the sea, 'Hush, be still.' And the wind died down and it became perfectly calm" (Mark 4:39).

The disciples had allowed fear of their circumstances to start dictating their theology, but at least they knew where to go for help. Jesus was asleep and they were desperate, so they came to Him and shook Him awake with their need. And they definitely came to the right person, because Jesus quickly and effortlessly calmed the wind and the sea. No problem there.

But notice that nothing happened until the disciples asked Jesus for help. They had tried rowing themselves out of trouble, but they got to the place where all their efforts at rowing were meaningless, and someone finally said, "Let's ask Jesus."

So they aroused Jesus. They didn't just gently whisper until He woke up or lightly tap Him, either. They made sure He was awake, because they were in a desperate situation.

Jesus wasn't going to do anything until the disciples asked Him. The apostle James wrote, "You do not have because you do not ask" (James 4:2). If you don't have a determination to get hold of God, don't be surprised if He seems to be sleeping through your storm.

The disciples had an external problem, the storm, that led to an internal problem, their fear and belief that Jesus didn't care about them. When they woke Jesus up, He dealt with the external problem. The elements immediately obeyed Him.

When Jesus fixes stuff, it's fixed. One way you know Jesus has done something is that it's done perfectly. Jesus doesn't do anything halfway.

A Lesson for the Disciples

The stilling of the storm was a miracle, but that's the kind of authority Jesus has. I'm surprised there are so many Christians who do not believe the authority of Christ still works miracles today. Sometimes we just do not understand the nature of the Christ whom we serve.

We serve a Christ who can tell the wind to stop blowing, because He made the wind. He can tell the sea to be calm, because He made the sea. So what is there in your life that Jesus cannot handle?

We would fare a lot better if we allowed Jesus to be Lord in our lives. He *is* Lord, make no mistake. But He will not rule as Lord in your life until you come to Him and say, "Jesus, I need You. I can't make it by myself."

Jesus wants to take control of our lives, but so many of us are like a wild mustang that needs to be broken. The first time the rider puts a saddle on the mustang and attempts to ride, the horse goes wild. The uncertainty and confusion of this new weight on its back sends the animal into hysteria, and so it begins to buck and resist the new pressure.

This goes on until the mustang learns to submit to the rider's will and discovers that the rider is not a threat but an ally. When God puts the saddle of trials on us, they are designed to bring us into submission to Him. But as long as we buck and resist, we are expending energy trying to throw off the very One who wants to help us realize the purpose for which we were created.

Having Jesus in your boat may not keep you out of the storm, but He is the provision you need to get you through the storm. Jesus is unique. He could be tired and fall asleep because He was human, and yet He could stand up and calm the wind and waves because He is God.

In other words, Jesus knows what you feel because He's man, and He can do something about it because He's God!

The disciples could empathize with each other, but they couldn't do anything about the problem. But Jesus could.

The disciples held a group counseling session and decided to try to get out of their mess by themselves. But that didn't work, so they had another very brief session and decided they had better take this mess to Jesus, because they needed Someone with authority over nature.

A NEW PERSPECTIVE

You can be sure the disciples got a new perspective on themselves and on Jesus after He quieted the storm.

A New Perspective on Themselves

Jesus performed the miracle, then He said to His disciples, "Why are you afraid? Do you still have no faith?" (Mark 4:40). Now Jesus was dealing with the *real* problem, which was not the wind or the waves or the water in the bottom of the boat.

The problem was the disciples' wimpy lack of faith. That's the idea behind the word *afraid.* The disciples wimped out on Jesus. Their faith collapsed in the face of the storm.

Men don't like to hear that they are wimps, that they are weak. So I can imagine the disciples thinking to themselves, *Wait a minute, Jesus. You obviously don't understand. This is the real world, and in the real world when your boat gets full of water, you get scared. It's just natural. We know how bad these storms can be.*

Why did Jesus rebuke the disciples for their lack of faith? Not just for becoming afraid in a bad situation. The problem was they had missed the whole point. Before they ever left, Jesus had said, "Let us go over to the other side."

Jesus was rebuking His men for allowing their bad situation to take over so that they reacted to the storm instead of believing what He said. They allowed their circumstances to dictate their theology, as we said above, and that's a very bad perspective. The disciples forgot what Jesus had told them.

He didn't say, "*I'm* going to the other side while you drown." And He certainly didn't say, "Let's all go out to the middle of the sea and drown." He intended to complete the trip with them. But Jesus also did not say the trip would be trouble free.

The disciples had the assurance of God's Word that they would be fine, because they had Jesus and He is the Word of God incarnate. But they forgot what God had said—and when circumstances come between you and God's Word, your fear of the storm will overwhelm your confidence in the Word.

What we need today is confidence in a Savior who has all authority. When you have that, your boat of circumstances may start taking on water, and it may look like you're going to drown. But you can go back to the Word with the confidence; "God says we are going to the other side."

The disciples had no faith. They didn't believe Jesus' word. They needed to see for themselves their lack of faith.

A New Perspective on Jesus

After Jesus gave the disciples a new look at themselves, they got a new perspective on Him. Seeing the miracle, "they became very much afraid and said to one another, 'Who then is this, that even the wind and the sea obey Him?'" (Mark 4:41).

At first the Twelve were afraid of the storm. But now they were afraid of the storm stopper. The Greek text says literally, "They feared with a great fear."

The disciples were afraid of Jesus because they did not yet fully understand or appreciate who it was in the boat with them.

They did not know that "very God of very God," to use the theologians' term for Jesus, was in the boat with them. They didn't realize what kind of person they were dealing with.

Our Need for Perspective

We lose sight of this too. That's why we need to keep our focus on Christ, especially when everything else breaks loose. Any carpenter will tell you that if you want to avoid hitting your thumb with the hammer, keep your eye on the nail you're driving, not on your thumb. If you take your eyes off Jesus, don't be surprised if you smash your spiritual thumb.

One day a farmer was teaching his son how to plow. He said, "Son, in order to plow a straight furrow, don't look down at the ground, look ahead. Find something on the other side of the field, fix your eye on it, and head toward it. That way, you'll plow straight furrows."

The farmer left his son to plow, but when he came back he saw crooked furrows going all over the field. The farmer asked his son, "What in the world happened?"

"Dad, I picked out something to keep my eye on just like you said. I kept my eye on the cow." The problem was, of course, that the cow kept moving. Keep your eyes on Jesus, because He's not going anywhere.

You don't have to deny your hard circumstances. A storm is a storm. Call it what it is, but don't yield to it. Remember that all the authority belongs to Christ.

That way, you can make your trials work for you. They can become stepping-stones to a new level of spiritual maturity and blessing, rather than stumbling blocks to take you to the bottom of the sea. The disciples were getting a new perspective on Jesus that they wouldn't have gotten if it had not been for the storm.

When the wind starts blowing, go to Jesus. Remind Him of the promises in His Word. Remind Him that He said that you're going to the other side, not that you will drown in the middle of the lake.

Once you know who's in charge, it doesn't matter whether your boat is rocking in the storm. Jesus is in charge of nature. He's the One with all authority. He can calm any storm. Does He have authority over your life?

PERSONAL APPLICATION FOR LIFE

1. As the disciples found themselves in a storm, we too find ourselves in various storms in our lives. Perhaps they are financial storms, family storms, or health storms. Never lose sight of the fact that Jesus is with you in your storm. As He did with nature, He can also calm the storm in your life or in your heart. Trust Him to provide.

2. Jesus slept in the boat while a storm was raging. The disciples concluded that He didn't care about their peril. Have you had similar experiences doubting God? Sometimes it seems God is taking too long, or that He just doesn't care. The disciples' problem was that they were being controlled by their circumstances rather than what they had learned about Jesus before the storm. The next time you go through a storm, remember to keep your eyes on Jesus, not your circumstances, and claim the promises of His Word.

3. Sometimes we go through storms because we disobey, as did Jonah in the Old Testament. But sometimes God sends us into a storm, as He did the disciples. Why? Because He wants us to grow in our faith. Remember that every storm God sends your way has a purpose. When one comes, ask God to help you grow from your experience.

4. Jesus' authority affects every force and power on earth and every realm of life. After their experience, the disciples confessed Jesus' total authority and lordship over nature. That same lordship should be evident in our lives as well. Ask God to reveal any hidden area or something you simply cannot let go of. Then ask Him to help you relinquish that area to Him.

FOR GROUP STUDY

Questions for Group Discussion

1. Read the account in Mark 4:35–41. We know that Jesus is uniquely the God-man. What do we see in this account that speaks of His humanity? What in this account that speaks of His Deity?

2. What key lessons did the disciples learn from their experience in the storm with Jesus?

3. To aid your discussion, read John 15:5 and James 4:2. Why does God allow us to go through trials and storms in our lives? Should we try to avoid our storms, or should we try to engage them? Why?

4. The disciples gained new perspectives after going through the storm. What new perspective did they gain about themselves? What new perspective did they gain about Jesus? Have the group members share stories about the life's storms they have faced. What new perspective did they gain from their storm experiences?

PICTURE THIS

An unexpected advantage the disciples' experienced was the new perspectives they gained. In Mark 4, Dr. Evans points out the two key perspectives below.

THE DISCIPLES' NEW PERSPECTIVES

FOCUS OF THEIR PERSPECTIVE	SCRIPTURE PASSAGE	NEW PERSPECTIVE
On themselves	Mark 4:40	The disciples learned that they lacked faith.
On Jesus	Mark 4:41	The disciples gained a reverential awe for Jesus after His exercise of authority.

23

THE AUTHORITY OF CHRIST OVER SATAN AND THE DEMONS

History may be defined as the outworking of the cosmic conflict between God and Satan in the realm of mankind. We see moves and countermoves between God and the Devil.

God made the first move by creating the world, which included all the angelic host. Satan, himself an angel with high ambitions (see Isaiah 14:12–14; Ezekiel 28:14–17), countered that move by rebelling and taking a third of the angels with him in his rebellion.

God countered that move by creating Adam, who would be His man to rule over planet Earth. Satan countered that move by tempting Adam and Eve to rebel against God's authority. God promised a coming Seed through the woman who would redeem mankind so we could be brought back into fellowship with Him.

Satan tried to counter that move by getting Cain to kill Abel, in order to cut off the godly line. But God blocked that move by creating Seth to reintroduce the godly line. So Satan induced the whole world to rebel against God.

But God found a righteous man named Noah and told him to build a boat on dry land, providing salvation for Noah and his family while wiping out the rest of the world.

Satan wasn't finished yet, though. He found a man named Nimrod and got him to lead a world movement that tried to declare its independence from God by building the Tower of Babel.

That's when God pulled off one of His great countermoves. He went to Ur of the Chaldeans to a man named Abraham and told him, "Through you I am going to build a nation that will obey Me."

Satan countered that move by sending Israel into bondage in Egypt. God, however, sent Moses to Egypt to tell Pharaoh, "Let My people go."

Satan tried to block that move by sending the Egyptian army to wipe out Israel. But God countered by opening the Red Sea for the Israelites and closing it over the Egyptians.

Throughout the Old Testament, this is the way it went. Israel rebelled against God, who raised up a prophet or a judge to bring the nation back to Him. But Satan would be there to tempt the nation to go back into idolatry and sin.

I'm not suggesting that God and Satan were equal foes, struggling for supremacy. There was never any question that God is absolutely sovereign in His power. But on the chessboard of biblical history, the outcome of the battle was still unclear to human observers by the time the Old Testament closed.

This was followed by four hundred silent years, a period in which there was no word from God. But that silence was broken with the birth of Christ. Up to this point, God had used men to counter the Devil. But now He was saying, "It is time to demonstrate My authority over Satan once and for all. I am coming down to take care of this Myself."

PREPARATION FOR THE GREAT BATTLE

So God became a man in the person of Jesus Christ, who took on Satan in head-to-head battle and emerged totally victorious. This battle is recorded in Matthew 4:1–11, the temptation of Jesus Christ in the wilderness.

This is the great contest between the authority of Christ and the authority of Satan, and there emerges a clear winner. Jesus had just been baptized by John the Baptist in preparation for ministry—His public coming out, if you will (Matthew 3:13–17). God the Father clearly identified Jesus as His Son, and Jesus was commissioned for ministry. The first step was His temptation, a time of testing and proving in which Jesus established His authority over Satan in no uncertain terms.

Jesus on the Offensive

Matthew 4:1 says, "Then Jesus was led up by the Spirit into the wilderness to be tempted by the devil."

Please notice that this confrontation did not come about by Satan's will, but by God's will. It's already clear who is calling the shots here. Jesus went into the wilderness on the offensive, not on the defensive. He was going to demonstrate His superior authority.

God also allows you and me to be tempted so that we might demonstrate the supreme authority of Christ through our lives. God does not permit Satan to tempt us to make us fall, but that we might prove the superiority of Christ.

The Battleground Decided

Why did God decide that His Son would be tempted in a hot, dry, barren wilderness instead of somewhere else? Because the purpose of Jesus' earthly ministry, which culminated in the cross, was to reverse the effects of Adam's sin and failure.

The first Adam was tempted in a garden. Satan came onto God's territory and got Adam to sin. As a result, Adam was kicked out of the garden into a world that was now a hot, dry, barren wilderness. It was now Satan's territory.

But Jesus Christ, the last Adam, paid Satan a return visit. He went onto Satan's territory and defeated him. Why? To bring us back into the garden, that which God intended mankind to have. Jesus gave us back what was taken from us by the sin of our forefather Adam.

Jesus' Spiritual Preparation

Jesus did not just rush into battle against Satan. What a lesson for us. The Bible says, "After He had fasted forty days and forty nights, He then became hungry" (Matthew 4:2).

Jesus knew that He was facing a test from His Father and a temptation from the Devil. He needed all the spiritual resources He could get. So He fasted, going without food for forty days. Jesus gave up a natural and normal need of the body in order to address a greater need of the spirit.

That's what fasting is all about. It is a reversal in priorities. We usually eat when we are hungry, but when we fast we ignore our hunger to feed our spirit. Fasting says to God, "The spiritual is more important to me than the physical."

THE FIRST ATTACK OF THE BATTLE

After Jesus had fasted for forty days and nights, it was time for battle. So the tempter came at Jesus with three powerful attacks.

The first is recorded in Matthew 4:3, where we read, "The tempter came and said to Him, 'If You are the Son of God, command that these stones become bread.'"

Why did Satan suggest that Jesus launch "Operation Breadbasket"? Because he knew Jesus was hungry! The Devil knew what was going on in the wilderness.

The Tempter's Suggestion

This first temptation hit Jesus where He was vulnerable physically. Remember, because Jesus became fully human, He experienced things the way we experience them. Jesus was just as hungry and weak as you and I would be if we fasted that long.

Since God had not stepped in and fed His Son for all that time, the Devil's first temptation was for Jesus to act independently of His Father and feed Himself.

The Devil was saying, "Jesus, You have been fasting for forty days and Your Father hasn't fed You yet. You have the power to turn these stones into bread. Why should You go hungry when You can do something about it? Your Father is really not that good because if He was good, You would have eaten by now."

The Answer of the Word

Jesus answered Satan, "It is written, 'Man shall not live on bread alone, but on every word that proceeds out of the mouth of God'" (Matthew 4:4). Jesus used the Word of God against the Devil.

"The word of God is living and active and sharper than any two-edged sword" Hebrews (4:12). When Satan shows up, we are to take the Word and say, "On guard!"

Jesus' answer to the first temptation was a quotation from Deuteronomy 8:3, where Moses was explaining to Israel how God brought the nation through the wilderness. "[God] humbled you and let you be hungry, and fed you with manna . . . that He might make you understand that man does not live by bread alone, but man lives by everything that proceeds out of the mouth of the Lord."

Manna was the little breadlike wafers God miraculously sent from heaven to feed the Israelites. The Hebrew word *manna* means "What is it?"

Why would anyone call a food by a name that's actually a question? Because it was a question God wanted Israel to answer. When the people saw these cornflakes coming down from above and asked, "What is it?" the correct answer was, "This is the supernatural provision of God."

In other words, Israel didn't make it through the wilderness just because the people had something to eat. They made it because they had a God who fed them. Jesus was hungry and needed bread, but He knew God would provide. He was not going to get it from the Devil.

Satan wanted Jesus to act independently of God by questioning His Father's provision. But Jesus dismissed the temptation because He has authority over the Devil.

THE SECOND ATTACK OF THE BATTLE

Satan wasn't through with Jesus yet. He fired the second volley in the battle when he took Jesus into Jerusalem and had Him stand at the highest point of the temple—some 450 feet above ground. From this high pinnacle Satan said to Jesus, "If You are the Son of God, throw Yourself down" (Matthew 4:6).

Satan's Pattern of Testing

The Devil said to Jesus, "Come with me so I can tempt you," and Jesus went. His authority was such that He did not put Himself in any danger at all by allowing Satan to take Him to a place of temptation.

We can't say that about ourselves, but the fact is that God still permits the Devil to take us on occasion to see whether we will be faithful to Him. The classic biblical example is Job. God allowed the Devil to take Job almost to the grave. The Devil took everything Job had and his ten children too, then he took Job's health. But Job's reaction was, "Though [God] slay me, I will hope in Him" (Job 13:15).

God's authority was never in doubt throughout Job's trial. God drew the line each time, and Satan had to stop (see Job 1:6–12; 2:1–6). But in the process, Job understood something we need to understand. After all his calamities had hit, Job said to his wife, "Shall we indeed accept good from God and not accept adversity?" (Job 2:10). Job understood that God was not what we might call today a "Santa Claus" God whose only reason to exist is to shower us with the things we want and never allow discomfort to touch us.

The Tempter's Suggestion

Satan took Jesus to the pinnacle of the temple and tempted Him to jump. Then look at what Satan said: "For it is written, 'He will command His angels concerning You'; and 'On their hands they will bear You up, so that You will not strike Your foot against a stone'" (Matthew 4:6).

Satan had been doing some reading in Psalm 91. He knew these verses and used them against Jesus to try to get Him to bypass God's plan, which included the agony of the cross. This was the second temptation, to get Jesus to take the easy way out.

Satan's idea was that if Jesus jumped off the temple in full view of Israel, the angels would ease Him to the ground, He would land safely, and the people would see the miracle and fall down before Jesus in awe and worship and say, "You are the Messiah."

Was Jesus Israel's Messiah? Of course. Did the nation need to fall at His feet and confess Him as Messiah? Certainly. Will they do that someday? Yes, someday *every* knee will bow and confess, "Jesus Christ is Lord" (Philippians 2:11). But it won't happen Satan's way.

Before we look at Jesus' second answer, let's talk about this thing of the Devil quoting Scripture. Satan knows the Bible. If he knows the Bible and you don't, you are in big-time trouble, right?

Satan tried "It is written" on Jesus because his first temptation failed. So he said to Jesus, "If I can't get You to act independently of God, let me try some religion on You." Don't get all ruffled when people use the Bible for their own twisted purposes. They're not being original. Hell uses the Bible.

The Answer of the Word

Jesus wasn't ruffled at all by Satan's quoting a few Scripture verses out of context. Instead, He countered the Devil by saying, "On the other hand" (Matthew 4:7). Don't believe everything you hear until you have checked out "on the other hand." This is where we get the rest of the story.

Jesus was saying, "Satan, if you are going to quote Scripture, tell the whole story." "On the other hand, it is written, 'You shall not put the Lord your God to the test.'" In other words, you can't back God into a corner so that He is obligated to perform a miracle for you.

That's what Satan tried to make Jesus do. But God had a plan, and when it was God's time for Jesus to be revealed and worshiped as Messiah, He would be revealed. The only way Jesus could gain the glory of the crown was by enduring the agony of the cross.

THE THIRD ATTACK OF THE BATTLE

In the third temptation Satan laid aside all the pretense of caring about whether Jesus was hungry or received the worship due Him. In his final attempt, we see Satan revealing himself in all his evil. Now he was standing there in his red jumpsuit, with two horns, a pitchfork, and a pointed tail.

The Tempter's Suggestion

"Again, the devil took Him to a very high mountain, and showed Him all the kingdoms of the world, and their glory; and he said to Him, 'All these things will I give You, if You fall down and worship me'" (Matthew 4:8–9).

This was Satan's bottom line. "Jesus, let me tell You what I've been trying to get at here. Bow!" This was Satan's attempt to get Jesus to bow down and hand over to Satan His authority and the worship due Him as God. This is what Satan has wanted since the day in eternity past when he rebelled against God and tried to take over heaven. He was tired of bowing to God and wanted God to bow to him.

It was impossible that Jesus Christ would yield to Satan and forfeit His divine authority. But today Satan is still trying to rob God of the worship due Him by coming to us as God's people, dangling things in front of us, and saying, "You can have it all. All you have to do is bow."

The Answer of the Word

Now that Satan had put aside his pretenses and revealed his true purpose of trying to dethrone God, the temptation was over. Jesus dismissed Satan with the Word. "Go, Satan! For it is written, 'You shall worship the Lord your God, and serve Him only'" (Matthew 4:10).

Here's a tremendous example of Jesus' authority. Satan had nothing in Jesus, as Christ Himself said (John 14:30). Jesus had no obligation to the Devil, and neither do you. Jesus' quotation, also from the book of Deuteronomy, puts the issue squarely.

A lot of people observe half of that command. They worship God on Sunday, but they serve all kinds of other agendas and other gods during the week. But if Jesus is the ultimate authority in the universe, then He deserves our exclusive worship *and* our service.

THE AFTERMATH OF THE BATTLE

According to Matthew 4:11, "Then the devil left Him; and behold, angels came and began to minister to Him."

Jesus resisted Satan, and Satan had to flee. Jesus had absolute authority to command Satan to leave, but we have His delegated authority against Satan because James says, "Resist the devil and he will flee from you" (James 4:7).

After Jesus' temptation, God sent angels to minister to Him. Where were those angels all that time? Waiting for the battle to be concluded. Those angels brought food to Jesus because He was hungry. They also brought Him spiritual strength from heaven because that's what He needed. And they brought Him worship because that's what He deserved.

The job of angels is to deliver the blessings of God according to the timetable of God when we are doing the will of God. When it comes to dealing with Satan, that means we are going to have to keep our eyes firmly fixed on Jesus, "the author and perfecter of faith" (Hebrews 12:2).

Jesus Christ is the One who has total authority over the Devil. You can't beat the Enemy on your own. It is the authority of Christ magnified through His Word that wins the battle.

SATAN'S EVIL EMPIRE

Christ's authority extends to the demons who have followed Satan in his rebellion. Revelation 12:4 indicates that one-third of heaven's angels defected with Satan. This was an enormous number of spirit beings, because the Bible pictures the angels as an innumerable host.

These fallen angels came to be known as demons, or unclean spirits. Like Satan, they have already been judged and one day will be consigned to hell, which Jesus said was created not for human beings, but for "the devil and his angels" (Matthew 25:41). Human beings go to hell because they choose to join Satan's rebellion.

Satan knows his doom is sure, but in the intervening time he is doing all he can to thwart the plan of God. He has emulated heaven by creating an organizational structure and hierarchy of his own among the demons. Satan has a demonic government whose job it is to carry out hell's agenda in attempting to defeat the program of God.

Satan's Organizational Structure

According to Ephesians 6:12, Satan's demonic hierarchy includes "rulers," "powers," "world forces of this darkness," and "spiritual forces of wickedness." These words denote governmental terms lifted out of the Roman world. Paul used them to describe the organization of demonic forces that do Satan's bidding.

Rulers are the princes who guide the affairs of the satanic realm. Then there are the powers who execute Satan's program. The next group is something like the officers and sergeants who make sure the program is properly implemented. The last group includes the troops who take the marching orders to the field of battle.

Notice the reach of Satan's government. It extends to all the world. When you become a Christian, you are targeted for Satan's attacks, because he does not want your influence working against his kingdom.

Since Satan is not God, he is neither omnipotent, omnipresent, nor omniscient. He doesn't have unlimited power, he can't be everywhere at one time, and he doesn't know everything. He's certainly more powerful than we are, but he must carry out his agenda through his organization of demons.

The Attributes of Demons

Satan has all the attributes of personality, and so do his demons. They exhibit intellect, emotion, and will. In fact, demons must have an intellect superior to ours because they can deceive people. They are master masqueraders.

Demons also have limited knowledge of future things. They can overpower men, interfere with the laws of nature, and pass through physical barriers. They can cause muteness, blindness, deformity, seizures, and insanity. So we are dealing with beings who, though they are invisible, are very powerful.

Since all of this is true, it's obvious that trying to battle demons using only our five senses will result in frustration and defeat. Demons are masters at getting people to fight and attack each other rather than recognize the true source of the problem. And as long as the demons can get us to do that, they win, because we are fighting the wrong enemy.

Our Need for Christ's Authority

I can't overemphasize the importance of taking seriously the reality of the demonic world. Part of Satan's strategy is to get us to think he is imaginary and that all this talk of an unseen spiritual world is sort of a fairy tale. If Satan can cause you to ignore him, he has won half the battle in your case. That's something of the nature and program of demons. They are formidable enemies, just like their commander.

But here's the good news. Jesus Christ has absolute, eternal authority over the demonic world. In fact, the only way we human beings can address the problem of demons is through the authority of Christ.

JESUS' CONFRONTATION WITH DEMONS

Demonic activity is evident all through the Bible, from Genesis to Revelation. But demons were particularly active during the ministry of Jesus Christ.

That shouldn't surprise us, since the Devil's overarching agenda is to oppose and thwart the program of God. Jesus came to do the will of God and to do it as no one else has ever done it. So we would expect the demons to show up where Jesus showed up, and that's the case throughout the Gospels.

The Initial Contact with the Demons

Of all Jesus' confrontations with demons, the incident described in Mark 5:1–20 is probably the most graphic illustration of Jesus' authority over demons.

Jesus and His disciples had crossed to the eastern shore of the Sea of Galilee when the action started. "When He had come out of the boat, immediately a man from the tombs with an unclean spirit met Him" (v. 2).

Here we are introduced to a man most people would call a madman. But the man's problem was not medical or psychological or environmental. He had "an unclean spirit," a demon. It turns out the man was possessed by a multitude of demons, but the bottom line is the same. He was under the control of demons.

Notice what demons produce when they take over a life. This man was living among the tombs that dotted the hillside of the area. He lived in the realm of death. Demon activity makes a person morbid. The person suffering from demonic oppression often has a fixation on death and self-destruction. This man was also "gashing himself with stones" (v. 5). He also possessed superhuman strength; no one could restrain him (vv. 3–4).

The Demons' Recognition of Jesus

In the middle of all this evil, Jesus showed up. "Seeing Jesus from a distance, he ran up and bowed down before Him; and shouting with a loud voice, he said, 'What business do we have with each other, Jesus, Son of the Most High God? I implore You by God, do not torment me!'" (Mark 5:6–7).

This man recognized Jesus, bowed before Him, and acknowledged His deity. Actually, this was probably the demons speaking through him, since the man had apparently never met Jesus before.

Demons have to acknowledge Jesus, and they have to bow before His authority. All they could do was beg Him not to command them to leave the man. Jesus had already told them, "Come out of the man!" (v. 8). Demons seek to inhabit a body through which they can express themselves. Otherwise, they are restless. The demons had taken such complete possession of this man that his identity had fused almost completely with theirs. Let me make a clarification: Believers in Jesus Christ cannot be demon possessed. The Holy Spirit inhabits our bodies and spirits. So a demon cannot take up residence in a believer's life. But believers can be oppressed and harassed by demons.

The Boldness of Demons

If demons won't leave us alone, they certainly aren't going to leave the unsaved alone. Demons are far more active and present than our secular world will ever admit. Many of the terrible evils we see today are the result of demon possession. The Bible makes it clear that hell can take over a life or a family.

Hell can also rule over nations. Daniel 10:13 talks about a demonic being called "the prince of the kingdom of Persia." In other words, this demon was assigned to the Persian government.

Hell can even dominate religion. Jesus referred to "a synagogue of Satan" in Smyrna (Revelation 2:9). In fact, "the whole world lies in the power of the evil one" (1 John 5:19). Satan is in the business of hostile takeovers. There is no human explanation for some of the things that are happening today.

The man from the tombs was a true split personality. He was demonically tormented, but a part of him was crying out for Jesus' help. The demons within him begged Jesus not to torment them, because when Jesus shows up they are exposed for who they are, and they know they have been placed under sentence.

The Demons' Need for a "Home"

These evil spirits did not want to leave the man's body, because demons seek a body through which to express themselves and carry out the Devil's agenda. They are only content when they are tormenting someone, not just floating around in space.

Jesus taught that demons seek a human home. "When the unclean spirit goes out of a man, it passes through waterless places seeking rest, and not finding any, it says, 'I will return to my house from which I came'" (Luke 11:24). The house is the body which the demon left. Evil spirits don't find rest until they have a body to inhabit.

This is why the demons begged Jesus not to make them leave the man from the tombs. What had sent them into a frenzy was the word of Jesus, "Come out of the man" (Mark 5:8). All it takes to bring the powerful, supernatural demonic world to its knees is the authoritative word of Jesus Christ.

The Destructive Nature of Demonic Activity

Let's pick up the story at Mark 5:9. "And He [Jesus] was asking him, 'What is your name?' And he said to Him, 'My name is Legion; for we are many.'"

Here's the dual-personality thing at work again. Jesus was simply asking the man for his name. But the demons were so totally in control that they answered with *their* name.

A legion in the Roman army was up to six thousand soldiers, so this was a horde of demons. Yet Jesus addressed the demons in the singular, and they answered in the singular. That's because this huge legion of demons was operating as one. They were unified. There is no defection among Satan's troops (see Jesus' words in Matthew 12:24–29).

Though a demonic legion was present, they understood the authority of Christ. When they realized Jesus was not going to rescind His command that they leave the man, "he [the demons] began to implore Him earnestly not to send them out of the country. Now there was a large herd of swine feeding nearby on the mountain. The demons implored Him, saying, 'Send us into the swine so that we may enter them'" (Mark 5:10–12). Remember, demons only fulfill their purpose when they are tormenting someone.

Jesus allowed the legion of demons to inhabit the pigs, and the pigs were driven to madness and self-destruction. In the meantime, the former madman was regaining his senses and his modesty. His problem was demonic, and only Jesus could do something about it.

The Commotion after the Cleansing

This scene caused quite a commotion. Those who were watching the pigs ran away and told everyone they met what had happened (Mark 5:14). So a crowd came out to see the excitement. They saw Jesus and "the man who had been demon-possessed sitting down, clothed and in his right mind, the very man who had had the 'legion'; and they became frightened" (v. 15).

When the authority of Christ moves into a situation, people are going to talk about what God is doing. The pig herders were certainly talking about it (vv. 14, 16), and the people from the city and the countryside must have been talking about it as they saw the former demon-possessed man sitting there completely healed.

Then they made the wrong decision, because they became afraid and asked Jesus to leave (v. 17). The man who had been healed and delivered wanted to follow Jesus, but Jesus sent him back to his own people to keep on talking about what God had done for him (vv. 18–20).

A STRATEGY FOR DRAWING ON JESUS' AUTHORITY

I want to reaffirm that Jesus' authority is the same today as it was two thousand years ago (see Hebrews 13:8).

But He also told His disciples, "I have given you authority . . . over all the power of the enemy, and nothing will injure you. Nevertheless do not rejoice in this, that the spirits are subject to you, but rejoice that your names are recorded in heaven" (Luke 10:19–20). Jesus was saying if you are going to get excited, get excited about what your salvation has done for you. Understand who you are in Christ, because it's in Christ that you find your authority. There are at least three things you need to know about your identity in Christ as it relates to the demonic realm.

Recall What Christ Has Done

First, you need to recall that Christ has completely and eternally smashed Satan and his realm on your behalf. Jesus made a very important statement about Satan's defeat in Luke 10:18. The seventy disciples He had sent out returned with testimonies of their power over demons in Jesus' name. Jesus responded: "I was watching Satan fall from heaven like lightning."

Of course, this was only a prelude to Satan's ultimate defeat at the cross. Through Jesus' death on the cross, God has "disarmed the rulers and authorities, [making] a public display of them, having triumphed over them through Him," that is, through Christ (Colossians 2:15). Even though Satan may still temporarily have an army, God has taken the bullets out of their weapons. Satan's government has no ultimate authority.

Peter said that Jesus is "at the right hand of God, having gone into heaven, after angels and authorities and powers had been subjected to Him" (1 Peter 3:22). Jesus' authority over demons did not end when He left the earth. He is still in total control from His place at the right hand of God.

The demons are still subject to Jesus. So the issue is not whether you have power over demons, but whether you know Jesus.

Resist the Devil

A second step in appropriating Christ's authority is to resist. James 4:7 is a familiar verse which says, "Submit therefore to God. Resist the devil and he will flee from you." This also applies to the Devil's underlings he may send to carry out his evil agenda.

Actually, what makes our resistance effective is our surrender to God. To submit to God is to reject compromise with the world, which lies in the control of the Evil One. We can stand against the Devil and his forces when we stand in the name and authority of Jesus Christ.

We do that by putting on the "full armor" of God as outlined in Ephesians 6:13–17. That includes the belt of truth, because the Devil is "the father of lies" (John 8:44); the helmet of salvation, because the Devil attacks us with doubt; and the sword of the Spirit, the Word of God. We need to wield the sword, because when Jesus speaks His authoritative Word, they have to go.

Rely on Jesus Christ

We must also depend on Christ to do in and through us what we could never do for ourselves. If God thought you could live the Christian life in your own power, He would not have sent the Holy Spirit to indwell you. You are indwelt by the Holy Spirit because you need a power bigger than anything you can muster yourself. You need Somebody who is experienced in spiritual warfare. The Holy Spirit is an experienced general in God's army. He has been fighting demons for eons. He knows how they move, when they move, and where they move.

So what you and I need is to be filled with the Spirit (Ephesians 5:18). We must give the Lord control of our lives and say, "Not my will, but Your will be done." That's what Jesus did, and it gave Him authority. When the Holy Spirit fills you, there is no place for demons to dwell.

APPLICATION FOR LIFE

1. Satan is the great deceiver. He is a master at twisting and counterfeiting the truth. He tried that tactic on Jesus. Be assured that Satan knows the Bible and is eager to introduce substitute "truth" into your thinking. Give him no room to operate. Be a student of God's Word and let His truth permeate your heart and mind. Here's a good exercise: Memorize a new portion of Scripture each week.

2. Our Lord used a very powerful strategy for resisting the temptations of the Devil. He countered Satan's temptations with Scripture. Jesus quoted the Old Testament Scriptures. Today, we have an entire Bible to learn and memorize. Hebrews 4:12 tells us that it is "sharper than any two-edged sword." When dealing with the Devil, be prepared to wield it like a sword.

3. Did you know that you have authority over Satan? When Jesus exercised His absolute authority to command Satan to leave, the Devil had to flee. According to James 4:7, Jesus has delegated to us that same authority. The next time the Devil tempts you, resist him on the basis of Jesus' absolute authority, and he will flee.

4. One of the steps in appropriating Christ's authority is to resist the Devil. This applies not only to Satan, but to any of his demons who do his bidding. When we stand against the Devil, we must do it in the authority of Christ by putting on the "full armor of God" (Ephesians 6:13–17).

FOR GROUP STUDY

Questions for Group Discussion

1. Read Matthew 4:1–3. What did Jesus do to prepare for His battle with temptation? How can we today prepare ourselves for the temptation that comes from the Devil?

2. Read the entire account, Matthew 4:1–11. For each of the three attacks, what was Satan's point of attack? What was Jesus' response to each attack? What truths can we learn from these attacks and apply to our lives?

3. What was the outcome of the great battle for authority between Jesus and Satan? Describe the aftermath. Why is James 4:7 a powerful passage for us?

4. Mark 5:1–20 is an illustrative chapter for our discussion, as it is an account of Jesus' authority over demons. From this account, what facts do we learn about Jesus' authority over demons?

PICTURE THIS

As believers, we face Satan and an organized army of demons who plot to deceive us and thwart the will of God for our lives. We need a strategy for winning the battle. The following strategy will ensure our victory.

Our Strategy for Drawing on Christ's Authority

STRATAGEM	SCRIPTURE PASSAGES	WHY IT WORKS
Recall what Christ has done.	Colossians 2:15; 1 Peter 3:22	Christ has already defeated Satan on our behalf.
Resist the Devil.	James 4:7	We can stand successfully against the Devil and his forces when we do so in the name and authority of Christ.
Rely on Christ.	Ephesians 5:18	Because of our human limitations, we must depend on Christ to do what we cannot do ourselves.

24

THE AUTHORITY OF CHRIST OVER DISEASE

Probably no area of Jesus Christ's authority is more discussed, debated, and disagreed about than the issue of Christ's authority over disease and how God intends that authority to be exercised in this age.

The disagreement isn't about whether Christ does or does not have authority over the diseases and deformities that ravage the human body. The Bible proves unmistakably that Jesus Christ has absolute control over the problem of disease.

The controversy is over whether God intended for every disease and illness to be miraculously healed by the power of Christ, or whether God sometimes allows and uses disease for His greater purposes in the lives of His children.

Two extremes operate here—both of which are a misrepresentation of what the Bible teaches. One is the extreme that *demands* healing from God for every sickness because all disease is from the Enemy and never part of God's will for believers. It seems that God can't make any decisions for Himself because He is controlled by what we want.

In reacting to this extreme, other believers wind up putting God in a box and restricting His power in such a way that He can't do anything about physical illness. It's all up to the doctors.

As with most extremes, the truth lies somewhere in between. What I want to do is try to let the Bible speak for itself as we go to Matthew 8:1–17, a passage in which Jesus healed three people in quick succession. I want to extract five key principles that will help us understand the authority of Christ over disease.

CHRIST'S AUTHORITY IS SOVEREIGN

The first principle Matthew 8 reveals is that Christ's authority over disease is exercised by His sovereign choice. The scene for these three healings is set in verse 1. Jesus had finished the Sermon on the Mount and was coming down from the mountain. Multitudes of people met Jesus at the foot of the mountain because He had developed quite a reputation.

Verse 2 says, "A leper came to Him, and bowed down to Him, saying, 'Lord, if You are willing, You can make me clean.'" Leprosy was such a feared disease in biblical days that a leper had to live apart from people. A leper was defiled from the standpoint of the Mosaic Law (Leviticus 13:44).

An Appeal to Sovereignty

This man was desperate for help. The leper may not have known the theological concept of *sovereignty*, but his appeal recognized that Jesus was the person with ultimate authority in his case. God's sovereignty means His freedom to act for His own purposes and glory. Jesus Christ has the right to choose what He will and will not do. None of us can presume on Him.

This flies in the face of a current theology that says, "God must heal, and if God does not heal you, the problem is you don't have enough faith." This view presumes on God. It puts man in the position of sovereignty and makes God our servant who is bound to carry out our demands.

Many times it is within the Lord's sovereign purpose to heal. The people in Matthew 8 all experienced healing. But it was by Jesus' choice and His initiative, not theirs or anyone else's.

It's very important that we understand God's sovereignty because, as you know, He does not always choose to do what we want Him to do.

The Part That Faith Plays

Luke says the man who came to Jesus was "covered with leprosy" (Luke 5:12). That's worth noting because it suggests his faith in Jesus was strong. When we say that Jesus' authority over disease is exercised sovereignly rather than on the basis of our faith or lack of it, this doesn't mean that faith plays no part in the process.

God still responds to our faith, just as Jesus responded to this man's request. But we can't make the mistake of saying that faith becomes the way we maneuver God into doing what we demand of Him.

Jesus exercised His authority immediately and comprehensively in healing this leper. "He stretched out His hand and touched him, saying, 'I am willing; be cleansed.' And immediately his leprosy was cleansed" (Matthew 8:3). There were no intermediaries, no delay, and no material used.

This is just one of the ways Jesus healed people. Once Jesus used saliva to heal a blind man, and He healed him progressively (Mark 8:22–26). Another time Jesus used clay, which the blind man had to wash off (John 9:6–7).

The point is that God may intervene directly or progressively, through full, instantaneous healing or through doctors and medication over a period of time. But in all cases, it is the authority of Christ that pulls off the healing.

CHRIST'S AUTHORITY IS POSITIONAL

The second principle we can learn from the healings in Matthew 8 is Christ's authority arises from His position. In Capernaum Jesus was approached by a centurion, a Roman commander, who said "Lord, my servant is lying paralyzed at home, fearfully tormented" (v. 5).

Jesus offered to come and heal the servant, but the man replied, "Lord, I am not worthy for You to come under my roof, but just say the word, and my servant will be healed" (v. 8)

Jesus' Position of Authority

This man paid high tribute to Jesus because he understood authority. He knew that when a person is in a position of authority, that person's presence is not necessary for his commands to be carried out. The people under him just need to know who gave the command.

This soldier was telling Jesus, "I know what it's like to be under authority and to have authority over others. And if I as a mere man can make things happen just by saying the word, I know You can do it by Your word. So if You will just speak from Your position of total authority, You can heal my servant."

Jesus Christ has authority over disease by means of His supreme position as Creator and Sustainer of the universe. He can simply speak away an illness or disease because He created the heavens and the earth (John 1:3; Colossians 1:16) and because the whole creation is held together by His power (Colossians 1:17).

So Jesus has total authority over any environment that can cause sickness, and He has authority over our bodies because He also created us. Christ's position of authority is such that He did not need to be present to heal the centurion's servant. All He had to do was speak the word.

Knowing Someone in the "Corporate Office"

One time I was in Miami, and my business there finished a lot earlier than expected, so I wanted to leave and return to my family. Another airline had a flight leaving two or three hours earlier than the flight on my airline, but I couldn't take the earlier flight because the ticket I had would not transfer between the airlines. The airline I was on said they couldn't transfer the ticket, and the airline I wanted to get on said I would have to buy a new ticket.

But then I remembered something. I knew somebody back in Dallas in the corporate office of the airline I was trying to fly home. So I picked up the phone and placed a call. I said, "I've got to get home. I don't want to wait around here three hours for the next flight. Can you help me?"

My problem was in Miami, but the person in Dallas was in a position of authority. It was all about position. This friend picked up the phone and dialed the airline ticket counter in Miami and said, "We have got somebody at the airport there who needs to be on your next flight. He doesn't have a ticket, but put him on the plane based on my word."

My friend did not have to be in Miami to help me. That position of authority within the airline solved my problem.

Let me tell you, when you know Christ, you know Somebody in the corporate office! You know Someone who is in heavenly places, but who has access to where you are. All Jesus has to do is speak the word, and your impossible situation becomes possible.

CHRIST'S AUTHORITY IS IMPARTIAL

After this Roman commander made his insightful statement about authority, the Bible says:

> Now when Jesus heard this, He marveled, and said to those who were following, "Truly I say to you, I have not found such great faith with anyone in Israel. And I say to you, that many shall come from east and west, and recline at the table with Abraham, and Isaac, and Jacob in the kingdom of heaven; but the sons of the kingdom shall be cast out into the outer darkness; in that place there shall be weeping and gnashing of teeth." (Matthew 8:10–12)

Jesus was saying that His authority is available to anyone in any place who exercises faith in Him. At this point in Jesus' ministry, He was ministering to the lost sheep of the house of Israel. The mission to the Gentiles had not yet begun in earnest, but incidents like this gave a sneak preview of what was to come.

Jesus marveled at the centurion's faith. No wonder. Remember that Jesus' own disciples had such little faith that they shook Him awake in the boat for fear they were going to die. But here was a Gentile saying, "Just say the word, and my servant will be healed."

So Jesus took this occasion to remind His Jewish hearers that in His coming kingdom, there would be many people at the banquet table from "east and west," from all corners of the earth.

Here's another principle about Jesus' authority over disease: He has come to deliver everyone who has faith in Him. He is impartial. The centurion was a Gentile who was not part of the covenant community of Israel. But he understood and believed in Jesus' authority, and his servant was miraculously healed.

CHRIST'S AUTHORITY IS POWERFUL

Fourth, Christ's authority displays His power. Jesus sent the centurion on his way and then went to Peter's house, where Peter's mother-in-law was sick with a fever. The Bible says Jesus "touched her hand, and the fever left her; and she arose, and waited on Him" (Matthew 8:15).

The power of Jesus' authority is seen in what happened after Peter's mother-in-law was healed. Usually, if you are down with a fever and you get better, you are left feeling weak. But after Jesus healed this woman of her fever, she immediately got up and was able to serve her special guest. Her healing was complete.

It doesn't matter what method Jesus used, the result was the same. Here He touched the sick person without saying anything. He touched and spoke to the leper but didn't see or speak to the sick servant He healed. The power of Christ's authority operates under any circumstances. It is not diminished by the severity of the disease or the greatness of the distance.

CHRIST'S AUTHORITY IS PROPHETIC

The fifth and final principle I want to talk about is more complicated than the others, so we need to address it more fully. It is a very important principle to understand if we are going to have a fully developed view of Jesus' authority over disease.

The setting is still Capernaum, the evening of the day that Jesus healed Peter's mother-in-law:

> When evening had come, they brought to Him many who were demon-possessed; and He cast out the spirits with a word, and healed all who were ill. This was to fulfill what was spoken through Isaiah the prophet: "He Himself took our infirmities and carried away our diseases." (Matthew 8:16–17)

Matthew quoted the prophecy of Isaiah 53:4 to explain what was happening that evening in Capernaum. Isaiah 53 is one of the prophet's Servant Songs, prophecies about the ministry and sacrificial death of the Messiah.

Prophecy Fulfilled in Jesus

These prophecies were fulfilled in the ministry of Jesus Christ, who is God's Messiah. In Isaiah 53:5, the prophet went on to say of the Messiah, "By His scourging we are healed."

Some people believe this verse teaches that in His substitutionary death on the cross, Jesus not only paid for and conquered sin, but took all our sicknesses on Himself so that no believer ever has to be sick anymore. Some also say that all you have to do is command your healing, because Christ purchased your healing on the cross.

It's true that Jesus' death is the basis on which someday all sickness and disease will be banned forever. The accomplishments of Christ's death were so comprehensive that they are the foundation upon which both your spiritual and your physical well-being rest. That's why John could write, "I pray that in all respects you may prosper and be in good health, just as your soul prospers" (3 John 2). The two areas are intricately related for the believer.

But the full realization of Christ's authoritative defeat of disease will come in His glorious kingdom. So I believe a better understanding of this passage is that Jesus' earthly healing ministry was a foretaste of the kingdom, when the full glories of all that His suffering purchased for us will be realized.

But whatever your view of the way Jesus' death has dealt with physical disease, the point is the same we have been making all along. That is, the power for healing can be found only in the person and the authority of Jesus Christ.

The Application of the Prophecy

Here's where it gets interesting and a little complicated. Jesus not only gave the people of His day a foretaste of this aspect of His kingdom, but He also has given us a foretaste too. The question with this quotation from Isaiah 53 is not whether it is true, but how we are to apply it.

Should we seek out so-called faith healers who can draw on the healing authority of Jesus' suffering as they touch us and make all our diseases go away? Should we go over to Israel and bathe in the Jordan River? What is the process today by which we can experience a foretaste of the blessing of healing that Jesus purchased in His death on the cross?

For the answer to that question, we need to leave Matthew 8 and spend the rest of our time in James 5:13–16, a powerful and controversial passage on healing that directs sick believers to Christ's body, the church.

The Sick Person's Responsibility

James begins with several questions:

> Is anyone among you suffering? Then he must pray. Is anyone cheerful? He is to sing praises. Is anyone among you sick? Then he must call for the elders of the church, and they are to pray over him, anointing him with oil in the name of the Lord. (James 5:13–14)

The Greek word *sick* here means "weak." This word could cover any of the different kinds of weaknesses, whether physical or psychological or emotional or spiritual.

James directs the sick or weak person to the elders of the church. If you are ill, you can go to Christ in prayer, but you cannot go to Christ physically. However, you *can* go to the church physically by calling for the elders.

The sick person must take the initiative, which shows that he or she really wants God to intervene in his or her situation. It's a demonstration of faith, the way the centurion sought out Jesus.

The Meaning of the Anointing

The elders are to "pray over [the sick one], anointing him with oil in the name of the Lord" (James 5:14). This was not oil as we normally think of it, but the oil used in biblical times for grooming and soothing of the body.

For example, Jesus told us to anoint ourselves when we fast so we won't appear to be fasting (Matthew 6:17). In other words, groom yourself with oil so you look good. Oil also had a medicinal use, as when the Good Samaritan poured oil on the wounds of the man lying by the side of the road (Luke 10:34).

In general, then, oil was used for refreshment and restoration. This is what the anointing of James 5 is referring to. The elders were to anoint the sick or weak person with oil as a symbol of the refreshment and restoration that God would bring into the person's life in fulfillment of the following promise: "And the prayer offered in faith will restore the one who is sick, and the Lord will raise him up" (v. 15).

The Promise of the Anointing

This verse is usually taught as promising full physical healing to anyone who follows the procedure. That interpretation is problematic for two reasons. First, it is obvious that not everyone who is anointed and prayed for is healed, and second, the focus of the verse is wider than just healing.

If an illness is the direct result of sin, and if the sin is confessed and removed, then the sick person can expect to be restored to health. That's why James says, "If he has committed sins, they will be forgiven him. Therefore, confess your sins to one another, and pray for one another, so that you may be healed" (James 5:15b–16).

But what about believers who are physically sick, or weak and weary in some other way, such as emotionally or spiritually? The promise is that if they will call for the elders and allow these representatives of Jesus to minister to them, they will be restored.

Why the anointing with oil by the elders? Because they are the formal representatives of the church, and it is the church's job to act on Christ's behalf. The anointing communicates the same kind of human presence and caring touch Jesus gave to people when He was here among us. The presence of the elders means the local church is there to help.

Jesus is no longer present with us physically, but His servants are. And when you're sick or weary, you need somebody you can touch. You need somebody who can relate to you face-to-face, person to person.

The elders may not be the means of your healing, but they can make sure the church brings you the restoration and refreshment that Jesus has for you. He wants you to feel His encouraging, grooming touch.

The anointing and prayer are a way of showing the same kind of immediate, personal concern that Jesus would show for a sick believer if He were here physically. And if healing results, praise God.

But let me emphasize again that James 5 is not saying that everyone will be healed. But it does promise that everyone will be restored, for the church is God's community of restoration.

Restoration and being free of a disease aren't necessarily the same thing. As an illustration of this, I would point you to Isaiah 40:31, which says, "Those who wait for the Lord will gain new strength; they will mount up with wings like eagles, they will run and not get tired, they will walk and not become weary."

Some people whom the Lord has touched will be like eagles. They will get well. They will soar out of their sickbed. Others may not soar, but they will be able to run. And still others will be able to walk—not quite like flying or running, but still a restoration.

When Matthew said that Jesus fulfilled prophecy by exercising His authority over disease, he was looking ahead to the complete application of that authority in the kingdom. But God gave the people in Jesus' day, and has given us today, a preview of Jesus' complete victory over disease.

ACCESSING JESUS' AUTHORITY

Jesus' authority is accessed by prayer, as seen in the pleas of the leper and the centurion (Matthew 8:2, 5–6).

This prayer is accompanied by an attitude of humility. The leper bowed before Jesus. The centurion came humbly, realizing that as a Gentile he had no claim on Jesus' time. He threw himself completely on God's will.

Access to Jesus' authority over disease must also be accompanied by active faith. God responds to faith. But it's not the amount of our faith, it's the focus of our faith that makes the difference.

Jesus' authority over disease is complete—and someday, it will be fully manifest in our bodies.

APPLICATION FOR LIFE

1. If you have ever had surgery, you know how much faith you placed in your surgeon. You want that professional to exercise any and all skills to perform the operation properly. Too often we tend to restrict God's power to meet our needs by placing Him in a sort of box. Let God have full reign in meeting your physical needs in the way He sees fit. Claim the promise of Ephesians 3:20 regarding He "who is able to do far more abundantly beyond all that we ask or think, according to the power that works within us."

2. God is sovereign and will heal according to His determination and purpose. The Bible teaches that we may access Christ's authority over disease. Humbly approach God in prayer, exercising your faith in Christ's sovereign will. Leave the final decision up to Him.

3. Ultimately, it is Christ's authority over disease that effects its healing. But keep in mind that God responds to our faith. He marveled at the Roman centurion's faith in Matthew 8. Although we can never maneuver God into doing something, He may decide that healing your illness has a purpose for bringing glory to Himself. Your faith could play a part in God's working His plan.

4. Have you ever wondered why God allows illness? Certainly, He could immediately rid the world of illness. The apostle John wrote that the blind man in John 9:2–3 was not blind because of sin. Rather, he was blind so "that the works of God might be displayed in him" (v. 3). Most of us will, at some point in our lives, live with some sort of physical impairment. Be encouraged that God gives us grace to endure such things as we grow in His grace. Also be encouraged that God can use your illness or its healing to bring glory to His name.

FOR GROUP STUDY

Questions for Group Discussion

1. What are the two extremes in thinking about God's power to heal physical illness and disease? Dr. Evans outlines five key principles related to Christ's authority over disease (see "Picture This" for summary). Which principle(s) are good reminders to you?

2. Read Mathew 8:15. What do we learn about Jesus' power when it comes to healing? How should the healings in this passage shape our thinking about Jesus' power to heal?

3. What is the significance of Jesus' healings and Old Testament prophecy? (See Isaiah 53:4–5.) Why is James 5:13–16 important to this discussion? What is the *anointing*, and why is it important?

4. We can access Jesus' authority over disease today. Read Matthew 8:2, 5–6; 2 Corinthians 12:9. From those passages, what do we learn about accessing Jesus' authority?

PICTURE THIS

The following five principles, drawn from Matthew 8, can aid in our understating of Jesus' authority over illness and disease.

KEY PRINCIPLES REGARDING CHRIST'S AUTHORITY TO HEAL
Matthew 8:1-17

PRINCIPLE	SCRIPTURE PASSAGES	WHAT IT MEANS
His authority is sovereign.	Matthew 8:3; John 9:6–7	Jesus heals according to His own purposes and glory.
His authority is positional.	Matthew 8:5–9; Colossians 1:16–17	Jesus has power to heal because of His position as Creator and Sustainer of the universe.
His authority is impartial.	Matthew 8:10–12	Jesus healed Jews and Gentiles alike.
His authority is powerful.	Matthew 8:14–15; Luke 4:38–39	Because of His authority over disease, Jesus could heal by His touch or His word.
His authority is prophetic.	Matthew 8:16–17; Isaiah 53	Jesus' earthly ministry fulfilled Old Testament prophecies about His authority to heal.

25

THE AUTHORITY OF CHRIST OVER SIN

A classic story in the gospel of Mark provides us with an in-depth understanding of the authority Jesus Christ wields over sin and its consequences.

The incident is found in Mark 2:1–12. It is a well-known story because of the unusual way the paralyzed man was brought to Jesus for healing. We included this account in the earlier discussion of Christ's authority over disease, since this man definitely had a serious physical problem.

This encounter came fairly early in Jesus' ministry. He was gaining a lot of attention, so when He came back to His headquarters in Capernaum, a huge crowd gathered (Mark 2:1–2).

Israel's religious leaders were also taking notice of this rabbi from Nazareth, and Jesus was demonstrating His authority. In fact, according to Mark 1, Jesus had already shown His power over demons and disease. The case of the paralyzed man gave Him an opportunity to demonstrate His authority to forgive sins.

THE NEED FOR CHRIST'S AUTHORITY

The man who was carried to Jesus that day definitely needed a physical touch. He was unable to walk, being carried on a pallet or stretcher by four friends (Mark 2:3).

The house in which Jesus was teaching was so packed with people that the four men had to take their sick friend up to the roof, dig a hole, and let him down through the roof (v. 4).

This is the part of the story most people remember, but we don't need to linger here. If you have ever seen drawings of houses in biblical days, you know that the roofs were flat. Because it was hot and the houses were small, the roof was used as a gathering place for family and guests. Usually an outside staircase on one wall led to the roof, so it was easy for these men to carry their friend to the roof.

The important thing is what happened when this man was lowered down to Jesus: "And Jesus seeing their faith said to the paralytic, 'Son, your sins are forgiven'" (v. 5).

The Pervasive Presence of Sin

It's obvious that Jesus had a bigger agenda than the rest of the people in this story. He dealt with the crippled man's soul before dealing with his useless legs. By pardoning the man's sins, Jesus put His authority on the line right up front.

Forgiveness did not seem to be this man's pressing need at the moment. But Jesus addressed his sins to underscore the fact that sin is at the root of all our problems, whether physical, emotional, environmental, or spiritual.

In fact, if Jesus had healed this man without addressing his spiritual need, this would have simply been a miraculous event whose deeper meaning would have been lost on the people watching and listening. Besides, Jesus did not want to leave the people He met in their sins without doing something about it.

Don't misunderstand. We are not saying this man's paralysis was the *direct* result of his own sins. But we can say that sin is at the root of all human suffering. Before Adam and Eve sinned, they had no problems. And when we are ushered into heaven where no sin is allowed, we will be free of all pain and suffering.

But between Eden and heaven, we have nothing but problems because this world is under the curse of sin. The first tree that Adam ate from messed us up. The second tree that Jesus Christ died on fixed us up. And in heaven there will be a third tree, the tree of life (Revelation 22:2) that will keep us fixed up.

When you get your trees straight, you understand how badly sin has infected the human race and what it takes to remove it. Sin is pervasive; it's everywhere, especially in the human heart.

The Fallout of Sin

Like radiation from a nuclear blast, sin generates fallout that continues to spread contamination long after the initial explosion.

Sin's fallout can reach across generations. I can't tell you the number of people I have talked to over the years who were abused as children by relatives or someone else, and who are still battling the spiritual or emotional paralysis caused by someone else's sin.

Sin not only pollutes individual lives; it can infect whole nations. "[If] My people who are called by My name humble themselves and pray and seek My face and turn from their wicked ways, then I will . . . heal their land" (2 Chronicles 7:14).

The connection between sin and sickness is also evident in Scripture. During the year or so that David hid his sin with Bathsheba, he suffered terrible physical effects. His body "wasted away." He groaned "all day long" (Psalm 32:3).

In Psalm 103:3 David praised the Lord as the One "who pardons all your iniquities; who heals all your diseases." Sin's fallout often affects our physical bodies, and if we only seek physical healing, we may miss the ultimate solution.

Treating Sin as Sinful

But instead of admitting sin and seeking a solution, our world tries to deny and ignore sin. Sin is not a popular topic today. We have substituted other terms. People make mistakes. They show bad judgment. They have a problem. Liars are merely withholding part of their testimony. Adulterers have affairs, or even worse, just relationships.

But when we refuse to call sin what it is, we forfeit the chance to deal with the real problem. Jesus' words to the paralytic in Mark 2, "My son, your sins are forgiven," seem to make a connection between the man's condition and his sin. We can't say for sure.

Some people are paralyzed physically because of sinful decisions they have made and sinful activity they have engaged in. Others are paralyzed emotionally because of sinful behavior patterns they have established.

But no matter what the consequences of a particular sin, Jesus always treated sin as something very serious. From His perspective, it was more important for this man to be forgiven than it was for him to be healed.

THE ACTIVATION OF CHRIST'S AUTHORITY

Jesus Christ's authority over sin was needed in that house in Capernaum. It was activated by the faith of the paralytic and the four friends who brought him.

Verse 5 says Jesus responded when He saw the faith of the sick man and his four friends. But it was their faith, not their demand, that moved Him.

Notice that Jesus *saw* their faith in action when a hole opened in the roof and this pallet came floating down. A lot of us have a good faith "rap." We say, "I'm trusting the Lord. I'm believing in God." But when it comes time to tear a hole in the roof, we back off.

The Importance of Cooperative Faith

At the heart of these men's faith was their decision to come to Jesus. The sick man said to his friends, "Take me to Jesus. He can help me." And they agreed to take him. The man was hanging around people who believed as he believed. These men exercised cooperative faith, and they tapped into Jesus' authority.

When you have been weakened in your faith, what you need are other folks who know where Jesus is and can help you get to Him. Some people say, "But I'm so weak." That's an unacceptable excuse if there are other strong people around. That's why we need the body of Christ. Paul called it "bear[ing] one another's burdens" (Galatians 6:2). We need to come alongside each other so we can help each other get to Jesus.

The Importance of Determined Faith

This paralyzed man and his friends also had determined faith. They said, "We are going to do whatever it takes to get you to Jesus." They did not let a room full of people stop them.

We need faith that isn't easily stopped. We need to be like Jacob, who wrestled with an angel all night and hung on, saying, "I will not let you go unless you bless me" (Genesis 32:26).

That sounds great, but you are not going to be determined in your faith unless you understand that Jesus Christ has authority over your problem. This paralyzed man and his pals realized that the solution to his physical need was in that house. What they got for their determination was the solution of his greater problem as well.

THE IMPLICATIONS OF CHRIST'S AUTHORITY

Beginning with Mark 2:6 we get to the deeper issue Jesus had in mind here. By pronouncing the paralyzed man's sins forgiven, Jesus was making a deliberate statement of His deity. And He knew the response this was going to bring from the scribes sitting before Him.

Jesus Claims to Be God

"But some of the scribes were sitting there and reasoning in their hearts, 'Why does this man speak that way? He is blaspheming; who can forgive sins but God alone?'" (Mark 2:6–7).

Give these men credit; they understood completely the implication of what Jesus Christ had just said. They knew that by claiming the authority of God to forgive sins, Jesus was claiming to *be* God. The scribes were correct in saying that only God can forgive sin. And they were correct in reasoning that for a mere man to make this claim was blasphemy against God—a capital offense in Israel (Leviticus 24:16).

All this reasoning was going on in the minds of these scribes, but they didn't say anything. So Jesus demonstrated that He was God by telling them He knew what they were thinking (Mark 2:8). Then He offered them further, irrefutable proof of His divine authority and power.

Since no one can see a person's sins being forgiven, Jesus knew the scribes didn't believe Him. So He said, "Which is easier, to say to the paralytic, 'Your sins are forgiven'; or to say, 'Get up, and pick up your pallet and walk'? But so that you may know that the Son of Man has authority on earth to forgive sins'—He said to the paralytic, 'I say to you, get up, pick up your pallet and go home'" (vv. 9–11).

Jesus' point was that for God neither the forgiveness of sins nor a miraculous healing is hard to pull off. So He did the latter to prove the validity of the former. Jesus was saying, "If I can heal this man's disease, I can also forgive his sins, because both are coming from the same authority."

Jesus Is Able to Restore

In response to Jesus' authoritative command, the crippled man got up, folded up his pallet, and walked out in full view of everyone (Mark 2:12).

This is good news. Because Jesus can deal with the root of our problem, He can also deal with the symptoms.

Many people are going through pain in their lives that finds its root in sin at some level. Because Jesus is the only one who can forgive sin, He is the one we need to get serious with when the symptoms show up.

The scribes didn't come to that house in Capernaum because they had heard that Jesus could deal with the root problem of sin. They came, like their buddies the Pharisees, to see Jesus perform a miracle or two. They wanted to see the show. If they had been serious about fixing their problem, they would have come to Jesus to be forgiven too.

Notice a key word Jesus used here. "Which is easier to *say*?" (v. 9, italics added). Because of who Jesus is, it doesn't matter whether the issue is the ability to forgive sins or the ability to bring about a physical healing.

Jesus can restore us internally and externally with just a word. The scribes were thinking, *It's easy for this man to say He can forgive sins. Anyone can say that. But only God can do it.*

But Jesus countered their reasoning by telling them it was just as easy for Him to produce a verifiable result, healing, with the same word of authority. In fact, Jesus put the issue to them point-blank. If He could heal this man with a word of authority, then the scribes would have to admit that His authority to forgive sins was real too.

Jesus then turned around and healed the sick man. We aren't told what the scribes thought, but the people loved it (v. 12).

THE RESULTS OF CHRIST'S AUTHORITY

What was the result of this exercise of Jesus' authority over sin? The man received two great things: a new relationship with God and strength for living.

A New Relationship with God

The paralyzed man received his healing. "And he got up and immediately picked up the pallet and went out in the sight of everyone" (Mark 2:12). That was wonderful. Thanks to Jesus' authority over disease, this man was cured.

But we are talking about Jesus' authority over sin. What this man received in addition to new legs was a new relationship with God. He was saved. His sins were forgiven. He became a child of God.

When Jesus addressed the man, He called him "son" (v. 5). The man not only got up and walked physically, but Jesus raised him up from the paralysis of sin.

God is free to release you from your paralysis when there is no more cause for judgment. If sin has judged you and paralyzed you, and then that sin is removed because you are forgiven, you have no reason to lie around in your sin. God calls you His son or daughter. You are family now. You are free from the crushing burden of sin.

If I recall correctly, I have only intentionally stolen one thing in my life. It happened when I was in the eighth grade. They had those wonderful creations called sticky rolls in our cafeteria in Baltimore. Those things were good!

I didn't have any money that day and the rolls were warm and dripping. So I looked this way and that way, and when I thought no one was looking I helped myself to a sticky roll.

But lo and behold, one of the cafeteria ladies came over and confronted me by saying, "I saw what you just did."

I will never forget the terror that engulfed me. I was petrified. She sat me down and proceeded to give me a lesson on theft and its consequences. She explained how stealing a sticky roll will lead to stealing money, stealing money will lead to robbing banks, and robbing banks will land a person in jail. And if you happen to rob a bank and shoot someone, you could get the death penalty.

This dear, caring woman had me in the grave over a sticky roll! She scared me to death. But then she took that roll out of my hand and said, "I'm going to take this and put it back, and we are going to forget that this ever happened."

I will never forget the feeling of relief that came over me when that woman forgave me. Once she had dealt with the root problem, my dishonesty, she was free to relieve the symptom, the trouble I was in for stealing the roll.

When God forgives you and you come into relationship with Him, He takes your sins from you "as far as the east is from the west" (Psalm 103:12). You will never meet them again.

New Strength for Living

Jesus told the man to get up, pick up his bed, and walk out of the house. The man couldn't get up until he had been healed. But he didn't know he had been healed until he obeyed Jesus, got up, and started walking.

Only Jesus can forgive and heal, but you must do the getting up and walking. Jesus didn't go over and lift this man off the pallet and help him out the door. Once Jesus has dealt with your problem, you must take responsibility for acting on what He's done. Once He has come in and taken care of the cause, you must move and claim the results.

Jesus healed this man to demonstrate His authority (Mark 2:10). That doesn't mean He didn't care about the man's condition and want to help him. That goes without saying. But the larger purpose of God in this healing was to show forth the identity and power and glory of His Son.

The people who saw the miracle got the idea, because Mark says they glorified God (2:12). They said, "We have never seen anything like this," which really means, "We have never seen Anyone like Jesus."

PERSONAL APPLICATION FOR LIFE

1. If you are suffering form the environment of sin—meaning simply the reality of the world in which we live—you can pray, "Lord, I believe You have power over the Evil One, and I commit myself to Your care and protection."

2. What paralysis has sin caused in your life? Sin may be causing you emotional, financial, moral, or some other kind of trauma. If the sin is yours and you can do something about it, get on the roof and start digging until you see Jesus. Forsake and confess your sin by claiming 1 John 1:9.

3. Sometimes the sin that is hurting you is not one you committed. If someone else's sin is hurting you in a way you have no control over, take that sin to Jesus Christ, forgive the sinner, and pray, "Lord, help me to get past this sin. Move me forward." God will provide you the strength and grace to do just that.

4. Whatever way you need to deal with sin, if you bring it to Jesus, He will release you from it. He may not always take away all the symptoms of that sin, but many times He will. We have all seen God take care of financial concerns, grant a miraculous healing, or lift the stress and put our minds at ease. He is still in the restoring business!

FOR GROUP STUDY

Questions for Group Discussion

1. What are some of the consequences of sin in the life of a believer? One of the greatest verses in all the Bible, and certainly one of the most often applied by believers, is 1 John 1:9. Read this verse as a group. What condition must we meet in dealing with sin in our lives? What promises from God can we claim?

2. When Jesus exercised His authority in the case of the paralytic in Mark 2, what activated His use of authority?

3. Dr. Evans mentioned *cooperative* faith and *determined* faith. What is unique about each? How does each play a part in activating Christ's authority?

4. When Jesus exercises His authority, results occur. What happens when He uses His authority on our sin?

PICTURE THIS

Sin has so permeated our world that we need Christ's authority to overcome sin's presence and control in our lives. Dr. Evans has outlined three reasons we need Christ's authority over sin.

THE NEED FOR CHRIST'S AUTHORITY OVER SIN
Mark 2:1–12

REASON	WHAT HIS AUTHORITY ACCOMPLISHES
The pervasive presence of sin	Christ's authority addresses spiritual need, not simply the physical consequences.
The fallout of sin	Christ's authority stops the spread of sin and its widespread fallout.
The need to treat sin as sinful	Christ's authority treats sin for what it is and gets to the root of the problem.

26

THE AUTHORITY OF CHRIST OVER CIRCUMSTANCES

Our study in this chapter centers on the only miracle of Jesus Christ that is recorded in all four Gospels: the feeding of the so-called five thousand. Actually, it was probably closer to fifteen thousand or twenty thousand people when the families were added in, because Mark 6:44 says the men alone numbered five thousand, and Matthew 14:21 says there were women and children besides.

This miracle came about two years into Jesus' ministry, when popular excitement over Him had reached a fever pitch. Messianic excitement was also at a fever pitch at this time, so when Jesus came doing miraculous things, the people began to flock to Him. They liked what they saw. But it was the goodies they were after, not the message Jesus came to deliver. As it turned out, they didn't want Him as their Messiah, their Lord, on His terms.

CHRIST EMPATHIZES WITH OUR NEEDS

The events leading up to this miracle are important not only because they set the context, but because of what they reveal about the heart of Jesus Christ.

Jesus' Compassion

The twelve disciples had just returned from the ministry trip Jesus sent them on (Mark 6:7–13). They were telling Him all they had done, but the crowds were so great they couldn't get any time alone. So they tried to get away in a boat:

> [But] the people saw them going, and many recognized them and ran there together on foot from all the cities, and got there ahead of them. When Jesus went ashore, He saw a large crowd, and He felt compassion for them because they were like sheep without a shepherd; and He began to teach them many things. (Mark 6:33–34)

Jesus saw all these spiritually lost and needy people coming to Him, many no doubt with crippled and broken bodies, and His heart went out to them. What a picture of Jesus Christ! He is not only a person of power, but He is a person of infinite compassion.

The Bible says Jesus had compassion on this huge crowd because the people "were like sheep without a shepherd." They were groping for direction. As we know, sheep left to themselves without a shepherd can stray away and get lost very easily, and they are totally defenseless against predators.

Things haven't changed much in two thousand years, have they? People today still don't know how to make the right choices. They are spiritually defenseless and directionless without Christ, vulnerable to the lures and attacks of the Enemy.

Jesus' Leadership

The job of the shepherd is to lead his sheep to safe pasture and then protect them. We often don't know which way to go and what decisions to make, but Jesus knows we are helpless and He leads us as our Great Shepherd. And He can lead us with authority, because no circumstance can thwart His word. Because Jesus Christ is man, He feels what we feel. Because He is God, He can do something about it.

That's why the old people could talk about Jesus as a lawyer in a courtroom, a doctor in a sickroom, a father to the fatherless, and a mother to the motherless. To the sick He was a balm in Gilead, to those who needed encouragement He was the Rose of Sharon, and to those who needed guidance He was the Bright and Morning Star.

The feeding of the five thousand makes clear that Jesus is Lord over any circumstance. Our need is to come to Him as our "merciful and faithful high priest" in our time of need (Hebrews 2:17; see 4:14–16).

CHRIST ACTS TO MEET OUR NEEDS

When you're facing a hungry crowd of fifteen to twenty thousand people, and it's getting close to dinnertime, you had better know where to turn for provisions. The disciples didn't know it yet, but Jesus was going to teach them that lesson. He had met the people's need for spiritual food by teaching them. Now He was going to meet their need for physical food.

The Disciples Identify the Need

As Jesus taught, the people gathered around Him, and as the day wore on, it became apparent to the disciples that something needed to be done if the crowd was going to make it home before it got too late.

So they came to Jesus and said, "The place is desolate and it is already quite late; send them away so that they may go into the surrounding countryside and villages and buy themselves something to eat" (Mark 6:35-36).

The disciples were basically saying, "Listen, Jesus, the markets will be closing pretty soon. Why don't You pronounce the benediction so these people can make it to a town before everything closes?"

Remember that the disciples and Jesus had been trying to get some time alone to rest. Jesus' men were tired and wanted to go home. Besides, they didn't have anything to feed a crowd that large.

Jesus Challenges the Disciples

So you can imagine the disciples' surprise at what happened next. "But He answered and said to them, 'You give them something to eat!' And they said to Him, 'Shall we go and spend two hundred denarii on bread and give them something to eat?'" (v. 37).

John's account tells us that that Philip and Andrew were the ones involved in this conversation with Jesus (John 6:5, 7–9). Jesus probably asked

Philip to take care of the situation because Philip was from Bethsaida (John 1:44), the closest town in that area. So Jesus asked a "homeboy" who knew the region better than anyone else. But Jesus knew Philip didn't have the money. This was a test (John 6:6).

The Disciples Take the Test

When Jesus asks a question, it is not to gain new information. When Jesus inquires of you, it is to test you.

Jesus was the one who could change water into wine and heal people. He was the one with supernatural power, yet He turned to Philip and asked, "What are we going to do?"

We can picture the look on Philip's face. It's the same look we would have if we were facing a seemingly impossible situation and, rather than Jesus meeting the need, He said to us, "What are you going to do?"

So Philip ran the numbers and panicked. A denarius was one day's wage for a laborer in that day. Two hundred denarii would have been about eight months' salary. Philip was saying, "You want to know how we are going to feed all these people? We can't. Pay attention now, Jesus. Let me get my calculator out here and show You something.

"Even if we had eight months' worth of wages, it wouldn't be enough for us to give everybody a few crumbs. Besides, we can't feed this crowd with crumbs. Some of these people are going to want a second helping. Jesus, we just don't have enough money in the budget to do this."

Philip was the logical one. "There's no way. This is impossible. It's too big. We can't afford it. Where are we going to find the money? Who are we going to get to do it?"

Most of us know someone like Philip—people who face the insurmountable circumstances of life and see only how it can't be done. People who bring out the bank statement and show you down to the denarius why it can't be done. People who can give you every reason in the world why they can't get victory over their circumstance and why their case is unsolvable. That's Philip.

The Disciples Search for a Solution

Standing next to Philip was Andrew, Peter's brother. Andrew was a little more optimistic than "It can't be done" Philip. Andrew said, "There is a lad here who has five barley loaves and two fish, but what are these for so many people?" (John 6:9).

Barley loaves were small round cakes. This was poor people's food, and there wasn't a lot of it. It would be about the equivalent of our having sardines and crackers for dinner.

Philip saw no way the crowd could be fed. Andrew had a little more vision, except that his hope was punctuated by a big negative right in the middle. "Well, we have some food here, *but* it can't do much."

Philip saw nothing. Andrew saw something. But neither was looking in the right direction, at Jesus and His authority over any circumstance.

Whether something can or cannot be done is never the question when God is in the formula. The only question is whether it is His will.

This was true at the feeding of the five thousand. The other person involved in this miracle was the boy who gave his lunch to Jesus. Andrew had found the boy and brought him to Jesus, so we can be sure the boy was willing to let Jesus have what he had.

This boy didn't have much, because this was a poor person's meal. But the little that he had, he gave to Jesus when he realized Jesus was asking for it.

The Danger of Holding Out on God

I don't know how old this boy was or what he was thinking. But I know how most boys are about food. We can imagine this boy saying to Andrew, "No, this is my lunch. My mama made it for me. It's all I have to eat. I'm not giving it to Jesus or anyone else. I won't have anything to eat."

This boy could have been like a lot of believers who talk a good game spiritually, but when it comes to letting go of what they have and making it available to Jesus, they want to keep it to themselves.

I need to ask you—as I need to ask myself regularly—are you holding something back from God? Jesus Christ has the power and authority just to take it from you, but He doesn't work that way. He wants you to bring it to Him willingly.

Otherwise, if you hold out on God you lose, and others He could have blessed through you lose too. This boy could have eaten his lunch, but thousands of other people would have gone away hungry.

CHRIST MEETS NEEDS THROUGH HIS PEOPLE

In Mark 6:39–40, the Bible says that when Jesus got ready to feed the crowd, "He commanded them all to sit down by groups on the green grass. They sat down in companies of hundreds and of fifties."

Jesus got the crowd organized because He was about to use the disciples to carry the food to the people. Jesus mediated His authority through the disciples so the people would be fed and the disciples would learn a vital lesson.

Jesus Uses His Workers

Society is always benefited when God's people understand and tap into Christ's authority.

Jesus was going to create the miracle of multiplying the bread and fish, but it was the disciples who were going to take the food to the multitude. Through the hands of the disciples, the miracle was going to reach the people who needed it.

Jesus took the boy's lunch and gave thanks for it (John 6:11). There was a lesson here for the disciples too. I can imagine that when Jesus began to pray, Philip and Andrew were looking at each other saying, "Pray for what? For this?" But Jesus gave thanks for what He had.

Being thankful doesn't mean you have to pretend that you don't have any needs. You may need a more dependable car, but thank God you are not walking. You may want a house, but thank God your apartment has a roof. You may want steak, but thank God the hot dogs are there.

Jesus gave thanks because He had something and because He was anticipating more. He could give thanks for that small lunch because He was "looking up toward heaven" (Mark 6:41). Jesus' focus wasn't on the food but on His Father, the Provider of food. After Jesus prayed, He broke the loaves and divided the fish until all the people in that huge crowd had eaten and all were satisfied (vv. 41–42).

Jesus broke the bread and divided the fish, and the food just kept multiplying. It wasn't as if they passed around the barley loaves and a bunch of people broke off a little nibble until the bread was gone. Mark says the people ate until they couldn't hold another bite. And don't forget, this was a hungry crowd. They had been out there almost all day with nothing to eat.

Philip and Andrew, and probably the other ten disciples too, may have been weak in their faith and small in their vision, but when it was all over, they were the ones God used to bring together the authority of Christ with the needs of the crowd. And when that happened, a miraculous provision occurred.

God still meets needs through His people. People are His method. But that means we have to be what He wants us to be and where He wants us to be so He can use us to the maximum. The good news is that God can do a lot with whatever we give Him, no matter how little it is. All through the Bible, we see God doing a lot with a little. A Hebrew baby crying in the Nile River is adopted by Pharaoh's daughter and becomes Israel's deliverer. A teenaged boy named David uses his sling to kill a giant of a warrior named Goliath and rout the Philistine army.

A widow with only one meal left to her name shares it with the prophet Elijah and has more food than she could ever eat for the rest of the famine (1 Kings 17) because when a little is given to God, He multiplies it and it becomes a lot.

Jesus Rewards His Workers

Jesus used the disciples to help meet the need for food, and then He taught them another important lesson. When everyone was full, Jesus told His disciples, "Gather up the leftover fragments so that nothing will be lost" (John 6:12). The disciples gathered up twelve baskets of fragments.

Who do you think those twelve baskets of food were for? The disciples! They had been busy helping to organize and serve the crowd, and they had not eaten yet. They were hungry too.

But Jesus was teaching them this principle: "Take care of My business, and I'll take care of you. Invest in My kingdom, and you will not lose. My authority will reach to cover your needs too."

God always picks up the tab for His servants who are fulfilling His will. If you try to fulfill your own will, you get to pay the tab. Jesus worked through the disciples, and then He rewarded them. They had a basketful of food apiece.

CHRIST MEETS NEEDS ACCORDING TO HIS AGENDA

Here's the final point I want you to see in this miraculous example of Christ's authority over circumstances. This story and the following events unfolded according to Jesus' agenda and no one else's. You and I cannot force Jesus to meet our needs whenever we feel like it.

No "Meal Ticket" Messiah

After Jesus had performed this great miracle in front of so many people, feeding the equivalent of a small city full of people with a poor boy's lunch, we shouldn't be surprised at what happened next:

> Therefore when the people saw the sign which He had performed, they said, "This is truly the Prophet who is to come into the world." So Jesus, perceiving that they were intending to come and take Him by force to make Him king, withdrew again to the mountain by Himself alone. (John 6:14–15)

The people were saying about Jesus, "He is the man! We have to grab this man and make Him our king. Anyone who can take sardines and crackers and turn them into Moby Dick sandwiches ought to be king!" In other words, the people saw in Jesus their meal ticket, a miracle worker who could keep them fed and satisfied.

But being the people's bread-making king was not on Jesus' agenda. The cross was. So He withdrew before the crowd could take any action.

Jesus is not interested in being our "Sugar Daddy." He did not come to build a new welfare system but to build the kingdom of God. Jesus has all the authority we will ever need for eternity, but it comes on His terms, as we have said before. Try to make Jesus function on your terms, and He will withdraw from you. He does not hang with people who only want His benefits.

Whose Authority?

It doesn't work to say, "Lord, I don't have time for the spiritual food You want me to have, but feed me with my daily bread anyway. Help me be successful at my job, but don't ask me to give You the glory in front of my coworkers. Give me more money, even though I'm not making any of my money available to Your kingdom."

God may bless you in spite of yourself, but over the long haul if you only want God's blessings with no real relationship, you won't see the power of His presence working in your life. Jesus came to exercise His authority as King of kings and Lord of lords, not to be a "meal ticket Messiah" who produced on command.

The question we need to answer is, Whose authority do we want operating in our circumstances? If we insist on having the final word, we won't see any insurmountable obstacles falling before us. But if we will bow to Christ's authority, there will be no need to panic even when a hungry crowd shows up.

APPLICATION FOR LIFE

1. The feeding of the multitude should be an enormous encouragement to us. We know the crowd included at least five thousand men, and likely thousands of women and children as well. What a provision! There is no need so great that Jesus' authority cannot handle it. Never hesitate to come to Jesus with your needs. He knows what to do. He is our merciful High Priest in our time of need (Hebrews 2:17; 4:14–16).

2. Jesus took a child's lunch and multiplied it to feed thousands of hungry people. After the multitude had been fed, Jesus had the disciples gather the fragments. Notice the attention He gave to the small things. Throughout the Gospels we see Him redeeming the fragment of a life, the fragment of character, or a fragment of time, and using it for His glory. This week either do a small act of kindness in His name or give a chunk of time for His service.

3. Who has the authority over the circumstances of your life? When you face that seemingly impossible obstacle, do you go it alone under your own power and authority? Or do you submit to Christ's authority over your circumstances?

4. We are people with needs and, as a result, our prayers focus on those needs. There is nothing wrong with getting up in the morning and praying, "Lord, give me what I need today." But here's a prayer God loves to hear: "Lord, make me what You want me to be today." Offer that prayer today.

FOR GROUP STUDY

Questions for Group Discussion

1. According to the discussion in this chapter, what two main channels does God use to meet our needs? How have you benefited from those channels?

2. Read Andrew's assessment of the situation in John 6:9. The other disciples were thinking in a similar manner. What does their assessment tell

us about the disciples' vision and their view of Jesus' authority over circumstances?

3. Read Mark 6:7–13. This passage speaks of Jesus' compassion and how He empathizes with our needs. When Jesus saw the multitude, how did He view them? How did both sides of the God-man's dual nature come into play in His feeding of the multitude?

4. Jesus used the feeding of the multitude to teach the disciples a few truths about the kingdom. What are some lessons Jesus taught the disciples? How might we apply those lessons to our lives today? To obtain a few more details for your discussion, read the accounts of this event as recorded in Matthew 14, Mark 6, and John 6.

PICTURE THIS

While the feeding of the multitude was a massive provision for thousands of people, it also served as a classroom for the disciples. Below are a few of the lessons they learned about Jesus' authority over circumstances.

The Disciples' Lesson in Christ's Authority over Circumstances

Mark 6, John 6, Matthew 14, Luke 9

STEP	DISCIPLES' LESSON
The disciples identified the need.	They underestimated Jesus' authority over circumstances.
Jesus challenged the disciples about providing the need.	They had a limited vision for Jesus' provision.
Jesus had the disciples take the boy's food so He could multiple it.	They learned about holding out on God with our resources (even limited resources).

27

THE AUTHORITY OF CHRIST OVER TRIALS

We should have put this notice at the end of the previous chapter: "To be continued. . . ." That's because we are going to study "part two" of the biblical drama that began when Jesus miraculously fed five thousand men plus thousands of women and children. Things got a little heady after that, since the people decided they wanted Jesus to be their king (John 6:14–15).

The disciples may have thought they had arrived too, because if Jesus became king of Israel they would be on easy street themselves.

But if the Twelve had any illusion like that, it didn't last long. Not only did Jesus reject the people's superficial adulation (John 6:15), but He put the disciples into a boat and sent them out onto the Sea of Galilee . . . and head-on into one of the scariest trials they would ever face.

You say, "Well, that was Jesus and the disciples. He had to teach them some special lessons because they were going to be His apostles and the founders of the church."

Sorry, but that's not the case. The apostles definitely had some things they needed to learn. But we need to learn the same lessons—and one way God has chosen to teach us and strengthen our faith is through trials.

Let me give you a definition of trials. A *trial* is an adverse circumstance that God either allows or brings into the lives of His children in order to deepen their faith and commitment to Him. Trials are designed to make us grow, even though we may groan in the process.

Trials can come from any number of sources. Some of the things we experience are the result of living in a sinful, messed-up world. A thief may rob your home, or a war overseas may take a family member, because we all suffer the effects of the world's evil.

At other times we suffer because of our own sin. A bad choice or yielding to temptation can lead to a result that is difficult to bear. But even our sins and their consequences can become God-ordained trials that He uses to grow us if we will repent and learn from them.

God may also send a specific trial because He wants you to learn a specific lesson. And, of course, trials can come about because you are under attack from your enemy the Devil.

Whatever the source of our trials, you and I need to understand that everything that happens to us is under the sovereign, total authority of Jesus Christ. Once you get this down, you can face any trial.

CHRIST CONTROLS THE ARRIVAL OF OUR TRIALS

The situation we are going to consider is described most fully in Matthew 14:22–33. Let's set the scene:

> Immediately He made the disciples get into the boat and go ahead of Him to the other side, while He sent the multitudes away. After He had sent the crowds away, He went up to the mountain by Himself to pray; and when it was evening, He was there alone. But the boat was already along distance from the land, battered by the waves; for the wind was contrary. (vv. 22–24)

Trials Are God's Idea

Notice that the whole trip was Jesus' idea. He controlled the creation of this trial. It was at His authoritative word that the disciples set out on the sea (the Sea of Galilee, the location of Jesus' calming a previous storm, described in chapter 23). Recall that Jesus had fed the crowd late in the day, so by the time the storm hit it was dark.

Mark says the wind was so strong the disciples were "straining at the oars" (Mark 6:48). The harder they rowed, the more the wind pushed them backward.

But even the most severe circumstances are subject to the authority of Christ. The Bible says Jesus "made" the disciples get into the boat. The implication is that they didn't want to go. After all, the people wanted to make Jesus their king. I can just hear the Twelve saying, "Jesus, we have been out here for several years telling these people that You are the king of the Jews. Now they finally have the picture. This is no time to leave!"

Jesus knew better, of course, since many of these same people would later cry out, "Crucify Him!" So He sent the disciples away and straight into a storm. There was a lesson waiting for them in the middle of the sea.

Trials Help Further God's Purpose

When the disciples had left, Jesus sent the crowd away and went up to a mountain to pray. That seemed to complicate things for the disciples, since Jesus was not there when the storm engulfed them.

Do you ever feel like you're in a storm and Jesus is nowhere to be found? That's never true for us, because even when there's more water in the boat than there is in the sea, Jesus is firmly in control.

This storm on the Sea of Galilee also proves that obedience to God does not necessarily remove obstacles. The disciples obeyed Jesus, and they still got rained on. Jesus wants to take us to the next level of spiritual experience, and that often means going through trials.

Trials Are God's Tests

Tests in school weren't usually fun, but it felt great when the test was over and we found out we had passed. The apostle James said, "Consider it all joy, my brethren, when you encounter various trials" (James 1:2).

Do we count the trial or test itself as a joy? No, the joy comes in knowing that God is doing something good through our trial. At times God tests us. He does so to see if we have learned the material, to see whether the "amens" we said with our mouths on Sunday get transferred to our feet the rest of the week.

What happens when you fail a test? You must take it again. And if you fail enough tests, you have to repeat the whole course. So the idea in trials is to pass the test the first time, to learn what God is trying to teach you.

At the next level of spiritual growth, there will be more tests. But they will be of a different character because you are being tested at a higher level of maturity.

CHRIST ENCOURAGES US IN OUR TRIALS

So the disciples were fighting a fierce storm, and it was now in the early hours of the morning. They were badly in need of Jesus' reassuring presence.

It was "the fourth watch of the night" when Jesus approached the boat, walking on the water (Matthew 14:25). That's from 3:00–6:00 A.M., so it was very dark. The disciples had been out there by themselves for a number of hours by now.

Jesus Can Find You

Matthew continues, "When the disciples saw Him walking on the sea, they were terrified, and said, 'It is a ghost!' And they cried out for fear. But immediately Jesus spoke to them, saying, 'Take courage, it is I; do not be afraid'" (vv. 26–27).

Jesus may not have come when the disciples wanted Him to come, but He came on time. God always shows up just in time. Jesus knew His disciples' predicament, even though they were several miles out on the sea engulfed in darkness and He was on a mountain somewhere else praying.

This kind of knowledge was no problem for Jesus, because Jesus is God. In the same way, Jesus had no problem walking straight to their boat in the darkness. God knows how to find you, even in the dark.

Jesus Can Calm You

Jesus showed up just when the disciples needed Him most, but at first they were anything but comforted and encouraged. The Greek text says they "stared intently" into the darkness when they saw this ghostlike figure coming toward them.

The Greek word for *ghost* in Matthew 14:26 is the word "phantom." The disciples thought that what they were seeing was a figment of their imaginations. The problem is all twelve of them saw it, so they figured they had a serious problem on their hands.

Jesus didn't let the disciples panic for long. He spoke to them "immediately" (v. 27). And when He said, "It is I," Jesus was using the Greek form of God's great statement of His deity to Moses, "I AM WHO I AM" (Exodus 3:14). Jesus answered their fear with a declaration of Deity.

Please note that the first thing Jesus did was calm the disciples on the inside, not calm their circumstances on the outside. He did not deal with the storm until after Peter tried walking on the water. Once Jesus calms you by His comforting and authoritative presence, it really doesn't matter if it's still raining and blowing hard.

Jesus walked on the water to demonstrate His power and His protection and to show the disciples there was no trial He could not penetrate. He walked *on* the problem to let them know He was bigger than the problem. When Jesus comes to you in your trial, He can walk on the mess you're in. He is the authoritative one.

Special Encouragement for Peter

The disciples recognized Jesus' voice, because Peter said, "Lord, if it is You, command me to come to You on the water" (Matthew 14:28). The Greek word translated "if" here means "since." It's an expression of fact, not of doubt.

Peter was ready to step out of the boat and trust himself to Jesus, something no one else was willing to do. And when Peter heard Jesus' word, "Come!" (v. 29), he was ready to cast himself on Jesus' authority. Now you know why Peter was the leader of the Twelve. Even when he was making mistakes and saying the wrong thing, Peter's desire was always to be close to Jesus. Here Peter was willing to take a risk to get to Jesus.

It took a lot of faith for Peter to step out into a raging sea. But when you are trusting Jesus and taking Him at His word, you can experience His power and authority to do what He does, which is walk on top of your trial.

Talk about encouragement in the middle of a storm. Peter figured it was better to be with Christ out in the storm than to be without Him in the boat.

CHRIST LOVES US IN OUR TRIALS

Peter started walking on the water toward Jesus, but then he hit a problem. "But seeing the wind, he became frightened, and beginning to sink, he cried out, 'Lord, save me!'" (Matthew 14:30).

Peter started out great, trusting in Jesus and His authority over the water. But then Peter did something we all do at times. He took his eyes off Jesus and started looking around. And when he did that, his trial started swallowing him up.

The interesting thing is that the circumstances had not changed for Peter. The sea was still raging, just as it had been when he was in the boat. The difference was in Peter. He began letting the trial control him, and he started going down.

At least Peter knew where to turn. His focus got shifted back to Jesus in a hurry when he cried out for help. When Peter turned back to Jesus and Jesus reached out to lift him up, Peter got back in the position he should have been in all along, which was walking on his trial and not under it.

The good part here is that Jesus loved Peter far too much to let him sink. "*Immediately* Jesus stretched out His hand and took hold of him, and said to him, 'You of little faith, why did you doubt?'" (Matthew 14:31, italics added). In other words, "Peter, you know how much I love you. How could you think I would let you sink?"

Peter learned his lesson too. Years later, in 1 Peter 1:3–9, he told his scattered and persecuted readers that they were protected by the power of God, even though they were suffering temporarily under hard trials. Once you've begun to sink under a trial and Jesus has reached down to you in love, you are never the same.

CHRIST IS SOVEREIGN IN OUR TRIALS

Another important principle can be found in the last two verses of this story.

Jesus rescued Peter, and the two of them walked to the boat. "When they got into the boat, the wind stopped. And those who were in the boat worshiped Him, saying, 'You are certainly God's Son!'" (Matthew 14:32-33). Everything was fine once Jesus got into the boat.

Jesus' Timetable

This raises several questions. Why didn't Jesus leave with the disciples in the first place? None of this trauma would have happened. Or, why didn't He come a lot earlier? He knew they were in trouble. Why did Jesus let the disciples twist in the wind for hours?

The only answer I can come up with is that Jesus came when He was ready. It was His prerogative all the way. He knew exactly how long to let the trial last, and when it was time to end it, He came walking on the water.

Jesus' delay here was as much an expression of His sovereign authority as His arrival and calming of the storm—which, by the way, was another miracle that only Deity could perform.

I don't know if the disciples fussed and fumed during those hours of futile rowing. I don't know if they kept asking each other, "Where in the world is Jesus? Why doesn't He do something?" But I do know this: If they did fuss and fume, it didn't hurry Jesus one bit. And guess what? Your fussing and fuming won't hurry Him either.

I hear people say, "I'm mad at God!" My response is, "Big deal." It's OK to be honest with God, but you have to understand that God is working His plan from the perspective of eternity, not your momentary emergency. Jesus is going to get into the boat when He's ready.

Reaching Their Destination

But the beautiful thing is that even if He is not in the boat with you, as long as He is in the vicinity you will be fine, because He can speak peace to you from the storm.

John's account of this trial includes an interesting detail. He wrote, "They [the disciples] were willing to receive Him into the boat; and immediately the boat was at the land to which they were going" (John 6:21).

Matthew also said they crossed over and reached their destination (Matthew 14:34), but John said the arrival was dramatic. As soon as Jesus boarded, they were on land. The disciples thought the storm was taking them down, when it was actually taking them where they wanted to go.

What a great illustration of Romans 8:28, which tells us that "God causes all things to work together for good to those who love God, to those who are called according to His purpose." Do you want to reach God's destination for your life? The fastest way to get there is to hang in there under trials, because if you are faithful Jesus has the authority to guarantee that you won't sink under the waves.

A New View of Jesus

The best thing of all that came from this trial was the way it changed the disciples' view of Jesus Christ. They saw Him for who He really is, and they worshiped Him.

These men had seen Jesus do miracles, but now it finally dawned on them, "You are really who You say You are. You are the Son of the living God!"

When you really discover who Jesus is, worship becomes a high priority. When you realize that He rules over all creation, that He wields the authority of God because He *is* God, and that He rules in authority in your life, you won't have any problem worshiping Jesus Christ.

As fast as the disciples could blink, they went from the middle of the Sea of Galilee in a raging storm to the calm of the other shore. They finally figured out that this man who could find them in the dark, walk to them on the water, and instantly calm the storm and propel them to land without so much as a word was no ordinary man. Nothing will change your perspective on your trials faster than worshiping God in the midst of them.

This does not mean the disciples had life all wired from there on out and never doubted or struggled again. We saw earlier that Mark included the disturbing note that the Twelve had not learned what God wanted them to learn from the feeding of the five thousand (Mark 6:52). This was one reason Jesus sent them into the storm for part two of the lesson.

Out there on the sea in the wee hours of the morning, the disciples forgot what Jesus had done the day before. So when He came and bailed them out of the storm, they were amazed that He could do something so miraculous.

We also tend to forget what God did for us yesterday, and last week, and last year. Worship helps to refresh our memories as we regularly praise God for who He is and what He has done and look to Him for what He is going to do in the future.

FLYING WITH GOD'S JET STREAM

The jet stream air currents were discovered after some airplanes began arriving at their destination far ahead of schedule. Scientists began to study this phenomenon after pilots discovered the jet stream, which propels a plane forward at a faster rate when the plane is flying in the same direction as the prevailing winds.

When you are in a trial, you need to learn how to use God's jet stream. You need to catch the "Jesus stream." When you catch the Jesus stream, He will propel you along to your destination faster than you could ever get there on your own.

But you have to be going in the same direction as Jesus to ride His jet stream. All the power, joy, and authority you need for any trial is in that stream. Get moving with Jesus by keeping your focus on Him, and He will carry you to your intended destination.

APPLICATION FOR LIFE

1. One result of our trials is that we learn something new about Jesus, and often something new about ourselves. The disciples saw Jesus in a new light, and it changed their view of Him. They worshiped Him in a new way. Is this your response after going through a trial? Thank God when He trusts you with a trial!

2. One of the great aspects of the account of the disciples in the storm is Peter's response. When Peter saw Jesus, he left the boat and began walking on the water, focused on Jesus. But then Peter took his eyes off Jesus and began looking at his circumstances, the wind and the waves, and he started sinking. When going through a trial, remember to keep your focus on Jesus and His authority to control your circumstances. Don't be controlled by your trial or you'll start sinking like Peter.

3. One of the reasons God sends us into trials is to help us grow spiritually. Previously, the disciples had been in a boat with Jesus near the shore on a clear day, in a storm on the sea with Jesus in the boat, and now in a storm and Jesus *not* in the boat. Remember that storms have a purpose. Ask Jesus to reveal the lesson He has for you!

4. Some of life's storms can be a bit more difficult than others. For example, a critical surgery can be a fearful prospect. Keep in mind that the disciples were experienced fishermen and had seen storms on the Sea of Galilee before. But with this one, because of the wind and the waves, they feared for their lives. But Jesus came to them in the storm, walking on the waves. Interestingly, the very thing they feared is what brought Jesus to them. Are you going through a difficult storm right now? Be encouraged that Jesus will come to you through that storm.

FOR GROUP STUDY

Questions for Group Discussion

1. Dr. Evans points out that Christ controls the arrival of our trials. Read Matthew 14:22–23. In what ways was this true with the disciples? What

purpose does Christ have for sending us into trials?

2. When we find ourselves caught up in the storms of life, as did the disciples, what are some of the ways Christ encourages us? What special encouragement did Peter receive? What special lesson did he learn? What lessons can we draw for ourselves from his experience?

3. In what way does Christ love us in our trials? Years later, when Peter wrote his first epistle, he alluded to this experience (1 Peter 1:3–9). What truth stuck in his mind?

4. Christ has authority over our trials. How do we see His sovereignty in the case of the disciples' trial?

PICTURE THIS

Trials are part of the believer's life in Christ. God brings them into our lives for a purpose. Below are several encouragements about our trials.

What Is True about Our Trials

Matthew 14:22–33

TRUTH	LESSON OF ENCOURAGEMENT
Trials are God's idea.	When God sends us into a trial, it is because we are obedient, not disobedient.
Jesus will find you.	Jesus found the disciples at night in the middle of the Sea of Galilee. Jesus will come to you in your trial.
Jesus will help us grow.	God's trials are His tests, and they further His purposes. With each test, we advance in our walk of faith to the next level.
Jesus will see us through to the end.	Jesus' delay in meeting the disciples in the storm was part of His timetable. He saw them to the other side of the lake.

28

THE AUTHORITY OF CHRIST OVER DEATH

Since death is "the last enemy that will be abolished" (1 Corinthians 15:26), it's appropriate that we end our discussion of Christ's authority by looking at His influence over death.

Christ conquers death. No chapter in the Bible brings this truth home more vividly than John 11, the story of Jesus' climactic miracle in raising His friend Lazarus from the dead. This miracle is climactic not only because it involves the conquest of death, but because this was the last miracle Jesus performed on His way to Jerusalem to die on the cross and Himself rise from the dead. So the apostle John used this miracle as an illustration of Jesus' power over death and His ability to make good on His promise of eternal life.

There is no question that death is an enemy. If you want to know how despicable sin is, look at death, because death is sin's reward (Romans 6:23). In Adam we all die (1 Corinthians 15:22).

But because Jesus Christ has exercised His authority over death, our last and greatest enemy need not hold any terrors for those who know Him. In this chapter I want to show you why we can make such a bold statement. Let's find out more about Jesus Christ's authority over death and what it means for us.

THE AUTHORITY OF CHRIST GIVES PURPOSE TO DEATH

The first thing I want you to see in John 11 is that Christ's presence and authority give meaning or purpose to death, an event that would otherwise be full of meaninglessness and despair. We are used to hearing that Christ gives us a purpose for life. The same is true of death. When Jesus is on the scene, death is not a random or meaningless event. That was true in the death of Lazarus. Jesus was firmly in command of the situation, as seen by His assurance to the disciples and to Martha that Lazarus would not remain in the grave (see John 11:4, 23).

Let's set the context of this story. Jesus was on His way to Jerusalem to be arrested, tried, and crucified. Bethany was a village only about two miles from Jerusalem (John 11:18), and it was the hometown of some of Jesus' favorite people—the sisters Mary and Martha and their brother, Lazarus (John 11:1).

Their home was like a second home to Jesus. He was always welcome there. Jesus loved these three people very deeply, and they loved Him. In fact, when Lazarus became ill, the sisters' message to Jesus was, "Lord, behold, he whom You love is sick" (v. 3). John added, "Now Jesus loved Martha and her sister and Lazarus" (v. 5).

So we know right up front that Jesus was acting out of deep love for these three followers of His. And we can have the same assurance that He is acting out of love in our lives. But at first glance, Jesus' love for these people doesn't compute with His actions upon receiving word of Lazarus's illness. "So when He heard that [Lazarus] was sick, He then stayed then two days longer in the place where He was" (v. 6).

It's obvious this was not what Martha and Mary expected. They sent for Jesus in the hope that He would hurry to Bethany before Lazarus died. When Jesus did arrive, they both said the same thing: "Lord, if You had been here, my brother would not have died" (vv. 21, 32).

But Jesus intentionally delayed His coming to Bethany, even knowing that Lazarus was deathly ill. In fact, Jesus delayed long enough that Lazarus died (vv. 11–14). Why did Jesus do this?

To Bring Glory to God

The first answer to the question why comes early in John 11, when He said, "This sickness is not to end in death, but for the glory of God, so that the Son of God may be glorified by it."

We've already established that Jesus loved Lazarus, so a lack of love wasn't the issue. The issue is that God was operating with a bigger program in mind. God had a bigger purpose in allowing Lazarus to die: Jesus would get more glory by raising a dead man than by healing a sick man. Mary, Martha, and Lazarus did not know this, but Jesus knew it.

To Increase Our Faith

Here's another purpose God often has when the issue is death. He wants to use our situation to increase our faith. Jesus said to His disciples concerning Lazarus's death, "I am glad for your sakes that I was not there, so that you may believe; but let us go to him" (John 11:15).

When Jesus arrived in Bethany, He said to Martha, "I am the resurrection and the life; he who believes in Me will live even if he dies, and everyone who lives and believes in Me will never die. Do you believe this?" (John 11:25-26). Martha's answer in verse 27 affirmed her faith in Jesus as "the Christ, the Son of God." Then at the grave Jesus said to Martha, "Did I not say to you, if you believe, you will see the glory of God?" (v. 40).

In delaying His trip to Bethany, Jesus would be able to strengthen the faith of everyone involved, including the disciples. Sometimes God doesn't do what you ask Him to do when you want Him to do it, so that you may learn to trust Him more.

To Save Sinners

We can see from the account in John 11 that God can also use death to bring sinners to salvation.

When Jesus prayed at Lazarus's tomb, He said, "I knew that You always hear Me; but because of the people standing around I said it, so that they may believe that You sent Me" (John 11:42). After Lazarus came out of the grave, "therefore many of the Jews who came to Mary, and saw what He had done, believed in Him" (v. 45).

Because of Jesus' delay and Lazarus's death, people got saved. I've conducted many funerals, and I don't know of any occasion when people are more receptive to the gospel, since they are face-to-face with eternity. God has used the deaths of many believers to bring unsaved relatives to Himself.

To Advance God's Prophetic Program

Another purpose for Jesus' delay was to further God's prophetic program in relation to His upcoming death. The miraculous resurrection of Lazarus stirred Jesus' enemies into action. Some of the Jews who witnessed the miracle went to Jerusalem and told the chief priests and Pharisees what Jesus had done (John 11:46).

These men got together in an emergency session to decide what to do about Jesus. One thing was not in doubt: This man had to be killed. They were afraid if they let Jesus go on, the Romans would have all their heads (vv. 47–48).

Caiaphas, the high priest, told the others to relax. Then he made a remarkable prophecy: "It is expedient for you that one man die for the people, and that the whole nation should not perish" (v. 50). Caiaphas was exactly right, but John added in verse 51 that Caiaphas made this prophecy in spite of himself.

Thus the decision was made. "So from that day on they planned together to kill Him" (v. 53). The order went out that "if anyone knew where [Jesus] was, he was to report it, so that they might seize Him" (v. 57).

In other words, the death and resurrection of Lazarus became part of God's larger plan because it moved Jesus' enemies to expedite their plans for His death. And since it was drawing near God's time for Jesus to die, these men's evil plans helped bring about the fulfillment of prophecy that Jesus Christ would die for the sins of the world.

THE AUTHORITY OF CHRIST OVERCOMES THE FEAR OF DEATH

Death is a fearful thing because it's unnatural. God created us to live, not to die. Death is part of the curse of sin, and so it brings fear and anxiety. But when you bring Christ into the equation, the sting of death is dismissed, because Christ has taken away our sins. As Paul said, "The sting of death is sin" (1 Corinthians 15:56). Remove the sin, and death loses its power to harm us.

This principle appears not in relation to Lazarus's death, but the impending death of Jesus. When Jesus announced He was going to Judea, the region of Bethany and Jerusalem, the disciples asked Him, "Rabbi, the Jews were just now seeking to stone You, and are You going there again?" (John 11:8). They couldn't understand why He would go into the backyard of the very people who were looking for Him. It was asking for a death sentence.

But Jesus said, "Are there not twelve hours in the day? If anyone walks in the day, he does not stumble, because he sees the light of this world. But if anyone walks in the night, he stumbles, because the light is not in him" (vv. 9–10).

Most of us aren't afraid to walk around in daylight, because we can see where we're going. But it's a different story at night, especially in that day when there were no lighting systems.

In the Bible, light and darkness often stand for the work of God and the work of the Devil. Jesus was saying that He was not afraid to go back to Judea, because He was going there to do the will of God. Jesus did not fear death, because He was living in God's will, and He knew He would not die one second before God's appointed time (see John 7:30).

You only have to fear death if you are not in the will of God. Why? Because when you are in God's will, you won't die until God's appointed time for you. The disciples were fearful for Jesus because the Jewish leaders were out to kill Him. But Jesus wasn't worried about that threat because He was walking in the light. The Pharisees were in danger of stumbling, not Him.

Death may seem ominous and beyond anyone's ability to control, but that's not true. Jesus holds our last enemy firmly in His authority. That's why when Paul's death was near, he talked not about his fear of dying, but about the reward Jesus had waiting for him (2 Timothy 4:6–8). Death is only the next step in God's will for His children. That was true for Lazarus too, by the way.

THE AUTHORITY OF CHRIST REDEFINES DEATH

Part of our problem in trying to cope with death is that it is sometimes hard to define. What constitutes death? To many unbelievers, death means the cessation of existence. They believe that people just lie down and die, and that's it. But the Bible teaches differently. Death is not the end of a person's existence. In fact, Jesus made an astounding promise to Martha concerning death. Let's go back to the story in John 11.

When Jesus arrived in Bethany, Martha came running up to Him and said, "Lord, if You had been here, my brother would not have died" (v. 21).

We have already quoted part of Jesus' reply, but I want to come back to it, because in the next few verses, Jesus redefines death on His terms:

> Jesus said to her, "Your brother shall rise again." Martha said to Him, "I know that he will rise again in the resurrection on the last day." Jesus said to her, "I am the resurrection and the life; he who believes in Me will live even if he dies, and everyone who lives and believes in Me will never die." (vv. 23-26)

Temporary Versus Eternal Death

At this point in the story, Lazarus had already been dead four days. So how could Jesus promise Martha, "Everyone who lives and believes in Me will never die"? Because Jesus does not define death the way we define it.

That's good news, because according to Jesus' authoritative definition of death, *you will never die* if you know Him as your Savior! Death is not in God's vocabulary. It is one of the things excluded from heaven (Revelation 21:4).

When people talk about death, they are referring to the temporary separation of the body from the soul and spirit, the immaterial part of a person. This is physical death, the kind Lazarus experienced and we will experience someday.

But as far as God is concerned, the only definition of death that matters is the eternal, spiritual separation of a person from God, which is hell. This is eternal death, which, unlike physical death, can never be reversed by resurrection.

The Sleep of Death

So if death is not the end of existence or the final step for a believer, what is it? Jesus had said of Lazarus, "Our friend Lazarus has fallen asleep; but I go, so that I may awaken him out of sleep" (John 11:11).

Jesus was talking about death, not slumber. Physical death is like going to sleep, because even when you are asleep and your body is inactive, the essential core of your being—your soul and spirit—are still functioning. Sleep doesn't change that fact. The soul is your self-consciousness. The spirit is your God-consciousness. Both are just as alive when you sleep as they are when you awake. The only thing that sleeps is your body.

When you close your eyes in death, you will be as alive then as you ever were when you were walking around. The only difference is that your body will be asleep. It is the body that sleeps, not the soul or spirit. And one day, the body will be awakened in resurrection to be reunited with the soul and spirit. Then the entire person will enter either heaven or hell.

I'll stick with God's definition of death! Let me say it again: On the authority of Jesus Christ Himself, death will never touch you if you are His child.

In fact, even the moment of physical death is nothing, because Paul said to be absent from the body is to be at home with the Lord (2 Corinthians 5:8). Paul was eager to depart this earth because it meant being with Christ (Philippians 1:23).

THE AUTHORITY OF CHRIST BRINGS COMFORT AT DEATH

What we just said above about death not really happening to a believer is not intended to ignore or minimize the sorrow and pain of physical death. Far from it. It hurts to be separated from friends and loved ones, even when we know we'll see them again someday.

Jesus did not minimize the pain Martha and Mary and the others were experiencing because Lazarus had died. On the contrary, He entered into their sorrow with them. When Mary learned Jesus had come, she ran and fell at His feet weeping (John 11:32). His response to her tears and those of other mourners? "He was deeply moved in spirit, and was troubled, and said, 'Where have you laid him?' They said to Him, 'Lord, come and see.' Jesus wept" (vv. 33- 35).

There are at least three reasons Jesus wept. First of all, He saw Mary and Martha and all their friends crying, and His heart went out to them in compassion. The Bible says Jesus sympathizes with our weaknesses (Hebrews 4:15).

You might ask, "Well, if Jesus hurts with me, why doesn't He do something about my pain?" Because the plan of God is not governed by emotions, but by what is best for us. It's like a father who spanks his child, even though the spanking hurts the father emotionally more than it does the child. A father cannot allow his feelings to dictate the program of discipline that he needs to carry out with his child.

The second reason Jesus wept was because of His love for Lazarus (v. 36). This man was Jesus' dear friend.

The third reason Jesus cried and was "deeply moved" (vv. 33, 38) is that He was disturbed by seeing once again the pain and devastation that sin had caused. Death is an unnatural intruder into God's perfect creation. So the presence of death meant that Satan was at work again.

Christ was troubled in His spirit because He knows the work of Satan is a horrendous thing (John 10:10). Satan rules in the realm of death, and Jesus was face-to-face with the kingdom of death and darkness once again. Jesus was stirred by another reminder of the reality of sin and death.

THE AUTHORITY OF CHRIST CONQUERS DEATH

But here's the best part of the story. Because He has supreme authority, Jesus can do something about the problem of death.

When He arrived at the grave of Lazarus, Jesus ordered the stone removed, prayed a prayer of gratitude and confidence to His Father, and then shouted "Lazarus, come forth" (vv. 39–43).

Martha was quick to remind Jesus that Lazarus had been dead four days. But Jesus is not limited to the laws of nature. In fact, it is incorrect to speak of the laws of nature. They are actually the laws of God that nature must obey. Jesus' authority is not subject to natural limitations. He can command a dead body to come out of the grave.

In response to Jesus' authoritative command, Lazarus came to life and walked out of his grave. He was still wearing his grave clothes and had to be untied. But Jesus' authority had conquered death once again.

THE SHADOW OF DEATH

Death is real, and it can be frightening, but it is not the last word, thanks to the authority of Jesus Christ.

Donald Grey Barnhouse, a great pastor and preacher from a previous generation, experienced the death of his wife. He told about coming back from the funeral with his small children in the car. They were asking, "Why did Mommy have to die?"

Dr. Barnhouse did not know what to say. He was thinking about the question when they came to an intersection and had to wait for a train to pass by. As the shadow of the train passed over their car, a thought suddenly occurred to Barnhouse.

"Children," he asked, "would you rather be hit by that train or by its shadow?" Of course, the children said they would rather be hit by the train's shadow.

Barnhouse then explained to his children that because their mother knew Jesus, she had only been struck by the shadow of death. They would see her again in heaven.

That's what the authority of Christ over death means for us too. The reality of death cannot hurt us when we belong to Him. *Not* to know Jesus is to be hit by the train, not its shadow. So my question to you is, When death comes for you, will just its shadow fall over you, or its reality?

APPLICATION FOR LIFE

1. Death may not be under our control, but it is firmly in Jesus' control. His authority over death has stripped it of its fear. If we had to face death alone, we would have a right to be afraid. However, with Jesus' authority over death, we need not fear it. In fact, as did the apostle Paul, we can anticipate and embrace it. When it comes your time to face death, place your trust in Christ's authority, for He has conquered death!

2. If you know Jesus, you have His new, resurrection life within you. But you need to shed those old ways of life that may still be binding you. You can't walk freely and unhindered in your Christian life and still practice the walk and talk of the world. If you can't get unwrapped from those graveclothes yourself, let the body of Christ help you. Seek the counsel of your pastor or a mature Christian.

3. The separation from loved ones is always a painful aspect of death. But death itself is no worry for the believer. We are going to get brand-new, perfect bodies after our current, decaying bodies are laid in the ground. Why should you be worried about dying? View death as it is: the sleep of the body in anticipation of the resurrection to eternal life!

4. Whenever our Lord faced the prospects of death or powerful people intent on destroying Him, He remained firmly in charge of each situation. His authority was never in doubt. Be encouraged that God always has something bigger in the works than we can see.

FOR GROUP STUDY

Questions for Group Discussion

1. As preparation for discussion, read John 11. In what ways does Christ's authority give purpose to death? (Use the "Picture This" chart as an aid to your discussion.)

2. What is the "sting of death" (1 Corinthians 15:56)? How does Christ's authority overcome the sting of death?

3. In what ways does Christ's authority redefine death? Read 2 Corinthians 5:8 and Philippians 1:23. Why was Paul so eager to depart this earth?

4. The death of Lazarus gives us unique insights into Jesus. When Lazarus died, Jesus wept. Focus on John 11:32–38. Discuss the three reasons He wept.

PICTURE THIS

In John 11, we find that the authority of Christ provides us with at least four purposes for death.

THE AUTHORITY OF CHRIST AND THE PURPOSE OF DEATH
John 11

PURPOSE	INTENDED RESULT
To bring glory to God.	Sickness and death are opportunities for God to bring glory to Himself.
To increase our faith.	Jesus used Lazarus' death as opportunity to strengthen the faith of those involved.
To save sinners.	Jesus used the raising of Lazarus from the dead to bring sinners to Himself.
To advance God's prophetic program.	Jesus' death was tied to God's prophetic program and larger plan for Jesus' sacrifice on the cross and His resurrection.

PART 3

PNEUMATOLOGY

The Doctrine of God the Holy Spirit

SECTION I

The Presence of the Holy Spirit

29. THE HOLY SPIRIT'S PROMISE
30. THE HOLY SPIRIT'S BAPTISM
31. THE HOLY SPIRIT'S SECURITY
32. THE HOLY SPIRIT'S FILLING
33. THE HOLY SPIRIT'S FREEDOM
34. THE HOLY SPIRIT'S ILLUMINATION

29

THE HOLY SPIRIT'S PROMISE

The Holy Spirit is not merely an addendum to the Christian faith. He is at the heart and core of it. Nor is the Holy Spirit merely a force or influence, but rather the third Person of the Trinity, who must be related to personally.

It is the distinctive role of the Spirit to make the reality of truth and the presence and power of the Godhead experiential, both in creation and in the life of God's people. Just as electricity brings living, functional reality to appliances, the Holy Spirit animates the person and power of God in history.

The Spirit's unique role is seen as He hovers over creation to bring order out of chaos, and light out of darkness and formlessness (Genesis 1:2). It is also seen as the Spirit oversees the virgin birth of Christ (Luke 1:35) and the writing of holy Scripture so that it was kept from human contamination (1 Peter 1:20–21). It is the Holy Spirit who supplies power to God's Word, giving it life and substance in the physical and spiritual realms (Genesis 2:7; Ezekiel 37:9–10, 14; Acts 2:1–4).

Therefore, if we are going to live the victorious Christian life, it is critical that we understand the person and ministry of the Holy Spirit. This doctrinal study of the Holy Spirit is known as pneumatology, taking its name from *pneuma*, the Greek word for "breath" or "spirit."

THE CENTRALITY OF THE HOLY SPIRIT

Even though the Holy Spirit is absolutely central to the Christian life, because of the mystery surrounding this third Person of the triune God, a great deal of confusion has been connected with the work of the Holy Spirit. This has led to a lot of misappropriation, as well as a lot of gross underappropriation of His power and gifts.

Usually, the Holy Spirit is approached from one of two extremes. Either we know very little about Him, or we try to make Him into a celebrity, someone we all think we know but don't really know at all. Neither is desirable, but we cannot let a lack of familiarity in some circles or excesses in others keep us from pursuing the knowledge of the Holy Spirit. The fact is, His role is the indispensable factor in determining whether you are a failure or a success as a Christian.

So I want to begin our study by looking at one of the foundational New Testament passages for understanding the person and work of the Holy Spirit. This is Jesus' Upper Room Discourse, which He delivered on the night of the Last Supper and His betrayal.

This was not one of the greatest moments in the lives of the disciples. This was what you would call a spiritual downtime. Everything was going wrong. Judas had shown himself to be a traitor. This was the tension-charged, late-night environment in which Jesus introduced His disciples to the ministry of the third Person of the Trinity:

> I will ask the Father, and He will give you another Helper, that He may be with you forever; that is the Spirit of truth, whom the world cannot receive, because it does not behold Him or know Him, but you know Him because He abides with you, and will be in you. (John 14:16–17)

THE SPIRIT'S PERSON

Jesus assured His followers that even though He would leave, they would not be left alone. There would be another divine Person who would take

His place in their midst. This Person would be with them as Jesus had been with them for comfort, strength, and guidance, but this Person would also be in them. Jesus wanted the disciples to know He was going to send them a Somebody, not a something.

A Real Person

How do we know the Holy Spirit is a person instead of just a force or an "it"? Because He bears all the attributes of personality: intellect, emotion, and will.

The Spirit's intellect is demonstrated by the fact that there are things He knows with His mind (Romans 8.27; 1 Corinthians 2:10–11). His emotions or feelings are seen in the fact that He can be grieved (Ephesians 4:30). His will is seen in the fact that He acts with intentionality or purpose (1 Corinthians 12:11). Only persons intend to do things.

In addition, the Bible uses personal pronouns for the Holy Spirit. Jesus referred to the Spirit as "He" (John 15:26; 16:13). The Spirit refers to Himself in the first person and also speaks His thoughts intelligibly to others, something only a person can do (Acts 13:2).

A Divine Person

The Holy Spirit is God, the third member of the Trinity. In theological terms, the Father, the Son, and the Holy Spirit are *homoousios*, "of the same essence or substance," not *homoiousios*, "of like or similar essence or substance." That extra Greek letter *i* in the second term makes a world of difference.

The thing I want you to see here is that the Holy Spirit is God. This truth is in abundant evidence in Scripture. He possesses the attributes of Deity. The Spirit is omniscient or all-knowing (Isaiah 40:13; 1 Corinthians 2:2), omnipresent or in all places at once (Psalm 139:7), and omnipotent or all-powerful (Job 33:4; Psalm 104:30). He does what only God can do, superintending Christ's virgin birth, inspiring Scripture, and creating the world.

The Spirit is also equally associated with the other members of the Trinity in the writing of Scripture (Isaiah 6:9; cf. Acts 28:25; Jeremiah 31:31–34;

cf. Hebrews 10:15–17). To lie to the Holy Spirit is the same as lying to God (Acts 5:3–4). Matthew 28:19 is especially crucial here because the singular "name" is used with the Father, Son, and Holy Spirit.

A Unique Person

Jesus called this Helper "the Spirit of truth" in John 14:17. In verse 26, Jesus called Him "the Holy Spirit." There is a lot in that second name.

The Spirit is holy because He is God, totally separate from all that is unlike who and what God is. This title also focuses attention on His primary work in the life of believers: to progressively conform us to the image of Christ, the process we call sanctification (1 Peter 3:15).

The Holy Spirit is spirit because He is nonmaterial, intangible, and invisible. Both the Hebrew and Greek words for *spirit* mean "wind, breath." The Holy Spirit is the very breath or wind of God. And like the wind, He wields great power even though He is invisible.

Now I'm not talking about Casper the friendly ghost. I mean the invisible reality of almighty God. So the Holy Spirit is not simply a power. Trying to explain an invisible reality is difficult, but Jesus made clear in John 14:17 that the Holy Spirit is knowable. We who know Christ can know the Holy Spirit.

Why doesn't the world know the Holy Spirit (v. 17)? For the same reason you cannot pick up radio stations if you don't have a radio. It has nothing to do with whether or not radio waves are going through the air. It has everything to do with not having anything with which to receive the signals.

The world does not have a spiritual receiver. But Jesus Christ has implanted a receiver within those who know Him that picks up heaven's signals so the believer can tune in to the heavenlies, to the very voice of God. So in the midst of discouragement, fear, loneliness, insecurity, or even sin, a believer can tune in to the Holy Spirit.

THE SPIRIT'S ENABLING

A second truth about the Holy Spirit we find in the text is this: The Spirit is the Helper, the Enabler.

Jesus was about to tell the disciples something very crucial: "Apart from

Me you can do nothing" (John 15:5). This blanket statement of inability without divine enabling made what Jesus was saying in John 14 even more critical. There would be no effective ministry or life that pleased the Lord by mere human effort.

An Internal Helper

Because the disciples' need was complete, Jesus promised them that "another Helper" would come after He left (John 14:16). The Greek word for "helper" is *paraclete*, translated differently in various Bible versions because it is a pregnant term. Some versions translate it "counselor."

One version translates it "advocate," because the word literally means "one called alongside to help," that is, to enable.

Jesus knew that after His resurrection, the disciples would need supernatural power to pull off what He wanted them to do. And He knew where they were going to get that power: from the enabling, internal presence of the Holy Spirit. Now this is very important, because whenever the disciples needed help, Jesus was always there.

So when they heard that Jesus was leaving, the question on the floor was "Who is going to help us?" That is, "Jesus, if we are going to keep on, who is going to help us when we are down and encourage us when we are discouraged? Who is going to strengthen us when we are weak? Who is going to lead us when we are confused? You did all that for us."

A Helper Like Jesus

Jesus' task on this night was to convince His fearful, confused followers that the Helper He was sending was just like Him, only this Helper would be able to do even more for them.

So Jesus told them, "I am going to leave you now. But I am going to send you Someone who is always going to be there for you. No matter what your problem, no matter what your circumstance, no matter what your trial, frustration, or irritation may be, no matter what you come up against, this Helper will be with you."

We call this the indwelling ministry of the Spirit of God. When a believing sinner comes to Jesus Christ, the Holy Spirit takes up residence in that person's life and becomes his Helper.

Again, the text helps us because in John 14:16, the Greek word Jesus used for "another" is *allos*, which means "another of the same kind." He did not use *heteros*, which means "another of a different kind."

Jesus' choice of words emphasizes the unique work of the Spirit in continuing what He had begun while on earth without any loss of character, quality, power, or intimacy. Jesus could promise this because the Spirit is of equal divine essence with Jesus Himself.

You do not get less when you get the Holy Spirit. You get all of God, for He is the third Person of the Trinity.

An Ever-Present Helper

The Spirit is not only our Helper, He is our ever-present Helper. It's very important to understand what's going on here because Jesus said later that night, "It is to your advantage that I go away; for if I do not go away, the Helper shall not come to you" (John 16:7).

Do you realize that if Jesus Christ were on earth today, we would actually be worse off as His people? If Jesus Christ were on earth today in His bodily presence, we would be a defeated, decimated people.

Why? Why did Jesus tell His disciples it was better for them that He leave and the Holy Spirit come? Because when Jesus was here on earth, He encased His deity in His humanity. Philippians 2:5–8 makes it clear that Jesus Christ willingly poured the totality of His deity into the location of His humanity.

The result was that even though Jesus is God, He could only be in one place at a time. His deity was always in the same vicinity as His humanity. Jesus never traveled more than a few miles from home or preached to more than a few thousand people. That's why He said we would do greater works than He did (John 14:12).

But because the Holy Spirit is ever present with us and indwells us, we can draw on the full power of deity wherever we go. When Jesus walked this earth, He limited His deity to the location of His humanity. He could only visit one village at a time. Today the Holy Spirit who indwells us can work through many believers at the same moment.

Why then are some Christians perpetually defeated? It is not because they have less of the Holy Spirit than victorious Christians. Jesus said in verse 26 of John 14, "The Helper, the Holy Spirit, whom the Father will send in My name, He will teach you all things, and bring to your remembrance all that I said to you."

Please notice the work of the Trinity in verse 26. The Father, in the name of the Son, sends the Holy Spirit. So we have the whole Trinity involved in the sending of the Spirit. If Christians are defeated, it is because the Holy Spirit has less of them.

THE SPIRIT'S PURPOSE

Here's a third truth I want you to see about the work of the Holy Spirit:

> But when He, the Spirit of truth, comes, He will guide you into all the truth; for He will not speak on His own initiative, but whatever He hears, He will speak; and He will disclose to you what is to come. He shall glorify Me; for He shall take of Mine, and shall disclose it to you. (John 16:13–14)

Glorifying Christ

The Holy Spirit has one overarching goal. If you want to sum up what the Holy Spirit is about, He is about glorifying Christ. What do I mean by glorifying Christ? The Spirit advertises Christ. He puts Jesus Christ on display.

The Spirit does not put Himself on display. He does not even speak on His own initiative. His job is to glorify Christ. So whenever you have anything that transcends the priority of Jesus Christ, it is not the Holy Spirit's doing. Anytime there is an emphasis on the Spirit that supersedes the centrality and priority of Jesus Christ, it is not the Holy Spirit doing it.

The Holy Spirit is not here to advertise Himself. His goal is to advertise Christ, to make us God's advertising agency by working in our hearts in such a way that our lives magnify the person of Christ. The Spirit is busy making Jesus preeminent.

No Glory, No Help

In fact, 1 John 4:2–3 says anything that diminishes Jesus Christ's glory as the incarnate Son of God is "the spirit of the antichrist." He is to be preeminent. Now this is very important because this means if your passion is not to glorify Christ, then you are not going to get help from the Holy Spirit.

THE SPIRIT'S BENEFITS

When you read John 16:7, where Jesus told His disciples, "It is to your advantage that I go away; for if I do not go away, the Helper shall not come to you," you know you're in for something good. Jesus doesn't make promises lightly.

In my wallet, I have an Advantage Club card from the airline I use when I travel. Every month, the airline writes me a personal letter to let me know the benefits I have as an Advantage member.

You see, I have established a very intimate relationship with this airline. It has been very close to my pocketbook, because I have flown so many miles. In the eyes of this airline, that makes me a preferred customer: I get certain rights and privileges the occasional flyer does not have. Advantage members are invited to board first, so I get to go on the plane earlier. I also get certain ticketing benefits. I don't have to stand in certain lines because I have an Advantage Club card. And I have the privilege to upgrade to first class.

Jesus says that, because of your relationship to Him, He is going to make you an Advantage cardholder. He is going to enroll you in the "Holy Ghost Club." If you will keep flying Jesus, He will make sure you stay in the club and accrue the Spirit's benefits.

Guidance

First of all, Jesus said the Spirit will "guide you into all the truth" (John 16:13). Isn't guidance something you need? Are there decisions you need to make that you wish somebody would advise you on? Don't you wish there was somebody who understood your situation perfectly and could guide you? You have that person in the Holy Spirit.

We can enjoy the Spirit's guidance today in the decisions of life. His guidance will always be tied to the truth, so we have an advantage because we have the completed revelation of God's truth in the Bible. So if you're seeking guidance from the Spirit, you can be sure it will align with Scripture and will glorify Christ.

Remembrance

Jesus also said the Holy Spirit would "bring to your remembrance all that I said to you" (John 14:26). Jesus had taught the disciples a lot. How were they going to remember it all? How could they remember every word and every event, how many people were there, and all of that? They couldn't, but the Holy Spirit would recall these things to their minds.

How are you going to remember every sermon you've heard and every word of the Bible you've read? You can't, and you don't have to. Your responsibility is to study to show yourself approved, to hide the Word in your heart.

When you do that, the Holy Spirit is your built-in computer system to pick up the words and illustrations and everything you need to know. Then at the proper time, He can punch the button and the information will show up on your mental screen. He will bring to your remembrance the things you need to remember. That's a benefit of belonging to the Spirit's Advantage Club.

Peace

Another benefit of the Holy Spirit is peace. "Peace I leave with you; My peace I give to you; not as the world gives, do I give to you," Jesus said. Therefore, "let not your heart be troubled, nor let it be fearful" (John 14:27).

What's your situation today? Whatever it is, if you have the Holy Spirit you can have peace in the midst of it because He lives within you. It's a peace that circumstances can't shatter.

PERSONAL APPLICATION FOR LIFE

1. The Christian life is a supernatural life. Therefore, as others look at us they ought to see something that can't be accounted for in purely natural terms: our love, our peace, our joy, our generosity, and so on. Ask yourself this question: Is there anything about my life that can't be explained except by the power of the Holy Spirit working in me?

2. Another good question to ask yourself is, Am I feeding the Spirit in my life? One way you can tell is to see what happens when you read your Bible, pray, or get in a conversation where the subject is spiritual things. Do these things feel strange to you? Are you comfortable or awkward in the Word, in God's presence, and among His people? Face those questions honestly, and you'll have a large part of your answer—and maybe a place to start turning things around.

3. The Spirit's purpose is to glorify Christ. Is that your purpose? Look at how you spend your time, abilities, and money, and ask yourself how many of these things have as their ultimate goal the exaltation of Christ in some way. The ones that don't may need to go. That's between you and the Holy Spirit.

4. Which benefit of the Holy Spirit do you need most in your life right now? If your life is lined up with His purposes, be bold in asking Him to meet your need.

FOR GROUP STUDY

Questions for Group Discussion

1. When we speak of the Holy Spirit being central to the Christian life, what does that mean? Read John 14:16–17. What in that passage defines His centrality in the life of the believer? From what two extremes do people approach the Holy Spirit?

2. The New Testament describes the Holy Spirit as a real person. What three attributes of personality does He possess? Why are those important to

our having a personal relationship with Him? What is unique about His work in the lives of believers?

3. What does the Greek term *paraclete* mean? In what ways is the Holy Spirit our Helper or Enabler?

4. For what purpose did God send the Holy Spirit? What is the Spirit's overarching goal? As believers, what benefits do we receive from the ministry of the Holy Spirit?

PICTURE THIS

The indwelling Spirit provides several benefits as He ministers to believers. In this chapter, Dr. Evans has focused on the three below.

THE BENEFITS OF THE HOLY SPIRIT

BENEFIT	SCRIPTURE PASSAGE	WHAT IT MEANS
Guidance	John 16:13	He guides us in the decisions of life, and in all truth, which is aligned with the Word of God.
Remembrance	John 14:26	He brings to remembrance those things we need to remember to accomplish God's will and bring glory to Christ.
Peace	John 14:27	He gives us peace in the midst of our circumstances, whatever they may be.

30

THE HOLY SPIRIT'S BAPTISM

If you're an observer of the current Christian scene, you can tell by the title of this chapter that we are about to enter turbulent waters.

Baptism is an indispensable ministry of the Spirit of God, one that is critical to our Christian experience. It marks the beginning of the Spirit's indwelling presence. The fact that much of the teaching about Spirit baptism has led to confusion, misunderstanding, and disharmony within the family of God—all the more reason to understand what God is saying to us.

Part of the controversy about baptism starts with the term *en pneumati* itself. Is it the baptism "of" the Spirit, "by" the Spirit, "with" the Spirit, or "in" the Spirit? The preposition in the original can be and has been translated all of these ways, and there is a difference in the meaning based on the translation you accept. Is the Holy Spirit the primary agent of the baptism, is He Himself the baptism, or is He the means by which believers are baptized?

How you answer that will probably depend upon your theological frame of reference. That little preposition has caused a lot of confusion, so in as clear and biblical a way as possible, I want to address this area of Spirit baptism.

My purpose, however, is not simply to settle an argument, but to help you experience the fullness of the Spirit's person and ministry in your life.

The verse I want to center on is 1 Corinthians 12:13, where Paul writes: "For by one Spirit we were all baptized into one body, whether Jews or Greeks, whether slaves or free, and we were all made to drink of one Spirit."

THE MEANING OF BAPTISM

Let's start by talking about the word itself, which is a transliteration of the Greek word *baptizō*. It means "to immerse" or "to dip." It was used to describe the process of dyeing cloth. If you wanted a piece of cloth to be purple, you would dip it in purple dye. When the cloth came out of the dye, you had a different-looking piece of cloth because it had been immersed or dipped into a colored dye.

This process of immersion, this baptism of the cloth, was not just an act. It was a transformation because the cloth took on a whole new color. When God wanted to describe the ministry whereby His Spirit places us into a whole new environment, this is the word He chose.

God chose the imagery of baptism to explain the Spirit's ministry of taking sinful people who believe on the Lord Jesus Christ and immersing them into a whole new dynamic of life, an entirely new realm or environment called the body of Christ.

When I speak of the Spirit's baptism, I am referring to the time when true believers become identified with Jesus Christ and placed into His body.

The distinguishing feature of baptism is that we are placed into another realm, a new family: the body of Christ, the family of God. This baptism occurs at the moment of our conversion. It is our initiation, if you will.

The indwelling of the Spirit refers to the Spirit's taking up permanent residence in the life of the believer, which continues throughout our lives here on earth. The filling of the Holy Spirit refers to His control and empowerment in the lives of believers to enable us to live the victorious Christian life.

So when the Bible talks about the indwelling of the Spirit, it means where the Spirit is. When the Bible talks about the filling of the Spirit, it means what the Spirit empowers us to do. When the Bible talks about the baptism of the Spirit, it means the new environment in which the Spirit places us when we come into a new relationship with Jesus Christ at salvation.

Jesus is the One doing the baptizing. He is the baptizer, not the Holy Spirit. The Spirit is the means by which this baptism takes place, the means by which believers enter into this new realm or environment called the body of Christ or the family of God.

So let me put the statement together. The baptism Paul refers to in 1 Corinthians 12:13 is a baptism by Christ, "by means of" the Holy Spirit, whereby we are placed into a new spiritual environment.

THE NATURE OF SPIRIT BAPTISM

A couple of important truths are found in the opening phrase of our text, 1 Corinthians 12:13: "For by one Spirit we were all baptized into one body." Notice especially the uniqueness and the universality of the Spirit's baptism.

It Is Unique

Nothing could be clearer than that there is only one baptism by one Spirit. Paul affirms the same thing in Ephesians 4:4–5: "There is one body and one Spirit . . . one Lord, one faith, one baptism."

What does this mean? It means you don't get a piece of Spirit baptism when you get saved and then a second helping of baptism later.

All of the Holy Spirit you are ever going to get as a believer, you received when Jesus baptized you by means of the Spirit into His body at your salvation. The Holy Spirit came to take up permanent residence in your life at that time.

Just as the Spirit's indwelling of us is a one-time, complete work of God's grace, so there is only one baptism by means of the Spirit. Based on Paul's absolute statement in 1 Corinthians 12:13, we could say that if the Spirit's baptism were not complete at salvation, then we would not be full members of the body of Christ at salvation.

It Is Universal

"We were all baptized into one body." The baptism by means of the Holy Spirit applies to every Christian.

All who have received Jesus Christ as their only God and Savior have been spiritually baptized by Him through the Spirit into the family of God.

In fact, Romans 8:9 says anyone who does not have the Spirit is not even a Christian.

Now it's interesting that Paul would say this to the church at Corinth because, according to 1 Corinthians 3, this was not the most spiritual church in town. It was a very carnal church, a church that lived by the flesh, a church soaked with immorality. There was litigation between members. People were choosing sides over personalities and leaving the Lord's Table drunk (chapter 11).

Yet Paul still says to them, "We were all baptized." What this shows is that baptism does not necessarily have anything to do with your present spiritual practice. It has to do with your spiritual position.

Baptism places you into spiritual relationship to Christ and His body. It gives you the Spirit, but by itself it does not guarantee the results.

I'm making this point for an important reason. People who want to make the baptism of the Spirit a later work, often called the second work of grace or the second blessing, emphasize that you must be spiritually prepared and primed to receive it. They may tell you that you need to get the baptism of the Spirit in order to ascend to a higher plane of spiritual life.

That's not why you need the baptism of the Spirit. You need the baptism of the Holy Spirit to get you into the family so you can live the spiritual life in the first place.

When we lose this vital distinction between the Spirit's baptism and His other ministries, great confusion abounds. And that's just what we are seeing today.

THE RESULTS OF SPIRIT BAPTISM

If the baptism of the Spirit is for every believer, and if it's an already accomplished fact, what are its results? What does the baptism do for us, since His work is experiential in nature?

A New Life

The first result of Spirit baptism is new life in Jesus Christ. You can see this in John 3, the well-known conversation between Jesus and Nicodemus.

Nicodemus was a model man, a Pharisee, a "ruler of the Jews" (v. 1), at the top of the religious order in Israel. Nicodemus is a Greek name, meaning this Jewish man also had gotten the finest in Greek culture.

So Nick was powerful, religious, and cultured. Yet when he came to Jesus that night, Jesus knew he wasn't there just to compliment Him on His miracles. In verse 3, Jesus told him, "Unless one is born again, he cannot see the kingdom of God" (v. 3b). Nicodemus did not understand, so Jesus clarified in verses 5–6: "Unless one is born of water and the Spirit, he cannot enter into the kingdom of God. That which is born of the flesh is flesh, and that which is born of the Spirit is spirit."

It is the Spirit who gives us spiritual life. In fact, there is no possibility of new life without Him.

A New Identity

The second thing the baptism of the Holy Spirit gives you is a new identity. In fact, identity is a major component of baptism in the New Testament. Romans 6:1–5 explains the identification aspect of the Spirit's baptism as having been "buried with Him through baptism into death, in order that as Christ was raised from the dead through the glory of the Father, so we too might walk in newness of life. For if we have become united with Him in the likeness of His death, certainly we shall be also in the likeness of His resurrection" (verses 4–5).

To be identified with Christ is to be so linked with Christ that we become like Him. We had an identity before we came to Christ, but it was nothing to brag about. We were totally identified with Adam as the head of a fallen, sinful race.

The Bible says that in Adam, all of us died (1 Corinthians 15:22). If your identity is still in Adam, then you inherit the destiny of Adam and his race. That was my identity and my destiny until, at the age of twelve, I heard the message of the cross, the good news that Jesus Christ satisfied the demands of a holy God against me. When I heard that message from my father, I put my faith in Christ and became identified with Him. I was baptized into the body of Christ, and the Holy Spirit came to live within me. He gave me a new identity.

A New Unity

The Spirit's baptism also gives us a new unity. "We were all baptized into *one* body" (1 Corinthians 12:13, italics added). We are to preserve "the unity of the Spirit" (Ephesians 4:3). It's already a reality. There is only one body of Christ, one family, one church. The whole point of our baptism is to create one new person out of a whole bunch of diverse individuals.

So if there is disunity in your home or in your other relationships, it's a spiritual issue. When your kids are fighting, one of the reasons you give as to why they have to stop is that they are family. "He's your brother. She's your sister. Why are you fighting like this? We're a family here." You are arguing that there is something bigger at stake than their personal desires.

The purpose of the Spirit's baptism is to bind us together in the community of the redeemed so that we function as family. That's why you can't have racism in the church. That's why you can't have sexism in the church. That's why you can't have division in the church. We're family now.

A New Ability

Not only do you get a new unity, you get a new set of abilities when you are baptized by the Spirit. They are called spiritual gifts, the empowerment to serve Christ and build up His body. Earlier in 1 Corinthians 12, Paul called spiritual gifts "the manifestation[s] of the Spirit" (v. 7). The gifts are His to distribute "as He wills" (v. 11).

Many Christians have gifts they have never used. Like Christmas gifts, they are under the tree but not opened yet. We will talk much more about this when we get to spiritual gifts. But the Spirit's baptism gives you a new enablement to serve Christ.

A New Nature

With the baptism of the Spirit, you also get a new nature. "If any man is in Christ, he is a new creature; the old things passed away; behold, new things have come" (2 Corinthians 5:17). You get a brand-new inner you.

The Bible says you are to put on Christ. You are to clothe yourself with Christ. When you trust Christ and are baptized into His body, you are given a whole new wardrobe.

So get dressed. Stop walking around with torn clothes when you have a brand-new pair of slacks. Stop walking around with a ragged jacket when He has purchased you a brand-new life by His precious blood. Stop talking about what you can't do and start talking about what the Holy Spirit can do in and through you. You have a new nature now.

Now, you look the same. You talk the same. You still have all the same features and characteristics, but as far as your identity is concerned, you are a brand-new person. That is what Christ does by the Holy Spirit.

BAPTISM AND SPEAKING IN TONGUES

Now there's still a fundamental question I need to answer: What is the indispensable and visible experiential proof that the baptism of the Spirit has taken place in a person's life?

Many in the charismatic and neopentecostal movements teach that the indispensable proof of the Spirit's baptism is speaking in tongues (called "glossalalia," after the Greek word for *language*, *glōssa*). They argue from events in Acts (2:1–4; 8:14–17; 10:44–46; 19:1–6) that baptism is a work of the Spirit subsequent to salvation and related to a special endowment of His power.

According to this position, then, a person may be saved and indwelt by the Spirit, but not baptized until sometime later when he is lifted to a new level of spiritual power and vitality. This event is validated by speaking in tongues.

There are a number of problems with this interpretation. First, not all Christians speak in tongues; not even all spiritually mature Christians do so. If speaking in tongues is necessary to prove the Spirit's power and fellowship in a believer's life, we have a problem. Why? Because it is possible to identify many believers from the beginning of the church to today who are being used powerfully by the Spirit, but who never spoke in tongues.

Second, Paul clearly stated that not all Christians speak in tongues (1 Corinthians 12:30). It's interesting, though, that Paul did expect all Christians to be spiritual (Colossians 1:28).

A third argument makes this position untenable: Nowhere does the Scripture teach that speaking in tongues is a necessary sign of the Spirit's baptism or that there has to be a time lapse between conversion and Spirit baptism.

Then how should we interpret the relationship between Spirit baptism and speaking in tongues in Acts? The answer lies in understanding the Old Testament prophecy that is the basis of the New Testament phenomenon.

In Numbers 11:16–17, God promised Moses that He would empower seventy men Moses chose to help him bear the burden of leading Israel. When this happened, the men prophesied when the Spirit rested on them (vv. 24–25). But two other men who were not there also received the Spirit and began to prophesy (v. 26). Someone ran and told Moses, and Joshua asked Moses to restrain the men (vv. 27–28). But notice Moses' response: "Would that all the Lord's people were prophets, that the Lord would put His Spirit upon them!" (v. 29).

The prophet Joel said it was in fact God's intention to put His Spirit upon all His people. Joel prophesied, "And it will come about after this that I will pour out My Spirit on all mankind" (2:28).

The day of Pentecost was the fulfillment of Moses' prayer and Joel's prophecy. Peter mentioned the fulfillment of Joel's prophecy in his sermon (Acts 2:16). He even quoted Joel directly. Pentecost was the fulfillment of this expectation that God would expand the outpouring of His Spirit from some to all of His people.

This happened initially only in Jerusalem and only to Jewish believers. But the rest of the book of Acts chronicles the spread of the fulfillment of this promise from Jerusalem to Judea to Samaria and ultimately to the Gentile world (Acts 1:8). Thus all believers in every group and every place received the gift of the Spirit. Peter revealed the significance of this event when he was in Cornelius's house and the Holy Spirit suddenly fell upon his Gentile listeners (Acts 10:44–48).

The point then is that all converts in Acts received full membership in the church, even though word of the fulfillment of the promise took some time to get around. There were no believers in Acts relegated to the back of the spiritual bus. There were no second-class Christians then, and there are none today.

So what was the significance of tongues? It became the outward sign that the Holy Spirit had descended as promised. The fact that the tongues experience in Acts was verbal in nature reflects the experience of Numbers 11, for we just saw that when the Spirit came, Moses' elders began prophesying.

What can we conclude, then? The reality of Spirit baptism is to be demonstrated by the common public confession and proclamation of the person and work of Christ (Romans 10:9–10). This confession may be in previously unknown languages (tongues) or known languages (prophecy). It is made visible by the inclusion of people who are racially, culturally, and socially different as equal members in the body of Christ (Acts 15:7–11) and who maintain the same confession of faith.

In this way, the baptism of the Spirit is in fact experiential. It affects our public confession and our personal relationship to the body.

A WORD ABOUT WATER BAPTISM

Water baptism is to salvation what a wedding ring is to a marriage. It is a visible symbol of a deeper reality. In Scripture, water baptism followed quickly on the heels of Spirit baptism (Acts 2:41; 8:34–38). Why? To give visible and experiential witness to the spiritual transaction that had occurred.

In addition, water baptism is designed to issue into visible participation in a local church, since water baptism is a picture of spiritual baptism. Spiritual baptism identifies the believer with the universal church, whereas water baptism identifies the believer with the local church (Acts 2:37–47; 1 Corinthians 12:7–14). This is because Spirit baptism places the believer into the universal body of Christ, which is given visible expression in the local church.

The failure to be baptized and become a functioning member of a local church means spiritual loss. It deprives the person of some of God's great blessing as well as preventing full participation in the experience of the Holy Spirit.

Water baptism also signifies believers' inauguration into a life of discipleship as they begin the process of walking "in newness of life" they possess as the result of their spiritual baptism (Romans 6:3–4).

APPLICATION FOR LIFE

1. Since the Spirit has given you a new identity, people who knew you before you became a Christian ought to see some difference. Imagine you have just met a friend from the old days. Write down some of the new things (attitudes, habits, etc.) you hope that person would see in you.

2. Since the Spirit has given you new abilities in the form of spiritual gifts, you should be seeing some results of that as you put your gifts to work in the body of Christ. List some ways you are using your spiritual gift(s) in Christ's service. If your list is really short, you may want to pray that God will help you make better use of the gifts He has entrusted to you.

3. Since the Spirit has given His people a new unity, we are called to treat one another as equals in the body of Christ. This is a tough one, because old attitudes are hard to root out. Search your heart, and if the Spirit points out a need or blind spot in this area, claim His power and authority to deal with it.

4. Since the Spirit has baptized you into the body of Christ, you need to be in fellowship with other believers in a local church. If you are in a church where the Bible is taught and Christ is honored, thank God for this blessing—and pray regularly for your pastor. Otherwise, ask God to lead you to a church where you can worship Him in Spirit and truth.

FOR GROUP STUDY

Questions for Group Discussion

1. What does it mean for a person to be baptized in the Holy Spirit? Why is baptism an indispensable ministry of the Spirit of God?

2. Read Ephesians 4:4–5. Discuss Dr. Evans's two key points about the nature of Spirit baptism. Why is each important?

3. Scripture teaches us about several of the results of Spirit baptism. (Use the chart in "Picture This" as an aid to your discussion.) Discuss each result. What changes do they bring to the life of a believer?

4. Read Numbers 11:16–17 and Romans 10:9–10. What is the indispensable and visible experiential proof that the baptism of the Spirit has taken place in a person's life? What are some of the interpretational problems associated with the position that speaking in tongues is a visible proof of the Spirit's baptism?

PICTURE THIS

Several results of Spirit baptism are evident in the life of the believer. Below is a list of those results and what they mean to the believer.

THE RESULTS OF SPIRIT BAPTISM

RESULT	SCRIPTURE PASSAGE	ITS SIGNIFICANCE
A new life	John 3:3b, 5–6	We receive spiritual life and all the supply we need to maintain our spiritual lives.
A new identity	1 Corinthians 15:22	We are now identified with Christ, rather than with Adam.
A new unity	1 Corinthians 12:13	We become part of the body of Christ, a community of believers.
A new ability	1 Corinthians 12:7, 11	We receive spiritual gifts that enable us to serve Christ.
A new nature	2 Corinthians 5:17	We receive a brand-new inner nature.

31

THE HOLY SPIRIT'S SECURITY

Many Christians are insecure about their salvation. They are insecure either because they are not sure they are saved at all or because they fear doing something that will cause them to lose their salvation.

Security is a very important component of salvation and one benefit of the Holy Spirit's presence in our lives. Therefore, it's tragic that so few believers seem to understand or experience the peace that comes from belonging to Christ forever.

Over the centuries, two basic, opposite positions have arisen as theologians have grappled with the doctrine of the believer's security. The first is known as Arminianism, the position that even the true child of God can in fact lose his or her salvation at any point due to sin or some departure from the faith. As a whole, Arminians tend to view eternal security as an unbiblical teaching that lures Christians into complacency in their walk with Christ.

The other position is called Calvinism, which holds that once a person is truly saved, he or she can never be lost. A more extreme form of Calvinism, often called Hyper-Calvinism, says that a believer is only secure if he or she perseveres in a life of obedience.

There is an element of truth in both of those teachings. What I hope to do is preserve these elements while articulating what I believe to be the clear biblical teaching on the believer's security.

Let me begin by stating my thesis: A true Christian can never lose his salvation. A true Christian is forever saved and is never again in jeopardy of eternal condemnation.

In light of the larger topic at hand, the indwelling presence of the Holy Spirit, let me add that the Spirit's task is to make real in the lives of true believers the comfort and joy of their security in Christ and to disturb those who are trusting anyone or anything other than Christ for their salvation. Thus security is a very experiential issue.

THE GROUNDS OF YOUR SECURITY

If the doctrine of security is biblical, then there ought to be plenty of biblical evidence for it. There is, and it's this evidence I want to consider first. We'll be treading some important and familiar biblical ground.

Christ's Finished Work

When you understand that Christ died on the cross in your place for your sin and rose bodily from the dead; when you respond to the truth and put your complete trust and confidence in Him; when you rest your eternal destiny on Jesus Christ alone for salvation; then the Holy Spirit comes to indwell you, you are baptized into the body of Christ, and the Spirit's presence is your guarantee of security, as we will see in a minute.

In Ephesians 1, Paul writes:

> He chose us in [Christ] before the foundation of the world, that we should be holy and blameless before Him. In love He predestined us to adoption as sons through Jesus Christ to Himself, according to the kind intention of His will, to the praise of the glory of His grace, which He freely bestowed on us in the Beloved. (vv. 4–6)

Christ alone must be your absolute basis of confidence for salvation if you would be born again into the family of God. Birth into God's family comes with your commitment to Christ as your only God and Savior.

Jesus' Resurrection

Consider first Romans 5:8–10:

> But God demonstrates His own love toward us, in that while we were yet sinners, Christ died for us. Much more then, having now been justified by His blood, we shall be saved from the wrath of God through Him. For if while we were enemies, we were reconciled to God through the death of His Son, much more, having been reconciled, we shall be saved by His life.

A lot of us can quote verse 8, but we tend to stop there. However, verses 9 and 10—especially verse 10—are tremendous statements of our security in Christ. The reason you can't lose your salvation is that Jesus not only died to save you, He arose to keep you saved.

Right now, at this moment, the resurrected and glorified Jesus is keeping you and me saved. Hebrews 7:25 says He is able to save us "forever" because "He always lives to make intercession for [us]." That means your salvation will only last as long as Jesus stays alive and keeps interceding for you—which is forever!

If sin can undo your salvation and cancel out the cleansing of Christ's blood, then you will spend more time being unsaved than saved, because we all sin every day even in ways we're not aware of. But even worse, if sin can break your saving relationship with Christ, then a doubt is cast on His sufficiency to forgive sin.

Jesus Himself said in John 6:39: "This is the will of Him who sent Me, that of all that He has given Me I lose nothing, but raise it up on the last day."

God's Keeping Power

Jesus is not going to lose one person given to Him by the Father. Here's why:

> My sheep hear My voice, and I know them, and they follow Me; and I give eternal life to them, and they shall never perish; and no one shall snatch them

> out of My hand. My Father, who has given them to Me, is greater than all; and no one is able to snatch them out of the Father's hand. (John 10:27–29)

Here is where many sincere believers make a great mistake. They think they remain saved because they hold on to God. Thus they are secure only as long as they hold on tight. No, Jesus is clear that you are secure because God holds on to you.

You are saved not because you hang on to Christ, but because you have trusted completely in His finished work. With that trust comes security. The security is built into the trust. When you got saved, when you trusted Christ, you were saved forever. That's the only kind of salvation He offers.

THE WITNESS OF YOUR SECURITY

In verses 13–14 of Ephesians 1, Paul says that those who hear, understand, and believe the gospel receive a very special witness, the seal and pledge of the Holy Spirit

Your Seal

One ministry of the Holy Spirit when He comes to indwell you at salvation is to be your seal, the guarantee of your salvation. The word *seal* is very interesting because it meant to stamp ownership on something, sort of like branding cattle to identify the owner. When you come to Jesus Christ, He sets His seal on you by sending the Holy Spirit to indwell you. The Spirit is the seal that locks you into the family of God.

Who is the sealer? Christ Himself, who came from the Father. And what is His seal? The Holy Spirit. So you would have to outdo the holy Trinity in order to lose your salvation. You would have to be more powerful than the Godhead to screw the cap of salvation off your life. When God saved you, He saved you with an eternal purpose and He sealed you with an eternal seal.

Your Down Payment

In addition to the seal, the Holy Spirit is also called your "pledge," or down payment. The Greek word here, *arrabōn*, means basically the same thing as a down payment in our culture. It's a first installment.

When you trust Christ alone for salvation, God gives you a down payment—the Holy Spirit—which means there is much more to come. The Spirit is your down payment or deposit on the life God is going to give you throughout eternity. The Spirit's abiding presence in your life is a promise that the transaction begun at salvation is someday going to be completed.

When a down payment is made, there is only one question left: Will the purchaser have the rest of the money necessary to redeem the merchandise? Many people fear they will lose their salvation because they don't think they can keep this thing going.

But the question here is, Can God afford to redeem what He has put on layaway: you and me? Absolutely! He is not expecting us to pay off the rest of our salvation. Why not? Because on the cross Jesus said, "It is finished!" (John 19:30). "It is finished" is one word in the original, *tetelestai*, meaning "paid in full." All the funds necessary to pay for our total redemption were put up by Jesus Christ on the cross.

THE FOCUS OF YOUR SECURITY

Why does God want you to know that you are secure in Him? Why does the Holy Spirit want to help you experience the truth of your security? Well, one reason is that if you are not sure you are saved, Satan will stay busy doing everything he can to keep your spiritual equilibrium upset and keep you from moving forward in terms of your growth in Christ.

Security is so important that the apostle John writes, "These things I have written to you who believe in the name of the Son of God, in order that you may know that you have eternal life" (1 John 5:13).

Pleasing Christ

If you have eternal life abiding in you and that life is lost, it can't be eternal. Now the first objection you usually hear to the doctrine of the believer's eternal security is this: If you teach people that they cannot lose their salvation no matter what they do, they will just go out and live any old way they want because they are guaranteed salvation.

Yes, God has secured us with His Holy Spirit. But God does not cover us eternally so we can go out and abuse His grace. Paul dismissed that nonsense idea in no uncertain terms in Romans 6:1–2, when he asked, "Are we to continue in sin that grace might increase? May it never be!"

Moving On to Maturity

Another blessing of security is that it allows us to move on from "the elementary teaching about the Christ" and "press on to maturity" (Hebrews 6:1).

This is a serious issue, not just a point to argue about. The writer of Hebrews specifically tells us not to keep on laying "a foundation of repentance from dead works and of faith toward God" (6:1b). That's salvation. Why are we to leave the basics and move on? Because the foundation is already laid. It's solid. Get on with the building.

Looking to Jesus

Your feelings are not your Savior. Some believers are constantly looking within themselves to make sure they are saved. But the problem with that is if you are messed up inside, you are going to get mixed signals.

When the Holy Spirit is living in you, He will constantly turn your focus away from yourself or anything else and put it on Christ. You do not experience the joy and peace of security by looking inside, but by looking to Jesus.

In John 3:14–15, Jesus said, "As Moses lifted up the serpent in the wilderness, even so must the Son of Man be lifted up; that whoever believes may in Him have eternal life."

The Bible says that Jesus was hung on a pole, a cross. Anybody who looks to Him in faith is granted eternal life. So the issue is not whether you feel saved, but who you are looking to for salvation. If you are looking to Jesus Christ alone as the only hope for your salvation, you are saved because Jesus is the Savior.

THE BENEFITS OF YOUR SECURITY

If the security of the believer is a biblical doctrine, if it is part of the redemption purchased for us on the cross of Christ, then it ought to have some real benefits that the Holy Spirit brings into our lives. And it does.

For example, the preserving work of the Spirit goes all the way back to the dawn of creation (Genesis 1:2). The purpose of the Spirit's "moving" over the waters was to preserve God's created material and prepare it for His further creative activity. The picture here is similar to an eagle hovering over its young to protect and preserve them (Deuteronomy 32:11).

In the same way, the Spirit hovers over and in God's children to preserve what God has redeemed. The Spirit's preserving work is not static or passive, however. Just as in the Creation, it is filling up emptiness, taking the barren wasteland and giving it life. Even so with us, the Spirit does not demonstrate His protective power just to make the Enemy stay put, but also to produce righteousness within; transforming the desert of our lives into an oasis of holiness.

Let me show you more of the Spirit's benefits in Romans 8:29–30. The process of your salvation began in eternity past when God "foreknew" and "predestined" you (v. 29), and it continues into eternity future with your glorification (v. 30).

The word "glorified" here is in the past tense. You are already glorified in the mind and plan of God. He has already fitted you for heaven. You are as good as there.

No Opposition

Paul comes out of the promises of verses 29 and 30 of Romans 8 with this question: "What then shall we say to these things? If God is for us, who is against us?" (v. 31). Now that is a heavy question. If God has made you His child, who can unmake you? Answer: nobody, because nobody can overrule God.

If God the Father didn't spare Jesus but gave Him up for us (Romans 8:32), then giving us eternal security as part of our salvation is no big deal.

No Condemnation

"Who will bring a charge against God's elect? God is the one who justifies; who is the one who condemns?" (Romans 8:33–34a). When you become a Christian, you become one of God's elect, His chosen. Who is going to "unjustify" you? We've already seen that Christ Jesus died and rose again for you and is in heaven today keeping you saved.

No Separation

The final benefit is found in Romans 8:35: "Who shall separate us from the love of Christ?" Love by its nature is experiential. We know when someone loves us. Christ will continuously demonstrate His love for us in tangible ways, thus validating our security in Him.

Neither Satan, sin, self, nor circumstances can separate us from Christ's love because, "in all these things we overwhelmingly conquer through Him who loved us" (Romans 8:37). Then Paul concludes by stating his conviction that nothing can separate us from Christ's love (vv. 38–39).

EXPERIENCING YOUR SECURITY

You may be saying, "I don't seem to have that internal sense of security. I know I have assurance based on the truth of Scripture and my faith in Christ. But how do I get that internal sense of assurance?" This is important because the internal is where the Spirit lives.

Grieving the Spirit

If the Spirit is not ministering the peace and joy of your security to you, it could be that He is grieved. Ephesians 4:30 says, "Do not grieve the Holy Spirit of God, by whom you were sealed for the day of redemption."

Notice first that even in this context, Paul still goes back to his earlier word of certainty in Ephesians 1:13 that you are sealed by the Spirit.

But whereas you can't lose the Holy Spirit, you can sadden or grieve Him. If you are an unhappy Christian, it is because living inside of you is an unhappy Spirit. It's pretty hard to feel secure when you know you've made the Spirit unhappy.

The Holy Spirit is grieved by sin. One of the ways you know you have the Holy Spirit is by your reaction to sin. Now you may sin the same sin you used to sin when you were a sinner, but you can't sin the same sin the same way as you did when you were a sinner. Your sensitivity to sin is a tremendous confirmation of the reality of His presence in your life.

Abiding in Christ

The experience of security (not security itself) can also be lost by a failure to focus on Christ (Hebrews 12:1–2). In 1 John 2:27 the apostle writes: "And as for you, the anointing which you received from Him abides in you, and you have no need for anyone to teach you; but as His anointing teaches you about all things, and is true and is not a lie, and just as it has taught you, you abide in Him."

John says you have the Holy Spirit. He is abiding in you, but are you abiding in Christ? You can lose the internal validation and enjoyment of your security when you are not developing an intimate walk with Jesus Christ.

Loving the Brethren

How we treat our Christians brothers and sisters also affects our sense or experience of security. John addresses this too: "No one has beheld God at any time; if we love another, God abides in us, and His love is perfected in us. By this we know that we abide in Him and He in us, because He has given us of His Spirit" (1 John 4:12–13).

The Spirit has made you part of the family of God, and He will make His presence felt when you are loving the members of His family the way He loves the members of His family.

Receiving the Witness

Here's one final passage, 1 John 5:9–10, that bears on this issue of security:

> If we receive the witness of men, the witness of God is greater; for the witness of God is this, that He has borne witness concerning His Son. The one who believes in the Son of God has the witness in himself; the one who does not believe God has made Him a liar, because he has not believed in the witness that God has borne concerning His Son.

The witness within you is the Holy Spirit, testifying to the truth about Jesus Christ and your faith in Him. When you seek to follow and focus on Christ, you engage the Holy Spirit in your heart and your walk with Christ becomes richer and more alive. His reality is being experienced subjectively because you keep your objective focus on Jesus Christ.

PERSONAL APPLICATION FOR LIFE

1. Most of us are familiar with down payments. When we make a down payment, we need to ensure that we are good for the remainder of the payment. God gave us the Holy Spirit as a down payment on our salvation. There is more to follow. And we can rest assured that God will deliver. Jesus' words from the cross were, "It is finished!" (John 19:30). That phrase is a one-word verb in the original Greek text, and it speaks of a completed action that remains completed. Praise God our salvation is finished!

2. One of the natural by-products of the Spirit's security is ongoing growth and maturity. Is your experience one that remains at the elementary levels? Or are you advancing in your faith and building upon the foundation, which is your salvation? Keep in the Word and ask God to help you "press on to maturity" (Hebrews 6:1b).

3. While we cannot lose the Holy Spirit, we can sadden or grieve Him by our sin. Ephesians 4:30 exhorts us to not grieve the Holy Spirit. Are you harboring sin in your life? Is it something that you are having a difficult time letting go? Courageously decide to let go of it, asking God for strength. Then ask God's forgiveness. Rejoice that you have a sensitivity to sin, as it is a confirmation that you are a child of God.

4. One way Satan tries to get us down is trying to make us believe we can lose our salvation. Don't let him get away with that! John 10:27–30 is a Scripture we can use against the Enemy. When you trusted in Christ's completed work on the cross, God saved you forever. Be encouraged by God's promise of Hebrews 13:5, "I will never desert you, nor will I ever forsake you."

FOR GROUP STUDY

Questions for Group Discussion

1. What do we mean by the Holy Spirit's security? Read these passages as preparation for discussion: Ephesians 1:4–6; Romans 5:8–10; and John 10:27–30. What are the three grounds of the believer's security?

2. Read Ephesians 1:13–14. In what ways does the Holy Spirit make our security real to us? What is the significance of the word *pledge*? What truth do we learn from John 19:30?

3. Discuss the benefits of the believer's security. What do we gain from each benefit? (Use the "Picture This" chart as an aid to your discussion.) What is the "sin leading to death" (1 John 5:16)?

4. Read Ephesians 4:30. How do we as believers grieve the Holy Spirit?

PICTURE THIS

Because of the security the Spirit provides, believers receive several benefits. Below are three key benefits as we learn from Romans 8.

THE BENEFITS OF THE HOLY SPIRIT'S SECURITY

Romans 8:28–39

BENEFIT	SCRIPTURE PASSAGE	WHAT IT MEANS
No opposition	verses 28–29	We are God's children, and no one can overrule God.
No condemnation	verses 33–34a	Because Jesus died for our sins, we are justified and no one can condemn us.
No separation	verses 35–39	Nothing can separate us from God's love.

32

THE HOLY SPIRIT'S FILLING

The Holy Spirit can be in you, and yet you can know very little of His power and influence. The issue we always have to deal with is not how much of the Holy Spirit we have, because we have all of Him. The issue is how much He has of us. In fact, we're going to get to this issue right off as we consider the filling of the Spirit.

OUR NEED OF THE SPIRIT'S FILLING

Paul's classic treatment of this subject is in Ephesians 5:

> For this reason it says, "Awake, sleeper, and arise from the dead, and Christ will shine on you." Therefore be careful how you walk, not as unwise men, but as wise, making the most of your time, because the days are evil. So then do not be foolish, but understand what the will of the Lord is. And do not get drunk with wine, for that is dissipation, but be filled with the Spirit." (vv. 14–18)

The Spirit of God wants to control our lives so that we wake up spiritually, we become wise spiritually, and we stop being foolish spiritually; that's how we can know God's will for us. God gave us the Holy Spirit because He knows something we tend to forget. It is impossible to live the Christian life on our own.

I cringe a little bit when I hear Christians say something like, "I'm going to stop doing that. I am going to change." Now don't misunderstand. There's nothing wrong with a determination to change. God can use that. But I fear that often behind statements like that lies a misunderstanding of the Christian life.

If you could do it, you would not need the Holy Spirit. His energy would not be necessary. But Jesus said in John 15:5, "Apart from Me you can do nothing." That's why He sent us "another Helper," the precious Holy Spirit.

The Christian life is a supernatural life, so we need supernatural help to live it. The only thing that makes you more powerful now than you were before is "He who is in you" (1 John 4:4). It's not a matter of doing your best and letting the Holy Spirit make up the difference.

FOUR OBSERVATIONS ABOUT THE SPIRIT'S FILLING

Every word in the phrase "be filled with the Spirit" is packed with meaning, so let me make four observations that will help us understand what God is saying to us.

God's Command

The first thing to note is that this is a command, not a suggestion. God is not saying, "If you want to, it would be nice if you were filled with the Spirit." God is not into suggestions. He is only into commands.

Interestingly, there is no command in the Bible to be baptized by the Spirit or indwelt by the Spirit. Those are blessings we receive automatically when we come to Christ. But we are commanded to be filled with the Holy Spirit, because this relates to our daily experience of His influence.

For Every Believer

The command of Ephesians 5:18 is plural in the Greek text. It applies to every believer. That means the Spirit's fullness is not reserved for an elite group of Christians.

You look at some Christians and say, "Oh, they are so spiritual. They love Jesus so, and they walk with Him so closely. The Spirit's power is so evident in their lives. Why can't I be like that?"

Well, it's hard to say what the difference is in individual cases. But it may simply be that you are seeing what happens when people allow the Holy Spirit to fill and control them.

The Spirit's filling is for every believer. But we have to appropriate or claim it, because it is not automatic. Every Christian has been baptized by the Spirit into the body of Christ, and every believer is indwelt by the Spirit. But not every Christian is filled with the Spirit.

God Does It

Notice that this command is passive. You are to "be filled," not fill yourself. Somebody else provides the action. You are the object of that action, the one acted upon. The content of the filling, of course, is the Spirit Himself. And you can resist the filling, but you cannot fill yourself. God does the filling.

Keep It Up

Also notice that this plural, passive command is in the present tense. This means it is to be a continuous process. An accurate way of translating it would be, "Keep on being filled with the Spirit." In other words, don't get filled with the Spirit today and expect the filling to cover you from here on out.

But even though the filling of the Holy Spirit is an experiential concept, don't ever think that if you are not filled with the Spirit, He leaves you empty. He doesn't leave you, period. The depletion of the Spirit's filling that I'm talking about is the loss of the experience and enjoyment of His full benefits in your daily experience.

WHAT IT MEANS TO BE FILLED

In order to understand what Spirit-filled people should look, act, and think like, I want to talk about the Greek word *plērousthe*, translated "filled" in Ephesians 5:18. This word occurs throughout the New Testament, and it has a lot to teach us.

In Luke 4:28, for example, the Bible says the people of Nazareth were "filled with rage" at Jesus when He challenged them for their unbelief. They tried to push Jesus off a cliff. Their rage took possession of them.

In Acts 13:45, the Jews in Pisidian Antioch became "filled with jealousy" at the success of Paul and Barnabas. They began to attack the two men verbally and even to blaspheme. Their anger possessed them and made them do things they would not ordinarily do.

A Matter of Control

These two examples give you the idea behind the word for filling. It means control. When you are filled in the New Testament sense, it means that somebody or something has taken over command in your life and is pulling the strings.

The purpose of the Spirit's filling is that He might control our lives. We know from Scripture and from experience that Satan also wants to control us. He wants to rule our emotions and our passions. He wants to set the agenda for our attitudes and actions.

So we have to replace the wrong control with the right control. That's why sincerity alone isn't enough. If the wrong person is in control, how sincere you are about wanting to live an effective Christian life is really irrelevant. It's not about sincerity, it's about control.

Controlled by Another

Ephesians 5:18 gives us an example of control we can understand when it says, "Do not get drunk with wine, for that is dissipation," or degradation.

We all know what it means for someone to be drunk. A drunken man doesn't get that way by looking at advertisements for liquor. He gets drunk by drinking. And the more he drinks, the drunker he gets and the more completely the alcohol controls him.

What alcohol is to the body negatively, the Holy Spirit is to the human spirit positively. He makes you walk in ways you would not normally walk and talk in ways you wouldn't normally talk.

When the Spirit takes over, a lot of our excuses are nullified. We say, "Well, that's my personality." But the Spirit can change our personalities. "But this is how I was raised." Well, when the Spirit takes over, He can change the way you were raised into the way you ought to be. "I've always been like this." That's because you have not always been under the control of the Spirit of God.

The Spirit transforms us supernaturally. That's why instead of spending our time and energy trying to change, we need to spend our time getting filled. A sober man doesn't have to try to stagger. All he has to do is get drunk. He doesn't have to try to change his personality. He just has to get drunk.

Now you can see why Paul drew the analogy between someone who is drunk and someone who is under the Spirit's control.

New Power

When you are filled with the Spirit, you will start hearing things like, "What in the world has happened to you?" They'll say that because when the Spirit takes control, you will start loving people you used to hate.

When people become intoxicated with the Spirit, men who used to hit their wives when they got angry will find the ability to tame their temper. When the Spirit takes control, people who had no control over their passion will be able to say no to immorality.

So, rather than saying, "I am not going to do that anymore," what we need to do is get intoxicated, or filled, with the Spirit. When we yield control to Him, He takes care of the transformation by releasing His power and influence in our lives.

When you get indigestion, you may open a little packet containing two tablets and drop them in water. Those tablets start to fizz because they are releasing power to solve your problem. But the power is in concentrated form. In order for that power to be released, you drop those two tablets in water and an explosion occurs. It's the power of the tablets being released in the water, so that the water is not plain water anymore.

When you were indwelt by the Holy Spirit, you received "Holy Ghost concentrate." The Spirit was placed in you in concentrated form. But when His power is released by your submission and willingness to be filled, He cures your spiritual indigestion and empowers you to pull off great things.

THE PROCESS OF BEING FILLED

How are we filled with the Holy Spirit? That's a crucial question, because there's a lot of confusion about the relationship between Ephesians 5:18

and verses 19–21 that follow. The issue is this: Are these things the result of being filled with the Spirit, or are they the means to His fullness?

It's important to understand what Paul is saying to us, so let's quote the verses and then we will see how they relate to our being Spirit-filled:

> Speaking to one another in psalms and hymns and spiritual songs, singing and making melody with your heart to the Lord; always giving thanks for all things in the name of our Lord Jesus Christ to God, even the Father; and be subject to one another in the fear of Christ. (vv. 19–21)

The Means of the Filling

Are these verses describing the how of being Spirit-filled, or its result? Although many Bible teachers believe these things are the result of the Spirit's filling, I want to suggest instead that they are the means to His filling.

Paul's concern here is not just to command you to be filled, but to tell you how to be filled. He does not skip the process to get to the results. I think Paul is saying that the way to be filled with the Holy Spirit is to make worship a lifestyle.

Making Worship a Lifestyle

Remember those wonderful times when you left church Sunday morning on "cloud nine"? You were spiritually full. What filled you was worshiping God in the holy environment of the family of God.

What did you do in that environment? You got filled up on God's Word. You got filled and inspired and lifted up by the music. You poured out your heart to God and you were filled with a sense of His holy presence as you communed with Him in the quietness and celebration of that hour.

All those things add up to a worship service. For one or two hours every Sunday, God's people gather in a worship service where we minister to one another and to Him. We hear His Word and we talk to Him. We worship and adore Him.

Well, who said that had to end at noon on Sunday? The way you learn to live a Spirit-filled life is to learn to do Monday through Saturday what you did on Sunday. The way you get filled with the Spirit as a day-by-day experience is to make worship a way of life

Taking Sunday Home

Here's the way it works. You leave church full of the Spirit, but when you go out on Monday and start jostling with people in a sin-soaked, sick world, your experience of the Spirit's filling can get depleted in a hurry. If He is going to continue ministering to and through you, you are going to need to refuel.

What Paul is saying in Ephesians 5:19–21 is that when worship becomes a way of life for you, when you begin to live in a spiritual environment on a day-by-day basis, you are going to be full of the Holy Spirit.

Four Ways to Get Filled

Paul gives us four specific ways we make worship a way of life, resulting in the ongoing filling of the Spirit. First, he says we are to communicate with one another: "Speaking to one another . . ." (v. 19). More believers aren't experiencing the Holy Spirit's fullness in their daily lives because their mouths and ears and hearts are so full of other stuff they don't have anything to say on the subject of the Spirit's work.

But Paul says that Christians should regularly be reinforcing others and being reinforced by others in order that their spiritual focus might be kept on track.

People in Dallas get "filled" with a certain football team every fall. Those Dallas Cowboys sure know how to throw a "worship service"! And it works. People all over town are wearing Cowboy clothes and talking Cowboy talk and squirming in the pew on Sunday so they can get home by kickoff. If your heart is set on the Cowboys, you become a Cowboys fan, but if your heart is set on Jesus, you become a Jesus fan.

How should we talk to each other? With psalms, the Word of God set to music; hymns, having to do with the expression of spiritual truth in song; and spiritual songs, having to do with our testimony, our experience with the Spirit.

Second, we are to communicate with the Lord by making melody in our hearts. This is the internal attitude of a heart that is in a continual attitude of worship.

Third, we are to give thanks for everything in Jesus' name (Ephesians 5:20). That means talking to God from a point of gratitude, not grumbling.

Fourth, when worship is a way of life, being subject to one another (Ephesians 5:21) won't be the kind of demeaning, subservient thing it is made out to be today. It will simply be an act of worship from a Spirit-filled heart to serve others, starting with our families. Servanthood reflects the spirit of Christ, so it is no wonder the Holy Spirit fills us as we reflect His attitude toward others.

GETTING THIRSTY

John 7:37–39 is a beautiful picture of the Holy Spirit's fullness. I love Jesus' invitation to the thirsty to come and drink freely.

That really nails what I have been trying to get across. Alcoholics don't just talk about drinking. They drink, long and deep. They have developed an overpowering thirst that they will sacrifice almost anything to quench.

The problem for many of us is that we are not yet thirsty enough. We are not yet tired of trying to pull off the Christian life with a maximum of our power and a minimum of Holy Ghost power. We don't see how empty we are, so we don't come to the Spirit to get filled.

So many Christians find personal devotions boring. That's because our devotions are not worship services. We're not singing in our hearts to the Lord. We're not reading the Word like God's love letter to us.

Begin your day entrusting your life to the Lord. Add a song and some Scripture, and after a while you are going to start being late for work because the worship was so good. Worship went overtime. That's what God does when you are full of Him.

APPLICATION FOR LIFE

1. The late Dr. Bill Bright, founder of Campus Crusade for Christ, helped many Christians appropriate the Spirit's fullness with his concept called "spiritual breathing." First exhale bad air. That's confession of sin. Then you inhale, claiming the Spirit's fullness as yours. It's a great concept—and, like physical breathing, you can do it as often as necessary.

2. One thing about those Pentecost Christians: they were doing things that couldn't be accounted for on merely human terms. Take a long look at your life and ask if that's true of you. If it isn't, ask the Spirit to do a new work in you.

3. Having a good hymnbook next to your Bible in your place of devotions is a great idea. Don't take one from the church pew—pastors don't like that! Many churches have extra hymnals for sale, and any Christian bookstore will have some. Make singing a regular part of your worship you never imagined possible.

4. For the next twenty-four hours, try to keep a record of what you fill your mind and heart with. Include your listening, viewing, reading, daydreaming, conversations—anything that affects your mind. Your list should tell you what you're giving the Spirit to work with and where you may need to adjust.

FOR GROUP STUDY

Questions for Group Discussion

1. Read Ephesians 5:18. What does it mean to be "filled" with the Spirit? What does 5:14–17 tell us about our need to be filled?

2. Drawing from the central passage for this lesson, Ephesians 5, Dr. Evans makes four observations about the Spirit's filling. Discuss those observations. How does each add to our understanding of the Spirit's filling?

3. Read Ephesians 5:19–21. How are we filled with the Holy Spirit? Discuss the process of being filled by the Spirit. What part does worship play in

the process? What are the four ways we get filled? (Use the "Picture This" chart as an aid for discussion.)

4. How is John 7:37–39 an excellent picture of the filling of the Spirit? What are some ways we can develop a spiritual thirst for the filling of the Spirit?

PICTURE THIS

As the apostle Paul shows us in Ephesians 5:19, when we make worship a way of life, we experience the ongoing filling of the Spirit in our lives. As worship becomes a lifestyle, we discover at least four ways we can become filled with the Spirit.

Four Ways to Get Filled with the Spirit

Ephesians 5:19–21

WAY OF FILLING	SCRIPTURE PASSAGE	HOW IT WORKS
We are to communicate with one another.	verse 19	Believers in the body fellowship with each other and help reinforce their spiritual focus.
We are to communicate with God by making melody in our hearts.	verse 19	When our heart is focused on Jesus, we become filled with the Spirit.
We are to give thanks for everything in Jesus' name.	verse 20	Speaking with God from a position of gratitude enables us to be filled with the Spirit.
We are to be subject to one another in a spirit of servanthood.	verse 21	When worship is a way of life, we reflect the Spirit of Christ and serve others.

33
THE HOLY SPIRIT'S FREEDOM

On New Year's Day, 1863, a proclamation was issued declaring that all slaves in the states of the Confederacy were now free. This document, known as the Emancipation Proclamation, resulted in the passage of the Thirteenth Amendment to the U.S. Constitution on December 18, 1865, when all slaves were formally set free.

However, for various reasons many slaves did not experience freedom. Some chose to stay enslaved to their masters because they preferred the security of slavery to the risk of freedom. Other slaves remained enslaved in their minds, even though they left the plantation, because they kept thinking and acting like slaves.

Still other slaves, like those in Texas, didn't get word until many months later that the Emancipation Proclamation had been signed.

My point is that it's a terrible thing to be free and not be able to enjoy it. Whether it's due to "Jim Crow" structures that seek to keep people in bondage, or simply a failure to understand that freedom has indeed been granted, it's a terrible thing to be free and yet not be able to throw off the chains.

That's true spiritually too, because when Jesus Christ saved you, He made you free (John 8:36). Therefore, one purpose of the Spirit's ministry is to help us experience the freedom Jesus purchased for us. This is part of the process of our sanctification, or becoming more like Christ as we grow in grace.

Experiencing the freedom of the Holy Spirit is a wonderful thing. But the process the Spirit uses to bring us to that point may not always seem so wonderful, because the Holy Spirit has to break us before He can release us.

By brokenness, I mean that work by which the Holy Spirit strips away our self-sufficiency. Now let me clarify something right here. Brokenness does not necessarily mean that everything goes wrong in our lives or that God takes everything away from us. But we all need this ministry of the Spirit because of our makeup as sinful human beings. Let me show you what I mean, because until you see how we are put together, you won't understand the need for brokenness and you won't be ready to truly experience the Holy Spirit's freedom.

THE NEED FOR BROKENNESS

First Thessalonians 5:23 says, "May your spirit and soul and body be preserved complete, without blame at the coming of our Lord Jesus Christ." We are both material and immaterial beings. Our material or physical part, the body, is that which allows us to interact with the physical world through our five senses. The immaterial is the invisible part of us, the soul and spirit.

The order in which the apostle Paul lists these elements is all-important. We are spirit, soul, and body—not body, soul, and spirit. Many people try to reverse the order as they live their lives, and they do so to disaster. If we look at ourselves as bodies first, we will work toward sanctification from the wrong direction: from the outside in, rather than from the inside out.

Our Makeup

When God formed Adam out of the dust of the ground, Adam was made a physical being. Then God breathed into Adam the "breath of life," and man became a living soul (Genesis 2:7). When man became alive, his being became fully integrated.

First of all, man developed God-consciousness because he has a spirit. This is what makes you different from an animal. You are created in God's image because you have a spirit, for God is spirit (John 4:24).

Man also developed self-consciousness because he has a soul. Animals have instinct, but not self-consciousness. That is, there is no eternal dimension to an animal because it has no soul and certainly no spirit.

Finally, man developed what you could call environmental or world consciousness because he has a body. We are aware of the world around us and can exist in it because we have bodies. Life is the ability to relate to these different levels of consciousness: the spirit to God, the soul to self, and the body to the outside world.

A Dead Spirit

But the day Adam sinned, something went wrong. His spirit died. He lost his God-consciousness. This is what God meant in Genesis 2:17 when He told Adam and Eve, "In the day that you eat from [the Tree of the Knowledge of Good and Evil] you shall surely die." Adam and Eve did not drop dead physically that day, but their spirits died. They were removed from the presence of God.

And in Adam all of us have died too (1 Corinthians 15:22). Because Adam sinned, we are all stillborn spiritually. We have no capacity to commune with God. We are dead in our sins (Ephesians 2:1). That's why we need to be born again. When you come to Jesus Christ, the Spirit of God brings your spirit alive. There is still a problem, however, because in saving you, God did not kill off your sin-scarred soul and give you a brand-new one. Your newly alive spirit is still surrounded by your soul.

A Scarred Soul

The soul is the self-conscious part of your being. It is your personhood. Your soul has to do with your mind. It's the seat of your will and emotions, your choices and decisions. All Christians have the same Holy Spirit, but it's through our souls that we express our distinct personalities.

When Adam sinned, his spirit died and he lost his ability to communicate with God, but he kept his soul. He was still a person (soul) even though he was spiritually dead.

The problem is, due to Adam's sin a negative component was added to his soul: what the Bible calls the "old man" or the sin nature. Theologians call it the Adamic nature. This sin nature affected both Adam's personhood and his personality.

Since Adam passed his sin nature on to the rest of us, we inherited his problems. The sin nature is the part of our soul that, like a magnet, gravitates to everything that is against God. Since we ourselves and those around us obey the sin nature so often, we get scarred by sin and build up scar tissue around our souls. The process of spiritual growth is peeling the scar tissue from around the soul.

I believe that if you are a Christian, your spirit is perfect. Why? Because your spirit is infused by the Holy Spirit, and God the Holy Spirit is perfect.

When you come to Christ, He gives you a brand-new spirit that is alive to God and under the control of the Holy Spirit. So there is no improvement for your spirit in the expression and demonstration of holiness. Your newly alive spirit is perfect and therefore cannot sin (1 John 3:9). Which is why Paul says that when we become believers we are already complete in Christ (Colossians 2:10). In the process of spiritual growth, the Holy Spirit is outworking our internal completeness.

Breaking the Shell

The spirit has a shell around it called the soul. The soul has a shell around it called the body. The spirit expresses itself through the soul, and the soul through the body. Your soul is what needs fixing, but you can't fix your soul just by fixing your body, because the body only does what your soul tells it to do.

That's why we need to deny our bodies the fulfillment of their sinful appetites (1 Corinthians 9:25–27), so that we can cooperate with the Spirit's program of soul transformation.

In order to fix the soul, we have to release or unleash our spirit by the ministry of the indwelling Holy Spirit. The spirit affects the soul. The soul affects the body. So if you want to live the way God wants you to live and become everything He wants you to become, His Spirit must do surgery on your soul. That's the message of Hebrews 4:12–13:

> The word of God is living and active and sharper than any two-edged sword, and piercing as far as the division of soul and spirit, of both joints and marrow, and able to judge the thoughts and intentions of the heart. And there is no creature hidden from His sight, but all things are open and laid bare to the eyes of Him with whom we have to do.

The goal of God's Word is not to make your body feel better. If that's all that happens, you have made no spiritual progress. The goal of the Word is not even to make your soul feel better, but to divide soul and spirit, to open up the soul and release the spirit.

Unless you get beyond the body to the soul and the soul is broken and transformed by the release of the spirit, you will never get to the core of who you are and you will never realize the Holy Spirit's power that can fix who you are. This is why the Word of God is so important. It alone can penetrate to divide the soul and spirit.

Your soul is still in need of Spirit surgery. God wants to grow you into the person He wants you to be, the process we identified earlier as sanctification.

But to do that, He has to remove the scar tissue from your soul. The way He does that is through the release of your spirit under the ministry of the Holy Spirit.

THE AGENT OF BROKENNESS

Paul writes in Galatians 2:20: "I have been crucified with Christ; and it is no longer I who live, but Christ lives in me; and the life which I now live in the flesh I live by faith in the Son of God, who loved me, and delivered Himself up for me."

In other words, Paul made a trade. He traded his soul life for his spirit life. He allowed the Holy Spirit to break his soul and bring forth his spirit life in such a way that it took over and began to dominate his existence. When it did, Paul became a transformed man.

The Revealer

Too many of us are trying to fix our souls ourselves. We can cover it and try to hide the scars, but the only way to fix the soul is to crack it open so that the spirit comes forth. Then, as we saw above, light will shine in the darkness.

There is only one way to fix darkness. You have got to penetrate it with light. Once you turn on the light, you have addressed the darkness. Many of us are trying to address the dark spots in our lives by trying to come up with a darkness remedy. But the only darkness remedy is light.

The Divine Surgeon

It is the Spirit's job to break open the soul by cutting into it like a skilled surgeon. The Spirit must cut away the accumulated scar tissue of your soul to set your spirit free.

There is only one part of you that is like God: your spirit. God is pure spirit (John 4:24). Your soul has been contaminated by sin, but the spirit is pure. It is totally under the control of the Holy Spirit.

If God ever broke open your soul and you experienced the Spirit's release, you would grow spiritually more than you ever thought you could, and you would become more than you ever thought you could be. You would find your personality changing because the Spirit broke you and released Himself in you through your spirit.

In other words, you would begin to experience the freedom of the Holy Spirit in ways you never imagined. I want to define freedom biblically before we go any further. Freedom never means you are free to do whatever you want. That's license. Freedom means that God has liberated us to fulfill the purposes for which He saved us. He has freed us up to become what He redeemed us to become.

FREE TO BECOME

In Galatians 5:1, Paul writes, "It was for freedom that Christ set us free; therefore keep standing firm and do not be subject again to a yoke of slavery."

God did not set you free so you could go back to slavery. He did not release you so that you could get bound up again. Paul states emphatically that when Christ set you free, He intended for you to stay that way by releasing you from the sinful bondage of the flesh, which hinders our day-to-day experience of God's power and presence in our lives.

Freedom within Rules

Freedom is becoming what God created you to be. It does not mean there are no rules. Without sidelines and foul lines, a football game or tennis match or baseball game would be nothing but chaos. The only thing that makes the game work is that there are restrictions.

Within those boundaries, there is still an awful lot of room for creativity and energy and action. That's what makes sports enjoyable for many people to watch. Within God's boundaries, we still have a lot of flexibility in how we go about becoming what He saved us to be. So don't let anyone tell you that Holy Spirit freedom is just another form of slavery.

There is a form of so-called freedom which is just that: a form of slavery. It's the kind of freedom the world peddles all the time. When a drug addict says he wants to be free to take drugs, what he is literally saying is, "I want the freedom to become a slave of drugs."

When a man without morals says, "I want to be free to pursue any and every woman I can find," he is saying he wants to be free to be a person who has no control over his passions and is, therefore, a slave of his passions.

There is a lot of confusion today about freedom. But God is not confused at all. When He talks about freedom, He means the ability to become what He created you and saved you to be. And God is not confused about where the dynamic of freedom is located. It comes to us "through the Spirit, by faith" (Galatians 5:5). Your freedom comes when the Holy Spirit is at work in your life.

The Supply Line

Paul writes, "Where the Spirit of the Lord is, there is liberty" (2 Corinthians 3:17). What a declaration of freedom! So if you are all bound up, the Spirit is not having His free flow in your life for some reason. The supply of freedom is there, but something is cutting off the supply line.

Some believers are, to use the psychological term, *codependent.* That is, they are slaves to somebody else. Somebody else is playing God in their lives.

If this is true for you, then one thing is sure. God can't be God in your life. And if God isn't God in your life, there is no Spirit control.

That explains why Paul tells the Galatians, "If you receive circumcision, Christ will be of no benefit to you" (5:2). If these believers let the Judaizers dictate to them—play God in their lives—they would forfeit their spiritual benefits.

In fact, the apostle didn't leave the issue there. He went on to say in verse 4, "You have been severed from Christ . . . you have fallen from grace."

What does Paul mean? He means the supply line of the Spirit who gave them the ability to be all that God wanted them to be had been cut off. They had allowed something to bring them into bondage.

It's easy to lose our focus. If you are in bondage as a believer, you are losing your spiritual focus. The Holy Spirit has not been allowed to set you free, even though Christ has purchased your freedom. But once you allow the Spirit to begin cutting away the scar tissue around your soul to release your spirit, you will experience the joy of Jesus' words: "If the Son make you free, you will be free indeed" (John 8:36).

APPLICATION FOR LIFE

1. Maybe you're saying, "I really don't see any need to be broken. I'm OK." If that is your position, it's time for you to change your position by dropping to your knees and asking God to show you yourself as you really are. Or if you say, "I see the need, but I can't honestly say I'm willing for God to do that," tell God about it. He can handle your lack of willingness. Ask Him to make you "willing to be willing."

2. Imagine a surgeon rushing through a operation because he wants to finish before the ball game starts, or trying to operate the last thing before he goes to bed when he's dead sleepy. That's how a lot of us handle our Bibles. The Holy Spirit is a skilled surgeon and the Word is sharp, but it takes more than a few hurried minutes for the Word to do its searching and dividing. How much time is in your schedule for the Word?

3. Nobody really enjoys being disciplined. But discipline is one way God breaks us and frees our spirits. Are you running from a difficult person or circumstance God is trying to use to teach you something? Better turn around because the second round of discipline is always harder.

4. Maybe you're still dragging around something from the old life, and it's pulling you down. Go somewhere alone, shut the door, and allow the Holy Spirit to poke around the corners of your spiritual attic until you've dealt with everything that could be holding you back from experiencing the Spirit's freedom.

FOR GROUP STUDY

Questions for Group Discussion

1. What does Dr. Evans mean by the term *brokenness*? Read 1 Thessalonians 5:23. Why do we have a need for brokenness?

2. Read Hebrews 4:12–13; James 1:2–3; and Romans 12:1. What is the process of brokenness, and what happens when we are broken? What are its benefits? (See the "Picture This" chart as an aid to discussion.)

3. Galatians 2:20 teaches us that the Holy Spirit is the agent of brokenness. In what ways does the Spirit strip away our self-sufficiency?
4. What happens when we experience the freedom of the Spirit? What do we learn from Galatians 5:1 regarding our freedom?

PICTURE THIS

The Spirit's stripping away of our self-sufficiency is a process that involves the three steps below. Only through this process may we experience the blessings of brokenness and freedom in the Spirit.

THE PROCESS OF BROKENNESS

STEP IN PROCESS	SCRIPTURE PASSAGE	WHAT IT MEANS
The Word of God	Hebrews 4:12–13	God's Word is alive and cuts into our innermost being with its transforming power.
Our discipline	James 1:2–3	God cuts through our souls and releases His Spirit through the trials He brings our way.
Our consecration	Romans 12:1	Our yielding to whatever the Spirit is doing in our lives to fix what is wrong.

34

THE HOLY SPIRIT'S ILLUMINATION

One benefit of the Spirit's abiding presence that believers enjoy is His ministry of illumination, or enlightenment. When I talk about the illuminating ministry of the Holy Spirit, I am referring to that process of spiritual enlightenment whereby the Spirit enables you to grasp, experience, and apply God's truth in your daily Christian life.

This ministry is critical because the Bible makes clear that the person without Christ, the unbeliever, has a darkened mind. That is, no matter how brilliant this person may be, he or she does not have the capacity to understand—or the access to—spiritual truth.

In His role as the Illuminator, the Spirit enlightens us so that we are able to grasp, experience, and apply God's Word to our lives. Anybody who can do that, we need to be close to. The Spirit can connect us to the mind of God.

SPIRITUAL DISCERNMENT

One way the Spirit illumines us is by giving us spiritual discernment—the ability to distinguish good from bad, right from wrong, to make sense out of what is happening. In 1 Corinthians 2:9–10, Paul talks about the great things God has for us and how He has revealed them to us by His Spirit.

Thus illumination is an experience because it involves our awareness.

The Depths of God

The Holy Spirit searches the very depths of the heart and mind of God. In fact, He is Himself God, the third Person of the Trinity. Paul says in 1 Corinthians 2:11 that the Spirit functions within the Trinity the way our human spirit functions within us. Our spirit is the innermost part of our being where our deepest, most private thoughts reside.

Because we have a spirit, we are usually our own best interpreter. That's why when two people get into an argument, one of them will often say, "Don't try to tell me what I mean. I know what I am saying."

The Holy Spirit is tuned in to the deepest thoughts of God. He has access to the innermost workings of the Godhead. And He is pleased to reveal them to us (v. 12).

Our Translator

In essence, the Holy Spirit acts as our translator. This is important for several reasons. Through the illuminating and revealing ministry of the Holy Spirit, we have access to the very heart and mind of God. That is a staggering thought.

God is speaking a language we can't interpret. We need a translator, somebody who can put God's words into words we can understand. But we don't just need a human translator like a pastor or a friend. We need a Spirit translator who can explain what it means deep down in our innermost being.

The Spirit of God knows the deep things of God. He is like a deep-sea diver who can go down into the depths and find out what's down there. That's why the Bible says that even when you don't know what is going on, the Spirit can help you because He dives down deep.

In 1 Corinthians 2:13, Paul says this all happens "not in words taught by human wisdom, but in those taught by the Spirit, combining spiritual thoughts with spiritual words."

We know we can trust the Bible because the thoughts that the authors' minds told them to record were the thoughts given to them by the Spirit. The result was truth without error.

We aren't guaranteed that degree of accuracy in our lives today, but I do think Paul is talking about a process of spiritual discernment that we have available to us. In 1 Corinthians 2:14, he writes: "But a natural man does not accept the things of the Spirit of God; for they are foolishness to him, and he cannot understand them, because they are spiritually appraised." Who among us could possibly know the mind of the Lord? Answer: nobody, except the Spirit. He alone knows the mind of God, so if you want to know God you must link up with the Spirit.

The Anointing

In 1 John 2:20, 27 the apostle writes:

> You have an anointing from the Holy One, and you all know. . . . The anointing which you received from Him abides in you, and you have no need for anyone to teach you; but as His anointing teaches you about all things, and is true and is not a lie, and just as it has taught you, you abide in Him.

All Christians are anointed. I know we say that about a particular preacher or musician, but if you are a Christian, you are anointed too because it is the capacity to know God's truth.

Every Christian has the same spiritual capacity when it comes to walking with God. We all have different IQs, but in the spiritual realm we have the same capacity for intimacy with God. That means you have the capacity to hear the voice of the Spirit.

I like to illustrate the anointing by pointing to something you may have in your backyard: a satellite dish. The anointing of God is like a satellite dish that points upward, pulls in a signal from the heavens, and translates the signal into a message you can see and understand.

As God transmits His message to you, the One who translates that message is the Holy Spirit. That's why your spirit needs to stay closely linked with the Holy Spirit. John calls it abiding in Christ (1 John 2:27). This illuminating or enlightening work comes to and through the human spirit.

John makes a statement in verse 27 that confuses a lot of people: "You have no need for anyone to teach you." John doesn't mean that the body of

Christ has no need for human teachers. Teachers are one of Christ's gifts to His church (Ephesians 4:11). I think John is referring to teachers who approach life from a non-Christian perspective—such as you would get from a horoscope, a psychic hotline, or any other non-Christian approach to life.

When the Holy Spirit has sensitized your human spirit, you know when something is not right spiritually. That's because Christians have a Witness, the Holy Spirit, who has anointed us to be able to understand the truth.

THE POWER OF RECALL

A second aspect of the Spirit's illuminating work is the power of spiritual recall. In John 14:26, Jesus says: "But the Helper, the Holy Spirit, whom the Father will send in My name, He will teach you all things, and bring to your remembrance all that I said to you."

The Authors of Scripture

Some of the books in the Bible were written forty years after Jesus died. So some people wonder, How could ordinary fishermen and tax collectors and laborers remember what Jesus said and write it down exactly as Jesus wanted it written?

Because the Holy Spirit enabled these men to think things they would not normally think and remember things they would not normally remember. Jesus told them, "When the time comes for you to remember what you need to remember, My Holy Spirit has it on file and will remind you of what I said."

You say, "I try to memorize verses, but I can't remember them." Oh, but the Holy Spirit remembers them. Haven't you had an experience in which you did not know exactly where a verse was found, and you could not quote it word for word, but you knew it was in the Bible and you were able to recall enough of it to use it in a given situation? That was the Holy Spirit

Christians Today

Let's not get mystical or mysterious here. The Holy Spirit won't remind you of something you never bothered to learn. Kids often ask their parents, "Why do I have to study the Bible? Why do I have to go to church?" Actually, a lot of adults are wondering the same thing. Answer: It gives the Holy Spirit something to bring up, some truth to work with.

There's a great example of this in Matthew 10. Jesus was giving His disciples instructions before sending them out to preach the good news. In verse 19 He told them, "When they deliver you up, do not become anxious about how or what you will speak; for it shall be given you in that hour what you are to speak."

Notice what Jesus said. The apostles would have what they needed when the time came that they needed it. He didn't give them a book of speeches ahead of time. Many of us want God to enlighten us now about what will happen a year down the road. We worry about stuff that God has no intention of giving us in advance.

The promise of the Spirit's teaching and reminding ministry is for all believers, because Jesus' condition for benefiting from the Spirit's indwelling presence is obedience to His commandments (John 14:21–24). That's a condition you and I can meet.

In addition, this promise is in the very same verse (14:26) as Jesus' promise of the Spirit's overall enabling ministry. So to limit the promise and experience of the Spirit's teaching and reminding ministry to the first century is to limit the Spirit's role as the divine Helper to the first century.

SPIRITUAL CONFIDENCE

Another aspect of the Spirit's illuminating ministry is that it gives you spiritual confidence. "For God has not given us a spirit of timidity, but of power and love and discipline" (2 Timothy 1:7).

Know Where You're Going

We don't have to be timid as Christians, because through the illumination or enlightenment of the Holy Spirit, we can know where we're going and what's happening.

I see an example of this in Acts 20:17–38, the story of Paul's farewell to the elders of Ephesus. In verses 22–23, Paul told these men that he was on his way to Jerusalem and that the Holy Spirit had revealed to him that he was in for a very rough time.

So why didn't Paul quit and turn back? Because, "I do not consider my life of any account as dear to myself, in order that I may finish my course, and the ministry which I received from the Lord Jesus, to testify solemnly of the gospel of the grace of God" (v. 24). Paul knew that God would see him through to the completion of his ministry. That's spiritual confidence.

Not Necessarily Easy

Now, confidence doesn't mean God is going to make everything easy. If it were all easy, you wouldn't need any confidence. You may be facing a rough time at home or at work right now. But when you are walking in the Holy Spirit and He tells you to go on anyhow, go on anyhow!

Seeing More

The reason many of us don't have confidence is that we are looking at the wrong people. We look at our boss as though he controls the bottom line. We look at the people who are against us as though they control events. But when you are full of the Spirit and He illumines you, you get to see things other people don't see. You get insights other folk don't have.

I love the story of the Emmaus disciples in Luke 24:13–35. The two were dejected and downcast. Jesus had been crucified. But along came a Stranger who opened the Bible to them and then opened their eyes to His identity. Their emotions changed because Jesus showed them something other people didn't see.

That's illumination, and that's what the Spirit has come to do in our hearts. When He turns on the light of God's glory in you, then you'll have the joy of the Lord even if things are bad.

SPIRITUAL DIRECTION

Here's a fourth aspect or benefit of the Holy Spirit's illuminating work: spiritual direction.

Life is full of tough decisions, the kind that make some people want to pull their hair out. Well, in the Holy Spirit you have a Guide who has been down this road before and knows where you are supposed to go and when you are supposed to get there.

Two Examples

In Acts 8, we meet Philip the evangelist, who went to Samaria and lit a revival. Just when things were going great, though, God pulled him out of Samaria and put him on a desert road, where the Spirit sent him to an Ethiopian official. Philip obeyed the Spirit, led the man to faith, and baptized him. Then the Spirit snatched Philip away for his next assignment (v. 39).

In Acts 10, a passage we keep turning to, Peter the racist who could not stand Gentiles was led by the Spirit to the house of Cornelius, where he wound up leading Gentiles into the kingdom. Now, God had to go some to enlighten Peter, but the illumination of the Spirit overcame racism and culturalism.

The beauty of the illuminating work of the Spirit of God is that He redirects your life according to God's agenda. And when you're following God's agenda, you're on your way!

God's Word

There are several things the Spirit uses to give us spiritual direction. The first is the Word of God. Here I am not talking about the specifics of whom to marry or where to work. I'm talking about the will of God for all believers that's clearly revealed in Scripture.

For example, the Spirit illumines the Word so we can see ourselves as we really are. He is going to use the Word to show us that we're not as good and as attractive as we thought we were.

The Spirit wants you to see that which is not what it should be so He can make it what it should be. He always starts with the Word. So if you do not have a commitment to the objective truth of Scripture, don't expect the subjective leading of the Spirit.

Don't expect Him to lead you to a godly mate if you don't have a biblical commitment to being holy while you are single. Don't expect the Spirit to reveal unknown facets of God's will if you aren't obeying the will of God revealed in His Word. Spiritual direction has to start with a commitment to the Word because Scripture reflects the Spirit's way of thinking.

Circumstances

The Holy Spirit also leads through circumstances. I remind you that Romans 8:28 says, "All things . . . work together for good" if we love God.

That's *all* things. So for the believer, there is no such thing as luck or coincidence or accident. All things work together for good. That means good things, bad things, up things, and down things work together for good.

God takes the good and the bad, stirs them together, and comes out with a pretty good meal on the other side. The negative thing you are experiencing right now is the thing He can use to achieve His positive results.

Common Sense

In Acts 15, the church had a controversy about what to do about Gentiles. James rendered a judgment, and verse 22 says it "seemed good" to the apostles and elders. It just seemed like the right thing to do.

But that's not all. It also "seemed good to the Holy Spirit" (v. 28). That's sanctified common sense. Now notice that it didn't seem good until they held a meeting of godly people and talked it over. In other words, if God is leading you in a way that makes good sense, He's going to tell someone else. This plan didn't make sense just to one person. If the Spirit doesn't seem to be telling anybody but you, better go slow.

Satan

God can even use Satan to help give you direction. I see it in 2 Corinthians 12, the well-known case of Paul's "thorn in the flesh" (vv. 7–9). He called it a "messenger of Satan" and asked God three times to take it away. God's answer was, "My grace is sufficient for you" (v. 9). So Paul rejoiced in that answer to prayer.

God used Satan to keep Paul humble before Him. God allowed Satan to inject a negative thing into Paul's life to achieve His positive purposes. God may use negative things to achieve His will in us—even if the negative thing comes from the Devil.

Other People

The Spirit's ministry of illumination may operate without human intervention. But He often uses other people in the process of illuminating us.

This happens, for instance, when the gospel is preached and the Spirit opens the eyes of unbelievers to their need for salvation (Acts 2:36–41). It also happens as Christians regularly place themselves under the ministry of a Spirit-filled teacher (1 Thessalonians 1:5–6; 2:9–13).

I can testify in my own life how God used other people to redirect me and help me see God's will from a different perspective. The Spirit used people in my life: a professor, a new friend. And He's used many others over the years.

He will do the same for you. The Holy Spirit is the Illuminator. His job is to help you understand God's Word and discern God's will. And He will shine the light of God on your path if you're committed to Him.

APPLICATION FOR LIFE

1. You've probably heard this before, but you'd be amazed how much of God's will, even His specific desires, is revealed for us in the Bible. Get out your Bible concordance—or go out and get one if you need it—and look up the word *will*. Then be prepared to obey what you find.

2. What situation or person do you feel the least confident in handling today? That may be exactly where you'll find the spiritual confidence we talked about. Try looking beyond just what you can see—the people, the events, the hurts, whatever. Ask the Holy Spirit to enlighten your spiritual eyes so you can see beyond the obvious to His purposes in your trial.

3. Dr. Evans used a satellite dish to illustrate our ability to receive and translate the things of God. You have the same capacity as every other believer to tune in, because you have the same Holy Spirit. Are you allowing outside interference, competing signals, to jam your spiritual receiver? Better do a "program check" to make sure God has your undivided attention.

4. When it comes to seeking direction, we usually just pray, "Lord, lead me today." That's not really what He wants to hear. Try praying this way and see what happens: "Lord, I am yours today. Bring those influences and people into my life that You can use to keep me close to You and walking in Your truth."

FOR GROUP STUDY

Questions for Group Discussion

1. What is spiritual discernment? Read 1Corinthians 2:9–10. What is the Spirit's role in our spiritual discernment?

2. John 14:26 speaks of the Spirit's power of recall. In what practical ways does He effect this power in our lives?

3. See 2 Timothy 1:7. Another aspect of the Spirit's illuminating ministry is that He gives us spiritual confidence. In what ways does the Spirit instill spiritual confidence in us?

4. In what ways do we receive spiritual direction from the Spirit? What resources may we draw from for direction? (Use the chart below as an aid to discussion.)

PICTURE THIS

The Holy Spirit uses many ways to provide us spiritual direction. Below are few of the most common methods.

How We Receive Spiritual Direction

METHOD	SCRIPTURE PASSAGES	HOW THE METHOD WORKS
God's Word	2 Timothy 3:16	God's will is revealed in His Word. Our spiritual direction must start with a commitment to His Word.
Circumstances	Romans 8:28	The Holy Spirit leads us through our circumstances. He can use any circumstance to achieve His positive results.
Common sense	Acts 15:22–28	The Holy Spirit leads in a way that makes good sense, not only to you, but to others as well.
Satan	2 Corinthians 12:7–9	The Holy Spirit may use negative things to achieve His will in us—even if the negative thing comes from the Devil himself.
Other people	Acts 2:36–41; 1 Thessalonians 1:5–6; 2:9–13	The Holy Spirit often uses other people in the process of illuminating us. Be open to direction from other believers in the body of Christ.

SECTION II

The Purpose of the Holy Spirit

35

THE HOLY SPIRIT'S CONVICTION

A young boy was at Disneyland enjoying Mickey Mouse and Donald Duck and the rides and the popcorn and the fanfare and didn't notice that he had become separated from his parents. He was enjoying the hustle and bustle of Disney life until he looked up and discovered that his parents were not there.

Once this boy discovered he was not in fellowship with his parents anymore, Disneyland turned into a Disney disaster. All of sudden, the cotton candy wasn't sweet, the rides were not fun, and Mickey Mouse was no longer cute, because Mom and Dad were nowhere to be found.

That's the great tragedy of our world: people so busy enjoying the rides and the thrills and the bright lights that they haven't even noticed they are not in fellowship with God. They are so busy sucking on the cotton candy of life, riding the Ferris wheel of entertainment, and going up and down the roller coaster of pleasure that they haven't even noticed God is not in the vicinity anymore.

That young boy at Disneyland needed to come face-to-face with two realities before he could get help. First, he needed to discover he was lost. And second, he needed somebody to lead him back to his parents.

The Bible declares that, apart from God, all people are eternally lost. They are forever separated from the life of God. They need to know they are lost, and they need to know the way back home.

Enter the Holy Spirit. He is the champion of the lost and found. His unique task is to bring men and women front and center before Jesus Christ: to bring the unregenerate and the unconverted into a saving relationship with Christ and to keep the regenerate in constant fellowship with Christ.

THE GREAT CONVICTER

One of the ministries of the Holy Spirit is that of conviction. That is stated quite clearly in John 16:8, particularly as it relates to the unregenerate world: "And [the Holy Spirit], when He comes, will convict the world concerning sin, and righteousness, and judgment."

The key word here is *convict.* When the Bible speaks of convicting someone of something, it is referring to a concept we could use synonymously with conviction—that of convincing. The job of the Holy Spirit is to make absolutely clear the spiritual issues of life and to call for a decision.

Unsaved people walk around in a spiritual fog or daze, not really understanding what God expects from them. You hear it every time you talk to an unbeliever. Just ask that person, "Are you going to heaven?"

"Well," he will usually say, "I sure hope so. I think so." When you ask him what he's pinning his hopes for heaven on, he may tell you, "I try to keep the Ten Commandments. I go to church. I'm doing the best I can." It's clear this person is lost in a deep fog.

So great confusion abounds when it comes to the things of God. The Holy Spirit's job is to make the issue clear and to jar people loose of their misconceptions about the good news of the gospel. And we'll see later that His job is also to jar us Christians loose of our misconceptions about intimacy with God.

The Spirit is the great Convicter, the great Convincer, the great Explainer. But in order to do this, He must get people's attention. He has to break through the fog that blinds the unsaved because of their darkened hearts (2 Corinthians 4:3–4), and He has to dispel the sinful distractions that get the saved off the track of fellowship with God.

CONVICTION OF SIN

In John 16:9–11, Jesus went on to explain more about the three areas in which the Holy Spirit must do His convicting work. The first of these is sin, "because they do not believe in Me" (v. 9). Unsaved people don't understand two realities about sin.

The Sinfulness of Sin

First, people do not realize how exceedingly sinful sin is. They will call it a mistake, a bad habit, a weakness—anything to soften the blow.

But God calls it sin. It is an affront to His holiness. The world does not understand that. Lost people do not understand that when you break one of God's commandments, you are held as guilty as though you had broken them all (James 2:10). People do not understand that salvation is not by works of righteousness they can do, and that they are powerless to cancel out their sin because they have offended a holy God.

And so the Holy Spirit must make clear to sinners the seriousness of sin. People must see that they have fallen short of the divine standard, that God is so infinitely holy there is no such thing as a "good" sinner versus a "bad" sinner. We are all sinners. Only the Holy Spirit can bring that conviction, because most people are convinced they aren't all that bad. The trouble is, people who do that are measuring themselves against the wrong standard. The measure of sin is not our neighbor.

When God measures us, He measures us against Himself and His standard of perfect righteousness. That's why all of us fall short of the standard (Romans 3:23). It takes the Holy Spirit to convince a sinner he's really as bad off as God says he is.

Rejecting the Savior

But there is something more specific the Holy Spirit wants to convict the world of: the ultimate sin of rejecting the Savior. This is vitally important to understand, so allow me a brief excursion into biblical theology.

Before Adam plunged the human race into sin, God had already prepared a way to reconcile sinners to Himself and bring them into relationship with Himself. The way God did this was by providing us a Savior, Jesus Christ.

What the cross of Christ did on behalf of all sinners everywhere was to satisfy the demands and the wrath of a holy God against sin. That's why the Bible says, "God was in Christ reconciling the world to Himself, not counting their trespasses against them" (2 Corinthians 5:19). In Romans 5:15, Paul says that in Adam the "many" died, but in Christ the same "many" have been made alive.

In other words, the death of Jesus Christ removed the barrier that kept sinners from being reconciled to a holy God, thus freeing God to save anyone and everyone who believes. Every person is still responsible to come to Christ in repentance and faith to be saved, but Christ's death makes that transaction available to all.

So the fact is that people do not go to hell simply because they sin. People go to hell because they reject the Savior. The lost are not separated from God forever because they did certain sins, because God provided a way of forgiveness for those sins by the death of Christ. The issue on the table is what a person does with Christ.

So the first thing the Holy Spirit does is convince men and women that they are sinners and convict them of the ultimate sin of rejecting Jesus Christ. That's why, when Peter stood up on the day of Pentecost and preached, the Bible says that the hearers were "pierced to the heart" (Acts 2:37). The Spirit convinced them, and all they could do was ask, "What shall we do?"

CONVICTION OF RIGHTEOUSNESS

The second area of the Spirit's convicting work is "concerning righteousness, because I go to the Father, and you no longer behold Me" (John 16:10).

Revealing the Standard

The Holy Spirit convinces the world of a new standard of righteousness, which is Christ. The reason the Spirit must convict men is that Jesus Christ is no longer on earth to demonstrate His righteousness. You can't see Him walk down the street. You can't watch Him cast out demons and make the lame walk. He has ascended to heaven.

It's the Spirit's job to convince people that Jesus Christ is the only perfectly righteous One who has ever lived, the only One who has perfectly measured up to God's holy standard. Others have claimed to be a savior. But Jesus died on Friday and got up on Sunday and showed Himself alive to more than five hundred brethren (1 Corinthians 15:6)!

The thing that sets Jesus apart, and the reason I am a Christian today, is that the grave is empty. Jesus Christ is the only One who has beaten death and can lay claim to being the righteous standard of God.

Accepting the Standard

Remember in school when you and almost everybody else messed up bad on a test? The teacher would throw a curve on those grades, which is what you were hoping for. But there was always one smart student who would ace the test. So you lost out because Mr. or Miss Know-It-All messed up the curve, which raised the scores needed for a really good test grade.

The problem with Jesus is He ruins the curve. You think you are OK spiritually until you run into Him. Then you find out that you and everybody else *failed* the test of meeting God's standard.

When I stand before God, I will have no excuse. I will not be able to cop a plea. There will be nothing I can offer God to pay for my sins.

My only plea on that day will be, "Father, I have accepted the righteousness of Jesus, your Son, as my righteousness. For You to reject me, You will have to reject Him, because I stand in Him. I have banked my eternal destiny on Your acceptance of Christ and His acceptance of me."

Christ is the only standard of righteousness that satisfies God's demands. The Holy Spirit must convince us of this truth, because we would never arrive at this conclusion on our own.

CONVICTION OF JUDGMENT

Jesus describes the third aspect of the Holy Spirit's convicting work in John 16:11. He convicts "concerning judgment, because the ruler of this world has been judged."

The Reality of Judgment

How do we know judgment is real? Because Satan, "the ruler of this world," has been judged. If Satan did not get away with his sin, neither will any of his followers. If Satan did not get away with rebelling against the holy standard of God, then neither will any who adopt him as their father.

Hell was not prepared for human beings. Jesus said hell was prepared for Satan and his angels (Matthew 25:41). God never intended people to be separated from Him for eternity. However, if that is your vote, He will not turn down your request.

Someone says, "I never voted to spend eternity with Satan." Oh, yes, you did! Every time you sin, that's a vote for hell. Every time you think an evil thought, every time you act outside the will of God, that's a vote for hell.

The Need for Judgment

You may wonder why Satan is still around bothering you if he has been judged. Well, Satan has been judged, but his full sentence hasn't been carried out yet (see Revelation 20:10). And he has a horde of demonic cronies who carry out his agenda in history. So his judgment becomes the judgment of anyone who rejects Christ.

CONVICTION OF THE SAINTS

The convicting and convincing work of the Holy Spirit is not limited to sinners. It is also the Spirit's work in the lives of the saints. This work takes a slightly different form and has a different purpose in our case, but it is still very real.

Making the Saints Uncomfortable

Because He is the Holy Spirit, His job is to make us uncomfortable with our sin. You have good reason to question your salvation if you never feel any guilt over sin. I don't care how many times you have walked down an aisle or how many forms you have filled out. If you can sin perpetually and never feel it, maybe your problem is not that you have backslid. Maybe your problem is that you have never "frontslid."

The Sin of the Saints

The Bible is clear that believers sin. That is why the Scripture says, "Do not quench the Spirit" (1 Thessalonians 5:19). Don't throw water on the fire when the Holy Spirit is convicting you of sin, because this is the way the Spirit pricks you.

We are told in Ephesians 4:30 not to "grieve" the Spirit by our sin. The Spirit is saddened by sinful speech, and He lets us know it because He lives within us. Your body is the Spirit's temple, and when your temple starts going places it ought not go and doing things it ought not do, the Holy Spirit, like a metal detector in an airport, goes off when He detects something illegitimate.

The Fellowship of the Saints

The issue we're talking about for true Christians is not that of salvation, but that of fellowship. The Holy Spirit convicts the saints of sin that we might draw closer to the Lord and please Him. This is made clear in the book of 1 John.

John says in 1:5, "This is the message we have heard from Him and announce to you, that God is light, and in Him there is no darkness at all." Now verse 7: "If we walk in the light as He Himself is in the light, we have fellowship with one another, and the blood of Jesus His Son cleanses us from all sin."

Please note: It is when we are walking in the light that the blood of Christ does its work of cleansing us from all sin. It is only when you are in the light that you see sin as sin. When you are in darkness, you don't see anything wrong with sin. It's only when you turn the light on that you see the stain.

The Action of the Saints

When the Holy Spirit reveals that you have displeased God, then you ought to take action. That's the whole point of 1 John 1:9, the classic verse on confession of sin for the believer: "If we confess our sins, He is faithful and righteous to forgive us our sins and to cleanse us from all unrighteousness."

The Greek word for "confess," *homologeō*, means to say the same thing, to agree. If you are going to be in fellowship with God, you have to say the same thing about your sin that the Holy Spirit says about your sin.

Far too many of us treat sin lightly. Like the unregenerate, we say, "Well, everybody does it." That's not what the convicting Holy Spirit says. He says, "You did it, and it's wrong." But confession is not simply saying glibly, "OK, so I sinned. I'm sorry." That's not the attitude of confession.

Confession means that I see this sin as God sees it, as something hideous and ugly, because I am measuring it against how God feels about it. When you have a conflict with someone and he or she blows it off as no big deal, that bothers you if it's a big deal to you.

Sin is a big deal to the Spirit, and He doesn't want us treating it like a little thing. When you do, you haven't practiced biblical confession. In fact, please note that the word in verse 9 is plural: "sins." John is talking about individual sins. That's how seriously God takes sin. He wants each one dealt with.

The reason the Holy Spirit is so faithful to convict us of sin the moment we sin is that He knows God cannot fellowship with sin of any size or on any level. So when I think a wrong thought, I am to confess that thought as sin. When I do an evil deed, I am to confess that deed when the Spirit alerts me to it.

Taking the Spirit Seriously

So the convicting work of the Holy Spirit lets you know when you are grieving Him or pouring water on the fire that He is placing on your conscience to bring you to confession.

The Holy Spirit is not to be trifled with. We must take seriously His call to holiness. None of us is perfect, don't misunderstand. We will always wrestle with sin. But we also need to be alert to His convicting and purifying work.

BROKEN OVER SIN

Real conviction should result in true confession. True confession is brokenness over sin. If that is not how you are treating your sin, no matter what you say you are not confessing it. When the Holy Spirit does His convicting work, He doesn't want a halfhearted confession.

When it comes to the conviction of the Spirit, we are like the general who was defeated in war and said to the victorious general, "I have come to negotiate the terms of my surrender."

The victorious general replied, "No, I will give you the terms of your surrender." On this matter of sin, God is not negotiating. He has set the terms of forgiveness and restoration of fellowship. Those terms are "a broken and a contrite heart" (Psalm 51:17).

The good news is that the convicting work of the Holy Spirit is designed to put us on our feet again—to restore us to the One we love, to draw us closer to our Lord. Let the Spirit do His work and experience anew the joy of God's sweet fellowship.

APPLICATION FOR LIFE

1. The first thing to remember is that the Holy Spirit is the convicter, not you. You just need to be faithful in presenting the gospel. So free yourself from the responsibility of trying to make people believe by the force of your persuasion.

2. Having said that, there are many things you can do to help your unsaved friends think clearly about the issues involved in salvation. Since most people try to justify themselves, jar them from their complacency by asking questions like, Just how good do you have to be to make heaven? How will you know when you've been good enough? What standard are you using to measure goodness? Do you live up to your own standard all the time? What happens when you don't?

3. Since the Holy Spirit's job is to convince unbelievers of sin, we had better keep the discussion centered on sin. People don't need Christ because they need fulfillment, joy, or peace. Those are the by-products of salvation. People need Christ because they are lost sinners under God's judgment.

4. What about your own sin? If you don't have a broken heart toward your sin, ask God to give you one. If you don't feel bad about your rebellion, ask God to make you feel bad about it so you can do something about it. God can handle your honesty, but He cannot tolerate sin.

FOR GROUP STUDY

Questions for Group Discussion

1. Begin by reading John 16:8 and 2 Corinthians 4:3–4. Describe the Holy Spirit's ministry as the Great Convicter. What does it entail?

2. Read John 16:9–11. What two realities about sin does the Spirit's ministry of conviction help us understand?

3. John 16:10 speaks of the Spirit's conviction of righteousness. How does He accomplish this ministry? Upon what aspects does He focus?

4. The Holy Spirit's convicting work is not limited to sinners but is also directed toward believers. Discuss the areas of focus of this ministry of the Spirit. (Use the chart below as an aid for your discussion.)

PICTURE THIS

The convicting work of the Holy Spirit is also at work in the lives of God's people. Although it takes a slightly different form and has a different purpose, it is still a very real focus and ministry of the Spirit.

THE HOLY SPIRIT'S CONVICTION OF GOD'S PEOPLE

AREA OF FOCUS	SCRIPTURE PASSAGES	REASON FOR THE SPIRIT'S CONVICTION
Making God's people uncomfortable	1 John 1:9	One of the Spirit's purposes in conviction is to make us uncomfortable with our sin so we will then confess our sin.
The sin of God's people	1 Thessalonians 5:19; Ephesians 4:30	We are not to quench the Spirit or grieve the Spirit when He convicts us of sin.
The fellowship of God's people	John 1:5, 7	The Spirit wants us to draw closer to God and walk in the light that we might fellowship with one another.
The action of God's people	1 John 1:9	The Spirit convicts us when we sin because He knows God cannot fellowship with sin.
God's people taking the Spirit seriously	1 John 5:16	God wants us to take seriously His call to holiness. We need to be alert to the Spirit's convicting and purifying work.

36

THE HOLY SPIRIT'S POWER

Wind is a good analogy for the Holy Spirit. In fact, the Hebrew and Greek words for "spirit" mean "wind." Wind is invisible and has a life of its own (John 3:8). Sometimes it is gentle and still. But at other times it blows so viciously that nothing can withstand its power. Trees, buildings, boats, and people are tossed around when the wind blows hard. So in likening the Holy Spirit to wind, Jesus was speaking of a Person with enormous power.

The power of wind is very real—but it is nothing compared to the power of the Holy Spirit. Let's talk about the Holy Spirit's power, beginning with a classic passage that addresses this topic:

> But you shall receive power when the Holy Spirit has come upon you; and you shall be My witnesses both in Jerusalem, and in all Judea and Samaria, and even to the remotest part of the earth. (Acts 1:8)

The clear implication of Jesus' words here is that the disciples would not have power until the Spirit came: Power is not simply a concept to be understood but a reality to be experienced. So you can't talk about spiritual power without simultaneously talking about the Holy Spirit.

A POWERFUL PRESENCE

Notice that the Spirit provides Christians with a powerful presence. In verse 4 of Acts 1, Luke says that after His resurrection Jesus gathered the apostles and "commanded them not to leave Jerusalem, but to wait for what the Father had promised, 'Which,' He said, 'you heard of from Me.'" Jesus then repeated the promise of the Spirit's coming: "You shall be baptized with the Holy Spirit not many days from now" (v. 5).

THE SPIRIT OF CHRIST

In John 14:16–19, Jesus told His disciples He would be leaving them soon, but would send them a Helper just like Him. In verse 18 He promised, "I will not leave you as orphans; I will come to you." The way Jesus was going to come to them was through the Holy Spirit. That's the way Jesus comes to us too.

That is why the Holy Spirit is often called "the Spirit of Christ." You can see the relationship between the Spirit and Christ in the letters to the seven churches of Revelation 2–3. In the letter to Ephesus, for example, the apostle John writes that "the One who holds the seven stars in His right hand" is the One speaking to the church (Revelation 2:1). We know from Revelation 1:16 that this person is the risen and glorified Christ. He delivers His message to the church, then He warns, "He who has an ear, let him hear what the Spirit says to the churches" (2:7). This same pattern is repeated in each of the seven letters. So here is Jesus Christ speaking to the churches by means of the Spirit. They speak with one voice.

The Holy Spirit can do what Jesus could not do in His flesh, since Jesus was limited by His human body. But the Holy Spirit is not subject to any limitations of location or time. Now the presence of God in Christ is with each of us equally through the Spirit. We are at no disadvantage for not having seen Christ. In fact, Jesus Himself said the Spirit's coming was to our advantage (John 16:7).

In 2 Corinthians 3:17–18, Paul writes: "Now the Lord is the Spirit; and where the Spirit of the Lord is, there is liberty. But we all, with unveiled face beholding as in a mirror the glory of the Lord, are being transformed into the same image from glory to glory, just as from the Lord, the Spirit."

Jesus Christ and the Holy Spirit are distinct persons in the Godhead, but Paul spoke of their work as synonymous because they belong to the same Godhead. So when you have the Spirit, you have Christ.

This is why the apostle John spent so much time reminding Christians to abide in Christ as well as in the Spirit (1 John 2:6, 24, 27; 3:24); that is, to live in the realm of the Spirit. It is the Spirit who brings you into the reality of the experience of the living, resurrected, and ascended Jesus Christ. If you want to be close to Christ, you must be close to the Spirit.

A Higher Realm

Our problem as finite human beings is that we need to be lifted to a higher realm—the realm of the spirit. The Holy Spirit, by His unlimited power, has already taken us in that realm, the very presence of God in "the heavenly places in Christ" (Ephesians 1:3).

If I were in the right realm, I could easily lift a ton. My problem, however, is that I cannot do it in this realm because there is a law that works against me called the law of gravity. But if only I could get on a space shuttle and travel in outer space, I could lift the weight.

Why? Because I would be living in a higher realm where the law of gravity does not operate. The reason some of us can't lift our heavy problems is that we are living in the wrong realm. The Holy Spirit wants to take you to the nongravitational realm of spiritual places.

A POWERFUL PROGRAM

The Holy Spirit not only provides a powerful presence; He is accomplishing a powerful program. Luke reports, "To [the apostles] He also presented Himself alive, after His suffering, by many convincing proofs, appearing to them over a period of forty days, and speaking of the things concerning the kingdom of God" (Acts 1:3).

We know that the kingdom was on their minds because they were asking Jesus, "Lord, is it at this time You are restoring the kingdom to Israel?" (v. 6). This is very important because this is the context in which Jesus promised the coming of the Holy Spirit.

Building the Kingdom

The question was not whether Jesus was going to establish His kingdom. It was just a matter of when. So the ultimate goal of the Spirit's coming at Pentecost to indwell believers is the building of God's kingdom.

One of the great problems we are facing today in the abuses regarding the Spirit, is that the Holy Spirit is made an end in Himself. But the Spirit is not an end in Himself. He did not come just so you could know Him and experience His power. The Holy Spirit came to provide you with power to accomplish a great program called the kingdom of God. So if you are one of those Christians who goes around Spirit-hunting, you need to know that God does not simply give His power to show off, to flex His muscles. God has a specific program in mind that He uses the Spirit's power to accomplish. Therefore, if you are not committed to God's kingdom purpose, you won't experience the Spirit's power.

The Bible declares that God's kingdom is the universe. Then the Scriptures narrow it down and say God's kingdom is the earth. "The earth is the Lord's, and all it contains, the world, and those who dwell in it," the psalmist declared (Psalm 24:1). But we live in a universe that does not recognize its rightful King.

That's going to change someday. God will set up His kingdom. Throughout the Old Testament, God's prophets kept prophesying that one day His Servant, who is Jesus Christ, would come to set up a kingdom where God Himself would rule and reign on planet Earth.

Even though the kingdom is not yet physically established on earth, the primary biblical concept of the kingdom is not a place. The Greek word for "kingdom," *basileia*, means "rule or authority." God's kingdom is first of all His sphere of authority, His rulership. So when you become part of God's kingdom, the concept is that you come under God's rule.

This whole world is God's kingdom, and it's a powerful program because it's energized by a powerful Holy Spirit. His job is to bring people to recognize God's right to rule as King and to submit to His authority. God does not want you bringing your rules into His house. The worst thing in the world, and you know this if you're a parent, is having kids who want to build their own little kingdoms in your house.

So Jesus told the apostles that God will indeed establish His kingdom someday, but in His own time. In the meantime, God has decided to set up His own kingdom within a kingdom. That is called the church, brought into being by the Holy Spirit.

The Church's Goal

The ultimate goal of the church is not itself, but the kingdom. The church has become ingrown when we equate the church with the kingdom. The church is the vehicle to deliver the kingdom that is to come. That is, we are to model, reflect, and illustrate the kingdom, so that anybody who wants to know what the kingdom that is to come will look like can look at the kingdom in miniature that has already come in the form of the church. That is why the witness of the church is so critical, and that is why the church has been given Holy Spirit power.

So the church is being established as the kingdom of God on earth to reflect the kingdom that is to come. God's kingdom is God's plan and program, and we as the church are the vehicle to deliver it. So if you want to see Holy Spirit power, make sure you are involved in the kingdom. If you are not doing kingdom business, don't expect Holy Spirit power.

If all you want is another miracle so you can feel better or have more money, that is not kingdom work. That's the problem with so-called prosperity theology. It is not about the kingdom. It is about me. The Holy Spirit is not interested in blessing you or empowering you. God and His Spirit are after the kingdom.

A POWERFUL PEOPLE

The power of the Holy Spirit is also evident in that He creates a powerful people who have His powerful presence carrying out His powerful program.

The disciples were a weak group of men. Peter denied Jesus. The other disciples left Him because they feared the Jews. They ran until the Spirit came.

The Holy Spirit Difference

But when the Spirit came upon them, those weak-kneed wimps who ran when the going got tough received some spiritual courage. They got Holy Spirit power, the Holy Spirit difference.

It didn't happen because of changes in their environment. They did not get it by taking a Dale Carnegie course or by enrolling in a class on the power of positive thinking. The only difference was Holy Spirit power, but what a change took place. Peter was drastically changed. Something happened to the apostle.

According to Acts 4:13, the Jewish authorities marveled at the courage shown by Peter—and John too. Those authorities knew both were "uneducated." I like that because it means they hadn't been to formal school. They hadn't been to Bible college or seminary. But they had been with Jesus.

The power of the Holy Spirit has nothing to do with the degrees you have on your wall. It has nothing to do with your theological training or background. You can have it all and still be a defeated Christian. But if you have been with Jesus, somebody else is going to know it. If you have been with Jesus, it's going to become evident that something powerful is at work in you

The Spirit's Control

The Holy Spirit will change your personality if He can get hold of you. So if you and I don't have a relationship with the Spirit, we are going to be defeated spiritual wimps, always running to the next conference or program to see if it can do for us what only the Holy Spirit can do.

The Spirit is infinitely bigger than all your attempts to fix yourself. He brings about a real change. He can change your personality. You may say, "I am a worrier. I was born that way. My mother was a worrier. I have worry in my genes."

That means you need a personality change. That's the Holy Spirit's specialty. He can make the insecure person secure, the fearful person confident. That's what He did with the apostles. But He only does it if you are doing kingdom work. He is not going to do it so you can win a personality or popularity contest. But when the Spirit goes to work, things change.

A POWERFUL PROCLAMATION

The Spirit of God also leads us to make a powerful proclamation. This is Acts 1:8, the Spirit-given power to be Christ's witnesses.

The first word of verse 8, *but*, is instructive, because in the original language this is a very strong adversative. When Jesus said, "But you shall receive power," He was telling the apostles in a strong way, "Get your minds off your preoccupation with My coming kingdom. I'm changing the subject."

Kingdom Power

The apostles wanted the kingdom to come because they knew that with the kingdom would come the power. After all, had not Jesus Himself taught them to pray, "Yours is the kingdom and the power and the glory forever" (Matthew 6:13)?

But Jesus said He was not going to give them the political kingdom they were looking for. Instead, He was going to give them the power of the kingdom in the person of the Holy Spirit. Now this was some power because the Greek word used here is the word from which we get our English word *dynamite*. Notice that this power would enable the apostles to become something, Jesus' witnesses. They were not just going out to do witnessing.

One of the ways you know the Holy Spirit is taking over is that you are being Christian when nobody is telling you to be Christian. You are representing Jesus when nobody is telling you to represent Jesus. You are taking a stand for Christ when nobody has to tell you because that is what you have become.

Christ's Witnesses

I like what happened to Peter when the Holy Spirit came upon him. On the day of Pentecost in Acts 2, the people were making fun of the disciples, accusing them of being full of "sweet wine" (v. 13), the good stuff.

But Peter took his stand, raised his voice, and boldly declared the Word of God to the crowd (v. 14). It was Peter's finest sermon, and God used His formerly wishy-washy witness to bring revival in Jerusalem.

Let me make an observation about the Spirit's power. He gave the gift of tongues on Pentecost so the apostles could proclaim "the mighty deeds of God" (v. 11). It's amazing to me how many people want the gift of tongues today so they can speak for God in heavenly languages when they aren't even speaking for Him in the earthly language He's already given them.

It does not make any sense to come to church and speak in another language if you are not willing to witness for Jesus Christ in English. The idea is that God has called us to represent Him, and He wants us to be witnesses.

People ought to know you have become intoxicated with Jesus. They ought to mistake your love for Jesus for a drunken man's obsession with alcohol because you are not ashamed of the gospel.

Turning On the Power

You don't need to go looking for power. You have all the power you need in the person of the Holy Spirit who lives within you. Many of us are going nowhere in our spiritual lives, not because there is something wrong with the Holy Spirit, but because we have not engaged His power.

If you are going to experience the benefits of the Holy Spirit's power, He must have more of you. You don't need more of Him. The key to enjoying the Spirit's power is obedience. This is why Jesus told His disciples that their love for Him would be measured by their obedience. When you and I obey, the Holy Spirit empowers, because through obedience we join with the Spirit's agenda of glorifying Christ.

GOD'S POWER AND MIRACLES

One of my concerns for the body of Christ is that when you look at the great God we serve, you see many of us living predictable lives. That's tragic because the Holy Spirit's presence guarantees that we are not limited to the ordinary or the natural. A miracle is the action of God that interrupts the normal course of events and produces a powerful and/or unusual result that would not have occurred otherwise. I call them the Spirit's surprises because a miracle is out of the ordinary. It is God's surprising power at work.

There ought to be more miraculous testimonies coming out of the body of Christ about what the Holy Spirit is doing among us. I don't necessarily mean big miracles. But whatever our need, I am convinced that the miraculous will be involved when the Holy Spirit is at work, but we have to get prepared.

If you and I are to be candidates for the Holy Spirit's miracles, then living for God and pleasing Him must become the passion of our lives. So if you need a miracle, the way to get it is not to go miracle-hunting. Instead, passion for Jesus Christ is the key to miracles by the Holy Spirit.

If Satan wants to keep you from experiencing the power of the Spirit, all he has to do is lower the flame on your "Christ burner." All Satan has to do is cool your passion for Christ, and the loss of power will follow.

I know that *passion* is an emotionally charged word. I chose it on purpose. God does not want our limp, lifeless religious activity. The Holy Spirit wants to cultivate within us a warm, throbbing passion for Jesus Christ. That's why Paul said, "That I may know [Christ], and the power of His resurrection" (Philippians 3:10). Paul was ready to forget everything else to know Christ (see 3:13). If the goal of your life is to know Christ, the power of the Holy Spirit will follow as surely as night follows day.

APPLICATION FOR LIFE

1. Wouldn't it be great to live in that spiritual realm where the gravitational pull of sin doesn't work against you? Well, the Spirit can take you there. He already lives within you. All He's waiting for is your cooperation. If you have any sin in your life pulling you down, confess it right now and claim Christ's cleansing (1 John 1:9). The Spirit will reveal any such sin if you'll ask Him to search your heart.

2. Jesus said we are to be His witnesses, beginning right in our own Jerusalem. The trouble is, most of us never get started where we are, so we can't move out to wider spheres of witness. Is there someone in your Jerusalem—your neighborhood, your street, maybe even your house—who you know needs the Lord? Put that person on your prayer list, asking God to give you a witnessing opportunity. Remember, you have the Spirit's power to help you be effective.

3. Maybe you can identify with the disciples in their fear of the Jewish authorities. But the Holy Spirit who replaced their fear with courage is the same Spirit you have within you. What or whom do you fear most today? Write down your biggest fear, then ask the Holy Spirit to give you a new dose of spiritual courage.

4. The Holy Spirit's power is totally available to you. Why not appropriate it in a new way by praying something like this: "Holy Spirit, I am Yours. I give my life to You. Have Your way with me. I will do what You want done as You want it done. I will seek to glorify Christ and build His kingdom. Be real in me because I want all of Your power expressed through me. I give You all of me."

FOR GROUP STUDY

Questions for Group Discussion

1. Dr. Evans points out that the Spirit is accomplishing a powerful program. What are the two purposes of that program? How do we, as believers, specifically relate to those purposes?

2. In what two key ways does the Spirit's power impact God's people?
3. In what ways is the Spirit's power proclaimed to the world? According to Acts 1:8, the Spirit gives us power to be Christ's witnesses. What are some ways we can proclaim the Spirit's powers in the course of our lives?
4. How are we to understand God's power as it relates to miracles? What was the apostle Paul's conclusion (Philippians 3:10)?

PICTURE THIS

The New Testament teaches that the Holy Spirit empowers the Christian witness to the world. The church, the body of individual believers, is Christ's witness to our world through the indwelling power of the Spirit.

THE PROCLAMATION OF THE HOLY SPIRIT'S POWER

PROCLAMATION	SCRIPTURE PASSAGE	WHAT IT MEANS
Kingdom power	Matthew 6:13	The power of the kingdom comes through the power of the Holy Spirit.
Christ's witnesses on the day of Pentecost	Acts 2	At Pentecost, the disciples were Christ's witnesses through the power of the Holy Spirit.
God's people	Acts 1:8	God makes all believers proclaimers of the gospel through the Spirit's power.

37

THE HOLY SPIRIT'S AUTHORITY

Someone has said that the Christian life is not a matter of our ability, but of our availability. The ability is all from above, made real to us in our day-by-day lives by the indwelling Holy Spirit.

I want to show you how you can experience the Spirit's authority by a brief survey of Romans 6–8, three of the most important chapters in the New Testament. In these chapters Paul sets forth the sanctification of the believer; that is, how we as Christians are set apart by the Spirit to a spiritually victorious experience.

YOUR NEW IDENTITY

Paul opens the sixth chapter of Romans with a handful of questions and a couple of powerful declarations:

> What shall we say then? Are we to continue in sin that grace might increase? May it never be! How shall we who died to sin still live in it? Or do you not know that all of us who have been baptized into Christ Jesus have been baptized into His death? Therefore we have been buried with Him through baptism into death, in order that as Christ was raised from the dead through the glory of the Father, so we too might walk in newness of life. (vv. 1–4)

At least a dozen times in Romans 6–8, Paul refers to what we do know, what we don't know because it's beyond us (see 8:26), and what we should know but don't. The point is that successful Christian living is predicated on what you know about how you ought to live because God has revealed it to you. It is our knowledge of our identity in Christ that allows us to interpret life from a divine frame of reference. So what is it we should know, and what should we do in response to what we know?

What You Need to Know

Many Christians either do not have this knowledge of their identity in Christ, or else they do not understand it, so they operate from a false identity. Whenever you identify yourself falsely, you will act falsely.

Your identity as a believer begins here in Romans 6. You must know and understand that you have been co-crucified, co-buried, and co-resurrected with Jesus Christ.

You are no longer a slave to sin. You no longer belong to this world order. Your old self was crucified (v. 6). That means dead. So you need to get this down: If you know Christ, you are not who you used to be. You are totally different.

What You Need to Consider

Not only must you know who you are in order to understand your identity in Christ, you must also consider who you are. "Even so consider yourselves to be dead to sin, but alive to God in Christ Jesus" (v. 11). You must count it as a reality.

The Greek word translated "consider" is an economic term that means to add up the figures and arrive at the proper answer. It's one thing to know something factually or academically. It's quite another thing to consider or count or reckon it to be true.

Paul is saying it's not enough to know who you are in Christ because the Bible tells you it's true. You can put it in the bank and count on it. In fact, it's crucial that you do so, for only then will you really start drawing on your new identity and experiencing it.

Let me illustrate. Every day when I put on my socks, I see the long scar running down my right leg from an old football injury in which they had to rebuild my leg. I can feel the lump of the steel plate that's in there. I not only know I have a repaired leg, but I consider it to be so. That is, I add up my memories of the event and the scar and the lump so that when I am tempted to try something that might jeopardize that repair job, I act on what I know and walk away.

Remember, we're talking about experiencing the Holy Spirit's authority to enable you to live a victorious Christian life. But before we can jump to that truth in Romans 8, we need to lay the foundation in chapters 6–7. It doesn't do much good to talk about the Spirit's authority until we have answered the question, His authority to do what?

What You Need to Do

Once you have considered the truth, then you're ready to take the third step: "Do not go on presenting the members of your body to sin as instruments of unrighteousness; but present yourselves to God as those alive from the dead, and your members as instruments of righteousness to God" (Romans 6:13).

The only way you will be able to stop living the way you used to live is when you get hold of the fact that you are not who you used to be. Where does that authority to know, consider, and do come from? From the ministry of the Holy Spirit in your life.

YOUR NEW PROBLEM

But you have a new problem too. The latter half of Romans 7 deals with a problem I call new because you've only had it since you've been a Christian:

> For we know that the Law is spiritual; but I am of flesh, sold into bondage to sin. . . . For I know that nothing good dwells in me, that is, in my flesh; for the wishing is present in me, but the doing of the good is not. . . . For I joyfully concur with the law of God in the inner man, but I see a different law in the members of my body, waging war against the law of my mind, and making me a prisoner of the law of sin which is in my members. (vv. 14, 18, 22–23)

Same Old Address

The problem is, only the inner you was made brand-new in Christ. Your spirit was dead in sin, and now it is alive in Christ. But this new you is still living in the same old house at the same old address: the flesh.

In other words, the new invisible you—your redeemed inner person, your spirit—is still hanging out in the old visible you—your body. Why is that a problem? Because the old you, which Paul calls the flesh, has been utterly contaminated by sin. It was born in sin. It is so messed up that God is not even going to try to fix it. We need to keep reminding ourselves that the flesh is only good for worm food.

Now don't misunderstand. Our physical bodies and our physical desires are not evil in themselves. God gave them to us. When Paul refers to the flesh, he's talking about our bodies and appetites under the destructive control of our old nature that is thoroughly ruined by sin.

Nothing Worth Saving

We have a hard time really believing what the Bible says about the flesh. We spend so much time making the outer shell look good that it's hard to believe it's all bad. Paul, you mean there's nothing of the flesh worth saving? "There isn't one good thing in my flesh" is Paul's answer in Romans 7:18.

So you may as well mark it down. There is nothing of value to God in your flesh. Your old address has been condemned. That's why it must die.

It's true you may be able to make a few minor improvements along the way. The authority to do what we're talking about, however, doesn't come from you. It comes from the authority of the Holy Spirit in you.

Growing the New You

You say, "Then why is my flesh so dominating?" Because it has been in control of you so long. That's why the only way to overcome the flesh is by growing the new you, not by trying to fix the old you.

How do you grow the new you while shutting down the old you? You do it by feeding your spirit while you starve your flesh—those old, corrupt impulses and desires and habits. You cannot feed the flesh, neglect the inner you, and expect to have victory over the flesh.

This is what happens to a lot of us. All week long we feed the flesh, then we come to church for worship, hoping that two hours on Sunday will cancel out all the feeding of the flesh we did Monday through Saturday. It won't work. The only answer for the flesh is "putting to death the deeds of the body" by the power of the Spirit (Romans 8:13).

"Putting to death the deeds of the body" is what I call starving your sinful flesh. You starve it by not feeding it the sinful stuff it craves and thrives on. The flesh is so bad that Paul cries out, "Wretched man that I am!" (7:24a). Notice this is present tense. This is the apostle Paul talking about his present struggles. So he asks, "Who will set me free from the body of this death?" (v. 24b).

You are trapped in your flesh until Christ releases you. That's what Paul gives thanks for in verse 25. Jesus alone can release you from "the body of this death." And He does it through the power and authority of the Holy Spirit. Once you realize the flesh can't be salvaged and is destined for dust, it will radically change your approach to the Christian life. You will give up trying to tame or fix the flesh and concentrate on building up your inner person by the power of the Spirit.

YOUR NEW LAW

Now we are ready to move to Romans 8 and the law of the Spirit, by which He gives us authority to live victoriously:

> There is therefore now no condemnation for those who are in Christ Jesus. For the law of the Spirit of life in Christ Jesus has set you free from the law of sin and of death. For what the Law could not do, weak as it was through the flesh, God did: sending His own Son in the likeness of sinful flesh and as an offering for sin, He condemned sin in the flesh, in order that the requirements of the Law might be fulfilled in us, who do not walk according to the flesh, but according to the Spirit. (vv. 1–4)

What God did when He saved you was to transfer His power from the outside of you to the inside of you.

A Power Transfer

Jesus has risen from the dead, so He has all the power we will ever need. When we are connected to Him by the Holy Spirit, we receive Christ's life as our dead spirits come alive.

You say, "Wait a minute. If I am connected to the living and powerful Christ by the living and powerful Holy Spirit, how come I still seem so dead? Why am I so weak? How come I am losing, not winning, the battle?"

Well, there is something you must do in order to authorize the benefits of the power and the authority that are being transferred to you by the Holy Spirit.

Walk by the Spirit

You'll find your responsibility in the latter half of Romans 8:4, where Paul says the Spirit's authority is made available to those "who do not walk according to the flesh, but according to the Spirit." There's that familiar word *walk*, a favorite euphemism of Paul's for our daily conduct, the way we live our lives. The imagery of walking has at least three concepts embedded in it.

First of all, walking assumes a destination. There's only one destination to pursue if you want to experience the Holy Spirit's power and authority, and that is the will and glory of God. If you are not committed to living for God's glory and doing His will, there will be no transfer of power (James 1:6–8).

Second, walking implies dependence. When you walk, you place one foot in front of the other, putting all your weight on each foot for each step. To walk by the Spirit, you must rest your weight on Him, depending on His power and not your own human resources.

One thing God hates to hear Christians say is, "Well, I'll try." You know why? Because that means you are going to use your own efforts to pull off what God has asked you to do. God wants to hear you and me say, "In dependence on Your power, I can."

He responds, "You're right. You can. Here's My power."

The third aspect of walking is that it is continuous. You don't take one step and sit down, not if you want to get anywhere. Walking is repetitive. Walking in the Spirit is something you are to do all the time. This is the way the Christian life is supposed to be lived.

That's why Paul calls it the "law of the Spirit of life" in Romans 8:2. A law implies authority, something that has real teeth in it. Well, the law of the Spirit is so powerful that even though your flesh has been enslaved to the "law of sin and of death" for ten, twenty, thirty, or more years, this law, this principle, this enabling from the Spirit is so strong it will release you from your slavery.

The Power to Soar

My favorite illustration of this principle is the law of gravity. Gravity pulls you down. It dictates that what goes up must come down. It's the reason we can't soar with the eagles. The gravitational pull of the earth always seeks to bring us down. The law of gravity demands it.

The law of sin and death seeks to pull you down too. It wants to send you crashing down mentally, morally, spiritually—every way possible. The law of sin wants to addict you to sin so it can drag you down, all the way to hell if possible.

Although you can't get rid of the law of gravity, you can transcend it. If you have ever been on an airplane, you have whipped gravity. When you move at a certain speed with a certain degree of power and upward thrust, you are propelled upward so that gravity no longer controls the agenda.

This works in the spiritual realm too. When the combustion of the Holy Spirit is combined with the power of an obedient life, you transcend the gravitational pull of sin and soar in your spiritual life. That's what God is after, but it only comes when you are walking in the Spirit as a habit of life, drawing on His power and authority. When you see the Spirit's authority at work giving you victory over sin, you will have experienced the Spirit.

Mind Control

"The mind set on the flesh is death, but the mind set on the Spirit is life and peace" (Romans 8:6). Paul says this because whatever controls the mind controls the feet. You walk where your mind tells you to walk. So if the flesh controls your mind, your feet are going to follow. If the Spirit controls your mind, your feet will follow the Spirit.

If you pump fleshly impulses into your mind all day long, don't be surprised if your feet turn aside to fleshly activities. But if your mind is being pumped with spiritual reinforcement all day long, don't be surprised if your feet start following in spiritual activity.

Whoever controls the mind runs the show. No wonder Paul says in Romans 8:12–13, "So then, brethren, we are under obligation, not to the flesh, to live according to the flesh—for if you live according to the flesh, you must die; but if by the Spirit you are putting to death the deeds of the body, you will live."

Fleshly Desires

Now let me try to correct a common misunderstanding. The Bible is not saying that when you walk in the Spirit, you will no longer have any of the desires of the flesh. What the Bible says is, "Walk by the Spirit, and you will not carry out the desire of the flesh" (Galatians 5:16).

There's a big difference between not having a desire and not acquiescing to that desire. All of us will go to our graves carrying fleshly desires. Our flesh still wants to sin. So don't feel bad that your flesh wants to sin. Feel bad when you don't draw on the power and authority of the Spirit to say no to your flesh.

Make sure you keep the order straight. The way to stop walking in the flesh is not to stop walking this way so you can start walking in the Spirit. The way to stop walking in the flesh is to start walking in the Spirit.

APPLICATION FOR LIFE

1. Maybe you realize you've got a dead body tied to you, some sin you've never really confessed or asked the Spirit's help to overcome. Cut that cadaver loose! Confess that sin as sin, turn from it, and claim your cleansing (1 John 1:9). Show the Devil Romans 8:2, and tell him to get out.

2. Want to starve your flesh and feed your spirit? Try putting down that remote control and picking up your Bible. Get off the phone and get on your knees. Turn your eyes away from the book or magazine and turn them on Jesus. Stop indulging your whims and start listening for the whispers of the Spirit.

3. Quit trying to subsist spiritually on "diet worship." Make time each day for a worship service. Sing a hymn to the Lord on your way to work. Use the last five minutes of your lunch hour to read a chapter of a Gospel, a psalm, or a chapter of Proverbs. Take a few minutes somewhere to be totally still in God's presence and allow the Holy Spirit to speak to your spirit.

4. Maybe it's time you looked around at the people you're hanging out with. If you're an eagle, you can't afford to spend a lot of time with those other birds! We're not talking about spending time with unbelievers so you can get to know them, care about them, and share with them the gospel of Jesus Christ. We're talking about letting yourself be unduly influenced by unsaved people who are pulling you away from your commitment to Christ.

FOR GROUP STUDY

Questions for Group Discussion

1. Read Romans 6:1–4. It is our knowledge about our new identity in Christ that allows us to interpret life from a divine frame of reference. What three aspects of our identity in Christ do we need to embrace?

2. When we become a believer, we have a "new" problem. Read Romans 7:14,

18, 22–23. What is this new problem? In what ways are we forced to deal with it?

3. According to Romans 8:1–4, Christians are subject to a new law—the law of the Spirit. How does this law differ from the old law of sin and death? What are the components of the law of the Spirit? (Use the chart on the next page as an aid to discussion.)

4. In Romans 8:4, the apostle Paul describes the believer's responsibility to "walk . . . according to the Spirit." What three concepts of this walk are embedded in this passage? In what ways does each concept serve to define the nature of this walk?

PICTURE THIS

Because of the security the Spirit provides, believers receive several benefits. Below are five key benefits when we are under the law of the Spirit, as declared in Scripture.

THE LAW OF THE SPIRIT

COMPONENT OF THE LAW	SCRIPTURE PASSAGE	HOW IT WORKS
A power transfer	Romans 8:4	The Holy Spirit lives within us and empowers us to live the life of Christ.
Walking by the Spirit	James 1:6–8	We no longer live according to the flesh, but rather according to the Spirit and His agenda.
Power to soar	Romans 8:2	No longer weighed down by sin, we experience the freedom that comes from the Spirit's power in our lives.
Mind control	Romans 8:6; 12–13	Our minds are now set on Christ, in whom is life and peace.
Fleshly desires	Galatians 5:16	We are able to live above the downward pull of these desires as we walk in the Spirit.

38

THE HOLY SPIRIT'S FELLOWSHIP

If you and I are powerless Christians, it is directly attributable to the lack of fellowship between us and the Holy Spirit. If you and I are anemic, if there is little joy and peace, if there is little of anything in our lives that seems to demonstrate the Spirit's reality, it is because our fellowship with the Spirit is not as it ought to be.

PRIORITIZE THE SPIRIT'S PASSION

If you want to enjoy the Spirit's fellowship, you need to make His passion your priority. What is the Spirit's passion? We have seen it repeatedly. Jesus said it best in John 16:13–14: "He will not speak on His own initiative. . . . He shall glorify Me; for He shall take of Mine, and shall disclose it to you."

The Spirit's passion is to glorify the Son. In the mysterious and wonderful inner workings of the Trinity that we talked about in an earlier chapter, it was determined that the Spirit would come to magnify Jesus Christ.

Putting Christ First

If Jesus Christ is a low priority in your life, then you will be a low priority in the Spirit's work. If Jesus Christ is an extra in your life, then you will be an extra in the Spirit's work. I'm not saying the Spirit will quit convicting and drawing you, and He certainly won't stop loving or indwelling you. But don't expect to enjoy dynamic fellowship with Him if your commitment to Christ is anemic.

So is Christ your passion? I don't mean is He your Sunday experience. I mean is loving and serving Christ your driving passion? Is glorifying Him what gets you up in the morning and keeps you going all day? If it is, you won't have to hunt for the Spirit. He has already tracked you down.

When Christ is your passion, He rewards you with the presence and power of His Spirit.

Living Water

Let me point you again to John 7:37–39. Recall that Jesus promises that those who believe on Him will experience a river of living water flowing out of their "innermost being" (v. 38). John then tells us in verse 39 that Jesus was talking about the Holy Spirit, who would come on the day of Pentecost to indwell and energize believers.

What I want to note is Jesus' description of the Spirit's presence as "living water." The Holy Spirit is a life-giving Spirit. When He dominates your life, He will make you more alive than you ever thought you could be. You will not only be fulfilled yourself, but the river of living water flowing out of you will overflow so others can drink from your life as well.

One reason we have so little spiritual power in the church of Jesus Christ today is that we are not thirsty Christians. God only satisfies folk who are thirsty. If you are not thirsty, you don't get to drink.

What we need is to develop our spiritual thirst. We need a generation of Christians who are passionate for Christ. Unless that is your goal, studying the Bible is a waste of time; coming to church will make little or no difference in your life. The life-giving, thirst-quenching fellowship of the Holy Spirit is enjoyed where the passion of Christ is sought.

Being Transformed

But when you prioritize the Spirit's passion, the provision is awesome:

> Now the Lord is the Spirit; and where the Spirit of the Lord is, there is liberty. But we all, with unveiled face beholding as in a mirror the glory of the Lord,

> are being transformed into the same image from glory to glory, just as from the Lord, the Spirit. (2 Corinthians 3:17–18)

Notice how the Lord and the Spirit are used interchangeably. This means that when the glory of Christ becomes your passion, the Spirit of God transforms your life. If you really want to see your life changed, let Christ become your passion. When the Spirit sees that you feel about Christ the way He feels about Christ, He will allow the glory of Christ to transform your life.

When you start making your decisions and your choices based on whether they bring Christ glory, you will automatically see the Spirit changing you. You will automatically see the fruit of the Spirit being developed in you. But don't get me wrong. Automatic does not mean immediate. We're talking about a process.

The Spirit's transformation is not instantaneous. But as you learn to make Christ the measure of your life, ever so surely you will find yourself being transformed into His image.

This transformation has some wonderfully practical benefits. You will start experiencing victories in areas where before you tasted one defeat after another. You will have joy where there was misery, harmony where there was conflict, and power where there was impotence. A passion to glorify Jesus Christ is transforming.

PRESERVE THE SPIRIT'S UNITY

A second thing we must do to enjoy the Spirit's fellowship is preserve His unity. This is critical because the Spirit of God only operates in a context of spiritual harmony. This is why Paul writes:

> [Be] diligent to preserve the unity of the Spirit in the bond of peace. There is one body and one Spirit, just as also you were called in one hope of your calling; one Lord, one faith, one baptism, one God and Father of all who is over all and through all and in all. (Ephesians 4:3–6)

Please note that we only "preserve" the Spirit's unity; we do not create it. This is because unity was already created for us when we were baptized by the Spirit into one body. Our job then is not to allow anything or anyone to divide the new family into which we have been placed. Since it is the Spirit's unity, then our relationship with the Holy Spirit is the essential ingredient that assures that our oneness goes undisturbed.

At All Costs

Paul says we should preserve at all costs the unity of the Spirit. In the Bible, unity does not mean uniformity. It does not mean trying to make everyone else like me. It does mean commonality of purpose, everybody going in the same direction.

God's relationship to you is inextricably linked to your relationship to other saints. Let me say again we're not talking about salvation here. We aren't saved in groups. We're talking about the day-by-day reality and experience of the Spirit's fellowship.

If you cause conflicts or divisiveness, not over issues of sin and righteousness but over preferences and opinions, you are breaking down the body rather than building it up. You are not preserving the unity of the Spirit. So if you are a cantankerous Christian, if you are a Christian who is bringing division to the body of Christ, the Spirit's fellowship is not yours until you use His resources to fix that mess.

The Spirit's Sensitivity

I want to let you in on a secret. The Holy Spirit is extremely sensitive. He is grieved when we engage in the activities Paul lists in Ephesians 4:25–32, which have to do primarily with our relationships with other members of God's family.

This is not talking about salvation, because verse 30 says we are sealed until the day of redemption. So to grieve the Holy Spirit is not to lose your salvation, but it is to lose the enjoyment of your salvation, which is the fellowship of the Spirit.

When you got saved, the Holy Spirit came to live within you and give life to your human spirit. There is a linking of your human spirit with the Holy

Spirit. What that means is when you grieve the Holy Spirit, who is now indwelling your human spirit, your human spirit is grieved too.

To put it another way, when the Holy Spirit within you is made joyful, He is going to give you joy. But when the Spirit within you has been saddened or wounded by sin, then of necessity you are going to be unhappy in your spirit. When fellowship with the Holy Spirit is blocked, when He is sensitive to sin in your life, His sensitivity will become your sensitivity.

Resisting the Spirit

In his bold message before the Sanhedrin, Stephen told the religious elite of Israel, "You . . . are always resisting the Holy Spirit" (Acts 7:51).

The unsaved can resist God and refuse to hear His Word, just as the Sanhedrin did in Stephen's case. They even stoned him in an attempt to silence the Spirit's witness through him of their condemnation.

As believers, we have already yielded to the call of the Spirit for salvation. But we can get ourselves into a state of mind and heart where we say no to the Spirit's promptings to deal with unconfessed sin and get back into intimate fellowship with Him. We can keep Him from giving us joy.

But when you resist the Holy Spirit, you are headed for a struggle. Why? For two reasons. First, for the sake of your own spiritual life. Second, because there are a lot of other kids in the family. The Spirit can't have you disrupting the family and making everyone else miserable. So He does whatever is necessary to break your rebellion and resistance. The job becomes misery, the marriage is drudgery, the kids start acting up.

Could it be that the Spirit is fighting against you because you are resisting Him? I certainly can't judge what is happening in your life. But I must point out the danger of resisting the Spirit, particularly in relationship to what He wants to do in the rest of the family of God. If you want to experience maximum fellowship with the Holy Spirit, make sure there are no walls of your making between you and your brothers and sisters in Christ.

PRACTICE THE SPIRIT'S DISCIPLINES

The third path to experiencing full fellowship with the Holy Spirit is to practice His disciplines. Let's return once more to Romans 8, this time to verses 5–7:

> Those who are according to the flesh set their minds on the things of the flesh, but those who are according to the Spirit, the things of the Spirit. For the mind set on the flesh is death, but the mind set on the Spirit is life and peace, because the mind set on the flesh is hostile toward God; for it does not subject itself to the law of God, for it is not even able to do so.

Here is the key to the successful practice of spiritual disciplines: Discipline your mind to focus on the realm of the Spirit. Discipline is a matter of setting your mind on "the things of the Spirit." The writer of Proverbs put it this way: "As [a man] thinks within himself, so he is" (23:7).

If I were to take out my pen and begin writing, I could record anything I wanted to record. But if I remove my hand, the pen would simply fall on the paper and lie there. My pen has no life of its own.

My pen contains all the raw materials I need to write with, but it has no writing ability of its own. In order for this pen to function, it must be joined to the life in my hand. When that happens, my pen can form letters it could never form by itself. It can compose clauses and phrases and put them together to make sentences because it is in my hand, and my hand is alive.

When you connect your life to the life of the Holy Spirit, He can write things that you could never write on your own. He can achieve things you could never achieve on your own.

Prayer

The first discipline is prayer. The simplest definition of prayer is communion and communication with God. Let me show you why the practice of prayer is so crucial as it relates to enjoying the fellowship of the Spirit.

Prayer takes you out of your realm, the realm of the flesh, and transports you into another realm, that of the Spirit. Remember, we are seeking the mind of the Spirit so that we might fellowship with Him. To do that, you must enter the Spirit's realm. Prayer takes you there.

As long as you are self-centered, you can't be God-centered. Prayer replaces your self-focus with a God-focus. Whether you pray silently or audibly, prayer lifts you out of yourself to a sphere inhabited by the Holy Spirit. When you enter His realm, He meets you for fellowship.

Our discipline of prayer should include thanksgiving, because that relates to what God is already doing for us. As the song says, "Count your blessings." Thanksgiving reminds us that we are talking to a God who keeps us when we want to throw in the towel, a God who stands by us when we do not think we are going to make it. If He hung with us yesterday, He'll be there today. Thanksgiving reminds us of that.

And when you pray, include confession. Confession brings you back into fellowship with the Spirit. Confession pleases Him because it means you feel the same way about your sin He feels about it—that it's wrong and has to be dealt with.

There is nothing mysterious about prayer. The only reason we don't feel more comfortable in prayer is that we don't pray enough. But if you are serious about cultivating the mind of the Spirit and entering the realm where He lives, you need to put some muscle in your prayer life. You need to practice the discipline of prayer.

The best way I know to keep prayer from becoming routine and automatic is to turn your focus from prayer to God. Here's an example of what I mean.

Eating is a duty in the sense that we have to eat to sustain life. But most of us don't approach eating as a chore. We take great delight in it. We eat when we need to eat, and we eat when we don't need to eat. Some of us even eat when we aren't supposed to eat.

When you start approaching prayer the way you approach eating, something will happen. Prayer is your time to gather around the table for warm, close fellowship with the Holy Spirit who can comfort and help you in any situation, with Jesus Christ your elder Brother, and with a Father who delights to hear from His children.

The Word

The second discipline of the Spirit is reading and studying the Bible. If you want to cultivate a mind set on the things of God, you need to get in the Spirit-inspired Word. The Spirit says, "If you want to fellowship with Me, spend time in My Word to you."

See, we often do with the Bible what we do with prayer. That is, we make it something other than what it was intended to be. The Bible was not written as a religious textbook. It is a love letter from the Holy Spirit to you. A lot of us won't read a textbook, but not many of us will pass up a love letter.

Try opening your Bible and saying, "God, what is it that You want to say to my heart today? What do You want to change about me today? What do You want me to understand about You today?" Now you have a love letter and not a textbook.

Trials

A third discipline of the Spirit is trials. Trials are what happens when God removes the "training wheels" from your spiritual life.

Training wheels give a child's bike a nice, steady feel. But they're meant to be temporary. When you remove them, there is a risk that your child may fall and get a skinned elbow or knee. But unless you take off those training wheels, your child will never learn to really ride a bike. Unless the Holy Spirit takes the training wheels off our spiritual lives, we will never learn how to get our balance. We will never learn to pedal for the glory of God. We will never learn to steer like we ought to steer our lives.

So the Spirit has to remove the training wheels. Far too many Christians are living off the spiritual success of others rather than developing spiritual vitality for themselves.

BY THE SPIRIT

Romans 8:13 says, "If you are living according to the flesh, you must die; but if *by the Spirit* you are putting to death the deeds of the body, you will live" (italics added).

There it is, the secret to a life of intimate fellowship with the Holy Spirit. It's you doing it, but not by your own power. You do it by the Spirit's power. So whatever you need to do on the positive side or put away on the negative side, you can do it because your human spirit is harnessed to the Holy Spirit.

PERSONAL APPLICATION FOR LIFE

1. Since the Spirit's passion is to glorify Christ, guess what your passion should be? If you can't honestly say the goal of your life is to exalt Jesus daily, better put that at the top of your prayer list.

2. Are you doing your part to preserve the Spirit's unity? We can hinder the unity of the body by our absence as well as by the wrong kind of presence. If you're not a full participant in a local church, you're leaving a void that causes the body to suffer. You don't just fellowship with other believers because you need it. You do it because the body needs it.

3. Prayer is a challenge for most of us, because it doesn't come naturally. Many people who have trouble focusing in prayer say that praying with a friend or praying out loud even in private helps a lot. You may want to try it if you find it hard to keep yourself focused.

4. Remember how good it felt as a kid when your dad removed the training wheels from your bicycle and you really took off? That's what the Holy Spirit longs to do for you spiritually, but He can't do it if you aren't willing to accept the scrapes and scratches too. Ask Him to help you see your trials through His eyes.

FOR GROUP STUDY

Questions for Group Discussion

1. What happens when we experience fellowship with the Holy Spirit? What happens when we do not?

2. Read John 16:13–14. What is the Spirit's passion? What is our goal for making the Spirit's passion our passion? To make the Spirit's passion our passion, we need to prioritize that passion in our lives. What are some ways we can make it a priority?

3. Ephesians 4:3–6 speaks of the importance of preserving the Spirit's unity. What does it mean to preserve His unity? What steps must we take to accomplish that?

4. Look at Romans 8:13. What is the "secret" to experiencing fellowship with the Spirit?

PICTURE THIS

If we want to enjoy intimate fellowship with the Holy Spirit, we must get serious about aligning our lives to carry out His purposes. Below are three paths we may take to establish fellowship with the Spirit.

Paths to Enjoying Fellowship with the Spirit

PATH TO FELLOWSHIP	SCRIPTURE PASSAGE	WHY IT'S SIGNIFICANT
Prioritize the Spirit's passion	John 16:13–14	To make the Spirit's passion our passion, we need to take the steps that make it a priority in our lives.
Preserve the Spirit's unity	Ephesians 4:3–6	Because the Spirit operates only within the context of spiritual harmony, we must preserve His unity among believers in the body of Christ.
Practice the Spirit's disciplines	Romans 8:5–7	We must discipline ourselves to focus on the realm of the Spirit and fix our minds on the Spirit.

39

THE HOLY SPIRIT'S RESTRAINT

One reason we do not get everything we deserve is the restraining ministry of the Holy Spirit.

The Holy Spirit's restraint of sin is like the atmosphere around us. It's helping to sustain this world as we know and experience it. The only reason sin isn't as bad as it could be worldwide is because of the Spirit's restraint.

In fact, the only reason you and I are not as bad as we could be is because of the Spirit's restraining ministry. So we need to understand and appreciate what the Holy Spirit is doing to hold back sin in this age so we can cooperate with rather than resist His work.

RESTRAINING SIN

The Spirit limits the operation of sin in the world. In 2 Thessalonians 2, Paul is comforting the believers in Thessalonica who had been scared to death by false teachers telling them the Lord had already come and they had missed it (vv. 1–2).

In the process of correcting this error, Paul unveils for the Thessalonians and for us the picture of a future time when, quite literally, all hell will break loose. There will be a great departure from the faith, culminating in the revelation of the "man of lawlessness" (v. 3)—Satan's false Christ, the

Antichrist—whose coming will usher in the time of the great tribulation that will devastate the earth.

The Principle of Restraint

That's the context of the verses I want us to examine. As Paul explains this future time, he makes reference to the restraining ministry of the Holy Spirit: "And you know what restrains him now, so that in his time he may be revealed. For the mystery of lawlessness is already at work; only he who now restrains will do so until he is taken out of the way" (vv. 6–7).

The word *what* in verse 6 is actually a neuter word, meaning that the restraint referred to here is not a person, but a principle. However, in verse 7 Paul uses the masculine equivalent of the term, "he who now restrains," so what we have here is a complete picture of the Spirit's restraint.

That is, the person of the Spirit uses a principle of restraint. There are different ideas as to what Paul means by this. Some say the reference is to the Spirit's restraint through the church or through human government or through some other agency. I think these are all included in the idea, and in fact I want to suggest below that the Spirit uses a number of means to hold back the full expression of sin in our world and in our personal lives.

The Spirit is not named as the restrainer here. But notice that this person and his means of operation were known to the Thessalonians (v. 6). Notice too that this restrainer is holding back the "mystery of lawlessness" which is already at work in the world and which will ultimately be given full expression when the man of lawlessness is revealed.

We know from elsewhere in Scripture that this lawless one is the emissary of the Devil, his imitation Christ (see Revelation 13:1–10). Satan would love to turn this guy loose on the world now. Satan would love to see sin have its maximum expression. But the restrainer is holding this back, so the restrainer has to be more powerful than the Devil himself.

The Benefits of Restraint

The Spirit's restraint keeps sin from overflowing its banks and flooding the world.

We often look at life backwards. If we get sick, we say, "Lord, why am I sick?" It's a natural response. But a more biblically accurate response would be, "Lord, as sinful as I am, why did You allow me to stay healthy for so long?"

Or if we are robbed, we say, "That's not fair, Lord. I don't deserve to get robbed." What should confound us is the fact that God allows us to live so long in this sinful world without getting robbed. The same holds true for tragedy and other painful circumstances that come upon us because we live in a very sinful world. The reason it isn't worse is that the Holy Spirit is restraining sin.

The time is coming when God will remove the restraints on sin by removing the Restrainer (2 Thessalonians 2:7). That's at the rapture. Until then the Spirit is restraining sin in a number of ways. Let's look at seven of them.

Seven Means of Restraint

The first way the Spirit restrains sin is by direct intervention. He will intervene in a circumstance and say to Satan, "No, you can't do that." In the case of Job, Satan wanted to bring total ruin to his life, but God intervened and told Satan exactly what he could and could not do. God controlled the agenda in Job's life. He limited what Satan could do to Job (Job 1:12).

A second means of restraint the Spirit uses is godly leaders. Time and again Moses intervened with God on behalf of Israel after the people sinned and God wanted to destroy them (Exodus 32; Numbers 14). In Exodus 32:11-35, Moses acted very directly to restrain the people's sin by breaking up their golden calf "worship service" and dealing out judgment to the offenders. His actions preserved the nation. The Spirit will often use God's appointed leaders to restrain sin.

The family is a third vehicle or means the Holy Spirit uses to hold back sin. One thing God expects the family to do is lay down guidelines for children to give them a track to run on and to keep them from doing everything they want to do. Most of us probably can't imagine what kinds of things our children would do if they thought they could. No, wait a minute. We can imagine it, because at one time or another in life, they try. But family is meant to exert a restraint.

Here's a fourth means through which the Holy Spirit restrains sin: our internal restraining mechanism called the conscience. In order for you to sin, you have to climb over your conscience. Now if you are a redeemed person whose conscience has been informed by God, the more sensitive your conscience is to sin the higher you have to climb to get over it.

That's good, because when you can sin and not think about it, feel it, or worry about it, you're in trouble. The Holy Spirit will sensitize your conscience to alert you to sin. The conscience can thus become a valuable restrainer.

A fifth means of the Spirit's restraint is through the church. In fact, many Bible commentators believe the church is what Paul had in mind in 2 Thessalonians 2:6. That fits the picture of the rapture in verse 7, because when the church is taken out of the world, the Holy Spirit will go too.

The Spirit won't cease being the all-present God, but the unique relationship He began with the church at Pentecost will end when the church's ministry on earth is complete and she is caught away.

Since every Christian is a temple of the Spirit, that means His restraining work will be wherever God's people are—and God's people are everywhere. By the way, this is why when we stop being salt and light in society, society deteriorates. We stifle the Spirit and His restraining work. So things begin to collapse because there is no more restraint.

A sixth mechanism of the Spirit's restraint is the Bible. When individuals, families, or entire cultures follow the Word of God, they will have guidelines to govern them that will help establish a righteous mentality in society, even if the people involved are not all Christians. Cultures that adopt biblical principles benefit from the application of those principles, one of the primary benefits being the restraint of sin that God's Word provides.

Government is the seventh means the Holy Spirit uses in His restraining ministry. Government is the God-ordained mechanism for the management of society and the maintenance of peace and order. Romans 13:1–7 makes it abundantly clear that the primary responsibility of government is to restrain evil.

I believe in limited government, but not because of my political preferences. I believe in limited government because I believe the Bible is very specific about government's role. Above all else, the Bible says that government is a "minister of God" to punish evil (v. 4). In other words, wrongdoers must fear the repercussions of their evil, or they will feel no restraint. Evil must be punished if society is going to be orderly.

The job of government is to bring terror to evildoers in order to restrain and prevent evil if possible and to deal with it when it is committed. The Holy Spirit uses government to create restraint in society.

When people, whether leaders or family or government or even the church, refuse to allow the Holy Spirit to carry out His ministry of restraint through them, the repercussions are staggering, because they are removing the only true source of restraint.

So we need to make sure we are not hindering, or quenching, the restraining work of the Spirit.

RESISTING THE SPIRIT'S RESTRAINT

We need to see that it is possible to resist the Holy Spirit's efforts to restrain sin. We noted in the previous chapter the occasion where Stephen, one of the original leaders in the church at Jerusalem, was hauled before Israel's governing council, called the Sanhedrin, to explain his ministry (Acts 6:12).

Beginning in verse 2 of Acts 7, Stephen launched into one of the most powerful sermons in the Bible. Then he concluded by laying the charge of resisting the Spirit at the feet of these men who were the religious authorities of Israel: "You men who are stiff-necked and uncircumcised in heart and ears are always resisting the Holy Spirit" (7:51).

The Danger of Resisting

So it is possible to resist the Holy Spirit, to tune out His voice. Have you ever been talking to someone who suddenly tuned you out? You are trying to communicate, but it's clear that the other person isn't paying any attention.

It is possible for someone to say no to the work of the Holy Spirit so often and so completely that He takes the person at his word, and his next no becomes his final no. It is very dangerous to say to the Holy Spirit of God, "No. I hear You and I know it's You. But I am not going to listen."

It's also possible for a society to resist the restraining work of the Holy Spirit—but as we said above, that society will pay a dear price. We in America should know, because this is exactly what is happening in our culture today.

People can resist the Holy Spirit's attempts to restrain their sin. This leads to the Spirit making a momentous decision. When sinful people resist Him to the point of no return, the Holy Spirit gives them over to practice their sin and suffer the awful consequences of their resistance.

Given Over to Sin

That's the picture we have in Romans 1:18–32. This passage is the epitome of what happens when sinful people resist the Spirit of God and He gives them over to their sin. This is a very important passage because of its repercussions, so I want us to note several things about these fifteen crucial verses.

Verse 18 is the key: "For the wrath of God is revealed from heaven against all ungodliness and unrighteousness of men who suppress the truth in unrighteousness." Notice that these people have the truth, but they hold it down. God is trying to speak, but they are saying, "I don't want to listen." So they try to put a lid on God's truth. They don't do it by accident; it's a purposeful act of unrighteousness. Suppressing the truth means that the people referred to here must stop their ears to the voice of the Holy Spirit, because He is the Spirit of truth (John 14:17).

The thing that increasingly marks Christians as unique is the fact that we believe in truth. We believe there is an unchanging standard by which all things can be measured. The interesting thing is that when it comes to their pocketbooks and their lives, people want truth to prevail.

But when it comes to issues of spiritual truth and morality, people suppress the truth and the Spirit whose job it is to reveal the truth to human hearts. And when you suppress the Spirit's ability to restrain sin, God takes the lid off and sin breaks loose.

Let's pick this up in Romans 1: "Therefore God gave them over in the lusts of their hearts. . . . God gave them over to degrading passions. . . . God gave them over to a depraved mind" (vv. 24, 26, 28).

Paul says that God gave these people over to sin in three basic ways. First, He gave them over to follow their lusts, to do their own thing. "You want to be your own God? Go right ahead." So the first layer of Holy Spirit restraint was removed.

Doing one's own thing may not sound like judgment to some people. It sounds more like fun. Yes, it is fun until it's time to pay up. Some people use credit cards like this. They go shopping, pull out all the cards, and just say, "Charge it."

If you've been caught in that trap, you know you will be paying for the stuff for years to come. That's true in the spiritual realm too. You may think you are free to indulge yourself, but the payment will always come due, with interest. So God says to those who refuse the Spirit's restraint, "You want freedom from Me? You've got it!"

Then they take a step down to the next level, "degrading passions." In this particular context, Paul talks about homosexuality. Notice that he doesn't argue lifestyle, hormones, what a person may be born with, or any of that. All of that is smoke to cover the real issue. The real issue, according to the Bible, is that homosexuality is a degrading sin that invites God's judgment.

Now, to many of us, this may sound like the bottom of the barrel. But according to verse 28, there's another step below degrading passions: "a depraved mind." You're in bad shape when you lose your mind concerning issues of sin and morality.

How do we know when people arrive at this point? "And although they know the ordinance of God, that those who practice such things are worthy of death, they not only do the same, but also give hearty approval to those who practice them" (v. 32).

That is, they want to legalize depravity. You know people have gone crazy when they try to wrap their depravity in a cloak of respectability by making it legal. So what do we have today? People wanting to make same-sex marriages legal, to make adoption by a homosexual couple legal, to give all same-sex practices the full protection of the law.

Paul says that when a society reaches this point, it has gone stark raving mad. If you want to see people who engage in degradation of every kind, just tune in to the talk shows. The people on the platform are bad enough. But the audience applauds their depravity, giving it "hearty approval."

What is the cause of this "devolution" of society? It's because people said no to the restraining influence of the Holy Spirit, and He said, "You want unrestrained sin? You've got it." It's like the prodigal son. His father said, "You want to leave? Go ahead. Call me when you are tired of the pigpen."

REAPING THE RESULTS

People can resist and refuse the restraining Holy Spirit for only so long. As we have seen, those who resist the Spirit are turned over by Him to the consequences of their refusal, until those consequences become their final judgment.

There is a great illustration of this in Genesis 6:1–13, the description of the society that fell under God's judgment in the flood. In verse 3, God says, "My Spirit shall not strive with man forever." The Hebrew word *strive* means to shield or protect. God is saying, "I am not going to keep on protecting mankind forever."

The people of the ancient world had thrown off all restraint of sin and were indulging themselves in degrading passions and violence (see especially vv. 5–7 and 11–13). It sounds like Paul's description of first-century Rome in Romans 1. And it sounds like much of the activity in the twenty-first-century modern world.

When God says, "My Spirit will not always be around to restrain sin," we had better take the clue! God isn't going to keep holding this messy world together forever.

PERSONAL APPLICATION FOR LIFE

1. This is another one of those occasions when it would be good to check around and make sure there are no influences coming into your home that you don't want to be there. For most of us, learning the restraint of the Spirit started at home.

2. You can also help your church be salt and light and a restraining influence in your community by your faithful prayer support and active involvement. Drop your pastor a note to encourage him in his preaching and teaching of the Word.

3. If you're like most Christians, you have some unsaved friends and family members on your prayer list. As along as they are still here, you know they haven't said their final no to the Holy Spirit, so keep up your prayers for their salvation.

4. A lot of Christians simply get angry or frustrated when they think of government. But let's not make the mistake of thinking that if we can't do something really big and noticeable, we won't do anything at all. If you need to get informed about the issues and know who your local leaders are, start there. If you need to make your voice heard on an issue, don't hesitate to speak up, but also be alert for an opportunity to turn the situation into a witness for Christ.

FOR GROUP STUDY

Questions for Group Discussion

1. Read 2 Thessalonians 2:1–6. What is the principle of restraint? What are the benefits of the Spirit's ministry of restraint?

2. Dr. Evans discusses seven means of the Spirit's restraint of sin. Have group members share examples of the Spirit's restraint they have experienced. (Use the chart in "Picture This" as an aid to your discussion.)

3. In what ways do we resist the Spirit's restraint of sin? What is the danger of doing so? Read Romans 1:18–32. What is the result of continually

resisting the Spirit's restraint of sin in one's life? Discuss the downward stages of giving oneself over to sin.

4. Read the illustration in Genesis 6:1–13. What is its message? How relevant is that message to today's society?

PICTURE THIS

The Spirit limits the operation of sin in the world, and He uses several means to effect His restraints. Below are seven of those restraints pointed out by Dr. Evans.

The Means of the Spirit's Restraint of Sin

MEANS	SCRIPTURE PASSAGES	HOW IT WORKS
Direct intervention	Job 1:12	God will intervene in our circumstances.
Godly leaders	Exodus 32:11–35; Numbers 14	God will use godly leaders to intervene on His behalf.
The family	1 Timothy 3:4	Families lay down guidelines for children to help keep them from doing everything they want to do.
The conscience	John 16:8	Because the conscience alerts us to sin, it can become a valuable restrainer of sin.
The church	2 Thessalonians 2:6	The body of Christ serves as a constant restraining force to sin in the world.
The Bible	2 Timothy 3:16	Its guidelines govern and help establish a righteous mentality in society.
Government	Romans 13:1–7	This is a God-ordained mechanism for the management of society and the maintenance of peace and order. Its primary responsibility is to restrain evil.

SECTION III

The Provision of the Holy Spirit

40

THE HOLY SPIRIT'S FRUIT

The fruit of the Holy Spirit consists of those qualities of the spiritual life that the Spirit will produce in us if we submit to His filling and control.

Paul delineates the fruit of the Spirit in Galatians 5:22–23, two tightly packed verses that are worthy of extended study. It would be great just to turn there and let the sweet juice of the Spirit's fruit run down our arms, so to speak, as we dig in and enjoy the good things He has for us. But we can't ignore verses 16–21, the context in which Paul's discussion of spiritual fruit occurs. What these verses do is whet our appetite for satisfying fruit of the Spirit by giving us a taste of the dry, rotten, and unsatisfying deeds of the flesh.

The believers in Galatia were trying to live the life of the Holy Spirit in the energy of the flesh, and Paul was astounded:

> You foolish Galatians, who has bewitched you, before whose eyes Jesus Christ was publicly portrayed as crucified? . . . Are you so foolish? Having begun by the Spirit, are you now being perfected by the flesh? (Galatians 3:1, 3)

This last question is one we all have to ask ourselves as Christians. Giving the correct answer is easy: No, we can't be perfected by the flesh. Living out that answer, however, is not always easy because we are engaged in a battle between the flesh and the Spirit.

We have already looked at the fact that the flesh, meaning our unredeemed humanity, is unfixable. This explains why Paul was so astonished at the foolishness of the Galatians. They were in danger of losing their moorings because of a serious misunderstanding of the spiritual life. The false teachers among them had convinced these believers that the way to pull off the Christian life was by taming the flesh and making it behave with a list of rules.

The Christian life does include rules. There are definite dos and don'ts. But the power for victorious Christian living is not in the rules. It's in the Spirit. Paul gives us a good taste of the bad fruit of the flesh so we will sincerely desire the fruit of the Spirit. We need to begin with Galatians 5:16–18:

> But I say, walk by the Spirit, and you will not carry out the desire of the flesh. For the flesh sets its desire against the Spirit, and the Spirit against the flesh; for these are in opposition to one another, so that you may not do the things that you please. But if you are led by the Spirit, you are not under the Law.

OLD HOUSE, NEW OCCUPANT

When you came to Christ, the Spirit of God came to take up residence in your life and give you a new nature. He placed your new nature in the old house of your flesh—and your old house doesn't want a new occupant!

But the Spirit of God comes in to set up a whole new program, take control of your body, and run the show. Your flesh says, "Not here, You won't. I have been running this show for all these years, and I am not about to give it over to You."

The flesh will desire to sin until it is laid in the grave. But the Holy Spirit gives you the ability not to give in to the cravings, appetites, and demands of the flesh. That's why we are told to walk by the Spirit (Galatians 5:16), a command Paul repeats in verse 25.

Notice how verse 17 describes the outcome of this war: "You may not do the things that you please." I think of it as being like a football game, where the other team opposes you across the line. As you try to go forward, this other team—captained by the flesh—says, "If we have our way, you will make no forward progress. In fact, try to run the ball this way and you are going to lose yardage."

Many of us have experienced that in our Christian lives, haven't we? We keep getting pushed back. We can't even seem to maintain our line of scrimmage because the flesh is opposing us. But that's not the way it has to be anymore because we have a powerful force on our team who opposes the flesh. We have the Holy Spirit, who knows how to resist the flesh.

IS THE LAW NECESSARY?

In Galatians 5:18, Paul says the Holy Spirit is so good at His job that if you are led by the Spirit, "you are not under the Law." Paul's contrast between the Law and grace goes all the way back to chapter 3. His point has been to show the Galatians that no amount of Law-keeping, which is really the effort of the flesh to live the life of faith, will do the job.

Law is good and necessary because we are rebellious. The Mosaic law, which is the revelation of God's perfect standard, was given to show us how sinful we are and how far short we fall of God's demands (Romans 3:23).

The problem with the law is that it doesn't give you the power to obey it. All it can do is give you the guidelines and punish you when you have broken them. That's why, if you try to live the Christian life by keeping a list of rules in the power of your flesh, you are doomed to failure and misery.

So law is necessary to restrain evil, but it's not the way to experience the Spirit-filled, Spirit-directed life. Paul says if you let the Holy Spirit take over in your life, then you are going to be pleasing God because you want to, not because you have to.

THE WORKS OF THE FLESH

In Galatians 5:19, Paul writes, "Now the deeds of the flesh are evident." You read the list that follows in verses 19–21 and you realize that no truer words were ever spoken. You can know whether you are a spiritual Christian or a fleshly Christian at any given moment. You don't have to wonder, because if you are producing the rotten "fruit" of the flesh, you will know it. Paul's list of the works of the flesh can be broken down into three categories of sins.

Moral Sins

The first category of fleshly deeds has to do with morality: "immorality, impurity, sensuality" (v. 19). Immorality is the Greek word *pornēia,* a word that should look familiar because it's the root of the English word *pornography.* You are definitely living in the flesh if you are seeking to satisfy your sexual desires either by direct, illegitimate sexual contact with another person outside the boundary of heterosexual marriage or by feeding yourself with illegitimate sexual material.

In this context sensuality has to do with flagrant sexual activity. Immorality can be now hidden, privatized—especially the Internet pornography that is an epidemic today among men. Nobody knows it but you.

But sensuality means that you have gone public. You have come out of the closet. When you "progress" to sensuality, you have little concern about who knows.

Religious Sins

Paul's next category is religious sin: "idolatry, sorcery" (Galatians 5:20a). Idolatry is worshiping other gods. Israel regularly did this. The nation went after other gods even though it knew the true God. Many of us go after other gods. We may even ride in them or live in them. Whatever takes the place of God in your life is your idol. When you fall into idolatry, worshiping the true and living God is not that big a deal anymore.

Paul's reference to "sorcery" is the Greek word *pharmakēia,* which should look familiar as the root of the English word *pharmacy.* In this context, it has to do with the use of drugs in religious ritual. Some Bible versions even translate the word as "witchcraft."

You may be old enough to remember the sixties, when hippies were using drugs and calling it a religious experience. They even used religious terms. But the "religious" use of drugs goes back to biblical days.

Social Sins

Paul's final, and longest, category is what I call social sins: how you relate to others (Galatians 5:20b–21). I count at least ten items on this list. One reason may be that these are the kinds of fleshly sins that Christians are most likely to fall prey to. Not too many true Christians are going to take a hit of crack cocaine to get high, but how many of us are guilty of "outbursts of anger," for example?

Paul says he is not giving us an exhaustive list (v. 21), but just a taste of the flesh. What living in the flesh does is disqualify us from inheritance in the kingdom, which I take to be a loss of full reward and full participation in the kingdom, not a loss of salvation.

THE FRUIT OF THE SPIRIT

Now we come to the Holy Spirit's fruit orchard (Galatians 5:22–23). The deeds of the flesh are evident, but so is the fruit of the Spirit. Here are three things you need to know about the Spirit's fruit.

Fruit Is Visible

The first thing you need to know about fruit is that fruit is always visible. Watch out for that tree in your backyard that is giving you invisible fruit! When fruit is ripe and luxurious, you know it.

So don't tell me that you are walking in the Spirit in your heart, or that you are full of the Spirit in your heart, if nothing is evident in your life but the works of the flesh. Jesus said that we can tell false prophets by the fruit they produce (Matthew 7:16, 20). The same is true for believers. If you are walking in the Spirit, others will know it.

Fruit Is Recognizable

The second thing you need to know about fruit is that fruit always reflects the character of the tree or vine that is bearing it. "Grapes are not gathered from thorn bushes, nor figs from thistles," Jesus said (Matthew 7:16). Apple trees produce apples, orange trees grow oranges, and so forth. The fruit that comes from a life controlled by the Holy Spirit will reflect the character of Jesus Christ.

Fruit Is for Others

A third fact about fruit is that fruit is always borne for the benefit of others. The seed in a fruit is designed for reproduction. So as you bear the fruit of the Spirit, others not only enjoy the "taste" of your life, but also the seeds of spiritual growth are planted in their lives.

Fruit is always meant for someone else's enjoyment. You never see fruit chewing on itself. In fact, fruit that only exists for itself gets rotten. One reason for fruit is so that somebody can take a bite.

The Holy Spirit wants to control us so that our families and friends can take a bite out of our lives and say, "Um, that's good!"

Although the word "fruit" in Galatians 5:22 is singular, Paul lists nine varieties or flavors, those wonderful qualities that grow out of a Spirit-controlled life. Why are the singular and plural together here? Because all of the Holy Spirit's fruit grows out of the same tree.

The Nine Spiritual Fruit

Paul says the fruit of the Spirit is *love* (Galatians 5:22). Godly love is the ability to seek the highest good for another, regardless of that person's response.

The fruit of the Spirit includes *joy*. The world can only offer you happiness, which is driven by circumstances. But the joy of the Spirit has nothing to do with happiness. It has to do with a well of living water on the inside, not the circumstances on the outside. Joy is the overflow of the life of God within you.

The fruit of the Spirit is also *peace*. The Holy Spirit can bring harmony where there is conflict. He can take two different personalities and cause them to live together in peace. He can take two factions that are at war and bring them together in harmony.

The fruit of the Spirit also consists of *patience*, that quality that allows us to be "long-fused" instead of short-tempered. It removes a vengeful spirit toward those who have wronged us.

Kindness is thinking of ways you can help others, not ways you can hurt them. *Goodness* means deeds that benefit others, not deeds that destroy. *Faithfulness* is the ability to be consistent, not there one day and gone the next. It means we are dependable.

Gentleness, or meekness (v. 23), is the ability to bring yourself under the control of another, the ability to submit to the will of God. Finally, *self-control* is the ability to say no to wrong and yes to right, no matter how tempting the wrong is.

WALKING BY THE SPIRIT

Go through that list and you'll understand why Paul concludes by saying, "Against such things there is no law." We won't need law to rein us in when the Holy Spirit is producing His life-transforming fruit in us.

In verses 24–25, Paul gives us two ways the Holy Spirit can get more of us. Verse 24 is a reminder instead of a command. If you are a Christian, you have already been crucified with Christ (Romans 6:1–11). Therefore, your flesh was put to death on the cross, and you were raised spiritually to a new way of life. What Paul is saying is that when it comes to this conflict between flesh and Spirit, you are already on the victor's side.

Then he says in Galatians 5:25, "If we live by the Spirit, let us also walk by the Spirit." This connects us back to verse 16, which is where we started.

BRINGING IT HOME

How do we bring all of this home? Consider Galatians 6:7–9:

> Do not be deceived, God is not mocked; for whatever a man sows, this he will also reap. For the one who sows to his own flesh shall from the flesh reap corruption, but the one who sows to the Spirit shall from the Spirit reap eternal life. And let us not lose heart in doing good, for in due time we shall reap if we do not grow weary.

To understand the spiritual life, look at farming, Paul writes. The principle is simple: What you plant is what you get back. If you sow to the flesh, if you feed the flesh, the flesh will grow and produce fleshly deeds. If you sow to the Spirit, you will reap the fruit of the Spirit.

The Greek word translated "mocked" means to thumb your nose at something. Don't thumb your nose at God, Paul says, because He will always have the last word.

How do you thumb your nose at God? By thinking you can wade around in the cesspool of the flesh without slipping and going under. If you are a drunkard today, it is because you have developed a habit of drinking. You are not a drunkard because you took one sip. It was that second sip, and third, and fourth, and so on, that got you hooked. Now drink controls you.

What you sow is what you reap. So if your life is marked by a conspicuous absence of spiritual fruit, it's because there has been an absence of sowing to the Spirit. But when you sow the right seed, you get the right result.

In fact, the beautiful thing about sowing to the Spirit is that you always get back more than you put in. When you sow a corn seed, you don't get just one ear. You get a stalk with many ears. What you sow is an investment that comes back many times.

So, do you want the Holy Spirit's brand of love, joy, peace, and so on? Then don't grow weary of sowing righteousness, of walking by the Spirit, because when the harvest comes "in due time," you'll reap a whole basketful of ripe, luscious spiritual fruit.

So how do we experience the Spirit's fruit? Many of us have sown bad things even as Christians. We have developed damaging habits or attitudes or addictions. Some of us are in our second or third marriages because of what we have sown.

Well, you may not be able to change what you have already reaped, but you can plow up your field! You may have some bad things in the ground even now, but the Holy Spirit knows how to plow that field and turn over the soil so you can sow new seeds in the same soil.

PERSONAL APPLICATION FOR LIFE

1. We seem to keep coming back to the importance of prayer. There are no easy formulas to help you develop a potent and consistent prayer life except that practice makes perfect. Ask God to help you approach prayer the way you do breathing. Insist on it!

2. Was there something on the list of fleshly deeds in Galatians 5:19–21 that really hit home with you? Or was your "pet" sin not listed? Either way, take that sin to God in prayer, stating it by name and asking the Holy Spirit to make you so sensitive to it that you react just thinking about doing it. Also, ask the Spirit to show you if there's some transgression you are doing without even being conscious of it.

3. Go through the list of the fruit of the Spirit in Galatians 5:22–23, and chances are that one of these qualities will leap out at you as something you need in a special way right now. Take your need for that fruit to the Holy Spirit in prayer, telling Him how much you want to see Him produce it in your life. Then be ready for Him to deal with whatever He needs to in order to prepare the soil of your heart for that fruit.

4. For many Christians, the biggest challenge is simply not to "lose heart in doing good." Are you growing weary in the process of planting the seed? Take a few minutes to sit under a shade tree and meditate on the harvest waiting for you. Read Revelation 21–22 and thank God that the harvest will be far greater in value than any effort we make in plowing and sowing!

FOR GROUP STUDY

Questions for Group Discussion

1. The apostle Paul speaks of the "deeds of the flesh" in Galatians 5:19. What three categories encompass the works of the flesh? What are some examples of how these works of the flesh manifest themselves?

2. What are some of the characteristics of the fruit of the Spirit? What is the purpose of fruit in the life of the believer?

3. Read Galatians 5:22–23. Discuss the fruit of the Spirit. (Use the chart on the next page as an aid for your discussion.) Have group members do a mental "report card" and evaluate the evidence of each fruit in their own lives.

4. In Galatians 5:24–25, Paul tells us two ways the Holy Spirit can get more of us. What are those two ways? What are the three components of walking in the Spirit?

PICTURE THIS

The fruit is the Holy Spirit consists of those qualities of the spiritual life that the Spirit will produce in us if we submit to His filling and control.

The Fruit of the Spirit
Galatians 5:22–23

SPECIFIC FRUIT	VERSE	HOW THE FRUIT BECOMES EVIDENT
Love	22	Through the ability of seeking the highest good for another, regardless of that person's response.
Peace	22	By allowing the Spirit to bring harmony where there is conflict.
Joy	22	By letting the life of God overflow within us.
Patience	22	By exercising the quality that allows us to be "long-fused" instead of short-tempered. It removes a vengeful spirit toward those who have wronged us.
Kindness	22	By thinking of ways we can help others, not ways we can hurt them.
Goodness	22	By doing deeds that benefit others, not deeds that destroy.
Faithfulness	22	By exercising the ability to be consistent and dependable.
Gentleness	23	By bringing ourselves under the control of another, the ability to submit to the will of God.
Self-control	23	By saying no to wrong and yes to right, no matter how tempting the wrong is.

41

THE HOLY SPIRIT'S INTERCESSION

I have been in enough foreign countries to know that if you don't know somebody who lives there and visit long enough, you are going to be in trouble, because there are a lot of folks who will take advantage of you and steer you the wrong way if they know you're new to the territory.

When it comes to functioning in the spiritual realm, we need somebody who lives there. Somebody who understands the terrain and can speak the language. Somebody who can point us in the direction we need to go and help us find the things we need. Somebody who can intercede, who can approach another person and make an appeal on our behalf. We need an intercessor.

We need that kind of spiritual help because as believers in Jesus Christ we are living in a world that is utterly foreign to our human nature. It's a world unlike anything the natural mind can see or understand, and we need a guide. Paul calls this realm "the heavenly places" (Ephesians 1:3; 2:6).

We have such a guide in the person of the Holy Spirit. He not only knows the realm, He knows the King of the realm. The Spirit intercedes on our behalf in the very presence of God the Father. Romans 8:26 is a key verse here: "In the same way the Spirit also helps our weakness; for we do not know how to pray as we should, but the Spirit Himself intercedes for us with groanings too deep for words."

OUR NEED FOR THE SPIRIT'S INTERCESSION

This is good news. How many of us have said, "I don't know what to say when I pray"? We all have. Well, here is the help we need, and it's not just a book of instructions. It's a person, the Helper Himself, the Holy Spirit.

The Holy Spirit helps us in prayer. He is God's agent of communication.

An Unfamiliar Language

If the world of the Spirit is a foreign realm to our fleshly minds, prayer is the unfamiliar language of that realm. When you're in a place you have never been before, among people whose language you don't speak, somebody needs to intercede for you.

Paul says we need help in our prayer lives because we are weak. God knows our weaknesses, so the Holy Spirit makes sure that what you need and where you get properly communicated to God. Paul says we don't know how to pray. That's obvious because we don't pray. We are so messed up in our weakness that coming before God is a job.

We aren't very adept at communicating with God, and the effort is a struggle. But the Spirit has the ability to take your cares and needs and hurts and confusion and so clarify, correct, and focus them that by the time they leave you and get to heaven, they have been fixed. So don't worry that you pray poorly. Worry that you don't pray at all.

I say that because Romans 8:26 assumes that we do pray. Not knowing how to pray is a lot different from giving up and not praying. We have no excuse for not praying, although there may be reasons for not praying well.

Whatever our prayer problem, the Holy Spirit's job is to help us by interceding for us. So you never have to worry that you didn't get your prayer just right. By the time the Holy Spirit takes it and gets it to the throne of God, that thing is cooking, because the Spirit's job is to carry it to God properly.

Learning the Language

If you want to learn a foreign language, the best way to do so is by hanging out in an environment where people speak it. It's amazing how many Christians say they want to pray but don't hang out in a prayer environment.

If you don't want to hang out in the environment, if you don't want to be around people who know the language, you don't really want to learn that language. The reason this is critical for prayer is that prayer is God's "two-way" system of communication.

As you pray, the Holy Spirit is there to interpret your prayer and clarify the meaning. That way, by the time your prayer arrives at the foot of the Father, the One who grants the request, that prayer has been corrected, fixed up, chopped off, and realigned so that, often, what you said does not look anything like what finally gets delivered in heaven.

Your prayer needed Holy Spirit reshaping. What you said needed a lot of help. When you prayed, you did not have all the information you needed. When you prayed, you did not understand all the related things that were going to happen down the line.

But the Holy Spirit added all the needed data to it so that it was ready for the Father to receive it. What happened was that your few-second prayer turned into a five-page petition because the Holy Spirit clarified it, fixed it up, and corrected it, bringing it into conformity with God's will.

The Need to Pray

If you really want to see some changes take place in your life, link up with the Holy Spirit in prayer. The apostle Jude tells us to "[build] yourselves up on your most holy faith; praying in the Holy Spirit" (v. 20). Prayer builds you up. Prayer keeps your love for God hot. Prayer can keep you hanging in there when you want to quit.

Now, if prayer is this powerful and you were the Devil, what would you do? Anything you could to keep people from praying. That's exactly what Satan does. He keeps us from coming face-to-face with God so that the Holy Spirit has nothing to grab hold of and deliver to the Father.

Then we don't experience the building up that occurs through "praying in the Holy Spirit," which means praying in the environment or realm of the Spirit. That's exactly where the Spirit's intercession is experienced, so let's find out what the terrain looks like and how to get there.

THE NATURE OF THE SPIRIT'S INTERCESSION

Paul gives us a look into the nature of the Holy Spirit's intercession in verses 26b–27 of Romans 8:

> But the Spirit Himself intercedes for us with groanings too deep for words; and He who searches the hearts knows what the mind of the Spirit is, because He intercedes for the saints according to the will of God.

Imagine the Holy Spirit engaged so deeply in prayer on your behalf that He enters into yearnings and groanings that cannot be expressed in words. This is not some type of heavenly language here. Paul is talking about the deep, quiet, inaudible prayer groanings of the Spirit.

The Spirit's Groanings

Now we all know what it is to feel something so deeply that we groan under the burden of it. That's the concept here, and it permeates all of creation. In Romans 8:22, Paul says, "We know that the whole creation groans and suffers the pains of childbirth together until now."

The whole creation groans and aches like a woman in childbirth, Paul says. A woman in labor groans as the baby serves notice on her that the nine months are up and he or she is ready to be born. But for that to occur, there must be a period of groaning as the contractions begin and pain sets in.

So the groaning is both good and bad news. The bad news is, it's going to hurt. The good news is, the hurt is worthwhile because it's going to produce something good.

The Bible says the entire universe groans under the curse of sin that expresses itself in things such as hurricanes and tornadoes and earthquakes. Those are not just random happenings in nature. They are "labor pains" as the creation groans to be delivered from the chaos into which sin has plunged it.

Now don't misunderstand. Paul is not talking about some kind of modern-day "Mother Earth" theology in which the earth is invested with a spirit and a soul and all of that. He's saying that even the unthinking natural creation feels the curse of sin and longs to be delivered from it because this is not what God created it for.

So the upheaval and violence of the created world is unnatural and will someday be reversed when the curse of sin is lifted. In other words, nature groans in expectation of something better ahead that will replace the groaning with joy. In this way, the groanings of nature illustrate the Holy Spirit's groanings for us in prayer.

Interpreting Our Groanings

But the natural world is not the only part of creation that's groaning. "And not only this, but also we ourselves, having the first fruits of the Spirit, even we ourselves groan within ourselves, waiting eagerly for our adoption as sons, the redemption of our body" (Romans 8:23).

Why do we have to go through the pains of life? Because we have been affected by the sin that has cursed our environment and cursed us as well.

Paul groaned when he cried out, "Wretched man that I am! Who will set me free from the body of this death?" (Romans 7:24). One reason God allows His children to experience pain at death is to cause them to want to leave earth and enter eternity (8:24–25). God wants us to desire heaven more than earth, eternity more than time.

Creation groans, the people of God groan, and the Holy Spirit groans. What's the connection? Creation groans to be relieved from the curse of sin. We groan because of sin's effects upon us. The Spirit groans in prayer in order to identify with our groanings, deliver them to God, and deliver to us from God what we need to be sustained in a world that produces pain.

In other words, the Holy Spirit identifies with our pain, clarifies that pain, and communicates it to the Father in a way we could never do ourselves. Then the Spirit brings out of that pain the will of God for us, "because He intercedes for the saints according to the will of God" (Romans 8:27b).

So the greater the groans, the closer we are to some kind of divine intervention and deliverance, either in time or eternity, or both. When we are experiencing the pains of life that produce groaning that cannot be uttered, that means God is sending something down the life canal.

Linking Up in Prayer

Now what does this say about prayer? The Holy Spirit only links with your prayer when it is tied to your heart, when it is tied to that which groans. If you just say a prayer because it's bedtime or mealtime, if your prayers never get deep enough to enter Spirit territory, you aren't experiencing the Holy Spirit's intercession.

Prayer has to come from within to be valid. Prayer is not valid just because words fall from our lips. The Lord said of Israel, "This people draw near with their words and honor Me with their lip service, but they remove their hearts far from Me" (Isaiah 29:13). Prayer must be rooted in who you are inside.

If God did not allow us to groan, we would never pray. We might say prayer words, but we would never pray from within.

One of the purposes of pain is to draw us to God. You appreciate the sun a lot more after a day of bad weather. When every day is good, you assume every day is supposed to be good and you take things for granted.

God is the most taken-for-granted person in the universe. That's not the way it is supposed to be, so to keep us from becoming complacent or self-sufficient, God allows us to groan under the weight of our sin and weaknesses. Then we're ready to seek His face.

THE RESULTS OF THE SPIRIT'S INTERCESSION

Did you notice where we have arrived in our study of Romans 8? We're at verse 28: "And we know that God causes all things to work together for good to those who love God, to those who are called according to His purpose."

Romans 8:28 is set in the context of the Holy Spirit's intercession. You can't get to verse 28 without going through verses 26–27. In fact, notice that this verse begins with a conjunction: "And." Verse 28 is very closely connected with verse 27.

The Divine Blueprint

This means that the people on whose behalf God is working all things together for good are the same people on whose behalf the Holy Spirit is interceding according to God's will. And these are the same people whose prayers the Spirit interprets with deep groanings (v. 26) as He prays according to God's will. The net result is bringing us into the experience of God's will.

So the Spirit is interpreting, redirecting, and reshaping our groanings in light of God's plan. He's following the divine blueprint, not just haphazardly bringing our requests before God. So you only get the Spirit's help when you are on God's program.

When you look at your world, it may seem chaotic and confusing. But once the Holy Spirit lifts you above your circumstances, you can see how God is aligning everything for your good according to His will. It's the difference between driving through farm country and seeing it from an airplane. From up high, things look orderly.

Conformed to Christ

So if God's will is the plan by which He is ordering our lives, then what is God's ultimate will or purpose for us? Paul answers that in Romans 8:29. God wants us "to become conformed to the image of His Son, that He might be the firstborn among many brethren."

God's optimum goal is to conform us to the character of Christ, and God is so passionate about this that He will stop at nothing to achieve it. So He is always answering prayer according to His will (1 John 5:14). Many times we don't pray because we don't think anything is happening. But with God, something is always happening. He is always working.

Don't ever think nothing is happening just because you haven't seen it happen yet. It's just not harvesttime. God is either moving to answer your request as you prayed it, or He is changing and reshaping the request to conform to His will.

According to God's Will

Someone might object, "Wait a minute. If I had wanted something different, I would have asked for something different." If that's the way you view prayer, you need a review of Romans 8. Prayer works "according to the will of God" (v. 27). That's because we are called "according to His purpose" (v. 28) that we might be conformed to "the image of His Son" (v. 29).

God only does what is in His will. So if what you are asking is God's will, the Spirit is interceding for it on your behalf, and God is doing something even though you haven't seen the answer yet. But if you are asking outside of God's will, the Spirit has to change your request because it is illegitimate. But to change your request, the Spirit has to change you, and sometimes that can make you groan.

Being Devoted to Prayer

So what's the best way to experience the intercession of the Holy Spirit? Colossians 4:2 says, "Devote yourselves to prayer." That means it should be abnormal not to pray. Is that the way it is in your life? If you pray abnormally, don't be surprised if you hear from God abnormally. If you pray every now and then, you are going to hear from God every now and then. Paul says prayer should be so important that not to pray is the exception.

But we have it backwards, because prayer interrupts our regular schedule. It should be that not praying interrupts our schedule, but we basically view prayer as something that intrudes into our day. If we were to give prayer the importance God gives it, we would see prayer as our normal routine and the other stuff we do as interruptions to prayer.

PERSONAL APPLICATION FOR LIFE

1. As is true for almost all the spiritual benefits God has for us, our sense of need determines how serious we will be about making the most of His blessings. That's true for intercession. The Spirit is ready to carry your deepest groanings to the Father, but you must engage Him in heartfelt prayer. How much do you long to experience the Holy Spirit's ministry of intercession on your behalf? That's how much you will experience it.

2. Take a close look at your prayer list. Any needs or situations there that seem beyond hope of any solution or supply? Those things are great candidates for intensive, Spirit-assisted prayer. Don't give up on the tough ones. It's just when you run out of answers and even words that the Spirit takes over.

3. Have you ever felt the pain of your sin and lack of conformity to Christ so deeply that your spirit groaned in its grief? You're on the right track, because the Holy Spirit can bring you to feel about your sin the way He feels about your sin; He'll do some amazing things with you. But don't get proud about your brokenness. Just ask the Spirit to keep you sensitive.

4. Do you really want God's will and Christ's image to be worked out in your life? Better make sure before you seek the Spirit's intercession, because these things are what He's after for you.

FOR GROUP STUDY

Questions for Group Discussion

1. Use Romans 8:26 as the basis for your discussion of these questions. As believers, why do we need the Spirit's intercession? In what ways is the Holy Spirit God's agent of communication?

2. Romans 8:26b–27 describes the nature of the Spirit's intercession. What does the apostle Paul mean by the Spirit's "groanings"? What is significant about the Spirit's interpretation of our groanings?

3. Romans 8:28 tells us, "And we know that God causes all things to work

together for good to those who love God, to those who are called according to His purpose." What are the results we see because of the Spirit's intercession? (Use the chart below as an aid to your discussion.)

4. Being conformed to the image of Christ is God's ultimate goal for us (Romans 8:29). It is also one of the results of the Spirit's intercession on our behalf. How does intercession play a part in this process of becoming conformed to Christ's character? Why is 1 John 5:14 significant in this regard?

PICTURE THIS

The Holy Spirit's intercession is purposeful and produces some genuine results. Below are four of those results Dr. Evans highlighted in this chapter.

Results of the Spirit's Intercession on Our Behalf

Romans 8:26–29

RESULT	VERSE	HOW IT WORKS
A divine blueprint	verse 26	The Spirit is interpreting, redirecting, and reshaping our groanings in light of God's plan, and aligning everything for your good according to His will.
Conformed to Christ	verse 29	God wants us to conform us to the character of Christ.
According to God's will	verse 37	If we ask for something that is God's will, the Spirit will intercede for it on our behalf.
Being devoted to prayer	Colossians 4:2	For us, prayer should be so important that not to pray is the exception. It should be a natural expression of our relationship with the Spirit.

42

THE HOLY SPIRIT'S GUIDANCE

When you open a road map to plan the route of your vacation or some other trip, it quickly becomes obvious that there are multiple ways to get to your destination. The map shows all the possibilities because the mapmaker has access to the big picture. He knows all the major highways, state roads, farm roads, and side roads.

The Christian life is like that. God is leading you from Point A to Point B, but He has the big picture in front of Him and He knows all the roads that can take you there. The problem is that you can't see the big picture, and more often than not, God doesn't issue detailed maps. So it's easy to get confused, even lost, when you're trying to get to Point B, because there are many ways to get there.

Being able to determine the Holy Spirit's guidance as we navigate through life's choices and decisions is a challenge for all of us. Every sincere Christian wants to find God's will, to know that He is guiding in the decisions we make.

SEEKING THE SPIRIT'S GUIDANCE

This matter of the Spirit's guidance is so important that people try a number of ways to discover it. They may ask for a miracle, resort to magic or rely on luck, or divide up the pros and cons of a decision and go with whichever list is longer.

The question people are seeking to answer is, How do I know when God is leading me? Well, I would like to suggest that spiritual guidance occurs when there has been a wedding between the objective revelation of Scripture and the subjective witness of the Holy Spirit—the witness of the Holy Spirit to our individual human spirit.

This definition reflects my belief that there are two extremes in the Christian community today. To go to either extreme is to miss the truth of the Spirit's guidance.

One extreme says just to read the Word. Now don't misunderstand; it is certainly not extreme to read the Bible. But anybody who has ever read the Bible knows that it does not give all the specifics for your life. What the Word does is give you certain specifics and a multiplicity of principles. So if you have the objective Word without any subjective verification, you are left with a lot of questions.

The other extreme is to look for subjective verification without an objective revelation. Then you get people counting anything they do as from God because they feel good about doing it, regardless of what the Bible says. That becomes a faulty witness, like when your house alarm goes off and there is no burglar.

THE SPIRIT AND THE WORD

There is no question that God wants to guide His people through the Holy Spirit. First Corinthians 2 tells us that the Holy Spirit searches the "depths" of God and reveals these things to us because the Spirit knows what God the Father wants (vv. 9–10). It is this revealing work of the Spirit to the believer that is experiential in nature.

Objective and Subjective

The Spirit does this in a unique way, "combining spiritual thoughts with spiritual words" (1 Corinthians 2:13), which I believe refers to the objective and subjective combination that must happen for spiritual guidance to take place. When the Holy Spirit connects with the human spirit, there is an illumination to the mind concerning the plan of God.

Notice how the Spirit and the Word are blended together in John 14:16–17:

> I will ask the Father, and He will give you another Helper, that He may be with you forever; that is the Spirit of truth, whom the world cannot receive, because it does not behold Him or know Him, but you know Him because He abides with you, and will be in you.

Here Jesus promises that the Holy Spirit will take up the leadership role Jesus had among His followers when He was on earth. Then in John 16:13, Jesus says that the Spirit's role will be to guide the believer in the light of God's Word to accomplish God's will.

If you go to the Holy Spirit and say, "Show me the way," but there is a question mark about whether you will go in the way He shows you, you can be assured that He will not guide you. The Spirit is not going to reveal God's will to you so you can debate whether you want to obey it.

Therefore, there must be a predisposition in your mind to obey the will of God once it has been revealed.

God Does Speak

It is possible to read the Bible and not hear the voice of the Spirit. I think this is why Paul says that when you pray, you ought to "pray at all times in the Spirit" (Ephesians 6:18). If we're not careful, we can pray words with no spiritual reality behind them.

So God speaks to His people. He speaks objectively through His Word, which means this is what God expects no matter what you feel or think about it, and whether you have a subjective witness or not. God also speaks subjectively to us through the Holy Spirit's witness within.

HOW THE SPIRIT GUIDES

That leads to a very important question. How does the Holy Spirit guide us? Assuming that we are not looking to violate the clear precepts and principles of Scripture, how do we know when we are hearing the guiding voice of the Holy Spirit? The Bible tells us in Romans 8.

The Spirit's Witness

In Romans 8:14, Paul says, "For all who are being led by the Spirit of God, these are sons of God." What does the Spirit do? He leads God's children.

Now look at verse 16: "The Spirit Himself bears witness with our spirit that we are children of God." If you have the assurance that you are saved, it's because you have heard the voice of the Spirit. I want to know that I know that I am saved, and God wants me to know it too (1 John 5:13). The way a person knows, Paul says, is by the witness of the Spirit.

So if you know what it is like to receive the assurance that you are saved, then you know what it is like to hear the Holy Spirit. If you have never had that experience, it could be you are not saved or that the scar tissue of your soul is blocking the voice of the Spirit.

The witness of the Spirit is the inner confirmation in your spirit of His direction. One way you know you are experiencing the Spirit's guidance is that He confirms to your human spirit that you are doing the will of God.

Access to Your Spirit

This means if you want to hear the Spirit's voice, He has to have access to your spirit. If there is no spiritual development in your spirit, there will be no understanding in your soul. And if there is no understanding in your soul, there will be no direction for your body. If you are not hearing anything in your spirit, your body does not know which way to go because your soul does not know which way to think.

Just as a parent gives a child his nature, so God has given you His nature. You are a new creation in Christ. You are brand-new in your spirit, and you are a temple of the Holy Spirit. So when He guides you, what He does through your human spirit is stamp on your soul an uncompromising confidence that this is what God wants you to do.

When you have that Spirit confidence, you don't care what the circumstances are. You don't care how many people say you can't do it. You don't care how many people say it has never been done before. When the Spirit has spoken to you, you have that inner confidence that you are in God's will.

When the Holy Spirit takes up His residence within you (1 Corinthians 3:16; 6:19), He does His talking inside of you, in your spirit, either confirming or convincing or convicting. He gives you a tenacious assurance of God's will for you. He tells you what God wants.

In Romans 9:1, Paul says, "I am telling the truth in Christ, I am not lying, my conscience bearing me witness in the Holy Spirit." Here we see Paul's subjective confirmation of the truth because the conscience is internal. His conscience now having been sanctified by the Holy Spirit, Paul was convinced he was speaking truth because He had that inner confirmation.

That is why you don't try to force other believers to conform to your standards (Romans 14:1–13). The Holy Spirit may be telling them something different in their spirits than He is telling you.

We must give people the right to hear the voice of God for themselves in the application of the truth of Scripture to their personal context. Thus Paul can write, "Let each man be fully convinced in his own mind" (Romans 14:5).

Trying to Disconnect You

Satan does not want your spirit to get connected with the Holy Spirit. Why? Because he can handle your body. He'll let you have all the New Year's resolutions you want. And to some degree he has already messed up your soul.

But Satan knows that he can't mess with your spirit. That's out of his realm because you have been made brand-new in your spirit. So Satan tries to cut off your communication with the Holy Spirit. He tries to distract you so you won't hear the guiding voice of the Spirit.

Applying the Word

So how does the Spirit lead us? Objectively, by the Word of God. If the Word has spoken, you don't have to listen to your spirit for a different message. The Holy Spirit will never contradict the Word He inspired (2 Peter 1:20–21). The only thing your human spirit will tell you once you hear the Word is how to implement God's truth in your life.

But He also leads us subjectively in the application of the Word. Have you ever heard someone say, "God gave me a verse"? That person finds an application of the verse to his life even though the verse itself may have been written about Moses or Abraham or someone else. How does this

Christian know that this verse can be applied this way in his life, when another Christian who is in the same situation may not be led to that verse? I believe the answer is the internal witness of the Spirit. He applies different verses to different Christians in different ways at different times.

THE GOAL OF THE SPIRIT'S GUIDANCE

The overarching goal of the Holy Spirit's guidance is to help us discover and do the will of God. That is where our experience of the Spirit of God comes in. He works from the inside out. Jesus promised in John 7:37–39 that there would come out of our innermost being a well of water. John says, "This He spoke of the Spirit" (v. 39).

Jesus was saying that you would have a reservoir called the Holy Spirit inside your human spirit. When you hear the voice of the Spirit in your human spirit, and that is transferred to your soul (intellect, emotion, and will) so it can be executed by your body, then you begin to live out the will of God.

To experience the Spirit's guidance, you must be committed to God's will. That is, you must say, "Lord, not my will, but Thine be done, because You are sovereign. I will search the Scriptures to know the parts of Your will that You have revealed to me. But I am also going to depend on You for guidance in my individual choices in life."

The reason you must ultimately trust the sovereign will of God is that you don't see all the facts. You never get all the details. So when you make a decision and the Holy Spirit blocks it, as happened to Paul in Acts 16:6, you have to trust that He sees something in the road ahead that you can't see. God's sovereign will must superintend your individual choices.

THE CHANNELS OF THE SPIRIT'S GUIDANCE

Now let me show you how the Holy Spirit intertwines these three aspects or tiers of God's will as He communicates with our spirits and gives us spiritual guidance.

Through the Word

First, the Spirit guides us through the Scriptures by clarifying and communicating to us God's moral will. The Bible is sufficient because it gives all believers everywhere the underlying principles God wants them to predicate their decisions on. So don't tell me the Spirit has ever led you to do anything that contradicts the Word of God.

God's moral will is clear, but in some cases God's moral will is also flexible. Here's what I mean. In 1 Corinthians 10, Paul was advising the believers about what to do if an unbeliever invites them over for dinner.

In verses 27–28, Paul said if somebody invites you to a dinner party and you want to go, feel free to go. It's up to you. But if an issue comes up that may hurt another believer or wound your own conscience, then back off. Not hurting another brother or wounding your own conscience is more important than your freedom.

The principle here is when you are operating in God's moral will, He gives you a lot of room for preferences in His individual will for you based on your personal desires. Paul says go to the party if you want to go. God's will in that case is that you choose. Paul even tells the Christian widow who is contemplating marriage to marry whomever she wants, "only in the Lord" (1 Corinthians 7:39).

God's moral will gives the parameters. As long as you are within those parameters, He gives you a degree of freedom in your choices. So you don't have to get up tomorrow morning and say, "Lord, do You want me to wear the blue suit or the black suit today?" When you go to buy a car, and you're looking at two possible purchases that are equal in cost and don't overextend your budget, I don't think you have to agonize in prayer over which one you should buy.

Through the Inner Witness

There are times within the moral will of God that our general choices do matter. In other words, it does not matter whether I wear the blue suit or the green suit tomorrow. But it matters very much whether I choose to take a loved one off life support. It matters whether I submit to a risky operation or try to live with my condition or illness as it is.

Decisions such as these are far different from choosing my suit for the day or deciding which color car to buy. There are decisions in your individual will that are not covered by God's moral will. For these, you need the

Holy Spirit's more specific guidance. Some decisions are easy. But others demand the leading of the Spirit—especially when there are kingdom implications involved.

Many Christians differ at this point. Some hold that as long as we are operating within God's moral will, we have total freedom in our decisions. But others argue that the Spirit gives specific directives to believers that go beyond what is recorded in Scripture.

My contention is that one of the Spirit's major roles is to provide us with specific guidance in the details of life. The reason we don't always think about it is that we are much more conscious of, and more concerned about, some details than others.

Those who reject individual guidance say you cannot equate impressions and hunches with the Spirit's voice. They argue that much that goes under the heading of spiritual guidance ("The Lord led me to . . .") is badly misguided and dangerous mysticism.

However, we don't need to throw the baby out with the bath water. I believe we experience the Spirit's guidance when there is a compelling inner conviction about a decision that is within the scope of God's moral will, be that decision large or small. The Spirit is guiding when my heart is gripped and stirred to make a certain decision or move in a particular direction. It is just that Christians differ in the degree to which they require or desire the Spirit's guidance, based on the value they place on the decision.

Even in the Old Testament, we see God guiding His people through the Spirit's work of stirring their hearts as well as through His objective revelation. In the building of the tabernacle, God filled Bezalel and Oholiab with His Spirit so that they might oversee the construction process (Exodus 31:1–6; 35:30–31; 36:1).

With God's objective command came the Spirit's presence, which produced the subjective stirring of the heart which, in turn, validated both the will and the empowering of God. This was true not just for these two men, but for the rest of the people too (Exodus 35:21–22, 26, 29; 36:1–2).

It is this same experiential work of the Spirit that Paul speaks about for the church when he tells the Corinthians that they are living letters, having been transformed by the Holy Spirit on the inside (2 Corinthians 3:1–3).

If the Holy Spirit does not provide a specific inner conviction or stirring of the heart regarding a matter, then He can speak through your personal preference. Sometimes He speaks louder than at other times. The greater the kingdom implications of the decision, the louder He speaks—which is why He is screaming in the book of Acts.

Another reason you need the Word of God is that it is the only thing that can distinguish between what is coming from you and what is coming from God. Have you ever asked, "Lord, is this You talking to me, or is this me talking to me?"

That's why Hebrews 4:12 is so vital. As I said in an earlier chapter, the Word can split the "unsplittable" soul and spirit. It can clarify what is coming from your humanness, which is the soul, and what is coming from God, which is the Holy Spirit. That's why you want to muse and meditate on Scripture so the Spirit can clarify it to you.

Since God's Word can separate soul from spirit, if you are confused about which way you ought to go on an issue that demands specific guidance, you want the Word. Perhaps you have been in church when the Word was preached, and it separated soul and spirit. You came in not knowing what you should do. You left saying, "Now I know what to do."

What happened was that the Spirit of God grabbed your human spirit and told your soul, "This is the way we are going." The Spirit can use the Word to do that. That's why you don't want to spend all your time listening to the world, because the world will tell the soul to boss the spirit. You want the spirit to boss the soul.

You say, "Well, I don't experience that kind of Spirit guidance." It's not God's fault. Remember, you have the anointing (1 John 2:20, 27), the teaching and illuminating ministry of the Holy Spirit.

Through Prayer

The Holy Spirit also guides us through prayer. I believe many Christians think prayer is a waste of time. Now you don't want to tell anybody that, because it will make you look bad. But I know that many of God's people think that way.

How do I know? Because they don't pray. They say, "I prayed for a while, and nothing happened"; so they give up. But James 1:5 reminds us, "If any of you lacks wisdom, let him ask of God, who gives to all men generously and without reproach, and it will be given to him."

That's a pretty awesome promise. God promises to give us wisdom, which is skill in living, if we will ask Him for it. Wisdom is basically the ability to make right choices, so it has to do with guidance. James says we must ask God for it—and as we ask, the Spirit begins to conform our thinking and desires to God's will. Paul calls this the renewing of the mind (Romans 12:2). We are often looking for God to do something externally when He is actually working within us, stirring us to move in a certain direction. This stirring is the experience of the Spirit's guidance.

If you have been praying and yet God is silent, let me give you some good news. Whenever God is silent over an extended period of time, it is generally because He has a big one coming through the pipe.

Through Circumstances

The Holy Spirit also guides through circumstances—but let me clarify something. Circumstances are to *confirm* the Spirit's inner witness, not *determine* it.

Here is where a lot of Christians get off track. They say, "This door opened, so it must be the will of God." Well, sometimes doors close in the will of God. That's why spiritual guidance must always start from the inside out. If you are not starting with the Spirit and moving out through the body, you are often going to misinterpret the message of outward circumstances.

We generally label only our good experiences as the will of God. If something negative happens, that can't be His will. But when a person has the inner witness of the Spirit, it doesn't matter how negative the circumstances are.

Through the Church

The Holy Spirit also guides through the church. That is why He made you part of a body that is vitally interconnected. If you are not a dynamic member of a Bible-believing church, you will miss a large element of the Spirit's guidance. One of the things God uses to guide us is the other members of the body. You will not be guided properly if you are not plugged in to the body of Christ through a local fellowship.

The great church council of Acts 15 is a classic example of the Spirit revealing His will to the church as a body. We have already looked at this passage in some detail, so I won't go over it again except to remind you how often you read the phrase "it seemed good" to someone (vv. 22, 25, 28, 34).

God brings people into your life who love the Lord and whose spirit witnesses with your spirit. That's why a church needs to seek unity and move with one accord.

GETTING READY TO HEAR THE SPIRIT

That leads to one final question: What must you do to position yourself to experience the Holy Spirit's guidance? Let me sum it up by pointing you to Acts 13:1–2. While these prophets and teachers were "ministering to the Lord," the Holy Spirit spoke a word of clear guidance (v. 2). He speaks most clearly when you are ministering to the Lord.

The more intimate your relationship with Christ, the clearer you will hear the voice of the Spirit. If you have only a Sunday relationship with Christ, don't expect to hear the Spirit on Monday. But if you have a daily relationship with Christ, you have an ongoing experience of the Spirit's guidance.

PERSONAL APPLICATION FOR LIFE

1. Even though people love to look for mysterious signs and happenings for spiritual guidance, our study of this subject keeps bringing us back to the Bible. Are you soaking your spirit in the Scriptures? If not, don't expect God to write you a message in the clouds. Get in the Word, and you'll be in touch with the Holy Spirit.

2. Circumstances will always affect us because they are highly visible. That's why it's important that you understand their confirming, not determining, nature in decisions. Are you up against something that seems to go against what God wants you to do? Before you turn around and head the other way, devote some special time in prayer to this thing. Ask God to show you specifically how to handle your problem.

3. If prayer is your "antenna" to tune you into the guiding voice of God through the Holy Spirit, guess what you should be doing a lot of? Praying! One lost art in prayer: the discipline of listening. Next time you pray, try beginning with total, focused silence. It may help to open your Bible and let your mind muse on Scriptures as you seek the face of God.

4. In 1 Thessalonians 5:17 we read that prayer is the will of God for our lives, no matter what our circumstances. Take your spiritual temperature today by asking yourself how well you're doing in these disciplines of the spirit: rejoicing, persistence in prayer, giving thanks, not quenching the Spirit, a willingness to hear God's Word, and keeping yourself from evil.

FOR GROUP STUDY

Questions for Group Discussion

1. What is the goal of the Spirit's guidance?

2. Read 1 Corinthians 2:9–10; John 14:16–17; and Ephesians 6:18. How is the Spirit's guidance related to God's Word?

3. How does the Spirit guide us? What are His methods of operation?

4. Discuss the channels of the Spirit's guidance. What can we do to keep those open and available to the Spirit's ministry of guidance? (Use the chart below as an aid to your discussion.)

PICTURE THIS

The following are channels the Holy Spirit uses to communicate with our spirit and give us spiritual guidance.

CHANNELS OF THE SPIRIT'S GUIDANCE

CHANNEL OF GUIDANCE	SCRIPTURE PASSAGES	HOW THE SPIRIT GUIDES
Through the Word of God	1 Corinthians 10:27–28	God uses the Spirit to guide us through the Scriptures, clarifying and communicating to us His moral will.
Through the inner witness	2 Corinthians 3:1–3	God will use the Holy Spirit's more specific guidance, especially when kingdom implications are involved.
Through prayer	James 1:5; Romans 12:2	God guides our thinking and desires according to His will.
Through circumstances	Acts 16:6–8	God guides us through our circumstances and uses those circumstances to confirm the Spirit's inner witness.
Through the church	Acts 15:22, 25, 28, 34	God uses other members of the body of Christ to guide us.

43

THE HOLY SPIRIT'S GIFTS

We can't talk long about the ministry of the Holy Spirit without coming to the subject of this chapter. Now, if it were just a matter of figuring out what gifts the Holy Spirit wanted to give us and then receiving them, our task would be easy.

But few topics generate more confusion, crisis, and criticism than the issue of the Spirit's work in gifting the church. My purpose is to help you experience the reality of a truth the Bible is crystal clear about: The gifts of the Holy Spirit are for every member of Christ's body, the church. That includes you and me.

What do we mean by the term *spiritual gifts*? A spiritual gift is a divinely bestowed ability given to every true believer in Jesus Christ in order to serve the church.

The reason the Spirit bestows His gifts on the church is that we are the ones charged with carrying out God's program in this age. When Jesus arose and ascended to heaven, He gave to His management team, the church, those tools necessary to pull off His kingdom work.

A spiritual gift is more than a human talent. All of us have talents, things we do well. Some of us are multitalented. But you don't have to be a Christian to be talented. When you become a Christian, you bring your talents with you. But they are not the same as spiritual gifts. Spiritual gifts are the sovereign bestowal of the Spirit. A natural talent may be involved in your spiritual gift, but the focus is not on your ability. The one overriding purpose of spiritual gifts is to serve the family of God, to enhance the body of Christ, to move the church forward.

The distinguishing feature of a spiritual gift is the blessing and empowering of God on it when it is used for Him. When a person has the spiritual gift of teaching, for example, you receive more than just facts for the mind to store. Your heart is stirred and moved to follow Christ.

In other words, spiritual gifts differ from natural abilities in the results they produce. There are three basic categories of spiritual gifts. In no special order, they are: *serving gifts*, such as service itself and showing mercy; *speaking gifts*, such as teaching and prophecy; and *sign gifts*, those more demonstrable gifts such as healing, miracles, and tongues that the Spirit of God bestows when He wants to make a "megapoint."

SPIRITUAL GIFTS AND SPIRITUAL MATURITY

Four primary New Testament passages discuss spiritual gifts. The first of these is 1 Corinthians 12:

> Now concerning spiritual gifts, brethren, I do not want you to be unaware. You know that when you were pagans, you were led astray to the dumb idols, however you were led. Therefore I make known to you, that no one speaking by the Spirit of God says, "Jesus is accursed"; and no one can say, "Jesus is Lord," except by the Holy Spirit. Now there are varieties of gifts, but the same Spirit. And there are varieties of ministries, and the same Lord. And there are varieties of effects, but the same God who works all things in all persons. But to each one is given the manifestation of the Spirit for the common good. (vv. 1–7)

Now, more is said about spiritual gifts in 1 Corinthians 12–14 than in any other place in the Scriptures. The reason? The Corinthians had more problems with spiritual gifts than anybody else.

No Necessary Correlation

I say that because most people who appeal to 1 Corinthians to defend their position on spiritual gifts appeal to it from the wrong vantage point. They say, "Let's go to 1 Corinthians to learn about spiritual gifts." It would be more accurate to say, "Let's go to 1 Corinthians to find out how to fix the mess we have made of spiritual gifts."

It wasn't because the Corinthians were lacking in the gifts. Just the opposite. They possessed every gift the church could possess (see 1:7). But despite their giftedness, the Corinthians were so spiritually immature and carnal that Paul said he had to feed them with milk like spiritual babies (see 3:1–3).

You can have all the spiritual gifts it's possible to have and be as carnal as you ever want to be. There is no necessary correlation between being gifted and being spiritually mature.

The Purpose of the Gifts

After introducing his subject in 1 Corinthians 12:1, Paul reminded the believers of their pagan background and dealt with a situation where false teachers among them were evidently denying Jesus' humanity, denying that He was fully human as well as fully divine (vv. 2–3).

His point is that nothing in the Corinthians' background or in the false teachers' heresies would help them in the matter of discerning the true activity of the Spirit.

So Paul begins setting the record straight (vv. 4–6). Notice the threefold contrast between "varieties" and "the same." All three Persons of the Trinity are unified in purpose when it comes to spiritual gifts.

The first indication of the purpose of spiritual gifts is in verse 7. They are to be used for "the common good" of the body. They are to flow through you to the benefit of others beyond you.

Too many Christians are like young children with their Christmas gifts. They have their stash, and they do not want their brothers or sisters to touch their gifts.

If the Spirit's gifts to you are not coming through you for the benefit of others, you get cut off from the blessing God intended for you. If you are a selfish Christian who is not willing to use your gifts for the common good, you lose out.

Let me highlight some key phrases in 1 Corinthians 12:8–27 and see if you detect a pattern emerging. Notice "the same Spirit" (vv. 8–9, 11); "one Spirit" (v. 13); "one body" (vv. 12–13, 20); "no division in the body" (v. 25); and "you are Christ's body" (v. 27).

The Unity of the Body

Do you see the pattern? What God is after in this matter of spiritual gifts is unity in the body of Christ. The analogy of the human body is critical because, although we only have one body, that body is made up of thousands of parts.

Whenever the body of Christ stops functioning as a harmonious whole, it demonstrates that the Spirit's gifts are not being used properly. The Corinthian believers were creating disunity in the body by comparing gifts and saying, "I'm more gifted than you." That led to jealousy over who had what gifts. And some were refusing to use their gifts for the benefit of the body.

SPIRITUAL GIFTS AND SPIRITUAL LEADERS

Ephesians 4 is another key passage, because it brings home the purpose of spiritual gifts in such a graphic way:

> But to each one of us grace was given according to the measure of Christ's gift. Therefore it says, "When He ascended on high, He led captive a host of captives, and He gave gifts to men." . . . And He gave some as apostles, and some as prophets, and some as evangelists, and some as pastors and teachers, for the equipping of the saints for the work of service, to the building up of the body of Christ. (vv. 7–8, 11–12)

Christ has gifted His church to equip the saints for service in order that the body might be built up. Paul refers both to the universal nature of spiritual gifts and to the gifted leaders that Christ has given the church.

The Role of Gifted Leaders

The job of church leaders is not to do all the ministry, but to equip the saints for ministry by helping them to understand and use their gifts. Nothing can replace the power, impact, and spiritual enrichment and development that occur when the body's giftedness is being used under the authority of the Spirit.

The goal of this service by gifted saints led by gifted leaders is found in Ephesians 4:13–16, which describes this goal in terms of the church being like a strong, mature body with all of its parts functioning properly.

The Role of Gifted Saints

The Holy Spirit has bestowed His gifts on us because God wants to accomplish His program through us. If we are negating the Spirit's work, the program of God is hampered. One reason the church's impact is not being felt is that too many members of the body have little interest in serving for the common good. So they are not interested in their spiritual gifts.

Cancer cells want to operate in your body, but on their own terms, for their personal benefit. The result is the deterioration of the body rather than its growth and development.

SPIRITUAL GIFTS AND SPIRITUAL SERVICE

The third passage on spiritual gifts is Romans 12:1–8, a classic text in a classic book. In these verses we learn that worship must lead to service, and that service is possible because of the Holy Spirit's gifts.

Verses 1–2 are Paul's great call to total commitment to God, the ultimate act of worship. Then he writes:

> For through the grace given to me I say to every man among you not to think more highly of himself than he ought to think; but to think so as to have sound judgment, as God has allotted to each a measure of faith. For just as we have many members in one body and all the members do not have the same function, so we, who are many, are one body in Christ, and individually members one of another. And since we have gifts that differ according to the grace given to us, let each exercise them accordingly: if prophecy, according

> to the proportion of his faith; if service, in his serving; or he who teaches, in his teaching; or he who exhorts, in his exhortation; he who gives, with liberality; he who leads, with diligence; he who shows mercy, with cheerfulness. (vv. 3–8)

Notice how Paul moves from the loftiest worship to the most mundane areas of service without any interruption. Worship always comes first. But it is always followed by service.

How does this relate to spiritual gifts? Well, you will never know what your gift is if you are sitting around saying, "God, show me my gift so I can get started serving You." You are going to be in the same spot for a long time with that kind of prayer, because God only hits a moving target.

As he introduces the subject of spiritual gifts, Paul cautions us not to think too highly of ourselves. Outside the doors of the church, you may have a big name or a big reputation. But when you come to God's house, you are a sinner saved by grace. We are all equal at the foot of the cross.

SPIRITUAL GIFTS AND SPIRITUAL STEWARDSHIP

Our fourth passage is 1 Peter 4:10–11:

> As each one has received a special gift, employ it in serving one another, as good stewards of the manifold grace of God. Whoever speaks, let him speak, as it were, the utterances of God; whoever serves, let him do so as by the strength which God supplies; so that in all things God may be glorified through Jesus Christ, to whom belongs the glory and dominion forever and ever. Amen.

Here's another truth we need to know about the Holy Spirit's gifts. Someday God is going to ask us whether we opened and used them for His glory.

Notice how Peter ties the concept of the stewardship of our gifts with what we were talking about earlier, the fact that our gifts are for the benefit of others. Peter says clearly we are to use our gifts to "serve one another," which is the definition of being good stewards of those gifts.

THE IMPORTANCE OF SPIRITUAL GIFTS

God has given spiritual gifts so those in the church can be built up and spiritually developed (1 Corinthians 12:7). But if spiritual gifts are not dynamically operating in the life of the local church, then the body of Christ is not being built up, regardless of how much the Bible is being preached.

Absolutely nothing can replace the power, influence, and impact of a church that is fulfilling God's kingdom agenda through the operation of the gifts of the body. Why? Because that's how the Spirit manifests Himself, and when the Spirit manifests Himself, powerful things happen.

This explains the unique influence of the church in Acts. Evangelism was at an all-time high (2:47; 5:14; 6:3–7). There was no need for welfare (2:44–46; 4:32–35). And racial disunity was overcome by racial harmony (10:17–23, 44–48; 15:1–35). All of this happened because the Holy Spirit took charge, expressing and manifesting Himself through the gifts and service not only of the leaders (4:33; 5:12), but of the whole assembly of believers (8:4).

Whenever this dynamic of the Spirit is absent, the church becomes anemic and our witness is compromised. Members who refuse to serve and thus fail to see the Spirit exercise His power for the benefit of the whole body are cancer in the church, receiving the benefits without incurring any of the responsibility. Unless the gifts of the church are unleashed for the building up of the body, the church will continue to limp along with a marginal influence on our world.

DISCOVERING YOUR SPIRITUAL GIFTS

It's interesting that nowhere in Scripture are believers urged or exhorted to discover their spiritual gifts. This reality flies in the face of the "gift inventories" being used in many churches today.

If gifts are so vitally important to the functioning of the church, it may seem odd that we are not commanded to discover them. That's because the discovery of spiritual gifts flows out of service, as we noted in our discussion of the Romans 12 passage. Whenever you see God gifting His people, it's because He has given them a task to perform, not vice versa.

One reason this principle is so often missed is that most studies on spiritual gifts begin and end in the New Testament. They should begin in the Old Testament, where we are first introduced to the manifestation of the Spirit for service.

The call of Moses is a clear example. Moses did not feel that he had the necessary gifts or abilities to lead the Israelites out of Egyptian bondage (Exodus 4:1–13). God's response to Moses' sense of "ungiftedness" was to let him know that the task would be accomplished by God's power (vv. 14–17). But Moses would not experience this power until he obeyed God and went before Pharaoh.

So the question now is, How do we know what task the Spirit is assigning to us? First, the Spirit stirs our heart toward fulfilling an area of need. This is what happened in the building of the tabernacle. The people wanted to be involved because their hearts were stirred (Exodus 35:21–22, 26, 29). When you are operating in concert with the Spirit, He brings joy along with the job.

Second, when the Spirit is leading there will be skill in the execution of the task (Exodus 36:1–2, 8).

Third, when the Spirit is leading in the assignment of the task, God's glory will always be manifested through its execution (Exodus 40:34–38; 1 Peter 4:11).

In none of the four New Testament passages we studied will you find a comprehensive list of the spiritual gifts. Why? Because giving you a "shopping list" of gifts is not the point. The point is to get us right with the Spirit of God, because when we are right with the Spirit, His gifts will find us.

The Holy Spirit has a gift for every believer, and the way you know it is a gift is that it is benefiting somebody else in the body of Christ. And since the Holy Spirit gives His gifts "just as He wills" (1 Corinthians 12:11), you don't need to go gift-hunting.

If you become so obsessed with possessing a certain gift that you start chasing after it, the real purpose for desiring the gift can get lost. So instead of going gift-hunting, go "Spirit-hunting" as you seek to live in tune with Him.

What about other people who know you well? Other people can help you discover your gift, and often they recognize your gift before you do.

But other people can't dictate what your gift should be, because the Spirit is the sovereign Giver of the gifts.

THE SPIRITUAL GIFT OF TONGUES

I suppose nothing related to the Holy Spirit is more controversial today than the issue of speaking in tongues. It has split churches, families, and friendships. It has created all manner of confusion. Yet it is clearly something the Bible deals with, and it is a facet of the Spirit's ministry.

I want to deal with this subject by raising and attempting to answer several issues or questions that come out of 1 Corinthians 14 and several related passages.

The Issue of Definition

The first thing we need to do is define the Greek word *glōssa*, translated "tongue" in 1 Corinthians 14:2. This word means "language."

Many people who speak in tongues speak in syllables unrelated to any known human language. They will tell you they are speaking a heavenly language. But does the Bible support such a view? Well, let's check the evidence, beginning where the New Testament gift of tongues began, on the day of Pentecost.

Every appearance of the word *tongue* in Acts, 1 Corinthians, and the rest of the New Testament, whether singular or plural, is a translation of this word.

The only exception is 1 Corinthians 14:21, where "strange tongues" is simply a compound of *glōssa*. What's more, in every reference outside of the discussion of the gift of tongues, the meaning of the word is clearly human languages or dialects (Acts 2:6, 8).

So the gift of tongues is the supernatural ability to speak in a human language that was previously unknown to the speaker.

The Issue of Priority

Those who want to make tongues a universal gift often argue this way. If you want to be really spiritual, you need to speak in tongues. Translation: If you don't speak in tongues, you won't reach "super-Christian" status.

Is the gift of tongues a priority experience for every believer? Well, if you go back to 1 Corinthians 12:28, you will see that in Paul's ranking, the gift of tongues is at the bottom of the list. Then he asks this question in verse 30: "All do not speak with tongues, do they?"

Here is evidence that the gift of tongues is not for every believer. In 1 Corinthians 14:5, Paul does say, "I wish that you all spoke in tongues." Does this contradict what we just read? No, Paul is expressing a wish, just like he said in 1 Corinthians 7:7 that he wished everyone was celibate like him. He didn't expect everyone to be celibate. Neither did he expect every believer to speak in tongues.

The Issue of Purpose

Why did the Holy Spirit give the gift of tongues in the first place? Paul said in 1 Corinthians 14:22, "Tongues are for a sign, not to those who believe, but to unbelievers."

The gift of tongues is a sign to unbelievers. But this gift has another purpose that relates to the body of Christ. Paul refers to it several times in the opening five verses of 1 Corinthians 14. That purpose is edification.

The word *edify* means "to build up," so we can conclude that anything that does not build up the church is illegitimate. The gift of tongues is given by the Holy Spirit to edify the assembled body of believers.

This is why the interpretation of a tongue in the gathered assembly was mandatory (1 Corinthians 14:27–28). It is also why prophecy, the forthtelling of God's Word, is preferred to tongues (14:4). Therefore, the use of a private prayer language is inappropriate in the gathered assembly of believers.

The Issue of Permanence

The final issue concerning the gift of tongues is that of its permanence.

Paul says in 1 Corinthians 13:8–12 there will come a time when the gift of tongues will cease. He describes that time in verse 10 as "when the perfect comes."

When Paul uses the word *perfect* (the Greek word *teleios*), he usually means "mature, complete," referring to the spiritual development process. This is clearly the case in his use of the word in 1 and 2 Corinthians (1 Corinthians 2:6; 14:20; 2 Corinthians 7:1).

Therefore, the "perfect" of 1 Corinthians 13:10 is consistent with Paul's normative usage of the term, namely, the maturing process in relationship to the completed Scriptures, not just a reference to the existence of the completed Bible. So I believe Paul is saying that tongues are basically for the immature. When you become mature, you will not need to see and hear continuous miraculous signs to sustain and build your faith.

Paul says in 13:12 that we are now looking in a mirror dimly, but someday we will see face-to-face. When you draw close to Jesus Christ and remove the steamy obstruction of worldliness and sin, you come before Him face-to-face. When you look into His face and He looks into your face, then you will say you don't need the miraculous revelatory gifts of others anymore because of your face-to-face relationship with the miraculous One.

PERSONAL APPLICATION FOR LIFE

1. Are you waiting for the Holy Spirit to drop your spiritual gifts in your lap before you get around to serving God? If so, you'll be sitting there a long time. If you don't know where to begin serving and finding your gift, ask your pastor what the needs are at your church. The Holy Spirit can use openings like these to reveal His plan to you.

2. Spiritually mature people whom you trust and who know you well can be a good source of encouragement and counsel as you seek the Spirit's place for you. If you feel the need, seek out the help of several godly people whose wisdom and spiritual maturity are evident to you.

3. Have you ever benefited in any way from the ministry of Spirit-gifted and Spirit-directed leaders? Why not tell them so, beginning with your pastor? Pastors need encouragement too.

4. Several hints in Romans 12:8 help answer the question, How will I know when I have found my gift? This is not ironclad, but verse 8 pictures people exercising their gifts with great enthusiasm and joy. One way to validate your gift is to ask yourself, What service brings me the greatest joy? What really gets me excited about serving the Lord? When the answers to these questions are combined with the fact that other believers are being helped by your service, you most likely are operating in the realm of your gift.

FOR GROUP STUDY

Questions for Group Discussion

1. What do we mean by the term *spiritual gifts*? What is the purpose of spiritual gifts? What is the distinguishing feature of a spiritual gift?

2. Read 1 Corinthians 12:1–7. How are spiritual gifts related to our spiritual maturity?

3. According to Romans 12:1–8, how are spiritual gifts related to spiritual service? Read 1 Peter 4:10–11. How important is the stewardship of our gifts?

4. How do we go about discovering our spiritual gift? In general, how important is your gift to the function of the body of Christ? How important is it to the function of your church? (Use the chart below as an aid to your discussion.)

PICTURE THIS

The Holy Spirit has a gift for every believer, and the way you know it is a gift is that it is benefiting somebody else in the body of Christ. And He gives His gifts "just as He wills" (1 Corinthians 12:11). The process below is a test to help you determine your spiritual gift.

THE PROCESS OF DISCOVERING YOUR SPIRITUAL GIFT

STEP	SCRIPTURE PASSAGES
1. The Spirit stirs your heart toward fulfilling an area of need.	Exodus 35:21–22, 26, 29
2. When the Spirit is leading there will be skill in the execution of the task.	Exodus 36:1–2, 8
3. When the Spirit is leading in the assignment of the task, God's glory will always be manifested through its execution.	Exodus 40:34–38; 1 Peter 4:11

PART 4

ANGELOLOGY

The Doctrine of Angels

SECTION I

THE HOLY ANGELS

44. THE EXISTENCE OF ANGELS

45. THE MINISTRY OF ANGELS

46. THE OPERATION AND ENLISTING OF ANGELS

44

THE EXISTENCE OF ANGELS

God's angels, both elect and evil, do exist. In fact, a foundational thesis of the doctrine of angelology, or the study of angels, is this: The physical, visible realm is greatly affected by the spiritual, invisible realm that the Bible calls the "heavenly places." What happens in the spiritual realm controls and influences what happens in the visible realm.

Currently angels are in vogue. But a lot of what we see about angels in the popular culture is inaccurate and trite when we compare it to what the Bible teaches about angels. They are an invisible army of beings who manage history for God. Angels have much more significance than the culture is giving them.

ANGELS ARE CREATED BEINGS

The first thing to know about angels is that they are created beings.

We will see later that several traits of the holy angels are also true of evil angels, or demons. That's because the demons are themselves fallen angels, created in purity and power until they followed Satan (himself an evil angel) in his rebellion. So we will see some similarities between good angels and evil ones.

Created for God's Purposes

According to Colossians 1:16, the angels were part of the original creation: "For by Him [Christ] all things were created, both in the heavens and on earth, visible and invisible, whether thrones or dominions or rulers or authorities—all things have been created by Him and for Him."

Notice that the object or focus of creation is Christ. Everything was created for Christ. The angels were not created as an end in themselves, but for God's divine purposes. In fact, in Colossians 2:18 the apostle Paul says that one tenet of false teaching is the worship of angels. One problem with all the attention being placed on angels today is that people get too focused on angels, watching for the angels to show up, and forget to focus on Christ.

This verse in Colossians reminds us that people can misuse divine truth. As people see and hear more about angels, the temptation may be to worship the created angels rather than the Creator of the angels. So Paul says, "Don't do it" (see 2:16–19). But that is not to deny the reality of the angelic realm and the truth the Bible teaches us about angels.

Created to Serve and Worship

Angels were created to be "ministering spirits" (Hebrews 1:14), to serve God and His people, not to be worshiped. Every time in the Bible when an angel appeared and a human being fell at that angel's feet, the angel told the person to get up and not worship him (see Revelation 22:8–9).

Angels were also created to give God endless worship around His throne. Far from wanting worship, the angels find their delight in praising God (Psalm 148:2). We can learn a lot about worshiping God from angels, His full-time worshipers.

When were the angels created? The Bible gives us a clue in Job 38, where God asks Job:

> Where were you when I laid the foundation of the earth! Tell Me, if you have understanding, who set its measurements, since you know? Or who stretched the line on it? On what were its bases sunk? Or who laid its cornerstone, when the morning stars sang together, and all the sons of God shouted for joy? (vv. 4–7)

The "morning stars" are the angels. Job is told that when the earth was made, the angels formed a choir and celebrated. Therefore, angels were created before the earth was created. We know this also because the angelic conflict began in heaven before it spilled over to the earth.

ANGELS ARE SPIRIT BEINGS

The second thing we need to know about angels is that they are spirit beings.

Hebrews 1:14 is just one of a number of Bible references that tell us angels are spirits. They are immaterial, invisible beings.

But even though this is true, angels can become visible to carry out specific, sovereignly directed supernatural activity on the earth. They did so on a number of occasions in Scripture. One of the most familiar examples of this is Genesis 18, when Abraham welcomed three strangers to his tent. One of the visitors was the Lord Himself, and the other two were angels. The Lord announced to Sarah that she was going to have a baby, the promised seed, Isaac (who, we might note, continued the righteous seed begun in the garden of Eden).

Abraham invited the three strangers to stay for a meal—and in the process of showing hospitality to them, he found the provision of God for the miracle he and Sarah needed to produce a child at their greatly advanced ages.

The two angels who visited Abraham were also God's provision for Abraham's nephew Lot, for it was the angels who went on to Sodom in Genesis 19 to warn and rescue Lot from destruction.

Occasions like this are why the Bible says, "Do not neglect to show hospitality to strangers, for by this some have entertained angels without knowing it" (Hebrews 13:2). The "strangers" the writer of Hebrews was talking about were fellow believers who traveled about from place to place in that day and often needed lodging. The writer is saying that we should not refuse our hospitality to other believers, because God may be sending us the answer to our prayers.

ANGELS ARE PERSONAL BEINGS

God's holy angels are personal beings as well. They exhibit the three qualities of personhood: intellect, emotion, and will.

Angels must have intellect or intelligence, because they are able to carry out God's commands and converse with human beings when the occasion demands it. They also use their minds in other ways, because Peter says the angels are intensely curious to understand human redemption (1 Peter 1:12). They have to look on from the outside because there is no redemption for fallen angels.

Angels have emotions too. When they see a human being get saved, they break out in rejoicing (Luke 15:10). Why do angels get so excited over each person's salvation? Because it means one more victory for God in the angelic conflict.

As personal beings, angels also have wills. At the time of Satan's rebellion, they were able to make a choice. It was through his will that Lucifer became the Devil, and it was through their wills that one-third of the angels became demons.

ANGELS ARE INNUMERABLE

In one of his visions, the prophet Daniel saw God take His seat on the throne of judgment. Attending God were "thousands upon thousands" and "myriads upon myriads" of His angels (Daniel 7:10).

A myriad is ten thousand, so we are talking about a minimum of tens of thousands of angels, but the vastness of this description suggests millions. And that number does not even begin to do justice to the scene Daniel saw.

Since angels do not procreate (Mark 12:25) and do not die, however many that God created initially is the same number that exists today. Try to imagine how many angels God created, and then recall that one-third followed Satan (Revelation 12:4). When it comes to spiritual warfare, the action must be heavy with untold millions of angelic beings engaged in the battle!

THE HOLY ANGELS ARE GLORIOUS BEINGS

Angels may be servants, but they are also glorious beings. In the Bible every appearance of heavenly angels is a glorious thing to behold.

One of the most glorious appearances of an angel is the angel who appeared to Daniel. The prophet writes:

> I lifted my eyes and looked, and behold, there was a certain man dressed in linen, whose waist was girded with a belt of pure gold of Uphaz. His body also was like beryl, his face had the appearance of lightning, his eyes were like flaming torches, his arms and feet like the gleam of polished bronze, and the sound of his words like the sound of a tumult. (Daniel 10:5-6)

This is a being of glory. Daniel's angelic vision was so overwhelming that he fell on his face (vv. 8-9). The sight was more than he could handle.

Because holy angels are glorious beings, when they show up, light follows them. This happened with the apostle Peter in a jail cell in Jerusalem. "An angel of the Lord suddenly appeared [in Peter's cell], and a light shone in the cell" (Acts 12:7).

Remember that Daniel said the angel he saw had the appearance of lightning. Throughout Scripture, the appearance of an angel has some sort of light or other glory associated with it. That's one reason angels are called stars, because like the stars in heaven they are flames of fire.

ANGELS ARE FUNCTIONAL BEINGS

Holy angels are also functional beings. That is, they have a job to do—three basic jobs, in fact.

Angels Worship God

The first job of angels is the one we mentioned above, that of worship. The evil angels were cast from heaven because they rebelled against such worship, choosing instead to honor Satan and his self-serving agenda. The myriads who remain include those who praise God continually, without ever ceasing (see Revelation 4:8). So when we come into the presence of God, we join the angels who are already there. This means that we never worship alone, because there is not one nanosecond of time in which God is not receiving the adoration of His angels.

Angels Execute God's Will

The second thing the holy angels do is execute the program of God. To put it another way, the angels are God's staff members, who carry out His will and His Word. The psalmist wrote, "Bless the Lord, you His angels, mighty in strength, who perform His word, obeying the voice of His word!" (Psalm 103:20).

Angels Minister to Saints

Hebrews 1:14 says that angels are sent "to render service for the sake of those who will inherit salvation." If you are a believer, you have one or more angels assigned to you, what we commonly call guardian angels.

Guardian angels are only sent to minister to saved people (Hebrews 1:14). The Bible is clear that angels are not just spirits out there floating around, waiting to rescue anyone who happens to need a hand. God uses angels for His specific kingdom purposes. Where angels are involved, they are ministering to the saints in cooperation with the will of God.

The Bible specifically says that children have guardian angels and that these angels "continually" behold the face of God (Matthew 18:10). Therefore, Jesus warned, don't despise these little ones, because they have some very powerful defenders.

ANGELS ARE POWERFUL BEINGS

The final trait of angels I want to discuss is their tremendous power. When Jesus Christ returns, He will return "with His mighty angels in flaming fire" (2 Thessalonians 1:7). The angel who rolled the stone from the mouth of Jesus' tomb (Luke 24:2, 4) did so without any trouble. Objects in nature are no problem for angels, because they have power.

Power over Nature

In fact, the Bible says that angels have power in nature. I want to look at a number of passages here and then draw some conclusions.

In the book of Revelation, angels are very active in the arena of nature. "After this I saw four angels standing at the four corners of the earth, holding back the four winds of the earth, so that no wind should blow on the earth or on the sea or on any tree" (Revelation 7:1). That's a tremendous picture of power over nature.

Manifestations in Nature

I believe that the elements of nature such as thunder and lightning are sometimes manifestations of God's angels.

Psalm 18:7–10 is a glorious statement of the power of angels. These verses are a virtual repetition of 2 Samuel 22:8–11, in which David described God's great deliverance from David's enemies. Psalm 18:10 says symbolically that God did this by riding "upon a cherub," one of the highest echelon of angels. The cherub's movements are connected with "the wings of the wind."

Verses 11–15 of Psalm 18 continue this description of God's movement in history being manifested through all manner of natural phenomena. You can read those verses and note all the references to meteorological activity and other occurrences.

When God moves in history, He often does it through angels. That's why angels play such a prominent role in the book of Revelation. The entire book is a record of God carrying out His end-time plan through the ministrations of angels.

ANGELS ARE GOD'S CREATURES

Here's a question that may have occurred to you, because it has occurred to a lot of other people. If angels are so great and so powerful, why not go looking for them? Why not seek an angelic visitation or an angelic blessing if they are God's servants just waiting to serve the saved?

I want to answer this from Hebrews 1, where the writer says concerning Jesus:

> And He is the radiance of His glory and the exact representation of His nature, and upholds all things by the word of His power. When He had made purification of sins, He sat down at the right hand of the Majesty on high, having become as much better than the angels, as He has inherited a more excellent name than they. And when He again brings the firstborn into the world, He says, "And let all the angels of God worship Him." And of the angels He says, "Who makes His angels winds, and His ministers a flame of fire." (vv. 3–4, 6–7)

The writer of Hebrews acknowledges that angels are awesome, but they are merely the servants and the worshipers of Jesus Christ, who is God.

We know the names of Gabriel and Michael, two angels who are mentioned in the Bible. They are glorious beings, but Hebrews says don't get too excited about angels' names. Get excited about Jesus' name, because His name is more excellent than that of any angel.

Don't go looking for angels; go looking for Jesus. Don't go looking for your guardian angel. He has already found you. Go looking for Jesus.

Angels are God's ministering servants, but when it comes to Jesus, God the Father says, "Thy throne, O God, is forever and ever" (Hebrews 1:8). When God addresses the angels, He says, "Give Me a little wind here. Give Me a little earthquake there. Give Me a little lightning over here." But when God addresses Jesus, He says, "O God."

Only Jesus is the Son of God. Only Jesus is God Himself, the second Person of the Trinity. Angels are Jesus' created, obedient servants, His worshipers who will exalt Him forever. Jesus is the name to know.

PERSONAL APPLICATION FOR LIFE

1. God deserves our praise and adoration. There are angels in the presence of God who unceasingly praise and adore the Creator. If you're like many believers, you can't think about who Jesus is for very long without singing a song of praise. If you have a favorite hymn that causes you to praise, worship, and adore God, sing it to Him now. God delights in our praise of Him.

2. If you are a believer, what a great encouragement it is to know that God has assigned you a guardian angel who watches over you! We know that God's angels minister to believers in cooperation with the will of God. Because we don't see them at work, it's so easy to take angels for granted. Take a moment to thank God for His personal provision of ministering angels.

3. Are you going through a difficult time? Perhaps you feel you are going it alone. Take comfort knowing that God knows your difficulty and is ministering to you even now. Not only do His angels constantly watch over you, but the indwelling Holy Spirit ministers to you as well. To top it off, Jesus intercedes for you at the right hand of God (Romans 8:34). Although we may feel alone, God sees to it we never are.

4. The apostle Peter tells us that the angels are intensely curious to understand human redemption (1 Peter 1:12). They have to look on from the outside because there is no redemption for fallen angels. Angels get excited when a person is redeemed through the blood of Christ. It represents another victory in the angelic conflict. Do you ever get excited about your redemption? During your next quite time, reflect on God's gift of salvation and thank Him for it.

FOR GROUP STUDY

Questions for Group Discussion

1. Discuss what we know about the origin of angels. For background, read Colossians 1:16; 2:16–19; Hebrews 1:14; Psalm 148:2. For what reasons did God create them?

2. We have all seen artists' conceptions of angels. Some of us place an angel ornament atop our Christmas trees. What does the Bible tell us about their appearance? Discuss Daniel's vision of an angel (Daniel 10:5–6). Discuss also Peter's angelic encounter in a jail cell (Acts 12:7).

3. As Dr. Evans points out, angels are functional beings. Read Revelation 4:8; Psalm 103:20; Hebrews 1:14; and Matthew 18:10. Discuss the three basic functions (or jobs) of angels. What do we learn about their duties? As believers, what encouragements can we lay hold of from those passages?

4. Scripture describes angels as very powerful beings. Discuss Psalm 18:7–15. What kind of power has God given His angels? How do they employ their power?

PICTURE THIS

God created His angels for very specific purposes. Scripture reveals at least some of the primary functions of God's angels.

The Primary Functions of God's Angels

FUNCTION	PASSAGE	DESCRIPTION
Angels worship God.	Revelation 4:8	Angels unceasingly praise the Creator.
Angels execute God's will.	Psalm 103:20	Various levels and orders of angels carry out God's plan for His universe.
Angels minister to saints.	Hebrews 1:14	Angels minister to believers in cooperation with the will of God.

45

THE MINISTRY OF ANGELS

Sometimes, when we need to get a package across town in a hurry either from our church office or from the Urban Alternative headquarters in Dallas, we call a local messenger service. The service sends a messenger, a courier, who picks up our package and delivers it for us. The messenger's only job is to deliver our message to the right person, without changing it in any way.

GOD'S MESSENGERS

That's exactly what angels do. The word *angel* itself means "messenger." God's holy angels are His divine messengers. This term gives you the fundamental, overarching picture of what they do, in at least five areas.

Angels Are Messengers of God's Word

First of all, angels are messengers of God's Word. They played a part in the delivery of the Law to Moses. In his defense before the Jewish council, the church leader Stephen said that the nation of Israel received the Law "as ordained by angels" (Acts 7:53; see also Galatians 3:19). According to Hebrews 2:2, the law was "spoken through angels."

When Moses sat down to write the Pentateuch, the first five books of the Bible, also called the Law, he was guarded from error by the superintending ministry of the Holy Spirit. That's true for every writer of Scripture (2 Peter 1:19–21).

But if the Bible says the angels are doing all of this, how does their work relate to the role of the Holy Spirit? The two relate in this way.

The Holy Spirit is fully God, the sovereign third Person of the Trinity. That means the angels are His messengers too. They act under His command. The Holy Spirit directs the angels in their ministry with and to God's people. So let's not confuse the Spirit's ministry with that of the angels.

The interplay between the Holy Spirit and the angels is evident in the recording of Scripture. The Spirit was the Guide when Moses wrote, but the angels were involved in the delivery of God's law. In some way, under the Spirit's direction the angels oversaw the transmission, protection, and integrity of the written Word.

Angels were also active in delivering the message concerning the coming of the living Word, Jesus Christ. Recall the Christmas story, and you'll remember that from beginning to end, angelic messengers were key to the unfolding drama of God's work.

Angels appeared to Zacharias, Mary, and the shepherds (Luke 1:11, 26; 2:9), and at least four times to Joseph (Matthew 1:20; 2:13, 19, 22).

Angels Are Messengers of God's Protection

Angels are also messengers of God's protection. There is a wonderful illustration of this in 2 Kings 6:8–23. The prophet Elisha had been advising the king of Israel concerning the movements of the king of Aram, or Syria.

The king of Syria became furious over this, so when he discovered that it was Elisha doing this, he plotted to capture Elisha. He found out Elisha was living in Dothan, so the king sent his army to surround Dothan and take Elisha (vv. 11–14).

Elisha's servant got up the next morning and went outside to see an army circling the city. He went to Elisha and said, "'Alas, my master! What shall we do?' So he answered, 'Do not fear, for those who are with us are more than those who are with them'" (2 Kings 6:15–16).

Then Elisha prayed that God would open the young man's eyes so he would see what Elisha saw. God answered Elisha's prayer, and his servant saw that "the mountain was full of horses and chariots of fire all around Elisha" (v. 17). Those were God's protecting angels, and they delivered Elisha from the Syrians in a supernatural way.

In Acts 12, an angel delivered Peter from prison. But this was actually the second time this had happened to Peter. Earlier, the high priest and his pals put all the apostles in prison (Acts 5:17–18).

But according to verses 19–20, "An angel of the Lord during the night opened the gates of the prison, and taking them out he said, 'Go, stand and speak to the people in the temple the whole message of this Life.'"

Here's another way God delivers His protection to us through the angels. In the middle of the story about the rich man and Lazarus (Luke 16:19–31), Jesus said this about the death of Lazarus: "It came about that the poor man died and he was carried away by the angels to Abraham's bosom" (v. 22). The angels transported Lazarus to heaven.

Why would Lazarus need an angelic escort into the heavenly realm? In order to get from earth to heaven, he had to pass through enemy territory.

Satan is the prince of the power of the air (Ephesians 2:2). Battles are going on in heavenly places between the forces of Satan and the forces of God in order to control the events of history. And if hell had its way, it would never let you out of that grave to get to heaven.

But you don't have to worry about hell winning even after you die, because you get an escort to glory. Lazarus was protected and escorted through enemy territory into heaven and the presence of God. That's protection!

Angels Are Messengers of God's Provision

In Psalm 78, the writer is rehearsing God's provision for Israel in the wilderness wanderings. The psalmist refers to the manna that God "rained down" on the people (v. 24). Then we read this statement: "Man did eat the bread of angels" (v. 25).

Manna was basically cornflakes from above, little white flakes that rained down from heaven to supernaturally supply the people's need. What

God did was tell the angels to deliver food to the Israelites.

Angels also ministered to Jesus after His temptation in the wilderness. I've seen that area. It's a dry, dusty, blazing hot place. I can imagine how emaciated Jesus must have been from forty days and nights of fasting in that desert, and how exhausted He must have been from dealing with the Devil. When it was all over, "The devil left Him; and behold, angels came and began to minister to Him" (Matthew 4:11). They brought Jesus food and water, God's provision for His weakness.

The prophet Elijah also experienced God's provision through angels—but in his case the help came after spiritual defeat. First Kings 18 tells the story of Elijah's incredible victory over Jezebel's prophets of Baal on Mount Carmel. But unlike Jesus, Elijah had a big letdown after Mount Carmel and ran for his life when Jezebel threatened him. Elijah even gave up and asked God to take his life (1 Kings 19:1–4).

Elijah had lost his spiritual equilibrium. He was afraid and defeated, but God was not finished with His prophet. So He sent the angel of the Lord to cook a little meal for Elijah and wake him to eat it. Elijah ate and drank and gained new strength (vv. 5–8).

Angels Are Messengers of God's Judgment

The popular idea of angels today is that they are little floating beings full of sweetness and light. Angels deliver God's protection and provision, but they are also messengers of His wrath and judgment.

We see an awe-inspiring picture of this in Revelation 15:1, where the apostle John records: "I saw another sign in heaven, great and marvelous, seven angels who had seven plagues, which are the last, because in them the wrath of God is finished."

Revelation 15 gives us a tremendous picture of God equipping His angels for fearsome judgment. They are given "seven golden bowls full of the wrath of God" (v. 7), and then in 16:1 they are commanded to go and pour out the bowls on the earth.

God has ordained that the angels deliver judgment against His enemies (see Matthew 13:41–42; 2 Thessalonians 1:7–8). In Psalm 78, the writer says God sent "a band of destroying angels" against Egypt when Pharaoh would not let the Israelites go (v. 49). You'll remember that the tenth plague against Egypt was the death of all the firstborn children.

What the psalmist is saying is that the plagues of Egypt were caused by angels. They are actively engaged in spiritual warfare today, and the Bible says that angels will execute God's final judgment against His enemies. This will be spiritual warfare raised to a higher level.

The Bible gives us some sobering examples of the angels delivering judgment against people who oppose God. One of the most amazing accounts is the death of Herod Agrippa that I mentioned earlier (Acts 12:20–23).

The people of Tyre and Sidon, the area north of Israel, wanted to make up with Herod. So he came one day in all of his royal finery and begin speaking to them. As he spoke, the people started shouting, "The voice of a god and not of a man!" (v. 22).

Herod said, "I like this."

But God didn't like it, because Herod refused to give Him the glory. So God dispatched an angel to strike Herod down, and he died an awful death. Angels will deliver someone to hell as surely as they will deliver someone to heaven.

Angels Are Messengers of God's Guidance

God uses angels again and again to guide His people.

We see two great examples of angelic guidance in the book of Acts: the ministry of Philip in Acts 8, and Peter's vision of the sheet full of unclean animals in Acts 10. In Philip's case, notice that he did not get specific instructions from the Holy Spirit until he had obeyed the angelic leading. The angel told Philip where to go, and then the Spirit took over.

An angel also appeared to Cornelius (Acts 10:3–8), and he obeyed. At the same time, the Spirit was dealing with Peter (vv. 9–16). The angels fulfill the guidance ministry that is delegated to them, and the Holy Spirit takes over the rest.

GOD'S MINISTERS

For the remainder of this chapter, I want to unfold a brief but very important passage of Scripture, John 1:45–51.

This story is important because in it Jesus reveals a truth about the work of angels that we need to understand and appropriate for our lives today. He does so by linking His ministry with one of the most well-known incidents in the Old Testament, what we know as Jacob's ladder.

The Ladder to Heaven

John 1 records Jesus' call of His disciples. One of the men He called was Philip (v. 43), who went immediately to his friend Nathanael and told him, "We have found Him of whom Moses in the Law and also the Prophets wrote, Jesus of Nazareth, the son of Joseph" (v. 45).

Nathanael was skeptical, so Philip invited him to come and meet Jesus (v. 46). Jesus saw Nathanael coming and said, "Behold, an Israelite indeed, in whom there is no deceit!" (v. 47).

Nathanael was taken back by this, and asked Jesus how He knew him. Jesus revealed to Nathanael that He had seen him earlier when he was sitting under a fig tree, before Nathanael ever thought about coming to see Jesus (v. 48). Nathanael knew he was dealing with Someone special, so he confessed, "Rabbi, You are the Son of God; You are the King of Israel" (v. 49). Then come the verses I want to focus on:

> Jesus answered and said to him, "Because I said to you that I saw you under the fig tree, do you believe? You shall see greater things than these." And He said to him, "Truly, truly, I say to you, you shall see the heavens opened, and the angels of God ascending and descending on the Son of Man." (vv. 50–51)

Jesus told Nathanael that because of his affirmation and his faith, he would see heavenly, angelic activity occurring in his life.

Why did Jesus call Nathanael an Israelite without deceit? I believe it wasn't only because He knew that Nathanael had a sincere heart. Jesus said this because He knew what Nathanael was thinking about as he sat under that fig tree.

Jesus' words grabbed Nathanael because they revealed to him that Jesus knew his thoughts, and that shook him up a little bit.

So what was Nathanael thinking about? He may have been thinking about an Old Testament Israelite in whom there was plenty of guile—Jacob the deceiver.

Specifically, Nathanael may have been pondering the incident in Genesis 28, when Jacob saw a ladder reaching into heaven and angels going up and down on it. Jesus referred to this event when He told Nathanael that he would see greater things in his life.

Jacob's dream of the ladder reaching into heaven occurred in a place he would later name Bethel. The reason Jacob was there was that he had deceived his father, Isaac, and stolen the blessing of his older brother, Esau. Esau got mad and threatened to kill Jacob, so his mother, Rebekah, told him to leave town until Esau cooled down.

So here was the deceiver Jacob—Mr. Guile himself—on the run, stopping to spend the night under the stars. He put his head on a stone pillow and went to sleep. Then "he had a dream, and behold, a ladder was set on the earth with its top reaching to heaven; and behold, the angels of God were ascending and descending on it. And behold, the Lord stood above it" (Genesis 28:12–13a).

In verses 13–15, God reaffirmed to Jacob His covenant promises to Abraham. God told Jacob He would give him a land and many descendants and make him a universal blessing. Then God left Jacob with a wonderful promise of His abiding presence until all of His purposes had been fulfilled.

Jacob did not deserve all of this, but God chose to bless him as an act of sovereign grace. God gave Jacob a glimpse into heaven as reassurance of His presence because Jacob was going to accomplish God's purposes.

Jesus promised Nathanael, and us, the same heavenly presence when we commit ourselves to living for Him and accomplishing His purposes.

Notice the Bible says that the ladder was set on earth, but its top reached to heaven. If we are going to be spiritually successful on earth, we must hear from heaven.

Jacob saw his ladder, and when he woke up from his dream he said, "Surely the Lord is in this place, and I did not know it" (Genesis 28:16). Jacob realized that he had been in God's presence.

This wasn't just a dream. God was making a supernatural disclosure of Himself. Jacob got God's ladder, and he received some awesome things with it. Let me tell you four things that come with God's ladder.

Four Blessings of the Ladder

First of all, God's promises come with His ladder. There at Bethel, God confirmed to Jacob the promise He had made previously to Jacob's ancestors Abraham and Isaac (Genesis 28:13–14). The Scripture says that God has many "precious and magnificent promises" (2 Peter 1:4).

A second thing that came with the ladder was God's presence. Jacob said God was there, and yet he didn't even know it (Genesis 28:16). God's ladder is there. The angels are there to minister to us. But sometimes it's easy to miss their activity.

A third blessing that comes with the ladder of God is the protection of God. "I will keep you," He told Jacob (see Genesis 28:15). When you are properly linked to heaven and the angels are ministering to you up and down the ladder, you can relax.

Why? Nothing can happen to you outside of God's will. When you are in God's will, He will keep you for whatever purpose He has for you. Nobody can take what belongs to you when earth is properly linked to heaven. God will keep you.

The fourth thing you get with the ladder is God's provision. We saw that above in the story of Elijah (1 Kings 19).

Elijah was scared and he ran, but God took care of him through an angel. The prophet even wanted to die. But even when you're at your worst, God can take care of you. And He can take care of you from beginning to end. So when you have a difficulty, don't run *from* God; run *to* God.

THE INVISIBLE WORLD

Let me give you a great verse to consider as we wrap up this chapter. Paul says in 2 Corinthians 4:18 that we need to keep looking "not at the things which are seen, but at the things which are not seen; for the things which are seen are temporal, but the things which are not seen are eternal."

The previous two verses, verses 16–17, help to set the context. The mature Christian is one whose life is guided by the unseen realities of the spiritual world, not by the five senses. It's not that these things are wrong; they just aren't enough.

The focus of your life must be derived from the invisible world. You say, "But how do I see that world?"

Paul tells us in Colossians 3:1–2. "If then you have been raised up with Christ, keep seeking the things above, where Christ is, seated at the right hand of God. Set your mind on the things above, not on the things that are on earth." God wants you to live on earth with a heavenly perspective. He wants you to see life through heavenly sunglasses. He wants the spiritual world to be the "tint" by which you look at the things of earth, so that your mind is functioning from a divine as opposed to a human perspective.

APPLICATIONS FOR LIFE

1. We know that one of the ministries of angels is guidance. God has a course for our lives. In the midst of spiritual warfare, we can become distracted and go off course. If this happens to you, stay committed to God and His Word—and thank God for His Spirit and His angels to help guide you.

2. Do you embrace the promises of God's Word? Satan would have us be ignorant of God's promises, because they become so important in the midst of the spiritual battle we are fighting. Our hope for the future is rooted in God's promises. Make it a point daily to get into the Word and claim one of God's promises for yourself.

3. Although we may struggle at times in our spiritual battle, Philippians 2:10–11 tells us that one day that "every knee will bow. . . and that every tongue will confess that Jesus Christ is Lord, to the glory of God the Father." Take comfort in the fact that God is in control and we are on His winning side. Allow that truth to shape your thinking the next time you feel the heat of the battle.

4. God wants you to live on earth with a heavenly perspective based on eternal values. Take to heart the words of Colossians 3:1–2: "Set your mind on the things above, not on the things that are on earth." Occasionally make a list of what you value the most in this world. Weigh your list against eternal and spiritual values taught in God's Word. You might find your values will need a few adjustments.

FOR GROUP STUDY

Questions for Group Discussion

1. Under the guidance of the Holy Spirit, God has provided us His written Word—an invaluable resource for every believer. As Dr. Evans points out, angels played a role in the transmission, protection, and integrity of the written Word. From Scripture, what other ways do we find that angels served as messengers of God's Word?

2. As God's messengers, angels were also called upon to deliver judgment against people who opposed God. The Bible gives us some sobering examples of the angels delivering judgment. As an example, discuss the account of Herod Agrippa's death in Acts 12:20–23. Other passages for discussion include Matthew 13:31–42 and 2 Thessalonians 1:7–8.

3. God uses His angels as messengers of provision. Read Psalm 78 and Matthew 4:11 for starters. Consider some of the promises of provision in Scripture. Discuss how God might even now be using His angels to minister provision for our physical and spiritual needs.

4. Read John 1:45–51. In this story, Jesus reveals a truth about the work of angels that we need to understand and appropriate for our lives today. What are the four blessings of the ladder? Why are they significant for us today?

PICTURE THIS

God created His angels for very specific purposes. Scripture reveals at least some of the primary functions of God's angels.

ANGELS: GOD'S MESSENGERS

SPECIFIC MINISTRY	SCRIPTURE PASSAGES	WHAT IT MEANS
Messengers of God's Word	Acts 7:53; Galatians 3:19; 2 Peter 1:19–21	Angels were involved in the delivery of God's Law, and they oversaw the transmission, protection, and integrity of the written Word.
Messengers of God's protection	2 Kings 6:8–23	God may choose to deliver His protection to us through His angels.
Messengers of God's provision	Matthew 4:11	God often sends His angels to minister to our physical and spiritual needs.
Messengers of God's judgment	Revelation 15	Angels deliver judgment against people who oppose God.
Messengers of God's guidance	Acts 10:3–16	Angels fulfill their guidance ministry as delegated, and the Holy Spirit takes over the rest.

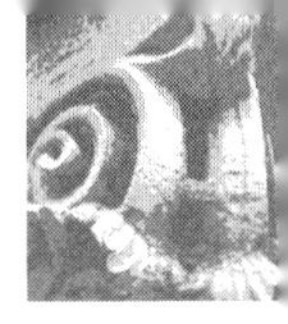

46

THE OPERATION AND ENLISTING OF ANGELS

How do angels operate on earth? The simple yet profound answer is this: Angels always operate along God-established and God-ordained lines of authority. Their actions are to serve and honor the Creator.

Angels follow these God-ordained lines of authority because of a fundamental principle about the nature of God. According to 1 Corinthians 14:33, "God is not a God of confusion." He's a God of order. So anything that originates from Him must be done "properly and in an orderly manner" (v. 40). Therefore, God's angels must operate in an orderly fashion.

ANGELS ARE ORGANIZED BY AUTHORITY

To operate effectively, angels are organized by authority. In Colossians 1:16, Paul explained, "By Him [Christ] all things were created, both in the heavens and on earth, visible and invisible, whether thrones or dominions or rulers or authorities—all things have been created by Him and for Him."

A couple of things are important here for our understanding of the way God's creation works. First, the fact that Paul talks about Christ creating both earthly and heavenly rulers and authorities underscores that parallel activity is going on in creation between the visible and the invisible world. These two realms operate in conjunction with each other, so that what happens in the invisible realm is mirrored in the visible realm. In other words, where there's a visible earthly king, spiritual rulers are also operating.

Not only that, but each realm is organized along definite lines of authority. Paul's reference to thrones and dominions refers to both the angelic and the demonic order because Satan mimics everything God does. God's angels are organized along a clear chain of command. The Enemy has his own ranks of demons too (Ephesians 6:12). As the anointed cherub (see chapter 51), Satan himself used to be at the top of the angelic chain of command. He was the ruler under God of the angelic realm.

Among the holy angels there are the cherubim, who are what we might call the angelic guard. It was two cherubim who were put at the gate of the garden of Eden to keep Adam and Eve from going back into the garden. Cherubim have a major role to play in protecting the glory of God.

The seraphim, another order of angels, are concerned with the holiness and worship of God. We met these awe-inspiring creatures in Isaiah 6. When they worshiped, the whole temple shook. They worship God twenty-four hours a day. A third order or tier of angelic beings is the living creatures of Revelation 4. They are unusual creatures engaged in serious worship.

This is the angelic order, with each rank of angels functioning under the higher rank. We get a good picture of this angelic order of authority in Revelation 12:7, which describes a war in heaven in which Michael and his angels went to battle against Satan and his angels.

ANGELS UNDERSTAND THE IMPORTANCE OF AUTHORITY

Angels are not only organized by authority, but they understand the importance of being under authority. Michael the archangel appreciated the importance of authority.

In Jude 9, we see the archangel Michael calling on God's authority to deal with Satan. "Michael the archangel, when he disputed with the devil and argued about the body of Moses, did not dare pronounce against him a railing judgment, but said, 'The Lord rebuke you!'"

As an archangel, Michael was Satan's counterpart. That's important because most people think God is Satan's counterpart or opposite. No, God has no counterpart. He is the all-powerful Creator. Satan is a created being.

If you want to find a counterpart to Satan, look in the angelic world, not at God. God is in a class all by Himself.

Notice that even though Michael is a powerful archangel, he was very careful in the way he dealt with the Devil. Michael knew that Satan had a higher authority than he had, even though both were archangels. Michael never forgot who he was, and he never forgot the position Satan held. So even though they were in face-to-face conflict over Moses' body, Michael never tried to leave or usurp his position of authority.

The angels understand authority, and that's why Michael invoked God's authority when he faced the Devil.

ANGELS ARE LOYAL TO THEIR AUTHORITY

Angels are also very loyal to their authority. This is true both for God's holy angels and for the demons. After the rebellion of Satan, there were no more defections on either side of the angelic world. The angels who followed Satan have already been consigned to eternal condemnation, and the angels who remained true to God were confirmed in righteousness.

We can see an illustration of this loyalty in Matthew 12. Jesus had cast a demon out of a man, and the people were saying, "This man cannot be the Son of David, can he?" (v. 23). They were wondering if Jesus might be Israel's Messiah. When the Pharisees heard this, they wanted to crush any talk like that because they hated Jesus. So they accused Jesus of casting out demons by the power of Satan.

Jesus replied, "Any kingdom divided against itself is laid waste; and any city or house divided against itself shall not stand. And if Satan casts out Satan, he is divided against himself; how then shall his kingdom stand?" (vv. 25–26). We should never expect Satan to go against himself.

Jesus went on to apply this to Himself in Matthew 12:28–29 when He said that He cast out demons by the Spirit of God. Then He used this illustration: "How can anyone enter the strong man's house and carry off his property, unless he first binds the strong man? And then he will plunder his house."

Jesus was saying that He was able to plunder Satan's house because He is stronger than Satan. And the reason He can overcome whatever Satan is trying to do in your life is that what He is doing is greater than what Satan is trying to do.

So when it comes to the angelic realm, there is complete loyalty. Satan will never betray himself, and God will never betray His kingdom.

Angels don't vacillate. Angels don't sit on the spiritual fence. You don't see angels with one foot in the world and one foot in heaven. Angels are full-time with God or full-time with Satan.

ANGELS EXERCISE AUTHORITY THROUGH PEOPLE

Here's a fourth principle by which angels operate. One of the primary ways they carry out their ministry in history is through people.

Again, this principle applies to both good and evil angels. Paul warns, "The Spirit explicitly says that in later times some will fall away from the faith, paying attention to deceitful spirits and doctrines of demons" (1 Timothy 4:1).

Demonic Control

This verse clearly says that some of the teaching that will come in the last days is demonic in origin. But how does this teaching come? Through liars (1 Timothy 4:2), men who try to get God's people to abstain from that which He has provided.

In other words, the demons are promoting Satan's agenda through people they control. These may even be people who don't know they are being controlled by demons. But they are teaching demonic doctrines and leading people astray from the truth.

This is why the Bible tells us to "test the spirits" (1 John 4:1). The first and most important test is found in verses 2–3. Every spirit that confesses Christ is from God, and every spirit that does not confess Christ is not from God. This test alone will help you sort out a lot of false teaching. We need to discern what is influencing people to do what they do and say what they say.

This is also important because even though we as believers cannot be demon-possessed, we can be demon-influenced. We can allow Satan's way of thinking and acting to control us.

Demonic Delays

I want to go back to Daniel 10, this time to look at the matter of angels exercising their authority through human beings. Daniel had been praying and fasting for understanding from God for three weeks when an angel appeared to him (v. 5).

The angel had to reassure Daniel and stand the prophet up so he could deliver his message. Then look at what the angel told Daniel:

> From the first day that you set your heart on understanding this and on humbling yourself before your God, your words were heard, and I have come in response to your words. But the prince of the kingdom of Persia was withstanding me for twenty-one days. (vv. 12–13a)

Here is a battle in heaven between an angel and a demon called "the prince of Persia." The demon had this title because he was exercising his power through people in the earthly kingdom of Persia, influencing this kingdom to oppose God's plan through Daniel and Israel.

Notice that the battle had begun the moment Daniel started praying three weeks earlier. The demon was able to delay the good angel in delivering God's answer to Daniel.

Angelic Help

As awesome as he was, the angel who appeared to Daniel had been unable to break through the demonic resistance. He couldn't get God's answer through to Daniel.

But then he invoked the principle of authority and sent for Michael to help him: "Then behold, Michael, one of the chief princes, came to help me, for I had been left there with the kings of Persia" (Daniel 10:13b). Michael overruled the resistance of the demon of the kingdom of Persia and got the answer through.

My point is that behind nations and events, there is angelic activity. Later in the book of Daniel, Michael is called the angel "who stands guard over the sons of your people" (Daniel 12:1). The reason the Arabs can't wipe out Israel is that Israel's wars are not just about human conflict. There is an archangel involved who says, "You will not be able to destroy this people."

ANGELS ARE ACTIVATED BY AUTHORITY

In 1 Corinthians 11:3, Paul sets down this foundational principle of authority: "I want you to understand that Christ is the head of every man, and the man is the head of a woman, and God is the head of Christ."

Then Paul goes into a discussion of praying and prophesying with and without head coverings. Whether this passage refers to a woman's long hair or to a covering over the hair is debated, but Paul's thesis is that the woman should have her head covered when engaging in these activities, as a sign of her submission to God-ordained authority.

Then Paul makes this summary statement in verse 10: "Therefore the woman ought to have a symbol of authority on her head, because of the angels."

First Corinthians 11 has to do with the church's worship and how that worship is supposed to work. What I believe Paul is saying here is that in order for the angels to do what they're supposed to do, the people for whom they are doing it must do what they are supposed to do.

Paul has argued that it is a disgrace and a sign of rebellion against authority for a woman to pray or speak in church with her head uncovered. If a woman did that and signaled her rebellion with the angels watching, she would rebuff the angels.

The woman is not the only person under authority here. Men are to operate under the authority of Christ. And Paul says that even Christ is subject to God the Father. Men and women are equal in essence, but they are distinct in function. And when you rebel against that chain of command, you lose access to the angelic involvement and activity in your life.

ANGELS ARE UNDER GOD'S AUTHORITY

Let's always remember that the holy angels are under God's sovereign authority. They worship and serve God alone, as should we.

The Temptation to Worship Angels

People in the Bible who saw angels often faced the temptation to worship them, because they are such overwhelming creatures. But angels know who is in charge, and they desire all worship be directed to Almighty God. Let me just note a couple of texts in the book of Revelation that should lay this temptation to rest.

When the apostle John saw the angel in Revelation 19, he said, "I fell at his feet to worship him. And he said to me, 'Do not do that; I am a fellow servant of yours . . . ; worship God'" (Revelation 19:10).

Again in Revelation 22:8, John fell at the feet of an angel to worship him. And again, the angel said, "Do not do that" (v. 9). No angel of God ever accepts worship. The angels know whose authority they are under and who is worthy of worship.

Only one angel ever tried to steal God's worship, and his name was Lucifer. No angel has tried it since. The angels always direct all worship to God.

A Demonstration of God's Authority

The holy angels accept the authority of God; the evil ones, while in rebellion, realize they cannot exceed such authority. Even Satan is limited by the authority of God, as shown in the story of the biblical patriarch Job.

God called the angels together for a conference in heaven, and He allowed Satan to attend the meeting (Job 1:6). Not only that, but God also took the initiative to point out His servant Job to Satan. "Have you considered My servant Job? For there is no one like him on the earth, a blameless and upright man" (Job 1:8).

This was not a case of Satan looking for Job. According to verse 7, Satan was just roaming around on earth, looking for someone to devour like the roaring lion he is (1 Peter 5:8).

So God pointed out Job, and Satan replied, "Does Job fear God for nothing? Have You not made a hedge about him and his house and all that he has, on every side? You have blessed the work of his hands, and his possessions have increased in the land. But put forth Your hand now and touch all that he has; he will surely curse You to Your face" (Job 1:9–11).

Satan issued a challenge to God as part of the angelic conflict. Satan wanted to embarrass God by proving to Him that Job was not the man God thought he was.

So God gave Satan permission to take everything Job had except his life or his health (Job 1:12). But Satan could not cross the line God had drawn, because God was firmly in control and Satan was under His authority.

Even later, when Satan again challenged God and was allowed to afflict Job with a terrible disease, God demonstrated His absolute control over the angelic realm by again drawing a line Satan could not cross (Job 2:6). Job's livestock was gone, his children had died, and now his health was failing, but God would not let Satan have Job's life.

So the angels operate by authority. They function along lines of authority that are clearly marked out by God, and the extent to which we will see the operation of angels in our lives is the extent to which we bring ourselves under God's authority as a way of life, like Job did. When we do that, then we can call on that authority for help in our time of need.

ANGELS ARE SENT AS MINISTERING SPIRITS

Angels are under God's authority to serve Him; at times God will release His angels to minister on our behalf. Of course, we have no authority in the angelic realm on our own. Yet Hebrews 1:14 tells us that angels are "ministering spirits sent out to render service [to] those who will inherit salvation." That is, angels have been given responsibility to serve those who know Jesus Christ. However, let me clarify: I do not mean to suggest that you and I can force the angelic world to do anything we want. The angels obey their boss, who is Jesus Christ.

Our authority to enlist the help of angels comes from our relationship with God through Jesus Christ. We have authority by virtue of our position, not our obedience; we cannot expect guidance or answers to prayer unless we are obedient to God. But when we are in right relationship with God, He is predisposed to release angelic activity on our behalf as we carry out His purposes. It's a matter of our putting ourselves in position for God to minister to us through the ministry of angels.

ANGELS ARE CREATED FOR WORSHIP

Keep in mind that when we come to worship God, we join the company of "myriads of angels" (Hebrews 12:22). Angels were created for the worship of God. In fact, they are always looking into the face of God (Matthew 18:10).

And when we join them in doing what they do best, God activates them on our behalf.

Isaiah 6 is a good example of this truth. In verse 1 we learn that the prophet had his great vision "in the year of King Uzziah's death."

That historical note may not mean much to you, but it meant a lot to Isaiah because under King Uzziah, Israel had finally flourished. It had come into its own. Under King Uzziah, Israel had become a power to be reckoned with. And yet, Uzziah had died.

Isaiah's vision came at just the right time, because he and his nation were hurting. But he did the right thing in that he bowed before the Lord. It was in recognizing his proper relationship before God that Isaiah joined the angels, and the angels moved on God's behalf in his life:

> In the year of King Uzziah's death, I saw the Lord sitting on a throne, lofty and exalted, with the train of His robe filling the temple. Seraphim stood above Him, each having six wings; with two he covered his face, and with two he covered his feet, and with two he flew. And one called out to another and said, "Holy, Holy, Holy, is the Lord of hosts, the whole earth is full of His glory." (Isaiah 6:1–3)

When Isaiah went into the temple in Jerusalem, he was suddenly transported to the temple in heaven, the realm that the New Testament calls heavenly places. And what did he see? He saw angels—the seraphim—doing in heaven what Isaiah came to the temple to do on earth, which was worship.

Whenever you and I worship God, we join the angels, because for them, worship is nonstop activity. The Bible says the seraphim had six wings. With two wings they covered their faces, because they could not look directly on the awesome glory of God. With two other wings they covered their feet, symbolizing humility in God's presence. And with two wings they flew, ready to do God's bidding.

ANGELS ARE ENLISTED BY OUR PRAISE

These opening verses give us the setting of the vision, and also reveal the first area of worship in which the angels are involved.

One of the fundamental elements of worship is praise. In the midst of his worship, Isaiah heard the seraphim calling out their praise to God. They spoke antiphonally, calling out to one another, perhaps from each side of the temple. One group spoke, and the other answered in response.

Transformed by Praise

Isaiah saw the Lord seated on a throne, "lofty and exalted." We call this attribute of God His *transcendence*, the fact that He is infinitely far above and distinct from everything in the universe.

But the angels also sang, "The whole earth is full of His glory" (Isaiah 6:3). This is the *immanence* of God, His nearness to His creation. Both are true of Him. He is "out there," and yet He is also right here.

Isaiah went to the temple to worship because King Uzziah died. Isaiah's earthly circumstances were a mess. But when he went into the temple, he learned something he couldn't learn in the newspaper. The newspaper headlines said, "The King Is Dead." But the temple "newspaper" headlines reminded him about another, eternal King: "The King Is Alive."

Cleansed by Repentance

When Isaiah saw and heard the angels worshiping, something happened: "The foundations of the thresholds trembled at the voice of him who called out, while the temple was filling with smoke" (Isaiah 6:4).

Isaiah—who was the most spiritual man in Israel—saw all of this and cried out, "Woe is me, for I am ruined!" (v. 5). He was saying, "I thought I was good until I came in here. I sing my songs, but I don't sing so that the building shakes. I believe in God, but I've never seen Him like this."

Isaiah got to see God as He really is, and as a result the prophet saw himself as he really was. He saw how unlike God he was.

The word *woe* means "undone," literally "coming apart at the seams." Isaiah saw his sin and the sin of his people, and he confessed, "I am a man of unclean lips, and I live among a people of unclean lips; for my eyes have seen the King, the Lord of hosts" (v. 5).

Commissioned by Praise

At this point the angels got active. After Isaiah let God and not the death of King Uzziah define his circumstances, the angels started to move. Verses 6–8 of Isaiah 6 describe the prophet's cleansing by a seraph that flew to him with a burning coal from the altar.

Why did God send an angel to purify Isaiah? God had a mission for him. "Then I heard the voice of the Lord, saying, 'Whom shall I send, and who will go for Us?' Then I said, 'Here am I. Send me!'" (v. 8).

Now Isaiah received his mission. He discovered what he was supposed to do with his life. Because he went into the temple to worship the Lord, he wound up joining the angels in bowing before God. And when God saw that, He sent the angels to prepare Isaiah for his mission.

ANGELS ARE ENLISTED THROUGH PRAYER

Here's a second element of worship that will enlist the angels on our behalf. When God's people pray, they move heaven.

Prayer and the presence of angels are tied very closely together in Scripture. Many times when God sent an angel down to earth, it was in response to someone talking to the Lord.

The experience of Peter in Acts 12 is a good example. Peter was in prison, and the church was praying. God sent an angel, and Peter was miraculously released. The only bad thing was that the church was shocked when God answered their prayer.

If you have a legitimate request or need, take it to God in prayer and expect an answer. Abraham interceded for Lot (Genesis 18), and two angels came to deliver Lot and his family from Sodom.

The angels also got involved when Daniel entered the lions' den. Remember that Daniel's enemies had persuaded the king to forbid prayer to any god but him for thirty days. They knew that Daniel would ignore the king's edict and pray to God (Daniel 6:4–9). They were right, and the king ordered Daniel to be tossed into a den filled with lions.

So Daniel wound up surrounded by lions, but God honored His praying servant and sent an angel to shut the lions' mouths. Daniel was able to announce his own deliverance to the king the next morning (v. 22). The lions lost their appetite through angelic intervention!

Jesus understood the importance of prayer because He functioned as a man while He was on earth. In Luke 22:41, we find Jesus in prayer in the garden of Gethsemane just before His crucifixion.

"And He withdrew from them about a stone's throw, and He knelt down and *began* to pray, saying, 'Father, if You are willing, remove this cup from Me; yet not My will, but Yours be done.' Now an angel from heaven appeared to Him, strengthening Him" (Luke 22:41–43, italics added).

Jesus was praying that He might be spared the cup of suffering that awaited Him at the cross. But then He submitted His will to the Father's will, and God the Father sent an angel to strengthen Jesus so He could accomplish the Father's will.

There's nothing wrong with praying that God will do certain things in your life. Jesus prayed fervently and specifically that God would remove the cross from His life. But then after He made His request, Jesus made it clear that what He wanted most was what God the Father wanted. Still, the angel came and gave Him strength to endure.

When you pray, God will either give you what you asked for, or He will give you strength to deal with what He wants. Jesus was strengthened by an angel after He submitted to the Father's will and needed strength to go to the cross.

So when you pray, "Thy will be done," God's strength will be yours. Prayer is a powerful way to enlist God's help, which may come through His angels.

ANGELS ARE ENLISTED BY SUBMISSION

A third aspect of worship that can bring you angelic assistance is submission, which simply means coming underneath appropriate, God-appointed authority.

Jesus in the garden of Gethsemane was also the perfect example of proper submission expressed in worship as He submitted to His Father's will.

In contrast, a group of Jewish exorcists who had not submitted to authority tried to imitate Paul's power over demons with violent results. We read about this unusual incident In Acts 19:13–16:

> But also some of the Jewish exorcists, who went from place to place, attempted to name over those who had the evil spirits the name of the Lord Jesus, saying, "I adjure you by Jesus whom Paul preaches." Seven sons of one Sceva, a Jewish chief priest, were doing this. And the evil spirit answered and said to them, "I recognize Jesus, and I know about Paul, but who are you?" And the man, in whom was the evil spirit, leaped on them and subdued all of them and overpowered them, so that they fled out of that house naked and wounded.

The angelic realm knows whether a person is functioning under authority. The demon knew that these men had no authority to be doing what they were doing. They had no right to be using the name of Jesus the way Paul used it. So the demon knew that they were totally unprotected, and he messed them up.

If you're not under authority, your own authority is limited. God does not trust full use of His authority to people who have not first learned submission. Even Jesus "learned obedience from the things which He suffered" (Hebrews 5:8).

The apostle James makes this crucial connection when he writes, "Submit therefore to God. Resist the devil and he will flee from you" (James 4:7). Most people start quoting this verse by saying, "Resist the Devil." But the first step is to submit to God. Come under His authority.

Why? Until you're submitted to God you won't have the power to resist the Devil. But when you are in submission to God, the Devil can't handle you because you are operating under God's authority.

Nathanael, our friend we met a few chapters ago, got to see the angels in action because he recognized Jesus for who He is and came under Jesus' authority by responding to His call to discipleship (John 1:46–51).

ANGELS ARE ENLISTED BY WITNESS

Let me mention one more thing, the issue of your witness.

In Luke 12:8–9, Jesus said, "Everyone who confesses Me before men, the Son of Man will confess him also before the angels of God; but he who denies Me before men will be denied before the angels of God."

Jesus said your witness, or lack thereof, is an issue that involves the angels. This is because the angels are messengers who wait for God's instructions to bring the answers to earth.

So if you are a Christian who can never seem to speak a word for Christ, He will deny you angelic assistance when you come with your needs and requests. But if you are not ashamed to be publicly identified with Christ, if you don't mind other people knowing that you belong to Him, He will not be ashamed to say before the angels, "She is one of Mine. Take her the answer."

I want to close with four powerful verses from Psalm 103:

> The Lord has established His throne in the heavens, and His sovereignty rules over all. Bless the Lord, you His angels, mighty in strength, who perform His word, obeying the voice of His word! Bless the Lord, all you His hosts, you who serve Him, doing His will. Bless the Lord, all you works of His, in all places of His dominion; bless the Lord, O my soul! (vv. 19–22)

This is an awesome picture of worship. Angels worship the Lord. His people worship Him. Even His works worship Him.

Worship is powerful because God is looking for worshipers (John 4:23). When you worship, you exalt the Lord. And when He is exalted, when He is lifted up, He sends the angels on your behalf.

APPLICATIONS FOR LIFE

1. "Thrones" and "dominions" (Colossians 1:16) refer to both the angelic and the demonic orders. That is because Satan mimics everything God does. Keep in mind that the Enemy is the master of lies and counterfeits, and we must not allow him to get us to settle for anything less than the truth. John warns us to "test the spirits" (1 John 4:1) so we do not fall prey to false teaching. Submit to God's Word and His Spirit, as they will guide your decisions and actions.

2. Michael, the awesome archangel of God, still called on God to rebuke Satan. We must also use God's authority—His holy Word, including its promises we can resist the Devil through God. If you have not yet done so, memorize key verses of promise and rebuke for dealing with Satan.

3. Prayer and the presence of angels are tied very closely together in Scripture. Read the accounts in Acts 12; Daniel 6:10; and Luke 22:41–43. Although God did not remove Jesus' "cup of suffering"—the Cross—God did send an angel to strengthen Jesus so He could accomplish God's will. When God has revealed His will, pray that God will give you strength to do it.

4. We find an excellent lesson in Acts 12. While Peter was in prison, and the church was praying for his release, God answered their prayer and sent an angel, and Peter was miraculously released. However, the church was shocked when God answered their prayer. Never doubt the power of your prayers! If you have a legitimate request or need, take it to God in prayer and *expect* an answer.

FOR GROUP STUDY

Questions for Group Discussion

1. Read Colossians 1:16 and Ephesians 6:12. What does this verse tell us about how God has organized the angels? How do angels view authority in the spiritual realm?

2. Dr. Evans teaches that one of the primary ways angels carry out their ministry in history is through people. From the Scripture passages in this chapter, what do we learn about the ways angels (both good and evil) operate with regard to people?

3. In the Bible, people who saw angels often were tempted to worship them. Why should we refrain from worshiping angels? (See Revelation 19:10.)

4. Hebrews 1:14 tells us that angels are ministering spirits assigned to those who will inherit salvation. For what reason does God release their activity on our behalf? What condition must we meet to be in position to receive angelic help? By whose authority do we receive their ministry?

PICTURE THIS

Whether for good or evil, one of the primary ways angels carry out their ministry in history is through people. Scripture tells us that they exercise their authority in at least three ways

HOW ANGELS EXERCISE THEIR AUTHORITY

AREA	SCRIPTURE PASSAGES	WHAT IT MEANS TO US
Demonic control	1 Timothy 4:2	Believers can be demon-influenced by allowing Satan's way of thinking and acting to control them.
Demonic delays	Daniel 10:5, 12–13a	Some evil angels have the power and authority to work through people to oppose God's plan.
Angelic help	Daniel 12:1	God might use angelic agents to help us.

SECTION II

The Evil Angels

47

THE CHARACTER OF SATAN AND THE DEMONS

There are two categories or types of angels in Scripture. We have studied the first group, the elect or holy angels who remained true to God when Satan rebelled and were confirmed in their holy estate. The second group includes one-third of the angels (see Revelation 12:4) who joined Lucifer, the anointed cherub of God, as he rebelled against God, was judged, and became God's archenemy. In the next chapter we will explore how Satan carries his battle against God today, assisted by his demonic forces. But first we need to learn more about the evil angels and their head. We'll consider Satan's character and that of his helpers.

THE CURSE UPON SATAN

Satan's evil character was formed the moment he let his pride cause him to rise up in rebellion against the throne of God.

This creature went from a beautiful, perfect being named Lucifer, living in the light and glory of heaven, to Satan the prince of darkness, banished to the earth. And he fell with the speed of lightning.

That's what Jesus said in Luke 10:18 when He told the seventy disciples He had sent out, "I was watching Satan fall from heaven like lightning." This is one of many Bible passages that speak of Satan's judgment by God and the curse imposed on him. Satan's curse was evident in his change of name and his change of destination.

A Change in Name

Before his fall, this angel's name was Lucifer (Isaiah 14:12 KJV). But in Luke 10:18 Jesus called him Satan.

The names given to Lucifer after his fall reflect his character. "Satan" is one of those names. It means *adversary* or *opposer*. His curse is revealed in the fact that he went from Lucifer, meaning *shining one*, to a name meaning *adversary*, the one who opposes everyone and everything associated with God.

Satan's character was corrupted so completely that God gave him a different name. Lucifer had lost his brilliance and his righteousness, so he got a name that reflected his fallen status.

Actually, the Bible has a number of names for our enemy. Satan is one name we are very familiar with. Another is the Devil, which means *accuser* or *slanderer*. The word *Satan* is used about fifty-five times in the New Testament, and *Devil* is used about thirty-five times.

The Devil is the great accuser of God's people. That's why the saints rejoice when the Devil is finally "thrown down" by God (Revelation 12:9).

The Devil's nature is revealed in the great contest of Job 1–2. By accusing Job of serving God for gain, Satan was slandering both Job's character and God's character. Remember, everything our enemy does is ultimately directed at God. The Devil hates God and wants to do anything he can to injure God's reputation so that He does not get the glory due Him.

The Devil can't touch God, so he seeks to destroy God's glory by attacking His people. This is why the Devil is regularly in God's presence, accusing and slandering the saints to hinder God's glory and keep us from being blessed.

The idea of an accuser suggests a legal setting, a court scene. We need to understand that God operates His universe like a court. He gave Israel His law, and throughout the Old Testament we find God bringing a charge against His people when they broke that law.

Lucifer himself was brought into the court of heaven, charged with rebellion, found guilty, and sentenced to the lake of fire, as we will discuss below. His fellow rebellious angels were also sentenced to eternal fire.

The Devil is on death row, even though he is being allowed to operate for a period of time. He has taken the role of prosecutor, bringing charges against us before God, accusing us of all sorts of things, slandering us and God.

The great thing is that we have a "defense attorney," Jesus Christ, to defend us by pleading His blood (1 John 2:1). The sad thing is how often we fail and do wrong things that give substance to the Devil's accusations.

So when the Bible calls our enemy "the devil," God wants us to understand that our adversary is also our accuser.

The Bible has many other descriptive names and designations for Satan. For example, he is called "the god of this world" (2 Corinthians 4:4) and "the prince of the power of the air" (Ephesians 2:2) because right now, he's in control of this planet. Satan has demonized this world.

Because of Satan, Adam and Eve died. Because of Satan, Cain killed Abel. And because of Satan, all the children of Adam will die someday. Satan would kill you and me if at all possible. He is a destroyer who wants to wreck everything and everyone God has made.

Here is one more name for the Devil that's very revealing of his character. It's found in Revelation 12:3, where the Devil is called the "great red dragon" (this is where people get the idea that Satan wears a red jumpsuit). He is then repeatedly referred to as a dragon in the verses that follow. John also calls the Devil "the serpent of old" (v. 9), a reference to his deception in the garden of Eden.

A dragon is basically a serpent on steroids. A dragon is an awesome, destructive creature. A dragon may be mythical and not an actual being, but the Bible draws on the imagery of a terrifying, destructive beast to characterize Satan.

A Change in Destination

Lucifer got something else hung on him besides new names. He also got an eternal death sentence.

Jesus said that the lake of fire "has been prepared for the devil and his angels" (Matthew 25:41). It is called "the lake of fire and brimstone" (Revelation 20:10), where the Devil will be cast along with his followers for eternity.

There was never any possibility of redemption for Satan or his angelic followers. Speaking of Christ's incarnation and death for sin, the writer of Hebrews says, "He does not give help to angels" (Hebrews 2:16). The cross did not include a provision for Satan's sin.

Why no provision for Satan? I believe that part of the reason is that he sinned against too much light. Lucifer was perfect in every detail. He had firsthand experience with God. He lived in God's very presence. He knew what he was doing. He wasn't seduced by any tempter. Satan entered into his rebellion with his spiritual eyes wide open. There was no remedy for him.

Satan's sin was so terrible that there was no grace for him. The result is that Satan is not only condemned to eternal death himself, but he is also defeated in his purpose of taking the entire human race with him to destruction. Salvation is God's statement to Satan that he is a beaten foe.

THE CONTEST OF SATAN

Even though Satan has been decisively and eternally defeated by Jesus Christ, he is not about to lie down and quit. He is still engaged in a great contest, a great war, against God for the souls of men and women. And he has some potent weapons at his disposal.

The Weapon of Power and Wealth

The Devil can give you a lot of stuff, because this world has been "handed over" to him temporarily. And as the Devil told Jesus in His temptation, "I give it to whomever I wish" (Luke 4:6).

Satan can give people power, wealth, friends, and fun on a mammoth scale. Scripture says that "the whole world lies in the power of the evil one" (1 John 5:19).

The Weapon of Deception

Everything Satan does is wrapped up in lies, because deception is at the heart of everything he does.

Jesus said concerning the Devil, "He . . . does not stand in the truth, because there is no truth in him. Whenever he speaks a lie, he speaks from his own nature; for he is a liar, and the father of lies" (John 8:44).

Satan is the ultimate deceiver. He will either make a promise that he doesn't deliver on, or else he won't tell you the whole story. When the thing gets delivered, you find out it isn't what you thought it was, and you don't like what you're getting.

In fact, Jesus called the Devil the "father of lies" because he gave birth to deception. He told the first lie to the angels who followed him in his rebellion. He continued lying in the garden of Eden, and he has been at it ever since. He's out to deceive the whole world (Revelation 12:9). And the people he controls are his deceivers too (2 John 7).

The Weapon of Opposition

If Satan cannot get you to believe his lies or fall into one of his traps, he will turn around and oppose and resist anything you try to do for God. You can bank on Satan's opposition in your efforts to live for Christ, but that's a good sign because it means that Satan considers you worth opposing! He doesn't waste his time messing around with people who aren't doing anything.

People who never feel the Devil's opposition probably are not doing much for God. See, the Devil knows he cannot touch you and me in terms of condemning us to hell. So he is content to let us go our way as long as we don't try to invade his kingdom and make an impact for Christ.

But when we get serious about serving God, the adversary shows up. He's not about to stand by and let us plunder his kingdom. Remember, he's still determined to steal God's glory, so he is going to oppose anything that brings God glory.

The Weapon of Accusation

Another potent weapon our enemy wields in his contest against God is accusation, the aspect of Satan's character and work underscored by the name *Devil*, the "accuser of our brethren" (Revelation 12:10).

To be effective, an accuser needs an opportunity to make an accusation. He needs something he can try to pin on the person being accused. Paul urges us, "Do not give the devil an opportunity" to accuse us (Ephesians 4:27). Paul chose the right name for the Enemy here, because the Devil is the accuser or slanderer who seeks to tie us up with guilt.

The Devil knows that God is so righteous and so holy He has to deal with sin. So when we sin we give the Devil the opportunity he needs to go into God's courtroom and lay a charge against us.

This is so important because God's justice demands that He always deal with sin. He can't just skip it. When we as believers sin, we break our fellowship with God and give the Devil an open door to operate in our lives. This is why the Bible urges us to deal decisively with sin (1 John 1:9).

THE CONQUEST OF SATAN

The goal of any contest is conquest, victory. In Revelation 12:11 the Bible gives us three powerful weapons for defeating our adversary Satan, the Devil who accuses us day and night.

The apostle John was looking ahead to that future day when Satan will be defeated once and for all, so the context of Revelation 12:11 is prophetic. But the weapons these tribulation saints used to defeat the Devil are the same ones we can use today. This great verse says, "They overcame him because of the blood of the Lamb and because of the word of their testimony, and they did not love their life even to death."

We need three things to keep the Devil from ruining us: the cross of Jesus Christ (which is absolutely foundational), our confession, and our commitment.

The Cross

The first thing you need to beat Satan is the cross, without which the other two weapons would not be possible. "The blood of the Lamb" is a reference to the death of Jesus Christ on the cross. The blood Jesus shed there not only purchased our eternal salvation, but it renders Satan powerless when we as believers are operating in the power of the Holy Spirit.

John 12:31–33 says that Satan was judged by the death—that is, the blood—of Christ. So if you are under the blood, you belong to Christ. And as Paul says in Romans 8:31, "If God is for us, who is against us?" Paul goes on to ask in verse 33, "Who will bring a charge against God's elect?" Then in verse 34 he asks, "Who is the one who condemns?"

The one who tries to condemn us is the accuser, the Devil. But look at

God's answer to the Devil's accusation: "Christ Jesus is He who died" (v. 34). So anyone, including Satan, who tries to condemn us has to undo and overcome what Jesus did when He died.

But that's not all Romans 8:34 tells us. Jesus not only died, but He was "raised" from the dead. So our accuser has to overcome the resurrection of Christ as well.

It gets even better. Christ is "at the right hand of God." That's a reference to His ascension back to heaven, so we have a crucified, raised, and ascended Savior to answer any accusation against us.

And here's the topper. Not only is Jesus Christ at the right hand of God, the place of God's favor, but Jesus also "intercedes for us" (Romans 8:34c).

Remember that when we sin, we give Satan a legal right to accuse us. But when we confess our sins (1 John 1:9), we are forgiven and cleansed through Christ's blood.

Our Confession

A second weapon we can use in our conquest of Satan is our confession, "the word of [our] testimony" (Revelation 12:11).

Our confession or testimony has to do with our public identification with Christ. It has to do with how we speak and live, whether we are adequately and accurately reflecting who Jesus is, acknowledging Him before the world, and pointing people to Him.

There is tremendous authority against Satan in our confession of Christ, because of what Jesus said in Matthew 10:32–33: "Therefore everyone who confesses Me before men, I will also confess him before My Father who is in heaven. But whoever denies Me before men, I will also deny him before My Father who is in heaven." Jesus was not talking about salvation, but about our willingness to confess before the world that we belong to Him.

The authority over Satan comes because when we confess Christ, He confesses us before His Father. That is, He says, "Father, this believer is faithful to Me. She needs power over the Evil One, and I am signing off on her request so You will know I approve it."

Our Commitment

The third weapon in our Revelation 12:11 "arsenal" is what I am calling our commitment. The saints in Revelation loved Christ more than they loved their lives. I'd say that is commitment.

Paul said, "I have been crucified with Christ" (Galatians 2:20). He also said, "For to me, to live is Christ, and to die is gain" (Philippians 1:21). Paul's only goal was that Christ be exalted in his life, even if it meant death (v. 20).

That's the kind of commitment we're talking about here. Jesus said something interesting to those seventy disciples in Luke 10:20: "Do not rejoice in this, that the spirits are subject to you, but rejoice that your names are recorded in heaven."

In other words, our authority doesn't come from our power. It comes from our relationship with Christ. Let's never forget that power belongs to Christ, not us. We can only conquer Satan as we stay fully committed to the Lord. The thing to rejoice about is that we know Him.

THE NATURE OF DEMONS

Assisting Satan in his war against God and God's people are the demons. Satan isn't operating alone. He has his own army of spirit beings called demons who obey him and carry out his agenda. A demon is a fallen angel who followed Satan in his rebellion (Revelation 12:4) and now assists Satan's program of opposition to God's purpose, program, and people.

In chapter 26 we looked at the well-known biblical story of Jesus' encounter with the demon-possessed man as told by Mark (5:1–20). Let's return to the story, this time considering Luke's account (8:26–39). It tells us pretty much all we need to know about the nature of demons.

Demons Are Personal Beings

Demons display all the primary attributes of personality.

For example, demons possess intellect. In Luke 8, they recognized Jesus and were able to speak and reason using this man's voice (v. 28).

Demons also have emotions. They begged Jesus not to torment them (v. 28). Since demons do not have bodies of their own, the torment they feel would apparently be in the spiritual or emotional realm.

Like people, demons also have a will. In verses 32–33, they expressed their desire to enter into the herd of pigs that was feeding nearby. We also know that demons have a will because they exercised that will when they chose to follow Satan in his rebellion. So it's not surprising that they were able to make a choice here, but note that they had no power to do what they wanted to do without Christ's permission.

Demons Are Spirit Beings

Demons are not only personal beings. They are spirit beings. Paul says specifically that our struggle is "not against flesh and blood" (Ephesians 6:12). Demons do not have bodies of their own, but as we saw above they are able to inhabit the bodies of others.

Jesus revealed more about the nature of demons when He said:

> When the unclean spirit goes out of a man, it passes through waterless places seeking rest, and not finding any, it says, "I will return to my house from which I came." And when it comes, it finds it swept and put in order. Then it goes and takes along seven other spirits more evil than itself, and they go in and live there; and the last state of that man becomes worse than the first." (Luke 11:24–26)

Notice what Jesus said about demons in the course of His teaching. They are restless when they have no one through whom to express themselves. "Waterless places" are places without life. Like the demons who inhabited the man in Luke 8, this demon became frustrated when it had no way to express itself, so it returned to the place of its former habitation—and it brought the brotherhood!

The demon called this man's body "my house" (Luke 11:24). Demons often seek a "house" to inhabit in order to find temporary peace and not be sent to the abyss. They are spirit beings who can use the bodies of humans and animals to express themselves.

Demons Are Powerful Beings

The demons of hell are powerful beings. The demons who possessed the man Jesus healed in Luke 8 were forcing him to do violent things, and they gave him superhuman strength. He could break chains as if they were string. No doubt the demons would have eventually killed him, since demons can even drive people to want to commit suicide (Revelation 9:3–6).

Demons Are Perverted Beings

Demons are also perverted beings. When they rejected God and lined up with Satan, they "earned" a special name. Not only are they called demons, but Jesus called them "unclean spirits." They pervert everything they touch.

For example, demons pervert the truth of God (1 Timothy 4:1). They want you and me to believe a lie because their leader, Satan, is the father of lies. Paul says they want to pervert God's goodness and make it into something that is all prohibition and denial of the good things God created.

Demons are also eager to pervert human sexual relationships (1 Corinthians 7:5; Revelation 18:2–3). Sometimes they have even been able to mix perversion with religious devotion, as in the worship of Aphrodite practiced in Corinth.

THE ACTIVITIES OF DEMONS

The Bible reveals two basic categories of demons: those who are not yet permanently judged and are free to move about doing Satan's will, and a subclass of demons who were imprisoned for their particular sin.

Demons Who Are Free

The first category of demons is the one we are most familiar with, those demons who are free to move about at Satan's bidding and carry out his purposes.

When I say they are free, I am using that term in a relative sense. Demons are under the ultimate control of heaven, as Jesus made clear on a number of occasions when He told demons what to do and they had to obey. In Luke 8, the demons Christ cast out of the man not only had to leave him when Jesus commanded them to, but they had to ask Jesus' permission to go into the pigs. But since God has chosen to let these "free" demons operate for the time being, they are able to carry out Satan's commands.

In Luke 8:32 the demons inhabiting this man begged Jesus "not to command them to depart into the abyss."

This is the place where all demons that are active now will ultimately be sent (Revelation 9:1). But these demons were worried that Jesus would send them there ahead of their time, we might say, so that they would be out of commission.

Jesus did not send them to the abyss, but allowed them to enter the pigs. There is no record in Scripture of Jesus consigning an active demon to this prison during His earthly ministry. But the demons knew that Jesus had the power to order them into the abyss, and they were worried.

Demons Who Are Imprisoned

The Bible refers to a second group of demons who are permanently imprisoned because of the exceptionally gross nature of their sin.

According to Jude 6, these are angels "who did not keep their own domain, but abandoned their proper abode." They are being "kept in eternal bonds under darkness for the judgment of the great day." Peter writes of these demons that "God did not spare angels when they sinned, but cast them into hell and committed them to pits of darkness, reserved for judgment" (2 Peter 2:4).

What is the "proper abode" of angels? Heavenly places, the spiritual realm. These angels left that sphere when they came down to earth to commit an especially wicked sin.

This occurred when these angels cohabited with women and produced a mutant race of giants (Genesis 6:1–4). For leaving their proper abode after creation and committing that sin, these angels were cast into eternal fire and eternal judgment, locked up with no possibility of release or parole forever.

Neither Satan nor the demons who follow him will ever change their character. Satan will never give up the contest until he is tossed into the lake of fire. But Satan and all his evil angels have been conquered by the blood of Jesus Christ.

APPLICATION FOR LIFE

1. When we sin, we give Satan a legal right to accuse us. More importantly, we break our fellowship with God. So righteous and so holy is God, He has to deal with sin. But when we confess our sins (1 John 1:9), we are forgiven and cleansed through Christ's blood. Be diligent daily to confess your sins and restore fellowship with God. The apostle Paul urges us, "Do not give the devil an opportunity" to accuse us (Ephesians 4:27).

2. Have you had one of those days where the Devil has gotten the best of you? If so, take the necessary steps to get back on course—confess sin, ask forgiveness from someone you have wronged, and so on. Never lose the perspective that, through Christ, you are victorious. Because of Christ's sacrifice on the cross, Satan has been defeated. Be especially encouraged that, even now, Jesus is interceding for you at God's right hand.

3. If you are living for Christ, you can be sure that Satan will oppose you. Commit to memory James 4:7, which exhorts us, "Submit therefore to God. Resist the devil and he will flee from you." It takes courage to stand against the Devil, but God will give you the strength to do it.

4. Is there something you've said yes to in your life that Jesus wants you to say no to? The Holy Spirit will show you what it is. I urge you, change your answer to Jesus' answer. Don't allow the Devil a base of operation in your life!

FOR GROUP STUDY

Questions for Group Discussion

1. After Satan rebelled against God, God judged him and imposed a curse on him. Because of that curse, what two things changed for him? What do these changes mean for Satan?

2. The Bible calls our enemy "the devil" because God wants us to understand that our adversary is also our accuser. The Bible uses many other descriptive names for Satan. Read 2 Corinthians 4:4; Ephesians 2:2; and Revelation 12:3, and discuss the different names for Satan. What do those names tell

us about Satan's character? What might they tell us about his activities?

3. What three weapons do we need to use to keep the Devil from ruining us? Why are these weapons so powerful in countering attacks from the Devil?

4. Dr. Evans points out that our commitment to Christ is a very effective weapon in fending off the attacks of Satan. Discuss what it means to be committed. To gain a biblical perspective on commitment, read Revelation 12:11; Galatians 2:20; Philippians 1:21; and Luke 10:20. What makes such commitment so powerful? Fashion your own definition of biblical commitment.

PICTURE THIS

Although decisively and eternally defeated by Jesus Christ, Satan relentlessly wars against God and His people. As believers who are targets of these weapons, we need to be ever watchful, lest we fall prey to them.

SATAN'S WEAPONS OF ATTACK

WEAPON	SCRIPTURE PASSAGE	IMPACT	OUR RESPONSE
Power and wealth	1 John 5:19	Satan can give people power and wealth.	Rely on God's generous provisions.
Deception	John 8:44	Satan tempts God's people with lies and deceptions.	Counter with the truth of God's Word.
Opposition	James 4:7	Satan opposes anything that brings God glory.	Resist the Devil, giving God the glory.
Accusation	Revelation 12:10	Satan seeks to tie up God's people with guilt.	Confess sin and maintain fellowship with God.

48

THE STRATEGY OF SATAN

A farmer was constantly having his watermelons stolen by thieves. Finally, he came up with a brilliant idea to thwart the thieves. He poisoned one watermelon, then put a sign in his watermelon field that read: "Warning: One of these watermelons has been poisoned."

The next day the farmer went out to find that none of his melons had been stolen, because the thieves didn't know which one was poisoned. He was quite satisfied that his idea had worked and that he would not have a problem with theft anymore.

But two days after the farmer put up his sign, he came out to his field to find that his sign had been altered. Someone had scratched through his message and had written, "Two of these melons have been poisoned." Our farmer friend had to destroy his whole crop because now he didn't know which other melon was poisoned.

That's what it is like dealing with the Devil. No matter what you come up with, he can come up with something better. No matter what sign you put up, he can change the wording. No matter what strategy you devise, you can't outwit this fellow.

Satan has a definite strategy, and it can be understood in one word:

deception. Satan's strategy for your life and mine is to deceive us. He is the master deceiver. He is the camouflage king.

The reason Satan has turned to deception is that he cannot outpower God. Satan tried to overcome God in heaven, and that gamble failed. Satan's power will never be a match for God's.

Evidently, in his rebellion Satan forgot that God can do something he cannot do, which is create something out of nothing by simply speaking it into existence. God looked at nothing and said, for example, "Let there be light." And light appeared.

Satan cannot create anything. All he can do is manipulate and maneuver what has been created. Since he cannot match God's power, Satan has to maximize the power he has, and deception is his strong suit. He has turned deception into an art form.

THE POWER OF SATAN'S STRATEGY

Just because Satan is no match for God, that doesn't mean he is powerless. In fact, I want to begin the discussion of Satan's strategy by looking at the power of his deception.

In 2 Thessalonians 2, Paul is correcting these believers' misconceptions about the day of the Lord:

> Let no one in any way deceive you, for *it will not come* unless the apostasy comes first, and the man of lawlessness is revealed, the son of destruction, who opposes and exalts himself above every so-called god or object of worship, so that he takes his seat in the temple of God, displaying himself as being God. (vv. 3-4, italics added)

Paul then says that this "lawless one," the Antichrist, will not be revealed until God's restraint is removed. Then, "That lawless one will be revealed . . . the one whose coming is in accord with the activity of Satan, with all power and signs and false wonders, and with all the deception of wickedness for those who perish" (vv. 8–10).

Satan's Authority

But we don't have to wait until the end times to see the power of Satan at work.

Where does Satan get the power he wields over people? He gets it from what I call his constitutional superiority over any man or woman. As an angel, a spirit being, Satan does not have the limitations of flesh and blood.

Therefore, you and I can't compete with the Devil in our own strength. We can't outsmart the master deceiver. He has authority by virtue of his person. Satan's authority is given by God and limited by God, but it is still a greater authority than you and I exercise.

Satan's Experience

Satan is also powerful by virtue of his vast experience. He has untold years of experience at being the Devil.

One thing Satan has learned during all these years is how to transform himself, as we will see later in 2 Corinthians 11:14. He is the master deceiver who the Bible says one day will deceive all the nations of the world (Revelation 20:8). This world is a puppet, and Satan holds the strings.

Satan's Organization

Another reason that Satan is so powerful in carrying out his strategy is that he commands a massive organization of evil (Ephesians 6:12). Satan's organization is well run and heavily disguised.

Satan heads a spiritual "Mafia" that controls people and even whole nations. People wonder how a nation can produce a Stalin or a Hitler. The explanation is the massive work and deception of Satan.

THE PROGRAM OF SATAN'S STRATEGY

What is Satan hoping to achieve by working his strategy of deception on the world and on God's people?

Satan's program is to produce such a wonderful counterfeit of God's works and ways that he leads us astray. Paul wrote to the Corinthians, "But I am afraid that, as the serpent deceived Eve by his craftiness, your minds will be led astray from the simplicity and purity *of devotion* to Christ" (2 Corinthians 11:3).

A Counterfeit View of Ownership

Satan told Eve she could be like God. He knew that was a counterfeit promise because he had tried it himself. But he's still tempting us to take things into our own hands, to set up our own kingdoms, to try to live independently of God.

Satan may temporarily control a lot of this world's assets and use them against believers, but he even does that within the limits of God's permission. Ultimately, it all belongs to God.

A Counterfeit View of Good and Evil

After telling her that she could be like God, Satan also told Eve that if she ate from the forbidden tree, she would know good and evil. In other words, "You can make your own decisions about what's right and wrong. You don't need God telling you what's right and making you feel guilty for doing what you want."

I once had a person tell me, "I'm never coming back to Oak Cliff Bible Fellowship." When I asked why, he said, "Because I want sermons that make me feel good. I don't need anybody telling me what to do." That is exactly what Satan told Eve.

A Counterfeit View of Life and Death

Satan also told Eve, "You won't die if you eat from this tree. God was lying to you."

In other words, "There are no consequences to your actions. You can do whatever you want without suffering any penalties. God won't do anything about it."

But the death God warned Adam and Eve about did come to pass. They lost their innocence, their relationship with Him, and their home in the garden. And physical death followed as the inevitable consequence of their spiritual death.

Counterfeit Views of Truth

Satan cannot stand truth. He does not want you to believe something simply because God said it. Our enemy has all kinds of systems in place to lead us away from objective truth, that which is independent of what we may think or what we may have experienced. Let me mention some of Satan's counterfeits for truth.

One is called *relativism*, the idea that truth is ever-changing, always on the move. In this view, what is true today may not be true tomorrow. You hear this when young people say, "Well, back in your day that may have been true. But that was then, this is now."

Another of Satan's counterfeits is *subjectivism*, which says that truth is strictly personal. You know you have encountered subjectivism when you hear the old line, "Well, that may be true for you, but it's not true for me." For these people, truth is a matter of personal choice, like choosing a dress or tie.

Empiricism is still another of Satan's phony substitutes for truth. Empiricism says that truth resides only in what we can see and feel and measure. Truth depends on evidence and data you can gather and evaluate.

Satan snares some people in the trap of *existentialism*, the teaching that truth is found in what you can experience. The idea that there is a revealed body of truth that never changes is irrelevant to existentialists. The only thing that matters to them is what is happening at the moment.

For still others, truth is purely logical. It can be arrived at through syllogisms. This is *rationalism*. If you can get the right formula, then you'll find the truth. This is the realm in which most science is conducted. Science proposes hypotheses and formulates equations, and based on logical deduction it announces, "Mankind is the product of evolution." Rationalism seeks to explain life on this planet without reference to God.

Whatever label you give to Satan's deception, the basis is the same. Satan hates objective truth, and he'll try to lead people astray from it every time.

A Counterfeit View of Christianity

Satan even has his own fake form of Christianity. He has phony doctrine (1 Timothy 4:1) as well as being able to produce phony miracles. The Devil even has a counterfeit communion table. That's why Paul said, "You cannot drink the cup of the Lord and the cup of demons" (1 Corinthians 10:21). Satan also offers a counterfeit spirituality (Galatians 3:2–3) based upon a counterfeit gospel (Galatians 1:11–12).

And to propagate his program, the Devil has his own false teachers. Paul warned the church at Corinth of men who were "false apostles, deceitful workers, disguising themselves as apostles of Christ" (2 Corinthians 11:13). Since Satan can make himself look like one of the good guys (v. 14), he can do the same for his servants.

THE PROCESS OF SATAN'S STRATEGY

Satan's strategy is powerful and purposeful. Our enemy has a well-laid-out program to deceive and destroy that proceeds in four distinct stages.

Stage One: Desire

The apostle James outlines the process by which Satan deceives people. It begins with the desire: "Let no one say when he is tempted, 'I am being tempted by God'; for God cannot be tempted by evil, and He Himself does not tempt anyone. But each one is tempted when he is carried away and enticed by his own lust" (James 1:13–14).

Stage one in Satan's plan is the arousal of a desire. Even legitimate desires become a problem when Satan tempts us to meet a legitimate desire in an illegitimate way. The process of temptation often means trying to get us to meet a good need in a bad way.

Stage Two: Deception

In stage two of the process, the illegitimate development of desire leads to deception, the moment when the person takes Satan's bait and finds out he has been deceived.

But Satan is far too smart to let his hooks show. He covers them with enticing bait. He invites a person down to the friendly neighborhood tavern for one drink, then two, three, and four, until that person's desire for alcohol overcomes all his other desires and commitments. He has been thoroughly deceived.

Satan deceives us by planting an evil thought or idea in our minds. He can't make us do anything, but he can build deceitful castles of desire in our minds. Satan knows how to intertwine our desires with his twisted plans to lure us into his deception. But we still have to bite on the hook.

Stage Three: Disobedience

So desire leads to deception, and deception leads to disobedience. "When lust has conceived, it gives birth to sin" (James 1:15).

James uses the analogy of conception, pregnancy, and birth because the birth process so closely parallels the process he is talking about. When an illegitimate desire is welcomed and acted upon, that act of conception produces a "child" called sin. And once a child has been conceived, its birth is sure to follow.

In other words, committing disobedience is like the act of procreation. The result will always show up after a while. The child of disobedience is sin, and like any other child sin will begin to grow once it has been born.

Stage Four: Death

The fourth and final stage in Satan's process is death. James says, "When sin is accomplished, it brings forth death" (1:15).

Sin certainly brings spiritual death. That is one of the fundamental truths we learn from the sin of Adam and Eve. Sin can also produce physical death. We have already mentioned several examples of that.

Satan brings nothing but death and destruction with him, but God is the source of "every perfect gift" (James 1:17). So James says, "Do not be deceived, my beloved brethren" (v. 16). When Satan deceives and leads us into sin, he causes us to miss the goodness of God. Don't ever think you have it better with Satan than you do with God.

Jesus is our perfect example here. When confronted by Satan's temptations in the wilderness, Jesus did not say, "Let Me think about it and I'll get back to you later." He said, "It is written." He dealt with the temptation on the spot, right in Satan's face. He didn't meditate upon the wrong desires Satan suggested and allow them to conceive disobedience.

THE PURPOSE OF SATAN'S STRATEGY

Now that we know the process Satan wants to take us through, we are ready to talk about the purpose behind his strategy. Satan has several major purposes behind his deceptions.

First Purpose: Prevent Salvation

When it comes to the unsaved, Satan's purpose is to keep them right where he has them, which is on their way to an eternity in hell. So he blinds the minds of nonbelievers to keep them from getting saved and bringing God glory (2 Corinthians 4:3–4). The more people who get saved, the more glory God gets.

Second Purpose: Make Believers Ineffective

When it comes to believers, one of Satan's purposes is to interrupt the process by which God gets glory through our lives. He wants to render us ineffective in terms of any real impact for Christ.

That's why the Devil keeps some believers depressed, some discouraged, and others underneath their circumstances. He wants you there because he knows you can do nothing for God if you're miserable.

Third Purpose: Frustrate God's Will

Finally, the Devil wants to deflect you and me from accomplishing the will of God by frustrating God's will for our lives.

Satan even tried to frustrate the accomplishment of God's will in Jesus' life. God the Father's will for His Son was the cross, but in the wilderness temptation the Devil tried to get Jesus to take the easy way.

Satan also used one of Jesus' own disciples to try to turn Him away from the cross (Matthew 16:21–22). Imagine Peter rebuking Jesus, trying to tell Him where He was wrong. Only Satan could have thought of an attack this bold. Jesus knew who was behind it, because He told Peter, "Get behind Me, Satan!" (Matthew 16:23).

Jesus was saying, "I have to go to the cross. Peter, Satan is using you, one of My children, to stop Me from doing My Father's will."

If Satan wasn't afraid to try to turn Jesus away from God's will in going to the cross, do you think he will leave us alone? Of course not.

As a matter of fact, Jesus went on to say in this same passage, "If anyone wishes to come after Me, let him deny himself, and take up his cross, and follow Me" (Matthew 16:24). Satan tried to get Jesus to focus on the suffering of the cross and thus to avoid it. Our enemy will do the same to us.

The cross does involve suffering. It's an instrument of death. Bearing my cross means I am willing to identify publicly with Jesus Christ and accept anything that goes with that identification. It means I will bear the scars of being identified with Christ.

But when we step onto the winner's stand and receive the crown from Jesus Christ, we will say, "It was worth it." Don't let Satan deceive and distract you from accomplishing God's will.

AGENTS OF SATAN'S STRATEGY

The demons assist in fulfilling Satan's strategy. They promote who Satan is and what Satan does; they oppose everything God is and God does. This is the essence of spiritual warfare.

Let's take these two items of the demonic program and study them in some detail, beginning with the promotion of Satan and his agenda.

HOW THE DEMONS PROMOTE SATAN

Demons Promote Satan's Doctrine

Demons promote the doctrine of Satan. They teach what their master wants taught so that people might live in the darkness of Satan's theology rather than in the light of God's truth.

In 1 Timothy 4:1, Paul talks about "deceitful spirits and doctrines of demons." In the end times, people will pay closer and closer attention to these teachings.

One particular doctrine demons propagate is the idea that God is not good (vv. 3–4). This ought to sound familiar, because this was the argument of the Devil back in Eden. Satan was saying to Eve, "If God were good, He wouldn't keep you away from that tree. He would share it with you."

Demonic doctrine hits at things God created to be enjoyed, such as marriage and food (v. 3). But those who know the truth know that God has not forbidden marriage or the eating of certain foods. Instead, He has created these things to "be gratefully shared in" by His people. . . . For everything created by God is good, and nothing is to be rejected, if it is received with gratitude" (v. 4).

Demonic doctrine wants to undermine the Son of God. In another familiar passage, Paul warned the Corinthians that the adversary wanted to undermine their devotion to Christ (2 Corinthians 11:3). Demons are also working hard to undermine the gospel of God by blinding people to its truth (2 Corinthians 4:3–4).

Demons Promote Satan's Destructiveness

Jesus said the Devil is in the business of destroying everyone and everything he can (John 10:10). All through the New Testament, we see demonic forces at work to debilitate and destroy people.

I am not saying that all illnesses and other serious problems are demonically orchestrated. However, a lot more physical and emotional illness is demonically orchestrated and influenced than most people are willing to admit.

For example, demons can cause blindness (Matthew 12:22), physical deformity (Luke 13:11), emotional and mental instability (Matthew 17:14–18), and even physical death (Revelation 9:13–15). If it were not for the grace of God, any one of us could have been killed before we came to Christ, because total and eternal destruction is Satan's goal.

Demons Promote Satan's Domination

Don't forget that Satan is a frustrated ruler. He tried to displace God from the throne of the universe, and he has been out to build his own kingdom ever since. The method he uses is one of seeking to dominate individuals, institutions, and ultimately entire nations. The demons are his primary henchmen.

Demon possession as one means of Satan's attempt to dominate the scene. The demons also seek to dominate organized religion on Satan's behalf. The risen Christ told the church at Smyrna, "I know your tribulation and your poverty (but you are rich), and the blasphemy by those who say they are Jews and are not, but are a synagogue of Satan" (Revelation 2:9).

Satan ultimately seeks to dominate nations that he might wage war against God and His people.

Demons Promote Satan's Distractions

Besides pushing Satan's doctrine, destructiveness, and domination, demons are also effective promoters of the Devil's distractions.

In this category I include all the cable television programs and psychic hotlines and newspaper horoscopes that purport to offer people spiritual guidance and advice. I am convinced that far too many Christians are dabbling in these things and are opening themselves up to the evil spirit world.

Whenever you appeal to the created order to do what is the prerogative of the Creator, you change gods. You are distracted from the true God—and you invite His severe judgment. "As for the person who turns to mediums and to spiritists, to play the harlot after them, I will also set My face against that person and will cut him off from among his people" (Leviticus 20:6).

HOW THE DEMONS OPPOSE GOD

Demons Oppose God's Position

One of the primary things that demons want to oppose is God's position.

Our God is a jealous God who will not share His glory with any other. He is supreme; we are to have no other gods before Him. So demons seek to oppose God's position primarily through idolatry.

In Deuteronomy 32:17, Moses said of Israel's rebellion, "They sacrificed to demons who were not God, to gods whom they have not known, new gods who came lately, whom your fathers did not dread." This is a New Testament problem too (1 Corinthians 10:20–22).

Demons Oppose God's Precepts

Demons also oppose God's precepts, the teachings of His Word.

I don't want to spend too much time here, because we have covered this point earlier. Let me just remind you that the Devil's opposition to God's precepts started very early when he challenged and denied God's word to Eve.

Eve had to choose whom she was going to believe. That's the choice we have to make too. God's Word is written plainly for us to know and obey. When the demonic world comes with its lies, we have a clear standard to measure its lies against.

Demons Oppose God's Purity

The opposition of demons extends to God's purity as well as His position and His precepts.

We have talked about the vileness and corruption that Satan and his demons seek to perpetrate. Jude referred to the case of demons who became involved in perverted human sexuality (v. 6), and also referred to *the* biblical epitome of impurity, Sodom and Gomorrah (v. 7). These cities practiced "gross immorality" and "went after strange flesh."

Then Jude turned to the reason for writing his short letter, the false teachers who were plaguing the church. These men "in the same manner . . . defile the flesh" (v. 8). In what manner does Jude mean? In the same manner as the demons and the people of Sodom and Gomorrah.

All of us have to battle with sin, which is why 1 John 1:9 is so important. We must confess our sins and cleanse them in the blood, because without the blood of Jesus Christ we can't get rid of sin's impurity. And if we can't get rid of the impurity, we can't have fellowship with God.

Demons want to keep us defiled and impure, away from the blood. They are unalterably opposed to God's purity.

Demons Oppose God's People

One way the demonic world opposes us is by slandering us to God. If Satan can use his henchmen to cause us to stumble and fall, then the slanderer has an accusation he can take into heaven's courtroom and fling in God's face. "Did You see what that man just did? Did You hear what that woman said? They claim to be Your children. What are You going to do about it?"

Demons oppose God's people by getting in their way. Paul said he wanted to come to the Thessalonians, but Satan hindered him (1 Thessalonians 2:17–18).

Demons also oppose us by tempting us to sin. Temptation is still the Devil's best weapon against us day in and day out. He is constantly dropping the seeds of thoughts that later on can produce a messy harvest if we yield to them.

The demons know what they are doing. They are not a house divided. Their strength is in their unity. They operate as one. If we can learn to operate as one with God, as one in the church, and as one in our homes, there will be no room for demons to work. That's why Paul pleaded, "[Be] diligent to preserve the unity of the Spirit in the bond of peace" (Ephesians 4:3).

SATAN'S DECOYS

The U.S. Army used to have pneumatic decoys, rubber units that could be inflated and made to look like tanks or trucks or whatever. The army would put these things in strategic locations so that when the enemy flew over doing reconnaissance, it would look like the army had a much larger and more powerful force than was actually the case.

Satan is busy inflating and placing his "pneumatic decoys" all over the place to make you think he's much stronger than is actually the case. The demons share in his strategies.

Since Jesus Christ's death and resurrection left Satan defeated, his only power is the power of deception. His only strategy is to deceive us. So tell him, "I know who you are and how you work, and I don't want any part of you or your works."

APPLICATION FOR LIFE

1. James 1:13–14 tells us that all of us are tempted when we are carried away and enticed by our own lust. Because a wrong desire is the starting point down the road to sin, don't let Satan get a handle on your desires. If you find yourself being aroused by impure desires, say no to those desires by changing whatever is influencing those desires—change your venue, turn off the TV, and so on.

2. Are you careful about what you accept as truth? We are inundated by counterfeit "truth" at every turn: The TV, the movie theater, and the media. What we allow into our minds is critical. The Devil can use his counterfeits of truth to influence your life and undermine your witness for Christ. And those influences often can be so subtle that we don't recognize them. That is why it is so important to begin each day in the Word, filling your mind with the mind of Christ and allowing God to anchor your thinking in the truth of His Word.

3. A Christian leader once said that the successful Christian life is a series of new beginnings. There are times when we stumble in our walk of faith, even falling prey to wiles of the Devil. Remember we have a forgiving Father. Call on Him, and He will restore you to fellowship and get you back on your feet.

4. "All of us have to battle with sin, which is why 1 John 1:9 is so important." Unconfessed sin in your life can grow like a cancer and reap great consequences not only to you, but to your loved ones and others. Do you need to clean your heart and mind of sin? If so, confess your sins now, and cleanse them in the blood of Jesus Christ.

FOR GROUP STUDY

Questions for Group Discussion

1. Dr. Evans points out that Satan's strategy of deception can be defined by four distinct stages. Read James 1. What are the four stages, and how does each dovetail into the next? What can we do to stop the progression of those stages?

2. Scripture shows us that Satan has at least three purposes behind his strategy of deception. In preparation for discussion of this question, read 2 Corinthians 4:3–4 and Matthew 16:21–23. How does each of those purposes impact us?

3. Discuss Satan's various counterfeit views. Why does Satan target these views? Share examples of where you see these counterfeits at play today.

4. We know that demons oppose the persons and work of God. What are the targets of their opposition? For discussion, cite examples where active opposition to God is very evident in our society.

PICTURE THIS

Satan is the master of counterfeit. The various counterfeit views he employs are designed specifically to lead us astray. His counterfeiting of truth has deceived countless people over the centuries, including God's people. An understanding of these will better equip us to counter Satan's falsehoods.

SATAN'S COUNTERFEIT VIEWS OF TRUTH

COUNTERFEIT VIEW	WHAT IT MEANS	CHRISTIAN PERSPECTIVE
Relativism	Truth is ever-changing; there are no absolutes.	God and His Word never change.
Subjectivism	Truth is strictly personal.	The inspired Word of God is objective truth.
Empiricism	Truth resides only in what we can see, feel, and measure.	God's truth exists infinitely and eternally beyond the physical realm.
Existentialism	Truth is found in what you can experience.	Truth is found in the written doctrine of Scripture.
Rationalism	Truth is based on logical deduction.	Truth originates with God and is independent of human logic.

49

THE DEFEAT OF SATAN

Let's make no mistake about it. Satan was defeated the instant he rebelled against God. That means he has been a loser for all of the ages since that rebellion, and someday he will taste his eternal defeat at the hands of Jesus Christ. As I look at what the Bible says about Satan's defeat, I see four ways in which God's Word declares the Devil to be a beaten enemy.

SATAN WAS DEFEATED STRATEGICALLY

The first way that Satan was defeated is what I call his strategic defeat. By this I mean that he devised a strategy—rebellion against God—that failed miserably. There was never a second that God's throne was in danger of toppling.

Satan made a fatal strategic mistake in that he as a creature rebelled against his Creator, the One on whom he depended to sustain his very life. Satan's "creatureliness" depended on God, yet Satan rose up in defiance of God.

God's Glory Seen through Satan

For His own sovereign reasons, God did not simply obliterate Satan when He defeated him. Instead, God decided to turn Satan's rebellion against

Him in a way that would bring God more glory. In other words, God is using Satan's rebellion and defeat to display His great glory and accomplish His good plan. In fact, God is using Satan to bring Himself more glory than He would have had if Satan's rebellion had not occurred.

Look at the way God used Satan's intentions to bring about His purpose and glory in the life of a prideful, independent Peter. God hates pride more than any other sin because it reminds Him of the Devil's rebellion. So He had to deal with the pride in Peter's heart.

Just before Jesus' crucifixion, the Lord stunned Peter by telling him: "Simon, Simon, behold, Satan has demanded permission to sift you like wheat; but I have prayed for you, that your faith may not fail; and you, when once you have turned again, strengthen your brothers" (Luke 22:31–32).

Notice first that Satan had to get God's permission to go after Peter, just as he did with Job. God granted him that permission because Peter was proud and needed to be humbled.

So Satan went right to work. First, he tempted Peter to brag about his faithfulness in response to Jesus' declaration (Luke 22:33). Then Satan got Peter to fail when the moment of truth came, and he denied Jesus three times. The only thing that kept Peter from falling apart completely was that Jesus was praying for him.

God not only defeated Satan, He turns Satan's strategy against him. The only thing the Devil knows how to do is get us to do what he did, to turn against God in rejection and rebellion. But God will not be outmaneuvered by the Enemy.

God's Judgment Using Satan

God also uses Satan's rebellion in the lives of His people in the matter of discipline and judgment.

One person whose life reveals this is King Saul of Israel. When Saul first became king, the Bible says that God changed his heart (1 Samuel 10:9). But as time went on, Saul proved to be disobedient and rebellious.

Things got so bad that God finally sent Samuel to anoint David as the next king (1 Samuel 16:1–13). Then we read this statement in verse 14: "Now the Spirit of the Lord departed from Saul, and an evil spirit *from the Lord* terrorized him" (italics added). So the king's attendants brought in David to play his harp for Saul and soothe him (vv. 15–23).

But the evil spirit began to drive Saul into madness, and in 1 Samuel 18:10–11, while David was playing for Saul, the king threw a spear at David to kill him.

Someone watching Saul might say he was just insane and needed to be put on medication or put away. But what Saul needed was to turn back to God and ask Him to lift His hand of judgment, because God was using Satan's kingdom to terrorize Saul.

But in Saul's case, the discipline of God did not bring repentance, as Satan drove Saul finally to destroy himself (1 Samuel 31). But even though Satan won a temporary victory in Saul's life, there was never any moment when God was not in sovereign control of the situation.

SATAN WAS DEFEATED PROPHETICALLY

A second way that Satan has been defeated is through the prophecy that God spoke back in Genesis 3:15 when He was pronouncing judgment on Adam, Eve, and the serpent for their sin.

God's "I Wills"

Satan issued five "I will" statements in Isaiah 14:13–14: "I will ascend to heaven . . . raise my throne above the stars . . . sit on the mount . . . ascend above the heights of the clouds . . . make myself like the Most High." The Devil declared what he was going to do, but he failed. In Genesis 3:15 God declares an "I will" of His own, and no one can stop Him.

Five times the Devil had said, "I will." Here God said, in effect, "Let's put your 'I will' statements against My 'I will' statements." God said He would put enmity or strife between the woman's seed and the serpent's seed.

This is the continuation of the struggle begun in heaven with Satan's fall. Satan produces his evil seed, and God produces His righteous seed. These two lines began their conflict with Adam's two sons, and the battle has been on ever since. God's righteous seed will win out, because no one can frustrate God's "I will."

The second part of God's "I will" declaration in Genesis 3:15 is implied rather than spoken, but it is no less powerful. It is the prophecy of the righteous Seed, Jesus Christ, who will crush Satan. We could state the middle phrase of the verse this way, "[I will see to it that] He shall bruise you on the head."

Genesis 3:15 also indicates that God's victory would not come without suffering. The bruising of God's righteous Seed on the heel is a cryptic, prophetic way of referring to Jesus' sufferings at His crucifixion. But even though Jesus died, it was Satan who received the fatal blow.

Why? Jesus rose again. A bruise on the heel is not fatal. But Satan got bruised or crushed on the head, which was a death blow. Satan's defeat was announced prophetically in Eden, and it was accomplished at Calvary and with the empty tomb of Jesus Christ.

Satan's Attack

The rest of the Bible unfolds the strife between the woman's seed and the serpent's seed. The conflict between the followers of God and the followers of the Devil begins immediately in Genesis 4.

When Abel was born, Satan probably thought he was looking at the fulfillment of God's prophecy, the one who would crush his head. Remember, Satan is not all-knowing. He can't see the future, and he can't know God's plan until it is revealed. So when Satan saw Abel bringing offerings that God accepted, he knew he had to do something to get rid of this seed. So he put murder in the heart of Cain, and Cain killed his brother Abel (1 John 3:12).

Even though Satan got Cain to kill Abel in an attempt to get rid of God's righteous seed, God had something Satan hadn't counted on. And in that part of His plan, God maintained His victorious edge.

God's Victory

What Satan didn't count on was the birth of Seth (Genesis 4:25–26). When Seth was born, Eve herself spoke of the significance of his birth: "God has appointed me another offspring in place of Abel; for Cain killed him" (v. 25). Seth was God's substitute for Abel.

Now you see what this has to do with the angelic conflict that began in heaven and was continued on earth. It was in the days of Seth's son Enosh that "men began to call upon the name of the Lord" (Genesis 4:26). God had someone else ready to take Abel's place. God always has someone prepared to make sure His will is accomplished.

Satan didn't know that God had a plan. All he knew was that when Seth was born, he got a divine curveball thrown at him. He decided that since he couldn't be sure which son was the righteous seed, he would do the job right and corrupt the whole human race. That brings us right back to Genesis 6 and Satan's grotesque plan to produce a demonic seed.

Verses 5-7 sound like the Devil's plan has worked, because God says He intends to wipe out the human race. But God knows something Satan didn't plan on. "Noah found favor in the eyes of the Lord" (Genesis 6:8). The righteous seed would be preserved through Noah.

Much later, Satan used the same strategy against the baby Jesus by driving Herod to kill all the boy babies in Bethlehem (Matthew 2:16-18). But our enemy didn't count on God sending His angels to lead Jesus and His family to Egypt.

SATAN WAS DEFEATED HISTORICALLY

We can thank God that Satan was defeated prophetically in Eden. Now here's the next stage in God's victory. Satan was also defeated historically at the cross.

Looking ahead to the cross, Jesus said, "Now judgment is upon this world; now the ruler of this world shall be cast out. And I, if I be lifted up from the earth, will draw all men to Myself" (John 12:31-32). The cross was the ultimate defeat that Satan did not anticipate.

The Judgment of the Cross

When Jesus Christ was on earth, He let the Devil know there was one Man he couldn't mess with. Jesus tied up the "strong man," the Devil, so He could plunder the Devil's house (Matthew 12:29). As we have already seen, Jesus had total control over Satan's demons. They had to do what He said, because He was and is infinitely stronger than the Devil.

But it was in His death that Jesus really crushed the head of Satan. Satan was judged at the cross (John 12:31; 16:7–11), because on the cross, God removed the curse of sin that Satan caused to be laid on mankind in the garden of Eden.

When Satan tempted Eve, he was banking on a fact he knew about God because he had experienced it himself: When you sin, you come under God's curse.

The Bible says that anyone who does not keep God's law perfectly is under a curse (Galatians 3:10). Sin is the failure to keep God's law. It is falling short of His standard, which is perfection. The reason unbelievers will spend eternity in hell is that sin puts men and women under the curse of God's broken law.

But Jesus removed the curse of sin, which was the curse of the law (Galatians 3:13). If Satan can't tempt us to go off into a life of overt sin, he will tempt us to go the other direction, that of trying to please God and earn His favor by our goodness. Satan doesn't care what it takes to distract us from Christ, just so we arrive in hell.

People go around reciting the Ten Commandments, but God didn't give them to be recited or memorized. He gave them to be obeyed. When we fail to keep God's commandments, we fall under His curse.

The Ten Commandments are good laws, but they are bad news for sinners like us, because the only thing the law can do is condemn us when we violate it. It has no power built into it to help us obey. The law can only condemn you when you break it.

So the Law of Moses gives the basis of condemnation, and because we sin and break it, we come under its curse. Satan loves to put people under the same curse he is under. But on the cross Jesus lifted the curse.

The Blessing of the Cross

Satan and his curse were judged and defeated at the cross. Jesus' cross turned what was our judgment into our blessing. That's reason enough for us to praise God, but let me give you more reasons that the cross has become a blessing for us.

One reason is that once we have been freed from the curse of sin, we cannot sin our way back under it. Satan has been defeated so royally and completely that he no longer has any claim on us once we belong to Christ. The writer of Hebrews says, "But [Jesus], having offered one sacrifice for sins *for all time*, sat down at the right hand of God. . . . For by one offering He has perfected *for all time* those who are sanctified" (10:12, 14, italics added).

God judged and defeated Satan at the cross, so Satan can no longer make sin an issue to separate us from God.

A second blessing of the cross is that it has removed the fear of death for those of us who know Jesus Christ (Hebrews 2:14–15).

SATAN WILL BE DEFEATED ETERNALLY

Here's a final way in which Satan is defeated. It is still future in terms of history, but it is as good as done from God's viewpoint. Someday, Satan will be eternally defeated.

Temporary Access to God's Presence

The beautiful thing about Satan's eternal defeat is that when his eternal sentence is executed, our enemy will be put away forever. The Devil, who has led countless millions to hell and has harassed and hurt God's people for eons, will be banished to hell. This is the final stage of his judgment.

Satan went from living in God's presence to having temporary access to God's presence after his sin. At the cross, Satan suffered another defeat because he was rendered powerless. His weapons were taken away from him.

Then in Revelation 12:7–12 we see the final war in which Satan will be "thrown down" (v. 9). No wonder this elicits great rejoicing on the part of God's saints. Finally, Satan will no longer have even temporary access to heaven.

Eternal Banishment

The last we hear of Satan is in Revelation 20, which describes the Devil's confinement during the millennial reign of Christ, his last gasp of rebellion, and his eternal judgment (see especially verses 1–3 and 7–8).

At the end of the millennium, those who didn't want Jesus to rule over them will get a final opportunity to rebel. Satan will be released to bring out the rebellion that they harbored in their hearts for the thousand years in which Christ reigned.

But the battle will be over quickly, because fire will come down from God and devour them (v. 9). Then will come the moment that God's people have been waiting for: "The devil who deceived them was thrown into the lake of fire and brimstone, where the beast and the false prophet are also; and they will be tormented day and night forever and ever" (v. 10).

The Bible calls this "the second death" (Revelation 20:14). Earlier in this verse it says that "death and Hades" are also thrown into the lake of fire. So not only is the Devil sent there for eternity, so are Hades and the people in it.

The *New American Standard* translation is helpful here because it renders the word used here as "Hades." This is the place of torment for people who have died without Jesus Christ, such as the rich man Jesus talked about in Luke 16:19–31. These people are awaiting the final judgment, described in Revelation 20:15. Hades is the place of punishment today.

But hades is not the final judgment. The holding cell for a death-row prisoner is not the final step. Execution is that prisoner's final judgment. And eternal hell is the final judgment for the Devil and his demons and his human followers.

Satan was judged a long time ago, and hell was prepared for him and his angelic rebels (Matthew 25:41). Jesus said He saw Satan fall from heaven like lightning (Luke 10:18). We can use the analogy of lightning and thunder to understand what is happening in Revelation 20.

Lightning and thunder occur at the same time, but we see the lightning before we hear the thunder because light travels faster than sound. Satan's judgment was pronounced in heaven in eternity past, and now in Revelation 20 we hear the "thunderclap" that follows the lightning as he is thrown into the eternal lake of fire. The point is that there is no question about Satan's defeat and eternal destiny.

APPLICATION FOR LIFE

Responding to the Defeat of Satan

1. God has sealed Satan's defeat in many ways. That is we why we need never concede to the Devil and his demons, no matter how severe his attacks. With God's help, we will always prevail. For "greater is He who is in you than he who is in the world" (1 John 4:4). Praise God that we have that assurance of victory!

2. For Satan, defeat means that eventually he will be cast into hell, which has been prepared for him and his rebellious angels. Tragically, those individuals who have refused to accept God's gift of salvation are bound for the same destination. Does your prayer include people you want to see bow to Jesus as Lord now rather than being forced to bow before Him later on their way to hell? If you can't name lost friends and loved ones you're faithfully praying for and reaching out to, don't get off your knees until God puts them on your heart.

3. As Satan goes down in defeat, he will be determined to take with him every person he can. Ask God to help you not become overly influenced by the world's standards for measuring greatness and reward. Those standards are nothing more that Satan's counterfeits to deceive you and distract you from what God has prepared for you.

4. We know that Satan was defeated historically. How remarkable that we possess recorded accounts of Jesus' birth, His sacrifice on the cross, and His resurrection! Those rate as the three greatest events in all of recorded history! If your heart needs a dose of joy, take a moment to reflect that.

FOR GROUP STUDY

Questions for Group Discussion

1. What do we mean when we say that Satan was defeated strategically? In what ways did God "turn the tables" on Satan?

2. How was Satan defeated prophetically? What is significant about the

account of Cain and Abel in Genesis 4? What did God do to defeat Satan?

3. Satan was defeated historically at the cross. Why was it a decisive defeat? Why was the cross a judgment on Satan? What makes the cross a blessing for us?

4. The Bible teaches that Satan will be defeated eternally. As preparation for discussion, read Revelation 12:7–12 and 20:1–3, 7–8. How is Satan eternally defeated? What is his status after this defeat?

PICTURE THIS

In Isaiah 14, Satan made five "I will" statements in defiance of God. But the Bible records God's own "I will" as He judges and defeats Satan.

God's "I Wills" Regarding Satan
Genesis 3:15

SPECIFIC "I WILL" STATED	IMPACT OF GOD'S WILL
"I will put enmity between you and the woman."	The prophecy that God's righteous seed will win out over Satan's evil seed.
"[I will see to it that] He shall bruise you on the head, and you shall bruise him on the heel."	The prophecy that the righteous Seed, Jesus Christ, will crush Satan.

SECTION III

The Reality of Spiritual Warfare

50

THE NATURE OF THE BATTLE

Remember that old newsreel that shows President Franklin Roosevelt addressing Congress the day after the Japanese attack on Pearl Harbor in December of 1941? Calling it "a day that will live in infamy," the president declared that, in reality, America was already at war. Roosevelt just needed a declaration of Congress to make it official.

I am not the president, but I have a declaration to make. You and I are at war! In fact, we are engaged in the mother of all battles. The war I am talking about is the spiritual warfare that you became a part of the day you trusted the Lord Jesus Christ as your personal Savior.

THE ESSENCE OF THE BATTLE

Because this warfare is first and foremost spiritual and not physical, the degree to which you and I will be successful is the degree to which we are prepared to understand and fight this battle on a spiritual level.

A Definition

Spiritual warfare is that conflict being waged in the invisible, spiritual realm that is being manifest in the visible, physical realm and affects you and me. The cause of the war is something you and I can't see. But the effects are very visible in the problems and day-to-day stuff you and I face all the time.

It's hard enough to fight an enemy you can see. It's much harder to fight someone you can't see. In his classic statement on spiritual warfare, Paul wrote: "For our struggle is not against flesh and blood, but against the rulers, against the powers, against the world forces of this darkness, against the spiritual forces of wickedness in the heavenly places" (Ephesians 6:12).

This verse identifies the enemy, Satan and his demons. We make a grand mistake if we think people are the real enemy.

What we need to understand is that what happens through people, including you and me, has its roots in something much larger. This fact does not excuse the wrong things people do. They are still responsible. But it helps us focus on the real enemy. Let me set down a foundational principle for spiritual warfare: Everything we see in the visible, physical realm is caused, provoked, or at least influenced by something in the invisible, spiritual realm. Your five senses are not the limit of reality.

Daniel 4:26–32 states that heaven rules over all the affairs of earth. So until we address the spiritual causes of a problem, we will never fix the physical effects of that problem.

Not only are your physical senses very limited, but they are often of little help in spiritual warfare. This means that if you are going to wage successful spiritual battle, you need a "sixth sense"—a keen awareness of the spiritual realm. This awareness begins with your worldview.

Two Worldviews

Your worldview is simply the lens through which you perceive reality. It is the presuppositions that determine what you believe and the way you look at life.

There are really only two categories of worldviews. One is a natural or materialistic worldview, what people today call the scientific worldview. This view says that man by his reason can figure out how the world works. People who hold this view seek life's answers in the natural realm. If you can put it in a test tube, examine it under a microscope, or explain it through natural processes, that's all you need.

This worldview has quite naturally led to agnosticism and atheism.

That is, you don't need God as long as you have test tubes, microscopes, and telescopes.

The second category of worldviews is the spiritual worldview, which says there is a realm outside of the physical. We have to recognize that there are competing spiritual worldviews, just as there are many variations of the naturalistic worldview.

A spiritual worldview is very popular right now, but unfortunately it is often not a biblically based, theistic view that believes in the one true God.

Instead, it is a man-centered view that believes in any form of spirituality that seems to pay off. This is the world of horoscopes, palm readers, and all sorts of New Age teaching. When people pick up their newspapers and turn to their horoscope for the day, they're looking for something outside of this world that will guide their lives and their decision making.

Obviously, this is not the worldview of the Bible. It is possible to have a spiritual worldview that is plugged into the wrong spirit. In order to understand spiritual warfare, we have to address it through the lens of the spirit, with the help of the Holy Spirit.

THE IMPACT OF THE BATTLE

Even though the battle we are talking about is spiritual in nature, it has very definite effects in the physical realm. You know you're in a battle when you get shot and start bleeding. We are seeing the "bleeding," the result, of spiritual warfare in at least four areas of life today.

Personal Impact

Many believers are seeing the wounds of spiritual warfare in their personal lives.

Our emotions can give the Devil an entry into our lives. To see the relationship between your emotions and spiritual warfare, look at several familiar verses in Ephesians: "Therefore, laying aside falsehood, speak truth each one of you with his neighbor, for we are members of one another. Be angry, and yet do not sin; do not let the sun go down on your anger, and do not give the devil an opportunity" (4:25–27).

Notice that failing to control anger grants the Devil an opportunity to get a foothold in your life. Then he can use it as a base of operations to launch more spiritual attacks against you. We could multiply these examples, but suffice it to say that the personal effect of spiritual warfare is great.

Family Impact

Many believers are also feeling the effects of spiritual warfare in their families. The Devil messed up the first family in the garden of Eden, and we have been dealing with the effects of Adam's and Eve's sin ever since.

One example of family relationships and spiritual warfare can be seen when Paul wrote to husbands and wives in 1 Corinthians 7:5, "Stop depriving one another, except by agreement for a time so that you may devote yourselves to prayer, and come together again so that Satan will not tempt you because of your lack of self-control."

Paul is saying that when a husband and wife don't have a fulfilling sexual relationship, the Devil sees that lack as an opportunity to come in and bring about moral destruction in the family.

Church Impact

Spiritual warfare also has an impact on church life. Paul told Timothy to watch out for "doctrines of demons" that will infiltrate the church (1 Timothy 4:1). The church is being undermined in many places today by teachers who purport to teach the Bible but are teaching doctrines from hell.

Anyone can quote the Bible. But we need to be like the Bereans, who checked out what Paul and Silas were teaching them to see whether their teachings agreed with the Scriptures (see Acts 17:11). The Devil will use, or misuse, the Scriptures when it is to his advantage to do so.

Cultural Impact

Finally, spiritual warfare affects the life of a nation, the culture in which we live.

According to passages like Daniel 10, entire nations are influenced by the invisible battle in the angelic realm. Satan is called "the prince of the power of the air" with good reason (Ephesians 2:2).

In other words, you and I are breathing this stuff. But Satan's job is to get us to ignore the spiritual realm or give it low value, or look at it inappropriately and worship spiritual beings other than God.

THE LOCATION OF THE BATTLE

Where in the universe is this great battle called spiritual warfare being fought? Paul tells us it is "in the heavenly places" (Ephesians 6:12), which means the spiritual realm.

The Heavenly Places

In the Bible, the word *heaven* describes three levels of existence (see 2 Corinthians 12:2). The first heaven is the atmosphere that surrounds the earth, the environment in which we live.

The second heaven is what we commonly refer to as outer space, the stellar heavens where the stars and planets exist. This is also a realm in which angels operate, because in the Bible angels are often called stars (Job 38:7).

The third heaven is the throne room of God, the place we normally think of when we hear the word *heaven*. It is about this heaven that the Bible has the most to say. In fact, the third heaven is a very busy place because it is the control center of the universe.

In the book of Ephesians alone, we find numerous references to heavenly places in addition to the reference in 6:12.

Ephesians 1:3 says, "Blessed be the God and Father of our Lord Jesus Christ, who has blessed us with every spiritual blessing in the heavenly places in Christ." This verse tells us that God resides in the heavenly places, and so do *all* of our spiritual blessings.

This is important because if you are engaged in a spiritual battle and need help to win, the help you need is with God the Father, who is in the heavenly places. But if you don't know how to get to heavenly places, you won't know how to get to the heavenly help you need to win the battle in earthly places.

According to Ephesians 1:20, when God the Father raised Jesus Christ from the dead, He seated His Son "at His right hand in the heavenly places." Not only are the Father and your blessings in heavenly places, Jesus Christ is there too. So if you need Christ's help in earthly places, you'd better know where He is hanging out and how to take a trip there to obtain His help in your warfare.

But it gets even better. God also "raised us up with [Christ], and seated us with Him in the heavenly places" (Ephesians 2:6). You and I as believers are also in heavenly places. Paul is saying that when you accepted Christ, you were transported to another sphere. Even though your body is limited to earth, your spirit that should be controlling your body is operating in a wholly different realm.

Too many Christians don't understand that. The most real part of our existence is what happens in our spiritual lives, not what happens in our bodies. We are residents of heaven, in our spirits now and someday in our bodies too. Once you understand how the heavenly sphere operates, you can begin changing what happens on earth.

What else is in heavenly places? Spiritual rulers and authorities are there, according to Ephesians 3:10. These are angels. This is important from the standpoint of spiritual warfare, because it takes an angel to beat an angel. Remember, Satan and his demons are also "in the heavenly places" (6:12).

See, if your problem originates in the heavenly places, you need a solution that originates in the heavenly places. Most of us have very little consciousness of angels because they're not part of our physical world. But we need to understand that the angels of God and the demons of hell are the "foot soldiers" in the cosmic battle between God and Satan.

When you hear believers say they are being attacked by the Devil, they probably mean they are being harassed by his foot soldiers. Satan is a limited being. He is not everywhere present, all-knowing, or all-powerful.

Satan is not God, but he has a whole host of evil angels called demons he can use for spiritual attacks. Anything that hell can bring against you is the result of satanic activity in the same realm in which God operates, called heavenly places.

You and I are no match for the power and deceptiveness of Satan and his army. We need the power of God to neutralize Satan's attacks against us.

A Spiritual "Capitol Hill"

In Washington, D.C., sits Capitol Hill, where Congress makes decisions about how our country will be run. What is decided there will affect you no matter where you live.

On Capitol Hill two parties are vying for power and control. These two parties have competing philosophies, and the party that is in control sets the basic direction for the country.

"The heavenly places" refers to the Capitol Hill of the universe. It is where decisions are made that affect our lives. There are two opposing parties, the kingdom of God and the kingdom of Satan, each seeking to promote its agenda.

Our party, headed by Jesus Christ, occupies the spiritual "White House," and He has veto power. Satan's party, however, seeks to undermine, sabotage, and destroy those who have aligned themselves with Jesus Christ. At the same time, Satan seeks to keep the members of his party from switching their allegiance to Christ.

Deciding Who Is in Charge

We can be thankful that God has established His throne in heavenly places. When it comes to the universe, there is no question that the kingdom of God and His King, Jesus Christ, are firmly in charge.

And Jesus' eternal victory is already assured. But God has allowed us to choose in our individual lives who will be in charge. Some people have decided for Satan, and they will spend eternity with him in hell. Those of us who have decided for Christ will live eternally with Him. But while we're here on earth, we still need to decide for Christ each day in terms of our spiritual warfare.

That's important because it is possible for children of God's kingdom to live as if they belong to the Devil. That's sort of like Republicans or Democrats who look and talk like loyal members of their party, but when they go behind that little curtain in the voting booth, they secretly vote for the other party. And it's the vote that counts, not the look or the talk.

THE ENEMY IN THE BATTLE

Revelation 12:7 depicts a day when the invisible warfare in the heavenly places will break out in a very visible form: "And there was war in heaven, Michael and his angels waging war with the dragon. And the dragon and his angels waged war."

The archangel Michael and the holy angels are fighting Satan and the angels who rebelled with him. The battle is angelic, but they are fighting over the earth.

So the war in heaven directly affects what is happening on earth. We are in the midst of an angelic conflict, a satanic rebellion, in which Satan is seeking to bring this whole world under his domain. That means when you were born into the kingdom of God, you were born into a war.

The Enemy's Goal

We are surrounded by our spiritual enemy, but the battle is not for anything physical. This cosmic battle is for *glory*. The issue is, Who is going to get the glory in this universe? Who is going to be worshiped?

Satan said to God, "You cannot have all the glory in creation. I want some of the glory for myself."

God's response was, "My glory I will not give to another" (Isaiah 48:11).

Satan said, "You are going to share glory with me. Let's go to war."

The battle is for glory, for the throne of creation. Praise God the outcome has never been in doubt, but the battle goes on every day in our personal, family, church, and community lives as to who will get the glory by what we do. That's why Paul told us, "Whatever you do, do all to the glory of God" (1 Corinthians 10:31; see Colossians 3:23). This is the essence of the battle.

The Enemy's Strategy

The fact that Satan has a plan is very clear. Ephesians 6:11 speaks of Satan's "schemes," and Paul said, "We are not ignorant of his schemes" (2 Corinthians 2:11).

Further on in 2 Corinthians, Paul outlined the schemes of the Devil. Speaking to this carnal church, the apostle wrote, "But I am afraid that, as the serpent deceived Eve by his craftiness, your minds will be led astray from the simplicity and purity *of devotion* to Christ" (11:3, italics added).

Satan's battle strategy is simple. He is out to deceive us, to trick us into buying his lies and temptations. He's been at his plan for countless years, and he's good at it. Paul even said that Satan can disguise himself as an "angel of light" (2 Corinthians 11:14).

The bottom line of Satan's strategy is that he wants you to think he is right; he wants you to follow him and not God. And not only is Satan good at what he does, he can give you a good time while he is deceiving you.

APPLICATION FOR LIFE

1. It is comforting to know that God is in complete control of His universe. But Satan desires to bring this world under his control. As part of his plan, he seeks to make our personal lives part of his domain. But as children of God, we must resolve to follow Jesus Christ and live for His glory lest we fall prey to the Devil's wiles. During your devotion time, ask God to cleanse your heart and mind and help you make certain you haven't given Satan any "handles" on your life.

2. As we know, temptation is part of our spiritual battle. Satan is a master at dealing out lies and counterfeit experiences. During the course of your daily routine, base your desires, thoughts, and decision making on the truth of God's Word. Give no inroads to Satan's deceptions and counterfeits. When temptation comes, as believers, we need to seek the counsel of the Scriptures and ask God for His help. Take to heart Ephesians 4:25–27.

3. Part of Satan's strategy is designed to catch us unaware, but God has equipped us for that part of the battle. Read over the Christian's list of armor in Ephesians 6:11–19 and "polish up" any piece of your armor that may have become a little rusty. Make it a point to continually guide your heart and mind by daily feeding upon Scripture reading and communing with God in prayer.

4. We know our flesh is weak, and we all have our unique weak spot. We can be assured that Satan is aware of those weak spots in our lives and can target those. If you don't know where you're prone to fall, ask God to show you your particular weak spot. Then go to God's Word and find verses to fortify you against it. Commit these verses to memory so they'll be available when you need them. A Bible concordance can help you find appropriate verses.

FOR GROUP STUDY

Questions for Group Discussion

1. In relation to the spiritual battle taking place, why is our worldview so important? Contrast the materialistic worldview with the spiritual worldview. In what ways does the materialistic worldview fail? How can we safeguard our worldview from being compromised by the world's materialistic influences?

2. Although spiritual in nature, the battle can have widespread impact in the physical realm. Dr. Evans mentions four areas on our lives where impact can occur. Examine Ephesians 4:25–27; 1 Corinthians 7:5; and 1 Timothy 4:1 As believers, what can we do in the course of our lives to minimize impact to those areas?

3. In Ephesians 6:12, Paul tells us that the battle takes place "in the heavenly places." Examine Ephesians 1:20; 2:6; and 3:10. In what ways are we, as believers, connected to the heavenly places? Why is this significant?

4. From Scripture, what do we learn about the Enemy's goals and strategy? (See Ephesians 6:11; 11:3; 2 Corinthians 11:14). Why is 1 Corinthians 10:31 the essence of the battle? (See also Colossians 3:23.)

PICTURE THIS

Without choice, we believers are engaged in a spiritual battle that impacts our physical lives. Although on the winning side, during the course of battle we can fall prey to the Enemy's strategy of deceit. But we need not be caught unaware, because God has given us provisions to resist the Enemy.

The Strategy of the Enemy

SATAN'S ACTIVITIES	THE BELIEVER'S RESPONSE
His title: "prince of the power of the air"	We are residents of heaven (Ephesians 2:6).
His goal: personal glory	We give glory to God (1 Corinthians 10:31; Colossians 3:23).
His strategy: lies and deception	We embrace the truth of God's Word and yield to the ministry of the Holy Spirit (1 Timothy 3:16; Ephesians 6:17; John 14:26).

51

THE ORIGIN OF THE BATTLE

I can honestly say I never felt safer than when I was in the Holy Land. The Israelis live with the realization that they are in a constant state of conflict. War could break out any day, even though everyone is talking about peace. Because the people of Israel live with the ever-present reality of physical conflict, everything they do takes that fact into consideration.

On the streets, civilians are practically surrounded by Israeli soldiers and various security people. The nation lives in a constant state of military readiness because its leaders understand that they are living on a battleground.

Even with this readiness, Israel still suffers some casualties. But imagine how the Israelis would suffer if they let down and started living as if they didn't have an enemy in the world.

When it comes to *spiritual* warfare, the reason there are so many casualties among believers is that we have lost sight of the fact that we are in a perpetual state of warfare, which demands constant alertness. There is another world, another dimension that sits outside our five senses, but it is equally real, equally dangerous. It is the spiritual realm, and there is a conflict under way in this realm that determines what happens in time and space.

To understand the origin of spiritual warfare, we have to go far back before recorded time, into eternity past, when God created a body of beings called angels. He created them like Himself, in that they are spirit beings and God is spirit (John 4:24).

We know that angels are magnificent beings from their appearances in Scripture. When a person saw an angel, he or she was usually overcome and fell to the ground. Angels are beings of great light, just as God's manifestations of Himself in the Bible are often accompanied by a bright light (see Acts 9). All the angels are awesome creatures, but one angel in particular was a special masterpiece—Lucifer, the "brilliant" or "shining one" or "star of the morning." We are introduced to Lucifer in Ezekiel 28.

Spiritual warfare began with Lucifer's rebellion against God in heaven.

THE CAUSE OF SATAN'S REBELLION

In Ezekiel 28:1–10, we are told of the king of Tyre, a human ruler who came under God's judgment because his heart was swelled with pride. He even tried to make himself like God.

Then in verse 12, we are introduced to the power behind this rebellious and prideful king. It was Lucifer himself, this great being who came to be called Satan, the Devil, Beelzebub, the accuser of the brethren, and so many other names and titles. Lucifer was the spiritual power influencing the king of Tyre.

Lucifer's Perfections

Ezekiel 28:12 begins a description of Lucifer before his rebellion against God. By understanding Lucifer before his rebellion, we'll have a better understanding of why he rebelled.

> You had the seal of perfection, full of wisdom and perfect in beauty. You were in Eden, the garden of God; every precious stone was your covering: the ruby, the topaz and the diamond; the beryl, the onyx and the jasper; the lapis lazuli, the turquoise and the emerald; and the gold, the workmanship of your settings and sockets, was in you. On the day that you were created they were prepared." (vv. 2–13)

This creature shone like the brilliance of the noonday sun. He was covered with every kind of precious stone. And he could sing! The Hebrew word *sockets* in verse 13 could be translated "pipes." Lucifer didn't just play the organ, he *was* the organ. When he opened his mouth to sing, he sounded like a million-dollar organ. After all, he was created to lead all the other angels in the praise of God. Lucifer was blameless, flawless, a masterpiece.

Lucifer's Exalted Place

Notice also that Lucifer occupied the most exalted place of all God's created beings. He was "in Eden, the garden of God." Verse 14 says, "You were on the holy mountain of God; you walked in the midst of the stones of fire."

Lucifer was near God's throne; he walked in God's holy presence. His access to God was awesome, greater than that of any of the other angels.

Lucifer's Lofty Position

Notice Lucifer's "job title": "the anointed cherub who covers" (v. 14). The cherubs, or cherubim, are the honor guard of the angels, the angels who have the responsibility to proclaim and protect the glory of God. They are the highest rank in God's hierarchy of angels.

Lucifer's Terrible Pride

But then came that terrible day when, like the queen in the children's fairy tale, Lucifer stood for too long in front of a mirror.

As Lucifer stood observing himself, he said, "Lucifer, you're *bad*. Look at that jasper. Look at these diamonds. You don't have to be number two up here. Look at all your glory. You don't have to lead the other angels in worshiping God. You deserve some of that worship yourself."

Ezekiel 28:15–17 tells us that Lucifer lost his perfections, his place, and his position because "unrighteousness was found in [him]" (v. 15). "Your heart was lifted up because of your beauty" (v. 17). Lucifer forgot that the only reason he was so beautiful was that God created him that way.

The angel who became Satan began to worship himself and wanted the rest of creation to worship him.

Lucifer's Diabolical Plan

When this shining angel chose to act on his pride, he began a plan of rebellion, a *coup d'etat*, against the throne of God.

Lucifer went to the angels and offered them the option of following him. He did this "by the abundance of [his] trade" (Ezekiel 28:16). What was his trade? His marketing effort among the angelic hosts, and one-third of the angels in heaven bought his plan (see Revelation 12:4).

Lucifer led a revolt of angels, but he failed because he found out that glory belongs to God alone. God says in Isaiah 42:8, "I am the Lord, that is My name; I will not give My glory to another."

The punishment Lucifer received is recorded briefly here in Ezekiel 28. He was thrown out of heaven and cast "to the ground" (vv. 16–17), the earth.

That's how Satan was in the garden of Eden, where he was apparently on hand when Adam and Eve were created.

THE CONTENT OF SATAN'S REBELLION

To understand the content of Satan's rebellion—the details of his plan—we need to look at Isaiah 14. We might describe the nature of the Devil's rebellion as negative volition. That is, Satan made some very bad decisions in his will. He exercised it five times when he said, "I will."

Isaiah 14 begins with God's pronouncement of judgment against a human king, in this case the king of Babylon (vv. 4–11). Then in verse 12 we read this statement: "How you have fallen from heaven, O star of the morning, son of the dawn! You have been cut down to the earth, you who have weakened the nations!"

This can be no one but the angel formerly known as Lucifer.

Why did God cut Satan down to the earth? God answers that in Isaiah 14:13–14. Satan reared up in rebellion and tried to tell God how things were going to be. Let's examine Satan's five volitional statements one at a time.

"I Will Ascend to Heaven"

"But you said in your heart, 'I will ascend to heaven'" (v. 13a). Satan didn't mean he wanted to take a tour of heaven. He already had access to the highest spot in heaven, the throne of God. He was already walking among the "stones of fire" (Ezekiel 28:14). But he wanted to take over.

"I Will Raise My Throne"

Satan's hostile intentions are obvious from his second boast: "I will raise my throne above the stars of God" (Isaiah 14:13b). Job 38:7 says the stars refer to angels. Satan wanted to rule over all the angels.

Satan wasn't in charge the way God was in charge. Lucifer was saying, "I'm tired of being the middle man between God and the angels. What I want to do is sit on the throne, give the orders, and accept some worship and glory."

"I Will Sit on the Mount"

Satan's third boast was, "I will sit on the mount of assembly in the recesses of the north" (Isaiah 14:13c). The Bible says that this mountain is the center of God's kingdom rule, where He controls the affairs of the universe (Psalm 48:2; Isaiah 2:2). Satan wanted to be managing the kingdom.

"I Will Ascend above the Clouds"

Then Satan said, "I will ascend above the heights of the clouds" (Isaiah 14:14a). The Bible associates clouds with the glory of God (Exodus 16:10; 40:34). His glory often appeared as a cloud. So the clouds are those things through which the glory of God is manifested.

Satan wanted glory. He wanted praise. He tempted Jesus by showing Him the kingdoms of the world and saying, "All these things will I give You, if You fall down and worship me" (Matthew 4:9). Satan wanted to be worshiped.

"I Will Be Like the Most High"

Here is Satan's fifth and last rebellious claim: "I will make myself like the Most High" (Isaiah 14:14b).

This is really the statement of a fool. Here is Satan, creature that he is, looking up at the all-knowing, all-powerful, all-present God and saying, "I'm going to be like Him."

For Satan to be like God would mean there would be two Gods. But that isn't going to happen. God says, "Before Me there was no God formed, and there will be none after Me" (Isaiah 43:10).

This idea of being like God was Satan's sin, and it was hideous. One reason it was so hideous is that he wasn't tempted to do this by anyone else. There was nobody around to tempt him. He came up with this plan all on his own.

THE CURSE OF SATAN'S REBELLION

God permitted Satan to carry out his rebellion, but He took control of the results. Satan raised himself up against God, but God slammed him to the ground. Satan learned that although he could control his decision, he couldn't control its consequences. We need to learn that too. You may do your thing, but after you do your thing God takes over. He controls the consequences.

The Devil's Immediate Sentence

Both Ezekiel 28 and Isaiah 14 address the judgment God carried out against His anointed cherub when Satan corrupted his character and sinned against God.

Let's go back to Ezekiel 28. When "unrighteousness was found" in Satan (v. 15), God expelled him from "the mountain of God" and took away his place amid "the stones of fire" (v. 16). "I cast you to the ground," God told him (v. 17).

We know that the mountain of God has to do with His throne, the place from which He rules. So Satan lost his privileged place near God's throne. He still has access to God's presence, as Job 1 reveals. But now he can only come to God as a "visitor." Satan has no place in heaven anymore.

The Devil lost his position as the "covering cherub" (Ezekiel 28:16). The stones of fire are the angels. Satan was removed from his exalted role as head of the angels.

He was also cast down to the ground, which Isaiah 14:12 tells us is the earth. Satan fell from heaven to earth, and he did not suffer his punishment happily. Revelation 12:12 warns those who dwell on the earth that Satan has come down with great anger, because he knows his time is short.

The Devil's Eternal Sentence

Isaiah 14:15 refers to Satan's ultimate sentence. "You will be thrust down to Sheol, to the recesses of the pit." Satan's eternal destiny is eternal fire.

Jesus stated this explicitly in Matthew 25:41. Speaking of His judgment on the Gentile nations at the end of the tribulation, Jesus said He will pronounce this sentence to those on His left hand: "Depart from Me, accursed ones, into the eternal fire which has been prepared for the devil and his angels."

The Devil's final judgment will be executed at the end of the millennial kingdom. "And the devil who deceived them was thrown into the lake of fire and brimstone, where the beast and the false prophet are also; and they will be tormented day and night forever and ever" (Revelation 20:10).

THE CONNECTION BETWEEN SATAN'S REBELLION AND SPIRITUAL WARFARE

What we have been talking about in this chapter is foundational to the reality known as spiritual warfare. This is such an important point that I want to show you how Satan's rebellion and his curse are related to the cosmic conflict in which we are engaged.

A Demonstration of God's Glory

When God permitted Satan's sin, and then judged him and his rebellious angels, He did more than just pronounce their curse. He decided in His eternal wisdom to demonstrate something very important to these rebellious heavenly creatures.

Satan attacked God's very throne and trifled with His glory. So God said to Satan, "I am going to demonstrate to you and to the angelic world My power and glory. I am going to unfold before your eyes a plan that will demonstrate I am not to be trifled with."

So Satan was expelled from heaven and demoted to the earthly realm. That's the situation when we come to Genesis 1 and the beginning of creation. This is where things get interesting, because this is where spiritual warfare really began.

Notice the familiar statement in Genesis 1:2 that "the earth was formless and void, and darkness was over the surface of the deep." How did the earth become that way? It likely happened when Satan was thrown out of heaven and down to the earth. Whatever Satan takes over becomes a garbage dump. The earth became a place of judgment because it became the holding cell for Satan and his angels until such time as their sentence is to be carried out.

Satan and his demons, the fallen angels, were limited to earth and its atmosphere as their primary realm of operation. They are still spirit beings, so they have access to the spiritual world. But their primary sphere of operation is earth.

So God decided to fix the wasteland called earth to demonstrate something very important to Satan and his demons and to the angels in heaven. Therefore, "the Spirit of God was moving over the surface of the waters" (Genesis 1:2).

God began to bring order out of the chaos. He created light to counter the darkness. He separated the waters from the dry land and began to dress the earth and fill it and the sea with all kinds of creatures.

Then God made a creature of lesser stature than the angels to demonstrate to all the universe that even though this creature did not have angelic ability, angelic power, or angelic experience, if this lesser creature would trust and obey God, he would go farther than an angel in heaven who refused to trust God.

Here, then, is the connection between Satan's rebellion and spiritual warfare. That lesser creature was mankind—you and me. God was saying to Satan, "I can take a creature of less beauty and ability than you, but who trusts Me, and I will do more with this weaker creature than you can do with all of your power." Psalm 8:5 can be translated, "You have made [man] a little lower than the angels," which is the translation and interpretation I believe is called for in the context.

With Satan listening, God said, "Let Us make man in Our image" (Genesis 1:26)—just as He had made Lucifer and the angels in His image in that they were spirit beings. And God announced to Satan, "I am going to put man in charge of your house. He will have dominion over the earth, and rule over the birds of the air and the fish of the sea."

A Demonstration of God's Justice

Let me give you a few more reasons that God permitted Satan to rebel and then judged him. God wanted to show His hatred of sin and His justice.

He wants us to see through all of this that He is a holy and perfect God who judges sin.

A Demonstration of God's Grace

Here's another key to God's plan. Satan and the angels who followed him spurned God's goodness and grace. So God wanted to show them the glory of His grace when it is received by repentant sinners. God permitted sin in order that His grace might be shown to be greater (see Romans 5:20).

A Demonstration of Hope

God also permitted sin to demonstrate that there is no meaning or hope in life apart from Him. He permitted Satan and us to have the ability to choose so that He could secure our obedience and service out of love, not out of fear.

This is spiritual warfare. God created mankind to rule the earth. Satan came to Adam and Eve to take it back. That's why God had to become a man in the person of Jesus Christ, because a man had to take the earth back from Satan. What we are experiencing on earth in terms of spiritual warfare has to do with something that is much bigger than we are.

APPLICATION FOR LIFE

1. The many negative and sinful influences of our culture are part of the spiritual conflict in which we find ourselves. Daily cultivate the mind of Christ by committing to memory verses of Scripture that provide strength for the battle.

2. Believers and unbelievers alike are all caught up in the spiritual conflict taking place. As believers, we should be doing and saying those things that bring glory to God and further His kingdom in this earth. Think of the people you associate with. Are they better off spiritually because of your influence on them, or are you worse off spiritually because of their influence on you?

3. Before you became a believer, your heart and mind were in rebellion against God. Do you know where Satan is most likely to trip you up and get you acting like the old you? Review your spiritual defense in this area and fortify as needed (e.g., avoiding certain places or turning off certain TV shows you know will be especially tempting to you).

4. The Bible tells us to humble ourselves before God (James 4:10; 1 Peter 3:6). Pride was Satan's sin, and it will bring us down as quickly as it brought him down. Because pride has a tendency to grow in our hearts, ask God to help you trim pride every day.

FOR GROUP STUDY

Questions for Group Discussion

1. Understanding the origin of the battle we face helps provide perspective. Read Ezekiel 28:1–10. It is our introduction to Lucifer. What insights do we gain into the character, power, and position of Lucifer?

2. From Ezekiel 28:1–10, what do we learn about the cause of Lucifer's rebellion against God? Is it possible that we might see some of the roots of Satan's rebellion manifested even in our hearts? What are some areas in which we are vulnerable?

3. Because of his rebellion, Satan was cursed with a twofold sentence. What were the immediate consequences of his rebellion? What are the long-term consequences? (See Isaiah 14:15; Matthew 25:41; Revelation 20:10.)

4. As Dr. Evans points out, Satan's rebellion and his subsequent curse and the cosmic conflict in which we are engaged are connected. What are some of the ways this connection is related to God's character and His eternal plan? Why is Romans 5:20 significant for us?

PICTURE THIS

Satan's rebellion was a choice—a conscious act of his volition. In fact, his hideous rebellion was played out in several stages. In Isaiah 14:13–14, we see the five "I wills" of Lucifer's rebellion.

REBELLION: THE "I WILLS" OF LUCIFER

SPECIFIC "I WILLS"	LUCIFER'S SINFUL DELUSIONS
"I will ascend to heaven"	He wanted to take over God's throne.
"I will raise my throne"	He wanted to rule over all the angels.
"I will sit on the mount"	He wanted to manage God's kingdom.
"I will ascend above the clouds"	He wanted God's praise and glory.
"I will be like the most high"	He wanted to be like God.

52

THE EXPANSION OF THE BATTLE

As we saw in the previous chapter, Satan launched a direct attack on the throne and the person of God. So God judged Satan and evicted him from his heavenly position.

But rather than just annihilate Satan, God decided to make him a spectacle before the entire universe. God wanted the angels and all of creation to see His wisdom and power in action.

God set His plan in motion when He created Adam and Eve and told them to rule over the earth. Satan had already been cast down to the earth, so the earth was now enemy territory as far as God was concerned. But God invaded Satan's territory by placing mankind on earth. Up to this point, the battle had been confined to the heavenly realm. Up to this point, the participants were all spirit beings.

But when Adam and Eve showed up, the battle expanded to the earth. And the list of combatants expanded to include the human race.

THE BATTLE LINES

According to Genesis 2:9, God filled Eden with every kind of tree imaginable for Adam's enjoyment and for food. In the middle of the garden God planted two particular trees, the Tree of Life and the Tree of the Knowledge of Good and Evil.

Genesis 2:16–17 records God's instructions regarding the forbidden tree. If Adam ate from it, he would "surely die." The Hebrew text is very strong. No question about it.

What God was doing was re-creating the conditions of the original spiritual battle in heaven. That is, He placed His perfect creatures, Adam and Eve, in a perfect environment, with everything they could ever want.

The point is that God now had a creature through whom He would demonstrate His power and His saving grace. But in order for God's grace to be made manifest, mankind had to have the power of choice. And in order for God to demonstrate His infinitely superior power, mankind had to be included in this angelic conflict called spiritual warfare.

This brings us to Genesis 3. Here was God's innocent couple, newly married, ready to serve Him and take planet Earth back from Satan. Satan had to make his move.

THE MODE OF ATTACK

So the Devil came at Eve with a subtle attack that cast doubt on the authority of God's word. "Now the serpent was more crafty than any beast of the field which the Lord God had made" (v. 1a).

Notice that the first conversation between a human being and the Devil was about God. Satan didn't ask Eve, "How is the weather?" He didn't want to know about her gardening, or how she liked being married to Adam. He said, "Let's talk about God."

Why? Because this is a spiritual battle. And mankind was about to be thrust right into the middle of it. God gave a command concerning the tree in Genesis 2:17. Satan challenged God's word in Genesis 3, and Eve was smack in the middle of the battle.

Questioning God's Word

Satan's first approach to Eve was to turn God's clear statement into a question. "Indeed, has God said, 'You shall not eat from any tree of the garden'?" (v. 1b).

Satan was saying, "Eve, has God placed any limitations on you? Has He said no to you about anything in the garden?"

God had said that Adam and Eve could eat freely from all the trees of the garden, except one. But Satan did not bring up the vastness of God's goodness. The Devil only wanted to discuss the one restriction God had placed on mankind.

Changing God's Word

When Satan asked Eve, "Has God put any limitations on you?" Eve responded, "From the fruit of the trees of the garden we may eat; but from the fruit of the tree which is in the middle of the garden, God has said, 'You shall not eat from it or touch it, or you will die'" (Genesis 3:2–3).

We know Eve is in trouble already, because she is talking with the Devil over what God said. In the process of doing so, she changes God's words at least three times.

First, Eve failed to mention that God said she and Adam could "freely" eat from all the other trees in the garden (Genesis 2:16). That omission minimized the provision of God. That word *freely* is very important, because God was saying, "All of creation is available to you at no cost. You may eat freely, abundantly, to your heart's content. I have provided all this for you." God wasn't just good to Adam and Eve, He was *very* good. It didn't cost them anything.

Second, Eve added the prohibition against touching the fruit. God never said anything about not touching it. Eve was turning God into a legalist. She was making God out to be a cruel killjoy who wouldn't even let her get near enough to the forbidden tree to feel its bark.

Eve's third change to what God said is a slight variation on the judgment He announced. God did not say, "Don't eat lest you die," as Eve repeated it to the Devil. That makes the judgment sound like merely a possibility. Eve weakened the penalty.

But God's word of judgment in Genesis 2:17 was much stronger than that. "You shall surely die." This is emphatic. Adam and Eve were *certain* to die if they disobeyed.

Contradicting God's Word

Now Satan was ready to deliver his major strike. He flatly contradicted what God said. "The serpent said to the woman, 'You surely shall not die!'" (Genesis 3:4).

Here Satan challenged God's truthfulness. "What God said won't really happen. He wasn't telling you the truth."

Satan didn't stop after delivering his frontal attack. He went on to tell Eve his version of what the real problem was. "God knows that in the day you eat from it your eyes will be opened, and you will be like God, knowing good and evil" (v. 5).

What did Satan want more than anything else? To be like God. He was trying to get Eve to repeat his sin. This was a powerful temptation.

Satan knew exactly what he was doing. The Tree of the Knowledge of Good and Evil, standing in the middle of the garden, was a daily reminder to Adam and Eve that they were creatures, not the Creator. They had to obey and answer to a higher authority. By offering Eve the forbidden fruit, Satan invited mankind to join him in his rebellion. The spiritual warfare Satan launched in heaven was about to be expanded to earth.

THE PLUNGE INTO SIN

As Eve listened to the serpent's line, she looked at the Tree of the Knowledge of Good and Evil. "When the woman saw that the tree was good for food, and that it was a delight to the eyes, and that the tree was desirable to make one wise, she took from its fruit and ate; and she gave also to her husband with her, and he ate" (Genesis 3:6).

This was not the first time Eve had seen this tree. But she had never seen it through Satan's eyes before. That was the difference.

The Entrance of Sin

The longer Eve looked at that tree, the more she just had to taste its fruit. She wanted to be what Satan wanted to be. She wanted to be like God. So she took the fruit and ate it. And then she said, "Adam, come here. I'm not going down by myself. This is a family thing." And he ate too.

The Results of Sin

The minute Adam and Eve ate the forbidden fruit, they died, just as God had promised. They became spiritually dead and alienated from God, just as Satan was alienated from God. And they fell under the curse of sin.

Our first parents knew right away that something was wrong. "The eyes of both of them were opened, and they knew that they were naked; and they sewed fig leaves together and made themselves loin coverings" (v. 7).

Sin produced immediate results. The Bible says that when Adam and Eve disobeyed, their fellowship with each other was broken. They were now conscious and ashamed of their nakedness. They hid their bodies from each other.

More important, their fellowship with God was broken, because the next time God came looking for them, Adam and Eve "hid themselves from the presence of the Lord God among the trees of the garden" (v. 8). They were now living in fear and shame. Their innocence was lost.

They had good reason to hide, because Adam's conversation with God in Genesis 3:9–12 brought out the truth: "I ate." The first pair disobeyed God because they let their feelings and desires take precedence over God's revelation.

The Curse of Sin

In one blink of time, the human race was handed over to the Evil One. Satan and mankind were now lined up against God in spiritual battle. So God began to take the situation in hand. He went down the line, pronouncing a curse against each participant in this first battle on earth.

The serpent was the first to be cursed. "On your belly shall you go, and dust shall you eat" (Genesis 3:14). God told this creature, "Do you want to be with the Devil? Fine. I am going to put you down on your face in the dust where Satan is. You are going to become like him—worm food."

Eve's curse was a painful one. "I will greatly multiply your pain in childbirth, in pain you shall bring forth children; yet your desire shall be for your husband, and he shall rule over you" (v. 16).

This last phrase of verse 16 is very controversial, but the curse fits the sin. Eve took over, grabbing the reins of leadership from her husband. She acted independently of Adam.

So God's judgment of Eve was twofold. She would experience pain in childbirth. Every labor pain would become a reminder of her rebellion. Every birth pang would remind Eve of what she forgot (which was the same thing Satan forgot): that she was the creature, not the Creator. She was not God.

Adam was the last to hear his curse. "Cursed is the ground because of you; in toil you will eat of it all the days of your life. . . . By the sweat of your face you will eat bread, till you return to the ground" (Genesis 3:17, 19).

Adam and Eve acted independently of God by eating the fruit. So God said to Adam, "Since you want to eat independently of Me, I am going to make it hard for you to eat now. You will have to work hard and sweat to earn your food."

When Adam and Eve let God feed them, He fed them abundantly and freely. But there were no more free meals now. Adam would have to go out and wrestle his food out of a cursed ground. He was going to have to work for a living. Although work itself was instituted before the fall, hard work is a perpetual reminder that when you rebel against God, there would be no more paradise.

This scene of judgment teaches us an important lesson for spiritual warfare: Rebelling against God isn't fun. All of a sudden, the thrill is gone. All of a sudden, that tree wasn't nearly as alluring to Eve as it had looked before. Now that chaos and destruction had set in, sin looked as ugly as it really is.

So God turned the earth over to mankind. But then Satan overturned that by tempting mankind to sin and bringing the human race and the earth back under his dominion. God could have wiped out the whole mess in judgment, but He had a better plan.

THE CURE FOR SIN

Now we're ready for the best part of the story.

God told the serpent, through whom Satan was working, "I will put enmity between you and the woman, and between your seed and her seed; he shall bruise you on the head, and you shall bruise him on the heel" (Genesis 3:15). A man from the seed of woman—Jesus Christ—would one day crush and destroy Satan.

In other words, God said, "Satan, this battle is not over. It may appear that you won this round. But I am not going to change My plan. I am still going to work through a human seed."

So the situation now is that the world contains two distinct seeds, two offspring, the children of the Devil who follow him, and the children of God who obey Him.

The Evil Seed

God guaranteed that His seed would win the final victory, but Satan—being the tireless adversary that he is—said, in effect, "We'll see about that, God. This war is not over. It will be my seed against Your seed from now on. I'm going to get started on my seed right away."

And he did. Genesis 6:1–4 describes a unique event. Satan sent "the sons of God," a group of his fallen angels, to cohabit with human women and produce a race of men called "Nephilim." Then the text says, "The wickedness of man was great on the earth" (v. 5).

The sons of God were the angels of Jude 6, those who did not keep to their own domain. They got together with women and had children who were evil and demonic. Satan was attempting to produce his own seed, his offspring. God judged these wicked angels by confining them in the abyss, but Satan has been trying to develop his seed ever since.

The Godly Seed

Adam had been judged, but God had another word for him (Genesis 3:20–21). Adam heard God's prophecy of a coming Savior (v. 15), and then the text says he named his wife Eve, "because she was the mother of all *the* living" (v. 20).

The last *the* in this verse is in italics, meaning it wasn't in the original language. Adam called his wife Eve because she was "the mother of all living." That's a powerful verse.

Adam was saying, "God, I believe that You are going to produce through my wife a seed that will crush the Devil's head. And the way You know I believe You is by the name I'm giving to my wife."

Then in verse 21, "The Lord God made garments of skin for Adam and his wife, and clothed them." God provided a sacrifice to cover their nakedness—and to cover their sin.

The Divine Covering

God judged Adam because he sinned. Adam would have to work the ground by his sweat until he died and returned to the dust himself.

But God also said there was going to be a seed of the woman who would engage Satan in spiritual warfare and, unlike Adam, emerge victorious.

Adam heard this and said, "God, I believe You. I'm going to name my wife in light of my belief that she will produce the seed who will fulfill Your promise."

So God said, "Because you have exercised faith, I am going to replace the leaves you sewed together by your own effort with My covering. Your covering will never work. Your covering will not solve the problem of sin. But I have a covering that will fix the problem."

Then God killed an animal, shedding its blood as a substitute for Adam and Eve. And God took the animal's skin and wrapped it around the two in the garden. Now they had divinely provided covering rather than humanly provided covering. God covered them in His righteousness, rather than letting them stay covered in their own righteousness.

This contest is the real heart of spiritual warfare—and the good news is that it's no contest! Because Jesus Christ is God, He could not help but emerge victorious. And to show us how we can win over Satan just as Jesus won over Satan, God allowed His Son to be tempted by the Devil (Matthew 4:1–11).

Jesus did everything right where the first Adam did everything wrong. Adam ate outside of God's will. Jesus refused to do so. Adam disobeyed God's word. Jesus obeyed it perfectly. So what the first Adam messed up, the last Adam fixed up.

So the *real* spiritual battle is already over and won. But Satan continues to fight, and he wants to take as many people down with him as he can. We must stand against him and defeat him the same way Jesus defeated him, through the power and Word of God. This is our battle.

The war is real, but isn't it great knowing you are on the winning side? If you know Christ, the curse of sin is lifted. You don't go from dust to dust. You go from dust to glory.

APPLICATION FOR LIFE

1. We live in a society corrupted by sin. As we battle a sin nature within and are constantly inundated by sinful influences, we are in the midst of the fray. But God has given us powerful resources to fight and win this battle daily. Make it a priority to set aside time (preferably at the start of the day) to feed upon the truth of God's Word and to commune with God in prayer. Aligning your heart and mind with God's truth will help you counter the attacks of the Devil and empower you to stay the course.

2. Many people are afraid to be alone and quiet because they have never learned how to think and meditate on the important things. Part of developing a new mind in Christ is spending time alone with the Lord so He can communicate His mind and heart to you. As soon as possible, finds some time to get alone and get quiet before the Lord. Listen for the "still, small voice" of the Spirit.

3. Because your mind absorbs whatever you put into it, you must also deal with any negative influences that are affecting your mind. Some are pretty easy to deal with. Turn off the TV, close the magazine, stop going to that place. Avoiding people who pull down may be a little harder, but if you know God wants you out from under their bad influences, ask Him to show you His "way of escape" (1 Corinthians 10:13).

4. As he did with Eve, Satan will go to any length with lies and falsehoods to tempt us to sin. We can be certain he knows our weaknesses. Jesus, when tempted by Satan (Matthew 4:1–11), countered each temptation by quoting Scripture. What an example for us! Make it a point to commit as much Scripture to memory as you are able, and lay hold of its truth as needed.

FOR GROUP STUDY

Questions for Group Discussion

1. Genesis 2:9, 16–17 sets the stage for the expansion of the battle—the human race. How has God set the stage for the inclusion of the human race?

2. In the garden of Eden, Satan used a subtle mode of attack with Eve. What was that mode of attack, and in what three distinct ways did he employ it? Can we see evidence that he still effectively employs this mode of attack today?

3. Read Genesis 3:1–19. How did the human race plunge into sin? What things changed immediately? What are the far-reaching effects of mankind's fall into sin?

4. God has provided a cure for sin. What are the two distinct seeds, and what is significant about each? Dr. Evans discussed the "divine covering." Why is this so important?

PICTURE THIS

In the garden of Eden, Satan attacked the actual word that God had given to Adam and Eve, attempting to corrupt its truth and intent. We need to beware, because the Devil uses the same strategy with us today.

SATAN'S ATTACK ON GOD'S WORD

God's Word: *"From any tree of the garden you may eat freely; but from the tree of the knowledge of good and evil you shall not eat, for in the day that you eat from it you will surely die" (Genesis 2:16–17).*

MODE OF ATTACK	SCRIPTURE PASSAGE	SATAN'S CORRUPTION OF THE WORD
Questioned God's Word	Genesis 3:1b	"You shall not eat from any tree of the garden?" (injected doubt)
Changed God's Word	Genesis 3:2–3	"From the fruit of the trees of the garden we may eat." (omitted the word "freely")
Contradicted God's Word	Genesis 3:4	"You surely shall not die!" (challenged God's truth)

53

THE SCOPE OF THE BATTLE

God created mankind to rule the earth and demonstrate His power to Satan and the angelic world. But now "the whole world lies in the power of the evil one" (1 John 5:19).

Satan has an agenda, which is to keep the world of unsaved people under his control and render Christians ineffective in spiritual warfare, bringing us down to daily defeat. Let's consider the scope of the battle.

SATAN'S FOUR FRONTS OF ATTACK

Satan is on the attack in four arenas of our lives. Since the garden of Eden, he has widened the battle to include all of life, and he is attacking on all four fronts simultaneously.

The Individual Front

The Devil's first battlefront is our individual lives. The apostle Peter said, "Be of sober spirit, be on the alert. Your adversary, the devil, prowls about like a roaring lion, seeking someone to devour" (1 Peter 5:8).

To put it bluntly, Satan is after you. No matter who you are or what your status, he wants to overthrow and defeat you. The Devil is after individual Christians, seeking to capture and destroy them spiritually.

The Family Front

The second front where Satan attacks the people of God is in their family life. When Satan tempted Eve, she gave the fruit to Adam, and the family came under the authority of hell. Then in Genesis 6, a group of fallen angels cohabited with women and produced offspring as part of Satan's plan to create a demonic family and race.

It should be obvious why the family is so important to Satan. According to God's curse on the serpent in Genesis 3, from then on the battle would be waged between the seed of the woman and the seed of the serpent. The offspring of these two lines, the godly line and the ungodly line, is key to the fight.

The Church Front

The enemy has also opened a third front, which is the church. Here he promotes disunity, division, and discrimination through things such as personality squabbles and power struggles, and through more serious problems such as doctrinal error, racism, chauvinism, and culturalism.

The Devil wants to split up the family of God, because Satan understands something that many Christians don't. He understands that God does not work in a context of disunity. There must be harmony in the body of Christ if we are going to see the power of God in action.

So if our enemy can split God's people along racial, class, gender, or cultural lines, if he can get people making decisions based on personal bias rather than on divine truth, he has won a major battle.

But when you're in a war, you don't care about the color, class, or culture of the person fighting next to you, as long as he is shooting in the same direction you are. Christians are in a common battle against a common enemy, so we'd better learn to get along.

The Society Front

Here's a fourth place where Satan has opened a battlefront. We get a glimpse of Satan's activity in the society at large in Daniel 10:13–14, where an angel reveals to the prophet Daniel that Satan is the energizing force behind the rulers of the nations.

Now don't misunderstand. I'm not saying that all human rulers are demonically inspired. It's easy to see Satan's power behind a Hitler or a Stalin and behind the various dictators and warlords who are destroying lives and nations today. Thankfully, not every nation is ruled by people like this. But it is important to recognize a spiritual warfare principle here. Since it's true that the whole world lies in Satan's power, then we have to recognize he exerts influence over the world's leaders and structures.

Once we understand this principle, we realize that the answer to our culture's woes lies much deeper than just electing the right person to office. That's certainly important, but there is a bigger battle going on here.

SATAN'S METHOD OF ATTACK

Satan not only knows *where* to get at us, but he also knows *how* to get at us. That's why we need to understand the method he uses to defeat us. In 2 Corinthians 10:3–5, the apostle Paul reveals the Devil's primary battle strategy. This is incredibly important information:

> For though we walk in the flesh, we do not war according to the flesh, for the weapons of our warfare are not of the flesh, but divinely powerful for the destruction of fortresses. We are destroying speculations and every lofty thing raised up against the knowledge of God, and we are taking every thought captive to the obedience of Christ.

The first thing Paul wants us to know is that we can't use secular or fleshly weapons to fight spiritual battles. The reason so many Christians are losing the battle is that they are trying to beat the Devil using the world's weapons. They are looking to the secular world to help them with their spiritual need.

Paul says our methods are not of the flesh because our enemy is not of the flesh. Some of us have been wrestling with things day in and day out for years. Those are battles, no matter what other name we may give to them.

An Attack on the Mind

The text we cited above tells us that Satan targets his attacks on our minds. We know that because Paul talks about "speculations," "the knowledge of

God," and "taking every thought captive" (2 Corinthians 10:5).

Where do speculations, knowledge, and thoughts come from? The mind. So the Christian must learn to think differently.

When Satan attacks a Christian's mind, he starts building what Paul calls "fortresses" ("strongholds" NIV). The Devil builds a place from which he can operate, and he means for that fortress to be permanent.

Satan makes himself at home, in other words, and he gets a grip on the mind until people begin thinking there is no way to overcome this problem, no way to save this marriage, no way to unify this church, no way to make a difference in our world.

A fortress or stronghold is a mind-set that holds you hostage. It makes you believe that you are hopelessly locked in a situation, that you are powerless to change. That's when you hear people saying, "I can't, I can't, I can't."

The only reason you say, "I can't," when God says, "You can," is that Satan has made himself at home in your head. In computer terms, he has you operating by the old information that was on the hard drive of your mind before you became a Christian. That's why Paul had to write this passage in 2 Corinthians. He wanted to help believers who had become trapped into thinking the Enemy's way—which all of us have done at one time or another.

The Formation of Partitions

How is Satan able to pull off this kind of influence in a Christian's mind? He does it by raising up "lofty thing[s]" (2 Corinthians 10:5). A lofty thing is a partition, a dividing wall.

Why does Satan want to raise up a partition in our minds? Because he wants us to be what James 1:8 calls "double-minded" people. He wants to divide our minds. When this happens, we keep that which is of God on one side, and that which is not of God on the other. We literally have two minds.

Satan's partitions are "raised up against the knowledge of God" (2 Corinthians 10:5). Satan wants to block divine information crossing over to the other side of your brain. He wants to block the knowledge of God in your life, to keep it from infiltrating the other side of the room.

Satan wants to block the knowledge of God in your life for the same reason he wanted to block the knowledge of God in Eve's life. He knows that if you ever take God seriously, you're going to live life as it was meant to be lived.

The Devil doesn't want you to do that. Instead, he wants to keep your mind divided. He wants to make you a spiritual schizophrenic.

A classic illustration of this kind of double-minded, partition thinking appears in Matthew 16:13–24, in the words and thoughts of the Peter the disciple.

When Jesus asked His disciples, "Who do people say that the Son of Man is?" (v. 13), they gave various answers. Then He asked, "But who do you say that I am?" (v. 15).

Simon Peter had the answer. "You are the Christ, the Son of the living God" (v. 16).

Peter was thinking with his right mind here. He knew who Jesus was, and he wasn't ashamed to say it. And Jesus not only commended Peter for his answer, but He also guaranteed that the church would be founded on Peter's confession, and He gave Peter the keys of the kingdom (vv. 17–19).

But then in the next breath, Peter became a tool of the Devil, when Jesus started telling His disciples that He was going to die and be raised again (v. 21). "Peter took Him aside and began to rebuke Him, saying, 'God forbid it, Lord! This shall never happen to You'" (v. 22).

Jesus' response to this schizophrenic saint was stunning. "He turned and said to Peter, 'Get behind Me, Satan!'" (v. 23). In other words, "I am not going to call you by your real name because right now you are thinking like the Devil. You are acting as his mouthpiece."

Peter thought he was speaking for God when he said, "God forbid it, Lord!" He thought he was representing God. But Satan had raised a partition in Peter's mind, and at that moment Peter had taken sides with the Devil.

THE GOAL OF OUR COUNTERATTACK

Satan wants to build his fortress in your mind, but he needs a piece of ground to build it on. He needs a corner of your mind where he can erect his stronghold.

But you don't have to yield any ground at all to the Enemy. God has given you and me the power to counter Satan's attack, to overrun and destroy his fortresses.

Tearing Down Fortresses

Back in 2 Corinthians 10:4, Paul says our spiritual weapons can destroy Satan's fortresses.

Weapons such as prayer, reading the Word, obedience, meditation on Scripture, fasting, and service can blow up the Devil's strongholds. And that's what we must do. These fortresses don't need to be remodeled. God doesn't tell us to capture them, change the locks, and use them for Him. Satan's fortresses must be torn down.

Destroying Partitions

We also need to pull down those lofty partitions (v. 5). These include "speculations," those rebel thoughts that take us far away from the knowledge of God. We must say, "This thought is from the Devil. I judge it in the name of Jesus Christ. Partition, come down."

You are not responsible for every thought that flashes into your mind. Satan can plant thoughts in our minds. But you are responsible for what you do with it once it is there. Our job is to recognize and dismiss evil thoughts.

Taking Our Thoughts Captive

That's the idea behind Paul's statement about "taking every thought captive to the obedience of Christ" (2 Corinthians 10:5). This is war language. When the Enemy sends us one of his thoughts, we need to grab that thought and take it hostage.

We can do this by telling ourselves, "This thought is not like God's thoughts. It is against God and His revealed will. No matter how good this thought makes me feel, no matter how much I may want to do it, it comes out of hell, sent from the Enemy. In Christ's authority I am going to make this thought my captive and dismiss it."

When we can do this successfully day in and day out, we are going to start winning some serious spiritual victories, because whoever controls the mind controls the battle. When you start taking all those roaming enemy thoughts captive, Satan no longer has any influence over you, and you are operating with the mind of Christ.

But you have to take each thought captive to Christ. No army can afford to have enemy troops running around loose behind its lines, wreaking havoc and sabotaging its weapons and defenses.

THE METHOD OF OUR COUNTERATTACK

This is the question we always face: Are we going to use human or divine methods? It saves a lot of time and grief to use God's method. Let's see what is involved in His method for countering Satan's attack on our minds.

Come to God in Faith

The apostle James has solid advice for us when we are facing a difficulty in life. If you need wisdom for your problem, James says, ask God (1:5). But you need to ask a certain way:

> But he must ask in faith without any doubting, for the one who doubts is like the surf of the sea driven and tossed by the wind. For that man ought not to expect that he will receive anything from the Lord, being a double-minded man, unstable in all his ways. (vv. 6–8)

The double-minded person, who is trying to operate from a human and divine viewpoint at the same time, knows what everybody else thinks and what God says, and is trying to entertain both views. That kind of person won't receive the answer he needs from God. You're wasting your time if you are trying to mix and match God's way with man's way.

Go to the Root

If we are going to counter Satan's attack with an offensive of our own, we need to address the root cause of the problem, not just the symptoms.

The root cause is not what someone is doing. A person may say, "I have a drug problem." No, you have a drug symptom. "I have a moral problem." No, you have a moral symptom. "I have an alcohol problem." No, you have an alcohol symptom. The symptom is what you do. The root is the thinking that makes you do it.

James says, "Draw near to God and He will draw near to you. Cleanse your hands, you sinners; and purify your hearts, you double-minded" (James 4:8). There are two things to do here.

Cleansing the hands refers to confessing and getting rid of the wrong things we are doing. This is why so many Christians' good intentions never get fulfilled. What they are doing is not the main problem. They need to fix the root that is producing the fruit.

See Sin God's Way

How do we fix our thinking? How do we cleanse our hearts?

James answers that in James 4:9–10. He says, "Be miserable and mourn and weep; let your laughter be turned into mourning and your joy to gloom. Humble yourselves in the presence of the Lord, and He will exalt you."

A lot of people misinterpret the promise at the end of verse 10. James is not saying that God will exalt you to some high position in society. He is saying that God will exalt you above your problem.

But before God can lift us up, He has to take us low. God wants us to weep and mourn over our sin. He wants us to start seeing our sin the way He sees it. When we do that, then we'll get the help that God gives. We will experience what the psalmist meant when he said, "The Lord is near to the brokenhearted and saves those who are crushed in spirit" (Psalm 34:18; see Psalm 51:17).

When God sees you go down low in mourning over your sin, He can reach down and pick you up. That's grace, God doing for you what you could never do for yourself.

Practice Warfare Praying

If all of this sounds foreign and even a little scary to you, I'd like to introduce you to a new way of praying. I want to help you begin to use God's Word like a sledgehammer to break down some walls and destroy some fortresses. Let me tell you about what is often called warfare praying. If we are going to be soldiers, we may as well learn to pray like soldiers.

This is a new way of praying for many believers. It is praying God's Word back to Him and standing on it for victory in spiritual battle and release for Satan's captives. God has such a high view of His Word that if you ever learn to pray His Word back to Him, you'll have power in prayer you never knew existed.

This kind of praying goes well beyond the safe, polite, general prayers that many people pray. We pray, "Bless me today, Lord. Be with me today." We make vague requests and offer bland sentiments that don't move the hand of God or make even a crack in Satan's fortress.

Are you praying about a problem or a situation that's so tough you wonder if it will ever be resolved? You say, "I hit it with the hammer of prayer one time, and nothing happened." Hit it again. Keep pounding on that wall with the Word of God until you see that first hairline crack. Then start praying even harder, because you know that wall is ready to come down.

Don't think I'm saying you have to do it all by your effort. Warfare praying is so powerful because our Helper is so powerful.

PERSONAL APPLICATION FOR LIFE

1. The family unit is one of Satan's targets of attack—Satan wants our families and the generations that follow. He loves to see divorce among Christian couples. If you are married, place God at the center of your relationship, and encourage each other in the Word. Never hesitate to take extra measures to guard the fidelity of your marriage.

2. As believers, we need to carefully guard our thoughts and cultivate the mind of Christ. When Satan attacks a Christian's mind, he starts building what Paul calls "fortresses," where he can continue to operate in our thinking. Guarding our minds at times requires that we courageously say no to certain activities and refuse to entertain harmful thoughts. Ask God to show you any areas of your thinking you may have left unguarded.

3. All believers are in a spiritual battle. Second Corinthians 10:4 speaks of the weapons of our warfare we may use to destroy the Devil's strongholds. They include prayer, reading the Word, obedience, meditation on Scripture, fasting, and service. The power behind these weapons is from God. Be watchful for any strongholds Satan be trying to build in your life.

4. Sin that lingers or is resident in our lives can be a sure foothold for Satan. There are times when we simply need to take inventory of our spiritual lives and ask God for forgiveness and to cleanse our hearts. If you don't know where to start, begin by praying Psalm 51:10–12 to God.

FOR GROUP STUDY

Questions for Group Discussion

1. Dr. Evans points out Satan's four fronts of attack (see 2 Corinthians 10:3–5). Discuss each of these. Why does Satan target those specific areas?

2. Read 2 Corinthians 10:4–5. What steps can we take to fortress our minds and build a stronghold that will withstand Satan's attack strategy?

3. As Dr. Evans states, "Our job is to recognize and dismiss evil thoughts."

What effective steps can we take to recognize and clear our minds of evil thoughts planted by the Devil?

4. What is "warfare praying"? Why is this kind of prayer so powerful in countering Satan's attacks? What would be a good example of this kind of prayer in Scripture?

PICTURE THIS

Spiritual warfare is ongoing; never static. It often requires that we take counteractive measures to guard our hearts and minds. The Word of God defines the counterattack measures we must take against Satan's attack strategy.

OUR COUNTERATTACK MEASURES AGAINST SATAN'S ATTACKS

COUNTERATTACK ACTION	SCRIPTURE PASSAGES	PURPOSE
Come to God in faith.	James 1:5–8	To ask God for wisdom.
Go to the root cause.	James 4:8	To correct the root cause of the problem.
See sin God's way.	James 4:9–10; Psalm 34:18; 51:17	To cleanse our hearts.
Practice warfare praying.	Matthew 4:1–10	To use the power of God's Word.

SECTION IV

The Authority for Spiritual Warfare

54

THE PURCHASE OF AUTHORITY

Satan is a powerful but defeated enemy, and we have authority over him in the name and the power of Jesus Christ. So we need to understand and put into practice all that Jesus has purchased for us by His death, resurrection, and ascension.

Therefore, I want to discuss three important things about Jesus and His purchase of authority for us: the person of Jesus, the payment of Jesus, and your position in Jesus.

THE PERSON OF JESUS CHRIST

When Adam sinned, God's promise of a seed from the woman who would crush the serpent's head (Genesis 3:15) was also a warning to Satan that the battle was not over. It appeared that Satan had won a big round, but someday a descendant of Eve would give birth to a baby who would crush Satan.

The Right Time for Jesus

The promise of Genesis 3:15 was made in the ancient past. But God made good on it one night in a stable in Bethlehem. Paul put it this way: "When the fullness of the time came, God sent forth His Son, born of a woman, born under the Law" (Galatians 4:4).

The One who purchased our authority over the Devil is God in the flesh. The Scripture is precise here. Paul said the Son was "sent," but the baby was "born." The Son existed before the baby was born. Isaiah said the same thing: "A child will be born to us, a son will be given to us" (Isaiah 9:6). The child had to come through the birth canal, but the Son already existed.

In the person of Jesus we have what theologians call the hypostatic union of deity and humanity, the two natures of Christ. The Son, the second Person of the Holy Trinity, was poured into humanity, the seed of the woman. The baby forming in Mary's womb was God in the flesh.

God had to have a man to fulfill the promise of Genesis 3:15—but this man had to be the kind of man who would not do what Adam did. He had to be the kind of man who could face the Devil one-on-one and never yield. What God needed was the God-man, Jesus Christ. So God sent His Son, born of a woman, to reclaim the dominion that Adam had handed over to Satan.

Satan's Attack on Jesus

Satan knew he was in trouble when the time came for Jesus to be born. So the Enemy pulled out all the stops in his warfare against the Savior.

Satan tried to foul things up before Jesus was born by subjecting Mary to humiliation and causing Joseph to divorce her. But the fullness of God's time had come, and Jesus was born. Then the Devil turned to King Herod for help, stirring him up to kill the babies in and around Bethlehem.

Remember, Satan does not possess all knowledge. He is not God's equal. In the birth of Jesus, God threw Satan the proverbial curveball. The Devil had been rolling along, defeating person after person because he knew there was no man who could handle him. But Satan didn't count on God becoming a man. That was part of the plan he didn't calculate. So the eternal God entered time and space as a Man. Satan tried to destroy Jesus, but none of his ideas worked.

When killing Jesus didn't work, Satan tried to overthrow Him by the temptation in the wilderness. The Devil tried to get Jesus to do the same thing Adam did, act independently of God.

And at one point Satan used the same tactic, food. Satan must be big on food. Satan told Adam and Eve, "Eat this fruit." He told Jesus, "Why don't You turn these stones into bread?" (see Matthew 4:3). Adam ate apart from God's will and failed. Jesus refused to eat outside of God's will and won the battle.

Jesus' Conquest of Satan

Why did Jesus have to go to all the trouble and suffering of fasting for forty days in the wilderness and then facing Satan head-on in intense spiritual combat? Why didn't Jesus just exercise His deity and destroy Satan right there in the wilderness?

For the same reason God did not crush Satan the moment he rebelled or in the garden of Eden. He had a different plan, one that would display His power and grace. Jesus had to win the battle as a man, as the seed of the woman.

In fact, Jesus lived His whole life on earth with the limitations of humanity. Jesus was fully God in His flesh, but He voluntarily submitted to the limits of humanity. Even when Jesus performed a miracle, He did it in dependence on His Father. Jesus lived as a man to demonstrate that He had the right to rule and to challenge Satan based on His obedience and dependence on God. Satan knew what Jesus was all about. So instead of just pulling out His deity, Jesus fasted in the wilderness for spiritual power, then pulled out God's Word and shut Satan down.

Satan wasn't finished, though. He had one more strategy to defeat Jesus—the cross. So according to Luke 22:3, Satan entered into Judas Iscariot, motivating him to betray Jesus Christ into the hands of His crucifiers.

Things looked bad for Jesus at the cross. But the cross did not catch God by surprise. He already had a plan in place that would turn what Satan thought was his finest moment into his worst defeat!

Jesus came "that He might destroy the works of the devil" (1 John 3:8). God would use the cross, an instrument of death and destruction, to destroy Satan's power and purchase for us all the authority we would ever need for spiritual victory.

THE PAYMENT OF JESUS CHRIST

In order to conquer Satan, Jesus had to conquer death, because death is Satan's weapon.

But to conquer death, Jesus had to pay for sin, since death is the consequence of sin. It was sin that brought death into the world, because God has decreed, "The soul who sins will die" (Ezekiel 18:4).

There's only one way to pay for sin, and that's through death. And there's only one way to conquer death, and that's through resurrection. You need resurrection power to conquer death. Somebody has to get up from the dead if death is going to be defeated.

This is what Jesus did in His payment for sin. He entered the realm of death, which is Satan's domain, and beat the Devil in his own territory. You know a person is powerful when he beats you on your own turf! Jesus said, "I will meet Satan at the place he owns, which is death."

Canceling Our Debt

Paul describes our problem and the payment Jesus made for sin:

> When you were dead in your transgressions and the uncircumcision of your flesh, He made you alive together with Him, having forgiven us all our transgressions, having canceled out the certificate of debt consisting of decrees against us and which was hostile to us; and He has taken it out of the way, having nailed it to the cross. (Colossians 2:13–14)

We were dead in sin and without hope, because we had a "certificate of debt" posted against us. This is a very significant phrase.

In Roman law, when a person was convicted of a crime and sent to prison, a list of his offenses was drawn up and posted on his cell door. This was his certificate of debt, showing why he was in prison. Anybody who walked by his cell could see why a person was in prison because of the certificate of decrees.

Jesus Christ had a certificate like this posted over His cross. Pontius Pilate had a sign posted on the top of Jesus' cross, written in Hebrew, Greek, and Latin: "Jesus of Nazareth, King of the Jews."

As far as the crowd was concerned, Jesus was being crucified for treason against Rome. The Jewish nation wanted Him put to death for blasphemy because He called Himself God. And as far as Satan was concerned, he was eliminating the seed of the woman who was going to crush him.

But little did Satan know there was another certificate of decrees posted above Jesus' cross. This was a divine certificate, drawn up by God, bearing the name of Tony Evans and every other person who has ever lived or who will ever live. This certificate contained every sin of every person, and every charge on that certificate was valid. We were hopelessly guilty—and the sentence for those sins was death.

But Jesus bore the punishment for all of those sins. He took our guilt. The Bible says that Jesus Christ did not die as innocent, but as guilty. "[God] made Him who knew no sin to be sin on our behalf, that we might become the righteousness of God in Him" (2 Corinthians 5:21).

Now we get to the good part. When a criminal had finished his sentence and paid his debt to society, his certificate of decrees was taken off his cell door and stamped with one Greek word: *tetelestai*, "paid in full." The certificate was canceled (Colossians 2:14) and handed to the former criminal, so he could prove to anyone who asked that he was now free. Those charges could never be brought against him again.

What were Jesus' last words on the cross? "It is finished!" (John 19:30). This was actually just one word: *"Tetelestai!"* The debt that you and I owed to God was paid by Jesus Christ, completely.

Announcing the Victory

Jesus' death took care of the sin problem. God's wrath against sin has been satisfied, and He is now free to declare us forgiven because the debt has been paid.

But there was still an authority problem. Jesus had to deal with the question of who is in charge in the universe. That brings us to what happened between the time of Jesus' death and His resurrection. This is "the rest of the story."

Jesus not only purchased the forgiveness for our sins by His death, but He also reclaimed the authority of the universe that Adam had relinquished by his sin (Matthew 28:18).

Satan and his demons in the underworld needed to hear the announcement of Jesus' victory. So did the saints who had died before Calvary and were in a place called "paradise" or Abraham's bosom (Luke 16:23). So while Jesus' body was lying in the tomb, Jesus in His spirit went to hades.

In the Bible, hades is not the same as the lake of fire, or eternal hell. Hades was the temporary abode of those who died before the coming of Christ. Everyone who died before Calvary went to hades because hades had two compartments in it.

Jesus' story of the rich man and Lazarus in Luke 16 is the clearest picture we have of this temporary arrangement. Lazarus died and went to paradise, but the rich man died and woke up in torment (Luke 16:23). The two could see each other, but they were separated by "a great chasm" (v. 26).

Why didn't Lazarus go to heaven as we know it, and the rich man to the eternal lake of fire? Because God was still operating on the "layaway" plan—the Old Testament system that provided only a temporary holding place. It was not until the death of Christ that the final matters relating to eternal destiny were settled.

But Jesus made the final payment on the layaway plan. What happens when you make the last payment on a layaway? You get to take the merchandise home with you. That's exactly what Jesus did, according to Ephesians 4:8. "When He ascended on high, He led captive a host of captives." Jesus went in spirit to the paradise compartment of hades and announced to those Old Testament saints, "I have paid the price. It's time to go home."

Then He led those saints in a great march to heaven in the greatest "shuttle service" in history. This is why Jesus could tell the thief on the cross, "Today you shall be with Me in Paradise" (Luke 23:43).

But that was not all. Jesus also visited the torment side of hades, where He announced His victory to the lost souls in hades and the Devil and his crew (1 Peter 3:18–20). Jesus' proclamation was, "Satan, I declare total victory over you."

Satan didn't count on the fact that the death of Christ would satisfy God's justice in such a way that God could show His love to sinners without compromising His holiness. To put it another way, Satan was aced by grace.

Getting God's "Receipt"

When you pay the price for something, you get a receipt to show that the purchase was made and the full price was paid. You don't want any doubt. You don't want anyone to think that you did not really pay for the merchandise. Your receipt is your proof. God gave us a receipt to prove that Jesus paid the price for sin and to show that His payment was accepted. That receipt is the resurrection.

Early on Easter Sunday morning, when Mary Magdalene came to anoint the body of Jesus, she discovered that He had risen. And then she met Him in the garden and ran to tell the disciples that the Lord had risen.

The resurrection was proof that God was satisfied with Jesus' death and payment for sin. Several times in the book of Acts, the apostles appealed to the fact that God raised Jesus from the dead to prove that He was the Christ. Peter said there were many witnesses who saw the resurrected Christ (Acts 2:32).

Disarming Satan

So what did Jesus' victory do to Satan? Go back to Colossians 2:15, where Paul writes: "When He had disarmed the rulers and authorities, He made a public display of them, having triumphed over them through Him [Christ]."

When Jesus rose from the dead, Satan was disarmed. He was stripped of his weapons (the literal meaning of "disarmed"). He lost all of his ammunition, and he was rendered powerless (Hebrews 2:14).

Jesus Christ went into Satan's territory of death and took away the captives of death who were waiting in paradise. Then Jesus beat death Himself by rising from the dead. And he took away the fear and the pain of death for all of those who believe in Him.

Satan's best weapon was deactivated. The roaring lion (1 Peter 5:8) had his teeth pulled out. The devouring lion was overcome by the Lion of the tribe of Judah, and now Satan is on a leash. We now have authority over Satan, not in and of ourselves, but because we belong to Christ.

APPLICATION FOR LIFE

1. Jesus' last words on the cross were "It is finished." This is actually one word in the original language: *tetelestai*. It carries the meaning of an act that is finished and that remains finished. Jesus' sacrifice may have occurred in time and space, but its results will last for eternity! We may never fully understand the depth and breadth of His sacrifice, but we can certainly take a moment to thank Him for His love toward us.

2. As believers on God's victorious side, we do not fight for victory. Rather, we fight *from* victory. As a believer, you may pray this prayer: "Lord, by faith I am going to live in Christ's authority, trusting in His blood to give me power over any attacks from the Evil One."

3. Tomorrow morning Satan is going to be in your face again. As always, he will try to devour you, to ruin your testimony, and to capture your children. So when you get up tomorrow morning, get up in the authority of Jesus Christ! Start your day in the winner's circle.

4. Here's an encouraging thought that will make your day. Jesus Christ wanted a love relationship with you so much that He pursued you for it! His sacrificial death on the cross gave you the greatest gifts ever—forgiveness for your sins and everlasting life.

FOR GROUP STUDY

Questions for Group Discussion

1. The apostle Paul uses the phrase "when the fullness of time came" (Galatians 4:4). What does it signify? What Old Testament promise does it fulfill?

2. Why did Jesus have to die? What did His death purchase? How did Jesus' sacrificial death directly impact Satan and his agenda? (See Hebrews 2:14.)

3. When Satan became aware that God was sending a Savior, in what ways did Satan try to attack Jesus? What was he trying accomplish with his attacks?

4. Jesus purchased the forgiveness of our sins by His death. What is the receipt that shows that the price was paid in full and that His payment was accepted?

PICTURE THIS

Because of Jesus' payment for our sins, we have a new position in Christ that brings some special benefits related to Christ's authority.

OUR POSITION IN CHRIST

"But God . . . raised us up with him and seated us with him in the heavenly places in Christ Jesus" (Ephesians 2:4, 6).

BENEFIT	WHAT IT MEANS
We share in Christ's triumph	God has partnered with us to share His victory with us.
We exercise Christ's authority	We can exercise our authority under God's authority to defeat Satan.
We fight from victory	By faith, we can live in Christ's authority and His power over the attacks of Satan.

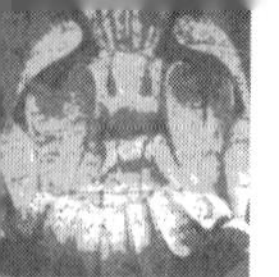

55

THE AGENCY OF AUTHORITY

A married woman's loyalty doesn't belong to her father anymore. Any demands he makes on her life are now illegitimate. The woman must give her allegiance to her husband, not her daddy. She is under a new authority because she has a new identity.

Before we knew Jesus Christ, we were the Devil's children. He dominated our lives; he told us what to do. But then one day we met Jesus, and there was a marriage. We transferred our identity to Him through salvation and came under His authority. Hell no longer had a claim on us.

But Satan is like a domineering parent who doesn't want to give up his ownership. He wants to maintain dominance in your life, even though you are now someone else's bride and you belong to Jesus Christ.

CHRIST HAS DELEGATED HIS AUTHORITY TO THE CHURCH

The first thing we need to understand is that Jesus Christ has delegated great spiritual authority to the church. In fact, let me say it in a stronger way. The church, *and only the church*, has been delegated spiritual authority by Christ.

The passage in which Jesus delegated His authority to the church is also the earliest mention of the church in the New Testament:

[Jesus] began asking His disciples, saying, "Who do people say that the Son of Man is?" And they said, "Some say John the Baptist; and others, Elijah; but still others, Jeremiah, or one of the prophets." He said to them, "But who do you say that I am?" And Simon Peter said to him, "You are the Christ, the Son of the living God." And Jesus answered and said to him, "Blessed are you, Simon Barjona, because flesh and blood did not reveal this to you, but My Father who is in heaven." (Matthew 16:13b–17)

The Delegator of Authority

Notice first who it is that is delegating this authority. The people were guessing that Jesus was one of the great prophets of the past.

Peter said to Jesus, "We've already discussed this issue, and let me tell You what we have concluded. You are the Messiah, the Christ, Son of the living God."

Jesus then told Peter and the other disciples, in effect, "You are right. Now let Me show you what I am going to do as the Messiah and Son of God." This is where we get to the church: "And I also say to you that you are Peter, and upon this rock I will build My church; and the gates of Hades shall not overpower it" (Matthew 16:18).

The Builder of the Church

This is the first occurrence of the word *church* in the New Testament. This Greek word, *ekklēsia*, was used of an assembly of citizens who gathered together to make governmental decisions in a city or district. It was also used of a congregation gathered for religious purposes in Israel, such as in a synagogue.

Here Jesus declares that He is going to build something so awesome that even hell won't be able to stop His building program. Since Peter was the one to confess Jesus as Lord and Savior, Jesus used a wordplay on Peter's name to specify the foundation on which He would build His church. Stay with me for a few paragraphs, because this is important.

The church was not built on Peter. In the Greek text, Peter's name is *Petros*. The rock on which Jesus promised to build His church is the word *petra*.

The word *Petros* means "stone." *Petra* is a feminine form of the word for rock or stone, so it couldn't refer to Peter. The classical Greek word *petra* meant a group of stones that had become connected to form a rocky cleft or a large slab. So this word has to do with the coming together of many stones.

Jesus was saying, "Peter, I am going to build My church on your confession of Me as Lord." The church is made up of people who confess the Lord Jesus as Savior, a group of individual stones who come together to form a solid rock that will roll over hell! Peter later described the church as "living stones [who] are being built up as a spiritual house" (1 Peter 2:5).

The only church that can overcome the onslaughts of hell is the church that Jesus is building—a community of believers who cross racial, cultural, and class lines (Ephesians 2:14). If you and I have our own agenda, call it what you want, but it is not a church. The church is Jesus' church. That means He sets the agenda. He must be the authority.

The one thing that hell can't stop is the church. It can stop anything and everything else, but it can't stop the church because it's what Christ is building.

On the Offensive

It would be great if Satan would stop tempting us. But that isn't going to happen, because the Devil isn't going to stop being what he is. He is always going to be the Devil.

But Jesus makes clear in Matthew 16 that it is hell, not the church, that is on the defensive. The church is moving out, on the offensive. It is hell's job to stop the church, not vice versa.

So instead of looking at what Satan is doing, we need to take a close look at what Christ has done in building His church. When you understand what Christ has done, you can be on the offensive. When you gather with other believers at church, you come to a place of victory, not a place of defeat.

Assaulting the Gates

The church has the authority of Jesus to assault "the gates of Hades." What does Jesus mean by the imagery of gates?

In the ancient world, the gates of a city were the place of authority. The elders of the city met at the gates to make decisions. It was like our city hall. So the gates of hades are the place where Satan and his demons have met together to try to set hell's agenda. Hades is the abode of the dead.

Whenever Satan moves against you, he always moves in the realm of death, because "the wages of sin is death" (Romans 6:23). And even if Satan doesn't kill you physically, he wants to ruin you spiritually. He wants you to live in the sphere of death.

The Keys of the Kingdom

Jesus said, "I will give you the keys of the kingdom of heaven; and whatever you shall bind on earth shall have been bound in heaven, and whatever you loose on earth shall have been loosed in heaven" (Matthew 16:19).

Keys are a symbol of authority in the Bible (see Isaiah 22:22; Luke 11:52). The one who has the keys has access, which translates to authority.

The keys Jesus was talking about belong to the kingdom of heaven. Why is the word *keys* plural? Because the gates of hades are plural. Keys can open locked gates. Jesus is saying that for every hellish gate, there is a corresponding heavenly key.

The church of Jesus Christ has been given the keys of the kingdom of God. It has been given access to heaven, so that whatever the church declares on earth, if it agrees with the kingdom of God, has already been determined in heaven.

In other words, there is a backup for the things you do on earth that are in concert with the kingdom. If you are doing kingdom business, if you are a kingdom Christian living a kingdom life, then you can have kingdom victory.

There's a good example of what it means to be on a kingdom agenda in Matthew 16. After Peter's confession, Jesus told His disciples that He was going to the cross.

Peter rebuked Jesus for saying this, but Jesus turned and said to Peter, "Get behind Me, Satan!" (v. 23). Jesus called Peter the Devil because Peter was trying to stop Jesus from carrying out God's agenda.

Jesus let Peter know that he was operating on Satan's agenda, not on

God's kingdom agenda. Peter thought he was helping God by trying to stop Jesus from going to the cross. But in reality, to try to turn Jesus away from the cross was to cooperate with the Devil, since Satan's goal was to keep Jesus from accomplishing what He came to do.

THE CHURCH HAS BEEN EXALTED TO A POSITION OF AUTHORITY WITH CHRIST

Here's a second principle you need to understand about the church. Jesus Christ has not only delegated His authority to the church, but He has elevated the church to a position of authority that takes us far above all other powers, including Satan.

Jesus Is in Charge

The reason Jesus can raise the church to such an exalted position of authority is that He Himself was raised triumphantly from the dead and enthroned in heaven over all principalities and powers. In other words, Jesus is firmly in charge.

Paul wanted the church at Ephesus to understand this, so he prayed this prayer for the church:

> I pray that the eyes of your heart may be enlightened, so that you will know what is the hope of His calling, what are the riches of the glory of His inheritance in the saints, and what is the surpassing greatness of His power toward us who believe. These are in accordance with the working of the strength of His might which He brought about in Christ, when He raised Him from the dead and seated Him at His right hand in the heavenly places. (Ephesians 1:18–20)

Paul was praying that the church at Ephesus would understand what they had and who they were associated with. He was praying that the church would understand what took place when Jesus Christ was raised from the dead.

What happened is that the risen and ascended Christ now possesses all authority in heaven and on earth (Matthew 28:18). He is in charge of the universe. Paul goes on to say that Christ is exalted "far above all rule and authority and power and dominion, and every name that is named, not only in this age but also in the one to come. And He put all things in subjection under His feet" (Ephesians 1:21–22a).

Like a conquering general, Jesus has His foot on the neck of His enemies. Everything and everyone on earth and under the earth is subject to Him.

God the Father raised Jesus and seated His Son at His right hand, the place of ultimate authority. He runs the show.

Many say that the United States is the only superpower left in the world today. That makes the president the most powerful man in the world.

But the reality is that there is only one superpower in this universe, and it's the kingdom of God. And since Jesus Christ is sitting in the position of authority in this kingdom, He is in charge.

We Are Raised with Jesus

According to Ephesians 2:6, believers have been raised up and exalted with Christ. God did not just give you new life when He saved you. God brought the church along when He raised Jesus from the dead and seated Him in the place of authority in the heavenly places.

So if Jesus Christ is in charge, and we are exalted with Him, then we ought to be exercising His power and His authority. If we aren't, something is wrong. Something is out of whack, because Ephesians 2:6 says that where Jesus is, you and I are. The church has been raised with Christ.

Jesus Has the Keys

By virtue of His death, resurrection, and ascension, Jesus Christ has gained possession of another important set of keys.

These are called "the keys of death and of Hades" (Revelation 1:18). They are possessed by the One who was dead and is now "alive forevermore."

Who had the keys of death and hades before Jesus died and rose again? Satan had them. We saw in the previous chapter that death is Satan's domain. Hades was his prison house for the spirits of the dead.

So how did Jesus take the keys of death and hades from Satan? While

Jesus' body was in the tomb, He went in spirit into hades itself, as we learned earlier, and freed Satan's captives. Jesus conquered death, and then He conquered him who had the power of death, the Devil (Hebrews 2:14).

No wonder Paul asks, "O death, where is your victory? O death, where is your sting?" (1 Corinthians 15:55). It's all gone, because Jesus Christ went into Satan's house and took that bad boy's keys away from him!

Jesus has all the keys, and all the authority. And He is sharing that authority with believers like you and me through the church, which is seated with Him in the position of authority.

Satan Is Powerless

If the church has been exalted with Christ above all authorities and powers, where does that leave Satan and his demons?

It leaves them defeated, disarmed, and totally powerless, that's where. Hebrews 2:14 says that although Satan once had the power of death, he has been "render[ed] powerless" by the death and resurrection of Jesus Christ.

This is why Satan must function largely by deception. Of course, Satan can still hurt us while we are on this earth, but ultimately his real weapons have been taken away from him. All the lion has left is his roar. With the resurrection of Christ, Satan's spiritual graveyard was robbed (Ephesians 2:4–6).

THE CHURCH IS TO EXHIBIT THE AUTHORITY OF CHRIST

Here's a third principle about Christ's church. As the agency of God's authority in this age or dispensation, the church is being called to put His authority and power on display to the world, to the angels, and to the Devil.

The Mystery of the Church

Paul says in Ephesians 3:9 that the church is "the mystery which for ages has been hidden in God."

For all the ages of history, God had a secret He wasn't telling anyone. A mystery in the Bible isn't something that's hard to figure out. A biblical mystery is something previously hidden that has now been revealed.

Paul says the church was God's mystery, kept hidden until His time to reveal it. And why was the mystery of the church revealed? Paul answers that in verse 10: "So that the manifold wisdom of God might now be made known through the church to the rulers and the authorities in the heavenly places."

God demonstrated His "multicolored" wisdom through the church. That's what the word *manifold* means. God's wisdom is multicolored.

What a tremendous statement! God has unveiled His great mystery—which is that by His grace He would save unworthy sinners of every race and language and bring them together into a brand-new community called the church.

Grace was the "curveball" God threw at Satan. The Devil didn't count on grace. All Satan knew was that all of us had sinned and rebelled against God the way he had sinned and rebelled. And Satan knew that a holy God could not tolerate sin but had to judge it—the way He judged Satan.

But God had a surprise for Satan: His grace. God demonstrated something marvelous to the entire angelic realm. He sent His Son to redeem lost people and bring them into a new relationship with Him through a new entity called the church.

Peter says the angels are looking at the church, trying to figure out how God's grace works (1 Peter 1:12). They had never seen grace before, and now they are looking at us in wonder.

Good Exhibitors

If the church is Exhibit A of God's grace and power and authority, guess what? We should be good exhibitors of His, showing off His power and authority over the world, the flesh, and the Devil. We should be exercising Christ's authority, because we are seated with Him above the "principalities and powers" that are causing our problems in the first place.

Since we have been raised with Christ, the church should be demanding its territory back from Satan. He's like a squatter who is illegally occupying ground he shouldn't be occupying. But Jesus Christ has issued Satan an eviction notice. It's time for the Devil to get off the property.

Jesus has sent the church to deliver the notice and evict the squatter. Jesus provided all the legal authority we need to overcome Satan. Our job is to exercise that authority—to invade Satan's territory, declare to him what the eviction notice says, and put his furniture out on the street.

Power Versus Performance

If you have ever seen a circus arrive in town, you have seen the elephants standing out in a parking lot or somewhere, tethered around one leg with a chain attached to a peg in the ground.

These elephants are huge, powerful beasts. Any of them could rip that peg out of the ground anytime they feel like it. They certainly have the power.

But the elephants don't budge. Do you know why? Because since they were little baby elephants, they have been taught that when the trainer puts that chain around their leg, they have no power to do anything. Why are the elephants chained up? Because they are in town to perform, not to demonstrate their power.

But the church is not in town to perform. Christ has delegated His incomparable authority to us. He has exalted the church with Himself and put us on display as Exhibit A of His grace and power. It's time for you and me to pull that peg out of the ground and begin walking, talking, and acting like who we are in Christ. He has set us free (John 8:32)!

PERSONAL APPLICATION FOR LIFE

1. Jesus said, "I am the way, and the truth, and the life" (John 14:6). As believers, we are alive in Christ! When Satan moves against us, he does so in the realm of death (see Romans 6:23). He wants us to live in the sphere of death where he can ruin us spiritually. But do not let the Enemy deceive you. You are a kingdom Christian living a kingdom life. Claim kingdom victory and don't allow sin a place in your piece of the kingdom.

2. Take the offensive! When Satan tempts us, God does not intend for us to be weaklings cowering in the corner. Jesus said that it is that hell is on the defensive, not the church (Matthew 16). Don't neglect to gather and worship with other believers. When you come together with other believers, you come to a place of victory, not defeat.

3. When God saved you, He gave you a new life in Christ. But there's more. You are also part of Christ's church, the body of believers. That means you are seated with Christ in the place of authority in the heavenly places (Ephesians 2:6). If you are not exercising His power and authority in your life, ask God to show the next thing to do so you can get started.

4. Hebrews 2:14 tells us that Satan has been rendered powerless by the death and resurrection of Jesus Christ. That means his real weapons have been taken away. But he is a master at deception, so don't underestimate the spiritual damage he can still inflict with his weapons of deception. Still, with God's help, you can resist temptation and choose not to be defeated.

FOR GROUP STUDY

Questions for Group Discussion

1. Jesus has delegated great spiritual authority to the church. Read Matthew 16:13b–17. What is the significance of *ekklēsia*, the Greek term for *church*? What is the main point of Jesus' teaching in these verses?

2. In Matthew 16:19, Jesus speaks of the "keys of the kingdom." Who holds the keys? What are these keys, and why are they important? (See Revelation 1:18.)

3. According to Ephesians 2:6, believers in Christ have been raised up and exalted with Him. What responsibility does that place on the church? Do you believe the church today is effectively doing its part in demanding back territory back from Satan?

4. What did Paul mean when he used the term *mystery* in Ephesians 3:9–10? To what was he referring? Why was this mystery a surprise to Satan?

PICTURE THIS

Because Christ has ascended, He now possesses all authority in heaven and on earth. The structure of Christ's authority includes His church.

THE CHURCH'S POSITION OF AUTHORITY WITH CHRIST

THE AUTHORITY	SCRIPTURE PASSAGE	WHAT IT MEANS
Jesus is in charge.	Ephesians 1:18–20	He was raised from the dead and is now enthroned in heaven.
We are raised with Jesus.	Ephesians 2:6	We are seated with Jesus in the place of authority in the heavenly places.
Satan is powerless.	Hebrews 2:14	The death and resurrection of Jesus Christ has left Satan defeated, disarmed, and powerless.

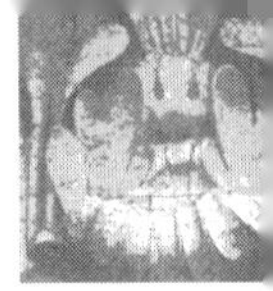

56

THE WEAPONS OF AUTHORITY

The source of our authority as believers is "the full armor of God" (Ephesians 6:11). We each need to know how to become equipped with this armor. To fully wear this spiritual armor, we need to unfold Ephesians 6:10–17. As we do so, you will learn about the nature of our armor, the need for our armor, and the names of the pieces of our armor.

THE NATURE OF OUR ARMOR

Paul doesn't waste any time in spelling out the nature of the armor you have for spiritual warfare. It's "the full armor of God" (Ephesians 6:11). The armor is something God gives us, not something we put together on our own.

But before Paul gets to the armor, he gives us an important exhortation: "Be strong in the Lord and in the strength of His might" (v. 10).

"Be strong in the Lord" is a passive command. That means God supplies the strength, not you. It's His battle. Your job is to put on the armor He supplies, to "dress for success."

The armor is all from God. Our job is to "dress up" in Jesus every day.

That's exactly what Paul says in Romans 13:11–14. He tells us to wake up from our spiritual sleep and put on "the armor of light" (vv. 11–12).

What is the armor of light? Paul explains it in verse 14 when he says, "Put on the Lord Jesus Christ." So if you want to dress for success in spiritual warfare, put on Jesus when you get up every morning, and the Devil won't be able to hang with you.

THE NEED FOR OUR ARMOR

Let's talk about our need for the armor of God as Paul explains it in Ephesians 6. He writes, "Put on the full armor of God, that you will be able to stand firm against the schemes of the devil" (v. 11).

The key phrase here is "stand firm," which Paul repeats in verses 13 and 14. The reason you need to put on your armor is because of your enemy, because of Christ's victory, and because of the coming "evil day" (v. 13).

Because of Your Enemy

The first reason you need God's armor is because of your enemy.

Satan's attacks come from the unseen realm of the spirit. Therefore, we can't use human weapons against him. The Devil is far too crafty for us. He has schemes and plans we can't even see. We need the armor of God because of the enemy we are up against.

Because of Your Victory

The second reason you need God's armor is because of the nature of the victory Christ has won for us.

Three times here in Ephesians 6, Paul tells us that our goal in spiritual warfare is to stand firm. That means to hold the ground Jesus has already won for us.

This does not negate what we said earlier about the church assaulting the gates of hell with the keys of the kingdom. The assault is led by the risen Christ, because Jesus has already invaded Satan's domain and won back all the territory Adam lost, and then some. So our job is to hold the ground Jesus has won, not to fight to win. Remember that we are fighting *from* victory, not *for* victory.

You need to understand that Satan is trying to rob you of spiritual victory and spiritual blessings *you already possess*. Ephesians 1:3 says God has already blessed us with every spiritual blessing it was possible to give us.

Because of the Evil Day

A third reason you need your armor is found in an interesting phrase in Ephesians 6:13. Paul says we need to stand firm and resist Satan "in the evil day."

What is the evil day? That's the day when your number comes up, so to speak. One translation puts it, "when things are at their worst" (NEB). That pretty well says it.

Ask Job about the evil day, when Satan unleashes everything he has against you. Job couldn't do anything about his horrible losses, but he stood firm by saying, "Though He slay me, I will hope in Him" (Job 13:15).

You need the armor of God to stand firm when the evil day comes. In 1 Corinthians 16:13 Paul writes, "Stand firm in the faith." That's the key. You can stand firm because your faith is in the One who provides you with the armor.

He has surrounded you with protection, so you don't have to worry about the Enemy's attacks. God wants us to hold our ground and not budge when the evil day comes.

THE NAMES OF THE ARMOR

I want to study each piece of the armor God has provided for us. These are important weapons you must know how to wear and how to wield if you are going to make the most of the spiritual authority you have in Christ.

The Belt of Truth

The first piece of armor Paul names is the belt of truth. "Stand firm therefore, having girded your loins with truth" (Ephesians 6:14a).

The spiritual armor Paul describes in this chapter is patterned after the armor and weapons of a Roman soldier of the day. Each soldier wore a long tunic that flowed down to the ground. But when it came time to fight, the soldier picked up that tunic and tucked it in his belt so he would have mobility for battle. A Roman soldier also carried his sword on his belt, and his breastplate connected to the belt too.

So the belt was fundamental, because everything else connected to it. Without his belt, a soldier couldn't keep himself together.

We men use our belts today to hold up our pants and keep our shirts tucked in. It gives us the look we want, keeps us neat, and holds everything together. That's what the truth is designed to do for us spiritually. The truth is an objective standard of reality that stands outside our experiences and above our opinions. That standard of truth is the Word of God.

We need to know God's truth because the Devil is a liar. He thrives on lies, so if he can get you in an environment where there is no objective standard of truth, he will milk it for all it's worth.

Truth is the beginning point of authority. The belt of truth holds your life together and protects you from the lies of the Evil One.

The Breastplate of Righteousness

The second piece of armor is also found in Ephesians 6:14. "Stand firm therefore . . . having put on the breastplate of righteousness."

The Roman soldier's breastplate protected his chest, his heart. What is the best protection for your heart in spiritual warfare? The best protection is to be covered in Christ's righteousness. If you know Jesus Christ as your Savior, not only were your sins forgiven, but Christ gave you His perfect righteousness. That is, God credited the righteousness of Christ to your spiritual account. You are righteous today as a Christian because of this transfer.

The theological term for this transaction is *imputation*. Christ's righteousness was put on your account. As a Christian, you are not simply a forgiven sinner. You stand as righteous in God's sight as Jesus Himself, because Jesus' righteousness is wrapped around you like a robe. When Satan accuses you, you can point to your righteous standing before God.

The breastplate of righteousness speaks of our exalted position in Christ. As we put it on each day, we have protection against Satan and his demons, because they can't hang out in an environment of righteousness.

The Gospel of Peace

The third piece of spiritual armor we need to wear are the shoes of "the gospel of peace" (Ephesians 6:15). If you are going to stand firm, you definitely need reliable footwear.

Earlier in Ephesians, Paul had said that Jesus is our peace (Ephesians 2:14). So we're still talking about getting dressed up in Jesus. The "gospel of peace," the good news of Jesus Christ, not only brings us truth and righteousness, it brings us peace of heart.

The Roman soldier wore shoes with cleats on them for sure-footedness in battle. A soldier had to be able to stand and fight without slipping and sliding around, because lost footing could be fatal.

Paul says we need to be prepared with peace because the world we are going to face is not always peaceful. In fact, since we are engaged in spiritual battle we should expect turmoil. But when we are wearing peace with Godlike shoes on our feet, we can handle whatever Satan brings against us—problems on the job, trouble with family—without stumbling. We don't need to pop a pill in the morning or do anything else like that to deal with life. God's peace is on duty.

The Shield of Faith

The fourth piece of armor Paul tells us to take up is the shield of faith, which allows us to "extinguish all the flaming arrows of the evil one" (Ephesians 6:16b).

The shield that a Roman soldier carried into battle was about four-and-a-half feet square. It was a huge shield that would even cover part of the body of the soldier fighting beside the shield-holder. So Roman soldiers lined up side by side in close formation with their shields together, and all of them were covered as they advanced.

What is this shield of faith that is able to protect you from anything Satan could ever fire at you? It is acting on the truth that you say you believe. You take up the shield of faith when you take the truth that you "amened" on Sunday and live it out on Monday.

One of the best examples of what I'm talking about is Joshua at the battle of Jericho (Joshua 6). God told Joshua to have the Israelites march around the city once a day for seven days, and then march around seven times on the seventh day.

That must have seemed like a foolish thing to do. It didn't make sense militarily. It certainly wasn't accepted strategy for warfare. But

God commanded Joshua to do it, and He promised to fight Israel's battle. So no matter how it looked to anyone else, Joshua took up the shield of faith and obeyed God. And God delivered Jericho into Joshua's lap.

I'm also reminded of Naaman, the Syrian commander who was covered with leprosy (2 Kings 5). Elisha told Naaman to go and dip seven times in the Jordan River to be cleansed.

Naaman felt insulted, because the Jordan is a dirty, muddy river. He didn't want to be embarrassed in front of his servants by having to dip in the Jordan. But his servants convinced him to do it, and Naaman did what God's prophet told him to do. He was healed because he chose to believe God.

Obeying God can sometimes seem foolish, difficult, or downright embarrassing. But God wants us to trust Him even when it doesn't make sense to trust Him. At times like these, we need to pick up our shield of faith and obey.

If you remember those old TV westerns, you know the damage that flaming arrows can do. The wagon train would be fighting off the Indians, with the wagons in a circle. But then a few Indians would set fire to their arrows and shoot them. Those arrows weren't aimed at the settlers behind the wagons. They were aimed at the canvas tops of the wagons, which would burst into flame.

Why did the Indians want to set the wagons on fire? First, to distract the settlers and get them fighting the fires, because they couldn't fight the fires and the Indians at the same time. But the main reason for setting the wagons on fire was to get rid of the settlers' protection. With the wagons burned down, they wouldn't have anything to hide behind.

Satan wants to hit us with as many flaming arrows as he can. That way, while we're fighting one fire he can hit us with another.

The question is, How can you put out Satan's fires? Answer: You can't. But the shield of faith can. If you will act on God's Word and believe Him, God will send His angelic host to snuff out Satan's fiery arrows as they come in.

The Helmet of Salvation

The helmet of salvation (Ephesians 6:17a) is the next piece of armor that can give you authority over the Enemy.

The helmet protects the head, the control center of the body. So the helmet of salvation covers a very key part. The purpose of a soldier's helmet was to absorb blows without causing damage to the head, much like a football player's helmet absorbs the shock of blows to his head.

Paul's reference to the helmet may imply our protection in a current spiritual battle, the way our salvation protects us from Satan's claim on our lives. Paul may also be thinking of the ultimate deliverance that salvation will bring, our hope for the future when our salvation is consummated. He uses the term *helmet* in this sense in 1 Thessalonians 5:8.

The helmet allows you to say to Satan when he hits you with his best shot, "I can do all things through Him who strengthens me" (Philippians 4:13). The helmet reminds you that God "is able to keep you from stumbling" (Jude 24). The helmet's visor allows you to see Jesus (Hebrews 2:9) and focus on Him. You won't get very far in spiritual warfare without your helmet.

The Sword of the Spirit

We complete the full armor of God when we take up "the sword of the Spirit, which is the word of God" (Ephesians 6:17b). The sword mentioned here is not the soldier's long sword, but a short, dagger-like weapon about ten inches long.

This sword had a needlelike point, and it was sharp on both sides. It was used for close-in fighting and could do some serious damage. It could cut an opponent coming and going. "The word of God is living and active and sharper than any two-edged sword," Hebrews 4:12 says.

What's interesting is that the term Paul uses for *word* here does not refer to the Bible as a written book of truth, the way we normally think of the Word of God. This is not the Bible sitting on your coffee table or bookshelf.

Instead, this is *rhēma*, the utterance of God, the Word as it is spoken. Paul is talking about the use of the Word, not just its existence. Many of us go to church every Sunday with our Bible under our arm, but we don't always know how to wield it like a sword to slice the Devil in half in spiritual battle.

The best example of wielding the Word was the temptation of Jesus. Satan attacked Jesus, but Jesus answered, "It is written," and then defeated Satan with the Word. Jesus didn't argue or dialogue with the Devil. Jesus simply hit him with the Word, and the battle was over.

That's the armor of God, the weapons of your authority. Is your armor in good shape? Are your belt, breastplate, and gospel shoes laid out when you go to bed, ready to be put on tomorrow? Are your shield, helmet, and sword close by, ready to be grabbed when needed? Then you're ready for the battle.

And if you can't remember all the individual pieces of your spiritual armor, then just remember Christ. For if you have an intimate relationship with Him, you also have the armor!

PERSONAL APPLICATION FOR LIFE

1. Are you having an "evil day"? When that happens, and the Devil is doing his worst, you can confidently "stand firm in the faith" (1 Corinthians 16:13) because God has surrounded you with protection. You need not worry about Satan's attacks when you are wearing the armor of God.

2. Ephesians 6:10 commands us to "be strong in the Lord." But it is a passive command, which means that God supplies the strength. What is our part? It is to make certain that we dress up in full armor to be ready for battle. What an encouragement that God provides not only the armor but also the strength for battle!

3. The victory in spiritual warfare is ours. We have already won. In Ephesians 6, three times we are told to "stand firm." That's actually a command to hold the ground Jesus has already won for us. Don't give back ground to Satan and allow him to rob you of the spiritual victory and blessings you already possess.

4. Is your spiritual armor is good shape? Are you missing any pieces? Is your armor laid out and ready to put on tomorrow? If not, do some armor maintenance. Never let down your guard in the face of the Enemy.

FOR GROUP STUDY

Questions for Group Discussion

1. Read Ephesians 6:10–17. What is the nature of our spiritual armor? Why do we need the "full armor of God"?

2. What is the "evil day" (Ephesians 6:13)? Have group members share their experiences with evil days. What new insights did they gain from their experiences?

3. What are the pieces of the armor of God? (See "Picture This.") Assign group members a piece of armor and have them describe what the piece is and its purpose or function.

4. Why is the breastplate of righteousness such a powerful piece of armor? What does the theological term *imputation* means? How might we fare against the Enemy without it?

PICTURE THIS

If we are to exercise our spiritual authority in Christ, we must know how to use the armor we wear to battle.

OUR SPIRITUAL ARMOR
Ephesians 6:14–17

PIECE OF ARMOR	VERSE	ITS FUNCTION
Belt of truth	verse 14	Protects us from the lies of the Enemy.
Breastplate of righteousness	verse 14	Gives us a righteous standing before God.
Gospel of peace	verse 15	Enables us to stand firm in the midst of battle.
Shield of faith	verse 16b	Protects us from the "arrows" of the Evil One.
Helmet of salvation	verse 17a	Gives us authority over the Enemy.
Sword of the Spirit	verse 17b	To defeat the Enemy with the use of God's spoken Word.

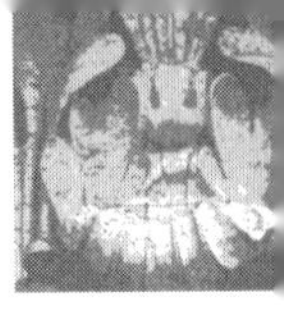

57

THE ACCESS TO AUTHORITY

In the previous chapter we studied the believer's spiritual armor, the six pieces of offensive and defensive weaponry God has equipped us with (Ephesians 6:10–17).

But the apostle Paul doesn't stop writing there, because in the very next verse he gives us the secret to using this great authority God has made available. We might say that after describing the Christian's battle dress, Paul tells us *how to get dressed*, how to access the authority we possess: "With all prayer and petition pray at all times in the Spirit, and with this in view, be on the alert with all perseverance and petition for all the saints" (Ephesians 6:18).

It is prayer that gains you access to the authority you need for victorious warfare. Prayer is the way you get dressed for battle. So let's talk about the vital place of prayer in spiritual warfare.

THE SIGNIFICANCE OF PRAYER

One of the first things a commander tries to do in warfare is to establish superiority in the air. Whoever controls the air war usually controls the war overall. If you establish air superiority, you'll suffer fewer casualties on the ground.

One of our problems is that the church is suffering a lot of casualties on the ground because we haven't established superiority in the air—in the heavenly places where the real warfare is taking place.

There's one big difference between an earthly army and the church. An earthly army has to go out and win the air war to establish superiority. But Jesus Christ has already won the spiritual war and established air superiority for all eternity.

Our task is to take the superiority we have and use it to win our battles. That's important, because it's possible to lose a battle even when you have superior weapons.

The Authority of Prayer

The significance of prayer to spiritual warfare is evident in the very first word of Ephesians 6:18: "*With* all prayer" (italics added).

With is a connecting word. Paul is saying that prayer is vitally connected to his discussion of spiritual warfare and the Christian's armor that has just preceded this verse.

Prayer is the atmosphere in which you are to fight. It's the way you stay in vital daily contact with your Commander. In other words, the way you activate the authority and use the armor described in Ephesians 6:10–17 is by prayer.

Remember, three times in this section (vv. 11, 13–14) the apostle has told us to stand firm. That means to hold the territory Jesus Christ has won for us and not let the Devil take any territory back.

But the problem is that the Devil has already taken back a lot of territory from many believers. He has taken back the territory of peace from some of us. From others, he has taken back the territory of our homes, our families, or our businesses. From still others, the Devil has taken back the authoritative position that God has given us.

Satan is always looking to take back territory that Christ has won. So if we are going to stand firm, we must know how to put our armor on and how to use it. And that authority is activated through prayer.

The kind of prayer Paul has in mind here is intense, fervent, knowledgeable prayer that enables you to reach into heaven and make withdrawals on your spiritual account.

The Protective Power of Prayer

Prayer is so potent because it provides us with spiritual protection even when the battle is at its hottest. It's in prayer that we locate the ground on which we can stand firm.

It is reported that the emperor Napoleon once looked at a map and said, "If it were not for that one red dot, I could rule the world." That red dot was the British Empire, the one place on the map Napoleon couldn't conquer.

Satan is a lot like Napoleon. He looks at the cross and says, "If it were not for that one red-stained cross, I could have conquered the human race." If God had not become a man and entered time and space in the person of Jesus Christ, Satan could have had his victory. He could have had us.

But we escaped Satan's clutches because of that one red-stained cross! Now what we need to do is stand on what Christ has done, protected from the Enemy by the power of prayer.

For a lot of us, however, prayer is like the singing of the national anthem before a ball game. It gets things started, but it has nothing to do with what follows on the field. We need to learn what warfare praying is all about so that prayer becomes vital to what is happening on the "field" of our lives.

The Essence of Prayer

Of course, the essence or heart of prayer is communication with God. As we all know, good communication involves both talking and listening.

If prayer is communication with God, then in order to communicate with God effectively, we need to know something about Him. We need to understand His greatness.

Many believers pray to a God who is too small. By their lack of understanding about God and their failure to appropriate His power, they reduce God to a microforce in their lives. And let me tell you, if your God is small, your prayers are going to be small. And if your prayers are small, you're a big target for the Enemy.

If our knowledge of God is anemic, our prayers won't get beyond, "Now I lay me down to sleep. . . ." Prayers like that will not enable us to stand against Satan. But if our knowledge of God is deepening by the time we spend in His Word and on our knees, when those deep problems come, we can go even deeper with God.

The Necessity of Prayer

Prayer is necessary because the battle we are fighting is spiritual. Prayer is necessary because it is through prayer that we engage the spiritual realm. When we pray, things happen in the heavenly places.

One of the best examples of a believer approaching God in prayer is the prayer of the prophet Daniel (Daniel 9:1–19). Daniel knew from his knowledge of Jeremiah's prophecy (v. 2) that the seventy years of Israel's captivity were about to end.

So Daniel proceeded to pray a great prayer in which he confessed his people's sins and called on God to remember His covenant with Israel and end His people's humiliation in exile from Jerusalem.

In other words, Daniel prayed God's own Word back to Him and called on Him to honor it.

One of the great things about prayer, especially if you know the Word of God, is that in prayer you can hold God to His Word. I don't mean you can coerce Him, but you can pray like Daniel, "O Lord, hear! O Lord, forgive! O Lord, listen and take action! For Your own sake, O my God, do not delay, because Your city and Your people are called by Your name" (v. 19).

Daniel was reminding God of what He had said about Jerusalem and its people. He was holding God to His Word. We have the same privilege to hold God to His Word in prayer. It's not a matter of His reluctance to fulfill His Word, but a test of our faith to believe and act on His Word.

Prayer is also necessary because of spiritual resistance in the heavenly realm. In Daniel 10:13, Daniel is told that the answer to his prayer was delayed three weeks by a demon called "the prince of Persia."

Daniel's prayer was heard and answered the first day he prayed. But it took three weeks of intercessory prayer and activity on the part of the angels, especially the archangel Michael, to break the demonic blockade and get the answer through.

Prayer is necessary because the battle is spiritual. When we pray properly, God puts out a restraining order against the powers of darkness.

THE SCOPE OF PRAYER

Prayer gives you access to your authority and your spiritual weapons. The scope of prayer is also included in Ephesians 6:18. We are to pray "at all times" and "with all perseverance and petition for all the saints."

A Full Agenda of Prayer

The key word here is pretty obvious. Prayer is to be made *all* the time, with *all* kinds of prayers, for all the saints.

So the scope of prayer is as wide as the world and as full as the hours in our day. God wants us to bombard the heavenlies with our prayers. In a war, an army doesn't fire just one shell or launch one missile at the enemy. An army pounds the enemy with repeated fire.

Paul tells us to pray with all kinds of prayer. In the Bible, we see people praying in all kinds of postures: standing, kneeling, lying prostrate, walking. They used all kinds of prayers: thanksgiving, praise, supplication, intercession. Whatever the prayer need is, there is a kind of prayer to meet it.

Paul also says to pray all the time, with perseverance. Don't "hang up" on God too soon. As Paul put it in 1 Thessalonians 5:17, "Pray without ceasing." If you and I are going to see this thing work, prayer cannot be an addendum to our day or week. It must be the controlling agenda of our lives. We need to pray when we feel like it and when we don't.

The Perspective of Prayer

When you pray, you enter into a whole other realm. You enter into the heavenlies. It gives you a different perspective.

Do you know how things look from the window of an airplane? When you're up that high, everything looks orderly. The fields all look perfectly laid out. No matter how chaotic things actually are on the ground, from high up everything looks great.

That's what prayer does for you. Our problem is that we've been on the ground too long. We've lost the divine perspective. When that happens, we begin operating according to the wisdom from below, not the wisdom from above.

Interestingly, James calls the wisdom from below "demonic" (James 3:15). That means Satan gets you thinking and acting the way he wants.

The only way you can find the wisdom from above, the heavenly wisdom, is by communicating with heaven.

THE SPHERE OF PRAYER

Let's go back to Ephesians 6:18 one more time and notice that Paul instructs us to pray "in the Spirit." This is the Holy Spirit, of course. We are to pray in His power, in the strength and spiritual insight He provides.

But this sounds rather ethereal. How do you know when you are praying in the Holy Spirit?

Praying in the Spirit

Let me answer that by first pointing out that in the Scriptures, being in the Spirit is always contrasted with being in the flesh. So Paul is talking about the spiritual environment in which we live. If we are going to pray in the Spirit, we must be immersed in the environment of the Spirit.

In 1 Corinthians 2:9–13, Paul shows us what it means to be in a Holy Spirit environment. Those who live in a Spirit-dominated sphere or environment are the ones to whom the things of God, even the deep things, are revealed. If we are going to pray in the Spirit and find authority and power for spiritual warfare, we will need the revealing work of the Spirit to our hearts.

Why is this so important? Because often we don't even know what to pray for, so the Spirit has to intercede for us (Romans 8:26).

Notice also that to pray in the Spirit, we must have "spiritual thoughts." If you and I think like the world, we'll pray like the world. If we learn to think like the Spirit, we'll pray in the Spirit. To pray in the Spirit requires a mind-set that comes from God.

Knowing the Word

How do believers get Spirit-directed thoughts? Paul says they come from being combined with "spiritual words" (1 Corinthians 2:13).

In other words, the only place you're going to find spiritual thinking is in a spiritual book. And there's only one perfect spiritual book.

A Biblical Example

One biblical example of praying in the Spirit appears in Acts 4:23–31, and it's right on target for our topic—the context of this prayer is intense spiritual warfare.

Earlier in Acts 4, Peter and John had been arrested for preaching Jesus. The Jewish authorities threatened them not to preach in that name anymore and let them go. Peter and John went back to the church and reported the threat they had received (v. 23). That's the setting for the prayer in verses 24–30.

The first thing you need to see about this prayer is that the disciples don't start right off praying about their problem. They start off talking about the greatness of God and quoting His Word back to Him (vv. 24–26).

In other words, this prayer begins with theology and the Word of God. The disciples were saying, "Lord, we're in a mess. But You are a big God. God, before we talk about the mess we are in, let us remind You what You have written in Your Word."

Only after the disciples had set the situation in its proper spiritual context did they get around to talking about their immediate problem (vv. 27–30). Here is their actual request: "And now, Lord, take note of their threats, and grant that Your bond-servants may speak Your word with all confidence" (v. 29). Notice that they didn't pray that they wouldn't be persecuted, but that they wouldn't let the fear of persecution hinder their witness.

Verse 31 tells what happened when they had finished praying. "The place where they had gathered together was shaken, and they were all filled with the Holy Spirit and began to speak the word of God with boldness." When God's people pray in the Spirit, something is going to shake!

YOUR APPLICATION FOR LIFE

1. How consistent is your prayer life? Have you learned to persevere in prayer? The Bible says to "pray without ceasing" (1 Thessalonians 5:17). This kind of praying goes beyond an occasional prayer for needs. It is an attitude of prayer that controls the agenda of your day. James 5:16 tells us that "the effective prayer of a righteous man can accomplish much." That includes thwarting the Enemy in spiritual warfare.

2. When we pray, we gain a unique perspective on our current situation. In a way, we enter the heavenlies and see things the way God sees them. A key to Spirit-directed thoughts in prayer is a knowledge of the Word of God. The Spirit has a way of bringing to remembrance Scripture that gives you guidance and wisdom. Never shortchange the power of prayer!

3. Unity is a key to answered prayer. If we are to be successful in tearing down powerful satanic strongholds in our society and families, we need to be a united body of believers. When the air is filled with prayer and praise, it becomes too uncomfortable for Satan to hang around. The next time Satan attempts to gain a foothold in your life or your church, gather a group of believers and draw near to God in prayer and praise—and the Devil will flee!

4. A key area of Satan's attack is the family. He will do whatever he can to undermine the unity and spiritual life of your family. Fight for your family! One of Satan's goals is to win over your family and generations that follow. Protect them by surrounding them with the protective power of prayer. Don't let the threats of the Enemy gain a stronghold.

FOR GROUP STUDY

Questions for Group Discussion

1. Why is prayer so important to the spiritual battle at hand? What is the key to our establishing superiority over the Enemy?

2. To what does prayer provide us access? What is the scope of prayer as

discussed in this chapter? What is its full agenda as related to our spiritual warfare?

3. Read 1 Corinthians 2:9–13. What does it mean to "pray in the Spirit"? How do we know when we are praying in the Holy Spirit? How is Romans 8:26 related to this discussion?

4. Read 1 Corinthians 2:13. What is the source of Spirit-directed thoughts in prayer? How do the Spirit of God and the Word of God work hand in hand?

PICTURE THIS

Prayer is a powerful weapon in the realm of spiritual warfare. When we use prayer properly, it serves to put a restraining order against Satan and his legions.

THE SIGNIFICANCE OF PRAYER IN SPIRITUAL WARFARE

Ephesians 6:10–18

SIGNIFICANT ASPECT	WHY IT IS SIGNIFICANT
Its authority	It activates spiritual authority and the use of our spiritual armor.
Its protective power	It provides us with spiritual protection in the heat of the battle.
Its essence	It is communication with God.
Its necessity	It is through prayer that we engage the spiritual realm, effecting action in the heavenly places.

PART 5

SOTERIOLOGY

The Doctrine of Salvation

SECTION I

Our Great Salvation

58. SIN: THE NEED FOR SALVATION
59. JUSTIFICATION: THE VERDICT OF SALVATION
60. REDEMPTION: THE PAYMENT FOR SALVATION
61. PROPITIATION: THE REQUIREMENT FOR SALVATION
62. RECONCILIATION: THE RELATIONSHIP OF SALVATION
63. REGENERATION: THE MIRACLE OF SALVATION
64. GRACE: THE GIFT OF SALVATION
65. SANCTIFICATION: THE PROGRESS OF SALVATION

58

SIN: THE NEED FOR SALVATION

It's safe to say that some words don't mean what they used to mean. Modern technology is responsible for a lot of these changes in meaning. For instance, if you stop a person on the street and ask what *windows* are, the chances are good that the answer will relate to a computer program instead of clear panes of glass that people look through.

The word *help* is another example. It used to mean a cry of desperation by someone in trouble. But today it's just an option on a computer's toolbar.

Here's one more example: the words *save* or *saved*. To a twenty-first century mind, "save" is a command whereby the data in a computer file is preserved, and "saved" describes the condition of the file after this command is performed. The world may consider the spiritual meaning of the word *saved* to be a relic from a previous generation, but it's a good biblical word that we ought not abandon.

The Philippian jailer who fell down before the apostle Paul and cried, "What must I do to be saved?" (Acts 16:30) knew that something was radically wrong and that he needed a radical solution. When the Bible says that people need to be saved, it communicates the message that they are lost.

Jesus Himself said He came "to seek and to save that which was lost" (Luke 19:10).

It is vital that people understand that they are eternally lost without Jesus Christ, and that they desperately need to be saved because they are totally lost and without hope for eternity apart from Christ. In this section we are going to study the doctrine called soteriology in theological circles, drawing from the Greek term *sōtēr*, meaning "savior."

THE CONCEPT OF SIN

One observer said that contemporary America has "defined deviancy downward." Our culture has made sin seem so acceptable that things that used to be considered deviant are now considered almost normal.

But make no mistake. God has not defined sin downward. His concept of sin is the same today as it was in eternity past when Lucifer and one-third of the angels rebelled against Him. Sin is anything that fails to conform to the holy and perfect character of God.

Failing to Measure Up

God said to Moses, "You shall be holy, for I the Lord your God am holy" (Leviticus 19:2). Sin becomes sin when it is measured against the standard of God. When the prophet Habakkuk encountered God, he said, "My inward parts trembled, at the sound [of God] my lips quivered. Decay enters my bones, and in my place I tremble" (3:16). Isaiah had a similar experience in God's holy presence. The prophet saw the Lord in His holy temple and cried out, "Woe is me" (Isaiah 6:5).

One reason we don't have a high view of sin today is that we have a low view of God. We haven't visited Him lately in His holy temple, because when we are in His presence we don't feel so good about ourselves anymore. We've become too comfortable living in an age that devalues God's standard and makes acceptable that which He hates.

The apostle John wrote, "God is Light, and in Him there is no darkness at all" (1 John 1:5). He is absolute perfection in every detail. Some theologians consider the holiness of God to be His controlling attribute. That is, all the other divine attributes are referenced from God's holiness. He is totally set apart from sin.

In the same epistle, John gave a more formal definition of sin. "Everyone who practices sin also practices lawlessness; and sin is lawlessness. You know that He appeared in order to take away sins; and in Him there is no sin" (1 John 3:4–5). These verses characterize sin as rebellion against God by the breaking of His law.

Sin makes us self-centered and self-dependent instead of God-centered and God-dependent. The less you need God, the more sinful you have become, because you are trying to function independently of the Creator.

Therefore, we can say that sin is the failure to reflect God's holy character and obey His righteous laws. "All have sinned and fall short of the glory of God" (Romans 3:23).

The Deep Roots of Sin

Where does sin finds its roots? This question takes us all the way back to some point in eternity past, before the creation of the world, when the angel Lucifer decided he was tired of being less than God. This beautiful being, the highest-ranking of all God's angels, led one-third of the angelic host in a rebellion designed to topple God from His throne.

Lucifer's rebellion is described in Ezekiel 28:11–19 and Isaiah 14:12–14. It was rooted in pride, the creature thinking more highly of himself than he ought to think (see Romans 12:3). Sin began in heaven, and it began with pride.

Pride is such a pervasive thing that it's good for us to remind ourselves regularly who is in charge here. If the Creator ever decided to withhold oxygen, water, or food, you and I wouldn't even be here, let alone start acting like we're the Creator. Everything we enjoy comes from something that God made.

Only pride could make any creature claim equality with God, as Satan did. Paul warned of this when he cautioned Timothy not to appoint a new believer to leadership in the church, "so that he will not become conceited and fall into the condemnation incurred by the devil" (1 Timothy 3:6).

God had commanded Adam and Eve not to eat of the Tree of the Knowledge of Good and Evil, because "in the day that you eat from it you will surely die" (Genesis 2:17).

This forbidden tree reminded our first parents that they could not do whatever they wanted to do whenever they wanted to do it, because they were limited, created beings who owed obedience and loyalty to their Creator.

When Satan approached Eve in the form of the serpent, he focused on the one prohibition God had made to teach Adam and Eve that they were not their own gods. Satan had tried to make himself equal with God and had failed, so he used the same tactic on Eve because he knew how seductive the temptation is to imagine that we can be like God, having His knowledge and power.

The serpent was too "crafty" (Genesis 3:1) to call God an outright liar. He questioned God's goodness in putting this tree off-limits for Adam and Eve (v. 5), suggesting that God was being selfish in keeping His deity to Himself. The serpent also promised Eve the opposite of death, the judgment God had decreed for disobedience. Eve was promised godlike status that would erase the Creator/creature distinction. Satan was saying to Eve, "There's no reason that God has to be up high while you're down low. You can erase that line by eating this fruit."

According to Genesis 3:6, Eve bought the lie and sinned. Not wanting to go down alone, she got Adam to sin with her. Adam allowed Eve to be god in his life at that moment, and it cost dearly. Anytime we let another human being become more important to us than God, that's sin.

Sin on Mankind's Charge Account

When Adam ate of the forbidden fruit and sinned against God, something very important happened. His sin was imputed, or charged, to the whole human race. Paul wrote, "Through one man sin entered into the world, and death through sin, and so death spread to all men, because all sinned" (Romans 5:12). This is the doctrine known as *imputation*, which simply means to post a charge against someone's account.

The reason is that Adam was acting as the covenantal representative of the human race. Adam was given a position of headship by God, so his sin affected all who would come after him. That's why Paul said sin passed to every person through Adam, the "one man" the apostle was talking about.

Adam sinned as the head of the human race, so his sin was imputed, or charged, to mankind's account. When this happened, Adam and Eve's sin was inherited by their offspring. We inherited a sin nature from our first parents, and that nature is passed on to every generation. We call this original sin, the nature that was transferred from Adam to every human being. David said in Psalm 51:5, "In sin my mother conceived me." Adam and Eve passed on their spiritual genes to their children.

THE CORRUPTION OF SIN

This inherited sin nature we possess brings us to another theological term that's important to understand. It's called *depravity*, which means that every facet of human nature has been polluted, defiled, and contaminated by sin. We are talking about inborn corruption.

Sin's Corruption Is Complete

Jeremiah 17:9 says of human nature, "The heart [the seat of our being] is more deceitful than all else and is desperately sick; who can understand it?" Jeremiah was referring to this capacity all of us have to function in rebellion against God.

Paul said of himself, "I know that nothing good dwells in me, that is, in my flesh" (Romans 7:18).

And Paul was not alone, because in Ephesians 2:1 he said, "You were dead in your trespasses and sins." The Bible declares that we are spiritually contaminated and are "by nature children of wrath" (v. 3). By nature we are destined to incur God's wrath because depravity also means that there is nothing within us to commend us to God or cause Him to accept us.

We never have to teach our children how to sin. No child ever needed a class on how to be selfish or disobedient. No, we have to teach children how to love, to share, to be kind to one another, to stop fighting. The bad stuff is automatic. The capacity for sin is present when a child is developing in the womb.

How many times have you told yourself you would never do something, but then you wound up doing that very thing? We all do things like this, and then we say, "I can't believe I did that. That just isn't me." Oh yes, it is. Let's not kid ourselves. Under the right conditions, we are capable of committing murder or any other terrible thing anyone else might do. Why? Because we all have the same corrupt human nature we inherited from Adam. It just doesn't express itself the same way in everyone.

God told Adam and Eve that on the day they ate from the tree He commanded them not to eat from they would die (Genesis 2:17). They died spiritually that same day, and eventually they died physically. In our sinful condition, the human race has been cut off from its life source and is dead. And the proof that we are dead spiritually is the fact that we will die physically someday.

The Bible says that all of us will die "in Adam" (1 Corinthians 15:22), just as Adam himself died. To put it another way, your birth certificate is also your death certificate. "The wages of sin is death" (Romans 6:23).

Sin's Corruption Is Obvious

Sin can also be collective, as when an entire nation or group of people systematically participates in and supports evil. Slavery is an example of collective sin. We see in the Bible that God judged whole groups of people for the sins they practiced. That doesn't necessarily mean that every person in that group was guilty of the particular sin, but that the group was so characterized by and corrupted by the sin that the people came under judgment collectively (Genesis 19:24–25). Sin is also collective in the sense that the entire creation has been affected by sin (Romans 18:19–22).

THE CONSEQUENCES OF SIN

The Bible is very clear about the consequences of sin. "The wages of sin is death" (Romans 6:23). Death in the Bible never means the cessation of our existence. Death means separation, and the Bible talks about three kinds of death, all of which have come about as a consequence of sin.

The Death That Results from Sin

One type of death is spiritual death, which we read about in Ephesians 2. Spiritual death is separation from the life of God. The first thing Adam and Eve did after they sinned was to hide from God because their fellowship with Him was severed (see Genesis 3:8–10). All of us are born spiritually dead.

The second manifestation of death, the one we're most familiar with, is physical death or the separation of the soul and spirit from the body. The proof that we are all sinners is the fact that we all die (Romans 5:12).

There's a third kind of death in Scripture, which is eternal death or separation from God for eternity in the place of punishment and suffering called hell. Spiritual death can be reversed by salvation, and physical death will be reversed by resurrection. But there is no reversal of eternal death. The horror of eternal death is total separation from God (Revelation 20:14–15).

In hell, there is no presence of God in the sense that there is no righteous provision of His goodness. God is everywhere, including hell, because He is all-present. But in hell there is no experience of God's goodness. There is nothing to balance or temper the presence of pure evil. Hell is the worst form of bondage because people are locked in their sin forever.

Sin's Devastation on the Creation

Sin has also devastated the whole of creation. Paul taught in Romans 8 that "the creation itself also will be set free from its slavery to corruption" when Jesus comes to complete our redemption (v. 21).

All of creation, what we call nature, was affected by sin. The reason we have all the disturbances and destructiveness of nature is that sin has spoiled God's creation. God's grace keeps sin from having total domination in nature, but even the natural world "groans" (Romans 8:22) under the weight of sin.

There is a direct relationship between man and nature. When God created Adam, He put him in the garden of Eden "to cultivate it and keep it" (Genesis 2:15). When Adam sinned, God cursed the ground as one of the consequences (3:17–18). Suddenly, nothing grew right anymore. Thorns and thistles appeared. Sin spoiled every part of God's good creation.

THE CURE FOR SIN

Sin is a dread disease from which all of creation is crying out for a cure. Now a terrible disease without a cure is bad news, but the news concerning a cure for sin is good. God has a remedy for this scourge, which is found in the atonement of Jesus Christ.

Atonement for Sin Is Necessary

Sin has to be atoned for, because God is too holy and just to ignore sin, and too loving to let us plunge headlong into judgment and hell. Christ is the only One who could pay the terrible price that sin demanded. Just saying "I'm sorry" doesn't atone for sin. Sin must be addressed in a way that is acceptable to the one who has been offended.

Atonement is paying what must be paid to settle the claim. Sin is an attack on the character of God, and, therefore, it must be atoned for by a payment that is acceptable to Him. The only payment that God ever accepted for sin is death (see Romans 6:23). God told Adam concerning the fruit of the forbidden tree, "In the day that you eat from it you will surely die" (Genesis 2:17). The Bible says, "The Lord will by no means leave the guilty unpunished" (Nahum 1:3).

God Permitted a Substitute to Die

Sin's death penalty would be very bad news for us, except for one exciting truth. Although God didn't lessen the penalty for sin, He did allow a substitute to bear the penalty for guilty sinners.

The principle of substitution also goes back to the beginning. After Adam and Eve sinned, God responded by slaying an animal to clothe them. Adam and Eve had their own substitute in mind, but it was a fig-leaf substitute, which was completely unacceptable to God. The only sacrifice that He accepts, and that will properly atone for sin, is the shedding of blood.

God's economy has always operated this way. According to Leviticus 17:11, "The life of the flesh is in the blood, and I have given it to you on the altar to make atonement for your souls; for it is the blood by reason of the life that makes atonement."

Blood is the only means of atonement that satisfies God's righteous retribution against sin. Before Christ came, God accepted the blood of sacrificial animals as a substitute for man's blood, and no sinner dared to approach God and seek forgiveness without an acceptable substitute. That's why the writer of Hebrews said, "Without shedding of blood there is no forgiveness" (9:22).

Jesus Is Our Substitute

When Jesus came, the sacrificial system came to an end as He became the final sacrifice for sin. We know that sin must be paid for, and that the penalty is death. We deserved to die on the cross, but Jesus Christ took our place by becoming our substitute and bearing the penalty for the guilt we had incurred (Romans 5:6–8).

This is why we refer to the atonement of Christ as substitutionary. Jesus didn't die just to leave us a good example, or show us how to bear up under suffering. Our guilt was transferred to Him and, therefore, He took the death stroke that should have fallen on us for all eternity. That's a great salvation!

PERSONAL APPLICATION FOR LIFE

1. Lucifer's original sin was one of pride. He wanted to be equal with God. That thinking is pretty much at the root of our own sin. Before we came to Christ, most of us operated as if we were our own gods. If you are not a believer and have never dealt with this issue of your heart, simply acknowledge your sinfulness before God (Romans 3:9–10). Believe that Jesus Christ, God's Son, died to pay for your sins on the cross and arose from the dead to save you (Romans 5:8). You can know the joy of forgiveness and eternal life.

2. Proverbs 14 gives a list of the social sins we can get ourselves into (including lying, mocking, being quick-tempered, and ignoring the weak and poor). Read this chapter of Proverbs. If any of these are problem areas for you, bring them to the Lord right now ands ask Him to remove these sins. Also, if He reminds you of anyone whose forgiveness you need to seek, do it as soon as possible.

3. Psalm 32 expresses David's joy at God's forgiveness after David repented of his sin. Read this wonderful psalm. If you cannot honestly say this is your experience right now, go before the Lord and stay there until you have dealt with anything that might be blocking your fellowship with Him.

4. God sometimes uses fellow Christians to draw us back. What would be your attitude if another believer came to you, with the right motive, to confront you in love about a sin in your life? Would your first response be anger and defensiveness, or openness and gratitude that someone cared?

FOR GROUP STUDY

Questions for Group Discussion

1. What is the biblical concept of sin? What is the essence of sin? What are its roots?

2. The term *depravity* deals with man's corruption of sin. What does the Bible tell us about the extent of sin's corruption? (Read Romans 3:9–20.)

3. Romans 6:23 tells us the consequences of sin—death. Read Ephesians 2. What is the nature of this death? How has sin impacted God's creation?

4. Why must there be a penalty for sin? What is the meaning of the term *atonement*? Discuss the three elements of the cure for sin. (Use the chart below as an aid to your discussion.)

PICTURE THIS

Although sin has corrupted our nature and permeated our existence, God has provided us a remedy—the atonement of Jesus Christ.

THE CURE FOR SIN

REMEDY	SCRIPTURE PASSAGES	WHAT IT MEANS
Atonement for sin is necessary.	Romans 6:23	Because God is holy, sin is an attack on His character. It must be atoned for by the only payment acceptable to Him—death.
God permitted a substitute to die.	Leviticus 17:11; Hebrews 9:22	Although God could not lessen the penalty for sin, He did allow a substitute to bear the penalty for guilty sinners.
Jesus is our substitute.	Romans 5:8	Jesus took the penalty for our sin for all eternity by dying on the cross.

59

JUSTIFICATION: THE VERDICT OF SALVATION

The human race has a huge predicament. We are sinners before God, and there is nothing we can do about it on our own. People may be able to tamper with or destroy the evidence of sin, and they may "beat the rap" in terms of human judgment even though they know they're guilty. But there is another court and another Judge we must deal with, and He is not impressed by our standards. Sin must never be measured by our viewpoint but by the standard of absolute perfection resident in a holy God.

Since God's verdict is the only one that matters, we need to answer the question of how guilty sinners can be made right before a perfectly holy and perfectly just God. Job asked, "How can a man be in the right before God?" (Job 9:2). The psalmist phrased the question this way: "If You, Lord, should mark iniquities, O Lord, who could stand?" (Psalm 130:3).

There are two ways God could deal with sin. He could simply issue a verdict condemning all sinners and be done with it, leaving us hopeless. However, God took a second option, providing the means to forgive sinners and declare them righteous in His sight without compromising His own righteousness and justice (Romans 3:24–26).

THE CONCEPT OF JUSTIFICATION

The biblical term for this glorious verdict is *justification*. I say "verdict" because the Greek word translated "justify" means to announce a favorable verdict, or to declare righteous. It is a legal term taken from the courtroom. A basic definition of justification is "a judicial act by which God declares righteous those who believe in Jesus Christ." The Bible is clear that justification comes from God alone, for "God is the one who justifies" (Romans 8:33).

Measured against the Law

The book of Romans is a good place to start, because Paul had a lot to say there about the doctrine of justification. In Romans 5 the apostle contrasted the disobedience of Adam in the garden and its effects with the obedience of Christ on the cross and its effects. In verse 18 we read, "So then as through one transgression there resulted condemnation to all men, even so through one act of righteousness there resulted justification of life to all men."

The opposite of justification is condemnation. Through Adam all people were condemned, but through Jesus Christ the righteous demands of God were met so that sinners can be justified before a holy God.

Justification as it is used in the Bible is a judicial term that sets it in the context of law. When you enter a courtroom, you are there to be measured against the law. It's the same in God's courtroom. Paul wrote:

> Now we know that whatever the Law says, it speaks to those who are under the Law, so that every mouth may be closed and all the world may become accountable to God; because by the works of the Law no flesh will be justified in His sight; for through the Law comes the knowledge of sin. But now apart from the Law the righteousness of God has been manifested, being witnessed by the Law and the Prophets, even the righteousness of God through faith in Jesus Christ for all those who believe; for there is no distinction; for all have sinned and fall short of the glory of God. (Romans 3:19–23)

Many people may not be aware of it, but all mankind has already been tried in the tribunal of heaven before God the righteous Judge and found guilty of sin. The sentence is pronounced. "The wages of sin is death" (Romans 6:23).

A New Plan Introduced in Court

This is serious because the Bible means eternal death, separation from God forever in hell, when it speaks of death as the penalty for sin. But God's court is unlike any human court, because God did what no human judge can do. He conceived the plan of salvation whereby we not only do not have to pay the penalty for our sins, but we are justified—given a declaration of righteousness that means God sees us the same way He sees His sinless Son. When we trust Christ, we move from being totally condemned to totally saved!

But God introduced a glorious plan called justification into His court. Therefore, sinners who accept Christ's payment for their sin can walk out forgiven, with their sin debt paid and the righteousness of Christ Himself credited to their account (2 Corinthians 5:21).

THE GIFT OF JUSTIFICATION

Perhaps you have noticed in this discussion that nothing has been said about our doing anything to earn this glorious justification. That's because we didn't earn it. The earlier quotation from Romans 3 ended at verse 23 with the statement of our shortcoming before God, but thank the Lord it is not the end of the story.

Candidates for God's Grace

According to Romans 3:24, the same people who fall short of God's glory are candidates to be "justified as a gift by His grace through the redemption which is in Christ Jesus." Paul then went on to say that Jesus made "propitiation" for our sins through His blood (v. 25). We are saving the concepts of redemption and propitiation for later chapters, because they are equally glorious facets of our great salvation.

So justification is a gift of God's grace. That's the only way it could happen, because we had nothing to offer God to make us acceptable to Him. The means by which God's declaration of righteousness is applied to us involves a biblical truth called imputation, or crediting something to someone's account.

Perfect Righteousness in Our Account

In the Bible *imputation* has both a negative and a positive application. We read in Romans 5 that Adam's sin brought death to all mankind because God charged the sin of Adam to every person's spiritual account (see Romans 5:12–14). But when Jesus died on the cross to satisfy God's righteous demands, He provided a means whereby those who receive His forgiveness could have His perfect righteousness credited to their accounts.

This is an incredible transfer, described this way by Paul: "He [God] made Him [Jesus Christ] who knew no sin to be sin on our behalf, so that we might become the righteousness of God in Him" (2 Corinthians 5:21). God imputed or charged our sin to Christ's account, even though He didn't deserve it. He paid the terrible debt for that sin, and God credited the righteousness of Christ to our account, which was formerly full of sin we couldn't do anything about.

Some people may think this transaction is not necessary because they are counting on the self-righteousness they have been depositing in their spiritual accounts. These are the people who believe they are accumulating enough goodness to pass God's bar of judgment and make it into heaven.

We don't know our true spiritual condition until God audits our account and says, "There is none righteous, not even one" (Romans 3:10). Until God imputes or credits the perfect righteousness of Christ to our lives, we are utterly bankrupt spiritually.

THE DEMONSTRATION OF JUSTIFICATION

Justification is a spiritual transformation that takes place in our hearts when we come to Christ for salvation. But that doesn't mean our salvation is strictly a private deal between us and God. Being declared righteous in the sight of God should produce changes in our attitudes and behavior that are visible in the sight of others.

That's what I mean by saying that our justification should be demonstrated. Christians ought to act differently than those who don't know Christ. That's the point the apostle James was making when he wrote, "What use is it, my brethren, if someone says he has faith but he has no works? Can that faith save him?" (James 2:14) .

A Faith That Works

This verse introduces a passage (James 2:14–26) that generated a lot of controversy in church history because James seems to be contradicting the biblical teaching of salvation by faith alone (see Romans 4:1–8; Ephesians 2:8–9). But James is complementing, not contradicting, the truth that we are justified in God's sight through faith alone. James is giving us the human perspective of a divine transaction.

This difference in perspective is the key to understanding James 2. His illustration of a brother or sister in need who is turned away without receiving what he or she needs (vv. 15–17) shows that James was writing about justification not in terms of our standing before God (which was Paul's focus), but in terms of our standing before other people, particularly fellow Christians. James was simply saying that justification should make a difference in the way we live.

Saints Who Look Like Saints

Paul was talking about how sinners become saints. James was talking about how saints can look like saints before others.

We can tell people that we are saved, but they can't see what happened in our hearts between God and us. They can only see what we do. A faith that stays private and never reaches our mouths and hands and feet isn't worth much if we're sending our destitute brothers and sisters away with nothing but a blessing when they're hungry and cold. There is definitely a sense in which our good works help to perfect our salvation.

Now, of course, it's possible for a person to act and look like a Christian and yet not be saved at all, just as it's possible to teach a chimpanzee to mimic human behavior. Chimps can perform all kinds of humanlike behaviors, but it's only an act because they lack the life principle of humanity within. So it is with non-Christians who do not have the life of Christ within but still look and act like Christians. They do not have the life principle in them. They have not been justified by faith, so their works have no meaning to God because they are not in a right relationship before Him. Therefore, let's be clear that justification by works is real only when it flows out of a life that has been justified before God by faith. It's not a matter of having one without the other. These two aspects of justification are not something we have to choose between.

THE BENEFITS OF JUSTIFICATION

If justification produces a radical change within us and leads to what should be a radical change in our behavior, there ought to be some benefits of this that we can enjoy. And there are.

Incredible Peace

Everybody wants peace at some level, but peace only comes as the result of a process. "Therefore, having been justified by faith, we have peace with God through our Lord Jesus Christ" (Romans 5:1). This is the peace that comes at the cessation of hostilities. This is the peace that makes friends out of former enemies.

Peace means that God is now our Friend because the reason for the hostility and the barrier between us—our sin—has been removed by Christ. And as Paul said, "If God is for us, who is against us?" (Romans 8:31). Paul went on to list a lot of things that could be against us: "tribulation, or distress, or persecution, or famine, or nakedness, or peril, or sword" (v. 35). But then he came back with the triumphant answer, "In all these things we overwhelmingly conquer through Him who loved us" (v. 37). If you have been justified, God is on your side, even when life seems to fall in on you.

Unlimited Access

Romans 5 continues with the benefits of justification, and it just keeps getting better. "Through [Christ] also we have obtained our introduction by faith into this grace in which we stand" (v. 2). This is the promise of access to God, because once you are at peace with Him and the door barring your way to Him has been opened, you are welcome to come into His presence anytime you want to come. God is ready to meet with you because you have gained access to Him through His Son.

Eternal Hope

We also have lasting hope through the salvation we have in Christ. Paul continued in Romans 5:2, "We exult in hope of the glory of God." And again, "Hope does not disappoint, because the love of God has been poured out within our hearts through the Holy Spirit who was given to us" (v. 5).

Hope means that even when it looks like it's all over, it's not all over yet. That's why the Bible says we can rejoice even in our tribulations. God is working in our hard times to produce proven character and hope in us (vv. 3–4). It's not over yet because "God causes all things to work together for good to those who love God, to those who are called according to His purpose" (Romans 8:28).

Restoration to Fellowship

Justification by the blood of Christ brings us permanently into a right relationship with God. We don't need to get saved again. The penalty for sin has forever been paid.

While we can never lose our relationship with God, we can disrupt our fellowship with Him due to sin. In order for fellowship to be restored, sin must be addressed. God's way of addressing our sin is through confession and repentance.

Confession means "to say the same thing." It is agreeing with God about a failure that is immediately addressed by saying the same thing that God says about the spiritual infraction. That's why John says, "If we confess our sins, He is faithful and just to forgive us our sins and cleanse us from all unrighteousness" (1 John 1:9). Such agreement allows harmony with God to continue uninterrupted.

Repentance, on the other hand, addresses the need to repair our relationships with God due to some prolonged unrighteous attitude or action in order to prevent or terminate His temporal judgment for our sins. The word *repent* means to change the mind in order to reverse the direction. It involves turning from sin. It's like traveling the wrong way on the highway and deciding to reverse your course. You exit, cross over the overpass, and enter the on-ramps going the other way. It is a change of direction. This change is illustrated in the return of the prodigal son after his prolonged departure from harmony with his father (Luke 15).

There is also a great picture of this cleansing in Zechariah, a vision the prophet had of the high priest Joshua, who was serving at that time. In the vision Zechariah saw Joshua standing before "the angel of the Lord, and Satan standing at his right hand to accuse him" (Zechariah 3:1).

This is a picture of us as believers standing before Christ, who appeared in the Old Testament as the angel of the Lord. Satan is our accuser too (Revelation 12:10), and he often has something to work with because we still sin. Joshua stood accused, but God reminded Satan in no uncertain terms that He had already redeemed Joshua. "The Lord rebuke you, Satan! Indeed, the Lord who has chosen Jerusalem rebuke you! Is this not a brand plucked from the fire?" (Zechariah 3:2). We have already been plucked from the fire of God's wrath, for remember that Paul said there is no wrath to come for those who have been justified by Christ's blood.

Now notice Zechariah 3:3. Joshua stood before the Lord "with filthy garments." Something wasn't right, but he had come to the Lord for grace, help, and forgiveness. And God responded, "Remove the filthy garments from him. . . . See, I have taken your iniquity away from you and will clothe you with festal robes" (v. 4). Then God told Joshua, "If you will walk in My ways and if you will perform My service, then you will also govern My house and also have charge of My courts, and I will grant you free access among these who are standing here" (v. 7).

We all get dirty as we live in the world, but because we have peace and access and hope, we can come to God and receive a cleansing and a new set of clothes . . . all because we have been justified as a gift of God's grace.

PERSONAL APPLICATION FOR LIFE

1. In our current post-Christian era, Christian norms are no longer widely acknowledged or accepted. In fact, views of Christianity are often distorted by our society. Even the Bible is not considered the Word of God. But how we conduct our lives in full view of the world can impact our culture.

2. Do you feel like people and circumstances are against you? Well, take encouragement. One of the great benefits of being justified by faith is that we have the peace of God that has removed the barrier of sin in our lives. Whatever is getting you down, keep this promise before you: "In all these things we overwhelmingly conquer through Him who loved us" (Romans 5:37). Claim your victory!

3. According to Romans 8:28, God has called us according to His purpose. That means we have hope for the future. The Word of God is replete with God's promises regarding the future. Embrace God's Word and His promises, and allow them to shape your present experience. Obedience to God's Word aligns us to His will.

4. Romans 3:10 is emphatic—none of us is righteous. Nothing you can do can make you righteous in God's eyes. But because you are justified by God, He credits His righteousness to you! It's an amazing spiritual transaction on your behalf, and one you don't deserve. Always try to demonstrate your justification in visible ways, or works, that point others to Christ.

FOR GROUP STUDY

Questions for Group Discussion

1. What is the meaning of the biblical term *justification*? According to Romans 8:33, from where does justification originate? Read Romans 3:19–23. What is our verdict when we are measured against the law?

2. Why is justification a gift? Who are the candidates for God's justification? Read 2 Corinthians 5:21. By what means does one receive His justification?

3. What are the results in the life of one who is justified by Christ? In what ways do we see the evidence of justification demonstrated in the life of one who has been justified?

4. What are the benefits of justification? What can we expect to receive after we have been brought into a right standing before God? (Use the "Picture This" chart as an aid to your discussion.)

PICTURE THIS

While the Bible teaches that justification produces radical changes in our behavior, it also provides many benefits. Below are four of the benefits of God's work of justification in the life of the believer.

THE BENEFITS OF JUSTIFICATION

BENEFIT	SCRIPTURE PASSAGE	WHAT IT MEANS
Incredible peace	Romans 5:1	The barrier (our sin) between us and God has been removed.
Unlimited access	Romans 5:2	We are welcome to enter into God's presence anytime.
Eternal hope	Romans 5:2–5; 8:28	"We exult in the hope of the glory of God." We will stand before Him as His justified saints.
Restoration to fellowship	1 John 1:19	By addressing our sins through confession and repentance, we can restore fellowship with God.

60

REDEMPTION: THE PAYMENT FOR SALVATION

One of the great heroes in African-American history is a woman named Harriet Tubman, a slave in Maryland who escaped to Philadelphia over the famous "Underground Railroad" and then became one of its most successful conductors in the years leading up to the Civil War.

Mrs. Tubman became known as "Moses" for her work in helping bring slaves to freedom. Altogether, she made nineteen trips back to the South and led about three hundred slaves from bondage to freedom. It was said that she worked between trips to get enough money to pay whatever it took for these slaves to reach freedom. The work of the Underground Railroad was a process of redemption, taking people out of slavery and setting them free no matter what the cost.

This story of redemption from human slavery forms an excellent backdrop for discussing the redemption that God accomplished when He sent His Son from heaven to lift us from our spiritual slavery to sin. Redemption involves paying a purchase price, and it was often used in the context of the slave market. This is how the biblical writers used the term to describe the purchase price that Jesus Christ paid on the cross.

The people of Jesus' day readily understood references to slavery because at that time the nation of Israel itself was under the heel of its Roman conquerors, and an estimated sixty million people were living as slaves throughout the Roman Empire. These people understood slavery very well. Jesus used the term *slave* on one occasion to startle His hearers with the reality of sin's bondage and their need for redemption.

This discussion took place in John 8, where a group of Jews came to believe in Jesus after hearing Him deal with the Pharisees (v. 30). Turning to the people around Him, Jesus said, "If you continue in My word, then you are truly disciples of Mine; and you will know the truth, and the truth will make you free" (vv. 31–32).

The suggestion that they needed to be free struck these people as a mistake, since as Jews they considered themselves to be no man's slave. So they said to Jesus, "We are Abraham's descendants and have never yet been enslaved to anyone" (v. 33). Then Jesus laid out the real deal. "Truly, truly, I say to you, everyone who commits sin is the slave of sin" (v. 34). The clear implication was that Jesus' hearers were included in this group that was enslaved to sin.

The people understood what Jesus was getting at so well that they became increasingly hostile until He finally said to them, "You are of your father the devil, and you want to do the desires of your father" (v. 44). These verses spell out the problem we all have that requires redemption, because all of us are born in slavery to sin. And as surely as the chains and shackles of slavery held their victims in an iron grip, the chains and shackles of sin hold every person in an iron grip until Jesus comes to the slave market with His precious blood and redeems us from the auction block.

THE CONCEPT OF REDEMPTION

With this understanding in place, we're ready to talk about the term *redeemed*, or *redemption*, and to explore the richness of its meaning in Scripture.

Making the Purchase

The Greek term for *redemption* means "to buy or to purchase." A person who wanted to purchase a slave would go to the slave market and bid on slaves as they were put on the auction block and offered for sale. And depending on how much potential buyers wanted to purchase a particular slave, the bidding price could go quite high. This process is important to keep in mind as we talk about Christ's redemption and the price He paid to redeem us from slavery to sin.

The Greek word usually translated "redemption" can also be translated "ransom," as in Matthew 20:28, where Jesus said, "The Son of Man did not come to be served, but to serve, and to give His life a ransom for many." We're familiar with the idea of paying a ransom for someone who has been kidnapped or taken prisoner and is being held in bondage until the payment that's demanded is met. Through the sin of our forefather Adam, you and I were kidnapped by sin and Satan and held in bondage until the price was paid to set us free.

We were held in bondage to sin—but the price Jesus paid to redeem us was paid to God, not to Satan. I make this clear because in the early centuries of the church, a heresy arose that said that Jesus' death on the cross was a ransom paid to Satan for our freedom. That heresy was thoroughly condemned. God is the offended party to whom payment for sin must be made, not the Devil.

Setting the Slaves Free

The concept of a ransom helps us to understand that when Jesus redeemed us, He did so for the purpose of setting us free, not re-enslaving us. The word Jesus used in Matthew 20:28 for ransom meant the redemption price for a slave. This word is closely related to the basic word for redemption, which we would expect. Emphasizing these words is important because what the New Testament writers did a number of times was take this word for redemption (*lutrosis*) and add a prepositional prefix to it (*apolutrosis*) that "super sized" it.

That is, when the Greek word for redemption is used with this prefix, it signifies more than that Jesus bought us from the slave market of sin. It emphasizes that we have been redeemed in such a way that nobody can ever enslave us again. It means we are redeemed completely and *permanently*.

This stronger word for redemption is used in Romans 3:24; Ephesians 1:7, 14; 4:30; and Colossians 1:14, among other places. It beautifully underscores the permanence of our redemption, which is also a compelling biblical argument for the eternal security of the saved, a truth we'll get to in time.

Pushing the Goat over the Cliff

The background of redemption goes all the way back to ancient Israel as the nation observed the Day of Atonement, the most solemn day of the year, in which the high priest would offer atonement for the people's sins for another year.

According to Leviticus 16:8–26, the high priest chose two goats, one to be sacrificed and the other to be released into the wilderness symbolically bearing away the people's sins. This live goat was called the "scapegoat." The high priest laid his hands on the head of the goat and confessed the nation's sins over the goat, and then it was released in the wilderness. This ritual signified the removal of sin, thus averting the judgment of God against sin for the next year.

Now the only problem was that this goat sometimes wandered back into the Israelites' camp, which nobody wanted to see because it was like having their sins come back on them. So according to some sources, the person who led the goat into the wilderness often took the goat to a cliff and pushed it off. That's a picture of complete redemption—the removal of sin in such a way that it will never show up again.

THE COST OF REDEMPTION

What was the cost Jesus had to pay to redeem us? Peter addressed this when he wrote to believers scattered across the empire. He urged them to live in the fear of the Lord, because "you were not redeemed with perishable things like silver or gold . . . but with precious blood, as of a lamb unblemished and spotless, the blood of Christ" (1 Peter 1:18–19).

If you're a slave on the auction block and someone wants to purchase you, your redeemer has to be able to afford the cost of your redemption. Jesus could afford the cost.

Jesus Had to Shed His Blood

Blood has always been the price for sin. "Without shedding of blood there is no forgiveness" (Hebrews 9:22). Money won't do the job. We can't buy our way out of the sin mess. Peter called silver and gold "perishable things" that have no purchasing power in heaven's economy. "In Him [Christ] we have redemption through His blood" (Ephesians 1:7).

Why blood? The Bible tells us in Deuteronomy 12:23, "The blood is the life." So the shedding of blood is another way of saying that the sacrifice had to die. Jesus had to die on the cross, not simply hang there and suffer for a while. Because He died, He was able to enter into the tabernacle in heaven to offer His blood as the payment for sin (see Hebrews 9:11–14). And what did His death purchase? "The redemption of the transgressions that were committed under the first covenant," according to Hebrews 9:15.

Jesus Had to Be Sinless

The redeemer also had to be someone who was not among the slaves himself. If you and I are both slaves, I'm not going to come to you saying, "Pay the price and set me free." If you can't set yourself free, you certainly can't buy my freedom. It's like the two men who fell into a deep ditch. One of the men panicked, turned to the other man, and said, "Get me out of here!" But the other man was in the same mess. What those men needed was someone from above the ditch reaching down to pull them out.

Whoever is going to redeem slaves has to be a free person. Transferring this to the spiritual realm, it means our redeemer has to be sinless. Why? Because we're enslaved to the sin that we inherited from Adam and the sin we commit ourselves. Since God is perfectly holy, He will not accept payment for sin from a sinner.

That's why Jesus was born of a virgin. Sin is passed on through the father, so Jesus could not have a human father. He had to be born without sin, and He also had to live a sinless life. Peter said God's sacrifice for sin was "unblemished" and "spotless" (1 Peter 1:19), just as were the animals used for sacrifice under the Law.

The mention of a lamb as the sin sacrifice again takes us back to the Old Testament. The lambs that the Israelites brought to offer for their sins had to be without any defects. Why? Because they were a picture of the coming Redeemer who would be totally sinless and blameless, and whose death, therefore, would pay the redemption price God demanded.

If Jesus had the same sin problem we have, He could not be our Redeemer because He Himself would need a redeemer. He had to be free of any blemish of sin. He had to live a perfect life and defeat the Devil. He had to be perfect so He could offer His "precious blood" to redeem us out of slavery.

Jesus Had to Become a Man

The author of Hebrews made a very important statement when he said, "It is impossible for the blood of bulls and goats to take away sins" (10:4). Animal sacrifices could only cover sins until God's perfect sacrifice came. In order to be a suitable substitute for mankind, Jesus had to be a man. That's why He left heaven's glory to take on human flesh. In light of the cost that Jesus paid, anything we could offer to God as a payment for our sins would be an insult to Him.

Nothing we can offer God will even begin to make up for what it cost Him to save us—His precious Son. The cost of our redemption is infinitely high.

THE ACCOMPLISHMENT OF REDEMPTION

What did Christ's redemption accomplish for us? In one sense, we've been answering this question throughout the chapter as we have discussed this aspect of our great salvation. But I want to give you two specifics here that are important in helping to fill out the picture of what Christ has done for us.

Jesus Freed Us from the Curse

The Bible says that we were under a curse before we came to know Jesus Christ. Paul explained the nature of the curse in Galatians 3:10: "For as many as are of the works of the Law are under a curse; for it is written, 'Cursed is everyone who does not abide by all things written in the book of the Law, to perform them.'"

God's requirement is perfect obedience. A person would have to keep all of God's law, without failure or exception, to merit His favor. Anything less than that, and the offender falls under God's curse. James put it this way: "Whoever keeps the whole law and yet stumbles in one point, he has become guilty of all" (James 2:10). The law is not a cafeteria where you can pick out what you want and skip the rest.

Since we have all failed to keep God's law, we are all under its curse. But here's the good news: "Christ redeemed us from the curse of the Law, having become a curse for us—for it is written, 'Cursed is everyone who hangs on a tree'" (Galatians 3:13). Of course, Christ hung on a tree when He died on the cross, and His death redeemed us from the law's curse, which was the sanctions and penalties the law imposed on those who disobeyed it.

In other words, the law of God had consequences attached to it. That's true even in human law. Wherever you have law and the possibility of violation, you have penalties attached for those violations. God is too holy to skip the penalty for sin.

That's what Christ did for us when He paid the redemption price to remove us from the law's curse, which was physical death and ultimately spiritual death. God couldn't just look the other way and ignore His law, because His holy demands are inextricably tied to His holy character. He can't skip the law, but He will allow somebody else to pay the debt we owe.

That's why Jesus came. In Galatians 4:4-5, Paul made this very interesting statement about Christ: "When the fullness of time came, God sent forth His Son, born of a woman, born under the Law, so that He might redeem those who were under the Law, that we might receive the adoption as sons."

God Adopted Us into His Family

Thanks to redemption, we're family! It's one thing to be bought off the slave market and set free. It's another thing entirely to be taken into the home of the person who freed you and given full status and inheritance as a member of the family.

That's what adoption meant in Paul's day. It was entirely different from adoption as we know it. Instead of adopting infants or children, families in those days took a child in and raised him to adulthood before adopting him. The adoptee became not only a full member of the family, but an heir of the estate.

When Christ redeemed us, He brought us into His Father's house and gave us all the rights and privileges that come with being members of God's family.

We Are Set Free from Fear

What do you think most people fear more than anything else? My guess is that most people fear death the most (see Hebrews 2:15).

There is fear in the thought of death, especially for those who don't know Christ. Death has a sting to it. "The sting of death is sin, and the power of sin is the law" (1 Corinthians 15:56). The law reveals our sin to us, and sin results in death. Death is the curse of the law. That's how it works, which is why you ought to be thankful every day that Christ has redeemed you from the curse of the law. You need not fear death if you know the Lord.

PERSONAL APPLICATION FOR LIFE

1. Are you motivated to serve Christ? Jesus bought us out of our slavery to sin and saved us from death, and He did so by paying a high price that we cannot fathom. If you are not serving Christ and using your gifts to further His kingdom, volunteer now to serve. If you don't know where to start, ask your pastor for help.

2. Colossians 1:28 exhorts us to proclaim Christ, "admonishing every man and teaching every man with all wisdom." Seize opportunities to proclaim the good news of our Lord. Keep in mind that we proclaim Christ not only by our words, but also by our actions.

3. Not only has our redemption set us free from our bondage to sin, Matthew 20:28 emphasizes that we have been redeemed completely and permanently. We can never be enslaved in such a way again! Give thanks to God for sending His Son to redeem us.

4. Since your relationship with Christ is first and foremost one of love, ask Him to keep your heart tender toward Him. If your focus is on loving the Lord, you won't have to worry about being sensitive to sin.

FOR GROUP STUDY

Questions for Group Discussion

1. What is the meaning of the biblical term *redemption*? What is the special significance of the Greek term (*apolutrosis*) Jesus used in Matthew 20:28?

2. First Peter 1:18–19 tells us that our redemption came at an enormous cost. For what reasons was Jesus the only person who could pay the cost of redemption?

3. What did Christ's redemption accomplish for us?

4. What do you believe should be our response to our redemption, to so great a salvation? (Use the chart on the next page as an aid to your discussion; what other appropriate responses come to mind?)

PICTURE THIS

The gift of redemption and eternal life should motivate us to several kinds of responses. Below are three responses we should have to our gift of redemption.

OUR PROPER RESPONSE TO REDEMPTION

SPECIFIC RESPONSE	SCRIPTURE PASSAGES	WHAT IT INVOLVES
We should serve Christ.	Titus 2:14	We should be motivated to serve Christ for all that He has done for us.
We should worship Christ.	Revelation 1:5–6	We will be worshiping Christ for eternity.
We should proclaim Christ.	Colossians 1:28; 1 Corinthians 1:23	We have a message to proclaim: "We preach Christ crucified."

61

PROPITIATION: THE REQUIREMENT OF SALVATION

Propitiation is necessary because our sin has offended the holiness of God and incurred His wrath, which must be satisfied or appeased before He can accept us.

This is the key to the meaning of propitiation. To propitiate means to render one person favorably disposed toward another. It signifies the averting of wrath by the offering of a gift to appease the offended party's anger. We could summarize this great concept with the word *satisfaction*. To propitiate means to satisfy. God is dissatisfied with the human race because sin is an affront to His holy character. So something must be done to appease God's righteous anger.

THE PRINCIPLE OF PROPITIATION

The Bible is filled with examples of one person propitiating another. Jacob sought to propitiate his brother Esau after stealing his blessing, bringing goats and camels as a gift (Genesis 32:13–20; 33:8–11). After Abigail's foolish husband, Nabal, insulted David and his men, Abigail took David an offering and pleaded with him not to kill Nabal (1 Samuel 25:14–35). In 2 Kings 18:13–16, King Hezekiah propitiated Sennacherib, the king of Assyria, with gold and silver in order to keep him from invading Jerusalem.

Two Problems with Human Propitiation

There are at least two questions that arise in any human attempt at propitiation. The first is whether the gift or offering is sufficient to turn away the other person's anger. The second is whether the offended party will accept the gift, no matter how great it is. David could have been so angry at Nabal that he wouldn't have been satisfied if Abigail had given him every penny she had.

I mention these conditions because we don't have to worry about the payment for sin being adequate or God refusing to accept it. Christ's death on the cross was a complete payment for sin, and God is completely satisfied with His Son's offering.

God's Nature Has Two Perfect Sides

God's satisfaction with this payment for sin is definitely good news. Yet a lot of people don't want to believe that God is all that upset with the human race and such a payment is necessary. These are the ones who say that God is too loving to judge sin or condemn anyone to hell, and they want to end the discussion of God's nature right there.

God is love, but He is also just. His response to sin is necessitated by His righteousness. The Bible teaches that there are two sides to God's character. Paul summarized them in Romans 11:22 when he wrote, "Behold then the kindness and severity of God." We could call these the polar caps of God's character. His kindness, or love, and His severity, or judgment, are in perfect harmony because they are both perfect attributes of His being.

If you understand a surgeon's "wrath" against contamination in a hospital operating room, you understand God's wrath against sin. He is perfect and sinless in every detail, and His character demands that He deal with the slightest contamination of sin. God also knows that sin leads to total corruption and infection, so for these reasons He must judge sin. As we read in Nahum, He will not let the guilty go unpunished.

God has already passed judgment on the world and declared all of us guilty because "all have sinned" (Romans 3:23). He has also pronounced the sentence against sin: "The wages of sin is death" (Romans 6:23). Therefore, we must either bear the full brunt of God's wrath against our sin, or someone must come in between us and God and provide an offering that is adequate to satisfy His demands so that we can go free.

THE PROVISION OF PROPITIATION

This brings us to a question. What do we give someone who already has everything? What can we offer to propitiate a Being whose only acceptable standard is perfection? When it comes to propitiation, we are in trouble on our own because whatever pitiful offering we could make is so far below what God requires that the only way He could accept it would be to compromise His holy character. And that is never going to happen.

God Paid the Price Himself

I don't want to pay the price for my sin, and neither does anyone else in his right mind. So what do we do? We have no gift costly enough or perfect enough to propitiate or satisfy God. The prophet Micah asked, "With what shall I come to the Lord and bow myself before the God on high?" (Micah 6:6).

This is the dilemma for every person, but there is good news. Knowing that we had nothing in ourselves with which to satisfy Him, God decided to take the initiative and provide His own sacrifice of propitiation. Think about what that means for you and me. Paul put it this way: "For while we were still helpless, at the right time Christ died for the ungodly" (Romans 5:6).

We have a wonderful biblical example of this principle in the offering of Isaac by his father, Abraham. As Abraham and Isaac were heading up the mountain where Abraham was going to offer Isaac in obedience to God, Isaac asked a very fundamental question. "Behold, the fire and the wood, but where is the lamb for the burnt offering?" (Genesis 22:7).

Abraham's answer summarized the heart of what God has done for us. "God will provide for Himself the lamb for the burnt offering" (v. 8). God Himself absorbed the awful cost to provide a sacrifice that would satisfy His righteous demands.

God Turned His Wrath on His Son

God looked at our spiritual bankruptcy and saw that we had nothing with which to pay the bill of sin. So in the person of Jesus Christ, God made Himself the answer to our problem. Since we could not satisfy God's wrath against sin, He decided to satisfy His wrath by turning it on His own Son.

God's judgment against sin had to be applied, but His love moved Him to devise a plan whereby the guilty would go free and His innocent Son would be punished. We could say that God drew on His love to pay His wrath—a divine transaction that we had no part whatsoever in helping to bring about.

God was propitiated by the offering of a sacrifice. In the Old Testament system, the place of propitiation for sin was the "mercy seat" that formed the lid on the ark of the covenant (Hebrews 9:1–5). The high priest entered the Holy of Holies, the inner sanctum of the tabernacle and later the temple, once a year to offer the blood of the sacrificial lamb on the mercy seat. If God accepted the sacrifice, the sins of the people of Israel were covered for another year.

We know that this sacrifice was an act of propitiation because the word translated "mercy seat" in Hebrews 9:5 is a form of the word for propitiation. The mercy seat was the place of propitiation.

This is significant because later in Hebrews 9 the writer said that Jesus Christ entered the Holy Place of the true temple in heaven as a once-and-for-all sacrifice for sin (vv. 24–28). He did this "by the sacrifice of Himself" (v. 26), offering His own blood on the mercy seat. Through Christ's death, God has been propitiated forever toward sinners, and the way of salvation is open.

THE POWER OF PROPITIATION

Propitiation was accomplished two thousand years ago on the cross. But it doesn't end there, because Jesus Christ is active today in heaven as our Great High Priest. The Bible says, "He is able also to save forever those who draw near to God through Him, since He always lives to make intercession for them" (Hebrews 7:25).

Our Defense Attorney in Heaven

Jesus Christ is called our "advocate," or defense attorney (1 John 2:1–2), who appears before the Father on our behalf. Why do we need a defense attorney? Because Satan, "the accuser of [the] brethren" (Revelation 12:10), is constantly bringing our sins before God, knowing that God cannot overlook sin and must respond to it. Satan is looking to get a judgment against us.

Satan understands the wrath of God because he has experienced it. He was banished from heaven and will spend eternity in hell, because of God's righteous wrath against sin. What Satan wants to do is take us down with him.

But he will never succeed, because our advocate is Jesus Christ, who has forever satisfied God's demands. The setting in 1 John 2 is a courtroom. God is the judge, and we are the defendants who have sinned and broken fellowship with Him. The prosecutor is Satan, who wants the Judge to throw the book at us for our sin.

But then our advocate steps forward and says, "Father, I object. While the accuser is correct on the sin, what has not been brought forth is the fact that I have already paid for this sin and satisfied Your demands through the blood I shed on the cross. And My blood will continue to pay for sin because the accused is one of those I have redeemed."

God's Only Program for Sin

This is our advocate, Jesus Christ, who Himself is the propitiation for our sins. Later in his epistle, John used this term again to describe Jesus when he wrote, "In this is love, not that we loved God, but that He loved us and sent His Son to be the propitiation for our sins" (1 John 4:10).

God only has one program to deal with sin, and that program is His beloved Son. God the Father is completely satisfied with Jesus' sacrifice for sin, which is why He doesn't want to hear about our plans for trying to make ourselves acceptable to Him. The only thing that satisfies God is His Son.

God doesn't want to know what you are going to do with your sin. He wants to know what you are going to do with His Son.

THE EXTENT OF PROPITIATION

I didn't deal with the last phrase of 1 John 2:2 earlier because I wanted to save it for special study as we close this chapter. John said that Jesus was not only the propitiation for our sins, meaning that of believers, "but also for those of the whole world." We need to find out what John meant by this, because at first reading it sounds like everyone is going to be saved.

But we know that the Bible does not teach universal salvation, so it's important to understand in what sense Jesus has made propitiation for the sins of every person. This raises the issue of the extent of Christ's atonement, a vital biblical doctrine.

The Reality of God's Love

According to Romans 5:8–9, "God demonstrates His own love toward us, in that while we were yet sinners, Christ died for us. Much more then, having now been justified by His blood, we shall be saved from the wrath of God through Him." Notice several things about the Bible's teaching concerning salvation.

First, God demonstrated His love. He didn't just talk about it. We often talk a better game than we play when it comes to love, but God put His love on the line by giving His Son for our sin.

How do you know God loves you? Because of Calvary. The proof of God's love is what Jesus suffered on the cross of Calvary when He took our place and suffered God's full wrath against sin to satisfy God's righteous demands.

Second, notice also that God's love in salvation is unconditional. God gave us His Son while we were still sinners in rebellion against Him. He didn't ask us to get better first or clean up our act before Jesus would receive us. Salvation comes without preconditions.

Third, the Bible also says that salvation is permanent. Paul asked, "Who will separate us from the love of Christ?" (Romans 8:35). Answer: No one and nothing! He gives a long list of possibilities; then, in case he missed anything, he adds, "nor any other created thing, will be able to separate us from the love of God, which is in Christ Jesus our Lord" (v. 39). Once you truly receive salvation, you can never lose it.

Fourth, the salvation God provided in Christ Jesus extends to all people. This is what John was saying in 1 John 2:2. The atonement of Christ is unlimited, in other words. The question is how the atonement is applied to believers and unbelievers, since the Bible also clearly teaches that many people will be lost for eternity despite the fact that sufficient provision has been made for their salvation if they will turn to Christ.

The Outworking of God's Love

The Bible is clear that Christ died for every man, woman, boy, and girl who was, is, and ever will be born. Jesus is the Savior of the whole world (see John 1:29; 3:16).

Paul made this important statement: "While we were still helpless, at the right time Christ died for the ungodly" (Romans 5:6). How many people are ungodly? Everybody. The Bible says Jesus "gave Himself as a ransom for all" (1 Timothy 2:6). We could multiply biblical examples that show that Christ died for every person.

Christ's salvation has a two-pronged effect. Because Adam was acting as our representative when he sinned in the garden, his sin was charged to the account of the human race. "Through one man sin entered into the world" (Romans 5:12). Then Paul said: "For if by the transgression of the one the many died, much more did . . . the gift by the grace of the one Man, Jesus Christ, abound to the many" (v. 15). The key phrase here is "the many." In relation to Adam's sin, "the many" are those who inherited his sin and the spiritual death it brought, which is every person. Paul said this same group has been given the gift of grace in Jesus Christ. As the apostle wrote in 1 Corinthians 15:22, "For as in Adam all die, so also in Christ all will be made alive."

The question is, Does this teach universal salvation? After all, John said that Jesus accomplished the work of propitiation for the whole world. I use the word *accomplished* for a reason, because the Bible teaches that Christ did not simply offer or make possible salvation for all. He accomplished salvation for all.

Some people see a conflict between this fact and the undeniable reality that not all people are saved. One group tries to get around this by saying that Christ died only for the elect. But that doesn't work, because Hebrews 2:9 clearly says that Jesus tasted death for every person.

Another group tries to solve the problem by arguing that Christ merely provided or offered salvation to everybody. But this weakens the power of salvation's offer because according to Romans 5:18, from Christ's "one act of righteousness there resulted justification of life to all men." This says that the work necessary for salvation has been accomplished, not just offered or made possible.

Why Everyone Is Not Saved

So if all of this is true, why are not all people saved? We need to look at Romans 5:17: "For if by the transgression of the one, death reigned through the one, much more those who receive the abundance of grace and of the gift of righteousness will reign in life through the One, Jesus Christ." Here is the key to what the Bible means when it says that all those who inherited Adam's sin have been brought under the saving death of Christ.

The answer is quite simple. Take note of the word *receive* in the middle of verse 17. Christ has accomplished salvation for all people regarding Adam's sin, but His atonement is effective for personal sin only for those who receive it. You didn't have a choice about inheriting Adam's sin, but you do have a choice to receive or reject God's grace in Christ for the sins you have committed. If you refuse Jesus as the propitiation for your sins, you are left with the impossible task of trying to satisfy God through your own merits and good works.

Two things must happen before we can be saved. First, God's holy and righteous wrath against sin must be satisfied by the shedding of blood, which is the act of propitiation we have been talking about. Because God is propitiated by the death of His Son, He is now free to forgive and save sinners.

But to get us into heaven, we not only need God's judgment against sin to be satisfied; we must have perfect righteousness to stand before Him because God is perfect. When we trust Christ, His righteousness is credited to our account, just the way Adam's sin was charged to our account. This wonderful transaction is called *imputation*, meaning that Christ imputed or transferred His righteousness to us, canceling out the sin that was charged against us from Adam (see chapter 58, page 710).

The implications of this are staggering. This answers the objection of those who say they don't think it's fair that they should die for Adam's sin. No one has to worry about that, because the fact is that nobody will go to hell for Adam's sin. Adam's sin was paid for in Christ's death for the whole human race. The sin for which people will have to answer is their own sin, not the sin nature they inherited from Adam.

This explains, for example, why babies go to heaven when they die. Babies are born with a sin nature inherited from Adam, but they have no personal sin to account for because they have not reached the age at which they can be held accountable. Babies go to heaven because what Jesus did on the cross took care of Adam's sin, that is, original sin.

So make no mistake. People will go to hell because they sinned, not because Adam sinned. The effects of his sin are still with us, to be sure. But Christ's death canceled the penalty of Adam's sin. Jesus said in John 3:18 that people are condemned because "[they have] not believed in the name of the only begotten Son of God." Jesus has done everything necessary for salvation. All we need to do is place our faith in His finished work, and He applies His righteousness to us.

PERSONAL APPLICATION FOR LIFE

1. In 1 John 2:1–2, Jesus Christ is called our "advocate," what we would call a defense attorney. Because Satan constantly accuses us by bringing our sins before God, we need an advocate. We could never win this battle ourselves. But Jesus wins the battle for us, as He paid the penalty and satisfied God's demands for payment. Salvation is a priceless gift. Take a moment now to thank God for His great gift.

2. Because of Christ's sacrifice and payment for your sin, you have a new life and a new identify in Christ. To help remember your new identity in Christ, memorize Galatians 5:24. Write it out and carry it with you, so you can pull it out at work, memorizing it when you get spare moments.

3. Christ paid an enormous price for your salvation. As believers, our natural response should be love toward Him. Perhaps you've gotten away from your first love for Jesus Christ and your faithful service to Him. Like a prodigal son, you need to return home to full commitment to Jesus Christ. Whatever it takes, put your love for Him back in first place where it belongs. God has a unique way of reweaving us back into His will.

4. As a visible reminder that you have taken off the old life and put on the new, find the oldest and most tattered piece of clothing you have and put it out where you'll see it every day for a while. Every time you look at it, thank God for the new you!

FOR GROUP STUDY

Questions for Group Discussion

1. What is the principle of propitiation? As preparation for discussion, review these biblical examples of propitiation: Genesis 33; 1 Samuel 25:14–35; and 2 Kings 18:13–16.

2. What are the two problems with human propitiation? How is divine propitiation different?

3. Read Romans 5:6 and Hebrews 9:24–28. Discuss the provision of propitiation. Why is the payment for our sin complete, and why is God completely satisfied with His Son's offering?

4. What is the power behind propitiation? How do we, as believers, benefit from that power?

PICTURE THIS

The extent of God's propitiation was not only for believers, but also for the whole world. The following points help us understand the true extent of His propitiation.

THE EXTENT OF GOD'S PROPITIATION

SUBJECT	SCRIPTURE PASSAGE	WHAT IT MEANS
The reality of God's love	Romans 5:8–9	God proved His love by giving His Son for our sin.
The outworking of God's love	John 1:29; 3:16	Through Christ's death, God removed the barrier between Himself and sinners.
Why not everyone is saved	Romans 5:15–17	Christ's atonement for sin is effective only for those who personally receive it.
A prayer we do not have to pray	Luke 18:10–14	We have no need to ask God to be propitiated toward Him with regard to our sin and salvation. He is forever satisfied through the death of His Son.

62

RECONCILIATION: THE RELATIONSHIP OF SALVATION

Reconciliation is another great transaction that took place when we were saved by the grace of God. Reconciliation has to do with the removal of hostility and the restoration of harmony in a relationship. It means that the wall separating the hostile parties has been broken down; the breach between them has been healed.

God took the initiative to reach out to sinners through the sacrifice of Jesus Christ. One of the things that Christ's death provided for us was the healing of the broken relationship between God and mankind that occurred in the garden when Adam sinned. As we will see, we have been reconciled to God through the death of His Son.

THE NECESSITY OF RECONCILIATION

Reconciliation is that work of God made possible through the death of Christ, by which sinners are brought from hostility toward God into a state of spiritual fellowship and harmony with Him. It is a movement from alienation to restoration.

Sin Alienated Us from God

The alienation that Adam's sin created in his relationship with God is evident in what happened immediately afterward. Whereas Adam and Eve had enjoyed intimate fellowship with God in Eden, they hid from the Lord after they sinned because they knew something was wrong (see Genesis 3:8–10). They had become alienated from God.

In Romans 5, the apostle Paul described our alienation as spiritual helplessness, a total inability to rectify the problem of our separation from God. Paul began this chapter by discussing what God has done to provide our great salvation, and then he proceeded to describe our situation that makes this salvation so great. "For while we were still helpless, at the right time Christ died for the ungodly" (v. 6). To be helpless means you can't do anything about your situation. To be ungodly means to be totally unlike God. We lacked any resources or merit to win His favor or overcome the barrier of hostility that sin had built between us and Him.

More than that, "we were yet sinners" (Romans 5:8). We stood guilty before a holy God, and that's not the end of the bad news. Paul said we were also God's "enemies" (v. 10), a term that graphically points out our need for reconciliation.

God Reached Out to Meet Our Need

It was when we were helpless, ungodly sinners and enemies of God that "we were reconciled to God through the death of His Son" (Romans 5:10).

Reconciliation is God's work and His initiative all the way. Christ's death brought our sin account into balance, so to speak, so that we no longer owe a debt of sin we can't pay. We talk about reconciling our bank statement with our checkbook to make sure the two figures agree and we aren't bouncing checks all over the place. The damage of an unreconciled bank account is obvious, as is the damage of an unreconciled relationship in which there has been broken fellowship.

THE DIMENSIONS OF RECONCILIATION

God's work of reconciliation is so complete that it reaches to every corner of creation and touches every relationship you will ever have. There are at least three crucial relationships that were restored when God reconciled the world to Himself.

Our Relationship with God Is Restored

We've established the fact that reconciliation involves a change in our relationship with God, which is where all true reconciliation begins. Paul gave this truth its classic statement when he wrote, "Now all these things are from God, who reconciled us to Himself through Christ" (2 Corinthians 5:18).

From God's standpoint, the chasm that separates sinful mankind from Him has been bridged by the cross. The only issue now is whether people will put their faith in Christ and be reconciled to God. That's why we are charged with the task of inviting sinners to be reconciled to God.

The results of this are awesome. Christ's death canceled the sin and rebellion of Adam. This means that the sin that was the original cause of our alienation from God has been removed—so that what God is upset about now, if I can use this term, is the fact that people refuse to believe and accept the message of reconciliation.

Our Relationship with Others Is Restored

When we are reconciled with God, we are in position to be reconciled with others. There is an important horizontal dimension to reconciliation.

People talk a lot about reconciliation between races, between nations, between husbands and wives, or between generations. But the problem with most attempts to bring harmony and peace is that there will be no true and lasting horizontal reconciliation without a proper understanding of vertical reconciliation between man and God.

The ancient world had a huge racial divide between Jews and Gentiles. The church at Ephesus felt the impact of this problem, so Paul addressed it in Ephesians 2:11–17.

The biblical principle established in this passage is that peace between people must be predicated on what God did for us in Christ. This means that since the world is lacking the basis of true peace we shouldn't be surprised if most peace efforts ultimately fail, whether on the individual or the national level.

Our Relationship with Creation Is Restored

Reconciliation also has a cosmic dimension. That is, the salvation Christ purchased at Calvary has implications for all of creation.

Sin was so devastating that it not only ruptured mankind's relationship to God; sin also marred the whole universe's relationship to God. Adam lived in a perfect Paradise until he sinned, and then all of a sudden the ground began producing thorns and thistles. Life became a struggle to survive in a sometimes harsh and hostile environment.

When God created the universe, He pronounced every part of it good, but sin threw the entire world out of order. Creation feels the alienation of sin and is waiting anxiously for the day of redemption (see Romans 8:19). Paul went on to say that the world is waiting in hope for the time when "the creation itself also will be set free from its slavery to corruption into the freedom of the glory of the children of God" (v. 21).

That's in the future, but for the present the reality is that "the whole creation groans and suffers the pains of childbirth together until now" (Romans 8:22). Creation is groaning from the burden of sin and the alienation it brought between God and His creation. Every time an earthquake occurs, we are witnessing the restless groaning of creation. Hurricanes are a result of creation groaning for the day when it will be reconciled with God. Nature is aching to be delivered from its bondage to the corruption of sin.

Who and what is going to reconcile nature once and for all? The answer is in Colossians 1:15–20, one of the greatest passages in Scripture about the deity and the redeeming work of Jesus Christ. His life, death, and resurrection have the power to reconcile the entire creation to God.

Jesus has this power because "He is the image of the invisible God, the firstborn of all creation. For by Him all things were created. . . . He is before all things, and in Him all things hold together" (Colossians 1:15–17). Jesus Christ was the active agent in the original creation, and the only thing keeping the molecules of this universe from flying apart is His eternal power. Therefore, His death and resurrection could not help but affect the creation.

Let's read on in Colossians 1, because it gets even better:

> He is also head of the body, the church; and He is the beginning, the firstborn from the dead, so that He Himself will come to have first place in everything. For it was the Father's good pleasure for all the fullness [of deity] to dwell in Him, and through Him to reconcile all things to Himself, having made peace through the blood of His cross; through Him, I say, whether things on earth or things in heaven. (Colossians 1:18–20)

That's as complete a statement of the extent of Christ's reconciliation as you will read anywhere in Scripture. How many things did Christ reconcile to God? All things.

Now let's put this great truth to work. If everything in the universe is held together by Jesus Christ, then that includes your life. So if your life is coming apart at the seams, if the stars and planets of your universe are flying out of their orbits, if your financial or marital or family world is spinning in chaos, then the cosmic reconciliation Christ accomplished on the cross has something to say to you.

You may be wondering, *If Jesus Christ has reconciled all of creation to Himself, why isn't the universe reconciled today? Why is there still chaos in nature?* Because as we read in Romans 8, nature won't be fully reconciled until Christ returns and the universe bows before Him as the One who has first place in everything. The universe has not yet recognized the "first placeness" of Jesus Christ.

But the Bible says that Christ's "first placeness" also includes the church. That's you and me. The natural world may not yet have Christ in His rightful place, but there's no reason that He should not be enthroned as Number One in our hearts.

It's only as He is first in everything that you enjoy the fullness of the reconciliation He has paid for. If you're tired of the thorns and thistles that are choking your spiritual growth and the earthquakes and hurricanes that are throwing you around and splitting your world apart, put Christ back in the place He deserves, which is "first place in everything."

THE BLESSING OF RECONCILIATION

We're getting a great picture of all that God has done to reconcile us. Let me summarize quickly the truths we have covered, not only in this chapter but in the previous chapters as we have been learning what it means to be totally saved.

The death of Christ gave God the legal grounds to declare us justified, freed from the charges that were posted against us. At the same time, we were redeemed or bought back from the slave market of sin by Christ's precious shed blood, which also propitiated God's wrath against sin so completely that He was free to reach out and end our rebellion and hostility against Him by reconciling us. Our justification provided propitiation, which made possible reconciliation.

Every aspect of the doctrine of reconciliation is a blessing, but there is one particular blessing or benefit that I don't want you to miss. It may be less obvious on a casual reading of Scripture, but it is powerful and important nonetheless.

We Are Saved by Christ's Life

For this we need to go back to Romans 5:10, especially the last phrase of the verse. After explaining all that Christ did in His death to reconcile us while we were His enemies and helpless to help ourselves, Paul added, "We shall be saved by His life."

This definitely broadens our understanding of salvation. We were reconciled to God by Christ's death, but Christ is now alive and sitting at the right hand of the Father in heaven (see Hebrews 1:3). There He is serving as our "great high priest who has passed through the heavens" (Hebrews 4:14), and He "always lives to make intercession for [us]" (Hebrews 7:25).

In other words, the idea behind Romans 5:10 is that if you put your trust in Christ's death to save you, now that He's risen from the dead you haven't seen anything yet.

If Christ can save you and reconcile you to God by His blood, wait until you see what He has in store for you now that He is alive forevermore. If He can take you from hell to heaven by dying, what more can He do for you by rising from the dead? If He can forgive you for all your sins and deliver you from judgment by His death, imagine the power that is at work on your behalf now that He lives!

Jesus Christ Is Our "Umpire"

The suffering patriarch Job made a very interesting statement as he was being harassed by his accusers. "For He [God] is not a man as I am that I may answer Him, that we may go to court together. There is no umpire between us, who may lay his hand upon us both" (Job 9:32–33).

Job knew that he was in no position to plead his case before God because God was so high and transcendent and he was merely a man. Job said he needed an "umpire," someone who could listen impartially to both God and him and make a ruling. But Job wound up disappointed because he knew of no one who could fill this role.

The umpire whom Job wished for would have had to understand Job so well that he could accurately represent him before God, and yet be as great as God Himself in order to accurately represent God. The umpire Job longed for, a mediator who could stand between us and God and represent each side perfectly, became flesh in the person of Jesus Christ. He is God Himself, yet He also knows the human condition intimately because He took on human flesh and experienced everything we have experienced.

Jesus Christ can reach out to God because He is God, and He can reach out to us because He is a man. Jesus brings the two together, explaining to the Father what we are experiencing, and explaining the otherwise invisible and unreachable God to us. And Christ is doing this now and every day as our High Priest who is alive forever! He is our Umpire, bringing God and man together.

THE DUTY OF RECONCILIATION

The Bible's teaching on reconciliation is exciting stuff, but, as always, we are called to do something more with the truth than merely sit on it and keep the good news to ourselves. The God who has reconciled the whole world to Himself has called us to be His ambassadors, taking this message to every corner of the earth.

We Are God's Mouthpieces

Our charge is found in 2 Corinthians 5:18–20. Paul began by saying that God "gave us the ministry of reconciliation" (v. 18), which is the message that God has taken the initiative to end our hostility toward Him by charging our sins to Christ and making peace with us through His blood.

Therefore, since God has "committed to us the word of reconciliation" (v. 19), our duty is clear. "We are ambassadors for Christ, as though God were making an appeal through us; we beg you on behalf of Christ, be reconciled to God" (v. 20). The duty of reconciliation is that we speak to others on God's behalf, telling them that they don't have to be alienated from Him any longer. An ambassador speaks for another, and we are to speak as if God were speaking through us.

We have the great duty and delight of telling sinners that in Christ God's anger has been appeased, and that if they will come to Him, the war will be over and they will find peace. We can say to sinners, "God told me to tell you that if you will believe in His Son, you will be safe from His judgment." What a great message for people who are at war with God!

Restoring What Has Been Disrupted

Reconciliation implies that something has been disrupted and divided, and it needs to be brought back together. Satan is the great alienator and the great divider. His only agenda is to tear families and marriages and churches and individuals apart so that they and others will fail to see God's power of reconciliation.

Jesus is the great Reconciler who wants to bring things together. But in order to accomplish His work of reconciliation in our lives, He must be at the center.

God has written the world a letter telling people of His love for them and His desire to have them reconciled to Him. It's our duty to open this letter, the Word of God, and help lost people understand how far God has gone to bring them back to Himself. Otherwise, if the message of His letter never gets through to those who need it the most, there will be no reconciliation. Let's make sure we are fulfilling our duty as ambassadors who have a great message to tell.

PERSONAL APPLICATION FOR LIFE

1. God's work of reconciliation means we can enjoy a harmonious relationship with God. He took the initiative to reach out to us—as sinners—and heal the broken relationship that separated us from Him. Take an inventory of the relationships that touch your life—friends, family, coworkers, other believers in the body. Ask God to give you the strength to take the initiative in restoring any broken relationships.

2. Are you going through a difficult time right now? Did you know that Jesus not only intercedes on your behalf, He also interprets your situations and specific needs to God? He knows what you are going through (Hebrews 4:15). Take your need to God in prayer, confident that He will work on your behalf and resolve things in ways that will bring glory to Himself.

3. The Good News of Christ's sacrifice on the cross should never become "old" news in the life of the believer. Second Corinthians 5:19 tells us we are "ambassadors for Christ." Make a list of those contacts we talked about above—friends, family, coworkers—and be Christ's ambassador to them. You might be the only witness for Christ those people have.

4. Is your life coming apart at the seams? Colossians 1:15–17 teaches that Jesus, through His power, holds all "all things" together, that is, all of creation. "All things" includes your life. If He can control the incredible forces of the universe, He can certainly work with you to control the chaos in your life. If something else taking first place in your life, start giving God first place. Let Him restore your life and bring it back into order.

FOR GROUP STUDY

Questions for Group Discussion

1. Describe the concept of reconciliation. Why do we need reconciliation? See Genesis 3:8–10 and Romans 5:6–8.

2. What three crucial relationships were restored when God reconciled the

world to Himself? See 2 Corinthians 5:18; Ephesians 2:11–17; and Romans 8:19–21. (Use the chart below as an aid to your discussion.)

3. What particular blessing does the believer receive as a result of reconciliation? (See Romans 5:10.) What is the result of that blessing? What exactly does Jesus do as our Great High Priest?
4. Second Corinthians 5:18–20 tells us that God "gave us the ministry of reconciliation" (v. 18). As believers reconciled to God, what is our duty to the world of unbelievers?

PICTURE THIS

God's work of reconciliation is far-reaching, including all of creation. Below are three crucial relationships that were restored when God reconciled the world to Himself.

The Dimensions of Our Reconciliation to God

DIMENSION	SCRIPTURE PASSAGE	WHAT IT MEANS
Our relationship with God is restored.	2 Corinthians 5:18	Because Christ's death canceled Adam's sin and rebellion, the original cause of our alienation from God has been removed.
Our relationship with others is restored.	Ephesians 2:11–14	God is working to remove the hostility between Jew and Gentile, reconciling both into one body.
Our relationship with creation is restored.	Colossians 1:15–20	When Christ returns, the universe will bow before Him as the One who has first place in everything.

63

REGENERATION: THE MIRACLE OF SALVATION

The biblical doctrine of regeneration is another of the great truths that help us appreciate what it means to be saved.

It's always helpful to begin with a definition of our terms, so let's talk about the meaning of the term *regeneration*. We can define it as the process by which God implants new spiritual life, His very life, in the heart of a sinner who believes on Jesus Christ for salvation.

EXPLORING THE MEANING OF REGENERATION

The Bible uses at least three figures to describe the process of regeneration. The first is the new birth, which we are most familiar with under the term "born again" (John 3:3, 7). When a new birth occurs, it means that there is life where life did not exist before. The moment a sinner places his or her faith in Christ, that person is born anew as the life of God is imparted to the new believer.

The Bible also describes regeneration as spiritual resurrection. Paul said that just as Jesus Christ was raised from the dead "so we too might walk in newness of life. For if we have become united with Him in the likeness of His death, certainly we shall also be in the likeness of His resurrection" (Romans 6:4–5).

A third important biblical figure for regeneration is a new creation. We have seen the apostle Paul's powerful statement in 2 Corinthians 5:17: "If anyone is in Christ, he is a new creature [or creation]; the old things passed away; behold, new things have come."

Salvation not only brings such a complete change that we are born again spiritually and raised from the dead, but we are completely remade people.

THE NECESSITY OF REGENERATION

The truths we have just reviewed describe radical changes of heart and life, because regeneration is a radical process. Nothing less will do the job when it comes to bringing life out of death.

We Are Born Spiritually Dead

The Bible declares that we are made up of three realities: body, soul, and spirit (1 Thessalonians 5:23). Our bodies give us the ability to communicate with our environment through the five senses. Our souls are the source of our self-awareness and our ability to communicate with others and to process the information we receive from our senses so that we can understand our world. Our spirits are designed to enable us to communicate with God, and it is here that the problem occurs.

When God told Adam, "In the day that you eat from [the forbidden tree] you will surely die" (Genesis 2:17), He was speaking of spiritual death. Of course, the human body also suffered from the effects of sin because all of us will eventually die physically. But our first parents died spiritually the day they disobeyed God, and every member of the human race is born dead in "trespasses and sins" (Ephesians 2:1).

We Are in Need of Eternal Life

Regeneration occurs when God imparts to us His very life, which the Bible calls eternal life. Jesus described this life in His great prayer the night before His crucifixion. Speaking of His followers, Jesus said, "This is eternal life, that they may know You, the only true God, and Jesus Christ whom You have sent" (John 17:3).

It's important to see that Jesus did not define eternal life solely in terms of its length. Eternal life certainly means that we are going to live forever;

that's why it's also called everlasting life. But there's much more to it than that. Even the lost will exist forever in hell. The eternal life that God gives is a quality of life that Jesus defined as knowing God the Father and Himself.

This is personal, intimate knowledge, not just a body of data, and it begins not when we arrive in heaven but the moment we trust Christ. Once we have been regenerated or made new by the power of the Holy Spirit, we can enjoy intimate, face-to-face fellowship with God because we have His life within us. And we will continue to have this relationship with Him for eternity. Heaven will be the uninterrupted knowledge of God, and we will never reach the end of that knowledge because God is infinite.

THE MEANS OF REGENERATION

Regeneration occurs by a sovereign work of God in the heart of the believing sinner. It could not be any other way, for salvation is God's initiative from beginning to end.

In fact, the entire Trinity is involved in the work of regeneration. According to James 1:18, God the Father brought us forth to new life through His Word, while John 5:21 says that God the Son gives life to whomever He wishes. Regeneration is also attributed to the Holy Spirit, whose work in salvation is to renew us to the point of salvation (see Titus 3:5).

What is the means by which God regenerates us? We have hints of it in James 1:18 and John 5:21, where the words "brought us forth" and "gives life" suggest that a new birth is the means by which we pass "out of death into life" (1 John 3:14). This is exactly what Jesus taught in John 3, a seminal passage on the new birth.

Jesus Announces the New Birth

John 3 is a story that many Christians know well: the night that a man named Nicodemus visited Jesus to find out what this man and His teaching were all about.

John identified Nicodemus as "a man of the Pharisees . . . a ruler of the Jews" (v. 1). We could call Nicodemus a model person of his day, which is important because Jesus was about to tell him that his religion and his goodness weren't enough to enter heaven. If correct religion could save a person and produce new life, Nicodemus would have been fine just as he was.

Apparently Nicodemus was too uncomfortable to start with the real issue, so he began by paying Jesus a compliment. "Rabbi, we know that You have come from God as a teacher; for no one can do these signs that You do unless God is with him" (John 3:2).

Jesus' responded in verse 3: "Truly, truly, I say to you, unless one is born again he cannot see the kingdom of God." I find this interesting because Nicodemus didn't ask a question for Jesus to answer. What Jesus did was get to the heart of the issue by answering the unspoken question on Nicodemus's heart.

Before we go any further, let me mention that the Greek term Jesus used for "born again" can also be translated "born from above," which points to the source of regeneration and the new life that it brings.

Religion Is Not the New Birth

Nicodemus was mystified by Jesus' answer, which is why he asked, "How can a man be born when he is old? He cannot enter a second time into his mother's womb and be born, can he?" (John 3:4). Now Nicodemus was ready to get down to the real deal. He forgot about his opening statement and pursued the discussion Jesus had begun.

When Jesus said that Nicodemus needed to be born again, that got him thinking about obstetrics. This was fine, because Jesus wanted to discuss obstetrics too—except that Jesus was talking about spiritual birth. The Lord moved the conversation along when He answered Nicodemus's question. "Truly, truly, I say to you, unless one is born of water and the Spirit he cannot enter into the kingdom of God" (v. 5).

There is some confusion about Jesus' use of "water" in connection with the new birth. A lot of people believe this is referring to the water of baptism. But the context here is birth and a mother's womb, not the rite of baptism. I believe Jesus is referring to the water that is released from a mother's womb at the start of the birth process, using the term *water* as a synonym for physical birth.

Jesus was telling Nicodemus that he needed to be born twice, not once, to enter the kingdom of God. Physical birth is not enough—even birth into the best family and the most dedicated religion and the highest culture. We must be born again because physical birth does not give us a relationship with God. It gives us a relationship with our environment and with ourselves because we have a body and a soul. But to relate to God we need to be made alive in our spirits, which only comes through spiritual birth.

Jesus made this clear by His next statement to Nicodemus: "That which is born of the flesh is flesh, and that which is born of the Spirit is spirit" (John 3:6). Flesh can only give birth to flesh. It cannot give birth to spirit. Only spirit can replicate spirit, which is why Jesus told Nicodemus, "Do not be amazed that I said to you, 'You must be born again'" (v. 7). Flesh and spirit reproduce after their own kind.

This is the problem with religion that does not call for regeneration. Religion can make you a better person, but only Christ can make you alive when your spirit is dead in sin.

Salvation Is from God Alone

Jesus then perplexed Nicodemus even more by using another analogy to illustrate the mysterious, sovereign nature of salvation. Nick was still trying to grasp the idea that God didn't operate according to the set rules of established religion when Jesus added, "The wind blows where it wishes and you hear the sound of it, but do not know where it comes from and where it is going; so is everyone who is born of the Spirit" (v. 8).

Nicodemus's head must have been spinning. His response in John 3:9 reveals that. "How can these things be?"

Nicodemus thought that all he had to do was scrupulously follow the religion of his ancestors and he was home free. He knew nothing about the need for the new birth of regeneration. He didn't even realize he was dead and needed to be reborn, although as we said he did sense that something serious was wrong in his life.

We've Been Bitten by Sin

So the means of regeneration is the new life. Jesus used an illustration in John

3:14–15, a story from the Old Testament that Nicodemus would have known. "As Moses lifted up the serpent in the wilderness, even so must the Son of Man be lifted up; so that whoever believes will in Him have eternal life."

On that occasion the people of Israel had grumbled against Moses and against God, and God sent serpents into the camp to bite them. God told Moses to erect a bronze serpent on a pole so that anyone who was bitten and looked to the serpent would live.

All of us have been bitten by the snake of sin and will die spiritually unless something is done. Jesus was lifted up on the cross to pay for those sins, and anyone who looks to Him will not die but will receive new life.

THE MANIFESTATION OF REGENERATION

Our New Life Will Show through the Spirit

If you are born again by the Spirit of God and the life of God is in you, there should be manifestations of that life that are unmistakably obvious both to you and to those around you.

How can you help ensure that your daily walk with Christ is marked by these manifestations? Paul gave us the key in Galatians 5:16–17: "But I say, walk by the Spirit, and you will not carry out the desire of the flesh. For the flesh sets its desire against the Spirit, and the Spirit against the flesh; for these are in opposition to one another, so that you may not do the things that you please."

If you want the new life that God placed within you at salvation to grow and produce the changes that God wants, you need to feed the Spirit while starving your sinful flesh. If you want to see God change your tastes so that sin doesn't taste as good as it used to taste; if you want to see God give you a love for the right kind of spiritual food; and if you want to see God reverse some things in your life, you have to grow in grace by chomping down on nourishing spiritual food such as prayer, study of God's Word, regular fellowship with other believers, and service to the Lord.

We Will Resemble Our Father

Another way that regeneration manifests itself is by the child bearing the characteristics of its parents. That's true in physical and spiritual birth. We have seen that when God saved us, He put His own nature within us.

With that in mind, I want to show you a characteristic of your heavenly Father you bear that may startle you. "No one who is born of God practices sin, because His seed abides in him; and he cannot sin, because he is born of God" (1 John 3:9).

This verse may throw you. It may make you wonder if you are saved, because John states clearly that the one who is born of God cannot sin. He's talking about you and me. John said the reason we cannot sin is that we have God's seed within us, and that seed "abides" or remains in us. John was also using birth language here, the seed being likened to a baby in a mother's womb that is alive and growing.

Now if you're like me, you have to admit that what John is talking about is not our experience. We sin every day in thought, word, and deed. But the new life or seed that we have from God is not the part of us doing the sinning. We know this because this new life is the very life of God Himself, and God is wholly perfect and utterly separate from sin.

While you're letting this settle in your mind, let me remind you that Peter said we became "partakers of the divine nature" when we were saved (2 Peter 1:4). We have a divine nature that is perfect and complete in every detail, for Paul said in Colossians 2:10 that we have been "made complete" in Christ. In other words, every Christian is born again perfectly. There are no spiritual defects in our new life.

But this raises a question. If we have the perfect life of God within us, why do we still have imperfect thoughts and say and do imperfect things?

The answer is that the life of God resident in our spirits exists in a body and soul that still bear the damage of sin. This is the principle of sin that Paul called the "sin which dwells in me" (Romans 7:20).

The Bible calls this old part of us the flesh, the soul that has been contaminated by the principle of sin that uses the body as the vehicle through which to express itself. The flesh is totally unlike God and completely opposed to God. The flesh wants to sin. The flesh does not want God.

Now our flesh or old nature is a burden and a drag that seeks to pull us downward, and it is going to be discarded when we get our new bodies in heaven. But since we're stuck with this flesh as long as we are in this life, how can we know that we are beginning to resemble our heavenly Father, who gave us new birth and wants us to reflect His nature?

Here's one important way: You'll know you are becoming more like your Father when you reflect His attitude toward sin. In other words, when you're saved, you may do the same sin you did before you were saved. But you won't do that sin the same way you did it when you were unsaved, because now you will run into a brick wall of resistance every time you sin. That brick wall is the presence of the Holy Spirit within you.

Someone explained the difference this way: Before we were saved we leaped into sin and loved it, but now we lapse into sin and loathe it. We used to sin without even thinking about it. But now the presence of sin in our lives causes us great distress and discomfort because we know it grieves our Father.

So don't misunderstand. Believers are still capable of sin, even terrible sin. But they have to climb over a wall of opposition to sin, and when they do, it is never their new divine nature that is doing the sin.

If you have been regenerated by the Spirit of God, you have the life of God within you. So the challenge is to make sure that the new you is growing so that the flesh can't dominate the scene. The way to do this is to feed the new you, the new life or seed that is within you from God, so that it grows to the point where you show!

PERSONAL APPLICATION FOR LIFE

1. Dr. Evans explains that sin left us spiritually dead with no ability to fellowship with God. Now, as a believer, you have been regenerated with new life and enabled to enjoy fellowship with God. Do you take that truth for granted? As a child of God, don't let a day go by without communing with your heavenly Father.

2. God's work of regeneration is one of the great truths of Scripture. It's one the many spiritual works and resources God provides for us. Take a moment to thank Him for all the resources He has given us for pressing on in the life of faith and living it victoriously.

3. Does your new life in Christ show? The Bible tells us that we are "made complete" in Christ because of our new birth (Colossians 2:10). Someday we will know that completeness fully. In our daily experience, we must always strive to grow in our new life and show the characteristics of Christ. When people see you, do they see Christ?

4. First John 3:9 tells us "no one who is born of God practices sin." In our experience, however, all of us fail and sin daily. Obviously, the new life from God is not the part doing the sin in our lives. Rather, we find ourselves influenced by our old sin nature. Do you have any sin in your life that you need to confess? If so, embrace 1 John 1:9 and clean that sin from your mind and heart. It has no place in your new life!

FOR GROUP STUDY

Questions for Group Discussion

1. Read 2 Corinthians 5:17 and Romans 6:4–5. What is the meaning of the term *regeneration*? What is involved wit the process of regeneration?

2. As Dr. Evans points out, regeneration occurs by a sovereign work of God in the heart of the believing sinner. By what means does God regenerate us? (See James 1:18 and John 5:21.) From the account of Nicodemus in John 3, what do we learn regeneration and the new birth?

3. How is regeneration manifested in the believer's daily walk with Christ? In this chapter, Dr. Evans points out at least two ways. Read the apostle Paul's words on this topic in Galatians 5:16–17.

4. To explain the new birth, Jesus used the analogy of physical birth. What parallels can we draw from that analogy? Discuss the four key truths Dr. Evans presents in this chapter to explain the characteristics of the new birth. (Use the chart as an aid to your discussion.)

PICTURE THIS

Regeneration is the sovereign work of God in the heart of the believer. As physical conception results in physical life, spiritual conception results in spiritual life. Below are four truths that help explain the work of regeneration.

GOD'S WORK OF REGENERATION IN THE BELIEVER
John 3

TRUTH	SCRIPTURE PASSAGE	WHAT IT MEANS
Jesus announces the new birth to us.	verses 2–3	Whereas Nicodemus got his message from Jesus, we have an entire Bible that proclaims the good news of the new birth.
Religion does not lead us to the new birth.	verses 4–7	Religious standing and cultural background do not give us a relationship with God; only a spiritual rebirth through Jesus Christ can do that.
Salvation is from God alone.	verses 8–9	One of Satan's deceptions is that religious practice can be a means of salvation. Only through God's work of regeneration can we be saved.
We have all been bitten by sin.	verses 14–15	All of us have the disease of sin. We will all die spiritually unless we are regenerated by the new birth through Christ.

64

GRACE: THE GIFT OF SALVATION

One day the great Christian apologist and author C. S. Lewis walked into a room where a group of men was debating what makes Christianity unique among all the world's religions. The question was posed to Lewis, who answered right away:

"That's easy. It's grace."

Then he went on to explain that no other religion teaches the concept of a God who takes the initiative to respond with undeserved favor to sinners.

He was right, of course. Every other religion is founded on the premise that mankind must do something to reach and please God. But the heart of Christianity is the good news of what God has done to bridge the gap of sin and make it possible for sinful human beings to have forgiveness and fellowship with Him. Grace is the unbridgeable divide between the Christian faith and every other religion, and it is a large part of what makes our salvation so great.

THE CONCEPT OF GRACE

Theologians have developed a classic definition of this great concept called grace. They define it as God's unmerited, or undeserved, favor toward sinners. I define grace as the inexhaustible supply of God's goodness whereby He does for us what we could never do for ourselves. Grace is "the gift of God" (Ephesians 2:8).

No study of grace can proceed very far without taking us to Paul's great letter to the Ephesians. Paul used the word *grace* itself twelve times in this letter, beginning with his trademark salutation, "Grace to you" (1:2).

Then the apostle said, "[God] predestined us to adoption as sons through Jesus Christ to Himself, according to the kind intention of His will, to the praise of the glory of His grace, which He freely bestowed on us in the Beloved" (1:5–6). Notice that God poured out His grace lavishly on those who are His elect in Christ. The only motivation for this outpouring of grace is God's kindness, which is why we will be praising God throughout eternity for the glory of His grace.

Paul knew whereof he wrote. He told Timothy that God called him into His service although Paul had been "a blasphemer and a persecutor and a violent aggressor" (1 Timothy 1:13). Despite this, "the grace of our Lord was more than abundant" to the apostle (v. 14). Grace overflowed to Paul. It came in waves.

Our concern here is God's grace in salvation, but we need to note that God is gracious to all people, including the lost. This is called "common grace," or God's kindness to all of His creatures. Jesus said of His Father, "He causes His sun to rise on the evil and the good, and sends rain on the righteous and the unrighteous" (Matthew 5:45). Paul said that the appearance of God's grace has brought salvation "to all men" (Titus 2:11), meaning that Christ's death is sufficient for the salvation of all people.

Your unsaved neighbor enjoys the same sunshine and rain that make your grass grow because God is gracious to all people. But only those who place their faith in the finished work of Christ for salvation experience God's special or saving grace.

THE NEED FOR GRACE

In order to appreciate grace to the fullest, we have to understand how badly we need it. The best way to do this is to contrast grace with its opposite, which Paul did in Ephesians 2. This chapter begins with our problem. "And you were dead in your trespasses and sins" (v. 1). We were "sons of disobedience . . . indulging the desires of the flesh and of the mind, and were by nature children of *wrath*" (vv. 2–3, italics added). God's wrath is the only alternative for those who reject His grace.

When the Bible says people are dead in sin, it doesn't mean they are incapable of doing good things. It means that none of their good deeds can raise them from spiritual death to spiritual life, because those deeds are done apart from a relationship with God. A corpse is a dead body no matter whether it's still dressed up and presentable or badly decomposed.

THE PROCESS OF GRACE

Romans 11:32 says, "God has shut up all in disobedience so that He may show mercy to all." All people are shut up in this container called sin, with no way out. The only way the container will be opened is if the One who shut it opens it.

God Has Two Great Words of Grace

Ephesians 2:4 begins with two of the most merciful, grace-filled words we will ever read. After establishing that we were sons of disobedience and children of wrath, Paul wrote, "But God . . ."

He continued: "But God, being rich in mercy, because of His great love with which He loved us, even when we were dead in our transgressions, made us alive together with Christ (by grace you have been saved)" (Ephesians 2:4–5). According to Paul, two attributes of God came together when He revealed His grace to us. Grace is the marriage of God's love and His mercy.

God's Grace Will Unfold for Eternity

Just how great is God's grace? According to Paul, it's so great that it will continue to unfold throughout eternity. God saved us by grace "so that in the ages to come He might show the surpassing riches of His grace in kindness toward us in Christ Jesus" (v. 7). God's supply of grace is so immense that it will take the ceaseless ages of eternity for you to grasp all that He has in store for you.

And the most amazing thing of all is that grace is a gift. Let's continue reading in Ephesians 2. "For by grace you have been saved through faith;

and that not of yourselves, it is the gift of God; not as a result of works, so that no one may boast" (vv. 8–9).

This means that God alone gets the credit for grace. Verse 7 said that the spotlight of eternity will be on the richness of God's grace, not anything we have done to deserve it. When you and I get to heaven, we'll be singing one song: "To God be the glory, great things He has done." Heaven will be a celebration of grace.

THE MECHANISM OF GRACE

Now that we've laid some foundation for the understanding of God's grace, I want to tackle a complex and important doctrine that belongs under the heading of grace because it is the essence of God's grace in action. This doctrine is *election*, which I call the mechanism by which God's grace operates to save sinners. Election is also the guarantee of grace, because no one whom He has chosen will be lost.

Election Raises Important Issues

The Bible's teaching on election seems to fly in the face of what we think is fair and right. For example, how is it fair that God has elected some sinners to salvation while passing over others? And how is it fair that these non-elect sinners are held accountable for not being saved? If God so loves the world, how can He choose some sinners and not others?

The Bible says that God chose or elected us in Christ "before the foundation of the world" (Ephesians 1:4). Election is based on God's eternal purposes and His prerogative to choose, not on our behavior.

Paul confirmed this in Romans 9 as he discussed God's choice of Jacob and rejection of Esau. "Though the twins were not yet born and had not done anything good or bad, *so that God's purpose according to His choice would stand,* not because of works but because of Him who calls, it was said to her, 'The older will serve the younger'" (vv. 11–12, italics added).

Some people think the fact that election is not based on human behavior or response to God is a problem, since it appears to make His choice arbitrary. But in reality, locating the motive for election in God's eternal, unchanging plan rather than in man's temporal, changing actions removes it from the category of arbitrary. Remember too that all have sinned and are deserving of God's wrath, so the fact that He chose to rescue some is an act of grace in the first place.

God Has a Gracious Purpose in Election

What was God's purpose in election? To demonstrate His grace by reaching down into the mass of lost humanity and redeeming a people for His name's sake, a people who will be trophies of His grace and bring Him glory for eternity. Paul told Titus that God's grace "has appeared" so that He might "purify for Himself a people for His own possession, zealous for good deeds" (Titus 2:11, 14).

Ephesians 1 contains a comprehensive statement on the electing work of God: "Blessed be the God and Father of our Lord Jesus Christ, who has blessed us with every spiritual blessing in the heavenly places *in Christ*, just as He chose us *in Him* before the foundation of the world, that we would be holy and blameless before Him" (vv. 3–4, italics added).

The key that unlocks the doctrine of election is found in those emphasized phrases. The words "in Christ," "in Him," or "in the Beloved" occur in verses 1, 3, 4, 6, 7, 9, 10 (twice), 12, 13 (twice). The centrality of the truth that we are chosen "in Christ" is too often overlooked in the discussion of election. God's electing purpose is centered in the life, death, and resurrection of Jesus Christ and His present ministry in heaven as our High Priest.

The point is that God has not elected believers in the abstract. He is not sitting in heaven deciding whom He loves and whom He does not love. The Bible is unmistakably clear that God loves all people. The cross of Christ was so powerful that it dealt with the sin of Adam and rendered the whole world savable so that anybody who believes in Christ will be saved. The doctrine of election must not be made to detract from God's love for all sinners or the lengths He went to in order to save every lost person.

But at the same time, we know that not everybody is saved. And we read in Scripture that God elected some in Christ before the world was created, and that those who are not saved will be judged and condemned for their sin.

God's purpose to call out a people who are "in Christ" is the key, because when it comes to mankind's condition, there are only two people as far as God is concerned: the first and last Adam (1 Corinthians 15:45). In God's mind all people are either still in Adam—that is, in their sin—or in Christ. Those who are in Adam are lost and condemned, while those in Christ are elected to salvation.

The difference between being in Adam and being in Christ is all-important because God imputed or charged Adam's sin to all of mankind. So we are born in sin, and we commit sin ourselves. Thus the whole world is shut up in sin, and God owes us nothing but judgment.

But because God is gracious, He chose to provide a bridge whereby sinful people could cross over from being in Adam to being in Christ. The bridge is the cross, and the offer of salvation is made to everyone on earth.

There Is Mystery in Election

Now this is where some of the mystery of God's work in election manifests itself. God's offer of salvation is valid to all, and yet those who respond do so because they are the elect of God before the foundation of the world was laid. And those who do not come to Christ are blameworthy because the Bible never says that people are lost because they are nonelect. The lost are lost because they refuse to believe.

These two truths may appear to us to be mutually exclusive, but the Bible teaches both and holds both in perfect balance. In Acts 13 Paul and Barnabas preached the gospel to the people of Pisidian Antioch on the first missionary journey. When they had finished their message, the Bible clearly says, "As many as had been appointed to eternal life believed" (Acts 13:48).

But Jesus said concerning Himself, "He who believes in Him [the Son of God] is not judged; he who does not believe has been judged already, because he has not believed in the name of the only begotten Son of God" (John 3:18).

The ones whom God has chosen to elect are those who respond in faith to the gospel, which places them "in Christ," the context of God's elective activity. The sovereign purpose of this election is that those who respond to the gospel would partake of the blessings God has predetermined to bestow on the redeemed throughout eternity (Ephesians 2:7).

We could sum it all up in these statements. God elects some to salvation for His own sovereign purposes and because He is gracious. The invitation to salvation is generously open for all, and "whoever will" may still come. All people are responsible for their response to Jesus Christ, and yet those who come can never take the glory for their salvation. The elect become so because of their attachment to Jesus Christ. We as believers are responsible to go and share the gospel with the world so that lost sinners will hear the good news and turn to Christ for forgiveness from their sins.

God Has Adopted Us

God's grace in election has a wonderful goal or end to it as far as we are concerned. "He predestined us to adoption as sons through Jesus Christ to Himself, according to the kind intention of His will" (Ephesians 1:5).

Adoption is a rich term in the New Testament because it means to be a fully privileged son or daughter. Adoption in the ancient world usually didn't happen until the adopted person was grown. At that time the adoptee was given the same rights, privileges, and inheritance as a birth child who grew up in the home.

The adopted child also had full access to his or her inheritance. For us as God's elect and His adopted children, this inheritance includes "every spiritual blessing in the heavenly places in Christ" (Ephesians 1:3).

Paul said that God did all of this "according to the kind attention of His will" (Ephesians 1:5). What is God's will? "To the praise of the glory of His grace, which He freely bestowed on us in the Beloved," who is Christ (v. 6). Election is another aspect of God's grace that results in salvation for those who believe and will bring Him eternal glory.

OUR RESPONSE TO GRACE

The grace of God calls for a commensurate response on our part—not to try to pay for what we have but out of overflowing gratitude for what God has done for us.

We Are Made for Good Works

One way we are called to respond to grace is by our works. Ephesians 2:8–9, the classic statement of salvation by grace alone, is followed by this statement: "For we are His workmanship, created in Christ Jesus for good works, which God prepared beforehand so that we would walk in them" (v. 10). The service we do for Christ is done out of gratitude for grace, not as our attempt to replace grace with works.

One of these works is daily self-sacrifice to the person and the will of God. "Therefore I urge you, brethren, by the mercies of God, to present your bodies a living and holy sacrifice, acceptable to God, which is your spiritual service of worship. And do not be conformed to this world, but be transformed by the renewing of your mind, so that you may prove what the will of God is, that which is good and acceptable and perfect" (Romans 12:1–2).

We Are to Grow in Grace

If a great man's last words are some of his most important, then 2 Peter 3:18 is a very important verse. It contains Peter's last recorded words to the church: "Grow in the grace and knowledge of our Lord and Savior Jesus Christ. To Him be the glory, both now and to the day of eternity. Amen."

Peter said you are to grow in your understanding of grace, because the better you understand grace, the better you will live the Christian life. And to grow in your understanding of grace means to grow in your knowledge of Jesus Christ, for grace is not an abstract concept but a person.

We Are to Draw on the Grace We Have

It's encouraging to read about how we can confidently approach Jesus Christ, our Great High Priest in heaven, to "receive mercy" and "find grace to help in time of need" (Hebrews 4:16; note vv. 14–15). But did you know that this great passage is set in a context of unbelief and failure to enter into everything that God has for us? Read Hebrews 4:1–13 and you'll understand this word of admonition: "Let us hold fast our confession" (v. 14). Our response to grace is to hold fast to our Lord and partake of His grace.

And what an invitation this is. The writer of Hebrews called it "the *throne* of grace" (italics added). A king sits on a throne, and Jesus is a King who has all authority in heaven and on earth (see Matthew 28:18). So when you come to Christ, you are coming to the final authority in the universe.

This is a tremendous promise, but don't miss the order in Hebrews 4:16.

God is ready to dispense all the grace we need when we need it, but it begins with our drawing near. You can't have a casual, long-distance relationship with the Savior and expect to find grace in your time of need.

But make no mistake about it. When we know the Lord and are growing in His grace, He dispenses His grace in an ever-flowing, ever-growing stream.

PERSONAL APPLICATION FOR LIFE

1. Ephesians 1:5 tells us that we are God's adopted children. As believers, we enjoy a family relationship as God's children, complete with an inheritance. The good news is that we can fully engage our inheritance now! Our inheritance includes "every spiritual blessing in the heavenly places in Christ" (v. 3). Are you still living in the ghetto of your old nature? As you grow in God's grace, discover your rights and privileges as a child of the King—and leave that old neighborhood!

2. God's grace is an interesting gift. Not only are we blessed with every spiritual blessing, but God also gives His grace abundantly. And His grace is "multicolored," that is, it is diversified. He has a version of grace for every need imaginable. As a believer, are you growing in His grace and experiencing its fullness?

3. One of the functions of grace is instructing us to deny ungodliness and worldly desires, and to live righteously (Titus 2:11–12). Are you struggling with an ungodly influence in your life that you need to get rid of? Take action! Close the magazine, turn off the TV, or avoid those who tend to bring you down. Let grace be your instructor in this arena. You will grow in grace and become more like Christ.

4. Spend the next five minutes listing all the things that are troubling you right now. Be specific. When your list is complete, take it to God. It is drawing near to the throne of grace that you find the grace to help you deal with each item on your list. It might seem overwhelming to you, but God is more than able to give you the grace to accomplish the task.

FOR GROUP STUDY

Questions for Group Discussion

1. Read Ephesians 1:5-6 and 2:8. Discuss the concept of grace. In what terms do we define it?

2. Why are we in need of God's grace? Read Ephesians 2:4–9. What is God's process of grace?

3. The doctrine of election is an important and complex doctrine. Dr. Evans gives it major attention in this chapter. What is the doctrine of election? Who are the elect? What is the doctrine of adoption, and what does it mean to the believer? To whom is grace available?

4. As believers and benefactors of God's grace, what should be our response to God's grace? (Use the chart below as an aid to your discussion.)

PICTURE THIS

We can never pay for God's gift of grace. Rather, our response should be rooted entirely in our gratitude for such an undeserving gift. Here are three specific responses we can have.

THE BELIEVER'S RESPONSE TO GOD'S GRACE

RESPONSE	SCRIPTURE PASSAGES	THE SIGNIFICANCE OF THE RESPONSE
Doing good works	Ephesians 2:8–9; Romans 12:1–2	One of our daily works is self-sacrifice to the person and will of God.
Growing in God's grace	2 Peter 3:18; John 1:14	When we grow in grace, we grow in the knowledge of Jesus Christ. The better we know Him, the more we experience His grace.
Drawing on the grace we have	Hebrews 4:14–16	God is ready to provide us all the grace we need when we need it.

65

SANCTIFICATION: THE PROGRESS OF SALVATION

Christians have been forgiven and are indwelt by the Holy Spirit, and God intends for us to progress in our faith from infancy to maturity, and from spiritual defeat to spiritual victory.

That much is beyond dispute. But translating these truths into daily life has become a challenge and a trauma for many Christians—even sincere believers who want their lives to make an impact for God. My thesis is that we need to understand what the Bible teaches about *sanctification*, another great word that opens up more of the depths of our great salvation.

Sanctification is an important biblical word that we don't hear used much anymore. Older believers would often say, "I'm saved and sanctified." That is a true statement because anyone who is saved is sanctified. But a more accurate statement might be, "I was sanctified the moment I was saved, I am being sanctified today, and one day I will be fully sanctified."

I say that because sanctification refers to the three tenses of salvation: past, present, and future. It deals with the progress that God wants us to make in our Christian lives from the moment we trust Christ until we are with Him in heaven.

Salvation is progressive. You were saved when you put your faith in

Christ. You are being saved today and every day as you walk with Him and grow in grace, and someday you will be saved when you step into God's presence. *Sanctification* is the term the Bible uses for this progression that encompasses what it means to be totally saved. It's a good place to wrap up this section of the book, because sanctification ends in the glory of heaven.

THE MEANING OF SANCTIFICATION

The word *sanctification* means "to be set apart." The concept isn't hard to grasp because all of us have utensils in our homes that are set apart, or dedicated, for a particular use.

I want to lay a common misconception to rest right here. In some circles, being sanctified was more or less equated with "being holy" in the sense of being a "super saint." That is, sanctified people looked and acted different than ordinary saints. Among some groups, sanctified people were those who experienced a further work or baptism of the Holy Spirit in their lives subsequent to salvation. And then there is the branch of Christendom that reserves the title of saint for people who reach a certain exalted status and are even said to be responsible for miracles.

But none of this is what the Bible means by sanctification. Sanctification is the normal experience of every Christian. God set us apart for Himself the moment Christ redeemed us. In fact, anyone who isn't sanctified, isn't saved. And every believer is a saint, a "holy one."

Set Apart from, *and Set Apart* to

Both the Hebrew and Greek terms for sanctification are at the root of words and phrases such as *holy, holiness, set apart, saint, consecrate,* and others that appear many times in the Bible.

Sanctification is a two-sided truth that includes being set apart *from* something and set apart *to* something else. As Christians we have been set apart from sin and to God. We are no longer to give ourselves over to evil to please our own flesh but to give ourselves over to God to please Him.

The most frequent use of sanctification in Scripture is to set something apart from a common or secular usage to a holy purpose for the service and glory of God. Ordinary people and ordinary things became sanctified when they were dedicated to God. Our modern practice of dedicating babies to the Lord, or dedicating a home or business to the Lord, reflects the biblical concept of setting someone or something apart for the Lord.

Sanctification is a way of acknowledging that God is to hold first place in the lives of His people. We are called to consecration today: "Sanctify Christ as Lord in your hearts" (1 Peter 3:15). If your heart is set apart for Jesus, there is no room for any other lord.

God's Special Purpose for Us

God's holiness, His total "apartness" from anything unholy, demanded that anything that belonged to Him be holy. We see this later in Israel as God prepared to give the nation His law:

> The Lord said to Moses, "Behold, I will come to you in a thick cloud, so that the people may hear when I speak with you. . . . Go to the people and consecrate them today and tomorrow, and let them wash their garments; and let them be ready for the third day, for on the third day the Lord will come down on Mount Sinai in the sight of all the people." (Exodus 19:9–11)

God also told Moses to have the priests consecrate themselves, and even to consecrate Mount Sinai by setting boundaries around it so the people would not touch the mountain and die (vv. 21–24).

"Consecrate" in these verses is the same word usually translated "sanctify." Sanctification involved a separation of holy things and holy people to God for a special purpose. With the Israelites at Sinai, the separation was visible in the form of the boundaries around the mountain. Our sanctification also has a specific purpose, as well as a definite beginning and a definite ending point.

THE THREE PHASES OF SANCTIFICATION

God's ultimate goal in our sanctification is stated for us in Romans 8:29, "Whom He foreknew, He also predestined to become conformed to the image of His Son, so that He would be the firstborn among many brethren." God has saved us and sanctified us—and is presently sanctifying us—so that we become more and more like Christ. And then in eternity, we will be like Him forever.

These are the three phases of sanctification. We have a past, a present, and a future as believers in Jesus Christ. It also helps to think of our sanctification as positional, progressive, and perfect.

Our Sanctification Is Positional

The Bible teaches that we have an exalted position in Christ, which we received at salvation and which is absolutely crucial to knowing who we are as Christians. That's why theologians have coined the term *positional* to describe this phase of sanctification.

What is the spiritual position we were given at salvation? We are seated with Christ "in the heavenly places" (Ephesians 2:6). We're already there spiritually, and someday we'll be there in person. This is an accomplished fact that occurred at salvation and is something we will never lose, so we can think of our position as the past tense of our sanctification. It happened at a definite moment in the past and is still in effect. From this standpoint, we are already sanctified.

Our Sanctification Is Progressive

Remember 1 Peter 3:15? "Sanctify Christ as Lord in your hearts." You are sanctified, but now you are told to do what you are. This is the essence of progressive sanctification, which involves acting in accordance with your position. This is the present tense of sanctification, relating to the day-to-day conduct of our Christian lives.

This is why I believe that one of the most important doctrines Christians can learn is their identity in Christ. Second Corinthians 7:1 says, "Therefore, having these promises, beloved, let us cleanse ourselves from all defilement of flesh and spirit, perfecting holiness in the fear of God."

The idea is that as believers who still retain the principle of indwelling sin, we are not there yet. We are holy in position but not always in practice. We can't improve on our position. It doesn't get any better than being seated with Christ. But we can definitely improve on our practice. In fact, the goal is to bring our practice in line with our position.

The way we do this is by cleansing ourselves. This refers to breaking sin's power over us. When we were saved, we were delivered from sin's penalty. Now we are in the process of being delivered from sin's power. And when we reach heaven, we will be delivered from sin's presence. Progressive sanctification means that we are now telling sin what to do and where to get off instead of sin bossing us around.

Our Sanctification Will Be Perfect

Our sanctification is not only positional and progressive, but someday it will be perfected. We're on our way to an eternal destination, and it's going to be glorious. The completion of our sanctification will be the completion of our salvation. When we leave this earth and these corrupt bodies behind and are ushered into the presence of Jesus Christ, we will finally be just like Him. And we will be delivered from the presence of sin forever.

Jesus' half brother, Jude, closed his short letter with a benediction of praise: "To Him who is able to keep you from stumbling, and to make you stand in the presence of His glory blameless with great joy" (v. 24).

How does the process of trading our sin-scarred bodies for new bodies take place? How do we leave behind these earthly lives of progressive sanctification for the perfection of heaven when we are with the Lord?

It will happen immediately at death when our perfect spirits—the new nature we received at salvation that is like God—deliver our blemished souls into His presence. John gave us a glimpse into how this will come about. "Beloved, now we are children of God, and it has not appeared as yet what we will be. We know that when He appears, we will be like Him, because we will see Him just as He is" (1 John 3:2).

John was referring to Christ's second coming, at which point all dead believers will be instantly raised and given new bodies, and all living believers will be transformed faster than the eye can twinkle. But until that day, every Christian who dies is immediately in the Lord's presence. We believe because of Paul's word of comfort and hope: "We are of good courage, I say, and prefer rather to be absent from the body and to be at home with the Lord" (2 Corinthians 5:8).

It's impossible to shoehorn any intermediate stages between death and glory into that verse. That may seem obvious to you, but there are entire segments of official Christendom that teach either an intermediate state called purgatory or a doctrine called soul sleep, which basically posits that the soul is still in the grave with the body, awaiting the resurrection. Thus, according to this teaching, there will be no conscious existence after death until Jesus comes.

Neither of these ideas is biblical. Paul's hope and expectation was that death meant being with Christ. He told the Philippians, "For to me, to live is Christ and to die is gain. But if I am to live on in the flesh, this will mean fruitful labor for me; and I do not know which to choose. But I am hard-pressed from both directions, having the desire to depart and be with Christ, for that is very much better" (1:21–23).

Paul's longing for heaven makes little sense if he knew that he would have to spend a thousand years in purgatory paying penance for his sins, or slumbering unconscious in the grave. Jesus told the dying thief on the cross, "Today you shall be with Me in paradise" (Luke 23:43). That was a promise of immediate glory in God's presence.

So don't worry if you have to go to the undertaker before you go to the "upper-taker." It won't matter where your body is or what condition it is in, because when God calls you home, you'll be raised as a perfectly sanctified, glorified saint fitted for heaven.

THE DYNAMIC OF DAILY SANCTIFICATION

There's another question I want to address in this matter of sanctification. It's wonderful to know that nothing can unseat us from our position in heaven with Christ, and it's great to think about the glories of heaven.

But the question many believers are asking today is, How can I get victorious sanctification working in my life right now? This is an issue for all of us, because every Christian has ingrained habits and sin patterns that need to be broken and a mind that needs to be reeducated.

God and You Are Working Together

I want to start with an important principle that will keep you from going off either end of an extreme when it comes to daily sanctification or Christian growth: Your growth in Christ is a cooperative effort between you and God. One extreme of this teaching is that the Christian life is all of God. Our only job is to "let go and let God." The other extreme says that the Christian life is basically a matter of self-effort, pulling yourself up by your own bootstraps. These are the "power of positive thinking" people.

But neither extreme gets at the truth of Scripture. Consider Romans 8:13, where we read, "If you are living according to the flesh, you must die; but if by the Spirit you are putting to death the deeds of the body, you will live."

Do you see the cooperative effort there? You are to put to death the sinful deeds of the body, but you do so by the power of the Holy Spirit. Don't misunderstand my use of the word *cooperative*. I don't mean a 50/50 partnership in which you put in your half and God puts in His half. The power is all His, but He does not act without our cooperation. The Holy Spirit will not levitate you to church if you decide you don't want to get up next Sunday.

But we can't miss the clear teaching of Scripture that the Christian life is a cooperative effort. Paul said of himself, "For this purpose also I labor, striving according to His power, which mightily works within me" (Colossians 1:29). Elsewhere the apostle declared, "I can do all things through Him who strengthens me" (Philippians 4:13). And just so we won't feel left out, here's a word for us: "So then, my beloved, just as you have always obeyed, not as in my presence only, but now much more in my absence, work out your salvation with fear and trembling; for it is God who is at work in you, both to will and to work for His good pleasure" (Philippians 2:12–13).

The Trinity Is at Work in You

Exodus 31:13 calls God "the Lord who sanctifies you." Jesus prayed to His Father, "Sanctify them in the truth; Your word is truth" (John 17:17). God the Father uses the Word to bring cleansing in the Christian's life. He is also "the God of all grace" (1 Peter 5:10). He supplies us with all the grace we will ever need to live as the sanctified people we are.

God the Son is also involved in our sanctification. He provides our cleansing, as John explained: "If we walk in the light as [God] Himself is in the Light, we have fellowship with one another, and the blood of Jesus His Son cleanses us from all sin" (1 John 1:7). And even when we fall into sin, the blood of Christ continues to cleanse us, as verse 9 promises: "If we confess our sins, He is faithful and righteous to forgive us our sins and to cleanse us from all unrighteousness."

Jesus Christ is our Cleanser and Sanctifier, because even on our most sanctified day, dirt still shows up. So we come into His presence each day for what I call general cleansing, which is the cleansing effect of the Word and prayer as we spend time with the Lord in our personal devotions, learning from Him what He wants us to do.

But we also need specific cleansing for specific sins. This is the cleansing addressed in 1 John 1:9. Confession of sin is vital to sanctification and fellowship with Christ.

God the Holy Spirit has a transforming role to play in our sanctification. "But we all, with unveiled face, beholding as in a mirror the glory of the Lord, are being transformed into the same image from glory to glory, just as from the Lord, the Spirit" (2 Corinthians 3:18). We have seen that the goal of sanctification is to make us more and more Christlike. Now we learn that the Spirit provides the dynamic for this transformation.

You Have a Role in Your Sanctification

Let me remind you that the Bible tells us in Philippians 2:12 to work out our own salvation. In other words, I can't work out your salvation for you, or vice versa. We can encourage and pray for each other and be faithful in teaching the Word, but this is an individual process.

This is an important word because of all the Christian television, books, seminars, and other resources available to the average believer today. It's easy to develop a secondhand faith reading about other believers' experiences or watching people shout and jump and claim miracles on TV. But the Christian life is a walk, not a piggyback ride.

Here is a principle that may encourage you as you work out your salvation and seek to live as the sanctified person you already are. The principle is that rate multiplied by time equals distance.

What I mean is that you can control your own rate of spiritual growth. You can speed it up by devoting the time and energy and commitment it takes to obey Christ and walk with Him in holiness. If you want to accelerate the rate of your growth in grace, give God all of your time, talents, and treasures. Make each day count for Him.

PERSONAL APPLICATION FOR LIFE

1. Give your inner resident, Jesus Christ, a scrub brush, mop, bucket, and whatever else He needs to scrub you clean and make you look good. Yield any known area of disobedience to Him. Give Him the key and the permission to enter any room of your heart that may be locked now.

2. Galatians 2:20 is a verse every Christian should memorize and quote every day. Write it down and review it daily. Say it to yourself until the truth of it becomes part of your permanent memory bank.

3. The present tense part of your sanctification has to do with the daily conduct of your Christian life. One of the ways we improve on our practice is by spiritually cleansing ourselves. Sin present in your life will prevent fellowship with God. Make it a point to claim the promise of 1 John 1:9 daily and stay clean before God.

4. Is your heart divided between the Lord and the world? Only you can answer that. Sometime soon, get alone with God and read through James 4:1–10 prayerfully. Ask the Holy Spirit to show how your love life with the Lord is doing.

FOR GROUP STUDY

Questions for Group Discussion

1. What does the Bible mean by the term *sanctification*? Why is sanctification considered a progressive work in the life of the believer?

2. Read Romans 8:29; Ephesians 2:6; 2 Corinthians 7:1; Jude 24; 1 John 3:2. Discuss the three phases of sanctification. How does each help complete the picture of sanctification?

3. The Trinity is at work in the believer. Each member of the Trinity has a part in the sanctification of the believer. Read Exodus 31:13; John 16:13; 17:17; and 1 Peter 5:10. What role does each member play in our sanctification?

4. How does daily sanctification work in the life of the believer? Philippians 2:12 instructs us to take a role in our own sanctification. What is that role, and what does it accomplish? What are the steps of working out our individual salvation? (Use the chart below as an aid to your discussion.)

PICTURE THIS

The sanctification of the believer is a dynamic, ongoing process. The believer has a strategic part in the process. Philippians 2:12 instructs us to work out our own salvation. Below are three steps we can take to work out our salvation and grow in grace.

THE BELIEVER'S DAILY STEPS TOWARD SPIRITUAL VICTORY

STEP	SCRIPTURE PASSAGES	WHAT THIS STEP MEANS
Walk by faith.	2 Corinthians 5:7; Galatians 2:20	Faith living is based on what God has said in His Word, not by what we see or feel.
Deny yourself.	Mark 8:34–35	This involves laying down our lives to follow Christ, even if it requires sacrifices on our part.
Abide in Christ.	John15:5	Abiding is focusing our lives and our heart's passion to please God.

SECTION II

The Assurance of Salvation

66

THE FOUNDATION OF ASSURANCE

A great spiritual malady permeates the church of Jesus Christ today. I call it ADD: Assurance Deficit Disorder.

The proportions of this spiritual affliction are gigantic. Many Christian ministries consistently list the lack of assurance of salvation as the Number One issue they deal with. The problem affects millions of sincere Christians who have little or no assurance that their eternal destiny is secure in Christ. When asked if they are on their way to heaven, they might answer if they're being honest, "I think so," or "I certainly hope so." But they would stutter to say, "I know so."

The symptoms of Assurance Deficit Disorder include an inordinate fear of death and hell, a questioning of God's love or of the believer's worthiness to be His child, a sense of real insecurity concerning eternity, and—not surprisingly—a lack of spiritual victory in daily Christian living.

Assurance of salvation is not a minor issue, for several reasons. First, it's important because the Bible addresses it in a number of places, which makes assurance a vital part of Christian doctrine and teaching. It must have been important to Jesus, because His last words to His disciples included this statement: "Peace I leave with you; My peace I give to you; not as the world gives do I give to you. Do not let your heart be troubled, nor let it be fearful" (John 14:27). That was a foundation they could stand on, so I want to address first the foundation of our assurance.

ASSURANCE AND CERTAINTY

Why do so many Christians lack assurance of their salvation? Some people are simply chronic doubters. They are so used to doubting that they are willing to doubt the clear teaching of God's Word before they are willing to doubt their doubts.

Other people have unconfessed sin in their lives, which will always undercut assurance. Still other believers suffer from Assurance Deficit Disorder when they are undergoing the stress of trials. This is chronic among believers in our culture because we have this persistent idea that if we were really God's children, we wouldn't be going through these things.

And then there are those Christians who, because they can't remember the exact day and hour they were saved, often doubt the reality of their salvation.

Faulty Theology Erodes Assurance

The reasons for a lack of assurance may vary, but unfortunately bad theology is a leading cause of this malady. A faulty understanding of the gospel of God's grace will play havoc with a believer's confidence in the power and promises of God.

We are not the first generation of believers to experience this problem. The Christians at Thessalonica were shaken and uncertain because they feared they would never see their dead loved ones again. Paul wrote to assure them with the truth of the church's rapture (see 1 Thessalonians 4:13–18).

But the most common reason for a lack of certainty among those early Christians was the presence of false teachers who followed the apostles around to the various churches, upsetting some people's faith and undermining their assurance. The writings of the apostles contain many references to these deceivers (see Romans 16:17–18; 2 Corinthians 11:13; Galatians 1:6–7; Ephesians 4:14; 2 Peter 2:1; 1 John 3:7; Jude 3–4).

Those who fell victim to the deceivers were deeply distressed. If you believe in an eternal heaven and an eternal hell, and if you aren't sure you are going to make heaven and miss hell, that will ruin some good nights' sleep.

The early church dealt with false teachers, and so do we today. And the antidote we need today is the same as it was in the days of the apostles: the clear teaching of God's Word.

Your Assurance Is Found in Christ

Where is assurance to be found? Very simply, our assurance is found in Christ. In other words, we don't look to Christ for salvation and then look elsewhere for the certainty of that salvation.

My premise for saying this is that assurance is bound up in the promise of the gospel. It is not an afterthought or a separate issue.

John, whom we could call the apostle of assurance, built a powerful case for this doctrine: "The testimony is this, that God has given us eternal life, and this life is in His Son. He who has the Son has the life; he who does not have the Son of God does not have the life" (1 John 5:11–12).

Then John clinched his teaching with verse 13: "These things I have written to you who believe in the name of the Son of God, so that you may know that you have eternal life."

Notice how salvation and assurance are woven together in this passage. God not only gives us eternal life in Jesus Christ; He also gives us the knowledge or certainty of that eternal life. The God who saves us through His Son is the God who secures us and testifies of our assurance through the Holy Spirit.

Paul told the Colossians, "Therefore as you have received Christ Jesus the Lord, so walk in Him" (2:6). We received Christ by faith, and we live by faith. The same principle is true for assurance. We could paraphrase Paul by saying, "Just as you have received Christ alone as your Savior, find your assurance in Him alone as well."

God's Testimony to Us

If our certainty is located in God's objective promise and not in our subjective experience, then what does John mean by the statement, "The one who believes in the Son of God has the testimony in himself" (1 John 5:10)? This sounds subjective.

But the testimony we have within us as believers is not just a warm, fuzzy feeling or a sense of security that we have to work up within ourselves by self-talk. The testimony we have internally is "the testimony of God" (v. 9) about who Jesus is and what He has done. This truth may generate good feelings of assurance and joy—and it should. But the feelings are not what John is talking about here.

We also know that this internal testimony is not just self-talk because of Romans 8:16: "The Spirit Himself testifies with our spirit that we are children of God." This is the Holy Spirit, whose job it is to inform your human spirit of the certainty of your salvation.

For some true Christians, the issue is not only that they are looking in all the wrong places for assurance, but that they simply can't believe real certainty is possible. As far as they're concerned, expecting to have certainty about things we can't see and feel and measure is just too much to ask.

John met this objection when he said, "If we receive the testimony of men, the testimony of God is greater" (1 John 5:9). The argument is from the lesser to the greater. We believe other people all the time about all kinds of things we can't see or measure for ourselves. So why should we have such a hard time believing what God tells us is true?

In John 5:24 Jesus said, "Truly, truly, I say to you, He who hears My word, and believes Him who sent Me, has eternal life, and does not come into judgment, but has passed out of death into life." There is certainty in this. You hear, you believe, and you have eternal life. Jesus did not add any qualifiers to His promise. There is no "may have" or "might have" here. Jesus never brought anyone from spiritual death to eternal life only to let that person fall back under God's judgment.

This is a tremendous word of assurance to all believers, but the key is to look to Christ both for salvation and the guarantee or assurance of salvation.

The Promise of Assurance

The bottom line of verses like 1 John 5:13 is so clear. You can *know* that you have eternal life. If you know Jesus Christ as your Savior, you are as certain of heaven today as if you had already been there ten thousand years.

One of the greatest believers in the certainty of salvation was the apostle Paul. Believers have quoted and even sung about his great declaration of confidence in God: "I know whom I have believed and I am convinced that He is able to guard what I have entrusted to Him until that day" (2 Timothy 1:12). In another place, Paul said that for him departing this life meant being with Christ (see Philippians 1:23).

And Jesus Himself spoke with certainty to His disciples when He told them, "Rejoice that your names are recorded in heaven" (Luke 10:20). It would be hard to rejoice if you had to worry about doing something that could cause your name to be erased from the Book of Life in heaven!

ASSURANCE AND GRACE

We also need to understand the relationship of saving grace to the doctrine of assurance. We dealt with grace's role in salvation, and I would urge you to review that chapter if you need to refresh yourself on the way grace operates.

My purpose here is to develop a twofold thesis. First, the grace of God that saves us totally apart from any merit of our own is the same grace that keeps us saved, totally apart from any merit of our own. Second, the God who saves us by His grace totally apart from anything we can do to earn it is the same God who guarantees the uninterrupted flow of that grace, totally apart from anything we can do to earn or keep it.

As Christians we often tend to get our Bible doctrines confused and start mixing truths that were never meant to be mixed. The relationship between grace and works is Exhibit A of this tendency. If the truth about salvation is compromised, our assurance will also be compromised.

Compromising Our Assurance

The early church also became confused about the nature of grace even though they heard the truth straight from the apostles themselves. The Christians in Galatia got sidetracked because a group of people called the Judaizers had confused them about the relationship between the gospel of grace and the works of the law.

Paul brought up the issue right at the beginning of the letter.

> I am amazed that you are so quickly deserting Him who called you by the grace of Christ, for a different gospel; which is really not another; only there are some who are disturbing you and want to distort the gospel of Christ. But even if we, or an angel from heaven, should preach to you a gospel contrary to what we have preached to you, he is to be accursed! (Galatians 1:6–8)

This was a serious issue to Paul. Even if he, or the angel Gabriel himself, showed up in Galatia with a message other than the gospel of grace, the Galatians were to show the person or angel the door. This was a reference to the Judaizers and their message that people needed to add law-keeping to grace to truly be saved and sanctified.

Paul summarized the problem this way: "I do not nullify the grace of God, for if righteousness comes through the Law, then Christ died needlessly" (Galatians 2:21). To try to win salvation by the works of the law ruins grace. Law and grace are an unholy mixture. That's why Paul called his readers "foolish Galatians" (3:1) for thinking they could begin the Christian life by grace and then progress in it by works (see v. 3).

Confusion's Road to Trouble

How confused can people become concerning the proper relationship between grace and the law or works? The answer to that is in Galatians 5:1–4, where Paul addressed the issue of circumcision in relation to salvation.

One of the law's requirements that the Judaizers insisted on was that Gentile believers become circumcised. But Paul warned that if the Galatians submitted to this rite as a means of seeking God's favor, then they were assuming the obligation to keep the whole law, which is what God demands and yet is impossible for anyone to do.

More than that, those who sought to be justified by law-keeping cut themselves off from Christ. Phrases like "severed from Christ" and "fallen from grace" (Galatians 5:4) sound like it is possible for believers to lose their salvation, which if true would fly in the face of everything the Bible says about our security in Christ. So let's find out what Paul meant by these severe warnings.

The first thing to remember is the context of Galatians 5:1–4. The teachings of the Judaizers had thrown these believers into such confusion that at least some of them were ready to take a giant step backward and place themselves under an impossible burden. Paul spared no severity or sternness in warning them against making this mistake.

So the very nature of the gospel as a gift of God's grace was at stake in this Galatian controversy. Those who were on the verge of "seeking to be justified by law" (5:4) were setting themselves up to be severed from a connection they had and to fall from a height they had reached. Did Paul mean that these believers would lose their salvation and fall back under God's judgment if they submitted to circumcision?

No, for at least two reasons. First, loss of salvation is not the subject under discussion here. The subject is the basis upon which a person is saved. Second, the Bible is clear that those who belong to Christ are kept by Him forever. If you or the Devil or anyone else could remove you from Christ's hand, then that entity would be greater than Christ and the eternal life He gave you would not be eternal at all. That's an impossible equation.

The issue Paul was addressing in Galatians 5 was the ground, or basis, upon which a person is saved. In other words, we can choose either "works of the law" righteousness or "by grace through faith" righteousness to be acceptable to God. But the Bible wants us to understand that these two paths are so mutually exclusive that the person who chooses to try to work his own way to heaven is cut off from the grace of Christ. It has to be either/or, not both/and.

To exchange grace for law is to trade a life of peace, joy, spiritual power, love, and confident assurance for one of guilt, frustration, exhausting effort, spiritual ineffectiveness, and restless uncertainty. A believer who decides to live like this in a misguided attempt to please God will still make it to heaven, but he won't enjoy the trip.

The Bible says in Colossians 2:6, "Therefore as you have received Christ Jesus the Lord, so walk in Him." How did we receive Christ? The Bible answers that for us. "For by grace you have been saved through faith; and that not of yourselves, it is the gift of God" (Ephesians 2:8). So how does God want us to live our Christian lives? By grace.

The Cost of Grace

God's grace is incredibly costly because He had to give His only Son to save us. But what does the cost of grace have to do with the issue of assurance?

It has everything to do with it, because when God gives us His complete package of grace in Christ and says, "This is My gift to you; it is free of charge, and I will never take it back," we can react in one of two ways. We can receive the gift with gratitude, thank the Giver, and rest in His promise that the gift really is ours forever. Or we can insist on trying to pay for that gift despite the Giver's assurance it already belongs to us.

The Impossibility of Paying for a Gift

But when we say to God, in effect, "Lord, I believe Your grace is enough to save me but not enough to keep me saved. Thank You for the gift of my salvation, but now I'm going to work hard for You and try to do everything right so You'll be satisfied with me and I won't lose my salvation," we insult Him (see Hebrews 10:29).

The point is that if God went to all of that trouble and paid such a dear price to save us, why should we think that it's too hard for Him to guarantee the eternal life He gave us? Paul asked the question this way: "He who did not spare His own Son, but delivered Him over for us all, how will He not also with Him freely give us all things?" (Romans 8:32). Assurance is part of the "all things" of the gospel.

I'm aware that many people get jittery when the subject turns to assurance and security because they're afraid that some will abuse grace and use it as permission to live in sin without having to worry about missing their trip to heaven. Paul anticipated that problem and answered it with an exclamation point: "Are we to continue in sin so that grace might increase? May it never be! How shall we who died to sin still live in it?" (Romans 6:1–2). Next question!

Our "Thank-You" Note to God

If our salvation and assurance rest solely in Christ and what He has done for us, where do our good works fit into the picture? After all, immediately after saying that salvation is a gift, Paul added, "For we are His workmanship, created in Christ Jesus for good works, which God prepared beforehand so that we would walk in them" (Ephesians 2:10).

The answer is quite simple. Grace inspires and empowers works while at the same time being distinct from works (see Romans 11:6). Good works are our thank-you note of gratitude to God for what He has given us. We serve the Lord not to get saved or make sure we stay saved but in appreciation for His grace and because He has promised to reward us for the things that we do in His name and for His glory.

ASSURANCE AND FAITH

I wish I could say that the confusion surrounding the doctrine of our assurance in Christ was just an academic debate among theologians. But I've seen too many believers who live in a "netherworld" of constant, nagging doubt regarding their salvation, and it's crippling to their spiritual growth.

The problem for many Christians is that they don't fully understand what it means to trust Christ and then live by faith. The trouble usually starts when people add human effort either to salvation by faith or to the life of faith.

Getting Paid Versus Receiving a Gift

There is a huge difference between getting paid for the work you do and accepting a gift. In the first case, you earned your salary and you get the credit for it. In the second case, you contributed nothing while someone else paid the price and he receives your gratitude for such generosity. The gift-giver gets the credit. Salvation belongs to the latter category.

There is a great example of this difference in Romans 4, where Paul reached back to Abraham to illustrate the truth that salvation comes by faith:

> If Abraham was justified by works, he has something to boast about, but not before God. For what does the Scripture say? "Abraham believed God, and it was credited to him as righteousness." Now to the one who works, his wage is not credited as a favor, but as what is due. But to the one who does not work, but believes in Him who justifies the ungodly, his faith is credited as righteousness. (vv. 2–5)

God is not going to let anyone take credit for His salvation, because if we earned it by our own efforts, we would have something to brag about in heaven. But God will not share His glory with anyone. Jesus paid it all, and He's the One we will be praising in heaven.

As Bad Off As We Can Be

If salvation is a faith proposition totally apart from works, why should it surprise us that assurance is also a faith proposition totally apart from works?

The world, and too often the church, operates on a basic misconception about the nature of human works that says that the good things people do, especially if they're done in a religious cause, make the doer acceptable to God.

Let me be extremely clear about this. The Bible has a very graphic term for the "righteous deeds" that human beings do apart from faith to try to win God's favor. These things are like "a filthy garment" (Isaiah 64:6; "filthy rags" KJV)—a reference to the cloths that a woman used during her menstrual period. It is not an attractive picture.

According to Jesus, many people who thought they were pleasing to God are going to stand before Him at the judgment and say, "Lord, Lord, did we not prophesy in Your name, and in Your name cast out demons, and in Your name perform many miracles?" (Matthew 7:22).

But Jesus' response to them is sobering: "I never knew you; depart from Me, you who practice lawlessness" (v. 23). This may not make sense to some people, but it does if you understand the doctrine of human depravity. The fact is that on the best day we ever had, our finest works are like a soiled garment in God's sight.

The Nature of Faith

Many people are unclear as to the nature of true faith. They think that if they "just believe," or "hope against hope," that's good enough. But no amount of wishful thinking can change the truth that the object of a person's faith is more important than the size of that person's faith. This is a biblical principle that is crucial to our understanding of assurance.

The Bible urges us to believe in Christ and receive His offer of salvation, and we are responsible to believe. But nowhere does the Bible assign any saving merit to our faith. When Jesus healed a man who was deaf and mute, the people who witnessed the miracle didn't congratulate the man. The Bible says they were astonished at Jesus and said, "He has done all things well" (Mark 7:37).

The Bible doesn't define faith precisely, but the famous description of faith in Hebrews 11:1 is a good starting point: "Now faith is the assurance of things hoped for, the conviction of things not seen." Faith is an inner conviction and persuasion that *what God says to us is true.*

I want to emphasize the second part of my definition because without this, faith loses its shape and becomes vague and nebulous. When you're hurting or in need of comfort, the statement "Just have faith" with no object or reasonable ground for that faith won't help you much.

Again, the object of our faith is far more important than the intensity of our faith. People often say, "I wish I had more faith." But that's not our need, and I have Jesus' testimony on that. "The disciples said to the Lord, 'Increase our faith!' And the Lord said, 'If you had faith like a mustard seed, you would say to this mulberry tree, "Be uprooted and be planted in the sea"; and it would obey you'" (Luke 17:5-6). And just in case there's any doubt about that, Jesus also said, "Believe in God, believe also in Me" (John 14:1).

We don't need more faith per se; we need either the right object to put our faith in or a deeper understanding of the object we have already put our faith in.

When you go to a doctor whose name you can't pronounce and receive a prescription you can't read and then take that prescription to be filled by a pharmacist you don't know and ingest a medication you never heard of before, you are exercising faith.

So everyone operates by faith on some level. The problem is a lot of people think saving faith is a special, "religious" faith that's entirely different from everyday faith. I don't find that distinction anywhere in Scripture. What separates saving faith from everyday faith is its object.

The Object of Faith

When the Jewish religious leader Nicodemus came to Jesus one night (John 3), Jesus told him, in summary, "Believe in Me and you will have eternal life." As part of that discussion, note that John 3:15 is followed by the wonderful promise of John 3:16. Jesus is the object of faith, and if your faith is in Him, you are His for eternity.

The Confidence of Faith

If you're still full of doubts as you read this, let me give a word of hope and a suggested solution to that nagging sense of uncertainty. There were doubters in the Scripture, who had all kinds of doubts. In fact, several prominent people in the Bible had serious moments of doubt.

One biblical doubter was the father who brought his demon-possessed child to Jesus and said, "If You can do anything, take pity on us and help us!" (Mark 9:22). We'll call this the doubt of desperation.

John the Baptist is probably the leading example of a powerful figure of faith who fell into doubt. John had been arrested, and he began to wonder if Jesus really was the Messiah (see Luke 7:18–19). In other words, John became overwhelmed by negative circumstances. He was isolated, and all kinds of questions began running through his mind. Why was he in prison and facing death if Jesus was the Messiah? Had he misplaced his trust? We might call this the doubt of defeatism.

Then there was the most famous doubter of all, the disciple Thomas. Ten of his fellow apostles testified to Thomas, "We have seen the Lord!" (John 20:25a). But Thomas insisted, "Unless I see in His hands the imprint of the nails, and put my finger into the place of the nails, and put my hand into His side, I will not believe" (v. 25b). The man had ten reliable eyewitnesses and rejected them all. Thomas's problem was deliberate doubt.

Take Your Doubts to Jesus

When Jesus challenged the unbelief of the father with the sick child, the man cried out, "I do believe; help my unbelief" (Mark 9:24), and Jesus healed his son. John sent his disciples to ask Jesus, "Are You the Expected One, or do we look for someone else?" (Luke 7:20). Jesus performed miracles and preached the gospel, and then told John's disciples, "Go and report to John what you have seen and heard" (Luke 7:22). John never raised another doubt.

And we know what happened to Thomas. Jesus invited Thomas to touch His wounds and said to him, "Do not be unbelieving, but believing" (John 20:27). Thomas's response is the one we need to make when we realize who Jesus is and what He has done to save us: "My Lord and my God!" (v. 28).

If you have doubts you can't shake, bring them to Jesus. He is still there, and He is your security.

APPLICATION FOR LIFE

1. One reason we need to rid our lives of known sin immediately is because the Enemy may try to convince you that your sin can cause you to lose your salvation. Remember, if you are a believer, your salvation is a work of God's grace—it is a gift that you can neither earn nor lose. Never allow false teaching that might come your way to conflict with what you know to be the truth. Take a moment to read and meditate on 1 John 5:6–13, and ask God strengthen your heart with its truth.

2. There are going to be times when you don't feel saved. There are going to be times of doubt and confusion when you wonder if you are on the right train. And there are going to be times when you have sinned and failed and don't even feel worthy to be on the train. Memorize 1 John 4:11–13, so that when such times come you can rest in the truth that "God has given us eternal life, and this life is in His Son. He who has the Son has the life."

3. Do you ever have doubts about the security of your salvation? Remember that your salvation is not dependent on your feelings or circumstances. Rather, its security rests with a person who is your Savior. Take to heart the admonition: "Do not be unbelieving, but believing" (John 20:27) and take your doubts to Jesus.

4. One blessing of assurance we ought to be thankful for is the fact that it lifts a heavy weight from our shoulders. We could never secure our own salvation. As a result, we are free to serve Him out of gratitude and love. What motivates your service to God? A fear that you might lose your salvation, or gratitude that God is holding you firmly in His grasp?

FOR GROUP STUDY

Questions for Group Discussion

1. For what reasons is the assurance of salvation an important doctrine and issue in the church today?

2. What was the main reason for the lack of certainty of salvation in the early Christian church? (See Romans 16:17–18; 2 Corinthians 11:13; Galatians 1:6–7; Ephesians 4:14; 2 Peter 2:1; 1 John 3:7; Jude 3–4.) What is the antidote to false teachers?

3. Read 1 John 5:11–13 and Luke 10:20. For those who lack an assurance of salvation, where can they find that assurance? (Use the chart below as an aid to your discussion.)

4. For what reasons is it important for salvation to be the result of the grace of God? (See Hebrews 10:29.) What part does faith play in our assurance of salvation?

PICTURE THIS

As believers, we need not lack assurance of our salvation. There are several assurances from Scripture we may mention, four of which are listed below.

THE BELIEVER'S CERTAINTY OF ASSURANCE

CERTAINTY	SCRIPTURE PASSAGES	WHY THIS CERTAINTY IS IMPORTANT
We find our assurance in Christ.	1 John 5:11–12	Because we received Christ by faith and live by faith, we find our assurance in the person of Jesus Christ.
God's testimony to us.	1 John 5:9	Our certainty of assurance is rooted in God's objective promise, not in our subjective experience.
God's testimony is reliable.	John 5:24	God's testimony is true, and the key is to look to Christ for both salvation and the guarantee or assurance of salvation.
The promise of assurance.	1 John 5:13; 2 Timothy 1:12	If you know Jesus, you can know that you have eternal life.

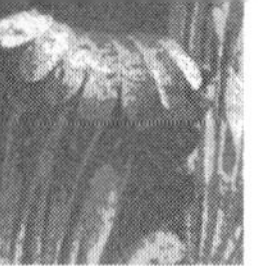

67

THE DEMANDS OF ASSURANCE

False security is always dangerous. The last thing I want to do is give anyone who doesn't really know the Lord a false sense of assurance. That's why we keep coming back to the central truth that our assurance rests in nothing but the finished work of Jesus Christ and the witness of the Holy Spirit that we are truly children of God (see Romans 8:16).

I also do not want to see Christians develop a false sense of security that often manifests itself in one of two ways: either the belief that we are above falling into temptation and failure because we are secure in Christ, or the equally mistaken notion that our eternal security means we can live in unrepentant sin or spiritual lethargy because we will make it to heaven anyway. There are demands that Christ has the right to make of us, based on the incredibly high price He paid to redeem us.

Thus the truth that we are forever secure in Christ doesn't give us an excuse for failure and spiritual lethargy and coldness. Nor does it mean that spiritual failure is a small thing. It's a real issue in the Christian life, and it will erode your sense of assurance faster than anything I can think of. I want to explore this issue, and then discuss how we can fortify ourselves against the very real danger of spiritual stumbling.

ASSURANCE AND SPIRITUAL FAILURE

There is no denying the fact that saved people who are sealed by the Holy Spirit until the day of redemption and secure forever in Christ can still fall into sin and failure. The Bible contains many examples of people who fell, some for short periods and others for a good part of their lives. These examples range from spiritual insensitivity and coldness to moral failure and even outright denial of the truth.

The Possibility of Spiritual Failure

David is an example of moral failure in his adultery with Bathsheba and murder of Uriah (2 Samuel 11–12). David covered his sin for about a year until confronted by the prophet Nathan. Then David immediately confessed and repented, and he told the Lord, "Against You, You only, I have sinned and done what is evil in Your sight" (Psalm 51:4). That's an important truth, because all spiritual failure ultimately is against the Lord.

The early church also contained examples of spiritual failure. The incestuous man in Corinth fell into deep moral failure (see 1 Corinthians 5:1–5), yet even in this case the man's eternal salvation was not at stake. Paul pronounced his discipline with the expressed desire that the man's soul would be saved (v. 5).

Spiritual failure doesn't have to be a huge leap into doctrinal error that denies the truth of Scripture. We can deny the faith by the way we live, failing to fulfill our biblical responsibilities or allowing the world to pull us away from faithfulness to Christ. I think of Demas, one of Paul's ministry companions who deserted the apostle because he "loved this present world" (2 Timothy 4:10).

The Road to Spiritual Failure

Admitting the possibility of spiritual failure is the first step to being on guard against it. None of us is perfect, but that doesn't mean we have to live in spiritual mediocrity, stumbling along from one setback to another. There are plenty of warning signs along the road that leads to spiritual failure.

The first sign is spiritual neglect. We don't have to curse the Lord or teach false doctrine to get into trouble. We can simply neglect our faith. "For if the word spoken through angels proved unalterable, and every transgression and disobedience received a just penalty, how will we escape if we neglect so great a salvation?" (Hebrews 2:2–3).

Spiritual neglect is so subtle that we can fall into it without feeling particularly sinful. People in this situation may console themselves by the fact that they aren't really doing wrong. It's not like they're lying or cheating or being unfaithful to their spouses. They still pray and read their Bibles and attend church sometimes. But no Christian ever "neglected" himself or herself into spiritual growth.

A second warning sign is spiritual insensitivity. If allowed to persist, spiritual neglect leads to spiritual insensitivity. Hebrews 3 contains this warning: "Take care, brethren, that there not be in any one of you an evil, unbelieving heart that falls away from the living God. But encourage one another day after day, as long as it is still called 'Today,' so that none of you will be hardened by the deceitfulness of sin" (vv. 12–13).

Insensitivity sets in when Christ stops being real to you and you stop looking to Him for your life. When you stop looking to Christ, unbelief sets in. And when unbelief sets in, you become susceptible to the deceitfulness of sin.

The third warning sign on the road to spiritual failure is spiritual stagnation. If you've ever seen a clouded, stagnant pond, you know what happens when the flow of freshwater is cut off. Nothing gets in or out. Even if you poured a bucket of freshwater into a stagnant pond, the new water would soon become green too.

In Hebrew 5, the author began teaching some deep truths about the priesthood of the Old Testament character Melchizedek, who was a type of Christ. But then it's as if the author realized whom he was addressing in his letter, because he stopped and said, "Concerning him [Melchizedek] we have much to say, and it is hard to explain, since you have become dull of hearing" (v. 11).

The phrase "dull of hearing" means mule headed, or stubborn as a mule. These believers had been saved long enough to be spiritually mature. But they had stagnated in their development because they had quit practicing the faith.

That doesn't mean they had quit being Christians. But eternally secure

Christians can become so dull and stagnant that they are basically useless to the kingdom of God. And when that happens, we shouldn't be surprised that there is no sense of assurance and peace of heart concerning salvation.

Here's a fourth warning sign: spiritual defection. If we miss the warning sign of stagnation, we're really heading into some serious territory on the road to spiritual failure. The Hebrews were on the verge of spiritual defection, so they received this admonition:

> Let us hold fast the confession of our hope without wavering, for He who promised is faithful; and let us consider how to stimulate one another to love and good deeds, not forsaking our own assembling together, as is the habit of some, but encouraging one another; and all the more as you see the day drawing near. (Hebrews 10:23–25)

Forsaking the local church is tantamount to spiritual defection. The Bible knows nothing of a Christian who is severed from the church and going it alone. If you're slipping toward spiritual failure and lethargy, the body of Christ can reel you back in.

The Consequences of Spiritual Failure

God takes spiritual defection very seriously, as He does spiritual failure on any level. There is always forgiveness available when we repent and come back to God, because we are still God's children even when we fail.

One of these consequences is divine discipline. In Hebrews 6:4–6a we read, "For in the case of those who have once been enlightened and have tasted of the heavenly gift and have been made partakers of the Holy Spirit, and have tasted the good word of God and the powers of the age to come, and then have fallen away, it is impossible to renew them again to repentance."

This is the passage that causes such confusion and is a favorite of those who deny the truth of eternal security. Some people try to get around the problem by saying that the people in question were not real believers because they only "tasted" of salvation.

But that view doesn't stand up, because Hebrews 2:9 uses the same Greek term to say that Jesus tasted death for every person. Did He just nibble at death, or did He die? If Jesus didn't really die on the cross, we have a major problem. But He drank the cup of death down to its dregs. The word "taste" means "to appropriate, not to dabble with." The people of Hebrews 6 were believers.

If that's true, don't these verses clearly teach that believers can lose their salvation? If this is true, then the text is also clear that it is "impossible" for them to get it back again—a view that no one who denies the possibility of assurance wants to hold.

So if the text is talking about true Christians and it is not talking about them losing their salvation, what is the author's point? He is saying that Christians can become so hardened in spiritual failure and departure from the truth that it becomes impossible to renew them again to repentance.

This is certainly not impossible for God, because the Bible says nothing is impossible for God. But believers who turn away from God can become so hard other people can't win them back, and their lives may end in spiritual ruin as far as their earthly service is concerned—even though they are saved.

Death is the most severe consequence of persistent spiritual disobedience and unrepentant sin. The book of Hebrews also addresses this issue in 10:26-29. The writer pointed out that an offender against the Mosaic law was stoned to death. That's how seriously God takes His character and His Word. The punishment for the offending Christian isn't specified, except that it is "much severer" than stoning. We don't see this kind of judgment carried out very often, because God is gracious and it brings Him no pleasure to have to judge His erring children.

The Cure for Spiritual Failure

Many people who agonize over whether they have lost their salvation need to be reminded that their deep concern is one of the best signs that they are truly saved. Lost people don't usually lose any sleep wondering if they are saved or not.

The same principle applies to spiritual failure. If you are concerned about your walk with God and you agonize over your sin, that's the best sign of all that you have not become hard of heart and uncaring. A good place to begin in renewing your spirit is to practice self-examination.

ASSURANCE AND SELF-EXAMINATION

Every coach who has ever lived has probably yelled in frustration to one of his players: "Get in the game!"

This doesn't mean the player is on the sidelines and needs to get up and get on the field. Any sports fan knows that this expression means the player in question is messing up. Maybe he's not giving it his full effort, or he's not paying attention and needs to do a little mental self-examination and wake up. "Get in the game!" means that although the player may be filling his position, he's not fulfilling the responsibilities of his position.

As Christians we need to be told to get in the game sometimes. The Bible tells us again and again to examine our spiritual condition.

Self-Examination and Spiritual Failure

Sometimes when you misbehaved as a child, your mother might have said something like this: "What is wrong with you, child? You didn't learn that in this house. You're acting like one of those wild kids down the street!"

God has the same problem with some of His children, and there's nothing humorous about it. Consider the spiritually ill-mannered Corinthian believers who were making a sham of the Lord's Supper by being gluttonous and even getting drunk (see 1 Corinthians 11:21). Paul took on that mess in no uncertain terms and warned the church, "For this reason many among you are weak and sick, and a number sleep" (v. 30).

We don't have to guess about the judgment Paul was talking about, because he provided that information. The judgment was physical discipline in the form of illness and even death (v. 30). The judgment mentioned in verse 32 must be read the same way. God was spanking His children for rebellious living, even destroying some of them physically the way the unbelieving world will also be destroyed someday.

Like a good father, God disciplines His children—and sometimes the discipline may be severe. The Bible says, "Those whom the Lord loves He disciplines, and He scourges every son whom He receives" (Hebrews 12:6). We would be wise to examine ourselves to make it unnecessary for God the Father to spank us.

Self-Examination and Spiritual Productivity

Given the spiritual track record of the Corinthian church, it's not surprising that Paul had to come back again and urge them to examine themselves. As he wrapped up his second letter to this church, the apostle wrote: "Test yourselves to see if you are in the faith; examine yourselves! Or do you not recognize this about yourselves, that Jesus Christ is in you—unless indeed you fail the test?" (2 Corinthians 13:5).

This passage is a little stickier to explain because it seems so obvious that Paul is saying, "Check yourselves out to see if you are Christians or not." In other words, "Check to make sure you are born again."

But 2 Corinthians 13:5 is not about our eternal standing before God. The theme of 2 Corinthians is Paul's vindication of his ministry and his love for the Corinthians. In answer to those who opposed and criticized him, and the Corinthians' own fickleness, Paul opened up his heart to demonstrate the sincerity and authenticity of his love and his apostleship.

This is key to understanding the test of faith Paul referred to in chapter 13. This was not a test of salvation but a test of whether God was really at work in a believer's life.

How do we know this was the apostle's focus? Because he used the same Greek term translated "fail the test" in 2 Corinthians 13:5 to refer to the productivity of his ministry. "I discipline my body and make it my slave, so that, after I have preached to others, I myself will not be *disqualified*" (1 Corinthians 9:27, italics added). To be disqualified is to fail the test, lose the race, and forfeit the victor's reward.

Paul was not afraid that he was going to lose his salvation. He was the champion of the eternal security of the believer. But he was afraid that he would be unapproved and unrewarded by God because he had not been faithful to his calling. Paul wanted to finish the Christian race so that he would not appear before Christ empty-handed and receive no rewards in heaven.

Self-Examination and Spiritual Growth

The apostle Peter also addressed the need for self-examination in 2 Peter 1:10. This is an interesting text because in one sense, we as believers don't make our calling and election certain. These are God's action to save us, and He is the One who guarantees our salvation.

Yet Peter has written that we are to "be all the more diligent to make certain about His calling and choosing you." So what did Peter mean? In the context of spiritual growth, he was saying that by being diligent to grow in our faith, we produce for ourselves something like a deed that a homeowner has to prove that he owns his home. This is the background meaning of the Greek word translated "certain" in verse 10.

In other words, if you are growing in your faith and producing the qualities listed in verses 5–8, that's a proof of the reality of your salvation. This is very different from saying that your growth guarantees or secures your salvation. Salvation is not dependent upon your spiritual growth but upon the finished work of Jesus Christ.

Interestingly, the word *certain* in 2 Peter 1:10 is translated "guaranteed" in Romans 4:16 and "assurance" in Hebrews 3:14, strongly suggesting that Peter used it here to convey certainty with regard to salvation. It's in this context that we must evaluate the word *stumble* at the end of verse 10. It cannot refer to a loss of salvation but the failure to grow as we should.

Spiritual growth was definitely on Peter's heart when he wrote his second letter. His last word to the church was "Grow in the grace and knowledge of our Lord and Savior Jesus Christ" (2 Peter 3:18). Second Peter is a reminder that God wants us to get busy growing in the grace He has given us instead of fretting about whether we are still in God's grace.

With this in mind, go back to 2 Peter 1:5–7: "Now for this very reason also, applying all diligence, in your faith supply moral excellence, and in your moral excellence, knowledge, and in your knowledge, self-control, and in your self-control, perseverance, and in your perseverance, godliness, and in your godliness, brotherly kindness, and in your brotherly kindness, love." Applying diligence to supply the qualities that make for spiritual growth means that we must make a plan to grow and work that plan.

Where will these qualities take you as you grow in grace? Peter wrote, "For if these qualities are yours and are increasing, they render you neither useless nor unfruitful in the true knowledge of our Lord Jesus Christ" (2 Peter 1:8). Fruitfulness, usefulness, and the eternal rewards these will bring are the result of careful spiritual self-examination. Don't let yourself get sidetracked into fearful and paralyzing introspection over whether you're really saved—or even worse, whether Christ really meant what He said when He promised eternal life to all who trusted in Him.

ASSURANCE AND DISCIPLESHIP

Discipleship is not your ticket to heaven. Nor is it the source of your assurance of salvation, but a process of growth whereby we get on with the business of becoming like Jesus Christ. Jesus Himself said, "A disciple is not above his teacher, nor a slave above his master. It is enough for the disciple that he become like his teacher, and the slave like his master" (Matthew 10:24–25).

This statement alone makes it clear that discipleship is not instantaneous. Instead, it involves a lifetime of learning. The word *disciple* means "student" or "learner," and so discipleship describes the process by which students absorb their teacher's instruction and skill so completely that they become just like that teacher. A more formal definition is that discipleship is a process of the local church that brings people from spiritual infancy to spiritual maturity.

The Meaning of Discipleship

In the ancient world, students often attached themselves to a teacher or master until they had acquired both a body of knowledge and the skills to use that knowledge effectively, no matter how long the process took. True disciples immersed themselves in their learning; it was a way of life, which is one difference between being a disciple and having a hobby.

When we became followers of Christ, we were enrolled in Jesus' school of discipleship and introduced to its curriculum. This is a lifelong process of learning from which we will not graduate until we are promoted to heaven. And even there we will not stop learning, because we'll spend eternity discovering more and more about our great God (see Ephesians 2:7).

Our challenge as Christians, then, is to become such committed, excited, and teachable disciples of Jesus Christ that we begin to look and act like Him. The Bible calls it being "conformed" to the image of Christ (Romans

8:29). Assurance plays a key role in this process, because you can't be a focused, learning, and growing student when you're spending all of your time worrying about whether you're still enrolled in the course. Assurance of salvation makes effective discipleship possible.

How Discipleship Differs from Salvation

Now that we have defined our terms, we need to decipher the relationship between discipleship, which is a lifelong process of growth, and salvation, which is complete the moment we trust Christ. Our thesis is that confusing these two leads to a lack of assurance and sends us searching for it in the wrong places.

You may be surprised by one passage that shows that discipleship and salvation are distinct. The Bible says that Jesus had disciples who were not even saved. According to John 6:60, a group of Jesus' disciples became offended at His teaching about His flesh and blood. They objected to what Jesus said, to which He replied, "There are some of you who do not believe" (v. 64). And it gets worse, because John went on to say, "As a result of this many of His disciples withdrew and were not walking with Him anymore" (v. 66).

It's obvious from this text that the term *disciple* was applied broadly to anyone who wanted to learn more about what it meant to follow Jesus Christ. Jesus had a large following at one point, but He thinned out that crowd when He began showing them the true cost of being His disciple.

Whereas salvation is free, discipleship is costly. Jesus said on one occasion, "If anyone wishes to come after Me, he must deny himself, and take up his cross and follow Me. For whoever wishes to save his life will lose it, but whoever loses his life for My sake and the gospel's will save it" (Mark 8:34–35). It will cost you your life to become Jesus' disciple.

Another difference between salvation and discipleship is that salvation demands only faith (although faith is to issue in works [James 2:14]), while discipleship makes radical, ongoing, and long-term demands. Jesus said, "If anyone comes to Me, and does not hate his own father and mother and wife and children and brothers and sisters, yes, and even his own life, he cannot be My disciple" (Luke 14:26).

You don't have to hate your mother or your father to get saved. You don't have to hate yourself to come to Christ and find eternal life. But to become a disciple requires such radical self-abandonment to Christ that compared to your love for Him, your love for even the people closest to you looks like hate.

Another important contrast between salvation and discipleship is what we might call their observability. That is, salvation is a transaction of the heart. No one can see it take place. Salvation takes place in the privacy of a person's heart and soul.

But discipleship is always meant to be public and, therefore, observable. John 19:38 refers to Joseph of Arimathea as a disciple of Jesus who had followed the Lord secretly because he was afraid of his fellow Jews. But guess what happened to Joseph? There came a day when he had to declare himself publicly, and you can read about it in the same verse. He went to Pilate and asked for Jesus' body to bury, and he laid Jesus in his own tomb. It would have been impossible to do something like that in Jerusalem without making his true allegiance known.

Jesus may have some "secret-agent saints," but He does not want disciples who function as covert operatives when there are no restrictions on the practice of their faith. "Therefore everyone who confesses Me before men, I will also confess him before My Father who is in heaven. But whoever denies Me before men, I will also deny him before My Father who is in heaven" (Matthew 10:32-33).

Salvation is unconditional, but discipleship is conditional. "Jesus was saying to those Jews who had believed Him, 'If you continue in My word, then you are truly disciples of Mine; and you will know the truth, and the truth will make you free'" (John 8:31-32). To continue means to abide or remain in the truth.

Many people want truth without the abiding that it takes to get the truth inside of them. If someone says, "I know the truth, but I'm not free," then we have an abiding problem.

John 8:32 is one of the most quoted verses in the New Testament, but don't forget the Bible study principle we learned earlier: the importance of context. The problem comes when people want to skip verse 31 and claim verse 32. We want to be free of our problems, our addictions, our vices, or our circumstances. But in order to be free, we have to know the truth. And in order to know the truth, we must continue or abide or remain in Christ and so prove to be true disciples.

How Discipleship Relates to Assurance

Salvation gives us new life, and assurance gives us the security and confidence to develop that new life as we follow Christ in discipleship.

There is a tremendous interplay of salvation, assurance, and discipleship in Titus 2:11–13. "For the grace of God has appeared, bringing salvation to all men, instructing us to deny ungodliness and worldly desires and to live sensibly, righteously and godly in the present age, looking for the blessed hope and the appearing of the glory of our great God and Savior, Jesus Christ."

Notice that the grace of God appeared to us and brought us salvation (v. 11). And that same grace will be manifested to us at the end of this age when Jesus appears and takes us to be with Him in glory (v. 13).

Verse 12 speaks to our discipleship "in the present age" and the way we should conduct ourselves on our journey from earth to heaven. It's like a sandwich, with the "meat" of discipleship in between the two pieces of bread called grace. The bread holds the meat in place, and the meat fills out the sandwich. Assurance is an integral part of the formula.

Assurance is the motivation and the power of discipleship. God wants us to be grateful for our eternal salvation. He wants us to be thankful that because of Christ's death on the cross, heaven is our home. If we will look at what God has given us and stop fretting about whether He is going to take back His gift of salvation, we'll be ready to follow Him in committed discipleship here on earth. If we can trust Christ with our eternity, can we not trust Him with our few days on earth?

PERSONAL APPLICATION FOR LIFE

1. When is the last time you did a spiritual self-examination? The Bible encourages us to do this on a regular basis. Examine your heart and ask God to help cleanse your life of sin, claiming 1 John 1:9. Should you neglect this responsibility, be assured that God disciplines His children.

2. Beyond monitoring sin in our lives, spiritual self-examination means monitoring our spiritual productivity. This is a test to confirm that God is working in our lives. If you are not seeing spiritual fruit and God's blessing in your life, perhaps you have allowed the world's substitutes for God to creep into your life. Take inventory and clean house if necessary. Ask God to help you keep things on a proper spiritual course in your life.

3. Whereas salvation deals with our legal relationship to Christ and is unconditional, discipleship is conditional, and has to do with the level of intimacy we have with the Savior who guarantees our eternal life. Maybe you became a Christian when you were ten years old; now you're forty-five, and you're still asking to see God. Maybe the intimacy you're missing is waiting for you in a deeper commitment to Christ in discipleship.

4. Discipleship for the believer is a costly commitment. The assurance of your salvation is the motivation and the power of discipleship. Are you ready to follow Him in committed discipleship here on earth? If you can trust Christ with your eternity, can you not trust Him for your days on earth?

FOR GROUP STUDY

Questions for Group Discussion

1. Dr. Evans discusses "spiritual failure." What does he mean by that term? Of the four warning signs that a believer is on the road to spiritual failure (see chart on page 822), which do you fear the most, and why?

2. Read Hebrews 6:4–6a. What serious consequences can result from spiritual failure? What is the cure for spiritual failure?

3. Why is spiritual self-examination a good preventive measure against spiritual failure? Read 2 Corinthians 13:5. How can it be a catalyst for spiritual productivity?

4. What is discipleship? (See Romans 8:29.) How does discipleship relate to our assurance of salvation?

PICTURE THIS

Since the Hebrews were on the verge of losing their spiritual confidence (not their salvation) and turning back, the letter to the Hebrews contains some clear warning signs we can read and heed as we seek to avoid going into the ditch in our Christian lives.

THE WARNING SIGNS OF SPIRITUAL FAILURE

WARNING SIGN	SCRIPTURE PASSAGE	ITS IMPORTANCE
Spiritual neglect	Hebrews 2:2–3	If we are neglecting things like time with God in the Word and prayer, and time with God's people in fellowship and service, this should be a warning sign that we are on the road to spiritual neglect.
Spiritual insensitivity	Hebrews 3:12–13	Spiritual insensitivity sets in when Christ stops being real to us and we stop looking to Him for our lives. We become susceptible to the deceitfulness of sin. Sin isn't as painful as it used to be.
Spiritual stagnation	Hebrews 5:11	This happens when we allow our hearts to become insensitive toward the things of God. We become dull and stagnant and useless to the kingdom of God.
Spiritual defection	Hebrews 10:23–25	As we are a part of the body of Christ, we need to be in fellowship with other believers. Forsaking the assembly of the local church is tantamount to spiritual defection.

68

THE BLESSINGS OF ASSURANCE

There are incredible benefits to being a Christian. When Jesus said of His children, "I give eternal life to them, and they will never perish" (John 10:28), that's exactly what He meant. As desperate and as hopeless as we would be without Christ, that's how secure we are in Him. Jesus made the promise of eternal life to a desperate woman one day, and we need to hear again what He said.

The story of the woman at the well is one of the most familiar in the New Testament. This Samaritan woman who came to Jacob's well to draw water had her life changed forever because Jesus was there that day. Since Jesus wanted to get a discussion started about water, He said to her, "Give Me a drink" (John 4:7). That got her attention because she was shocked that Jesus would want to put His Jewish lips to her "unclean" Samaritan cup and take a drink.

The woman expressed her surprise that a Jew would have anything to do with a half-breed Samaritan, but Jesus had something much more shocking and surprising in mind. In response to her comment, He said, "If you knew the gift of God, and who it is who says to you, 'Give Me a drink,' you would have asked Him, and He would have given you living water" (v. 10).

The woman didn't realize yet that Jesus was offering her eternal life, so she questioned His ability to give her a drink when He had nothing to draw water with. I want to focus on Jesus' answer to her confusion. "Everyone who drinks of this water will thirst again; but whoever drinks of the water that I will give him shall never thirst; but the water that I will give him will become in him a well of water springing up to eternal life" (vv. 13–14).

Jesus promised the woman at the well that if she drank of His living water, she would not need to keep drinking. Her response in John 4:15 indicates that she was still thinking of physical water, but whatever it was Jesus was offering her, she definitely wanted it: "Sir, give me this water, so I will not be thirsty nor come all the way here to draw."

THE WATER OF ETERNAL LIFE

This water of life that Jesus gave us at salvation is a special gift. Jesus didn't say it would well up within us as long as we toe the line and don't do anything to displease Him. Neither did He say that once the flow of eternal life was interrupted, we would have to come and drink and start the process all over again. He said the well He places within us will flow eternally. Assurance of salvation is built into the gift of eternal life.

The Essence of Eternal Life

Jesus defined the essence of eternal life as a relationship with Him. If the "man on the street" was asked to define eternal life, he would probably say that it means to live forever. But length of existence is an insufficient definition of eternal life. Lost people are going to exist forever in hell, so there has to be more to eternal life than just its "foreverness." You and I were created as eternal beings.

Jesus gave us the "more" of eternal life in His prayer to the Father in the Upper Room just before His crucifixion. "This is eternal life, that they may know You, the only true God, and Jesus Christ whom You have sent" (John 17:3). Eternal life is the knowledge of God, the kind of intimate relational knowledge between a parent and child that people in hell will not be able to experience because they will be separated from God for eternity.

No wonder the Bible tells us to "[fix] our eyes on Jesus" (Hebrews 12:2).

We don't focus on Christ just to gain assurance. It is actually a by-product of our commitment to look to Christ as our life and develop the eternal life that God has placed within us.

You won't have an assurance problem if you are growing and developing in your relationship with Jesus Christ, "who is our life" (Colossians 3:4). And by the way, this verse also ties our life with Christ to the certainty of our spending eternity with Him, because Paul wrote, "When Christ, who is our life, is revealed, then you also will be revealed with Him in glory."

The Experience of Eternal Life

Have you ever looked at something and yet not really seen it in terms of realizing it was there? It happens all the time, especially as we get older. Something similar can happen with the eternal life we have been given by Christ. It's there, but we have to realize it and do something with it to fully experience all that God has for us.

The Bible says, "Do not be deceived, God is not mocked; for whatever a man sows, this he will also reap. For the one who sows to his own flesh will from the flesh reap corruption, but the one who sows to the Spirit will from the Spirit reap eternal life" (Galatians 6:7–8). The reaping of eternal life here is not salvation, because this was written to Christians ("brethren," v. 1).

Paul's point was that in order for us to experience—not achieve—eternal life, we must sow to eternal life. In other words, we must starve the flesh and cultivate the Spirit.

Paul chose the most common metaphor of his day to illustrate what he meant. A farmer has to prepare the ground before he can sow the seed. It takes work to sow good seed and reap a harvest. If we want to experience and enjoy the benefits of eternal life, we must "sow to the Spirit." Paul told Timothy, "Take hold of the eternal life to which you were called" (1 Timothy 6:12). Timothy already possessed the gift of life in Christ. But that gift needed to be cultivated.

If you sow to the flesh, the unrighteous part of you that doesn't want to please God, you will die. That means we will be spiritually impoverished. The eternal life within us will begin to shrivel and become unproductive, like a crop that is sown but then neglected.

That's because the flesh is like an in-law you can't get rid of. The flesh is never satisfied. Even when you give the flesh what it wants, it always wants more. That's why God has consigned these sin-contaminated bodies of ours to the grave and will give us new bodies in the resurrection. But in the meantime, the Bible says that to get rid of sin we must feed the Spirit, or sow to the Spirit, and starve the flesh. By the way, this is the opposite of the ancient heresy of Gnosticism, which said the material body itself was bad and therefore it didn't matter what you did with it, which gave Gnostic followers permission to indulge in sin and debauchery.

Jesus also used an agricultural metaphor to describe the way He wants us to experience eternal life, "Abide in Me, and I in you. As the branch cannot bear fruit of itself unless it abides in the vine, so neither can you unless you abide in Me" (John 15:4). To abide in Christ means to maintain intimate connection and fellowship with Him. That's essential because Jesus is the vine, another way of saying that He is our life.

Jesus will affect and empower you no matter where you are, because He is your life and your power source. All you have to do is put yourself in His abiding presence.

Jesus will change you, develop you, encourage you, strengthen you, and empower you. He'll give you victory because "greater is He who is in you than he who is in the world" (1 John 4:4). And you won't have to wonder whether God still loves you enough to keep you in His care now and for eternity.

ASSURANCE AND REWARDS

Teachers are always eager for signs that their students are maturing and ready to get on with the business of learning. One sign that students are progressing is when they quit asking questions such as "Is this going to be on the exam?" or "What time does this class end?" or "Are you going to grade on the curve?" and start asking things like "What does this mean?" and "How can I use this knowledge?" and "How should I adjust my life in relation to what I'm learning?"

There is a spiritual parallel to this phenomenon. One sign that we are maturing and progressing in our Christian lives is the kind of questions we ask and the thoughts that occupy our minds. For instance, some believers are still hung up on what I call "ABC" questions of the faith such as "How can I know that I'm really saved?" or "Could I ever sin so badly that God will reject me?" or "Are my doubts a sign that I've lost my salvation?"

Don't misunderstand. These issues are important, and it's not necessarily wrong to have times of doubt. But these periods of uncertainty should become shorter and less frequent as we grow in the grace and knowledge of our Savior. And one area in which we can grow spiritually is in our understanding of the connection between our assurance and the service we offer to God in gratitude for His great salvation.

Therefore, I want to close this section of our study by discussing assurance as it relates to our service and rewards. My thesis is that the fact of our eternal salvation, and our knowledge of that fact, should spur us to please God by offering Him a life of grateful service. And the amazing thing is that when we do this God turns around and rewards us based on our faithfulness.

Our Motivation to Serve Christ

I fear that too often we fail to appreciate our great salvation. We lose our sense of awe and wonder that Jesus would die for us. A good reminder is the story of the woman who came to Jesus at a dinner party and wept in repentance at His feet, washing His feet with her tears and wiping them with her hair.

You can read the story in Luke 7:36–48. I want to focus on Jesus' response to the self-righteous Pharisee who was His host for the dinner and who was appalled that Jesus would allow this sinful woman to approach Him. Jesus said to the Pharisee, "Her sins, which are many, have been forgiven, for she loved much; but he who is forgiven little, loves little" (v. 47). The message to all of us is that we are in the same predicament as this woman, needing much forgiveness. And those who are forgiven much should love much.

In his second letter to Timothy, Paul included a great statement that may have served as a confession of faith for the early church: "It is a trustworthy statement: For if we died with Him, we will also live with Him; if we endure, we will also reign with Him; if we deny Him, He also will deny us; if we are faithless, He remains faithful, for He cannot deny Himself" (2 Timothy 2:11–13).

Endurance here means more than just hanging on until the end. It means enduring the way a skilled and well-conditioned runner runs a race: not barely making it to the finish line but running a strong race and blasting through the tape with a final burst of speed. Those are the kinds of runners who "reign" in a race, who win the crown and the prize.

Similarly, our endurance in running the Christian race results in our winning the crown and reigning with Christ.

Paul was looking ahead to the reward that comes with faithful service for Christ. Paul was motivated by the promise of rewards from Christ. He was expecting not just to squeeze through the door of heaven but to reign with Christ in a place of honor, authority, and responsibility. The Bible contains many hints of what that position will entail, but for our purposes now, it is enough to note that those who endure with Christ in service on earth reign with Him in glory in eternity.

In 2 Corinthians 5:11, Paul wrote, "Therefore, knowing the fear of the Lord, we persuade men." (We'll see below what "therefore" refers to.)

The King James Version translates the word "fear" in verse 11 as "terror," which is closer to the idea that Paul was trying to convey. He wasn't terrified of the Lord, but he knew some things about God that we forget too easily. For example, "Our God is a consuming fire" (Hebrews 12:29). "It is appointed for men to die once and after this comes judgment" (Hebrews 9:27). "It is a terrifying thing to fall into the hands of the living God" (Hebrews 10:31).

In other words, Paul was highly motivated to rescue the perishing from the burning fires of God's judgment. And even if we interpret the "fear of the Lord" to be reverence for Him, the motivation is still there because we serve God out of reverence for His person and His great love for us.

Second Corinthians 5:11 begins with the transitional word "Therefore," which points back to the previous thought. There is another reason that Paul was motivated by the fear of the Lord: the knowledge that he would have to stand before Christ and give an account of his life. "For we must all appear before the judgment seat of Christ, so that each one may be recompensed for his deeds in the body, according to what he has done, whether good or bad" (v. 10).

The judgment seat of Christ is not a judgment of our eternal destiny but an evaluation of Christians to determine our rewards, or lack thereof, for the way we have served Christ.

The Glory of God's Rewards

Jesus made a very important promise to His apostles in Matthew 19:28–29, after they had watched the rich young man come to Jesus and leave rather than give up his wealth as Jesus had told him to do:

> Jesus said to them, "Truly I say to you, that you who have followed Me, in the regeneration when the Son of Man will sit on His glorious throne, you also shall sit upon twelve thrones, judging the twelve tribes of Israel. And everyone who has left houses or brothers or sisters or father or mother or children or farms for My name's sake, will receive many times as much, and will inherit eternal life."

Obviously, part of the reward Jesus promised to the disciples was unique to the Twelve. You and I are not going to sit on thrones judging the twelve tribes of Israel. But this promise illustrated the basic principle of rewards Jesus announced in Matthew 19. When you give yourself and everything you have to serve Christ, you always get back far more than you give up. None of the apostles gave up a throne for Christ, but that's what they received in return.

Every believer will make it to heaven, but believers will not all have the same level of reward and honor in heaven. All Christians will enjoy eternal life, but they will experience that life at different levels.

God's Grace and Our Rewards

The grace that God displayed in salvation is always the foundation for our service. The God who saved us by grace alone through faith also crafted us as His workmanship to do good works (see Ephesians 2:8–10). The Bible exhorts us, "Therefore, since we receive a kingdom which cannot be shaken, let us show gratitude, by which we may offer to God an acceptable service with reverence and awe" (Hebrews 12:28).

In other words, in light of all that God has done for us, we need to express our gratitude in our service. Have you ever been offended when you've done something for someone and never heard a word of thanks? We teach our children to say thank-you for what they are given because we don't want them to be ungrateful, grasping people and because givers want to know that their gifts are appreciated. The greatest Giver in the universe wants us to show our gratitude by our reverent service—and then He turns around and rewards us for that service with blessings even beyond the unspeakable gift of eternal life.

In 1 Corinthians 3:10–15, Paul compared our Christian lives to builders erecting a building. Paul himself was laying the foundation of this building through his own apostleship as "a wise master builder" following God's blueprint (v. 10). The foundation is none other than Jesus Christ Himself (v. 11).

With the foundation in place, Paul turned to the work we do in building on that foundation: "Now if any man builds on the foundation with gold, silver, precious stones, wood, hay, straw, each man's work will become evident; for the day will show it because it is to be revealed with fire, and the fire itself will test the quality of each man's work" (vv. 12–13).

The difference between these building materials is all-important. The first three materials are costly, permanent, and of the highest quality. The next three materials are cheap, temporary, flammable, and easily obtained on a scrap pile or by the side of the road. It's obvious that the materials you use to construct the "building" of your Christian life and service will reflect the value you place on the grace God has bestowed on you.

When Jesus turns His attention to our works, they will be tested by fire. "If any man's work which he has built on it remains, he will receive a reward. If any man's work is burned up, he will suffer loss; but he himself will be saved, yet so as through fire" (1 Corinthians 3:14–15). That's both a tremendous promise and a very sobering reminder that God demands our best.

Paul closed this section with a word of assurance, but we need to remember that the doctrine of assurance is not meant to be an excuse for us to sit back and coast our way to heaven. The person whose works are consumed by fire at Christ's judgment seat while he is saved through the fire will feel the sting of that loss. Job said, "I have escaped only by the skin of my teeth" (Job 19:20). That's the idea here. I don't want to barely make it to heaven smelling of smoke. I want to inherit the rewards God has for me, and I want the same for you.

PERSONAL APPLICATION FOR LIFE

1. Take a minute to read and reflect on 2 Timothy 2:11–13. How are you running the race of endurance? Those who endure and finish the race will be rewarded by reigning with Christ. Be encouraged that your salvation is unconditional. Be motivated that your rewards are conditioned upon your response here on earth. Are you game enough to endure the race until the end?

2. How is your relationship with Christ? Since He is your life, are you abiding in Him so you can experience the continued flow of life? Perhaps you have been out of contact with that flow for some time. If so, take a moment to place yourself into His abiding presence, and begin experiencing anew His empowering in your life.

3. We may not all be equal in our gifts, abilities, and opportunities, but all of us can be faithful to God's call in our lives. Even though we do our best, God knows we all fail at times. The important question is, Has dependability been the pattern of your life?

4. People in this life are slaves to many things—money, power, hobbies, sports, and so on. Are you willing to get serious about being a slave for Christ? You'll never be embarrassed if you invest your service in God's kingdom. God always gives back more than we could ever give up for Him. Throw yourself into God's service, and give it your all!

FOR GROUP STUDY

Questions for Group Discussion

1. Read the account of the woman at the well in John 4:7–14. What did Jesus require of the Samaritan woman that she might receive eternal life? Upon what does our entrance into eternal life depend?

2. Read John 17:3 and Colossians 3:4. What two points does Dr. Evans bring out that define the essence of eternal life?

3. What do we learn from Galatians 6:7–8 with regard to eternal life and

the here-and-now? In addition, what do 1 Timothy 6:12 and John 15:4 tell us about our current calling to eternal life?

4. Read Luke 7:36–48 and 2 Timothy 2:11–13. Assurance is an essential part of our foundation for serving God. How does it play into our motivation to serve God?

PICTURE THIS

Do you ever want to gauge the quality of your service to Christ and His kingdom? Scripture provides us at least four ways we can measure the quality of our Christian service.

FOUR WAYS TO TEST OUR SERVICE TO GOD

TEST OF SERVICE	SCRIPTURE PASSAGES	ITS IMPORTANCE
Our dependability	1 Corinthians 4:2	God will reward us according to our faithfulness and trustworthiness.
Our declarations	Matthew 12:36; Luke 12:3	Every careless word we speak is recorded. Use your words to bless God and build up others.
Our deeds	Revelation 22:12	Someday the risen Christ will reward every person according to that person's works.
Our desires	1 Corinthians 4:5	Make certain that in the secret place of your heart, your desires reflect the desires of God's heart.

SECTION III

Our Eternal Security in Christ

69

THE IMPORTANCE OF ETERNAL SECURITY

There is nothing wrong with feeling the need for a sense of spiritual security. That's the way God made us. In fact, Romans 4:25 says that the resurrection of Jesus Christ was God's assurance that He had accepted His Son's payment for salvation. The resurrection is our "receipt" to show that that debt of sin has been paid. So the issue of eternal security is important to our spiritual lives for a number of reasons beyond that of helping us to deal with doubt and get on with living for Christ.

THE NEED FOR ETERNAL SECURITY

As we study the truth of eternal security in its various aspects and applications, there will be some inevitable repetition from the assurance section since these two doctrines dovetail so closely. But I think you'll see these passages in a slightly different light.

Eternal Security and Evangelism

Many people would not necessarily put these two subjects together because they seem to be at opposite ends of the spiritual spectrum. But eternal security bears on the message of evangelism that we deliver because it is built into the nature of the gospel.

I know there aren't any verses in which we find the apostles saying to someone, "Let me show you how you can know for certain that you are saved and eternally secure." But if it is not possible to know that we have eternal life, and if salvation is contingent upon anything within us, then the offer of the gospel in evangelism is compromised whether the subject ever comes up or not.

Eternal Security and the Fear of Judgment

One of the great promises in the Bible is in John 5:24. Jesus said, "Truly, truly, I say to you, he who hears My word, and believes Him who sent Me, has eternal life, and does not come into judgment, but has passed out of death into life."

I don't know of any fear that is greater than the fear of judgment. Those who deny the truth of eternal security have to admit the possibility that a believer who fell from grace and lost his salvation, and died in that condition, would face God's judgment. It's no wonder that in some churches people are at the altar every week, begging God to save them again.

You can get people to do a lot of things out of fear, especially if they fear that their eternal destiny depends on what they do. I'm not suggesting that legitimate Christian groups and denominations intentionally instill fear, but the result of instilling fear, even without intentionally doing so, is that people spend their Christian lives walking on eggshells to make sure they don't mess up and cause God to loosen His grip on them. If eternal security is not true, then we cannot fully obey the biblical command, "Be anxious for nothing" (Philippians 4:6).

Eternal Security and the Cross

When we understand the finality of the transaction that took place when Jesus died on the cross, the truth of eternal security comes into clearer focus. Understanding the cross also lifts the issue above all the wrangling about whether people can sin their way out of God's grace, or whether they will abuse their security and live any way they want.

Paul wrote concerning the cross:

> When you were dead in your transgressions and the uncircumcision of your flesh, He made you alive together with Him, having forgiven us all our transgressions, having canceled out the certificate of debt consisting of decrees against us, which was hostile to us; and He has taken it out of the way, having nailed it to the cross. (Colossians 2:13–14)

Notice that God speaks in the past tense of our sin debt being completely paid for by Jesus Christ on the cross, so much so that the "certificate" containing our sins has been "paid in full." This is what Jesus was referring to when He cried out from the cross, "It is finished!" (John 19:30).

Paul teaches that all of our transgressions—past, present, and future—have been forgiven. But those who deny eternal security cannot really affirm this because their position necessitates the view that only those sins that we committed before we became Christians were really forgiven at the cross.

How can I say that? Because if we can commit a sin tomorrow, next week, or next year that can cause us to be severed from God's grace and pass from life back into death, then that future sin is not truly paid for at the cross. The problem with that view is that all of our sins were still future when Jesus went to the cross. Yet the Bible makes no distinction between past, present, and future sins, speaking of all our sins as though they are already under the blood.

Eternal Security and God's Character

One Sunday I asked the people at our church, "Who wants to be the first person to stand up and call God a liar this morning?" No one took me up on my offer. Who would want to accuse our great God of lying to us or breaking His Word? But if God says He has given us eternal life and nothing can separate us from Him (see Romans 8:38–39), and yet we try to say that He will take back His eternal life under certain circumstances, then we are in effect calling God a liar. Why? Because we are denying the clear teaching of His Word.

I also believe that to deny that we are secure in Christ has the effect of making Jesus' work on the cross a failure. Why? Because it means that He died to give you and me something, eternal life, that He is ultimately unable to deliver or guarantee.

More than that, if our salvation can be lost the first time we sin or slip along the way, then the Holy Spirit would be found to be impotent. Why? Because it is through His power and on the strength of His seal on us that we are supposed to be kept and guarded and secured until the day of redemption (see Ephesians 1:13).

You can see why I call a denial of the biblical doctrine of eternal security an attack on God's character. The work of every member of the triune Godhead in salvation is undermined if God doesn't really mean it when He says we are His forever.

Eternal Security and God's Promises

I want to review some tremendous promises from Jesus' lips that you know well. He said, "All that the Father gives Me will come to Me, and the one who comes to Me I will certainly not cast out. . . . This is the will of Him who sent Me, that of all that He has given Me I lose nothing, but raise it up on the last day" (John 6:37–39). Again, Jesus said, "My sheep hear My voice, and I know them, and they follow Me; and I give eternal life to them, and they will never perish; and no one will snatch them out of My hand" (John 10:27–28).

Jesus also told Martha, "I am the resurrection and the life; he who believes in Me will live even if he dies, and everyone who lives and believes in Me will never die. Do you believe this?" (John 11:25–26).

If Jesus had not done His Father's will, He wouldn't be the perfect Son of God. And if He's not the perfect Son of God, He's not qualified to be our Savior. And if He's not qualified to be our Savior, we don't have a Savior. And if we don't have a Savior, we might as well quit church and go home. And if Jesus could lose some of those who have come to Him, then He would not have been the perfect Savior we love and follow.

Speaking of promises from God's Word, here's one that motivates me every day: "Therefore, my beloved brethren, be steadfast, immovable, always abounding in the work of the Lord, knowing that your toil is not in vain in the Lord" (1 Corinthians 15:58). I am so excited that God looked at this sinner and not only forgave me but secured me forever. I am so excited that I am unshakable in Him that I want to be unshakable in my service for Him.

THE PASSION OF ETERNAL SECURITY

Having taken a very difficult course at Dallas Seminary on the theology of Karl Barth, I enjoy the story of the time this great Swiss theologian visited America. A reporter asked Barth, "What is the greatest thought that has ever come across your mind?"

I can see this young man sharpening his pencil (this was more than fifty years ago) and getting ready to write furiously as the great theologian cut loose with some grand and complicated thought. Dr. Barth paused for a moment and replied, "The greatest thought that has ever come across my mind is this: 'Jesus loves me, this I know, for the Bible tells me so.'"

Karl Barth was not being facetious. He understood in a profound way the importance of a very simple truth that is a cornerstone of the Christian faith. We've sung about Christ's love since we were little children, but sometimes we forget the basics. If we fully understood the enormous scope of that love, we wouldn't have any problem with the doctrine of eternal security.

The Meaning of God's Love

One reason so many people struggle with the concept of eternal security is because they struggle with the concept of God's love. It's important to remember that our definitions of love and God's definition aren't always the same. If you grew up in a loveless environment, in an environment in which the love you received was conditional on your behavior, then you may be using a human definition of love to define an infinite divine attribute.

Starting with human definitions of love leads to statements such as, "I don't see how God could love me perfectly and eternally in spite of what I do. I don't even like myself all that much at times." It's true that human love is often inconsistent, misplaced, and bestowed for the wrong reasons—the very opposite of God's love. Let's take a quick refresher course in the nature of God's love and see how it relates to the doctrine of security.

One aspect of God's love is that it is visible. By this I mean that God did something to show us how much He loves us. Jesus said, "Greater love has no one than this, that one lay down his life for his friends" (John 15:13). Paul gave a classic statement of the atonement when he wrote, "God demonstrates His own love toward us, in that while we were yet sinners, Christ died for us" (Romans 5:8).

Sacrifice is another word for love as far as defining God's eternal, saving love. The *agape* love that God lavished upon us in Christ is characterized by a commitment to act in the best interest of the person loved, regardless of the cost or self-sacrifice demanded of the one doing the loving.

God's love also comes without conditions. This doesn't mean that He never has any demands to make on us but rather that we don't have to be a certain kind of person to merit His love. The only condition for receiving God's love is being a sinner, and we all qualify.

This is very important for eternal security. God loved us despite the fact that we were "helpless," "ungodly," and "sinners" (Romans 5:6, 8). In other words, we weren't very pretty at all when God saved us. In fact, we were downright ugly in our sin.

So here's the question: If God was not too repulsed by our sin to reach down into the pit and save us, why should it be so hard to believe that He is not too repulsed by our sin now to keep us by His grace? Don't misunderstand. This is not permission to live unfruitful, lackadaisical Christian lives. Just the opposite, in fact. Knowing the great price God paid to save us, and our unworthiness to be saved, should make us want to serve the Lord with everything we have.

Besides being visible, sacrificial, and unconditional, God's love is also judicial. Here's a corrective to the mistaken view that teaching the security of the believer leads to license and lazy Christian living. Being judicial means to act as a judge, to weigh both sides of a case and come to a firm decision. The human race has already been put on trial in the court of heaven and the verdict has been announced: "There is none righteous, not even one"; "For all have sinned and fall short of the glory of God" (Romans 3:10, 23).

The fact that God's love is judicial is good news for us, because He didn't just let us go in our sin to be condemned to eternal hell. He brought us up on charges and alerted us to our need. Then He did something very judicial and very loving. He exacted payment for those sins, as a righteous judge must do, but He carried out that judgment on His own Son so we could be forgiven and go free.

Let me tell you one more thing about God's love that bears on eternal security. God's love is eternal because God Himself is love. "Love is from God . . . for God is love" (1 John 4:7–8). The statement "God is love" has been twisted and abused to mean all kinds of things, but don't let the distortions obscure what the Bible is saying. God loves because He is love. Love is an integral part of God's being. His love for us is eternal because God is eternal. His love toward us will never cease, because God cannot contradict who He is.

The Greatness of God's Love

In the book of Ephesians, the apostle Paul explained the greatness of the love God has bestowed on us in Christ. Two of the most important words in the Bible are "But God" (Ephesians 2:4). We were dead and hopeless in our sins, but God did something about it. Why? That's the rest of verse 4. God acted because He is "rich in mercy" and "because of His great love with which He loved us."

In Ephesians 3:17–19, Paul invited us to explore all the dimensions of God's love. Breaking in at midsentence, we read, "That you . . . may be able to comprehend with all the saints what is the breadth and length and height and depth, and to know the love of Christ which surpasses knowledge, that you may be filled up to all the fullness of God."

The context of these verses is worth noticing. All three members of the Godhead are involved in delivering our salvation and securing us in the love of Christ: God the Father (v. 14), God the Spirit (v. 16), and God the Son (v. 17). We are joined together with each member of the Holy Trinity in a relationship of love that is so deep it is beyond anything we can understand.

God's love is also tenacious, with a reach you can't outrun.

The Old Testament prophet Hosea is a powerful example of the tenacity with which God loves His people. Hosea's story and prophecy are about

God's determined, everlasting love. God told Hosea to marry a prostitute named Gomer and settle down with her (see Hosea 1:1–2). Hosea married Gomer and loved her, but after their children were born, Gomer forsook Hosea and her family and went back to her old ways.

But in spite of Gomer's unfaithfulness and the pain and humiliation it must have caused Hosea, God told him, "Go again, love a woman who is loved by her husband, yet an adulteress, even as the Lord loves the sons of Israel, though they turn to other gods" (Hosea 3:1). So the prophet bought his wife back from whatever bondage and degradation she had fallen into, took her to their home again, and restored her to his love.

God told Hosea to do all of that to serve as a picture of His pursuing, tenacious love for Israel. God had entered into a covenant with the nation of Israel like a marriage covenant between a husband and wife. Israel was God's wife, and no matter how far the people strayed from Him, no matter how far they sank into sin and degradation, God was telling them that He would not let them go.

The Finality of God's Love

God's love is the love to end all loves. When God sets His love upon a person, He does not change His mind and He doesn't quit until His purposes have been fulfilled—whether we're talking about His chosen people Israel or individuals in the church like you and me. John 3:16 says that God gave "His only begotten Son" so that we might have eternal life. We've talked a lot about the price that God paid to save us, so let me put it in a little different context.

Jesus testified to the finality of God's love on the cross when He uttered His final words before releasing His spirit and dying: "It is finished!" (John 19:30).

You may know the background of that phrase. It meant, "Paid in full!" Jesus was announcing to the angels in heaven, to the people of earth, and to Satan and the demons of hell that no more debt was owed for sin. I don't know how anything could be clearer than that. Even the tearing in half of the temple's huge veil from top to bottom (see Matthew 27:51) was a visible testimony to the fact that no more sacrifices for sin would ever be needed again. Well, when Jesus demonstrated His love for you and me on the cross, God was signaling to every person and every power on earth and under the earth that the transaction was complete. This is the wonder of God's love.

PERSONAL APPLICATION FOR LIFE

1. Failing to look to Christ and trust Him for your security is tantamount to putting yourself under the law in terms of putting yourself on a performance basis with God. Skip following your own performance list—or someone else's. Rather, be on the grace standard and please the Lord by your performance (2 Peter 3:18).

2. It's always an edifying experience to contemplate God's character. It becomes an exercise in awe and worship of our God. One aspect of His character is that He always acts true to His Word. When God says He has given us eternal life, we can believe it! Next time you have a quiet time, thank Him for being a God who means what He says.

3. Since your relationship with Christ is first and foremost one of love, ask Him to keep your heart tender toward Him. If your focus is on loving the Lord, you won't have to worry about being sensitive to sin; you'll feel it right away!

4. John 3:16 is so often quoted and so well known that we might tend to overlook its profound message. Take a few minutes to read and meditate upon its message. What a statement of the securing lover of God!

FOR GROUP STUDY

Questions for Group Discussion

1. What are some of the reasons eternal security is important to our spiritual lives? Dr. Evans discusses at least five reasons.

2. Read John 6:37–39; 10:27–28; 11:25–26; 1 Corinthians 15:58. Discuss these promises from the lips of our Lord in the New Testament regarding the eternal security of the believer. As believers, what encouragements can we take away from these promises?

3. Read Romans 4:22–25. What do the theological truths in this passage tell us about God's eternal love for us? What does Ephesians 3:17–19 tell

us about the dimensions of God's love? (Use the chart below as an aid to your discussion.)

4. John 15 is important for all believers. Read the first six verses as preparation for discussion. What does it mean to abide in Christ? When we abide in Christ, what can we expect to take place in our spiritual lives?

PICTURE THIS

God's love eclipses any kind of human love. The dimension of His love listed below can give us a better handle on the greatness of its depth and breath.

THE DIMENSIONS OF GOD'S LOVE RELATED TO OUR SECURITY

DIMENSION	SCRIPTURE PASSAGE	WHAT IT MEANS
It is visible.	John 15:13	God shows us how much He loves us by His actions.
It is sacrificial.	Romans 5:8	God acts in our best interest, regardless of the cost.
It is unconditional.	Romans 5:6, 8	Despite the ugliness of our sin, God still saved us.
It is judicial.	Romans 3:10, 23	God's love carried out judgment on His own Son so we could be forgiven and go free.
It is eternal.	1 John 4:7–8	God's love is eternal because God Himself is love. His love toward us will never cease.

70

THE PROCESS OF ETERNAL SECURITY

My purpose in this chapter is to demonstrate several more key facets of a reassuring truth: Your salvation and mine are part of a divine program that is so incredible it reaches from eternity to eternity and encompasses both the human and angelic realms. And since God's salvation program has never been in danger of failing at any time, we are as secure as we could possibly be.

God's program of salvation involves His electing purposes, as the Bible states in Ephesians 1:4: "[God the Father] chose us in [Christ] before the foundation of the world, that we would be holy and blameless before Him."

THE OUTWORKING OF ETERNAL SECURITY

The exciting thing is that we get to participate in our salvation. By this I don't mean that we help God along in His plan, although we are responsible to respond in faith to the gospel. The Bible sets these two truths in perfect balance, as Paul wrote to the Thessalonians: "We should always give thanks to God for you, brethren beloved by the Lord, because God has chosen you from the beginning for salvation through sanctification by the Spirit and faith in the truth" (2 Thessalonians 2:13). God's work is to choose and to save; our response is to put our faith in the truth.

I'm using the term *participation* simply to mean that our salvation is tied to our participation or identity with Jesus Christ.

In 2 Timothy 1, the apostle Paul urged Timothy to stand with him unashamedly in the work of the gospel and even to suffer by the power of God, "who has saved us and called us with a holy calling, not according to our works, but according to His own purpose and grace which was granted us in Christ Jesus from all eternity" (v. 9).

The Program of Election

Here Paul located the origin of our salvation in eternity past, as he did in Ephesians 1:4. We can't pinpoint the exact beginning of God's electing plan because eternity doesn't have a beginning or an end. Paul even said that God's plan to display His grace in Christ was "from all eternity," which takes the process back farther than our limited minds can comprehend.

We need to go back into eternity because we humans are not the first beings God created to praise and glorify Him. In eternity past God created the myriads of angels in heaven to execute His will and to lead heaven in His praise and worship.

But when Lucifer, the chief of angels, declared, "I will make myself like the Most High" (Isaiah 14:14) and rebelled against God, one-third of the angels joined him in his rebellion (see Revelation 12:4). But God defeated Lucifer and his angels, and he was cast to earth as Satan with the fallen angels becoming his demons.

Those angels who remained true to God were then called "chosen" (1 Timothy 5:21). This is the same Greek root as the word *elect* and could just as easily be translated that way (as in the NIV). While judging the angels who rebelled, God also confirmed the two-thirds of the holy angels who remained true to Him in their holiness.

So the principle of divine election was established with the angels. It has to do with the permanent blessings God chooses to bestow on those who choose Him. This is crucial because what happened to the angels happened to mankind, with one very important difference.

Satan's attempt to usurp God's throne was smashed before it ever got started. But the rebellion in heaven also gave God a unique opportunity, if you will. This was the opportunity to receive greater glory by demonstrating that He could do more with lesser beings, when those beings were dependent on Him, than He could do with superior beings (the angels) when those beings rebelled against Him. This new creation would also allow God to express a part of His nature that had never been fully revealed before: namely, His grace.

So God decided to create the human race, a group of beings temporarily made a little lower in rank than the angels (see Hebrews 2:7), as creatures to do what the fallen angels failed to do, which is bring Him praise. Human beings sinned and fell from their original position and purpose too, but in grace God redeemed a body of people who will be with Him in heaven for all eternity and render Him the praise and glory due His name.

The Purpose of Election

We referred earlier to Ephesians 1:6 as stating the purpose of God's election. Let me begin with verse 5: "He predestined us to adoption as sons through Jesus Christ to Himself, according to the kind intention of His will, *to the praise of the glory of His grace*, which He freely bestowed on us in the Beloved" (italics added).

The focus of election is what we are elected to: a new relationship with God that involves all the special blessing and security God has promised those who believe (1 Peter 5:10).

In accomplishing His elective purposes, God the Father decided to present a redeemed humanity as a love gift to His Son. Every person in God's gift to His Son receives salvation. No one is overlooked. And it gets even better, because Jesus not only saves the elect; He keeps them. (Election also reflects Good's gracious love, as discussed in chapter 64, pages 774–75).

"Keep them in Your name," Jesus prayed (John 17:11). Then He asked the Father to keep His people from "the evil one" (v. 15). And in case you think He was only talking about the disciples who were with Him in the Upper Room, Jesus prayed "for those also who believe in Me through their word" (v. 20). That's you and me. And then Jesus asked of His Father, "I desire that they also, whom You have given Me, be with Me where I am" (v. 24).

Jesus was asking His Father to protect the gift He had given His Son, and to make sure that every believer whom the Father elected and the Son redeemed would be with Christ in heaven. We are as secure as we could possibly be.

The Predestination of Election

Once you understand that God's plan of salvation encompasses eternity past and eternity future, and not just these few years of earth's history, then doctrines such as election and its companion truths that have caused so many people so much confusion should not be hard to accept. Our range of vision and understanding is very limited, but God sees everything in one complete package.

The doctrine of predestination is one of those teachings that we ought to be able to accept and believe even if we don't fully understand it. The Bible says clearly, "[God] predestined us to adoption as sons through Jesus Christ to Himself" (Ephesians 1:5). That should communicate security to you because your salvation is the result of careful planning on the part of the eternal God.

To predestine means to preplan, or to plan beforehand. Before He brought the world into being, God conceived a plan to save those who would believe in Jesus Christ and appoint them to a special position of blessing because of this new relationship. This suggests an issue that is for most people the biggest stumbling block in believing the truth of election. If God chose some people for salvation, that means He did not choose others. The Bible is clear that many people will wind up in hell, although the Bible also says that God loved the world so much He sent His Son to die for the world. We must remember that election and predestination do not rule out human responsibility.

But even though the human race exercised its option to sin and fell under God's condemnation, God has given mankind a way to "opt back" into His favor. But each person must still accept or reject God's offer of grace that forgives the sins they have committed. Those who accept God's grace do so because they are His elect, but those who refuse His plan of salvation are held accountable for their rejection. In the councils of eternity, God predetermined to provide salvation for all and secure it for those who are in Christ.

There is still an element of mystery to election and predestination. (See pages 775–76 for more about this "mystery.")

But the Bible teaches them plainly and also says that we are responsible to respond to God's call. The beauty of grace is that God gives us a way back to Him from our sin and rebellion. That's what it means to be elected.

THE PAYMENT OF ETERNAL SECURITY

The issue of eternal security must bring us back to the cross, to the tremendous price that Jesus Christ paid to save you and keep you. Paul's prayer for the Thessalonians speaks powerfully about God's intention to keep all of those who belong to Christ and deliver them to heaven: "Now may the God of peace Himself sanctify you entirely; and may your spirit and soul and body be preserved complete, without blame at the coming of our Lord Jesus Christ" (1 Thessalonians 5:23). It is Jesus' death—and His life before that death—that offer us eternal security.

The Saving Death of Christ

Since the Bible says that Jesus is "the author and perfecter [or completer] of faith" (Hebrews 12:2), can you think of anything that can crop up between the beginning and the end of salvation that can interrupt the work Jesus has begun and will complete? I can't either.

The heart of what Jesus Christ did for us in His saving death is captured in two great passages of Scripture, one from Paul and the other from the lips of Jesus Himself on the cross, which tell us the debt of our sin has been fully paid. The apostle wrote:

> When you were dead in your transgressions and the uncircumcision of your flesh, He made you alive together with Him, having forgiven us all our transgressions, having canceled out the certificate of debt consisting of decrees against us, which was hostile to us; and He has taken it out of the way, having nailed it to the cross. (Colossians 2:13–14)

Paul was referring to the bill of indebtedness that was prepared against a prisoner in Roman days and posted outside his cell, often having been signed by the prisoner himself as an admission of his debt. The bill stayed there until the debt was fully paid and the prisoner was set free, at which time the bill was taken down and, according to some ancient sources, was first blotted out and then canceled.

The word that was written across a debt to cancel it after all its demands were met was the Greek word *tetelestai*, which means "paid in full." You may not recognize this word, but you are probably familiar with Jesus' usage of it on the cross. It was the last word He spoke before dismissing His spirit and dying: "It is finished!" (John 19:30). In other words, the sin debt of the world had been settled.

Tetelestai is an accounting term. By using it at that dramatic moment on the cross, Jesus was announcing to every authority and power in heaven and on earth and under the earth that every demand of God against sinners like you and me had been met. From that day forward, the sin bill of every child of God would read zero on the line labeled "Amount due." The death of Christ was so complete that it totally and completely satisfied God's righteous demands. In the wording of a great term we learned in an earlier chapter, God has been propitiated or satisfied with regard to us.

The Saving Life of Christ

Most Christians are familiar with the saving death of Christ because it is one of the pivotal truths of our faith. Peter told the Jewish enemies of Christ, "There is no other name under heaven that has been given among men by which we must be saved" (Acts 4:12).

But the salvation Jesus Christ has provided is even more wonderful than a lot of people realize, because it encompasses His life as well as His death. Concerning this, Paul made a very interesting comparative statement: "For if while we were enemies we were reconciled to God through the death of His Son, *much more*, having been reconciled, we shall be saved by His life" (Romans 5:10, italics added). You are not only saved by Christ's death; you are also saved by His life.

What does the life of Christ have to do with our security? To answer that, we need to note an important doctrinal statement that Paul made in 2 Corinthians 5:21. Speaking of what God did for us in Christ, Paul wrote:

"He [God] made Him [Christ] who knew no sin to be sin on our behalf, so that we might become the righteousness of God in Him."

This great verse actually encompasses both the saving death and the saving life of Christ. God made Christ to be sin on our behalf when Christ bore the sin of the world on the cross. The cross took care of our sin problem forever, because our sins were charged to Christ's account and His death was credited to our account, His blood washing our sin debt away.

But we have another problem or need as sinful creatures. We not only need to have something subtracted from our lives, our sins which separated us from a holy God, but we need to have something added to our lives. We need an infusion of perfect righteousness in order to be able to stand before a perfectly righteous and holy God and find acceptance. The life of Christ has to do with providing us with the perfect righteousness we must have to come into God's presence.

Righteousness in the New Testament refers to a rightness of life or a right standing before God. Sin is wrong, and getting rid of sin is good. But getting rid of sin does not automatically ensure that we will start doing what is right. We not only need a positive infusion of righteousness to be right before God, but according to Paul we need the very "righteousness of God," which means being as righteous and holy as God Himself.

Jesus lived a sinless life on earth for thirty-three years to provide you and me with the righteousness we need to be acceptable to God. This is why Jesus wasn't born as a full-grown adult who appeared suddenly on earth one day, died on the cross, and then went back to heaven. He had a specific mission to fulfill through His life. Jesus announced that mission during the Sermon on the Mount: "Do not think that I came to abolish the Law or the Prophets; I did not come to abolish but to fulfill. For truly I say to you, until heaven and earth pass away, not the smallest letter or stroke shall pass from the Law until all is accomplished" (Matthew 5:17–18).

What Jesus did during His earthly life was to completely and perfectly obey the righteous law of God without any sin or failure at all, which qualified Him to be our sin-bearer. Jesus had to satisfy all of God's demands for perfect obedience and perfect righteousness in order for His death to be an acceptable payment for our sins.

People sometimes wonder why Jesus lived the number of years He lived and why He died at the particular time He died. Both His ministry and His life were short by our standards, but He lived just as long as He needed to live to satisfy the demands of God's law. Jesus also had to face every kind of temptation we would face so that we would have a High Priest in heaven who can "sympathize with our weaknesses" (Hebrews 4:15). That's one reason His temptation by Satan was so important.

So what God does when we are saved is not only credit Christ's atoning death to our account but also credit Jesus' perfect righteousness to our account. The former takes away our sin, and the latter clothes us with Christ's righteousness so that when God looks at us now, He sees not our sin but the perfection of His Son.

Everything we have talked about to this point applies to Christ's life on earth prior to His death. But He is also alive from the dead today and ministering on our behalf in heaven to keep us saved. The writer of Hebrews said:

> The former priests [under the old system], on the one hand, existed in greater numbers because they were prevented by death from continuing, but Jesus, on the other hand, because He continues forever, holds His priesthood permanently. Therefore He is able also to *save forever* those who draw near to God through Him, since He always lives to make intercession for them. (7:23–25, italics added)

This is one of the many references in Hebrews and other parts of the New Testament to the high priestly ministry of Jesus Christ in heaven today.

There are several reasons that Jesus' priestly intercession is necessary for us today. One reason relates to the passage we noted above referring to Jesus as our understanding and sympathetic High Priest (Hebrews 4). If Jesus had gone back to heaven and simply detached Himself from everything on earth until His return, you and I would not have a merciful and faithful High Priest we could call on in times of need.

There's another way in which Christ's life in heaven today saves us. This has to do with His role as our Advocate or defense attorney before the Father.

"My little children, I am writing these things to you so that you may not sin. And if anyone sins, we have an Advocate with the Father, Jesus Christ the righteous" (1 John 2:1).

The reason we need Jesus to defend us is that Satan is our accuser (see Revelation 12:10). The Devil's self-appointed job is to bring our many sins and failures before God in the court of heaven to see if he can get our salvation reversed, so to speak, and get our acquittal in Christ overturned.

It's not as if Satan doesn't have any evidence to work with, because we sin and fail God every day. But every time Satan shows up as our accuser and prosecutor, Jesus shows up as our Defender, opens the Book of Life, and reminds the Father that our sins have been paid for and that we are clothed in His perfect righteousness.

PERSONAL APPLICATION FOR LIFE

1. You can wonder if and when you are going to disappear from God's care and be lost, or you can relax and rest in the reassuring knowledge that He holds you securely for eternity! If feelings of doubt come, remember that your salvation is not determined by your feelings. Rather, it is founded on the finished work of Christ on the cross and supported by the promises of God's Word.

2. It's a great encouragement to know our salvation is secure and we will one day be with the Lord. We hope your prayer list includes people you want to see become Christians. If you can't name friends or loved ones who need Christ, ask God to put them on your heart.

3. Although our salvation is secure, we still need to work it out before we go to be with the Lord and receive our rewards. Ask God to help you not be overly influenced by the world's standards for measuring greatness and reward. It may help you to write the words "Not Home Yet" on a card and set it on your table as a reminder that you're operating on a different system.

4. Eternal security is a great gift. It's so easy to be consumed with Christ's benefits rather than the person of Christ. One way you can tell whether you are consumed with Christ or just seeking His benefits is what happens to the flame of your love for Him after He tells you no to something you've been praying for. Does the flame of your love flicker and grow weaker because you're either upset or disappointed, or does your love stay strong because you know that He said no in love?

FOR GROUP STUDY

Questions for Group Discussion

1. What do we mean by the term *election*? Use 2 Thessalonians 2:13; 2 Timothy 1:9; and Ephesians 1:4 as the basis for your discussion.

2. What is the purpose of election? (See Ephesians 1:6 and 1 Peter 5:10.) How does election make our salvation secure?

3. What is the doctrine of *predestination*? What is the role of human responsibility in predestination?

4. What does the saving life of Christ have to do with our security? (Use the chart below as an aid to your discussion.)

PICTURE THIS

Our salvation in Jesus Christ encompasses His life as well as His death. Romans 5:10 tells us that we are "saved by His life." Below are three truths related to how Jesus saves us through His life.

The Saving Life of Christ

TRUTH	SCRIPTURE PASSAGE	WHAT IT MEANS
We need righteousness.	2 Corinthians 5:21	As sinful creatures, we need the perfect righteousness of Jesus Christ to stand before God.
Jesus' righteousness covers us.	Matthew 5:17–18; 3:13–14	Jesus provides us with the righteousness we need to be acceptable before God.
Jesus' intercession keeps us.	Hebrews 7:23–25	Jesus intercedes for us as our High Priest in heaven because our sins are forgiven and we on our way to heaven.

71

THE PROTECTION OF ETERNAL SECURITY

Most people have a security system of some kind on their property, especially in large urban areas such as Dallas. But security systems that afford protection are nothing new. God devised the first security system before the universe was created when He drew up the plan of salvation in eternity past. We have seen that each member of the Trinity was involved in delivering salvation to the human race, and we have spent a considerable amount of time discussing the roles that God the Father and God the Son play in the divine drama of salvation.

The Holy Spirit also plays a key role in salvation as the One who convicts us of sin and the truth of the gospel and implants the life of Christ in us through the miracle of regeneration (see chapter 63). I want to discuss two other ministries of the Holy Spirit relative to salvation because they are crucial to the security system God designed to protect and ensure our redemption. These are the Spirit's work in the baptism and sealing of every believer.

THE SPIRIT'S WORK IN ETERNAL SECURITY

The Spirit's Work of Baptism

If you want to get a lively discussion going among a group of Christians, bring up the subject of the baptism of the Holy Spirit. Just mentioning the subject in today's Christian circles invites controversy, because if you get four people together, you'll have five opinions about the nature and significance of the Holy Spirit's baptism. The fundamental statement of the Spirit's work in baptism is found in 1 Corinthians 12:13, where Paul wrote: "For by one Spirit we were all baptized into one body, whether Jews or Greeks, whether slaves or free, and we were all made to drink of one Spirit."

Baptism is the Spirit's ministry by which He places a believer into the body of Christ at salvation. The Spirit's baptism is universal and equally applied to all believers. As a matter of fact, anyone who has not been baptized by the Holy Spirit is not saved. This is discussed in greater detail in chapter 30.

The key thought behind the doctrine of baptism in the New Testament is that of complete identification and unity with Christ. The Spirit's baptism of a new believer into the body of Christ identifies that believer with Christ and brings him or her into an organic union with Christ (Galatians 3:27–29). The church practices water baptism as an outward symbol of the inward spiritual reality that takes place when we are born again.

Our baptism into Christ by the Holy Spirit creates a new union so indivisible that God can already tell us what we are going to experience in the future with Christ. For example, the Bible says that we will be "revealed with Him in glory" (Colossians 3:4). According to 1 Corinthians 15:51, we will be changed when Christ returns. And in 2 Corinthians 4:14, we are told that God will raise us up with Jesus.

The Spirit's Work of Sealing

One reason that genuine believers tend to doubt their salvation is that they don't receive all of it at once. Our full redemption is "reserved in heaven for [us]" (1 Peter 1:4). Until then, "we ourselves, having the first fruits of the Spirit, even we ourselves groan within ourselves, waiting eagerly for our adoption as sons, the redemption of our body" (Romans 8:23). The salvation we enjoy is just a small taste of the glory we will share with Christ in heaven.

But in the meantime, we have to live in this sin-ruined world in these sin-contaminated bodies. God has given us "His precious and magnificent promises" (2 Peter 1:4) concerning the certainty of our salvation and future glory, but being human we can forget these and begin to doubt ourselves and even God.

So what God has done is give us a down payment on His promises, a pledge or a reminder that our redemption is secure and will be consummated someday. This down payment is described in Ephesians as the sealing of the Holy Spirit: "In Him, you also, after listening to the message of truth, the gospel of your salvation—having also believed, you were sealed in Him with the Holy Spirit of promise, who is given as a pledge of our inheritance, with a view to the redemption of God's own possession, to the praise of His glory" (1:13–14).

The Holy Spirit's presence in our lives is our witness that God will fulfill all His promises. We know how a pledge or down payment works. It's a promise that the purchaser will pay the full price and take ownership of the property or whatever is being bought. God does not want His children to doubt either His capability or His willingness to redeem those whom He has purchased for Himself at the cost of His Son's life.

A seal also indicated protection because no one dared break it except the person whose insignia was in the wax or his duly authorized representative.

In addition, God's seal represents ownership. When the Holy Spirit takes up His residence in our hearts at salvation, one of His ministries is to testify to us that we belong to God. "The Spirit Himself testifies with our spirit that we are children of God" (Romans 8:16). And because we are His children, God takes responsibility for our future.

If you belong to Jesus Christ, you are identified, marked, protected, and purchased by God for all eternity, and you have the Holy Spirit as a guarantee that every promise God made you will come to pass.

Let me also remind you of a responsibility we have as sealed believers. If God's seal means ownership, who owns our lives? Not us but the One who bought us. We forget sometimes that we belong to God body and soul, which can lead us not only into doubt but into sin.

The first half of Ephesians 4:30 says, "Do not grieve the Holy Spirit of God." And Paul asks this pointed question: "Do you not know that your body is a temple of the Holy Spirit who is in you, whom you have from God, and that you are not your own? For you have been bought with a price: therefore glorify God in your body" (1 Corinthians 6:19–20). There is so much wrapped up in the Bible's teaching that the Spirit is our seal guaranteeing full redemption.

Likewise, the Holy Spirit's presence within us is a promise and a foretaste of good things to come. When God gave us the Holy Spirit as a pledge of our coming inheritance, we can be sure that He will provide all the good things He has promised us. God is saying to us, "When I saved you, I gave you a pledge of My commitment because I want you to be My bride. You belong to Me, and even though we are not together yet in heaven, I will come for you and fulfill all My promises to you."

THE POWER OF ETERNAL SECURITY

When you accepted Jesus Christ, He made a reservation for you in heaven. And to pay for your reservation, Jesus paid the price with His own precious blood.

Two thousand years ago Jesus Himself told us about the reliability of the reservation He has made for His people. "This is the will of Him who sent Me, that of all that He has given me I lose nothing, but raise it up on the last day" (John 6:39). As far as Jesus is concerned, our "last day" reservation in heaven is confirmed. And just to make sure we don't misunderstand, Jesus said the same thing three more times in the same discourse: "I will raise him up on the last day" (vv. 40, 44, 54).

The Certainty of God's Securing Power

A hotel reservation, like all plans that we make for the future, is really a promise that certain things will happen at a certain time. Political candidates may make election promises that they have every intention of keeping. The problem is that they don't always have the clout to bring their promises into being, or they are unable to control circumstances that make the fulfillment of their promises possible.

The difference between our plans and promises and God's plans and promises is that He has the power to pull off every promise He makes. The Bible affirms, "You know in all your hearts and in all your souls that not one word of all the good words which the Lord your God spoke concerning you has failed; all have been fulfilled for you, not one of them has failed" (Joshua 23:14).

The Purpose of God's Securing Power

God is going to deliver you safely to heaven because He has invested too much in you to let you fall away and be lost. God has a lot more at stake in this salvation business than we do. It cost Him everything to save us, and His character and integrity are on the line in His promise to glorify every believer whom He has predestined, called, and justified (see Romans 8:30).

God's purpose in securing His people is clearly stated in the opening verses of 1 Peter. The apostle addressed his letter to those "who are chosen according to the foreknowledge of God the Father, by the sanctifying work of the Spirit, to obey Jesus Christ and be sprinkled with His blood" (1:1–2). To these elect saints Peter said:

> Blessed be the God and Father of our Lord Jesus Christ, who according to His great mercy has caused us to be born again to a living hope through the resurrection of Jesus Christ from the dead, to obtain an inheritance which is imperishable and undefiled and will not fade away, reserved in heaven for you. (vv. 3–4)

These verses contain some wonderful descriptions of our "inheritance," which is another way of talking about our salvation. It's a living hope because Jesus Christ rose from the dead never to die or perish again, which makes our inheritance imperishable. Imperishable applies to something that is not subject to decay and cannot be spoiled. There is nothing else in life you can say that about.

This salvation and inheritance in heaven we have received from God also "will not fade away" (1 Peter 1:4). This means it won't lose its luster over time.

Peter also referred to the fullness of salvation we will experience when we see Christ because our inheritance is "reserved in heaven for [us]" (1 Peter 1:4). The salvation that Christ purchased and secured for His own is being stored up in heaven for us. Paul said it so well: "I know whom I have believed and I am convinced that He is able to guard what I have entrusted to Him until that day" (2 Timothy 1:12). Notice that the One who is guarding our inheritance is the One we have believed in, who is Jesus Christ.

The Bible also affirms that we are being reserved for our salvation. Peter continued talking about the greatness and the security of our salvation by saying that we are "protected by the power of God through faith for a salvation ready to be revealed in the last time" (1 Peter 1:5). The word "protected" is a military concept that pictures a garrison on guard to protect a city against the enemy.

Verses 4–5 form a strong one-two punch for the truth of eternal security. Verse 4 refers to that which is being reserved, while verse 5 has to do with the people who are being reserved. Verse 4 is all about the inheritance, while verse 5 speaks of the heirs. Verse 4 assures us that a reservation has been made in heaven. Verse 5 assures us that the reservation is in our name. God is saying to us in every way possible that He is not going to let anything happen to us or to our inheritance until He brings the two together in heaven.

The Power of Being in God's Hands

There is power in the blood of Jesus Christ to save and keep His own. Jesus Himself had some very important words to say about the security of those who belong to Him. One of the most notable passages is in John 10, a tremendous chapter in which Jesus assured His followers that as the Good Shepherd, He knows His own sheep.

Earliy in the chapter Jesus gave us a great word picture of His power to save and guard His sheep. "I am the door of the sheep. . . . If anyone enters through Me, he will be saved, and will go in and out and find pasture. The thief comes only to steal and kill and destroy; I came that they may have life, and have it abundantly" (vv. 7, 9–10). Note the contrast between any intruder who would try to harm one of Christ's sheep and His assurance that they will find salvation and life in Him.

When you received Christ, you placed your eternity into the hands of God the Father and God the Son for safekeeping until Jesus returns for you. Jesus chose the imagery of hands for good reason, because whenever you read about the hand or hands of God in the Bible, you're reading about His power (see Deuteronomy 26:8 and Jeremiah 21:5 for just two of many examples).

If keeping ourselves saved was in our hands, we'd mess it up for sure. But if we put our security in God's hands, it's a completely different story. Now we can talk about heaven as our home as though we were already there.

I love the phrases "no one will snatch" and "no one is able to snatch" of John 10:28–29. No one includes every "someone" in the universe. That means neither the Devil nor any of his legions of fallen angels can take you out of your Father's hands. You can't even take yourself out of God's hands, because you are also a someone who is part of the "no one" of John 10. We've said it before, but it needs to be emphasized again. Instead of living in fear that you might mess up and slip from God's grasp, get on with loving and serving Him with all of your being, and He will minister assurance to your heart.

Let's face it. If we could forfeit our salvation, most of us would already be in deep trouble because of things we have said and done. You may feel as if you're holding God's hand but He isn't holding yours, but that's not the case. Both the Father and the Son are committed to your security.

The best antidote for worry and insecurity is commitment to Christ. I believe that the folks who have the most trouble serving God and who constantly worry about their security are those who don't really understand all that Christ has done for them. If He has promised never to let us go, who are we to tell Him we don't really believe Him? If we understand how much we are loved, returning that love will not be a chore or duty but the delight and the consuming passion of our lives.

PERSONAL APPLICATION FOR LIFE

1. A seal in the ancient world referred to the wax with which a letter or other important document would be sealed. God has given you the Holy Spirit as His down payment on your salvation, and with the Spirit Himself as the seal. What a promise to each believer! Be assured that God is true to His Word and fulfills His promises.

2. The Holy Spirit's presence in your life is witness that God fulfills His promises. The reality of God's presence should renew your confidence in prayer. Look at your prayer list today and pick out your toughest circumstance, greatest need, or biggest fear. Thank God that He is present in this situation, and ask Him for the grace to continue praying about it and awaiting His answer.

3. Never allow the certainty of your salvation to be an excuse to "slide by" in your walk with God. He requires of us that we live holy and blameless lives before Him. Ask God to help you live each day in a healthy awareness of His awesome holiness. Pray that God will make the truth of 1 Peter 1:15–16, "Be holy yourselves also" a reality in your heart and life.

4. God's power to secure your salvation should be a source of excitement each day. Since God has promised to carry you from spiritual birth (no condemnation) all the way to heaven and His presence (no separation), nothing in between can take you out! If that assurance makes you just a little bit happy, why not spend the next few minutes telling God how wonderful His love is.

FOR GROUP STUDY

Questions for Group Discussion

1. Read 1 Corinthians 12:13. What is the baptism of the Holy Spirit?

2. Discuss the power behind our eternal security. What is the purpose of God's securing power? How secure is our salvation in the hands of God?

3. What is so significant about the Holy Spirit's work of sealing? (Use the chart below as an aid to your discussion.)

4. Read John 10:19–30. What assurances do we find in this passage about our salvation and its security in the hands of God?

PICTURE THIS

There are several truths and promises upon we which we can rest our assurance of salvation. Below are a few the Dr. Evans discussed in this lesson.

THE SPIRIT'S WORK OF SEALING

TRUTH	SCRIPTURE PASSAGES	WHAT IT MEANS
The Holy Spirit is our down payment.	Ephesians 1:13–14	The Holy Spirit is a seal that protects our salvation and guarantees it forever.
The Holy Spirit is our protection.	Revelation 7:1–8	Scripture teaches us that God protects those He seals.
We are sealed for God.	Romans 8:16	God's seal means He has ownership of us. As a result, He takes responsibly for our future.
We have God's "seal of approval."	John 6:27; Ephesians 4:30	Because God placed the Holy Spirit as a seal of approval on us, He has also approved us.
We belong to God.	1 Corinthians 6:19–20	Because God owns us, we have a responsibility to keep our body (the temple of the Holy Spirit) clean.
We have God's engagement ring.	Ephesians 1:13–14	His ring is a down payment and a promise of good things to come.

72

THE PRIVILEGES OF ETERNAL SECURITY

The grace necessary to finish well is one of the privileges we have the opportunity to enjoy because we have been saved, sealed, and secured forever by the precious blood of Christ. I want to talk about some of these privileges that can be ours in Christ, in the hope that you will come to appreciate and value your salvation in new ways and determine that nothing will keep you from serving Him faithfully and running your race to His glory.

I refer to these privileges as opportunities because they are not automatic. That is, these things we're going to discuss are tied to our faithfulness in living for Christ. They don't determine how much salvation we get, because we get all of it. But they do help to determine how much we will enjoy our salvation.

THE MANY PRIVILEGES OF ETERNAL SECURITY

The Privilege of Becoming Partakers with Christ

One of the privileges available to us as believers is the opportunity to become "partakers" of Jesus Christ. The writer of Hebrews addressed his readers as "partakers of a heavenly calling" (3:1), and then he told them, "For we have become partakers of Christ, if we hold fast the beginning of our assurance firm until the end" (v. 14).

Let me deal with the last part of verse 14 first, because on first reading, it sounds as if the writer is making salvation conditional. We've covered enough biblical ground in this book to demonstrate that these conditional phrases refer to the potential loss of privilege and reward, not salvation. So let's lay that issue to rest right here.

The Greek word translated "partakers" in this text has a tremendous meaning. In biblical days it referred to a ruler's cabinet or inner circle of friends and advisers. Interestingly, this same word is translated as "companions" in Hebrews 1:9 in reference to Christ's preeminence. These companions are believers, the same ones who are later called "brethren" (Hebrews 2:11). That makes Jesus Christ the most special person among those who are His partakers or companions.

We have pointed out before that when it comes to our service and usefulness for Christ here on earth, all believers do not have the same depth of relationship with Christ. Nor does He commit Himself equally to all believers (John 2:24). He is the Savior of all who believe, so that's not the issue. But the privilege of being a partaker with Him is for those who prove themselves worthy, who "hold fast the beginning of [their] assurance firm until the end" (Hebrews 3:14).

The problem is that being human, we can get sidetracked from the work God has called us to do. Although in one sense that's understandable, and although it happens to all of us at one time or another, it's not an excuse for a failure to be faithful.

Jesus made some strong statements about what it takes to have a place close to Him in terms of our earthly service. "Whoever does the will of My Father who is in heaven, he is My brother and sister and mother" (Matthew 12:50). "You are My friends if you do what I command you" (John 15:14). Again, these are not conditions for salvation but conditions for being what the book of Hebrews calls a partaker of Christ.

The Privilege of Entering God's Rest

If you've studied the book of Hebrews, you know that one of its key themes is what is called God's rest. Hebrews 4:1 contains a conditional statement regarding God's rest: "Let us fear if, while a promise remains of entering His rest, any one of you may seem to have come short of it."

Then in verse 4 we read: "For He has said somewhere concerning the seventh day: 'And God rested on the seventh day from all His works.'" This takes us all the way back to Genesis 2:2, where we read, "By the seventh day God completed His work which He had done, and He rested on the seventh day from all His work which He had done." God did not rest because He was tired and needed some sleep. The idea here is that God sat back, if you will, beheld His creation, and felt complete satisfaction in what He had done. In other words, God thoroughly enjoyed what He had created.

God offers you and me the privilege of feeling the same way about our work as He felt about His work. Not because our work is perfect, by any means, but because when we are fully participating in His plan for us and are serving Him to the limits of our ability and faithfulness, we can enjoy a tremendous sense of satisfaction and spiritual fulfillment. The opposite is that sense of guilt and frustration so many Christians testify to because they are knocking themselves out trying to please God.

The Privilege of Earning Great Reward

I've referred to Jesus' parable in Matthew 25:14–30 that teaches the principle of reward for faithful service. We don't have the space here to quote the entire passage, which you can read for yourself. I want to summarize the story and highlight the principle.

The parable involves a man who goes on a long trip and leaves various amounts of his money to three of his servants to manage and invest for him. You may recall the story, in which the first two servants double their money while the third hides his allotment in the ground and does nothing with it.

When the master returns and calls for an accounting, he commends the two diligent servants and gives them a reward that is described as being put "in charge of many things" (vv. 21, 23) and the extra blessing of entering into his joy. Whatever this involved, it was very good. But the third servant is judged and stripped of his money because he was faithless with what the master had given him. He had nothing to present to the master in return for the privilege of having charge of some of the master's money.

It's true that the servants were given different amounts of money to work with. But the reward for those who were faithful is identical. And the third servant had the same opportunity to hear the master say, "Well done, good and faithful servant" (vv. 21, 23 KJV). The only difference was that this servant didn't persevere in faithful service.

God is watching what we do with the salvation we have been given. Rewards await those who are faithful.

The Privilege of Finishing Well

Aren't you glad that God gives us the privilege of finishing well? That's important because as so many have said, the Christian life is a marathon and not a short sprint. This takes us back to Hebrews 3:14 and the exhortation to "hold fast the beginning of our assurance firm until the end."

In one sense, the truth of eternal security assures us that we will finish well, because every person whom God saves makes it to heaven. But there's something even better than making it to heaven. It's finishing well and entering heaven with a lifetime of rewards from Christ instead of merely making it through the fire of Christ's judgment seat (see 1 Corinthians 3:15).

Finishing well should be our response to the grace of God. Grace is what God gives us; good works are what we can—and are called to—do in response. And as God's grace gains you heaven, so your works gain you reward in heaven.

THE PERSEVERANCE OF ETERNAL SECURITY

We've said a lot about this great salvation and what it means to be totally saved. The Bible is clear that what God wants from His children is a life of faithfulness in gratitude for what He has given us. And, as noted above, the Bible is equally clear that God desires to reward His children when they are faithful to Him.

We conclude our study of eternal security and the doctrine of soteriology by looking at that life of faithfulness to which God calls us.

The Importance of Perseverance

In 2 Timothy 2:12, the apostle Paul made a very important statement about the great value of our endurance or perseverance in the faith: "If we endure, we will also reign with Him [Jesus Christ]." We've dealt with this verse and the crucial passage of which it is a part, so let me remind you that it deals with reward or the loss thereof in heaven, not the loss of salvation. The principle being taught is that the degree of our eternal reward depends on our faithfulness to Christ.

There is a major difference between being a son or daughter and being an heir. Jesus had a lot to say about our service for Him and the reward it brings. One of the most concise summaries of His teaching on this subject comes in Jesus' Sermon on the Mount, found in Matthew 6:1–21. In verses 1–18, the Lord taught us how to do our giving, our praying, and our fasting in a way that honors Him and brings His reward.

It's not that the hypocrites Jesus was talking about go unrewarded. It's just that their reward, human praise and recognition, is so temporary and totally restricted to earth. It makes no impact whatsoever in heaven. That's why Jesus closed this section of the Sermon on the Mount by saying:

> Do not store up for yourselves treasures on earth, where moth and rust destroy, and where thieves break in and steal. But store up for yourselves treasures in heaven, where neither moth nor rust destroys, and where thieves do not break in or steal; for where your treasure is, there your heart will be also. (Matthew 6:19–21)

The Test of Perseverance

It doesn't take much perseverance to reap a temporary earthly reward if that's what you're willing to settle for. But storing up treasures in heaven demands a mind-set of faithfulness that believes God when He says He will reward us for the service we do in His name and His power, and for His glory. The deposits we lay up in heaven are long-term investments, like the deposits people make in their retirement accounts.

In order to enjoy these blessings, you have to take the long view and see the unseen, like the apostle Paul:

> Therefore we do not lose heart, but though our outer man is decaying, yet our inner man is being renewed day by day. For momentary, light affliction is producing for us an eternal weight of glory far beyond all comparison, while we look not at the things which are seen, but at the things which are not seen; for the things which are seen are temporal, but the things which are not seen are eternal. (2 Corinthians 4:16–18)

Now don't misunderstand. I'm not saying that if we just get the right spiritual attitude, then a life of fruitful, consistent service will flow easily from our lives with no struggles. The interesting thing is that of all of Paul's letters, 2 Corinthians is the most poignant and revealing in terms of Paul's human weakness and struggles. He had "conflicts without, fears within" (2 Corinthians 7:5). But he was able to serve God consistently in spite of his weakness because he had learned how to access God's grace and the power of the Holy Spirit.

The church is built and God's work is advanced by faithful believers who have the long view and serve Christ to the best of their ability. I love what Paul said in 1 Corinthians 1:26–27:

> For consider your calling, brethren, that there were not many wise according to the flesh, not many mighty, not many noble; but God has chosen the foolish things of the world to shame the wise, and God has chosen the weak things of the world to shame the things which are strong.

That should encourage us, because, let's face it, most of us fit in the category of the foolish and the weak as far as greatness in this world is concerned. You may not be able to bring the crowd to its feet, but you can be faithful and persevere in the place where God has put you.

I'm convinced that the people who will enjoy the greatest reward in heaven are those who didn't give up when the storms came.

When Questions Come

What about those times when we are tempted to question our salvation as doubt takes hold of us? The best example I can give you in this case is what John the Baptist did as he languished in prison and began to wonder if Jesus really was the Messiah. John sent two of his disciples to Jesus with the question: "Are You the Expected One, or do we look for someone else?" (Luke 7:19). Jesus demonstrated His power to John's disciples, then sent them back with the unmistakable testimony of His deity (vv. 21–22).

God is not afraid of your questions, so if you're struggling He knows it, and you might as well talk to Him about it. Don't hide when you have questions and doubts, because God can deal with them if you'll be honest with Him. Now let me point out that Jesus' answer to John didn't get John out of jail. His circumstances didn't change, but it makes a big difference in trials whether you know that Jesus is the One and you belong to Him, or whether you're not sure. That can make the difference between persevering and giving up.

Now let me turn this issue of questions around and talk about what happens when God has questions to ask of us. God would ask some of us, "I have given you a great salvation and secured your future in heaven. What are you doing with what I've given you?" We've promised God that if He would meet this need or get us out of that tight spot, we would serve Him faithfully. Have you ever done that?

This question of what we are doing with our salvation is one that all of us need to ask ourselves. We're secure in Christ, but what are we doing for Him in gratitude and love for what He has given us? If you are a spiritual dropout, then get back in the race. Pick up the pace to make up lost ground. Every day you delay is another day of lost opportunity. "Let us not lose heart in doing good, for in due time we will reap if we do not grow weary" (Galatians 6:9).

OUR UNSHAKABLE KINGDOM

Here's a final word from Scripture to encourage us with the truth of our security in Christ and urge us to persevere: "Therefore, since we receive a kingdom which cannot be shaken, let us show gratitude, by which we may offer to God an acceptable service with reverence and awe; for our God is a consuming fire" (Hebrews 12:28–29).

This world may be shaking, and things may get a lot worse before God decides it is enough and Jesus returns for His own. But as believers in Christ, we are in the most secure position we could possibly be in. We are part of a kingdom that cannot be shaken by the instability around us, because our kingdom is not of this world.

What can we do to express our appreciation for this secure position? The answer is in the text. We need to show gratitude to God by serving Him "with reverence and awe." In other words, God is like loving parents who take care of their children and meet all of their needs, but who have to say sometimes, "How about a little gratitude here? How about a little help with the chores and the responsibilities around the house?"

We are saved and secure, and God wants us to be grateful for our privileges by serving Him in a way that is acceptable to Him. God will not make us be grateful, but neither can we make Him reward us for our lack of gratitude. There's a whole lot of shaking going on out there in the world, and if anything ought to make us grateful, it is our security in Christ.

PERSONAL APPLICATION FOR LIFE

1. God has saved and secured you and brought you into His unshakable kingdom. He has promised to keep you from falling. He loves you that much. His question is, How grateful are you for His presence in time and His promise for eternity?

2. In any task, it's important to finish well. Our faith is no exception. Hebrews 3:14 exhorts us to "hold fast the beginning of our assurance firm until the end." God gives us not only the opportunity, but the grace to finish our course well. How well are you holding to your confession of faith? If you need help, ask God to give the grace you need to finish the course well.

3. We look forward to an eternity with God. As a child of God, are you ready for the coming kingdom? Matthew 6:33 exhorts us to make it a priority to seek God's kingdom and righteousness. Is kingdom living the top priority in your life?

4. In 2 Timothy 2:12, the apostle Paul made a very important statement about the great value of our endurance or perseverance in the faith: "If we endure, we will also reign with Him [Jesus Christ]." Staying the course can certainly be difficult at times. Never forget that God is capable of helping you do whatever He's called you to do. Are you finding the road difficult right now? Lay claim to the affirmation of Philippians 4:13 and ask God to give you a special measure of strength to get through the current storm in your life.

FOR GROUP STUDY

Questions for Group Discussion

1. What does it mean for believers to be partakers of Christ with regard to their eternal security? What does being a "partaker" involve?

2. Read Hebrews 4:1. What is "God's rest"?

3. Read 2 Timothy 2:12. What does it mean to "persevere" in our faith?

What is the test of our perseverance? (See 2 Corinthians 4:16–18.) (Use the chart below as an aid to your discussion.)

4. What is the reward of our perseverance? (See Galatians 6:9; Matthew 25:14–40; Hebrews 12:28–29.)

PICTURE THIS

There is great value in our persevering in the faith. If we endure, we will reign with Christ in His kingdom. The degree of our eternal reward depends on our faithfulness to Christ.

THE IMPORTANCE OF OUR PERSEVERANCE

TRUTH	SCRIPTURE PASSAGE	WHAT IT MEANS
Perseverance is part of being an heir.	1 Peter 4:12–13	The degree of our reward is tied to the measure of our sharing in Christ's suffering.
Perseverance determines the greatness of our reward.	Matthew 6:19–21	The greatness of our reward is commensurate with the goal of our service for Him.

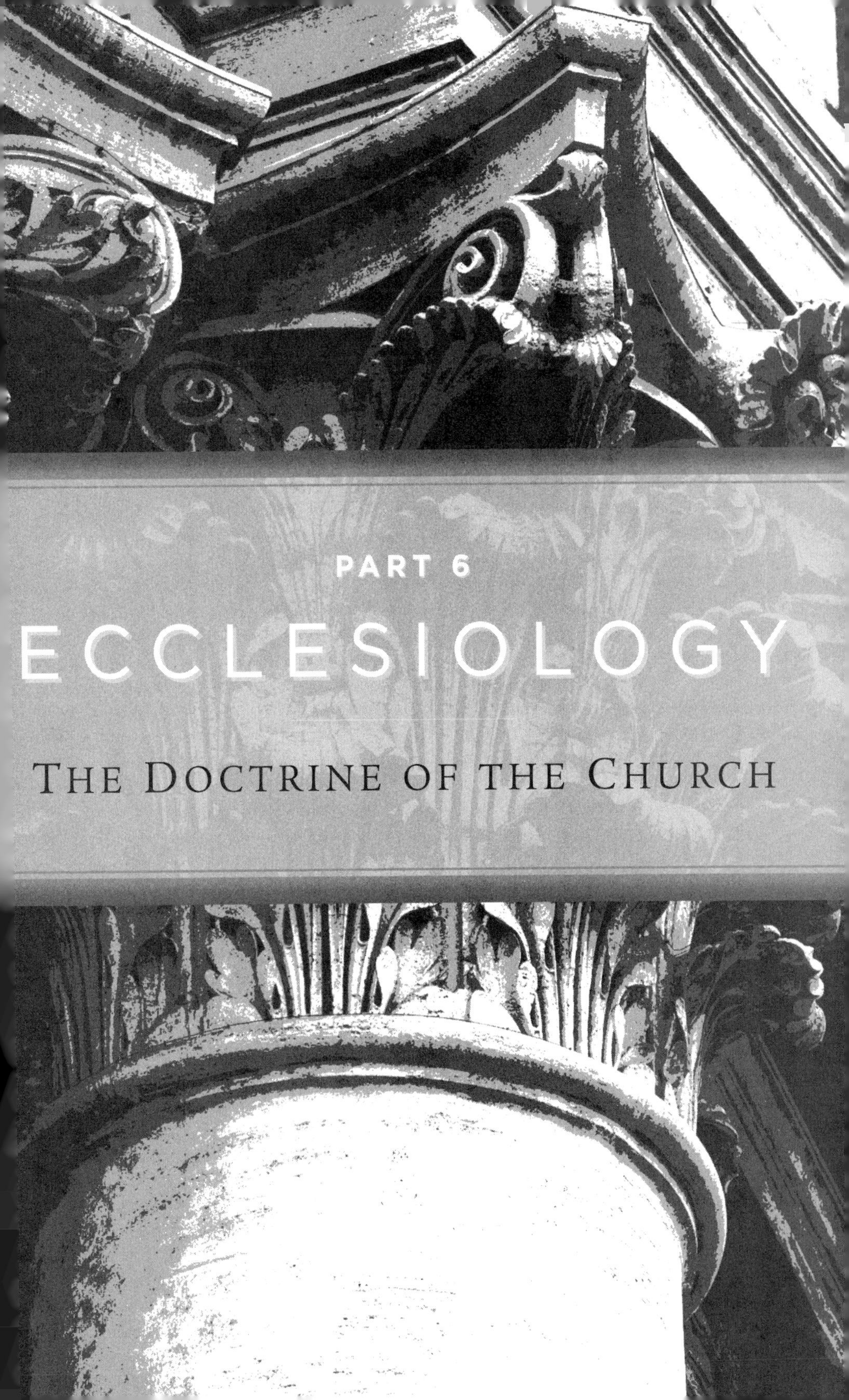

PART 6

ECCLESIOLOGY

The Doctrine of the Church

SECTION I

The Nature of the Church

73. THE IMPORTANCE OF THE CHURCH
74. THE PURPOSE OF THE CHURCH
75. THE MISSION AND DISTINCTIVES OF THE CHURCH
76. THE POWER OF THE CHURCH

73

THE IMPORTANCE OF THE CHURCH

The study of the church is known as ecclesiology, from the Greek word *ekklēsia*, which is a common term the New Testament uses for the church. What we believe about ecclesiology is very important, because in God's economy, the church is the most important institution on earth. The church, and only the church, has been commissioned by the sovereign Lord to be His representative agency in history. It has been given sole authority to unlock the treasures of the spiritual realm so that they can be brought to bear on the realities of earth.

Thus, as the church goes, so goes everything else. God designed the church to be the epicenter of culture, and the church's strength or weakness is a major determining factor in the success or failure of human civilization. When the church is strong, the culture is impacted positively—even if the "powers that be" in a particular place don't realize that impact and seek to marginalize and persecute the church. But when the church is weak, its influence deteriorates and so does the culture.

A GOD-SIZED PROBLEM

Talking about the church may bring certain verses from the Bible to your mind. But I want to begin our discussion of the church in what seems like an unusual place—not in the words of Jesus or the writings of Paul, but in an obscure Old Testament passage in which we find a God-sized problem that will help us answer the question of why the church is so important in God's plan today.

A Time of Great Chaos

Less than fifty years after King Solomon died and the kingdom of Israel had divided, King Asa had begun reforms in Judah. In 2 Chronicles 15, the prophet Azariah was urging the king to continue those reforms. To reinforce his message, Azariah reminded Asa of the sad condition God's people were in during an earlier age, which many Bible commentators believe was the period of the judges. If so, Azariah was speaking of Israel's low point spiritually when he said, "For many days Israel was without the true God and without a teaching priest and without law" (v. 3).

Verse 4 refers to those times when Israel sought God during that period, but in verses 5–6, the prophet summarized those days of chaos and God's judgment: "In those times there was no peace to him who went out or to him who came in, for many disturbances afflicted all the inhabitants of the lands. Nation was crushed by nation, and city by city, for God troubled them with every kind of distress."

Several things from these verses are worth noting. For instance, the description of a society in the grip of violence, crime, and conflict between nations sounds like our world today, so we know there's a lesson for us here. Like the world of ancient Israel, our culture is also in chaos and confusion.

But what ought to grab your attention is the statement in verse 6 that this all came about because "God troubled" the people. We might have expected Azariah to say that this mess was the result of satanic activity and influence in the world. According to the prophet, however, God was the author of this confusion among the people, although He was not in any way the author of their sin that provoked His judgment.

In other words, these problems that were tearing apart the fabric of society had a spiritual cause. So to address the lack of peace on a social level, to try to deal with violence and crime through more law enforcement, or even to meet at the bargaining table in an effort to settle conflicts between governments would not be enough, because the people's problem was with God. And when God is your problem, God alone is your solution.

What was it about this period of Israel's history that caused God to "trouble" His people with distress at so many levels? The root of the problem is found in 2 Chronicles 15:3. Three key elements that are necessary to keep God's people on track spiritually were missing.

A Lack of True Knowledge

The first of these elements was the lack of "the true God." This does not say that God had withdrawn Himself from Israel so that the people forgot who He was or could no longer find Him. Even in the days of the judges, there was religious service going on in Israel. People were offering sacrifices to God. But it was not the kind of authentic religion that pleased God or produced the right kind of response from Him.

A Lack of Biblical Teaching

What could have caused God's people to get all confused about the nature of God and start mixing the true with the false? In the case before us, the second phrase of 2 Chronicles 15:3 gives us a large clue. In those days, "Israel was . . . without a teaching priest." We would say today that the nation had a very serious pastoral problem—a mist in the pulpit that became a fog in the pew, as we'll see later.

The priests were doing an inadequate job of providing a divine viewpoint through which the people could interpret all of life and make God-honoring decisions. There was a systemic spiritual failure at the heart of Israel's spiritual leadership that kept the people uninformed and ill-informed about their responsibility before God and the consequences of failing to meet it.

A Lack of Correct Application

The third problem mentioned in 2 Chronicles 15:3 follows as a natural consequence of the first two. Because the people didn't know their God intimately and were not hearing His Word taught, they were "without law." That is, they didn't know how to apply God's law to the situations they faced. The divine rules weren't being applied, so people made up their own.

The last phrase of the last verse of the book of Judges illustrates this problem perfectly: "Everyone did what was right in his own eyes" (Judges 21:25). Everybody had an idea of what to do, but nothing worked because God's government of His people was not being upheld and enforced.

A GOD-ORDAINED SOLUTION

Because the basic realities of spiritual conflict and the superior power of the spiritual world haven't changed since the days of the judges in ancient Israel, we see the same principle of the visible world being controlled by the invisible world at work today. Paul gave us one of the clearest statements of this reality in Ephesians 6:12 when he said, "Our struggle is not against flesh and blood, but against the rulers, against the powers, against the world forces of this darkness, against the spiritual forces of wickedness in the heavenly places."

This is also a great statement of why the church is central to God's plan. God has always had a vehicle or an agency on earth to make His presence manifest, carry out His will, and bring what is invisible and spiritual down to the world of the visible and the physical.

Jesus' Promise of the Church

Jesus Himself revealed His future plan in a crucial discussion with His disciples that took place early in His ministry. The first time the Bible mentions a subject is very significant, and the first time the church is mentioned is on the lips of Jesus in His time with the disciples (Matthew 16:13–19) as He prophesied the church's coming. The Greek word Jesus used here is *ekklēsia*, the word we mentioned above, which means "called out ones." It was also used of an assembly; so the idea is that the church is a special assembly of people called out from the world to become part of God's family. This definition is critical for our understanding of the church as people instead of just an institution or a collection of buildings.

In the broadest sense, the church refers to all believers of all times, from the church's birth on the day of Pentecost to the rapture, when Christ will remove the church from the world. This is often referred to as the universal church, using the term *universal* in its best sense of meaning "all-encompassing." However, the universal church is to be visibly manifested in local assemblies that live out the principles given to the universal church in their individual churches. Just as America has embassies in foreign countries that represent the presence and values of the United States, so God has His embassies—His church—spread out around the world to represent His presence and rule in history.

My purpose in looking at these familiar verses in Matthew 16 is to focus on Jesus' teaching concerning the church and the authority He gave the church to carry out His plan. Jesus had taken the disciples and traveled north for a time of retreat to get away from the crowds. It was while they were alone that Jesus raised the all-important question, "Who do people say that the Son of Man is?" (v. 13). Then He asked, more specifically, "But who do *you* say that I am?" (v. 15, italics added).

The disciples offered several names in answer to the question of what the people at large were saying about Jesus (v. 14). The important thing was who Jesus' disciples believed Him to be. So Peter stepped forward as the leader and declared, "You are the Christ, the Son of the living God" (v. 16). The clear implication is that the other eleven disciples agreed with him. Peter was saying, "Lord, we've just been discussing this and have come to the conclusion that You are Israel's promised Messiah and Savior."

Jesus blessed Peter for this confession (v. 17), which the disciples didn't really arrive at on their own, but which came to them by revelation from God the Father.

Now we come to the heart of the passage as far as the church is concerned. In Matthew 16:18, Jesus followed up His affirmation of Peter's confession by saying, "I also say to you that you are Peter, and upon this rock I will build My church; and the gates of Hades will not overpower it."

The Church's Foundation

This is not only one of the most important statements about the church in the Bible, but also one of the most controversial. Some people teach that Peter himself is the rock on which the church is built, but that's not what Jesus said. He used a play on words here that is important to understand because it gives us the clue to Jesus' meaning.

"Peter" is the word *Petros*, a masculine form of the word for a stone. But the word *rock* that Jesus used next in Matthew 16:18 is *petra*, which is a feminine form of the same root word. This word was used in classical Greek of a collection of stones knitted together to form a larger rock, such as a ledge or a slab. It meant many stones joined together to form a rock that is far larger and more significant than any one stone could be.

This is a great picture of the church. Elsewhere Paul likened it to a human body in which all the individual parts are knit together to form one whole (see 1 Corinthians 12:12; Ephesians 4:16). The analogy is different, but the point is the same. The church is not built on Peter alone, but on Peter, the other apostles, and all those who believe and confess that Jesus is "the Christ, the Son of the living God" coming together to form this larger entity called the church.

Of course, in the ultimate sense the church is built on Jesus Christ. The church is, and always will be, His church. But it doesn't have to be either/or. Both Paul and Peter later taught that Christ was the church's one and only "corner stone" (Ephesians 2:20; 1 Peter 2:6). But Paul still referred to the apostles as the church's foundation stones, and Peter said that the church was being built out of all the stones. Peter's ministry was indispensable to the church, but he was not the cornerstone.

Jesus' Promise of Victory

The last phrase of Matthew 16:18 is worthy of separate treatment because it is loaded! Jesus said, "I will build My church; and the gates of Hades will not overpower it."

Please notice that Jesus is on the offensive here, not the forces of Satan. Jesus is not trying to stop hell. Hell is trying to stop Jesus. A lot of ministry today has missed this point as people spend an inordinate amount of time trying to defeat the Devil. But Jesus knew we could never defeat the Devil on our own. That's why He came to live a perfect life, die on the cross for our sins, and be raised to life by God the Father three days later. That's why Jesus spoke of the church as yet future in Matthew 16. He had not yet been to the cross, but when He arose our Savior presented His church with a defeated Satan.

It's not that Satan and his forces won't attack and try to overcome the church. We know that our real battle is against evil spiritual forces. But Jesus guaranteed that hell will not win this battle because it has already been fought and won at the cross. Sometimes we "do church" as if we are struggling for all we're worth to be victorious. But that's not the image of the church Jesus gave us.

Jesus chose His words carefully when He spoke of the "gates" of Hades, or hell. In the biblical world, the gate of a city was the place of authority. The city's elders would sit at the city gate to conduct the city's business and render decisions on behalf of the citizens. The gate was their city hall.

Jesus was speaking of satanic authority to act against the church. God has given Satan some room to operate for now, and we are going to learn the reason for that. But the word here is that Satan's authority will not prevail against the church—which also has real implications for society at large because the invisible and spiritual world controls the visible and physical.

Thus, when the church is doing its job, all of society benefits. This is what makes the church the most important entity in the world, whether the world realizes it or not. Actually, the world will not realize the restraining and sanctifying influence of the church until God raptures His church away and all of hell breaks loose on the earth.

THE KEYS OF THE KINGDOM

Jesus finished His response to Peter with these words: "I will give you the keys of the kingdom of heaven" (v. 19a).

Notice right away that Jesus did not give Peter the keys of the church. Many people today misunderstand this verse because they think that the church and the kingdom are synonymous. But Jesus was careful to distinguish between the two, using a completely different word for "kingdom." This word refers not to a called-out body of believers, which is the church, but to God's comprehensive rule over all of His creation. The church is limited, whereas the kingdom is comprehensive.

Keys stand for access, so what Jesus was giving His people is access to the resources of His all-encompassing kingdom. We can be grateful that Jesus did not limit our access to the resources of the church, because the kingdom is much bigger than the church. In fact, the church exists for the kingdom and not just for the church. I say that because our job is to help establish the rule of God in the hearts of people and bring the values and priorities of God's kingdom to bear on every aspect of our culture.

God created the church to be His agency in this age representing His bigger plan, which is the kingdom. Satan knows this, which is why he works so hard to keep churches divided. He knows that if God's people ever really get together, his influence will be severely limited.

The kingdom keys of Matthew 16:19 are plural because the gates of hell are plural. This means that for every hellish gate Satan throws open against us, there is a corresponding kingdom key that opens a kingdom door behind which are the resources we need to meet that challenge.

So every time hell tries to stop Jesus from building His church, the church is supposed to pull out its kingdom key ring and find the key that corresponds to the gate hell just opened. This is a tremendous gift from Christ to His church.

The access and authority Jesus has given to the church is also underscored by the last phrase of Matthew 16:19, where Jesus said, "And whatever you bind on earth shall have been bound in heaven, and whatever you loose on earth shall have been loosed in heaven." This is another gift from Christ, speaking of the authority the church has to carry out His agenda.

Satan cannot stand against the authority that Christ has given the church to wield in His name and His power. The church is God's only authorized representative in the world today.

PERSONAL APPLICATION FOR LIFE

1. We need the gathered body of Christ because it is the context in which spiritual growth occurs. You may grow some without the family of God, but you cannot develop into a fully mature disciple of Christ without the family of God. If you are not part of a body of believers, don't delay in joining a local church. And get involved with that church's ministry. Family life calls for dynamic participation and involvement.

2. Look at our nation today. How is it that we have churches on every corner with their programs and ministries, and yet our nation is in such moral and spiritual chaos? The church is to be salt and light to the world. Be part of a fellowship of believers who are committed to bringing God's Word and its power to bear upon their community.

3. What is true of the physical body is also true of God's spiritual body. We are to show the same kind of care for one another that the body shows for itself. Are you making a contribution to your local body of believers?

4. All of us as God's children need discipline, but we don't need to go so far that we lose His blessing and benefits. Take a close look at your life and try to determine if that nagging problem, troublesome relationship, or persistent trial is a normal discipline from God designed to strengthen your faith—or a result of disobedience.

FOR GROUP STUDY

Questions for Group Discussion

1. What is the New Testament concept of the church? What has been the church's place in history?

2. Read 2 Chronicles 15:3–6. What problems gave rise to the need for the church?

3. Read Jesus' prophecy about the coming church in Matthew 16:13–19. When describing the church, Jesus used the Greek word *ekklēsia*. What is the significance of that term?

4. Read Jesus' promise regarding the church in Matthew 16:18. What was Jesus teaching with His imagery of a church foundation?

PICTURE THIS

As a people, the children of God faced many growth problems in the Old Testament. The church was God's solution. The points below help illustrate why the church is so important in God's plan today.

GOD'S PLAN FOR THE CHURCH
2 Chronicles 15:3–6

PROBLEM	SOLUTION
God's people were experiencing a time of great chaos.	The problems that were tearing apart society had a spiritual root cause and God needed to restore order.
God's people lacked true knowledge.	God's people needed a better understanding of the one true God they were serving.
God's people lacked biblical teaching.	God's people were confused and mixing the true with the false. They needed to be anchored in sound teaching.
God's people lacked correct application.	God's people did not know how to bring God's truth to bear upon their world. They needed to learn how to bring God's Word ands its power to bear upon their world.

74

THE PURPOSE OF THE CHURCH

Jesus made a very important declaration to His disciples the night before He was crucified. As they reclined at the Last Supper, Jesus said, "Truly, truly, I say to you, he who believes in Me, the works that I do, he will do also; and greater works than these he will do; because I go to the Father" (John 14:12). We are certainly not greater than our Lord, but we can do greater things than He did in terms of our outreach because the church has taken the gospel around the world and has brought countless numbers of people to faith in Christ. We are also able to do greater works because the Holy Spirit has come to indwell and empower each believer. This could not happen until Jesus returned to His Father (see John 16:7).

Notice that the church is not called to do *different* works than Jesus did, only greater works. I want to break this definition down into its component parts using the book of Ephesians, which perhaps more than any other book in the Bible is dedicated to explaining the mystery and the ministry of the local church.

THE COMPLETION OF CHRIST'S PERSON

First of all, the church is the completion of Christ's person. Paul ended Ephesians 1 by saying that the church is "[Christ's] body, the fullness of

Him who fills all in all" (v. 23). I want to start here so you won't think I'm announcing heresy by implying that the Son of God is incomplete in His divine essence without us. Jesus fills all things as the second Person of the Godhead, but Paul also said that the church is Christ's fullness.

We Are His Body

The key is to distinguish between Christ's divine essence and His functioning as the Lord of history and head of the church. We complete His person in the way that a body completes a head by carrying out the head's orders and giving it hands and feet with which to express itself. Disembodied heads only work in horror films. Of course, Christ could have carried out His work from heaven without our help, because He is God. But He commissioned the church to finish His work after He rose from the dead and ascended back to heaven.

By the way, the body is Paul's favorite term for the church. He used it more than any other word to picture the way the church is designed to function in relation to Christ. As we said, the only job of a body is to do whatever the head tells it to do. The head is where the command center is located. If any part of your body ever disobeys the signals from your brain and starts acting independently, get yourself to a doctor right away because something is wrong. As Christ's body, the church is to move to His orders and make His presence visible as it was when Jesus was on earth Himself.

Everybody Is Important

When we say that the church is to complete Christ's person, let's acknowledge that no local church fulfills this assignment perfectly. Yet each local church does have a vital role to play. The church in Paul's mind was not some amorphous concept or an ideal with no real substance. Every local church is a visible expression of the universal church, and every believer is a visible expression of Christ in his or her world.

I want to go back to the last phrase of Ephesians 1:23, which says that the church is "the fullness of Him who fills all in all." That sounds like a tongue-twister, but it means that as we complete Christ, He completes us. As the church is faithful to be the visible, physical expression of the Lord of eternity, He will involve Himself in that process to make sure we are completing the task that He has assigned us.

THE COMPLETION OF CHRIST'S PRESENCE

As Christ's body, which completes His person on earth, the church also becomes the completion of His presence on earth. These two are related because it's obvious that wherever a person's body is, that's where his presence is. In the old days students used to answer "Present" when the teacher called their name on the roll. It was their way of saying, "Yes, I'm here. I am making my presence known."

That's the idea here. Jesus makes His presence known in a special way through the church. Now don't misunderstand. As the eternal God, Jesus Christ is omnipresent, or present everywhere. He fills every atom of creation, so let's be clear on that. But He is uniquely present in the church.

A New Kind of Temple

In Ephesians 2:19–23, Paul summarizes his teaching on grace by saying that God has created a new kind of temple in which His presence will dwell:

> So then you are no longer strangers and aliens, but you are fellow citizens with the saints, and are of God's household, having been built on the foundation of the apostles and prophets, Christ Jesus Himself being the corner stone, in whom the whole building, being fitted together, is growing into a holy temple in the Lord, in whom you also are being built together into a dwelling of God in the Spirit.

When Paul called the church a "holy temple," he was using Old Testament terminology to explain how the church is supposed to function as the expression of God's presence today. The temple in Jerusalem was the place where God was uniquely present among His people. The temple was where the special cloud of His glory appeared, and where His presence was manifested in the inner sanctum called the holy of holies.

In the temple the people came into the presence of God's glory; were reminded of His holiness, His law, and His expectations; and had their priorities adjusted so they could go back into society and reflect His glory.

Taking Jesus' Presence Everywhere

The church is called to fulfill this function for God's people today. I'm not talking about the church as the building on the corner or down the street. I'm talking about the church as the people of God, who are called to manifest His presence wherever we go. Yes, Christians usually gather in a building for worship, praise, and instruction in the Word, and when the church is gathered, God's presence is evident. But we take His presence with us because the church is God's human temple. God no longer limits His presence on earth to a building made of wood and stone.

THE COMPLETION OF CHRIST'S PLAN

This is the third way in which the church completes Christ, and I love this one! According to Ephesians 3, the church is the culmination of God's plan for the ages that will demonstrate to the entire angelic realm His infinite wisdom in choosing weak vessels like us through whom to manifest His glory.

Paul was explaining to the Ephesians his ministry as the one whom God called to reveal the mystery of the church. This mystery had been "hidden" for ages (Ephesians 3:9), but was now being revealed with the intent that "the manifold wisdom of God might now be made known through the church to the rulers and the authorities in the heavenly places" (v. 10).

The plan God set in motion to redeem fallen humanity and call out a people for His name culminating in the church, was all a big surprise to Satan. He must have thought he outwitted God when he deceived Adam and Eve and plunged the race into sin. But Satan didn't understand what Christ was going to achieve on the cross.

So the church is the climax of God's plan and purpose that He set in motion in eternity past. The church is God's way of saying to the angelic realm, "This is the plan and purpose I have been carrying out on earth." It is through the church's action on earth that God gives instruction to the spiritual realm.

THE COMPLETION OF CHRIST'S PROGRAM

Here's another facet of the church's purpose that boggles the mind. The church is to complete Christ's program by which His eternal plan is carried out in history. Ephesians 4:7–16 is a powerful passage that teaches that every believer is gifted for service and that Christ has also given the church gifted people to lead it. The Bible says, "To each one of us grace was given according to the measure of Christ's gift" (v. 7).

Christ Led a Triumphant Procession

The way Christ did this is worthy of a study all by itself. Paul used an Old Testament quotation to describe the Lord's activity prior to His ascension: "When He ascended on high, He led captive a host of captives, and He gave gifts to men" (v. 8; taken from Psalm 68:18). Then verses 9–10 are added as a parenthesis explaining what Paul meant by this intriguing statement.

This passage answers the question of what happened between the time Christ died on the cross and rose from the dead on the third day.

While His physical body lay in the tomb, Jesus Christ descended in His spirit into *Sheol*, the realm of the dead, to proclaim His victory to the demons that are locked up there and to empty the paradise side by leading the saints there up to heaven in a triumphal procession. Paradise was moved to heaven because the temporary plan of covering sin with the blood of animals was over. The final payment for sin had been made.

In the process of completing His triumph, Jesus was authorized by the Father to hand out gifts. This is a very picturesque phrase, which was used of a Roman general who defeated his enemy and brought back the spoils of the conquered kingdom to be used for the benefit of his own land. Jesus so completely defeated Satan by His death on the cross that He was able to march into Satan's own domain and rob him of the spoils—all the redeemed saints with their gifts, talents, and abilities—which are now transferred from Satan's use to Christ's kingdom and His service.

This gifting also includes gifted leaders for the church (see Ephesians 4:11). These leaders, including pastors and teachers, have this assignment: "The equipping of the saints for the work of service, to the building up of the body of Christ" (v. 12). The church does not pay pastors to do all of the church's work, but to prepare the members of the body for their ministry.

Jesus Wants a Mature Church

For the church to operate properly, each part of the body has to function properly. The goal of Christ's gifting of His body is that the body might grow up into full maturity, "to the measure of the stature which belongs to the fullness of Christ" (Ephesians 4:13). Its members stop being an infantile body that is always fighting and fussing when someone upsets us; they grow up.

Paul used another great word picture in Ephesians 4. As we grow up into Christ, the whole body, which is "fitted and held together by what every joint supplies, according to the proper working of each individual part, causes the growth of the body for the building up of itself in love" (v. 16).

A healthy body builds itself up and wards off disease. So when a cell decides to quit doing its assigned job and start doing its own thing, the body will malfunction. When rogue cells replicate, the result can be cancer.

It's the same way in the church. When members of Christ's body decide they don't want to cooperate with the program, they go off and start doing their own thing. That's bad enough, but these "rebel cells" want to replicate, and now you have a lump in the body. And it doesn't stop there, because those cancerous cells want to metastasize and spread throughout the body. The result is to weaken and eventually shut the body down.

But a healthy body draws strength from every part because every part is doing its job. You and I must understand that for the church to complete Christ's program, all of the members need to function using the spiritual gifts He has given. First Corinthians 12:12–25 teaches that some gifts are exercised in public while others are more private. Some gifts are visible while others are hidden, but the church needs each person or the body of Christ will be deformed.

THE COMPLETION OF CHRIST'S PORTRAIT

There's a fifth way that we complete Christ, which I'm calling His portrait. When Paul discussed the relationship between wives and husbands in Ephesians 5:22–33, he said that he had a large purpose in mind: "This mystery [of a one-flesh relationship] is great; but I am speaking with reference to Christ and the church" (v. 32).

In fact, throughout this section the apostle likened the husband-wife relationship to Christ and His bride, which is the church. The wife's responsibility is to submit to her husband's leadership the way the church submits to Christ, and the husband's responsibility is to love his wife with the selfless, sacrificial love that Christ shows to the church. Then in Ephesians 6 Paul went on to teach about the proper relationship between parents and children and employers and employees.

We can't hand someone a "portrait" of Christ and say, "This is what Christlike married couples, children, parents, or employers are supposed to look like." But God has provided a visible portrait of these relationships through the way the church is supposed to conduct its relationships. In this sense we complete Christ's portrait.

In other words, husbands are portraying Christ when they love their wives "just as Christ also loved the church and gave Himself up for her" (v. 25). And wives are portraying Christ when they are "subject to [their] own husbands, as to the Lord" (v. 22). They recall the humble Son, who while on earth was completely submissive to His Father's will, even to the extent of submitting to the cross. When husbands love their wives more than themselves, when wives submit to their husbands (without losing their exalted identity, even as Jesus did not lose His deity on earth), they give the world a clear portrait of Christ.

THE COMPLETION OF CHRIST'S POWER

We're ready for the climax of this brief study of Ephesians related to the church's purpose—and what a finish it is! The church is called and equipped to complete Christ's power. Paul wrote:

> Finally, be strong in the Lord and in the strength of His might. Put on the full armor of God, so that you will be able to stand firm against the schemes of the devil. For our struggle is not against flesh and blood, but against the rulers, against the powers, against the world forces of this darkness, against the spiritual forces of wickedness in the heavenly places. (Ephesians 6:10–12)

If the church ever grasped the full reality of what God is telling us here, there would be no holding us back. Notice that we are told to "stand firm" (which is repeated twice in vv. 13–14), to stand our ground. Why didn't God tell us, "Go fight"? Because we are not fighting *for* a victory, but *from* a position of victory, and there is all the difference between those two positions. Christ has already won the victory over the Devil and his schemes. Our job is to do the mop-up and hold on to the ground that Christ has already captured.

PERSONAL APPLICATION FOR LIFE

1. God has equipped His church—through gifts, talents, and abilities—to carry out Christ's work. Is there some gift or ability you know God has given you, yet you are hiding it for whatever reason? Then get your shovel out! Dig up your "talent" (see Matthew 25:25) and ask God for an opportunity to serve Him with it. Then be alert for the answer.

2. One problem in today's church is that we have too many saints on the sidelines and not in the game. It's easy to sit in the stands and call the plays. But we are here to carry on Christ's work, and the church needs more disciple-makers. God has not called you to be a bystander; He has called you to build His truth into somebody else's life. Ask God to open the door for you to help disciple another believer in the body of Christ.

3. For those times when life collapses, we need the fellowship of the body of Christ. The ministry of those who are following Christ can be invaluable. The question is, Are you too busy in your own world to become part of the circle of Christian fellowship? If so, you are too busy to become a disciple of Jesus Christ! Perhaps "Rearrange priorities" should appear on your next to-do list.

4. As the body of Christ, we are Christ's presence in a dying world. People should look at us in the church and see what Christ would look like and what He would do in a given situation. As we grow spiritually and mature in Christ, we become more like Him. When people see you, do they see Jesus Christ?

FOR GROUP STUDY

Questions for Group Discussion

1. In Ephesians 1:23, the apostle Paul referred to the church as the body of Christ. How does the church function as a body? How does the church complete Christ's fullness?

2. Read Ephesians 2:19–23. How does the church function as the expression of God's presence today? How does the Holy Spirit's indwelling of believers contribute to the church's function as the temple of God?

3. How is the church the culmination of God's plan for the ages? Why is the church considered a "mystery"?

4. In what ways is the church the completion of Christ? (Use the chart on the next page as an aid to your discussion.)

PICTURE THIS

The local church is a community that has been given every spiritual gift and blessing we will ever need to carry out the work of Christ on earth. There are least six ways that God designed and equipped the local church to complete Christ's incarnation.

THE MULTIFACETED PURPOSE OF THE CHURCH

SPECIFIC PURPOSE	SCRIPTURE PASSAGE	WHAT IT ACCOMPLISHES
It completes Christ's person.	Ephesians 1:18–23	With the help of the Holy Spirit, the body of Christ carries out the work of Christ.
It completes Christ's presence.	Ephesians 2:19–23	The church is the human temple of God—Christ's presence on earth and where the Holy Spirit dwells.
It completes Christ's plan.	Ephesians 3:9–10	The church is the culmination of God's plan for the ages. It will demonstrate God's wisdom by displaying His glory through such weak vessels as ourselves.
It completes Christ's program.	Ephesians 4:7–16	God is using the church to complete Christ's program by using it to carry out His eternal plan in history.
It completes Christ's portrait.	Ephesians 5:22–33	God is entrusting the church to carry out the climactic relationship between Christ and His church.
It completes Christ's power.	Ephesians 6:10–12	The church is the means by which Christ's power over Satan and his forces is manifested on earth.

75

THE MISSION AND DISTINCTIVES OF THE CHURCH

Entire books have been written on the church's mission, but perhaps the most comprehensive summary of our calling is the text commonly called the Great Commission (Matthew 28:16–20). These are the last words of Jesus Christ before His ascension to heaven, which makes them crucial for that reason alone. But these are also very important words because they contain Christ's final instructions to His church, which is to "make disciples of all the nations" (v. 19).

DISCIPLE-MAKING DEFINES OUR MISSION

I want to give you two basic definitions of *discipleship* because the word has both a personal and a corporate dimension in terms of our place in Christ's body. Discipleship is the growth process by which we as Christians learn to progressively bring all of life under the lordship of Jesus Christ. This doesn't happen overnight, even though your salvation is complete the moment you trust Christ. Becoming a disciple means that Jesus Christ wants more of you today than He had yesterday, and He wants more of you tomorrow than He has today.

But there's more to discipleship than the personal dimension of our growth in grace. There is also the corporate dimension of discipleship.

That's why I define discipleship as a developmental process of the local church by which Christians are brought from spiritual infancy to spiritual maturity, so that they can reproduce the process with others, which the Bible calls being "conformed to the image of [God's] Son" (Romans 8:29). This verse is crucial because it goes on to explain the goal of our becoming like Jesus Christ: "So that He would be the firstborn among many brethren." It is the church's job to encourage and equip saints for this task.

The process of discipleship that leads to believers becoming Christlike is designed to be repeated again and again until Jesus has many brothers and sisters who look like Him. You and I can't do this if we are living as isolated Christians. Someone has said that Christianity was never meant to be "Jesus and me, under a tree." God placed us in a body of people called the church so that together we can accomplish the mission. The church is God's place to produce disciples who think and talk and act so much like Jesus that the world can look at us and say, "This must be what Jesus is like." Jesus Himself said, "It is enough for the disciple that he become like his teacher" (Matthew 10:25).

Jesus' Final Meeting

Jesus articulated the church's mission when He met with His followers in Galilee after the resurrection. Matthew 28:16 says, "The eleven disciples proceeded to Galilee, to the mountain which Jesus had designated" (see Mark 16:7). This was the only organized meeting He called during the forty days He was on earth between His resurrection and ascension. There were actually three groups at this meeting, including the eleven apostles (Judas was dead) and a second group that Paul called the "more than five hundred brethren" who saw the risen Christ at the same time (1 Corinthians 15:6).

The third group at this all-important meeting was there in spirit. This includes all believers from that day until Jesus comes again. How do I know we are part of the Great Commission meeting? Because Jesus said His commission to make disciples is in effect "even to the end of the age" (Matthew 28:20), which hasn't come yet. So the Lord's instructions are for us too.

Jesus' Declaration of Authority

Jesus' first words to His disciples in Matthew 28:18 are indispensable to the church's ability to execute its mission. I love this declaration: "All authority has been given to Me in heaven and on earth." Evans translation: "I am in charge now."

The word Jesus used for authority means "authority in legitimate hands." In other words, Jesus is not only in charge of the universe, but He is *rightfully* in charge. Christ's authority was given to Him by God the Father by virtue of Christ's death and resurrection in victory over sin, death, and the Devil. And Jesus is now in charge both "in heaven and on earth," in time and eternity. His authority is complete and eternal.

Jesus' Commission to Us

With His disciples worshiping Him and His authority established, Jesus gave us a commission to carry out until the end of the age: "Go therefore and make disciples of all the nations" (Matthew 28:19). Making disciples is not part of the gospel in the sense that it is not an integral part of what a person needs to know to get saved. But we need to understand that our salvation is not the be-all and end-all of what God wants to do with us. It is not the end of the process, but the beginning. Our calling isn't complete until the church is making disciples who can go and make more disciples.

We stopped our reading at verse 19 because it is the core of the commission. The phrase "make disciples" is a command in the Greek, and in fact it is the only command in this text. The other three activities—going, baptizing, and teaching—are actually participles that explain and expand the command to make disciples. (This is true even though the phrase "Go therefore" sounds like a command and is translated this way in many English versions.)

We have Jesus' authority and command to make disciples. This is exciting because it means that He is with us in the process to ensure that it works when we do it correctly.

MAKING DISCIPLES IS AN AWESOME CONCEPT

I'm afraid that too many Christians have become so familiar with our spiritual jargon that we have forgotten what an awesome concept making disciples really is. Jesus committed His entire enterprise for this age to the church—to people like you and me. What's more, He told us to take it to "all the nations." Discipleship is so big that when we are obedient to God and faithful in discipling people, the church will impact the world.

In today's world we are familiar with another kind of "discipleship" in the form of terrorists who are willing to give their lives for their religion. Referring to committed members of other religions as disciples has a precedent, because the Greek word translated "disciple" in the New Testament was not a uniquely Christian term. It means "student" or learner, and the practice of making disciples was well known in the Greek world hundreds of years before Christ.

The Greek philosopher Plato developed a system of thought that bears his name. Then he trained his young disciple Aristotle in this system of Platonic philosophy. Aristotle built on Plato's teaching and developed his own system known as Aristotelian logic. Aristotle then established schools called academies to train more disciples.

This Greek discipleship system was very effective, because even after Rome conquered Greece, the Romans could not eradicate Greek influence. So while Rome wielded military power, the Greeks wielded power over the culture because well-trained Greek disciples were functioning at every level of the society. These people lived under Roman rule, but their thinking was Greek. And in the end, what people think is a lot more important and powerful than what an external power can force them to do.

This helps us understand why Jesus commissioned the church to make disciples. When disciple-making is done correctly, the disciple becomes a follower for life because the real battle for souls is waged in the mind. A well-trained disciple can live in a foreign, hostile culture without succumbing to that culture because his mind is fixed on another world.

God has called out of the world a body of people known as the church, men and women and young people who live under the lordship of Jesus Christ. He wants us to become disciples who make other disciples, who can then be sent out into this satanically controlled world to infiltrate its structures and bring the thinking of Christ to bear on every part of society until every nation has been discipled.

FULFILLING THE MISSION: JESUS TELLS US HOW TO MAKE DISCIPLES

We've come to the final portion of the Great Commission, in which Jesus spelled out how to make disciples: "*Go* therefore and make disciples of all the nations, *baptizing* them in the name of the Father and the Son and the Holy Spirit, *teaching* them to observe all that I commanded you; and lo, I am with you always, even to the end of the age" (Matthew 28:19–20, italics added). The emphasized words are the three participles I mentioned earlier that support and expand Jesus' command to make disciples.

We Must Go to People

The first of these involves going. Let me point out again that this is not a command, but that doesn't mean our going is insignificant. On the contrary, the idea here is "As you go, make disciples." In other words, Jesus expects us to be going out. We could even say that our going is assumed.

What we are talking about is the ministry of evangelism. Discipleship begins with evangelism. You can't make disciples out of sinners. The nations are not told to come to Christians for the gospel. We need to go to them. The church is not doing the work of the church if we are not winning souls to Christ. I often tell our church people that I don't want Oak Cliff Bible Fellowship to grow just by people transferring their membership. There will always be some of that growth, but I want our church to grow primarily because we are bringing people to Christ and discipling them. The church should be like a hospital nursery in which you hear the sound of new babies crying to be fed and eager to grow.

That's why we must keep evangelism front and center in the life of the church. If the church is going to grow by making disciples, we have to have people who are willing to go into the whole world as Christ's witnesses. That's one reason Jesus sent us the Holy Spirit. "You will receive power when the Holy Spirit has come upon you; and you shall be My witnesses . . . even to the remotest part of the earth" (Acts 1:8).

We Must Help People Identify with Christ

Jesus said that another part of making disciples is baptizing those to whom we have gone and who have accepted Christ. He was not telling us simply to get folks wet. The problem in too many cases is that people go into baptism as dry sinners and come out as wet ones. There is much more to baptism than just undergoing a ritual involving water.

In fact, the primary meaning of the Greek word for baptism is "identification." This was a very picturesque word in New Testament days. It was used of dipping a cloth into a dye so that the cloth became completely identified with the dye by absorbing its color. The cloth was immersed in the dye until it took on the character of the dye. The cloth underwent a complete identity change.

This is the picture behind Romans 6:3–4, where Paul wrote, "Do you not know that all of us who have been baptized into Christ Jesus have been baptized into His death? Therefore we have been buried with Him through baptism into death, so that as Christ was raised from the dead through the glory of the Father, so we too might walk in newness of life."

When we put our trust in Christ, we became so completely identified with Him that His death and resurrection to new life became our death and resurrection. When we immerse believers in the waters of baptism, we are picturing their death to the old life and resurrection to a new way of life. That happened the moment they trusted Christ, but the ordinance of water baptism was given to the church as an outward testimony to this inward change.

Every believer is baptized by the Holy Spirit into the body of Christ and becomes identified with Christ and His family, the church, as we learned earlier (1 Corinthians 12:13). This spiritual reality is to be made visibly manifested in history through the believer's identification and involvement with a local church body. But many Christians struggle in their daily lives because they don't understand their new identity. They don't know who they are in Christ. We have to realize that being "in Christ" is such a radically new way of life that whatever happens to Christ happens to us. That's why the Bible says that when Christ died, we died, and when Christ arose from the dead, we arose.

Notice also that we are to baptize people in the *name* of all three persons of the Godhead. This is a tremendous statement of both the Trinity and yet the oneness of God. Three persons are mentioned, but They share one divine name. This may be the greatest of all the mysteries of Scripture, because no one can explain the Trinity adequately. But Jesus was clear that as His commissioned followers, we go in the power and authority of the Godhead.

We Must Teach People

Once people have believed the gospel and have been identified with Christ, we must teach them "to observe all that I commanded you" (Matthew 28:20).

Our teaching must have solid content, because Christians are people of the truth and people of the Book. Jesus' commands that we are to obey are contained in the Word. But the goal is not content alone. The church today has too many "spiritual bulimics" who take in the Word at church on Sunday, but then throw it up as soon as they get home so it doesn't do them any good.

The goal of biblical teaching is to combine information and knowledge with skill in applying the truth to daily life.

We Must Rely on His Presence

Jesus closed the Great Commission with a tremendous promise of His presence (Matthew 28:20). The promise is made even stronger by that little word translated "lo," one of those "King James"-sounding words that we just glide over. But a more accurate translation of the phrase "lo, I" would be "I, even I," or "I Myself," because "lo" is actually another form of the first-person pronoun.

As the Lord of the church, Jesus promises us His abiding presence and power to carry out His commission. To make disciples, first and foremost, we must rely on His presence and power as we go.

THE DISTINCTIVES OF THE CHURCH

Every company in the marketplace wants us to think that their product or service is distinctive—totally unlike anything else being offered. I'm not a marketing expert, but I can confidently state that there is really only one entity that is totally distinctive and set apart from everyone and everything else. No other organization except the church has been called into being by God Himself through the supernatural ministry of the Holy Spirit and charged with the specific task of carrying out Christ's work here on earth.

In fulfilling its mission of making disciples, the church has several distinctive elements, including a unique motivation, master, and mission. Several of the church's important distinctives are found in a key passage that the apostle Paul wrote to Timothy, his son in the faith, fellow worker in the gospel, and the person Paul left in Ephesus to pastor the local church there. Paul also sent Titus to oversee the local churches on the island of Crete, which is why the books of 1 and 2 Timothy and Titus are called the Pastoral Epistles.

The church was established in Ephesus despite intense opposition by those who worshiped the Greek goddess Artemis, whose beautiful temple stood over the city. (The temple was one of the Seven Wonders of the ancient world and one of the largest temples the Greeks ever built.) In this hostile setting the church became a voice for the truth. Paul drew on this background in his instructions to Timothy. His purpose was to tell Timothy how people who belong to Christ and are part of His church ought to behave "in the household of God" (1 Timothy 3:15), which he identified as the church, the only truly distinctive entity on earth.

We Have a Distinctive Motivation

The church's first distinctive trait relates to our identity as members of God's household. The Bible uses several metaphors for the church, one of which is a family. Because God has redeemed us and adopted us into His family, we have a distinctive motivation to act rightly. One reason the church comes together is to learn how to live differently under the lordship of Jesus Christ.

We are members of God's household, His children, whom Christ purchased with His own blood. Talk about something to motivate a person to right conduct! No one else on earth is offering the deal God is offering folks through His body, the church. Instead of constantly telling Christians that they need to stop doing wrong and start doing right, we need to help them understand who they are in Christ. That doesn't mean that there won't be problems, but understanding our identity in Christ is a far higher motivation for right conduct than just the fear of messing up.

We Have a Distinctive Master

"The household of God, which is the church of the living God" (1 Timothy 3:15) not only has a distinctive motivation. It also have a distinctive Master—God Himself in the person of Jesus Christ. The Bible leaves no doubt as to who is in charge in this house. Make sure all the family knows who is the master of the church, because the church is God's assembly. It's a divine institution. Let the family of God know who the head of the house is, lest we start doing what a lot of teenagers do and insist on living by our own rules while we're living in someone else's house.

The church is God's house, not ours. My job as a pastor is not to make up the rules for the church, but to announce and teach God's rules outlined in His Word. His name is on the title deed to the church, because "He purchased [it] with His own blood" (Acts 20:28). When the risen Christ appeared to His disciples, "He showed them both His hands and His side" (John 20:20). These are the marks of His ownership.

Paul's reference to the church as a household is important because believers are to relate to one another as family. Later in 1 Timothy, the apostle instructed Timothy: "Do not sharply rebuke an older man, but rather appeal to him as a father, to the younger men as brothers, the older women as mothers, and the younger women as sisters, in all purity" (5:1–2).

We Have a Distinctive Mission

You would expect a living body with a distinctive motivation and Master to have a distinctive mission, and that's what we find with the church. The mission, of course, is disciple-making. The distinctive of this mission is to proclaim truth. Paul pointed to this distinctive when he called the church "the pillar and support of the truth" (1 Timothy 3:15).

There is only one source of truth in the universe, which Paul said elsewhere is found "in Jesus" (Ephesians 4:21). And since Jesus has entrusted His Word of truth to the church, the church is to be the guardian and disseminator of the truth. No other body of people on earth has been given this assignment to uphold truth.

The church simply needs to convey God's truth in all of its clarity and power. Yes, we must also defend the truth from distortion and misrepresentation, but the best defense of truth is a good offense in which we are taking God's Word to the ends of the earth. Jesus said, "I am truth," not "I know the truth" or "I have access to the truth." He is the personification and embodiment of all that is true, so when we proclaim Him to the world we are giving people a sure standard against which to measure and judge all reality. Therefore, anything that does not line up to Jesus is false.

The church is distinctive in its message because we are obligated to proclaim the truth even when no one else agrees or stands with us.

But along with learning goes the need to live the truth. When Paul urged Titus, "Speak the things which are fitting for sound doctrine" (2:1), he explained why it was so important for Titus to teach sound doctrine. God was interested in the way the believers on Crete lived their lives. The goal of Titus's instruction was that Christians would "[show] all good faith so that they will adorn the doctrine of God our Savior in every respect" (v. 10).

To adorn means to decorate or dress something up in a way that makes it look nice and people are attracted to it. Local churches are to teach their members to "wear" God's truth by putting it on display in their daily lives. It's true that not everyone is looking for the truth, but many people will be attracted to believers whose lives correspond to truth.

We Have a Distinctive Message

The church's fourth and final distinctive in 1 Timothy 3 is our distinctive message. "By common confession, great is the mystery of godliness," Paul began in verse 16. This was a play on the worship of Artemis, because her followers in Ephesus used to chant, "Great is Artemis of the Ephesians."

The church's message is great too, summarized here as "the mystery of godliness." In the Bible, a mystery is not a puzzle or dilemma that no one can figure out, but a truth previously hidden that has now been revealed. The mystery that the church has been called to uphold and proclaim is all about the person and work of Christ, as the rest of verse 16 makes clear.

Most Bible teachers believe that the remainder of this verse was an early hymn that the church learned and recited to remind themselves of the truth. Notice that each line or stanza of this hymn is about Jesus. He is the mystery of God, "He who was revealed in the flesh, was vindicated in the

Spirit, seen by angels, proclaimed among the nations, believed on in the world, taken up in glory."

The church's message is Jesus from beginning to end. That's the only thing that makes us distinctive from any other body of people.

In 1 Timothy 3:16, Jesus was "revealed in the flesh." That's very important, because it does not say that Jesus originated in the flesh. He simply became visible in the flesh when He was born of the virgin Mary, but Jesus existed before His birthday. We call His conception and birth the incarnation because in it God took on human flesh. Isaiah said of the Messiah that a child would be born, but a Son would be given (see Isaiah 9:6). The child born in the manger of Bethlehem was already the Son of God. "The Word became flesh, and dwelt among us" (John 1:14).

Another declaration in the hymn of 1 Timothy 3:16 is that Jesus was "seen by angels." Angels were active at every important stage of Jesus' life. An angel foretold His birth, a whole choir of angels showed up at His birth, and angels guided Joseph at crucial points in the birth and early life of Jesus. Angels ministered to Jesus when He was tempted in the wilderness and on the cross. Angels were also there at the tomb to roll the stone away and announce His resurrection, and when Jesus returns the angels will be with Him.

When Jesus is proclaimed, the truth of the next stanza of 1 Timothy 3:16 follows. The Bible says that He is "believed on in the world." This is what we've been saying, that when the church presents the message of Christ in the power of the Holy Spirit, people will respond. People today are dying for something to believe in, and we have a unique Word to present about a unique Person.

Paul ended this great statement of faith by saying that Jesus Christ was "taken up in glory." This was His ascension, when He went up in the sight of the disciples and was lifted back to heaven (see Acts 1:9–11). Jesus' ascension was bodily, not just a spirit. He will also return bodily, because the angels at His ascension told the watching disciples, "This Jesus, who has been taken up from you into heaven, will come in just the same way as you have watched Him go into heaven" (Acts 1:11). Jesus is the distinct and unique message of the church. An old church in England had this sign on it: "We preach Christ crucified." But as time went on, some ivy began to grow over the sign and obscure part of it. Soon the only part of the sign that could be seen was, "We preach Christ." The ivy continued to grow, and before long the sign said, "We preach." But then even the word "preach" was blocked out, and all that was left was the word "We."

Unfortunately, what happened to the sign also told the story of what happened to this church. It began to surrender its calling of preaching Christ crucified, and the church began to die. By the time the sign out front showed just the one word "We," the church was a dark, empty building.

When all that a church has left is "We," that church is in trouble. For like a boxcar that has been disconnected from its train, when the church gets disconnected from Christ, it isn't going anywhere. Let's make sure that the church does not surrender its distinctive motivation, Master, mission, and message.

PERSONAL APPLICATION FOR LIFE

1. Who is the last person you shared Jesus Christ with? If you can't remember, you need to consider whether you're growing as a disciple the way you should. One mark of a person who wants to follow Christ, one absolute necessity for being His disciple, is to be His witness.

2. Sometimes it's difficult to get Christians to go into the world with the gospel. But the cults are going out with their message, and they are not apologizing. It may not mean going overseas or door-to-door in your neighborhood, but are you ready to ask God how you can tell others about your transformed life and the good news of Jesus?

3. There is no shortcut to being a disciple. It's difficult and it's costly. But the rewards are incredible both in this life and the next. Are you ready to go?

4. Have some of the truths of faith become "old hat" to you? Does the truth no longer strike you with the force it used to? Then it's time for you to get back into the Bible and start rediscovering God's timeless truths. One way to ignite the power of God's Word in your life is to act by faith on its promises and precepts.

FOR GROUP STUDY

Questions for Group Discussion

1. In Matthew 28:19, Jesus gave what is called the Great Commission. What does that commission involve? What must we do to fulfill it?

2. Discuss the concept of discipleship. What makes it such a powerful concept? How would you define a disciple of Jesus Christ?

3. Drawing from Matthew 28:19–20, what instructions did Jesus give us for making disciples? What did Jesus promise He would do that would enable His church to carry out the Great Commission? (Use the chart on the next page as an aid to your discussion.)

4. Read 1 Timothy 3:16. What makes the church's message so distinctive? What does the apostle Paul mean by the term "mystery"? Why does he refer to the church as a mystery?

PICTURE THIS

In Matthew 28:19–20, Jesus spells out how we are to go about making disciples. The process is based on three participles in His commission: going, baptizing, and teaching.

THE GREAT COMMISSION IN ACTION
Matthew 28:19–20

ACTION	SCRIPTURE PASSAGES	IN DETAIL
We must go to people.	verse 19; Acts 1:8	We must be willing to go out into the whole world to be Christ's witnesses.
We must help people identify with Christ.	verse 19; Romans 6:3–4	Baptizing those who have accepted Christ identifies them with Christ's death and resurrection to new life. Their identification with Christ brings them the benefits of His new covenant.
We must teach people.	verse 20; Mark 8:14–21	Making disciples is a process of spiritual development. The content of this teaching is the Word and its application to daily life.
Jesus promised us His presence.	verse 20	Jesus enabled us by giving us permission to use His name, authority, rights, and privileges. In addition, He promised us His abiding presence and power to carry out His commission.

76

THE POWER OF THE CHURCH

The church as the visible body of Christ on earth has been endowed with incredible, supernatural power. That power is activated when the Holy Spirit applies the Word of God to the hearts and minds of His people and energizes us for a life of godliness and service.

The Holy Spirit is the power of the church, in the same way that the engine in a car supplies the power to make the car go. Without this power source the church may look good, like a new car sitting in the parking lot. But we won't get anywhere. That's because living the Christian life without the active participation of the Holy Spirit is impossible. It is possible to know the Bible and not know the Lord, to memorize Bible verses and yet not be transformed, because only the Holy Spirit can make what is true in the Bible become real for you and me.

It is also impossible for the church to be the church that God intended us to be apart from the dynamic ministry of the Holy Spirit. That's because Jesus said, "Apart from Me you can do nothing" (John 15:5), and Jesus is the One who sent the Spirit to indwell and empower the church.

THE HOLY SPIRIT WAS PROMISED TO THE CHURCH

It was Jesus Himself who alerted us to the absolutely critical role that the Holy Spirit was to play in the church, and it was Jesus who promised to send the Spirit after His ascension back to the Father. On the night before His crucifixion, Jesus told the disciples, "It is to your advantage that I go away; for if I do not go away, the Helper will not come to you; but if I go, I will send Him to you" (John 16:7).

The Promised Spirit of Truth

Jesus then referred to the Spirit as "the Spirit of truth . . . [who] will guide you into all the truth" (v. 13). This is key to the Spirit's ministry since we have already seen that His basic job is to make God's truth come alive within us.

We could use many analogies for this process. The Spirit's work is like taking the still photographs of the Bible and turning them into a motion picture in our lives. Of course, the Bible is living and true and powerful whether we believe it or not. But the Word will lie dormant until the Holy Spirit comes and makes dead people alive and then plants the truth in their hearts.

The Promised Spirit of Power

Jesus also indicated that no Spirit equals no power. Just before His ascension, the Lord made another great promise to His apostles: "You will receive power when the Holy Spirit has come upon you; and you shall be My witnesses both in Jerusalem, and in all Judea and Samaria, and even to the remotest part of the earth" (Acts 1:8). This promise was fulfilled just a matter of days later at the birth of the church in Acts 2.

Think about what Jesus' promise really meant. The apostles had spent more than three years listening to Jesus teach and watching Him work. They had spent three-plus years absorbing truth from the eternal Son of God, who was preparing them to be foundation stones in His church (see Ephesians 2:19–20). Peter and the other apostles were not lacking for information to do what God wanted them to do.

But Jesus knew they were lacking in power. And even though He had been their Bible teacher, He told them that they wouldn't have power until the Holy Spirit came. According to Acts 1:4–5, Jesus prefaced His promise by telling the disciples not to leave Jerusalem until the promised Spirit had been given. The disciples did that, and then we read in Acts 2:

> When the day of Pentecost had come, they were all together in one place. And suddenly there came from heaven a noise like a violent rushing wind, and it filled the whole house where they were sitting. And there appeared to them tongues as of fire distributing themselves, and they rested on each one of them. And they were all filled with the Holy Spirit and began to speak with other tongues, as the Spirit was giving them utterance. (vv. 1–4)

Pentecost was the church's birthday, and it was the power and activity of the Holy Spirit that brought the church into being. The Spirit's presence was manifested as wind and fire, a powerful invasion from heaven that the disciples had never known before. The secret of the church's power lies in the filling, or empowering, of the Holy Spirit, a topic dealt with on the personal level in chapter 32. This chapter looks at its significance for the church's ministries.

When the Holy Spirit came with power, the disciples were able to speak in a way they had never been able to speak before, declaring the message of God in a number of languages they hadn't learned (Acts 2:5–11). They were able to do things they had never done before because they were filled with the Holy Spirit.

THE SPIRIT IS ACTIVE IN THE CHURCH

Since the day of Pentecost, the church as the people of God has been indwelt and energized by the Holy Spirit. I want to look briefly at several of the Spirit's distinct ministries to and through the church as they relate to our thesis, which the Bible clearly teaches, that the church's power resides in the Holy Spirit's person and work.

The Spirit Indwells Us

There is no saved member of the church of Jesus Christ who does not have the Holy Spirit living inside him or her. When the Spirit takes up residence in your life, He will never leave you. Jesus said of the Spirit's coming, "He . . . will be in you" (John 14:17). The Holy Spirit baptizes every believer into the body of Christ at the moment of salvation (see 1 Corinthians 12:13).

The Spirit Is Our Teacher

This is one of the Holy Spirit's most crucial, and yet too often overlooked or undervalued, ministries to the church. The Spirit is the church's divine Teacher. As we noted in the first paragraph, the Spirit's job is to take the Word of God and bring it alive in our lives. With all his Bible education, even your preacher is informed and taught the Word through the Spirit.

During His discourse in the Upper Room before the crucifixion, Jesus referred to the Spirit's future teaching ministry. "The Holy Spirit, whom the Father will send in My name, He will teach you all things, and bring to your remembrance all that I said to you" (John 14:26). And again, "When He, the Spirit of truth, comes, He will guide you into all the truth" (John 16:13). If you want to know the Word of God in all its power, you need God's Spirit for your Teacher.

We need to know the Bible, because the Holy Spirit only teaches and applies the Word. He is not interested in applying our philosophy or human reasoning. But the "letter" of the Word without the Spirit kills instead of bringing life.

The Spirit Equips Us for Ministry

The Bible teaches that the Holy Spirit is the source of the spiritual gifts that make it possible for the church to execute its ministry.

The apostle Paul wrote to the Corinthians concerning spiritual gifts, "Now there are varieties of gifts, but the same Spirit" (1 Corinthians 12:4). Going on to verse 7 we read, "But to each one is given the manifestation of the Spirit for the common good." And then after mentioning a number of gifts, Paul clinched his point that the Holy Spirit is sovereignly in charge of the gifts: "But one and the same Spirit works all these things, distributing to each one individually just as He wills" (v. 11).

THE SPIRIT FILLS THE CHURCH

The Bible says, "Do not get drunk with wine, for that is dissipation, but be filled with the Spirit" (Ephesians 5:18). This command is written in the plural, which means it is addressed to the whole church. More than that, it is a conditional command that requires us to continually be filled with the Spirit on an ongoing basis because the filling can be lost.

When we say that the Holy Spirit fills the church, we mean, of course, the believers who make up the church—both individually and in our corporate life when we come together as the body of Christ. The Holy Spirit's filling is commanded for every Christian, because the Word of God is designed to lead us to experience His supernatural power for holy living and ministry.

The Necessity of the Spirit's Filling

If this is true, we need to ask why more of us are not experiencing the supernatural—and by this I don't mean the spectacular stuff, but such an obvious power of God in our lives and in our churches that no natural explanation for what's happening will suffice. The short answer is that individual Christians and churches are not Spirit-filled. Why are more churches not seeing the supernatural power of God at work in their midst? Because they are not Spirit-filled churches made up of Spirit-filled people.

The word *filled* means "to come under the control of." That should give us a clue to the difference between indwelling and filling. The issue in filling is not how much of the Spirit we have, but how much of us the Spirit has. We need to be filled with the Spirit for the same reason we need to stop at a gas station if we plan to drive somewhere. We need fuel to energize the motor in our car.

Who Is Filling You?

If you are going to be filled with the Holy Spirit, you can't also be full of yourself, because the Spirit isn't going to take second place to your ego. What are the characteristics of people who are full of themselves? All they can think about and talk about is themselves, because they are all wrapped up in themselves.

Now turn that self-centeredness around and you have the characteristics of Spirit-filled people. All they can talk and think about is God and what He is doing because He is continuously flowing through them in the power of the Spirit. I love the way Jesus pictured the Spirit's ministry as a constantly flowing stream of water (see John 7:37–39). The Holy Spirit does not want to minister to us in little spurts, but as a continuously flowing stream that is constantly refreshing and renewing us. In other words, the Spirit's filling is meant to be a way of life.

How to Get the Filling

If it is so important for us as the church to be filled with the Holy Spirit, the next logical question to ask is how we can get the filling that God commands us to have. God would not give us such a command without telling us how to fulfill it. The question of how to be filled with the Holy Spirit is answered in the three verses that follow Ephesians 5:18.

After giving the command to be filled, Paul went on to write, "Speaking to one another in psalms and hymns and spiritual songs, singing and making melody with your heart to the Lord; always giving thanks for all things in the name of our Lord Jesus Christ to God, even the Father; and be subject to one another in the fear of Christ" (vv. 19–21).

As noted in pages 404–407 (chapter 32), it is in the act and the attitude of worship that believers are filled with the Spirit. A church that wants to be a Spirit-filled church must be a worshiping church. A family that wants to be Spirit-filled must be a worshiping family. And if you want to be Spirit-filled as an individual believer, you must know what worship means and know how to worship.

I'm not saying that you have to go to church in order to be filled with the Holy Spirit. You can go to church and not be a worshiper. You can go to church, sit back, and let the "professionals" on the stage do your worshiping for you.

But having said that, we shouldn't be surprised that the Spirit would grant His filling in the context of the church at worship. The Christian life was never intended to be a solo act. The Bible tells us to sing, not to and for ourselves alone, but "to one another" and to "the Lord." Our thanksgiving is to be directed to God the Father, and we are to be subject to one another, which means putting the interests of others ahead of our own and submitting to one another.

These things mentioned in Ephesians 5:19–21 are all forms of worship that put us in a dependent position in one way or another. They also require that we reach out to others for their benefit and blessing, not just our own. This is where the problem comes in, because too many believers don't want to be dependent worshipers. They want to be in control of their lives. They aren't that interested in blessing others because they're too caught up in themselves and their needs. But we've already seen that being filled with the Spirit means yielding to His control. Therefore, no worship means no Spirit filling.

You see, God is not interested in filling and blessing you just for you. He wants to work through you. That's why the Bible brings the saints into the equation when it talks about the Holy Spirit's filling.

Jesus told the woman at the well that God the Father is seeking people who will worship Him "in spirit and truth" (John 4:23). These are the kind of people on whom God is eager to pour out His power and blessings through the ministry of the Holy Spirit. This is the kind of church God wants us to be, so we can know the Spirit's power for ourselves and turn this world upside down for Him, just like the early church did (see Acts 17:6).

PERSONAL APPLICATION FOR LIFE

1. The church's power—both individually and corporately—resides in the Holy Spirit's person and work. As we are filled with the Holy Spirit, we are empowered to do God's work. The problem is that sometimes we are too filled with ourselves to be filled with the Spirit. If you're missing the Spirit's power in your life, pray this prayer: "Lord, I am desperate for You because I cannot be the person You want me to be and do what You have asked me to do without the filling and empowering of Your Holy Spirit." Then do what He tells your heart.

2. If you want to have an interesting family conversation at your next meal together, ask each member to try to identify his or her spiritual gift(s) (Romans 12, 1 Corinthians 12), and then talk about the ways God can use each of you to put your gifts to work for Him. Read Jesus' parable in Matthew 25:14-30 and stress the importance of using what He entrusts to us.

3. You don't have to know the Bible through and through to be witness for Christ. All you need to know is that you were lost in sin, that Jesus died for you, and that He lifted you out of your sin. Of course, you need to learn more, but don't wait unto you have it before you start doing something for the cause of Christ. Make yourself available, and God will use you.

4. Believers in the body of Christ have varying gifts and abilities, and we all benefit from each other's unique contributions. Look around and take note of the people whose faithfulness to the Lord and to His people blesses your life. Make it a point to let three people you know how much you appreciate them.

FOR GROUP STUDY

Questions for Group Discussion

1. The Holy Spirit is the power behind Christ's church on earth. Why did Jesus promise to send the Holy Spirit? What is the Spirit's role in the church?

2. What was the significance of Pentecost? Why was it such an important event for the church?

3. Read John 14:17, 26; 16:13; 1 Corinthians 12:4, 11. In what ways does the Holy Spirit minister to the church? (Use the chart below as an aid to your discussion.)

4. How are believers filled with the Spirit? What happens when God's people are filled with the Spirit?

PICTURE THIS

The Holy Spirit indwells and energizes God's people through several distinct ministries He performs to and through the church as shown below. It is through the Spirit's person and work that the church receives its power.

THE HOLY SPIRIT'S WORK IN BELIEVERS

SPECIFIC WORK	SCRIPTURE PASSAGE	WHAT IT DOES FOR US
The Spirit indwells us.	John 14:17	The Spirit's abiding presence in God's people gives them the power to accomplish the church's mission.
The Spirit is our teacher.	John 14:26; 16:13	The Holy Spirit teaches and applies the truth of God's Word to the lives of God's people.
The Spirit equips us for ministry.	1 Corinthians 12:4, 11	Because the Holy Spirit is the source of the spiritual gifts, He empowers God's people to exercise their gifts within the church.

SECTION II

THE MINISTRY OF THE CHURCH

77. THE WORSHIP OF THE CHURCH
78. THE FELLOWSHIP OF THE CHURCH
79. THE PROCLAMATION OF THE CHURCH
80. THE WITNESS OF THE CHURCH

7

THE WORSHIP OF THE CHURCH

People get together all the time to celebrate a friend or family member who is having a birthday or an anniversary, or who has earned a job promotion or some other honor. At these gatherings we expect to hear the invited guests speak well of the person being honored. The host or hostess may even ask several of the guests to tell what the honoree means to them or has done for them.

Celebrating special people on special occasions is in keeping with one of the primary definitions of the word *celebrate*, which is "to hold up for public acclaim." What we have just described is what the church is supposed to do when we come together as a body to worship our God and Head of the church. Corporate worship is the collective celebration of God for who He is, what He has done, and what we are trusting Him to do.

WORSHIP LIFTS UP THE LORD OF THE CHURCH

A phrase in the opening verses of Ephesians captures the basic content of the church's worship. There are a number of individual components to worship, but Ephesians 1:3 gives its foundation: "*Blessed* be the God and Father of our Lord Jesus Christ" (italics added).

Offering God Our Praise

The word *blessed* is from the Greek word *eulogia*, which means "to speak well of." You may recognize this as the source of the English word *eulogy*, which unfortunately we have come to associate only with funerals. But although the world may reserve its eulogies for the dead, the Bible calls the church to eulogize or speak well of our living God, and we do this when we gather for worship. "It is good to give thanks to the Lord and to sing praises to Your name, O Most High" (Psalm 92:1).

You can see these elements of worship in a classic passage from Psalm 100, in which the psalmist calls us to worship: "Enter [God's] gates with thanksgiving and His courts with praise. Give thanks to Him, bless His name. For the Lord is good; His lovingkindness is everlasting and His faithfulness to all generations" (vv. 4–5).

Thanksgiving in the Bible is usually associated with worshiping God for what He has done, while blessing the Lord or praising Him often speaks about who He is. That's not a hard-and-fast rule, but it helps us see the various ways that we are to worship God.

In Ephesians 1, Paul gave us a great clue about what our worship should focus on. Paul rejoiced in the salvation God provided in Christ and also rejoiced that He did it "to the praise of the glory of His grace" (v. 6). Later Paul said that God designed it so that we who have trusted in Christ would be "to the praise of His glory" (v. 12).

Magnifying God's Glory

Our job as worshipers in the church is to praise and exalt the glory of our great God.

In Psalm 34:3, David issued this invitation to corporate worship: "O *magnify* the Lord with me, and let us exalt His name together" (v. 3, italics added).

What happens when something is magnified? It is made to appear bigger in the eye of the person looking through the magnifying glass. God already fills the universe and eternity. There is no lack in God that requires us to magnify Him so He will look big.

Instead, the key is what I said above, that when we magnify something it looks bigger to us. The idea of magnifying the Lord is that when you focus your praise lens on Him, you see Him for the great and awesome God that He really is, and suddenly God looks bigger than your problems or your circumstances—which is the way things are supposed to look to believers.

That's the power worship has to change us when we go together into God's presence in His house. Have you ever gone to church when God seemed small and distant, and left with Him seeming big and close because you were drawn closer to Him in worship? That's what happens when we magnify the Lord and bless His name together.

The Power of Collective Praise

It's true that any believer can worship God anywhere. But God never meant that to be a substitute for the church's collective worship. That's why the Bible exhorts us not to forsake assembling ourselves together (see Hebrews 10:25). The fact is that a lot of good things happen when the church gathers that are missing in private worship.

Two of those good things are found in the two verses immediately preceding Hebrews 10:25. "Let us hold fast the confession of our hope without wavering," and, "Let us consider how to stimulate one another to love and good deeds" (vv. 23–24). You will hold fast to your confession in Christ a lot better when you have other Christians around you holding up your hands in encouragement and calling you to accountability. Also, it's pretty hard to stimulate other believers to love and good deeds when you're not with them. And since God also promises to meet with His people (see Matthew 18:20), there is a definite sense in which the presence of God is among His people in a special way when we join together to worship Him.

Showing God Off

We are told in Psalm 29:2, "Ascribe to the Lord the glory due to His name; worship the Lord in holy array." To ascribe glory to the Lord means to show Him off, to put Him on display so everyone can see how glorious and wonderful He is. Glorifying the Lord means that you want His name to become greater and greater.

The Bible calls us to give God the glory that is due Him. God has intrinsic glory that is an essential part of His person. God is glorious because His nature is filled with glory. "May the whole earth be filled with His glory" the psalmist declared (Psalm 72:19). God calls His church together to recognize who He is, worship Him, and magnify His glory. We go to the house of the Lord to meet with the Lord of the house. His name is due all the glory, and the church has been given the glorious task of declaring God's glory to the world.

WORSHIP LIFTS THE CHURCH TO A HIGHER SPIRITUAL EXPERIENCE

Another reason the church gathers for worship is that when we lift the Lord up, He lifts us up to a higher place that only those who know and worship Him can reach. This higher place is described in Ephesians 1:3, which we need to look at again, this time adding the second phrase: "Blessed be the God and Father of our Lord Jesus Christ, who has blessed us with every spiritual blessing in the heavenly places in Christ."

Reaching the Heavenly Places

We bless the Lord who has already blessed us with every spiritual resource we will ever need to live the way He wants us to live and do what He wants us to do. But notice where these blessings are located. They are in "the heavenly places," which refers to the spiritual realm where the capital of the universe is located and where God rules. That's where you and I need to go for our blessings, and worship takes us there.

One of the fundamental principles of Scripture is that everything in the physical realm is initiated in or influenced by the spiritual realm. Most of our problems, struggles, and needs are in the physical realm, but if we never access the heavenly places where our Lord and our spiritual blessings are located, then our solutions will be limited to the physical level, which is always temporary. If you want to fix something that's wrong in the physical realm, but affected by the spiritual realm, you have to go to the spiritual realm for your solution.

Seeing God Face-to-Face

A lot of Christians don't ever get to heavenly places because they don't know how to worship. In the opening chapters of the book of Revelation, the risen Lord Jesus is moving among the golden lampstands that represent the church. He is moving among His people, and He has a message that He wants the angel, or the pastor, of each church to deliver to the people.

But the Lord also knows that not everyone in the church is listening to Him or seeking Him, which is why He ends each message of Revelation 2–3 with these words: "He who has an ear, let him hear what the Spirit says to the churches" (see Revelation 2:7 as an example). God is speaking to the whole church, but only those who are tuned to God in worship will respond to the message.

Worship transforms you to a higher place, where the Holy Spirit moves and works. But this is not just an individual thing with you and Jesus and no one else. Paul said the church is "being fitted together, [and] is growing into a holy temple in the Lord, in whom you also are being built together into a dwelling of God in the Spirit" (Ephesians 2:21–22). God wants us to understand that we are part of something bigger than our own small world.

When the people of God join in His praise, worship, and adoration, His Spirit is free to work in mighty ways. He lifts us to another kingdom, where there is peace, joy, power, goodness, grace, and mercy. This is a totally different world than any you have ever known before, and it can be accessed as you bless the Lord in community with the saints.

WORSHIP SHOULD BE THE CHURCH'S PRIORITY

Knowing this ought to make worship a priority for all of us, something we do first instead of last. The psalmist who wrote Psalm 73 in despair over the seeming prosperity of the wicked was about ready to give up. Things didn't change for him until he made his way to God's sanctuary to enter His presence. Then his perspective on earth changed because he saw the spiritual reality behind the physical world around him.

The church experienced the same thing in Acts 4 when Peter and John had been arrested for preaching Christ. They were released with threats, but the church members came together and lifted up their voices to God in praise and supplication (see Acts 4:23–30). When they finished their prayer the Bible says, "The place where they had gathered together was shaken, and they were all filled with the Holy Spirit and began to speak the word of God with boldness" (v. 31). The church was lifted to heavenly places and got the real story on the situation, which caused them to preach Christ rather than fear the authorities.

When you go to church, you ought to go hungry to worship God and enter the heavenly realm. One reason God allows things to go wrong during the week is to make you hungry for Him. He'll make you dependent to drive you to His house where you can meet Him. When you are in desperate need of God, then you are ready to worship Him because you know you have a hunger and a need that He alone can satisfy.

WORSHIP CONNECTS THE CHURCH WITH GOD'S POWER

Worship that lifts the name of the Lord and lifts you to a higher realm also puts you in connection with God's power. I love the way Paul linked worship with power in his prayer of Ephesians 3:

> I bow my knees before the Father, from whom every family in heaven and on earth derives its name, that He would grant you, according to the riches of His glory, to be strengthened with power through His Spirit in the inner man, so that Christ may dwell in your hearts through faith; and that you, being rooted and grounded in love, may be able to comprehend with all the saints what is the breadth and length and height and depth, and to know the love of Christ which surpasses knowledge, that you may be filled up to all the fullness of God. (vv. 14–19)

Most of the time when we quote this passage, we quote it as a personal and private promise of God's power. But that's not what the text says. This is plural, written to the church as Christ's body when we gather to worship Him. Verses 20–21 also make this very clear. "Now to Him who is able to do far more abundantly beyond all that we ask or think, according to the power that works within us, to Him be the glory in the church and in Christ Jesus to all generations forever and ever. Amen."

Experiencing God's Power Together

There is power in our worship, because when the saints of God bless His name together He is able to do abundant things, far beyond anything we can imagine.

When the family of God worships and prays together, then we can get ready to see something happen. Then we will see God doing "far more abundantly beyond all that we ask or think." It's the difference between one person standing in the darkness with a little candle, and a whole group of people lighting the candles of the people next to them. Many churches have a service like this at Christmas or some other special time when they give everyone candles and then turn out the lights in the sanctuary. As each candle is lit, the light grows. It's a powerful reminder of why we need the body of Christ.

Experiencing God's Blessings Together

Zechariah 14:17 is an amazing passage of Scripture. The prophet was speaking of Christ's millennial kingdom when He will rule over all the earth from His throne in Jerusalem: "And it will be that whichever of the families of the earth does not go up to Jerusalem to worship the King, the Lord of hosts, there will be no rain on them."

Rain is symbolic of God's blessings. God says that people who don't have time to worship Him will not experience His blessings. But when His glory is important enough for people to acknowledge through worship at His house, then those people's needs will be answered not with a few sprinkles here and there, but with showers of blessing.

PERSONAL APPLICATION FOR LIFE

1. God wants to hear you say, "I will bless the Lord at all times; His praise shall continually be in my mouth" (Psalm 34:1). Are you ready to worship God? Do you desire above all to praise Him, to give Him the glory due His name? Worship is an absolute necessity if you are going to follow Christ.

2. God wants you to advertise Him. He wants you to show forth His qualities and His nature. Why? Because He is the invisible God. People can only see what God look like by watching us. Do you advertise God well?

3. When you worship, you draw near to God. Drawing near to Him is like putting yourself under an X-ray machine—it exposes your sin. That's why in worship we need to pray, "God, search me and show me what I really am." When you worship God, you need to be ready to come clean with Him and approach Him with a sincere heart.

4. How hungry are you to encounter God in worship and be transported to heavenly places? The degree of your hunger will determine the degree of your satisfaction. Often, when we are in desperate need of God, we are ready to worship Him. Do you have a hunger and need that only He can satisfy?

FOR GROUP STUDY

Questions for Group Discussion

1. According to Ephesians 1:3, what is the foundation of true worship? What is the significance of the word *blessed*? How does that relate to worship?

2. Read Psalm 34:3. What happens when we magnify the Lord? Why is there power in collective praise of God? What does it accomplish? (Use the chart on the next page as an aid to your discussion.)

3. What does it mean for believers to be in the "heavenly places in Christ"? What do we find there?

4. Read Ephesians 3:14–19 as preparation for discussion. In what ways does worship connect us with God's power?

PICTURE THIS

Ephesians 1:3 provides us the foundation of worship: "Blessed be the God and Father of our Lord Jesus Christ." Dr. Evans identifies four different ways we lift up God in our worship.

When We Lift Up God in Our Worship

OUR ACT OF WORSHIP	SCRIPTURE PASSAGE	WHAT HAPPENS
We offer God our praise.	Psalm 92	When we praise God and offer our thanksgiving, we speak well of Him.
We magnify God's glory.	Psalm 34:3	When we magnify God, all else diminishes, and we see His greatness as it really is.
We collectively praise God.	Hebrews 10:23–25	When we worship collectively, the presence of God is among His His people in a special way.
We show off God.	Psalm 29:2; 72:19	We show off God when we give Him His due glory and declare His glory to the world.

78

THE FELLOWSHIP OF THE CHURCH

One of the most fundamental realities about the church of Jesus Christ is that anyone who is a child of God is also related to the rest of God's children, because the Bible says, "We are members of one another" (Ephesians 4:25). Believers are knit together in a bond of family fellowship that is critical to the church's function. None of us is in this thing alone.

The church's fellowship is a relational reality that reflects the relational nature of God. God has never known what it is like to be alone, because one of the foundational truths of our faith is that God is a triune being, eternally existing as Father, Son, and Holy Spirit in a perfect fellowship of distinct Persons who share the same essence. Jesus said at one point in His earthly ministry, "He who sent Me is with Me; He has not left Me alone, for I always do the things that are pleasing to Him" (John 8:29).

So we ought not be surprised that relationships are very important to God. The only thing that God said was not good about His creation was that Adam was "alone" (Genesis 2:18). The first relational statement made about the human race was that God did not design us to function as isolated units. When Jesus chose His twelve disciples, Mark noted that one of Jesus' purposes was "so that they would be with Him" (Mark 3:14).

THE REALITY OF OUR FELLOWSHIP

Fellowship is so important to the church's proper functioning that it stands as one of the foundational activities we are to engage in, along with discipleship, worship, proclamation, and evangelism. The Greek term for the church's fellowship is *koinonia*, which basically means "to share" or "hold in common." What we hold in common as the church, the thing that brings us together from a myriad of cultures and races and backgrounds, is our faith in Jesus Christ.

So let me give you a more formal definition of Christian fellowship. It is the mutual sharing of the life of Christ among believers. The church is a family affair, a group of people coming together so all can partake of our mutual faith in Christ.

Fellowship in the Truth

The Bible has a lot to say about the church's fellowship, and no book is more important on this subject than 1 John. In fact, John the apostle made this statement about his purpose in writing this letter to the church: "What we have seen and heard we proclaim to you also, so that you too may have fellowship [*koinonia*] with us; and indeed our fellowship is with the Father, and with His Son Jesus Christ" (1:3).

The rest of 1 John makes it abundantly clear that John's concern was not just that believers enjoy some good times together. He wanted to make sure that the church's coming together was anchored in the truth about who Jesus Christ is and what He did for us on the cross.

One interesting clue to the important place that fellowship holds in the body of Christ is found in Galatians 2:9. Paul said that when the church in Jerusalem recognized that God was working through him and Barnabas, then "James and Cephas and John, who were reputed to be pillars, gave to me and Barnabas the right hand of fellowship." That is, these leaders signaled that they were one in unity and purpose with Paul and Barnabas, and members of the same body. The word *fellowship* here is almost a synonym for the church.

The Two Dimensions of Fellowship

Biblical fellowship has two dimensions, the vertical and the horizontal. John said, "Our fellowship is with the Father, and with His Son Jesus

Christ." This is the vertical aspect of fellowship, while the horizontal concerns our relationship with one another. Both aspects are crucial.

For instance, if there is no vertical fellowship with God, then whatever we do on earth is without real meaning because it is not based on truth. John wrote, "If we say that we have fellowship with [God] and yet walk in the darkness, we lie and do not practice the truth" (1 John 1:6).

If we have horizontal fellowship but no vertical fellowship, then we are not holding to a common faith, which is the very basis of biblical fellowship. But if we have vertical fellowship without horizontal fellowship, then the thing we're holding in common is not benefiting anybody but us. If God only had one spiritual child, he or she wouldn't have to worry about fellowship on earth. But God's family is full of children from every corner of the world.

How Fellowship Reveals the Unseen

Why is fellowship so important to the church? Why does God place us in an environment of *koinonia*? One reason is that He wants to make the invisible visible through you and me. Later in his first epistle, John made an important statement: "Beloved, if God so loved us, we also ought to love one another. No one has seen God at any time; if we love one another, God abides in us, and His love is perfected in us" (1 John 4:11–12).

You can't see God, who is invisible. But His presence in your life becomes real as you love your brothers and sisters in Christ's body. God will make Himself at home in your life through the Holy Spirit, and His presence will become visibly real to you—not through your physical eyes, but in terms of your spiritual experience. He will give you the vertical reality you're looking for as you make the horizontal connection with other believers.

How Fellowship Validates Our Faith

Our participation in the body also validates the reality of our relationship with God. That's what 1 John 4:11–12 is saying. You cannot have intimate fellowship with God if He cannot have intimate fellowship through you to somebody else. Someone has said that the only Jesus some people will see is the Jesus they see in us. That's true not only for lost people, but it's true in the church as well. God becomes real to us, and to others, when He works through us to touch their lives.

So if your life is a spiritual cul-de-sac, with no outlet, instead of a conduit, you are cutting off a large portion of God's blessing to and through you. If you don't have time to minister to somebody else, God says He doesn't have time to minister to you. God is so big that we cannot possibly see or comprehend even a small portion of the totality of His being. But the quality of our fellowship gives us a valve or gauge that indicates whether God is working within us.

THE POWER OF OUR FELLOWSHIP

There is power in authentic, biblical fellowship. The Holy Spirit works uniquely when believers are in dynamic relationship with God and with one another. The early church's experience is a classic example of this power.

The Power of a Shared Commitment

As those first disciples waited for the coming of the Spirit that Jesus had promised, the Bible says, "These all with one mind were continually devoting themselves to prayer" (Acts 1:14). Then on the day of Pentecost "they were all together in one place" (Acts 2:1) when the Spirit came with the sound of a rushing wind.

And in the days following Pentecost as the church ministered and grew, the believers faithfully devoted themselves to fellowship along with the teaching of the Word, sharing the Lord's Supper, and prayer (see Acts 2:42). Verse 44 also makes a very insightful statement: "All those who had believed were together and had all things in common," which is another form of the word *koinonia*.

Because these Christians practiced true fellowship, they had no problem sharing their possessions with anyone who was in need (see v. 45; Barnabas is the great example of this generosity, as we'll see later). The church was also of "one mind," and the believers "were taking their meals together with gladness and sincerity of heart" (v. 46). No wonder Acts 2 concludes, "And the Lord was adding to their number day by day those who were being saved" (v. 47). This church had power with God and power with people.

True *koinonia* let's God do more for us, and it lets His Holy Spirit do more among us. When the church is united in spirit and purpose, we will see God do things among us and through us that we are not likely to see happen apart from that dynamic relationship of believers. We saw that Ephesians 5:18 commands us to be filled with the Holy Spirit and then sets that filling in the context of our ministry to one another in the body of Christ. The church in the books of Acts was together when they were filled with the Spirit. The Spirit invaded the whole environment.

The Power of Generosity

There is one especially powerful example of the church's *koinonia* at the end of Acts 4 and the beginning of Acts 5. These verses are a study in contrasts between the church at large and Barnabas in particular, and a couple named Ananias and Sapphira.

Acts 4:32 tells us, "The congregation of those who believed were of one heart and soul; and not one of them claimed that anything belonging to him was his own, but all things were common property to them." The believers in Jerusalem were so closely knit together in heart, so drawn together as members of one another, that they didn't even bother to distinguish one person's possessions from another's.

The result was "there was not a needy person among them" (v. 34). These Christians were all on the same page when it came to meeting needs in the congregation. They were all pulling in the same direction.

Notice the impact of the church's fellowship: "And with great power the apostles were giving testimony to the resurrection of the Lord Jesus, and abundant grace was upon them all" (Acts 4:33). The power of God was greatly evident among them, and His abundant grace rested upon them. These people got to see God do things that were far beyond church business as usual. And they experienced grace that was, as the hymn says, greater than all their needs. God's power and grace show up when the church is fellowshiping according to His standards.

Barnabas stepped out of this context and distinguished himself by an extraordinary act of generosity. He sold a piece of land he owned, then "brought the money and laid it at the apostles' feet" (Acts 4:37). That's the end of his part, because nothing else needed to be said. Barnabas gave it all.

But then we come to Ananias and Sapphira (see Acts 5:1–11), who tried to enjoy God's full blessing while holding out on Him and their fellow believers in need. You can read the story of how they lied to the Holy Spirit and paid for their sin with their lives. Ananias and Sapphira were struck dead because they lied to God and because of the damage that their lie did. These two were pretending to minister to their fellow Christians who were hurting, but by their actions they hurt the body of Christ.

THE CONTEXT OF OUR FELLOWSHIP

The Bible makes it clear that the church's fellowship occurs in the context of our assembling together. There are three important admonitions to the church in Hebrews 10, which the writer sets in this context: "Since we have a great priest over the house of God" (v. 21). In other words, he is speaking to the collective church as the household or family of God. In other words, we do not assemble just to hear good sermons, but also to form meaningful relationships that build one another up in the faith.

Since we have Jesus Christ ministering as our great high priest, we need to do three things. First, "Let us draw near" together before Him in worship (Hebrews 10:22), "Let us hold fast" to our common faith (v. 23), and "Let us consider how to stimulate one another to love and good deeds, not forsaking our own assembling together" (vv. 24–25). This is a powerful formula for a church that wants to establish a context or environment in which dynamic, biblical fellowship can flourish.

We could summarize these commands by saying, "Let us not stay at home and draw back from one another in isolation, but let us draw near to God and to one another so we can hang in there together and be strong." Hebrews 10:25 says it is "the habit of some" to forsake the assembly. This is the Easter and Christmas crowd, the people who have little experience of the life and power of God because they have forsaken the family.

Notice what happens when the church is united in true fellowship. We not only stimulate each other to love and good works, but we encourage each other (see Hebrews 3:13; 10:25b). If the Devil's favorite weapon is discouragement, then we had better be encouraging one another. If you want to become discouraged and tempted to give up, just try going it alone day after day and week after week. This is why it is crucial that churches develop mechanisms to teach people on an intimate individual level. Whether it be through home groups, ministry groups, or Sunday school classes, every church must make sure it facilitates biblical fellowship for every member of the body.

The church's fellowship reminds me of a wicker chair. One or two strands of a wicker chair could not hold a person's weight by themselves, but when enough strands are woven together, the chair can easily bear a person's weight. It's the sum total of the wicker strands joined in "fellowship" that makes the chair work. No pastor can bear the weight of a congregation alone without collapsing. That's why all of us have to work hard at developing *koinonia*.

Paul wrote, "Blessed be the God and Father of our Lord Jesus Christ, the Father of mercies and God of all comfort, who comforts us in all our affliction so that we will be able to comfort those who are in any affliction with the comfort with which we ourselves are comforted by God" (2 Corinthians 1:3–4). As God meets us in our need for comfort or encouragement, He also enables us and even expects us to meet someone else's need.

You see, too many people look at the service of fellowship as an irritation or an interruption instead of an opportunity to serve others. But God meets our needs so that we can be ready when it's our turn to comfort someone else. You know a church is growing and making progress when in addition to its "official" ministries of helping the sick and lonely and hurting, individual believers are being led by the Holy Spirit to reach out to others in unofficial ways.

Whenever the Spirit brings someone to mind and tugs on your heart to help that person, He is saying, "It's your turn to serve." That's why when we gather as the church, it's not just to pray and sing and hear the Word, but to allow the Holy Spirit opportunities to sensitize our hearts toward others and show us how we can serve the body.

APPLICATION FOR LIFE

1. In the Upper Room, the disciples were arguing over who was the greatest among them. Without a word, Jesus picked up a towel and began washing the disciples' feet. He did so to serve them. True fellowship demands that we serve each other without waiting to be told. When was the last time you picked up a towel and did whatever you had to do to serve someone else?

2. God wants us to be mature disciples, but that won't happen without meaningful fellowship. This means you must do two things. You must carve out time to be with God, and you must carve out time to be with others. Unfortunately, convenient time to do either one will not simply fall into your lap. Are you willing to take the steps to make both a priority?

3. The church is a household, a family. When it comes to family, everyone has to contribute. Each family member relates to other members of the family. That is the way the church is supposed to work. It is to be an environment of shared lives where each other's spiritual needs are met. Are you pulling your weight in God's household of believers?

4. No one said it would be easy to confront a brother or sister living in sin. But it is crucial. If you know someone who is making Jesus Christ look bad and risking God's judgment, pray for the courage and opportunity to confront the problem. If a third party is close enough to the offender to help, you might consider taking along a brother or sister in Christ.

FOR GROUP STUDY

Questions for Group Discussion

1. What is the definition of *koinonia*, or Christian fellowship? What are the two dimensions of Christian fellowship, and how do they function?

2. Read John 4:11–12. How is it that in the environment of Christian fellowship, the invisible becomes visible? What realities emerge in this environment?

3. In what ways does the Holy Spirit work within believers to give fellowship its power?

4. Read Hebrews 10:25. The New Testament stresses the importance of believers assembling together. What are some of the reasons believers need to assemble in worship and fellowship? What benefits come from the gathering of believers?

PICTURE THIS

The content of Christian fellowship may be summed up by at least four key exhortations given to us in Scripture. They are critical to the concept of fellowship.

THE CONTENT OF OUR CHRISTIAN FELLOWSHIP

MINISTRY OF FELLOWSHIP	SCRIPTURE PASSAGES	WHAT IT INVOLVES
Love one another.	John 13:34–35	Biblical love is truth in action and is at the heart of Christian fellowship.
Serve one another.	1 Corinthians 9:10; 2 Corinthians 4:5; Galatians 5:13	This involves using our spiritual gifts to minister to one another within the body of Christ.
Restore one another.	Galatians 6:1-2	This involves bearing the burden of an erring brother or sister in such a way that he or she is restored.
Comfort one another.	1 Thessalonians 4:18; 5:11; Romans 15:14	This involves building up and encouraging fellow believers when circumstances have torn them up or worn them down.

79

THE PROCLAMATION OF THE CHURCH

The Bible is amazingly clear and concise when it comes to the heart of the church's proclamation. Talking about God's Word in the context of the church's ministry takes us back to the Pastoral Epistles, the books of 1 and 2 Timothy and Titus that tell us how the church of God ought to function.

WHAT WE NEED TO PROCLAIM

In this chapter I want us to consider several passages from 2 Timothy, particularly 2 Timothy 4:1–4, which addresses the church's proclamation. This is the Bible speaking of itself, for the apostle Paul instructed Timothy, the pastor at Ephesus, "I solemnly charge you in the presence of God and of Christ Jesus, who is to judge the living and the dead, and by His appearing and His kingdom: *preach the word*" (vv. 1–2a, italics added).

The Centrality of God's Word

I love the Bible's simplicity. When Paul told Timothy, and all the pastors and teachers who would follow him, to declare God's Word, it was like taking a Bible, putting it into his hand, and saying, "This is your message." I know that the whole Bible had not been revealed, written down, and conveniently bound together in one volume in Paul's day, but the message to the church is the same. Whatever else the church does, we need to proclaim the Word of God in its entirety.

In fact, we have no excuse whatsoever for failing to preach the Bible, because we do have the entire Word of God in our hands. Years before writing 2 Timothy, Paul had told the elders at Ephesus, "I did not shrink from declaring to you the whole purpose of God" (Acts 20:27). Any church that can say this is doing a lot of things right. The Word must be central.

We live in a world where everybody wants to have things their own way. But the authoritative word has not been spoken until God has said it. And God has spoken in His Word. Our job is simply to deliver the message, the way a king's herald in medieval days would ride into a town, unroll the scroll of the king's message, and read it to the king's subjects, who were then obligated to obey. To preach is to declare what God has to say to His people, that they might understand the expectations and demands of the King.

The Power of Biblical Preaching

Biblical preaching confronts men and women with God through His Word, inspired and energized by the Holy Spirit, filtered through the personality of the pastor, so that the church will understand and respond to Him. Proclamation involves reading, explaining, and applying the Word.

God want His church to preach the Word because we spend too much time listening to and studying the words of men, and too little time coming to grips with what God has said to us. You aren't going to find the world grappling with the Word, but there ought to be one place where you can go and get the real deal about what God thinks on the issues of life. That place is the church, the only entity on earth specifically charged with the responsibility of holding forth God's Word. The Bible is like a telescope. If you look through it, you can see the world far beyond. But if you just look at it, you don't see anything. The great danger is that the church will look at the Word and not through it.

So we need to make sure that the message we are delivering to the church is "Thus saith the Lord," not "Thus thinketh the pastor." I tell our people at church that if they want to know my personal opinions, call me at home, because in the pulpit my job is to deliver the King's message. I need to be evaluated as a pastor by how faithfully I preach the whole Word of God, not by whether I can move people to tears or shouts or impress them with my eloquence. The question is, Does what I say agree with what God says?

WHEN WE NEED TO PROCLAIM GOD'S WORD

Second Timothy 4:2 contains another needed word to the church concerning our biblical proclamation. Paul wrote, "Preach the word; be ready in season and out of season."

The Greek word *season* literally means "convenient." The answer to the "when" question concerning the church's proclamation of the Word is at any and every time, whether it's convenient or not.

That has a lot of applications. For a pastor it means to preach the Word no matter whether the congregation is saying amen or sitting and glaring. Preach the Word whether doing so reaps praise or anger. Preach the good parts that make everyone smile, but don't neglect the tough passages that have a hard message for God's people.

God commands His church to preach His Word all the time because there is no season and no time when God's people do not need to hear from Him. There is a reason that we don't go through the Bible once and then move on to something else. An old advertising slogan used to say, "You never outgrow your need for milk." I can't comment on the nutritional accuracy of that statement, but I can say with authority that we will never outgrow our need for God's Word. In fact, most of us need the inconvenient, "out of season" messages more than we might like to admit.

With today's increased emphasis on "praise and worship" in the church, one of the things we have to be careful of is that the declaration of God's Word doesn't become devalued. With all the talented worship teams and catchy worship choruses the modern church has, it might be "convenient" for a pastor just to read a verse or two and offer a few thoughts at the end of the service and send the people home. But the church is not a performance center; it is a guardian of the truth.

Earlier in 2 Timothy, Paul wrote, "Retain the standard of sound words which you have heard from me. . . . Guard, through the Holy Spirit who dwells in us, the treasure which has been entrusted to you" (1:13–14), which is the Word of God. We have learned from 9/11 that we need to be on guard at all times, even when it's not convenient.

HOW WE NEED TO PROCLAIM GOD'S WORD

When the church is faithful to proclaim the Word of God, lives will be changed, because the Bible deals with the central issues of life through its principles and examples. We're not left in the dark as to how to preach the Word, thanks to our key verse in 2 Timothy 4:2 and another passage just above it in verse 16 of chapter 3.

There are a lot of important terms in these two texts that describe the effect the Word of God will have when it is applied to people's lives. Obviously, this doesn't have to be done exclusively by preaching, but the church's public proclamation of the Scriptures was Paul's concern in 2 Timothy 4, and that's our focus. In that context the apostle instructed Pastor Timothy, "Preach the word . . . reprove, rebuke, exhort, with great patience and instruction" (v. 2). Before we look at these terms, let's add 3:16: "All Scripture is inspired by God and profitable for teaching, for reproof, for correction, for training in righteousness."

There is some overlap in these two lists, but when we put them all together, what emerges is an amazing picture of the power the Word has to shape and correct people's lives. The Word, and only the Word, has this power, because it is "inspired by God." From cover to cover the Bible is true or inerrant, which means without any error at all. Since the Author of Scripture is perfect, it is impossible for the product not to be perfect. The God of truth can only produce truth.

Proclaim the Word as Truth

So the fundamental answer to the question of how the Bible is to be preached and taught is that we are to present it as truth—absolute truth—without apologizing or stuttering. Remember that the church is "the pillar and support of the truth" (1 Timothy 3:15).

We know the Bible is true because this is the testimony God gives us concerning His Word. We need to keep coming back to Jesus' statement, "Your word is truth" (John 17:17). And because the Word is truth without any mixture of error, it can do what no other book can do. God's Word produces lasting results when it is faithfully and fully taught. Let's look at some of these results.

Preach the Word for Results

The apostle began with the word *reprove* (4:2), the same Greek word translated in a slightly different form in 2 Timothy 3:16 as "reproof." This means basically to tell someone what is wrong, not just to chastise but with a view to changing the wrong behavior. The Bible has an incredible ability to point up areas of sin and shortcoming in our lives. A preacher doesn't have to know what is happening with all the people in the congregation. All he has to do is preach the Word, and the Holy Spirit makes the application.

Timothy was also told to *rebuke* when necessary. This is a different word that means to bring a person under the conviction of guilt.

The next word in the list of 2 Timothy 4:2 is *exhort*. Although reproof and rebuke are negative, this is the term for encouragement, the arm around the shoulder in support, urging the person along the right path. Biblical encouragement is more than just saying, "Hang in there" to someone. It has content because it is based in the Word. The best way I can encourage people as a pastor it to preach and teach God's Word faithfully and consistently.

The content of our rebuke, reproof, and encouragement is found in the words *instruction* (2 Timothy 4:2) and *teaching* (3:16). These are two forms of the same word, with the emphasis on what is taught and not so much on the method of teaching. We've already seen that the Scriptures themselves are the church's textbook for living.

When we preach the Word in the power of the Spirit, we can expect the results of such preaching, for the Word is more than adequate to rebuke and convict.

Preach It with Authority

One other verse is important here because it provides a further clue as to how the church should proclaim the Word. Paul instructed Titus, his other pastoral representative, who was assigned to the island of Crete, "These things speak and exhort and reprove with all authority. Let no one disregard you" (Titus 2:15). The church's preaching must be done with authority because in the Bible we have the truth, the whole truth, and nothing but the truth.

No pastor who is preaching the Word needs to apologize for the message. People need an absolute and absolutely reliable standard by which to measure their lives.

WHY WE NEED TO PROCLAIM THE BIBLE

Why must we preach the Word in all of its convicting and teaching power? Because people need to hear the truth and feed on healthy spiritual doctrine, and because they aren't likely to get this if left on their own.

This is the positive side of Paul's admonition concerning the necessity of preaching the Word: "For the time will come when they will not endure sound doctrine; but wanting to have their ears tickled, they will accumulate for themselves teachers in accordance to their own desires, and will turn away their ears from the truth and will turn aside to myths" (2 Timothy 4:3–4).

Human nature is such that people will get itchy ears and begin to gravitate toward teachers who will only say what they want to hear. If all you care about is attracting a crowd, start a "doughnut" church whose primary goal is to make people feel good and be happy about themselves. In a church like this people can get any kind of doughnut they want, with as much glaze over the truth as they want, and it will all taste sweet. But the result will be a group of people on a temporary "sugar high" who will stumble and falter someday for lack of solid spiritual nourishment.

Now I'm not saying it will always be easy to preach the truth, or to hear and obey it. When my granddaughter and I make our morning run to the doughnut shop, there is usually a line of people ahead us crowding in to get their sugar fix. But did you ever notice that you don't see long lines at the health food stores?

There is a message here for the church, because the Greek word for "sound" in verse 3 means "healthy." By and large, people won't gravitate toward either healthy food or healthy doctrine if left on their own. That's why the church has to make sure that there is one place where people are being fed a healthy, balanced diet of the truth as it is found in God's Word.

There will always be things in the Word of God that go against what we would like to believe, or what we have been taught. There may be something we want to do, and would do too, if it weren't for the Word standing there saying, "Thou shalt not." People with ears itching for what they want to hear and what agrees with their prejudices can always find a teacher willing to scratch the itch, to make the Word fit conveniently into their plans and their ideas.

But the nature of truth is that it doesn't matter whether you agree or what you think. Truth doesn't change, so the church's job is to help people keep their ears turned toward the truth—which, by the way, will not only scratch the real itch inside but satisfy with solid spiritual nourishment.

Changing the analogy, the church's proclamation should hold up the mirror of God's Word to our faces so we can see what we really look like and make any adjustments necessary (see James 1:23–25). Let's make sure that we are holding up the Word of truth for all to see. "Preach the word" is God's charge to the church.

PERSONAL APPLICATION FOR LIFE

1. This week, look for opportunities to recite Scripture to someone. Never underestimate the power of God's Word to affect the lives of others. Every word that comes from God's mouth is infused with His propose. And because God's Word is also infused with His life, it has the power to bring His purpose to pass.

2. The nature of truth is that it doesn't matter whether you agree or what you think. Truth doesn't change. So the church's job is to help people keep their ears turned toward the truth. Are you doing your part by holding up the Word of truth for all to see?

3. Psalm 119 is an incredible tribute to God's Word and what it can do in our lives. It is divided into twenty-two sections of eight verses each. Why not start a reading program of reading one eight-verse section a day until you finish the psalm. Ask the Holy Spirit to enlighten your eyes and open your heart to the Word. As you read, meditate on what you are reading and reflect on what God is saying to you. You just may find a huge spiritual payoff in the process.

4. The gospel is the power of God to everyone who believes. Don't be ashamed to proclaim the gospel using God's Word. Make a list of those you typically meet during the week who are not believers and put them on your prayer list. Ask God to create opportunities to present the gospel to them using the Scriptures.

FOR GROUP STUDY

Questions for Group Discussion

1. What happens when God's people proclaim God's Word?

2. Using 2 Timothy 3:16 as the basis for your discussion, what kinds of results are we to strive for when proclaiming God's Word?

3. Why is it important how we proclaim God's Word? What key points do we need to keep in mind while we proclaim? (Use the chart below as an aid to your discussion.)

4. Read 2 Timothy 4:3–4, which teaches that the church needs to proclaim God's Word to the world. What is the apostle Paul's admonition for the necessity of preaching the Word? What happens when the truth of God's Word impacts human nature?

PICTURE THIS

Effectively proclaimed, God's Word changes lives because its message deals with the central issues of life through its principles and examples. The methods below help us to apply the Word's life-changing power to the lives of people.

HOW WE NEED TO PROCLAIM GOD'S WORD

METHOD	SCRIPTURE PASSAGES	WHAT IT MEANS
We need to proclaim the Word as truth.	1 Timothy 3:15; John 17:17	We are to proclaim the Bible as the absolute truth with no apologies.
We need to preach the Word for results.	2 Timothy 3:16	We are to preach the Word with a view to changing wrong behavior.
We need to preach the Word with authority.	Titus 2:15	We are to authoritatively preach the truth of God's Word as the standard by which we measure our lives.

80

THE WITNESS OF THE CHURCH

People who are facing certain disaster need a rescuer to lead them out of harm's way, no matter what the cost or inconvenience to the rescuer. And people who are facing certain spiritual disaster without Jesus Christ also need someone to lead them to safety, which is to the cross of Jesus Christ where sin is paid for and forgiven. This is why God has called and mobilized the church as a "rescue unit"—to go out into the world and be His witnesses, to turn people on their way to hell toward heaven. "You shall be My witnesses," Jesus said (Acts 1:8).

It is our calling as followers of Jesus Christ to lead lost people through the fire and smoke to the safety of the cross. Evangelism is a priority with God. You are never closer to the heart of God than when you are telling your unsaved friends and loved ones about the gospel and the eternal life that Jesus gives.

Jesus has called the church to have a major impact on the lost of this world through the witness of our words and our actions. We should be different than those without a Savior; Jesus said we should be salt and light to those in a thirsty and dark world. When we are, those bound for hell often are willing to listen to the good news of deliverance.

PRAYING FOR LOST PEOPLE

Having just read that people are lost and on their way to hell unless we reach them, and that God wants us to be His witnesses, you might expect me to say, "So let's get out there in the unsaved world and start witnessing."

Well, we need to do that, to be sure. But God has an order within His priority of evangelism. The heading of this section tells you where we're going first, so let's look at what Paul wrote to Timothy, his spiritual son and pastoral representative in Ephesus. In 1 Timothy 2, the apostle laid down key principles for the church that wants to reach its world for Jesus Christ. Notice Paul's emphasis in the opening verses:

> First of all, then, I urge that entreaties and prayers, petitions and thanksgivings, be made on behalf of all men, for kings and all who are in authority, so that we may lead a tranquil and quiet life in all godliness and dignity. This is good and acceptable in the sight of God our Savior, who desires all men to be saved and to come to the knowledge of the truth. (vv. 1–4)

Before we get into the specifics of these and the following verses, please note God's desire that all people come to the knowledge of Christ. Peter said of God's desire, "The Lord is not slow about His promise, as some count slowness, but is patient toward you, not wishing for any to perish but for all to come to repentance" (2 Peter 3:9).

Praying with the Right Priority

So what does the God who desires all people to be saved want His people to do about it? He wants us to pray for a lost world "first of all." These are priority words. That's why I want to begin by considering the church's prayer ministry in relation to evangelism. I don't believe I need to convince you that the church is supposed to go into the world.

But I do believe that our biblical calling to pray before we go and as we go is sadly lacking in emphasis in the church at large. We need a renewed understanding that God wants prayer to be at the center of the church's life and evangelistic efforts. In fact, the priority of prayer is such that it comes before a lot of other programs and projects the church gets caught up in that, when all is said and done, have an inward, "us-centered" focus.

Since God's priority in prayer is evangelism instead of us and our concerns, we may have an answer as to why more of God's people are not seeing more of their prayers answered. It's because they have their priorities out of order. People who are facing a life-or-death situation need a rescuer, and you can only become a rescuer when you put aside your agenda.

Praying for the Right People

The Bible makes us understand that no one is left out when the church goes to prayer for the lost. This is obvious from the "all men" at the end of 1 Timothy 2:1. When we pray evangelistically for unsaved people, we are saying it's not enough that we are saved. We want to help more dying people get into the lifeboat and be saved.

The issue in evangelism isn't whether those who are drowning know they are in trouble and are crying out for help. The issue is that they are lost and facing eternity in hell without Christ, and the church has the responsibility to reach them with the gospel. So the important thing is not so much what is happening in the ocean, but what's happening in the lifeboats that are on the ocean.

The church needs to be stirred up in the area of evangelism, and the thing that will stir God's people more than any evangelistic "pep talks" or guilt trips or programs is prayer. If you ask me, "How can I get a burden for lost people and overcome my fear of witnessing?" my answer would be to start praying. Pray for unsaved family members, friends, and coworkers by name. Ask God to break your heart over their condition and give you "divine appointments" to share Christ with them and the boldness to speak for Him.

And, by the way, if you feel fearful at times, you are not alone. Even Paul, the great evangelist, asked the Ephesians to pray that he would have the boldness necessary to proclaim the gospel. Paul's prayer request is worth quoting here because it would make a great prayer for you to pray: "Pray . . . that utterance may be given to me in the opening of my mouth, to make known with boldness the mystery of the gospel . . . that in proclaiming it I may speak boldly, as I ought to speak" (Ephesians 6:19–20).

The Bible says that Christians are no longer to live for themselves (see 2 Corinthians 5:15). Many of us are not seeing the power of God at work because we're living for ourselves when God wants us to have a heart for others that's as big as the needy world we live in. When we start praying for people, we won't have a hard time reaching out to the spiritually dying and making room for them in the lifeboat, because we will realize that the church's witness is a life-and-death issue.

Praying for the Right Conditions

At first glance, Paul's request in 1 Timothy 2:2 may not seem to fit with the theme of praying for the lost. The apostle urged the church to pray in particular "for kings and all who are in authority, so that we may lead a tranquil and quiet life in all godliness and dignity."

But it makes perfect sense in the context because it's clear that the main reason Paul wanted us to pray for a peaceful environment is to enhance the spread of the gospel. Over the past ten years we have witnessed enough riots and rebel attacks and dislocations of entire populations to know that as a rule, social and political upheaval do not make a conducive environment in which to share the gospel. In fact, in many of the world's troubled countries the most endangered people during a riot or attack, and among the first to be evacuated, are the missionaries in that area.

So a priority reason that we are to pray for "domestic tranquility," as the preamble to the U.S. Constitution puts it, is to enhance the spread of the gospel. The blessing of being in America is that we can talk about God freely. Now don't misunderstand. Domestic peace is not absolutely necessary to the spread of the gospel, as we have witnessed in countries where the church is growing despite oppression and persecution. But I don't know anyone who wishes or prays for turmoil and persecution so the gospel can grow. Paul certainly didn't. The hostile environment in which Paul ministered added pain and burden to his work, and he had no problem telling the church to pray for quiet and tranquil lives.

Another benefit of praying for peace in the context of evangelism is that it helps you to see your life and the world from God's perspective—a perspective that we don't come by naturally. If you ever used those old 3-D glasses they used to give out at special movies, you know that the audience needed them to see what was happening on the screen. Without those glasses, the picture was blurry. God wants His church to see the world through His "glasses," because without them we can get things out of focus and begin to think that He is blessing us with peace for our enjoyment alone.

This prayer for tranquility also applies to other spheres of authority. Pray for peace at work and favor with your employer so that you will have opportunity to share Christ without people getting upset. Pray for an environment at home, in your extended family, and in your neighborhood that is conducive to spreading the gospel.

GOING TO LOST PEOPLE

Whenever the Bible addresses any subject, it does so with perfect balance. We can see that in 1 Timothy 2. Paul said to begin with prayer for the lost, but he didn't say that this is all the church has to do. In verses 5–7, he drew on his personal example to show that praying for the lost must be accompanied by going to the lost with the good news of salvation. This is what I call pray-ers—that is, people who pray—becoming proclaimers.

We have the essence of the gospel in verse 5, where Paul wrote, "For there is one God, and one mediator also between God and men, the man Christ Jesus." The Word of God tells us that there is only one way to reach God, and that is through Jesus Christ. This basic truth has become a flash point of controversy, because since the 9/11 terrorist attacks, everyone is bending over backward to show that we're all just one big family and that Christians and Muslims in particular worship the same God.

No way. It doesn't matter if the world thinks the gospel is narrow or intolerant. Neither Buddha nor Mohammed, nor any other religious figure can bridge the gap between sinful people and a holy God. That chasm from hell to heaven was bridged by Jesus, and only by Jesus, on the cross.

I like the way Job put it in reference to the gulf between him as a human being and God: "There is no umpire between us, who may lay his hand upon us both" (Job 9:33). Job was painfully aware of his inability to stand before a holy God, and lamented the lack of an "umpire," or mediator, who was qualified to step in.

But now that need has been met in Jesus Christ. He fits the criteria perfectly because He is both holy God and a sinless man. Paul continued in 1 Timothy to describe this uniquely qualified mediator: "[Jesus] gave Himself as a ransom for all, the testimony given at the proper time" (2:6). To ransom people means to pay the price to set them free, to rescue them from their predicament. He came to rescue people, and if you and I aren't in the rescuing business, we aren't in Jesus' business. He said, "As the Father has sent Me, I also send you" (John 20:21). Where did the Father send the Son? He sent Him into the world to hang out with sinners and bring them to Himself.

If we really believe Acts 4:12, then there is no excuse for not telling others about Jesus. Speaking of Jesus Christ (see 4:10), Peter said, "There is salvation in no one else; for there is no other name under heaven that has been given among men by which we must be saved."

Jesus is not looking for spectators, but folks who are "players." These are the ones who are in the game, praying for the unsaved and willing to go out into the world to reach them. It's easy to have our priorities straight on Sunday morning when we are together in God's house praising Him. But we need to take our prayers and our actions outside the doors, getting on our knees before God on behalf of unsaved people and then moving our feet to go to them with the gospel.

A WITNESS TO THE WORLD

The church's impact should not only open people to the gospel but also have an influence on society. Indeed, as goes the church so goes the society. If we want strong communities, then there must be strong churches at the heart of those communities. A healthy community needs an intact immune system standing against the evil that would debilitate and destroy society.

Unique People with a Unique Purpose

The Bible teaches that the people of God are unique. Peter called us "a spiritual house for a holy priesthood" and "a chosen race, a royal priesthood, a holy nation, a people for God's own possession" (1 Peter 2:5, 9). That makes us different and set apart, yet we are also created for "good works" (Ephesians 2:10) that impact the world around us.

There is a lot of confusion here. Some churches are so heavenly minded they are of no earthly good. They sing, shout, and pray while the community outside continues to spiral downward into social and moral decay. People in churches like this love God, but they don't take that love outside the church's walls to the neighborhood. The other extreme is what has happened to so many churches since the 1920s battles with liberal churchmen and secularists. That is, many churches have become so earthly minded that they are no heavenly good. Ironically, they've become secularized, surrendering the truth of the gospel and the demands of the life hereafter for the here-and-now. Churches like this have turned the house of God into a political forum rather than a place where people learn the divine viewpoint.

Both of these extremes are wrong. The church is made up of people who are called to live out heaven's values in the midst of a very unheavenly world. We receive instructions from above, with our feet firmly planted here below. We are to think heavenly, and let it show in our earthly walk. We are looking for the return of Jesus, but we have a lot to do while we're waiting for Him to come.

Jesus Himself expressed the biblical viewpoint for the church in His parable of the man who went away on a long journey and left his estate with his servants to manage. In Luke's version of the parable the owner of the estate told his servants, "Do business with this until I come back" (19:13).

Here is the balance the church needs to strike. The man's servants knew he was coming back, so they had to live in light of that certainty. But, at the same time, they were left with his resources and his charge, "Do business with this." The answer was not to sit down and do nothing until the master returned or to get all wrapped up in the business of life and forget that he was coming back.

Later in 1 Peter 2, the apostle struck this balance with a marvelous description of how the church should impact the world while staying true to Christ: "I urge you as aliens and strangers to abstain from fleshly lusts which wage war against the soul. Keep your behavior excellent among the Gentiles, so that in the thing in which they slander you as evildoers, they may *because of your good deeds, as they observe them*, glorify God in the day of visitation" (vv. 11–12, italics added).

Notice the heavenly part of this exhortation. We are "aliens" down here. This world is only a seventy- or eighty-year pit stop on the way home. And as we're passing through this world we are called to be holy, or set apart, in body and spirit. And yet, our lives are to be so influential that non-Christians can't help but glorify God for what they see in us.

The Salt of the Earth

How, then, should the church influence society? One of the most concise yet comprehensive statements on this subject is from the lips of Jesus in Matthew 5:13–16. In the Sermon on the Mount, the Lord used two key metaphors to communicate the impact He wants us (the church) to make for Him. The first one is salt.

You could probably recite the first half of verse 13 from memory. Jesus told us, "You are the salt of the earth." (The second half of the verse adds a needed word about the importance of retaining our influence, which we'll deal with in a moment.)

By declaring His people the salt of the earth, Jesus was making a clear statement about the decaying condition of this world and the role of Christians in delaying the decay. Of course, salt has been used as a preservative for thousands of years. Rubbing it into a piece of meat helps to preserve the meat from decay, because salt is an antibacterial agent.

Jesus put His church on earth to act as a preserving influence on a rotting world, to slow down the decay of sin. If Jesus had nothing on earth for His people to do, He would have taken us out of here the moment we trusted Him as Savior. Evil ought to slow down and take notice when it gets in the vicinity of the church, because we are being salt.

Jesus finished His illustration on salt by saying, "But if the salt has become tasteless, how can it be made salty again? It is no longer good for anything, except to be thrown out and trampled under foot by men" (Matthew 5:13b). In the culture of Jesus' day when salt was so crucial in preserving food, there was nothing worse than salt that had lost its usefulness. (In biblical days salt was distilled from marshes and other places where it was mixed with all manner of impurities; when the salt was used up, the impurities would remain and render the mixture useless.)

God's people can become so diluted by the world that they lose their impact. The world walks right over us without feeling any effect.

Besides its preserving qualities, salt also creates thirst. As believers gather together in the name of Jesus Christ, the church's impact should not only have a preserving influence against the decay of evil, but the quality of our lives should also make people so thirsty for what we have that they are drawn to Christ like a parched man to water.

The job of the church is to create a thirst in the culture that can only be satisfied by the living water of Jesus Christ. We don't have to worry about trying to make Christianity attractive or palatable or relevant to the world. All we have to do is make people thirsty for Jesus. And don't forget that when lost people feel their thirst, they will be looking for a thirst-quencher. When Jesus offered the woman at the well a water that would quench her thirst forever, her response was, "Sir, give me this water, so I will not be thirsty" (John 4:15).

The Light of the World

Jesus used a second familiar metaphor in Matthew 5 when He said of His people, "You are the light of the world. A city set on a hill cannot be hidden; nor does anyone light a lamp and put it under a basket, but on the lampstand, and it gives light to all who are in the house" (vv. 14–15).

The last time I checked, the role of light was to shine, and in so doing to drive back the darkness. The world needs light because it sits in spiritual darkness. We were saved out of that darkness, and now our job is to shine the light of Christ back on the world's darkness. Paul told the Ephesians, "You were formerly darkness, but now you are Light in the Lord; walk as children of Light" (Ephesians 5:8).

When we are walking through this world as children of light, the world has a better chance to see things as they really are. "All things become visible when they are exposed by the light, for everything that becomes visible is light" (Ephesians 5:13). You know how hard it is to sleep when someone comes in and turns the light on in your face. That's the effect we should have on unbelievers who are sleeping the sleep of eternal death (see v. 14 of this same passage).

Jesus went on to say, "Let your light shine before men" (Matthew 5:16a). In other words, carry your light out where it's dark so that unsaved people can see it. It would be ridiculous to turn on a lamp and then put something over it to hide its glow. If you say you want your house to be a welcoming place on a dark night, it would be foolish to turn the lights on and then close all the curtains so no one can tell you're home.

Yet, all too often that's what we do in the church. Our lights burn brightly inside the church, but we are the only ones benefiting from them. Meanwhile, the world outside goes on in its darkness. But lights are designed to be displayed, not hidden. It's impossible to hide a light that's "set on a hill," and the farther the beam reaches, the more people are affected by it. A local church that wants to measure its effectiveness only has to look into its community to see how far its light is penetrating the darkness.

Don't misunderstand. We are not the light, but simply the reflector of Christ's light. It's interesting that before Satan fell into pride and rebelled against God, he was Lucifer, "the shining one" or "light-bearer." He was called "star of the morning" and "son of the dawn" (Isaiah 14:12). As the highest-ranking angel, Lucifer's job was to reflect God's glory by leading heaven's worship. But Lucifer decided he wanted to *become* the light instead of just reflecting it, and God cast him out of heaven into darkness. Satan has been the prince of darkness ever since, and he's still trying to put out the light of God's glory. But God has set the church in the world as a "city on a hill" to reflect His glory.

This is what Jesus said in Matthew 5:16. The full verse says, "Let your light shine before men in such a way that they may see your good works, and glorify your Father who is in heaven." Jesus not only mentioned good works here, but Paul said of us, "For we are His workmanship, created in Christ Jesus for good works, which God prepared beforehand so that we would walk in them" (Ephesians 2:10). God also wants us to be "equipped for every good work" (2 Timothy 3:17).

So what are the good works Christians are called to do? They are the visible demonstration of Christ's love and power within us. Good works are the deeds of kindness and blessing that we do to benefit others, in the name of God and for His glory. They are important for the same reason that no one wants a television with sound only. People want a picture to go with the sound. People don't just want to hear us talk about God. They want to see actions that back up our faith.

The good works that we're talking about are based on God's Word and are done to give Him the credit, to shine the light on His glorious person. They are also to be done with surpassing excellence, which doesn't mean just bigger and better. Paul said, "[This] one thing I do" (Philippians 3:13), not "These ten things I dabble in." When we show His light, those in the dark will notice—and our witness will be bright and attractive to those who need rescuing.

PERSONAL APPLICATION FOR LIFE

1. The opportunities we have in history to win people to Christ will be unavailable in eternity, because people's eternal destiny is sealed when they exit this planet. So if you are serious about following Christ and being His disciple, you must be willing to tell the good news about Him to dying men and women so they can come to faith in Christ. Ask God to open doors for witnessing, and seize all opportunities He sends your way for sharing the gospel!

2. If you are following Christ the way you should, and if you are strong and growing in your faith, your influence will flow from you and impact unbelievers for Christ. That influence starts with delivering the gospel message. Always be ready to share the good news.

3. Perhaps you are fearful of rejection if you were to present the gospel. Yet unsaved people don't shutter when they swear. They come right out with it. They are not ashamed of evil words; so we ought not to be ashamed of the gospel. Imagine the benefit of seeing a hell-bound sinner turned around and put on the right road to heaven. That's an eternal payoff!

4. Matthew 5:16 exhorts us to "let our light shine before men." Does your local church penetrate the spiritual darkness in your community? Are you doing your part in your local fellowship to ensure that the light shines brightly?

FOR GROUP STUDY

Questions for Group Discussion

1. Read 1 Timothy 2:1–4. What are the key principles to which the church must adhere while reaching out to a lost world?

2. As we seek to be God's witnesses to the world, how should we focus our praying for the lost? What specifics must we keep in mind?

3. With the apostle Paul's emphasis in 1 Timothy 2:1 on praying for the lost, he mentioned four kinds of prayer. What is the significance of each

kind of prayer as it relates to lost people? (Use the chart below as an aid to your discussion.)

4. The content of our proclamation is the gospel of Jesus Christ. What is the essence of our message?

PICTURE THIS

The apostle Paul urged us to pray on behalf of all people. To help us understand how God wants us to pray, Paul mentioned four kinds of prayer we can engage in for the unsaved of the world.

PRAYING FOR THE LOST
1 Timothy 2:1

KIND OF PRAYER	WHY IT'S IMPORTANT
Entreaties	This kind of prayer addresses a need. Our entreaty is that the unsaved would meet their need for Christ.
Prayers	This kind of prayer refers to worship before God. Praying for the lost is an act of worship.
Petitions	This kind of prayer is a request on the behalf of others. It requires that we get close enough to people to know their needs and feel their pain.
Thanksgivings	This kind of prayer means to be grateful. It involves thanking God for His saving grace and for responding to the prayers of His people.

SECTION III

THE FUNCTION OF THE CHURCH

81

THE LEADERSHIP OF THE CHURCH

The Bible has clear principles and guidelines for leadership in the church. We need to know these so that the church is functioning biblically, leaders are being identified and developed as God intended, the body of Christ is being served, and the church is being equipped to take its ministry out into the streets where lives can be changed.

A good working definition of leadership is to know the right way to go, to go that way yourself, and then to show the way for others. Leaders are people who know the way, go the way, and show the way. Leadership also implies "followership." A shepherd who has no sheep is not really a shepherd.

There is another element we need to add to our definition of leadership, because spiritual leadership is different from secular leadership. Jesus articulated this further element when He said, "Even the Son of Man did not come to be served, but to serve" (Mark 10:45). Spiritual leaders are servant-leaders, setting the example by loving service rather than by cracking the whip and barking out orders to the rank-and-file.

Leadership is critical to the church, because God's people need leaders who can stand before the church and say, "Thus saith the Lord." We call this process expository preaching, which is expounding the Word of God in such a way that His people understand it and know how to apply it. This is the pastor's primary calling as the shepherd of God's flock.

Biblically informed leadership is also necessary due to the limitation of human resources. One person has only so much time and energy. When there is ministry to be done or people who are hurting and need help, these things can't wait for months until the pastor can get to them.

A third reason that leadership is important is that people do have needs and problems. Any pastor can tell you that folks don't leave their struggles and messes at home when they join the church. They drag all that stuff with them into the family, and things can become very complex.

But despite all of these challenges, God has a will for His people and a direction He wants them to move in. Church leadership is designed to guide God's people toward their divinely ordained objectives. Leadership involves both instruction and modeling, teaching people what God expects and then showing them by example how to achieve it.

A MODEL FOR CHURCH LEADERSHIP

The issue of spiritual leadership doesn't begin in the New Testament, because the basic paradigm or model for church leadership was established in Exodus 18, long before the church came into existence. And the idea for this model did not come from Israel's leaders, but from a man named Jethro, a priest from North Africa who was the father-in-law of Moses.

An Impossible Assignment

The situation in Exodus 18 was that Moses was trying to act as the "pastor" to a congregation of more than two million people who had left Egypt in the Exodus. His father-in-law Jethro came to visit Moses (see vv. 1–13), watched him trying to deal with the people all by himself, and offered some wise advice:

> Now when Moses' father-in-law saw all that he was doing for the people, he said, "What is this thing that you are doing for the people? Why do you alone sit as judge and all the people stand about you from morning until evening?"

> Moses said to his father-in-law, "Because the people come to me to inquire of God. When they have a dispute, it comes to me, and I judge between a man and his neighbor and make known the statutes of God and His laws." (vv. 14–16)

Moses was getting up every morning at dawn and staying up until dark, trying to render decisions for a long line of people. They streamed to him with their problems, and woe be to anyone who needed a follow-up session or further counseling. They were in for a long wait.

Ever since they left Egypt, the Israelites had been charging Moses with not caring about them. So Moses was wearing himself out trying to act as pastor, judge, and counselor because he was trying to show the people that he did care. And this was one way he could prove his concern for them.

Wearing Out the Pastor

Jethro watched Moses knock himself out, and then gave him this counsel: "The thing that you are doing is not good. You will surely wear out, both yourself and these people who are with you, for the task is too heavy for you; you cannot do it alone" (vv. 17–18).

The Hebrew words for "wear out" mean to fade away. Moses was going to put himself in the grave trying to deal with all these problems, and the people were going to suffer too. Jethro was saying, "Moses, people who are in conflict and crisis can't wait a month or two for your schedule to open up."

This, unfortunately, is the case with too many pastors. Some poor pastor wears himself out trying to do everything and see everybody, and then the people stand at his funeral and say, "Oh, wasn't he a good pastor? He was down there at the church from dawn to dusk every day. He did everything for us. We sure are going to miss him."

That's not the way the ministry is supposed to work. So Jethro told Moses:

> Now listen to me: I will give you counsel, and God be with you. You be the people's representative before God, and you bring the disputes to God, then teach them the statutes and the laws, and make known to them the way in which they are to walk and the work they are to do. (vv. 19–20)

The Principle of Representation

Jethro told Moses to bring the people's disputes before God, get God's answers for those problems, and then communicate God's Word to the people in such a way that they would know how to apply God's truth to their lives. Today in the church this is expository preaching, which we talked about earlier as a pastor's primary calling and responsibility.

When a pastor goes before God to seek His Word and His will for the people, he is serving as a representative. This is the role that Jethro counseled Moses to take in the verses quoted above. Representation is a fundamental principle of Scripture that is often overlooked when we talk about the church, but it is crucial to understand if we are going to do church God's way.

Jethro's advice to Moses drew on this great principle of representation. Moses was in a mediatorial position between God and the people, the same position a husband is to take in his home and the pastor is to take in the church. Biblical church leadership is impossible without God's representatives.

Delegating to Godly Leaders

This is critical to the functioning of the church today because the basic principle is the same. A pastor should be spending time with his leaders instilling God's Word in their hearts. The church doesn't need leaders primarily to administer budgets, although that is part of leadership. The church needs leaders who can provide biblical answers and effective ministry to the needs and challenges that the people face.

The selection of the seven deacons in the church at Jerusalem provides an early example of church leadership principles at work (see Acts 6:1–7). There was a legitimate need that had to be addressed, the neglect of the Hellenistic or Greek widows in the daily administration of food. The apostles said it was not right for them to leave their primary calling as the people's representatives before God to address this need, so they directed the church to put forward spiritual men who could administer this task.

THE LEVELS OF CHURCH LEADERSHIP

With this backdrop we are ready to look at the church's leaders and their qualifications. The Bible identifies three distinct leadership roles for the church, which are pastor, elder, and deacon.

The Office of Pastor

The pastor, or pastor-teacher as described by Paul in Ephesians 4:11, is the church's spiritual leader. The senior pastor is charged with the primary responsibility for the church's spiritual health and direction. I would summarize the pastor's role as proclaiming the Word and overseeing the work, which includes developing leaders who are qualified to serve as elders and deacons.

Make no mistake about it. No matter how big a church's staff may be, there is always a primary leader who has been invested by God with authority and responsibility. This leader is not a despot, and he is accountable to the body of elders (see 1 Timothy 5:17 NIV, where the elders are said to "direct the affairs of the church"). The church's leadership does not rest in committees. There has to be a place where "the buck stops," and there has to be a leader who leads the way in formulating and implementing the church's vision. God always transfers leadership to a person, whether it be from Moses to Joshua, Elijah to Elisha, or Paul to Timothy. God places His vision in the hands of a person.

The Office of Elder

The second New Testament classification of leaders is the elders—which are always talked about in the plural, by the way. These are the spiritually qualified men who form the governing body of the church and in whose hands the final policy decisions rest. (The pastor is an elder also, for Paul talked about elders "who work hard at preaching and teaching," 1 Timothy 5:17.)

The Bible does not teach congregational rule. However, the Bible clearly teaches congregational involvement, but not congregational government in which the church body at large has the final authority. Why is this? Because you don't want to have carnal people voting on the will of God. There is this assumption in the church that if we put a matter before the people, they will have the spiritual insight and biblical knowledge to make a right decision. Now this may be the case with some of the people, but God's will should never been subject to majority vote.

The Bible also teaches that elders must be men. "If any man aspires to the office of overseer, it is a fine work he desires to do" (1 Timothy 3:1). The word for "man" is the gender-specific word for males. The principle of male leadership in the church is established earlier in 1 Timothy: "I do not allow a woman to teach or exercise authority over a man" (2:12). Paul's statement in 1 Corinthians 14:34–35 that women are to be silent in church doesn't mean they can't speak. The issue there is authority.

The clear pattern in Scripture is a plurality of elders in each church. For example, Acts 14:23 says that Paul and his missionary team appointed "elders [plural] for them in every church [singular]." James tells us that if anyone is sick, he should "call for the elders of the church" (James 5:14), the same pattern as in Acts. Paul left Titus in Crete to "appoint elders in every city" (Titus 1:5). Timothy's spiritual gift was bestowed by "the presbytery," or the governing board of the church at Ephesus (1 Timothy 4:14).

The plurality of elders solves the problem of who is in charge and who has the final authority in the church. There is often a lot of jockeying for power, but I believe the answer to the problem is fairly simple. The board of elders establishes the policies that govern the church's ministry, in line with Scripture. The pastor works within these guidelines and is accountable to the elders, with the freedom to set the church's vision and ministry direction.

The Office of Deacon

The Greek word for "deacon" means "servant." This office is interesting because nowhere in Scripture do we find a deacon board. There is the presbytery, or elder board, but no corresponding formal organization of deacons. This is because the deacons only have one basic job, which is to execute the church policies and ministries that have been established by the elders and the pastor.

Deacons are to do more than serve communion and count the offerings. They must be spiritually mature and responsible men and women. Women can be deacons because of 1 Timothy 3:11, which says, "Women must likewise be dignified, not malicious gossips, but temperate, faithful in all things." In the context Paul is talking about women who serve as deacons, since he mentions deacons' wives in verse 12. Paul called Phoebe "a servant," the same word for deacon (Romans 16:1).

The job of deacons is to fan out among the flock to make sure that the ministry gets done. They are the church's foot soldiers. Deacons are accountable to the elders, but the biblical pattern indicates that deacons do not come together as a separate governing board.

THE QUALIFICATIONS OF CHURCH LEADERS

One thing is clear concerning the qualifications of church leaders. The lists in 1 Timothy 3:1–13 and Titus 1:6–9 deal first and foremost with character and the pursuit of a godly lifestyle on the part of those who aspire to lead in the body of Christ. Having skilled but carnal people doesn't help the church. Neither is it helped by people who have their own agenda to push.

There are well over a dozen qualifications for elders and deacons mentioned in 1 Timothy 3, some of which are repeated in the qualifications for elders outlined in Titus 1. For example, both elders and deacons must be temperate or self-controlled. This quality not only means freedom from excess in their personal habits, but also in their attitude toward things such as money. The other side of this coin is prudence, or a well-ordered life. The goal is a person whose personal and family life is solid, showing depth of character and the ability to manage a family and a household well. The need for these qualities is obvious. "If a man does not know how to manage his own household, how will he take care of the church of God?" (1 Timothy 3:5).

Paul used a number of terms to refer to the fact that elders and deacons also need to be people of even temperament. They cannot have a violent temper or be "pugnacious," the kind of people who are always ready for an argument or a fight and pound their fists on the table when things don't go their way.

Church leaders must also have good reputations. Nobody is perfect, but "above reproach" (1 Timothy 3:2) means that no one can lay a charge of improper behavior against them. The other side of this is the quality of hospitality and unselfish generosity, someone whose home and heart is open to others. Being above reproach also means a leader who is just and impartial in his decisions, not allowing himself to be swayed by the opinions of others.

An elder must also be "able to teach" and "not a new convert" (1 Timothy 3:2, 6), meaning that he must have a track record of demonstrated spiritual maturity, commitment to the truth of Scripture, and an ability to handle the Word. These qualifications reflect the teaching office of elders, a qualification that is not repeated for deacons because they are in a different role. Deacons can teach, of course, but it is the elders who are responsible for what is taught in the church.

Elders and male deacons need to be faithful husbands, literally "a one-woman man." The reference to the conduct of a leader's children doesn't mean there are never any problems in the home. It may even be that an elder or a deacon must deal with a rebellious child. The issue isn't the problem itself, but the way the leader handles it.

One other area of qualification deals with the honesty and integrity of leaders. We mentioned earlier the need for church leaders to be free from greed and honest in their financial dealings. They must also "lov[e] what is good" (Titus 1:8). This means pursuing the best things in life, not the sordid or questionable. God wants His leaders to be able to stand up to the scrutiny of the church and have a good reputation with the unbelieving world.

PERSONAL APPLICATION FOR LIFE

1. Every church congregation has its needs, and your pastor requires the help of godly leaders within his church to meet those needs. Do you possess leadership skills but "sit on the sidelines" instead of becoming more involved? Do you know someone in your fellowship who is hurting and needs a shoulder to lean on? Perhaps an erring brother or sister needs to be restored to the fellowship. The needs can be endless, and your skills and talents might prove very effective. Consider making yourself available to your pastor and his leaders for training and service.

2. Are you praying for your church leaders? As your representatives, your pastor, elders, deacons, and others, need your prayer support as they seek wisely to lead your church. Pray for them on a regular basis.

3. How well does your church address needs and problems? Those in need must have the proper direction spiritually and biblically, which the church leadership has an obligation to provide. Do your church leaders give the right instructions and offer the best examples for achieving God-ordained objectives?

4. When was the last time you wrote your pastor a note of thanks and encouragement for his ministry? Do it the next chance you get. He will appreciate it more than you can imagine.

GROUP STUDY

Questions for Group Discussion

1. What is the definition of leadership within the context of the church? How does biblical leadership differ from secular leadership?

2. For what reasons is leadership critical to the church? What does Mark 10:45 reveal about this?

3. Read Exodus 18:1–20. What issues were God's people facing at that time? What solutions did they find? How is the basic paradigm for church leadership established in Exodus 18 a good model for the church today?

4. Dr. Evans discusses three distinct leadership roles for the church. Why is each level important?

5. Read 1 Timothy 3:1–13 and Titus 1:6–9. What are the key qualifications of church leaders? How does a church maintain a high standard for its leaders?

PICTURE THIS

In this chapter, we identified three distinct leadership levels for local churches. Below are those levels and their associated roles.

THE LEVELS OF CHURCH LEADERSHIP

LEADERSHIP LEVEL	SCRIPTURE PASSAGES	ITS ROLE
The office of pastor	Ephesians 4:11	The pastor proclaims the Word of God and oversees the work of the local church.
The office of elder	1 Timothy 5:17; 3:1	The elders form the governing body of the local church, upon which final policy decisions rest.
The office of deacon	Romans 16:1; 1 Timothy 3:11	Deacons execute church policies and ministries that have been established by the elders and the pastor.

82

THE UNITY OF THE CHURCH

In our individualistic society some may lose sight of the fact that Christians are bonded together in a relationship of unity. God takes this relationship so seriously that the Bible warns us to watch out for people who cause division in the church, because they are harming Christ's body. And those who withdraw from the community of believers will find their relationship with God limited by their failure to participate in the fellowship of the saints.

The Bible teaches that the unity of the church is the Holy Spirit's assignment and ministry. The Spirit extends this unity to each new believer, as Paul explained in 1 Corinthians 12: "For even as the body is one and yet has many members, and all the members of the body, though they are many, are one body, so also is Christ. For by one Spirit we were all baptized into one body, whether Jews or Greeks, whether slaves or free, and we were all made to drink of one Spirit" (vv. 12–13).

THE CONCEPT OF OUR UNITY

The word *unity* means "oneness," but that is different from sameness. Over the centuries the church has suffered from the misguided efforts of those who try to make everyone conform to their standards and keep their lists of dos and don'ts.

God doesn't do that, which makes life in the body of Christ a lot more exciting and challenging. Unity in Christ is possible because we are united around Him—bowing to His lordship and obeying His commands. True unity is finding oneness of purpose and commitment, moving toward a common goal, despite our differences. Unity doesn't require that we all be the same, but that we all head in the same direction.

Paul spent the rest of 1 Corinthians 12 showing how the church's unity functions in the midst of our differences (see vv. 14–31). His illustration of the human body reminds us that the body's various parts are designed to work together as a harmonious whole to accomplish the body's tasks.

A Big Job to Do

The fact that the church's unity is an organic reality wrought by the Holy Spirit doesn't mean it's easy to pull off. The problem isn't the Spirit's lack of power, of course, but the flawed human beings who make up Christ's body. There's no better example of this than the Spirit's work of bringing Jews and Gentiles together in the church.

The Jew-Gentile problem of the first century was the epitome of racial, religious, and cultural divisions. Jews wanted nothing to do with Gentiles. Gentiles were "dogs" to the Jews. The Gentiles didn't want to deal with the Jews either.

But in the church, the Holy Spirit was blending Jews and Gentiles together into one body. The Bible says that this process involved having to overcome hostility and break down walls. It's worth quoting Paul's classic statement of what God did through Christ:

> Remember that formerly you, the Gentiles in the flesh, who are called "Uncircumcision" by the so-called "Circumcision" . . . remember that you were at that time separate from Christ, excluded from the commonwealth of Israel, and strangers to the covenants of promise, having no hope and without God in the world. But now in Christ Jesus you who formerly were far off have been brought near by the blood of Christ. For He Himself is our peace, who made

> both groups into one and broke down the barrier of the dividing wall, by abolishing in His flesh the enmity . . . thus establishing peace. (Ephesians 2:11-15)

The immensity of the task of uniting Jews and Gentiles into one harmonious body cannot be overstated. As Peter preached to the Gentile household and friends of the Roman centurion Cornelius, the Holy Spirit fell on the people, and the Jews with Peter were "amazed" (Acts 10:45). Later, when Peter was called to answer for his actions in going to Gentiles (a forbidden thing under the old rules), he explained that it was God's doing and quieted the objections (see Acts 11:18).

When the church came into being and the Holy Spirit began uniting a crowd of different people into one body, all of a sudden a person's religious standing, racial background, or social class was no longer preeminent. The early church not only contained Jews and Gentiles, but also slaves and slave owners, rich and poor people, the cultural and educational elite alongside folk from the "sticks."

The Holy Spirit is the divine emulsifier, binding together people of different colors and personalities in the family of God. The Spirit's indispensable role in church unity is obvious from the opening verses of 1 Corinthians 12. Notice how many times Paul emphasized the unifying work of the Spirit amid the wide variety of gifts among believers: "the same Spirit" (vv. 4, 8, 9), "the one Spirit" (v. 9), and "one and the same Spirit" (v. 11).

Jesus' Prayer for Unity

We've seen that the church's unity is a divine operation, coming down from above and working from within rather than being imposed from the outside. This is clear in Jesus' great high priestly prayer in the Upper Room the night before His crucifixion. The first discussion of the church's unity was not between Jews and Gentiles, or any other group of people. It was between the Father and the Son.

In the middle of His prayer, Jesus prayed on behalf of the people who believed in Him, "Holy Father, keep them in Your name, the name which You have given Me, that they may be one even as We are" (John 17:11). Then in verses 20–23 we read:

> I do not ask on behalf of these [the apostles] alone, but for those also who believe in Me through their word; that they may all be one; even as You, Father, are in Me and I in You, that they also may be in Us, so that the world may believe that You sent Me. The glory which You have given Me I have given to them, that they may be one, just as We are one; I in them and You in Me, that they may be perfected in unity, so that the world may know that You sent Me, and loved them, even as You have loved Me.

This prayer shows how much is at stake in the church's unity. God's name, His glory, and His love are tied to the unity in which His people are to live. Our bond as believers in Christ is much more than something to keep us from fussing and fighting among ourselves. It is a testimony to the world that the Lord and the faith we preach are real.

There is no doubt that the Father answered the Son's prayer for unity, because God the Father and Jesus exist in complete unity.

The church's unity is key to our blessing, service, and effectiveness for Christ, both corporately and individually. So if we are functioning in conflict and disunity rather than unity, God will limit His work in our lives. If we have time to be blessed but not be a blessing, if we are selfish saints who want things from God but don't want to mess with being a functioning member of a local church, or if we are causing disruption in the church by our attitudes or words, then we are wasting our time on our knees, asking God to answer our prayers.

The Attack on Unity

If you were the Devil and you knew that unity was the key to answered prayer and effectiveness among Christians, what would you do? You would sow disunity and cause a mess. You would create scenes in which people aren't talking or are glaring at each other out of the corner of their eyes. You would do everything possible to split believers apart, knowing that the power of God would be hindered.

That's why the Bible says watch out for anybody in the church who causes disruption. "I urge you, brethren, keep your eye on those who cause dissensions and hindrances contrary to the teaching which you learned, and turn away from them" (Romans 16:17). Elsewhere Paul said concerning the church, "If any man destroys the temple of God, God will destroy him" (1 Corinthians 3:17). And among those things God hates is this: "One who spreads strife among brothers" (Proverbs 6:19). This is not a small issue, because God responds to His people's unity.

THE POWER OF OUR UNITY

The apostles and the rest of the disciples went to an upper room in Jerusalem after Christ's ascension, where "these all with one mind were continually devoting themselves to prayer" (Acts 1:14). They were all on the same page and heading in the same direction, and the Spirit came in power at Pentecost.

When this happened, three thousand people were saved in one day (see Acts 2:41). Acts 2:42–47 is a portrait of a church united. These believers worshiped and enjoyed fellowshipped together; they even shared their possessions with anyone in need. They were still of "one mind" (v. 46), and the results were powerful. There was "a sense of awe," and the apostles were performing many wonders (v. 43). And people were getting saved daily (see v. 47). God not only showed up in the church's midst, but He showed out to the people outside the assembly. Sometimes we forget that even though we must express our individual faith in Christ in order to get to heaven, it takes more than us by ourselves to get some heaven here on earth.

Those in the early church understood the power of the corporate body. That's why when the apostles were threatened by the authorities, the church came together and "lifted their voices with one accord" (Acts 4:24). And when they were through, the building shook (see v. 31).

THE FUNCTIONING OF OUR UNITY

The church's unity did not originate with us, but with God. It is the Holy Spirit who places every believer into a dynamic relationship with others in the body of Christ. Therefore, our job is to guard and preserve the unity that God has already given us.

Preserving Our Unity

That's why Ephesians 4:3 is so important. We quoted part of it earlier, but it's time to give the whole verse. Let me start with verse 1 to set the context: "Therefore I, the prisoner of the Lord, implore you to walk in a manner worthy of the calling with which you have been called." A big part of this worthy walk is "being diligent to preserve the unity of the Spirit in the bond of peace" (v. 3).

"Being diligent" means to make unity a top priority. The church's unity is already a reality. Our job is not to mess it up. Now, if God is this serious about the church's unity, what would you call it when a believer decides this doesn't apply to him or her and blows off the fellowship of God's people? I would call it sin, because the church is not optional. It is essential.

Verses 11–16 of Ephesians 4 highlight the importance of the church in God's plan and the importance of every believer contributing to its strength. Christ gave gifted people to the church (see v. 11) "for the equipping of the saints for the work of service, to the building up of the body of Christ; until we all attain to the unity of the faith" (vv. 12–13a). The emphasis throughout this section is on the growth of "the whole body" (v. 16) until every member of the church reaches spiritual maturity. That's a lifelong assignment because there is always room for growth and because this growth requires the participation of every member of the body for it to occur as it should.

Comparing the church to a human body really helps us to see how vital unity is to the church's health and growth. An earlier generation used to say that if someone wasn't in church, something was missing. They understood in a more profound way than we do today that it takes "the proper working of each individual part" (Ephesians 4:16) to make the church go and grow. So if Sister or Brother Jones was absent, the rest of the body felt the loss of the missing part.

So it is with the faith of Jesus Christ. Every part of Christ's body has to cooperate with the program if the church is going to be everything that God wants us to be.

"Cruise Ship" Christians

One of the problems in the church today that threatens our unity and effectiveness is what I call the "cruise ship" approach to Christianity.

Do you know why it's so wonderful to go on a cruise? Because somebody else does everything for you. You don't even have to handle your luggage. The crew provides recreation and serves you about eight meals a day with fabulous food. And if you don't want to get out of bed, that's fine. They'll bring the food to your room. They'll even wash and iron your clothes. Every detail on a cruise ship is designed to pamper you, and all you have to do is decide how much you want to enjoy.

The problem is that this cruise ship mentality has invaded the church, so people expect to be fed and entertained. They say, "I think I'll cruise on over to church this morning and see what they have for me. I'll check out the music menu and see if there's anything I like. I'll find out what they're serving on the Bible study menu and sample the sermon buffet."

This is a problem because the church is a battleship, not a cruise ship. When a battleship engages the enemy, what is the call that goes out? "All hands to their duty stations."

Loving One Another

One final passage that's important for this study is Colossians 3:14, where Paul wrote: "Beyond all these things put on love, which is the perfect bond of unity." Notice the language of priority again. Love is not optional because the church's unity is not optional.

This verse answers the question of how we can practice true Christian unity with people we may not particularly like. Our likes and dislikes are personal preferences, which is why the Bible never commands us to like anybody. We are commanded to love one another, however, because biblical love transcends our preferences and feelings. It is a decision of our will to act in the best interest of another person, even at our expense. Biblical love is passionately and righteously pursuing the well-being of others.

The Bible is so radical on this that the apostle John told the church, "The one who does not love his brother whom he has seen, cannot love God whom he has not seen" (1 John 4:20). If you say, "Tony, down deep in my heart I just don't feel the importance of this unity thing," then it's time to test your "love quotient" for your fellow believers. Unity is the result of genuine love. Paul said unity is perfected in love.

PERSONAL APPLICATION FOR LIFE

1. When you join a local church, you join a family. We all have the same Father (Ephesians 3:14–15). We have all experienced the same spiritual birth and have the same spiritual blood flowing through our veins. Our relationship in the church transcends ethnic, clan, or earthly family relationships. That's built-in unity! Are you "cruising" along in your church, or are you actively working to preserve that unity?

2. Read Matthew12:46–50. Jesus tells us that His real brothers and sisters are His disciples—those who committed to doing His will. This ought to be all the motivation you need to serve Jesus. Are you following Him as you should?

3. God has so constructed the spiritual body that growth and maturity only occur in the context of attachment. Development also requires the context of unity. For the body to progress, there must be unity of purpose. Are you aligning yourself with God's objectives for His church? Are you finding your guidance from God's Word? Are you involved in dynamic fellowship with other believers? If not, it's never too late to begin realigning yourself with God's purposes for you.

4. There is great diversity with the body of Christ. That means what you do really counts. In fact, the body can feel pain if you don't do your part. Are you using your spiritual gift(s) to build and maintain the unity of the church?

FOR GROUP STUDY

Questions for Group Discussion

1. Read 1 Corinthians 12:12–31. Describe the concept of church unity. What makes it unique?

2. What are some of the challenges to church unity?

3. In His great high priestly prayer in the Upper Room the night before His crucifixion, Jesus addressed unity of believers. What did He pray in this

regard? Why was unity such a high priority to Jesus?

4. How does unity function within the church? (Use the chart below as an aid in your discussion.)

PICTURE THIS

The Holy Spirit places every believer into a dynamic relationship with others in the body of Christ. It is our job is to guard and preserve the unity that God has already given us. Below are three activities that help us guard and preserve our unity.

How Christian Unity Works

DYNAMIC	SCRIPTURE PASSAGE	WHAT IT DOES
We must work to preserve our unity.	Ephesians 4:3	As members of the body remain true to their calling, they preserve the church's unity.
We must all contribute to the church.	Ephesians 4:11–16	As each member contributes with gifts and talents, the church grows, strengthens, and matures.
We must love one another.	Colossians 3:14	As we bond with fellow believers in love, we build and grow the church.

83

THE SERVICE OF THE CHURCH

For those of us who know Jesus Christ, our salvation and our trip to heaven are free, paid for in full by the blood of Christ. In gratitude for what God has given us, we ought not mind at all serving Him on the way. Among all the names and titles we carry as believers, we are "bond-servants of Christ Jesus" (Philippians 1:1).

In this chapter I want to consider four aspects of the church's calling to serve God, other believers, and the people around us. Serving others is not just a nice thing to do at the holidays or during times of special outreach. It's a way of life for those of us who claim the name of Christ. Jesus said, "Whoever wishes to become great among you shall be your servant; and whoever wishes to be first among you shall be slave of all. For even the Son of Man did not come to be served, but to serve, and to give His life a ransom for many" (Mark 10:43–45).

OUR MANDATE TO SERVE

Service for Christians is a mandate from God, which means it is mandatory. We love to talk about how we are free in Christ from all the restraints and restrictions of the Mosaic law, and that is absolutely true. But Paul cautioned the believers in the churches of Galatia not to take their freedom too far: "You were called to freedom, brethren; only do not turn your freedom into an opportunity for the flesh, but through love serve one another" (Galatians 5:13).

Elsewhere, Paul told Christian slaves, "With good will render service, as to the Lord, and not to men" (Ephesians 6:7). The Greek word for "slaves" is the same as "bond-servants" in Philippians 1:1, which includes every believer regardless of our status on earth. All of us are mandated, or commanded, to serve.

Serving the Right Person

Being a servant or a slave may not sound like a really exciting calling—but it is, when you are serving the right person with the right tools.

Ephesians 4:7–16 is a passage that has much to teach us about the divine nature and proper functioning of the church. The Bible says, "To each one of us grace was given according to the measure of Christ's gift" (v. 7). Every believer is gifted for service, which is why Paul said that Christ gave His gifts "for the equipping of the saints for the work of service, to the building up of the body of Christ" (v. 12). There is no such thing in the Bible as a saint who doesn't serve.

Serving with the Right Tools

The tools we have are the spiritual gifts that God has given to every member of the church. The Bible clearly teaches that every saint has been gifted for service, without exception. Some may have more gifts than others, but all of the gifts are to be used to strengthen the church "until we all attain . . . to a mature man, to the measure of the stature which belongs to the fullness of Christ" (Ephesians 4:13).

The body of Christ grows to the extent that each part is working properly. This means that every saint is critical. No believer is an addendum or an afterthought in the body of Christ. Your contribution and mine, through our divine enablement or gifting, are important if the whole body is to grow and reach maturity.

THE MEASURE OF OUR SERVICE

You may have noticed in Ephesians 4 that Paul twice used the word *measure* in relation to the giving of spiritual gifts for the building up of Christ's body. One reference is to the "measure of Christ's gift" and the second is "the measure of the stature which belongs to the fullness of Christ" (vv. 7, 13).

Christ Is Our Standard

The point is hard to miss. The measure, or the standard, of our service is Christ Himself. This means, for instance, that we don't have to compare ourselves to other Christians and wonder why they were given certain gifts that we didn't get. It also means that Christ is the One we are working to please, not someone else. More on that later.

Of course, true service done in Christ's name and power will be pleasing to others, but their reaction is not the standard. Christ alone is the measure—or more specifically, the "fullness of Christ," which basically means that our service should make us and those we serve as much like Christ as it is possible to be in this life.

Measuring Ourselves for Service

Christ is our measure in terms of the goal or standard we are to work toward. But there is another sense in which we are told to measure our service for Christ, and for that we need to look at Romans 12. This is the great passage that begins with our responsibility to worship God by presenting ourselves to Him as a "living and holy sacrifice," ready to "prove what the will of God is" (vv. 1–2).

Most people stop reading with verse 2 because these two verses are so familiar. But verse 3 begins with "for," which is a connecting word. Paul has more to say to the Romans, and to us, on this subject. And what he is going to say in verses 3–8 is that our commitment to worship and seek God's will isn't complete until we are ready to serve. In other words, if your worship does not lead to service, then you haven't finished worshiping yet.

In verse 3 we are told, "For through the grace given to me I say to everyone among you not to think more highly of himself than he ought to think; but to think so as to have sound judgment, as God has allotted to each a measure of faith." This is not saving faith, but a capacity to serve. Every

Christian has been given grace that is designed to lead to God-honoring service in the church. But before we can serve effectively, there is a standard of thinking we must adopt by which to measure our service.

Paul called this thinking with "sound judgment" so that we do not get inflated egos and begin to think more highly of ourselves than we should. The other side of the coin is thinking more lowly of ourselves than we should, but that's not a problem that most believers wrestle with. However, there is such a thing as false humility that causes people to insist that they really can't do anything when God has gifted them in some measure. If God has given you a gift to use in His service, use it and don't apologize for it.

Finding Our Place to Serve

Thinking with sound judgment also means that we are realistic about our gifts and our ability to serve.

It's important that all of us serve in our capacity, because this thing of being a Christian is not just about us. Paul continued in Romans 12: "For just as we have many members in one body and all the members do not have the same function, so we, who are many, are one body in Christ, and individually members one of another. Since we have gifts that differ according to the grace given to us, each of us is to exercise them accordingly" (vv. 4–6a).

Find the area of service where God has called and gifted you. Once you find it you will know, for there will be a joy and freedom and blessing in that service. Find the area of service and serve there for the glory of God.

THE MANIFESTATION OF OUR SERVICE

Another key passage that addresses our service in the context of God's gifts is 1 Corinthians 12. I want to pick up two verses that we need to fix in our minds as we talk about the church's service, the first of which is verse 7. After saying that there are varieties of gifts, ministries, and effects (vv. 4–6), Paul added the clincher: "But to each one is given the manifestation of the Spirit for the common good" (v. 7).

The Holy Spirit's Imprint

It is the manifestation of the Holy Spirit that makes any gift or ability unique. When you and I are trying to operate outside of our giftedness, or when we are exercising our gifts in our fleshly strength apart from the Sprit's enabling, nothing happens because the Spirit is not manifesting Himself. And when there is no manifestation of the Spirit, we will not see God at work in supernatural power in and through us.

And when the Holy Spirit is manifesting Himself through your service, you will not be the only one who sees it. The people you are serving will know that you have been used of God for their benefit. That's why the corporate ministry of the church is indispensable, for at least three reasons.

First, the church provides the context in which we serve each other and the world around us. The Holy Spirit is going to have a hard time manifesting Himself in the life of a Christian who is living in spiritual isolation.

Second, the church is also indispensable because when a local body of believers in whom the Spirit is working comes together, His power is multiplied and expanded.

Third, we need the church because it is a group of people in whom the Holy Spirit is able to manifest Himself in many different ways. This gets back to the church's connectedness. We need the whole body so that the whole ministry of Christ is accomplished. If everyone in the church was a preacher, there's a lot that would never get done. In 1 Corinthians 12:14–21, Paul addressed this issue by saying that if the body were all eyes, ears, or feet, vital functions would be left undone. A local church with nonserving saints is suffering like a human body that is missing an eye, an ear, or a foot.

The Holy Spirit's Choice

There is another way that the Spirit manifests Himself in the church's service. According to 1 Corinthians 12:11, "One and the same Spirit works all these things, distributing to each one individually just as He wills." The "things" mentioned here are the spiritual gifts of verses 8–10, which of course is just a partial list. The Spirit sovereignly gives each believer the exact gift or combination of gifts He wants that person to have.

So don't get mad or jealous if the Christian next to you at church has a spiritual gift you wish you had and are convinced you could do a better job with anyway. Take it up with the Holy Spirit. He decides who receives what gift, because He knows each one of us intimately, far better than we know ourselves, and He can see how we will best serve the kingdom with our personality and background. The Spirit doesn't need our counsel or input on His decision—and besides, remember that the goal of the church's spiritual gifting is to promote "the common good" (1 Corinthians 12:7), not our personal preferences.

THE MOTIVATION FOR OUR SERVICE

Along with all of the other blessings that accompany our service to and with the body of Christ, there is a wonderful motivation that can keep us going when all the other props are knocked out from under us.

Peter gave us this motivation when he wrote,

> As each one has received a special gift, employ it in serving one another as good stewards of the manifold grace of God. Whoever speaks, is to do so as one who is speaking the utterances of God; whoever serves is to do so as one who is serving by the strength which God supplies; so that in all things God may be glorified through Jesus Christ, to whom belongs the glory and dominion forever and ever. Amen. (1 Peter 4:10–11)

Serving for God's Glory

We need to understand that our service for the Lord, and the gifts with which to do it, are a stewardship from God, the One for whose ultimate glory we serve. Of course, we are called to serve one another, as we talked about earlier. But we have to be straight about our true motivation, because if you and I are serving only for people, we are going to crash at some point.

Why? Because not everyone will appreciate us, even in the church. Not everyone is going to say thank-you or treat us right, even when our motivation is to do right. Unless we serve with our eyes on the Lord, some people somewhere along the line are going to make us want to quit. That's just the truth of human nature, even redeemed human nature. Our motive to serve has to be for God and His glory. And the great thing is that He never misreads our motive or overlooks the least act of service done for Him.

Receiving God's Reward

There is also a great motivational principle for us in Colossians 3:22–24. Paul exhorted slaves to serve their masters well, not simply to please them "but with sincerity of heart, fearing the Lord. Whatever you do, do your work heartily, as for the Lord rather than for men, knowing that from the Lord you will receive the reward of the inheritance. It is the Lord Christ whom you serve."

This speaks directly to our work, but it also has application to our service in the church. If you're content to have people reward you with a pat on the back or nice words, then you will serve with that temporary reward in view. There's nothing wrong with being recognized and appreciated for faithful service rendered, but we have a much greater prize to keep our eyes on—the reward that Jesus will give us when we stand before Him.

Another great thing about serving with the goal to please God is that He doesn't use the world's measure to judge our service. The world may reward those who are out front or who make the biggest splash, but God considers those in the background to be equally valuable and important. That's why Jesus said the last will be first someday.

PERSONAL APPLICATION FOR LIFE

1. Failing to serve when God has given us the capacity is to disobey His will. The list of spiritual gifts in Romans 12 makes it clear that whatever your gift may be, the thing to do is to exercise it with everything you have. If you know your gift, then exercise it for the glory of God. If you need help discovering your gift, ask your pastor for help.

2. You may be saying, "Being a servant or a slave doesn't sound like a really exciting calling." However, when you are doing your service "as unto the Lord, and not men," that changes everything. Recognize that you have no greater calling than to serve your Lord.

3. There is a problem we have in our churches today: too many part-time Christians. We have too many SMOs—"Sunday Morning Only" Christians—who want to play the religious game. If you're a part-timer, perhaps it's time switch to full-time service and get more active in your church.

4. If there is a breakdown in your fellowship with Christ, there will be a breakdown in your fellowship with others. If you stop communing with Christ vertically, there will be a loss of fellowship with others horizontally. Don't become detached from the body, or your spiritual gift will stay "on the shelf" until you reestablish fellowship. If something is keeping you from fellowship with Christ, go before God and ask Him to help you fix it.

FOR GROUP STUDY

Questions for Group Discussion

1. What do we learn about serving Christ from Mark 10:43–45; Galatians 5:13; and Ephesians 6:7?

2. Read Ephesians 4:7–16. How does God equip each believer in the church to serve?

3. In Ephesians 4:7 and 13, Paul speaks of measuring our service to Christ. In what ways are we able to measure our service?

4. What should be our motivation for service? (See 1 Peter 4:10–11 and Colossians 3:22–24.)

PICTURE THIS

In Ephesians 4, Paul uses the word *measure* in relation to the giving of spiritual gifts for the building up of Christ's body. Below are three standards of measure from Scripture we may use for measuring our service.

MEASURING OUR SERVICE FOR CHRIST

STANDARD OF MEASURE	SCRIPTURE PASSAGE	HOW IT WORKS
We look to Christ as our standard.	Ephesians 4:7, 13	We look to Christ alone as our standard, not fellow believers.
We measure ourselves for service.	Romans 12:1–8	We need to measure our service with sound judgment and with humility.
We find our place to serve.	Romans 12:4–6a	We discover our spiritual gifts and understand the most effective way to use them within the body of Christ.

84

THE ACCOUNTABILITY OF THE CHURCH

Because life brings problems, one of the church's important ministries is to call its members to be accountable for the way they live. This may involve teaching and encouraging the saints in their walk with the Lord, and at times it may involve applying biblical discipline to a sinning saint for the purpose of correction and restoration.

But whatever form accountability takes, the church cannot escape its responsibility to see that its members are living lives worthy of Christ (see Ephesians 4:1). When we do this, we are imitating our Lord: "For whom the Lord loves He disciplines, and He scourges every son whom He receives" (Hebrews 12:6).

THE NECESSITY OF ACCOUNTABILITY

The work of discipline and restoration is part of the church's discipleship training, but it is also one of the most difficult and neglected areas of church ministry. We are terrified by the very thought of having to practice discipline. We're afraid of what people might think or do, which is why some parents are afraid to discipline their children. But discipline is a non-negotiable in Scripture.

I am going to make a strong statement here that I believe can be substantiated biblically. A church that does not practice discipline of its members is not yet functioning properly as a church, just as a family that does not discipline is not a fully functioning family. The writer of Hebrews went on to say, "It is for discipline that you endure; God deals with you as with sons; for what son is there whom his father does not discipline? But if you are without discipline, of which all have become partakers, then you are illegitimate children and not sons" (12:7–8). A church that lets its people go around undisciplined has no real claim to be part of God's family.

Directive Discipline

Accountability in the church can take two basic forms, which we could call directive and corrective. Directive discipline has to do with the church pointing out the way that people should go, directing them in the way of godliness. The church does this by exercising its ministry of teaching, encouraging, and exhorting the saints to deal with sin and live holy and fruitful lives, as well as lovingly supporting them during times of struggle (Hebrews 10:24–25).

This may involve correction in the form of pointing out what is wrong so people can fix it and get back on the right path. But I'm reserving the term *corrective discipline* for the action that needs to be taken when a believer refuses to go in the right direction and persists in sin. Directive discipline has a much more positive implication. It's what happens when believers respond to the church's ministry and seek to get their lives lined up with Christ.

This is why local churches that are serious about accountability should have church courts set up to settle issues and resolve disputes between its members. In this way the church is calling them to biblical and spiritual accountability to the authority of the church in accordance with Paul's teaching in 1 Corinthians 6:1–8.

Corrective Discipline

When a believer rejects the church's directive discipline and decides to continue in a sinful direction, the church is to apply corrective discipline. This application of discipline revolves around the refusal to deal with sin, what the Bible calls "presumptuous sin." The Old Testament law made this stipulation: "The man who acts presumptuously by not listening to the priest who stands there to serve the Lord your God, nor to the judge, that man shall die; thus you shall purge the evil from Israel" (Deuteronomy 17:12).

The saint who will not listen to the church and its duly appointed leaders is a candidate for corrective discipline. If a person won't hold himself accountable for his sin, it's up to the church to hold him accountable. It's the spirit of rebellion behind the sin that needs to be dealt with as much as, or perhaps more than, the fact of the sin.

THE DETAILS OF DISCIPLINE

The basic rules for carrying out discipline in the church were established before the church ever came into existence. The Savior and Lord of the church set this standard in Matthew 18:15–20, the central passage for church discipline. Other texts speak to the subject, but Jesus' teaching here is foundational because the responsibility given to the church is clearly spelled out.

The Participants in Discipline

First of all, look at the participants in discipline. Jesus said, "If your brother sins, go and show him his fault in private" (Matthew 18:15). Sin in the church is a family matter. The discipline that Jesus outlined is not for outsiders. I don't discipline the neighbors' children or expect them to live by my rules. But it was a different story for my kids when they lived at home.

The offender is not the only participant, of course. Any believer who sees a brother or sister fall into sin is responsible to go to that person and seek his or her restoration. Church discipline is not something to leave for the pastor or elders. If the offender refuses private discipline, then the process becomes more formal and involved because it requires "one or two more" people who can act as witnesses against the sin (v. 16).

These may be church leaders or members of the congregation. But if nothing else works to bring the sinner back, and if the church's leaders have not been involved to this point, they get involved now because the problem is brought "to the church" (v. 17). And if all avenues of discipline fail to bring about repentance and restoration, the leaders are the ones who announce to the church that this brother or sister is under discipline and is banned from the church's fellowship (see 1 Corinthians 5:9–11). So the level of participation goes in ever widening circles until the full church is involved if that becomes necessary.

The Problem Requiring Discipline

Jesus also gave the conditions under which discipline is to be initiated. It is sin that needs to be judged. Now, that may seem obvious on paper, but in real life it isn't always so clear. In other words, what is not being judged here is personal preferences or biases, or hearsay about a person's alleged behavior with no proof. The issue is always sin, which is anything that violates the law of God. Discipline is not applied because someone did something that someone else doesn't like. Discipline is applied because someone did something that God doesn't like and refuses to repent and come back.

The Bible distinguishes between the sins that we all commit and a lifestyle of persistent spiritual rebellion. For example, in Galatians 6:1, Paul advised, "Brethren, even if anyone is caught in any trespass, you who are spiritual, restore such a one in a spirit of gentleness; each one looking to yourself, so that you too will not be tempted."

This is a picture of someone being snared in a trap. In other words, the person Paul talked about here didn't set out to sin, but through the weakness of the flesh fell into the Devil's trap. The sin is still serious, and the sinner needs to be restored. But he needs, and is often open to, the intervention of someone to cut him loose from the snare and set him free. And the one who is cutting him loose is warned to do this gently because he can also fall into a trap and be snared. The believer who is ensnared doesn't need discipline as we are talking about it, but loving release.

But in the case of open rebellion and known sin, the church's job is to bring the sin to light and deal with it. This begins with private rebuke and expands from there if that is not successful. Notice that this reproof is to be done face-to-face with the offender. Jesus said go to your brother, not to someone who knows your brother or to everybody else in the church but your brother.

Proper church discipline leaves no room for gossip or involving people who are not related to the problem, at least not until the whole church has to be notified of the discipline. The circle is kept as small as necessary because the objective at every level of discipline is restoration, not further harm. The goal is to win the offender back before things get worse.

This is serious stuff. Paul instructed Timothy, "Do not receive an accusation against an elder except in the presence of two or three witnesses. Those who continue in sin, rebuke in the presence of all, so that the rest will be fearful of sinning" (1 Timothy 5:19–20). Even if the offender is an elder, he is to be publicly exposed and rebuked if necessary to deal with the sin.

The Reasons to Discipline

We've touched on some of the reasons the Bible commands us to carry out discipline in the church. The first and most obvious is to teach the sinner the error of his ways. In 1 Timothy 1:20, Paul referred to two men named Hymenaeus and Alexander, "whom I have handed over to Satan, so that they will be taught not to blaspheme." Discipline has a teaching element to it. We must teach people not to take God or His Word lightly.

Discipline also teaches the rest of the body the seriousness of sin and the holiness of God. When I heard my brother getting a spanking, it made me change my mind about some of my plans. We read earlier that an elder who continues in sin is to be rebuked in the presence of everyone, so that others will fear.

A third reason for discipline is to restore the sinner. This may involve having to expose the person to public shame if everything else fails. We see this in 2 Thessalonians 3, where Paul was dealing with unruly members of the church: "If anyone does not obey our instruction in this letter, take special note of that person and do not associate with him, so that he will be put to shame" (v. 14). There is shame in being publicly rebuked and disciplined. But don't miss the purpose of the shame: "Yet do not regard him as an enemy, but admonish him as a brother" (v. 15).

Here's a reason for discipline we don't think much about today. Discipline shows the unrighteous world the church of God at work, so that the unrighteous will also fear God and His holiness. The discipline enacted in response to the sin of Ananias and Sapphira, described in Acts 5, not only had a profound effect on the church, but on everyone else in Jerusalem.

THE PROCESS OF DISCIPLINE

The process of discipline is outlined clearly in Matthew 18:15–17. The first step is private confrontation of the offender by a caring fellow believer. The ideal situation is for the offender to respond to this loving and courageous act of caring.

Bringing Along Witnesses

But if the sinning saint does not respond, then the next step is to go to him in semi private; that is, taking one or two others with you. This principle of requiring two or three witnesses to confirm a matter was well established in the Law (see Deuteronomy 19:15). This step validates the offender's sin and his refusal to repent. This rebellious attitude that refuses to address the sin, as opposed to struggling to deal with it, is the ultimate basis for church discipline.

Bringing in several other people protects against the process being a personal vendetta or making too much of a minor issue. If an accuser was simply trying to ruin another believer's reputation, or was overreacting, he should not be able to find other witnesses to help him. Now, of course, it is possible for people to get together and make something up. That happened with the false witnesses at Jesus' trial (see Mark 14:56). But multiple witnesses are still the best safeguard against one person trying to trump up a charge against someone. Otherwise, it could just be one person's word against another's.

Telling the Church

However, if the sinning saint refuses to listen to the two or three people who confront him and try to win him back, then the issue becomes a matter of public record. Jesus said, "Tell it to the church" (Matthew 18:17). I don't think this necessarily means announcing to the entire congregation that a member of the church is under discipline for unrepentant sin. The issue of how much of the church should be informed is a tough question. I believe the answer is that those people in the church who have the most direct access to and possible influence with the offender should be told so they can bring their influence to bear in trying to end the sin and turn the sinner back to the Lord.

If there is a dispute about whether something does or does not qualify as a matter for church discipline, or if extenuating circumstances need to be considered, this is where the church court comes into play. The biblical basis for this court is in 1 Corinthians 6, where Paul clearly tells the church to take care of its own disputes, because it is a spiritual defeat and a mark against the name of Christ to take these things to the unrighteous.

If a person under discipline repents under the church's ministry, that's wonderful. But, in cases of extreme rebellion and refusal, the entire church may have to be informed, because the final stage of the church's judgment is to treat the offender "as a Gentile and a tax collector" (Matthew 18:17). Gentiles were outcasts because they were pagans. Tax collectors were Jews who were considered traitors because they served the Roman government by taking money from their fellow Jews.

So a stubbornly unrepentant believer is to be considered an outcast from the church, someone with whom the body is not to fellowship. This would seem to require that the congregation be informed of the rebellious person's judgment and banishment from the local body of Christ.

However the discipline is carried out, it has a formal side because the steps are endorsed and carried out by the leadership. Discipline is also informal because it involves the members going to each other as the need arises for confrontation.

THE POWER OF DISCIPLINE

Some people object that church discipline is a waste of time today because the disciplined person can just go down the street and join another church without changing his behavior. That may be true, but the objection misses the point that God commanded the church to practice discipline and that the power of church discipline is not limited to what we can see.

The Offender's Punishment

When Paul pronounced judgment on the man in Corinth who was having an affair with his stepmother, the apostle said: "I have decided to deliver such a one to Satan for the destruction of his flesh, so that his spirit may be saved in the day of the Lord Jesus" (1 Corinthians 5:5). If the offender will not listen to the church, maybe he will listen to the Devil.

Some people who have been disciplined by the church don't seem to suffer the destruction of their flesh. But this phrase may mean more than just physical death, although that can certainly happen in extreme cases. There is a point of no return in sinful rebellion. John said there is a "sin leading to death" for which even prayer is useless (1 John 5:16).

The Church's Excommunication

A believer who has resisted and refused the church's every effort at his repentance and restoration is a candidate for the very serious step of excommunication. I believe there is only one place where this step of discipline should be carried out, and that is around the communion table at the Lord's Supper. Why? Because the Bible makes it clear that this is where we deal with sin (see 1 Corinthians 11:27–32). This is one of the fundamental purposes of communion. The goal is always restoration of the offender, but whether that happens or not, the church must be diligent to exercise discipline.

The Church's Restoration

Just as the prodigal son was restored to his loving father when he repented and returned home (Luke 15:11–24), even so the church must open its arms to those who want to turn from their sin and return to the fellowship of Christ and His body. This is why Paul encouraged the church at Corinth to receive back the brother whom they had previously disciplined and removed from the fellowship (2 Corinthians 2:6–8). The goal of church discipline is always the restoration of the erring believer who repents.

PERSONAL APPLICATION FOR LIFE

1. No one said it would be easy to confront a brother or sister living in sin. But it is crucial. If you know someone who is dishonoring Christ and inviting God's judgment, pray for the courage and opportunity to confront the problem. If a third party is close enough to the offender to help, include that person as the Lord leads.

2. If there is a Christian you know whose lifestyle is an embarrassment to God, make sure you are not doing anything to help it along, such as pretending nothing is wrong, continuing to fellowship with that person, or dodging the issue when it comes up. It is your responsibility as a fellow believer to confront the problem and bring the erring believer to accountability.

3. Restoration of a sinning believer is part of the church's responsibility. To help prepare yourself to be a restorer, ask yourself how you'd want to be dealt with if you were caught in a trespass. Then determine that you will deal with an erring brother or sister the same way when the need arises.

4. If you are in the position to confront an erring believer, pray that God will make you sensitive. Pray also that you will have the discernment to know whether the issue is a preference or a biblical absolute.

FOR GROUP STUDY

Questions for Group Discussion

1. Within the body of Christ, why is accountability critical?

2. Read Matthew 18:15–20. What are the church's basic responsibilities for carrying out its discipline?

3. Read Matthew 18:15–17. Describe the steps of the process for disciplining a fellow believer in the body of Christ.

4. What is the extent of the power of church discipline? What is the church's responsibility if a believer resists the proper discipline?

PICTURE THIS

Matthew 18:15–17 outlines the steps in the process of bringing discipline to an erring fellow believer.

THE STEPS OF CHRISTIAN DISCIPLINE

Matthew 18:15–17

STEP	SCRIPTURE PASSAGE	WHY IT'S IMPORTANT
Bring along witnesses.	verses 15–16	Bringing in several other people protects against the process being a personal vendetta or making too much of a minor issue.
Tell the church.	verse 17	Should a sinning saint refuse to listen to the two or three people who confront him and try to win him back, then the issue becomes a matter of public record in the church.

85

THE ORDINANCES OF THE CHURCH

The word *ordinances* refers to those rites that Jesus commanded the church to observe to remind us of our relationship with Him, as well as the benefits that accrue to us because of this relationship.

The Bible recognizes two ordinances to be observed by the church: baptism and communion, or the Lord's Supper. (Some Protestant denominations teach foot washing as a third ordinance, citing Jesus' example during the Last Supper (John 13:3–15)).

These ordinances are not merely pictures to remind us of spiritual realities. They are also channels the Holy Spirit uses to confer the benefits of the new covenant to the body of Christ.

THE KEY TO THE SYMBOLS

On the night before His crucifixion, Jesus instituted the ordinance of communion in the Upper Room with His disciples. As He blessed and passed the cup, the Lord said, "This cup which is poured out for you is the new covenant in My blood" (Luke 22:20).

The mention of a new covenant presupposes an old covenant. *Covenant* is the word that God uses to describe His relationship with His people. A covenant can be defined as a spiritually binding relationship that God has with His people, bringing them the benefits of His kingdom. The old covenant was the Mosiac law that God gave to Israel. The new covenant is the covenant of grace that God has given to the church. This new covenant is based on God's new relationship to the church through the death and resurrection of Christ.

Under the old covenant, God related to His people by the principle of law. In the new covenant, God relates to His people by grace through the Holy Spirit. To help us understand and demonstrate His new covenant, God has given us the two biblical symbols of communion and baptism. These are a picture of Christ's death and resurrection, and our actual participation with Him. In other words, these pictures have an experiential reality tied to them.

The bread of communion pictures Christ's body that was broken for us. The apostle Paul quoted Jesus' words as he explained the significance of communion in 1 Corinthians 11: "This is My body, which is for you; do this in remembrance of Me" (v. 24). The juice represents Christ's blood shed on the cross for our salvation. And in baptism, we see a picture of our burial and resurrection with Christ (Romans 6:3–4). It's important to understand that we are not saved by getting baptized or by taking communion. They are *symbols* for the saved to understand and experience our spiritual connection to, and the benefits of, this new covenant God has with us. These ordinances are then both meaningful in what they represent and powerful in what they convey.

THE ORDINANCE OF BAPTISM

Baptism is connected in Scripture to the old covenant of circumcision. Under the old covenant of the Mosaic law, all males had to be circumcised to become members of the covenant and share in its benefits; circumcision was the sign or symbol of the covenant.

A Symbol for All Believers

But in the new covenant, the symbol is no longer physical in the sense of a cutting of the flesh, and it applies to all believers, not just males. This symbol is baptism, as we read in Colossians 2: "In [Christ] all the fullness of

Deity dwells in bodily form, and in Him you have been made complete, and He is the head over all rule and authority; and in Him you were also circumcised with a circumcision made without hands, in the removal of the body of the flesh by the circumcision of Christ; having been buried with Him in baptism" (vv. 9–12).

God is saying that in the new covenant, you don't have to do something physical to enter into the covenantal relationship. It is a spiritual transaction that is demonstrated or symbolized through baptism. Thus baptism is the new circumcision whereby the believer publicly identifies with Christ. Such public identification is critical for us to experience the blessings and benefits of the new covenant that are conferred by the Holy Spirit.

Because baptism is a spiritual covenant, Jesus said told His disciples in the Upper Room: "I will ask the Father, and He will give you another Helper, that He may be with you forever; that is the Spirit of truth, whom the world cannot receive, because it does not see Him or know Him, *but* you know Him because He abides with you and will be in you" (John 14:16–17, italics added).

A Public Witness to Christ

The ceremony of baptism is the point at which you go public with your testimony that you belong to Christ. Marriage is a good illustration of this relationship. When you get married, you are declaring that your mate is the person you will stay with and be faithful to your whole life. One way you publicly declare this new relationship is by wearing a ring that tells the world you are married and you are not ashamed to say it and be identified with your mate. Baptism is the Christian's "wedding ring" that tells everyone you are married to Christ and that you are not ashamed of this relationship.

And just as marriage takes you out of the single world and places you in an entirely new world and a new relationship, baptism disconnects you from the world that you were a part of and connects you with a new world, a new kingdom, a new family, and a new Lord.

THE ORDINANCE OF COMMUNION

The second biblical ordinance of the church is communion. Communion is the renewal of the new covenant, just as Passover was the renewal of the old covenant. The Bible makes this connection in 1 Corinthians 5:7, where Paul said, "Christ our Passover also has been sacrificed." Passover, of course, was the meal the Jews ate in Egypt the night the death angel came and killed the firstborn sons in all the homes of Egypt (Exodus 12).

Communion, then, is the renewal of what was instituted at baptism, just as regular physical intimacy in marriage is the renewal of the commitment made on the wedding day.

A Symbol of God's Salvation

God's people avoided this plague by killing a lamb and putting its blood on the doorposts of their homes, because God had said, "When I see the blood I will pass over you, and no plague will befall you" (Exodus 12:13). The blood of the lamb was a symbol of the blood that Christ would shed on the cross to save us from the eternal spiritual death of eternal separation from God—and so Paul could refer to Christ as our Passover lamb.

Jesus consciously connected Passover with communion when He told the disciples at the beginning of the Last Supper, "I have earnestly desired to eat this Passover with you before I suffer" (Luke 22:15). Jesus knew that the time had come for Him to become the final sacrifice for sins, which had been pictured and symbolized for so long through Israel's annual Passover observances in which a lamb was killed to represent God's covering of the people's sins. Jesus came not to cover sins, but to take them away.

As noted earlier, communion is also referred to as the Lord's Supper. It may also be called the Lord's Table, a reference to 1 Corinthians 10:21: "You cannot drink the cup of the Lord and the cup of demons; you cannot partake of the table of the Lord and the table of demons."

That's an amazing statement. Paul had just said in verse 20: "The things which the Gentiles sacrifice, they sacrifice to demons and not to God." Did you realize there are two tables in the world? There is the table of the Lord and the table of demons. You can sit at one table or the other, but not at both. To sit at the table of the Lord is to sit in God's presence and remind yourself of His covenant and become a partaker of the benefits of being part of it. You cannot do that and still fellowship at the table of the world. When you take communion, just as when you are baptized, you also identify yourself publicly with Christ and actually participate in a spiritual reality. Paul put it this way: "As often as you eat this bread and drink the cup, you proclaim the Lord's death until He comes" (1 Corinthians 11:26).

A Regular Reminder

The Bible says that the church met on the first day of the week "to break bread" (Acts 20:7). That is, the church observed communion weekly to remind themselves of God's new covenant relationship with His people through Christ. The early church understood the spiritual significance of the Lord's presence at the table, not in His literal body as some teach, but the spiritual presence of Christ in the midst of His people.

If you read Paul's full teaching on communion in 1 Corinthians 10–11, you will see that this ordinance involves both blessing and judgment—another example of how the church's ordinances convey an experiential reality to the participants.

Paul said, "Is not the cup of blessing which we bless a sharing in the blood of Christ? Is not the bread which we break a sharing in the body of Christ? (1 Corinthians 10:16). The blessing of communion is the impartation of the gracious benefits of the new covenant to the body of Christ.

But the communion table also involves discipline, and thus it demands that we examine and judge ourselves. It's worth looking at this portion of Paul's teaching in some detail:

> Therefore whoever eats the bread or drinks the cup of the Lord in an unworthy manner, shall be guilty of the body and the blood of the Lord. But a man must examine himself, and in so doing he is to eat of the bread and drink of the cup. For he who eats and drinks, eats and drinks judgment to himself if he does not judge the body rightly. For this reason many among you are weak and sick, and a number sleep. But if we judged ourselves rightly, we would not be judged. But when we are judged, we are disciplined by the Lord so that we will not be condemned along with the world. (1 Corinthians 11:27–32)

The Seriousness of the Symbol

We've been saying that communion is a symbol of a spiritual reality that is powerful in its ability to impart grace or judgment, and thus is not to be taken lightly! Sickness and even death were two consequences the Corinthians were experiencing because they had approached the Lord's Table and the meal that went with it in a casual and even sinful manner (see 1 Corinthians 11:27–30). The Lord's Table is a place of blessing, but it is also a sacred moment when we are to examine ourselves and confess our sins in order to be worthy of taking the bread and the cup, and in so doing be in the right spiritual position to receive and experience the benefits of the new covenant.

The celebration of communion is also a declaration of Christ's victory over sin, death, and the grave. In John 6:51, Jesus said, "'I am the living bread that came down out of heaven; if anyone eats of this bread, he will live forever; and the bread also which I will give for the life of the world is My flesh." Jesus' death and resurrection mean that we who know Him have been made victors over sin and death. Paul gave us this connection when he wrote: "When we were dead in our transgressions, [God] made us alive together with Christ . . . and raised us up with Him, and seated us with Him in the heavenly places in Christ Jesus" (Ephesians 2:5-6).

Too many times we as Christians forgot where we're really sitting. God says that while we are physically on earth, spiritually we are already seated with Him in heaven. At the communion table, you're supposed to recall your spiritual identity and position in Christ—and rejoice in our daily participation in His victory!

PERSONAL APPLICATION FOR LIFE

1. Communion is intended to be a picture of spiritual realities about Christ's death and resurrection. When believers come together for communion, it not simply an observance of Christ's death and a celebration of His resurrection. It is a participation in the benefits that accrue to believers through the new covenant. When you celebrate communion, do you recall your spiritual position in Christ—and rejoice in His victory?

2. The ordinances of the church serve to remind us of our relationship to God through His new covenant in Christ. How is your relationship with Christ? Since He is your life, are you abiding in Him so you can experience the continued flow of life? Perhaps you have been out of contact with that flow for some time. If so, take a moment to place yourself into His abiding presence, and begin experiencing anew His empowering in your life.

3. Those who are married publicly declare their new relationship to their spouse by wearing a ring that tells the world they are married and not ashamed to be identified with their mate. Believers in Christ embrace baptism as our symbolic "wedding ring" that tells everyone we are married to Christ. Take a moment to thank God for the reality behind the biblical symbol of baptism—a new kingdom, a new family, and a new Lord.

4. The ordinance of baptism symbolizes a very real spiritual transaction that is part of our spiritual covenant with God (see Colossians 2:11–12 and John 14:16–17). Jesus commanded baptism for all who believe in Him (Matthew 28:19–20). Although not a requirement for salvation, baptism is necessary if you are to be obedient to Him. If you have not been baptized, consider taking part in this ordinance. By doing so, you declare publicly that you are no longer part of this condemned world but are now connected to a new world, a new kingdom, a new family, and a new Lord!

FOR GROUP STUDY

Questions for Group Discussion

1. What are the two "ordinances" of the church? Why do we observe these ordinances?

2. Read Colossians 2:9–12. What does baptism represent? How the significance of baptism change after the establishment of the new covenant? Why do we perform the ceremony of baptism in the church today? What does it symbolize?

3. Read Luke 22:20. What is the significance of the word *covenant*, and why is it important to us as we observe the ordinance of communion? What is the different between the old and new covenants? Why does Jesus stress the "new" covenant?

4. What does the ordinance of communion symbolize? Read 1 Corinthians 11:26. According to 1 Corinthians 10:16; 11:27–32, what does the celebration of this ordinance involve? Also read John 6:51. What key truth does our celebration of communion declare?

PICTURE THIS

The ordinances of the church symbolize spiritual realities. To help us understand and demonstrate His new covenant, God has given us the two biblical symbols of baptism and communion. These ordinances are a picture of Christ's death and resurrection.

THE ORDINANCES OF THE CHURCH

ORDINANCE	SCRIPTURE PASSAGES	WHAT IT REPRESENTS
Baptism	Colossians 2:9–12	Because of the new covenant, we no longer need a physical symbol like circumcision to enter into the covenantal relationship with God. Baptism is the new circumcision.
Communion	Luke 22:20; 1 Corinthians 11:26	The celebration of communion is a declaration of Christ's victory over sin, death, and the grave. The bread of communion pictures Christ's body that was broken for us, whereas the cup is a symbol of the blood that Christ shed on the cross.

86

THE ORIENTATION OF THE CHURCH

The church of Jesus Christ is designed to be a grace-oriented fellowship rather than a law-oriented group. When a local church bases its ministry on law and rule-keeping rather than grace, spiritual growth is stunted and the church becomes an unpleasant, negative place to be. But when a church ministers the grace of God in all of its facets, it becomes an exciting, life-giving environment in which spiritual growth is nurtured.

THE EMBODIMENT OF GRACE

One of the Bible's greatest statements to churches and pastors on grace is found in Titus 2:11. Paul told Pastor Titus to teach the churches under his charge this truth: "For the grace of God has appeared, bringing salvation to all men." What does Paul mean by the appearing of God's grace? The apostle answered that in another place when he spoke of the grace that was granted to us "from all eternity, but now has been revealed by the appearing of our Savior Christ Jesus" (2 Timothy 1:9–10).

God's grace has existed from all eternity. Some liberal theologians used to talk about the contrast between the God of wrath, vengeance, and judgment in the Old Testament and the God of love, grace, and forgiveness in the New Testament. No, God has always been a God of grace. The Old

Testament is filled with stories of His gracious dealings with mankind. But before Christ appeared and sin was fully dealt with, we could say that God's grace was in the shadows. Like the sun on a cloudy day, God's grace was fully present before Christ, but it was not fully visible to us.

But when Christ came, it was like the clouds parting to reveal the sun shining in all of its glory. The grace of God appeared when Jesus came to earth. Jesus is the full-orbed expression of God's grace. John said of Jesus, "There was the true Light which, coming into the world, enlightens every man" (John 1:9). Jesus brought the saving purposes of God out of the shadows.

John then continued: "The Word became flesh, and dwelt among us, and we saw His glory, glory as of the only begotten of the Father, full of *grace* and truth" (v. 14). And finally: "For of His fullness we have all received, and *grace upon grace*. For the Law was given through Moses; grace and truth were realized through Jesus Christ" (vv. 16–17, all italics added). Grace is embodied in the person of Jesus Christ.

THE TEACHING OF GRACE

The job of the local church is to teach its members the awesome truth of grace and help enable them to experience its reality and power in their lives. That's a big job, because the grace of God that has appeared in Christ has a lot to teach us. According to Titus 2:12, this grace "instruct[s] us to deny ungodliness and worldly desires and to live sensibly, righteously and godly in the present age." Grace not only redeems us, it reforms us. Living by grace opens up to us a whole new series of data that we were unaware of before. That's why we need to be instructed in the grace of God. It's an entirely new way of thinking and living. Churches that are not grace-oriented defeat, rather than develop, their members.

One reason I know that many churches need to be taught about grace is that so many Christians still try to relate to God based on law, as we said earlier. Another reason grace needs to teach us is that we are quick to forget that God's grace is free. One way you can test any preacher or any movement in the church is whether he or it wants you to pay for your manifestation of grace.

By that I mean if you have to send a gift to get a bottle of water from the

Jordan River so you can experience God's blessing, something is wrong. If you have to send for an anointed handkerchief if you want to see God work in your life, that's not of God because He relates to you in grace, and His grace is free. The Bible says, "He who did not spare His own Son, but delivered Him over for us all, how will He not also with Him freely give us all things?" (Romans 8:32). God freely gave us Christ, which was the most expensive grace gift ever given. If God did not charge us for that, He is not about to start charging us now.

Grace also has a lot to teach us because some people in the church will take God's free grace to its illogical conclusion and say, "Since we are under grace and nothing can change that, let's live it up. Let's sin to our hearts' content because we're already forgiven."

That argument ought to sound familiar, for it's as old as the church. Paul addressed this issue in a classic passage that begins with these questions: "What shall we say then? Are we to continue in sin so that grace may increase?" (Romans 6:1). Then he gave the ringing answer: "May it never be! How shall we who died to sin still live in it?" (v. 2). Anyone who thinks grace is a license to sin doesn't understand the first thing about it.

This is why it's so important for churches to teach their members how to live the Christian life from a grace orientation. Grace is different from law not only because the basis of acceptance is different. Grace is also different because it has built into it the power to enable you to fulfill God's perfect, righteous standards as embodied in the law. In other words, grace enables what it expects.

That's important because God's expectations have never changed. God has always required that people say no to sin and yes to righteousness. But as we said above, the law of Moses had no inherent power to enable our obedience. But, in grace, God writes His law on our hearts by the Holy Spirit and gives us the Spirit to indwell and empower us. The church should be a powerhouse of obedient Christians who know how to tap into the Spirit's enabling grace to live for Christ. The world should be looking at us and saying, "If that's what living by grace can do, I want in on it!"

You see, the world is used to living by rules. But rules alone don't change the human heart. If your heart is diseased and beyond repair, no number of rules about eating right and not smoking will fix it. But if you receive a new heart through a transplant, nobody should have to lecture you about how to keep that heart working like new. You will respond in gratitude for your heart, which was a gift of grace that someone else provided.

Responding in obedience out of a relationship will always accomplish more than guilt-laced lectures rooted in rules alone. Most Christians aren't experiencing this truth because the churches they attend don't teach it.

THE FOCUS OF GRACE

Once we experience the grace of God in Christ, everything changes, including our focus. If you are looking for grace, you won't find it by looking in the mirror or anywhere else except to Jesus. The writer of Hebrews called us to "[fix] our eyes on Jesus, the author and perfecter of faith" (Hebrews 12:2).

Paul had the same idea in Titus 2:13, which continues the great sentence he began in verse 11: "Looking for the blessed hope and the appearing of the glory of our great God and Savior, Christ Jesus." Jesus is the focus of grace; our eyes need to be firmly fixed on Him.

You may say, "But this verse tells us to be looking for Christ's return. What does this future hope have to do with our living by grace today?" Oh, that's the best part. It has everything to do with today because Christ wants His church to keep Him first in its focus. Jesus' parable of the talents teaches us to conduct our lives as if the Master of the house could return at any moment (see Matthew 25:14–30).

In other words, looking for Christ's return in glory does not mean that we sit around doing nothing because He might come back today, or live any old way we please because He might not come back for a long time. When we live with our eyes on Jesus, looking for the blessed hope of His return, we will start to become more like Him. John said this about people who hope to see Jesus someday: "Everyone who has this hope fixed on Him purifies himself, just as He is pure" (1 John 3:3).

In Titus 2:11, Paul said that God's grace appeared in Christ at His first coming as Savior. Now we look for the second appearance of Christ, who will bring grace to fulfillment when He gathers the church to Himself and we celebrate the marriage supper of the Lamb (see Revelation 19:1–9).

Besides the fact that Jesus is our glorious God and Savior, there is another reason for us to keep our focus on Him. Jesus is also the perfect Man who knows exactly where you are and where you are coming from because He has been there. There is no tight spot you will ever be in, and no temptation you will ever face, that Jesus did not face Himself (see Hebrews 4:14–16).

You say, "Yes, but that was Jesus. He's the perfect Son of God. I don't have His ability to be victorious over sin."

Yes, you do. Jesus is ministering in heaven today as your Great High Priest to enable you to be an overcomer. Listen to this incredible invitation: "Therefore let us draw near with confidence to the throne of grace, so that we may receive mercy and find grace to help in time of need" (Hebrews 4:16).

The reason more believers aren't living in the victory that is ours by grace is that we are looking through the wrong end of the binoculars, so to speak. If you have ever tried that, you know how impossible it is to see what you want to see. We look at ourselves and see how weak and small we are, instead of looking at Christ and how mighty and all-glorious He is.

Now if you're wondering how you can get Christ in focus, the answer is found in your worship. I'm not just talking about what you do on Sunday morning, although that's important. I'm talking about a lifestyle of worship in which you learn the secret that the psalmist knew: "I will bless the Lord at all times; His praise shall continually be in my mouth. My soul will make its boast in the Lord; the humble will hear it and rejoice" (Psalm 34:1–2). You look to Christ by faith in your praise. You look to Him by faith in giving Him the glory that He deserves.

And when you do that, something important comes into focus. I love the next verse of Psalm 34: "O magnify the Lord with me, and let us exalt His name together" (v. 3). Using a magnifying glass, you can make an object look bigger. But you can't make God any bigger than He is. He already inhabits and rules the universe. But you can make Him look bigger to you when you praise and worship Him.

Local churches, then, should not only bring their members out of their homes to worship, but also send them back home as worshipers who have a passionate desire to live under the umbrella of God's grace.

THE FREEDOM OF GRACE

If there is anything still holding you in bondage, the message of grace is a message of freedom for you. It's found in Galatians 5:1: "It was for freedom that Christ set us free; therefore keep standing firm and do not be subject again to a yoke of slavery." If you have been set free from sin and death by Jesus Christ, stand firm in your freedom and don't let the Devil put his yoke around your neck again. That was Paul's message to the church in Galatia, and it's a message that churches desperately need to understand and preach today.

The Burden of the Law

A lot of people misunderstand the nature of true freedom. To many people, freedom means they have the right to do anything they want. But biblical freedom is liberty from the bondage of sin to enjoy a new relationship with Christ and do what is right. Freedom doesn't mean the absence of boundaries, but the ability to use your full potential within the boundaries God has set.

Biblical freedom is the ability and the privilege God gives you to fulfill your divinely ordained purpose. Jesus called it having life "abundantly" (John 10:10). Paul raised the issue of freedom in Galatians 5 because he was being pursued and harassed by a group of people called Judaizers, or legalists, who wanted to hold Gentile believers hostage to the Mosaic law. These people had come to the local churches of Galatia and were tying the believers there in knots with their teaching.

Church-based and church-sanctioned legalism is a lethal approach to the Christian life. It is a self-sufficient way of living because it all depends on you following the rules and checking off your obedience. The legalism that the Judaizers wanted to impose on Gentile Christians involved submitting to circumcision as a sign that the person was coming under obligation to the law. So Paul continued: "Behold I, Paul, say to you that if you receive circumcision, Christ will be of no benefit to you" (Galatians 5:2).

When grace is our motivation, there is joy in keeping God's commands. But the Galatians were being burdened and troubled (see Galatians 5:12) by the Judaizers' attempts to bring them under the law's yoke. Law-keeping frustrates God's people and robs them of their freedom and joy and purpose. Paul had made a profound statement about the law earlier in Galatians: "If a law had been given which was able to impart life, then righteousness would indeed have been based on law" (3:21). The issue of whether any person can be made right before God by the law was settled a long time ago, and the verdict was no, not one.

Freedom from the Law

So how do we experience the freedom Christ purchased for us on the cross? We need to get rid of that plantation mentality. Don't let anyone put a yoke of religious legalism on your neck.

Paul told the Galatians not to abandon grace. There is no need to, because God's grace is inexhaustible. James says He gives "a greater grace" (James 4:6). Paul said that grace abounds to cover sin (see Romans 5:20). Remember when that police officer pulled you over for a violation? Your palms became sweaty as you handed the officer your license and waited for the ticket that you knew was coming because you knew you were guilty. But when the officer said, "Just be careful" and let you go free with a warning, there was a sense of relief because you had just experienced grace. At that moment you were probably more than ready to give testimony to the joy and freedom that grace brings.

PERSONAL APPLICATION FOR LIFE

1. If your heart is diseased and beyond repair, no list of rules about eating right and not smoking will fix it. But if you receive a new heart through a transplant, nobody should have to lecture you about how to keep that heart working like new. You will respond with gratitude for your new heart, which was a gift of grace that someone else provided. Doesn't that want to make you take a moment and thank Jesus for His great gift of grace?

2. God is very generous with His grace. He can provide grace for any situation you might encounter. What have you received—or avoided!—in the last month or so that was purely a gift of grace from a good God? Reflect on it, and thank Him again for it.

3. God's grace is a wonderful gift. For we humans, its depths are unfathomable. Don't try to figure it out; just accept His gift of grace. Thank God that He knows you so thoroughly and loves you so completely. No one will ever know you better or love you more!

4. If you were asked if Jesus Christ was first in your life, could you say yes? Could you say He is first in every area of your life? Now that's a bigger question. The final question is, Where is Jesus Christ *second* in your life . . . and what are you going to do about it?

FOR GROUP STUDY

Questions for Group Discussion

1. What is the difference between a grace-oriented fellowship and a law-oriented group?

2. Read Titus 2:11 and 2 Timothy 1:9–10. What does the apostle Paul mean by "the appearing of God's grace"? Why is John 1:14–16 a revelation about grace?

3. Read Titus 2:12. Why is teaching grace a necessary activity within the church? What can happen in churches without a grace orientation?

4. Read Galatians 5:1. Contrast the burden of the law and the freedom that comes with grace.

PICTURE THIS

God designed the church of Jesus Christ to be grace-oriented. When a church ministers the grace of God in all of its facets, it becomes an exciting, life-giving environment in which spiritual growth is nurtured. To ensure spiritual growth, it's important that the church diligently teach certain truths about God's grace.

TEACHING GOD'S GRACE IN TODAY'S CHURCH

TRUTH	SCRIPTURE PASSAGE	WHY IT'S IMPORTANT
We must teach about the truth of grace.	Titus 2:12	So that believers may experience the reality and power of God's grace in their lives so they might live righteously.
We must teach about the freedom of grace.	Romans 8:32	So that believers will not try to relate to God based on law rather than grace.
We must teach about grace and committing sin.	Romans 6:1–2	Believers need to be reminded that a grace orientation does not give them a license to sin.

PART 7

BIBLIOLOGY

The Doctrine of the Bible

SECTION I

THE NATURE OF THE BIBLE

87. THE BIBLE IS UNIQUE
88. THE BIBLE IS TRUTH
89. THE BIBLE IS AUTHORITATIVE
90. THE BIBLE IS POWERFUL
91. THE BIBLE IS SUFFICIENT

87

THE BIBLE IS UNIQUE

No other book on earth can compare with the Bible. It stands apart from and is unique among all other books and so-called sacred writings, because it alone is the very Word of God with the power to transform individual lives and entire cultures. One of the great statements the Bible makes about itself is found in Isaiah 55.

> For as the rain and the snow come down from heaven, and do not return there without watering the earth and making it bear and sprout, and furnishing seed to the sower and bread to the eater; so will My word be which goes forth from My mouth; it will not return to Me empty, without accomplishing what I desire, and without succeeding in the matter for which I sent it. (vv. 10–11)

You will never find an unconditional guarantee like this in any other piece of writing—especially a guarantee that is still good some 2,600 years after it was first made. In fact, you will never find another book that can compete with the Bible in any form or fashion whatsoever. As we study the doctrine of bibliology, or what the Bible teaches about itself, this fact will become clear.

THE BIBLE IS UNIQUE IN ITS ORIGIN

Everything we are going to talk about in this study of the Bible hinges on the fact that this book came from God. Scripture is unique because it is not the word of man, but of God.

Some people will challenge this claim because they say their book is the Word of God. Mormons make that claim for the Book of Mormon, and other cults say the same about their founders' writings. And of course, Muslims make a similar claim for the Qur'an.

The problem is that anyone can step forward and claim that he or she has received a revelation from God. So how do we know which claim to believe? Thankfully, we don't have to guess, because there are stringent tests that any writing must meet to be validated as the true Word of God.

Jesus Testified to the Bible's Uniqueness

The most important proof of the Bible's uniqueness is Jesus' testimony to the Scriptures. The main reason we know the Bible is God's Word is that Jesus said so. He used the word *Scriptures* on a number of occasions to describe the Old Testament writings, whether the Law or the prophets (see, for example, Matthew 21:42; 22:29; 26:56).

Jesus also made a statement in the Sermon on the Mount that no one can ignore. "Truly I say to you, until heaven and earth pass away, not the smallest letter or stroke shall pass from the Law until all is accomplished" (Matthew 5:18). To reject the Bible is to reject Jesus Christ, since it is the Bible that speaks of Him (Luke 24:27).

The Bible Testifies to Its Own Uniqueness

Hundreds of times in the Old Testament the prophets said "the word of the Lord" came to them. Many other times God spoke directly through the patriarchs or the prophets to His people, who never failed to acknowledge that it was God who spoke.

One great statement of God's uniqueness is found in Isaiah 43, where the Lord said: "Before Me there was no God formed, and there will be none after Me. I, even I, am the Lord, and there is no savior besides Me" (vv. 10–11). If God is unique among all so-called gods, then His Word is unique.

A classic argument for the Bible's validity is the way that the Word so naturally and continually, without the slightest self-consciousness or apology, refers to itself as the Word of God.

Another proof of the Bible's uniqueness is the very nature of the truths it teaches. The Bible gives unmistakable evidence that its thoughts come from God and not man. Consider Isaiah 55:8–9, which makes a strong case for the Bible's uniqueness: "'For My thoughts are not your thoughts, nor are your ways My ways,' declares the Lord. 'For as the heavens are higher than the earth, so are My ways higher than your ways and My thoughts than your thoughts.'"

That's a very strong claim; so if the Bible is indeed unique, then its thinking should be so far higher than our thinking that we could never figure it out on our own. And that is exactly the case with Scripture. This argument may not satisfy the skeptics, but the fact is that the doctrines of Scripture, such as man's total ruin in sin and helplessness to save himself, and the incarnation of God Himself to save mankind, are utterly apart from any other religious teachings. Someone has said that the Bible is the only book that has the courage to tell us the truth about ourselves.

The Bible's Perfect Unity Testifies to Its Uniqueness

The Bible is also unique in the way it has come down to us. The Bible's unity of message is nothing short of a miracle, given that it was written over a period of about fifteen hundred years by forty or more different people, who lived in several different countries with different cultures and came from every kind of background imaginable.

The thin red line of our Redeemer and His blood runs all the way through the Bible—from the first prophecy of a Savior and God's slaying of animals to cover Adam and Eve (Genesis 3:15, 21) to the last chapter of Revelation that invites the redeemed to spend eternity with God (Revelation 22:17). The Bible's message is consistent and unified from beginning to end. I love the psalmist's statement: "The sum of Your word is truth" (Psalm 119:160).

History Testifies to the Bible's Uniqueness

Let's think about the Bible as a work of historical literature. The point here is that if people accepted the same standards of validity for the Bible that they readily accept for other historical documents, they would have to admit that the Bible is the most widely attested book ever written.

One test of the validity of any historical record is its proximity to the life of the person whose history it records. One reason the history of George Washington is considered reliable is that much of it was written during his lifetime by people who did see and know him, and more of it was written in the years very soon after his death.

The principle? The closer the historical record is to the person's life, the more valid it becomes.

Well, guess what? The very latest part of the New Testament, the book of Revelation, was written in the 90s A.D., about sixty years after Jesus' death. And the writer was an eyewitness of Jesus' life, the apostle John, so that gives the record added weight.

This is amazing testimony to the Bible's trustworthiness. By comparison, some of the famous writings of antiquity, such as those that tell of people like Julius Caesar, were recorded hundreds of years after the events they describe. Many critics attack the early dates for various books of the New Testament, because they know that if they admit the Gospels and Epistles were written so soon after Jesus' life and death—mostly by eyewitnesses—their case against the Bible is greatly weakened.

Another test of the Bible's historical validity is the number of existing manuscripts that corroborate it. We are told that ten copies exist of the account of Julius Caesar crossing the Rubicon, one of the most famous events of ancient history. Yet the fact of Caesar's crossing has never been seriously questioned by historians.

But the Bible puts that record, and almost any other historical record, to shame. We have about five thousand copies of the New Testament in existence, from fragments of a single verse to entire books. These copies agree on the basic doctrines of the faith and the important facts of Jesus' life, although there are many differences of words and the order of events. This record is unheard of in historical circles, yet the Bible continues to come under attack.

THE BIBLE IS UNIQUE IN ITS TEACHING

A book that is unique in its origin should also be unique in its content and what it teaches. The Bible qualifies on this point because it teaches what no other book does. The Bible claims to teach the whole truth and nothing but the truth about God, man, creation, sin, salvation, and any other subject it touches on. Let's consider some of the Bible's unique truths.

Only the Bible Teaches about a Divine Trinity

Other religious books may teach that there is a God, but only the Bible teaches that God is a triune Being. God's Word is unique in affirming that God is "one in three"—three distinct persons who share the same divine essence (see Matthew 28:19).

We know the persons of the Godhead are distinct because of statements like this by Jesus: "My Father is working until now, and I Myself am working" (John 5:17). Jesus also promised that God would send the Holy Spirit after Jesus' resurrection (John 14:26). But at the same time Jesus also said, "I and the Father are one" (John 10:30). Three yet one is the glory and the mystery of the Trinity, and only the Bible teaches it.

Only the Bible Teaches the Divine Truth about Jesus

Jesus testified to the truth of Scripture, and the Scripture also testifies to the truth about Jesus. The Bible's teaching of Christ's virgin birth, sinless life as perfect man and eternal God in a human body, atoning death, and triumphant resurrection are enough to set this Book apart from all others.

The Bible presents Jesus as the God-man, totally unlike anyone else in history (Philippians 2:5–11). One minute He was hungry because He was man, but the next minute He was creating enough food to feed five thousand people because He is God. He slept because He was tired, yet He also raised people from the dead. He died on the cross because He was man, yet He walked out of the grave because He is God. The guards who were sent to arrest Jesus one time came back so awed that all they could say was, "Never has a man spoken the way this man speaks" (John 7:46).

Only the Bible Teaches the Whole Truth about Man

The Bible's teaching about the origin and nature of mankind also sets it totally apart. Other religious writings have their stories and myths about how the human race began, but the Bible is alone in portraying man as not only the unique creation of God, but as utterly ruined by sin and completely helpless even to improve himself, to say nothing of saving himself, apart from God's intervention.

Because it is the revealed truth of God, the Bible explains and probes the depth of human nature in a way no other book does. The testimony of countless people is that even though they thought they were reading the Bible, they realized that the Bible was reading them. This is so because the Bible is alive. Hebrews 4:12 says that God's Word is "living and active and sharper than any two-edged sword, and piercing as far as the division of soul and spirit, of both joints and marrow, and able to judge the thoughts and intentions of the heart."

You cannot get any deeper into a person's life than to divide between the soul and spirit, the immaterial part of man.

Only the Bible Teaches the Whole Truth about Salvation

Here's another unique characteristic of Scripture. Every other religion known to mankind tells you what you must do to make yourself acceptable to God. But the Bible tells you what God has already done to save you.

There are really only two religions in the world—the kind in which you do your best to reach up to God, and the kind in which He gave His best to reach down to you. Unlike any other religious book, the Bible says we are saved by grace and not by works (see Ephesians 2:8–9).

Only the Bible Teaches History in Advance

Teaching history in advance sounds like an oxymoron—and it would be for any book but the Bible. God's Word teaches about history hundreds of years before it happens, which is called prophecy. If we had no other validation of Scripture but its fulfilled prophecies, we would still be on very solid ground.

There have been many so-called prophets in history, and some of them seemed to make some accurate prophecies. But the Bible's standard is 100 percent accuracy, whether the prophecy is one hundred or five hundred years in advance of its fulfillment. For example, the prophecy that Jesus would be born in the village of Bethlehem was written (in Micah 5:2) about seven hundred years before Christ's birth. Its fulfillment is recorded in Matthew 2:5–6.

It's not even worth discussing other prophets' records, because no prophet in any holy book has ever claimed to prophesy the future on the scale of the Bible.

THE BIBLE IS UNIQUE IN ITS IMPACT

In some ways we have already made the point that the Bible has had, and continues to have, an influence that is unequaled by any book in history. My point here is simply to reinforce the incredible impact that God's Word has made on the world. God promises in Isaiah 55:11 that His Word will always accomplish the purpose for which He sends it. That is obvious from the influence the Bible has in this world.

When I was a student at Dallas Seminary, we used to hear a story that was told about the late Dr. Harry Ironside, who was one of the great Bible teachers in the early half of the twentieth century and a frequent lecturer at the seminary.

The story goes that Dr. Ironside was preaching in a town once when a local atheist challenged him to prove the existence of God and tried to argue that atheism was as beneficial a way of life as Christianity.

Dr. Ironside challenged the man to a contest. "I want you to find one hundred people whose lives have been changed and made better by atheism, and I will find one hundred people whose lives have been radically changed by the gospel of Jesus Christ. We'll meet here tomorrow and see which way is the true way." Needless to say, the man couldn't meet the challenge, because only the Bible has life-changing power.

The Bible has also changed entire cultures. I love the story of the unbelieving anthropologist who visited a primitive tribe that had accepted the gospel, seeking evidence against Christianity. The chief told the scientist that he knew Christianity was true. When his visitor asked the chief how he knew that, he replied, "Because if it weren't, we would eat you."

The United States is far from perfect, but perhaps more than any other nation, many of our laws and ideas were intentionally based on the teachings of God's Word. And even though our nation has strayed far from God, His Word still has a deep impact on our culture and ways of thinking.

THE BIBLE IS UNIQUE IN ITS PRESERVATION

The Bible has survived for several thousand years, even though kings and the world's mightiest powers and intellects have been trying to destroy it for centuries.

Think about it. How many books have not only survived for several thousand years, but are still being read, debated, and sold around the world today? I can only name one. Bible societies tell us that when they go into a country where Bibles are scarce, people stand in line for hours and even days to receive a copy. Chinese university students pass around any portion of the Bible they can get their hands on and memorize all they can. Would to God that American college students would start doing this!

No book in history has been preserved like the Bible. Why wouldn't it be, if God is the author? He is going to take care of His Book. Nations have outlawed the Bible, tried to destroy every copy, and killed people for translating and printing it.

But God says His Word will stand forever (see Psalm 119:89; Isaiah 40:8). "Heaven and earth will pass away, but My words will not pass away," Jesus declared (Matthew 24:35). There is no destroying the Bible, because it is the eternal Word of God.

PERSONAL APPLICATION FOR LIFE

1. The Word of God is alive with the power of God to change lives. Have you allowed its message of truth to grip your heart and transform it? If not, meditate upon John 3:16 and believe that Jesus Christ, God's Son, died to pay for your sins on the cross, and rose from the dead to save you (Romans 5:8, 10). Give your heart and life to Him, and become a child of God. You can know the joy of forgiveness and eternal life.

2. Approach your Bible as if it were God's love letter to you, because that's exactly what it is. Before you begin reading, ask the Holy Spirit to open your heart and help you make a heart response to what you read.

3. One of the most easily accomplished, and most overlooked growth exercises in the Christian life is simply *reading* the Bible. Too often we neglect to pick up our Bibles and read them every day. One way you can remind yourself to read your Bible is to keep it out where you put your other reading materials: on the coffee table, by the recliner, in the kitchen, or wherever. Once you get in the habit of reading the Bible, you'll get hooked!

4. If your spiritual life is experiencing a growth problem, perhaps you need to start feasting on some choice biblical meat. Your pastor or local Christian bookstore can recommend a number of good basic Bible study tools that will help you get started on the exciting, lifelong adventure of chewing and digesting God's Word.

FOR GROUP STUDY

Questions for Group Discussion

1. Read Isaiah 55:1–10. What does this passage reveal about the transforming power of God's Word?

2. Discuss the unique origins of the Bible. What is the most important proof of the Bible's uniqueness? What are some ways in which history testifies to the Bible's uniqueness?

3. The Bible is unique in its teachings. Discuss some of its unique teachings. (Use the chart on the next page as an aid in your discussion.)

4. What is unique about the Bible's impact on individuals and cultures who engage its message?

PICTURE THIS

The Bible is like no other book. It claims to teach the whole truth and nothing but the truth about God, man, creation, sin, salvation, and any other subject it touches on. Below are some of its unique teachings.

THE UNIQUE TEACHINGS OF THE BIBLE

SPECIFIC TEACHING	SCRIPTURE PASSAGES	WHY IT IS UNIQUE
Only the Bible teaches about the Trinity.	Matthew 28:19	The Bible teaches that God is a triune Being. God's Word is unique in affirming that God is "one in three"—three distinct persons who share the same divine essence.
Only the Bible teaches the whole truth about Jesus.	John 7:46	The Bible presents Jesus as the God-man. It teaches Christ's virgin birth, sinless life as perfect man and eternal God in a human body, atoning death, and triumphant resurrection.
Only the Bible teaches the whole truth about man.	Hebrews 4:12	The Bible explains and probes the depth of human nature in a way no other book does.
Only the Bible teaches the whole truth about salvation.	Ephesians 2:8–9	The Bible tells us what God has already done for us, and that we are saved by grace and not by works.
Only the Bible teaches history in advance.	Micah 5:2; Matthew 2:5–6	God's Word teaches about history hundreds of years before it happens, which is called prophecy.

88

THE BIBLE IS TRUTH

The Roman governor Pontius Pilate asked the question of the ages when truth incarnate in the person of Jesus Christ stood before him on trial. Jesus said to Pilate, "For this I have been born, and for this I have come into the world, to testify to the truth. Everyone who is of the truth hears My voice" (John 18:37).

Pilate responded, "What is truth?" (v. 38).

If that Roman governor had been an honest seeker, he would have found the answer to his question. In fact, Jesus had definitively answered Pilate's question the night before at the Last Supper, during His prayer to the Father on our behalf: "Sanctify them in the truth; Your word is truth" (John 17:17). The Bible is truth—the whole truth and nothing but the truth.

THE INESCAPABLE ISSUE OF TRUTH

There may have been a day when affirming among ourselves as Christians that the Bible is true would have been enough, and we could close this chapter and go on to the next one. But if that simpler day ever existed, it doesn't anymore. Not only is the world today more confused about truth than ever, but the church is confused too. That's why we need to talk about the implications of Jesus' statement that the Bible is truth.

Looking for Truth in All the Wrong Places

The world has always been confused and divided on the question of truth. There have been a myriad responses to the question, What is truth? We have just talked about the denier, for the lack of a better term. This is the person who simply dismisses and rejects the very concept of truth.

The agnostic says that absolute knowledge on issues such as God's existence cannot be attained in this life. Since the word *agnostic* literally means "without knowledge," the agnostic's answer to Pilate's question would be "I don't know." This person is supposedly the perpetual questioner and seeker after truth—although in reality, many people who claim to be agnostics aren't working very hard to search out the truth. They are content to say that truth can't be known and leave it at that.

The rationalist says that human reason and experience are the ultimate criteria for determining truth. Rationalism focuses on the mind and simply says that whatever the mind conceives of as being reality is, in fact, truth. Rationalism thus limits the search for truth. It is one of the theories that came into play during the eighteenth-century movement known as the Enlightenment when the truths upon which Christianity is based came under sustained attack and were largely abandoned.

Pragmatism is yet another means of seeking to arrive at truth. Pragmatism appeals to a lot of people because it says that truth is whatever works. This kind of approach is tailor-made for our American love of "common sense" thinking that looks at a problem and wants to produce solutions.

I need to mention one other significant route people have taken to try and arrive at truth. This is man-made religion, defined as humanity's best attempts to reach up to and understand God—or even deny that He exists or cares about what happens to us. The religionist may be the hardest person of all to deal with, because he's the guy who claims to be a follower of God and a seeker after spiritual truth. But more often than not, religion begins by denying the absolute truth that God has spoken with finality in Jesus Christ (see Hebrews 1:1–2).

Beginning at the Beginning

As you can see from our brief list, the problem is not that people refuse to search for truth. They just refuse to begin with the real source of truth. Jesus said to those who opposed Him and His message, "You search the Scriptures because you think that in them you have eternal life; it is these that testify about Me; and you are unwilling to come to Me so that you may have life" (John 5:39–40). Paul also spoke of people who are "always learning and never able to come to the knowledge of the truth" (2 Timothy 3:7).

THE NATURE OF TRUTH

A definition of truth that most people on the street would agree with is this: Truth is that which conforms to reality, the way things actually are. Truth is an accurate statement of the facts. My generation grew up with Sergeant Joe Friday of the television program *Dragnet*, whose famous statement was, "The facts, ma'am, just the facts." The opposite of truth in this definition is falsehood, and the opposite of telling the truth is lying.

The Bible says clearly that truth not only exists, but that it is knowable if we truly desire to know it. Both halves of this claim may have been normative in our grandparents' day, but they sound radical in today's increasingly truth-less world. Jesus said in John 8:32, "You will know the truth, and the truth will make you free." Jesus said that truth was not only knowable, but powerful since it is the door to true freedom.

There Are Many Claims to Truth Today

Now if you're tracking with me, you may already see the problem that our culture has with truth today. The man on the street may not disagree with you that there is such a thing as truth, but he may passionately believe that there is no such thing as truth that is the same for every person in every place and time. More than likely, he will tell you that there are many kinds of truth that are different for everyone. In other words, truth is whatever is right for you.

I am not saying that people cannot discover certain truths on their own. But the problem with the world's "truth" is that it often has to be revised or discarded when new facts are uncovered. Hundreds of years ago, people were convinced the earth was flat. It was feared that if explorers sailed to the edge of the earth, they might fall off. But that "truth" had to be discarded as new evidence was found.

Truth Conforms to the Nature of God

The only reason we can know any truths at all is that God is God. Truth is not just that which conforms to reality, because there is no reality apart from God. Truth is that which conforms to His nature. We as Christians can make an unapologetic, uncompromising, definitive statement about truth because of the perfectly true nature of God. The Bible calls God the Father "Him who is true" (1 John 5:20), and Jesus made the astounding statement, "I am the way, and *the truth*, and the life" (John 14:6, italics added).

Here's one example of the way God's nature is the standard for what is true. The Bible says, "God is not a man, that He should lie" (Numbers 23:19). Lying is wrong not just because it messes people up and causes harm, but because it violates God's very nature. The same can be said for murder and theft and adultery and coveting. These things are out of line with God's character. Truth and purity are part of His eternal attributes.

THE SOURCE OF TRUTH

If truth is a fixed standard of reality, and of right and wrong, which has been determined by the God who is true and unchanging, then we had better be giving careful attention to the Book He gave to communicate His truth to us.

The Holy Spirit directed the revelation of Scripture in such a way that what was produced is pure truth from God. It could not be any other way if God is pure truth at the core of His being. Don't tell me that God wrote the Bible but at the same time try to tell me that there are mistakes in the Bible. That is a contradiction in terms. God the Holy Spirit safeguarded the Bible, and how He did it is amazing.

God Used Human Authors to Record His Word

Whenever we say that the Bible is God's Word, the argument we often get is, "But the Bible was written by imperfect human beings who were limited in their knowledge, and they were subject to all manner of errors and mistakes."

We need to answer this charge. How is it that a perfect Bible can be the product of imperfect authors? We do have an answer to that charge, which is that God did with the Bible what He did with His own Son in the virgin birth.

The Bible declares Jesus was sinless, even though a human being was the vehicle, so to speak, of His birth. How could an imperfect human being like Mary give birth to a sinless Son? Because the Holy Spirit came upon Mary (see Luke 1:35), which meant that the child in her womb was conceived by God. This ensured that Jesus was free from the contamination of sin, since the Bible says that sin entered the human race by Adam (see Romans 5:12–21). God safeguarded the purity of His Son, so that it was possible for a human being to produce a perfect result.

God Safeguarded the Truth of His Word

God did the same thing with the Bible through the process called divine inspiration. The apostle Peter, who experienced this inspiration, said the Holy Spirit oversaw the writing of Scripture so that there was no contamination in it (see 2 Peter 1:20–21). This is why we can say that God is the Bible's true Author.

But even though the Bible's human authors were "moved" or "carried along" by the Holy Spirit, they often appealed to their own experiences and witness as reliable. Peter said, "We did not follow cleverly devised tales when we made known to you the power and coming of our Lord Jesus Christ, but we were eyewitnesses of His majesty" (2 Peter 1:16). Peter went on to relate the transfiguration of Jesus, which Peter saw and heard (vv. 17–18). John, another apostolic eyewitness, wrote about "what we have heard" and "what we have seen with our eyes" (1 John 1:1).

The writers of Scripture were safeguarded from error by the Holy Spirit, who moved them to write and bore them along in the process. These men were so convinced of the truth that they were willing to die for it—which is a strong argument for the Bible's truth, by the way.

THE TRUTH WITHOUT ERROR

We have said that the Bible is the complete truth (John 17:17), and now I want to give you an important term for this doctrine. That word is *inerrant*, which means "without error." Some people will say the Bible contains truth or contains the Word of God. But that's only half the truth, because it leaves open the possibility that the Bible also contains other things.

The inerrancy of Scripture means that the Bible is true no matter what the subject. At this point some Bible critic will be quick to point out that the existing manuscripts we have of the Bible vary one from another in thousands of places. So the argument goes that we can't talk about the Bible being inerrant because we don't have the original manuscripts, called the autographs.

There are two solid answers to that objection. The first has to do with human nature, and this simply is that God knows that if we had the original autographs of Scripture, we would be tempted to make an idol out of the Book and worship it instead of its Author, which would be a sin. If you don't think humans have an incurable need to make something visible to worship, go to Israel and see all the religious shrines with ornate altars and thousands of lights and candles that various Christian groups have built over the centuries at holy sites.

Second, although the copies of Scripture we do have contain tens of thousands of variations in words and phrasing, these copies do not contradict each other on the basic tenets of the faith, such as the person and work of Christ. This in itself is astounding.

It's Important to Know We Have a Perfect Standard

But the reason we still affirm the Bible's inerrancy in the autographs even though we don't have them is that it is absolutely crucial to believe and know that we have a perfect standard to work against as we compare the various existing manuscripts. Where the texts of biblical manuscripts differ, scholars work to reach the closest consensus possible on what the original said. All this work is worthwhile because it matters what the original said.

It's Important to Let the Bible Speak for Itself

Although the Bible is inerrant, it still contains normal figures of speech at times to make its point, just as we do. It talks about the rising and setting of the sun; it describes the hand or face of God. We know the sun does not rise or set, and we know that God is pure spirit. The Bible's writers wrote what God told them to, without trying to say that the sun literally rises or that God really does have hands.

If you want a good exercise, read all of Psalm 119 in one sitting. It contains 176 verses, making it by far the longest chapter in the Bible, and it has only one subject: the majesty and wonder of God's Word. The Scriptures themselves say God's Word is unique.

After you have finished reading Psalm 119, close your Bible and spend some time thanking God for the gift of His Word, and ask Him to let it saturate your mind and heart. There is no limit to what the Word can do when we allow it to take root in our hearts, because it is always right. It will never adjust to you, but it will do wonders for you when you adjust to it.

PERSONAL APPLICATION FOR LIFE

1. One of the greatest gifts to us is the Bible. It is loaded with timeless precepts and examples from history that will help you stay on the right road, learn from the triumphs and tragedies of others, avoid their pain, and enjoy God's best. Make sure nothing keeps you from reading and heeding your Bible. The Holy Spirit is eager to be your teacher. Open your Bible, and ask God to open your spiritual ears and eyes.

2. The Bible is a source of truth that God will use to guide, strengthen, and nurture you. Our enemy, Satan, is clever and has many of his own perverted versions of the "truth." They are really lies, as he is the Father of Lies. Make a point daily to fill your mind and heart with the truth of God's Word. Never allow Satan to invade your life with his substitutes for truth.

3. People in the New Testament had the Old Testament Scriptures and the teachings of Jesus to guide them. They obeyed the truth they had. When Peter walked on the water, he banked his obedient faith on only one Word from Jesus—"Come." Today, we are privileged to have an entire Bible. Yet, instead of "walking on the water," some of us still stumble on the sidewalk because we haven't learned to obey the precepts of God's Word. Follow Peter's example. Place your faith in the truth of God's Word—and obey it!

4. Take Dr. Evans's advice: Read all of Psalm 119 in one sitting. After you have finished reading Psalm 119, close your Bible and spend some time thanking God for the gift of His Word, and ask Him to let it saturate your mind and heart.

FOR GROUP STUDY

Questions for Group Discussion

1. As preparation for discussion, read 1 John 5:20; John 8:32; 14:6. What is the nature of truth? What power does it hold for those who engage its message?

2. How did the Bible come to us? How do we know its message has been preserved over time? What makes the Bible, apart from all other books, our source of truth? (Use the chart below as an aid to your discussion.)

3. Dr. Evans comments that truth conforms to the nature of God. What are some of the implications of that statement? What impact does that have on those who appropriate the truth of God's Word?

4. When discussing the content of the Bible, what do we mean by the term *inerrant*? What value is it to us that the Scriptures are inerrant?

PICTURE THIS

God has seen to it that the Bible we have and use is His truth. The Holy Spirit directed the revelation of Scripture in such a way that what was produced is pure truth from God.

OUR REVELATION OF TRUTH

2 Peter 1:20–21

"Men moved by the Holy Spirit spoke from God."

GOD'S ACTION	ITS IMPORTANCE
God used human authors to record His Word.	The Bible was written by human authors whose lives and work were attested to by history.
God safeguarded the truth of His Word.	The writers of Scripture were safeguarded from error by the Holy Spirit, who moved them to write and bore them along in the process.

89

THE BIBLE IS AUTHORITATIVE

The supreme authority that kings held over their subjects in ancient days by virtue of their office, the Bible continues to hold by virtue of its Author, who is the King of creation and thus Ruler over all the earth. The Bible's authority is inherent in its every word and even every portion of a word, as we will see. The Bible is supremely authoritative because it is God's revelation in history. Just as there was no higher authority that King Frederick's subjects could appeal to, there is no higher authority you and I can appeal to than the Word of God. And although the Bible may not be taken as seriously in society as it once was, a witness who takes the stand in court must still lay a hand on the Bible and take a solemn oath to tell the truth.

The Bible, of course, can inspire and lift us up. But God does not simply want to inspire us by His Word. He wants us to put ourselves under its authority as the very voice of God.

THE BIBLE IS GOD'S VOICE SPEAKING TO US TODAY

When I say the Bible is God's voice, I mean that the words of Scripture come from His mouth. This is the doctrine of inspiration, which we'll consider later. Christians talk about hearing God's voice in His Word, or hearing

God speak to them through His Word. This is the Holy Spirit's ministry of illumination, another upcoming chapter in this book.

God's Voice Is Timeless in Its Authority

I want to use the term *God's voice* here to help you grasp what we might call the immediacy of the Bible's authority. That is, the Bible's authority is timeless. For example, when we read in Exodus 20:3, "You shall have no other gods before Me," this command has the very same force behind it today that it had when God first thundered these words to Moses more than three thousand years ago. This is important because one problem I see as a pastor is that people disregard God's Word because to them, it's just ink on a page.

Our problem is that we weren't there when God first spoke His Word—because if we had been there, we wouldn't be so casual about it. To get an idea of the terror that gripped Moses and all of Israel when God gave His commandments, read Hebrews 12:18–21. Even Moses said, "I'm so scared my knees are knocking together" (v. 21, Evans translation).

Receiving the Bible as God's voice speaking directly to us is important because of another common problem among God's people. These are the folks who know what God said, and can even repeat it back to you, but they aren't doing anything about it. Every parent is familiar with this scenario. Your child disregards your direct instructions, and when you confront that child later and say, "What did I tell you to do?" he or she can repeat your words verbatim. But for some reason your command didn't carry any weight with that child, so the result was disobedience. And a good parent won't let that go without appropriate discipline (see Hebrews 12:5–6).

Jesus Used the Bible to Affirm His Deity

Jesus was being challenged by His opponents one day when He tried to tell them that He was God. They objected, accused Him of blasphemy, and got ready to stone Him (see John 10:31–33). Jesus turned to the Scripture to make His case, and the way He used the Word has a lot to teach us about the Bible's authority.

> Jesus answered them, "Has it not been written in your Law, 'I said, you are gods'? If he called them gods, to whom the word of God came (and the Scripture cannot be broken), do you say of Him, whom the Father sanctified and sent into the world, 'You are blaspheming,' because I said, 'I am the Son of God'?" (vv. 34–36)

Jesus was using a powerful argument here. He said that if the Bible—in this case through the writing of the psalmist Asaph (Psalm 82:6)—used the term *gods* for men who were merely God's representatives, then those who were accusing Jesus should not object if He called Himself God. Why? Because they had just seen Him heal a blind man (John 9) and do other miracles, for one thing.

What I want you to see here is the binding authority of Scripture. Not even one word can be changed. Let me give you a term you may not have encountered before. Scripture is irrefragable, which means it cannot be voided or invalidated. How important is this trait of Holy Writ? It was important enough to Jesus that He built a critical argument around it.

The Lord's opponents might have wished they could nullify or get around the word *gods* in Psalm 82:6, because it is the Hebrew word *Elohim*, which is one of the names of God. But Jesus had them, because God's Word called His representatives "gods," and nothing could change the Scripture. Paul used a similar tactic in Galatians 3 to prove that Jesus is Abraham's promised seed. The validity of Paul's entire point hung on the difference between the singular "seed" and the plural "seeds" (v. 16). Not only each letter of the Bible, but even the smallest part of each letter (see Matthew 5:18), is vital and carries God's authority.

Jesus Said the Bible Carries His Authority

Jesus Christ also said that the Bible carries the imprint of His divine authority. He announced to His disciples, "Heaven and earth will pass away, but My words will not pass away" (Matthew 24:35). That statement on the lips of anyone other than Jesus would be heresy, but He alone can claim, "All authority has been given to Me in heaven and on earth" (Matthew 28:18). Therefore, Jesus' words, which are recorded in Scripture, will outlast history, because the Word is eternal. I love the way the psalmist put it: "Forever, O Lord, Your word is settled in heaven" (Psalm 119:89).

Rejecting the Bible Means Rejecting Jesus

If Jesus Christ tied His authority so closely to the Bible's authority, then the logical conclusion is that to reject the authority of Scripture is to reject Christ.

In John 10:34–36 Jesus appealed to the authority and inviolability of the Bible to argue that He was correct in saying, "I and the Father are one" (v. 30). His detractors understood very clearly that Jesus was claiming to be God, and they wanted to stone Him for blasphemy (vv. 31–33) because Jesus was claiming an authority they said no one but God should be able to claim. And they were exactly right. Jesus could only claim this authority because He was God in the flesh.

Jesus answered their charge by showing them that they could not reject Him without rejecting the Word of God they professed to believe. He pointed to the works He had done (vv. 37–38) as proof of His deity, knowing the Jews believed that Messiah would do great miracles when He came (see John 3:2).

You can't say you love and believe God's Word without loving and believing the Savior whom God has sent. It is said of Jesus in the Gospels that He spoke "as one having authority, and not as [the] scribes" (Matthew 7:29). The scribes had opinions and their Jewish traditions, but Jesus spoke with the voice of God, and we have His words in the Bible.

WE MUST RESPOND TO GOD'S VOICE TO US IN THE BIBLE

The fact that the Bible is completely authoritative and cannot be broken is a wonderful doctrine of the Christian faith. But the truth and power of God's Word can be nullified in your experience if you refuse to let the Word speak to you as it is or you start mixing it up with your human viewpoints.

Now, please notice that I did not say the Bible can lose its power or authority. That will never happen because God said His Word is "forever settled in heaven." But the Bible's power is blunted in our lives when we do not respond to God in humility and obedience.

Don't Mix the Bible's Words with Your Words

This is probably the Number One travesty that people who claim to believe and follow God's Word commit against it. A lot of people who try to mix their own thoughts with the Bible's teaching have many degrees after their name. Education is fine, and the church has benefited from well-trained commentators and scholars who seek to understand what the Word means.

This is not what I'm talking about. There's a big difference between an honest attempt to understand the Bible as it reads and diluting its teachings with human thinking. The best example of this is in Scripture itself, when the Pharisees and scribes came to Jesus to accuse His disciples of breaking "the tradition of the elders" (Matthew 15:1–2).

But Jesus came back at them with a much more serious charge, that of nullifying the Word of God (vv. 4–6), using the example of God's commandment to honor one's father and mother. Jesus showed how the scribes and Pharisees allowed people, mainly themselves, to get around this clear command with a hollow promise to give those resources to God while actually not having to give them away at all.

Jesus gave the bottom line of this kind of thinking when He said at the end of verse 6, "And by this you invalidated the word of God for the sake of your tradition." The point is that God never meant for the commandment to honor your father and mother to be skirted on a technicality.

The Jews added so many traditions and regulations to the law that they ended up creating a barrier around the Word so people couldn't get to it. Now, let's give them enough credit to say that they were trying to help God out. And there were questions that had to be worked out in everyday life. But these rules became more important than what God said.

The Bible says, "Let God be found true, though every man be found a liar" (Romans 3:4). The issue Jesus dealt with was the authority of God's Word. If God says we are to honor our parents, then trying to find a "loophole" in that command is a sin against the truth.

Don't Poison the Pot of Stew

There's an interesting story in 2 Kings 4:38–41 about the prophet Elisha and the "apprentice prophets" who were under his tutelage. There was a famine in the land, and these student prophets were hungry. Elisha told his servant to make a pot of stew for everybody, and one of the prophets gathered some wild gourds for the stew. The gourds looked fine to him, and he probably thought they would add a little spice to the stew. So he decided to help out by tossing the gourds into the stew.

But as everyone ate, some apparently began to feel sick and said the stew was poisoned. Someone cried out to Elisha, "O man of God, there is death in the pot" (v. 40). Elisha took care of the problem, and the stew was fine.

Unfortunately, every Sunday in churches all across this nation there are plenty of pastors and teachers who are tossing "wild gourds" into the pot—adding human wisdom to God's Word or even allowing human views and opinions to replace the Scriptures.

Some attend good churches where this is not a problem, yet they still get sick spiritually by tossing into the Word their own wild gourds of human opinion. I often hear people say, "My mama taught me," or "All my friends say." Before you listen to what other people say, even friends and family, check it against what God actually says in His Word. Don't let someone else spoil the effect of the Word with the poison of human opinion.

Let God Set Your Life's Agenda

Biblical authority means that God has the supreme right to determine our decision making and set the agenda for our lives. God doesn't want our rationalizations, but our response. He wants us to do like we do when we're driving and come up over a hill only to see a police car sitting on the side of the road.

That police car is a symbol of the officer's authority—and we know the officer also has the clout to back up that authority. So if we are doing wrong by speeding, we don't just say, "Big deal. So what if I'm doing eighty in a fifty-five zone? I don't need to do anything."

No, when we see the police car and we know we are not living right at that moment, our heart starts to palpitate and we hit the brake. Why? Because we have run into a legitimate authority that we respect, and we respond. In other words, the presence of this authority creates a response, not just an analysis.

Paul told Timothy to preach the Word whether it was convenient or not because people would want to have "their ears tickled" instead of hearing the truth (2 Timothy 4:2–3). There's nothing wrong with feeling good, as long as it's the truth that is making you feel good. But when a lie is making you feel good, it's illegitimate.

Too many people treat the Bible the way Great Britain treats the queen. The British people give great honor to the queen, and she is involved in many impressive and elaborate displays of her power and authority. But when it comes to governing the country, the queen is for show only, because England is a constitutional monarchy. The queen is the representative head of the land, but she is just a figurehead. She doesn't make or veto laws, and she doesn't formulate policy. The queen has no real authority. She doesn't set the agenda for her country.

People can have Bibles in every room of the house, in their cars, and even at their offices and yet still want to have their ears tickled by the latest religious fad or clever deceiver. But God wants to occupy the place of supreme authority in your life, and He wants to set your life's agenda as you submit yourself to His Word.

PERSONAL APPLICATION FOR LIFE

1. Make no mistake. The Bible can inspire you and lift you up. But God does not simply want to inspire you with His Word. He wants you to put yourself under its authority as the very voice of God. When you read God's Word, submit to its authority by letting it search your heart and change you.

2. Have you ever run into something God is asking you to do but you don't want to do? Perhaps it doesn't even make sense to you. But if God is calling you to obey, don't try to figure it out. Don't go around asking everyone else what you should do. Don't take a vote and see how many other folks would agree with you. Just do what God says.

3. Before you listen to what other people are saying about a problem or issue, check it against what God says in His Word. A lot of "advice" we get from others is given by those who aren't even living out their own advice. Don't let someone else spoil the powerful effect of the Word in your life with the poison of human opinion.

4. Have you ever wished God would speak to you directly—as He did to Abraham or Moses? But God *has* spoken to you. The Bible is His direct communication to you. It is His voice. So when you open your Bible, start by saying, "I am going to listen to God's voice speak to me today."

FOR GROUP STUDY

Questions for Group Discussion

1. What makes the Bible authoritative? Discuss the four points Dr. Evans presents.

2. Why does Dr. Evans refer to the Bible as "God's voice"? Read the account in Hebrews 12:18–21. What authority did Moses ascribe to the voice of God? Does the church today have the same level of respect for God's voice?

3. What was Jesus' view of the Bible's authority? See Matthew 24:35; 28:18.

4. Why is rejecting Jesus tantamount to rejecting the Bible? How was rejection played out by Jesus' detractors?

PICTURE THIS

The Bible is completely authoritative. We can experience its truth and power as we properly respond to it. It is important that, as we respond, we are careful not to add our thoughts and opinions, or those of others, to God's voice.

RESPONDING TO GOD'S VOICE

OUR RESPONSE	SCRIPTURE PASSAGE	WHY IT'S IMPORTANT
Let the Bible speak for itself.	Romans 3:4	Rather than imposing your own thoughts upon Scripture, listen for God's voice.
Do not add to what God says.	2 Kings 4:28–31	Embrace the pure truth of God's Word without allowing human opinion to poison it.
Let God set your life's agenda.	2 Timothy 4:2–3	Give God supreme authority in your life and allow Him to set your life's agenda as you submit to His Word.

90

THE BIBLE IS POWERFUL

The Word of God can transform any situation or person, because built into it is the ability to pull off whatever God desires it to accomplish. Power is the ability to effect change or produce the desired effect. That is the power within God's Word.

God declares this truth in a verse that opened our look at bibliology: "So will My word be which goes forth from My mouth; it will not return to Me empty, without accomplishing what I desire, and without succeeding in the matter for which I sent it" (Isaiah 55:11).

The unstoppable power of God's Word is another attribute that sets it apart from anyone else's word. When God had finished giving Job a lesson in His awesome power, Job confessed: "I know that You can do all things, and that no purpose of Yours can be thwarted" (Job 42:2). The prophet agreed, saying, "For the Lord of hosts has planned, and who can frustrate it?" (Isaiah 14:27).

God's Word cannot be frustrated or stopped, and God never goes around showing off His power just because He can. His Word is always purposeful when it goes out from His mouth, and that purpose is always achieved. God's power is never random or out of control. He always has a plan that He intends to fulfill.

I want to give you two great biblical examples of the power that God's Word has to accomplish His purposes. We could call these the Bible's external and internal power, because they refer to the creation around us and our soul and spirit at the innermost recesses of our beings. The word that God spoke, as revealed and preserved in the Bible, can bring a world into being and cut to the core of our hearts.

THE POWER TO CREATE A UNIVERSE

When the writers of Scripture wanted to illustrate the awesome power of God, they often pointed to His creation of the world. The psalmist declared, "By the word of the Lord the heavens were made, and by the breath of His mouth all their host" (Psalm 33:6). Then he added in verse 9, "For He spoke, and it was done; He commanded, and it stood fast," referring to the earth and all of its mighty oceans.

God Can Make Something Out of Nothing

To simply speak a world into existence is power beyond anything we can imagine. Theologians have a phrase for the creative act of God whereby He made the universe out of nothing. It is called creation *ex nihilo*, or "out of nothing." In other words, God did not need any raw materials to work with when He created the world. He created the raw materials and everything else with His word.

Genesis 1 records again and again that "God said . . . and it was so." This is creation *ex nihilo*, making not just something out of nothing, but everything out of nothing (Hebrews 11:3).

No human being can literally make something out of nothing. Nor can we just speak and make whatever we want happen. You may be able to make lemonade out of a lemon, but at least you have to start with a lemon.

But God spoke just two words in the Hebrew text of Genesis 1:3, which could be translated "Light be," and light appeared. He spoke again and the dry land appeared. Time after time, God said the word and whatever He commanded came into being. There were no gaps or lapses. God simply worked out His will through His word.

God Can Create Life Out of Death

I like the way Paul put it. He said that God "calls into being that which does not exist" (Romans 4:17). The apostle made this great statement of God's power in the middle of discussing Abraham's faith in God's promise to give him a child even though he and Sarah were way too old to become parents. In fact, the Bible says that in terms of their ability to bear children, both Sarah and Abraham were as good as dead (v. 19).

That was no problem for God. His word to Abraham was, "I will surely return to you at this time next year; and behold, Sarah your wife will have a son" (Genesis 18:10). This was God's promise to Abraham, and it came to pass.

The power of God's Word was on display in an even greater way in the birth of Jesus Christ, who was the fulfillment of the promised Son of which Isaac was a type. Luke 1:26–38 is an incredible passage of Scripture that tells of the angel Gabriel announcing to Mary that she was going to have a baby. Mary was stunned at this word, and wondered how this could be since she was a virgin. This was an impossible situation as far as Mary was concerned.

During this announcement, Gabriel also revealed that Elizabeth was expecting a child, telling Mary, "for nothing will be impossible with God" (Luke 1:37). Mary had hardly had time to absorb the startling news that she was going to conceive and bear the Savior of the world, and now she was being told that Elizabeth was going to have a baby too.

At least Elizabeth had a husband, and her baby had come about by means of human conception, just as Isaac was fathered by Abraham. However, Elizabeth's conception of John the Baptist was still a miracle because she was old and her womb was as dead as Sarah's. But when it came to the virgin Mary and the birth of Jesus, we have the miracle of all miracles.

The angel had the message that made sense out of all this for Mary: "For nothing will be impossible with God." Now let me show you something interesting about this verse. The word *nothing* here actually translates three words in the Greek text that literally mean "not any word." The idea is that no word God speaks is too hard for Him to fulfill. So the fact that Mary was a virgin was no obstacle to God.

God Can Make Something Where You See Nothing

It doesn't matter who tries to stop God from carrying out the word He has spoken. The Enemy can throw up a lot of defenses, and may even appear to be winning sometimes because God allows human choices and failings to be part of His plan. But God guarantees that even these things will be incorporated into His divine program. No matter how long it takes or what has to happen to get there, God will accomplish His objective. His Word is sure and effective.

Now don't misunderstand. I'm not saying there is some kind of special power in the pieces of paper stitched together between leather to make a Bible. One charge that liberal theologians and churchmen make against evangelicals is that we worship the Bible instead of worshiping God.

No, we worship the God who has revealed Himself to us in His Word. The Bible is like the electrical outlet in your home that puts you in touch with the power source when you plug into it. Without the power, the plug would be dead—which, by the way, is the problem with every other so-called holy book in the world. They lack power because they are just human words on a page. The plug is dead, so to speak.

God's Word Sustains What He Has Created

God not only brought the universe into existence by the power of His word, but that same word also sustains His creation. The writer of Hebrews said of Jesus, "He is the radiance of [God's] glory and the exact representation of His nature, and upholds all things by the word of His power" (1:3). God is able to sustain what He brings into being (see 2 Peter 3:5–7).

This is part of the good news of our salvation. As the gospel song puts it, God didn't bring you this far just to leave you. The reason you can't lose your salvation is that what God creates, He keeps. If you are a Christian, you are a new creation in Christ (see 2 Corinthians 5:17), and no one can snatch you out of God's hand (see John 10:28–30).

THE POWER TO SEARCH US

Now we're getting down to the nitty-gritty. From the vastness of creation we are going to focus down to the inner workings of the human soul and spirit. God's Word has the power to pierce into the deepest recesses of our being with laserlike power and precision.

We know this from a great passage of Scripture that I hope is familiar to you: "For the word of God is living and active and sharper than any two-edged sword, and piercing as far as the division of soul and spirit, of both joints and marrow, and able to judge the thoughts and intentions of the heart. And there is no creature hidden from His sight, but all things are open and laid bare to the eyes of Him with whom we have to do" (Hebrews 4:12–13).

God's Spirit Is Active in His Word

The Bible is not dead words on a page but is alive and powerful, which is the idea behind the word *active*. The Bible is a living document because it is the Word of the living God, animated by the living Holy Spirit. Genesis 1:2 says that God's Spirit was "moving," or hovering, over the waters of the earth at creation, breathing life into the creation.

The Holy Spirit does the same thing with the Word that He did with creation. The Spirit hovers over the Word and breathes life into it, with the result that we are not to read the Bible the way we read a novel, a history book, or any other book. We read other books to get information or to be entertained, but we should read the Bible to get life from it and allow it to penetrate our hearts.

God's Word Cuts to the Heart

The writer of Hebrews likened the Bible to a two-edged sword that cuts on both sides as it is thrust into the target. Roman soldiers carried these swords, which were kept very sharp. When a Roman soldier used his two-edged sword on an enemy, it penetrated deeply for maximum effect.

God's Word is so sharp and powerful that it can plunge into our spirits like a sharp sword that cuts not even just to the bone, but into the marrow inside the bone. No other book can reach down into a person that deeply and bring about the effects that the Bible can.

In other words, God wants His Word to do spiritual surgery on us. He wants to lay bare our souls so He can show us what's on the inside of us.

Have you ever said or done something that seemed out of character for you, and you wondered later where in the world that came from? Maybe it was there all the time.

All of us are capable of reacting in ways that are unusual for us, but at the same time we don't really know our own hearts very well. The Bible says, "The heart is more deceitful than all else and is desperately sick; who can understand it?" (Jeremiah 17:9). The answer is that no one can understand the human heart perfectly—no one, that is, except God. He knows our deepest thoughts because our souls and spirits are completely exposed before Him.

This explains why people testify that when they read the Bible, they feel as if it is looking into the deepest recesses of their minds and hearts. They feel this because the Word is alive and powerful, constantly probing us. It's a good thing to be probed and exposed by the incision that God makes in our lives by His Word, because that's when we really deal with deep-rooted sin and begin to grow.

Let God's Word Do Its Work in You

Hebrews 4:12 says that God's Word can probe our deepest being. It critiques "the thoughts and intentions of the heart." That's what the word *judge* means. It is the word for a critic. A drama critic watches a play and then makes judgments about what is good, what needs to be improved, and what needs to be discarded.

We may assume that most of our thoughts and intentions, or plans, are fine. But we are ultimately not capable of making that judgment. We need the Holy Spirit to take the sword of the Word and slice us open right down to the core of our being. We need to separate what is good from what is worthless, the way a person in Bible times would winnow wheat to separate it from the chaff, so the good wheat would be saved and the bad chaff would blow away in the wind.

The Word of God is living and powerful, and what God wants to do is show us the power of His Word. Through the Word you will come to see yourself as God sees you, which is as you really are. You will also come to see God in ways that you could not see Him otherwise. And when God begins to stitch you up after performing spiritual surgery, you will come back from the operation stronger than ever.

Experience the Power of God's Word

Someone may say, "I'm not sure if I know what you're talking about. I read the Bible, but I've never experienced anything like what you've been describing."

If we are reading the Word just so we can say we've had our devotions, because we feel like we're supposed to, or because the preacher said we should, then we are going to miss the purpose God has for us. God's purpose is that His Word goes into our deepest parts and begins to remake us from the inside out, conforming us to the image of Christ (see Romans 8:29).

The power of God's Word is discovered as we cooperate with the purposes for which God gave us His Word. The Word will always accomplish God's will, which is good and perfect (see Romans 12:2). The only question still on the floor is whether we are going to get in on the action.

APPLICATION FOR LIFE

1. It was God's word that spoke the universe into existence. According to John 1:14, the Word (Jesus) became flesh and dwelt among us. Through Christ's sacrificial death, we become a new creation in Him. The same power that speaks creation into existence also sustains creation, and that includes your salvation. Although it's difficult for us to comprehend all that God does on our behalf, we can certainly thank Him for what we can grasp and understand. Take a moment to give thanks to God for the power of His Word at work in your life.

2. God's Word cuts to the heart like no other book can (Hebrews 4:12). Brokenness and contrition of the heart can be a cure for spiritual insensitivity. Psalm 51 is David's great prayer of confession and cleansing. Pray Psalm 51 regularly and let the power of God's Word keep your heart clean before Him. Do you need to make this your prayer today?

3. As humans, we spew out a lot of words. A lot of what we say never comes to pass, thankfully. And our plans are often frustrated. Be encouraged that with God, His powerful Word always accomplishes its purpose. As you engage His Word, God will accomplish His purposes in your life.

4. A wonderful cleansing agent for a stagnant spiritual life is the blood of Christ. Ask the Holy Spirit to search your heart. Be ready to confess any sin He puts His finger on, claming the promise of 1 John 1:9.

FOR GROUP STUDY

Questions for Group Discussion

1. What are some of the characteristics of God's Word? Read Isaiah 55:11. What truths does it give us about the power of God's Word? (See also Job 42:2 and Isaiah 14:27.)

2. Read Psalm 33:6, 9. Discuss the creative power of God's Word. Dr. Evans uses the Latin term *ex nihilo*. What is its significance as it relates to this discussion? (Use the chart on the next page as an aid to your discussion.)

3. Dr. Evans explains that the Holy Spirit is active in God's Word. In what ways does the Holy Spirit work in conjunction with the Bible to minister to us?

4. Read Romans 8:29. What is God's purpose for using the Word to work in believers? How can we realize this purpose in our lives?

PICTURE THIS

One of the themes that runs throughout the Bible is the power of God's spoken and written Word. Below are examples of the creative power of God's Word.

THE AWESOME CREATIVE POWER OF GOD'S WORD

GOD'S WORD IN ACTION	SCRIPTURE PASSAGE	WHAT IT MEANS
God can make something out of nothing.	Genesis 1–18	God can create everything out of nothing, without the benefit of any raw materials.
God can create life out of death.	Luke 1:26–38	God can create life when it appears to be physically impossible.
God can make something where we see nothing.	Romans 4:17	Because His Word is powerful, God needs nothing else to do His work.
God's Word sustains what He has created.	2 Peter 3:5–7	The same Word that spoke creation into being also sustains that creation.

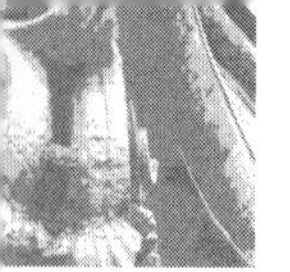

91

THE BIBLE IS SUFFICIENT

Go into almost any bookstore today and you will probably find books that include the word *Bible* in their title. You'll also find books that, while they might not contain the actual word, have been called "the bible" on their particular subject, such as the vegetarian's bible or the fashion bible. I understand there is even a hunter's bible.

Why would an author or a publisher want to call a book the such-and-such "bible"? Why would a reviewer refer to a book, or perhaps a magazine or some other publication, as the "bible" in that field? They do it because the Bible is associated with the final word on a subject.

There is no issue we will ever face that is not addressed either by direct command or by general principle in the Word. In the Bible, God has given us "everything pertaining to life and godliness" (2 Peter 1:3).

Paul put this doctrine into a compact statement when he wrote: "All Scripture is inspired by God and profitable for teaching [or doctrine], for reproof, for correction, for training [or instruction] in righteousness; so that the man of God may be adequate, equipped for every good work" (2 Timothy 3:16–17).

One magnificent passage of Scripture lays out the sufficiency of the

Word in very beautiful and clear terms. In Psalm 19:7–14, the psalmist David made six statements about the ability of God's revelation to address every area of human existence, and in particular every area that we as believers need to know if we are going to please God. These verses also speak to the all-consuming desire we should have for the Word and remind us that God's Word can keep us from sin.

Verses 1–6 of Psalm 19 form a backdrop to this poetic tribute to the Word, and we need to review them briefly. They deal with general revelation, the truth about God that He has written, so to speak, into every atom of creation and made available to every person. The psalm begins with a declaration of this truth: "The heavens are telling of the glory of God; and their expanse is declaring the work of His hands" (v. 1).

Just reading Psalm 19:1–6 makes it clear that God's revelation of Himself in creation is powerful and profound. But general revelation is also limited. It is enough to condemn the sinner, as Paul said in Romans 1:18–23. In fact, those who reject or pervert this witness in nature are "without excuse" (v. 20) because they did not follow it to its logical conclusion, which is to seek the God of whom it speaks.

THE BIBLE IS GOD'S PERFECT GUIDE FOR US

General revelation is limited because it is not sufficient in and of itself to save the sinner. Psalm 19:3 says of the heavens as God's witness, "There is no speech, nor are there words; their voice is not heard." We can look at the stars or the oceans and know that the creator God must be great and powerful. But we must go to His Word to learn that He has spoken to us and revealed that He is altogether righteous and judges sin, and is the Father of our Lord Jesus Christ.

David began what we could call this hymn of praise to God by saying, "The law of the Lord is perfect, restoring the soul" (Psalm 19:7a). *Law* is another term for the Scripture. David must have wanted to begin at the top, because he described the Word of God as perfect. This term refers to that which is whole, complete, not lacking in any area. The Bible is complete in its revelation of divine truth.

There Are No Flaws in God's Word

Now let me clarify something here before we go any further. To say that the Bible is complete is not to claim that God has told us everything. We know that isn't so. The apostle John said that if everything Jesus did while He was on earth was recorded, even "the world itself" could not contain the books this would require (John 21:25). And John was just talking about a three-year slice of time.

The Bible says, "The secret things belong to the Lord our God" (Deuteronomy 29:29). His knowledge is inexhaustible. If God told us everything, we would be like Him. Much of what the Lord has for us will have to wait until we are with Him in heaven. But in the meantime, God's revealed Word has everything we need to know to be all that God expects us to be.

God's Word Has Power to Restore Us

The second half of this phrase in Psalm 19:7a gives us the blessing or benefit of His perfect Word: It restores the soul. This is a picture of something being brought back to its original condition. It speaks of being revived or refreshed. The Bible is sufficient to take what is broken and restore it, much like you might restore an old piece of furniture to its original beauty. God's Word can make old things new.

What is your soul? The Hebrew word *nephesh* refers to the essence of your being, who you are at your core. Most of us spend most of our time trying to fix what we do rather than who we are. But we only do what we do because we are who we are. God's Word deals with our whole being, and it has the power to turn us inside out so we can see ourselves the way He sees us.

THE BIBLE CAN MAKE US WISE

Psalm 19:7 goes on to make a second statement about the Word of God. "The testimony of the Lord is sure, making wise the simple."

God's testimony refers to His truth as revealed in Scripture. The statements a witness makes in court are supposed to be nothing but the truth, but only God's witness is 100 percent true. Thus it is completely solid, or trustworthy. You can build your life on it. That's what the psalmist meant when he said the Word is "sure" like a rock, as opposed to something unstable and flimsy.

We need the sure Word of God to guide us. Psalm 19 is a reminder that the Bible can save us a lot of heartache by giving us the ability to discern situations with godly wisdom and make God-honoring choices.

THE BIBLE GIVES US THE DETAILS OF GOD'S WILL

The third of the psalmist's six declarations in Psalm 19 about Scripture is also packed with good stuff. "The precepts of the Lord are right, rejoicing the heart" (v. 8a). Here David described the Bible using a word that means the particulars of divine instruction. God's *precepts* spell out things in more detail so that we can live a well-ordered life.

God's Precepts Are Always on Target

One example of a biblical precept is in Proverbs 6:1–5, where we are told not to become "surety," or what we would call a cosigner, for another person's debts. The reason is obvious: If the borrower defaults on the debt, we will be left holding the note and the debt. God's Word tells us by way of principle to be wise in how we handle our finances, but Proverbs 6 gets down to a specific case of avoiding the trap of guaranteeing someone else's debts.

The great thing about the Lord's precepts is that they are always "right," or on target. They never miss the mark. This word in Hebrew means to show someone the correct path, the right way, the road he or she ought to take. Now in the case of avoiding surety, most folk would agree that this is the right thing to do because the risks of taking on another person's debts are enormous. In fact, Proverbs 6 advises the person who has done this not to allow himself any rest until he gets out of that mess.

But God's precepts are right even when nobody else agrees. If the Bible says one thing and everybody else is saying another thing, then everybody else is wrong. The gospel is "foolishness" to the unsaved world (1 Corinthians 1:21), but it is the right path to take. Jesus spoke about two roads, the broad road that is crowded but leads to destruction, and the narrow road that has plenty of room because there are so few people on it (see Matthew 7:13–14).

There Is Joy in Following Jesus

When you obey God's precepts, they rejoice your heart. When you follow the biblically prescribed path, you will be happy you took that road.

How do you know when you're on the right path, especially when everyone else seems to be going the other way? You know the path is right cognitively when it is the path that the Bible prescribes. But you know you are on the right path experientially when you have God's indescribable joy in the midst of the journey, no matter how difficult or painful.

THE BIBLE GIVES US COMMANDS TO ENLIGHTEN US

There is more good news in Psalm 19, because the Word tells us, "The commandment of the Lord is pure, enlightening the eyes" (v. 8b). This statement expresses the fact that the Bible's teachings are divine mandates, which means they are not optional. God is not writing down suggestions for us to consider. Most people think the Bible contains ten commandments, but here David described all of God's revelation as a commandment that is binding on us.

God isn't the only one looking for our obedience. The trouble with obeying others is that if you aren't careful whom you obey, it can lead to disaster, because people's commands are not pure. But God's commandments are free of all contamination. Following them will enlighten our eyes and help remove the impurities from our hearts so we can see things clearly.

The opposite of having our eyes enlightened is to have them darkened or blinded. God blinds the eyes and hearts of those who refuse to listen to or obey Him. Jesus prayed in Matthew 11:25, "I praise You, Father, Lord of heaven and earth, that You have hidden these things from the wise and intelligent and have revealed them to infants." The intelligent here are those who are wise in their own eyes and don't feel they need God's Word to enlighten them. But people who are dependent on God get to see life in the blazing light and truth of His Word.

THE BIBLE WILL ENDURE FOREVER

We have two more statements about God's transforming Word to consider from Psalm 19, and they just keep getting better. Beginning in verse 9 we read, "The fear of the Lord is clean, enduring forever."

The word *clean* is similar to *pure* in that it speaks of an absence of impurity or defilement. God conveys His truth without flaw or blemish. In an earlier psalm, David declares, "The words of the Lord are pure words . . . refined seven times" (12:6).

The fear of the Lord is the reverential fear or awe that the Bible inspires in the hearts of those who love Him and seek to live by His commandments and precepts. The fear of God will last forever, because even when we are in heaven with Jesus, God will not lose any of His majesty, and we will not lose the awe in which He wants us to hold Him. In fact, our awe of the Lord will be infinitely increased when we are with Him in His uninterrupted, holy presence.

As the pure expression of God's heart and mind, the Bible will also last forever. "Forever, O Lord, Your word is settled in heaven" (Psalm 119:89). The Bible is permanent and always relevant. It will never go out of date or out of print.

THE BIBLE REVEALS GOD'S RIGHTEOUSNESS

The last of David's six declarations about the Word of God certainly does not mean least. It too is great: "The judgments of the Lord are true; they are righteous altogether" (v. 9b). *Judgments* refer to the ordinances or divine verdicts issued from the bench of the Supreme Judge of the earth. The Bible is our infallible standard for judging all of life's situations.

God's Word produces righteousness in the life of the believer who seeks to live by it. Because the Bible is the unadulterated truth of God, you become right with God when you apply it.

God's Word Is Surpassing in Its Value

The remaining verses of Psalm 19 may be read as expanding this final statement about God's Word as His judgments. But more likely they refer to all that David has said in the previous section about the Bible and its value. But whatever the case, let's look at them in closing because they answer an important, if unspoken, question: If the Bible is this incredible and sufficient for all of our needs, what priority should it have in our lives?

The psalmist spoke to this, and he didn't stutter. The words of God are "more desirable than gold, yes, than much fine gold" (v. 10a). It would be news to many people in our culture that there is something more important than money. I would like to think that we as believers know that, but we unfortunately don't always act like we know it.

The first time some people realize there are more important things in life than money is on their deathbed. That's when they want a Bible or someone who can tell them what life and death are all about.

God's Word Is Sweet in Its Effect

Psalm 19:10 also says the Word of God is "sweeter also than honey and the drippings of the honeycomb." That means it is better than any dessert you can dream of. Have you ever read a passage that became sweet to you? There's nothing else like it. That's why the Bible invites us, "O taste and see that the Lord is good" (Psalm 34:8).

God wants you to taste and savor His Word. For David, the Word was something to be experienced as well as to be known. The Bible is true, but you want more than just the facts of Scripture. You want the reality of it. You want the Bible to take on life, which is the ministry of the Holy Spirit who gives life to the words on the page in front of you. And when that happens, the Scripture will become flavorful to you.

God's Word Is Powerful in Its Protection

In verses 11–13 of Psalm 19, the psalmist continued with a tribute to the Bible's ability to protect believers from sin of every kind. These include "hidden faults" (v. 12), those deep-down flaws we may not always be aware of that can trip us up, and "presumptuous sins" (v. 13), those we plan and deliberately commit. David's goal in all this was to be "blameless" and "acquitted of great transgression."

The psalm closes with a great prayer that expressed David's desire to respond properly to the wonderful truth that God's Word was all he would ever need. "Let the words of my mouth and the meditation of my heart be acceptable in Your sight, O Lord, my rock and my Redeemer" (v. 14).

God's Word is sufficient for every area of life. All the ingredients you need to be acceptable to God are there in the Scripture. You don't have to mess with the recipe. Just dig in and enjoy it.

PERSONAL APPLICATION FOR LIFE

1. Sometimes God explicitly states what He does and does not want us to do, while at other times He gives us general principles that apply to a multitude of situations. Both are designed to govern our character and conduct, and both are equally authoritative. Obey the precepts of the Word, and you will live a well-ordered life aligned with God's will.

2. God's Word has an enduring quality about it. Psalm 119:89 tells us, "Forever, O Lord, Your word is settled in heaven." Have you ever tried to keep a record of how God has remained faithful to the promises of His Word in your life? It's so easy to take God for granted. When you get a chance, reflect on God's provisions and how faithful He has been to His Word. Make a list or journal your thoughts. It can be an eye-opener!

3. Psalm 19:14 reads, "Let the words of my mouth and the meditation of my heart be acceptable in Your sight, O Lord, my rock and my Redeemer." This was David's response to the truth that God's Word was all he would ever need. Let this be your response as well.

4. Is your life falling apart? The help you need is already in the Bible. You say, "I'm worried. Does God have a word for me?" Yes, He does. "I don't know how I'm going to pay my bills." It's in His Word. "I just found out I have cancer." The Bible has a word for you. Whatever your need, God's Word is sufficient to address any need you will ever have.

FOR GROUP STUDY

Questions for Group Discussion

1. Discuss 2 Timothy 3:16–17 and 2 Peter 1:3. To what extent is God's Word sufficient? What does God's written Word reveal that is beyond His general revelation of Himself in nature?

2. Read Psalm 19:7a. For what two reasons is the Bible a perfect guide for us? How do those two reasons serve to guide us? How does the Bible make us "wise"?

3. What is a biblical precept? Read the example of a biblical precept in Proverbs 6:1–5. How do we discover God's will by reading the Bible?

4. Read Psalm 19:7–9. The Bible reveals God's righteousness. As we engage God's Word, what features does it possess that produce righteousness in God's people? (Use the chart below as an aid to your discussion.)

PICTURE THIS

God's Word produces righteousness in the life of the believer who seeks to live by it. As we apply the Word to our lives, we grow in His righteousness and become right with God.

GOD'S WORD PRODUCES RIGHTEOUSNESS IN HIS CHILDREN

Psalm 19

TRUTH	SCRIPTURE PASSAGE	WHAT IT MEANS
God's Word is surpassing in its value.	verse 10a	Because it is sufficient to meet all our needs, the Word is more desirable and valuable than money or gold.
God's Word is sweet in its effect.	verse 10b; Psalm 34:8	When we engage the truth of the Word in our lives, it becomes flavorful, and we can taste and savor it.
God's Word is powerful in its protection.	verses 11–13	The Bible is able to protect us from sin of any kind, even those hidden faults that can trip us up.

SECTION II

The Communication of the Bible

92. THE REVELATION OF THE BIBLE

93. THE INSPIRATION OF THE BIBLE

94. THE ILLUMINATION OF THE BIBLE

95. THE INTERPRETATION OF THE BIBLE

96. THE CANONICITY OF THE BIBLE

92

THE REVELATION OF THE BIBLE

Like a master playwright, God had a great drama that He wanted to present to the human race. When His time was right He raised the curtains and unveiled what had not been known before. The biblical word for this unveiling or curtain-raising is *revelation*, or *apocalypse*. This latter word is simply a transliteration of the Greek term that means "revelation." The revelation to John is the title of the last book in the Bible, which we could also call the final act in God's great cosmic drama of sin and redemption.

In this section I want to consider five aspects of the Bible that have to do with God's once-only delivery of His Word to us, and His ongoing work in aiding our understanding and application of it. God's revelation has been recorded and preserved for us in written form, but when it was first revealed to its authors and other "actors," a good portion of the Bible was also accompanied by a visual display.

This interplay between the visual and verbal aspects of revelation helps to give us a working definition of this doctrine of Scripture. Revelation is the supernatural work of God whereby He makes known, either by verbal disclosure or visible display, that which was previously unknown or hidden. God does this so that we might come to know the truth He wants us to know—and which we desperately need to know in order to be rightly related to Him—but which we could never discover on our own apart from Him.

GOD HAS CHOSEN TO MAKE HIMSELF KNOWN TO US

It is critically important that you grasp how utterly and completely dependent we were upon God's grace to reveal Himself to us. Remember, general revelation in nature is enough to condemn the one who ignores it and doesn't seek God.

God Is Higher than We Can Conceive

Without God's self-disclosure to us in His Word, we would be hopelessly lost. This is true not only because God is infinitely higher than anything or anyone we can imagine, but also because if God had not lifted the curtain of heaven and revealed Himself, there would have been no divine story and no salvation for lost sinners like us.

You can read Isaiah 55:8–9 to refresh yourself on how God and His thoughts are totally above and apart from us and our thoughts.

Paul made a strong statement of this truth as he concluded a magnificent section in Romans 9–11 about God's dealings with Israel: "Oh, the depth of the riches both of the wisdom and knowledge of God! How unsearchable are His judgments and unfathomable His ways! For who has known the mind of the Lord, or who became His counselor?" (Romans 11:33-34).

The fact is that God is not like us. He doesn't think or operate the way we do. Older theologians used to refer to God as the "Wholly Other." Since this is true, God has to make sense of Himself for us. We can't figure Him out, because our only reference point for trying to understand God is ourselves.

Sin Darkens Our Ability to Comprehend God

There is another reason that God must reveal Himself in order for us to know Him. Ephesians 4:18 says that our hearts have been "darkened" by the plague of sin. This is true of our minds as well. Sin has messed up our thinking so badly it's as if we are wearing blinders that limit our spiritual perception and ability to understand God. Besides, our first inclination as sinners is to hide from God in an attempt to keep Him from knowing us. It was only after Adam and Eve had sinned that they tried to hide from God when He came to take His daily walk with them in the garden (see Genesis 3:8).

Before this, they had walked with God in Eden, which suggests they had an intimate relationship with Him. That relationship changed drastically when Adam and Eve sinned. And ever since, people have been blinded to the reality of God by their sin and trying their best to hide from Him.

GENERAL REVELATION SHOWS GOD'S EXISTENCE AND POWER

We're talking about revelation in broader terms than just the Bible because it's important to see where the Scripture fits in God's ages-long, unfolding plan to reveal Himself to the human race. Paul said that God "did not leave Himself without witness" (Acts 14:17).

Paul made this statement during his sermon to the pagan people of Lystra, and it refers to God's witness in nature through the general revelation He gives to all men. But everything God did to disclose Himself to us is His witness.

God Has Left Himself a Witness in Nature

In our discussion of general revelation in the previous chapter, we learned that God has written the message of His existence with an unmistakable hand in the heavens above and the world around, so that all men have a clear picture that He exists. Creation manifests the reality of God even without words (see Psalm 19:3).

People Have No Excuse

People can walk through a museum, view its works of art, realize that great masters created them, and then walk out of the building without having to make any decisions about the way they are living. But that's not true of God's revelation in nature. It is clear enough that God can demand that people do something about it.

This was the thrust of Paul's famous message in Acts 17:22–31 to the idolatrous Greeks in Athens when he saw them ignorantly worshiping an "unknown God." Paul was deeply disturbed by their foolish ideas, and he used God's witness in nature to argue that they needed to seek the true

God in repentance. I want to note some of the highlights of that message, and then we'll deal with special revelation.

Paul's argument to these idol worshipers followed this line of reasoning. First, the creator God who made everything is not at all like us in that He cannot be reduced to living in man-made temples, nor does He need anything from us (Acts 17:24–25). Not only that, but He cannot be represented by man-made images of gold, silver, or stone (v. 29).

Second, this God who made the world and everything in it gave men His witness in nature in order that "they might grope for Him and find Him" (v. 27). I love the way Paul stated the goal of general revelation: "Therefore having overlooked the times of ignorance, God is now declaring to men that all people everywhere should repent" (v. 30).

Third, the reason people need to seek God in repentance is that He is going to convene a court of judgment someday and hold them accountable for their unbelief (v. 31).

The Bible says that all alike are "without excuse" before God (Romans 1:20). Like a gigantic billboard staring at us on the highway, creation is a witness to God's glory that is plain to everybody. People who ignore it do so at their own peril.

SPECIAL REVELATION SHOWS GOD'S CHARACTER

Suppose you attend a great orchestra concert with thousands of other people. Everyone gets to see the performers on stage at a distance and hear the beautiful music they create, but the audience can't interact with the musicians and conductor. But your family has received a backstage pass that allows all of you to go behind the scenes and meet the musicians ands the conductor. You learn their names and all about their families, hear them explain how the musical compositions you just enjoyed came into being and their plans for future concerts.

Your backstage pass, an "upgrade" from the general admission pass, is like the difference between someone receiving general and special revelation. Special revelation takes us from being in the "audience" at creation to intimate fellowship and interaction with God.

When we see what God has done in nature, we should want to know more about Him. We should be asking, "Who is this Being that is so awesome and powerful He can make all of this, and what is He like?" Special revelation answers this question; it takes up where general revelation ends. Special revelation has come to us in two forms we can see and read and understand—Jesus, the Son of God, and the Bible, the written Word of God.

People often refer to Jesus and the Bible as the living and the written Word. But both are actually the living Word, because the Bible is "living and active" (Hebrews 4:12). So it would be more biblically and theologically accurate to say that the Bible is the living written Word of God, and Jesus is the living incarnate Word of God—referring to Jesus' coming to earth when "the Word became flesh, and dwelt among us" (John 1:14).

These two revelations agree as one, for the written Word testifies to the truthfulness of Jesus, and Jesus testifies to the truthfulness of the written Word. Jesus is the visible display of God, and the Bible is the verbal display of God. Both are heaven's answer to the question: Who is this God of creation, and what is He like? Let's consider Jesus first.

God Has Revealed Himself in the Person of Christ

The apostle John opened his gospel by teaching us that Jesus is the eternal God who came down from heaven to take on a body and live among us. John called Jesus "the Word" (1:1) because He is the perfect expression of God. Jesus is also the Word because He came to deliver God's message.

The author of Hebrews opened his letter with a tremendous explanation of Jesus' uniqueness: "God, after He spoke long ago to the fathers in the prophets in many portions and in many ways, in these last days has spoken to us in His Son, whom He appointed heir of all things, through whom also He made the world. And He is the radiance of His glory and the exact representation of His nature, and upholds all things by the word of His power" (vv. 1-3a).

Hebrews 1:1-3 makes the same basic point as John 1, which is that God sent His one and only Son to demonstrate who He is and what He is like by bringing us His final and climactic message. Jesus Christ came to give us the details about God—doing so by His life, death, and resurrection, which were visual, and by His teachings, which were verbal.

God Has Revealed Himself in the Pages of His Word

The written Word of God is the other aspect of God's self-revelation to us. The Bible is the verbal manifestation of God, His "authorized autobiography" by which we get to know Him personally. Since Jesus is no ordinary man but the invisible God supernaturally made visible to us, His Word is no ordinary book but the supernatural Word of God to us.

Jesus told the people of His day that they searched the Scriptures in hopes of finding eternal life. There's nothing wrong with that, because the Bible is the Word of eternal life. But then Jesus said, "It is these that testify about Me; and you are unwilling to come to Me so that you may have life" (John 5:39–40). What Jesus was saying is that there is no contradiction or disconnect between Him as the incarnate Son of God and the Scriptures as the Word of God. They both convey the same message.

Jesus and the Bible speak the same message from God. Jesus said on another occasion, "It is the Spirit who gives life; the flesh profits nothing; the words that I have spoken to you are spirit and are life" (John 6:63). The Bible's words are the living words of the living God.

It's also important to mention that the moment the last word of the last book of the Bible was recorded under the Holy Spirit's inspiration, God's revelation was completed. There is no "second" or "expanded" edition of the Bible. We'll deal with this important issue in an upcoming chapter on the canon of Scripture, or how the books of the Bible were chosen to be included in the sacred text before it was closed. Suffice it to say here that the Bible is the complete Word of God to us.

One of the traits of almost every cult is the claim to have extrabiblical revelation from God that supposedly explains the Bible more fully, or more often contradicts what the Bible teaches. But those claims are absolutely, categorically false. God illumines Scripture to us, but He has said His final Word in the Person of Jesus, as Hebrews 1:1–3 says so eloquently. Be careful of folk who claim that God told them something He hasn't told anyone else in the two-thousand-year history of the church. If it isn't in the Bible, it is not God's Word.

GOD'S WORD HOLDS MANY VALUABLE BENEFITS FOR US

This is another one of those topics that could fill a book, but I want to show you several benefits that the Bible provides for your encouragement as we wrap up the discussion on the Scripture as God's revelation, or self-disclosure, to us.

God's Word Teaches Us to Worship God

The Bible reveals the priority that worship should have in our lives and teaches us how to worship properly. "Ascribe to the Lord the glory due to His name; worship the Lord in holy array" declares the psalmist (Psalm 29:2). Psalm 89:5–7 says that God's creation and His holy angels praise and fear Him. We ought to be doing the same because He redeemed us.

I would encourage you to get a Bible concordance if you don't already have one. A concordance lists every word in the Bible and gives the reference, so you can trace a thought or concept through the entire Scripture. If you want to revolutionize and energize your worship, start tracing words like *worship*, *praise*, and *glorify* through the Bible and see what God has said about the kind of worship He desires. We know He is seeking worshipers because Jesus said so (see John 4:23).

God's Word Gives Us a Perfect Standard

Another benefit of God's revelation is that it gives us a completely reliable standard by which to assess and measure divine reality. The Bible is a new pair of glasses through which God wants us to look at Him and all of life.

Many people think it's cool to say, "I'm a natural man." Well, from God's perspective it isn't. The Bible says, "A natural man does not accept the things of the Spirit of God, for they are foolishness to him; and he cannot understand them, because they are spiritually appraised" (1 Corinthians 2:14). Then Paul made a contrast: "But he who is spiritual appraises all things, yet he himself is appraised by no one. For who has known the mind of the Lord, that he will instruct Him? But we have the mind of Christ" (vv. 15–16). The spiritual person sees everything from a different perspective because he appraises or evaluates life from God's perspective.

Having "the mind of Christ" tells us that when we judge everything by the standard of God's Word, we are looking at things the way Jesus would look at them. Now we don't do that perfectly, of course, but the only way to get God's view on life is to look at it through the lens of His Word. The mind of Christ, as revealed in the Scripture, gives us the ability to see the invisible realm through the eyes of faith. And that divine perspective changes everything.

God's Word Reveals His Ways and Means

The United States Congress has a committee known as "Ways and Means." God means every word of what He says. The Bible reveals God's ways and means, or His purposes, so that we can know the right path to take. Proverbs 14:12 is a very sobering verse to me: "There is a way which seems right to a man, but its end is the way of death." In other words, use your human logic alone to chart the course of your life, and it will eventually take you down a path that's headed straight into hell. The best example of this I can think of is Israel under the judges, a dark and disastrous period when "everyone did what was right in his own eyes" (Judges 21:25).

The remedy to keep us from making this kind of mess out of our lives is also found in the proverbs: "Trust in the Lord with all your heart and do not lean on your own understanding. In all your ways acknowledge Him, and He will make your paths straight" (Proverbs 3:5–6). God doesn't want us coming to crucial crossroads in our lives with nothing to guide us but human opinions and ideas. He wants us to know His ways.

PERSONAL APPLICATION FOR LIFE

1. It's so easy to develop our own, erroneous concepts about God. Our efforts are often based on a human characteristic or some other unworthy representation of God. The problem is that our finite minds can only conceive that which is finite. One of your daily "thank yous" to God should be because He loved us so much that He reached down to make Himself known to us. Why not take a moment to thank Him right now. He always enjoys our praise and thanks.

2. God's special revelation reveals His character. Do you ever take a few minutes to think about the character of God as revealed in the Scriptures? The God who reveals Himself in the Bible also reveals Himself to you as He works in your life. A good question to ask yourself during your quiet time is, What new truth have I learned about the character of God today?

3. Read Luke 8:15. If your true desire is to be the good soil Jesus described, tell Him so in prayer. Write in the flyleaf of your Bible the day you made the commitment to soften the soil of your heart, pull out the thorns, and deal with the choking effects of this world's concerns. Refer to that page often as you seek to live out your commitment.

4. "And the Word became flesh, and dwelt among us, and we saw His glory, glory as of the only begotten from the Father, full of grace and truth" (John 1:14). As undeserving humans, we have benefited by God's revelation through His spoken Word, His written Word, and through His Son, the Word incarnate. Praise God for reaching out to us and revealing Himself to us in so many unmistakable ways. That should get you on your knees in thanks to such a gracious God.

FOR GROUP STUDY

Questions for Group Discussion

1. What is the meaning of the biblical word *revelation*? What is the difference between general revelation and God's special, or recorded, revelation in the Bible?

2. Read Ephesians 4:18 and Romans 11:33–34. Why are we so dependent on God's revealing Himself to us? What obstacles can cloud one's perception of God?

3. What does general revelation reveal to the non-believer? Read Paul's famous message in Acts 17:22–31. In his argument, what three key points did the apostle make to his audience?

4. What truths does God's special revelation reveal that His general revelation does not? What special benefits do we receive from God's written revelation? (Use the chart below as an aid to your discussion.)

PICTURE THIS

God's Word is an invaluable resource for the believer. It provides several benefits for those who engage it and live by its message.

THE BENEFITS OF GOD'S WRITTEN REVELATION

BENEFIT	SCRIPTURE PASSAGES	ITS IMPORTANCE
God's Word teaches us to worship God.	Psalm 29:2; John 4:23	The Bible teaches us how to praise and worship God.
God's Word gives us a perfect standard.	1 Corinthians 2:14-16	The Bible gives us a reliable standard to live by and the ability to gain a divine perspective through the eyes of faith.
God's Word reveals His ways and means.	Proverbs 14:12	The Bible reveals God's purposes, so that we can know the right path to take.

93

THE INSPIRATION OF THE BIBLE

If you were to ask people on the street for their definition of inspiration, most would probably talk about that feeling of exaltation, of being carried or lifted up, that a person gets when his spirit is raised to a higher level. Other people might use words like *encouragement, motivation,* or *stimulation* to describe the experience of being inspired.

It's interesting that two dictionaries from two different but authoritative publishers show a marked difference in the way the word *inspiration* is defined. One dictionary's first definition is a "divine influence" that a person receives that allows him to "receive and communicate sacred revelation." The second dictionary lists this aspect of inspiration as its last definition and begins with the basic definition of inspiration as the act of breathing in air, or inhaling. This physical meaning is not far removed from the emotional or spiritual side of inspiration, as we will see.

When discussing what inspiration means, more theologically aware people may even cite the Bible as an example of inspiration. The Bible is certainly inspired, but not in the way that any other work has ever been inspired before, or ever will be again. Inspiration takes on a unique meaning when applied to God's Word.

THE MEANING OF INSPIRATION

The Greek word translated "inspired" (2 Timothy 3:16) is *theophneustos*, which means "God-breathed." It is a compound word made up of the words for God and breath or spirit. The New International Version translates this word literally when it says, "All Scripture is God-breathed." Thus inspiration is the breath of God as He breathes out His Word. Scripture came from God as words come from the mouth of a person who is speaking (see Romans 3:2; 16:25).

Thus the Bible does not simply contain the Word of God; it is the very words of God. The Holy Spirit inspired His chosen men to write the Bible, and the result is the only Book in history that flawlessly communicates God's Word and will to man.

With this information, let's put together a biblical definition of inspiration and then consider its process and its product. The doctrine of inspiration refers to the process by which God oversaw the composition of Scripture through its authors in such a way that they recorded its message exactly the way God wanted it recorded, without error or omission. Inspiration guarantees that God's revelation, that which He disclosed concerning Himself, has come to us without contamination.

THE PROCESS OF INSPIRATION

The reason we can study truths like the inspiration of the Bible is that, unlike all other so-called gods, our God speaks. One appropriate name or title for the true and living God is "the God who speaks."

The psalmist said of idols that are the work of human hands, "They have mouths, but they cannot speak" (Psalm 115:5). The prophets often mocked the impotence and silence of the false gods that the nations around Israel, and ultimately Israel herself, came to trust in. "Like a scarecrow in a cucumber field are they, and they cannot speak" (Jeremiah 10:5). No god but our great God has anything to say. In the Old Testament alone, you will encounter the phrase, "Thus saith the Lord," or some derivative thereof, more than three thousand times.

Inspiration Applies to the Words of the Bible

The doctrine of inspiration addresses the relationship between the God who speaks and the human writers who recorded what the God who speaks had to say. The place where God's words were written and collected is the Bible. Again, it is critically important that we understand that inspiration is the process by which "men moved by the Holy Spirit spoke from God" (2 Peter 1:21). Over and over again, the authors of Scripture declared their message to be the Word of God given through them to their readers, not just their best thoughts about God. And because their message was from God, it carried His authority.

For example, consider what Paul wrote to the church at Corinth, which was full of proud people and those who challenged the apostle's authority. Speaking of this church's misuse of the gift of tongues and his correction for this abuse, Paul said, "If anyone thinks he is a prophet or spiritual, let him recognize that the things which I write to you are the Lord's commandment" (1 Corinthians 14:37).

Notice the thrust of Paul's argument. He was bold enough to say that when the Corinthians read his letter, they were reading a letter written by the hand of God as surely as if it had come sealed and addressed straight from heaven. The doctrine of inspiration means that every word in the original autographs or manuscripts of Scripture is from God. He didn't waste any words or leave out anything He wanted to say, and neither did the Bible's writers toss in their own ideas here and there.

Inspiration Is the Breath of God as He Speaks

I said earlier that the basic definition of inspiration as the act of breathing in air is related to the biblical use of this word to describe God's "breathing out" of His Word.

This was as much a creative act on God's part as when He breathed the "breath of life" into Adam's nostrils and he came alive (Genesis 2:7). What happened when God inspired holy men to write the Bible is that they were carried along, as it were, by God's breath. That is, they were inspired or lifted up by God. I'll have more to say about this later because there is another biblical word for this process that is very picturesque and interesting.

When Paul said that all Scripture is God-breathed, he was asserting that the Scripture came from God's mouth the way a person's breath leaves his body when he speaks. This concept emphasizes the immediacy and directness of

God's speaking, rather than just hearing from someone that God said something.

GOD'S WORDS ARE FOUND IN THE BIBLE

Back in 2 Timothy 3:16, where Paul said all Scripture is inspired by God, the word *Scripture* emphasizes that the words God spoke did not just float away, but were written down. The Greek word is *graphe*, which is a familiar component of many English words. It means a piece of writing. Not only does God affirm again and again in Scripture that He speaks or breathes out His Word (see Deuteronomy 9:10), but you will also read that these words were recorded by men (Exodus 17:14; Deuteronomy 31:19; Revelation 1:10–11). For example, John writes, "These things I have written unto you" (1 John 5:13).

Notice something else important in 2 Timothy 3:16. The verse does not say that the writers of Scripture were inspired, but that what they wrote is inspired. This takes the emphasis off of questions such as whether the authors of Scripture drew on their own vocabulary to express the thoughts the Holy Spirit gave them, or whether the Spirit simply dictated the Bible to them word by word the way a boss dictates a letter to his secretary.

The fact that each writer's style and vocabulary are different shows that the Spirit drew on the authors' personalities as He revealed the Word to them. But we are not told the details of how the process of inspiration was carried out, because God wants us to know that the finished product is His Word, spoken from His mouth. And the Word is not only God's thoughts, but also His very words that make up those thoughts (see Exodus 4:15; Deuteronomy 4:2).

The Holy Spirit Is the Agent of Inspiration

The closest we come to a description of the process of inspiration is 2 Peter 1:20–21, where the apostle wrote: "But know this first of all, that no prophecy of Scripture is a matter of one's own interpretation, for no prophecy was ever made by an act of the human will, but *men moved by the Holy Spirit* spoke from God" (italics added). We have the Bible because the Holy Spirit acted in a unique way upon the prophets and apostles, or their assistants, to record God's words.

The word *moved* (*pheromenoi*) is very interesting because it pictures a sailboat on the water with the sail catching the wind and moving or carrying the boat along. The word is used this way in Acts 27:15, where Luke said that when Paul was in the storm on his way to Rome, the wind blew his ship along with such force that the ship had to go wherever the wind wanted it to go.

What wind is to a sailboat, Peter said the Holy Spirit was to the writers of Scripture. The image of the Spirit, who is Himself the wind or the breath of God, moving the biblical writers to record what God wanted fits well with what we said earlier about Scripture coming from God's mouth as His very breath. All that men like Peter, John, and Matthew had to do was keep their sails up and the Holy Spirit would catch them and move them in the right direction.

This principle also has application to us today as the people of God. When we gather as the church to hear the Word of God proclaimed, our prayer should be, "Lord, I want to hear from You today through the sermon."

Now don't misunderstand. The pastor is not speaking new revelation, but he is proclaiming the Word that God spoke to His people for our spiritual correction, growth, and benefit. Paul said that the same "all Scripture" that is inspired by God is also "profitable for teaching, for reproof, for correction, for training in righteousness; so that the man of God may be adequate, equipped for every good work" (2 Timothy 3:16–17).

You Need to Keep Your Sails Up

You and I have spiritual sails too, which the Bible calls "ears" to hear what the Holy Spirit is saying to us. We are not writing Scripture today; God's revelation is complete. But you and I need the Spirit's wisdom and guidance to properly understand and apply the Scriptures to our daily lives.

How does the Holy Spirit lead you to choose which job to take, or which person to marry? You may have several choices, any one of which would be within the boundaries of God's will. The name of a person's future mate is not in the Bible, but the Word of God does say to believers, "Do not be bound together with unbelievers" (2 Corinthians 6:14).

Clear biblical principles like this are part of the "wind" of the Holy Spirit to move you along in the right direction concerning a marriage partner. The same process applies to making other life decisions. God wants to lead you each day by His Holy Spirit, but you have to be ready to hear Him. If you are a Christian and yet you are not experiencing the Spirit's leading, it's because your sail is down. That means it's time to get into your prayer closet and shut the door, and not come out until you have a clear word from God.

THE PRODUCT OF INSPIRATION

We have spent most of our time in this chapter on the process of inspiration, and that is by design. We have already presented arguments and proofs for the inerrancy of Scripture, so I don't need to spend too much time demonstrating that the product of inspiration is exactly what God wanted. But here are several important truths to consider under this heading.

God Still Has His Secrets

The Bible doesn't tell us everything there is to know about God, just what He wants us to know. Deuteronomy 29:29 says, "The secret things belong to the Lord our God, but the things revealed belong to us and to our sons forever, that we may observe all the words of this law." The Bible has everything you need to know to obey and please God. Don't worry about the stuff you don't know or the questions that are still unanswered.

We Have a Perfect and Complete Bible

Because of the Holy Spirit's work of overseeing and superintending the inspiration of Scripture, in the Bible we have a perfect and complete text of everything God desired to reveal to men. If this teaching of the care and attention that God gave to every word of Scripture is somewhat new to you, here is a good passage to meditate on: "Every word of God is tested. . . . Do not add to His words or He will reprove you, and you will be proved a liar" (Proverbs 30:5–6). God has weighed and examined every word to get just the ones He wanted. Our job is to explain and teach the Scriptures, not to try to figure out which of its words are inspired and true and which ones aren't.

God's Word Will Last Forever

Not only can we put our faith in every word of Scripture, but we also don't have to worry that the truths and promises of the Word will ever expire. "Heaven and earth will pass away, but My words will not pass away" is our Lord's assurance to us (Matthew 24:35). That milk in your refrigerator has an expiration date on it, after which the guarantee of freshness is over and you are on your own. The company that packaged this milk knows how long it should be good for, based on the nature of milk and the method of processing.

Jesus was saying about the Word, "Based on what My Father and I have put into this product, it is going to last forever." This is why all attempts to destroy the Bible have always failed, even though there have been many throughout history. People have given their lives to make sure that we would have a Bible in our hands, in our own language, because they believed that nothing was more important than making God's eternal Word accessible to all.

PERSONAL APPLICATION FOR LIFE

1. Second Timothy 3:17 tells us that God gave us the Bible that we "may be adequate, equipped for every good work." That word "adequate" means "sufficient to the need." When we allow the Holy Spirit to apply the Word of God to our hearts, we experience its power. There is nothing God asks you to do that His Word does not give you the tools to accomplish!

2. Is your "spiritual sail" up or down? Are you getting clear sailing direction from God's Word? If you are a believer and not experiencing His leading, perhaps you need to get some private time with the Lord until you get clear direction from Him.

3. Second Timothy 3:16 shows us how sufficient the Scriptures are. "All scripture is given by inspiration of God, and is profitable for doctrine, for reproof, for correction, for instruction in righteousness." "Reproof" tells us where we have gone off the path, "correction" shows us how to make it right, and "training in righteousness" is what we need to live life the way God intended us to live. When was the last time you took inventory of the condition of your heart? Maybe it's time to get on your knees and ask God to use the Word to search your heart. Be sensitive to what God tells you about your heart, and allow Him to make any necessary changes.

4. Is there anything in your life you're working hard to change these days? Only God can change hearts. Get into the Word and allow the Holy Spirit and the Word's transforming power to work in your heart. Whatever your need, God's Word is sufficient.

FOR GROUP STUDY

Questions for Group Discussion

1. Read 2 Timothy 3:16. What does the term *inspiration* mean? What significance does the Greek term *theophneustos* add to the meaning of inspiration?

2. What do we know about the process of inspiration? How were God's words communicated, written, and collected in the Bible?

3. What was the Holy Spirit's specific role as the agent of inspiration?

4. Read Deuteronomy 29:29; Proverbs 30:5–6; and Matthew 24:35. As a result of inspiration, what are some important truths we know about the Bible? (Use the chart below as an aid to your discussion.)

PICTURE THIS

Because of God's work of inspiration, there are several truths about the Bible we use as God's divine revelation to us. Below are four of those truths.

THE PRODUCT OF DIVINE INSPIRATION

TRUTH	SCRIPTURE PASSAGE	ITS SIGNIFICANCE
God still has His secrets.	Deuteronomy 29:29	Although there is more to know about God, we have what we need to obey and please Him.
We have a perfect and complete Bible.	Proverbs 30:5–6	Because of the Holy Spirit's work of inspiration, the Bible contains a perfect and complete text of everything God desired to reveal to mankind.
God's Word will last forever.	Matthew 24:35	We can put our faith in every word of Scripture, because the truths and promises of the Word will never expire.
God's Word meets our every need.	2 Timothy 3:16–17	The Bible is designed and shaped to mature us so God can use us to accomplish the work of His kingdom.

94

THE ILLUMINATION OF THE BIBLE

The illumination of Scripture follows naturally in the sequence of God's self-disclosure. *Revelation* is what God has said about Himself, *inspiration* is the recording of what God said, and *illumination* is the process by which God's revelation ceases to be just words on a page and comes alive in our hearts and minds. Here is a more formal definition: Illumination is the work of the Holy Spirit that opens up believers' minds to the Word of God, enabling them to understand the meaning and personal application of divine revelation. It allows believers to hear God's personal Word to them through the Scriptures.

THE IMPORTANCE OF ILLUMINATION

The illumination that a student receives in school could be called natural enlightenment. The difference between this human activity and supernatural, Holy Spirit–directed enlightenment is crucial for several reasons. One is that the word *illumination* is often misused by unbelievers. Some people who have no relationship to Jesus Christ use terms that sound very similar to biblical terms to describe their religious experiences, while others turn to the Bible to support all manner of heresies and offbeat ideas, and then claim that they have biblical reasons for their views.

Anyone Can Read the Bible

We need to understand illumination from a biblical standpoint because nonbelievers can read the Bible and claim to understand and follow its message. I'm thinking here of those who try to use the Bible to support heretical teachings. These false teachers very often claim that their views came directly from God in the form of special revelation or illumination.

Only the Spirit Can Illumine the Bible

For those of us who believe in the Savior, the Spirit's illumination of Scripture may result in a new and deeper understanding of truth we already know, lead us to see truths we never grasped before, cause us to change our beliefs or behavior —or possibly all three. Saul of Tarsus qualified on this score.

Saul was a brilliant young rabbi who knew the Old Testament backward and forward. But it wasn't until Jesus struck Saul down on the Damascus Road (Acts 9) that he really began to understand the Scriptures he had studied all his life, saw new truths about Jesus as the fulfillment of the Mosaic law, and radically changed his behavior by going from persecutor of Christians to the leading Christian of his day.

We are instructed in the Bible to pray for illumination. A great verse you ought to memorize and pray each day as you open your Bible is this: "Open my eyes, that I may behold wonderful things from Your law" (Psalm 119:18). The psalmist was saying, "Lord, I want to encounter You face-to-face in Your revelation." The entire text of Psalm 119, the longest chapter in the Bible, is an expression of the psalmist's deep love for God's Word and his intense desire to know God.

THE PROCESS OF ILLUMINATION

The apostle Paul said in 2 Corinthians 3 that in contrast to the veil that covers the Jews' eyes when they read Scripture, believers have "unveiled" faces with which to see the Lord (v. 18). We meet Christ when we come to Him in salvation, but there is another face-to-face meeting with God waiting for us in the pages of His Word. This occurs when we read the Bible and the Spirit turns on the light in our hearts and minds.

God's Light Is Not Automatic

The teaching of illumination reminds us again that nothing is automatic in the Christian life. Have you ever wondered why two Christians can be sitting beside each other in church, hearing the same message with their Bibles open to the same passage, and yet one person is staring blankly into space, not really getting anything, while the other is alive with excitement about what God's Word has to say?

Part of the reason may be the two people's personalities, but there's more to it than that. If the Bible is nothing more than dead words on a page to a Christian, that person may be suffering from a lack of illumination—and it isn't God's fault. (We'll talk shortly about problems that can hinder the Holy Spirit from illuminating God's Word to us.)

The Spirit's Work in Illumination

Paul explained 1 Corinthians 2:9–16 that, left on our own, we would never be able to know God: "As it is written, 'Things which eye has not seen and ear has not heard, and which have not entered into the heart of man, all that God has prepared for those who love Him.' For to us God revealed them through the Spirit; for the Spirit searches all things, even the depths of God" (vv. 9–10).

Praise God for the revelation of His Word that opens our spiritual eyes and ears to things that would otherwise be hidden from us. The Holy Spirit was the active agent in communicating the Scripture to its writers, because He is the One who knows "the thoughts of God" (v. 11).

Today the Spirit's primary role in relation to the Bible is illumination, which Paul explained as helping us "know the things freely given to us by God" (v. 12). Only the Spirit can do this, because only the Spirit can teach us "not in words taught by human wisdom, but in those taught by the Spirit, combining spiritual thoughts with spiritual words" (v. 13).

Problems That Can Block the Spirit's Illumination

What can hinder God's work of illumination in a person's life? Sin has obscured man's view of God. This is certainly true for unbelievers who are spiritually blind. Paul said that people who are separated from God are "darkened in their understanding" of the truth (Ephesians 4:18). Just as a blind man can't see the sun no matter how much you explain it to him, so the sinner cannot "see" and experience God, because his spiritual receptors are dead.

Paul gave us a classic statement of this fact in 1 Corinthians 2:14: "But a natural man does not accept the things of the Spirit of God, for they are foolishness to him; and he cannot understand them, because they are spiritually appraised."

This is the nonbeliever's condition. But sin can also interrupt a believer's ability to understand and experience God's Word. Sin blocks our ability to experience God's Word in a life-changing way.

Another problem that can hinder God's work of illumination in a believer's heart is an unwillingness to respond. Someone may say, "Well, it's fine to talk about the need to see beyond the physical. But even though I go to church and read my Bible, I'm not getting any illumination. I'm not getting what other people seem to be getting from the Bible."

If there is no willingness on our part to apply the Word, God will not illumine the Word to us. Jesus said, "Take care how you listen; for whoever has, to him more shall be given; and whoever does not have, even what he thinks he has shall be taken away from him" (Luke 8:18). Jesus was talking about our response to God's truth. Believers who respond in obedience to the Word are given more light, while those who hear the Word but don't obey it can actually be worse off for hearing it.

Reaching the Highest Possible Level

Illumination is something like reaching the highest level of the three levels of hearing that human beings are capable of. The first level consists of simply receiving the auditory waves that come into our ears. In other words, we hear the sound but it doesn't register in our minds. Parents and married people often get frustrated with their children and spouses when they realize that what they said went in one ear and out the other, as the old saying goes.

We hear on this first level all the time, but we screen out most of the noises or voices around us. This ability is necessary to keep us from being constantly distracted by all the noises of modern-day life—but it's not so helpful when we tune out people we really need to listen to.

The second level of hearing is what we could call the understanding level, when we go beyond just picking up sound waves to focusing our minds on what the sounds mean. At this level we can say, like a soldier in the field talking to his commander at headquarters, "Roger, message received." This is obviously an important level of hearing that takes us beyond the first, but there's another level that is much more critical.

This third level is reached when the message not only gets into our brains, but down into our bones, so to speak. A parent will often say to his child, "Do you understand what I'm saying to you?" The child may say yes, and even repeat back what was said with great detail and clarity. But until the child responds by obeying the message, he or she hasn't really heard it at all.

God wants to get us to this third level of hearing in which we connect with His Word so completely that we change and arrange our lives in obedience to Him because we see the Word's relevance to our lives. But it takes more than just reading or even studying the Bible to reach this level. It takes the Holy Spirit illuminating the Word in a personal way that reaches us at the core of our being.

THE APPLICATION OF ILLUMINATION

Do you know why so many Christians are discouraged and want to throw in the towel? Because all they see is what they can see with their physical eyes. Look at the secular world around you for a minute. Do you see much out there to make you think God is winning the battle? Probably not, which is why God says we must be able to see beyond the physical realm.

You Have an Anointing from God

Many Christians tend to think that this kind of enlightenment is only for people like pastors, teachers, and other spiritual leaders in the body of Christ. Not so. The apostle John wrote, "You have an anointing from the Holy One, and you all know" (1 John 2:20). All believers are anointed in terms of their ability to receive, understand, and apply truth from the Holy

Spirit. In this sense, the anointing is another word for illumination. John went on to say, "The anointing which you received from Him abides in you, and you have no need for anyone to teach you; but as His anointing teaches you about all things, and is true and is not a lie, and just as it has taught you, you abide in Him" (v. 27).

This is the anointing, the divine capacity to receive from God the understanding and personal application of His truth. We can't leave out this step if we want to discover all that God has for us.

Does this mean believers don't need anyone else to help them understand and apply the Word? No, this statement in no way eliminates the need for Bible teachers, who are part of God's gift to the church (see Ephesians 4:11–12). John was writing here about false teachers who were trying to deceive the church (see 1 John 2:18–19), and his point was that believers have the Holy Spirit within to guide them in distinguishing truth from error, and that He can do that even if no human teachers are involved.

If you are a believer in Jesus Christ, you have the capacity to distinguish truth from falsehood because the anointing of God is within you to turn on the light and help you see with the eyes of faith what is not visible to your physical sight. It would help a lot if these cultists came around dressed up like demons or something so everyone could see that they are peddling the Devil's lies. That way, even when unbelievers who don't know the Bible opened the door, they would scream in fear and slam it shut.

But it doesn't work that way. The Bible says, "Even Satan disguises himself as an angel of light. Therefore it is not surprising if his servants also disguise themselves as servants of righteousness" (2 Corinthians 11:14–15).

You Don't Need a Guru

The anointing also means that Christians don't need to run all over the place looking for someone to tell them what God wants them to do in applying His Word to their lives.

Now again, I'm not saying that because we are Christians with the Holy Spirit as our illuminator and teacher, we don't need to be under the regular teaching of the Word. After all, you can't live out what you don't understand.

But God says the anointing is within you in the person of the Holy Spirit, who according to Jesus "will teach you all things, and bring to your remembrance all that I said to you" (John 14:26). We also learn, "He will guide you into all the truth" (16:13).

Just as the biblical writers were given what God wanted them to write, in a similar way the Holy Spirit gives us what we need to know from the Word to address specific areas in our lives.

Abiding Brings the Anointing

The key to experiencing the illumination of God's Spirit through His Word into your life is "abiding" (1 John 2:24, 27). The abiding of the believer is the assurance we find in the presence and power of Christ when we are living in intimate fellowship with Him and obedience to Him. The anointing flows from abiding.

John used "abide" as his relational term for staying closely and intimately connected to God through His Word. When you abide, you don't just read the Bible as words, but you are looking for the person behind the words. Abiding says to God, "I want to know and love You more each day and to become more like You." When reading or studying the Bible for knowledge becomes an end in itself rather than the vehicle to cultivate an intimate relationship with God, we miss the power of the anointing.

Look at 1 John 2 again. "The one who says he abides in Him [Christ] ought himself to walk in the same manner as He walked" (v. 6). Again, "The word of God abides in you, and you have overcome the evil one" (v. 14). And then, "As for you, let that abide in you which you heard from the beginning. If what you heard from the beginning abides in you, you also will abide in the Son and in the Father" (v. 24).

PERSONAL APPLICATION FOR LIFE

1. God wants to see some motion from us in the form of obedience to His will, as expressed in His Word. Don't be a stagnant Christian, never advancing in the life of faith. Ask God to make you sensitive to the Spirit's illumination in your heart. Start enjoying the growing blessings and presence of God.

2. Are you experiencing the spiritual realm firsthand? God wants you to discover "the things freely given to [you] by God" (1 Corinthians 2:12). When you are illuminated by the Holy Spirit, the truth of God becomes real to you because it gets down to the deepest levels of your being. Is that your experience? If not, ask God to help you see and know a whole new level of seeing and knowing.

3. If you are a believer in Jesus Christ, you have the capacity to distinguish truth from falsehood because the anointing of God is within you. Are you still walking by "sight," allowing your circumstances and emotions to dictate your walk? Ask the Holy Spirit to turn on the light and help you see with the eyes of faith what is not visible to your physical sight.

4. Are you experiencing in your life the kind of illumination and enlightenment Dr. Evans describes in this chapter? If you ask God with an honest and open heart to make His Word real to you, you'll find that the words of Scripture will start jumping off the page and into your heart, even when the world around you is dark. You'll read God's Word so that He can speak to you personally as His Spirit connects with your human spirit.

FOR GROUP STUDY

Questions for Group Discussion

1. With regard to God's revelation to us, what is the definition of *illumination*? How does it differ from the process of inspiration discussed in the previous chapter?

2. Why is the doctrine of illumination so crucial to a proper understanding of the supernatural, Holy Spirit–directed nature of God's Word?

3. How does illumination work in the life of the believer? What is the Holy Spirit's role in the process? What are some problems that can block the Holy Spirit's work of illumination?

4. What happens in the life of a believer who experiences the Spirit's illumination? What is the importance of abiding discussed in 1 John 2? Why is abiding so crucial to a believer in Christ? (Use the chart below as an aid to your discussion.)

PICTURE THIS

The Spirit's work of illumination helps us to see beyond the physical realm into the spiritual realm. Below are three truths regarding the work of illumination in the life of the believer.

HOW ILLUMINATION WORKS IN THE LIFE OF THE BELIEVER

TRUTH	SCRIPTURE PASSAGE	WHAT IT MEANS
We have an anointing from God.	1 John 2:20, 27	As believers, we are anointed in our ability to receive, understand, and apply truth from the Holy Spirit.
The Holy Spirit is our Illuminator and Teacher.	John 14:26	The Holy Spirit teaches us what we need to know from the Word to address specific areas in our lives.
Abiding brings the anointing.	1 John 2:6–27	The abiding of the believer is the assurance we find in the presence and power of Christ as we live in fellowship with Him and are obedient to Him. Our anointing flows from our abiding.

95

THE INTERPRETATION OF THE BIBLE

If you have ever tried to communicate with someone in another language, you know how difficult that can be. Even with an interpreter who knows both languages, there are always times when you are stymied either because the interpreter is groping for the right word in the other language to accurately convey your English word, or vice versa. And interpretation is almost never just a matter of doing a straight word-for-word translation.

I can illustrate this by mentioning the word *lead*. You have no way of knowing for sure which meaning I have in mind until I give it some context by using it in a sentence. That's because these four simple letters can be a verb that means "to direct," a noun that means "a position in front," or an adjective that means "to act or serve as the lead," as in the lead story in a newspaper.

These meanings are at least related in concept, but they don't exhaust the possibilities for confusion. The word *lead* has an entirely different meaning, and even a different pronunciation, when it refers to a soft metal. And even beyond this we have the word *led* that sounds just like the soft metal, but is the past tense of the verb *lead*.

According to one linguistic expert, the five hundred most often used

English words have an average of twenty-three meanings each. It's no wonder that communication demands understanding to be effective, even between people who are speaking the same language.

Now let's take this one step further and think about how totally ill-equipped sinful human beings are to understand God's message from heaven without someone to interpret it to us. If you think you have problems trying to understand your teenager or your spouse, you haven't seen anything yet. How could a perfectly holy God communicate with a sinful race on a tiny speck of His creation called Earth? He did it in two ways: by becoming a man Himself in the person of His Son, and by giving us His written Word in human languages that were designed to be read and understood.

THE HOLY SPIRIT IS THE BIBLE'S DIVINE INTERPRETER

We don't have to worry that the message got distorted during the transmission of the Bible from God's mouth to our hands. God Himself is the encoder in the person of the Holy Spirit, and the message is His Word sent to the "decoders," the human writers of Scripture.

These men would have been the fallible link in this infallible chain, but the Spirit took care of that by moving them to write under His inspiration in order to deliver the exact message God wanted to communicate. From Moses, who wrote the first five books of the Bible around 1400 B.C., to the apostle John, who wrote Revelation in about A.D. 90, the Holy Spirit made sure there was no accuracy lost in the transmission of Scripture.

We Need to Know What the Bible Is Saying

I said in the previous chapter that our task is not to receive new revelation, but to understand the revelation God has given us. This task is interpretation, or the work of determining what the Holy Spirit meant by what He inspired the Bible's authors to record. Many people avoid the Bible because they say they can't understand it.

When people say they can't understand the Bible, they are usually talking about the issue of interpretation. The technical word for this is *hermeneutics*, a word that comes straight from the Greek and is related to the god Hermes of Greek mythology, whose job was to communicate the language of the gods to human beings. Hermeneutics is the science and art of interpreting the Bible.

Interpretation is a science because words have meanings that we can rely on, and languages follow certain rules of grammar and composition that can be observed and cataloged. But interpretation is also an art because language is not that precise.

The Holy Spirit Knows What the Word Means

There is a great example of our need for interpretation in the evangelist Philip's encounter with the Ethiopian eunuch, as recorded in Acts 8:26–40. You can read the entire story, which only takes a minute and may be familiar to you. This Ethiopian was an official of the royal court who had come to Jerusalem to worship the true God and was returning home, sitting in his chariot and reading from the book of Isaiah (v. 28).

The Holy Spirit told Philip to go meet this man, and, when Philip did, he heard him reading aloud from Isaiah 53. Now, Isaiah 53 is a passage that begs for interpretation. We understand it to be speaking of Christ, because the suffering described there matches what happened in His crucifixion to such an amazing degree that this can be nothing else but a prophecy of Jesus' death. Besides, this one is easy because this is the interpretation that Philip gave to the eunuch (v. 35), which means we have the Bible interpreting itself. And when it comes to understanding Scripture, it doesn't get any better than that.

We Need an Interpreter to Understand the Bible

But the court official had none of this background. So the deacon Philip asked the Ethiopian, "Do you understand what you are reading?" (Acts 8:30). When we talk about the meaning of a Bible text, we are after the original author's intent and not just what it says to us. Many Christians think that doing Bible study consists of going around the room while people tell one by one what the verse or passage in question means to them.

But that's not interpreting the Bible, because one of the principles of good biblical interpretation is that a text has one primary meaning. It may have many personal applications, but the Bible does not mean whatever anyone wants it to mean. Most heresies begin with a twisted interpretation of the Scripture. Building a spiritually healthy faith has to begin with the correct interpretation of God's Word.

The goal of accurately interpreting the Bible is not just understanding for its own sake, but understanding so as to apply the Word correctly to our lives. Our church in Dallas has a ministry to people who are hearing impaired so they can join fully in the ministry of the Word. We do this because our goal is not to fill the pews, but to help every believer understand and obey God's Word. The exciting thing is that when you arrive at the right understanding of the Bible along with the right application, there is no issue in life that cannot be addressed victoriously. Understanding and application join together to bring about transformation.

THERE ARE PREREQUISITES TO INTERPRETING SCRIPTURE

The Bible is meant to be an open book to anyone who wants to know the truth. But this does not mean that God simply throws His treasure chest of truth open to anyone who comes along so the person can look it over and take whatever he wants. Jesus called that "throw[ing] your pearls before swine" (Matthew 7:6). This means to give something valuable to folks who don't value it and, therefore, treat it with contempt. Certain prerequisites must be present in our lives before the Bible becomes an open book to us.

We Must Know Christ as Our Savior

The Bible teaches that every believer is a priest before God. Peter called the church "a royal priesthood" (1 Peter 2:9). A priest's job was to stand between the people and God and intercede for them, while also bringing back God's message and will to them. But the office of priest is no longer needed now that Christ's death has opened the way into God's presence for every believer.

The doctrine of the priesthood of the believer means that we do not need someone else to hear from God for us and tell us what He said. All Christians have the anointing and don't need a teacher in the sense of someone to represent them before God while they stand by and wait to see what

God says (see 1 John 2:27). God gives us pastors and teachers to guide us, but all true believers are qualified to hear from God by virtue of their salvation and the gift of the indwelling Holy Spirit.

We Must Be in Fellowship with the Holy Spirit

A second prerequisite is intimate communion with God through the Holy Spirit. The closer you are to the Spirit, the more clearly you will understand the Word. This follows because the Holy Spirit is "the Spirit of truth" (John 16:13) whom God sent to continue the teaching Jesus began while He was on earth. One of Jesus' titles was Teacher (see Mark 4:38 and John 11:28), a ministry that was handed over to the Spirit when Jesus went back to heaven.

The Holy Spirit's job is to interpret and clarify the truth—to reveal to you what it means and how you need to apply it to your life. But the Spirit does not do His work of teaching in a heart and mind that are closed to Him. I am referring to a believer who is out of sync with the Spirit for whatever reason. Since the Holy Spirit is the illuminator and the interpreter of Scripture, it makes sense that the closer you are to Him, the clearer the Bible will become to you, while the farther you are from the Spirit, the fuzzier God's Word will become (see John 16:13).

We Must Be Willing to Grow as We Learn

A third prerequisite to understanding the Bible has to do with our willingness to respond in obedience to what the Spirit shows us (see Psalm 119:34). Peter wrote, "Therefore, putting aside all malice and all deceit and hypocrisy and envy and all slander, like newborn babies, long for the pure milk of the word, so that by it you may grow in respect to salvation" (1 Peter 2:1–2). God wants us to get rid of any sinful attitude that prevents us from growing as we feed on His Word.

One aspect of this involves a crucial spiritual principle we encountered earlier. This is what we could call the "obey before you know" principle; that is, we must be committed to obey God even before He reveals the specifics of His will and Word to us. You may take a car out for a test-drive to see if you like the way it handles and feels before you commit yourself to buy it, but you don't take God's truth out for a test-drive to see if it's something you want to do.

An unwillingness to obey God helps to explain why some Christians can go to church for decades, and yet their understanding is muted and their growth is stunted. God's Word is transforming, but they aren't transformed by it because they are not willing to submit to God. Some of these people may know the Bible in terms of being able to quote it or find the stories. But knowledge is not equivalent to obedience. In fact, Paul said that without spiritual transformation, "Knowledge makes arrogant" (1 Corinthians 8:1).

INTERPRETING THE BIBLE INVOLVES SPECIFIC STEPS

Having said that knowledge of the Bible alone is not enough, let me add that knowledge of the Word is the right place to start. Learning the Bible takes work. That's why Paul told Timothy, "Be diligent to present yourself approved to God as a workman who does not need to be ashamed, accurately handling the word of truth" (2 Timothy 2:15).

The First Step Is to Read the Bible

A lot of Christians don't advance in their knowledge and understanding of Scripture because they simply don't take the first and seemingly obvious step, which is to read the Bible with consistency and concentration.

These are the folks who read a verse a day to keep the Devil away, or who turn to the Bible during a crisis for a word of hope or direction. It's OK to ask God to give you a word from the Word when you are in a crisis. But make no mistake; this kind of approach to the Bible is the exception, not the pattern. But a lot of people just want a little bit of Bible here and there to get them through the tough spots because they don't want to be consistent workmen.

The Second Step Is to Ask Some Questions

Another step is to ask some very basic interpretive questions about the passage you are reading. For instance, what does the text say? That is, try paraphrasing it back to yourself or summarizing what the passage says.

Then you might ask to whom this passage was written, and under what circumstances. Knowing a passage's original recipients and context can help unlock its meaning. Many Christians can quote Philippians 4:19, the promise that God will meet all of our needs according to His riches in Christ.

But this is part of a larger context in which Paul thanked the Philippians for their faithful and sacrificial giving in support of his ministry (vv. 14–18). So the promise of God's supply is tied to our faithfulness in giving to His work.

It's amazing how many times people overlook the context or the recipients of a Bible text. Many of the twisted Bible teachings floating around today could be untwisted really fast if these basic principles of interpretation were applied. Cults love to rip individual Bible verses out of their context.

Other basic interpretive questions to ask of any Bible passage include these: Is there a command here to be obeyed, a sin to avoid, a promise to claim, or a warning to heed? These are just some of the questions you can use to understand the Word. You should also have some basic Bible study tools such as a concordance that lists every word in the Bible, a good Bible commentary, and a Bible dictionary. There are available several excellent one- or two-volume commentaries on the whole Bible.

The Most Important Step Is to Look for Jesus

I have saved the most important interpretive key for last because it deserves special treatment. The key to understanding the Bible is to see how it relates to Jesus Christ. Christ is the key to the Scriptures (see John 5:39).

The Old Testament points to Jesus Christ. John the Baptist made that clear when he said of Jesus, "Behold, the Lamb of God who takes away the sin of the world!" (John 1:29). What John was saying is that the entire sacrificial system of the Mosaic law pointed forward to Jesus. Today, the entire New Testament points backward to Jesus. He is the living incarnate Word of God, and He and the living written Word always agree. Find Jesus in your passage, and you will be on the right track to its meaning.

Jesus Himself made this emphatically clear when He taught the disciples on the road to Emmaus. Jesus began at the beginning of Scripture and "explained to them the things concerning Himself in all the Scriptures" (Luke 24:27).

PERSONAL APPLICATION FOR LIFE

1. God wants us to grow in our salvation. If you are a believer and growth is not happening, then you need to find out what is wrong and deal with it. You can be sure your problem is not with the Word itself, as it is filled with all the right nutrients and free of impurities. If you're not growing, it's time you started cooperating with the Holy Spirit and letting Him teach you. Are you ready to respond in obedience to what He shows you?

2. If you have never gotten lost in the wonder of the Word, then you are missing one of the great delights of the Christian life. There is tremendous power in simply reading the Bible. As you read, the Holy Spirit weaves truths together, and the Bible makes sense. Reading the Bible is the first step to interpreting it. Make daily time in the Word and with God one of your highest priorities.

3. Are you struggling with a problem right now that is causing a sense of hopelessness, fear, or depression because it seems like nothing is going to work out right? Get into the Word! When God opens the truth of the Bible to your understanding, your heart will burn with new excitement and new insight. A heart on fire with God's Word will lift from the deepest despair. Take that first step and start reading the Word, listening for God's voice.

4. When it comes to interpreting the Bible's truth, we never have to go it alone. God the Holy Spirit wants to guide you into "all the truth" (John 16:13). He doesn't just want you to be *under* the teaching of the Word, but to also be *in* the Word. He wants to make His Word burn in your heart, because when that happens and you apply what the Holy Spirit of God is teaching you, you will be changed by the power of His transforming Word. Are you engaging that power?

FOR GROUP STUDY

Questions for Group Discussion

1. What is the role of the Holy Spirit in the interpretation of Scripture? What part do humans play in the interpretation of Scripture?

2. What is *hermeneutics*? Why is it a critical discipline?

3. What are the prerequisites for the human interpretation of Scripture? Why is each a prerequisite? (Use the "Picture This" chart as an aid to your discussion.)

4. What are the steps for a believer's proper interpretation of Scripture? How does each step get us closer to the proper interpretation of God's Word?

PICTURE THIS

Although the Bible is meant to be read by anyone who wants to know the truth, certain prerequisites must be present in our lives before the Bible becomes an open book to us. Below are three prerequisites provided in God's Word.

The Prerequisites for Interpreting Scripture

PREREQUISITE	SCRIPTURE PASSAGE	ITS IMPORTANCE
We must know Christ as our Savior.	1 Peter 2:9	The first qualification for understanding the Bible is to be saved. A nonbeliever does not have the capacity to interpret divine truth.
We must be in fellowship with the Holy Spirit.	John 16:13	We need to be in intimate communion with God through His Holy Spirit. The closer we are to the Spirit, the more clearly we will understand the Word.
We must be willing to grow as we learn.	1 Peter 2:1–2	We must be willing to respond in obedience to what the Spirit of God teaches us.

96

THE CANONICITY OF THE BIBLE

The canonicity of the Bible and the Bible canon form a topic you don't hear much about, but as you can tell by the spelling of the word, it has nothing to do with weapons. The canonicity of Scripture is a very important part of bibliology, the doctrine or study of the Bible.

The word *canon* is from the ancient world and basically means a rule or standard. It referred to a reed that was used to measure things, much as we would use a ruler today. The classic definition of canon in church life is "rule of faith." Over the centuries of church history, many denominations and church bodies have drawn up canons that help to determine belief and practice for their people.

In the process of time, the canon also came to mean a catalog or list—in this case, the authoritative list of books that make up the Bible. Canonization tells how the Bible received its acceptance as men recognized the authority of God's inspired writings. It is the process by which God's inspired Word was recognized by men of God and then collected and preserved by the people of God. This subject is as intriguing as it is important, because the process by which the books of the Bible were included is an amazing story in itself and one that's filled with drama. But my primary concern is the product that we have in our hands today, the thirty-nine Old Testament books and twenty-seven New Testament books that make up God's inspired, inerrant Word.

THE BOOKS OF THE BIBLE WERE DISCERNED

The first question that needs to be answered concerning the Bible's canonicity is how some writings were chosen to be included in the Scripture, while others were excluded. The key is in the heading above: *discerned*. What the early church did was discern, under the guidance of the Holy Spirit, which books *already* carried the stamp of the Spirit's inspiration and which did not. In other words, a body of church leaders did not sit down and read, say, the Gospel According to Matthew, and then take a vote as to whether they thought it was inspired or not, with the majority vote winning.

The Bible's Books Have Their Own Authority

That may sound confusing at first, because in fact the church did have to draw the line and either include or exclude particular books. But there is all the difference in the world between discerning what is already true and deciding whether it's true or not by human judgment and majority vote. The determining authority for the canon of Scripture was God Himself, not any church body or individual leader. God decided the canon of Scripture; men simply recognized it.

Let's consider Matthew, which was written by one of Jesus' twelve apostles. There was also a text floating around in the early church that claimed to be a "gospel" written by the apostle Thomas, who was just as authentic an apostle as Matthew. And the gospel of Thomas was just one of dozens of so-called gospels and epistles in existence that claimed divine authority. How did the early church know that the gospel of Matthew was part of God's authentic revelation, while the gospel of Thomas was a fraud? And how can we be sure today that we're not missing something God wanted us to know, but that got left out of the Bible?

The answer is that the church ran both books under the "scanner" of the Holy Spirit's sovereign guidance and direction, and the gospel of Thomas didn't cut it. Church leaders examined the books carefully for internal evidence of inspiration, and checked out the external evidence for their authenticity, following specific criteria by which a book claiming to be Scripture either authenticated or disqualified itself.

We must understand this fundamental principle that God the Holy Spirit, and not man, determined the canon of Scripture. If we do not believe and affirm that the God who guided human beings to write Scripture also guided other human beings to collect it into one book, then our entire doctrine of Scripture crumbles like a house of cards.

Canonicity Is a Critical Issue Today

Someone might say, "Tony, is this really a big deal? I mean, come on. The Bible has been the way it is for hundreds and hundreds of years. This is not something we need to get worked up about, is it?"

Absolutely. Canonicity is not just a musty issue from ancient history. American founding father Thomas Jefferson, who was a deist, took a pair of scissors to the Gospels and cut out the parts he didn't accept. But we have a much more recent example than that.

The mega-bestselling novel entitled *The DaVinci Code* claimed that there was an entire period of Jesus' life that was written down but later was suppressed by the church because it conflicted with the "official" story of Jesus as recorded in Scripture. The issue of the Bible's canonicity has been hotly debated on all the TV networks and talk shows, although the word *canon* was not used very often.

The canon is something like gravity. You and I didn't create the law of gravity, and we can't control it. All we can do is recognize, use, and submit to this law that God created. You don't have to like the law of gravity for it to be in effect. Your decision to demonstrate your freedom from gravity by jumping out of a tenth-floor window won't change anything except the way your body is arranged. So it is with those who have tried to ignore, defy, and deny the truth that God superintended the process by which each of the sixty-six inspired books was admitted into the Bible's canon.

THE BIBLE HAD STANDARDS OF ADMISSION

Just as college administrators have admission standards that applicants must meet before being accepted at the school, church fathers had admission standards for each book of the Bible. These strict standards of admission had to be met for a piece of writing to be recognized as Spirit-inspired and admitted to the canon of the New Testament. During this process, the early church used several critical tests. The two basic criteria were that a book (1) had to carry the authority of an apostle and (2) had to be recognized and accepted by the church. Within these standards there are various subpoints, which we will discuss as we go.

A Book Had to Have the Right Authority

For a book to be admitted into the Bible, it had to have been written by a true prophet or apostle, or by someone in direct contact with them. The legitimacy and authenticity of this message was confirmed by accompanying supernatural acts of God (Acts 2:22; 2 Corinthians 12:12; Hebrews 2:4). Thus Matthew, and John's and Peter's writings, met that standard. Books like Mark, Luke, Acts, James, and Jude qualified because they were written by firsthand associates of the twelve apostles, men who carried the apostles' stamp of approval. Paul's epistles bore the stamp of apostolic authorship because God called him to be the apostle to the Gentiles. Hebrews is the only New Testament book whose author we don't know for sure.

Just as a contender for the New Testament had to meet the standard of apostolic authority, the standards were extremely high for inclusion in the Old Testament canon. The writer of Hebrews affirmed that God "spoke long ago to the fathers in the prophets in many portions and in many ways" (1:1).

God established very strict guidelines for His prophets that help us draw the line between true and false prophets even today. God said to Moses:

> I will raise up a prophet from among their countrymen like you, and I will put My words in his mouth, and he shall speak to them all that I command him. It shall come about that whoever will not listen to My words which he shall speak in My name, I Myself will require it of him. But the prophet who speaks a word presumptuously in My name which I have not commanded him to speak, or which he speaks in the name of other gods, that prophet shall die. (Deuteronomy 18:18–20)

If someone tried to claim a true prophet's authority falsely, it would cost him his life. A prophet had an awesome responsibility because he had to speak the very words of God, just as he received them from God, and the words he received from God became the standard by which God's people would be judged. Thus, for a book to be recognized as canonical it had to tell the truth from God and had to be true about God (Deuteronomy 13:1–3).

When it comes to the Old Testament canon, we have a witness to the authenticity of the books that goes back even before the beginning of the church. The Jews had recognized and brought together the books of the Hebrew canon many years before the days of Jesus and the apostles. In other words, God led the Jews to assemble their inspired canon—and the fact that God's people rejected a batch of other Jewish books, called the Apocrypha, is critically important, as we will see in a minute.

Each of the New Testament books except Hebrews carries the name either of an apostle or a personal associate of an apostle. And the apostles, particularly Paul, were not reluctant to claim God's inspiration for their writings. (See Galatians 1:11–12 and 1 Thessalonians 2:13.) The apostles knew their writings were authoritative and said so. But even Luke, who was not an apostle, was bold to say that he received the material for both volumes of his writings from the apostles (see Luke 1:1–4 and Acts 1:2). And in a very important passage, Paul's writings received the apostolic seal of approval from Peter, who called Paul's letters "the Scriptures" (2 Peter 3:15–16).

A Book Had to Be Accepted by the People of God

Another test of canonicity was whether the people of God recognized it as authoritative and accepted it as the Word of God. In other words, a book had to win a hearing from God's people as the Holy Spirit witnessed within them that the book's message was from God (see Nehemiah 8:9, 14–18; 1 Thessalonians 2:13).

As already noted, the Hebrew canon was already established by the time of Jesus. Our Lord quoted extensively from the Old Testament during His earthly ministry, and in so doing validated the writings of the patriarchs and prophets (Matthew 26:56; Luke 24:27). The appearance of Moses and Elijah with Jesus on the Mount of Transfiguration (see Matthew 17:3) was a powerful testimony of their authority as representatives of these two categories of Old Testament authors, and also a powerful testimony that all of the Old Testament points to Jesus.

Notice how Paul also testified to the authority of the Old Testament and urged the church to make use of it in learning how God wants us to live. Paul wrote, "For whatever was written in earlier times [the Old Testament] was written for our instruction, so that through perseverance and the encouragement of the Scriptures we might have hope" (Romans 15:4). Elsewhere Paul said the events in the Old Testament "happened to them as an example, and they were written for our instruction" (1 Corinthians 10:11). The New Testament quotes the Old Testament more than 250 times, and alludes to it another 900 times. This is overwhelming evidence that the apostles considered the Old Testament to be God's authoritative Word.

The Gospels came to the church bearing the stamp of inspiration. The New Testament epistles were used in the church and circulated among the churches, and they gained instant recognition as the Word of God. The teachings of the apostles were considered authoritative for the church (see 1 Corinthians 14:37; 1 Thessalonians 2:4). The authors of these books often claimed inspiration for themselves (see Galatians 1:11–12; 1 Thessalonians 2:13). And the apostles' doctrines are consistent with one another—another key test of canonicity.

THE DOUBTED BOOKS IN SCRIPTURE

A few additional observations that are important to this study. The canon of Scripture was compiled over time, not being fully settled until about four hundred years after Christ. And even then some books continued to be questioned by various leaders and councils, including 2 Peter, 2 and 3 John, James, Jude, Hebrews, and even Revelation.

Some people point to these things as evidence that the process of assembling the canon was a subjective human work. Actually, they prove just the opposite. The fact that the canon of Scripture existed by informal recognition for so long shows the staying power of the books that God inspired. For instance, the gospel of Thomas had basically several hundred years to convince the church that it was real, yet it did not make it into the canon because it is not Scripture. The lateness of the final canon is testimony to the fact that what the church had recognized and accepted all along as Scripture was valid.

Some Christians get uncomfortable when they learn that some of the New Testament books were questioned for many years. If you feel that way, you have nothing to worry about. Again, the fact that each of the books named above survived its doubters and was either accepted into or allowed to remain in the canon is very significant.

Most of the doubts had to do with the apostolic authorship of these books, but they proved their inspiration. Many of the doubts about James stemmed from a misunderstanding of James's teaching that we are saved by works and not by faith alone. Careful study and exposition of James has shown that those who thought James contradicted Paul's ringing declaration, "The righteous man shall live by faith" (Romans 1:17), were simply wrong. James complements Paul by telling us that we are justified in the eyes of others by our works.

Each book in Scripture meets the rule or canon of the faith, and carries the Holy Spirit's stamp of approval. You don't need to worry that anything good was left out. On the contrary, you can be sure that what you hold in your hands is "the whole purpose of God" (Acts 20:27)—the very Word of God.

PERSONAL APPLICATION FOR LIFE

1. As you approach your Bible, you must understand the fundamental principle that God the Holy Spirit, and not man, determined the canon of Scripture. Thank God that you can partake of His Word, which He has preserved throughout the centuries.

2. Do you pray for your pastor? Each week your pastor must correctly and faithfully interpret the Bible so its message can be heard and believed in all its power. Ask God to help your pastor deliver the truth in ways that will cause his congregation to see only Jesus.

3. Isn't it great that God the Holy Spirit has provided us with an authoritative provision of His timeless truth? Never take for granted the precious Bible that we have. It enables us not only to know God's will, but also to know Him in a personal relationship. When you drink from the Word, drink deeply. Its depths are inexhaustible!

4. Every time you open your Bible, acknowledge its authority and power to change your life. Before you begin reading, ask God to open every area of your heart to the Word's power. Be ready to make a heart response to what God shows you.

FOR GROUP STUDY

Questions for Group Discussion

1. What is the *canon*? How did the church determine the canon? Who ultimately decided the canon?

2. Why is canonicity a critical issue today?

3. What factors determine a book's authenticity? What were the admission standards? (Use the chart in "Picture This" as an aid to your discussion.)

4. Some books in our Bible were questioned as to their authenticity. Which books are they, and why were they eventually accepted into the canon?

PICTURE THIS

Of the several critical tests carried out by the early church during the admission process, the two basic criteria are listed below.

THE CANON'S ADMISSION STANDARDS

STANDARD	SCRIPTURE PASSAGES	WHY IT WAS IMPORTANT
A book had to have the proper authority.	Acts 2:22; 2 Corinthians 12:12; Hebrews 2:4	For a book to be included, it had to have been written by a true prophet, an apostle, or a direct contact.
A book had to be accepted by the people of God.	Nehemiah 8:9, 14–18; 1 Thessalonians 2:13; Matthew 26:56; Luke 24:27	This involved a hearing from God's people as the Holy Spirit witnessed within them that the book's message was from God.

SECTION III

THE BENEFITS OF THE BIBLE

97

THE BIBLE PRODUCES SPIRITUAL LIFE

The apostle Peter said this about the Bible's power to bring new spiritual life: "You have been born again not of seed which is perishable but imperishable, that is, through the living and enduring word of God. For, 'All flesh is like grass, and all its glory like the flower of grass. The grass withers, and the flower falls off, but the word of the Lord endures forever.' And this is the word which was preached to you" (1 Peter 1:23–25). God's Word is so powerful it can bring life out of death.

In this section of the book we want to answer the "So what?" question that every preacher ought to address as he delivers a sermon. This is the payoff, so to speak, the part that answers this question in the listeners' minds: "So what? Now that I know this truth, what difference does it make? What should I do about it?"

THE WORD OF GOD IS LIFE-GIVING

Talking about the Bible's life-giving power is the right place to start, because no other spiritual benefit would do us any good if we had not been given new life.

When the apostle John wrote his first letter to teach believers how to have intimate fellowship with God, he referred to Jesus Christ as "the Word of Life" (1 John 1:1). John went on to say that this Word was "manifested" (v. 2) to him and the other apostles who saw Jesus in His flesh. We do not have that privilege now, but we have the same Word of Life because we have the completed Bible that embodies and reveals Jesus to us. There is no division or contradiction between the Bible and Jesus Christ, who is also called "the Word" in the first verse of John's gospel. Jesus gives life and His Word gives life because the two operate in concert with each other.

Jesus declared in John 6:63, "The words that I have spoken to you are spirit and are life." Peter responded in that same chapter when everyone but the Twelve had deserted Jesus, "Lord, to whom shall we go? You have words of eternal life" (v. 68). The book of Hebrews reminds us, "The word of God is living" (4:12), and thus it can impart life.

We Were Dead without the Life-Giving Word

How grateful should we be for the fact that we have been made alive by the imperishable seed of God's Word? We should be eternally grateful, since the news in the divine coroner's report was as bad as it gets. This is what God said about us before we were saved: "You were dead in your transgressions and sins" (Ephesians 2:1 NIV).

This is a chapter about life, so we don't want to dwell too long on the subject of death. But the blessing of spiritual life only shines in all of its glory when we see it against the dark backdrop of the spiritual death that had us in its grip. Besides, all of us have family members or friends who are still living in the realm of spiritual death, and we need to be reminded of their desperate condition to spur us to reach out to them with God's life-giving Word.

Probably the hardest thing for unbelievers to grasp is that outside of Jesus Christ, they are dead. Not just a little bit ill or even barely alive, but as dead now as they will be throughout eternity apart from God's saving grace.

This is the true condition of lost people. They are the living dead because death in Scripture is separation, never mere cessation of existence. We will never stop existing, for our souls and spirits are immortal. The problem most unbelievers have is that they don't understand the Bible's definition of death. Of course, the Bible recognizes physical death as the moment when the body is separated from the soul and spirit. But the Bible's overriding concern is with spiritual death, in which the unsaved already exist, and which will become irrevocable when they die and are separated from God forever.

We can see this crucial distinction in Jesus' word to a would-be disciple who wanted to wait until his father died before following Jesus: "Allow the dead to bury their own dead; but as for you, go and proclaim everywhere the kingdom of God" (Luke 9:60).

In other words, Jesus told this man to let the spiritually dead bury their physical dead. The Lord wasn't being coldhearted, but He knew that if this man went back to live in that realm of spiritual death from which he had come, he would succumb to his environment and not follow Jesus.

Jesus Came to Give Us Abundant Life

The classic statement of God's life-giving purpose for us is in John 10:10. Jesus said, "I came that they may have life, and have it abundantly." Notice that Jesus does not just give life, but multiplies it into abundant, overflowing life. We could paraphrase John 10:10 as, "I came that they might live—and I mean really live!" And we know from 1 Peter 1:23 that the means God uses to give us abundant life is His eternal Word.

Most people miss the abundant life God promises because they look for life in the physical realm. But all that material things can do is provide people with more camouflage to hide the fact that they are dead and empty on the inside. What I mean is that a person can buy a lot of toys and nice clothes and good times that may bring temporary enjoyment and keep him from thinking about how dead he feels deep within. But other people can't fill a person's spiritual emptiness.

There is only one place and person we can look to for real life. Jesus prayed on the night before His crucifixion, "This is eternal life, that they may know You, the only true God, and Jesus Christ whom You have sent" (John 17:3). This verse makes it clear that life is found in knowing God through Jesus—and we know this message of life because it is recorded in God's Word.

Even in the world of the dying, God says you can be among the living because of what His Word can do. Even if everyone around you is dying, you can be fully alive. I like how Paul puts it: "Though our outer man is decaying, yet our inner man is being renewed day by day" (2 Corinthians 4:16).

THE BIBLE GIVES EVIDENCE OF BEING ALIVE

The consistent testimony of the Bible's authors is that the Word they wrote is alive and has the ability to produce life in anyone who will receive it. God's witness to His Word is the most important proof of its life-giving power. But there are other proofs that provide validating evidence that the Word of God is alive.

The Word of God Has Given Life to Millions

One of these proofs is the legions of Christians throughout the ages who have found new life as the Spirit applied the Word to their lives (see James 1:18). Only living things can produce life. Inanimate objects do not have the ability to bring life out of nothing, as God did when He spoke creation into existence with His Word. Neither can inanimate objects bring life out of death, as God does through His Word whenever a person is born again.

The Word of God Is Eternally Fresh

Another evidence of the Bible's life is its incredible, inexhaustible freshness. I have been preaching for about thirty years, and in some ways I feel as if I am just beginning to understand the Bible. I have not even begun to explore all of its depths, and I am confident that any other biblically based pastor would say the same thing.

It is impossible to imagine studying any other book for decades, and preaching from it every week, without exhausting both yourself and your hearers. But the Bible is preached, taught, read, and otherwise examined in detail thousands of times every week across the world, and no one has ever been able to say, "OK, that's it. I've covered the whole Bible and there's nothing left to say about it."

The Bible never loses its life. It is forever fresh (Isaiah 40:8). You may be looking at your Bible today and seeing no signs of life, but be assured that the life is there. The best thing you can do is stay in the Word until the winter is past and God's revelation bursts forth with new life in your heart.

The Word of God Makes Things Grow

Another evidence that the Bible is alive is that it produces growth. "Therefore, putting aside all malice and all deceit and hypocrisy and envy and all slander, like newborn babies, long for the pure milk of the word, so that by it you may grow in respect to salvation" (1 Peter 2:1–2).

Why is it that growth doesn't take place in some believers' lives, if the Word is capable of producing growth and God wants us to grow? As I was thinking about this, the answer hit me in verse 1 of our text. We tend to read over it quickly to get to the part about growing by the milk of the Word. But look again at 1 Peter 2:1. Here is a list of "dirty laundry" we need to do something about—sins and poor attitudes that we have to rid ourselves of before the milk of the Word can flow freely and provide its nourishment.

Some people say to me, "Pastor, I don't know what's wrong. I read my Bible every day. I go to church on Sunday and Wednesday. I read Christian books, listen to Christian radio, and watch Christian television. But I still feel spiritually weak, like I'm not getting what I need to grow."

The answer could be that these believers are not removing the hindrances to their growth. Feeding on the "junk food" of sin kills our legitimate hunger for the Word. The problem for many nongrowing Christians is not that they need more Bible study or the latest book on spiritual growth. Their biggest need is for some spiritual dialysis.

If you are in need of kidney dialysis, for example, it does not matter how much healthy food you eat. The quality of your diet becomes irrelevant because there is no filtering of the impurities, and the best diet in the world won't keep you alive when your kidneys are not functioning properly.

The same is true in our spiritual lives. If the impurities of sin are not cleansed by the blood of Christ, don't be surprised if you don't experience growth even though you may be reading your Bible regularly and going to church.

The Word of God Has Unbelievable Power

We also know the Word of God is alive because of its power. People who had no relationship to God and knew nothing of His grace have picked up a Bible, begun reading it, and fallen on their faces crying out for God's mercy and grace. Then they have testified that whereas they were dead in their sins, they are now alive in Jesus Christ.

The last time I checked, no other book has this life-changing, life-giving power. The testimony of those who have been transformed by God's Word is that the Bible is the only Book that reads you as you read it. But sometimes we don't like the Bible's power because it makes us uncomfortable by slicing us open, as Hebrews 4:12 says, and exposing our deepest thoughts and attitudes. It works the other way too, and there is nothing like the excitement of reading a passage that has your name on it as the Holy Spirit speaks directly to you through the Word. But whether the Bible convicts or confirms you, you are experiencing its power.

YOU CAN TAP INTO THE BIBLE'S LIFE-GIVING POWER

It wouldn't be fair to talk about the Bible's ability to produce life without helping you tap into this life. There is a very important verse that gives us three basic ways we can use and enjoy the power of God's Word: "Blessed is he who reads and those who hear the words of the prophecy, and heed the things which are written in it" (Revelation 1:3).

Everybody wants to be blessed, which means to be full, satisfied, and happy. John said that the state of being blessed that we seek comes when we read, "seed," and heed God's Word.

You Need to Read the Word

We don't need to say much here, because we have already talked about the importance of reading the Bible on a regular, systematic basis (1 Timothy 4:13). There are many daily reading plans available that will take you through the entire Bible in one year. Someone has calculated that if we would cut out one thirty-minute television program per day and devote that time to the Word, we could read through the Bible twice in one year.

You Need to "Seed" the Word

Revelation 1:3 promises a blessing to those who "hear" the Word of God. I call this "seeding" the Word because in biblical terms, hearing doesn't mean simply letting the words of Scripture penetrate your consciousness. It means internalizing what God tells you, letting the Word take root in your heart like a seed that produces a harvest.

This is why Jesus said on more than one occasion, "He who has ears to hear, let him hear" (Matthew 11:15). This statement would not make sense were it not for the fact that it is possible for us to hear something without letting it get down inside of us. But to really hear the Word is to say, "Dear God, I'm reading, so please talk to me." If you develop that mind-set as you read your Bible or sit under its teaching, you'll hear, because now you're asking God to speak to you, and you're ready to really listen.

You Need to Heed the Word

The third requirement for the blessing God promised in Revelation 1:3 is to heed, or obey, the Word. "Prove yourselves doers of the word, and not merely hearers who delude themselves" (James 1:22). Now don't be thrown off by this statement about hearing the Word. The key is "merely," meaning those who let the Word go in one ear and out the other without taking seed.

Some people read the Bible but don't hear it because the Word doesn't "register" with them. Others read and hear the Word, but don't get up and obey it. Some don't do any of these—but the blessing comes in doing all three (1 Thessalonians 2:13).

PERSONAL APPLICATION FOR LIFE

1. To lead a healthy spiritual life, you need to keep it clean. If sin's impurities are not cleansed by the blood of Christ, don't be surprised if you don't experience growth even though you may be reading your Bible regularly and going to church. Make claiming 1 John 1:9 an ongoing exercise—as often as is necessary!

2. We may be assured that Satan knows where the power is, and that he will do anything to keep you from reading and studying your Bible. When you become detached from your spiritual power too long, you no longer hear God. It's like turning off your cell phone. Stay connected to your power source so you can always hear His voice.

3. "Seeding" the Word of God in our hearts involves opening our hearts unconditionally before His truth and letting it penetrate every level of our being. Are you guarding that locked room in your heart you don't want God to see? Unlock every door and let Him in. As you read your Bible, pray, "Dear God, I'm reading, so please speak to me."

4. How is your appetite for the Bible? Get yourself a good taste of God's life-giving Word, and you will develop an appetite that won't be satisfied with anything else as you continue to be transformed into the image of Jesus Christ (2 Corinthians 3:18).

FOR GROUP STUDY

Questions for Group Discussion

1. Read John 6:63, 68. Discuss the life-giving power of the Word of God. How does God use the Bible to give us life? What is the nature of this life?

2. What evidence do we see that the Bible is alive and has the ability to produce life in anyone who will receive it?

3. Read 1 Peter 2:1–2. What kind of growth does the Word produce in the life of believer? Why is it that some believers fail to grow?

4. What must we do to tap into the Bible's life-giving power? (Use the chart below as an aid to your discussion.)

PICTURE THIS

Revelation 1:3 gives us three basic ways we can use and enjoy the power of God's Word. Each step can be fruitful, but the real blessing comes by doing all three.

TAPPING INTO THE BIBLE'S LIFE-GIVING POWER

OUR ACTION	SCRIPTURE PASSAGE	WHAT IT DOES
We need to read the Word.	Revelation 1:3	We must actively engage the Word by reading it on a regular basis.
We need to "seed" the Word.	Matthew 11:15	We must internalize what God tells us and let the Word take root in our hearts.
We need to heed the Word.	James 1:22	We must act upon the Word and obey it.

98

THE BIBLE PROVIDES SPIRITUAL DIRECTION

Our need for God's guidance is as old as the human race. Throughout the Bible, God's people cried out for His help when they were either at a fork in the road or had their backs against the wall. Moses and the Israelites were trapped between the Red Sea and the Egyptian army in Exodus 14 when God told them to move forward into the sea. He commanded Moses to stretch his staff out over the water. Solomon prayed as he assumed the throne of Israel, "I am but a little child; I do not know how to go out or come in" (1 Kings 3:7). Solomon then asked for wisdom to guide God's people.

I'm sure you know what it feels like to be in an "I don't know what to do" dilemma. There are situations in which you simply don't know which way to go. During such times you need a light to guide you, which makes the psalmist's ancient statement so relevant today: "Your word is a lamp to my feet and a light to my path" (Psalm 119:105).

GOD'S GUIDANCE IS PERSONAL AND SPECIFIC

One of the first things that stands out about this great verse is how personal and specific the guidance is that we receive from God's Word. We can see this, for instance, in the psalmist's use of the word *lamp*.

Watch Each Step You Take

Lamps in biblical days were a far cry from the kind of lighting we have today. Our lights can illuminate an entire room or a large area. And if we are walking in the dark, we have flashlights that can really brighten up the path and show us any hidden obstacles.

But in biblical days a small oil lamp was a personal item, providing only enough light for a person to see the next step as he walked, or to illuminate a small corner of a room. So a person walking along a path had to go deliberately, watching each step. This is true of so many decisions and choices in life. Rarely if ever do we see an entire issue in one grand moment of illumination and know instantly everything to do. God has designed life in such a way that we have to trust Him one step at a time, and so the Bible's assurance is that He will give us light for the next step.

Find Guidance from God

The first-person pronouns of Psalm 119:105 also reveal that this issue of guidance is personal. It's amazing how one Christian can open the Word and find clear guidance, while another can read the same passage and see nothing. This is true even though all believers have the same Bible and the same Holy Spirit. God does not play favorites, but He reveals Himself to those who seek Him with all their hearts (see Jeremiah 29:13). Two Christians can be very different in their sensitivity to the Spirit and His ministry of illuminating the Word.

Spiritual direction works something like the passenger reading-lights in airplanes. Each passenger's light is focused directly over his or her seat so as not to shine in the faces of the other passengers in the row. If you want to see what you're doing, you have to use the light that is provided specifically for you. You can't borrow someone else's light for your purposes.

The personal nature of spiritual guidance is another testimony to the fact that God wants to have a deeply personal and intimate relationship with you through His Word.

FIND DIRECTION AND BLESSING IN GOD'S WORD

Why is it so important that the Bible be the source we go to first for our spiritual guidance and decision making? Because God has promised to bless only His Word, not our own ideas or the opinions of others.

Be Careful of Counselors

Please don't think that I am putting down human counselors. As a pastor, I have spent literally thousands of hours seeking to help married couples, families, and individuals work through problems, make decisions, and find God's best for their lives. What I am saying is that any counselor or adviser who does not anchor that counsel in God's Word is suspect, because "the foolishness of God is wiser than men, and the weakness of God is stronger than men" (1 Corinthians 1:25).

Beware of the Enemy's Fortresses

There is another reason we need the wisdom and guidance found only in God's Word. This has to do with the nature of our human mind and the way it has been corrupted by sin. We have a serious problem when it comes to figuring out what we should do and where we should go. Paul explained this dilemma in a crucial passage of Scripture:

> For though we walk in the flesh, we do not war according to the flesh, for the weapons of our warfare are not of the flesh, but divinely powerful for the destruction of fortresses. We are destroying speculations and every lofty thing raised up against the knowledge of God, and we are taking every thought captive to the obedience of Christ. (2 Corinthians 10:3–5)

This is spiritual warfare language, which may seem out of place in a discussion of spiritual guidance. But not in this case, because there is someone out there who does not want you and me to find God's direction.

You know what a fortress looks like with its high, seemingly impenetrable walls. The problem we face in seeking God's direction for life is that we have a formidable enemy called the Devil whose job is to erect fortresses in our minds. These are things such as ungodly and unbiblical ways of thinking, ingrained habits and attitudes, or even addictions that keep us from hearing from God and finding His will.

WATCH OUT FOR THE ENEMY'S PARTITIONS

Paul also said we need to destroy speculations and every "lofty thing" that is raised up against the knowledge of God. We need to resist and tear down anything that hinders our ability to get God's viewpoint. The Greek word translated "lofty thing" is very interesting. It refers to a partition, or even an obstacle.

Let God's Word Be "At Home" in You

So how do we tear down the Devil's fortresses and destroy the "Berlin Walls" of partition that he builds in our minds? Paul gave us the answer: "Let the word of Christ richly dwell within you, with all wisdom teaching and admonishing one another with psalms and hymns and spiritual songs, singing with thankfulness in your hearts to God" (Colossians 3:16).

Comparing this passage to its parallel in Ephesians 5:18–21 reveals that letting God's Word dwell in us is a synonym for being "filled with the Spirit" (Ephesians 5:18). This is important because when we talk about the Word doing this or that in our lives, we are talking about the Holy Spirit's ministry of making the Word real to us. When the Holy Spirit fills a person, He brings with Him the Word.

The key word in Colossians 3 is *dwell*, which means to let the Spirit and the Word of God make themselves at home in your heart. The person who wants God's direction must let His Word move in and go wherever He wants it to go in the house.

Let God's Word Do the Talking

When you have this attitude of submission to God fixed in your mind, then you are ready for Colossians 3:17, which says, "Whatever you do in word or deed, do all in the name of the Lord Jesus, giving thanks through Him to God the Father."

We have to understand that God's direction comes as His Word permeates our minds. Do you want to know God's will for you? Then heed Romans 12:2, "Be transformed by the renewing of your mind, so that you may prove what the will of God is, that which is good and acceptable and perfect." To renew your mind is to change your thinking, which is vital because every decision in life is related to the way you think. There is no choice without thought.

Let God's Word Guide You Safely

The Word of God is meant to be a lamp and a light for you. To what end? Psalm 119:133 tells us: "Establish my footsteps in Your word, and do not let any iniquity have dominion over me." Your footsteps—your thinking, choices, and decisions—must be grounded in the Bible so you will not be controlled by sin.

In order for an airplane to land safely and arrive at the proper gate at the terminal, at least three things must happen. First, an air-traffic controller must maintain contact with the plane and give the pilot clearance and instructions to land. Second, if the landing is at night, the runway lights must be lit to guide the pilot down onto the right runway. And third, once the plane is on the ground the guy with the red batons must guide the plane to the right parking spot at its gate.

The same thing is true in being directed by God. God must be able to stay in contact with you, so He can tell you when it's safe to land. Then, you need the illumination of His Word to show you where to land. And you need the Spirit to show you the specific parking spot where you need to stop.

Let the Great Physician Give You a Checkup

If you haven't memorized Psalm 37:4, you should. David wrote, "Delight yourself in the Lord; and He will give you the desires of your heart." When your thinking and heart and desires are in agreement with God and His Word, you will hear from Him, because now you both have the same desires. And you have nothing to fear from God's desires, because He wants to give you His best even more than you want to receive it.

But God does want to X-ray our inner being using His Word until our hearts are "open and laid bare to the eyes of Him with whom we have to do" (Hebrews 4:13). Only when we get the true diagnosis can we be sure that the decisions we make are the ones God wants us to make. If we don't give the

Great Physician permission to examine our hearts, all we really do when we read His Word or go to church is take an over-the-counter medicine. Instead, we need to take what God would prescribe.

Make Sure You Listen to the Right Voice

What we need is someone to take us by the hand and lead us in the way we should go. And we'll find that guiding hand when we reach out our hands and pick up our Bibles. You've got to open the Book and look intently into the Word, which James called "the law of liberty" (James 1:25). The benefit of doing this is found in the last part of the verse, "This man will be blessed in what he does."

But as I suggested earlier, many Christians don't want to make the effort to search the Word. They want an easy, quick answer, even if they have to pay someone for it.

SOMETIMES WE NEED BIBLICAL COUNSELING

Whenever we talk about the Bible's ability to provide us with the guidance and wisdom we need to live complete, fulfilling lives, an important question always comes up: Does this mean it is unspiritual, or even wrong, for a Christian to seek out a human counselor for help with a serious problem?

People in some Christian circles would answer yes, it is wrong for Christians to go to counselors because these individuals rely too much on human wisdom and the principles of psychology to arrive at their diagnoses and offer solutions. Other Christians would say that there is nothing at all wrong or unspiritual about seeking help for a problem that is beyond the person's ability to handle alone.

The Key Is the Foundation for the Counseling

My answer falls between these two poles of absolute rejection and absolute acceptance of the need for counseling. I do not chastise people who need help. We are complex beings made up of body, soul, and spirit (see 1 Thessalonians 5:23), and things can go wrong in our souls and spirits just as they can in our bodies. To condemn somebody for seeking soul healing is like condemning that person for seeking physical healing for an illness or pain.

My concern with this issue is that we had better make sure the counseling we receive is *biblical* counseling. By that I mean far more than the counselor tossing a few Bible verses into the conversation. I am talking about using the Bible as the primary diagnostic tool in getting to the root of the ache in our souls and spirits. The problem with a lot of counseling is that it incorrectly diagnoses the problem because the root issue never gets dealt with.

The problem is that too much counseling, even Christian counseling, is focused on cleaning out the spider webs in people's lives when God wants to kill the spiders. That's why I say that any counseling that is not deeply embedded in Scripture is ultimately going to be ineffective. Biblical counseling is using the Word of God as the foundation for diagnosing and addressing what people need to know to bring healing to their souls (Matthew 7:24–27).

The Church Needs to Be a Counseling Center

Talking about counseling usually raises another question, which is, Great, sounds like just what I or my loved one needs. So where do we find this kind of counseling?

My answer is the church of Jesus Christ—and in particular, mature believers whom God has placed in the body—are equipped to counsel others.

Paul told the Romans, "Concerning you, my brethren, I myself also am convinced that you yourselves are full of goodness, filled with all knowledge and able also to admonish one another" (Romans 15:14). This may be the most important verse in Scripture on counseling, because that is exactly what the term *admonish* involves. The Bible says that we are to counsel one another, guided by the Holy Spirit and using the knowledge of God's Word that He has placed within us.

Professional counselors have their place in the body of Christ. My point is that the church has a crucial ministry of counseling to perform that is largely going undone today. We need to raise up a body of mature, godly believers who are equipped to skillfully employ and apply God's truth to other Christians.

If we truly believe that "all Scripture is inspired by God and profitable for teaching, for reproof, for correction, for training in righteousness" (2 Timothy 3:16) and that "His divine power has granted to us everything pertaining to life and godliness" (2 Peter 1:3), then we need to go to the Bible to diagnose, address, and correct the pain in our souls.

PERSONAL APPLICATION FOR LIFE

1. If you listen to all the voices around you, you will be confused and eventually misled. You can be certain some of those voices are coming from Satan and his helpers. Look intently into the Bible for your direction from God's voice, and block out all others.

2. When was the last time you allowed the Great Physician to give you a spiritual checkup? Keep in mind that God doesn't accept our academic degrees or self-help formulas as a substitute for the real thing. God wants us to X-ray our inner being until our hearts are laid bare to Him. Don't delay. Dig into the Word and let God diagnose the condition of your heart, and then follow up on His prescriptions.

3. Maybe you're the type who believes in guiding yourself in certain areas of your life, rather than giving full control to God. Can you find any area of your life where you've excluded God, even unconsciously, because you feel perfectly capable of handling that area? Perhaps you need to focus on letting go of that part of your life and giving it to God. Give this question some prayerful, heart-searching thought, and be prepared to respond to whatever God shows you.

4. As fallible human beings, we all make mistakes. When looking for direction, if we start with the Bible instead of relying on ourselves or others, we might save ourselves a lot of grief and cost. To help your thinking and desires be in agreement with God and His Word, memorize Psalm 37:4 and learn to "delight yourself in the Lord."

FOR GROUP STUDY

Questions for Group Discussion

1. God has been guiding His people throughout history. How is His guidance both personal and specific?

2. Read 1 Corinthians 1:25 and 2 Corinthians 10:3–5. Why is it so important to make the Bible our first source for our spiritual guidance and decision making?
3. Satan will throw any obstacle in our way to keep us from God's Word. What steps can we take to ensure the Enemy doesn't trip us up with his "partitions"?
4. When is it appropriate to seek biblical counseling? What are its benefits? What are some guidelines we should observe in the area of biblical counseling?

PICTURE THIS

There are some safeguards we can observe to resist the Enemy's efforts and ensure that we receive the guidance we need from God's Word. Below are safeguards we can employ.

Receiving Guidance from God's Word

TRUTH	SCRIPTURE PASSAGES	WHAT IT MEANS
Let God's Word be at home in you.	Colossians 3:16; Ephesians 5:18–21	If the Spirit and the Word of God make themselves at home in our heart, there will be no foothold for Satan.
Let God's Word do the talking.	Colossians 3:17	God's direction comes as His Word permeates our minds. We must renew our minds with its transforming power.
Let God's Word guide you safely.	Psalm 119:133	We must ground ourselves in the Bible to avoid being controlled by sin.
Let the Great Physician give you a spiritual checkup.	Psalm 37:4; Hebrews 4:13	We must allow the Word to X-ray our hearts. Only the Great Physician can give us the true diagnosis of the condition of our hearts.
Make sure you listen to the right voice.	Isaiah 30:21; James 1:25	God uses His Word to guide us. Make certain you are listening for His voice only.

99

THE BIBLE BRINGS SPIRITUAL BLESSINGS

It would be almost impossible to get one hundred people to agree on anything. But chances are good that if you asked one hundred people, "Do you want to be blessed?" you would get few if any refusals. I've never met anyone who has told me flat out, "No, Pastor, I really don't want to be blessed." There's something wrong with anyone who doesn't want to be blessed.

GOD WANTS YOUR BLESSINGS TO BE MULTIPLIED

Psalm 1:1–3 is a formula for blessing that is both timeless and rich. It doesn't contain any tips on how to get ahead in the stock market or how to land that dream job. What it offers is infinitely better—a pattern for spiritual living that pleases God and opens the treasure stores of heaven.

When You Seek God, You Have Abundant Blessings

The psalmist put the "goodies" right at the front door in these verses. It isn't immediately evident in the English version, but the phrase "how blessed" in verse 1 is a plural word in Hebrew that could be translated, "How many are the blessednesses of. . . ." That may not be very smooth English, but it's great theology! When you seek God, you get blessings multiplied, an abundance of blessings. You roll from one blessing to another.

The Hebrew verb "to be blessed" means basically "to be happy." We all want to be happy, and God wants us to be happy too. It's just that our concept of happiness does not always match His. Biblical happiness is neither the world's idea of happiness as a carefree sail through life with everything coming up roses, nor is it the "name it, claim it" theology of the prosperity teachers who say that God's greatest desire for you is that you be healthy and wealthy.

You Are Blessed When You Enjoy God's Goodness

What does it mean, then, to be blessed or to receive a blessing in the biblical sense? Here is a simple definition: A blessing is the God-given capacity to enjoy His goodness in your life.

A lot of people would look at this definition and think it misses the mark. They believe the blessing is the thing itself, not the capacity to enjoy it. In other words, the blessing is good health, the bonus at work, or the big promotion.

Those are certainly nice things to have, but they are not necessarily blessings in the biblical sense. Why? Because there are plenty of people who have all of that, and a whole lot more, and yet aren't enjoying it. That is, they have no sense of God's peace or satisfaction in their hearts, and thus even "good" things can become a source of unhappiness or just drive them to want more.

But when God pours out His goodness to you, He gives you joy and peace and satisfaction with it, regardless of the particular form His goodness may take. And He adds no sorrow to it (Proverbs 10:22).

ENJOY THE BLESSINGS GOD HAS FOR YOU

The psalmist's instruction on how to enjoy God's blessings actually begins with a statement concerning the people and the places among whom we will not find a true blessing. "How blessed is the man who does not walk in the counsel of the wicked, nor stand in the path of sinners, nor sit in the seat of scoffers!" (Psalm 1:1).

This is not how most people would begin a discussion about what it means to be blessed. Most people would talk about what they do and have, or where they go and who they know. But the psalmist lets us know right off that it is important to know what a blessing looks like and where it can be found. He wants us to be able to spot the difference between the real thing and the world's counterfeit.

Happiness Is Not the Possession of Wealth

Maybe the most common definition of happiness is to equate it with material wealth. Certainly our possessions can be a blessing—if they are gained in a God-honoring way by honest work, we don't destroy our relationship with God and our families to acquire them, and they do not become our god. But you probably know people who have a lot and yet are miserable. The more some people get, the more discontent they are.

There are many problems with this definition of blessing. One is a problem that most people continue to ignore even though thousands of years of human history validate it: Riches alone do not guarantee happiness, peace of mind, security, or any other benefit people seek after. At best, material wealth is a temporary side benefit, although you'd have a hard time convincing most Americans of that. But Jesus said a person's life does not consist of the things he possesses (Luke 12:15).

Happiness Is Not Freedom from Pain

Another very popular, but very unbiblical, idea of what it means to be blessed is to be free of any major hassles, problems, and setbacks, including pain or serious illness. In this definition of blessedness your wife adores you, the roof never leaks, your kids go from being ideal children to responsible and well-behaved teenagers, your mother-in-law is your biggest fan, the job is rolling along, and your worst health problem is a little heartburn. In other words, you may not have it all materially, but at least the sun is shining every day.

The Bible's consistent witness is that blessedness has little to do with the absence of trouble or pain in our lives. In fact, many of God's best blessings are hidden inside a painful trial, like the chewy chocolate center of a sucker with a hard outer shell.

James wrote: "Consider it all joy, my brethren, when you encounter various trials" (James 1:2). Later, he used the New Testament equivalent of the Hebrew word for "blessed" when he said, "Blessed is a man who perseveres under trial; for once he has been approved, he will receive the crown of life" (v. 12). This is the biblical pattern.

Biblical Blessings Allow Us to Enjoy God's Goodness

The Bible is clear that happiness does not depend upon our financial, emotional, or physical circumstances. And yet, God's Word says He wants every one of His children to be blessed. That's why I like the definition of blessedness as the God-given capacity to enjoy His goodness. This definition provides the common denominator that allows any Christian in any age and any circumstance to be a full-fledged candidate for God's blessings.

Paul addressed this in Philippians 4:11–12: "Not that I speak from want, for I have learned to be content in whatever circumstances I am. I know how to get along with humble means, and I also know how to live in prosperity; in any and every circumstance I have learned the secret of being filled and going hungry, both of having abundance and suffering need."

THE BLESSED PERSON FINDS DELIGHT IN GOD'S WORD

False views of happiness are typical of the kind of "counsel" or advice that the world offers us, and that Psalm 1:1 counsels us to avoid. We are not to "walk," or conduct our lives, according to the perspective of people who have a man-centered instead of a God-centered worldview.

The "wicked" are not just terribly evil people, but those who do not take God and His Word into account. If you want to enjoy God's goodness, don't go to folks who have no regard for God to get advice on how to live. A lot of us aren't blessed because we're talking to the wrong people.

You Have to Follow the Right Path to Be Blessed

Now that we know that the path to blessedness is not found in following the world, where can God's blessings be found? The psalmist answered this with a clear declaration that God's blessings are inextricably tied to His Word. "But his delight is in the law of the Lord, and in His law he meditates day and night" (Psalm 1:2).

The word *delight* refers to things or people that bring you pleasure and make you smile just thinking about them. When you delight in someone, you want to be with that person all the time—and when you're not together, you can't stop thinking about that person. When you delight in a song, you play the tune again and again in your mind even when the song isn't playing. In other words, these things are messing with your mind.

Meditating on God's Word Brings Blessings

When God talks about the importance of meditating on His Word, don't necessarily assume that to do this you have to sit down in a quiet room trying to focus your mind on Scripture. That's not a bad idea, and most of us do far too little of that. But meditating on the Word can be done wherever you are—just as you can think about a person or an object that brings you great pleasure wherever you are.

To *meditate* means to chew on the Word, to keep bringing it up and rolling it over in our minds. When you meditate, you are fantasizing over Scripture and what it can do in your life, just as a boy standing out in his backyard with a baseball bat and a ball fantasizes about winning the World Series with a home run and feels the exhilaration of being a hero. Meditation is musing on Scripture until its truth and application to our lives has been clarified by the Holy Spirit. Anyone who knows how to worry knows how to meditate.

So let's not use the "I don't know how to meditate" excuse as a reason for not focusing our minds on God and His Word.

WE ARE BLESSED TO FIND OUR DELIGHT IN GOD'S WORD

We've seen how to avoid places where God's blessing is not found, and where to locate it. Now let's consider what the blessing of God does for the person who knows how to enjoy it. Psalm 1:3 says of the blessed person, "He will be like a tree firmly planted by streams of water, which yields its fruit in its season and its leaf does not wither; and in whatever he does, he prospers."

You Will Be Well Rooted

A tree is a great word picture of someone who is enjoying God's goodness and blessings in spite of circumstances. The Bible uses grass to illustrate something that is transitory (see Isaiah 40:7–8 and Matthew 6:30). But a tree illustrates that which is meant to last. You cut down grass when it begins to grow too long, but you don't mow down a tree. Grass is tied down tight to the ground, but a tree soars above it.

You Will Be Firmly Established

The psalmist continued to describe the blessed person as a tree "firmly planted." This is a picture of stability, being firmly anchored. I can get a very tall ladder, lean it against a building, then climb to the top of the ladder and stand there. But there is a fundamental, all-important difference between me on a ladder and a tree. Unless Superman is holding that ladder for me, I am not firmly planted. The next puff of wind could blow me over. In fact, I am not about to climb to the top of a tall ladder and stand there just to demonstrate the truth of this illustration!

When you are firmly planted, the stuff that used to blow you over doesn't knock you down anymore. You may bend in the wind, but your root system will hold you if your roots are planted deeply in God's Word. The writer of Hebrews called our hope in Christ "an anchor of the soul" (6:19). Guess where we learn about that hope? In God's revealed Word.

You Will Be Well Nourished

The blessing of God doesn't just leave you planted in the middle of a desert, either. Instead, you are planted "by streams of water," an Old Testament phrase for irrigation ditches. If you have ever been to Israel, you know that irrigation has been the key to making the desert over there blossom like a rose.

The beauty of an irrigation system is that it carries water to the tree regardless of the external circumstances. The important thing is not what is happening on the surface but underground, where water runs deep and the tree can drink. Similarly, being blessed means the internal is fine even if the external is under great hardship. You can drink of God's goodness because your roots are attached to the ever-flowing spring of His eternal Word.

You Will Be Fruitful

The middle of Psalm 1:3 says further that a blessed person will "yield" or produce fruit. This refers to being productive, taking that internal refreshment and turning it into something that other people around you can enjoy too. Someone has said that Christians are blessed to be a blessing. That's a good way to put it. If you're being blessed but all you are passing on to others is a sour, dried-up piece of fruit, your blessing is stopping at the wrong station. Fruit always reflects the character of the tree it comes from.

Your capacity to enjoy God should give you something to share. A tree doesn't yield fruit for its own consumption. This is the problem with so much of today's teaching on how to get God's blessings. It tends to turn Christians into self-focused, "gimme, gimme" people. The emphasis is on how I can get my goodies from God, never mind you.

But fruit always exists for the benefit of another. So one way you know you're blessed is that you are being a blessing. Other folks can take a bite out of you and be blessed. When fruit starts eating itself, that means disease has set in and corrective action is required.

You Will Prosper

Now look at the summary statement of this great passage. Whatever the blessed person does "prospers." Whatever this person touches comes back to life if it was dead. God can make such a great promise because the person who is delighting in and meditating on His Word will reflect God's mind and heart in what he or she desires and does. God's blessing will prosper you in that you will know His smile of pleasure on your life.

That's quite a package of blessing. Do you want to be blessed? I believe you do, and so do I. There is no question about God's desire to deliver His blessings. The only question is whether we are putting ourselves in a position to receive His goodness. To be blessed, you need to go deep in God's Word. Meditate on it. Let it penetrate your mind and hit your heart. Let God take you deep into His Word, and you will find the place of true blessing.

PERSONAL APPLICATION FOR LIFE

1. How do you know you're on the right track to receive God's blessing? Compare your pursuit to the weary working man in Ecclesiastes 4:8. He was working himself to death and depriving himself of all pleasure; is that a snapshot of you? Don't get caught up in the world's methods of chasing happiness. You don't need to shred your soul and exhaust yourself to enjoy God's true blessings.

2. Be careful where you get advice. The "wicked" mentioned in Psalm 1:1 are those who do not take into account God and the counsel of His Word. If you want to enjoy God's goodness, don't go to people who have no regard for God. If you need advice, seek out your pastor or a mature believer. Ensure that you involve those with a God-centered worldview.

3. Do you tend to box God in? We can't say to God, "I'll give to Your work with the understanding that You will bless my finances." God may want to bless you anyway, but He won't be part of any bargaining. God's blessings are not tied to their temporal benefits. He has eternal purposes in mind and is far more generous than we can imagine.

4. Are you craving spiritual nourishment? Why not try a main course of meditation on God's Word? Jump-start yourself by asking these questions: God, how does your Word affect what I'm facing right now? What does it say about my response to what I'm facing? How can your Word change what I'm thinking and feeling right now if my attitude is not right? How does your Word equip me to deal with the things I'm facing?

FOR GROUP STUDY

Questions for Group Discussion

1. Read Psalm 1:1–3. Discuss its formula for blessing. Why is it such a good pattern for spiritual living? Contrast the biblical concept of happiness with the world's ideas.

2. What kind of mind-set must we have to enjoy God's blessings? What is the definition of a true blessing? What is not a true blessing?

3. What part does God's Word have in our finding God's blessings? What does it mean to "delight" in the law of the Lord? What is involved with our meditating on God's Word?

4. What blessings do we receive when we delight in God's Word? (Use the chart below as an aid to your discussion.)

PICTURE THIS

God's blessings come to those who delight in God's Word. Below are four specific blessings we find in Psalm 1:3 that result from delighting in His Word.

The Blessings of Delighting in God's Word
Psalm 1:3

GOD'S BLESSING	SCRIPTURE PASSAGES	OUR BENEFIT
You will be well rooted.	Isaiah 40:7–8; Matthew 6:30	We are transplanted by the water where we can grow strong, deep spiritual roots.
You will be firmly established.	Hebrews 6:19	With a healthy root system, we can withstand even the strongest winds of adversity.
You will be fruitful.	Psalm 1:3	Because our roots draw nourishment from the sure source of God's Word, we will produce spiritual fruit.
You will prosper.	Psalm 1:3	God's blessing ensures our prosperity.

100

THE BIBLE BRINGS SPIRITUAL FREEDOM

Freedom is a prize that people have treasured, fought for, and guarded throughout history. In Jesus' day, the people of Israel longed for freedom from the Roman armies who had invaded the land of Israel, conquered it, and made it a part of their kingdom.

Jesus knew that Israel was chafing under the rule of Rome and that many Jews were looking for a liberator who would drive out the Romans and set them free. Jesus was intensely interested in the subject of freedom, and He was well aware that some of His followers and others who had seen His power and miracles were hoping that He was the Messiah/Conqueror they wanted. But Jesus had come to bestow a totally different kind of liberty on people who were in bondage to Satan, the true oppressor, whose tool of oppression and tyranny is sin.

JESUS TAUGHT THE TRUTH THAT SETS US FREE

The apostle John records that as Jesus spoke to a crowd of Jews that day, He told some people who believed in Him, "If you continue in My word, then you are truly disciples of Mine; and you will know the truth, and the truth will make you free" (John 8:31–32). This provoked angry reaction from the crowd, particularly the idea that Jesus' hearers did not really know what it meant to be free.

Whenever you tell people they need to be free, an assumption is being made that they are in slavery of some kind. The only people who need to be set free are those who are enslaved to someone or something, or under tyranny, and need to be liberated. It's bad enough to be a slave, but it's even worse to be ignorant of your slavery. Jesus was talking to people who didn't realize they were slaves and so did not recognize their need for Jesus' offer of freedom. They did not realize how bad their slavery really was.

Spiritual Freedom Is a Special Kind of Freedom

Let's define the concept of freedom from a biblical standpoint. To be spiritually free is to be liberated from slavery to sin in order to become all that we were meant to be. Notice that this definition says nothing about being able to do whatever you want whenever you want, without any restraints or restrictions at all. This is often the world's idea of freedom, but people who live like this are actually in the worst slavery of all, which is slavery to their own sinful desires. Freedom in the Bible has nothing to do with the removal of all boundaries or limitations, but with the ability to be and to do what God wants within His boundaries.

Many people also have the mistaken idea that freedom means having no master, no one who can tell them what to do. But true freedom is having the right master, one who knows how to help you reach your potential and not limit you to less than you were created to be. The importance of having the right master was the crux of the message that Jesus delivered to the crowd that stood around Him in John 8 as He taught them about the real nature of spiritual slavery and freedom.

Jesus' implication that His hearers were not yet free brought this angry reaction: "We are Abraham's descendants and have never yet been enslaved to anyone; how is it that You say, 'You will become free'?" (v. 33). That was quite a statement coming from people whose nation had endured a long history of bondage. These Jews said they had never been anybody's slaves, but their ancestors were in bondage in Egypt for four hundred years. Later generations had been conquered and carried off into captivity by the

Assyrians and Babylonians, and then they came under the rule of Persia.

Sin Is the Cause of Spiritual Slavery

The kind of slavery Jesus had in mind had nothing to do with political boundaries or human kingdoms. He answered the boast of the people that they had never been slaves with a description of true slavery: "Truly, truly, I say to you, everyone who commits sin is the slave of sin. The slave does not remain in the house forever; the son does remain forever" (John 8:34–35). Here Jesus clearly identified sin as the cause of slavery.

This is true even in the natural realm, because all human slavery is the result of the sinful domination of one people by another. And in the spiritual realm, all bondage can either directly or indirectly be traced back to the presence of sin. Slavery comes because people reject God and rebel against Him and His plan of salvation. This is the type of sin Jesus meant when he told the Jews that whoever commits sin is the slave of sin. That indictment covers every person today, regardless of our pedigree or status in the world.

God's Truth Applies to Our Lives Today

How does this freedom apply to us today? If you are not spiritually free, it is either because you have never embraced the truth of the gospel and come to Jesus for salvation, or because as a Christian you are not continuing in the truth. Remember Jesus said, "If you continue in My word, then you are truly disciples of Mine" (John 8:31). We'll get into this issue later.

Notice also where true freedom is located. Jesus said freedom is found in knowing "the truth" (v. 32), which is another way of describing His Word, the Bible. Don't miss the fact that just having a Bible in your house or under your arm at church is not enough to bring freedom. You must know the truth. You must allow the Word of God to unlock your mind and fill it with the knowledge of God that brings salvation.

God's True Children Know His Truth

This was the problem with the people Jesus was talking to in John 8:31–36. Their argument was that they were Abraham's children (see also v. 39) and therefore free, not slaves of anyone. The Jews saw themselves as the true sons and Jesus as the illegitimate son (see v. 41), but Jesus moved the conversation into a whole new realm when He told them they were slaves of sin. In fact, He did not even wait for them to answer or make another protest, but He hit them with the ringer by saying, "So if the Son makes you free, you will be free indeed" (v. 36).

TRUE FREEDOM MEANS ABIDING IN GOD'S WORD

Let's double back to John 8:31 and abide there for a while, because it is easy to read over what Jesus said and focus on the controversy that followed. He said that His true followers are those who "continue" in His Word. This is the Greek verb that means "to abide, to stay, to remain." Jesus used this same verb again in John 15:7, a great promise for abiders: "If you abide in Me, and My words abide in you, ask whatever you wish, and it will be done for you."

God Wants His Word to Be Fully at Home within Us

There are basically two ways you can abide or stay. You can stay because you have to, as when a father says to his teenager, "You're grounded for two weeks! You aren't going anywhere but to school and straight home!" Or, you can stay because you want to, like your daughter's boyfriend who thinks he's part of the family and wants to hang out at your house all the time.

This second picture is what Jesus meant by abiding. It means to feel completely at home, to be comfortable with, to hang out with because there's no place you'd rather be and no one you'd rather be with.

This is a convicting question, but I need to ask it: Does this describe your passion for God's Word and the anticipation of meeting with Him in the pages of the Bible? If not, you're not really abiding in His Word—and the consequences of failing to abide are devastating.

We are new creations now in Christ, but we are still carrying the scars of sin—which you realize when you try to do the right thing and wind up doing the wrong thing. As the bumper sticker says, "Christians aren't perfect, just forgiven." At least we're in good company, because in Romans 6–7 the apostle Paul wrestled with the question, "If I'm a Christian, why am I doing the very things I don't want to do?" His answer was that it was "the law of sin which is in my members [of his body]" (Romans 7:23).

But keep on reading, because Paul wasn't making excuses for himself or for us. Here is his conclusion to the matter: "Thanks be to God through Jesus Christ our Lord!" (v. 25). Why? Because "the law of the Spirit of life in Christ Jesus *has set [me] free* from the law of sin and death" (Romans 8:2, italics added).

We Can't Let Anyone Enslave Us Again

This is the Christian's "emancipation proclamation." But Paul also told the Galatians, "It was for freedom that Christ set us free; therefore keep standing firm and do not be subject again to a yoke of slavery" (5:1). How can someone who has been set free by Jesus Christ be in danger of becoming a slave again?

We can rule out the loss of salvation, because that can never happen to true believers. Salvation was not the issue in Galatians 5, but whether these Christians would allow themselves to be subjected to the demands of the Mosaic law instead of living by grace. One of the ironies of the Christian life is that the Bible tells us to be what we are. God says we need to behave like His children because that's what we are. And we are told to make sure we live in the freedom that Christ purchased for us because we are, in fact, free people.

The Galatians were in danger of being brought under bondage by a group called the Judaizers, who ran around following Paul into each city where he preached and tried to make Gentile Christians put themselves under the Jewish law. So the issue was the very nature of God's salvation. The Galatians had heard the truth from Paul and knew that salvation was by grace alone through faith.

The antidote to bondage for the Christian is abiding in the Word. It's pretty hard for the Devil or anyone else to put one over on you when God's Word is so integral a part of your being that you automatically think and react biblically. But that kind of discipline only comes from hanging out in the Word until you start to absorb it through every pore in your body.

We Don't Want to Abide in God's Word

The lack of desire or commitment to abide in the Word helps to explain a question that a lot of Christians have. When they look around, it seems that everybody is growing and enjoying victory but them. So they conclude that God must relate to other believers better than He relates to them. They figure other Christians have an inside track to God that they don't have. But that's not the case at all.

The answer can be found in an incident recorded in John 2:23–25. The Bible says that many people believed in Jesus when they saw His miracles. "But Jesus, on His part, was not entrusting Himself to them, for He knew all men, and because He did not need anyone to testify concerning man, for He Himself knew what was in man" (vv. 24–25).

Someone may read that and say, "See, it's true. Jesus doesn't relate to all believers equally. He kept these people at arm's length even though they believed in Him." But the issue here is why He did that. Based on His perfect knowledge of the human heart, and the fact that many of His early disciples later deserted Him when things got tough (see John 6:64, 66), Jesus knew who was real and who wasn't. He doesn't play favorites; it's just that He is not going to commit Himself to someone who only wants a casual relationship.

Read the Bible as God's Love Letter to You

I'm sure you've heard it said that we should read the Bible the way we would read a love letter. I know you didn't just read a "verse" or two of love letters and then lay them aside for a few days until you had a free minute or there was nothing good on television. You devoured each letter, weighing the nuances and deeper meanings of every word because the relationship behind those letters was more important to you than your food or other comforts.

When the Bible becomes that precious to us, then we will begin to experience what Jesus meant when He said, "If the Son makes you free, you will be free indeed" (John 8:36). "Indeed" means "sho 'nuff," or certainly. It means this is the real deal, because the Son has the authority to set us free and keep us free. It means to look for Jesus, because when He shows up, you know everything is going to be OK.

Don't Rush Your Time in God's Holy Presence

I remember talking once with a greatly respected Christian author and speaker who is well-known for his deep, intimate relationship with God. I asked him for his secret, and he said, "Well, if there is a secret it boils down to one phrase: unhurried time in God's presence."

God didn't just set you free on Calvary so you could avoid hell. He wants to set you "free indeed" to enjoy a life in His presence. He gave you His Word so you can abide in it until His truth oozes from every pore of your being and changes you from the inside out.

PERSONAL APPLICATION FOR LIFE

1. It is possible to be a Christian and yet not live in the freedom Christ gave us. Are you struggling with something that is keeping you in bondage? Is there unconfessed sin in your life? If so, immediately ask God's forgiveness and restore fellowship with Him. Then get into the Word! The antidote to bondage for the believer is abiding in the Word.

2. God wants you to spend as much time with Him as you want to spend. Don't get caught up in the notion that time spent with God means less time for more "productive" activities. The truth is, the more time you spend in His presence, the more problems get solved before you even get to them. The next time you get alone with God, take off your watch or hide the clock. Watch what happens when being with God and His Word is not a hurried event.

3. Are the worries, riches, and pleasures of daily life choking off your desire to focus more on God's Word? Try this. The next time you find yourself dwelling on a problem or worry, stop and take a moment to redirect your thoughts by reading a portion of the Bible. Claim a promise or take an encouragement from Scripture, and act on it by faith. You'll find that the power of God's Word will free you from those daily distractions.

4. Be sure that the Bible is much more to you than simply a collection of chapters and verses that you visit occasionally. As Dr. Evans suggests, read the Bible as if it were God's love letter to you, because that's exactly what God intends it to be. Before you begin reading, ask God to open your heart to receive His truth and to respond to it in a personal way.

FOR GROUP STUDY

Questions for Group Discussion

1. What does it mean to be spiritually free? In what ways might spiritual freedom differ from the world's view of freedom?

2. Read John 8:31–36. How does God's spiritual freedom apply to us today?

3. Read the promise of John 15:7. Why does our spiritual freedom relate to abiding in Christ? What happens when we allow the Word to abide in our hearts?

4. How can we tell when we are enjoying God's company through the Word? (Use the chart below as an aid to your discussion.)

PICTURE THIS

When we are abiding in Christ, and His Word is abiding in us, then we are enjoying His company through the Scripture. The confirmations below help confirm the quality time with God and His Word that occurs when we are abiding in Christ.

HOW WE KNOW WE ARE ABIDING IN THE WORD

CONFIRMATION	WHAT IT REVEALS
We read the Bible as God's love letter to us.	We find ourselves weighing the nuances of meaning and seeking the deeper meanings because of the relationship behind the letter.
Don't rush our time in God's holy presence.	We desire to spend time in God's presence—worshiping and praying—without hurrying.

101
THE BIBLE GIVES SPIRITUAL VICTORY

It's a tragedy to make people fight a battle that shouldn't have to be fought at all, especially when it drains their time and energies that are needed elsewhere. This is exactly the strategy that our enemy the Devil uses when he comes at us in spiritual warfare. He tries to discourage and distract us from the real battle and convince us that we have to fight him on his terms, not God's, and in the power of our own flesh, not in the strength that God provides. Tragically, Satan succeeds in this strategy far too often, the proof of which is the number of defeated Christians who are wondering what hit them.

But God's Word has an announcement for the Devil. In the words of David to Goliath, "The battle is the Lord's and He will give you into our hands" (1 Samuel 17:47). The enemy Goliath, who stood for all that was evil, was a terrifying presence with his huge size, heavy armor, and gigantic weapons. But like our enemy Satan (see 1 Peter 5:8), Goliath was a toothless lion despite his roaring because David was fighting in the Lord's name and strength. In the end, it was no contest. David's little stones and slings were the mighty weapons, not Goliath's huge spear, because this was not really a battle of the flesh but of the spirit.

THE BIBLE IS OUR PRIMARY WEAPON FOR SPIRITUAL WARFARE

In Ephesians 6, Paul explained the nature of our battle and the armament God wants us to use. The specific pieces of the Christian's armor are described in verses 14–17a, which you can review for yourself. I want to focus on the one offensive weapon available to us in this battle, "the sword of the Spirit, which is the word of God" (v. 17b).

Our Battle Is Spiritual, Not Physical

Now the reason this is the Spirit's sword instead of a steel blade is that "our struggle is not against flesh and blood, but against the rulers, against the powers, against the world forces of this darkness, against the spiritual forces of wickedness in the heavenly places" (Ephesians 6:12; see also 2 Corinthians 10:3–4). If you're fighting with other people because you think they are the enemies keeping you from enjoying the victory God promises to His people, you are on the wrong battlefield. Our real battle is in the spiritual realm against Satan and his array of demons, who can use people to harass and wound us.

Our Victory Is Already Assured

Ephesians 6 makes it crystal clear that when it comes to spiritual warfare and the issue of our victory, the matter has already been settled. How do we know? Well, if you read the spiritual warfare passage in Ephesians 6:10–17, you will notice that nowhere are we told to attack the Enemy and try to overcome him. Instead, our job is to "stand firm" (v. 11; see also vv. 13–14).

Now why would a soldier be told to stand firm instead of attack and advance? Because he already has the territory his commander wants to take, and his job is to hold on to it. Jesus Christ defeated the Devil and all of his army on the cross, and nothing can cancel out that victory. The result is that we are not fighting for victory, but from a position of victory. Satan is a defeated foe.

I know the next question someone usually asks: "Well, if Satan is whipped already, why is he pounding away on me? He doesn't feel like a defeated enemy the way he's attacking me."

Satan may be able to sting you once in a while, but he's firing a BB gun and not a lethal weapon. Knowing this ought to turn our fear into courage, because once you realize your enemy has a popgun instead of a Howitzer, it dawns on you that you have nothing to be afraid of. And you can turn around, face the Enemy, and stand firm.

God Tells Us How to Wield the Sword of His Word

We said earlier that "the sword of the Spirit," the "word of God," is the only offensive weapon in our Christian armory. Paul likened it to a particular kind of sword that Roman soldiers carried, and that all of his readers in Ephesus would be very familiar with.

The sword mentioned in Ephesians 6:17 is not the long sword we usually see in the old movies hung at a soldier's side in a sheath. The word for "sword" here refers to a much shorter, daggerlike weapon that a soldier carried in his belt for quick access in case he got into closer combat and needed a precision weapon to strike a decisive blow. A soldier sometimes used both hands to wield his long sword, flailing and slashing away at the enemy. But his short, daggerlike sword could be applied much more directly and with deadly result.

We Must Have God's Word Ready at Hand

Another Greek word in Ephesians 6:17 is very enlightening as we seek to understand how to win at spiritual warfare. Paul called the Spirit's dagger "the word of God"—but we need to stop here, because this is not the ordinary word for Scripture. Paul did not use the familiar Greek word *logos*, which looks at the Bible in its entirety as the received body of God's truth.

Instead, Paul used the word *rhema*, which means "an utterance," and looks at the Bible not as a bound volume of sixty-six books, but as a weapon ready at hand to be used in a definite way at a definite time of need.

This is where it gets exciting! Paul was saying that if we want to be victorious in spiritual warfare, we must be able to draw on specific truths from the Bible in specific situations to counter specific temptations and attacks from the Enemy.

GOD'S WORD IS POWERFUL IN BATTLE

You have the entire *logos* of God on your shelf, the very Word of God that is complete and true in every syllable, and yet not be well armed for spiritual warfare because you don't know how to draw on the *rhema* of God when you are under attack. You can own a Bible factory and yet be basically defenseless against Satan if you are not well practiced in handling the Word of truth.

Until the logos of God—that Bible under your arm at church—also becomes the *rhema* in your hand to defeat the Enemy, you won't see the Bible's power at work. As long as the Bible is just a bunch of general statements to you, you'll be a general Christian knowing general truth, and you'll get general results. But a believer who is filled and controlled by the Holy Spirit and who knows how to handle the sword of the Spirit in specific spiritual encounters, can win any battle in any realm.

THE BIBLE IS POWERFUL—REGARDLESS

Now don't misunderstand. We're not saying that the Bible only becomes sharp and powerful when we start using it properly. In fact, one of the foundational verses of this entire study says exactly the opposite. "The word [logos] of God is living and active and sharper than any two-edged sword" (Hebrews 4:12). Guess what word for "sword" the writer used here? You got it—the Roman short sword/dagger we've been talking about. So here is a text that joins the logos with this concept of a sharp, precision weapon, just as Ephesians 6:17 does with the *rhema*. God's Word is sharp regardless of whether we ever discover that reality for ourselves.

The reason you want to learn the Bible generally is so that you can use it specifically when the need arises for victory in spiritual warfare. You want to be victorious in your Christian life, not just barely hang on until you die or Jesus returns with angelic reinforcements. The great thing about the *rhema* of the Spirit is that it can keep you out of unnecessary battles so you can save your energies for the real warfare.

JESUS USED THE WORD TO DEFEAT THE DEVIL

Of course, the best example of someone using the sword of Spirit to slice up the Devil was Jesus in His wilderness temptation (Matthew 4:1–11). We've been through this account before, but let me make a few important observations about what was going on here.

Don't Be Surprised by the Time of the Enemy's Attacks

Notice that Jesus had a great spiritual triumph just before Satan launched his attack. Jesus was baptized by John the Baptist and God the Father declared, "This is My beloved Son, in whom I am well-pleased" (Matthew 3:17). In other words, Jesus was heading directly from a great spiritual victory into a great spiritual battle.

Don't be surprised if some of your hardest times of struggle and temptation come on the heels of some of your greatest victories. That's the nature of spiritual warfare. The Devil knows that our human tendency is to lay down our sword, take off the armor, and put our feet up after we've been through a battle. But when we relax our guard we are most vulnerable to attack.

Here's another important principle of spiritual warfare and victory. Jesus was "led up by the Spirit into the wilderness to be tempted by the Devil" (Matthew 4:1). The battle Jesus was about to face was God's perfect will for Him. And remember, Jesus also faced crushing agony and temptation in the garden of Gethsemane when His human spirit wanted to avoid the pain and suffering of the cross (see Matthew 26:39).

If the perfect, sinless Son of God had to undergo the most severe kind of testing, what do you think we need to experience? We often think that if we were just better Christians, we wouldn't be facing all these battles. Nothing could be further from the truth. God allows the Enemy to attack us precisely so that we can learn to use the sword and armor He has provided us with. You'll never know that your weapons can stand the test until you're tested.

Jesus' temptation not only came after a great victory (Mark 1:12 says the Spirit "immediately" sent Jesus into the wilderness), and was permitted and ordained of God, it also came when He was physically weak after fasting for forty days (see Matthew 4:2). But Jesus answered each of the Devil's temptations with the sword of the Spirit, the *rhema* of God. "It is written," Jesus said three times (vv. 4, 7, 10), quoting Deuteronomy 8:3; 6:16; and 6:13.

Jesus Knew Where to Get the Word He Needed

Let's explore the first of these temptations to see how the Master used His sword to counter a specific attack in face-to-face spiritual combat and emerge victorious. The Devil tempted Jesus to meet His legitimate need for food by making bread from stones—but at the Devil's will and command, not God's.

Here is the full text of Deuteronomy 8:3, the verse Jesus drew on to deliver His precision blow to Satan. Moses said, "[God] humbled you and let you be hungry, and fed you with manna which you did not know, nor did your fathers know, that He might make you understand that man does not live by bread alone, but man lives by everything that proceeds out of the mouth of God."

Jesus did not pull out a random verse and swing it at the Devil. In fact, His use of Deuteronomy 8:3 was so precise that He only quoted to the Devil the part of the verse He needed. The Lord cut right to the heart of the issue. He was hungry, so He drew on a scriptural occasion when the Israelites in the wilderness were hungry and cried out to God, who answered by sending them manna.

Jesus knew that it was His Father's will for Him to fast for forty days to the point that He was really hungry, and He also knew that when His Father was ready, He would feed His Son. Satan tried to short-circuit that connection, but Jesus sliced the Devil's argument to ribbons by saying He would eat only when God said it was time.

This same principle of Jesus' reliance on God's power and His refusal to act independently of His Father runs through the other two temptations He faced. The Devil offered Jesus instant recognition and fame by jumping off the pinnacle of the temple in Jerusalem, because the Devil had read the Bible and knew that God had promised to protect His Son. Satan even quoted Psalm 91:11–12 to prove his point—an attempt to use the *rhema* of God that was completely illegitimate. Then he showed Jesus the kingdoms of the world and offered them to the Lord in exchange for His worship.

But Jesus refused in each case, because He knew something we have to know too. Jesus knew that everything the Devil offered Him was going to be His already in the will of God. Here's the principle: The victories and blessings God has for you are yours, and nobody can take them away from you if you will pursue them in His will and way. Satan can't offer you anything good that God can't give you if it is in His perfect will and pleasure to give it to you.

God Will Show Up When You Use His Word

What happened when Jesus had defeated Satan? "Then the devil left Him; and behold, angels came and began to minister to Him" (Matthew 4:11). That's exciting, but I have a question: Where had those angels been, and why did they show up after the battle was over? Because sometimes God wants us to be alone with His Word, that we might learn to trust what He said and learn how powerful and sufficient His Word actually is.

If you want the power of God's Word to transform you, and you want it more than you want to mess around with the Devil and his toys, then take your Bible off the desk or coffee table and start hiding it your heart. God's Word is sufficient for anything you will encounter this side of heaven!

PERSONAL APPLICATION FOR LIFE

1. We may take encouragement that God gives us the power to overcome temptation. Satan will go to any length with his lies and falsehoods to tempt us to sin. We can be certain he knows our weaknesses. Jesus, when tempted by Satan (Matthew 4), countered each temptation by quoting Scripture. What an example for us! Make it a point to commit as much Scripture to memory as you are able, and lay hold of its truths as needed.

2. Our Lord was tempted by Satan. If you are living for Christ, you can be sure that Satan will oppose you as well. Commit to memory James 4:7, which exhorts us, "Submit . . . to God. Resist the Devil and he will flee from you." The more Scripture you memorize, the better equipped you will be to chase away the Enemy.

3. Perhaps the most effective weapon demons use against believers is tempting us to sin. Do not underestimate the power Satan and his helpers have in their attacks on our areas of weakness. They know them and will attack them relentlessly. During your next quiet time, take a bold step and list the weaknesses that are a struggle for you. Ask God's wisdom and power to gain victory. Then act on Ephesians 6 and put on the full armor of God so you are equipped to deflect the Enemy's attacks.

4. James 1:13–14 tells us that we are tempted when we are carried away and enticed by our own lust. Because a wrong desire is the starting point down the road to sin, don't let Satan get a handle on your desires. If you find yourself being aroused by impure desires, say no to those desires by changing whatever is influencing those desires. Then get into God's Word, cleanse your heart and mind, and claim victory.

FOR GROUP STUDY

Questions for Group Discussion

1. Read 1 Samuel 17:47; 1 Peter 5:8; Ephesians 6:12; and 2 Corinthians 10:3–4. What is the nature of the spiritual battle in which we find ourselves?

2. Why is this battle already won? Why are we still battling against the Enemy and his army of evil angels?

3. God has given the "sword" of the Word as our weapon to fight against the Enemy. Why is the Bible so effective in countering and chasing away the Enemy?

4. Read Matthew 4:1–11. What method did our Lord use to engage the power of the Scriptures to defeat Satan? See also Ephesians 6:12 and James 4:7. How can we use God's Word to ward off attacks from the Enemy?

PICTURE THIS

In Matthew 4:1–11, Satan tempted Jesus three times, but Jesus answered each of the Devil's temptations with the sword of the Spirit, the Word of God. We would do well to follow our Lord's example when facing similar attacks from the Devil. When engaged in spiritual battle, we can be certain of the following truths.

USING THE SWORD OF THE SPIRIT IN BATTLE

TRUTH	SCRIPTURE PASSAGE	WHAT IT MEANS
Don't be surprised by the time of the Enemy's attacks.	Matthew 3:17; 4:1	Satan attacked Jesus after a great spiritual victory in His baptism. Don't be surprised if some of your hardest struggles and temptations come on the heels of some of your greatest victories. It's the nature of spiritual warfare.
Jesus knew where to get the Word He needed.	Deuteronomy 8:3	As we memorize Scripture and hide the power of God's Word in our minds and hearts, the better prepared we will be to resist the Devil.
God will show up when you use His Word.	Matthew 4:11	Jesus gave us the supreme example for defeating the Devil's attacks. God's Word is our most effective weapon during spiritual battle.

PART 8

ESCHATOLOGY

The Doctrine of the Last Things

SECTION I

The History of Fulfilled Prophecy

102

THE IMPORTANCE OF PROPHECY

The reason we can study Bible prophecy is that the eternal God has chosen to unfurl His plan for creation in time. Therefore, the doctrine of prophecy or eschatology—a compound of two Greek words meaning "last things"—is very important.

Most of us have a natural desire to know the future, to try to find out what tomorrow will bring. That's why the phony psychic networks are raking in the money. People desire to put together the jigsaw puzzle of life, whether it's the collective history of a nation or an individual life. People want to know how things are going to unfold.

But Bible prophecy is not designed to satisfy our curiosity about tomorrow or the next day, nor is it designed to fill our heads with information so we can get together and debate the details of God's plan. Gaining information has its place in the study of prophecy. It's important that we understand as fully as we can what God is saying to us. But at the heart of God's purpose for prophecy is changing our hearts and affecting the way we live our lives. Bible prophecy is important. The Bible's final chapter warns:

> I testify to everyone who hears the words of the prophecy of this book: if anyone adds to them, God shall add to him the plagues which are written in this book; and if anyone takes away from the words of the book of this prophecy, God shall take away his part from the tree of life and from the holy city, which are written in this book. (Revelation 22:18–19)

This thing called prophecy is very serious business with God. Mess with His prophetic Word, and it will mess up your eternity. God's prophetic message is so important that He announced a curse on anyone who tampers with it.

Let me say right up front that I know everybody does not agree on every jot and tittle of God's prophetic program. There are various views within the Christian community about exactly when Jesus will come back and the shape His kingdom will take. But these varieties of interpretations, if they remain within the sphere of orthodoxy, do not have to hamper us from gaining a broad-based understanding of what God has in store for His people.

PROPHECY HELPS AUTHENTICATE THE BIBLE

One of the questions people often ask is how we Christians can claim that the Bible is true as opposed to any other holy book. What makes the Bible distinct from other writings that claim to be from God?

The Bible's Prophetic Accuracy

There are many answers to that question, but one thing that sets the Bible apart is its prophetic accuracy. A large portion of biblical prophecy has already been fulfilled with flawless accuracy. Events that one author wrote about were fulfilled precisely hundreds of years later.

One of the classic examples is the prophecy of Jesus' birth in Bethlehem by the prophet Micah more than seven hundred years before the event (Micah 5:2; cf. Matthew 2:1–6). If Bethlehem had been a major metropolis in Israel, someone could argue it was a good guess. But Micah pinpointed an obscure village because he spoke the mind of God. The fulfillment of prophecies like this helps to validate the truth of the Bible.

The Divine Origin of Prophecy

In 2 Peter 1:20–21, the apostle wrote, "Know this first of all, that no prophecy of Scripture is a matter of one's own interpretation, for no prophecy was ever made by an act of human will, but men moved by the Holy Spirit spoke from God." The accuracy of the Bible's predictions should not surprise us, because this was not human writers doing guesswork. Prophetic Scripture is accurate in all of its details because God moved the authors to record what was said.

Someone who was good with numbers and probabilities figured out that it would require 200 billion earths populated with four billion people each to come up with one person who could achieve one hundred prophecies accurately without any errors in sequence.

In other words, it would be impossible. But the Bible contains hundreds of prophecies that have already come true. That's because it's not based on chance, but on the eternal knowledge of God.

PROPHECY REVEALS GOD'S CHARACTER

The second reason prophecy is important is that it reveals to us the character of God. When you understand God's program, you get to know more about Him.

The prophet Isaiah made a powerful statement of God's character and knowledge as it relates to His prophetic program:

> Remember this, and be assured; recall it to mind, you transgressors. Remember the former things long past, for I am God, and there is no other; I am God, and there is no one like Me, declaring the end from the beginning and from ancient times things which have not been done, saying, "My purpose will be established, and I will accomplish all My good pleasure." . . . I have planned it, surely I will do it. (46:8–10, 11c)

Whatever God plans, He accomplishes. No part of His will can ever be outwitted or thwarted by the mind of man. God was not caught off guard by human sin, because His plan for this universe was drawn up and nailed down in eternity past. But this raises a question for a lot of people. If God planned everything and nothing can change His plan, why should we do anything? Why not just sit back and take it easy, because what's going to happen is going to happen anyway?

The answer is that God's sovereignty does not relieve us of our human responsibility. We are still obligated to live righteously, because God is holy and just and cannot tolerate sin. And God will use our obedience to help accomplish His plan.

I realize there is plenty of mystery here, because God's knowledge of the future includes not only everything that actually happens, but everything that could potentially happen. God knows all possibilities in any circumstance, but He chooses what *will* happen according to His will and purpose.

Prophecy not only reveals the character of God in terms of His perfect knowledge and power, but also in terms of His purpose to bring Himself glory and bless His people. Paul said of his trials, "I consider that the sufferings of this present time are not worthy to be compared with the glory that is to be revealed to us" (Romans 8:18).

The apostle knew that the suffering God was allowing in his life would work out to God's greater glory and his greater reward. Paul could say this because he believed Christ's message about a future hope that was laid up for Paul, and "not only to [him], but also to all who have loved His appearing" (2 Timothy 4:8).

A knowledge of prophecy gives you confidence to trust God for what's ahead. If God knows tomorrow already because He has been there and taken care of it, then you can go to sleep tonight confident that He is in control.

PROPHECY PROMOTES HOLINESS

A third reason for studying prophecy is that it is designed to promote holy living. The more conscious we are of Christ's return, and of the fact that we could be standing face-to-face with Him at any moment, the more this knowledge will affect us. But if we forget that Jesus is coming back, we will start living like He's not coming back.

John gave a classic statement of prophecy's purifying purpose. "We know that, when He appears, we shall be like Him, because we shall see Him just as He is. And everyone who has this hope fixed on Him purifies himself, just as He is pure" (1 John 3:2–3).

A Prize to Be Won

Paul said, "I press on toward the goal for the prize of the upward call of God in Christ Jesus" (Philippians 3:14). Paul was determined to remain faithful to Christ because there was a heavenly prize to be won when Christ returned.

God's prophetic program included a reward for Paul, one that was worth all of his commitment on earth. And he urged all believers to adopt the same attitude (v. 15). There's a lot we will do if there's a big enough prize at the end of the process. Paul went on to explain his perspective: "Our citizenship is in heaven, from which also we eagerly wait for a Savior, the Lord Jesus Christ; who will transform the body of our humble state into conformity with the body of His glory" (vv. 20–21).

Paul said, "I'm really a citizen of heaven. I just have a temporary address here on earth." Because Paul had such a high consciousness of eternity, he pressed on in history.

A Perspective to Gain

Peter also had something to say about the way prophecy ought to promote holy living:

> The day of the Lord will come like a thief, in which the heavens will pass away with a roar and the elements will be destroyed with intense heat, and the earth and its works will be burned up. Since all these things are to be destroyed in this way, what sort of people ought you to be in holy conduct and godliness, looking for and hastening the coming of the day of God. (2 Peter 3:10–12a)

Peter said a day is coming when your house, your car, the clothes in your closet, and the money in your bank will burn. The malls at which you shop for your clothes will burn. The earth as we know it is going to melt away. So a good understanding of prophecy can give us a reference point for living.

A Future to Prepare For

Paul also said he lived in light of one inescapable fact. Speaking of the judgment of believers for kingdom reward, or the lack thereof, he wrote, "We must all appear before the judgment seat of Christ, that each one may be recompensed for his deeds in the body" (2 Corinthians 5:10).

This is how I picture the judgment seat of Christ taking place. Most stores today have security cameras recording a customer's every move. Some stores even alert people to that fact as they enter the store.

Why tip off would-be shoplifters? Because people who know someone is watching their every move will probably think twice before trying anything funny.

Similarly, our lives are being recorded on God's cosmic video camera. At Christ's judgment seat, He will sit down with us to view the tape. That's a good reason to prepare for the future. Further, a bride doesn't wait until the wedding day to prepare for her marriage. She begins preparing far in advance in anticipation of that special day. When you have a prophetic mindset, it will affect your preparation for eternity.

PROPHECY BRINGS STABILITY IN TRIALS

Stability in times of difficulty is a fourth reason prophecy is important to us. Knowing what tomorrow holds for us can help us be strong in the storms of today.

A Calm in the Storm

In the Upper Room, as He celebrated the Last Supper with His disciples, Jesus told them He was about to leave them. Their response was, "How are we going to make it?" To reassure His faithful followers, Jesus spoke these well-known words of comfort:

> Let not your heart be troubled; believe in God, believe also in Me. In My Father's house are many dwelling places; if it were not so, I would have told you; for I go to prepare a place for you. And if I go and prepare a place for you, I will come again, and receive you to Myself; that where I am, there you may be also. (John 14:1–3)

Jesus' prophecy of His own return helped produce calm in the midst of the disciples' panic.

Good News in Grief

One of the best examples of the use of prophecy to calm troubled hearts is in 1 Thessalonians 4:13–18, another familiar passage in which Paul comforted the Thessalonians concerning their fellow Christians who had died.

Verses 13–17 are Paul's teaching on the rapture, the moment when Christ will return in the air to take His people home to be with Him forever. This is one of the great, central passages of prophecy in the Bible. Yet Paul wasn't just dispensing doctrine. He closed this section by saying, "Therefore comfort one another with these words" (v. 18).

Hope for the Future

We've mentioned this benefit of studying prophecy: The prophetic Word of God also brings us encouragement and hope for the future.

The Thessalonian church was shaken by the death of some of its members, because the believers weren't sure what had happened to these brothers and sisters. The church was also shaken by a false word from someone that the day of the Lord had already come. Paul answered that charge and put their fears at ease:

> Now we request you, brethren, with regard to the coming of our Lord Jesus Christ, and our gathering together to Him, that you may not be quickly shaken from your composure or be disturbed either by a spirit or a message or a letter as if from us, to the effect that the day of the Lord has already come. (2 Thessalonians 2:1–2)

Paul proceeded to give them details by which the day of the Lord can be recognized, and we'll cover these in a subsequent chapter. What I want you to see here is the way Paul used this teaching to restore their hope. He concluded in verse 15, "So then, brethren, stand firm and hold to the traditions which you were taught, whether by word of mouth or by letter from us."

God wants to teach us about prophecy so we will stand firm today and not be thrown off by Satan or false teachers. If you're not alert, people will throw you off. The Devil will throw you off. Together they can make your knees wobble. But if you know God's Word you have a firm hope to hold on to even in the changing wind of circumstances.

A Right View of Life

In 2 Corinthians 5:8, Paul said, "We . . . prefer rather to be absent from the body and to be at home with the Lord." If you prefer heaven, you'll make it on earth. But if you prefer earth, you'll have a misperception of heaven. In other words, be heavenly. Colossians 3:2 says, "Set your mind on the things above, not on the things that are on earth." Your life should have such a heavenly dynamism about it that earth shrinks in significance.

If you have a firm grip on the truth that God has a program that nothing on earth can override, then you don't have to worry about what might happen.

PROPHECY PROMOTES WORSHIP AND PRAISE

When he came to the end of Romans 11, Paul was concluding a complex discussion of God's plan for Israel. We'll have a lot to say about Israel in this study of future events, because Israel is so key to the unfolding of prophecy. Here I just want to touch on a few highlights as we see how Paul concluded this section.

The Blessing of Our Position

Paul was clear in Romans 11:25–27 that God is not finished with Israel. His chosen people have a distinct place in His plan for the future. The world saw a partial fulfillment of this prophecy when the modern nation of Israel was born on May 14, 1948. No nation had ever before disappeared and come back with its native language intact. This was a first in human civilization, and it happened because it was prophesied in the Bible.

Earlier in this chapter, Paul had pointed out that we as Gentiles are "grafted in" to God's program and His blessings, the way wild olive shoots are grafted to an olive tree. We were grafted into God's covenant with Abraham, so that we too might enjoy the spiritual blessings of the Abrahamic covenant.

Paul was building his case that the blessings Gentile believers enjoy are the result of being grafted in with Israel. We are beneficiaries of Israel's blessings through Abraham.

The Praise for Our Position

With that privileged position of the Gentiles in mind, Paul then went on to say that someday Israel will be turned back to God and play a role in His prophetic plan.

Paul came to the end of this teaching, took one look back at the magnificent way God had worked to bring all things into harmony with His will, and was overwhelmed with awe and praise. "Oh, the depth of the riches both of the wisdom and knowledge of God! How unsearchable are His judgments and unfathomable His ways!" (Romans 11:33).

For several more verses, Paul poured out his doxology to God. The apostle burst into praise when he grasped the plan of God for the future. He was so overcome with the greatness of God that he concluded, "For from Him and through Him and to Him are all things. To Him be the glory forever. Amen" (v. 36).

PROPHECY PROMOTES WITNESSING

When we study prophecy, God is letting us know what is going to happen tomorrow, and far beyond that.

But God does not tell us about the future so we can argue about it or show how much we know. He wants us to know the truth about tomorrow and about eternity, because people on their way to hell need to know God today, before it's too late for them.

Let me show you several verses that underscore what I'm talking about. "It is a terrifying thing to fall into the hands of the living God" (Hebrews 10:31). "Our God is a consuming fire" (Hebrews 12:29). "Therefore knowing the fear of the Lord, we persuade men" (2 Corinthians 5:11). As we learn a lot about prophecy of end times in this final part of the book, let us go beyond knowing to doing. Let's make sure we are ready to tell others the good news of God's plan.

PERSONAL APPLICATION FOR LIFE

1. As we learned in this chapter, a knowledge of prophecy enhances our understanding of God's character. In the apostle Paul's letters, we can see how he became so overwhelmed with God's character, he couldn't help but worship when he considered God's powerful plan for the future. During your next quiet time, take a few minutes to simply reflect on God. Focus on new truths have you learned about the character of God.

2. The apostle Peter said that we can hasten Christ's return by our holy conduct. How? Stay busy doing God's work. Are you a spectator on the sidelines, or are you a player? If you want to draw nearer to Christ's return, get busy serving Him and the time will fly by.

3. As disciples of Christ, we look forward to the day when Christ will return for us. Can you see how consciousness of our tomorrow keeps us on track today? We should we living righteously as we await the final revelation of God's prophetic plan.

4. There's lot to worry about today from a human standpoint. But if you have a firm grip on the fact that God has a prophetic program that nothing on earth can override, then you don't have to have a coronary worrying about what might happen. Memorize and follow the exhortation of Colossians 3:2: "Set your mind on the things above, not on the things that are on the earth."

FOR GROUP STUDY

Questions for Group Discussion

1. Why is it important for believers to study prophecy? What does the warning of Revelation 22:18–19 tell us about the serious nature of biblical prophecy? What two ways does prophecy serve to authenticate the Bible?

2. Dr. Evans points out that prophecy reveals to us the character of God. What key truth do we learn from Isaiah 46:8–10, 11c? What does a proper understanding of prophecy reveal about God's character?

3. Read 1 John 3:2–3. In what ways can studying prophecy motivate us to holiness? (Use the chart below as an aid to your discussion.)

4. Read John 14:1–3 and 1 Thessalonians 4:13–18. How does knowing what the future holds serve as a stabilizing factor when we go through the trials of life?

PICTURE THIS

The notion that we could be standing face-to-face with Jesus Christ at any moment should be an enormous motivation for holy living. Prophecy is designed to promote holy living, and below are four motivations for doing so.

A Motivation to Holiness

MOTIVATION	SCRIPTURE PASSAGE	WHAT IT MOTIVATES US TO DO
There is a prize to be won.	Philippians 3:14	We should remain faithful to Christ because there is a heavenly prize to be won when He returns.
There is a hope to be realized.	Titus 2:11–13	We should be living righteously as we await the final revelation of God's plan.
There is a perspective to be gained.	2 Peter 3:10–12a	If we focus our hope on Christ's coming, that perspective on tomorrow can help us walk a straight line today.
There is a future to prepare for.	2 Corinthians 5:10	We should prepare for the future as if every day were the day of Christ's return.

103

THE KEY TO PROPHECY

The doctrine of eschatology involves a lot of details, and they're important. Libraries full of books have been written to discuss and examine the details of God's prophetic drama. In fact, we are going to examine many of these details in part 8.

But before we put God's prophetic Word under the microscope, we need to put it up on the big screen, so to speak, and see the full picture. We need to get the program in proper focus, and to do that we need to understand the key to Bible prophecy.

A key is important because it gives you access. A key that will unlock Bible prophecy, helping you see the individual details in their proper relationship and keeping them in proper perspective, is hanging at the "door" of Revelation 19:10. After another awe-inspiring revelation by an angel, John was about to fall at the angel's feet in worship. But the angel told John, "Do not do that; I am a fellow servant of yours and your brethren who hold the testimony of Jesus; worship God. For the testimony of Jesus is the spirit of prophecy."

That's a profoundly important statement. It tells us that the key that unlocks the door to prophecy is not a thing or an idea, but a person. Jesus

Christ is the key to God's prophetic revelation.

By this I mean that the degree to which prophetic details are related properly to Christ is the degree to which we will understand prophecy. God did not simply string together a series of prophetic events that happen one after another. There's a point, a definite climax, to God's plan. Prophecy, like history, is taking us somewhere. And that destination is Jesus Christ. So if we study all the details and yet miss Christ, we have missed the point of prophecy.

JESUS CHRIST IS THE CENTERPIECE OF PROPHECY

The first thing we need to understand is that Jesus is the centerpiece of biblical prophecy.

Paul began the book of Titus by saying, "Paul, a bond-servant of God and an apostle of Jesus Christ, for the faith of those chosen of God and the knowledge of the truth which is according to godliness, in the hope of eternal life, which God, who cannot lie, promised long ages ago" (1:1–2).

The phrase "long ages ago" refers to eternity. Long before He created the world, God promised eternal life to those who would be chosen of Him. But to whom did God make this promise? It wasn't to you and me, because we didn't yet exist. God the Father made this promise to His Son, the Lord Jesus. In 2 Timothy 1:9, Paul said the grace that saves us "was granted us in Christ Jesus from all eternity." In other words, we as believers were promised or given to Christ by His Father in eternity past.

Jesus Himself confirmed this when He said, "All that the Father gives Me will come to Me, and the one who comes to Me I will certainly not cast out" (John 6:37). The Word could not be clearer. Every Christian is a gift from God the Father to God the Son.

JESUS CHRIST IS THE CAUSE OF PROPHECY

All of this raises a question: Why did God craft this plan, before there was ever a creation, to redeem a portion of humanity by His sovereign choice and present these people as a gift to His Son? A lot is mystery here, because we were not present when the Trinity held its eternal council. But at least part of the answer goes back to another event that took place before creation—the rebellion of the angel Lucifer in heaven and his judgment by God. The rebellion of this angelic being who became Satan led to God's gift to Christ of a redeemed humanity.

Lucifer's Terrible Downfall

This is not a chapter on spiritual warfare. See section 3 in part 4 (angelology) for that. But Satan's conflict with God and subsequent fall explain why Jesus Christ came to be the key and the focus of God's prophetic program.

This awesome angel called Lucifer occupied a unique place in the heavenly realm before he led an open rebellion against God. As Ezekiel 28:12: "You had the seal of perfection, full of wisdom and perfect in beauty." This being was created flawless by God. He was the head angel, the "anointed cherub who covers" (v. 14), and he led the myriads of angels in the worship and adoration of God. He was the greatest of all God's created beings.

But Lucifer's great beauty and exalted status were his downfall. They led him into pride. "Your heart was lifted up because of your beauty; you corrupted your wisdom by reason of your splendor" (Ezekiel 28:17). In other words, Lucifer forgot he was created, not the Creator.

The five "I will" pronouncements (see pages 634–36) show how Lucifer tried to usurp God's throne. God judged his rebellion and expelled Lucifer from heaven. Once "the shining one," Lucifer now became Satan, "the adversary." He was consigned to eternal punishment (see Matthew 25:41), a sentence that will be carried out as the last stages of God's prophetic plan are unveiled.

The Connection to Prophecy

How does the rebellion of Satan tie together with Jesus' central place in prophecy? The Bible declares that Jesus was revealed to "destroy the works of the devil" (1 John 3:8). In reference to Satan's judgment, Jesus said, "I was watching Satan fall from heaven like lightning" (Luke 10:18).

A trial was held in heaven in which Satan and his cronies were found guilty of cosmic treason, rebellion against God. Jesus was saying, "I was at the trial when Satan was judged." Jesus saw Satan booted out of heaven "like lightning." The trial didn't last long, and the sentence was carried out in a hurry.

When Satan was kicked out of heaven, he took up temporary residence on the earth. His presence is evident from the fact that the earth was "formless and void, and darkness was over the surface of the deep" (Genesis 1:2). The earth became a garbage dump, because wherever Satan lives he produces garbage, including your life or mine.

The important thing is that the Godhead decided to use Satan for a very crucial purpose. God the Father said to Jesus Christ, "My Son, Satan's rebellion and judgment present an opportunity to accomplish two very important purposes.

"To show You how much I love You, I am going to create mankind, a race of beings inferior to Satan and the angels. Satan will mess with these beings and try to get them to follow him. I will redeem from this race a body of humanity I am going to give You as My love gift to You. And I am going to redeem these people right out of the hand of Satan. This redemption will bring Me eternal glory. It will prove that I can take mankind, the lesser creature, and do more with lesser beings who obey Me than I can do with angels who rebel against Me.

"My second purpose is to demonstrate to the angels and all of creation what happens when anyone rebels against Me. I am going to allow Satan to continue his operations on earth, and yet in the end I will utterly defeat him and his associates and gain the final victory for all eternity."

What I'm saying is that God's prophetic program is His response to Satan's rebellion. When the smoke of the final battle clears, when every prophetic event in the Bible has been fulfilled and time is no more, Jesus Christ has His redeemed throng rejoicing with Him forever in heaven, and Satan is totally defeated and thrown into the lake of fire.

Giving It All Back to God

Paul wrote of the final resurrection, "Then comes the end, when He hands over the kingdom to the God and Father, when He has abolished all rule and all authority and power. . . . when all things are subjected to Him, then the Son Himself also will be subjected to the One who subjected all things to Him, so that God may be all in all" (1 Corinthians 15:24, 28).

Guess what God is going to do? When His program for this earth is finished, when the goal of defeating Satan and redeeming a special people for His Son has been achieved, when Christ has ruled in His millennial kingdom, then the Son is going to say, "Father, You have loved Me so much to give Me this. Now let Me show My love to You by giving it all back to You."

When it's all over and eternity is ushered in, God will be all in all. There is such an equal love affair and equality of essence between the Father and the Son that they will share equally in the fruit of the prophetic plan that was conceived before the world began.

JESUS CHRIST IS THE CONTENT OF PROPHECY

There is no question that Jesus is the centerpiece of prophecy. And He is the cause of prophecy in the sense that the purpose of God's plan was to present a gift of redeemed humanity to His Son.

Jesus is also the content, the subject, of prophecy. There's no guesswork about this either, because we have Jesus' word on it. He said so Himself, to two of His discouraged disciples on the road to a little village called Emmaus.

Missing the Message

You probably know this story well. It's a familiar account in the Gospels, occurring at evening of the most important day in history, the day of Christ's resurrection. The two disciples were returning home discouraged because they didn't believe the reports that Jesus had risen. Jesus joined them on the road, although they didn't know it was He.

When Jesus asked the two what they were discussing, they explained that it concerned "Jesus the Nazarene, who was a prophet mighty in deed and word in the sight of God and all the people" (Luke 24:19). They went on to explain that they had hoped this Jesus would be Israel's Messiah. But since He had been crucified, and since it was now the third day since His death, they figured they had been wrong, and they were heading home.

This is amazing unbelief on the part of these two disciples, considering they also told Jesus all about the women's reports of the empty tomb and how other disciples had checked it out (vv. 22–24). They apparently did not believe the reports.

Jesus in the Old Testament

No wonder Jesus said to them, "O foolish men and slow of heart to believe in all that the prophets have spoken! Was it not necessary for the Christ to suffer these things and to enter into His glory?" (Luke 24:25–26).

And then, "beginning with Moses and with all the prophets, He explained to them the things concerning Himself in all the Scriptures" (v. 27). This is a very important verse, because it's here that Jesus demonstrated to these two men how He was the subject of all the prophetic Scripture.

"Moses and the prophets" was another term for the Old Testament. Moses takes us all the way back to the beginning and the first five books of the Bible. Jesus was saying that Moses talked about Him, the writers in the poetic books talked about Him, and the prophets talked about Him.

FELLOWSHIP WITH CHRIST

If you don't see Christ, you become spiritually blind, like these disciples were that night on the Emmaus road. And when you become spiritually blind, circumstances rule your emotions. That was their problem. They were depressed because they thought their Messiah was gone, and He was walking with them.

So Jesus gave these two an unforgettable Bible study as they walked along. Notice Luke 24:28–29: "They approached the village where they were going, and He acted as though He were going farther. But they urged Him, saying, 'Stay with us.'"

Why did Jesus act as if He was going to keep going when they arrived at Emmaus? Why did He give the two disciples an opening to invite Him to stay with them? I think Jesus was testing them to see what they were going to do with what they had heard.

They invited Jesus to dinner, and He accepted their offer. But as soon as He had broken bread, they recognized Him, and He disappeared from their sight (Luke 24:30–31). "They said to one another, 'Were not our hearts burning within us while He was speaking to us on the road, while He was explaining the Scriptures to us?'" (v. 32).

Don't miss the sequence of events here. Even though Jesus had taught them a wonderful "series" on prophecy, they didn't get the message until they sought fellowship with the Teacher. If you miss Jesus, you have missed everything.

JESUS CHRIST IS THE CULMINATION OF PROPHECY

In Ephesians 1 we read, "He made known to us the mystery of His will . . . with a view to an administration suitable to the fullness of the times, that is, the summing up of all things in Christ, things in the heavens and things on the earth" (vv. 9–10).

Clearly, the culmination of God's program is found in the person and work of Jesus Christ. We saw that God's plan started with Christ in the councils of eternity, and it is going to end with Christ. Every knee is going to bow at the name of Jesus (see Philippians 2:10).

The Climax of God's Program

The book of Revelation, which describes the culmination of God's prophetic program, opens with this declaration: "The Revelation of Jesus Christ" (1:1). This book, with all that it has to say about the future, is fundamentally about Him.

Then Christ made this statement: "I am the Alpha and the Omega . . . who is and who was and who is to come" (v. 8). *Alpha* and *omega* are the first and last letters of the Greek alphabet, so Jesus was saying He is the whole show. All things climax, or culminate, in Him.

Therefore, we can say that prophecy is about the exaltation, glorification, and adoration of Jesus Christ. God has placed all of history in the lap of Jesus Christ. And that's why to miss the Son is to miss the point of everything, including life itself.

The Subject of Our Praise

In the book of Revelation, John said:

> I looked, and behold, a great multitude, which no one could count, from every nation and all tribes and peoples and tongues, standing before the throne and before the Lamb, clothed in white robes, and palm branches were in their hands; and they cry out with a loud voice, saying, "Salvation to our God who sits on the throne, and to the Lamb." And all the angels were standing around

> the throne and around the elders and the four living creatures; and they fell on their faces before the throne and worshiped God. (Revelation 7:9–11)

This is quite a picture of praise. Redeemed people from every corner of the earth, the myriads of angels, and the special beings in heaven whose job is to praise God were all gathered before God the Father and Jesus the Lamb, pouring forth their praise and adoration.

God has created millions, and perhaps billions, of creatures who will sing praises to the Son. We who know Christ as our Savior will have the privilege of being in this eternal choir. If we are going to be singing the praises of Jesus Christ in heaven for all eternity, doesn't it make sense that we should be getting our voices in practice down here? He is the culmination, the capstone, of God's program—and the object of His Father's attention and love. Jesus Christ is the key to prophecy.

PERSONAL APPLICATION FOR LIFE

1. As we learned in this chapter, Satan tries to defeat God's prophetic plan. Scripture tells us that "greater is He who is in you than he who is in the world" (1 John 4:4). Praise God that we have His assurance of victory!

2. Because of his rebellion, Satan eventually will be cast into hell. Nevertheless, he has done his damage. God sent His Son to redeem the human race. Tragically, those individuals who have refused to accept God's gift of salvation are bound for the same destination as Satan. Do your daily prayers include people you want to see come to saving knowledge of Jesus as Lord? Are names of lost friends and loved ones on your list?

3. Join in God's plan. Be part of the work of Christ in taking the gospel to the people in your world. As Satan goes down in defeat, he will be determined to take with him every person he can. And he is determined to get you off your course of service for Christ. Ask God to help you not become overly influenced by the world's standards for measuring greatness and reward, which are simply Satan's counterfeits to deceive you and distract you from what God has prepared for you.

4. God has revealed many aspects of His prophetic plan through His Word, the Bible. How remarkable that we possess recorded accounts of Jesus' birth, His sacrifice on the cross, and His resurrection. Those rate as the three greatest events in all of recorded history! If your heart needs a dose of joy, take a moment to reflect on those truths.

FOR GROUP STUDY

Questions for Group Discussion

1. For what reasons is Jesus Christ the key to prophecy? Why is it important that we understand Jesus to be the key? (Use the "Picture This" chart as an aid to your discussion.)

2. Read the remarkable promise God gave the Son in Titus 1:1–2. See also 2 Timothy 1:9. What significance does that promise hold for us as believers?

3. As Dr. Evans point out in this chapter, Jesus is the content, or subject, of prophecy. For what reason do people miss that message?
4. Read Ephesians 1 and Philippians 2:10. From what we read in those passages, how will Jesus be the culmination of prophecy?

PICTURE THIS

"The testimony of Christ is the spirit of prophecy" (Revelation 19:10). God's prophetic plan has a beginning and a definite ending. Its climax and destination is Jesus Christ. To miss Him is to miss the point of prophecy.

JESUS CHRIST AS THE KEY TO PROPHECY

REASON	SCRIPTURE PASSAGES	WHAT SCRIPTURE TEACHES
He is the centerpiece.	Titus 1:1–2; 1 Timothy 1:9	Jesus is the focus of God's eternal promise to His Son.
He is the cause.	John 3:16; 1 John 3:8; 1 Corinthians 15:24, 28	As the key part of God's plan to redeem the lost human race, Jesus is God's gift to us.
He is the content.	Luke 24:25–29	Jesus is the subject of biblical prophecy, both Old and New Testaments.
He is the culmination.	Philippians 2:10; Ephesians 1:9–10	We find the culmination of prophecy in the person and work of Jesus Christ.

104
PROPHECY AND HUMAN HISTORY

The unfolding of human history is really the outworking of God's plan to demonstrate His glory and defeat Satan forever using lesser creatures, human beings, who would serve and obey Him. We're going to see how biblical prophecy ties in to this, because the Bible's earliest prophecy occurs in connection with the dawn of human history.

THE CREATION OF MAN

King David addressed the reason for our creation in Psalm 8. After asking the question, "What is man that You take thought of him?" (v. 4), David answered in these classic verses:

> Yet You have made him a little lower than God ["the angels" KJV], and You crown him with glory and majesty! You make him to rule over the works of Your hands; You have put all things under his feet. (vv. 5–6)

Our Position in Creation

I believe David was talking about our position in relation to the angels, not to God, despite the New American Standard reading here. Although we are "a little lower" than the angels in their intrinsic being as eternal creatures, we were created to rule over all creation–including angels–on God's behalf.

The writer of Hebrews confirmed this view when he quoted Psalm 8 and said mankind was created "a little while lower than the angels" (Hebrews 2:7). Then he added, "For in subjecting all things to him, He [God] left nothing that is not subject to him" (v. 8).

Why was mankind created inferior to the angels? So God could get greater glory in our redemption–because when the lesser defeats the greater, then He gets all the praise.

The Act of Creation

The opening chapters of Genesis look at the creation account as the beginning of human history and the setting for the beginning of the cosmic conflict between God and Satan. Man's creation was first recorded in Genesis 1:26. "Then God said, 'Let Us make man in Our image, according to Our likeness.'" Verse 27 then describes the fulfillment of God's intention. "God created man in His own image, in the image of God He created him; male and female He created them."

The fact that we are created in God's image and likeness is very important. Since it cannot refer to our physical makeup, it means we are created with the attributes of intellect, emotion, and volition or will, just as God has these attributes. We bear the image or stamp of God in our souls and spirits.

We are also like God in our ability to produce new life. The first thing God said to His new creatures was, "Be fruitful and multiply" (Genesis 1:28). Adam and Eve were also told to "subdue" and "rule over" the earth (v. 28). That is, they were to rule as God's representatives on the earth, which was Satan's domain.

A Reminder of Creation

God placed one tree in the middle of the garden of Eden and commanded Adam and Eve concerning it, "From the tree of the knowledge of good and evil you shall not eat, for in the day that you eat from it you shall surely die" (Genesis 2:17).

The Tree of the Knowledge of Good and Evil was a daily reminder that it was God who set the rules in the garden. The prohibition on eating from it was a statement that God never wants knowledge to be investigated independently of Him—which is exactly what we have today in the heresy of humanism.

Another tree in Eden was called the Tree of Life. Adam and Eve were free to eat from it. These two trees were probably right next to each other, presenting mankind with a clear choice. Would it be obedience, or rebellion and disobedience like Satan?

THE COLLAPSE OF MAN

In Genesis 3, human history took a terrible plunge downward, appropriately called the fall. This pivotal chapter is actually the beginning of prophecy, because from the moment Adam and Eve rebelled and sinned against God, the divine plan has been focused on the battle between God and Satan and God's ultimate triumph.

The drama began with the arrival of another character on the scene. "Now the serpent was more crafty than any beast of the field which the Lord God had made" (v. 1).

Focusing on the Prohibition

Satan's approach was to focus on the one prohibition God had made in the midst of all the abundance of Eden. God had commanded Adam not to eat from the Tree of the Knowledge of Good and Evil, under penalty of death (Genesis 2:17). So the serpent asked Eve, "Indeed, has God said, 'You shall not eat from any tree of the garden'?" (3:1).

Satan knew what God had said to Adam and Eve about the trees in the garden. The Devil brought up that conversation because he knew he had to get God's command out of Eve's mind if he was going to seduce her.

Satan cannot defeat the Word of God. But he can manipulate us so that we begin to doubt or disregard the Word, and when that happens he can defeat us.

In answer to the serpent's question, Eve said, "From the fruit of the trees of the garden we may eat; but from the fruit of the tree which is in the middle of the garden, God has said, 'You shall not eat from it or touch it, or you will die'" (Genesis 3:2–3).

Eve added to God's prohibition. She told the serpent that God commanded her not even to *touch* the forbidden tree. But God didn't say that. So again, she was making God look narrow and restrictive and harsh and legalistic. In addition, Eve failed to mention the absolute certainty of the penalty for disobeying God. She said, "You will die." But God had said, "You shall *surely* die" (2:17, italics added).

Denying God's Word

These little subtleties crept into Eve's conversation with the Devil, and God's Word was weakened. Satan jumped on the opportunity and came out with a flat denial of that Word. "The serpent said to the woman, 'You surely shall not die! For God knows that in the day you eat from it your eyes will be opened, and you will be like God, knowing good and evil'" (Genesis 3:4–5).

A Deceptive Offer

Now Satan had made Eve an enticing offer. Since God was holding out on her and Adam, Satan implied, and since they couldn't really enjoy life to its fullest under God's restriction, Satan offered to help Eve get all she deserved. He made the forbidden tree look all the more appealing. "When the woman saw that the tree was good for food, and that it was a delight to the eyes, and that the tree was desirable to make one wise, she took from its fruit and ate; and she gave also to her husband with her, and he ate" (Genesis 3:6).

The tree looked good, and the idea of being liked God sounded good, so she rebelled against God. And Adam followed right along with her.

This set the scene for the first and most basic statement of biblical prophecy, a statement that described the contest between God and Satan that would last throughout human history and take Jesus to the cross.

THE CONFLICT OVER MAN

The fall of Adam and Eve brings us to the verse we've been referring to, what I'm calling the conflict over mankind and his eternal destiny.

In the process of judging the serpent, God said, "I will put enmity between you and the woman, and between your seed and her seed; he shall bruise you on the head, and you shall bruise him on the heel" (Genesis 3:15).

This is the Bible's first prophecy, and it foretells the basic outcome of God's prophetic drama. Satan's seed, those opposed to God, would deliver a crippling blow to Christ, the seed of a woman (named Mary), on the cross (the bruise on the heel).

However, Christ would ultimately deliver a fatal blow to Satan (the bruise on the head). Part of this blow came when Jesus Christ rose from the dead, redeeming mankind and guaranteeing Satan's eternal judgment. God used this prophecy to explain the conflict that was about to unfold in human history and that is still in progress today. This important verse is prophetic because God was talking about the Seed, or offspring, who had not yet come.

God's "I Will" Statement

The first thing I want you to notice is God's declaration, "I will . . . ." Does that sound familiar? It should. We've seen that Lucifer made this same statement five times in Isaiah 14 as he declared his rebellion against God. But the moment the Devil exercised his independent, rebellious will, he lost and got booted out of heaven. But when God says, "I will," nothing can stop Him. The triumph of His will is being worked out in history, and we can watch it unfold through prophecy.

The War in History

So the battle was on, and all of history is now the outworking of this struggle. What we will see from this point on is the unfolding of prophecy as it relates to the fulfillment of the Bible's first great prophecy—the earthly life, death, and triumphant return of Jesus Christ.

The Next Generation

It didn't take long to see this conflict between God and Satan really break out. Adam and Eve had their first two children, Cain and Abel (Genesis 4:1–2). And "in the course of time," as Cain's offering was rejected by God while Abel's was accepted, that evil Cain killed righteous Abel (vv. 3–8).

So here was Cain operating under Satan's influence, attempting to wipe out God's righteous seed before it even had a chance to become established. As we will see, attempting to destroy God's seed has been the focus of Satan's program throughout history.

Even though Cain fell under Satan's influence, Cain used religion to try and make himself acceptable to God. Religion is trying to please God on your terms. Cain brought an offering to God, but it wasn't the offering God required. Religion is man's attempt to make his own way to God, as opposed to salvation, which is coming to God on His terms, in His way based on His Word.

THE CONQUEST BY A MAN

The human race may have collapsed into sin and been conquered by Satan, but there's one Man whom Satan could not defeat.

The Right Man at the Right Time

Galatians 4:4 is a great summary of what happened in history when God's program of crushing Satan was fulfilled. "But when the fullness of the time came, God sent forth His Son, born of a woman, born under the Law."

Jesus came at just the right time in history. When all the factors of history had come together to make it the right time, God sent Jesus Christ to be born of a virgin.

Jesus came under the Law, the Old Testament system of sacrifices God put in place temporarily after the fall of man, because Jesus was the fulfillment of that Old Testament system. He was the final sacrifice toward which all the Old Testament sacrifices pointed.

Jesus Christ came for this express purpose: "To destroy the works of the devil" (1 John 3:8). He accomplished that purpose on the cross. Because of His conquest, when we put our faith in Him, we regain our original created purpose, which, as we learned in Psalm 8, is to rule over God's creation.

Satan's Defeat at the Cross

Satan knew he had to get rid of Christ. He tried to kill Him as a baby when Herod had the baby boys of Bethlehem put to death. Then Satan tried to get Jesus to fall in the wilderness temptation.

Neither of those worked, but Satan must have thought he had reached his goal when he inspired wicked people to crucify Jesus on the cross. Satan did not know that the cross was going to be the instrument of Jesus' triumph over him. Paul wrote in Colossians 2:13–14 that Jesus canceled our sin debt at the cross by shedding His blood to pay for sin. Then he continued, "When [God] had disarmed the rulers and authorities, He made a public display of them, having triumphed over them through [Christ]" (v. 15).

That's the key verse. Satan was disarmed at the cross. His weapons were rendered useless at Calvary. The cross was the defining moment in history. On the cross Christ defeated Satan.

Our Conquest in Christ

The writer to the Hebrews said this of Jesus Christ: "We do see Him who was made for a little while lower than the angels, namely, Jesus, because of the suffering of death crowned with glory and honor, so that by the grace of God He might taste death for everyone" (Hebrews 2:9).

In other words, because you and I were humans, God had to become a human to save us. Christ had to die for our sins, because God's righteousness demanded payment for sin. But in His death Jesus was able to "render powerless him who had the power of death, that is, the devil; and might free those who through fear of death were subject to slavery all their lives" (Hebrews 2:14–15).

When you confess Christ and His sacrifice on the cross, you will beat Satan every time. He will have no more authority in your life. So while you are waiting for the future realization of Christ's full and final conquest of Satan, you can experience that victory now because of the cross.

I like what Paul told the Romans: "The God of peace will soon crush Satan under your feet" (Romans 16:20). Though this hasn't happened yet, you're still dealing with a defeated enemy. Christ is already victor over Satan because of the cross. If you are a child of God, Satan should not be stepping on you anymore. He should be dust under your feet. And when he tries to tell you he's in charge, you can tell him, "You're a liar. The cross says Jesus is in charge. His blood is your defeat. I overcome you in the power of Jesus' blood."

How can puny, sinful people like you and me talk to Satan like that?

Because "God has chosen the weak things of the world to shame the things which are strong" (1 Corinthians 1:27). He has chosen to take weak bundles of human flesh like us and put us up against the mightiest of the angels, Satan, to demonstrate what He can do with a lesser creature who will obey Him.

God has chosen to do things this way because He gets the greater glory when we conquer sin and Satan in His power. And we give God all the glory because we know it was " 'not by might nor by power, but by My Spirit,' says the Lord of hosts" (Zechariah 4:6).

PERSONAL APPLICATIONS FOR LIFE

1. We are victors over Satan in Christ, but activating our victory requires something of us. Read Revelation 12:11. That verse tells us that believers must live their lives based upon the accomplishment of Christ. If you have confessed Christ, you are His disciple. Are you living up to your commitment to Christ as the Lord of your life?

2. How consistent is your prayer life? The Bible says to "pray without ceasing" (1 Thessalonians 5:17). This is not occasional praying, but rather an attitude of prayer that controls the agenda of your day. James 5:16 tells us that "the effective prayer of a righteous man can accomplish much." That includes thwarting the Enemy in spiritual warfare.

3. Hebrews 2:14 tells us that Satan has been rendered powerless by the death and resurrection of Jesus Christ. That means the Devil's real weapons have been taken away, and he is pretty much left with the weapon of deception. But he is a master at deception, so don't underestimate the spiritual damage he can still inflict in your life. When tempted, resist the Devil! When we resist the Devil on the basis of Christ's authority, Satan must flee. If you need help resisting an attack from the Enemy, call upon God and He will help you.

4. When God saved you, He gave you a new life in Christ. But there's more. You are also part of Christ's church, the body of believers. That means you are seated with Christ in the place of authority in the heavenly places (Ephesians 2:6). If you are not exercising His power and authority in your life, ask God to show the next thing to do so you can get started.

FOR GROUP STUDY

Questions for Group Discussion

1. Read Psalm 8:3–6. What does this passage teach? What position does the human race hold in God's creation?

2. As revealed in Genesis 3:2–5, what was the cause of mankind's collapse in the garden of Eden? How did Satan misrepresent God's Word?

3. What was the cause of the conflict over mankind? Read the Bible's first prophecy in Genesis 3:15. What truths does it reveal to us?

4. Read Galatians 4:4 and Hebrews 2:9, 14-15; 1 Corinthians 1:27. Why was it important that Satan be defeated by a man? Why was Christ's work on the cross effective in defeating Satan? (Use the chart below to aid your discussion.)

PICTURE THIS

Although the human race collapsed into sin and was conquered by Satan, God sent the one man whom Satan could not defeat—the God-man, Jesus Christ. Because of Christ's work on the cross, Satan's defeat is sealed. Below are three reasons this is true.

THE GOD-MAN'S CONQUEST OF SATAN

REASON	SCRIPTURE PASSAGES	WHY IT WAS IMPORTANT
He was the right man at the right time.	Galatians 4:4; 1 John 3:8	According to God's prophetic plan, Jesus came at just the right time in history to carry out His redemption of mankind.
Christ's work on the cross defeated Satan.	Colossians 2:13–15	Jesus' sacrifice on the cross canceled our sin and completely disarmed Satan.
Because of Christ's victory, we have victory over Satan.	Hebrews 2:9	When we confess Christ and His cross, Satan can have no authority over us and is powerless to control us.

105

PROPHECY AND THE COVENANTS

A covenant is a relationship or agreement between God and His people in terms of the plan of action God is going to follow to carry out His program. All of the biblical covenants that are important for prophecy were initiated by God, and in the sense that they are God's statements of what He is going to do, they were prophetic or predictive at the time they were made.

The most serious covenant of all is the covenant ratified by blood, of which there are several examples in Scripture. The earliest of these covenants is the Adamic covenant, in which God killed animals in order to cover Adam and Eve and then promised that a future Redeemer would come to crush Satan (Genesis 3:15).

Cain's murder of Abel was the next step in the battle between the seed of God and the seed of Satan (Genesis 4:1–8). This act of violence set a tone of evil that escalated the battle until wickedness dominated the earth. God moved decisively to deal with this intolerable situation, and in the process of bringing worldwide judgment He also established a covenant with Noah that is still in effect.

THE COVENANT WITH NOAH

The Domination of Evil

The "sons of God," a group of the fallen angels who followed Satan in his rebellion, infiltrated the human race by using unrighteous men to have illicit sexual relationships with women and producing a demonic seed (Genesis 6:1–4). This pollution of the race was enough to bring God's judgment, so we read this declaration:

> Then the Lord saw that the wickedness of man was great on the earth, and that every intent of the thoughts of his heart was only evil continually. The Lord was sorry that He had made man on the earth, and He was grieved in His heart. The Lord said, "I will blot out man whom I have created . . . for I am sorry that I have made them." (vv. 5–7)

God determined to judge mankind with the flood because the human race was contaminated by this demonic seed produced through the unrighteous. However, "Noah found favor in the eyes of the Lord" (v. 8). Noah was a righteous man, and he became the one through whom God would continue the human race and preserve the righteous seed.

The Promise of the Covenant

After the flood waters subsided and the animals and Noah's family had left the ark, Noah offered burnt offerings to the Lord. God smelled the "soothing aroma" of Noah's sacrifice and made an unconditional, unilateral promise—or covenant—never to destroy the entire earth by water again (Genesis 8:20–22).

God ratified the covenant by saying, "Now behold, I Myself do establish My covenant with you, and with your descendants after you" (Genesis 9:9). Again, God said, "I establish My covenant with you; and all flesh shall never again be cut off by the water of the flood, neither shall there again be a flood to destroy the earth" (v. 11).

In His covenant with Noah, God instituted human government for the first time. That's implied in the commandment to carry out capital punishment for murder. Noah and his descendants were charged with establishing righteousness in civilization through government, which was a new thing on the earth.

This is why Paul called duly constituted government "a minister of God to you for good" (Romans 13:4).

But mankind soon corrupted God's program as Nimrod led the world in rebellion against God at Babel (Genesis 10:8–10; 11:1–9), with the result that God judged the people and scattered them over the face of the earth.

THE COVENANT WITH ABRAHAM

The rebellion of the nations at Babel produced a major shift in God's program. Whereas God had been dealing with mankind in general, beginning in the last portion of Genesis 11, He turned His attention to one man.

The Covenant Promised

Genesis 11:31–32 records the beginning of Abraham's trek from Ur to Canaan. Evidently God had already called him to leave home and go to Canaan before we read about it in Genesis 12:1.

Abraham obeyed, but only partially, because the family settled in Haran. God did not call Abraham to enter the Promised Land until his father, Terah, had died in Haran.

Once Terah had died, God called Abraham and gave him some incredible promises:

> Now the Lord said to Abram, "Go forth from your country, and from your relatives and from your father's house, to the land which I will show you; and I will make you a great nation, and I will bless you, and make your name great; and so you shall be a blessing; and I will bless those who bless you, and the one who curses you I will curse. And in you all the families of the earth shall be blessed." (Genesis 12:1–3)

God gave Abraham both personal and national promises that would later be ratified by God in a covenant ceremony. First of all, look at the personal promises. Abraham (still Abram at this time) would have a great name and great blessing from God. In fact, his new name (Genesis 17:5) was a witness to the blessings God had in store for him.

God also made the promise that Abraham would become the father of a great nation. This promise was restated at a later time, but here is the first prophecy of the birth of the nation of Israel, who would become God's chosen people.

At this point, Abraham probably didn't know what all of this meant or how all of it was going to be fulfilled. He was basically a converted pagan who had acted in faith and traveled to a barren, dusty land where he lived in tents.

So here we have this great man Abraham with these great promises. God repeated His covenant promises to Abraham time and again. One of these was in the very next chapter, Genesis 13:14–16. Another restatement of the promise comes in Genesis 17.

The Covenant Ratified

Genesis 15 describes the ceremony by which God ratified His covenant with Abraham. Abraham (then called Abram) had just defeated the federation of kings who had kidnapped Lot and his family. "After these things the word of the Lord came to Abram in a vision, saying, 'Do not fear, Abram, I am a shield to you; your reward shall be very great'" (v. 1).

In other words, "Keep trusting Me, Abraham." Don't just look for the signs or other things God gives; look for God. He is your reward, not anything else.

But Abraham saw a problem. "O Lord God, what will You give me, since I am childless?" (v. 2). That's a definite problem for a man who is supposed to have so many descendants they can't be counted.

It seemed impossible for Abraham and Sarah to have a child. But God restated His promise. He took Abraham outside and said, "Now look toward the heavens, and count the stars, if you are able to count them. . . . So shall your descendants be" (Genesis 15:5). At that point, Abraham believed God and was justified by his faith.

Then Abraham asked God, "O Lord God, how may I know that I shall possess it?" (v. 8). God's answer was the covenant ratification ceremony we read about in the rest of Genesis 15.

God instructed Abraham to bring certain animals and prepare them for the ceremony by cutting them in half and laying the two sides on the ground opposite each other (vv. 9–10). Abraham prepared everything and then sat down to wait for God to show up for the ceremony. But as time passed, Abraham fell into a deep sleep (v. 12). God was preparing Abraham for the ratification ceremony, but Abraham would not be part of the process except as a witness to the event.

With Abraham watching and listening, God gave him a prophetic summary of Israel's future bondage in Egypt and deliverance in the Exodus under Moses, and also of Abraham's future (Genesis 15:13–16).

A Unilateral Agreement

The manifestation of God to Abraham in Genesis 15:17 was the *shekinah*, the glory of God, His visible presence. God passed between the pieces of the animals by Himself, not with Abraham, as the act of covenant ratification.

Normally, when two parties cut animals in half to make a blood covenant, both parties walked between the pieces to seal their pledge to keep the covenant. It was something like the Indians and the cowboys cutting their fingers and pressing them together to make a blood covenant.

But God did something unique here. He took the walk between the animals by Himself, signifying that this covenant would be totally dependent upon Him, not upon Abraham. God was saying, "Abraham, I'm going to fulfill this covenant through you and with you. But this is My covenant, and I am going to fulfill it without any conditions. I am going to do this by Myself."

The Abrahamic covenant was unconditional. God made the agreement unilaterally. Abraham was a party to the covenant, but its fulfillment was not dependent upon his keeping up his end of the agreement. That's different from the Mosaic covenant, the law at Sinai, which was conditional upon the people's obedience and faithfulness to God.

God promised to fulfill His covenant of an heir and a land for Abraham. But as we know from the following chapters, Abraham and Sarah decided to try to help God by producing a son through Sarah's maid Hagar. The child born was named Ishmael, and Abraham later had to drive Hagar and Ishmael out of his home because Ishmael was not the son of promise.

Of course, Ishmael's birth was very important for Bible prophecy because he became the father of the Arabs, who are still fighting with their Israeli "cousins" today. The Arab nations will play a role in the final unfolding of God's prophetic plan.

THE PALESTINIAN COVENANT

Since we are talking about the land of Israel in relation to God's promises and prophetic program, I want to step ahead in the biblical text and look at a covenant that was made later in Israel's history, as the children of Israel were on their way from Egypt to Canaan under Moses (Deuteronomy 29–30). This is a conditional covenant often referred to as the Palestinian covenant.

The Condition of Obedience

The fact that the Abrahamic covenant was unconditional did not mean that Abraham himself, or the people of Israel, had no responsibility to God. His people cannot simply live any way they want and expect to bask in His blessings with no consequences. When it comes to both the Mosaic and the Palestinian covenants, blessing is conditioned on obedience.

We can see this element in the Palestinian covenant. It's clear that this agreement is separate from the Mosaic covenant, because the text clearly says, "These are the words of the covenant which the Lord commanded Moses to make with the sons of Israel in the land of Moab, *besides* the covenant which He had made with them at Horeb" (Deuteronomy 29:1, italics added).

It's plain from Deuteronomy 29–30 that this covenant is conditional all the way. Obey God, and dwell in peace and safety and prosperity in the land of Israel. Disobey God, and suffer His judgment.

When He had finished announcing the covenant provisions, God put the choice squarely to Israel. "I have set before you life and death, the blessing and the curse. So choose life in order that you may live, you and your descendants" (Deuteronomy 30:19).

Israel's Dry Bones

In Ezekiel 37:1–14, we have one of the most powerful and stark prophecies in all the Bible, the prophet's vision of the valley of dry bones.

We don't have the space to quote all of these verses here. If you are familiar with the prophecy, you know that Ezekiel was puzzled by the vision. But God gave him the answer in verses 11–14. God would take a land full of dead, dry bones and form them into a nation. This would be impossible, humanly speaking, but in May 1948 the impossible occurred. After being scattered among the other nations since A.D. 70, Israel became a nation again. This has never happened before or since in human history—but then no other nation is the subject of biblical prophecy the way Israel is.

Now Israel's Arab neighbors also claim the land as theirs, and this is where the battle is today. The struggle in the Middle East today turns on the fundamental question of who owns the land.

THE COVENANT WITH MOSES

The Mosaic covenant, the law given at Mount Sinai, was another conditional covenant between God and His people.

We don't need to spend a lot of time on this covenant except to note its conditional nature, and also to recall its prophetic significance in that the entire sacrificial system of the law was designed to point to Jesus, the Lamb of God who was the full and final sacrifice for sin.

The ratification of God's covenant with Moses shows its conditional nature. The ratification ceremony is described in Exodus 24:1–8. We need to note two verses here. "Then Moses came and recounted to the people all the words of the Lord and all the ordinances; and all the people answered with one voice and said, 'All the words which the Lord has spoken we will do!'" (v. 3). Again in verse 7 we read, "[Moses] took the book of the covenant and read it in the hearing of the people; and they said, 'All that the Lord has spoken we will do, and we will be obedient!'"

Deuteronomy 28 also speaks to the conditional nature of the Mosaic covenant, emphasizing that its blessings were conditioned on obedience, whereas curses and judgment awaited the people if they disobeyed. It's interesting that the blessings run from verses 1–14 of this chapter, while the warnings about the curses stretch from verses 15–68.

THE COVENANT WITH DAVID

Another biblical covenant is crucial for the unfolding of prophecy. This is the Davidic covenant relating to the kingdom and the throne of Israel. God made a promise to David in 2 Samuel 7 concerning the continuation of his dynasty. Verses 1–11 were something of a prelude to the covenant, in which David expressed a desire to build a temple for God and God reviewed His faithfulness to David. Then God said:

> When your days are complete and you lie down with your fathers, I will raise up your descendant after you, who will come forth from you, and I will establish his kingdom. He shall build a house for My name, and I will establish the throne of his kingdom forever. I will be a father to him and he will be a son to Me; when he commits iniquity, I will correct him with the rod of men and the strokes of the sons of men, but My lovingkindness shall not depart from him, as I took it away from Saul, whom I removed from before you. And your house and your kingdom shall endure before Me forever; your throne shall be established forever. (vv. 12–16)

God said He was going to establish Israel, a nation that will last forever, and give this nation Palestine, a land that will be theirs forever. Then He promised to establish a kingdom that will last forever.

The immediate reference in the verses above is to Solomon, David's descendant. But the ultimate Ruler who will sit on David's throne forever and fulfill the Davidic covenant is the Messiah.

THE NEW COVENANT

The final covenant we need to review is the new covenant, first mentioned in Jeremiah 31. This agreement deals with the reestablishment of God's relationship with His people Israel. From Israel's standpoint, the provisions of this covenant are still future, being fulfilled when Jesus returns.

In Jeremiah 31:31–34, God told His covenant people that someday His relationship with them would be different. The former covenant God spoke of here was the covenant of Moses, the law, which was conditional on Israel's obedience. Israel failed to keep its end of the agreement, and God brought down the curses of the covenant on His people.

But in the future, God is going to establish a new relationship with Israel that will be so rich and so dynamic the nation won't need to have His law written on stone tablets. It will be inscribed on their hearts.

Remember, the problem with the Mosaic law wasn't the law itself but the condition of the people's hearts. The law of Moses revealed God's holy will and showed the people their need of regeneration.

The church partakes of the benefits of the new covenant. On the night of His betrayal, at the Last Supper, Jesus gave the cup to His disciples and said, "This cup which is poured out for you is the new covenant in My blood" (Luke 22:20). We are told to partake of this cup and the bread as part of the new covenant Jesus instituted in His death (1 Corinthians 11:25–26). The new covenant is lived from the inside out, not from the outside in like the law of Moses. We as believers today are living under the new covenant—and the day is coming when the people of Israel will also follow their Messiah, Jesus Christ, with all of their hearts when He comes to reign on David's throne in His millennial kingdom.

PERSONAL APPLICATION FOR LIFE

1. A covenant is only as good as the people making it. Whenever God makes a covenant, He fulfills it. It is a function of His perfect character. As children of God, we can always rely on God fulfilling His Word. Are you trusting the promises of God's Word for help with a problem or a decision? Bank on His character and His Word, and claim Hebrews 10:23, remembering that God is the God who keeps His promises to us.

2. God's promise to Abraham reminds us of the way God often works. He will not always tell you everything He's doing at the beginning, or where He's taking you. He may give you a little bit now and little bit later, and then a little more after that. That why the Bible says, "We walk by faith, not by sight" (2 Corinthian 5:7). Never run from God's lessons in faith; embrace them!

3. You can be an eternally secure Christian and yet be a miserable, defeated, and unfruitful Christian because you are disobedient. You can actually be unhappy on your way to heaven! Don't get the idea that God's unconditional promise of salvation means you have no responsibility to obey and serve Him.

4. When a person isn't right with God internally, no external statute can give that person a right relationship with God. But when a person loves God with all his heart, that person is enabled to fulfill the demands of God's law because that person's motivation is to please and obey God. Why? Because God has replaced the old heart with a new one. If you don't know Christ as your Savior, ask Jesus to forgive your sins and put your trust in Him to save you. Only through Jesus can you establish a right relationship with God.

FOR GROUP STUDY

Questions for Group Discussion

1. As recorded in Genesis 12:1–3 and repeated in Genesis 13:14–16, what was God's covenant with Abraham? What promise did God give Abraham? How is this covenant unconditional?

2. What was God's covenant with Moses as recorded in Exodus 24:1–8? In what way was it conditional?

3. Read 2 Samuel 7:1–16. What is the content of God's covenant with David, and how does relate to God's prophetic plan?

4. What does Jeremiah 31:31–34 reveal to us as God's people? When will the provisions of the new covenant be fulfilled?

PICTURE THIS

All of God's covenants are His agreements with His people to carry out His program. They were all prophetic at the time they were made, and as they unfold, they reveal not only God's plan but also His perfect character.

God's Prophetic Covenants with His People

COVENANT	SCRIPTURE PASSAGE	ITS PROPHETIC SIGNIFICANCE
God's covenant with Noah.	Genesis 6:1–7: 8:21–22	Because of God's impending worldwide judgment, He established a covenant with Noah. That covenant is still in effect.
God's covenant with Abraham.	Genesis 12:1–3; 15:13–16	God promises Abraham that he would become the father of a great nation. This is the first prophecy of the birth of the nation of Israel, who would become God's chosen people.
The Palestinian covenant	Deuteronomy 29–30	This covenant promised God's people peace, safety, and prosperity in the land of Israel. However, its blessings were conditioned on obedience.
God's covenant with Moses.	Exodus 24:1–8	Another covenant conditioned on obedience, it was prophetically significant as it recalled that the entire sacrificial system of the law was designed to point to Jesus, the Lamb of God, who was the full and final sacrifice for sin.
God's covenant with David.	2 Samuel 7:1–16	A covenant crucial for the unfolding of prophecy, it relates to the kingdom and the throne of Israel.
The new covenant	Jeremiah 31:31–34	This covenant deals with the reestablishment of God's relationship with His people Israel—a kingdom that will last forever. From Israel's standpoint, the provisions of this covenant are still future, being fulfilled when Jesus returns.

106

PROPHECY AND THE TIMES OF THE GENTILES

Bible prophecy is like the course syllabus we used to get in college that outlined the requirements for the semester. God doesn't give us every detail of His program, but He gives us enough so we can know where history is going and what He expects of us.

We have already seen that God is in charge when it comes to Israel's future. Now we will learn, from the book of Daniel, that God is firmly in charge when it comes to the unfolding of His prophetic plan for the other nations on earth.

GENTILE WORLD HISTORY

Daniel's prophecy deals in depth with the progress of Gentile world history, and the amazing thing is that we can verify much of Daniel's prophecy by laying our history books alongside Daniel's prophecies, written hundreds of years earlier.

It's obvious to anyone who knows history and the Bible that Israel long ago lost its dominant place in God's program. Gentile world powers have been dominating the scene for many centuries; they continue in power today, and they will continue in power until Jesus returns and Israel enters into a new covenant relationship with Him.

This long period of Gentile domination is no accident, but a predetermined part of God's prophetic plan. Jesus called this period "the times of the Gentiles" (Luke 21:24). Israel has been set on the sidelines in God's redemptive program, under His discipline for their disobedience to His law and their rejection of His Messiah.

As we said, Israel will one day be restored in the new covenant. But between their disobedience and discipline, and the future time of their restoration, we have a period of history known as the times of the Gentiles. That is the time we are living in. The church today is predominantly Gentile, and for the most part the Jews remain in their unbelief and rejection of Jesus Christ as their Messiah.

Many Bible scholars agree that the times of the Gentiles began with the conquest and destruction of Jerusalem by the Babylonians under King Nebuchadnezzar and the deportation of the people to exile in Babylon (Daniel 1:1–7). God allowed Babylon to destroy Israel because the people had rebelled against Him. God had warned them that if they disobeyed, the ultimate penalty would be removal from their land. You can review those warnings in Deuteronomy 28:49–68. So a Gentile power took control over Israel. The Gentiles were still in control six hundred years after Daniel in Jesus' day, and Revelation 11:2 shows that Israel will continue to be under Gentile domination during the great tribulation. (More on the tribulation in chapter 112).

One of the Jewish exiles deported to Babylon was Daniel, a young teenager of exceptional character and ability. He was trained to be one of Nebuchadnezzar's court advisers, and when the king had a dream that no one could interpret, God gave the meaning to Daniel.

NEBUCHADNEZZAR'S DREAM

The prophetic portion of Daniel begins in chapter 2 with Nebuchadnezzar's dreams. This mighty king was so disturbed by this recurring dream, and so eager to know what it meant, that he called all his wise men together to interpret it for him (Daniel 2:1–3).

The problem was that the king couldn't, or wouldn't, tell these men what the dream was. But being the king, he demanded an explanation anyway, and he ordered all his counselors in Babylon to be killed when the sorcerers and magicians couldn't tell him the dream (vv. 4–15).

The Answer from God

That death order included Daniel and his three friends—who hadn't been present when the king originally asked for an interpretation of the dream; so Daniel asked for some time. Then he and his three Hebrew friends went to prayer, and God revealed the interpretation of the dream to Daniel (Daniel 2:16–19).

Notice that "Daniel blessed the God of heaven" (v. 19) for this answer to prayer. Five times in this book, God is called "the God of heaven." Why? Because when there's chaos on earth, it's good to remind ourselves that there's still a God in heaven who is reigning over the confusion on earth.

Daniel received his answer from God and went before Nebuchadnezzar. The exchange leading up to Daniel's interpretation was a powerful testimony on his part, which you can read for yourself (Daniel 2:24–30).

Daniel told the king that he saw a great statue in his dream, a statue whose "appearance was awesome" (v. 31). I want to summarize the statue's makeup because we need to focus our attention on the interpretation, which is the key to all of this. Daniel described this magnificent statue as having a head made of gold, a chest and arms of silver, a belly and thighs of bronze, legs of iron, and feet made of a mixture of iron and clay.

Then Daniel said a stone "cut out without hands" struck the statue on its feet and crushed them (v. 34). After that, all of the statue was crushed and the metals blown away completely like chaff in the wind. But "the stone that struck the statue became a great mountain and filled the whole earth" (v. 35c).

Interpreting the Dream

As Daniel began to interpret the dream, he explained that Nebuchadnezzar himself was the head of gold because as far as earthly powers were concerned, he was currently "the king of kings" (Daniel 2:37). But God made it clear that the king's power wouldn't last forever. In fact, the eventual demise of the Babylonian Empire was contained in the rest of the statue. Daniel continued:

> After you there will arise another kingdom inferior to you, then another third kingdom of bronze, which will rule over all the earth. Then there will be a fourth kingdom as strong as iron; inasmuch as iron crushes and shatters all things, so, like iron that breaks in pieces, it will crush and break all these in pieces. (vv. 39–40)

Daniel's prophecy of the four major Gentile empires of the ancient world is so accurate that many critics claim he had to have written his book after the fact. Daniel wrote in the sixth century B.C., hundreds of years before the rise of the Greek or Roman Empires. Yet we can verify his prophecy with a history book.

The kingdom illustrated by a chest and arms of silver was the Medo-Persian Empire that overthrew Babylon many decades later, when Daniel as an old man was serving the Babylonian king Belshazzar. The Medes and the Persians defeated Babylon on the very night of Belshazzar's drunken feast (Daniel 5:20–31).

The third kingdom of bronze was the kingdom of Greece under Alexander the Great, who destroyed the Medo-Persian Empire and did in fact "rule over all the earth" (Daniel 2:39). It's obvious that when Daniel came to the fourth kingdom something was different, because it occupied more of the vision than any of the other kingdoms. This was the great Roman Empire that crushed Greece and became the most dominant empire in the ancient world. The Roman Empire ruled the known world when Jesus arrived on the scene.

But even though Rome's military might was unmatched, it had a flaw, a weakness, as described in Daniel 2:41–43. From God's perspective, the thing that distinguished the Roman Empire was its mixture of iron and clay, two substances that cannot stay together. In other words, the flaw in the Roman Empire could not be fixed. Something would cause this kingdom to come apart.

This prophecy was fulfilled because the Roman Empire did come apart, but not by military conquest. Rome was brought down by decay from within as immorality, wanton luxury, and loose living mixed with Rome's governmental structures to weaken the kingdom's moral will and desire to rule effectively.

God's Kingdom

The revelation of the four great world empires is now followed by the revelation of another kingdom, the eternal kingdom of God:

> And in the days of those kings the God of heaven will set up a kingdom which will never be destroyed, and that kingdom will not be left for another people; it will crush and put an end to all these kingdoms, but it will itself endure forever. Inasmuch as you saw that a stone was cut out of the mountain without hands and that it crushed the iron, the bronze, the clay, the silver, and the gold, the great God has made known to the king what will take place in the future; so the dream is true, and its interpretation is trustworthy. (Daniel 2:44–45)

This kingdom is yet future, being fulfilled when Jesus Christ returns to set up His millennial kingdom. He is the stone cut out without hands, which means He is from God.

Jesus is called a stone throughout Scripture (1 Peter 2:4–8), and in this dream the stone becomes a mountain, which in the Bible symbolizes a kingdom. At His return, Christ will crush all earthly powers, and His kingdom will rule over the earth.

DANIEL'S VISION

Many years after interpreting Nebuchadnezzar's dream concerning the times of the Gentiles, Daniel himself had a dream and a vision related to the same four earthly kingdoms (Daniel 7).

The interesting thing about this is the difference in perspective between the dream of a pagan king and the vision God gave His holy prophet. The sequence of the kingdoms is the same, and their eventual destruction, but what a difference in the way they are presented.

In Nebuchadnezzar's dream, these world powers were magnificent to behold in their glory, an awe-inspiring statue that was "large and of extraordinary splendor" (Daniel 2:31). But in Daniel 7, from God's perspective, these kingdoms are wild beasts, meant to be destroyed. Their true nature as sinful, rebellious empires is revealed when God shines His light on them.

Daniel wrote, "I was looking in my vision by night, and behold, the four winds of heaven were stirring up the great sea. And four great beasts were coming up from the sea, different from one another" (Daniel 7:2–3).

The "four winds" is a reference to angelic activity, when angels address the wickedness of men (see Revelation 7:1–3). The "great sea" in the Bible is always the Mediterranean Sea, so what we have in Daniel 7, as in Revelation 7, is God addressing Gentile rulers. Daniel saw four beasts, four Gentile kingdoms in the area around the Mediterranean Sea, which was the center of the world at that time.

The First Beast

The first beast in the vision "was like a lion and had the wings of an eagle. I kept looking until its wings were plucked, and it was lifted up from the ground and made to stand on two feet like a man; a human mind also was given to it" (v. 4).

We just saw that the first great Gentile world empire addressed in prophecy is Babylon, particularly under Nebuchadnezzar. He was the golden head of the great statue in Daniel 2.

But Nebuchadnezzar got into trouble when he started looking at himself as the master of the universe. His arrogance was obvious in his threat to the three Hebrew boys, Shadrach, Meshach, and Abednego, concerning bowing to his image or being thrown into the fiery furnace. "What god is there who can deliver you out of my hands?" asked this proud king (Daniel 3:15).

But according to Daniel's vision, the eagle got his wings plucked. Daniel 4:28–37 tells the story of Nebuchadnezzar's judgment by God. The king was on his rooftop, looking over the city of Babylon and boasting about his own glory. Immediately, the Bible says, God struck Nebuchadnezzar with insanity.

This is a sobering lesson for any of us who are tempted to develop a "theo-ego," a God complex. Whenever you get so big that you don't think you need God, people may as well get your room in the sanitarium ready, because you have already lost your mind.

Daniel's vision depicted Nebuchadnezzar getting his sanity back after seven years when he was stood back up on his feet after crawling around like a beast (7:4).

Eventually, though, Babylon got its wings plucked by the Medo-Persian Empire. In the reign of Belshazzar, at the end of his drunken party, the Persian army under King Darius launched a surprise attack.

The Second Beast

The Medo-Persian Empire is the second beast of Daniel's vision. Of this beast the prophet wrote, "And behold, another beast, a second one, resembling a bear. And it was raised up on one side, and three ribs were in its mouth between its teeth; and thus they said to it, 'Arise, devour much meat!'" (Daniel 7:5).

Why is the bear raised on one side? Because the Persians defeated the Medes and absorbed them into the Medo-Persian Empire. Persia was the greater of the two empires, and combined they were able to defeat Babylon.

The three ribs in the bear's mouth symbolized the three great enemies that Persia defeated in its conquest: Egypt, Assyria, and Babylon. All of them were gobbled up by the Medo-Persian Empire, which ruled for some two hundred years.

The Third Beast

In verse 6 of Daniel 7, Daniel described the third beast of his vision, the Greek Empire established by Alexander the Great. "After this I kept looking, and behold, another one, like a leopard, which had on its back four wings of a bird; the beast also had four heads, and dominion was given to it."

A leopard is fast on its feet, so when you add that image to one of a bird with four wings instead of the normal two, you have the picture of lightning speed. The Greeks under Alexander the Great defeated the Medo-Persian Empire in a matter of a few months in 334 B.C., and Alexander the Great had conquered the world by the time he was thirty years old.

The end of verse 6 is another example of the accuracy of Bible prophecy. The four heads of the Greek Empire that Daniel saw refer to the four kingdoms into which Alexander's domain was split after his death.

Alexander's four generals fought among themselves for power, and the

Greek Empire was split four ways. These commanders were able to divide the kingdom because the strong leader who had held it together was gone. So eventually the Greek Empire passed off the world scene as a ruling power.

The Fourth Beast

The fourth beast of Daniel's vision corresponds to the fourth part of Nebuchadnezzar's statue, the Roman Empire symbolized by iron. But here God gave Daniel a much more complete picture of the progression of Gentile world domination, because we find that the Roman Empire will appear in history again, except in a different form.

Daniel said of the fourth beast, "I kept looking in the night visions, and behold, a fourth beast, dreadful and terrifying and extremely strong; and it had large iron teeth. It devoured and crushed and trampled down the remainder with its feet; and it was different from all the beasts that were before it, and it had ten horns" (Daniel 7:7). This beast was horrifying to see.

The statue in Nebuchadnezzar's dream had ten toes, which were said to be kings (Daniel 2:44). Now we read about ten horns, which are also ten kings or kingdoms that were coming out of this kingdom.

Daniel said that as he was studying this terrifying image, trying to figure it out, "Behold, another horn, a little one, came up among them, and three of the first horns were pulled out by the roots before it; and behold, this horn possessed eyes like the eyes of a man and a mouth uttering great boasts" (7:8).

Look ahead to verse 11. "Then I kept looking because of the sound of the boastful words which the horn was speaking; I kept looking until the beast was slain, and its body was destroyed and given to the burning fire."

The "little horn" of Daniel 7 is called the Beast in Revelation 13:1. This is the Antichrist, the final world ruler whose reign of terror during the tribulation will bring to a completion the times of the Gentiles, when Israel is trodden down by the nations.

God in Control

There are two other persons in Daniel 7 we haven't mentioned yet: the Ancient of Days (vv. 9–10), and the Son of Man (vv. 13–14). These are God the

Father and God the Son. The story isn't over, and Daniel's vision of Gentile world powers isn't complete, until these two have acted. This is the good stuff.

God is called the Ancient of Days here because He's the timeless One. He takes His throne while all of this chaos is happening on earth. The scene Daniel was shown is the great tribulation, when the Antichrist will have his way with the world for three-and-one-half years. But just as things get to their worst, the Ancient of Days takes His throne. God is still in control.

Then Daniel saw "One like a Son of Man" coming up to the Ancient of Days, God the Father (Daniel 7:13). The Father presents this Son of Man with an everlasting kingdom that cannot be destroyed (v. 14). This is a prophetic picture of God the Father handing over to His Son, the Lord Jesus Christ, the kingdoms of this world for Him to rule.

So Jesus receives His eternal kingdom from the Father, the Antichrist is utterly crushed and handed over to God's court for his eternal doom (v. 26), and Christ establishes His kingdom (v. 27). Daniel wanted his people, and us, to know that God alone is sovereign over world affairs (4:31–37).

PERSONAL APPLICATION FOR LIFE

1. We live in the period referred to as the times of the Gentiles. The church today is predominantly Gentile, and for the most part the Jews remain in their unbelief and rejection of Jesus Christ as their Messiah. Take an inventory of the relationships that touch your life—friends, family, and coworkers. Ask God to give you opportunities and the strength to take the initiative in reaching them for Christ

2. One of the concluding events of Christ's future millennial rule is the defeat and judgment of Satan. In our present age, however, we battle against Satan and his army of evil angels. Whatever Satan throws your way, remember that, because of Christ's work on the cross, you stand on the victorious side of the battle. In your daily walk with God, ask Him to enable you to fight Satan's deceptions and temptations so you can claim victory.

3. Someday Christ will return to establish His kingdom. As a child of God, are you ready for the coming kingdom? Matthew 6:33 exhorts us to seek God's kingdom and righteousness. Is kingdom living the top priority in your life? It's never too late to get into practice by establishing the kingdom of God in your life.

4. Whereas our salvation deals with our legal relationship to Christ and is unconditional, our discipleship is conditional. It has to do with the level of intimacy we have with the Savior and our obedience to God's Word. Maybe the intimacy you're missing is waiting for you in a deeper commitment to Christ in discipleship. Take some time soon and get into His Word and spend some quiet time with Him.

FOR GROUP STUDY

Questions for Group Discussion

1. Why is understanding Daniel's prophecy of importance to us today?

2. Read the account of King Nebuchadnezzar's dream in Daniel 2:1–45. Discuss Daniel's interpretation of the king's dream. What did it prophesy about future Gentile kingdoms?

3. What does Daniel 2:44–45 reveal about God's future eternal kingdom? Who is the "stone . . . cut out of the mountain"? (See 1 Peter 2:4–8.) What is the significance of this prophecy?

4. Discuss Daniel's vision in Daniel 7:1–14. What do the four beasts represent? (Use the chart below as an aid to your discussion.)

PICTURE THIS

Many years after interpreting Nebuchadnezzar's dream concerning the times of the Gentiles, Daniel himself had a dream and a vision related to the same four earthly kingdoms. Below is a snapshot of his vision and its prophetic significance.

THE "BEASTS" OF DANIEL'S VISION

Daniel 7:1–14

BEAST	VERSES	ITS SIGNIFICANCE
First beast	verses 1–4	This is the kingdom of Babylon under Nebuchadnezzar, toppled by the Medo-Persian Empire.
Second beast	verse 5	This represents the Medo-Persian Empire. The three ribs in the bear's mouth are enemies Persia defeated in its conquest.
Third beast	verse 6	This beast represents the Greek Empire established by Alexander the Great.
Fourth beast	verses 7–8	This beast represents the Roman Empire, symbolized by iron. The "little horn" is the Antichrist of Revelation 13:1.

107

PROPHECY AND ISRAEL'S TIMETABLE

In today's world life often seems chaotic, out of control. At times like this, we may wonder where God is.

But we who know God and His Word understand that He is in charge even when that doesn't seem to be the case. And when God blows the whistle to signal the start of an event, everything comes together according to the purpose of His own will.

The prophecy of Israel's timetable is found in Daniel 9:24–27, where we are going to spend the bulk of this chapter. We'll also look at several other passages that relate to Daniel 9 since this passage is what we might call a hub in the prophetic wheel.

BACKGROUND TO THE PROPHECY

Israel's seventy weeks are detailed in the final four verses of Daniel 9. Before we plunge into the details, we need to see this prophecy in the context of the entire chapter. Verse 1 indicates that this prophecy was given to Daniel many years after the prophecies of Gentile domination written in Daniel 4 and 7.

Daniel's Discovery

Daniel was an elderly man at this time. He had been in exile for about sixty-seven years—a number that's very important, as we will see below. He was now serving in the court of Darius, king of the Medo-Persian Empire.

Daniel recorded that in the first year of Darius's reign, he "observed in the books the number of the years which was revealed as the word of the Lord to Jeremiah the prophet for the completion of the desolations of Jerusalem, namely, seventy years" (Daniel 9:2).

In other words, Daniel was having his devotions one day when he read something in the prophecy of Jeremiah that apparently startled him. Daniel was probably reading Jeremiah 25:11–12:

> "This whole land shall be a desolation and a horror, and these nations shall serve the king of Babylon seventy years. Then it will be when seventy years are completed I will punish the king of Babylon and that nation," declares the Lord, "for their iniquity, and the land of the Chaldeans; and I will make it an everlasting desolation."

Later Jeremiah recorded this promise from the Lord: "For thus says the Lord, 'When seventy years have been completed for Babylon, I will visit you and fulfill My good word to you, to bring you back to this place'" (29:10). Daniel was almost certainly aware of this prophecy too.

Here's what jumped off the page to Daniel. He was reading this in 538 B.C., sixty-seven years after Nebuchadnezzar had come to Jerusalem in 605 B.C. and taken Daniel and other Israelites as captives to Babylon. God said through Jeremiah that Israel's captivity would last seventy years—so Daniel realized that Israel's captivity was about to end.

Daniel's Repentance

After reading Jeremiah, Daniel immediately fell on his face and poured out his heart to God in an incredible prayer of confession and repentance on behalf of his nation Israel (Daniel 9:3–19). In this prayer, Daniel personally identified with the sins of Israel more than thirty times.

It's obvious from the way Daniel prayed that he knew the law: "Indeed all Israel has transgressed Your law and turned aside, not obeying Your voice; so the curse has been poured out on us, along with the oath which is written in the law of Moses the servant of God, for we have sinned against Him" (Daniel 9:11).

Israel's Exile

Judging by Daniel's prayer, the exile was for seventy years because Israel had failed to observe seventy Sabbath years. The language of the curse suggests that Israel would be in exile until the land received all the rest it had missed during their years of disobedience. So God decreed one year of exile for each Sabbath year missed.

THE PROPHECY REVEALED TO DANIEL

It was while Daniel was praying that God sent the angel Gabriel to him with the prophecy of the seventy weeks.

The Prophecy's Duration

The question Gabriel was sent to answer (vv. 20–21) was one Daniel may have wondered about: What happens when Israel's captivity in Babylon is over? The angel told Daniel, "I have now come forth to give you insight with understanding . . . so give heed to the message and gain understanding of the vision" (vv. 22–23).

What follows in verses 24–27 is the prophecy called the seventy weeks, literally "seventy sevens." The idea is not seventy units of seven days each, but seventy units of seven years each. This fits the context, because Daniel had just been reading in Jeremiah about the seventy years of captivity. Also, the prophecy covers far too much time to be anything but seventy units of seven years, or a total of 490 years.

The prophecy begins, "Seventy weeks have been decreed for your people and your holy city, to finish the transgression, to make an end of sin, to make atonement for iniquity, to bring in everlasting righteousness, to seal up vision and prophecy and to anoint the most holy place" (Daniel 9:24).

The Prophecy's Specifics

Gabriel gave Daniel six specific things that would be accomplished during the period of the seventy weeks. This 490-year period would "finish the transgression," a reference to ending Israel's rebellion and bringing her to repentance. God would also "make an end of sin," imparting to the Israelites new spiritual life through the new covenant.

Gabriel also said the seventy weeks would "make atonement for iniquity," pointing forward to the death of Christ as the final atonement offered for Israel's sin. The fourth item on the list is "to bring in everlasting righteousness" (Daniel 9:24). This is a reference to Christ's millennial kingdom when He will rule in righteousness and the righteous will rule with Him (Jeremiah 23:5–6).

The final two items on the angel's list are "to seal up visions and prophecy," to fulfill all the prophecies concerning Israel, and to "anoint the most holy place." Since the word *place* is not in the original, I take it Gabriel is referring to the anointing of the Messiah.

The Prophecy's Starting Point

That's the panorama of the entire period. Then the angel revealed to Daniel how the seventy weeks would unfold. "So you are to know and discern that from the issuing of a decree to restore and rebuild Jerusalem until Messiah the Prince there will be seven weeks and sixty-two weeks; it will be built again, with plaza and moat, even in times of distress" (9:25).

The angel said the seventy weeks would begin when a decree was issued to rebuild Jerusalem. From that moment until the appearance of the Messiah would be seven plus sixty-two weeks, which in the formula of the weeks is 483 years.

The decree referred to in Daniel 9 would not be issued until more than one hundred years after Daniel, in 444 B.C. by the Persian king Artaxerxes. The decree came about because of the burden for Jerusalem and the mighty prayer of Nehemiah, a Jewish exile and the king's trusted servant (Nehemiah 1:1–11).

You probably know the story. Artaxerxes noticed Nehemiah's distress and asked him what was wrong. When Nehemiah explained his agony over the desolate condition of Jerusalem, Artaxerxes sent him back to Jerusalem with permission to rebuild the city and gave him official letters to acquire what he needed. This was the decree referred to in Daniel 9:25.

Nehemiah 2:1 pinpoints the date for us on this decree because he said it came in the twentieth year of Artaxerxes' reign. So we can establish the date as 444 B.C. That's when the clock started counting down on Daniel's seventy weeks.

Some Jews in exile had gone back to Jerusalem prior to this time, but from the standpoint of Israel's prophetic timetable it was the decree of Artaxerxes that got the clock moving. Within the first seven weeks of Daniel's prophecy, or forty-nine years, the city was rebuilt "even in times of distress" (Daniel 9:25). Nehemiah experienced some of those times in Jerusalem himself as his enemies first taunted him and then tried to kill him.

The Prophecy's Messiah

The next distinct segment in the seventy weeks is the sixty-two weeks from the time of Jerusalem's restoration until the appearance of Messiah. Altogether, then, the angel said we are to count off sixty-nine weeks, or 483 years, from the decree concerning Jerusalem to Messiah.

Now we're ready for Daniel 9:26, the next piece of the prophecy. "Then after the sixty-two weeks the Messiah will be cut off and have nothing, and the people of the prince who is to come will destroy the city and the sanctuary. And its end will come with a flood; even to the end there will be war; desolations are determined."

This is where we see a clear break between the end of the sixty-ninth week and the beginning of the seventieth week. Messiah's cutting off was a prophecy of Jesus Christ's death on the cross, after which Jerusalem would suffer another destruction by a different people.

The "prince who is to come" is a reference to the Antichrist, the final world ruler who will reign over a restored Roman Empire. This is the "little horn" (Daniel 7:8) who seizes world power. Therefore, the "people of the prince" has to be referring to the Romans, who did in fact come against Jerusalem and so completely destroy the city and the temple in A.D. 70 that there wasn't even one stone left on another, as Jesus Himself prophesied (see Matthew 24:2).

The Prophecy's Accuracy

The key to plugging Daniel's prophecy into history is to know that he was writing about prophetic years, which are different from our calendar years. Whenever the Bible speaks of prophecy, it measures time in prophetic years, which are thirty days a month for twelve months, for a total of 360 days a year. This concept of the 360-day prophetic year is arrived at by comparing the last half of Daniel's seventieth week (Daniel 9:27b), which is three-and-a-half years, with the 1,260 days of Revelation 11:3 and 12:6 and the forty-two months of Revelation 11:2 and 13:5. The number of days works out to thirty days a month, or 360 days a year. Using this figure of 360 days per year, multiplied by the 483 years of Daniel's first sixty-nine weeks, gives us a total of 173,880 days. This is the length of time from the decree to rebuild Jerusalem in 444 B.C. to Messiah being cut off.

Many Bible students have done the calculations, which show that this length of time brings us from 444 B.C. to March A.D. 33, the month in which Jesus was crucified. So at the end of the sixty-ninth week as prophesied in Daniel 9:26, the Messiah was cut off. Jesus was crucified, and He had nothing. He was a King, but He had no earthly kingdom.

After Christ's death, the clock stopped ticking on Daniel's prophecy. The nation of Israel entered a time of parenthesis that actually continues until this day, and will continue until the tribulation, a seven-year period that will constitute Daniel's seventieth week.

Just before His crucifixion, Jesus said, "Jerusalem, Jerusalem, who kills the prophets and stones those who are sent to her! How often I wanted to gather your children together, the way a hen gathers her chicks under her wings, and you were unwilling. Behold, your house is being left to you desolate!" (Matthew 23:37–38).

Then in Matthew 24:2, Jesus prophesied the destruction of Jerusalem and the temple that occurred in A.D. 70 under the Roman general Titus. Speaking of the temple, Jesus said, "Do you not see all these things? Truly I say to you, not one stone here will be left upon another, which will not be torn down."

The Prophecy's Gap

One series of sevens, the seventieth week, stands out as distinct in the prophecy of Daniel 9. The prophet marks a clear division between the first sixty-nine weeks and the seventieth week, but what Daniel didn't reveal is the nature or the length of the gap separating the sixty-ninth and seventieth weeks. We have to turn to the New Testament for that information.

When Jesus told His disciples, "I will build My church" (Matthew 16:18), He was announcing the start of a new program in God's plan of the ages. What we learn is that the final week of Israel's prophetic program was being put on hold. The clock has stopped for Israel, and God's primary focus will now be upon the building of a new entity called the church.

The church is different from national Israel because the church is made up of Jews and Gentiles, coming together to form one new body called the body of Christ (Ephesians 2:11–22). God hasn't ceased His program with Israel, but because Israel did not repent and receive its Messiah, the nation was put on the sidelines, prophetically speaking.

God called a "time-out" on Israel for a period of time called the church age. So far, that time-out has lasted for nearly two thousand years, and it continues for Israel today.

DANIEL'S SEVENTIETH WEEK

Now let's go back to Daniel 9 and finish the prophecy of the seventy weeks:

> And he will make a firm covenant with the many for one week, but in the middle of the week he will put a stop to sacrifice and grain offering; and on the wing of abominations will come one who makes desolate, even until a complete destruction, one that is decreed, is poured out on the one who makes desolate. (v. 27)

The Israelites were restored to their land after the captivity, but the people did not really repent. Jesus Christ came preaching this message: "Repent, for the kingdom of heaven is at hand" (Matthew 4:17). But instead of receiving their Messiah, the nation rejected Him and cut Him off. They put Christ to death on the cross. The crucifixion marked the end of Daniel's sixty-ninth week and stopped the clock on Israel's prophetic program.

Starting the Clock Again

That clock will start ticking again during the seven-year period known as the tribulation, as we said above. During this yet-future period, God will complete His program with Israel to bring the nation to repentance, cleanse her of her sin, fulfill His promises, and accomplish all the other things the angel outlined in Daniel 9:24.

A Covenant Made and Broken

So Israel is out of the spotlight in God's program until Daniel's seventieth week. This week will begin when he "make[s] a firm covenant with the many for one week" (Daniel 9:27), that is, for seven years.

The person making this covenant is the "prince who is to come" (Daniel 9:26). We saw above that this is the Antichrist, making a covenant of peace with Israel. This marks the beginning of the tribulation, when God resumes His program with Israel.

But according to Daniel 9:27, this leader will break the covenant at the halfway point. In Revelation 11:1, the apostle John was told to measure the temple of God in Jerusalem. This is the temple that apparently will be built during the tribulation period. The Jews will again be offering sacrifices during the first half of this seven-year period.

But when the Antichrist breaks his covenant, Daniel says the sacrifices will stop. Daniel's prophecy anticipates the temple John saw in his vision because the Bible is perfectly consistent with itself.

John was told to measure the temple, but not the "court," which is the court of the Gentiles. Why was John told not to measure this part? Because "it has been given to the nations; and they will tread under foot the holy city for forty-two months" (Revelation 11:2). That's three-and-one-half years, the second half of Israel's seventieth week.

When the Antichrist first comes on the scene, everybody is going to be excited because, finally, there will be peace in the Middle East. But halfway through the covenant Antichrist is going to reveal himself for who he really is.

His real identity is terrible because Daniel 9:27 says he will come "on the wing of abominations." The Antichrist will set himself up as god in Israel's temple. Anyone who doesn't acknowledge and worship him by having the number 666, the mark of the Beast, imprinted on his forehead or right hand will be subject to persecution and death. The only reason people would refuse that number is because they believe in Jesus Christ.

GOD IS IN CONTROL

But if Daniel's prophecy of the seventy weeks tells us anything, it's that God has this whole thing under control. His prophetic program is timed so exactly that He can pinpoint the arrival of Jesus Christ and His crucifixion down to the day.

If I were the Devil, I'd quit fighting. Since the Devil can read, he may think he's got the program scoped out, but God doesn't reveal all of His plans. So even when the Devil makes a move that seems to thwart God's plan, God makes a countermove that messes up Satan's plan!

PERSONAL APPLICATION FOR LIFE

1. Occasionally, we need to be reminded that this world is not our final home, that we're laboring for something far better. As we wait for Christ's return, Hebrews 10:23 give us this encouragement: "Let us hold fast the confession of our hope without wavering, for He who promised is faithful." God is always true to His word. Are you remaining faithful to Him?

2. Waiting for Christ's return is not something we sit still waiting for. We must be up and about the Lord's business. Don't be so inactive that you allow yourself to get stagnant spiritually. If your love for Christ seems stagnant right now, you can bring it back to sparkling beauty. A wonderful cleansing agent for a stagnant heart is the blood of Christ. Ask the Holy Spirit to search your heart and cleanse it from any sin you might be harboring.

3. One thing we can observe with God's prophetic plan is that He is a patient God. Over and over He gives people and nations the opportunity to repent. Isn't it like our Lord to give the opportunity to repent and come back to Him of our own accord? If you have a need concerning repentance, don't delay. Deal with it now!

4. One day every knee will bow to Jesus. What a privilege we have to worship Him as our Lord and Savior now. When we worship God, we must prepare ourselves for worship by coming before the Lord with a clean heart, one that has been "sprinkled clean from an evil conscience" (Hebrews 10:22). If you have sin in your heart, confess it and come clean!

FOR GROUP STUDY

Questions for Group Discussion

1. Discuss the prophecy of Israel's timetable found in Daniel 9:24–27. Why is it a "hub" of the prophetic wheel?

2. Read Daniel 9:2 and Jeremiah 25:11–12. What was Daniel's discovery? What was Daniel's response to it?

3. Discuss the prophecy of the seventy weeks in Daniel 9. What are the specifics of this prophecy? When does it begin? When does it end? What do we know about its accuracy?

4. Read Daniel 9:27. What are the key events of the seventieth week? What do the accuracy and the timing of this prophecy convey to us?

PICTURE THIS

In Daniel 9:24-27, we see Daniels' prophecy of the seventy weeks. The prophecy culminates in the seventieth week with several key prophetic events. Below is a snapshot of these events as revealed in Daniel 9:27.

THE KEY EVENTS OF DANIELS' SEVENTIETH WEEK

Daniel 9:27

EVENT	ITS SIGNIFICANCE
Restarting of the prophetic clock	The clock resumes ticking with the advent of the tribulation.
The Antichrist's covenant	The Antichrist will make a covenant of peace with Israel.
The breaking of the covenant	Halfway through the week, the Antichrist breaks the covenant with Israel and reveals his true identity.

SECTION II

End Times Prophecy

108. PROPHECY AND THE CHURCH

109. PROPHECY AND THE RAPTURE

110. PROPHECY AND THE JUDGMENT SEAT OF CHRIST

108

PROPHECY AND THE CHURCH

When Israel rejected and crucified its Messiah in fulfillment of Daniel's sixty-ninth week, God hit the clock for Israel and stopped the movement of the nation's prophetic program.

But when God stopped the clock on Israel, He started the prophetic clock ticking for the Gentile world—and it's still running. The times of the Gentiles began with Israel's desolation in the sixty-ninth week when Jesus the Messiah was cut off, and they will continue until the tribulation. At that time, God will start the clock for Israel again and Daniel's seventieth week will unfold in the great tribulation.

What has God been doing since He stopped one prophetic clock and started another one? The primary thing He has been doing is building the church of Jesus Christ, a brand-new entity made up of Jews and Gentiles.

THE REJECTION OF ISRAEL

When Jesus Christ was ready to begin His ministry, John the Baptist came on the scene proclaiming, "Repent, for the kingdom of heaven is at hand" (Matthew 3:2) in fulfillment of Old Testament prophecy (Isaiah 40:3–5; Malachi 3:1).

In other words, the kingdom promised to Israel in the Old Testament was ready to be handed over because the King had arrived. Everything Israel had been hoping for, looking for, and longing for was within the nation's reach.

Announcing the Kingdom

Jesus Himself began His ministry by proclaiming the same message. "Repent, for the kingdom of heaven is at hand" (Matthew 4:17). The kingdom was being offered to Israel, but the condition was repentance.

Jesus' announcement of the kingdom was even more explicit in the familiar scene of Luke 4, in which Jesus went back to His hometown of Nazareth and attended the synagogue on the Sabbath. It was customary to allow a visiting rabbi to read the Scripture and speak, so the book of Isaiah was handed to Jesus (Luke 4:16–17). This is what He read from Isaiah 61:1–2:

> The Spirit of the Lord is upon Me, because He anointed Me to preach the gospel to the poor. He has sent Me to proclaim release to the captives, and recovery of sight to the blind, to set free those who are oppressed, to proclaim the favorable year of the Lord. (Luke 4:18–19)

The "favorable year of the Lord" was the Year of Jubilee. It was a time when God would make society right (Leviticus 25:8–55). In the Year of Jubilee, Israel would begin to live out its God-ordained purpose. But the people could not enjoy Jubilee until they had first celebrated the Day of Atonement (v. 9), in which their sins were atoned for. Atonement involved repentance for sin, but Israel in Jesus' day wanted the societal benefits of Jubilee without repentance and acceptance of Jesus as their Messiah.

Validating the King

Back in Luke 4, Jesus closed the book after reading this passage and sat down in the synagogue at Nazareth. Then, with every eye riveted on Him, Jesus announced, "Today this Scripture has been fulfilled in your hearing" (vv. 20–21). This was stunning, because Jesus was saying, "Messiah is here with you today. I am the One you have been waiting for."

Everyone thought Jesus was doing well until He said that. Then they said,

"Wait a minute, this is Joseph's son. We know Him. He's claiming to be Messiah." They got so mad they tried to throw Jesus off a cliff (see vv. 28–29).

But Jesus had the right to make this claim. His miracles were validation to Israel of His messianic claims. That's why on several occasions Jesus told people He had healed to show themselves to the priest (Luke 5:14; 17:14). It was a testimony to the nation's leaders that Jesus was, in fact, the Messiah.

Rejecting the King

But those leaders rejected Jesus in a dramatic way after He performed a miracle by healing a demon-possessed man who was blind and mute (Matthew 12:22). The crowd saw the miracle and began asking in amazement, "This man cannot be the Son of David, can he?" (v. 23). In other words, Could Jesus be the Messiah?

Jesus answered by saying that if the Jewish leaders admitted He did His work by the power of God, they would have to admit that He was the Messiah. But since they didn't want to admit that, they were willing to accuse Jesus of acting by Satan's power (vv. 25–28). These men rejected what their own eyes had seen, which led them to commit the so-called unpardonable sin (vv. 31–32).

This was determined rejection. In the face of truth, when there was no way of denying what they had seen, this group of Israel's leaders rejected the light that was thrust upon them.

Crucifying the King

Jesus' rejection by the nation of Israel led ultimately to His crucifixion. Jesus foresaw this, of course, and with the cross ahead, He told "the chief priests and the elders of the people" (Matthew 21:23) a series of parables illustrating their rejection.

At one point, Jesus said, "Did you never read in the Scriptures, 'The stone which the builders rejected, this became the chief corner stone; this came about from the Lord, and it is marvelous in our eyes'? Therefore I say to you, the kingdom of God will be taken away from you and given to a nation producing the fruit of it" (vv. 42–43).

Scripture is clear that the Jews weren't the only people who crucified Jesus (Acts 4:26–28). When it comes to our sin, all of us are guilty of nailing Him to the cross. But Israel's rejection was especially significant, and because of it God was going to temporarily remove the kingdom from them.

THE FORMATION OF THE CHURCH

We've spent a lot of time on the subject of Israel's rejection because it is so important as the background for the formation of the church. We'll spend the rest of the chapter unfolding the church's place in God's prophetic program.

Announcing the Church

To find the first mention of the church, we have to turn back to Matthew 16:13–19. Jesus Christ went to Caesarea Philippi with His disciples and asked them what people were saying about Him.

After hearing the disciples' answers, Jesus asked, "But who do you say that I am?" Peter gave the right answer. "You are the Christ, the Son of the living God" (vv. 15–16). The truth Peter spoke led to a new prophecy from Jesus. "I also say to you that you are Peter, and upon this rock I will build My church; and the gates of Hades will not overpower it" (v. 18).

In this verse, Jesus announced for the first time the new plan of God that would unfold because of Israel's rejection. God was going to take a detour around Israel's unbelief, because He will never allow man's rebellion to thwart His kingdom program.

The church is a brand-new entity that had never existed before. The church is different from Israel because a person was an Israelite by virtue of physical birth and religious heritage. The Jews are a physical race of people. But the church is made up of people from all races who belong to Jesus Christ.

Access to Heaven

In Matthew 16:19, Jesus said, "I will give you the keys of the kingdom of heaven; and whatever you shall bind on earth shall be bound in heaven, and whatever you shall loose on earth shall be loosed in heaven."

Keys give access, and the church has the keys to the kingdom—which means access to God's program—because Israel refused the kingdom. The church is now the entity in history that has access to God, that can unlock heaven's doors. Those who refuse to accept Christ have no access to heaven. Only the church has the keys to God's kingdom.

The Church and Israel

This raises a question of the relationship between the church and Israel during this period called the church age when the prophetic clock has been stopped for Israel. Paul dealt with this important question in Romans 11:15–18, using the illustration of an olive tree.

The olive tree is God's program or blessings. Israel was the natural branch because it was the first to enjoy God's blessings through Abraham. But Israel's branch was cut off due to unbelief, and the Gentiles were grafted in as a new branch. This new branch is the church, made up of Jews and Gentiles who have come to Christ and are brought together in a new body (Ephesians 2:11–14).

Even though most believers today are not Jewish, we are enjoying the blessings of the Abrahamic covenant because God told Abraham, "In you all the families of the earth shall be blessed" (Genesis 12:3). God promised to bless the whole world through Abraham. But now instead of bringing the blessing through Israel, He is doing it through the church.

Israel's Temporary Rejection

Paul explained that Israel's unbelief is not permanent. "For I do not want you, brethren, to be uninformed of this mystery—so that you will not be wise in your own estimation—that a partial hardening has happened to Israel until the fullness of the Gentiles has come in; and so all Israel will be saved" (Romans 11:25–26a).

In the Bible, a mystery is something that wasn't understood in the past, but is now revealed. The mystery Paul wanted the church to understand is that Israel's unbelief is temporary. He has not completely rejected His chosen people. Once the full number of Gentiles "has come in," or is born, God will bring Israel to Himself.

Israel was supposed to be the light of the world to bring the Gentiles to faith in God. But when Israel failed its mission, God set the nation aside and is now using the church to reach the world until all the Gentiles God has ordained to be born are born.

The Gentiles are an integral part of God's creative purpose and occupy a specific place in His program. Therefore, when God's purpose for the Gentiles has been accomplished, the curtain will close on the Gentile era in God's program (Romans 11:25). At that time, Israel will once again occupy center stage in the prophetic drama of the ages. And even though the rapture of the church will usher in a time of terrible suffering and persecution for Israel, God is going to turn the hearts of His chosen people to Christ. Then "all Israel will be saved."

So Israel and the church are related, even though they are distinct entities in God's program. They are both part of God's olive tree. Israel's unbelief and rejection of Christ is a temporary situation. God is not finished with Israel.

THE ILLUSTRATIONS OF THE CHURCH

Besides talking about the church's relationship to Israel and its formation by Jesus Christ, recall several of the key figures the Bible uses to describe Christ and, by extension, His church. Let's summarize seven, which are detailed in chapter 20 (pages 256–65)

The Head of the Body and the Author of Creation

Jesus Christ is the *head*, the one who provides direction and guidance to the church, His body (Ephesians 1:22–23; 2:16; 4:15–16). He is also the *author* of the new creation called the church (Ephesians 2:10, 15; Hebrews 12:2). That's us; believers who come to Christ in salvation are made new creations in Christ (2 Corinthians 5:17) and are joined with each other in Christ's body.

The Shepherd, the Vine, and the Cornerstone

Jesus Christ Himself said that He is *the Shepherd* of His sheep (John 10:11). He provides for and protects his sheep.

Christ also is *the vine*: "I am the vine, you are the branches; he who abides in Me and I in him, he bears much fruit; for apart from Me you can do nothing" (John 15:5). That's why Jesus says we can do nothing without Him.

Jesus Christ is also "the *cornerstone* [of the church], in whom the whole building, being fitted together, is growing into a holy temple in the Lord," in whom you also are being built together into a dwelling of God in the Spirit" (Ephesians 2:20–21; see also 1 Peter 2:6). The cornerstone was the most important stone in a building in New Testament days because it was the stone on which all the other stones were aligned. The church must be properly aligned with Christ if it is to be a solid citadel for the kingdom.

The High Priest

Jesus Christ is also *the High Priest* of the church (see Hebrews 4:14–16), the one who represents us before God. Just as the Israelites couldn't just come into the presence of God without a priest opening the way by offering sacrifices, Christians still need a *High Priest*, because if Jesus' blood didn't keep on working we could lose our salvation. I believe in the security of believers, but our security is based on the fact that Jesus is "a high priest forever" (Hebrews 6:20).

The Bridegroom

The final figure is the one that is the most future oriented. The Bible says that Jesus Christ and the church are the Bridegroom and his bride.

Paul said in Ephesians 5:25–27, "Husbands, love your wives, just as Christ also loved the church and gave Himself up for her; so that He might sanctify her, having cleansed her by the washing of water with the word, that He might present to Himself the church in all her glory, having no spot or wrinkle or any such thing."

Jesus is the purifier of the church. He is getting His bride ready for her wedding day, the marriage supper of the Lamb. Right now we are in the betrothal period, the engagement, waiting for the Bridegroom to return for His bride.

THE FUTURE OF THE CHURCH

I want to close this chapter with a brief preview of the church's future, which is all glorious.

Jesus said at the Last Supper, "Little children, I am with you a little while longer. You shall seek Me; and as I said to the Jews, I now also say to you, 'Where I am going, you cannot come'" (John 13:33). Christ knew the disciples were deeply troubled. They had staked their whole lives on Him. So He immediately gave them a promise of His return.

The Rapture

That promise is found in John 14:1–3. Jesus said He was going away to prepare a dwelling place for His people and that He would come back for them so they would be with Him forever.

We know this promise to be the rapture of the church. When Jesus Christ has finished preparing His bride the church for her wedding day, He is coming to take her to the greatest wedding party anyone has ever seen. (More on this rapture in the next chapter.)

The Reception

Jesus Christ is making ready a magnificent wedding reception for His bride. It's called the millennial kingdom, and it's going to be a one-thousand-year-long party. We are going to rule by Christ's side in His kingdom as His bride.

This is the church's future, and it is all given to us in prophecy so we can look forward to it and serve and love Christ faithfully here on earth in preparation for it.

And when the kingdom is completed, then Christ will hand the kingdom over to the Father (1 Corinthians 15:24), and we will enjoy eternity in the presence of God. If you are a child of God, you have a lot of good stuff coming your way as God's prophetic program unfolds.

PERSONAL APPLICATION FOR LIFE

1. As an illustration of Christ and His church, John15:5 refers to Jesus as the Vine. Of course, the purpose of a vine is to provide nourishment and life to its branches that they may produce fruit. When you are fruitful, you impact others for Christ. To put it another way, you produce fruit so that somebody else can take a bite of you and be blessed. Are you a fruit-producing branch?

2. Take a moment to go through the list of the fruit of the Spirit in Galatians 5:22–23, and chances are that one of these qualities will leap out at you as something you need in a special way right now. Take your need for that fruit to the God in prayer, telling Him how much you want to see Him produce it in your life. Then be ready for the Holy Spirit to deal with whatever He needs to in order to prepare the soil of your heart for that fruit.

3. As believers, we are all part of the body of Christ. Because the Spirit has given His people a new unity, we are called to treat one another as equals in the body. This can be a tough one, because old attitudes are hard to root out. Search your heart, and if the Spirit points out a need or a blind spot in this area, claim His power and authority to deal with it.

4. You need to be in fellowship with other believers in a local church. If you are in a church where the Bible is taught and Christ is honored, thank God for this blessing–and pray regularly for your pastor and other church leaders. If you are not part of a fellowship of believers, ask God to lead you to a church where you can worship Him in spirit and truth.

FOR GROUP STUDY

Questions for Group Discussion

1. Israel's rejection of Jesus Christ as King was not a single event, but the culmination of a series of events. Discuss the path of Israel's rejection of Jesus, ending in His crucifixion. Why did Israel reject Jesus?

2. Read Matthew 16:13–19. What is the church's place in God prophetic program? Why did the apostle Paul refer to the church as a "mystery"? (See Ephesians 3:3–11 and Colossians 1:26–27.) Use the chart on the next page as an aid to your discussion.)

3. Read Romans 11:15–18. What is the relationship between the church and Israel during this period we call the "church age"?

4. Discuss the various illustrations and figures we find in the New Testament for Christ and His church. Read Ephesians 5:25–27. How does the church as the bride fit into God's future prophetic plans?

PICTURE THIS

Israel's unbelief and rejection of Jesus as the Messiah required a twist in God's plan—which only God could foresee—the church. The apostle Paul described it as a hidden "mystery." God would not allow man's rebellion to thwart His kingdom program, and so unfolded His plan for the church. Below are a few of the key events associated with the church's place in God's prophetic program.

THE CHURCH IN GOD'S PROPHETIC PROGRAM

KEY EVENT	SCRIPTURE PASSAGES	ITS SIGNIFICANCE
The church announced	Matthew 16:13–18	Jesus first announced the church to His disciples.
The church's access to heaven	Matthew 16:19	Because of its belief, Jesus has given the church access to God and His programs.
The relationship of the church and Israel	Romans 11:15–18; Ephesians 2:11–14; Genesis 12:3	Because of Israel's unbelief, only the church is currently enjoying the blessings of the Abrahamic covenant.
Israel's temporary rejection	Romans 11:25–26a	Israel's period of rejection will end. Israel and the church both occupy a specific place in God's program.

109

PROPHECY AND THE RAPTURE

The rapture is the next event in God's prophetic program, as we fast-forward to the end of the church age. The term *rapture* comes from the Latin word for the Greek term translated "caught up" in 1 Thessalonians 4:17. We'll deal with this central passage as we unfold the doctrine of Christ's return in the air to take His bride, the church, home for the wedding.

THE IMPORTANCE OF THE RAPTURE

In the Upper Room the night before He was crucified, Jesus announced to His disciples that He was going to leave them. This threw them into consternation and fear, so Jesus gave them the reassuring promise of John 14:1–3, which concludes, "If I go and prepare a place for you, I will come again and receive you to Myself, that where I am, there you may be also."

This is the first clear reference to the return of Jesus for His own, the event described in 1 Thessalonians 4:13–18 that we call the rapture. The fact of Jesus' prophetic promise, and the conditions under which He made it, make the rapture a very important teaching for the church.

A Reason to Be Secure

One reason the rapture is so important is that the expectation of Christ's return means we don't have to be troubled (John 14:1).

We have a secure future in Christ even though we have to face troubling times, troubling situations, and troubling people. We can be calm in the face of trouble because Jesus Christ is coming back for His bride, and we'll be with Him forever.

The Answer to Jesus' Prayer

The rapture is also an important part of biblical prophecy because it is the answer to Jesus' prayer in John 17:24: "Father, I desire that they also, whom You have given Me, be with Me where I am, so that they may see My glory."

Jesus asked His Father to make arrangements so that those whom the Father had given to the Son—His bride the church—could live with Christ. Jesus is going to claim His bride at the rapture. We will be the first to be with Him because the rapture will occur before the end time events we have been studying.

Hope in the Face of Death

A third reason the rapture is important takes us to 1 Thessalonians 4:13–18, the key passage on this concept. Notice the purpose for which God gave the revelation of the rapture: "Therefore comfort one another with these words" (v. 18; see also 1 Thessalonians 5:11).

The truth of the rapture is designed to bring hope at what would otherwise be the most hopeless moment in life, when someone you love is taken into eternity.

A Glorious Future

First Thessalonians 4 was written in response to a concern these Christians had in relation to those who had died. One reason the Thessalonians were unclear about this question is that Paul was only able to spend a short time in Thessalonica (Acts 17:1–9). Paul's preaching caused quite a stir, and he had to leave town after a few weeks because the Jews were very upset that he was preaching Jesus Christ.

That's why Paul started this section by saying, "But we do not want you to be uninformed, brethren, about those who are asleep, so that you will not grieve as do the rest who have no hope" (1 Thessalonians 4:13). Paul wanted the Thessalonians to understand what God had in store for them. A glorious future awaits for those loved ones who have "fallen asleep in Jesus (v. 14)—and all of us know Jesus and are alive when Christ returns.

CHRIST'S RETURN FOR HIS CHURCH

Now that we have seen something of the importance this doctrine holds for us, let's dig a little deeper into 1 Thessalonians 4 and find out what's involved in the rapture of the church.

No Reason for Confusion

We don't want to get the rapture confused with what is usually called the second coming of Christ, which will occur at the end of the tribulation as He comes to earth to set up His kingdom.

There are a number of differences between these two appearances. At the rapture, Christ comes in the air, and believers rise to meet Him and go back to heaven. There is also a resurrection of the dead.

At His second coming, Christ rides out of heaven on a white horse with an army following Him, and He comes to the earth to judge, make war, and overthrow all earthly powers. He then rules for a thousand years from His throne in Jerusalem, and no resurrection occurs at the moment of His coming. The rapture and second coming are different events.

No Reason to Fear Death

If you asked people whether they feared death, most would probably say they do. It's a natural human fear. Paul calls death "the last enemy" (1 Corinthians 15:26). But for Christians, death is a defeated enemy, so for us to be gripped by the fear of death is irrational.

That's what the Bible teaches, because "to be absent from the body" is "to be at home with the Lord" (2 Corinthians 5:8). That's why the Bible calls death "sleep" for believers. Death is not the cessation of existence. The moment a Christian dies, that person's spirit leaves the body and is immediately with the Lord. If you know Christ, before the doctor has a chance to pronounce you dead, you will be in the Lord's presence. You will not experience death for even one portion of a second, as we will see later.

No Reason to Doubt the Word

Paul wanted the Thessalonians to know that what he was telling them was authoritative revelation from God: "For this we say to you by the word of the Lord" (1 Thessalonians 4:15).

The reason Paul said this is that the rapture was not prophesied in the Old Testament. It is truth for the church age, which the Old Testament prophets did not foresee clearly or write about in detail. But the word of the Lord was just as authoritative through Paul as it was through the prophets, and the Thessalonians could bank on it.

THE REUNION AT THE RAPTURE

The truth Paul was about to reveal was the order of events in the rapture and the fact that, when it was all over, believers both dead and alive would be reunited with each other and with the Lord.

Remember, the problem here was the Thessalonians' distress over friends and family members who had died. So the good news Paul had to bring was that there is going to be a reunion for Christians someday. He continued:

> We who are alive, and remain until the coming of the Lord, shall not precede those who have fallen asleep. For the Lord Himself will descend from heaven with a shout, with the voice of the archangel, and with the trumpet of God; and the dead in Christ shall rise first. (1 Thessalonians 4:15b–16)

Not only do dead believers not miss out on the rapture, they get a head start on everybody else!

The Call to the Reunion

Three distinct steps, or events, are mentioned here that signal the arrival of the rapture.

The "shout" was a military command from an army officer, giving instructions on what should be done. What will the Lord's shout at the rapture do? The best way to answer this is by looking at an actual biblical event in which Jesus shouted for a dead person to come alive. The incident is the resurrection of Lazarus of Bethany in John 11.

Jesus' dear friend Lazarus had died, but Jesus came to Bethany four days later to do something about it. After they had removed the gravestone, Jesus prayed and then "cried out with a loud voice, 'Lazarus, come forth.' The man who had died came forth, bound hand and foot with wrappings, and his face was wrapped around with a cloth. Jesus said to them, 'Unbind him, and let him go'" (John 11:43–44).

The second event Paul revealed in 1 Thessalonians 4:16 is the "voice of the archangel." Michael is the only archangel specifically mentioned in the Bible. What does he have to do with this?

Well, "archangel" means the chief angel, the one in charge. Satan was the original chief angel in heaven when he was named Lucifer. But when he rebelled against God and was judged, Michael was apparently promoted and given the post.

So throughout the Bible we read of conflict between Michael and Satan at key points in biblical history (see Daniel 10:13, 21; Jude 9; Revelation 12:7–9). Michael as the head of the righteous angels seeks to carry out the will of God, and Satan as the head of the unrighteous angels seeks to stop God's will.

Michael is going to be on the scene with Christ at the rapture. When Jesus issues the command for the resurrection, Michael is going to tell his righteous angels, "You heard what the Lord said. Go get those dead believers and escort them through Satan's territory to heaven."

Then we have the third event in the rapture, the sounding of "the trumpet of God" (1 Thessalonians 4:16). In the Bible a trumpet was used for two reasons, to call the people either to worship or to war. This trumpet call is to both.

It's a call to worship because once we get to heaven our occupation for eternity will be worshiping God. But the trumpet of God is also a call to war because we will come back with Him at the battle of Armageddon, when the armies of heaven will ride out with Jesus in the lead (Revelation 19:11–16).

I don't know exactly how the shout, the voice of the archangel, and the trumpet will occur, whether they happen in order or all at once. But they summon us to the reunion: "The dead in Christ will rise first. Then we who are alive and remain will be caught up together with them in the clouds to meet the Lord in the air, and so we shall always be with the Lord" (1 Thessalonians 4:16b–17).

Our New Bodies

Being caught up, or raptured, and meeting Jesus in the clouds won't be a problem for our resurrected bodies, since they will be like Jesus'. This issue of the resurrection usually raises the question of what our new bodies will be like.

You will still fundamentally look the way you look now, except without any flaws. The Bible also indicates that we will retain our racial and ethnic identities in heaven. John said he saw in heaven "a great multitude . . . from every nation and all tribes and peoples and tongues" (Revelation 7:9). The similarity between our earthly and heavenly bodies is also seen in Mary's reaction to Jesus at the tomb after His resurrection. At first she thought Jesus was the gardener (John 20:15), which may have happened because it was still somewhat dark. But as soon as He spoke to her, she recognized Him (v. 16). Jesus' voice was the same as it was before He was raised.

Together Forever

The last phrase of 1 Thessalonians 4:17 is the crowning jewel in the joyful event called the rapture: "Thus we shall always be with the Lord." All believers, living and dead, will be reunited with Christ and with one another. And we will never be separated from Him, or from each other, again.

No wonder Paul said in closing this section, "Comfort one another with these words" (v. 18). It's comforting to know that we will never really die. If our physical body dies before Christ returns, the people visiting us at the funeral home may think we are dead. But we won't be there. We'll be with the Lord!

THE TIME OF THE RAPTURE

Let me say a closing word about the time of the rapture. By this I mean when it will occur in the unfolding of God's prophetic plan.

Three Basic Views

There are three basic views on the timing of the rapture. Some believe it will occur before the tribulation and mark the beginning of this prophesied seven-year period. Others believe the rapture will come at the midpoint of the tribulation, just as the Antichrist breaks his peace treaty with Israel, eradicates religion and demands to be worshiped as God, and all hell breaks loose on earth. The third position is that the church will have to go through the tribulation, but will be supernaturally protected during that time and raptured at the end of the tribulation.

These three positions are logically known as pre-, mid-, and posttribulationalism. I am a pretribulationalist because I believe the Bible teaches that Christ is coming for His church prior to the beginning of the tribulation.

Jesus' Promise to the Church

This is the promise Jesus made to the faithful church of Philadelphia, which is representative of the true church in all ages. The Lord said in Revelation 3:10, "Because you have kept the word of My perseverance, I also will keep you from the hour of testing, that hour which is about to come upon the whole world, to test those who dwell upon the earth."

The "hour of testing" is the tribulation. Jesus used this terminology to describe the tribulation because He was saying the church is going to be kept from the very time frame in which the tribulation will occur.

To be kept "from," or "out of," a situation is different than being kept "through" it. The preposition translated "from" in Revelation 3:10 suggests the church will not be around when the tribulation breaks loose.

The Church in Heaven

It's also worth noting that immediately after this promise, Revelation 4 begins describing the time of God's final judgment on earth. But the church is nowhere to be found amid all the horrors that a righteous God is going to unleash on a sinful earth and the people who dwell on it.

The best explanation for the church's absence from Revelation 4 until the kingdom and the marriage supper of the Lamb in Revelation 20–21 is that the church will be raptured before the tribulation begins.

The Bible also promises that as God's people, we will be delivered "from the wrath to come" (1 Thessalonians 1:10). God's wrath here is not only hell, but the tribulation period. Later in 1 Thessalonians, Paul said, "The day of the Lord [the day of God's judgment in the tribulation] will come just like a thief in the night" (5:2). But then Paul said to the church, "But you, brethren, are not in darkness, that the day would overtake you like a thief" (v. 4). And finally we have this promise: "For God has not destined us for wrath, but for obtaining salvation through our Lord Jesus Christ" (v. 9).

The Revelation of the Antichrist

Let me offer another proof for the pretribulational position. When Paul wrote 2 Thessalonians, the believers there were all shook up again, this time because false teachers there were saying the day of the Lord had already started (2 Thessalonians 2:1–2). But Paul said:

> Let no one in any way deceive you, for it will not come unless the apostasy comes first, and the man of lawlessness is revealed, the son of destruction, who opposes and exalts himself above every so-called god or object of worship, so that he takes his seat in the temple of God, displaying himself as being God. . . . And you know what restrains him now, so that in his time he may be revealed. For the mystery of lawlessness is already at work; only he who now restrains will do so until he is taken out of the way. And then that lawless one will be revealed. (vv. 3–4, 6–8a)

The Thessalonians were rattled because if the tribulation had begun, that meant they had been left behind in the rapture. But Paul set their end times theology straight, and in the process made clear the order of events.

The tribulation will not begin until the Antichrist, who is described so vividly in these verses, is revealed. And he won't be revealed until the restrainer, the Holy Spirit, is taken off the earth.

Follow the reasoning here. The Holy Spirit dwells in the church. He came at Pentecost to take up His residence in the body of believers who make up the church. In fact, it is Holy Spirit baptism that marks a person as a member of Christ's body the church (1 Corinthians 12:13).

So if the tribulation doesn't begin until the Antichrist is revealed, and if he won't be revealed until after the Holy Spirit leaves, guess who leaves when the Spirit leaves? The church!

PERSONAL APPLICATION FOR LIFE

1. The knowledge of Christ's return should motivate us to serve Him fully and faithfully. It should lead to holiness of life on our part. We don't know when Christ will return, but Scripture tells us it is soon. When Christ comes, will He find you busy doing His work?

2. According to Colossians 2:17, those things that are a mere shadow of what is to come found their substance in Christ. The writer of the book of Hebrews spoke of the "better things" of Christ. Among the many better things we have is a better covenant, a better hope, and a better salvation. Take on a special confidence in your walk of faith, allowing the promises of God's Word to anchor your hope and shape your future in Christ.

3. Wouldn't it be great to live in that spiritual realm where the gravitational pull of sin doesn't work against you? Well, when Jesus returns for His church, we will experience such a realm, free from the effects of sin. For the present, the Spirit can take you there. He already lives within you. All He's waiting for is your cooperation. If you have any sin in your life pulling you down, confess it right now and claim Christ's cleansing (1 John 1:9). The Spirit will reveal any such sin to you if you'll ask Him to search your heart.

4. We can read about Christ in prophecy and see the many ways the prophetic Word about Christ was fulfilled in His first coming. Do you also have confidence in the prophecies about His second coming and glorious rule? (See Daniel 7:14; 1 Peter 1:10–11.) Not only is our future shaped by God's prophetic promises, it is also rooted in past salvation. If we learn anything from God's past dealings with His people, it is that He is always true to His Word. Ask God to help you live confidently and victoriously now in view of His second coming.

FOR GROUP STUDY

Questions for Group Discussion

1. Read John 14:1–3 and 1 Thessalonians 4:13–18. What is the doctrine of the rapture? Why did Jesus give this teaching to His disciples? Where does it fit into God's prophetic plan?

2. What does 1 Corinthians 15 teach about our resurrection bodies? Discuss the apostle Paul's illustration in verses 35–38.

3. Read 1 Thessalonians 4:15b–16. What three distinct steps or events does this passage mention regarding the rapture?

4. Discus the three basic views of when the rapture will occur. What does the promise of Revelation 3:10 teach us?

PICTURE THIS

In 1 Thessalonians 4:15b–17, the apostle Paul gives us the order of events of the rapture. Below is a list of those events.

The Events of the Rapture
1 Thessalonians 4:15b–17

EVENT	VERSES	WHAT IT MEANS
There will be a call to the reunion.	verse 16	The Lord will descend from heaven with a shouted command of resurrection, and believers in Christ will be escorted to heaven.
We will receive our resurrected bodies.	verses 16–17	At the moment of the rapture, all believers will be given their resurrected bodies.
We will be united with Christ forever.	verse 17	All believers will be united with Christ, never to be separated from Him or each other again.

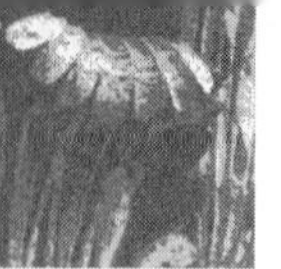

110 PROPHECY AND THE JUDGMENT SEAT OF CHRIST

The "judgment seat of Christ," so named by the apostle Paul (2 Corinthians 5:10), pertains only to Christians, and is not related at all to the final judgment in which all nonbelievers are sent to their eternal destiny. If you know Jesus Christ as your Savior, your judgment in terms of heaven and hell has already been decided. So what is the purpose of Christians appearing at Christ's judgment seat?

THE PURPOSE OF CHRIST'S JUDGMENT

In the verse prior to 2 Corinthians 5:10, Paul had said his all-consuming ambition was to please Christ. Why? The answer is, "For we must all appear before the judgment seat of Christ, so that each one may be recompensed for his deeds in the body, according to what he has done, whether good or bad."

The purpose of Christ's judgment seat is to judge or evaluate us for the way we lived our Christian lives, for the quality of our service. The question here is not whether you are a Christian, but what kind of Christian you are. At the judgment seat, Christ will determine our degree of faithfulness to Him and the eternal rewards (or lack thereof) we have earned.

The Bema of Christ

The word translated "judgment seat" is the picturesque Greek word *bema*. An ancient athletic competition held near Corinth called the Isthmian Games was something of a forerunner to the Olympics. The *bema* at the Isthmian Games was a raised platform where the honored citizens sat to watch the events, and where the rewards were given to the winners in the games.

Not only was the *bema* the place of recognition for victory, but it was also the place where a judgment was rendered if there was a question about the rules. Paul used this descriptive word to describe what happens when the church goes to be with Christ.

Reaching for the Prize

Did you know it's fine with God if part of your motivation for serving Him is to get a reward?

Some Christians say, "You should serve Christ because you love Him, not to get a reward." That's only half right. We serve Christ because we love Him, but that's not all the Bible says. Jesus told us to lay up treasures in heaven (Matthew 6:20). The book of Hebrews says God "is a rewarder of those who seek Him" (11:6).

Christ Himself looked ahead to the reward that was before Him when He endured the cross (Hebrews 12:2). He anticipated the joy on the other side that made Calvary worth all the suffering.

Nobody works without expecting to be rewarded. When you have worked hard all year and done a good job, you hope to get a raise at your annual review. If you are a worthy candidate for a vacancy above you, you hope to get the reward of a promotion. This is a normal part of life—and of eternity too.

THE PARTICULARS OF CHRIST'S JUDGMENT

The Bible gives us several important clues about the particulars, the details of the evaluation we will all face as believers.

A Test of Our Individual Quality

One aspect of Christ's judgment at the *bema* will be the sincerity of our lives. Paul said in Romans 14:

> But you, why do you judge your brother? Or you again, why do you regard your brother with contempt? For we will all stand before the judgment seat of God. For it is written, "As I live, says the Lord, every knee shall bow to me, and every tongue shall give praise to God." So then each one of us will give an account of himself to God. (vv. 10–12)

The context of this passage is very important in helping us understand what Paul was saying. In verses 4–9, he addressed Christians who were judging their brothers and sisters on the basis of their preferences in diet and the observance of certain special days. Since neither of these things is central to the life of faith, Paul told the critics to stop judging other believers and recognize that each Christian will stand before Christ alone.

A Test of Our Motivation

Here's a second particular of the judgment seat. It will be a test of the motivation behind our service for Christ. The things we do out of sincerity and love for Christ will stand the test and be rewarded, while the stuff we do to impress others will burst into flames before our eyes.

The passage I want to unfold with you is 1 Corinthians 3:10–15, a familiar text in part because Paul used the imagery of a building to illustrate the Christian life and our judgment as believers.

The apostle wrote, "According to the grace of God which was given to me, like a wise master builder I laid a foundation, and another is building on it. But each man must be careful how he builds on it. For no man can lay a foundation other than the one which is laid, which is Jesus Christ" (vv. 10–11).

Paul said he was the "contractor" to whom God gave the responsibility of laying the foundation for the Christian faith. Paul, more than anyone else, set down the doctrine upon which the church is built. That foundation is the truth about the person and work of Jesus Christ. Everything must be built on this foundation—or it's illegitimate to begin with.

You and I didn't get to help lay the foundation, but we can definitely contribute to the building's superstructure. That's why Paul continued, "Now if any man builds upon the foundation with gold, silver, precious stones, wood, hay, straw, each man's work will become evident; for the day will show it, because it is to be revealed with fire; and the fire itself will test the quality of each man's work" (1 Corinthians 3:12–13).

God's concern is that we use the right materials as we build our Christian lives. We have two choices. Gold, silver, and precious stones are indestructible, whereas wood, hay, and stubble will go up in smoke when the fire hits them. The first materials are valuable, but the second are of little or no value.

It's here that we learn the means by which Christ will test our work. It will pass through His refining fire, and only what's worthwhile will survive the flames. This passage concludes, "If any man's work which he has built upon it remains, he will receive a reward. If any man's work is burned up, he will suffer loss; but he himself will be saved, yet so as through fire" (1 Corinthians 3:14–15).

Paul said that service that passes the test will receive a reward, but a person whose chicken coop goes up in flames at the judgment seat will "suffer loss" (1 Corinthians 3:15).

That sounds pretty serious to me. Some people have the attitude, "Oh well, rewards aren't that big a deal. I just want to make it to heaven. Just build me a cabin in the corner of glory land." That wasn't Paul's attitude. He said the person whose works don't pass the test will be saved, "yet so as through fire." That phrase actually means "by the skin of his teeth." We are talking about unhappiness in heaven. To suffer loss means a person is going to feel the pain of his loss if he has little or no spiritual fruit to present to Christ.

A Test of Our Discipline

The third and final particular of the judgment seat of Christ is the test of our spiritual discipline—or if you prefer, our endurance in the contest. I say that because Paul often used athletic imagery for the Christian life, as he did when he described his service for Christ as both a race and a boxing match (1 Corinthians 9:24–27).

Here's the good news about the Christian race. Unlike an athletic contest, we're not competing against each other. Every Christian can win the prize at Christ's judgment seat.

But discipline requires making the right choices. The writer of Hebrews said, "Let us also lay aside every encumbrance [weight], and the sin which so easily entangles us, and let us run with endurance the race that is set before us" (12:1).

The race God has set before you is different from my race, but we can both win the prize. But it will take discipline. Nobody runs a 100-meter race wearing ankle weights. We must deal with the things that hinder us from running the race.

Sometimes people can be a hindrance. They can slow us down. Playthings can be a hindrance. There's nothing wrong with a lot of the things we do for enjoyment or leisure, but if these activities override our spiritual priorities, then we had better get rid of them.

Paul said he didn't want to be disqualified from winning his rewards. In the Isthmian Games, as in all competition, the athletes had to compete according to the rules in order to win. Our rule book is the Word of God. If our Christian service conforms to God's rules for sincerity, quality, motivation, and discipline, we qualify for the prize.

PREPARATION FOR CHRIST'S JUDGMENT

From the standpoint of God's prophetic plan, the judgment seat of Christ is the first order of business for the church after the rapture. Since we know we are going to be evaluated, how can we prepare for the *bema*? What is Christ going to judge?

Judging Our Deeds

We've already seen that the Lord is going to judge our deeds "according to what [we have] done, whether good or bad" (2 Corinthians 5:10). That's why Jesus warned us not to do righteous acts just to impress people (Matthew 6:1).

Our service for the Lord also needs to be consistent day in and day out. Some Christians are what I call "big-play" believers. A big-play person is the guy who comes into the game and makes one big splash, but that's all he can do. But that's not usually how games are played and won.

Judging Our Declarations

We will also be evaluated at the judgment seat of Christ for our declarations—our words.

Jesus' statement of warning to unbelievers in Matthew 12:36–37 is relevant for us. "I say to you, that every careless word that men will speak, they will render account for it in the day of judgment. For by your words you will be justified, and by your words you will be condemned."

The judgment of believers will surely include the words we say. No word of profanity or gossip will slip past Jesus' review, and neither will the encouraging words we have said. James cautioned us not to be too quick to become teachers (James 3:1), since those who instruct others will be judged by a stricter standard.

Judging Our Desires

Paul said that God is going to judge "the secrets of men through Christ Jesus" (Romans 2:16). For many people, the deepest desires of their hearts are secret, hidden things. That doesn't necessarily mean these are all bad. It's just that most people don't go around revealing their deepest secrets. But at Christ's judgment seat, our desires will be on the video screen for us to see.

Judging Our Dependability

We've already talked about this to some degree when we discussed endurance. Let me just note that Paul said, "It is required of stewards that one be found trustworthy" (1 Corinthians 4:2).

Another way to describe the Christian life is the term *stewardship*. All of us are stewards, or managers, of the things God has entrusted to us. How well we do as His managers determines the rewards we will receive. The importance of our stewardship also comes out in the parable of the talents, which we'll deal with next.

Dependability is another of those characteristics that any Christian can achieve and be rewarded for, regardless of how long that person has known Christ. Let me say it again. At the judgment seat, you will only be held accountable for what you have been given.

PLEASURE AND PAIN AT CHRIST'S JUDGMENT

For many believers, the judgment seat of Christ is going to be a time of profound joy and delight. They will be lavishly rewarded for their faithfulness. But for others, the evaluation at the bema will produce shame, tears, and pain as they see their life's work burned up in their presence.

We can see how these two elements of reward and judgment come together in a familiar parable Jesus taught in Matthew 25:14–30. It's the story of a man who goes on a long trip and entrusts his "talents," or money, to his servants while he's gone.

The Servants' Assignment

The story line of the parable is pretty straightforward. Let me summarize verses 14–18 for you. The man in the parable, who represents God, entrusted the servants with certain sums of money based on their ability.

The first servant proved why he was worthy of being trusted with five talents, because he doubled his money. So did the second slave. But the third one panicked and hid his master's money in the ground. He didn't do anything with what the master had given him.

The Servants' Evaluation

Finally, the master came back after a long time (Matthew 25:19)—just as the Lord will come back for us in the rapture. At that time, the servants were called in to be judged, just as we will stand before the judgment seat of Christ.

Let's look at the end of the story, and then we'll get into the heart of what this parable teaches about reward and judgment. The master called each slave to account, and rewarded the first two for doubling the funds he had given them. But when the third slave gave the master back his money with nothing to show for it, the master condemned the slave and gave his one talent to the guy who already had ten talents (Matthew 25:19–28).

Principles of Reward and Judgment

That's the story Jesus told to illustrate what His kingdom is like. Now let's talk about what it means, and then we'll deal with Matthew 25:29–30, which are critical to understanding what's being illustrated here.

The first two slaves were praised and promoted. The master said the same thing to each one: "Well done, good and faithful slave; you were faithful with a few things, I will put you in charge of many things, enter into the joy of your master" (vv. 21, 23).

But then we come to the third slave. Look at the excuse he gave to his master. "Master, I knew you to be a hard man, reaping where you did not sow, and gathering where you scattered no seed. And I was afraid, and went away and hid your talent in the ground; see, you have what is yours" (Matthew 25:24–25).

In other words, this slave may not have gained anything with his master's money, but he didn't lose it either. The master was no worse off than before.

But that wasn't the criterion for serving this master. "You wicked, lazy slave," he said (v. 26). Then he judged the slave by his own words. "You knew that I reap where I did not sow, and gather where I scattered no seed. Then you ought to have put my money in the bank, and on my arrival I would have received my money back with interest" (vv. 26b–27).

Let me tell you why this slave was condemned for his actions. This guy was a smooth operator. He figured, "My master has gone on a long trip. I don't even know if he's coming back, so I'm not going to break my neck trying to double his money. I'm going to look out for number one.

"What I'll do is bury my master's money in the ground. That way, if he never comes back, I know where it is. If he does return, I can give him his money back and we'll be even. But if I put it in the bank, there will be a record of it, and besides I'll have to manage the account. In the meantime, I've got my own life to live."

Loss at the Judgment Seat

Now we come to the point Jesus wanted to make, the point of the parable. The master said, "Take away the talent from him [the wicked slave], and give it to the one who has the ten talents. . . . And cast out the worthless slave into the outer darkness; in that place there will be weeping and gnashing of teeth" (Matthew 25:28, 30).

The evil servant not only lost what he had, but he was judged and cast out of the master's presence. Most people assume the slave was condemned to hell.

But this is not a parable of heaven and hell. Jesus was not talking about people's eternal destiny, but about rewards or lack thereof in His kingdom when He returns. The graphic expressions above speak of profound regret over the loss of rewards.

That's what it will be like in the kingdom for believers whose works are burned up and who suffer a loss of rewards. You may be asking, "But if I'm in a perfect place with a perfect body, how can I feel regret?"

It's precisely because you will be perfect that you can feel regret, because you will be very sensitive to that which displeases God. Sin makes God unhappy and sad, yet He is a perfect Being who never sinned. God's perfection is what makes Him so sensitive to sin.

There will be profound regret at the judgment seat for a person who was saved for fifty years and yet had nothing of any value to present to the Savior who gave up heaven to save him.

The apostle John had a profound word for us on this issue. "Little children, abide in Him, so that when He appears, we may have confidence and not shrink away from Him in shame at His coming" (1 John 2:28).

PERSONAL APPLICATION FOR LIFE

1. Being disciplined in your Christian life doesn't mean being straitlaced, sober, and sad. It means measuring everything you do by the goal of pleasing Christ. Discipline means asking, "Is what I'm doing now going to help me win my Christian race?"

2. One sure sign of a person's maturity is when he begins to seriously consider the future repercussions of his actions. Immature people care only about immediate gratification. Every Christian can win the prize at Christ's judgment seat. We're not competing against each other. If your Christian service conforms to God's rules for sincerity, motivation, and discipline, you qualify for the prize.

3. In case you're discouraged or feel like it's too late to get going, here's a word of encouragement from the apostle Paul: forget what's behind and press on for the prize (see Philippians 3:13–14). Get back into the game!

4. Christian service that has no lasting value is like junk food. It may look good and taste good and fill your stomach, but when it's melted down, there is nothing left but grease, sugar, calories, salt, and fat. So the next time you go to the donut shop or hamburger drive-through, think of the judgment seat of Christ and take a few minutes to evaluate the quality of your service for Him.

GROUP STUDY

Questions for Group Discussion

1. The word translated "judgment seat" in 2 Corinthians 5:10 is the picturesque Greek word *bēma*. What special nuance of meaning does that word carry in the Greek language? What is the purpose of Christ's judgment seat?

2. As preparation for discussion, read Romans 14:10–12, 1 Corinthians 3:10–15, and 1 Corinthians 9:24–27. What kind of evaluation will believers face at the judgment seat of Christ?

3. How can we, as believers, prepare for the *bēma*? On what should we focus in order to be ready for Christ's judgment? (Use the chart below as an aid to your discussion.)

4. Read Jesus' parable in Matthew 25:14–30. What is the point of the parable? What lessons and applications might we draw from this parable? What are the principles of reward and judgment?

PICTURE THIS

There will be both reward and judgment at the *bēma*. The New Testament provides us a preview of how Christ will evaluate us. Below are at least four of those areas of evaluation.

PREPARING FOR CHRIST'S JUDGMENT

BASIS OF JUDGMENT	SCRIPTURE PASSAGE	WHY IT'S IMPORTANT
Our deeds	2 Corinthians 5:10	Our deeds will be judged according to our faithfulness and what we have done.
Our declarations	Matthew 12:36–37	Our speech will be evaluated and judged.
Our desires	Romans 2:16	Our heart's secrets and deepest desires will be revealed.
Our dependability	1 Corinthians 4:2	We will be judged according to our stewardship of what God has entrusted to us.

SECTION III

THE RETURN OF CHRIST

111

PROPHECY AND THE ANTICHRIST

Now that we've spent some time concentrating on the church's place in the prophetic plan of God, including the future awaiting us in the rapture and Christ's judgment seat, we need to bring our attention back to earth, so to speak.

So for the next two chapters I want to examine the events that will unfold once the restraining influence of the church and the Holy Spirit is removed from the earth.

It's not a pretty picture, because what we're talking about here is the tribulation, the seven-year period of God's judgment that begins after the rapture and constitutes the seventieth week of Daniel's prophecy. More specifically, this period will feature the unveiling of the person first mentioned in the book of Daniel—the incarnation of Satan himself, the Antichrist.

We'll do some review of Daniel along the way, but you may want to go back and refresh yourself on his prophecy of the seventy weeks (see chapter 107). This is Israel's prophetic history, a 490-year span of time that began with the decree given to Nehemiah to rebuild Jerusalem and that ground to a halt when Messiah, Jesus Christ, was "cut off" (Daniel 9:26) at His crucifixion.

We pointed out that the seventieth week of Daniel's prophecy—the final seven years of God's prophetic plan for His people—has never been fulfilled. That's because God stopped the clock and called "time-out" on Israel after Calvary. The tribulation starts Israel's clock ticking again.

A ticking clock is a good analogy for the seven-year period called the tribulation, because Satan's time bomb is just waiting to explode in unrestrained evil on the world, and on Israel in particular. This will happen at the midpoint of the seven years when his "star," the Antichrist, reveals himself for who he is and all hell breaks loose on the earth.

Satan's "superstar" who will rule in the tribulation is known by several names. Daniel called him "another horn, a little one," "a king [who is] insolent," and "the prince who is to come" (Daniel 7:8; 8:23; 9:26). He is also called "the man of lawlessness" and "the son of destruction" (2 Thessalonians 2:3), and the Beast (Revelation 13:1).

But the name that sums up this person's character is "the Antichrist" (1 John 2:18). He will be against Christ and will seek to undermine and imitate the Son of God. Let's look at the Antichrist's rise to power, the evil nature of his rule, and the condemnation in store for him.

THE CONTEXT FOR THE ANTICHRIST

History teaches us that powerful rulers don't just arise out of nowhere. They come to the fore within a certain context, a set of conditions that prepares the way for their coming.

The Biblical Context

We've already discussed Daniel 7 in some detail, but we need to review some verses to set the context for the rise of Antichrist. Daniel wrote:

> After this I kept looking in the night visions, and behold, a fourth beast, dreadful and terrifying and extremely strong; and it had large iron teeth. It devoured and crushed and trampled down the remainder with its feet; and it was different from all the beasts that were before it, and it had ten horns. While I was contemplating the horns, behold, another horn, a little one, came up among them, and three of the first horns were pulled out by the roots

> before it; and behold, this horn possessed eyes like the eyes of a man and a mouth uttering great *boasts.* (vv. 7–8, italics added)

As we discussed earlier, God gave Daniel a vision of four powerful beasts that would arise and rule the world. This prophecy was fulfilled in the Gentile world powers of Babylon, Medo-Persia, Greece, and Rome. King Nebuchadnezzar had had a similar dream earlier, seeing a statue of a man with legs of iron and feet of iron and clay (Daniel 2:33).

This statue also outlined the four major Gentile powers that would dominate the Middle East. The ten toes of Nebuchadnezzar's statue, which symbolized the breakup of the Roman Empire, are called the "ten horns" in Daniel 7. It is out of these horns, or rulers, that the little horn, the Antichrist, will arise.

The Revival of Rome's Empire

The old Roman Empire was divided and eventually fell apart in fulfillment of biblical prophecy. The ultimate result of this breakup was the formation of the various nations in Europe, as we noted in the chapter on Daniel's prophecy. But the Bible also prophesies a future revival of the Roman Empire.

For many years skeptics dismissed this prophecy because for hundreds of years Europe has been divided into sovereign kingdoms and nations that fought each other to maintain their independence and/or conquer and rule their neighbors. Even Germany was divided into east and west after World War II.

But all of a sudden in 1989, the Berlin wall fell and Germany soon was reunified. Then the European economic union emerged, and we now have something called the Euro, a common currency to be used over most of Europe. The nations in the union have surrendered their currencies to unite under one standard. Suddenly, the picture of a reunified Europe is taking shape.

The Technology for Control

People also used to wonder how the Antichrist would ever be able to imprint the number 666 on people so that he could wield absolute economic control.

But with the technology we are seeing emerge today, that question doesn't come up as much. A technological context is being created in which the right person at the right time could not only control the economies of entire nations, but track the whereabouts of each person in a nation twenty-four hours a day.

Chaos and a Desire for Peace

The deterioration of civilization we are seeing today will increase greatly after the church has been raptured. The chaos will become such that the human race will cry out for a leader who can impose order and bring peace to the world.

Our world today is longing for peace. Imagine how the world would embrace a leader who could step up and settle the age-old conflict in the Middle East with one stroke of brilliant diplomacy. Imagine how people would welcome someone who could give them economic stability in return for a little more control over their lives. History proves that people will surrender their rights for stability and a sense of peace in times of chaos.

The Antichrist will be able to deliver peace and stability, and the unbelieving world will welcome him as he spends the first three-and-a-half years of the tribulation solidifying his power and gaining control.

This leader will be able to bring all peoples together and appear to be able to end racial conflict, ethnic cleansing, class destruction, and religious tension. The conditions are ripe for the emergence of such a dictator.

THE CHARACTER OF THE ANTICHRIST

The world kingdoms that Daniel saw were characterized as beasts. It was out of the fourth beast that the Antichrist arose, and he is more beastly than all the others.

Satan's "Incarnate One"

"And I saw a beast coming up out of the sea, having ten horns and seven heads, and on his horns were ten diadems, and on his heads were blasphemous names. And the beast which I saw was like a leopard, and his feet were like those of a bear, and his mouth like the mouth of a lion" (Revelation 13:1–2).

The Beast John saw is the Antichrist—fast like a leopard, strong like a bear, and boastful like a lion roaring to assert its power. He comes out of the sea, which in this kind of setting refers to the Gentiles as opposed to the Jews, who come from the land of Israel.

So the Beast will be a Gentile, possibly a European because Europe contains the remnants of the old Roman Empire and will be the center of the revived empire. The "diadems" or crowns the Beast will wear are ten nations over which he will rule.

It's clear where the Antichrist gets his power. "The dragon gave him his power and his throne and great authority" (v. 2b). The Dragon is none other than Satan, so identified by John in Revelation 12:9.

The Antichrist's program is described in the following verses of chapter 13. "And I saw one of his heads as if it had been slain, and his fatal wound was healed. And the whole earth was amazed and followed after the beast; and they worshiped the dragon, because he gave his authority to the beast" (vv. 3–4a).

A Prideful Beast

The Antichrist will also inspire worship (Revelation 13:4b), and will spew out his pride:

> And there was given to him a mouth speaking arrogant words and blasphemies; and authority to act for forty-two months was given to him. And he opened his mouth in blasphemies against God, to blaspheme His name and His tabernacle, that is, those who dwell in heaven. (vv. 5–6)

Why does the Antichrist blaspheme God? Because the great sin of the Beast's spiritual father, Satan, was pride. So the Beast is going to reflect his father's character. That's why God hates pride above all other sins (Proverbs 6:16–17). It reminds Him of Satan and his rebellion in heaven.

The Beast is granted power for forty-two months, the three-and-a-half years that make up the last half of the tribulation. This period is the great tribulation, as we noted above, the time when evil incarnate breaks loose on the earth.

A Lawless Beast

Paul said that when the restraint of the Holy Spirit and the church has been removed, "then that lawless one will be revealed" (2 Thessalonians 2:8).

This lawless one is the Antichrist, the offspring of the Devil. Notice that he can work miracles. Some people get all excited about miracles, but don't jump too quickly. The Devil can produce miracles and signs, for the wrong purpose: "And with all the deception of wickedness for those who perish, because they did not receive the love of the truth so as to be saved" (v. 10).

THE CONDUCT OF THE ANTICHRIST

Let's look at the conduct of the Antichrist. What will he do during his time on the earth? The Bible shows that the Antichrist is a true "Dr. Jekyll and Mr. Hyde," because when he first appears on the scene he comes as a man of peace, a Nobel Peace Prize winner, bringing peace to the Middle East. Everybody will love him.

A Deceitful Peacemaker

Daniel wrote concerning the Antichrist's activity, "He will make a firm covenant with the many for one week" (9:27). This "week" is Daniel's seventieth week, the final period of seven years, which is still future. The covenant is a seven-year peace treaty the Antichrist will make with Israel that will seem to settle the Middle East conflict.

This charismatic, powerful, attractive leader will do what other world leaders couldn't do—get the Arabs and Israelis to the peace table and hammer out a treaty. And guess what else he will do? He will give the Jews back their temple and make it possible for them to start offering sacrifices again.

This is very important to understand. The Jews lost their temple and their ability to offer sacrifices when the Roman general Titus destroyed Jerusalem in A.D. 70.

The only part of the temple left standing today is the Western Wall. But there's one huge problem. A Muslim mosque sits on the temple mount, Mount Moriah where Abraham offered up Isaac.

During the Gulf War, the orthodox Jews were praying that a Scud missile would hit that mosque because it has to go before the temple can be rebuilt. Orthodox Jews are praying for Messiah to come and give them back their place of worship. Of course, since Messiah has come, worship is no longer tied to a place but to a person (John 4:21–24). But the Antichrist will give the Jews what they ask for. They will be allowed to rebuild their temple and offer sacrifices once again.

When all of this comes to pass, the world will be saying, "Peace and safety" (1 Thessalonians 5:3) and singing the Antichrist's praises because finally there is peace. He will be a hero. People will wonder where this man has been all their lives. He will appear out of nowhere and do astounding things.

Solidifying His Power

The Antichrist will also use the first half of the tribulation to solidify his power in preparation for his world takeover. He will be a masterful schemer, because he will control the powerful forces of politics and religion, fusing them into one entity to serve his will.

We mentioned above that the Antichrist's political and economic control will be so complete that anyone who does not accept his mark cannot carry on a normal life (Revelation 13:16–18). He we will also use religion to further Satan's plan, as described in Revelation 17.

Once the Antichrist has total political and religious control, he will be ready for his unveiling, the great tribulation, when Satan pulls off the mask and shows the world his true nature. It is as though God is saying, "You wanted a world without Me. Now you have it. Satan, the earth is yours."

At this point human civilization will come full circle back to the goals of those who built the Tower of Babel (Genesis 11). There mankind came together to build a one-world government without God. But what the builders of Babel failed to do, the Antichrist will pull off for a while.

Once the Antichrist has solidified his power, he won't need organized religion anymore. So later in Revelation 17 we learn, "And the ten horns [ten kings] which you saw, and the beast, these will hate the harlot and will make her desolate and naked, and will eat her flesh and will burn her up with fire" (v. 16).

Demanding Worship

In the middle of Daniel's seventieth week (Daniel 9:27), or the midpoint of the tribulation, the Antichrist will use his control to demand worldwide worship (Revelation 13:8).

This in itself is not unusual. The ancient Romans worshiped their emperor as a god. To be a loyal Roman citizen, you had to offer a pinch of incense to Caesar and declare, "Caesar is Lord." It's not unusual today to see people worshiping their political leaders. But the Antichrist will take this further than anyone.

The Antichrist's sudden attack on religion will commence with his desecration of the rebuilt temple in Jerusalem, the halting of the daily sacrifices, and the establishment of "the abomination of desolation" (Daniel 11:31; cf. 9:27). Jesus warned His listeners to run for the hills when they saw this abomination standing in the temple (Matthew 24:15–16).

Now the wraps are off and the Antichrist is revealed in all of his evil. In the holy place of the temple, where the sacrifices are offered, an image of the Antichrist will be set up and he will be proclaimed as God. He will demand not only political loyalty, but worship. And the penalty for anyone who refuses will be death. Satan will finally have his false Christ and the worship he has always wanted (Revelation 13:4).

THE COMPANION OF THE ANTICHRIST

So far we have met two unholy beings, Satan and the Antichrist. But there is a third member of this evil trinity, because Satan wants to imitate God in every way. God is Father, Son, and Holy Spirit, so Satan has his version of the Trinity, the unholy trinity of himself, the Antichrist, and the False Prophet.

The Antichrist's "Energizer"

In Revelation 13, we are also introduced to this third member of the evil trio, later called "the false prophet" (Revelation 16:13).

John wrote: "And I saw another beast coming up out of the earth; and he had two horns like a lamb, and he spoke as a dragon. And he exercises all the authority of the first beast in his presence. And he makes the earth and those who dwell in it to worship the first beast" (Revelation 13:11–12).

The job of this Satan-inspired creature will be to mimic the Holy Spirit's relationship to Christ. The Holy Spirit's role is to bring praise and worship to Christ, so the False Prophet's assignment will be to bring praise and worship to the false Christ, the Antichrist.

John saw this beastly figure coming up out of the earth as opposed to the Antichrist, who arose out of the sea. The sea represents the Gentile nations in prophecy, but the earth refers to the land of Israel. So this probably means the False Prophet will be of Jewish origin, or at least come out of the Middle East.

A Miracle Worker

How will the False Prophet inspire people to worship the Antichrist openly? Please take careful note of his method.

> He performs great signs, so that he even makes fire come down out of heaven to the earth in the presence of men. And he deceives those who dwell on the earth because of the signs which it was given him to perform in the presence of the beast, telling those who dwell on the earth to make an image to the beast who had the wound of the sword and has come to life. And it was given to him to give breath to the image of the beast, so that the image of the beast would even speak and cause as many as do not worship the image of the beast to be killed. (Revelation 13:13–15)

The False Prophet's next assignment is to oversee the application of the mark of the Beast (vv. 16–18). By this time, very few people will have the courage to resist the Antichrist, and those who refuse the mark, the number 666, will pay with their lives.

Everybody loves to speculate about the meaning of the number 666. People have tried to tie it to the names of various figures in history so we will know who the Antichrist is. But I have a much simpler explanation for the significance of 666. In the Bible, six is the number of man. Man was created on the sixth day. He was commanded to work six days, and to rest on the seventh day and worship God. Six is close to seven, the number of

God and the number of perfection in the Bible. The number 666 is man trying to be God but never arriving.

THE CONDEMNATION OF THE BEAST

The Antichrist's reign as Satan's world ruler will come to an abrupt end after three-and-a-half years. (We'll deal with this in more detail later, so let's just review it briefly for now.) Defeat for the Antichrist will come swiftly and totally when Jesus Christ rides out of heaven with His armies:

> And I saw the beast and the kings of the earth and their armies, assembled to make war against Him who sat upon the horse, and against His army. And the beast was seized, and with him the false prophet who performed the signs in his presence, by which he deceived those who had received the mark of the beast and those who worshiped his image; these two were thrown alive into the lake of fire which burns with brimstone. (Revelation 19:19–20)

When Jesus comes back, that will be it for the Antichrist. His beastly days will be over because number six will have run into number seven! Jesus Christ will destroy the Antichrist with the sword that comes out of His mouth (v. 21).

PERSONAL APPLICATION FOR LIFE

1. Satan is the master of disguise, and his substitutes always look like the real thing at first. He can disguise himself as an angel of light (2 Corinthian 11:14). But shine the light of God's truth on Satan, and you'll see the "horns and pitchforks." Don't ever let the Enemy fool you with his old tricks. Resist him with the truth and power of Scripture.

2. Satan is out to destroy the church, but he can't handle the blood of Christ. Matthew 12 tells us that Jesus was able to plunder Satan's house because He is stronger than Satan. In 1 John 4:4 we read, "Greater is He who is in you than he who is in the world." Be encouraged that the reason Jesus can overcome whatever Satan is trying to do in your life is that what He is doing is greater than what Satan is trying to do.

3. Satan has subtle ways of prying his way into our lives if we let him. Is there something you've said yes to in your life that Jesus wants you to say no to? The Holy Spirit will show you what it is. Change your answer to Jesus' answer. Don't give the Devil a foothold in your life that he can make into a stronghold!

4. Hebrews 2:14 tells us that Satan has been rendered powerless by the death and resurrection of Jesus Christ. That means his real weapons have been taken away, and he is pretty much left with the weapon of deception. But he is a master at deception, so don't underestimate the spiritual damage he can still inflict in your life. With God's help, we can always resist temptation and choose not to be defeated.

FOR GROUP STUDY

Questions for Group Discussion

1. What world conditions will make it ripe for the emergence of a dictator such as the Antichrist? What does Daniel 7:7–8 reveal about the context for the Antichrist?

2. Read Revelation 13:1–6 and 2 Thessalonians 2:8. What does Scripture

teach us about the character of the Antichrist? (Use the "Picture This" chart as an aid to your discussion.)

3. Read Daniel 9:27 and Revelation 13:16–18. What agenda does the Antichrist carry out? What kind of power does he gain? In what evil and deceptive activities does he engage?

4. Read Revelation 13:11–15. What do we know about the False Prophet? What is his role?

PICTURE THIS

The Antichrist's program is an evil one. As Satan's "incarnate one," he is the ultimate denial of every truth about Christ. Below is a glimpse of his evil character.

THE CHARACTER OF THE ANTICHRIST

CHARACTERISTIC	SCRIPTURE PASSAGE	ITS SIGNIFICANCE
He is Satan's "Incarnate One."	Revelation 13:1–4a	The Antichrist will be Satan's false messiah.
He is a prideful beast.	Revelation 13:1–4b, 6	Full of pride, the Antichrist will inspire worship of himself.
He is a lawless beast.	2 Thessalonians 2:8–10	With the Holy Spirit removed, the Antichrist will have no restraints on his lawlessness.

112

PROPHECY AND THE TRIBULATION

We should have put the notice "to be continued" at the end of the previous chapter, because this is really part two of our study on the tribulation period. We couldn't talk about the Antichrist, the major figure of the tribulation, without covering some of the events that will take place during these seven years.

So with that background, let's take another brief overview of this prophetic time when the wrath of God falls on rebellious man. When you realize that most of the book of Revelation is devoted to the tribulation, it becomes obvious that all we can do here is survey some of the highlights and give you an overview of God's prophetic plan as it unfolds.

IMAGES OF THE TRIBULATION

The tribulation was prophesied in the Old Testament, particularly in its impact upon Israel. Jeremiah says it is a time of "terror" and "dread," and compares the pain to a woman in labor. No wonder the prophet says this period will be "the time of Jacob's distress" (30:5–7). In the second three-and-a-half years, the Antichrist will unleash his fury on Israel.

Jesus also used the imagery of birth pains in His classic teaching on the tribulation (Matthew 24:4–28). The early warning signs include "wars and rumors of wars," along with "famines and earthquakes" (vv. 6–7). Then Jesus said, "But all these things are merely the beginning of birth pangs" (v. 8). This is the first half of the seven-year period.

The Lord's reference to "the abomination of desolation" (v. 15) marks the start of "great tribulation" (v. 21). We know this to be the midpoint of the tribulation, when the Antichrist crushes apostate religion and sets up his image in the rebuilt Jerusalem temple, demanding to be worshiped as God.

CONDITIONS IN THE TRIBULATION

In the previous chapter, we mentioned the fact that the tribulation will actually begin peacefully for those on earth. After giving us the comforting word that the church will be caught away by the Lord (1 Thessalonians 4:13–18), Paul continued: "The day of the Lord will come just like a thief in the night. While they are saying, 'Peace and safety!' then destruction will come upon them suddenly like birth pangs upon a woman with child; and they will not escape" (5:2–3).

A Time of Deceptive Peace

When the tribulation begins, people will actually be positive. We saw that the main reason for this feeling of security is that the Antichrist will come as a champion of peace and solve the unsolvable conflict in the Middle East.

But there may be other reasons for a deceptive sense of well-being. It could be that the stock market will be hitting all-time highs. It's also possible that as the tribulation begins, there will be no major wars. Maybe the United Nations will be doing its thing more successfully than ever.

Remember, the world won't know who the Antichrist really is when he appears on the scene. Even though the church will be gone, life will continue, as is obvious from chapters 4–18 of Revelation. These chapters describe the judgments of the tribulation on those left on earth, and Revelation 17–18 in particular show that commercial and even religious life will have carried on after the rapture.

There will also be a sense of euphoria in Israel in the first half of the tribulation. The Antichrist's covenant will allow for the rebuilding of the temple in Jerusalem and the resumption of the sacrificial system. So the Jews will have their temple and their worship restored. Go to Israel today and you'll find a lot of people eagerly waiting for the day they can rebuild the temple and offer sacrifices again.

The Outpouring of God's Wrath

The time of tribulation is referred to in both the Old and New Testaments as "the day of the Lord" (cf. Isaiah 13:6; 1 Thessalonians 5:2). This period is the opposite of the day of man, which is in effect today and during which God's grace limits the full expression of His wrath. But when the day of the Lord comes, there will be no holding back His judgment.

Then the world's false sense of peace is going to end as suddenly as a pregnant woman being stabbed awake in the middle of the night by her first labor pain. The outpouring of God's judgment on earth during the tribulation begins in Revelation 6 with the breaking of a seal. This is the first of seven seals, followed by seven trumpets and then seven bowls—overlapping judgments that contain the fullness of God's wrath against sin.

These judgments are so detailed and so complete that we would need to do a separate book to cover them in detail. What I want to show you here is just the beginning of this process. You can read Revelation 6–18 for yourself and see how the horror of the tribulation builds until Jesus returns to defeat the Antichrist (Revelation 19:11–21).

John begins in Revelation 6, "I saw when the Lamb broke one of the seven seals, and I heard one of the four living creatures saying as with a voice of thunder, 'Come.' And I looked, and behold, a white horse, and he who sat on it had a bow; and a crown was given to him; and he went out conquering, and to conquer" (vv. 1–2).

The rider going forth on the white horse is Jesus Christ leaving heaven to begin the process of delivering God's wrath and conquering rebellious mankind. I believe the rapture also occurs at this moment, as Christ comes to deliver God's judgment on the earth. The church is called up to meet the Lord in the air as "the day of the Lord" begins.

This rider has a bow, which can be used for long-range warfare. This fits with the picture of the rapture, in which Christ comes not to the earth, as

He does at the end of the tribulation, but in the air to call His people home. So He fights Satan long-range, so to speak, from His position in the heavenly places.

You can see the contrast here with the Lord's second coming, because in Revelation 19:15, He comes with a sharp sword for close-up battle. The first seal is really preliminary to the outbreak of chaos in the tribulation. But the opening of the second seal (Revelation 6:3–4) brings the Antichrist on the scene, the one to whom "it was granted to take peace from the earth." Notice that he carries a sword because this is going to be a time of furious conflict, with death on a massive scale.

From this point on, the story is one of total destruction and chaos, all the way to the end of the tribulation. Conditions just continue to get worse. The fourth seal, for example, destroys one-fourth of the world's population. That will be more than one-and-one-half billion people. We can't even imagine death on this kind of scale.

The Antichrist is going to march on Israel during this time (Daniel 11:40–45), striking out at nations such as Egypt on his way to the "Beautiful Land" (v. 41). Then Israel will become his command post and the center of the world's activities. The second half of the tribulation is a horrific time, the likes of which the world has never seen.

SALVATION IN THE TRIBULATION

Despite all the judgment and destruction and horror being unleashed on the earth, God will not leave Himself without a witness during the tribulation.

In fact, the world is going to witness the greatest "evangelistic campaign" in history. Masses of people will be saved during the tribulation, but it won't be easy because they will have to accept Christ in the day of His wrath rather than in the day of His grace. And they will face the fury of the Antichrist for their commitment to Christ.

God's Two Witnesses

Even though the Holy Spirit and the church will be gone, God will send two special witnesses to the earth during the tribulation. We're introduced to these two figures in Revelation 11: "I will grant authority to my two witnesses, and they will prophesy for twelve hundred and sixty days, clothed in sackcloth" (v. 3). These men have supernatural powers. They can kill anyone who tries to hurt them with fire from their mouths, and they can stop the rain, turn the waters into blood, and strike the earth with plagues (vv. 5–6).

This description of their powers will sound familiar if you know your Bible. Elijah stopped the rain in Israel for three-and-a-half years, and Moses brought the plagues on Egypt. Interestingly, both Moses and Elijah also appeared with Jesus at His transfiguration (Matthew 17:3).

In other words, these men have unique ministries to fulfill even after their departure from earth. Elijah was raptured to heaven in a chariot of fire, and Moses' body was buried by God so that no one knows where it is. The evidence suggests that the two witnesses of Revelation 11 are Moses and Elijah.

The content of their witness is not specified, but the miracles Moses and Elijah did were testimonies to the true God in the midst of paganism. That may be the type of witness they will bear in the tribulation, pointing people to the true God who is still willing to save.

When the two witnesses have finished their ministry, they will be overcome and killed by the Antichrist. The world will see their dead bodies lying in the streets of Jerusalem and throw a party (Revelation 11:7–10).

The 144,000 Jews

The 144,000 are introduced in Revelation 7:1–8. They are called "the bond-servants of our God," and they are clearly Jewish (vv. 3–4). And later, they are said to be male virgins, specially consecrated to God, and blameless (Revelation 14:4–5). Besides, they aren't even chosen until the tribulation.

Now that should be enough information to eliminate a lot of misguided teaching about the 144,000. You don't need to join a group and go knocking on doors to try and make yourself worthy to be in this group. You probably don't qualify, and neither do I.

These witnesses will be converted during the first half of the tribulation, and they will serve as evangelists for the gospel during this time. They are the "first fruits" (Revelation 14:4) of many other Jews who will be saved by the time the tribulation ends.

So the gospel is going to be preached to the whole world during the tribulation, and everybody on earth will hear the message because everything these witnesses say and do will be televised, courtesy of the satellite networks. Their ministry will lead to a great multitude of Gentiles being saved during the tribulation—a number so large no one can count it (Revelation 7:9; cf. v. 14). The cost in suffering for following Christ will be tremendous, but many will choose Him over allegiance to the Antichrist.

THE OUTBREAK OF THE GREAT TRIBULATION

As the tribulation approaches its midpoint, there comes an escalation of judgments and chaos and warfare as events move toward the final half, "the time of Jacob's distress."

Satan's Defeat and Attack on Israel

Israel's distress in the tribulation is obvious from the opening scene of Revelation 12:

> A great sign appeared in heaven: a woman clothed with the sun, and the moon under her feet, and on her head a crown of twelve stars; and she was with child; and she cried out, being in labor and in pain to give birth. Then another sign appeared in heaven: and behold, a great red dragon having seven heads and ten horns, and on his heads *were* seven diadems. And his tail swept away a third of the stars of heaven and threw them to the earth. And the dragon stood before the woman who was about to give birth, so that when she gave birth he might devour her child. (vv. 1–4, italics added)

The woman in this vision represents Israel, who gave birth to Jesus Christ. And there is no mistaking the identity of the Dragon. This is Satan trying to destroy Christ, the offspring of Israel. Satan knows that if he can kill God's Redeemer and King, there will be no kingdom. But that attempt failed (v. 5).

So Satan escalates the war, and what follows is war in heaven between Satan and the archangel Michael and their forces. Satan is defeated and thrown down to the earth (vv. 7–9), where he will operate directly for the remainder of the tribulation in the physical realm. Satan's banishment from heaven marks the beginning of the great tribulation.

After Satan is thrown down to the earth, he will be unhindered in his operation against the earth dwellers. And he will have "great wrath" (Revelation 12:12), which he will vent on Israel. This will be the Devil's last chance to defeat God by destroying Israel, so he is going to pull out all the stops.

Satan will persecute the woman, Israel, "pour[ing] water like a river out of his mouth after the woman" to sweep her away (vv. 13–16). Those Israelites who flee (vv. 6, 16) will be protected by God, but those who stay will come under Satan's attack. That's why Jesus warned His listeners to flee Jerusalem immediately, not stopping for anything, when they saw the abomination of desolation in the temple (Matthew 24:15–18).

The Antichrist's "Fatal Wound"

This brings us back pretty much full circle to where we began in the previous chapter, the appearance of the Antichrist in Revelation 13. We have presented a lot of information about the Antichrist's person and program, but we haven't dealt with his fatal wound. "And I saw one of his heads as if it had been slain, and his fatal wound was healed. And the whole world was amazed and followed after the beast" (Revelation 13:3).

We don't know for sure what this wound is a reference to, but apparently the Beast is going to receive a deathblow and then be brought back to life by Satan as a miracle to further deceive the world. And it will work. By this time God is going to help people be deceived who insist on being deceived (see 2 Thessalonians 2:10–12).

The Antichrist will gradually assume power by bringing peace to the Middle East and building up apostate religion. But if anyone is reluctant to believe him or hand over the reins of world power to him, his resurrection will make a tremendous impression. People are going to listen to someone who can get up out of the grave. Satan even counterfeits Christ's resurrection by bringing his false Christ back to life.

The Antichrist's Allies

As we saw previously, the Antichrist is going to have some powerful allies. First, he will be empowered by Satan (Revelation 13:4–7). He will also be assisted by the False Prophet, whom we have discussed (vv. 11–18) and who has some awesome satanic powers of his own in his ability to perform miracles. Together, Satan, the Antichrist, and the False Prophet form the satanic trinity in imitation of the triune God.

The Antichrist also has plenty of human beings who will be more than willing to align themselves with him. We reviewed the fact that he will acquire religious control, becoming the "sugar daddy" of the apostate church by encrusting it with jewels and gold and all sorts of wealth (Revelation 17:1–4). Organized religion will do the Antichrist's will, until such time as he turns on this false system and destroys it.

He will also accumulate enormous political power. He will be in charge of ten kings, the reunited Roman Empire, who "receive authority as kings with the beast for one hour. These have one purpose and they give their power and authority to the beast" (Revelation 17:12–13). In other words, Europe will say to the Antichrist, "We will follow you wherever you want us to go." And he will say like Adolf Hitler, "Today Europe, tomorrow the world." The Antichrist wants to be a world ruler, not just a European ruler.

The Response of Stubborn Unbelief

You might think that when all the horrors prophesied in the Bible begin unfolding on earth, people would run to God crying for mercy and salvation. You'd think that once people realize they are in the last days of God's judgment, and they see all these terrifying things unfolding before their eyes, they would repent and beg God's forgiveness.

Not so. According to Revelation 9:20–21, "The rest of mankind, who were not killed by these plagues, did not repent of the works of their hands, so as not to worship demons, and the idols of gold and of silver and of brass and of stone and of wood, which can neither see nor hear nor walk.... They did not repent."

Then in Revelation 16:9 we read, "And men were scorched with fierce heat; and they blasphemed the name of God who has the power over these plagues; and they did not repent, so as to give Him glory" (see also v. 11).

God is warning the world today to repent and flee His wrath to come. The day of His grace is still upon us, and whoever will may come to the cross and find forgiveness. But when the day of God's judgment falls, sinners will not be inclined to seek forgiveness. Don't let anyone you know be left behind to face the blast of God's judgment.

PERSONAL APPLICATION FOR LIFE

1. When God saved you, He gave you a new life in Christ. But there's more. You are also part of Christ's church, the body of believers. That means you are seated with Christ in the place of authority in the heavenly places (Ephesians 2:6). If you are not exercising His power and authority in your life, ask God to show the next thing to do so you can get started.

2. Are you having an "evil day"? When that happens, and the Devil is doing his worst, you can confidently "stand firm in the faith" (1 Corinthians 16:13) because God has surrounded you with protection. You need not worry about Satan's attacks when you are wearing the armor of God.

3. Jesus said, "I am . . . the life" (John 14:6). As believers, we are alive in Christ! The apostle Paul tells us in Romans 6:23 that the "wages of sin is death." When Satan moves against us, he does so in the realm of death. He wants us to live in the sphere of spiritual death where he can ruin us spiritually. But do not let the Enemy deceive you. You are a kingdom Christian living a kingdom life. Claim kingdom victory, and don't allow sin a place in your piece of the kingdom.

4. We know that Satan was defeated historically. How remarkable that we possess recorded accounts of Jesus' birth, His sacrifice on the cross, and His resurrection! Those rate as the three greatest events in all of recorded history. If your heart needs a dose of joy, take a moment to reflect on that.

FOR GROUP STUDY

Questions for Group Discussion

1. Read Jeremiah 30:5–7 and Matthew 24:4–28. What images do these passages provide us of the tribulation?

2. What conditions will characterize the tribulation? Jesus returns as the rider of the white horse. What will be His agenda?

3. Who are the 144,000 of Revelation 7:1–8? What will be their purpose during the tribulation?

4. What does "the time of Jacob's distress" signal? Drawing from Revelation 12—13, discuss the key events that occur during the great tribulation. (Use the chart below as an aid to your discussion.)

PICTURE THIS

As the tribulation approaches its midpoint, there comes an escalation of judgments and chaos and warfare as events move toward the final half. Below are three keys events that will occur in the final half.

THE EVENTS OF THE GREAT TRIBULATION

EVENT	SCRIPTURE PASSAGE	ITS IMPACT
Satan's defeat and attack on Israel.	Revelation 12:1–4	Satan will be defeated and thrown down to the earth, where he will attempt to destroy Israel.
The Antichrist's "fatal wound."	Revelation 13:3	The Antichrist will receive a deathblow and then be brought back to life by Satan as a miracle to further deceive the world.
The Antichrist's allies.	Revelation 13:4–18	His allies will include Satan, the False Prophet, and many humans.

113

PROPHECY, THE BATTLE OF ARMAGEDDON, AND CHRIST'S SECOND COMING

Since God never leaves anything undone or half-finished, we can be sure that He will not leave any loose ends in bringing the great tribulation to a close. In fact, this period during which Satan has been in command and evil has run rampant will end with the Devil's most foolish move of all. It's an all-out attempt to use his evil forces to defeat Jesus Christ and the armies of heaven in head-on combat.

The Bible says this awesome, climactic battle will occur in "the place which in Hebrew is called Har-Magedon" (Revelation 16:16). We know this as the battle of Armageddon, the time when God's wrath against sin and sinners will be unleashed and the Antichrist's reign in the great tribulation will be ended.

The world has been interested in the subject of Armageddon for a long time because a lot of people believe that the next big war, which some call World War III, will be so cataclysmic it will be history's final conflict. Some think it will be a nuclear holocaust that will annihilate mankind.

The hill of Megiddo overlooks the massive plain of the valley of Jezreel, an area that extends for miles. The ancient city of Megiddo lay on the strategic north-south trade route between Mesopotamia and Egypt, and therefore it came to be important militarily. The Greek general Alexander the Great is reported to have said that Megiddo is the most natural battlefield in the world. This will be the staging area and command center for a series of conflicts that make up the battle of Armageddon—the war to end all wars, prophetically speaking.

Revelation 16 briefly describes the preparations for the conflict, and then in Revelation 19 we see Jesus riding out of heaven to engage the Devil, the Antichrist, and the False Prophet, Satan's unholy trinity.

PREPARING FOR ARMAGEDDON

Preparations for Armageddon begin as the angel pours out the sixth bowl of God's judgment on the earth (Revelation 16:12–16). God's wrath on the unbelieving world during the great tribulation will be executed in a series of judgments that include seals, trumpets, and then bowls.

There are seven bowls altogether, so at this point we are near the end of the tribulation. John wrote:

> The sixth angel poured out his bowl on the great river, the Euphrates; and its water was dried up, so that the way would be prepared for the kings from the east. And I saw coming out of the mouth of the dragon and out of the mouth of the beast and out of the mouth of the false prophet, three unclean spirits like frogs; for they are spirits of demons, performing signs, which go out to the kings of the whole world, to gather them together for the war of the great day of God, the Almighty. (vv. 12–14)

When the time comes for Armageddon, the great Euphrates River is going to be turned into a wading pool so the armies of Eastern powers can come to Israel to wage war against God.

The Reason for the Battle

The reason for this monumental battle is clear: This battle is inspired by the false trinity wanting to overthrow the true Trinity. The demons that call the kings to battle come from each member of this unholy trio. This is all-out, desperate war against God and His Son (Revelation 19:19). Armageddon is the climax of the angelic conflict that began in heaven, was transferred to earth, and now has come full circle as Satan tries to defeat God by force.

Armageddon is also the world's final response to God's call for repentance. Throughout the tribulation, God will be calling on mankind to repent. But most will refuse (Revelation 16:9, 11) and align themselves with the Antichrist, with the result that God will allow Satan to gather together the world's armies for God's swift judgment.

It won't surprise you to learn that Armageddon was prophesied in the Old Testament. Joel 3:9–17 is one of those passages in which the place of battle is called "the valley of decision" (v. 14). The prophet used that term because this is the place where unbelieving men will make their decision to join Satan in making war against God.

Satan's Attempt to Destroy Israel

The key to Armageddon is Satan's attempt to defeat God by destroying Israel (Revelation 12:13–17). The battle takes place in the Holy Land, with the focus on Jerusalem. This is because even though Satan knows it is futile to wage war against God because the outcome was decided at the cross, he believes that if he could eradicate Israel, he would destroy God's covenant promises. That would make God a liar.

God made covenants with Israel to give them their land, to redeem them, to bless them, and to give them an eternal King through David's line. Some of these promises were fulfilled with Christ's first coming, and the rest of them will be fulfilled when Christ returns to take the throne of David.

Satan can't get at God directly, so he will go after God's people. That's why he wants Israel, and that's why Israel will never know real peace until Jesus Christ sits on the throne of David. The Devil will always keep some nation or group stirred up to come against Israel.

In Revelation 12:1–6, John described Satan's attempt to devour Israel's "child," Jesus Christ, at His birth (v. 4). But since that failed, the Devil will unleash intense persecution on Israel for "one thousand two hundred and sixty days" (v. 6), the last three-and-a-half years of the tribulation (see also

Revelation 12:13–17). By protecting Israel, God is also protecting His covenant promises.

THE DETAILS LEADING TO ARMAGEDDON

Let's focus in a little closer on the details of Armageddon, particularly the armies that will be arrayed against Jesus Christ and the armies of heaven.

An Islamic Invasion

One of the battles that will lead into Armageddon is an Islamic invasion of Israel. The Middle East is a tinderbox because of the conflict between the Jews and Muslims, and one reason for the ongoing tension is the Muslim mosque that sits directly on the site in Jerusalem where the Jewish temple stood.

We've mentioned this problem before. The reason it will become so critical is that the Bible indicates the Jews will resume their sacrificial system during the tribulation. If the Antichrist somehow aids the Jews in restoring their temple and sacrifices, that will cause an incredible amount of tension, leading to open warfare.

The invasion of Israel by an Islamic army is prophesied in Ezekiel 38–39. Let's line up the major nations that will be part of this invasion from the Islamic world. Gog was probably a ruler over the land of Magog, which is part of modern-day Turkey. Meshech and Tubal were also part of Asia Minor. Persia is modern-day Iran, Ethiopia is actually part of modern-day Sudan, and Put is Libya. Gomer and Beth-togarmah are also part of Turkey today.

The Iranians are Persians, not Arabs, but all of these areas have one thing in common: the Islamic religion, which is firmly entrenched against Judaism. When the time comes for Armageddon, Satan will use Islamic hostility toward Israel as a pawn in his rebellion against God and his desire to destroy Israel. But God will work above it all to accomplish His prophetic purpose.

God's Intervention

Today's tensions in the Middle East are simply the precursor to this massive invasion that will take place in the end times. Peace efforts between Israel and its neighbors may slow the pace of the hostilities or delay the outbreak of open conflict, but just before Armageddon the Islamic nations will see the chance they've always wanted to annihilate Israel.

But God will intervene in a decisive way:

> My fury will mount up in My anger. . . . And I will call for a sword against him on all My mountains. . . . Every man's sword will be against his brother. . . . And I will magnify Myself, sanctify Myself, and make Myself known in the sight of many nations; and they will know that I am the Lord. (Ezekiel 38:18, 21, 23)

Verses 20 and 22 refer to an earthquake, hailstones, fire, and brimstone that God will rain down on the invaders. So when this massive coalition of Islamic nations comes against Israel, God will use natural phenomena to wipe them out. The slaughter will be so great that Revelation 14:20 refers to the blood running several feet deep for several hundred miles as God supernaturally imposes Himself on this battle. So the nations of Islam will fall just prior to the battle of Armageddon.

Israel's Repentance

This battle will accomplish another objective besides the destruction of God's enemies. It will be the beginning of Israel's repentance and spiritual awakening. Speaking of the events of Armageddon, God said in Ezekiel 39:22, "And the house of Israel will know that I am the Lord their God from that day onward."

Remember that Israel will welcome the Antichrist in the first half of the tribulation because he will be the great peacemaker in the Middle East. He will appear to be Israel's friend and protector, and the nation will be allowed to rebuild its temple and reinstitute the Mosaic sacrifices.

But when Antichrist turns on Israel in his fury, the nation will undergo intense persecution. When God reveals Himself at Armageddon, the Jews will see that the Lord God alone is their God.

SUMMONING THE NATIONS TO ARMAGEDDON

We're now back to our starting point in Revelation 16:12–16, when the demons draw the kings of the earth to Megiddo, or the Valley of Jezreel.

These kings will have no allegiance to God, so they will readily come under demonic influence.

The numbers here are staggering. Megiddo is an area two hundred miles long, so it will have no problem accommodating the leaders of the armies that will mass for Armageddon. Revelation 9:16 pictures an army of two hundred million mounted troops. Joel prophesied the battle of Armageddon as the biggest bloodbath in human history (Joel 3:9–17).

Let me show you who's coming to this battle. We know that the European confederation is going to be there because the Antichrist will be over the ten nations of Europe. The "kings of the east" will also come because the Euphrates River will be dried up to make it possible for them to cross and attack Israel (Revelation 16:12).

Euphrates is a seventeen-hundred-mile river that runs from Turkey all the way down to the Persian Gulf. On the east side of the Euphrates is communist China, which could easily assemble an army of two hundred million mounted troops all by itself. God is going to let China mobilize an army of this size and bring it against Israel to fulfill His prophetic plan.

China will lead the satanic coalition that comes against Jesus Christ and the armies of heaven at Armageddon, aided by Europe and its allies, which may bring another two hundred million troops. These great armies will gather at Megiddo in preparation for the second coming of Jesus Christ.

THE PURPOSES OF CHRIST'S SECOND COMING

Jesus Christ's return to earth is the climax of history and the event anticipated in so much of Bible prophecy. Jesus Christ will return at the end of the great tribulation, the last half of Daniel's seventieth week, to conquer His enemies and usher in His thousand-year millennial kingdom.

His appearance will come once the armies have assembled for the battle of Armageddon. The second coming of Jesus Christ is initiated with this brief but powerful word from the apostle John: "I saw heaven opened" (Revelation 19:11).

This announcement signals Christ's return to earth, specifically to Megiddo and the battle of Armageddon, to accomplish God's purposes for Satan and his allies and for His chosen nation Israel. The second coming will also fulfill mankind's destiny in God's plan as He reverses the curse of sin and ends the angelic conflict that began with Satan's rebellion in heaven. Let's see how these purposes will be brought about when heaven opens and Christ rides forth.

The Gathering at Armageddon

When heaven opened, John saw an awesome sight. "Behold, a white horse, and He who sat upon it is called Faithful and True; and in righteousness He judges and wages war" (Revelation 19:11).

The image of a conqueror riding a white horse was something that anybody in New Testament times could have readily related to. When a victorious Roman general returned from battle with his captives and the spoils, he rode through Rome in a victory parade on a white horse. A white horse was a symbol of victory in that day.

So the Bible pictures Jesus Christ as returning to earth for His day of conquest, the day when He lays claim to the ultimate and final victory in history. In Zechariah 14:2 the Lord says, "I will gather all the nations against Jerusalem to battle." Here at Megiddo Satan and his unholy trinity draw the nations together to do battle at Armageddon. And here Christ the King will accomplish God's purpose of judgment against them.

God's Defense of Israel

Zechariah 14:4 describes Satan's attempt to destroy Israel at Armageddon and God's defense of His people, as Jesus comes and "his feet will stand on the mount of olives, which is in front of Jerusalem on the east; and the Mount of Olives will be split in its middle from east to west by a very large valley, so that half of the mountain will move toward the north and the other half toward the south."

This is going to be some event. We know that God is going to intervene supernaturally at Armageddon, and this prophecy gives us more of the details. The Mount of Olives is situated right in front of Jerusalem, only about a long stone's throw from the city. Jesus Christ ascended from the Mount of Olives, called "Olivet" in Acts 1:12, and He will return to that spot to defend His people as the battle rages against Jerusalem—the focal point of Armageddon.

But things are going to change when Jesus' feet touch down on the Mount of Olives. The mountain will divide all the way down to the Dead Sea. In fact, Ezekiel 47:1–10 says when this happens, the Dead Sea will become a place of life instead of a place where nothing can live because of the salt content. Nature itself will respond and come alive at the return of Christ (see Romans 8:19–22).

When Jesus Christ comes back as Israel's defender at Armageddon, the tide of battle will suddenly change. Zechariah 12:2–4 describes this:

> Behold, I am going to make Jerusalem a cup that causes reeling to all the peoples around; and when the siege is against Jerusalem, it will also be against Judah. And it will come about in that day that I will make Jerusalem a heavy stone for all the peoples; all who lift it will be severely injured. And all the nations of the earth will be gathered against it. "In that day," declares the Lord, "I will strike every horse with bewilderment, and his rider with madness. But I will watch over the house of Judah."

When Jesus enters the battle, things will change in a hurry. This prophecy is very graphic in describing the injury that Israel will inflict on its attackers when the Lord comes to strengthen His people and fight for them.

THE DESCRIPTION OF CHRIST'S COMING

Revelation 19 offers a magnificent description of Jesus Christ returning in power and glory. Here comes Jesus—not the baby of Bethlehem we sing about, or the gentle Jesus who holds children in His lap. This is the God-man of heaven coming to judge and make war.

And what a return His coming will be. John said that "every eye will see Him" (Revelation 1:7). How will this be possible for people who don't have television? I believe that Christ and His accompanying armies will travel around the globe, passing in front of the sun during the daylight hours so that every person on earth will witness this incredible sight.

The Names He Bears

The Bible says that the One who is coming from heaven on the white horse "is called Faithful and True" (Revelation 19:11). Jesus is called Faithful because as perfect man, He is perfectly obedient to the will of God—unlike the first Adam, who failed and plunged the human race into sin. Christ is also called True in contrast to Satan and his cohorts, who are liars. Because He is God, Jesus is the embodiment of truth (see John 14:6). It takes a person like this to judge righteously.

I'm intrigued by the name Jesus carries that "no one knows except Himself" (Revelation 19:12). It is a very powerful thing whenever God gives you a name, because in the Bible names always reflect character. So apparently there is some aspect of Christ's character that is still unrevealed, and something special about Him we are yet to learn.

Then in verse 13 we read, "His name is called The Word of God." Jesus Christ is the ultimate expression of God's character and person because He is God in the flesh.

There's still another name given to Christ in this passage. "On His robe and on His thigh He has a name written, 'King of kings, and Lord of lords'" (v. 16). Jesus is the King of anybody else called a king and the Lord of anybody else called a lord because all of earth's rulers will bow to Him.

The Garments He Wears

At His return Jesus will also wear "many diadems" (Revelation 19:12). These crowns are emblems of His conquest because He is coming to put down rebellion and take over.

The Lord will also be "clothed with a robe dipped in blood" (v. 13) because He is coming for judgment. There will be no question whatsoever about Jesus' authority or His purpose when He returns to this earth.

The Armies He Commands

Jesus is not coming back alone. "The armies which are in heaven, clothed in fine linen, white and clean, were following Him on white horses" (Revelation 19:14). These are the saints in heaven, including the church that was raptured at the beginning of the tribulation. That means we're in this army.

These saints are dressed in white linen, which is symbolic of righteousness

—in this case, the "righteous acts of the saints" (v. 8). Why will we be in righteous dress? Because after the rapture, we will go through the judgment seat of Christ where our unworthy acts will be burned up. Only the good will remain, so when we return with Christ to reign with Him in the kingdom, we will appear in righteous clothing.

The Sword He Wields

Jesus is also not coming back unarmed. "And from His mouth comes a sharp sword, so that with it He may smite the nations; and He will rule them with a rod of iron; and He treads the wine press of the fierce wrath of God, the Almighty" (Revelation 19:15).

The sharp sword in Jesus' mouth is God's Word, which the writer of Hebrews said is capable of discerning the deepest thoughts and motives of our lives (Hebrews 4:12). This sword speaks of judgment. So does the imagery of the "wine press" of God's wrath. He will grind His enemies into pulp.

Jesus Christ will judge and rule the nations by His Word. So certain is this judgment, in fact, that before the battle of Armageddon even begins, an angel appears to announce the outcome and invite the birds to "the great supper of God" (Revelation 19:17) at which they will feed on the carcasses of all God's enemies.

Those gathered against God at Armageddon are people who have refused to repent throughout the tribulation, even though God has been demonstrating that He alone is God. When you refuse to repent, judgment is all that awaits you.

John said, "I saw the beast and the kings of the earth and their armies, assembled to make war against Him who sat upon the horse, and against His army" (v. 19). The armies are massed together for what they think is a great battle during which they will overthrow God. But what they are really gathering for is a great judgment in which they will become vulture food when Christ simply speaks the Word from His mouth.

THE POWER OF CHRIST'S SECOND COMING

With the two sides at Armageddon drawn up against each other, the next thing we see is the lightning-quick, awesome power that Christ displays at His return.

The fact is that Armageddon isn't much of a battle. It's decided very quickly, over almost before it starts. And by the way, Jesus Christ is used to fighting these kinds of quick battles. He fought one as the "angel of the Lord," the way He appeared in the Old Testament before His incarnation.

A Certain Doom

There is certain judgment in store for the participants of Armageddon who try to overcome Christ, as described in Revelation 19:20–21. Jesus will kill the human kings and their armies at Armageddon, and they will later face God at the great white throne judgment. But He has swifter judgment in store for the Antichrist and his False Prophet. They will go directly into the lake of fire without even experiencing death.

This is a terrifying picture of judgment, of God's wrath poured out on sinful man. The slaughter is beyond our comprehension, armies with hundreds of millions of troops wiped out in a single blast from the mouth of Jesus Christ.

This brings us back to what we said above. If you refuse to repent, you fall into the hands of the living God—and that, the Bible says, is "a terrifying thing" (Hebrews 10:31).

Satan's Binding

With two-thirds of the satanic trinity taken care of, Jesus will turn His attention to Satan himself, the ringleader of this rebellion. Armageddon will be followed by the Devil's "arrest" and incarceration for one thousand years. This is how John described it:

> Then I saw an angel coming down from heaven, holding the key of the abyss and a great chain in his hand. And he laid hold of the dragon, the serpent of old, who is the devil and Satan, and bound him for a thousand years; and he threw him into the abyss, and shut *it* and sealed *it* over him, so that he would not deceive the nations any longer, until the thousand years were completed; after these things he must be released for a short time. (Revelation 20:1–3, italics added)

This imprisonment is not Satan's final, eternal doom, because at the end of the millennium he will go out once more to deceive the nations and make his very last stand against Christ. This brief rebellion will also result in Satan's defeat and his being cast into the lake of fire forever (Revelation 20:7–10).

Satan is going to be locked away for a thousand years because that's how long Christ is going to rule in perfect righteousness on earth. The Devil's absence is one thing that will make the kingdom so wonderful. Jesus is running the show, and the Devil will be nowhere to be found.

THE NATIONS JUDGED AT CHRIST'S SECOND COMING

It's obvious that the second coming of Jesus Christ means judgment for His enemies and blessing for those who know Him. This is evident in another event that will take place when Christ returns—the judgment of the nations in Matthew 25:31–46. A lot of Christians are confused about this, for several reasons.

One reason is that these verses are quoted so often as a standard of how we should be treating people right now. There's no denying that we ought to treat others as we would treat Christ. But that interpretation ignores the specific context Jesus Himself gave for the teaching: "When the Son of Man comes in His glory" (Matthew 25:31).

Another reason for the confusion is that this judgment is harder to fit into the sequence of end times events. It seems to stand alone. But that fact shouldn't keep us from trying to understand this passage and the judgment Christ spoke about here.

The Nature of the Judgment

In Matthew 25, Jesus answered the question of what will happen to millions of people around the world who will survive the tribulation and still be alive "when the Son of Man comes in His glory."

According to Jesus, the people of the nations will be judged at this point. Jesus will be sitting "on His glorious throne" (v. 31), which speaks of His roles as King and Judge. He told us what will occur:

> All the nations will be gathered before Him; and He will separate them from one another, as the shepherd separates the sheep from the goats; and He will put the sheep on His right, and the goats on the left. Then the King will say to those on His right, "Come, you who are blessed of My Father, inherit the kingdom prepared for you from the foundation of the world." . . . Then He will also say to those on His left, "Depart from Me, accursed ones, into the eternal fire which has been prepared for the devil and his angels." (vv. 32-34, 41)

This is the judgment the King issues for these two groups. Now let's go back and notice the criteria for this judgment.

The Criteria for the Judgment

Jesus gave the righteous group of people, the sheep, a number of reasons by which they qualify to inherit His kingdom:

> For I was hungry, and you gave Me something to eat; I was thirsty, and you gave Me drink; I was a stranger, and you invited Me in; naked, and you clothed Me; I was sick, and you visited Me; I was in prison, and you came to Me. (Matthew 25:35-36)

The rest of the passage helps us to understand the central elements and see what Jesus was talking about here. The righteous are surprised by this commendation from King Jesus, and they ask when they did this (vv. 37-40). Jesus gave them this classic answer, which is the main reason for the confusion surrounding Matthew 25: "Truly I say to you, to the extent that you did it to one of these brothers of Mine, even the least of them, you did it to Me" (v. 40).

Then the people on the King's left are judged by the same criteria, except that they fail the test and receive eternal condemnation in hell (vv. 41-45).

The fact that the people standing before Jesus are either sheep or goats, saved or lost, has been determined by the time He makes the separation. Those He places on His right hand are already His sheep. That is, they already belong to Him. What they did was demonstrate they belonged to Christ by their kindness to His "brothers." We'll talk about who those brothers are in a moment. So this passage is not talking about how people can be saved. It's not talking about the present day either, but about Christ's return in glory. That takes us to the end of the tribulation, which is the key to the identity of Jesus' brothers.

These brothers are the 144,000 Jewish evangelists who go out worldwide to preach the gospel during the tribulation, and the sheep among the nations are all the people they have led to Christ during this terrible period of suffering and persecution.

So the decision to help, or refuse to help, these specially designated Jewish evangelists in the tribulation will become a test of a person's true faith. Those who prove their faith in Christ by remaining true to Him will enter the kingdom, while the goats, those who refused to accept Christ, are banished to hell.

Israel's Repentance

At Christ's second coming, Israel will not be included in the judgment of the nations. This is instead a Gentile judgment. According to Ezekiel 20:33–38, God will separate Israel out and enter into judgment personally with His chosen people.

At this time the Israelites will look upon Christ, the One whom they have pierced (Zechariah 12:10), and will mourn over Him. Israel will recognize Jesus Christ as its Messiah, and all the years of rejecting Him will end. Christ will sit on David's throne as the acknowledged King of Israel and King of the world.

PERSONAL APPLICATION FOR LIFE

1. Just as he is out to destroy Israel, Satan has it in for all of God's people. If you are living for Christ, you can be sure that Satan will oppose you. Commit to memory James 4:7, which exhorts us, "Submit therefore to God. Resist the devil and he will flee from you."

2. Armageddon will be a horrible day of slaughter, worse than anything we could imagine. If you are a believer, you will be there as a member of Christ's army, riding at God's side, riding out of heaven, when His fierce wrath against evil is unleashed. Which side will you be on?

3. At Christ's coming, Scripture speaks of the sharp sword in His mouth, which is God's Word. The writer of Hebrews said the Word is capable of discerning the deepest thoughts and motives of our lives (Hebrews 4:12). At His coming, this sword speaks of judgment. Your Bible has the same power, as it also is God's Word. Are you willing to let it search your heart and "judge" your desires and motives?

4. Do you embrace the promises of God's Word? Satan would have us be ignorant of God's promises, as they become so important in the midst of the spiritual battle we are fighting. Our hope for the future is rooted in God's promises. Make it a point daily get into the Word and claim one of God's promises for yourself.

FOR GROUP STUDY

Questions for Group Discussion

1. In God's prophetic program, what is the purpose of this battle? Read Revelation 12:13–17. What is Satan's goal in this battle?

2. According to Ezekiel 39:22, what will be the key result of Israel's battle against the surrounding Islamic nations?

3. According to Revelation 19:11–14, what will Christ look like when He returns?

4. How will Christ display His power when He returns? Read Revelation 20:1–3. What becomes of Satan? (Use the chart below as an aid to your discussion.)

PICTURE THIS

With the two sides at Armageddon drawn up against each other, the next thing we see is the lightning-quick, awesome power that Christ displays at His return. Scripture describes three results of His awesome power.

THE POWER OF CHRIST'S COMING

DISPLAY OF POWER	SCRIPTURE PASSAGE	ITS SIGNIFICANCE
A quick decision	Hebrews 10:31	The battle will be decided quickly and decisively.
A certain doom	Revelation 19:20–21	There will be certain judgment for the participants of Armageddon who try to overcome Christ. Hundreds of millions of troops will die.
Satan's binding	Revelation 20:1–3	Satan will be imprisoned for one thousand years, during the entire millennial kingdom of Christ.

114

PROPHECY AND THE MILLENNIAL KINGDOM

The millennium is the perfect way to end time. Only God could have conceived of a program that brings His creation called time to an end in such a way that everything messed up by sin and Satan is restored, God's promises are fulfilled, His righteousness is fully vindicated and displayed, and every legitimate human longing for peace and justice is met.

All of that and more will come to pass when Jesus Christ establishes His thousand-year kingdom on earth. We call it the "millennium" from the Latin term for the Greek word *chilias*, which means "thousand."

Some people think this is just a symbolic term for time, so that the thousand-year kingdom is not literal but merely a way of speaking about eternity. However, John used this term six times in Revelation 20:1–7 to describe this period that follows the tribulation, and he gave no indication that it is to be taken metaphorically. The millennium is a specific period of time.

The millennium is the perfect way to end time because it is followed immediately by the eternal state. During Christ's millennial reign, God will set creation right again, and man will have what he has always wanted, a utopia on earth.

But there will be no utopia until Jesus Himself brings it, and He will do so on His terms. His enemies will be destroyed at Armageddon, Satan will be locked away for a thousand years, and the Antichrist and the False Prophet will be sent to hell. No one will be able to stop Christ from taking over. Let's look at what the Bible says about this glorious period of time.

THE COMPLETENESS OF THE MILLENNIUM

Because the millennium is the completion of time and the culmination of history, God will bring His purposes for Jesus Christ, for mankind in general, and for Israel in particular, to completion during this golden age. We've talked about this before, so I just want to review it briefly.

Rightful Rule Restored

Christ's millennial reign will restore the creation to its rightful order that was interrupted and thrown into disarray when sin entered the human race. The most important purpose achieved in the millennium is that Jesus Christ will take His rightful throne as Ruler of the earth. He was ordained by God to rule, and that purpose will be gloriously fulfilled during this time.

Mankind's purpose and divine destiny will also be realized during the millennium. God told Adam and Eve to have dominion over the creation (Genesis 1:26–28; see Psalm 8:6–8), a dominion they forfeited when they sinned.

But then Jesus Christ, the last Adam, replaced the first Adam as head of the human race when He died for sin and rose victoriously over sin and death and Satan. So when Christ rules, we will rule with Him as God reverses the effects of sin and restores to mankind the dominion He commanded the human race to exercise back in Eden.

In fact, the Bible often compares Christ's kingdom to Eden. The prophet Ezekiel wrote, "And they will say, 'This desolate land has become like the garden of Eden; and the waste, desolate, and ruined cities are fortified and inhabited'" (36:35; see Isaiah 51:3).

The first Adam was created in a perfect environment of absolute innocence. But the kingdom will be even better, because the last Adam will reign in a perfect environment of absolute righteousness.

Fulfillment for Israel

The millennium will also mean the completion and fulfillment of God's purposes for Israel. God promised concerning Israel, "'I will also plant them on their land, and they will not again be rooted out from their land, which I have given them,' says the Lord your God" (Amos 9:15).

God not only promised Israel that He would give them their land, but that they would be permanent residents of all the land. That's not the case today. Israel inhabits only a portion of the land God promised to Abraham. But in the millennial kingdom, Israel will get all of its land back. There will be no trading of land for peace with the Arabs.

Israel will also have its rightful King in the millennium. Jesus was rejected when He came the first time to present Himself to the Jews as their King. His birth in Bethlehem fulfilled God's promise of a King, as the religious leaders of Israel acknowledged when the magi came to them (Matthew 2:6).

But Jesus illustrated Israel's rejection of Him in His parable of the nobleman who went away to receive a kingdom. His subjects sent the nobleman this message: "We do not want this man to reign over us" (Luke 19:14). That was the official position of Israel concerning Jesus. But God had promised David that his Son would rule on his throne forever. Jesus Christ is that Son of David, and He will take the throne in Jerusalem and reign in His kingdom.

By the way, Christ's rule in Jerusalem will be a righteous dictatorship. "It will come about that in the last days, the mountain of the house of the Lord will be established as the chief of the mountains, and will be raised above the hills; and all the nations will stream to it" (Isaiah 2:2).

Jerusalem will be the capital of the world in the millennium (Isaiah 2:3; Jeremiah 3:17–18; Zechariah 14:16), which is why at Armageddon the battle will be for control of Jerusalem. The kingdom will be Israel's golden age of restoration and the realization of all that God promised and purposed for His chosen people.

THE CHURCH IN THE MILLENNIUM

We've already noted that the church occupies a special place in the kingdom, the place next to Jesus Christ as His bride. We will enter the kingdom with glorified bodies given us at the rapture, as opposed to survivors of the tribulation who enter in their normal human bodies.

The Marriage Supper

Revelation 19:7–9 describes the great event awaiting the church when Christ comes for His bride:

> Let us rejoice and be glad and give the glory to Him, for the marriage of the Lamb has come and His bride has made herself ready. And it was given to her to clothe herself in fine linen, bright and clean; for the fine linen is the righteous acts of the saints. And he said to me, "Write, 'Blessed are those who are invited to the marriage supper of the Lamb.'"

The marriage supper of Jesus Christ, at which He will receive His bride, the church for which He died (see Ephesians 5:25–27), is going to be a glorious occasion. To understand just how glorious it will be, we need to compare it to an Oriental wedding, the kind the apostle John would have been writing about.

In biblical days, marriages in the Orient consisted of four distinct parts. The marriage began with the betrothal or engagement, an arrangement made by a father to acquire a bride for his son. The engagement was a legal contract and was considered as binding and sacred as the marriage itself. That's why Joseph was ready to divorce Mary when he discovered she was pregnant, even though they were only "betrothed" or engaged (Matthew 1:18–19).

A father could arrange his son's wedding long before the son was of marriageable age by reaching an agreement with the father of the future bride. The agreement would mean that when these two young people came of age, they would be married to each other and were to save themselves for one another. The agreement was legally recognized.

Paul drew on this concept to describe the church's relationship to Christ and Paul's role in that bond. "I am jealous for you with a godly jealousy; for I betrothed you to one husband, that to Christ I might present you as a pure virgin" (2 Corinthians 11:2).

Every Christian becomes a part of Christ's bride, the church, and becomces engaged to Him at the moment of our salvation. We belong to Christ, even though we have not yet come to the wedding ceremony. Therefore, to give ourselves to anyone or anything else is spiritual adultery.

There was often a long time between the betrothal and the actual marriage. For most believers, there is a long time between salvation and the time when they are united with their Beloved at the rapture. Paul was concerned that false teachers would slip in and lead the Corinthians away from their faithfulness to Jesus Christ during their betrothal period.

We were actually betrothed to Christ by God the Father "before the foundation of the world" (Ephesians 1:4), so we have been engaged for a long time from heaven's perspective.

Our betrothal to Christ will last until He comes for His bride at the rapture. This corresponds to the second stage of an Oriental wedding. The bridegroom went to the bride's home to take her back to his father's house, so that she would be with her husband where he was. That's why Jesus told us He was going to His Father's house to prepare a place for us, so we could be with Him where He is (see John 14:1–3).

The third stage of the marriage was the wedding reception itself, in which the bridegroom introduced his bride to her new family and new life. The bridegroom invited his family and friends to the wedding reception, which could last for a long time and become quite a celebration.

People in that culture didn't have a brief ceremony in front of an official and then go to a reception that lasted a few hours. Depending on the wealth of the bridegroom's father, the reception could last for days or even weeks and include elaborate dinners.

Well, guess what? Our heavenly Daddy is very rich! So His Son's wedding reception, the marriage supper of the Lamb, is going to last one thousand years. The ultimate focus of this wedding party will be on the Bridegroom, Jesus Christ. He is the One who will take people's breath away as He appears in all of His glory. The radiance of the bride will simply be a reflection of His glory.

Reigning with Christ

As Christ's bride in the kingdom, we will also reign with Him the way a king's wife shares his throne. Paul said the church will judge the world and even angels (see 1 Corinthians 6:2–3), and in Revelation 20:4, John said the resurrected saints will reign with Christ for a thousand years.

The Bible says we are "fellow heirs" with Christ (Romans 8:17), and our level of authority in the kingdom depends on our faithfulness to Him on earth. That explains why in His parable of the servants, Jesus rewarded the first two servants with authority over ten cities and five cities, respectively (Luke 19:15–19). Jesus is going to administer His kingdom through us. Changing the imagery from that of a bride, we will be Christ's governors in the millennium. We will rule with Him.

THE CHARACTER OF THE MILLENNIUM

What will the millennium be like? What can we look forward to during the rule of Christ on earth?

We have called the millennium the golden age of man, and that's what it really is because, as we said above, everything that's wrong with this world will be set right.

A Time of Long Life

The first thing I want us to see is that during the millennium, mankind will enjoy the long life people have always wished for. Length of life will be immaterial to the believers who are raptured and come back with Christ, because we will have our resurrection bodies. But those who are saved at the end of the tribulation, the ones Jesus calls His sheep (Matthew 25:31–40), will enter the millennium in their natural bodies and procreate, as we have already seen.

They will live on an earth returned to its original perfection and beauty and fruitfulness, an environment in which long life will be the norm:

> No longer will there be in it an infant who lives but a few days, or an old man who does not live out his days; for the youth will die at the age of one hundred and the one who does not reach the age of one hundred will be thought accursed. (Isaiah 65:20)

The only reason people will die young and not live out their days in the millennium is if they are foolish enough to rebel against Jesus Christ. And that brings us to another feature of this thousand-year period.

No Rebellion Permitted

When Jesus Christ sits on His throne, no rebellion or disobedience will be allowed. Christ will rule "with a rod of iron" (Revelation 19:15). That's how it should be, because we are talking about a perfect King who rules in perfect righteousness and justice. Jesus will demand obedience, and He will have it. Those who don't conform out of love for Him will do so because they rightly fear His iron rod.

Even nature and the animal kingdom will be brought under Christ's control. "'The wolf and the lamb will graze together, and the lion will eat straw like the ox; and dust will be the serpent's food. They will do no evil or harm in all My holy mountain,' says the Lord" (Isaiah 65:25).

Nothing in nature will be allowed to rebel or express itself in an unrighteous way. Even little children will be safe with formerly wild animals (see Isaiah 11:6–8) because the dominion over nature that was given to the first Adam will be restored by Christ, the last Adam, in the millennium.

A Time of Total Fulfillment

I love this characteristic about the millennium. All of the limitations and frustrations we experience here on earth will be lifted. Isaiah says:

> They will build houses and inhabit them; they will also plant vineyards and eat their fruit. They will not build, and another inhabit, they will not plant, and another eat; for as the lifetime of a tree, so will be the days of My people. . . . They will not labor in vain, or bear children for calamity. (65:21–22a, 23)

Your work won't be in vain in the kingdom. You won't see your best efforts fail or go up in smoke, or build something only to watch someone else take it over. You'll enjoy the fruit of your own work in the kingdom. There will be no unfulfillment.

A Time of Perfect Righteousness

We've made this point about the millennial kingdom several times already, but let me show you a wonderful passage that captures the character of Jesus Christ's reign.

The prophet Isaiah said of the king who will rule, "The Spirit of the Lord will rest on Him" (11:2). Isaiah then went on to describe the fullness of the Spirit that will rest on Christ.

People say they want justice and honesty from their rulers. We have a hard time today finding people of integrity who can occupy the offices of government. But that will not be a problem when Jesus Christ takes the reins of government.

His administration in the millennial kingdom will result in a thousand years of perfect justice and righteousness. The earth will also abound with health and prosperity (Isaiah 29:18; 32:2–4; 33:24; 35:5–6).

All of this will take place because the earth will be filled with the knowledge of God (Isaiah 11:9; 32:15; 44:3), and God will personally communicate to the hearts of His people (Jeremiah 31:33–34).

THE CULMINATION OF THE MILLENNIUM

When the millennium comes to an end and the thousand years are completed, the Bible says that "Satan will be released from his prison" (Revelation 20:7) to gather all the rebels for one more run at overthrowing God.

Satan Released and Judged

Satan will "come out to deceive the nations" and will amass an army of rebels so great its number "is like the sand of the seashore" (Revelation 20:8). Satan's army will surround Jerusalem, but this fight will be over before it starts, because "fire [will come] down from heaven and [devour] them" (v. 9).

Then the Devil will finally and forever get his due. "The devil who deceived them was thrown into the lake of fire and brimstone, where the beast and the false prophet are also; and they will be tormented day and night forever and ever" (v. 10).

Rebels Identified and Judged

We know that there will be people in the millennium who refuse Christ and want to rebel against His rule. But even when we read it in Scripture, it seems hard to believe that people will rebel in a perfect environment.

Out of that mass of humanity, Satan will find enough sinners to gather an army that can't be counted. He will bring out the sin that these unbelievers were holding on the inside. The huge size of this army isn't hard to explain when you think about all the babies that will be born over a thousand-year period. And the fact that people will live a lot longer means the population in the millennium will be enormous.

This brief rebellion will be the final expression of Satan and the final expression of sinful man. These rebels will have lived in a perfect world, with no worries about crime or violence. Their children could have lions as pets because nature will be under the dominion of man. But some people don't want God even when things are perfect.

So history will culminate in Satan's final rebellion and his eternal judgment. Those who belong to Christ will be ushered into eternity, and those who refuse Him will come up before God for the great white throne judgment. History will end with God's final and complete victory.

Handing Over the Kingdom

According to 1 Corinthians 15:24–26, at the end of the kingdom Jesus Christ will hand over the reins of authority to God the Father. Paul described this amazing moment:

> Then comes the end, when He delivers up the kingdom to the God and Father, when He has abolished all rule and all authority and power. For He must reign until He has put all His enemies under His feet. The last enemy that will be abolished is death.

Christ will defeat all His enemies in a perfect reign as King, and then deliver His kingdom to the Father to extend the rule of heaven into eternity.

What was true of the millennial kingdom will become the normal, eternal operation of heaven. Jesus Christ will turn to His Father and say, "I have fulfilled My reign. The kingdom is now Yours."

PERSONAL APPLICATION FOR LIFE

1. The Bible doesn't tell us about the kingdom so we can sit and daydream about the future and escape the hard realities of the present. Our job as the church is to model the kingdom on earth here and now in such a way that people will be drawn to Christ and long to be part of His kingdom. Does your life model Jesus Christ and make others want to know more about Him?

2. The church's calling is to set in place the mechanisms of the kingdom. Read 1 Corinthians 6:2–3. The apostle Paul used the reality of a future kingdom to show the body of Christ how we should be functioning in the present. If you are not part of a local church where you can be a functioning part of the body of Christ, then get busy and find a fellowship where you can start doing the work of Jesus Christ!

3. We cannot remind ourselves too often that Satan is a defeated enemy. His total defeat will be evident to all in the kingdom when the Devil is chained up for a thousand years. But he's free to roam today, so don't let your defeated foe bring you down to spiritual defeat in your daily Christian life. Claim kingdom victory today and every day.

4. The reason we study prophecy is not to satisfy our curiosity, but to learn how we are to function while we wait for Christ to return. The church is designed to be God's preview of the coming attraction. People are supposed to look at us and say, "Wow, if the preview is this good, the full show must be something!" Is your life giving people a preview of the kingdom?

FOR GROUP STUDY

Questions for Group Discussion

1. In what ways does the millennium function as the culmination of time as we know it?

2. Read Revelation 19:7–9 and Ephesians 5:25–27. What roles does the church have in the millennium? What is the Marriage Supper of the Lamb?

3. What will be the characteristics of the millennium? (Use the "Picture This" chart as an aid to your discussion.)

4. Read Revelation 20:7–10 and 1 Corinthians 15:24–26. How will the millennium end? What are the key events of its culmination?

PICTURE THIS

The Bible gives us a preview of what the millennium will be like. The rule of Christ will be completely different than anything the world has ever seen. Below are a few characteristics of this coming golden age.

The Millennium

CHARACTERISTIC	SCRIPTURE PASSAGE	WHAT IT MEANS
A time of long life	Isaiah 65:20	Those with resurrection bodies will not die, and those with natural bodies will live long lives in a restored earth.
No rebellion will be permitted	Isaiah 65:25	Christ will permit no rebellion or disobedience, as He will rule "with a rod of iron" (Revelation 19:15).
A time of total fulfillment	Isaiah 65:21–22a, 23	All limitations and frustrations of earthly experience will be lifted.
A time of perfect righteousness	Isaiah 11:2–5	Christ will rule in the fullness of the Holy Spirit with perfect justice and righteousness.

15

PROPHECY AND THE GREAT WHITE THRONE

The great white throne judgment is the last event in time before God ushers in eternity, and so in one sense it is the termination point of His prophetic program for mankind. It is best known by the description of the seat upon which the Judge will sit.

John said, "I saw a great white throne" (Revelation 20:11). The white throne judgment is the event most people are referring to when they talk about "judgment day" in terms of having to face God. Let's look at the details of this judgment in which unrepentant sinners "fall into the hands of the living God" (Hebrews 10:31).

THE PARTICIPANTS IN THE JUDGMENT

The most important participant in this final judgment of mankind is the Judge Himself—although interestingly enough, He is not identified by name. But this is an awesome person "from whose presence earth and heaven fled away" (Revelation 20:11). That can only be a description of Deity, and so we understand that the Judge is a member of the Godhead.

The Judge is Jesus Himself, who has already been sitting on the throne in Jerusalem ruling and judging the world for one thousand years. Besides, He has just defeated Satan and his rebellious forces at the climax of the millennium (v. 10), so He is already exercising judgment. The whiteness of the throne speaks of Christ's purity and holiness.

Why is Jesus Christ seated on the throne executing God's judgment? Because He is the Son of Man, who paid the price for man's sin and can relate to the people He is judging since He also took on human flesh. Of course, Jesus is also the Son of God, so He can relate to God's justice. He is the perfect Judge to sit on this great white throne.

Who else is present at this judgment? "I saw the dead, the great and the small, standing before the throne. . . . And the sea gave up the dead which were in it, and death and Hades gave up the dead which were in them; and they were judged" (Revelation 20:12–13).

The defendants at this judgment are the unbelievers of all the ages, the people whose names are not found in the Book of Life (v. 15). No Christians are anywhere to be found at this judgment. The penalty for their sins has been laid on Christ, and their names written in His Book of Life. At this point, Christians have already been evaluated for their service at the judgment seat of Christ prior to the kingdom.

Notice that those unbelievers who had died before this judgment will be raised from the dead to face their condemnation. This is the "resurrection of judgment" Jesus spoke about (John 5:29). Death is no barrier to God. Nothing will be missed or overlooked as unsaved people from throughout history appear before Christ in the final judgment of the ages.

THE PURPOSES OF THE JUDGMENT

What purposes of God will be accomplished when Jesus sits on the great white throne at the end of time? I see at least four reasons for this judgment.

To Purge Sin from the Universe

When Christ finishes judging the world from His white throne, the world will be finally and forever purged of the sin that has plagued it since the day Eve was seduced by the tempter.

We have seen that at various points in God's prophetic plan, He will deal with sin and judge sinners. But even during the millennium, sin and rebellion will be brewing in the hearts of multitudes of people. And at the end of this time, Satan will still have one last gasp.

But all sin will be swept into hell forever at God's great white throne judgment. Revelation 21:1 shows that immediately after the final judgment, the new heaven and new earth appear. The order of events is important here, because God can't introduce His new creation while sin is still polluting the environment.

To Vindicate God's Perfect Justice

Since God's judgment is never unfair or arbitrary, the sinners who stand before Christ at the great white throne will be judged "according to their deeds" (Revelation 20:12–13). God says it twice to emphasize the justice of this trial. At the final judgment, sinners will finally see the awfulness of their sin because it will be revealed in the blazing light of God's justice.

Now having said this, let me back up and affirm that the reason people will be sent to hell is their lack of a saving relationship with Christ. Revelation 20:15 says they will be thrown into the lake of fire not because of their deeds, but because they weren't in the Lamb's Book of Life. And the only way you can get your name in this book is by accepting Christ.

To Determine People's Punishment

A third purpose of the white throne judgment is to determine the degree of punishment unbelievers will receive in hell. This aspect of the judgment isn't found explicitly in Revelation 20, although it is suggested by the fact that the books of people's deeds are opened. But there is abundant evidence in Scripture that people will be judged based on the knowledge they had and the opportunities they had or didn't have to repent and receive Christ.

We're not talking about whether people are punished, but how severely. Any sin will disqualify a person from heaven. But because God is just, there will be degrees of judgment in hell just as there will be degrees of reward for believers in heaven. Some sinners are more blatant and vile than others.

People often wonder if murderous tyrants like Adolf Hitler and Joseph Stalin will be punished more severely for their horrible sins. I believe the Bible teaches that they will be. We need to distinguish between the effect sin has on our standing before God and the impact of our sin on others.

Satan, the Antichrist, and the False Prophet will receive the most severe punishment because they led so many others astray. That's why the Bible warns that spiritual teachers will be judged by a stricter standard (James 3:1).

All sin is equally sinful to God, and no sinner can stand in His presence. But sins are not all equal in their impact. Stealing a cookie is not as devastating in its effect as murder. God's law allowed differing levels of punishment for differing levels of crimes, and God will apply the same standards at the great white throne.

To Reveal Man's Responsibility

A fourth purpose of this judgment is to show once and for all that people are responsible for their sins. We have already suggested this purpose in our discussion of the books that contain people's deeds. No one will be able to dodge responsibility or blame God for his or her sins, because the records of all deeds will be there in perfect order. Someone might say, "That's not fair. What about all the good deeds these people did?" There are at least two answers to that question.

First, remember that when it comes to God's perfect standard, there are no good deeds acceptable to God apart from Christ. The best that people can do on their own is in reality "a filthy garment" in God's sight (Isaiah 64:6). So there won't be any good deeds people can present in their defense at the judgment.

Second, even if unbelievers could bring their good deeds to the judgment, these would still be irrelevant to the issue at hand. Standing before Christ at His great white throne, their sin will appear "utterly sinful" (Romans 7:13) and their supposed goodness will evaporate. People will see God as He is and see their sin for what it really is. And they will know they are responsible for their sins, without any excuse to offer.

THE PATTERN OF THE JUDGMENT

What pattern will Jesus Christ follow in His judgment at the great white throne? What standard will He use in executing judgment? I want to suggest that three books will be present at this tribunal.

The Word of God

Jesus said in John 12:48 that the word He spoke will be the standard by which those who reject Him will be judged "at the last day." When the ruler came to Jesus seeking eternal life, Jesus cited the Ten Commandments, thereby suggesting that these were the standard by which this man would be judged (Luke 18:20).

The Bible is God's standard of judgment because it is the only revelation of His will and His commands. A person cannot be judged and condemned for breaking a law that doesn't exist. God will judge people by His Word.

The Book of Deeds

We've discussed the contents of this book previously, so I just want to mention the book of deeds as the second volume to be used in the process of final judgment.

Ecclesiastes 12:14 says God will bring every act into judgment. The Word of God will pronounce the doom of unbelievers, and being faced with the record of their sins will have the effect of confirming the rightness of God's judgment.

The Book of Life

We have also mentioned the Book of Life, which is sometimes called "the Lamb's book of life" (Revelation 21:27). This is Jesus' book, filled with the names of the people whom He purchased with His precious blood. As we said, none of the people in this book will have to appear at the great white throne. This book is only there to verify the lost condition of those whose names are not in it.

As John was describing the New Jerusalem, he said the only people who will be allowed to enter the Celestial City are those whose names are in the Book of Life (Revelation 21:27).

Believers are told to rejoice in their salvation (see Luke 10:20), but the tragedy of the great white throne is that no one there will be found in the book. Those who come to Christ by faith have their names eternally recorded in His book (Luke 10:20), where no eraser can ever remove them.

THE PUNISHMENT AT THE JUDGMENT

The punishment Jesus Christ will mete out at the great white throne judgment has a definite sense of finality to it. "Death and Hades were thrown into the lake of fire. This is the second death, the lake of fire. And if anyone's name was not found written in the book of life, he was thrown into the lake of fire" (Revelation 20:14–15). This is the final and eternal punishment for sin.

The Second Death

John said the lake of fire is "the second death." To experience a second death, there must have been a first death. The first death that mankind experienced was original sin, which takes us back all the way to the beginning of time in Eden.

When God commanded Adam not to eat from the Tree of the Knowledge of Good and Evil, He added this warning, "In the day that you eat from it you will surely die" (Genesis 2:17). Adam and Eve ate from the tree and died the same day—not physically, but spiritually. They were driven from the garden and from God's presence and saddled with the curse of sin.

This was the first death. It consisted of lost fellowship with God. When our first parents sinned, the human race was banned from Paradise, cut off from God, and sent out to live in a world cursed by thorns and weeds and sickness and physical death.

In His death on the cross, Jesus Christ provided redemption from the curse of sin by taking the curse on Himself and paying the price for sin (see Galatians 3:13). Therefore, if you are a Christian, you are removed from the curse.

In other words, the effects of the first death can be reversed. But the second death is irreversible. It is eternal. Like the first death, the second death involves removal from God's presence, except that this removal is forever. The second death is permanent separation from God's grace and mercy.

The Absence of God's Goodness

God is omnipresent. He is everywhere. He fills all of creation. David asked, "Where can I flee from Your presence?" (Psalm 139:7). Answer: nowhere. The presence of God, then, is a reality even in hell. When we say people in hell are eternally separated from God, we are talking about His grace and mercy and salvation. Those who suffer condemnation at the great white throne will find none of these attributes of God in hell. They are unavailable.

This horrific, devastating fact is the real torment of hell. Imagine being in a place totally devoid of God's goodness. Do you realize that every good thing we enjoy in life is possible only because God is good (see James 1:17)?

An Eternity of Evil

Here's another terrible aspect of the second death. "Let the one who does wrong, still do wrong; and let the one who is filthy, still be filthy; and let the one who is righteous, still practice righteousness; and let the one who is holy, still keep himself holy" (Revelation 22:11). Whatever a person's nature, that person will be locked into it for all eternity.

So a filthy, vile person on earth will exist eternally as a filthy, vile person. There is no moral improvement in hell because hell is not restorative punishment. It will be too late for that. Hell is retributive punishment.

You may wonder why it matters what people will be like in hell. It matters because the Bible is giving us the real deal so no one in his right mind would refuse Christ for eternity in hell. Along with the absence of God's goodness, hell will be torment because sinners will have all of their same evil cravings with no capacity to satisfy them. A sexually immoral person will burn for sex, but there will be none. The jealous person will burn with jealousy, but there will be no way to fulfill those jealous longings. Sinners will be confirmed in their evil character and their lostness.

Unfit for Heaven

Here's something else to consider. Because people who are judged at the great white throne will remain in their sinful condition in hell, they wouldn't be able to enjoy heaven even if God allowed them to enter. Sinners in hell are totally unfit for heaven, in other words. It would be too painful, like a person whose eyes are dilated suddenly stepping out into brilliant sunlight. If you have ever been in that condition, you know that darkness is preferable to light because the light is too painful.

That's what would happen if an unredeemed sinner from hell were ever to enter heaven. It wouldn't be relief and joy. It would be incredibly painful, and the sinner would want to run back to the darkness.

Hell is the final punishment that will be pronounced on unrepentant sinners at the great white throne judgment.

USHERED INTO ETERNITY

When the great white throne judgment is completed at the end of Christ's millennial kingdom, the kingdom will be over and we will be ushered into eternity, as described in Revelation 21–22.

PERSONAL APPLICATION FOR LIFE

1. It was God's Word that spoke the universe into existence. According to John 1, the Word (Jesus) became flesh and dwelt among us (v. 14). The Word of God will one day be the standard for judgment (John 12:48). Although it's difficult for us to comprehend all that God does on our behalf, we can certainly thank Him for what we can grasp and understand. Take a moment to give thanks for the power of God's Word at work in your life.
2. Have you brought your sin record to Jesus and trusted Him to pay the bill for your sins? If not, don't delay! Accept His gift of salvation made possible by His sacrifice on the cross for your sins. Trust Jesus now to save you from the penalty of your sin.
3. Here's a way to test your "faithfulness quotient." Figure out how much time you've spent in fellowship with Christ through prayer, worship, and study of His Word the last week. How does that match how much time you've spent on other activities during the same period of time? If that ratio doesn't look very healthy for your relationship with the Lord, it may be time for some schedule changes.
4. The certainty of God's judgment means that the best thing we can do today is make sure our affairs are in order in terms of our relationship with Christ. If you want to enjoy heaven with Jesus Christ for all eternity, accept Him today, and do all you can to make sure that everyone you know knows Christ!

FOR GROUP STUDY

Questions for Group Discussion

1. Read Revelation 20:11 and Hebrews 10:31. What is the great white throne judgment?
2. According to Revelation 20:11 and John 5:29, who will be participating in this judgment?

3. What is the fourfold purpose of the great white throne judgment? (Use the chart below as an aid to your discussion.)
4. What pattern will Jesus Christ follow in His judgment at the great white throne? What standard will He use in executing judgment?

PICTURE THIS

What purposes of God will be accomplished when Jesus sits on the great white throne at the end of time? There are at least four things this judgment will accomplish.

THE FOURFOLD PURPOSE OF THE GREAT WHITE THRONE JUDGMENT

PURPOSE	SCRIPTURE PASSAGES	WHAT IT MEANS
To purge sin from the universe	Revelation 21:1	The world will be finally and forever purged of the sin that has plagued it since the fall in the garden of Eden.
To vindicate God's perfect judgment	Revelation 20:12–13	Sinners who stand before Christ at the great white throne will be judged "according to their deeds."
To determine people's punishment	Revelation 20; James 3:1	This judgment will determine the degree of punishment unbelievers will receive in hell.
To reveal mankind's responsibility	Isaiah 64:6; Romans 7:13	This judgment will show once and for all that people are responsible for their sins.

116
THE ETERNAL STATE

Those who accept Jesus as Savior will enjoy heaven with Him for all eternity, we noted in the previous chapter. What is heaven like—or for those who reject the Savior, what is hell like? Our discussion of eternity will focus on heaven and hell, the two realities of the eternal state. The Bible is clear that all people will be resurrected to spend eternity in one of these two places (John 5:28–29). This is what the future holds for all of us after death . . . or when Jesus comes.

I want to begin with a survey of the Bible's teaching on hell, so that we can close out this book in the best place—heaven, the eternal home of believers

THE REALITY OF HELL

The first fact we need to establish about hell is its undeniable reality. Let's start with a basic definition. Hell is the place of eternal exile where the ungodly will eternally experience God's righteous retribution against sin.

Jesus believed hell was a real place, and He taught its reality throughout His ministry. While teaching on the judgment awaiting the Gentiles, Jesus called hell "eternal fire" and "eternal punishment" (Matthew 25:41, 46).

These are just two of many verses in which the Bible clearly teaches the reality of hell as a place of punishment. Jesus Himself said more about hell than He did about either heaven or love, and He taught that hell is a place to be avoided at all costs (Matthew 18:8–9).

THE RESIDENTS OF HELL

The next fact about hell we need to understand is who will end up in this place of torment. Who will be the residents of hell?

Jesus made perhaps the most important statement in this regard when He said the unrighteous Gentile nations will hear this pronouncement of judgment: "Depart from Me, accursed ones, into the eternal fire which has been prepared for the devil and his angels" (Matthew 25:41).

Hell's Intended Occupants

Hell was not originally created for human beings, but as a place of eternal exile and punishment for Satan and the fallen angels who joined him in his rebellion against God in heaven. Remember the five "I will" statements Satan made in his attempt to usurp the throne of God (Isaiah 14)?

But Satan and his angels, who became the demons, failed in their rebellion. So God prepared a place to eternally remind them of the consequences of spiritual rebellion.

Satan chose to set himself in opposition to God. The fundamental fact about hell is that going there is a choice, a decision. There will be no resident in hell, demonic or human, who did not opt for spiritual rebellion against God.

A Place for Unrepentant People

Although God did not create hell for people, those who make the same choice Satan made will suffer the same judgment. Just as we have to choose Christ and heaven, unrepentant sinners will go to hell by choice, not by chance.

Hell is the built-in consequence of rejecting Christ. Human beings in their natural state are already alienated from God and under His wrath. They don't have to choose hell in the sense of making a conscious choice. They make their choice to reject heaven when they refuse to repent and receive Christ's forgiveness for sin.

THE REASON FOR HELL

God always responds to evil in one of two basic ways. We might call them His passive and His active wrath. Romans 1 is a good example of passive wrath because when people persisted in sin, God "gave them over" to follow their evil desires (vv. 24, 26, 28). God removed His protection from them and turned them over to the consequences of their evil.

Paul later referred to God's active wrath when he warned, "Because of your stubbornness and unrepentant heart you are storing up wrath for yourself in the day of wrath and revelation of the righteous judgment of God" (Romans 2:5). God's fierce wrath against sin is as much a reflection of His character as His love is (Romans 11:22).

THE LOCATION OF HELL

The Bible also relates this terrible place to "the lake of fire and brimstone" (Revelation 20:10). Later we read, "Death and Hades were thrown into the lake of fire. This is the second death, the lake of fire" (v. 14). Hell will be placed in the lake of fire, similar to the way Alcatraz prison is surrounded by the waters of San Francisco Bay. The lake of fire will make escape from hell impossible.

Even though hades and hell are distinct terms in the New Testament, hades is clearly a place of torment and, therefore, is more or less a synonym for hell (the NIV translators use "hell" in Luke 16 in recognition of this fact). Hades is the place where the unrighteous go at the moment of death. Jesus' story of the rich man and Lazarus in Luke 16 shows that hades is a place of conscious suffering and torment. But right now it is more of a "holding cell" for unbelievers until their final judgment at the great white throne. That's why hades as a place that holds condemned sinners is also said to be thrown into the lake of fire.

THE PHYSICAL TORMENT OF HELL

In Luke 16:24, Jesus said that when the rich man looked up into heaven and saw Lazarus being comforted in Abraham's bosom, he cried out, "Father Abraham, have mercy on me, and send Lazarus so that he may dip the tip of his finger in water and cool off my tongue, for I am in agony in this flame" (Luke 16:24).

Revelation 20 says that the sea, the grave, and hades itself "gave up the dead which were in them" (v. 13) so these people could be judged and sent to hell. The fact is that just as believers will receive new bodies that will prepare them for eternal life in heaven, so the lost will receive resurrected bodies that will allow them to endure eternal punishment in hell.

THE MENTAL TORMENT OF HELL

The Bible teaches that the suffering of hell will also include the mental torment of memory and regret.

When the rich man of Luke 16 asked for a drop of water to cool his tongue, Abraham gave him this answer. "Child, remember that during your life you received your good things" (v. 25).

Jesus said of hell that it was a place where "their worm does not die, and the fire is not quenched" (Mark 9:44, 46, 48). He was speaking literally of the unquenchable fire. The worm refers to the mental suffering of hell, which will be so intense that people will be able to recall specific occasions when they may have heard the gospel of Jesus Christ and rejected it. They will remember the day that a pastor or Sunday school teacher or friend asked them about the condition of their soul, and they laughed and walked away.

THE SPIRITUAL TORMENT OF HELL

I wish we could say that the physical and mental suffering of hell were the limits of its misery. But we need to talk about two more elements that are actually far worse.

Glimpses of Heaven

According to Luke 16:23, the rich man could see Lazarus and Abraham far off in heaven. He could actually see the eternal life and joy he was missing.

Jesus said the rich man could see Lazarus in Abraham's bosom, so we can legitimately talk about what it would be like if a person in hell was able to catch glimpses of heaven. That would be incredible spiritual torment. It would heighten the pain of being in hell.

Spiritual Emptiness in Hell

For a sufferer in hell, the torment of knowing and seeing what is being missed in heaven is one thing. But the Bible also declares that there is no fulfillment or peace of any kind in hell itself. God says in Isaiah 48:22, "There is no peace for the wicked." There is no fulfillment in hell, no dreams, only bitter regrets.

So besides being cut off from any relationship with God, people in hell will also not find any solace from other sufferers. Sinners will only be confirmed or "locked in" to their sin. There will be lots of people in hell, but they won't be any company to anyone. Instead, people will be contemptuous toward one another (Daniel 12:2).

THE ETERNAL TORMENT OF HELL

The most intense and agonizing of all the aspects of hell is that it is an eternal place (Revelation 14:9–11). We need to grasp the awful, eternal consequences of rejecting Christ. God has done everything necessary to keep anyone from going to hell. He has an "anti-hell" vaccine, the blood of Christ, available to all who trust Christ alone for their eternal salvation.

THE JOYS OF HEAVEN

Heaven is God's eternal home, the place where His program began and where it will end. Heaven will also be our future home for all eternity, so it makes sense that we try to get as clear a picture as possible of what heaven is like.

Heaven Is a Promised Place

Jesus told His disciples in John 14:1–2, "Do not let your heart be troubled; believe in God, believe also in Me. In My Father's house are many dwelling places; if it were not so, I would have told you; for I go to prepare a place for you."

If you ever doubt the reality of heaven, believe in the God who cannot lie. The only way heaven can be a lie is if God is a liar—and that's impossible (Numbers 23:19; Hebrews 6:18). This God who cannot lie has told us in His Word that when our earthly bodies collapse like an old tent, we have new bodies prepared for us that are eternal in heaven (2 Corinthians 5:1).

Heaven Is a Particular Place

Here's another feature or characteristic of heaven. It's a particular place. By that I mean heaven isn't some nebulous, indistinct concept floating out there in the universe.

God is not a nebulous concept, but a distinct person. His house, heaven, isn't fuzzy either. This place has an address. It's a particular location.

The apostle John wrote, "[An angel] carried me away in the Spirit to a great and high mountain, and showed me the holy city, Jerusalem, coming down out of heaven from God, having the glory of God. Her brilliance was like a very costly stone, as a stone of crystal-clear jasper" (Revelation 21:10–11).

John went on to describe this awesome city that is fifteen hundred miles in each direction (v. 16). We will deal with the indescribable beauty of the New Jerusalem a little later in the chapter, so I just want to note it here. It's no wonder Paul said that when he was taken to heaven and given a vision of God's dwelling place, he saw things he was not permitted to talk about.

Heaven Is a Populated Place

Hebrews 12:22–23 says, "You have come to Mount Zion and to the city of the living God, the heavenly Jerusalem, and to myriads of angels, to the general assembly and church of the firstborn who are enrolled in heaven, and to God, the Judge of all, and to the spirits of the righteous made perfect."

You will be in heaven with all of these people, and with the saints of the New Testament. God created heaven to be inhabited. John said he saw "a great multitude which no one could count" (Revelation 7:9).

Heaven Is a Place of Perfect Beauty

It's interesting that when John first saw the vision of the New Jerusalem coming down from God, he described the city as "a bride adorned for her husband" (Revelation 21:2).

That's a great analogy, because when a bride enters the church and comes down the aisle on her wedding day, everyone stands and looks at her in awe. She has gone into great detail in preparing for her wedding, and she is flawless in her beauty. That's how the apostle John saw the New Jerusalem in his vision. This city is not all of heaven, but the capital city of the new heaven and the new earth.

According to Revelation 21:16, the New Jerusalem is as tall as it is wide, fifteen hundred miles in each direction. That's a lot of space.

The city has twelve gates emblazoned with the names of the twelve tribes of Israel, and twelve foundation stones emblazoned with the names of the twelve apostles (vv. 12–14). These represent all the Old Testament and New Testament saints. And just for good measure, it is all enclosed by a wall that is 216 feet high (v. 17).

John went on to say that the entire city is pure gold, the foundation stones of the wall are adorned with every kind of precious stone, each of the twelve gates is a single pearl, and the street is pure gold (vv. 18–21).

But that's not all. These are transparent jewels. Look back at Revelation 21:11, where John said the New Jerusalem is like "a stone of crystal-clear jasper." Then in verse 18 he wrote, "The material of the wall was jasper; and the city was pure gold, like clear glass."

Heaven Is a Place of Perfect Worship

Heaven is every preacher's dream because it is a place of perfect worship.

During his vision of heaven, John wrote, "I heard a loud voice from the throne, saying, 'Behold, the tabernacle of God is among men, and He will dwell among them, and they shall be His people, and God Himself will be among them'" (Revelation 21:3).

The tabernacle in the Old Testament served the same basic purpose as the church in the New Testament. It was the place where people went to worship God, whether New Testament believers met in the temple or in a private house.

But in heaven there will be no tabernacle or temple (Revelation 21:22), no place we need to go to be reminded of God. It's not necessary, because heaven is permeated by the all-consuming presence of God. You won't need to go to church in heaven, because you will be surrounded by and engulfed in His presence.

Heaven Is a Place of Perfect Service

Revelation 5:10 indicates that part of our service will be spiritual or religious in nature, in that God will make us "to be a kingdom and priests to our God." Jesus' parable in Luke 19 suggests that His faithful servants on earth will be put in charge of "cities" in heaven (vv. 17, 19), so we will also have administrative or governmental responsibilities.

If you're like me, the more you talk about heaven, the more you wish you could experience some of heaven right now. Well, we can. The Bible says God has given us the Holy Spirit as the "pledge" or down payment on our redemption (Ephesians 1:14). The Spirit's daily presence in our lives is God's assurance that someday He will complete our salvation by taking us to heaven.

But in the meantime, it's the Holy Spirit's job to give us a taste of heaven while we wait for our final redemption. The Spirit wants to lift our spirits to the third heaven so we can have a heavenly experience even while we're living on earth (Romans 14:17).

PERSONAL APPLICATION FOR LIFE

1. Do you know a friend of family member who isn't a believer? Have you considered where they might spend eternity? The message of the gospel is too good to keep to ourselves. That's why Jesus told us to go into all the world and announce the good news. Each of us has a unique circle of contacts and influences. Have you missed sharing Jesus with anyone you know who is lost?

2. As believers, our true citizenship is in heaven. God's Word tells us that our total identity and worth as believers is linked to heaven, a promised place. We can be assured that God's promises in His Word are based on His perfect character. Are you laying up for yourself treasures in heaven? (See Matthew 6:20.)

3. God wants you to remember that while you are ironing clothes and scrubbing floors, Jesus Christ is coming back someday to take you to be with Him forever. Take that encouragement with you today as you engage in the routines of your day.

4. The church's power—both individually and corporately—resides in the Holy Spirit's person and work. As we are filled with the Holy Spirit, we are empowered to do God's work. The problem is that sometimes we are too filled with ourselves to be filled with the Spirit. It would not be a bad idea occasionally to clean house of any of our accumulated self-centeredness. If you're missing the Spirit's power in your life, pray this prayer: "Lord, I am desperate for You because I cannot be the person You want me to be and do what You have asked me to do without the filling and empowering of Your Holy Spirit." Then do what He tells you to do.

FOR GROUP STUDY

Questions for Group Discussion

1. Read Matthew 25:41. What did Jesus say about hell? Who will be the residents of hell?

2. What is hell like? Read Revelation 21:8; 22:15.Why did God create hell?
3. Read John 14:1–3; Philippians 3:20; and 1 Peter 1:4. What did Jesus tell us about heaven? On what two key spiritual pillars does the promise of heaven rest?
4. From what we know through Scripture, what is heaven like? (Use the chart below as an aid to your discussion.)

PICTURE THIS

In this chapter, Dr. Evans discusses the kind of place heaven is. Scripture gives us many glimpses of what heaven is like. Below are a few of the snapshots we have of our future abode with Christ.

HEAVEN ACCORDING TO GOD'S WORD

WHAT HEAVEN IS	SCRIPTURE PASSAGE
Heaven is a promised place.	John 14:1-3; Philippians 3:20
Heaven is a particular place.	John 14:2; 2 Corinthians 12:2
Heaven is a populated place.	Hebrews 12:22-23; Revelation 7:9
Heaven is a beautiful place.	Revelation 21
Heaven is a place of perfect worship.	Revelation 21:3
Heaven is a place of perfect pleasure.	Revelation 21:4
Heaven is a place of perfect life.	1 John 3:2
Heaven is a place of perfect service.	Luke 19:17, 19; Revelation 5:10; 22:3

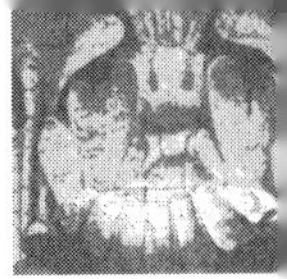

SUBJECT INDEX

SCRIPTURE INDEX

The Understanding God Series

Totally Saved

Understanding, Experiencing and Enjoying the Greatness of Your Salvation

Tony Evans explores justification, propitiation, redemption, reconciliation, forgiveness, and other biblical truths.

ISBN-10: 0-8024-6824-1
ISBN-13: 978-0-8024-6824-6

Our God Is Awesome

Encountering the Greatness of Our God

Tony Evans has done a masterful job of unfolding the rich truth about God . He writes with uncommon clarity, accuracy and warmth. A treasured resource for all who desire to know God better.

– John MacArthur, Pastor, Grace Community Church of the Valley.

ISBN-10: 0-8024-4850-X
ISBN-13: 978-0-8024-4850-7

The Promise

Experiencing God's Greatest Gift the Holy Spirit

"Here is a book that points us to the Spirit's way to purity and power. Every chapter is appropriately titled 'Experiencing the Spirit's. . . .' May this work help all who read it to do so."

—Dr. Charles Ryrie

ISBN-10: 0-8024-4852-6
ISBN-13: 978-0-8024-4852-1

The Battle Is the Lord's

Waging Victorious Spiritual Warfare

Tony Evans tackles the difficult and theologically complex issue of spiritual warfare with the intensity, skill, and biblical foundation readers have come to expect. He systematically reveals Satan's strategies and helps readers fight back.

ISBN-10: 0-8024-4855-0
ISBN-13: 978-0-8024-4855-2

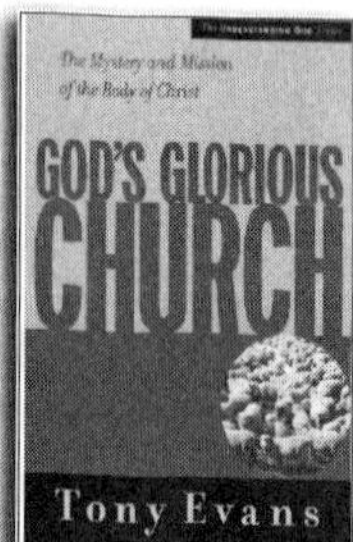

God's Glorious Church

The Mystery and Mission of the Body of Christ

Tony Evans shows how the church is nothing less than the ongoing incarnation of Christ on earth—a living body with a mission, a purpose, and an ultimate call to disciple the whole world.

ISBN-10: 0-8024-3951-9
ISBN-13: 978-0-8024-3951-2

Who Is This King of Glory?

Experiencing the Fullness of Christ's Work in Our Lives

In this practical, biblically-based volume, Tony Evans examines Jesus, "the greatest of all subjects," from three different perspectives: His uniqueness, His authority, and our appropriate response to Him.

ISBN-10: 0-8024-4854-2
ISBN-13: 978-0-8024-4854-5

The Transforming Word

Discovering the Power and Provision of the Bible

Much is at stake when we don't fully understand what the Bible is and why God gave it to us. In *The Transforming Word*, Tony Evans invites readers to discover why knowing the Bible matters so much—and how it can transform our lives.

ISBN-10: 0-8024-6820-9
ISBN-13: 978-0-8024-6820-8

The Best Is Yet to Come

Bible Prophecies Through the Ages

Tony Evans propels you past the hype and confusion of prophecy, straight to the Source. He skillfully unlocks the secrets of the prophetic program, simultaneously unveiling the future for all to read and understand.

ISBN-10: 0-8024-4856-9
ISBN-13: 978-0-8024-4856-9

What Matters Most

Four Absolute Necessities in Following Christ

God's goal for believers is that they become more like Christ. But what does that mean? In *What Matters Most*, Tony Evans explores the four essential elements of discipleship: worship, fellowship, education and outreach.

ISBN: 0-8024-4853-4
ISBN-13: 978-0-8024-4853-8

Returning To Your First Love

Putting God Back in First Place

Tony Evans has done to us all a service in focusing the biblical spotlight on the absolute necessity of keeping our love of Christ as the central passion of our hearts.

– Charles Stanley, Pastor, First Baptist Church in Atlanta, Author

ISBN-10: 0-8024-4851-8
ISBN-13: 978-0-8024-4851-4